A BIOGRAPHICAL DICTIONARY OF CANADIAN JEWRY 1909-1914

from
The Canadian Jewish Times

by Lawrence F. Tapper

Avotaynu, Inc.
P.O. Box 1134
Teaneck, NJ 07666

Copyright © Lawrence F. Tapper

All rights reserved. No part of this publication may be reproduced or transmitted in any form or by any means, electronic or mechanical, including photocopy, recording, or any information storage and retrieval system, without the prior written permission of both the copyright owner and the publisher. Brief passages may be quoted with proper attribution. Request for permission to copy any part of this publication should be addressed to:

Avotaynu, Inc.
P.O. Box 1134
Teaneck, NJ. 07666

Printed in the United States of America

First Printing

Library of Congress Cataloging-in-Publication Data

A biographical dictionary of Canadian Jewry, 1909–1914 from the Canadian Jewish times / compiled, edited, and abstracted by Lawrence F. Tapper
    p.   cm.
   Includes indexes.
   ISBN 0-9626373-0-0
    1. Jews—Canada—Biography—Dictionaries. 2. Canada—Biography—Dictionaries. 3. Jews—Canada—Genealogy. 4. Canada—Genealogy. 5. Registers of births. etc—Canada. I. Tapper, Lawrence F. II. Canadian Jewish times.
F1035.J5F76 1992   920'.0092924071—dc20   92-18521
       [B]   CIP

In memory of my father, Murray Harvey Tapper, of Winnipeg

1929-1991

with love and admiration

Table of Contents

Foreword vii
Preface viii
Abbreviations x

PART ONE — TOPICAL ENTRIES

Bar Mitzvah and Confirmation Announcements 2
Biographical Essays 5
Birth Announcements 8
Deaths and Obituaries 13
Engagements and Marriages 22
General News Items 42

PART TWO — GEOGRAPHICAL ENTRIES

New Brunswick and Newfoundland 56
Nova Scotia 57
Quebec 59
Montreal 60
Ottawa Region 148
Toronto 154
Northern Ontario 170
Ontario — Other Centers 171
Winnipeg 175
Saskatchewan 182
Alberta 183
British Columbia 185

Index 188

Foreword

History is about people. Their lives constitute the fabric of the past; they supply history with the substance of ideas and events that historians interpret for their own contemporaries and, they hope, for future readers of their works. Mr. Tapper's volumes of material drawn from the columns of the *Canadian Jewish Times* constitute major tools for reconstituting the history of the Canadian Jewish community in a most significant period. The history of the Canadian Jewish people is filled with a rich variety of persons who created a fascinating and in some ways distinctive grouping of communities in the Dominion of Canada.

The Jewish experience in Canada began at the British Conquest in 1760 with the arrival of a number of Jewish traders in the wake of the Army that conquered Quebec, a community was organized in Montreal and a synagogue built in 1768. This served as the foundation for what became, in time, Canada's largest, most diverse and politically active, and culturally dynamic Jewish community. In Montreal the battle for political equality was fought in the early nineteenth century and, later, the issue was joined for equal civil rights in the Quebec school system. By the mid-nineteenth century, Jewish communities had emerged in Toronto, Hamilton, Quebec, and Victoria and, by the 1880s, there were numerous others across the Dominion, as immigrants, mainly from the Russian empire, sought economic opportunity on the urban frontier, in the cities and towns in the Maritimes, southwestern Ontario and, very soon, on the Prairies. Thus, a truly national and geographically differentiated Jewish community, now enriched by the culture of the new immigrants, was beginning to emerge. Some Jews, meanwhile, seeking a new style of life, began to settle in farming colonies out on the Prairies in the 1880s and 1890s.

By the early, 1900s, the metropolitan communities of Montreal, Toronto, and Winnipeg were becoming transformed by the enormous and overpowering flood of new immigrants. These transitions were not always easy or pleasant. Class conflict surfaced within the community as Jewish workers in the Jewish-owned clothing factories struck for better conditions and union recognition, causing street violence and searing tensions. Jewish philanthropies had to cope with overwhelming problems of crime, juvenile delinquency, broken families, and poverty, as the underside of the migration process manifested itself. More serious, perhaps, was the emergence of deep cultural divisions within Canadian Jewry, notably in the metropolitan centers, as the outlook—so diverse, rich and complex—of many newly-arrived Russian and Polish Jews clashed in nearly every sphere with that of the older community. Many in the former group pursued survival strategies through trade unionism, socialism, Yiddish, Zionism, and other routes to accommodation within the Dominion of Canada at the same time that they sought to express themselves in the Dominion of the Lord, in secular literature, or in daring political agendas.

The study of the Canadian Jewish experience must be set within its contexts, first of this nation—before 1867 a collection of colonies, to be sure—that sought to develop within the British family and which, with its biracial symbiosis, fostered a constitution that celebrated both national growth and provincial autonomy in local matters. Montreal, the location of about half of the dominion's Jews until recent years, was therefore a special place for them because the major battles for civil and political rights took place in a context that was becoming increasingly tense over the same kinds of issues affecting French and English Canadian concerns. Between the interstices of such competing interests (not to minimize the intracommunal tensions) the Jews sought accommodation to their Canadian environment. In these socio-political contexts lies the distinctiveness of the Canadian Jewish experience. In the early 1900s, meanwhile, Jews were exposed to poisonous antisemitism in both English and French Canada.

By 1914, the Jewish people in Canada had attained self awareness through national organizations, such as the Federation of Zionist Societies of Canada and the foreshadowing of the Canadian Jewish Congress. They had achieved also political representation in legislatures of all levels, strong communal institutions for local needs, and an emerging cultural expression in English and Yiddish. All of these represented over a century and a half of interplay between the Jewish and non-Jewish communities and suggested an equally complex evolution in the future. But what had emerged by the end of World War I was a Jewish community that was sensitive to its specific national agenda and its distinctiveness as an ethnic group within the Dominion beset by French-English differences, regional tensions, and political disruptions; and its intracommunal divisions.

Gerald Tulchinsky
Department of History
Queen's University

Preface

This volume is the sequel to *A Biographical Dictionary of Canadian Jewry, 1897-1909: From "The Jewish Times"* on the ancestry of early twentieth century Canadian Jews. With the publication of these two volumes genealogists now have quick and ready access to published information concerning the personal lives of several generations of many early Canadian Jewish personalities and families provided by Canada's first English-language Jewish newspaper. Recorded here are their familial and social relationships, their communal activities and synagogal involvements, all kinds of happy occasions and family celebrations — especially the births of their children and the celebration of Bar Mitzvahs, engagements and marriages — as well as information concerning their occupations, personal and business addresses, and of course, their deaths.

A Biographical Dictionary of Canadian Jewry, 1904-1914: From "The Canadian Jewish Times" takes us from 1909 to April 1914, the fateful year which saw the outbreak of World War I. The year 1914 also represented an important watershed for Jewish life in Canada. The cessation of large-scale Jewish immigration from Europe to Canada during the second half of the year had a major impact on the Jewish community here and, as well, far reaching consequences for world Jewry. Immigration from overseas came to an abrupt halt with the outbreak of hostilities in Europe and the docking of the last trans-Atlantic passenger ship at the port of St. John. The war marked the transition from relatively easy entry into the country to one of ever-tightening immigration policies, eventually slowing down the rate of European arrivals to a virtual trickle with the onset of the Great Depression in 1929. By the time the flow of immigrants had finally dried up, the Jewish population of Canada stood at 100,000. While many remained permanently in Canada, for others it was merely a brief stopover. Large numbers would eventually make their way overland by rail to the United States.

The year 1914 also marked another turning point for Canadian Jewry. *The Canadian Jewish Times* was sold during the same year to the noted publisher Hirsch Wolofsky, of Montreal, and was renamed *The Canadian Jewish Chronicle*. Mr. Wolofsky founded the *Keneder Odler*, the first Yiddish language newspaper in Canada in 1907. *The Jewish Times* was co-founded by two prominent Montrealers Lyon Cohen and S.W. Jacobs, K.C., in 1897, not as a business venture, but to counteract antisemitic influences in the French Canadian press which were being stirred up by the Dreyfus Affair. Both were Canadian-born young men descended from prominent well-established Canadian Jewish families. With Messrs. Jacobs and Cohen at the helm, the newspaper continued to promote and defend the community's interests on the local and national level, whether on the Montreal Jewish School Question, the Halifax Schecita trial or the Sunday Observance Laws. Thereafter the newspaper changed hands in rapid succession. In November, 1911, the newspaper was sold to Marcus M. Sperber. A year later, it was sold to Leon Goldman and Max Sanders who published it until its final sale to Mr. Wolofsky. *The Jewish Times* appeared as a bi-weekly until November, 1909, when it changed to a weekly format. This, too represented another significant landmark in the history of the Jewish presence in this country. Indeed, the paper's increased frequency of publication as well as its broadening content and coverage underscored the transformation of its Jewish readership from a rather localized, close-knit pioneer society into a widely dispersed, urban and urbane national community.

The Canadian Jewish community, whose roots extend back well into the 1700s, thrived during the heyday of the British Empire. So, by 1914, the Jewish presence in Canada was already firmly established. Perhaps this can best be seen in the fact that the composition of the Canadian Jewish community's leadership was now multi-generational. As a consequence, the community could begin to feel a sense of continuity in its existence here.

In the early twentieth century, Montreal, with its large nucleus of Jewish communal organizations served as the center of Canadian Jewry. That city, by far, had the best established and influential Jewish community in the country. With a large network of synagogues and communal organization, it far surpassed Toronto and Winnipeg in relative importance. Of all the urban Jewish communities across the land, the activities of Montreal Jewry's old leading families were the best documented and recorded in *The Canadian Jewish Times* (the effect of which is also strikingly apparent in this volume). The newspaper's preoccupation with their doings and goings-on occured quite naturally because it was Montreal-based and most of its readers were from that city.

As a result, *The Canadian Jewish Times* features important information on many first-generation immigrants of Ashkenazic descent who had come from western Europe or the Russian Empire and settled in the Canadas in the early to mid 1800s. The issues published between 1897 and 1914 — that is, the ones dealt with in these volumes - are laden with data on the immigrants from the early pioneering days. The death notices, in particular, provide an important source of information on the earliest immigrants because most were then well advanced in years and subject to a high mortality rate. The obituaries of these pioneers are valuable sources for genealogists, especially because many of them contain the names of surviving siblings and offspring.

Also recorded in *The Canadian Jewish Times*'s columns are the hundreds of births, Bar Mitzvahs and marriages of their Canadian-born children. Their sons and daughters, who were raised and educated here, assimilated quickly into Anglo-Canadian society. However, as these native-born Jews entered into adulthood and began choosing mates from within the community, the marriage bonds uniting their families had the further effect of strengthening the community too. As the newspaper attests, many of the younger, upwardly mobile generation ultimately achieved a measure of commercial and business success as well as social prominence within the community. It also records the achievements of the grandchildren of the original settlers who, in turn, began entering and graduating from university before joining the ranks of the professions or family businesses, and marrying and having children of their own.

Of special interest to genealogists is *The Canadian Jewish Times* and its companion volume's recording of large numbers of single Jewish women. In no other single source do we find so many of them identified. Also worth noting are the comings and goings of foreign Jewish visitors to Canada, mostly from the north-eastern United States and Britain. Most travellers were visiting relatives here, some had come for purposes of marriage, while others came on business trips. In certain fortunate cases, the wealth of biographical material provided on the life of family or individual is substantial; in others it consists of as little as a single reference to a given surname.

From "The Canadian Jewish Times", in digesting data gleaned from *The Canadian Jewish Times* between 1909 and April 1914, unavoidably shares in that newspaper's informational virtues and deficiencies. Much the same comment applies to the companion volume, which covers *"The Jewish Times"*. Although both of these volumes will assist many Jewish genealogists in search of their Canadian ancestors, they will not benefit everyone. Researchers should be aware of the fact that, just as frequently occurs today, not all personal announcements and news of life cycle events were published in the newspaper. Therefore, these volumes do not provide a definitive account or complete record of every Jewish person resident in Canada in those days.   As well, references to those recently arrived in the country are not as numerous as one would hope, except perhaps for those who married into the established community. What the paper reported also reflects the bias of its editors who sided with the established lay and rabbinical leadership in a power struggle against those Orthodox newcomers such as the influential Rabbi Simon Glazer who sought to carve out a power base amongst the immigrants. For example, most of the Montreal marriages found in these volumes were performed by Canada's leading "establishment" clerical leaders, Rabbi Hirsch Cohen, an uncle of Lyon Cohen, Rabbi Herman Abramowitz, of the Shaar Hashomayim Synagogue and Rabbi Meldola de Sola, of the Spanish and Portuguese Synagogue and not Rabbi Glazer who, no doubt, performed a great many himself. Researchers may also be disappointed with the heavy emphasis on Montreal entries to the exclusion of other cities. This deficiency is due to two factors. First, as was noted before Montreal was the largest Jewish community and therefore the Montreal-based paper's first priority was to serve its local constituency and advertisers. Second, it was a reflection of the newspaper's spotty record in securing the services of competent provincial correspondents for any length of time.

Like every good reference work, both of these dictionaries frequently pose more questions for the genealogist than they answer. For that reason they should be used together with other reference tools. Researchers will find them to be particularly helpful when used in conjunction with two major biographical reference works on Canadian Jewry: Arthur Daniel Hart's *The Jew in Canada : A Complete Record of Canadian Jewry from the Days of the French Regime to the Present Time* (1926) and Zvi Cohen's *Canadian Jewry: Prominent Jews of Canada* (1933). While quite rare these volumes are still found in major Canadian university and public libraries. Biographical references to later generations of some of these families are also found in Eli Gottesman's *Who's Who in Canadian Jewry* (1965). Researchers should also bear in mind that whatever source is used innacuracies are bound to be discovered and are therefore advised to make every effort to verify the information provided by cross-checking it against other primary and published sources. Nevertheless, it is hoped that they will provide researchers with some of the clues and answers to help solve the larger puzzle, that of solving and piecing together historic family relationships.

These dictionaries are also intended to help researchers in coping with the uneven state of official and private record sources, many of which suffer from inaccuracy and incompleteness and are often difficult to use. Genealogists world-wide are familiar with the problems and pitfalls associated with using state-created records. Unfortunately, Canadian government records have proved no exception to those difficulties. We find that the federal government's pre-World War I immigration, census and naturalization records were either poorly kept, lost or destroyed — and, of those still extant, many are subject to stringent privacy laws. Its naturalization records, for example, were lost in the Parliamentary fire in Ottawa in 1917. As well, the original census records and passenger lists were destroyed after microfilming. These microfilms, some of which were poorly filmed, have not been indexed. Many entries suffer from the illegible hand-writing of court clerks, census takers, and ship stewards.

Provincial record-keeping fares a little better. Even so, depending on the jurisdiction in question, a search may be time-consuming and costly. As well, it may be difficult or next to impossible to obtain certain types of provincial vital records under the existing freedom-of-information laws. Too often, researchers will find that synagogal and cemetery records of the pre-1914 period are incomplete or provide information that is either inaccurate or misleading.

While all this suggests that researchers must consult a wide variety of sources, my years of experience as a professional archivist and genealogist have told me just how difficult this can often be. As I have also learned too well, the carrying out of research on Jewish family history in this country has been made even more onerous by the dearth of specialized reference works dealing exclusively with Canadian sources. With that in mind, I was finally persuaded to undertake the work of compiling a biographical dictionary based on the pages on the *The Jewish Times and The Canadian Jewish Times*. It is hoped that the fruit of that labor — *From "The Jewish Times"* and *From "The Canadian Jewish Times"* — will assist other researchers of the Canadian Jewish heritage.

HOW TO USE THIS VOLUME:

Within each chapter, surnames which appear in blocked characters are arranged alphabetically rather than chronologically. Researchers searching for a surname of a person should first consult the general nominal index to locate the appropriate page number. Then they should scan the entire page to find every reference to that surname. Note that the surname may constitute the sole subject of an entire entry or, in other cases, it may comprise but one of several surnames within a given entry. It is very important to check the entire page because the surname can occur more than once on the same page. The date of publication, volume and issue number for each entry have been provided in that order. This information will enable researchers to examine the original newspaper issue from which the entry was taken.

I am most indebted to Sallyann Sack and Gary Mokotoff, who are respectively the editor and publisher of *Avotaynu*, for their encouragement of this project. I should also like to extend my sincere thanks and appreciation to the National Archives of Canada whose encouragement and support has gone along way to make this work possible. I would like to thank Stephen D. Smith of the Informatics and Records Services Branch for his technical assistance. I am also grateful to Dr. Edward Laine, the Ethnocultural Historian, Canadian Museum of Civilization for his incisive comments and advice.

ABBREVIATIONS

BdHI & HBS	Baron de Hirsch Institute and Hebrew Benevolent Society
HSBA	Hebrew Sick Benefit Association
IOBB	International Order of B'nai B'rith
IOSB	International Order of Sons of Benjamin
JCA	Jewish Colonization Association
LHBS	Ladies' Hebrew Benevolent Society
YMHBS	Young Men's Hebrew Benevolent Society

TOPICAL ENTRIES

BAR MITZVAHS AND CONFIRMATION ANNOUNCEMENTS

ABINOWITZ, Philip, son of Mr. and Mrs. L. Abinowitz, St. Agnes St., St. Henry, Montreal, celebrated his Bar Mitzvah on Sat. April 17, 1909, in the Shaar Hashomayim Synagogue (30 April 1909, 12, 20)

BECKER, Master, son of Mr. and Mrs. I. Becker, of Sydney, N.S., celebrated his Bar Mitzvah on Dec. 28, 1913 in the Glace Bay Synagogue. "Master Becker read a portion of the Holy Law and also delivered a nice impressive speech." (9 Jan. 1914, 17, 5)

BERNSTEIN, Ruben, son of Mr. and Mrs. J. Bernstein, St. Lawrence Blvd., Montreal, celebrated his Bar Mitzvah on Sat. (20 June 1913, 16, 28)

BIRNBAUM, H., a Talmud Torah student, celebrated his Bar Mitzvah last Sat. in the Shaar Hashomayim Synagogue, Montreal (15 Sept. 1909, 12, 40)

BLOCK, Julius, son of Mr. and Mrs. M. Block, celebrated his Bar Mitzvah last Sat. in the Chevra Kadisha Synagogue, St. Urbain St., Montreal. Mr. and Mrs. Block hosted a banquet Sun. in Auditorium Hall (31 Jan. 1912, 15, 12)

BLOUT, Mildred, Eva Claman, Howard Claman, Muriel Goldstein, Irving Levine and Sybil Youngheart were confirmed in Temple Emanu-El, Westmount, Que., during the Shebuoth morn. service, Mon. at 10.30 a.m. A. Goldstein and B. Kortosk led the confirmation class and Rabbi Nathan Gordon delivered the confirmation sermon on the duties of children to their parents and parents to their children. Miss Eva Claman gave the opening prayers and Miss Mildred Blout, the flower prayer. Howard Claman read the ten commandments in Hebrew and Irving Levine read the Haftorah. Sybil Youngheart recited the Declaration of Principles of Judaism and Miss Muriel Goldstein delivered the closing prayer (17 June 1910, 13, 31)

BLUMENTHAL, Joseph, son of Mr. and Mrs. T. Blumenthal, of Hamilton, celebrated his Bar Mitzvah last Sat. morn. in the Anshe Shalom Synagogue (18 June 1909, 12, 27)

COHEN, Lawrence Z., son of Mr. and Mrs. Lyon Cohen, 25 Rosemount Ave., Montreal, celebrated his Bar Mitzvah on Sat. Sept. 27, 1913 in the Shaar Hashomayim Synagogue. Mr. and Mrs. Cohen were "at home" after the ceremony. Guests were received by Mrs. Cohen and Mrs. C.L. Friedman. "Master Lawrence has the example of his father, Mr. Lyon Cohen, and his grandfather, Mr. Lazarus Cohen, who have both distinguished themselves in communal work, before him. On the occasion of his Bar Mitzvah, the "Canadian Jewish Times" extends its heartiest congratulations to him, and trusts that he too, as he grows, will devote himself in the cause of Judaism and keep up the family tradition of steadfastness to our faith, associated with a deep love of race." (1 Oct. 1913, 16, 42-43)

COOPER, Abraham, son of Moses Cooper, 144 Laurier Ave. W., Ottawa, celebrated his Bar Mitzvah. "...Rabbi Fyne addressed the lad at the end of the Sermon on the duty devolving upon every Jew to see that the Jewish name does not suffer through his conduct..." David Epstein collected ten dollars for the National Fund at the celebration last Sun. (4 April 1913, 16, 17)

COSSMAN, Eddie, second son of Mr. and Mrs. D. Cossman, 75 Pleasant St., North Sydney, N.S., celebrated his Bar Mitzvah on Sat. Dec. 21, 1912 in Publicover Hall, Sydney, where the Hebrew Educational Society of Sydney meets and worships. Master Cossman read from "Vaychee" and addressed the congregation taking for his text, Leviticus 19, 3. The following spoke at the reception:- Rev. G. Sakuto, minister of the congregation and the Bar Mitzvah's tutor; I. Becker, the congregation's president; P. Cohen, the congregation's hon. sec.; M. Bonavitskty, G. Ein, H. Green, M. Lubchansky, B. Michael, L. Shlossberg, and L. Silverman, Mrs. Cossman's brother, of New Waterford, N.S. Telegrams were received from his older brother, Jack Cossman, Mr. and Mrs. Mendelsohn and sons, Malca Kirsch, of Montreal, and Mr. and Mrs. S.L. Levitz, of St. John's, Nfld. (3 Jan. 1913, 16, 4)

DARWIN, S., son of Mr. and Mrs. R.A. Darwin, Stanley St., Montreal, celebrated his Bar Mitzvah on Sat. Dec. 16, 1911. At the reception held on Sun. "...the Bar Mitzvah delivered a fine speech in Hebrew. Rev. Dr. Abramowitz, in a few words of praise, spoke of the parents' attachment to our national cause and was glad to hear their son speak Hebrew." H. Lozinsky, Henry V. Bye, A. Falick, M. Wexler, Dr. Ortenberg, M. Gelbman, Dr. Wortsman and Mr. Darwin made donations to the Herzl Wald in honor of the Bar Mitzvah (29 Dec. 1911, 15, 7)

DAVIS, A., son of Mr. and Mrs. Morris Davis, of Lachine, Que., celebrated his Bar Mitzvah (10 March 1911, 14, 17)

DIAMOND, Jacob, son of Mr. and Mrs. J. Diamond, 582 St. Denis St., Montreal, celebrated his Bar Mitzvah on Sat. Dec. 18, 1909, in the Chevra Kadisha Synagogue, St. Urbain St. The Diamonds were "at home" on Sun. Dec. 19 to 125 guests (31 Dec. 1909, 13, 7)

DIAMOND, Max, son of Mr. and Mrs. J. Diamond, 582 St. Denis St., Montreal, will celebrate his Bar Mitzvah on Sat. Jan. 11, 1913 in the Chevra Kadisha Synagogue, St. Urbain St. (3 Jan. 1913, 16, 4)

FELSEN, Mr. and Mrs. O., their eldest son celebrated his Bar Mitzvah in Temple Emanu-El, Westmount, Que., on Sat. March 29, 1913. Rabbi Nathan Gordon and Mr. and Mrs. Bernzweig, of New York, were present at the reception on Sun. (4 April 1913, 16, 17)

FISCHEL, Leon, son of Mr. and Mrs. Gustave Fischel, 51 Winchester Ave., Westmount, Que., celebrated his Bar Mitzvah in Temple Emanu-El, Westmount, on Sat. Jan. 1, 1910 (7 Jan. 1910, 13, 8)

FISCHEL, Leon, will celebrate his Bar Mitzvah in Temple Emanu-El, Westmount, Que., on Sat. Jan. 1, 1910 (17 Dec. 1909, 13, 5)

FLORENCE, Jacob, son of Mr. and Mrs. A.E. Florence, of Ottawa, celebrated his Bar Mitzvah on Dec. 17, 1911. Rabbi Berger spoke at the banquet afterwards. Some of the out-of-town guests were:- Mr. and Mrs. M.D. Pullan, A. Pullan, E. Pullan and Mr. Saks (Toronto), D. Florence (Peterborough, Ont.), and M.J. and I. Saxe (Montreal) (29 Dec. 1911, 15, 7)

FRAID, Louis, son of Mr. and Mrs. Fraid, Sherbrooke St. E., Montreal, celebrated his Bar Mitzvah in the Chevra Kadisha Synagogue, St. Urbain St., of which Mr. Fraid is the treasurer. A banquet for two hundred couples was held Sun., New Year's Eve, in the Auditorium Hall (5 Jan. 1912, 15, 8)

FREEDMAN, Louis, son of Mr. and Mrs. B. Freedman, will celebrate his Bar Mitzvah in the Shaar Hashomayim Synagogue, Montreal, on Sat. Dec. 17, 1910 (9 Dec. 1910, 14, 4)

FRIEDMAN, Arthur, eldest son of Mr. and Mrs. I. Friedman, will celebrate his Bar Mitzvah next Sat., Oct. 23, 1909, in the Shaar Hashomayim Synagogue (22 Oct. 1909, 12, 45)

FRIEDMAN, Norman, son of Mr. and Mrs. D.S. Friedman, of Montreal will celebrate his Bar Mitzvah Sat. morn., June 14, 1913, in the English-German-Polish Synagogue. His parents will be "at home" to their friends at the Montefiore Club, Sat. aft., from 3 to 5 p.m. (13 June 1913, 16, 27)

FROMSON, Mr. and Mrs. M., 68 Colonial Ave., Montreal, gave an "at home" in honor of the Bar Mitzvah of their eldest son, Abraham Fromson, on Sat. and Sun., Nov. 22 and 23, 1913. Guests were received by Mrs. M. Fromson, assisted by Mrs. D.M. Chorlton. Refreshments were served by the Misses Rae and Myra Marks and Sadie Rutenberg. The Bar Mitzvah's name was inscribed in the Golden Book by his father. The Agudath Zion Society purchased five dunams of land in Palestine in his name as well as several trees in the Herzl Wald which were purchased by his friends (12 Dec. 1913, 17, 1)

GELDZAELER, Alfred B., youngest son of Mr. and Mrs. M. Geldzaeler, celebrated his Bar Mitzvah on Feb. 7, 1914 in the Holy Blossom Synagogue, Bond St., Toronto. "On Sunday, Feb. 8th, a reception was held at the Home of Mr. Geldzaeler, Walmer Road, where besides relatives, many friends came to extend their best wishes to Mr. and Mrs. Geldzaeler." (27 Feb. 1914, 17, 9)

GLICKMAN, Lawrence, son of Mr. and Mrs. T. Glickman, of Montreal, celebrated his Bar Mitzvah, Sat. Jan. 25, 1913 (24 Jan. 1913, 16, 7)

GOLDBERG, Israel, son of Mr. and Mrs. Z. Goldberg, Notre Dame St., Montreal, will celebrate his Bar Mitzvah tomorrow morn. in the Shaar Hashomayim Synagogue (21 May 1909, 12, 23)

GOLDENSTEIN, Dana, son of Mr. and Mrs. I.S. Goldenstein, 225 Clarke Ave., Montreal, will celebrate his Bar Mitzvah. Mr. and Mrs. Goldenstein will be "at home" Sat. aft., Sept. 30, 1911 (20 Sept. 1911, 14, 45)

GOLDMAN, Arthur Zion, the eldest son of Mr. and Mrs. Leon Goldman, of Montreal, celebrated his Bar Mitzvah, Sat. June 1, 1912 in Shaar Hashomayim Synagogue. At the reception the following day, Clarence I. de Sola, president of the Zionist Federation council " S.made a present of the title to thirteen dunam of land in Palestine, purchased in the name of Master Arthur Zion Goldman, and they also presented him with an entry of his name in the Golden Book of the

National Fund." (7 June 1912, 15, 26)

GOLDSTEIN, Edgar, son of Mr. and Mrs. J. Goldstein, Dorchester St. W., Montreal, celebrated his Bar Mitzvah on Sat. Dec. 25, 1909. The Goldsteins were "at home" to their friends on Sun. Dec. 26. Mrs. Goldstein was assisted in receiving by her sister, Mrs. H. Myers and the Misses Hyman, Levinson and Goldstein (31 Dec. 1909, 13, 7)

GOLDSTEIN, Edgar, will celebrate his Bar Mitzvah in Temple Emanu-El, Westmount, Que., on Sat. Dec. 25, 1909 (17 Dec. 1909, 13, 5)

GOLDSTEIN, Joe, son of Mr. and Mrs. M. Goldstein, of Hamilton, Ont., celebrated his Bar Mitzvah (8 Jan. 1909, 12, 4)

GOLDWATER, Ephraim, son of Mr. and Mrs. A. Goldwater, of Lachine, Que., will celebrate his Bar Mitzvah in Beth Israel Synagogue, Lachine, on Sat. June 17, 1911 (9 June 1911, 14, 30)

GREENBERG, Gilbert, son of Mr. and Mrs. Albert Greenberg, 4 the St. St. Charles Apts., Dorchester St. W., Montreal, will celebrate his Bar Mitzvah on Sat. March 28, 1914 in the Spanish and Portuguese Synagogue, Stanley St. Mr. and Mrs. Greenberg will be "at home" to their friends at their residence from 4 to 7 p.m. (20 March 1914, 17, 12)

GREENFORD, Isidore, son of S. Greenford, celebrated his Bar Mitzvah in the Austro-Hungarian Synagogue, Milton St., Montreal, last Sat. morn. A reception was held that aft. and Sun. at Mr. Greenford's home, 911 Cadieux St. (4 March 1910, 13, 16)

GROSS, Samuel, son of Mr. and Mrs. Gross, Prince Arthur St., Montreal, read a "parsha" in the Shaar Hashomayim Synagogue, on Sat. April 21, on the occasion of his Bar Mitzvah (30 April 1909, 12, 20)

HARRIS, Jacob, son of Mr. and Mrs. A. Harris, of Montreal, celebrated his Bar Mitzvah last Sat. Friends and colleagues of A. Harris, who is a member of the Federation of Zionist Societies of Canada, entered the Bar Mitzvah's name in the Golden Book by planting twenty-one trees in the Herzl Wald, purchasing ten dunams of land, and erecting a house for the Yemenite Jews in Palestine (6 June 1913, 16, 26)

HARRIS, Mr. and Mrs. Max, Dorchester St. W., Montreal, were "at home" on Sun. March 1, 1914 in honor of the Bar Mitzvah of their son, Hesse Harris. (6 March 1914, 17, 10)

HIRSCH, Percy T., son of Mr. and Mrs. Michael Hirsch, will celebrate his Bar Mitzvah in the Shaar Hashomayim Synagogue, on Sat. morn. May 8, 1909 (7 May 1909, 12, 21)

HOLDENGRABER, Sol., son of Mr. and Mrs. Adolph Holdengraber, 1690a St. Urbain St., Montreal, celebrated his Bar Mitzvah (14 Nov. 1913, 16, 49)

HYMAN, Mr. and Mrs. I.E., 2232 Park Ave., Montreal, will be "at home" on Sun. Jan. 5, 1913 from 3 to 6 p.m. on the occasion of their youngest son's Bar Mitzvah (3 Jan. 1913, 16, 4)

ISSEN, Joseph, youngest son of Mrs. Mark Issen, celebrated his Bar Mitzvah in the Odessa Synagogue, Montreal. "A speech was rendered by him and much praise and thanks were extended to Mrs. S. Berman, St. Lawrence Blvd., for the able manner in which Master Joseph had been taught to chant the Haphtorah." (9 Jan. 1914, 17, 5)

JOSEPH, Jacob, son of Mr. and Mrs. M. Joseph, 236 Elm Ave., Westmount, Que., celebrated his Bar Mitzvah on Sat. Oct. 25, 1913 in the Chevra Kadisha Synagogue, St. Urbain St., Montreal (31 Oct. 1913, 16, 47)

JOSEPH, Michael Joseph, son of Mr. and Mrs. Andrew C. Joseph, of Quebec City, celebrated his Bar Mitzvah in the Spanish and Portuguese Synagogue, Stanley St., Montreal, last Sat. morn. Mr. and Mrs. Horace Joseph, 47 Mance St., hosted a party (11 June 1909, 12, 26)

KAPLANSKY, David, youngest son of Mr. and Mrs. A.L. Kaplansky, celebrated his Bar Mitzvah on Sat. Feb. 21, 1914 in the Spanish and Portuguese Synagogue, Stanley St., Montreal. "Master David ably read a portion of the law and the Haphtorah, after which Rabbi de Sola addressed him on the duties to his race and religion." (27 Feb. 1914, 17, 9)

KAPLANSKY, William, fourth son of Mr. and Mrs. A.L. Kaplansky, 68 Park Ave., Montreal, will celebrate his Bar Mitzvah Sat. March 2, 1912 in the Spanish and Portuguese Synagogue, Stanley St. Julius A. Kaplansky the Bar Mitzvah's brother is in town for the celebration (1 March 1912, 15, 16)

KELLNOR, Louis, son of Mr. and Mrs. Kellnor, celebrated his Bar Mitzvah on Sat. Sept. 27, 1913 in the Shaar Hashomayim Synagogue, Montreal (1 Oct. 1913, 16, 42-43)

KIRSCHBERG, David, son of Mr. and Mrs. Joseph Kirschberg, Tupper St., Montreal, celebrated his Bar Mitzvah last Sat. in the Spanish and Portuguese Synagogue, Stanley St. At the reception last Sun. evening, Joseph Fineberg raised $50.00 to inscribe the Bar Mitzvah's name in the Jewish National Fund Golden Book. The Misses Miriam and Annie Kirschberg, Elizabeth Bernstein, Agnes Fineberg, Mildred Gorfinkle and Dorothy Leo were in charge of the tables and refreshments (13 Dec. 1912, 16, 1)

KIRSCHBERG, David, was inscribed in the Golden Book on the occasion of his Bar Mitzvah (28 March 1913, 16, 16)

LANG, Jacob David, son of Mr. and Mrs. H. Lang, 365 Bleury St., Montreal, celebrated his Bar Mitzvah last week. "After the service, a large number of friends assembled at the parent's residence where refreshments were partaken of and speeches indulged in. The Bar-Mitzvah responded to the toast in his honour, in Hebrew which brought forth much praise from the guests." David Levy acted as toast-master. Among those present were:- Rabbi Herman Abramowitz, Clarence I. de Sola, M.A. Levine, Rabbi Hirsch Cohen, Mr. and Mrs. A. Levin, A. Lozinsky, Max Levin, Mr. Jackell, Dr. Ortenberg, Mr. and Mrs. H. Levy and A. Harris. Twenty trees were subscribed in the Herzl Wald (18 March 1910, 13, 18)

LANG, Jacob David, son of Mr. and Mrs. H. Lang, 365 Bleury St., Montreal, will celebrate his Bar Mitzvah in the Shaar Hashomayim Synagogue, Sat. March 12, 1910 (11 March 1910, 13, 17)

LANG, Jesajahu Richard, son of Mr. and Mrs. H. Lang, 677 St. Urbain St., Montreal, will celebrate his Bar Mitzvah on Sat. Sept. 28, 1912 (20 Sept. 1912, 15, 41)

LOZINSKY, Ezra, son of Mr. and Mrs. Adolph Lozinsky, St. Urbain St., Montreal, celebrated his Bar Mitzvah in the Adath Yeshuran Synagogue last Sat. Among those present at the reception afterwards were:- Rabbis Herman Abramowitz and Hirsch Cohen, Lazarus Cohen, Lyon Cohen, E. Guilaroff, Clarence I. de Sola, A. Levin, M. Talpis, M. Silverman, H. Bernstein A. Harris, H. Lang, L. Teplitzky and Rev. M.A. Levin, Principal of the Talmud Torah. At the suggestion of R.A. Darwin, the gathering subscribed $50.00 for the inscription of the Bar Mitzvah's name in the JNF Golden Book (7 Jan. 1910, 13, 8)

LOZINSKY, Ezra, son of Mr. and Mrs. H. Lozinsky, will celebrate his Bar Mitzvah on Sat. Jan. 1, 1910 in the Adath Yeshuran Synagogue, Montreal. The family will receive at their home, 821 St. Urbain St. after the service (31 Dec. 1909, 13, 7)

LYONS, Harry, youngest son of Mr. and Mrs. F.H. Lyons, 144 Walmer Road, Toronto, was confirmed in Holy Blossom Synagogue, Bond St., on Sat. Oct. 14, 1911. "Rabbi Jacobs spoke feelingly of the responsibilities attached to being a good Israelite." A reception was held the following day at the home of the parents (17 Nov. 1911, 15, 1)

MARKUS, Ernest, son of Mr. and Mrs. M. Markus, will celebrate his Bar Mitzvah in the Shaar Hashomayim Synagogue, Montreal, on Sat. Dec. 3, 1910 (25 Nov. 1910, 14, 2)

MORRIS, Jake, celebrated his Bar Mitzvah last Sat. in the Shaar Shalom Synagogue, Hamilton. A reception was held at the home of his parents, John St. N., on Sat. aft. (16 July 1909, 12, 31)

MOSKOVITCH, Harry, son of Mr. and Mrs. S. Moskovitch, 11 Sherbrooke St. E., Montreal, will celebrate his Bar Mitzvah on Sat. Dec. 14, 1912, in the Chevra Kadisha Synagogue, St. Urbain St. (6 Dec. 1912, 15, 52)

MYERS, Phillip, son of Mr. and Mrs. S.P. Myers, 202 Bishop St., Montreal, celebrated his Bar Mitzvah. His parents were "at home" Sun. Mrs. Myers received, assisted by her sister, Mrs. C. Sessenwein. Young ladies assisting at the table were :- Miss Belle Leah Sessenwein and Mesdames Solomon Silverman and Max Jacobs (1 Nov. 18, 1910, 14, 1)

NEWMANN, Harold, son of Mr. and Mrs. J.N. Newmann, Laval Ave., Montreal, celebrated his Bar Mitzvah in the Austro-Hungarian Synagogue, Milton St., where Mr. Newmann is a member. Mr. and Mrs. Newmann hosted a reception at their home on Sun., New Year's Eve. A dance was held afterwards at the home of Mr. and Mrs. M. Dubrofsky, Esplanade Ave. (5 Jan. 1912, 15, 8)

OSTROGURSKY, Joseph, will celebrate his Bar Mitzvah in the Shaar Hashomayim Synagogue, tomorrow, Sat. Feb. 19, 1910 (18 Feb. 1910, 13, 14)

RAFOLOVITCH, Moses, son of Mr. and Mrs. M. Rafolovitch, Park Ave., Montreal, celebrated his Bar Mitzvah on Jan. 31, 1914 in the Chevra Kadisha Synagogue, St. Urbain St. "The young Bar-mitzvah after his "Haphtorah" delivered an address in Hebrew." A reception for friends and relatives was held at the home of Mr. and Mrs. Rafolovitch on Sun. (20 Feb. 1914, 17, 8)

RIPSTEIN, Isadore, son of Mr. and Mrs. S.A. Ripstein, celebrated his Bar Mitzvah on Sat. morn., Jan. 15, 1910, in the Shaarey Zedek Synagogue, Winnipeg (28 Jan. 1910, 13, 11)

RITTENBERG, Mr. and Mrs., Mance St., Montreal, will be "at home" Sun. Feb. 13, 1910, in honor of their son Alfred's Bar Mitzvah (4 Feb. 1910, 13, 12)

RITTENBERG, Mr. and Mrs. Moe, will be "at home" in honor of the Bar Mitzvah of their son, Aubie Rittenberg, Sun. Jan. 11, 1914, at their residence, 228 St. Joseph Blvd. W., Montreal (Jan. 2, 1914, 17, 4)

ROBINSON, Sydney, eldest son of Mr. and Mrs. R.S. Robinson, of Winnipeg, celebrated his Bar Mitzvah, on Sat. June 19, 1909. The date also marked the Robinson's twentieth wedding anniversary (25 June 1909, 12, 28)

RUBINOVICH, Irwin, son of Mr. and Mrs. J.B. Rubinovich, 448 Argyle Ave., Westmount, Que., will celebrate his Bar Mitzvah in the Shaar Hashomayim Synagogue on Sat. May 7, 1910 (6 May 1910, 13, 25)

SAMUELS, Solly, celebrated his Bar Mitzvah in the Spanish and Portuguese Synagogue, Stanley St., Montreal, last Sat. (4 June 1909, 12, 25)

SHALINSKY, David, of Montreal, celebrated his Bar Mitzvah Sun. evening, Dec. 24, 1911 (29 Dec. 1911, 15, 7)

SHAPIRO, Julius, son of Mr. and Mrs. D.H. Shapiro, Mt. Royal Ave., celebrated his Bar Mitzvah last Sat., in the Shaar Hashomayim Synagogue, Montreal. On Sun. evening, Mr. and Mrs. Shapiro gave a dinner for twenty-five couples (relatives) in honor of the Bar Mitzvah (Dec. 12, 1913, 17, 1)

SHAPIRO, Samuel, son of Mr. and Mrs. L. Shapiro, of Montreal, celebrated his Bar Mitzvah. A reception was held Sun. evening last week in the Auditorium Hall. At the reception the Chevra Kadisha Congregation, St. Urbain St., presented Mr. Shapiro with a testimonial in appreciation for his services to the synagogue (3 Nov. 1911, 14, 51)

SIEGLER, Max, son of Mr. and Mrs. F. Siegler, 1683 Notre Dame St. W., Montreal, will celebrate his Bar Mitzvah tomorrow, Sat., in the Shaar Hashomayim Synagogue (11 June 1909, 12, 26)

SILVER, Alexander, son of Mr. and Mrs. N. Silver, Souvenir St., Montreal, will celebrate his Bar Mitzvah. His parents will be "at home" on Sun. Sept. 11, 1910 (26 Aug. 1910, 13, 41)

SILVERMAN, Charles, son of Mr. and Mrs. S.J. Silverman, 30 Versailles St., Montreal, will celebrate his Bar Mitzvah on Sat. Feb. 1, 1913, in the Shaar Hashomayim Synagogue (24 Jan. 1913, 16, 7)

SILVERMAN, Samuel, son of Mr. and Mrs. J. Silverman, Bonaparte St., Montreal, will celebrate his Bar Mitzvah in the Shaar Hashomayim Synagogue tomorrow morn. (10 Sept. 1909, 12, 39)

SIMON, Jake, son of Mr. and Mrs. M. Simon, celebrated his Bar Mitzvah on Sat. Feb. 14, 1914 in the B'nai Jacob Synagogue, Montreal. "The Bar Mitzvah read the Haftorah, and also delivered a speech in Hebrew." On Sun. Feb 15th, a dinner for 450 guests was given in Prince Arthur Hall (20 Feb. 1914, 17, 8)

STEINE, Ben Zion, son of Mr. and Mrs. M.B. Steine, of Montreal, was inscribed in the Golden Book on the occasion of his Bar Mitzvah (28 March 1913, 16, 16)

STEINE, Mr. and Mrs. M.B., 819 University Ave., Montreal, will be "at home" to their friends, Sun. Nov. 24, 1912, in honor of the Bar Mitzvah of their son, Ben Zion Steine (22 Nov. 1912, 15, 50)

TEPLITZKY, Mrs. L., was "at home" in honor of the Bar Mitzvah of her son, Bernard Joseph Teplitzky, on Sun. Dec. 28, 1913. Out-of-town guests included:- Mr. and Mrs. M. Shapiro, Mr. and Mrs. N. Shapiro, Mr. and Mrs. S. Shapiro, Mrs. E. Shapiro and Miss Sophie Shapiro from New York (Jan. 2, 1914, 17, 4)

WALKER, Isaac, of Hamilton, celebrated his Bar Mitzvah recently (11 July 1913, 16, 31)

WEEKSLER, Joseph, son of Mr. and Mrs. Chas. Weeksler, 69 Winchester St., Toronto, celebrated his Bar Mitzvah recently in the Holy Blossom Synagogue, Bond St. (22 Oct. 1909, 12, 45)

WEINROCH, Joseph, son of Mr. and Mrs. L. Weinroch, of Montreal, celebrated his Bar Mitzvah last Sat. (25 Nov. 1910, 14, 2)

WEISSBURGH, Isaac, son of the late Mr. E. and Mrs. Weissburgh, Bleury St., Montreal, will celebrate his Bar Mitzvah tomorrow morn. in the Spanish and Portuguese Synagogue, Stanley St. (21 May 1909, 12, 23)

WENER, Lawrence, celebrated his Bar Mitzvah on June 11, 1910 in the Shaar Hashomayim Synagogue, Montreal. The Misses Nellie, Malca and Sadie Vineberg and Florence Wener were in charge of the dining room at the reception held at the home of Mr. and Mrs. H. Wener later that day (24 June 1910, 13, 32)

WENER, Lawrence, son of Mr. and Mrs. H. Wener, 85 St. Famille St., Montreal, will celebrate his Bar Mitzvah tomorrow morn. in the Shaar Hashomayim Synagogue (10 June 1910, 13, 30)

WOLOFSKY, Felix, son of Mr. and Mrs. H. Wolofsky, Berri St., Montreal, celebrated his Bar Mitzvah last Sat. At the reception Sun. evening, Dec. 8, 1912, Max Sanders, manager of The Canadian Jewish Times, raised $50.00 to inscribe the Bar Mitzvah's name in the Jewish National Fund Golden Book. Speeches were made by M. Sanders, M. Wolofsky and Reuben Brainin (13 Dec. 1912, 16, 1)

WOLOFSKY, Philip, was inscribed in the Golden Book on the occasion of his Bar Mitzvah (28 March 1913, 16, 16)

WYMAN, Nathan, of Sydney, N.S., celebrated his Bar Mitzvah (23 Aug. 1912, 15, 37)

Be Particular About Your Druggist!

No one is better qualified to act in that capacity than we are   Our prescription department has the endorsement of the very best physicians, as nothing but pure Drug are used in the dispencing of your prescriptions and graduate chemists are always in charge of this department.

Let us send our messenger for your prescriptions and deliver them to you promptly as our service is the best in the city.

A. H. Jassbey & Morris Ginsberg
CHEMISTS & DRUGGISTS.

Dispensing Dept. Tel Up 1067
Sundries   Tel Up 5115

Jassbey's Drug Store
Guy & St. Catherine Sts.
Successors to F. E. Morgan.

BIOGRAPHICAL ESSAYS

ALEXANDER, George L., age 25, has obtained his law degree this year from Indiana University. He received his elementary education in London, England and attended the University of London where he received his B.A. at age 18. After graduation, he joined the Bishopsgate Press, of London where he soon became assistant editor to Sydney H. North, the well known London editor of the Playgoer. In May 1904, he went to South Africa for the Central News Agency and was associated with the South African News of Cape Town before becoming dramatic and news editor for the Daily Express of Johannesburg. Following his legal studies in Indianapolis, Mr. Alexander was a law editor for Bobbs-Merrill Law Book Publishing Co. In 1907 he came to Canada on a visit but was forced to remain and it is here that he decided to study law (10 June 1910, 13, 30)

ALEXANDER, Maurice, is the McGill University student who saved two people from drowning last summer at Ste. Agathe, Que. while on vacation. Mr. Alexander was born in Cape Town, South Africa in 1887. He will receive his B.C.L. degree next year. The Recorder of McGill University presented him with a diploma of the Royal Canadian Humane Society for his act of heroism. "In doing so, the Recorder dwelt upon Mr. Alexander's heroism, and pointed out this young man is the first McGill student to gain this distinction." (14 May 1909, 12, 22)

ANSELL, David A., the Mexican Consul-General in Montreal, has not resigned his office and will not leave Canada permanently as was erroneously reported in the Montreal Star this week. Mr. Ansell admitted to being older than sixty-four years but would not give his age. He remembers his Hebrew school days in Germany where he studied under the late Dr. Samson ben Raphael Hirsch, of Frankfurt. Once active in the life of the Canadian Jewish community, he devoted much time to the development of Jewish education in Montreal and through his efforts was responsible for securing funds from the late Baron de Hirsch to build the Baron de Hirsch Institute. Mr. Ansell prizes highly his letters from the Baron and was proud to have laid the cornerstone of the Institute. A past president of the Institute, he ceased involvement in community affairs when the school was ousted from the Institute. An Orthodox Jew, his office was never open on the Sabbath. He comes from a scholarly family and possesses many family heirlooms. His grandfather was the famous Dayan Solomon, of London, England. He intends to leave his Book of Esther to the Jewish Theological Seminary of New York and other valuables to the Chevra Kadisha Synagogue, St. Urbain St. (5 Jan. 1912, 15, 8)

BALLON, David, has graduated in medicine from McGill University. Dr. Ballon came to Canada with his parents fifteen years ago. He attended Ann Street School, Montreal. He and his brother each received a scholarship for four years free tuition at high school. He entered McGill six years ago and received his B.A. degree. (4 June 1909, 12 25)

BALLON, Miss Ellen, age 12, Montreal's "wunderkind", will play a recital in Windsor Hall, on Thurs. evening, April 7, 1910. "Born in Montreal, the daughter of Mr. and Mrs. Samuel Ballon, Ellen showed marked musical talent at the age of three, and made her first public appearance at the Windsor Hall at five." (1 April 1910, 13, 20)

BERCOVITCH, Peter, a Montreal lawyer, has been appointed a King's Counsel. He is the third Jewish lawyer to receive this honor, preceded by Maxwell Goldstein and S.W. Jacobs. Mr. Bercovitch has been in practice for eleven years. He was born in Montreal on Sept. 17, 1879, the son Mr. and Mrs. Hyman Bercovitch, of Montreal. He was educated at the local grammar and high schools. He graduated from McGill University with a B.C.L. degree in 1900 and was admitted to the Bar in Jan. of the following year. After serving an apprenticeship, he entered Laval University where he graduated with an L.L.B. in 1904. He practiced alone for four years and then joined the firm of Trihey, Bercovitch and Karney. He is very active in politics and was mentioned as a possible candidate in the recent elections. He is president of the Laurier Political Club. Mr. Bercovitch married Miss Florence Levine, of San Francisco, in 1908 (3 Nov. 1911, 14, 51)

ETERNAL BLOOM.

A Sonnet by Hyman Edelstein.

One time there bloomed upon an arid waste
A little flower of wondrous loveliness,
A dew of heavenly manna was its dress,
Sweet incense bathed its head divine and chaste;
And starving birds flocked round about to taste
Its nectar, and, unpitying its distress,
The manna-robe they plucked with each caress,
Then from the little blossom fled in haste.

Once Israel dwelt beneath her own fair sky,
While clamorous foes assailed her sacred bower;
But God had sworn: "My child, thou shalt not die!"—
Then breathed His saving wind upon the flower,
Blowing its petals over all the earth
To blossom in a new almighty birth!

COHEN, Arthur, age 29, the son of Jacob Cohen, J.P., of Toronto, has been appointed an Examiner of the Law School for a five year term by the benchers of the Law Society of Upper Canada. A native of Toronto, he graduated from the University of Toronto with a law degree. He won first scholarships each year and the gold medal on graduation. Mr. Cohen was a student with Beatty, Blackstock and Co. and later a student and partner in the firm of Ritchie, Ludwig and Balantyne. He is now practicing law on his own (10 Dec. 1909, 13, 4)

DAVIS, Mr. and Mrs. Z., of Montreal, celebrated their fiftieth wedding anniversary on Tues. Mr. Davis is one of the oldest cigar maufacturers in Canada. Born in London, England in 1834, he came to New York in 1858 and then moved to Boston where he married. His wife, age 72, was born in London. They have spent 45 years in Montreal. "Mr. Davis, senior, was one of a family noted for its probity and charity and one of the traditions was that a member should serve in the synagogue. To such an extent had this prevailed that for three hundred years a member of the family had acted as usher in the Great Synagogue, the father of Mr. Z. Davis being the last member of the family to hold office." Mr. Davis has a brother, age 82, in London and a sister age 68 still surviving. They have two sons, one in Detroit and one in the Old Country and four daughters (13 May 1910, 13, 26)

DE SOLA, Clarence I., Belgian vice-consul in Montreal, has been appointed consul by the Belgian government. Mr. de Sola, who has been vice-consul for six years, has had close ties to Belgium. He has been managing director of the Comptoir Belgo-Canadien for twenty-two years. He was responsible for increasing trade between Canada and Belgium. One of his major achievements was his role in negotiating a treaty which granted Belgium tariff concessions. He is also the Canadian representative of Swan, Hunter and Wigham Richardson, the world's largest ship builders which built the "Mauretania", the largest vessel afloat. Through his connections many ships have been built for Canadian shipping lines and the Canadian government. He has also carried out large construction contracts including the Soulanges and Trent Canals and the retracking of the Intercolonial Railway. He has been parnass of "Shearith Israel" for many years (20 Oct. 1911, 14, 49)

EDELSTEIN, Hyman, is founder of the Ottawa Jewish Literary Debating and Dramatic Society. Mr. Edelstein was born in Dublin, Ireland in 1889 and was educated at the famous High School there. He obtained the very highest distinction in the Irish Intermediate Examinations, for which over ten thousand students compete. In 1905, he was first in classics in all Ireland, winning $160 and medals. In 1908, he entered Trinity College, Dublin University and won several scholarships in classics and mathematics. "In 1911 he was included among those who were awarded the annual Vote of Thanks for Oratory by the University Philosophical Society of Dublin, before whom he had also read a paper. Mr. Edelstein is a young poet of great distinction, whose poems have appeared in the columns of the "Canadian Jewish Times."" (20 June 1913, 16, 28)

ELZAS, Rev. Dr. Barnett A., former rabbi of Holy Blossom Synagogue in Toronto from 1890 to 1893, is a physician working for the Anti-Tuberculosis Society in Charleston, S.C. He is a brother-in-law of Mrs. Meldola de Sola, of Montreal. Dr. Elzas was born Dec. 7, 1867 in Eydkuhnen, Germany. He studied for the rabbinate at Jew's College, London. He was one of the first to receive a B.A. from University of London. Upon graduation, he went to Holy Blossom. While in Toronto, he graduated from the University of Toronto in 1893. Later that year he received the call to Sacramento, Cal. where he remained for one year before taking the pulpit of the historic Beth Elohim Congregation, of Charleston which he still occupies. In Charleston, Rev. Elzas graduated medicine in 1900 and pharmacy in 1901. He has written extensively on Jewish history in South Carolina (7 Jan. 1910, 13, 8)

FINEBERG, Nathan, recently passed the Quebec Bar examination and was admitted to the Bar. Mr. Fineberg is the second son of Z. Fineberg, president of the Hebrew Free Loan Association. He is a member of Z. Fineberg & Sons, St. James St. and studied law while carrying on his business duties. A Montreal High School graduate, he entered the McGill University, Faculty of Arts in 1914 and graduated in 1908 with first rank honors in history and economics. He was awarded a scholarship to Yale University where he received his M.A. He returned to Montreal where he entered business before taking up law at McGill in 1910. Mr. Fineberg was one of the founders of the Maccabean Society and was three times president (11 July 1913, 16, 31)

FINEBERG, Nathaniel S., received his M.A. in economics and sociology from Yale University. "The study of economics occupied most of Mr. Fineberg's time. Canadian economics proved his favourite topic of research, and soon some views on this subject will be published in America's leading economic and financial journals." Nathaniel Fineberg graduated from McGill University Faculty of Arts in the spring of 1908 with first rank honors in history and economics. He was chairman of the Maccabean Literary Club for two years while at McGill. He will spend the summer in Montreal. (9 July 1909, 12, 30)

FISH, Dr. Joseph, the superintendent of the Mount Sinai Sanatorium, is one of America's leading authorities on tuberculosis. Born is Warsaw, he is a member of one of the best Jewish families in Russia. Trained in Europe and America, he headed the Montefiore Consumptives' Hospital in Bedford, N.Y. after graduation. He then became superintendent of the Jewish Consumptives' Relief Society of Denver, Col. for two years before taking charge of the Mount Sinai Hospital at Ste.

Agathe, Que. (7 June 1912, 15, 26)

FITCH, Louis, has won the Gold Medal and Macdonald Scholarship in his final year law at McGill University. Born in Suezawa, Austria, in 1889, he came to Canada with his parents in 1891, who settled in Quebec City where they still reside. Mr. Fitch came to Montreal in 1904 to study Arts at McGill. He graduated with first rank honors in history and economics. In 1910 he won the Silver Medal for oratory at MGill. Mr. Fitch was one of the founders of the Maccabean Literary Circle and served as president for two years (12 May 1911, 14, 26)

FRAID, Nathan J., is the president of the Board of Trade, Cornwall, Ont., age 45, who came to Canada about twenty years ago settling in that city. He started with a small store and has built a large business. He has served as alderman of Cornwall for several terms. He is a governor of the Cornwall General Hospital. He is "an example of the class and calibre of our co-religionists who landed on these hospitable shores some twenty to thirty-five years ago. These men were respected and esteemed in their own town or village in Eastern Europe, and it is, therefore, only natural that the same good feeling should exist for them in

---

Hebrew Consumptive Aid Association

ILLUSTRATED LECTURES

on

"TUBERCULOSIS" by Dr. J. B. Fish

Supt. Mount Sinai Sanatorium

and

"Jewish Activities—Montreal and Canada"

By Maxwell Lightstone.

at the

BARON DE HIRSCH INSTITUTE

SUNDAY, JUNE 1st, 1913, at 8 p. m.

Tickets, - - 25c. and 50c.

SUMMER DANCE

Under the auspices of the

Young Ladies Zionist and Literary Society

and the

Young Men's Zionist and Literary Society

on

THURSDAY, JUNE 12th, 1913

at the

AUDITORIUM HALL

Tickets from Members   Price, Fifty Cents

---

this country of their adoption." He is married to the former Rebecca Friedman, daughter of Mrs. N. Friedman, of Montreal (26 Feb. 1909, 12, 11)

GOLTMAN, Dr. Max, has been elected head of health department in Memphis, Tenn. where he now lives. Dr. Goltman lived in Montreal fifteen years ago. He moved to the coal districts of Pennsylvania where he gained experience as a surgeon before locating to Memphis. He was a lecturer at the university and was attached to the city hospitals (11 Feb. 1910, 13, 13)

GORDON, Rabbi Nathan, is the spiritual leader of Temple Emanu-El, of Montreal, who was appointed a lecturer in the Department of Oriental Languages and Literature at McGill University last Mon. night. Rabbi Gordon is a graduate of Hebrew Union College and the University fo Cincinnati. He came to Montreal in Sept. 1906 and is chairman of the FZSC Press Bureau. Simon Kirsch, M.A., is the only other Jewish member of the teaching staff at McGill (8 Jan. 1909, 12, 4)

GREEN, S. Hart, was elected to the Manitoba Legislature for North Winnipeg. Mr. Green was born in St. John, N.B. twenty-four years ago and is the son of Louis Green, of that city. About ten years ago, he came to Montreal with his father and was in the cigar business for three years. He left Montreal and returned to St. John to study law which he graduated with honors. He then moved to Winnipeg two years ago and commenced practice. Mr. Green is believed to be the youngest member of any legislature in Canada. He won by over 500 votes taking the seat from the Conservatives. "Of fine appearance, a fluent speaker and sincere manners, he has gained the confidence of his electors and we feel sure that this has not been misplaced." Mr. Green is a nephew of Mrs. Gustave Fischel, of Montreal (15 July 1910, 13, 35)

HARRIS, Major Samuel, son of Mr. and Mrs. Nathan Harris, of Perth Australia, who saw service in the South African war, is a Vancouver businessman. At the outbreak of hostilities, he was a lieutenant in an Australian regiment. He volunteered for service in the 5th Victorian Mounted Rifles and was mentioned in despatches on several occasions. "Before peace was proclaimed, he had acted as president of the military Court Martial at Cape Town and also as officer in charge of the Forts. Major Harris was at that time only in his 24th year, which we believe to be one of the youngest, if not he youngest, Major in the British forces." (16 July 1909, 12, 31)

HIRSCH, Michael, was elected president of the

Montefiore Club in Montreal for the fifth time at the thirty-first annual meeting held last Mon. evening. Born in Richmond, Que. on Feb. 7, 1864, the son of Mr. and Mrs. Jacob Hirsch, he came to Montreal with his parents in 1875. Mr. and Mrs. Hirsch moved to Montreal "...in order to secure a proper education in religion and Hebrew for his children. After graduation from the McGill Normal School in 1879, Michael Hirsch went to New York where he trained in the cigar manufacturing industry. He returned to Montreal in 1882 and entered the retail cigar business. He then entered the wholesale manufacturing business and for the past seventeen years has been in business with his father and brothers in the well-known Canadian firm of J. Hirsch & Sons Ltd. In 1885, he married Miss Estelle Jacobs, the daughter of Morris Jacobs, of Montreal. They have two sons. Mr. Hirsch served as secretary of the Shaar Hashomayim Congregation for several years and has been an active member of the Montefiore Club almost from its inception. He was vice-president of the Dominion Cigar Manufacturers' Association at its founding and has served as president on several occasions (29 Sept. 1911, 14, 46)

KIRSCH, Simon, son of Mr. and Mrs. Abraham Kirsch, of Montreal, received the degree of Doctor of Philosophy at the McGill University annual convocation on May 11, 1910. Dr. Kirsch was educated at Dufferin school and the Montreal High School. He finished his fourth year arts in biology at McGill. He received his M.A. in 1907. That year he wrote a thesis which was read before the Royal Society of Canada and later published. During the summer of 1908 he was appointed botanist at the Marine Biological Laboratory at St. Andrews-by-the-Sea. His research work will soon be published by the government. Dr. Kirsch leaves soon for Madison, Wisc., where he has been appointed to the United States Dept. of Agriculture in the Forestry Service (27 May 1910, 13, 28)

LAUTERMAN, Major M., has been appointed medical officer in charge of Mounted Troops on the Canadian Coronation Contingent. His contingent sails on the Empress of Ireland from Quebec on June 2, 1911. Dr. Lauterman has served in the militia for ten years. He joined the 6th Duke of Connaught's Royal Canadian Hussars as a subaltern. It "...can never be said of him that he shirked his duty no matter how irksome or inconvenient. This he did from a high sense of duty, and in the hope that by his actions he would encourage other Jewish young men to join the Militia." Major Lauterman was born in Ontario in 1873. He has lived in Montreal with his parents since 1878. He graduated McGill University and is Jewish House Surgeon at the Montreal Maternity and Royal Victoria Hospitals. Dr. Lauterman studied in the leading hospitals of Europe. He believes the time is right for the establishment of a Jewish hospital in Montreal (19 May 1911, 14, 27)

LEVIN, Rabbi J.K., has been minister of Shaarey Shomayim Congregation in Winnipeg since 1907. Rabbi Levin was born in 1880 and received his early education at the Liverpool Hebrew School. He graduated from Liverpool High School and in 1896 was awarded the Moses Marsden entrance scholarhip to Jews' College, London, England. In 1900 he obtained the practioner's certificate for Hebrew at Jews' College. In 1904 he received his B.A. from London University. From 1904 to 1907, Mr. Levin was visiting chaplain to the Aldershot Jewish community and chaplain to Jewish soldiers stationed there. During this time, he studied Gemara and Poskim with Rabbi Avigdor Chaikin, the spiritual head of the Federation of Synagogues in East London and renowned Talmudic scholar. Rabbi Levin served as prison chaplain at Pentonville for a brief period in 1907. Then on the recommendation of Chief Rabbi Dr. Herman Adler, he received the call to Winnipeg. The day before sailing for Canada he was married to Miss Minnie Sumeray by his brother, Rabbi Walter Levin, minister of the North London Synagogue. Since coming to Winnipeg, Rabbi Levin has done much to foster good relations between Christians and Jews and has frequently addressed non-Jewish audiences on Jewish subjects. He has also fought the influence of apostate Jews. Rabbi Levin was elected a member of the Protestant Ministerial Association and is secretary of the local B'nai Brith Lodge (17 Feb. 1911, 14, 14)

LIGHTSTONE, Bernard, of Montreal, graduated at the head of his class in the final year of dentistry at McGill University. He obtained seven honors in various dental courses in the Faculty of Dentistry and has been appointed a demonstrator at the dental clinic in the Montreal General Hospital. Dr. Lightstone is the son of Michael Lightstone, of Montreal, and a brother of Dr. Lightstone, now living in England (9 Aug. 1912, 15, 35)

SAMUEL, Jacob L., profile of the longest serving trustee and honorary officer of the "Shearith Israel", the Corporation of Spanish and Portuguese Jews in Montreal. Mr. Samuel was born in London, England and came to Montreal as a young man in 1855. "Probably no man living among the Jews of Montreal to-day has had so long a career in communal activities, and there are few men who have been more popular or more richly merited the high esteem of the Jewish citizens of this city than Mr. Samuel." He was a long-time board member and past president of the Young Men's Hebrew Benevolent Society. Mr. Samuel posesses an exceptional tenor voice and has sung in the congregational choir for the past fifty-five years. In 1860, he sang before the present King Edward, when as Prince of Wales, he visited Montreal. Among those attending a testimonial last Sun. in his honor were:- Mr. and Mrs. Clarence I. de Sola, Mr. and Mrs. David Levi, Israel Rubenstein, Harris Vineberg, Miss K. Morris, I. Rose, Israel Blumenthal and M. Levitt (10 Dec. 1909, 13, 4)

SAMUEL, Jacob L., was elected president of "Shearith Israel" the Corporation of Spanish and Portuguese Jews of Montreal at the annual meeting held Sun. aft., May 7, 1911. Mr. Samuel "...is a veteran Jewish communal worker, he having held various communal offices in this city uninterruptedly for a period of fifty-six years. Mr. Samuel is an excellent example of that highest type of Jew known as a "shool man;" for his whole life has been largely devoted to shool work." Mr. Samuel was born in London, England. He came to Montreal in 1855 as a young man and immediately joined the Spanish and Portuguese Congregation. He was soon elected to the Board of Trustees and has served for fifty-six years. He has been honorary secretary for fifty-one years (12 May 1911, 14, 26)

SIMON, George, of Alexandria, Ont., is the only Jewish alderman holding office in Canada this year, according to a search made by The Canadian Jewish Times. Others have been A. Rosenthal, of Ottawa, Mr. Fraid, of Cornwall, and M. Finkelstein, of Winnipeg. At age 24, Alderman Simon is probably the youngest city father in Canada, having been elected Dec. 27, 1909. He was born in Brantford, Ont., in 1886, the son of Mr. and Mrs. Isaac Simon, who moved thirteen years ago to the town of Alexandria, Glengarry County. George Simon is not only a prosperous merchant in this town of Scottish descent, but also a free-mason and secretary of the local hockey club. "It is said that there are no Jews in Scotland, because the canny Scot is too shrewd for the Jew, and in fact is the only man who can beat him in business. In this instance, however, our co-religionist has held his own with them." (28 Jan. 1910, 13, 11)

VINEBERG, Solomon, age 24, son of J.L. Vineberg, of Montreal, has been appointed instructor of political economy at the State University of Iowa. He takes up his duties there next month. Mr. Vineberg studied at the Sherbrooke High School before entering McGill University in 1909 where he specialized in political economy. He then entered Columbia University in New York where he obtained his M.A. "Mr. Vineberg's brilliant scolastic successes must be as keen a source of pleasure to his parents and many relatives, as it is to his numerous friends. Born in Montreal, he is well known among us, and his progress has been watched with interest and admiration...That he will adorn the profession he has adopted, cannot be doubted, and the good wishes of Montreal Jewry will follow him wherever he may be." (20 Aug. 1909, 12, 36)

BIRTH ANNOUNCEMENTS

ABRAMOVITZ, Mr. and Mrs. D., on Oct. 9, 1910, at 161 York St., Toronto, a son (11 Oct. 1910, 13, 48)

ABRAMOWITZ, Mr. and Mrs. Leon, in Winnipeg, a son. The Brith Milah was held Sat. Jan. 16, 1909 (29 Jan. 1909, 12, 7)

ABRAMSKY, Mr. and Mrs. Alex., in Kingston, Ont., on Jan. 4, 1912, a son. The Brith Milah took place on Jan. 12th at their residence, 104 Queen St. The mohel was Rev. Berkovitz, of Toronto (26 Jan. 1912, 15, 11)

ADELSTEIN, Mr. and Mrs. L., 961 St. Hubert St., Montreal, on May 28, 1909, a daughter (11 June 1909, 12, 26)

ADELSTEIN, Mr. and Mrs. Louis, at 961 St. Hubert St., Montreal, a son (19 May 1911, 14, 27)

ADELSTEIN, Mr. and Mrs. Michael, 27 Esplanade Ave., Montreal, on Feb. 13, 1911, a son (17 Feb. 1911, 14, 14)

ALBERT, Mr. and Mrs. S., on Aug. 6, 1911, at 1719 Park Ave., Montreal, a daughter (25 Aug. 1911, 14, 41)

ALBERT, Mr. and Mrs. Sam, 1719 Park Ave., Montreal, on Dec. 20, 1912, a daughter (3 Jan. 1913, 16, 4)

ALEXANDER, Mr. and Mrs. Joseph, at Ottawa, on Nov. 4, 1909, a daughter (12 Nov. 1909, 12, 48)

ARAKIE COHEN, Mr. and Mrs. E., (née Ruth Hast Jacobs) on June 20, 1910, at 143 Polson Ave., Winnipeg, a son (8 July 1910, 13, 34)

ARON, Mr. and Mrs. A., on Feb. 26, 1910, at 217 St. Lawrence St., Montreal, a son (4 March 1910, 13, 16)

ARON, Mr. and Mrs. A., on Fri. Feb. 10, 1911, at 219 St. Lawrence Blvd., Montreal, a daughter (17 March 1911, 14, 18)

ARON, Mr. and Mrs. Adolph, on June 26, 1912, at 108 St. Lawrence St., Montreal, a daughter (28 June 1912, 15, 29)

BACAL, Mr. and Mrs. A., of Montmagny, Que., on Aug. 5, 1913, a son (15 Aug. 1913, 16, 36)

BALINSKY, Mr. and Mrs., at 86a Rivard St., Montreal, on Aug. 9, 1909, a daughter (20 Aug. 1909, 12, 36)

BAZAR, Mr. and Mrs., 25 Esplanade Ave., Montreal, celebrated the Brith Milah of their infant son, Benjamin B. Bazar. Rev. Judelson collected $10 for the Talmud Torah Anshe Sephard. Two trees in the Herzl Wald were subscribed for in the name of Benjamin Bazar and one by Lyon Hoffman in the name of his daughter, S. Rachel Hoffman (27 Jan. 1911, 14, 11)

BEAR, Mr. and Mrs., of Saskatoon, celebrated the Brith Milah of their infant son, Myer (29 Nov. 1912, 15, 51)

BERCOVITCH, Mr. and Mrs. Peter, on Feb. 6, 1911, at Selby Ave. W., Westmount, Que., a daughter (10 Feb. 1911, 14, 13)

BERNSTEIN, Mr. and Mrs., 2515a Clarke St., Montreal, on Nov. 12, 1913, a daughter (14 Nov. 1913, 16, 49)

BERNSTEIN, Mr. and Mrs. D.H., on May 10, 1910, at the Montreal Maternity Hospital, a son (20 May 1910, 13, 27)

BERNSTEIN, Mr. and Mrs. E.G., Henri-Julien St., Montreal, celebrated the Brith Milah of their infant son, Hillel at their residence on Sun. Sept. 29, 1913. "A very notable Zionistic gathering participated in this celebration, and many appropriate speeches were delivered, the principal one by Mr. Hyam Bernstein, the Doyen Zionist of Canada." Twenty-nine olive trees in the Herzl Wald were subscribed for in the name of Hillel (10 Oct. 1913, 16, 44)

BILSKY, Mr. and Mrs. A.M., on July 6, 1910, a daughter (15 July 1910, 13, 35)

BLANKSTEIN, Mr. and Mrs. M., 258 Ontario St. E., Montreal, celebrate the Brith Milah of their infant son today at 12 noon (11 Feb. 1910, 13, 13)

TEL. EAST 3568

Rev. M. Bloomenfeld

PRACTICAL MOHEL

פראקטישער מוהל

Residence, 456 St. Dominique St. - Montreal

BLOOMFIELD, Mr. and Mrs. David, at 200 Cherrier St., Montreal, on March 23, 1909, a daughter (9 April, 1909, 12, 17)

BLOOMFIELD, Mr. and Mrs. Harry, on April 10, 1910, at 92 Pine Ave. E., Montreal, a daughter (15 April 1910, 13, 22)

BLOOMFIELD, Mr. and Mrs. Samuel (née Jeanette Davis), on June 9, 1911, at 22 Cameron Road, Seven Kings, Ilford, Eng., a daughter, Hannah Bessie (30 June 1911, 14, 33)

BLUMENTHAL, Mr. and Mrs. S., on Fri. April 7, 1911, at 1630 Mance St., Montreal, a daughter (21 April 1911, 14, 23)

BLUMER, Mr. and Mrs. D., on Thurs. Sept. 8, 1910, at 233 Prince Arthur St., Montreal, a daughter (16 Sept. 1910, 13, 44)

BLUMER, Mr. and Mrs. L., on March 17, 1911, at 476 Sanguinet St., Montreal, a daughter (31 March 1911, 14, 20)

BLUMER, Mr. and Mrs., of Montreal, celebrated the Brith Milah of their infant son, Moses (29 Nov. 1912, 15, 51)

BOULKIND, Mr. and Mrs. S., on May 2, 1911, at 679 City Hall Ave., Montreal, a son (19 May 1911, 14, 27)

BRUKER, Mr. and Mrs. D.S., of Ottawa, on Oct. 23, 1909, in Montreal, a son (29 Oct. 1909, 12, 46)

CHAMPAGNSY, Mr. and Mrs., celebrated the Brith Milah of their son, Moses Clarence Champagnsy, on Sun. Sept. 5, 1909, at the home of Mr. and Mrs. R. Ness, 1726 St. Catherine St., Montreal (10 Sept. 1909, 12, 39)

CHORLTON, Mr. and Mrs. D. Marks, at 119 Union Ave., Montreal, on Aug. 28, 1909, a son (3 Sept. 1909, 12, 38)

CHORLTON, Mr. and Mrs. David M., 119 Union Ave., Montreal, on Sept. 23, 1913, a daughter (1 Oct. 1913, 16, 42-43)

CHORLTON, Mr. and Mrs. David Marks, on Aug. 29, 1911, at 119 Union Ave., Montreal, a daughter (1 Sept. 1911, 14, 42)

CIPIN, Mr. and Mrs. Joseph, of Glace Bay, N.S., celebrated the Brith Milah of their infant son at their home on Sun. aft., Oct. 26, 1913. The Brith was performed by Rev. Levin, assisted by Rev. Abramowitz. Messrs. Lurie and N. Michael collected $5.00 for the Zionist National Fund (21 Nov. 1913, 16, 50-51)

COHEN, Mr. and Mrs. A., 24 Durocher St., Montreal, at the Maternity Hospital on Fri. Nov. 7, 1913, a daughter (14 Nov. 1913, 16, 49)

COHEN, Mr. and Mrs. A.Z., on Thurs. May 19, 1910, at 4219 Western Ave., Montreal, a daughter (20 May 1910, 13, 27)

COHEN, Mr. and Mrs. I., at 4262 Western Ave., Westmount, Que., on Jan. 22, 1910, a daughter (28 Jan. 1910, 13, 11)

COHEN, Mr. and Mrs. J., at the Maternity Hospital, Montreal, on Oct. 23, 1909, a daughter (5 Nov. 1909, 12, 47)

COHEN, Mr. and Mrs. Lyon, on Mon. Sept. 19, 1910, at 8 Tower Ave., Montreal, a daughter (23 Sept. 1910, 13, 45)

COHEN, Mr. and Mrs. S., on March 9, 1912, at 1365 Cadieux St., Montreal, a daughter (15 March 1912, 15, 18)

COHEN, Mr. and Mrs. Samuel, on Aug. 13, 1912, at 2014 St. Lawrence Blvd., Montreal, a daughter (16 Aug. 1912, 15, 36)

COHEN, Rev. Louis and Mrs., on Sat. July 30, 1910, at Huron St., Toronto, a son (5 Aug. 1910, 13, 38)

DAVIS, Mr. and Mrs. Harry E., Elm Ave., Montreal, on April 13, 1910, a son (15 April 1910, 13, 22)

DE SOLA, Mr. and Mrs. Clarence I., of Montreal, on Tues. Aug. 9, 1910, a daughter (12 Aug. 1910, 13, 39)

DIAMOND, Mr. and Mrs. F., in Montreal, on Jan. 27, 1910, a daughter (28 Jan. 1910, 13, 11)

DIAMOND, Mr. and Mrs. S., of Ottawa, celebrated the Brith Milah of their first born son. "Rabbi S. Fyne spoke impressively upon the initiation of the child into the covenant of Abraham." (4 July 1913, 16, 30)

DIRECTOR, Mr. and Mrs. I., in Prince Rupert, B.C., on April 11, 1910, a daughter (6 May 1910, 13, 25)

DRAIMIN, Mr. and Mrs. Chas., on Sun. April 9, 1911, at their residence, Beatrice St., Toronto, a son (21 April 1911, 14, 23)

DWORKIN, Mr. and Mrs. A.J., on Oct. 6, 1910, at 64 Elizabeth St., Toronto, a daughter (11 Oct. 1910, 13, 48)

DWORKIN, Mr. and Mrs. H., her first child, a daughter, "Chano Elke", named after Mrs. Dworkin's maternal grandparents (28 June 1912, 15, 29)

DWORKIN, Mr. and Mrs. L., of Ottawa, celebrated the Brith Milah of their infant son, on Sun. March 19, 1911. L. Petegorsky, vice-president of the Young Men's Zionist Association, raised $8.05 for the National Fund (31 March 1911, 14, 20)

ELKIN, Mr. and Mrs. J., on March 28, 1911, at 61 Esplanade Ave., Montreal, a son (31 March 1911, 14, 20)

ELLISON, Mr. and Mrs. E., at 417 Sanguinet St., Montreal, on March 19, 1909, a son (26 March, 1909, 12, 15)

EPSTEIN, Mr. and Mrs. J., of Edmonton, celebrated the Brith Milah of their infant son, Gershon Abraham Epstein (14 April 1911, 14, 22)

FINKELMAN, Mr. and Mrs. Harry, formerly of Eyebrow, Sask., now of Winnipeg, celebrated the Brith Milah of their second son on Sun. April 30, 1911 (5 May 1911, 14, 25)

FINKELMAN, Mr. and Mrs. Harry, of Eyebrow, Sask., on Mon. Sept. 12, 1910, a son (23 Sept. 1910, 13, 45)

FINKLEMAN, Mr. and Mrs. Harry (née Dolly Isaacs), in Selkirk, Man., a son (15 Jan. 1909, 12, 5)

FINKLESTEIN, Mr. and Mrs. M., of Winnipeg, a daughter (26 March, 1909, 12, 15)

FISCHMAN, Mr. and Mrs., on July 27, 1912, at 422 Gladstone Ave., Ottawa, a son (2 Aug. 1912, 15, 34)

FISHMAN, Mr. and Mrs. P., on Feb. 23, 1910, at 849 St. Hubert St., Montreal, a son (4 March 1910, 13, 16)

FRAENKEL, Mr. and Mrs. H., on Mon. Dec. 6, 1910, at 460 Strathcona Ave., Westmount, Que., a son (9 Dec. 1910, 14, 4)

FRAID, Mr. and Mrs. N.J., in Cornwall, Ont., on Sun. March 6, 1910, a daughter (11 March 1910, 13, 17)

FRANKLIN, Mr. and Mrs. F., 89 St. Genevieve St., Montreal, a daughter (London, Eng., papers please copy) (13 May 1910, 13, 26)

FRANKLIN, Mr. and Mrs. Harry B., (née Miss B. Abrahams, of Montreal), at Allston, Mass., on Oct. 11, 1909, a daughter (15 Oct. 1909, 12, 44)

FRANKLIN, Mr. and Mrs. W.A., in Ottawa, on Dec. 19, 1909, a son (31 Dec. 1909, 13, 7)

FREED, Mr. and Mrs. Harry, on Nov. 3, 1912, at 354 Lafontaine Park, Montreal, a son (8 Nov. 1912, 15, 48)

FREEDMAN, Mr. and Mrs., 1336 Notre Dame St. West, Montreal, on Jan. 17, 1909, a daughter (St. John, N.B., papers copy) (22 Jan. 1909, 12, 6)

FREEDMAN, Mr. and Mrs. Albert, on March 2, 1911, at 354 Oliver Ave., Westmount, Que., a daughter (10 March 1911, 14, 17)

FREEDMAN, Mr. and Mrs. H.W., on Sat. April 23, 1910, at 764 St. Joseph Blvd., Montreal, a son (29 April 1910, 13, 24)

FREEDMAN, Mr. and Mrs. Harry, 124 Clandeboye Ave., Westmount, Que., on Jan. 23, 1912, a son (26 Jan. 1912, 15, 11)

FREEMAN, Mr. and Mrs. Hyman, at 25 Cuthbert St., Montreal, on Aug 28, 1909, a daughter (Manchester, Liverpool and Glasgow papers copy) (3 Sept. 1909, 12, 38)

FRIEDMAN, Mr. and Mrs. B., on Fri. June 9, 1911, at 26 Guilbault St., Montreal, a son (16 June 1911, 14, 31)

GABRIEL, Mr. and Mrs. J.S., (née S.R. Livinson), on April 14, 1913, at the Montreal Maternity Hospital, a daughter (18 April 1913, 16, 19)

GABRIEL, Mr. and Mrs. J.S. (née Miss S.R. Livinson), at 189 Craig St., Montreal, on June 4, 1909, a daughter (11 June 1909, 12, 26)

GELBER, Mr. and Mrs. Louis, on Sun. Dec. 4, 1910, at 293 Huron St., Toronto, a daughter (9 Dec. 1910, 14, 4)

GLICKMAN, Mr. and Mrs. P.B., 320 Elm Ave., Westmount, Que., on July 25, 1913, at Beloeil, a son (1 Aug. 1913, 16, 34)

GLICKMAN, Mr. and Mrs. Philip, at 40 St. Louis Square, Montreal, on June 12, 1909, a daughter (18 June 1909, 12, 27)

GLICKMAN, Mr. and Mrs. S.M., at 47a St. Famille St., Montreal, on Oct. 3, 1909, a daughter (8 Oct. 1909, 12, 43)

GLUCK, Mr. and Mrs. Samuel, of Ottawa, on Nov. 15, 1913, a daughter (21 Nov. 1913, 16, 50-51)

GODINSKY, Mr. and Mrs. N.H., at 11 Souvenir Ave., Montreal, on Feb. 6, 1910, a daughter (11 Feb. 1910, 13, 13)

GOLD, Mr. and Mrs. J., at 1434 Simard Ave., Montreal, on Feb. 5, 1910, a daughter (11 Feb. 1910, 13, 13)

GOLDBERG, Mr. and Mrs. H., on Aug. 10, 1911, at 352 Cadieux St., Montreal, a son (11 Aug. 1911, 14, 39)

GOLDBERG, Mr. and Mrs. Max, at 54 Dorchester St. W., Montreal, on Aug. 17, 1909, a daughter (20 Aug. 1909, 12, 36)

GOLDBERG, Mr. and Mrs. S. (née Miss R. Diamond, of Sault Ste. Marie, Ont.) on Oct. 31, 1910, at 2003 W. Division St., Chicago, Ill., a son (2 Dec. 1910, 14, 3)

GOLDENBERG, Mr. and Mrs. J.S., on Tues. July 26, 1910, at Terauley St., Toronto, twin sons (5 Aug. 1910, 13, 38)

GOLDENBURG, Mr. and Mrs. M., of Three Rivers, Que., on Sun. Jan. 15, 1911, a son (27 Jan. 1911, 14, 11)

GOLDNER, Mr. and Mrs. A., on Jan. 29, 1911, at 1748 Mance St., Montreal, a son (24 Feb. 1911, 14, 15)

GOLDNER, Mr. and Mrs. A.J., 591c Berri St., Montreal, on March 16, 1914, a son (20 March 1914, 17, 12)

GOLDNER, Mr. and Mrs. A.J., at 591c Berri St., Montreal, on Nov. 20, 1909, a son (3 Dec. 1909, 13, 3)

GOLDNER, Mr. and Mrs. L., on April 1, 1910, at 559a Berri, Montreal, a daughter (8 April 1910, 13, 21)

GOLDSTEIN, Mr. and Mrs. Edward, on Oct. 4, 1910, at Elgin Ave., Westmount, Que., a daughter (7 Oct. 1910, 13, 47)

GOLDSTEIN, Mr. and Mrs. Rueben (née Minnie Tobias), on Jan. 20, 1911, a son (stillborn) (3 Feb. 1911, 14, 12)

GOLTMAN, Mr. and Mrs. Robert, on Dec. 26, 1910, at 4637 Sherbrooke St., Westmount, Que., a son (30 Dec. 1910, 14, 7)

GREEN, Mr. and Mrs. S. Hart, of Winnipeg, celebrated the birth of their first born son (Louis), on Mon. June 23, 1913. Mr. Green is a prominent lawyer and MPP for North Winnipeg in the Manitoba Legislature (18 July 1913, 16, 32)

GREENBERG, Mr. and Mrs. F.F. De Young, celebrated the Brith Milah of their infant son at their residence, 197 Grace St., Toronto, on Tues. Feb. 7, 1911 (10 Feb. 1911, 14, 13)

GREENBERG, Mr. and Mrs. M., at St. Hyacinthe, Que., on May 4, 1909, a daughter (14 May, 1909, 12, 22)

GUILAROFF, Eugene and Annie, on Mon. Jan. 13, 1913, at 288 Laval Ave., Montreal, a daughter (17 Jan. 1913, 16, 6)

HAID, Mr. and Mrs. M., formerly of Halifax, N.S., now of Winnipeg, a son (26 March, 1909, 12, 15)

HALTER, Mr. and Mrs. Samuel (née Kitty Isaacs), in Winnipeg, on April 23, 1911, a son, Benjamin (5 May 1911, 14, 25)

HARRIS, Mr. and Mrs. G., 21 Craig St. E., Montreal, celebrated the Brith Milah of their infant son. $22.50 was collected for the two Talmud Torahs (16 June 1911, 14, 31)

HARRIS, Mr. and Mrs. H., on Thurs. June 8, 1911, at 71 Colonial Ave., Montreal, a son (16 June 1911, 14, 31)

HART, Mr. and Mrs. Allen J., on Wed. Aug. 3, 1910, at 600 Argyle Ave., Westmount, Que., a daughter (12 Aug. 1910, 13, 39)

HART, Mr. and Mrs. H.G., of Montreal, celebrated the Brith Milah of their infant son. $1.50 was collected for the FZSC Land Fund (17 Feb. 1911, 14, 14)

HAYES, Mr. and Mrs. B.J., on Sat. Dec. 3, 1910, at 889 Mount Royal Ave., Montreal, a daughter (9 Dec. 1910, 14, 4)

HEINSHEIMER, Mr. and Mrs. Arthur, at 426 Mt. Stephen Ave., Montreal, on Sept. 18, 1909, a daughter (24 Sept. 1909, 12, 41)

HERMAN, Mr. and Mrs. L., at 731 St. Lawrence St., Montreal, on Jan. 24, 1909, a son (29 Jan. 1909, 12, 7)

HERMANT, Mr. and Mrs. Percy, Sussex Court, Toronto, on Dec. 27, 1912, a son (3 Jan. 1913, 16, 4)

HOFFMAN, Mr. and Mrs. Harry, in Prince Rupert, B.C., on Feb. 4, 1910, a son (11 March 1910, 13, 17)

HORWITZ, Mr. and Mrs. A., on Dec. 25, 1910, at 686 Berri St., Montreal, a daughter (30 Dec. 1910, 14, 7)

ISSENMAN, Mr. and Mrs. S., on March 5, 1910, at 56 Shearer St., Montreal, a daughter (11 March 1910, 13, 17)

JACKSON, Mr. and Mrs. A.H., on Sun. June 12, 1910, at 141 Stanley St., Montreal, a son (17 June 1910, 13, 31)

JACOBS, Mr. and Mrs. J.A., on Sat. Feb. 4, 1911, at 1014 Dorchester St. W., Montreal, a daughter (10 Feb. 1911, 14, 13)

JACOBS, Mr. and Mrs. Lyon W., on Aug. 20, 1913, at 408 Henri Julien Ave., Montreal, a daughter (29 Aug. 1913, 16, 38)

JOSEFO, Mr. and Mrs. Julius, 144 Elgin St., Montreal, on Jan. 31, 1911, a daughter (3 Feb. 1911, 14, 12)

KAMMAN, Mr. and Mrs. Maurice J., 322 Yonge St., Toronto, on Sun. Sept. 11, 1910, a daughter (23 Sept. 1910, 13, 45)

KARP, Mr. and Mrs., 39 St. Lawrence St., Montreal, on Thurs. Dec. 4, 1913, a son (12 Dec. 1913, 17, 1)

KAUFMAN, Mr. and Mrs. R., at Lake Macaza, Que., on April 15, 1911, a son (12 May 1911, 14, 26)

KEYFITZ, Mr. and Mr Arthur, 19 Staynor Ave., Westmount, Que., on June 29, 1913, a son (4 July 1913, 16, 30)

KIRSCH, Dr. and Mrs. S., on May 21, 1911, at 181 Esplanade Ave., Montreal, a son (26 May 1911, 14, 28)

KITZ, Mr. and Mrs. Harry, on Nov. 29, 1910, in Halifax, N.S., a daughter (16 Dec. 1910, 14, 5)

KLINEBERG, Mr. and Mrs. L., 917 St. Denis St., Montreal, on Oct. 27, 1913, a daughter (31 Oct. 1913, 16, 47)

KONEL, Mr. and Mrs. M., of Glace Bay, N.S., celebrated the Brith Milah of their infant son, on May 19, 1913. Three olive trees were purchased in the Herzl Wald in the name of the family (30 May 1913, 16, 25)

KORNFELD, Rabbi and Mrs. Joseph, in Columbus, Ohio, on Nov. 15, 1909, a daughter (3 Dec. 1909, 13, 3)

KOWALSON, Mr. and Mrs. Max, in Winnipeg, on April 28, 1911, a son (5 May 1911, 14, 25)

KREHM, Mr. and Mrs. H., on Thurs. Dec. 29, 1910, at Cameron St., Toronto, a daughter (6 Jan. 1911, 14, 8)

LANDE, Mr. and Mrs. I., at 513 Grosvenor Ave., Montreal, on March 29, 1909, a daughter (2 April 1909, 12, 16)

LANDE, Mr. and Mrs. Nathan, in Montreal, on Sun. May 16, 1909, a son (Ottawa and Hamilton papers copy) (21 May, 1909, 12, 23)

LANDE, Mr. and Mrs. Nathan, of Montreal, celebrated the Brith Milah of their son, on Mon. May 24, 1909. Mr. and Mrs. H. Freiman and Mr. and Mrs. A.J. Freiman, of Ottawa, were present (28 May 1909, 12, 24)

LANDE, Mr. and Mrs. Nathan, on March 29, 1911, at 482 Strathcona Ave., Montreal, a daughter (7 April 1911, 14, 21)

LANG, Mr. and Mrs. H., on Wed. Aug. 30, 1911, at 667 St. Urbain St., Montreal, a son (8 Sept. 1911, 14, 43)

LANG, Mr. and Mrs. Harry, Bleury St., Montreal, celebrated the Brith Milah of their son Joshua Joseph Lang, on Sept. 30, 1909. Seventeen trees were subscribed for in his name in the Herzl Wald (8 Oct. 1909, 12, 43)

LASKY, Mr. and Mrs. B., at Ste. Hyacinthe, Que., on May 9, 1911, a son (12 May 1911, 14, 26)

LAUER, Mr. and Mrs. Ben, in Winnipeg, their first born son, Harold Isadore (3 Nov. 1911, 14, 51)

LEHBERG, Mr. and Mrs., in Winnipeg, on April 15, 1911, a daughter, Ruth May (5 May 1911, 14, 25)

LEHRER, Mr. and Mrs. L., 448 Mt. Stephen Ave., Westmount, Que., on Sun. Dec. 7, 1913, a daughter (12 Dec. 1913, 17, 1)

LEVI, Mr. and Mrs. William, of St. John, N.B., on Aug. 1, 1913, a daughter (8 Aug. 1913, 16, 35)

LEVIN, Mr. and Mrs. M.L., (née Coviensky) on Wed. Nov. 1, 1911, at 1576 Esplanade Ave., Montreal, a son (3 Nov. 1911, 14, 51)

LEVIN, Mr. and Mrs. M.L., 1576 Esplanade Ave., Montreal, on Sun. May 11, 1913, a son (16 May 1913, 16, 23)

LEVIN, Mr. and Mrs. Philip, at 968 St. Urbain St., Montreal, on Tues. Dec. 21, 1909, a son (31 Dec. 1909, 13, 7)

LEVIN, Rabbi and Mrs. J.K., of Winnipeg, on Sept. 17, 1910, a son (23 Sept. 1910, 13, 45)

LEVINE, Dr. and Mrs. S., on Sun. April 16, 1911, at 159 Beverley St., Toronto, a daughter (21 April 1911, 14, 23)

LEVINSON, Mr. and Mrs. B., 482 McDermott Ave., Winnipeg, a son (10 Dec. 1909, 13, 4)

LEVINSON, Mr. and Mrs. I., of Winnipeg, a son (1 Oct. 1913, 16, 42-43)

LEVITT, Mr. and Mrs. Joseph, (née Florence Tannenbaum), at 542b Mance St., Montreal, on Jan. 7, 1909, a son (Rochester, N.Y., papers copy) (15 Jan. 1909, 12, 5)

LEVITT, Mr. and Mrs. M.B., 2144 St. Hubert St., Montreal, on Sat. Sept. 3, 1910, a daughter (9 Sept. 1910, 13, 43)

LEVY, Mr. and Mrs. William, at Western Ave., Montreal, on March 27, 1909, a son (2 April 1909, 12, 16)

LITWIN, Mr. and Mrs. H., at 1537 Mance St., Montreal, on Aug. 16, 1909, a son (20 Aug. 1909, 12, 36)

LITWIN, Mr. and Mrs. Samuel, 771 City Hall Ave., Montreal, on Aug. 21, 1911, a son (25 Aug. 1911, 14, 41)

LIVSHITZ, Mr. and Mrs. J., at 12 Albina St., Montreal, on Sun. April 18, 1909, a daughter (30 April, 1909, 12, 20)

LONN, Mr. and Mrs. J., on Fri. April 7, 1911, at 135 Duference St., Montreal, a son (14 April 1911, 14, 22)

LONN, Mr. and Mrs. J.S., on Sun. May 1, 1910, at 6 Dorchester St. W., Montreal, a daughter (27 May 1910, 13, 28)

MANUEL, Mr. and Mrs. Louis, of Glace Bay, N.S., celebrated the Brith Milah of their infant son on Sun. March 15, 1914 at their home. $9.50 was subscribed for the purchase of olive trees in Palestine (27 March 1914, 17, 13)

MARGOLIES, Mr. and Mrs. G., in Winnipeg, on Sun. April 25, 1909, a son (30 April, 1909, 12, 20)

MARGOLIES, Mr. and Mrs. G., of Winnipeg, celebrated the Brith Milah of their first-born son, on Sun. May 2, 1909 (7 May, 1909, 12, 21)

MARGOSCHES, Mr. and Mrs. Max. B. (née Miss Anna Wolfe), 508 Besserer St., Ottawa, at the Maternity Hospital, on Sat. Aug. 17, 1912, a daughter (23 Aug. 1912, 15, 37)

MAROM, Mr. and Mrs. Morris, 380 Mitchison St., Montreal, celebrated the Brith Milah of their infant son. Rev. S. Goldstein raised $16.00 to be distributed equally among the three Talmud Torahs and the Mount Sinai Sanatorium for Consumptives (16 Aug. 1912, 15, 36)

MAYBACK, Mr. and Mrs., at their residence, McCaul St., Toronto, a son (5 May 1911, 14, 25)

MENDELSOHN, Mr. and Mrs. E., of Glace Bay, N.S., celebrated the Brith Milah of their infant son, on May 21, 1913. The ceremony was performed by Rev. Mr. Levin, assisted by Rev. Abramowitz (30 May 1913, 16, 25)

MENDELSOHN, Mr. and Mrs. M., on May 2, 1910, at 262 St. Elizabeth St., Montreal, a daughter (6 May 1910, 13, 25)

MICHAELS, Mr. and Mrs. C., on Mon. Jan. 23, 1911, at their residence, Villeneuve St., Montreal, a son (27 Jan. 1911, 14, 11)

MICHAELS, Mr. and Mrs. M., on June 21, 1911, at their residence, Elm Ave., Westmount, Que., a son (23 June 1911, 14, 32)

MICHAELS, Mr. and Mrs. Michael A., in Montreal, on March 29, 1910, a daughter (1 April 1910, 13, 20)

MILLER, Mr. and Mrs. H., of Sackville, N.B., celebrated the Brith Milah of their infant son, on Sun. April 23, 1911. Among those present were:- Mrs. R. Amder, of St. John; Mr. and Mrs. Charles Hoffman; Mr. and Mrs. Philip Corten;

Myer and Charles Sharpe; Abel Allen; Joseph Erron; M. Abrahams, of Amherst; E. Harris; Arthur Shaleck; Morrice Hoffman; Harry Ness and daughter Mrs. David Miller, of Montreal; Mrs. Max Litwick, of Ottawa; and Mrs. Landy, of Sackville (5 May 1911, 14, 25)

MITCHELL, Mr. and Mrs. M., on Thurs. Nov. 9, 1911, at 1438 St. Dominique St., Montreal, a son (17 Nov. 1911, 15, 1)

MORRIS, Mr. and Mrs. Arthur C., on April 24, 1910, at 84 St. Luke St., Montreal, a daughter (6 May 1910, 13, 25)

MOSES, Mr. and Mrs. Henry, 81 Beverly St., Toronto, celebrated the Brith Milah of their infant son on Mon. Feb. 28, 1910 (4 March 1910, 13, 16)

MOSS, Mr. and Mrs. I., on Sun. May 22, 1910, at 612 Cadieux St., Montreal, a daughter (27 May 1910, 13, 28)

MOZORE, Mr. and Mrs. J., at 40 Pine Ave., Montreal, a son (11 June 1909, 12, 26)

MYERS, Mr. and Mrs. Ben, on June 3, 1911, at 171 Main St. E., Hamilton, Ont., a son (16 June 1911, 14, 31)

NACHMANSON, Mr. and Mrs. Benjamin, at 40 McCaul St., Toronto, on Tues. Jan. 3, 1910, a son (14 Jan. 1910, 13, 9)

OGULNICK, Mr. and Mrs. L.M., 438 Clairmont Ave., Montreal, on Feb. 14, 1912, a daughter (16 Feb. 1912, 15, 14)

OGULNIK, Mr. and Mrs. S.M., at 438 Claremont Ave., Montreal, on Dec. 19, 1909, a son (24 Dec. 1909, 13, 6)

ORNSTEIN, Mr. and Mrs. I., of Roberval, Que., on Oct. 21, 1909, a son (29 Oct. 1909, 12, 46)

OSTROGURSKY, Mr. and Mrs., on March 15, 1914, at the Homeopathic Hospital, Montreal, a daughter (20 March 1914, 17, 12)

PHILIPS, Mr. and Mrs. J.F., at 430 Laurier Ave. West, Ottawa, on June 3, 1909, a son (11 June 1909, 12, 26)

POLONSKY, Mr. and Mrs. Billy, 10 Dorchester St. W., Montreal, on Sept. 20, 1913, a son (1 Oct. 1913, 16, 42-43)

POPKIN, Mr. and Mrs. H., 1461a St. Urbain St., Montreal, had a Brith Milah for their son, on Thurs. Jan. 28, 1909. J. Crown and M. Denenberg collected for charity (5 Feb. 1909, 12, 8)

POYANER, Mr. and Mrs. Myer, on Dec. 25, 1912, at 99 Elizabeth St., Montreal, a son (27 Dec. 1912, 16, 3)

PRESSER, Mr. and Mrs. Phillip, in Winnipeg, a daughter (Zippy Helen) (27 Jan. 1911, 14, 11)

RABINOVITCH, Dr. and Mrs. M., on Oct. 15, 1911, at the Montreal Maternity Hospital, a daughter (20 Oct. 1911, 14, 49)

RABINOVITCH, Mr. and Mrs. George, celebrated the Brith Milah of their infant son on Thurs. Dec. 11, 1913. Carl Rosenberg was chairman of the gathering and Rabbi Simon Glazer made a speech. I. Rabinovitch, father of the Baal Brith, inscribed the name of the new-born son in the Golden Book (19 Dec. 1913, 17, 2)

RILL, Mr. and Mrs. A., of 400 Mitcheson St., Montreal, on Thurs. March 7, 1912, a son (15 March 1912, 15, 18)

RILL, Mr. and Mrs. Abraham, 1637 Mance St., Montreal, on June 10, 1913, a son and daughter (13 June 1913, 16, 27)

RIPSTEIN, Mr. and Mrs. I., of Winnipeg, a son (26 March, 1909, 12, 15)

RIPSTEIN, Mr. and Mrs. Max, (née Adeline Pulver), in Winnipeg, on April 5, 1911, a son, Jerome (5 May 1911, 14, 25)

ROGUL, Mr. and Mrs. S., of Toronto, celebrated the Brith Milah of their son on Sun. Sept. 12, 1909 (1 Oct. 1909, 12, 42)

ROMAN, Mr. and Mrs. Marcus, at 1 St. Joseph Blvd., Montreal, on Oct. 14, 1909, a daughter (22 Oct. 1909, 12, 45)

ROSEN, Mr. and Mrs. E., in Winnipeg, a son (12 Sept. 1913, 16, 40)

ROSEN, Mr. and Mrs. J., 863 City Hall Ave., Montreal, on Sept. 14, 1909, a son (1 Oct. 1909, 12, 42)

ROSEN, Mr. and Mrs. J.S., on Oct. 30, 1911, at 44 Drolet St., Montreal, a son (10 Nov. 1911, 14, 52)

ROSENBERGER, Mr. and Mrs. M., on Sat. April 23, 1910, at 1120 Cadieux St., Montreal, a son (29 April 1910, 13, 24)

ROSENTHAL, Mr. and Mrs. Samuel, on Jan. 3, 1911, at 98 Carling Ave., Ottawa, a son (6 Jan. 1911, 14, 8)

ROST, Mr. and Mrs. Julius, 1340 St. Urbain St., Montreal, on March 16, 1913, a daughter, Malca Esther (18 April 1913, 16, 19)

ROTHMAN, Mr. and Mrs. A., on Wed. May 25, 1910, at 62 Lagauchetiere St. E., Montreal, a daughter (27 May 1910, 13, 28)

ROTSTEIN, Mr. and Mrs. A., 55 Oxford St., Toronto, celebrated the Brith Milah of their infant son at their home. Fourteen dollars was raised for the Jewish nursery (11 April 1913, 16, 18)

ROUTTENBERG, Mr. and Mrs. I., in Montreal, on April 9, 1912, a daughter (12 April 1912, 15, 22)

RUBIN, Dr. and Mrs. J., on Mon. Oct. 28, 1912, at Prince Arthur Apts., Montreal, a daughter (1 Nov. 1912, 15, 47)

RUBIN, Dr. and Mrs. J., Prince Arthur Apts., Montreal, on Tues. June 29, 1909, a son (2 July 1909, 12, 29)

RUBIN, Dr. and Mrs. J., Prince Arthur Apts., Montreal, on Tues. Sept. 29, 1911, a son (6 Oct. 1911, 14, 47)

RUBIN, Mr. and Mrs. C.S., at 65 Argyle Ave., Montreal, on Wed. Nov. 17, 1909, a son (3 Dec. 1909, 13, 3)

RUBINOVITCH, Mr. and Mrs. I.M., 4480 Sherbrooke St. W., Montreal, a daughter (24 May 1912, 15, 25)

RUBINOVITCH, Mr. and Mrs. J.B., at 989 St. Urbain St., Montreal, on April 26, 1909, a son (30 April, 1909, 12, 20)

RUSKIN, Mr. and Mrs., in Kingston, Ont., on Wed. Sept. 14, 1909, a son (24 Sept. 1909, 12, 41)

SAINER, Mr. and Mrs. C.B., on March 22, 1911, at 970 St. Urbain St., Montreal, a daughter (24 March 1911, 14, 19)

SAMUELS, Mr. and Mrs. Morris, at 57 Argyle Ave., Montreal, on Jan. 28, 1910, a son (4 Feb. 1910, 13, 12)

SAPERY, Mr. and Mrs. Louis, in New York, on May 2, 1910, a son (6 May 1910, 13, 25)

SCHLEIFER, Mr. and Mrs. H., 63 Mount Royal, Westmount, Que., a son (31 Oct. 1913, 16, 47)

SCHLEIFER, Mr. and Mrs. Hyman, 63 Mount Royal, celebrated the Brith Milah of their new born son on Thurs. Nov. 6, 1913 (14 Nov. 1913, 16, 49)

SCHWARTZ, Mr. and Mrs., celebrated the Brith Milah of their infant son (24 March 1911, 14, 19)

SCHWARTZ, Mr. and Mrs. F., in Montreal, on April 28, 1909, a son (7 May, 1909, 12, 21)

SCHWARTZMAN, Mr. and Mrs. Harry, on Mon. May 29, 1911, at 372 Rivard St., Montreal, a son (9 June 1911, 14, 30)

SHANKMAN, Mr. and Mrs. W., in Ottawa, Ont., a son (12 Aug. 1910, 13, 39)

SIEGEL, Mr. and Mrs. I.H., 129 Bathurst St., Toronto celebrated the Brith Milah of their son David, on Tues. July 6, 1909. Rev. M. Kaplan performed the ceremony (9 July 1909, 12, 30)

SILBERMAN, Mr. and Mrs. Harry, on May 18, 1910, at 100 Bridge St., Quebec City, a daughter (27 May 1910, 13, 28)

SILVER, Mr. and Mrs. Lazarus, Tupper St., Montreal, on Aug. 30, 1910, a son (2 Sept. 1910, 13, 42)

SILVERMAN, Mr. and Mrs. M.A., on March 1, 1913, at 191 Mount Royal Ave., W., Montreal, a son. Toronto, New York, Newark and Worcester papers please copy (14 March 1913, 16, 14)

SILVERSTONE, Mr. and Mrs. S. (née Stone), on Tues. Aug. 23, 1910, in Carbondale, Pa., a daughter (26 Aug. 1910, 13, 41)

SIMON, Mr. and Mrs. John, of Halifax, N.S., on Dec. 6, 1909, a daughter (10 Dec. 1909, 13, 4)

SINGER, Mr. and Mrs. Herman, 198 Park Ave., Montreal, on April 18, 1912, 15, a son (26 April 1912, 15, 24)

SINGER, Mr. and Mrs. Israel, at the Renfrew Apts., 205 Simcoe St., Toronto, on Oct. 31, 1909, a daughter (5 Nov. 1909, 12, 47)

SINGER, Mr. and Mrs. Israel, in Toronto, on Nov. 24, 1909, a daughter (10 Dec. 1909, 13, 4)

SINGER, Mr. and Mrs. L., on Sun. April 9, 1911, at their residence, Kendall St., Toronto, a son (21 April 1911, 14, 23)

SINGER, Mr. and Mrs. M., in Toronto, on Nov. 20, 1909, a daughter (10 Dec. 1909, 13, 4)

SIVITZ, Mr. and Mrs. H.N., 34 Cecil St., Toronto, celebrated the Brith Milah of their infant son last Tues. in the presence of nearly one hundred and fifty relatives and friends. Rabbi Sivitz, of Pittsburgh, the grandfather, was there for the occasion (3 Feb. 1911, 14, 12)

SOCIETY, Mr. and Mrs., celebrated the Brith Milah of their infant son (3 Feb. 1911, 14, 12)

SOLIN, Mr. and Mrs. M., celebrated the Brith Milah of their infant son last Tues. $34.44 was collected for the Talmud Torahs (3 Feb. 1911, 14, 12)

SOLOMON, Mr. and Mrs. A., at 1 Mountain St., Montreal, on March 18, 1909, a son (26 March, 1909, 12, 15)

SOLOMON, Mr. and Mrs. A.E., at Granby, Quebec, on Mon. April 19, 1909, a son (30 April, 1909, 12, 20)

SOLOMONS, Mr. and Mrs. Louis, 1128 St. Urbain St., Montreal, celebrated the Brith Milah of their infant son, Reginald Solomons, on Sun. March 29, 1914 at their residence. Six trees in the Herzl Wald were donated in the name of the newborn, as well as a share in the Jewish Colonial Trust by R.A. Darwin, president of the B'nai U' Bnoth Zion Kadimah Society (3 April 1914, 17, 14)

STEINBERG, Mr. and Mrs. Frank, of Montreal, on Oct. 29, 1913, two boys (31 Oct. 16, 47)

STEINBERG, Mr. and Mrs. J., 548 St. Urbain St., Montreal, on Jan. 6, 1913, a daughter (10 Jan. 1913, 16, 5)

STEINBERG, Mr. and Mrs. J., 548 St. Urbain St., Montreal, on Sat. Dec. 13, 1913, a son (19 Dec. 1913, 17, 2)

STEINBERG, Mr. and Mrs. J., on Sat. May 27, 1911, at 548 St. Urbain St., Montreal, a daughter (1 June 1911, 14, 29)

STEINBERG, Mr. and Mrs. Joseph, at 548 St. Urbain St., Montreal, on Wed. Nov. 17, 1909, a daughter (3 Dec. 1909, 13, 3)

STEINE, Mr. and Mrs. M.B., at 279 University St., Montreal, on Sept. 16, 1909, a son (24 Sept. 1909, 12, 41)

STEINE, Mr. and Mrs. M.B., of Montreal, celebrated the Brith Milah of their son, Zusman Behr Steine, last Wed. $6.00 was collected for four trees in the Herzl Wald in his name (1 Oct. 1909, 12, 42)

STEINKOPF, Mr. and Mrs. Max (née Hedwig Mayer), in Winnipeg, their first born, a daughter (3 Feb. 1911, 14, 12)

VENIS, Mr. and Mrs. S., of Ottawa, on Dec. 22, 1913, a son (9 Jan. 1914, 17, 5)

VINEBERG, Mr. and Mrs. H., at 513a Esplanade Ave., Montreal, on Jan. 12, 1909, a son (15 Jan. 1909, 12, 5)

VINEBERG, Mr. and Mrs. Louis I. (née Holstein), on July 13, 1911, at Ontario St., Montreal, a daughter (14 July 1911, 14, 35)

VOLK, Mr. and Mrs. A., 445 Mitcheson St., Montreal, celebrated the Brith Milah of their son on June 25, 1909. $4.40 was collected for the Talmud Torah (9 July 1909, 12, 30)

WEINFELD, Mr. and Mrs. Henry, in Montreal, on March 3, 1909, a daughter (5 March 1909, 12, 12)

WEINFIELD, Mr. and Mrs. John J., 245 Sherbrooke St. E., Montreal, celebrated the Brith Milah of their infant son. Rev. S. Goldstein took up a collection for charity (18 Oct. 1912, 15, 45)

WEINFIELD, Mr. and Mrs. John J., of Montreal, a son (11 Oct. 1912, 15, 44)

WEINSTEIN, Mr. and Mrs. P. (née Bessner), on Aug. 14, 1911, at 1754 Mance St., Montreal, a daughter (18 Aug. 1911, 14, 40)

WEINTRAUB, Mr. and Mrs. M., of Winnipeg, on Aug. 26, 1910, a son (23 Sept. 1910, 13, 45)

WEISMAN, Mr. and Mrs. S., 91 Vitre St., Montreal, celebrated the Brith Milah of their son, on Jan. 31, 1909 (5 Feb. 1909, 12, 8)

WEISS, Mr. and Mrs. Adolph, on Aug. 2, 1911, at 1128 St. Urbain St., Montreal, a daughter (4 Aug. 1911, 14, 38)

WEISS, Mr. and Mrs. Adolphe, 158 Ontario St. E., Montreal, celebrated the Brith Milah of their son on Sept. 19, 1909 (1 Oct. 1909, 12, 42)

WEISS, Mr. and Mrs. Adolphe, at 158 Ontario St. E., Montreal, on Sept. 12, 1909, a son (24 Sept. 1909, 12, 41)

WENER, Mr. and Mrs. Harry, St. Famille St., Montreal, a son (6 May 1910, 13, 25)

WEXLER, Mr. and Mrs. Louis, 28 Colonial Ave., Montreal, on Sept. 12, 1913, a daughter (19 Sept. 1913, 16, 41)

WEXLER, Mr. and Mrs. Marcus, 434 Berri St., Montreal, on June 1, 1912, a son (7 June 1912, 15, 26)

WIRTZ, Mr. and Mrs. George (formerly Miss Gertrude Veld), in Brooklyn, N.Y., on Nov. 6, 1909, a son (3 Dec. 1909, 13, 3)

WISEMAN, Dr. and Mrs. Max, on Sun. March 13, 1910, at 489 St. Lawrence Blvd., Montreal, a daughter (18 March 1910, 13, 18)

WOLFE, Mr. and Mrs. Louis, on Sat. Feb. 1, 1913, at 1960 St. Urbain St., Montreal, a son (7 Feb. 1913, 16, 9)

ZAID, Mr. and Mrs. S., celebrated the Brith Milah of their infant son at their residence, 15 Cameron St., Toronto, on Mon. Dec. 5, 1910 (9 Dec. 1910, 14, 4)

ZEMAN, Dr. and Mrs. B., in Hartford, Conn., a son (6 May 1910, 13, 25)

Rev. J. M. Judelsohn
PRACTICAL
מוהל ומסדר קדושין
1166 Clark   **MONTREAL**
PHONE ST. LOUIS 6601

Rev. D. Epstein,
פראקטישער מוהל ומסדר קדושין
PRACTICAL MOHEL.
Marriage Licences Issued.
1049 St. Urbain St.   Montreal, P.Q.

DEATH NOTICES AND OBITUARIES

ABRAHAMS, Samuel, age 68, died suddenly Sat. morn. at his residence, 530 Argyle Ave., Westmount, Que. For the past thirty years Mr. Abrahams was well-known in Montreal commercial circles as a manufacturer's agent for several New York firms. He was one of the oldest members of the Dominion Commercial Travellers' Association. "Mr. Abrahams was in his usual good health and spirits and the news of his death was a great shock not only to his family but to his many friends." He was born in Russia and came to the United States as a child, settling in Montreal at age thirty-two. Mr. Abrahams was a member of the Montefiore Club and Temple Emanu-El. Rabbi Nathan Gordon conducted the funeral service. Mr. Abrahams is survived by his wife and five children:- Leonard and George Abrahams, the Misses Grace and Estelle Abrahams and Mrs. H.B. Franklin, of Boston, Mass. Mack Abrahams and the Misses Abrahams, of Boston also attended the funeral (5 Dec. 1913, 16, 52)

ACKERMAN, Charles L., age 59, of San Francisco, and brother-in-law of Mrs. Mortimer B. Davis, of Montreal, died in San Francisco, after a lingering illness. Born in New Orleans and graduated from Harvard College, Mr. Ackerman was one of the most prominent members of the San Francisco Bar (19 Feb. 1909, 12, 10)

ALBERT, Mrs. William, of Montreal, has passed away. "The deceased lady was a native of Canada, having been born in Toronto some forty years ago, and was well known in this and her native city." Mrs. Albert is survived by her husband and four children, two boys and two girls. The funeral took place from the residence of her brother-in-law, H. Albert, 184 St. Catherine St. W., yesterday aft. Burial took place in the Shaar Hashomayim Cemetery, Mount Royal (26 Aug. 1910, 13, 41)

ANTHONY, Mrs. Bertha Ollendorf, widow of the late Louis Anthony, died on April 13, 1909 at the home of her daughter, Mrs. J.C. Sampliner, in Cleveland. Born in Breslau, Germany, in 1834, she settled in Montreal in 1840 and was married there in 1858. She had lived with her daughter in Cleveland for the past fourteen years. Mrs. Anthony is survived by three children: - Mrs. J.C. Sampliner, Cleveland; J.R. Anthony, Chicago; and M.O. Anthony, New York; and five grandchildren. Montreal relatives are Samuel Roman and Mrs. Jacob Hirsch. Referring to Mrs. Anthony, a Cleveland contemporary said "The story of the life of this venerable lady was a most beautiful poem and impressive sermon. The home was her prime arena of usefulness. She embodied the virtues of a loving wife and devoted and watchful mother; a sympathetic nature, responsive to the misfortunes and trials of others; a keen intelligence, a gentleness of character and sweetness of nature made all who knew her feel that they were in an ennobling presence." (23 April 1909, 12, 19)

ANTIPITZKY, Moses, senior member of the Antipitzky Metal Co., died last week at the family residence, 76 Grange St., Toronto, after an illness lasting ten weeks. Mr. Antipitzky was one of the earliest Russian Jewish settlers in Toronto. He came to Toronto in 1881 from Regula. "After many years of hardship he finally succeeded in establishing the business which subsequently became one of the wealthiest of its kind in the city. Besides, he was extensively interested in real estate." Active in Jewish fraternal and benevolent societies, he was a member of the Goel Tzedek and McCaul Street Synagogues. Mr. Antipitzky is survived by his wife, four daughters, Mrs. A. Grassman, of Vancouver; Mrs. Louis Korn, the Misses Annie and Lillie Antipitzky, and two sons, Herman and Samuel Antipitzky, all of Toronto (20 Sept. 1912, 15, 41)

ARON, Miss Emma, died on May 4, 1913 at the residence of her sister, Mrs. M.L. Rose, 146 St. Joseph Blvd., Montreal. Miss Aron is survived by her mother, sister, and brothers Adolph and Lewis Aron (6 June 1913, 16, 26)

ARON, Mr., of Montreal, in loving memory of our beloved father who died Jan. 18, 1913. "Gone but not forgotten." (16 Jan. 1914, 17, 6)

ARON, Simon, age 71, an old and respected member of the Montreal Jewish community, died last Sat. A native of Germany, he was one of the oldest members of Temple Emanuel and was a member of the IOSB for the past twenty-five years. He is survived by his wife, Adolph and Louis Aron, Mrs. M.L. Rose, and Miss Emma Aron. Mr. Aron was buried Mon. morn. in the IOSB Cemetery, Rabbi Nathan Gordon officiating (3 Jan. 1913, 16, 4)

AUERBACH, Fischel, second son of Mr. and Mrs. Z. Auerbach, of Montreal, died last week in Port Arthur, Ont. A resident of Toronto, he leaves a widow, son and daughter. He was buried in Toronto last Mon. Marcus Auerbach and Z. Auerbach, of Montreal, were present at the funeral (19 Feb. 1909, 12, 10)

BACHRACK, Mrs. Jennie, wife of Maurice Bachrack, president of the Bachrack Company Ltd., of Toronto, died Sat. morn. from shock after undergoing an internal cancer operation in the Toronto General Hospital. Mrs. Bachrack was born in New York fifty years ago and came to Toronto with her husband about 1885. She is survived by eleven children and her husband. Her sons are boot and shoe merchants on Yonge St. She also leaves several brothers and sisters living in New York, and one brother, A. Levy, of Toronto. The funeral was held Sun. at 3 p.m. with Rabbi S. Jacobs conducting the service (14 Jan. 1910, 13, 9)

BARRETT, Alexander, late son of Mr. and Mrs. A. Barrett, of Glasgow, Scotland, died May 16, 1913 in the Royal Victoria Hospital, Montreal. Deeply mourned by his brothers and friends (30 May 1913, 16, 25)

BERCOVITCH, Bernard, age 62, died at his residence, 1082 St. Urbain St., Montreal on Aug. 13, 1913. Deeply mourned by his three daughters, Mesdames M. Dobrofsky, J. Epstein and S. Levy (22 Aug. 1913, 16, 37)

BLAUSTEIN, Mrs. Fannie, 898b City Hall Ave., Montreal, died on Sept. 5, 1913 and left-$500.00 in legacies to be distributed to the Royal Victoria Hospital, the General Hospital, Mount Sinai Sanatorium, Hebrew Sheltering Home, Hebrew Ladies' Aid Society, her old servant and for religious purposes (1 Oct. 1913, 16, 42-43)

BLOCK, Anna, wife of Joseph Block and mother of Mrs. M. Felsen, died Mon. Sept. 15, 1913 in the Montreal General Hospital. Mr. Block is survived by three sons and four daughters (19 Sept. 1913, 16, 41)

BLUMENTHAL, Mrs. Esther, one of the oldest Jewish residents of Montreal, died on Wed. midnight, June 29, 1910. The wife of Myer Blumenthal, she died after an illness of nine weeks duration. The funeral was held July 1, 1910 from her daughter's residence, 451 St. Denis St. Besides her husband, Mrs. Blumenthal is survived by four daughters: - Mesdames A. Solomon and A. Blumenthal, of Montreal; Mrs. N. Forcimmer, of Nanaimo, B.C.; and Mrs. F. Josephson, of Malone, N.Y. Rabbi Herman Abramowitz officiated at the funeral. Burial took place in the Shaar Hashomayim Cemetery, Mount Royal (1 July 1910, 13, 34)

BOAS, B.A., died Mon. morn. at the "Sherbrooke", corner of Crescent and Sherbrooke Sts., Montreal. "Deceased has suffered from frequent attacks of bronchitis, which affected his heart, and from the attacks of Saturday he became unconscious and for twenty-four before his death he lingered in that state." Mr. Boas was born in Westphalia, Germany, in 1839. He came to New York at age 8 and later moved to Montreal. Forty-two years ago he entered the importing business, dealing in dry goods. He retired from active business fourteen years ago and gave up the building at the corner of McGill and Notre Dame. Mr. Boas was the founder of Reform Judaism in Canada and was one of the prime movers behind the establishment of Temple Emanu-El in Montreal about twenty-seven years ago. He served as president for fifteen years and retired from the position two years ago. He also served on the Board of the Baron de Hirsch Institute. He is survived by his wife, two sons and two daughters:- A.B. Boas, of Boas, Felsen & Co.; Bernard Boas, of the Imperial Tobacco Co.; Mrs. M.H. Davis, of Montreal; and Mrs. Alfred Oppenheimer, of Chicago. The funeral was on Wed. at 9.30 to the Mount Royal Cemetery with Rabbi Nathan Gordon officiating (9 Dec. 1910, 14, 4)

BRODY, F., a leading wholesale drygoods merchant in Des Moines, Iowa and one of the most prominent men in the state, died recently. He was a life-long friend of Rabbi Simon Glazer, of Montreal. Rabbi Glazer received the message of Mr. Brody's death last Tues. night and that the remains would be held till Fri. so that he could preach the funeral sermon. Mr. Brody was an officer of B'nai Israel Synagogue in Des Moines during the time that Rabbi Glazer was the spiritual leader. Rabbi Glazer returns Wed. next week (19 Jan. 1912, 15, 10)

BROWN, Phillip, the oldest Jewish resident of Winnipeg, died at his home last Sat. "The deceased had just returned from the Sharey (sic.) Zedek Synagogue, where he had been attending the Sabbath services, when he suddenly succumbed." Mr. Brown settled in Winnipeg in the early 1870s and operated a clothing store at the corner of Main and Water Sts. He later became a senior partner in the firm of Brown & Coblentz, at the corner of Logan and Main Sts. He was later employed by the government's immigration dept. He was one of the founders of Shaarey Zedek Synagogue and was one of the oldest members of B'nai Brith. He was an Odd Fellow and a Mason of high degree. "He founded the Carmen congregation a few years ago, which now has a flourishing synagogue." Mr.

Brown is survived by his wife, one daughter, Mrs. Krolick, of Winnipeg, and several grandchildren. He was buried Tues. aft. in the United Hebrew Cemetery, Kildonan. Services at the synagogue were conducted by Chief Rabbi Israel Kahanovitch and Rev. E. Cashdan and the synagogue officers acted as pallbearers (14 Feb. 1913, 16, 10)

BROWNSTEIN, Samuel, of Winnipeg, died in the Winnipeg General Hospital on Dec. 10, 1909 after much suffering. The funeral took place Sun. Dec. 12, Rev. J.K. Levin officiating (17 Dec. 1909, 13, 5)

COHEN, Hiam, age 93, of Verballen, Russia, Poland, died there last Sat. "The deceased gentleman, who was born in that town, always took a deep interest in the communal doings in his midst. As a pious and God-fearing man he brought up his children as such, and it is therefore not surprising that his immediate descendants are so devoted to the communal affairs in their midst." Mr. Cohen is survived by four sons, Lazarus, Fischel and Rabbi Hirsch Cohen, all of Montreal and Jacob Cohen, of Verballen, and three daughters, Mesdames F. Phillips and M. Coviensky, of Montreal, and Mrs. Levine, of Verbalen. Lazarus Cohen last saw his father seventeen years ago and Rabbi Cohen had not seen him since his departure from Russia twenty-five years ago (27 Jan, 1911, 14, 11)

COHEN, Lawrence, young son of Rabbi Hirsch Cohen, of Montreal, died last Tues. The funeral was on Wed. morn. (30 Dec. 1910, 14, 7)

COHEN, Mark, formerly of Toronto, died in Chicago on Fri. Oct. 7, 1910. "The old gentleman who celebrated his 80th birthday on the 12th of January last, was a resident of many years standing in this city and was eminently and influentially connected with the insurance world both in Canada and the United States." Mr. Cohen was past president of Holy Blossom Congregation and the Anglo-Jewish Association headquartered in London, England. He was predeceased by his wife sixteen years ago and is survived by his children:- Moses M. Cohen and Jacob S. Cohen, both of Toronto; Isaacson Cohen, of Baltimore; and Mrs. L.J. Isaacs, wife of Dr. Isaacs, of Chicago (11 Oct. 1910, 13, 48)

COHEN, Mrs. F., eldest daughter of the late Max Rubenstein, of Montreal, died in Fort Wayne, Ind., on Jan. 18, 1911 (3 Feb. 1911, 14, 12)

DAVIDSON, Mrs. Elizabeth, age 40, died suddenly Tues. Sept. 24, 1912 at her residence 500 Besserer St., Ottawa. She was the daughter of Mr. and Mrs. I.D. Holofcener and the wife of M. Davidson. She is survived by her husband and two daughters, the Misses Rose and Lillian Davidson. The funeral took place Wed. Sept. 25, 1912 to the Jewish Cemetery, Rabbi S. Fyne officiating (2 Oct. 1912, 15, 43)

DAVIS, Eugene H., age 50, died Sat. morn. in the Royal Victoria Hospital, Montreal. "The deceased gentleman was the son of the late Mr. Samuel Davis, the founder of the cigar manufacturing establishment on St. Antoine street, which still bears his name. Mr. Davis, who had been at one time in partnership with his father, had lived during the past twenty years in New York City. About two months ago, feeling the need of change, the deceased gentleman came to Montreal on a visit but was here only a short time when it became necessary for him to go to the Royal Victoria Hospital." Mr. Davis was unmarried. He is survived by three brothers and two sisters:- Maurice B. and Mortimer B., of Montreal; David Davis, of the United States; Mrs. Cole, of Nice, France; and Mrs. Dr. Lustgarten, of New York City (13 Jan. 1911, 14, 9)

DAVIS, Zelic, age 75, a Montreal cigar manufacturer, died last Thurs. at his home 433 Sanguinet St., after a brief illness. Mr. Davis was born in London, England and was a member of the Shaar Hashomayim Synagogue. He is survived by his wife, a brother and sister, four sons and two daughters. His sons are A. Davis, of Flint, Mich.; D. Davis, of Z. Davis & Sons, St. Paul St., Montreal; Jack Davis, of the I. Davis Feather Mills Company, London, England; Sol. Davis, of Boston, Mass. His daughters are Mrs. S. Cochenthaler, of Montreal and Mrs. S. Klinsmith, of Detroit. The funeral took place from his late residence on Fri. aft., with Rabbi Herman Abramowitz officiating (30 Sept. 1910, 13, 46)

DE LA PENHA, Sarah, of Montreal, in loving memory of our beloved daughter who died Jan. 7, 1912. "Gone but not forgotten." (9 Jan. 1914, 17, 5)

DE LA PENHA, Sarah, only daughter of Rev. and Mrs. I. de la Penha, of Montreal, died. The funeral took place Mon. aft., Rabbi Herman Abramowitz officiating in the absence of Rabbi Meldola de Sola (12 Jan. 1912, 15, 9)

DOVER, Mrs. Minnie, 27 York St., Ottawa, was buried Feb. 26, 1914 in the Jewish Cemetery, Metcalfe township. The service was held at her residence by Rabbi S. Fyne. "The late Mrs. Dover was a great worker among the Hebrews of this city, and took a great interest in the welfare of the Hebrew community in Ottawa." She is survived by five sons, Harry Dover, a McGill University medical student, Joseph, Myer, David and Jacob Dover, and two daughters, the Misses Hettie and Sarah Dover (13 March 1914, 17, 11)

DOVER, William, died at his home, 268 Murray St., Ottawa, on Fri., after an illness of several weeks. Born in Russia in 1834, he settled in Ottawa in 1889. Mr. Dover organized the Hebrew Benevolent Society and was the oldest member of the King Edward Avenue Synagogue. He was an honorary member of the Ottawa Men's Zionist Society. He was buried in the Jewish Cemetery, Bank St. South. He is survived by five sons and one daughter:- John Dover, of Aylwin, Que.; Harry Dover, of Eganville, Ont.; David Dover, of Chalk River, Ont.; Julius Dover, of Detroit; and Phillip Dover, of Montreal; and Mrs. Abbie Spector, of Brandon, Man. (6 Aug. 1909, 12, 34)

ELIASOPH, Harry, son of Rev. and Mrs. M.I. Eliasoph, died at his residence, 239 Mentana St., Montreal, on Tues. Nov. 28, 1911, at age 23, after becoming ill with pneumonia and typhoid for three weeks (1 Dec. 1911, 15, 3)

ELKIN, Abraham A., died on Tues. July 15, 1913 in Joliette, Que. The funeral took place from his residence, 951 St. Urbain St., Montreal, on Wed. July 16 (25 July 1913, 16, 33)

ENGELBERG, Mrs. Leah, age 68, wife of the late A.J. Engelberg, died in New York, on Sun. Nov. 14, 1909. She is survived by four daughters, Mrs. Isidore Friedman, of Montreal, and Mesdames Lewis Smalowitz, B. Calashman and M. Zacharia, of New York, and two sons, S. and A. Engelberg, both of Montreal (19 Nov. 1909, 13, 1)

FEINGOLD, Louis, age 18, son of Mr. and Mrs. N. Feingold, died after a lengthy illness on Tues. Nov. 8, 1910, in the Royal Victoria Hospital, Montreal (11 Nov. 1910, 13, 52)

FELS, Mrs. Sarah (née Bois), of Montreal, died at her residence (3 Nov. 1911, 14, 51)

FEND, Mrs. Sarah, age 78, died at her home, 543 St. Antoine St., Montreal last Sat. She was a long time resident of Canada. She is survived by one daughter, Mrs. Rost. The funeral took place on Sun., to the Sons of Benjamin Cemetery. Rabbi Nathan Gordon officiated (12 Nov. 1909, 12, 48)

FINKLEMAN, S., a commercial worker in Winnipeg died there recently. "Though the deceased gentleman had been ailing for over sixteen years, he was never known to complain. His life was beyond reproach. His funeral was one of the largest ever seen in this city. Hundreds followed the cortege on foot through the streets of Winnipeg, as it slowly wended its way from the house of his son, Joseph Finkleman, to the Synagogue Adath Jeshurun, which the dead man had been instrumental in building. It was extremely pathetic to see the aged father of ninety years at the grave of his son of 62. The Finkleman family is said to be the largest in the Dominion of Canada." He is survived by his father, I. Finkleman, his widow and four sons, Joseph, Charles, Jacob, and Isadore, and two daughters, Mrs. L. Goldstein, of Winnipeg and Mrs. Lennis, of Vancouver (22 April 1910, 13, 23)

FINSTEIN, J., age 30, an employee of Eaton's in Toronto, was found dead in his room by his room-mate, Louis Rosenbloom. He died of heart failure (29 Oct. 1909, 12, 46)

FISCHEL, Sigmund, age 61, died at his residence, 344 Mackay St., Montreal last Wed. Mr. Fischel resided in Montreal for over twenty-five years. He was a partner in the cigar firm of Smith, Fischel & Co. which did business in Montreal and St. Jerome. In recent years he travelled for Neuberge & Co. and A. Cohen, of Ottawa. Mr. Fischel was a trustee of the old Stanley St. Temple Emanu-El. He was one of the congregation's founders. He is survived by his wife and a brother, Gus Fischel, of Montreal (29 Sept. 1911, 14, 46)

FORCIMMER, Nathan, formerly of Montreal, died in Nanaimo Beach, B.C., on Feb. 27, 1914, age 56 (6 March 1914, 17, 10)

FOSS, Louis, of Brookline, Mass., died suddenly in New York on Sun. Nov. 9, 1913 (14 Nov. 1913, 16, 49)

FRANKLIN, M., died Sat. Jan. 31, 1914 in Chicoutimi, Que. His body was taken to Montreal for burial. The funeral took place Mon. Feb. 2 (13 Feb. 1914, 17, 7)

FRANKS, Miss Cecile, of Chicago, niece of Mrs. Gus Fischel, of Montreal, died recently. Miss Franks visited Montreal during the last season and made many friends. "She was a very charming young lady and her Montreal friends were very sorry to hear of her death." (26 Dec. 1913, 17, 3)

FREEDMAN, Levi, age 65, died at his residence, 911 Cadieux St., Montreal, on Wed. Dec. 24, 1913 (9 Jan. 1914, 17, 5)

FREEMAN, Kalman, of Montreal, died Thurs. morn., Oct. 24, 1912, age 65. Mr. Freeman was for many years financial manager of the Baron de Hirsch Institute and a member of the Shaar Hashomayim Synagogue. He is survived by three daughters (1 Nov. 1912, 15, 47)

FREEMAN, Kelman, in loving memory of, who died Cheshvan 13, 5673 (Oct. 24, 1912) (14 Nov. 1913, 16, 49)

FREUND, Mr., of New York died there recently. He was the brother of Mrs. S. Fischel, McKay St., Montreal (5 Feb. 1909, 12, 8)

FRIEDLAND, Morris, son of Mr. and Mrs. Friedland, of Winnipeg, was killed when he "...was run over by the rear wheel of an automobile truck, to which he was holding whilst riding his bicycle." (18 April 1913, 16, 19)

FRIEDMAN, Hyman, an old respected resident of Montreal, died last week at 486 Cadieux St., age 72. Mr. Friedman was born in Austria and came to Montreal in 1897. He was a member of the Keyal Yeshuran and of the Baron de Hirsch Institute. He is survived by his wife and five children:- Isidore, Adolph and Jack Friedman and Mesdames L. Scharf and A. Goldschlager. The funeral was Sun. aft. and was conducted by Rabbi Hirsch Cohen and Rev. A. Signer (18 Aug. 1911, 14, 40)

GELIN, Mrs. Annie, wife of M. Gelin, Spence St., Winnipeg, died Jan. 1, 1911, age 29 (13 Jan. 1911, 14, 9)

GLASER, Morris, age 52, of St. Louis, Mo., died suddenly in the Chateau Frontenac Hotel, Quebec City, last week while on vacation with his wife, two daughters, Mrs. Eleanor and Mrs. Cora Swartz and a son, Lawrence Glaser. Morris Glaser was a founder and officer of Temple Israel and a director of the Mechanics-American National Bank. He is survived by his wife and six children:- Edwin V. and Walter, and Lawrence Glaser; and Mrs. Eleanor, Mrs. Cora Swartz and Miss Amy Glaser. Mr. Glaser is also survived by his brothers:- Louis, Adolph, Julius and Sigmund Glaser and sisters:- Mesdames Wm. Mendel and Sophia Sicher. His remains were taken to St. Louis for burial (10 Sept. 1909, 12, 39)

GLICKMAN, Alton, age 5 years and 2 weeks, youngest son of Tobias Glickman, 95 Shuter St., Montreal, died on Nov. 19, 1909 (26 Nov. 1909, 13, 2)

GLICKMAN, Ethel, youngest daughter of Mr. and Mrs. P.B. Glickman, 320 Elm Ave., Westmount, Que., died Nov. 15, 1911, age 6 years and five months (17 Nov. 1911, 15, 1)

GLICKMAN, Osher, the well-kown manager of the Lyric Theatre in Toronto, committed suicide three days after the accidental death of Louis Samuels. "Although it is commonly believed that Mr. Glickman's suicide was the result of straightened financial circumstances, yet there seems to be a great mystery behind his death than may be readily guessed. Notwithstanding the fact the deceased was so widely known, his private life and history were altogether obscure. Nobody knows with certainty whether he was married or not, though it is commonly believed that he was a bachelor. His private life was so secret that it was not even known where he resided. All sorts of tales have spread after his death. One of these is to the effect (I do not vouch for the truth of it) that Mr. Glickman was a man of exceedingly great consequence in his native country, where he is supposed to have possessed the title of baron." (7 June 1912, 15, 26)

GOLDBERG, Gittle, widow of the late Gershon Goldberg, of Montreal, has died. "Although the deceased was 80 years of age, she was hale and hearty until quite recently, and her death will be deeply regretted by all those who knew her." She is survived by four children, - one son and three daughters: Israel Goldberg, Mrs. Michael Lightstone, Mrs. William Rutenberg and Mrs. Casper Adelson. The funeral took place from Mrs. Adelson's home, 65 Bleury St., Montreal, on Wed. aft. at 2 p.m. Rabbi Meldola de Sola officiated (16 April 1909, 12, 18)

GOLDBERG, Goldie, wife of William Rutenberg, of Montreal, in loving memory of our dear mother who died 17 Kislev, 5673 (Nov. 26, 1913). "May her soul rest in peace." (19 Dec. 1913, 17, 2)

GOLDBERG, Julius, age 59, who was ailing for many months, died at his residence, 45 Drolet St., Montreal, on Wed. last week. Mr. Goldberg was a native of Germany. He came to America fifty years ago, spending twenty-five years in Montreal. He was in the hat and coat manufacturing business during his career and retired five years ago. He was a member of the Chevra Kadisha Synagogue, St. Urbain St. He is survived by his wife, four sons, Max, Morris, Jake and Isidore Goldberg, and three daughters, Mrs. S. Rosenthal and the Misses Julia and Goldie Goldberg. The funeral took place from his late residence with Rev. Bloomfield officiating (29 July 1910, 13, 37)

GOLDBERG, Max, died Thurs. June 30, 1910 at his residence, 427 Elm Ave., Westmount. The funeral took place the following day with Rabbi Herman Abramowitz, and Rev. S. Goldstein conducting the service. Mr. Goldberg was born in Pinsk, Russia forty-eight years ago and came to Canada in 1882. He entered the fur business and was head of the British Canadian Fur Company. His business frequently took him to Europe. He was a governor of the Baron de Hirsch Institute and the Montreal General Hospital and was a member of Shaar Hashomayim Synagogue. Mr. Goldberg is survived by his wife, and three nephews whom he raised, Benjamin, Myer and Samuel Isaacs. His will has been made public "... and as was to be expected from one so charitable during his lifetime, he made some handsome bequests to the charitable and philanthropic institutions in this city. He did not confine his benevolence to the Jewish organizations alone, but distributed a fair share of his wealth to non-sectarian institutions - such as the General Hospital, etc., as well. In all, he left about $10,000 to the Jewish and many non-Jewish institutions." (22 July 1910, 13, 36)

GOLDENBERG, Mrs. P., wife of P.M. Goldenberg, died at her home, 172 Mitcheson St., Montreal, last Sun. She had lived in Montreal for about eight years. She is survived by her husband, three daughters: Mrs. S. Rosenback, Misses Lottie and Molly Goldenberg, of Montreal and four sons: Benjamin Goldenberg, of Montreal; Joseph, Jacob and David Goldenberg, all of Campbellton, N.B. The funeral took place on Sun. aft. and interment was in the Chevra Kadisha Cemetery (10 Sept. 1909, 12, 39)

GOLDENSTEIN, Mrs. S., mother of I.S. Goldenstein, of Montreal, died Wed. July 23, 1913. The funeral took place at the Spanish and Portuguese Cemetery, Montreal (25 July 1913, 16, 33)

GOLDMAN, Joshua, age 78, died in Munich, Bavaria. Mr. Goldman was the father of Leon Goldman, of Montreal. "The late Mr. Goldman resided in this city [Montreal] for the last few years, and was greatly esteemed by all who knew him for his fine and venerable qualities." (3 April 1913, 17, 14)

GOLDMAN, Philip, eldest son of Mr. and Mrs. M.H. Goldman, 33 Kings Road, Brighton, England, died on April 22, 1910, at St. Leonards, Hastings, England, age 26. He is survived by his parents, brother and sister (13 May 1910, 13, 26)

GOLDSMITH, Leopold, of Cleveland, Ohio, father of Mrs. Clarence de Sola, of Montreal, died last Mon. evening of heart failure. Mr. and Mrs. Goldsmith were visiting their only daughter at the time of his death. Mr. Goldsmith was born in Altleining, a suburb of Mannheim. He moved to Cleveland about forty-five years ago and was prominent in Jewish circles. He was a member of the Anshe Chasid Congregation of Cleveland and the Spanish and Portuguese Congregation of Montreal. "He was a warm-hearted and sympathetic man and a devoted husband and father." He is survived by his wife, his daughter, Mrs. Belle Maud de Sola and three grandchildren. The funeral took place from the home of his son-in-law, Clarence de Sola, on Wed. aft. to the Spanish and Portuguese Cemetery on Mount Royal. The service was conducted by Rabbi Meldola de Sola (19 Nov. 1909, 13, 1)

GOLDSTEIN, Harold, son of Mr. and Mrs. I. Goldstein, 52 Cherrier St., Montreal, died on Oct. 1, 1909, age 5 years and 1 month (8 Oct. 1909, 12, 43)

GOLDSTEIN, Mrs. Esther, wife of Isaac Goldstein, died suddenly on Thurs. Nov. 11, 1909 in Montreal. "The deceased lady had only a few months ago lost her eldest boy of five years of age, and this grief no doubt was the main cause of her demise." She is survived by her husband and a child, age 2.5 years. The funeral took place from her residence, 52 Cherrier St., last Fri. to the Mount Royal Cemetery, Rabbi Nathan Gordon officiating (19 Nov. 1909, 13, 1)

GOLDSTEIN, Sigmund, of Winnipeg, died there on Sat. April 24, 1909 after an attack of meningitis. His "demise is a severe loss to Winnipeg Jewry. He was a true gentleman, a model husband and a tender and loving father. He was respected and beloved by all who knew him, and the sincere sympathy of all, goes out to the young widow and little children who are left to bewail his loss." (30 April 1909, 12, 20)

GOLDSTINE, Miss Ada Rose, eldest daughter of Mr. and Mrs. Max Goldstine, 123 Mayfair Ave., Winnipeg has died. She and her mother had recently returned home from Princeton, Ky. where they had visited relatives. "On Tuesday, Feb. 2nd, she retired, to rest, to all appearances, in fairly good health, though for some months past she had been under medical care. A few minutes afterwards she was heard calling, and when her parents entered her room, she was beyond medical aid, and passed away away almost immediately.

Miss Goldstine was a very accomplished young lady, and her untimely death at the age of 20, has caused a terrible shock to the whole Jewish community of Winnipeg. She was a clever pianist and an expert painter on China and miniatures, she having gained a number of prizes for this work. The sincere sympathy and condolence of the community goes out to the stricken family in their terrible sorrow." (26 Feb. 1909, 12, 11)

GOLTMAN, Mrs. S., wife of the late S. Goltman, of Montreal, died Fri. April 12, 1912 after a lingering illness at the home of her daughter, Mrs. Maurice Wormser in New York. Mrs. Goltman was buried in Montreal. She is survived by two sons, Charles E. Goltman, (Montreal), and Dr. Max Goltman, (Memphis, Tenn.), and one daughter, Mrs. Wormser (19 April 1912, 15, 23)

GOLTMAN, Solomon, age 72, of Montreal, died Wed. morn. He came to Canada about thirty-two years ago and entered the clothing business in Montreal. He was one of the old members of the Spanish and Portuguese Synagogue, Stanley St. He is survived by his wife and two sons: Dr. Max Goltman, of Memphis, Tenn. and Charles Goltman, of Montreal, and one daughter, Mrs. M. Wormser, of New York. The funeral will take place next. Sun. morn. from 4296 St. Catherine St. West at 11 a.m. (5 Nov. 1909, 12, 47)

GREENBERG, H., formerly of Montreal, has died in New York. He was the brother of Mrs. P. Myers, of Montreal. Mr. Greenberg leaves a widow, threes son and one daughter, Miss Sophie Greenberg (2 April 1909, 12, 16)

GREENBERG, Moses, an old Montreal resident who was connected to several families here, died after a short illness. "All his friends will deeply regret this sad news." (10 Jan. 1913, 16, 5)

HAAS, Henrietta, of Montreal, in loving memory of our dear beloved mother who died March 23, 1910. "May her soul rest in peace." (20 March 1914, 17, 12)

HAAS, Miss Carolina, of Buffalo, N.Y., has died. She was the sister of Mrs. C.A. Workman, Kensington Ave., Montreal (16 Sept. 1910, 13, 44)

HAID, Miss Clara, age 17, daughter of Mr. and Mrs. M. Haid, of Winnipeg, died. Prior to the funeral which took place Mon. June 30, 1913 at 3.30 p.m., a short service was performed by E.A. Cohen at the home of the parents. "As the funeral passed the Shaarey Shomayim Synagogue, of which the family are members, the prayer "El Mole Rochamim" was chanted by Cantor E. Cashden, and the cortege the proceeded to the United Hebrew Cemetery, where the last rites were performed. The deceased bore her long and painful illness with remarkable fortitude, and to the last remained sweet and composed." She is mourned by her parents, brothers and sisters, and her numerous friends (18 July 1913, 16, 32)

HARRIS, Miss Fannie, of Montreal, passed away after a tedious illness on June 22, 1910. "Miss Harris was well known for her kindly disposition, her many charitable acts, and untiring efforts in all matters she undertook for the welfare of the poor. The deceased young lady was an active member of the Ladies' Hebrew Benevolent Society, being on its Board for the past fourteen years, taking the place of her late mother." Miss Harris is survived by the Misses Harris, Samuel Harris and Aaron Harris, of New York (24 June 1910, 13, 32)

HAYES, Henrietta, in memory of our beloved mother who died March 23, 1910. Sadly mourned by her children (21 March 1913, 16, 15)

HENDLER, Mr. and Mrs., of Toronto, died in quick succession, leaving their son, age eight and their daughter, age six. Mr. Hendler was a middle-aged man "... and it appears that the early death of his wife was the cause of his sudden illness, from which he died." (11 Sept. 1912, 15, 40)

HIMMELSTEIN, Mr. and Mrs. Alfred Lewis, of Winnipeg, lost their ten year old son who was run over and killed by an automobile at the corner of Market and Main St., in the heart of the city. "He was at once taken to the Winnipeg General Hospital, where he expired a few minutes after his entrance." (7 Feb. 1913, 16, 9)

HOLOFCENER, Mrs. I.D., wife of I.D. Holofcener, of Ottawa, died Tues. Dec. 24, 1912 and was buried Wed. Dec. 25. Mrs. Holofcener was a member of the Ottawa Ladies' Hebrew Benevolent Society, the Ladies' Herzl Zion Society and the King Edward Synagogue Ladies' Auxiliary. "The memory of her good deeds will live as a shining star of credit to her sorrowing and devoted husband, as well as to her large circle of friends." (10 Jan. 1913, 16, 5)

HYMAN, William S., age 23, only son of Mr. and Mrs. H.J. Hyman, of Montreal, died Mon. this week. Mr. Hyman was a student at McGill University in third year science. He was a member of the Maccbean Literary Circle, the Jewish students' organization and Temple Emanu-El. "Although ailing for some time, his death was a shock to his many friends and acquaintances." The funeral took place Tues. aft. from his late residence, 29 Metcalfe St. (31 March 1911, 14, 20)

ISAACS, Abraham, of St. John, N.B., died at his residence on Sun. March 14, 1909. Born in London, England, he moved to New York as a young man where he was in the cigar business along with his father and brother. In 1878, he moved to St. John where he became a cigar manufacturer. In 1879, his brother, Israel Isaacs joined him and they established the firm of A. & I. Isaacs. Abraham Isaacs married the daughter of the late Solomon Hart in New York. He is survived by his widow and two sons and two daughters: Mrs. Samuel Lewis, of St. John, Miss Mildred Isaacs, at home, Lysle Isaacs, of the American Clothing House and Sydney Isaacs, owner of the Cigar Box. He is also survived by four brothers and two sisters: Israel Isaacs and Alfred Isaacs, of St. John; Joseph Isaacs and Emmanuel Isaacs, Mrs. Oscar Silberstein and Mrs. L. Marks, all of New York. "Mr. Isaacs was one of the eldest and most ardent workers in the Jewish community of St. John. Ten years ago when the first synagogue was organized there, Mr. Isaacs was chosen president. He held that position until three years ago, when he was appointed president of the New Hazen Avenue Synagogue, which post he held until his death." Rabbi Amdur officiated at the funeral. Mr. Isaacs was buried in the family plot in St. John (26 March 1909, 12, 15)

ISAACS, Mrs., of New York, mother of Mrs. Joseph Kellert, of Montreal, has died (11 June 1909, 12, 26)

JACOBS, Hannah, in memory of our mother who died April 18, 1907, corresponding to 4 Iyar 5667 (13 May 1910, 13, 26)

JACOBS, Miss Sarah, second daughter of the late William and Hannah Jacobs, died last Mon. in Montreal. "The deceased young lady was ill but a short time and the cause of her demise was rheumatic fever. The late Miss Jacobs was of a most amicable disposition and a general favorite amongst all who were fortunate enough to know her." The funeral took place from the family residence, 52 McGill College Ave. last Tues., Rev. I. de la Penha officiating in the absence of Rabbi Herman Abramowitz. Rabbi Abramowitz is conducting the Kaddish services (25 Aug. 1911, 14, 41)

JACOBS, Simon, brother of Abraham Jacobs (and of the late William Jacobs), of Montreal, died in Chicago, on Yom Kippur, Sept. 25, 1909 (1 Oct. 1909, 12, 42)

JACOBS, William, in loving memory of our father who died on Sept. 25, 1905, corresponding to 21 Ellul, 5665 (23 Sept. 1910, 13, 45)

JACOBSON, Bertha (née Sloves) in loving memory of our dear mother who died 6th day of Chesvan 6559, corresponding to Oct. 31, 1908 (3 Nov. 1911, 14, 51)

KAUFFMAN, Mrs., of Montreal, age 93, died on Tues. morn. at the residence of her daughter, Mrs. Levy Friedman. She was a resident of Montreal for twenty-five years, having come from Russian-Poland. "Up till the last, she enjoyed the best of health, and was in full possession of every faculty, death being due to old age. She was especially gifted with a wonderful memory, and could remember events as far back as eighty-five years ago." She is survived by one daughter, Mrs. Levy Friedman; two sons, Max Kauffman and Moses Kauffman, both of Milwaukee; 29 grandchildren and 35 great-grandchildren (20 Aug. 1909, 12, 36)

KAUFMAN, Max, of New York, father of Mrs. Isadore Elkin, of Montreal, has died. Mr. and Mrs. Elkin have gone to New York for the funeral (30 Sept. 1910, 13, 46)

KERT, Max, age 23, son of Mr. and Mrs. I. Kert, of Montreal, died suddenly at the residence of his fiancé, Miss Katie Stone, 153 Laval Ave., Montreal, last Sat. evening. "The young man and his bride-to-be, were fixing upon their wedding date, which was to be decided for January 18, next, when a sudden attack on the heart caused immediate death...He was gifted with remarkable business acumen, as witnessed by his success as a railway contractor, at such an early age." The funeral took place from his parents' home, Papineau Ave., on Mon. aft. at 2.30 with burial in the B'nai Jacob Cemetery. Rabbi Herman Abramowitz conducted the service (3 Dec. 1909, 13, 3)

KEYFITZ, Nathan, age 78, one of the oldest residents of Toronto, died at his home Thurs. morn. Aug. 29, 1912 in the presence of most of his children. He would have celebrated his golden wedding anniversary this week. "The deceased was the descendant of a line of celebrities in Russia, and was considered one of the most scholarly and best informed Jews in the city." Born in 1835, Mr. Keyfitz was educated in Russia. For several years he was employed by the government of Moghileff, his native town. At age 27, he married Rebecca Madorsky. Soon afterward he was appointed Crown Rabbi of Rogacheff, a position he held for eighteen years. From there he went to St. Petersburg where he was superintendent of the orphan asylum founded by Baron Ginsburg. On his return from St. Petersburg, he resumed the office of Crown Rabbi for the entire district of Moghileff, a position he held until he left for America twenty years ago. "In Canada Nathan Keyfitz led a life of retirement and seclusion, honored and respected by all who knew him. The deceased was known for his charitable work, and, especially, for frequent intercessions on behalf of Russian immigrants in their relation with the Russian consul." He was a "...man of inimitable character, known for his love of truth and justice. Though orthodox in his convictions and habits the deceased regarded with tolerance those who were not in agreement with his views." He is survived by his wife, four sons and four daughters:- Dr. Moses (Russia), Mark (Toronto), Arthur (Montreal), Samuel (Kinmount), Mrs. F. Wolfsohn (Winnipeg), Mrs. J. Andrews, Mrs. de Levinne and Miss Esther (all of Toronto) (11 Sept. 1912, 15, 40)

KIRSCHBERG, Miss Bella, the daughter of Mrs. and the late Abraham Kirschberg, of Montreal, died Wed. June 29, 1910 at 3 p.m. "She suffered very much from a long and lingering illness and expired conscious till the end in the presence of all her immediate relatives. Although she died young in years she yet did sufficient to win the favor and praise of all who knew her. Her accomplishments in many directions always received the highest admiration of her numerous friends." The funeral will be held this aft. at 2.30 p.m. from the residence of her mother, Mrs. A. Kirschberg, 451 Claremont Ave., Westmount. Miss Kirschberg is survived by her mother, two brothers, Joseph and Isaac Kirschberg and five sisters, Mesdames Z. Fineberg, Isaac Rose, Aaron H. Haskell (of New York), and the Misses Miriam and Annie Kirschberg (1 July 1910, 13, 34)

KOROTKIN, W., age 32, of Toronto, died there recently. Mr. Korotkin was born in Russia and was single at the time of his death. "Mr. Korotkin was a young man of the old type who are now very seldom to be found." An active communal worker, he was a member of the Canadian Zionist Federation, chairman of the National Fund for Toronto, and a member of the B'nai Zion and Nordau Zion societies and the Hebrew Free School. The funeral took place Wed. Oct. 23, 1912 and was in charge of the B'nai Zion Society. "The Toronto Zionist Institute will be draped in mourning for seven days and the Bnoth Zion Kadimah have postponed their reception owing to the death of this devoted Zionist." (25 Oct. 1912, 15, 46)

KREVEL, J.B., of Dominion City, died in Winnipeg, on May 9, 1909, age 74 (28 May 1909, 12, 24)

KUPPENHEIM, Mrs. Helene, of New York, formerly of Montreal, died on April 19, 1909. She had moved back to Montreal two months ago. She is survived by two sons, J.D. Kuppenheim and Joseph Kuppenheim. Rabbi Nathan Gordon officiated at the funeral which took place from her residence, 429 Mance St., Montreal, on Wed aft. (April 1909, 12, 19)

KUSSNER, I., age 36, of Kussner Bros., ladies' blouses manufacturers, 205 St. Catherine St. W., Montreal, died this week when he fell down the elevator shaft. "The fatal accident occurred on Tuesday evening, when Mr. Kussner desirous of descending from the seventh floor to the basement by the freight elevator, and receiving no answer to the bell, he bent over and lost his balance, falling down the shaft. His cries, as he descended, atracted (sic.) the workpeople, who carried him out, mortally wounded, from the basement. He was hurried to the Royal Victoria Hospital, where he died an hour later." Mr. Kussner is survived by his wife and four children. He was a member of the Shaar Hashomayim Synagogue. "Three weeks ago a workman of Mr. Kussner's was killed by falling down the elevator shaft from the sixth floor." (2 May 1913, 16, 21)

LAZARUS, Mrs. Dora, age 83, died at her daughter's house, 530 Argyle Ave., Westmount, Que., last Sat., after an illness of four months. Mrs. Lazarus came to Canada from Thorn, Germany forty-four years ago. She was one of the founders of Ladies' Hebrew Benevolent Society and was one of the oldest members of Shaar Hashomayim Synagogue, Montreal. She was an active member of the chevra kadisha. "The end came peacefully, surrounded by her entire family." She is survived by five daughters and one son. They are:- Henry Lazarus and Mesdames Lyon Silverman, B. Goldstein, R.H. Blumenthal, Abrams, and Bernstein, of New York, as well as thirty-three grandchildren and three great-grandchildren (22 Dec. 1911, 15, 6)

LEHRER, Bernice Isabelle, age 17 months, only child of Mr. and Mrs. L. Lehrer, 448 Mt. Stephen Ave., Westmount, Que., died Sun. Feb. 15, 1914 (20 Feb. 1914, 17, 8)

LEHRER, infant daughter of Mr. and Mrs. L. Lehrer, Mt. Stephen Ave., Westmount, Que., died Fri. Dec. 12, 1913 (19 Dec. 1913, 17, 2)

LEVI, David, of Montreal, died in Paris three weeks ago. The body arrived in Montreal by boat, on Tues. morn. He was buried in the Spanish and Portuguese Cemetery later that day, the funeral taking place from Wray's Undertaking Establishment, Mountain St. Mr. Levi, who was in the clothing trade, was born in Russian Poland. "His name was associated with communal charities. His death is a loss to our community." (20 June 1913, 16, 28)

LEVINSON, Goldie, in loving memory of our beloved wife and mother who died Adar 15th, 1912. Missed by her husband M. Ginsberg and children (21 March 1913, 16, 15)

LEVINSON, Goldie, the beloved wife of Mendel Ginsberg, of Montreal, and loving mother, who died 15th Adar, 1912 (in memory of) (13 March 1914, 17, 11)

LEVY, Gabriel, of Nancock, N.S., lost four of his children in a devastating fire. "His wife and another child were so dangerously burned that it is doubtful whether they will recover. Mr. Levy and three of his surviving children are now in dire circumstances. In Nancock over three hundred dollars was raised for the family, and in this city [Montreal] through the efforts of Mr. Louis Lewis a further sum of four hundred dollars was subscribed." (10 Feb. 1911, 14, 13)

LEVY, Louis, of Montreal, died in Montreal on Mon. March 23, 1914. Born in Russia, he came to Canada at age five with his parents. Mr. Levy settled in Montreal nine years ago and established a successful business. "He was a man beloved by all his employees, had hosts of friends, and was a member of many charitable institutions. Only a week ago the deceased donated a generous sum to be distributed among the different Jewish charitable institutions of this city." (27 March 1914, 17, 13)

LEVY, Rene Ernest, of Montreal, went down with the "Titanic". Mr. Levy came from an old Jewish family of Alsace which later emigrated to France. A chemist with a world-wide reputation, he developed the "Levy Oxygen Process" for cutting and welding iron and steel. S. Talpis, author of the obituary, wrote "As to the inventor himself, alas, we have lost in him a conscientious, noble and patriotic Jew. A Jew, though born and reared in an un-Jewish environment and atmosphere, where tendencies for assimilation prevailed, yet he was not influenced by them: on the contrary, his pronounced French sensitiveness had aroused within his innermost being a feeling and longing, equally as strong for his own Jewish people. His finer instinct of French patriotism did not deter him from being a true and devoted scion of his own less fortunate race." (26 April 1912, 15, 23)

LIVERMAN, Mrs. Annie, age 37, wife of Thomas Liverman and daughter of Mrs. S.J. Cohen, died in the Royal Victoria Hospital, Montreal on Fri. June 17, 1910 "...after many years suffering borne with great fortitude." (24 June 1910, 13, 32)

LONN, Miss Martha, age 13, eldest daughter of Mr. and Mrs. Harris Lonn, died in Dr. Boulie's private hospital. The funeral took place from the residence of her parents, 186 Laval Ave., Montreal on Sun. (15 July 1910, 13, 35)

MARKS, Alexander, age 19, son of Mr. and Mrs. R. Marks, Craig St., Montreal, drowned at a picnic at King Edward Park last Sun. aft. "It appears that about 1 p.m. when a large number of the events of the Progressive Literary and Debating Club picnic had been gone through, the deceased and another one of the party went for a bathe, and the deceased had hardly gone up to his waist in the water when he disappeared and his body was not discovered till some three hours later. It is difficult to understand how the fatal accident happened in but three or four feet of water, but the opinion generally is that a current caught him and dragged him along. His friend alongside of him dived after him, as did likewise many others who arriving at the scene, but without success and only by dragging the river was he found." Mr. Marks was secretary of the Young Men's Zionist and Literary Society and was involved with the YMHA, Malbush Arunim, the Consumptive Aid Society and other organizations. The funeral took place from his parents' residence with close to one thousand people attending. The Progressives wore mourning badges (1 July 1910, 13, 34)

MARKS, Nathaniel, formerly of Montreal, died in Ottawa, last Sun., age 78. His body was brought to Montreal on Tues. and he was buried in the Spanish and Portuguese Cemetery that aft. He is survived by his wife and five children:- Abraham Marks, of Montreal; Philip Marks, of Pittsburgh; Mrs. Duchan, of Winnipeg; Mrs. (Dr.) Goltman, of New York; and Mrs. J. Tieson, of Ottawa (23 July 1909, 12 32)

MARTIN, Mrs. A. (née Tena Bernstein), of Buffalo, N.Y., age 48, died after a short illness. "Mrs. Martin was well known to many in Montreal, who will deeply sympathize with her family in its bereavement." (26 Aug. 1910, 13, 41)

MATZ, Rev. Jacob, former first reader of the Manchester New Synagogue, England from 1890 to 1907, died Aug. 21, 1913. The funeral took place Fri. from his residence. Born in Rumshishock, Government of Kovno, he came from a family of rabbis. Rev. Matz compiled his musical compositions written over a period of thirty-seven years as a chazan into his book **The Voices of Jacob**. He married a daughter of his first tutor, Chazan Libovitz. Rev. Matz had several family members in Montreal, Canada including his son, B. Matts, his sister, Mrs. H. Kellert, and his brother, L.J. Matts, Oliver Ave., Westmount, Que. (10 Oct. 1913, 16, 44)

MENDELS, Isaac, who died last week, was an active member of the Young Men's Hebrew Benevolent Society of Montreal before it became known as the Baron de Hirsch Institute. He had been presented with an illuminated address on vellum in recognition of his services he rendered as administrator of the Hirsch agricultural colony in the North West Territories during the summer seasons of 1894 and 1895 (10 June 1910, 13, 30)

MENDELSSOHN, Mr., father of J. Felix Mendelssohn, of Montreal, died suddenly from heart failure, on board ship, on April 30, 1910. Mr. Mendelssohn is at present on the Pacific Coast (20 May 1910, 13, 27)

MEYER, Mrs. Leah, age 72, mother of Mrs. Mortimer B. Davis, of Montreal, died on Aug. 21, 1910 in San Francisco. Mrs. Meyer is survived by three daughters and one son. Funeral services were held at her residence, 2201 Van Nees Ave. with Dr. Jacob Nieto officiating. She was buried in Hills of Eternity Cemetery (23 Sept. 1910, 13, 45)

MILLMAN, Mrs. S., died at her residence, 268 Sherbrooke St. W., Montreal, on Sat. Jan. 28, 1910, after a year's illness. She is survived by three sons, L. and A. Millman, of Montreal and Solomon Millman, of Riviére du Loup, Que., and two daughters, the Misses Rose and Bena Millman. The funeral took place on Sun. aft., to the Spanish and Portuguese Cemetery, on Mount Royal, Rabbi Meldola de Sola and Rev. I. de la Penha conducting the service (4 Feb. 1910, 13, 12)

MINTZ, Isaac, of Hamilton, Ont., died last evening at 9 p.m. at his home, 244 South James St., age 58. Mr. Mintz had been ill with pneumonia for about eleven days. He was born in Charleston, S.C., in 1854 and moved with his parents to Toronto as a young man. He settled in Hamilton fifteen years ago where he has lived since. He was the head of a prosperous hair goods business and was well-known in the city. Mr. Mintz was an active member of the Hughson Street Synagogue from which he was buried Wed. aft. "The late Mr. Mintz was a man of reserved manner, but was of a very friendly nature. He was unfailing in his efforts to help others and the memory of his many acts will long remain with residents of Hamilton. He was also a great reader, and enjoyed the peace and quietness of home life. In the synagogue he was a tower of strength, and his loss will be keenly felt in the congregation." He is survived by his wife, Mrs. Amelia Mintz, two sons, Solomon and Myer Mintz and a daughter, Miss Sarah Mintz (15 March 1912, 15, 18)

MORRIS, Margaret, of Montreal, dearly beloved wife of Harry Albert, died on Aug. 4, 1913 at Old Orchard Beach, Me. The funeral took place from the home of her son, Moses Albert, Prince Arthur Apts., Montreal (8 Aug. 1913, 16, 35)

MOSKOVITCH, Esther, died May 15, 1912. "Ever fondly remembered and sadly missed by her father, mother, sisters and brothers." (16 May 1913, 16, 23)

MOSS, Charles, of London, England, who died there July 21, 1909, left 10 £ sterling to the McGill College Avenue Synagogue in Montreal. Mr. Moss was born in Montreal in 1852. He was the son of David Moss, a founder of the English, German and Polish Synagogue and one of the best known communal workers of his day. Charles Moss, who is survived by his wife, one son and two daughters, was a brother of Hyam D. Moss, formerly of Montreal (1 Oct. 1909, 12, 42)

NEISSER, Dr. Eugene Jacob, age 42, professor of political economy at the University of Berlin and a German government representative, died on Sat. Oct. 16, 1909, in the Winnipeg General Hospital, of typhoid fever. Dr. Neisser arrived in Winnipeg on Sept. 26 and registered at the Royal Alexandra Hotel. He became ill shortly thereafter and entered the hospital on Oct. 2. He was travelling through Canada and planned to visit the North West. "It was not known that Dr. Neisser was a coreligionist, till he expressed a wish on his deathbed, that he might be buried with Jewish rites. He was a member of the Reform Gemeinde of Berlin, and a cousin of Dr. Neisser, of the University of Breslau, the famous specialist on diseases of the skin." He is survived by his wife (22 Oct. 1909, 12, 45)

OBERNDORFFER, Simon, of Kingston, Ont., died last Fri. Oct. 24, 1913. Mr. Oberndorffer was born in Baden, Germany in 1830 where he was educated in the public school and the Jewish school attached to the Baden synagogue. He was well-travelled, was a good linguist and an excellent Hebrew scholar. He came to Kingston fifty-five years ago at age 28 where he was a cigar manufacturer with a factory on Ontario St. A staunch Conservative, Mr. Oberndorffer was already active in Kingston politics going back to the days when Sir John A. Macdonald, the former prime minister of Canada, was just beginning his political career. Mr. Oberndorffer briefly represented Cataraqui ward on Kingston city council. He was past president of the local synagogue and was actively involved with the Oddfellows as a member of the Cataraqui lodge. "But his religion was broader than the limitations defined by sect or cast, he being a man of profound humanitarian views who "went about doing good," regardless of nationality or faith." He is survived by his wife, five sons and three daughters (31 Oct. 1913, 16, 47)

ORNSTEIN, Isaac, age 66, died in Montreal on Mon. June 27, 1910. Mr. Ornstein came to Canada from his native Romania in 1887 and settled in Ottawa before moving to Montreal. He retired from business ten years ago. He was chairman of the Burial Committee of the Chevra Beth David Congregation with which he was affiliated since his arrival in Montreal. The funeral took place from his residence, 440 Sherbrooke St. E., to the Chevra Beth David Synagogue, Chenneville St. where the service was held. Over 150 people attended. He was buried in the Congregation's Cemetery at St. Laurent which he had planned and bought for the Congregation. Mr. Ornstein is survived by his widow and son, Osias Ornstein and a daughter, Mrs. Jacob Manolson (1 July 1910, 13, 33)

POLAKEWICH, Mrs. Joseph, died in Biddeford, Maine, last month. Her family was known to many Jewish Montrealers who visit Old Orchard Beach each summer. She is survived by her husband, Joseph Polakewich and six children:- Louis, William, George, Isaac, Dora and Emma. She is survived by her mother, Mrs. Goodkowsky, of Lewiston and six brothers and one sister. Of all the brothers, N. Goodkowsky is the best known to Montrealers. The funeral took place in Portland, Me. (5 Nov. 1909, 12, 47)

RABINOVITCH, Lazer, age 78, died in Montreal on Aug. 6, 1913. Deeply mourned by his wife and children, S. Rabinovitch, P. Rabinovitch and Mrs. A. Derosa (5 Sept. 1913, 16, 39)

RAM, Jacob, age 9, son of Mr. and Mrs. B. Ram, of Montreal, died suddenly on Wed. aft. (5 Jan. 1912, 15, 8)

RAPHAEL, A., late headmaster of the Jews' Hospital and Orphan Asylum in London, England has died. "He was beloved by all who came under his sway, and the news of his death will be received by many an old "boy" and "girl" now in Canada, with sorrow." (17 Jan. 1913, 16, 6)

RAPHAEL, William, one of the oldest and most distinguished artists of Montreal, died after a brief illness in that city. Mr. Raphael was born in West Prussia eighty-one years ago, and was a graduate of the Royal Academy of Art in Berlin. He came to Canada sixty years ago and settled in Montreal. He was a charter member of the Royal Canadian Academy, founded in 1880. Several of his works

---

The St. Lawrence Grocery
at 414 St. Lawrence Boulevard

A high-class line of Grocery, Delicatessen and Liquors of all descriptions always on hand. All city and country orders promptly attended to.

B. RAM, - Proprietor.
414 St. Lawrence Blvd.   Phones: E. 3381-3382

hang on the walls of the federal parliament. Mr. Raphael was married fifty-two years ago to Thina Danziger. Mr. Raphael is survived by his wife, six sons:- Randolph Raphael, of New York; Julius Raphael, of Montreal; Samuel Raphael, an artist in New York; Harry Raphael, of Montreal; Maurice Raphael, of New York; Walter Raphael, in Massachusetts; and three daughters:- Mrs. Kayton, of Norfolk, Va.; Mrs. H.M. Levine, of Montreal; and Miss Bertha Raphael, living at home (20 March 1914, 17, 12)

RILL, Mrs. Louis, age 65, died in the Royal Victoria Hospital, Montreal, Wed. morn., April 30, 1913 (2 May 1913, 16, 21)

RILL, Mrs. Louis, died last Wed. morn. in the Royal Victoria Hospital, Montreal. Mrs. Rill came to Montreal with her husband twenty-three years ago and was well-known by a large circle of friends and relatives. "She had been ill for the last two years, and her death, while not unexpected, has caused deep regret to those who knew her." Mrs. Rill is survived by her husband, three sons, seven daughters, and twenty-seven grandchildren. Her sons are Julius Rill (Winnipeg), Isidore Rill (Vancouver), and Abraham Rill (Montreal). Her daughters are Mesdames J. Ettenberg, I. Ressler, M. Lasker, L. Hirschorn and A. Schumann (Montreal), Mrs. Schwartz (Hamilton) and Mrs. L.W. Avner (Boston). The funeral was held last Thurs., Rabbi Meldola de Sola of the Spanish and Portuguese Synagogue officiating. Mrs. Rill was a member of that congregation (9 May 1913, 16, 22)

RITTENBERG, Phillip, son of Mr. and Mrs. Rittenberg, of Toronto, formerly of Montreal, died last week (9 April 1909, 12, 17)

RITTENBERG, Samuel, in memory of the dearly beloved son of Annie and Isaac Rittenberg, of Toronto, who died Nov. 22, 1912. "Gone but not forgotten." (5 Dec. 1913, 16, 52)

ROGERS, Mr., a peddler from Chicago, committed suicide in Black River, a town about fifty miles from Toronto. "It appears that the deceased suffered from occasional attacks of melancholia during which his state not infrequently approached that of insanity. It must have been during one of these fits that Rogers made the attempt at his life." He is survived by his wife and children (11 Sept. 1912, 15, 40)

ROMAN, Samuel, age 66, longtime resident of Montreal, died suddenly at his residence, 2155 Mance St. on Sat. after being confined to his bed for only a few days. Mr. Roman was a life-long member of the Shaar Hashomayim Synagogue and was a life governor of the Baron de Hirsch Institute as well as a life member of the Oddfellows, Royal Guardians and Royal Arcaniums. Mr. Roman was born in Prussia and came to Montreal with his parents when he was two years old. In 1869, he married Miss Fanny Levine, daughter of Marcus Levine, who predeceased him twenty years ago. Mr. Roman was engaged in the cigar manufacturing business most of his life. Ten year ago he sold his interest in the business and entered the Montreal Shirt & Overall Co. Ltd., of which he was president at the time of his death. He is survived by three sons and three daughters - Marcus, William and Abraham Roman and Mrs. Charles Redlich, of Montreal; Mrs. J.H. Mendles, of Perth, Ont.; and Mrs. Adam Klopot, of Boston. The funeral was held Mon. aft. and the service was conducted by Rev. S. Goldstein (22 July 1910, 13, 36)

ROSENBAUM, Mrs. Beatrice, (née Miss Ogulnik), wife of Harry Rosenbaum, of Montreal, died on Feb. 13, 1909, in the Western Hospital. The funeral took place, last Sun., from her residence, 430 Claremont Ave., Westmount, Que. (19 Feb. 1909, 12, 10)

ROSENTHAL, Aaron, a resident of Ottawa for thirty years, died there last Fri., age 78. Born in Germany in 1831, he lived in India, Ceylon and Australia before settling in Canada about forty years ago. He began his business career in Montreal but after a few years he moved to Ottawa. He founded a jewellery business now known as A. Rosenthal & Sons. He is survived by his widow and four sons: Arthur, Samuel, Harry and Martin Rosenthal. The remains were brought to Montreal on Sun. morn. Burial was in the Shaar Hashomayim Cemetery, Rabbi Herman Abramowitz officiating. In his eulogy Rabbi Abramowitz said, in part "With his removal from our midst, there has been removed one of the old landmarks, as it were, in Canadian Jewry. He came to this country many years before most of us; he was one of those who did pioneer work in establishing Jewish communities in this land, he was known for his interest in religious and philanthropic causes, and the communities of Ottawa and Montreal particularly, were benefitted through his generosity. Through his integrity in the commercial world, his high sense of honour displayed in all his dealing he won respect and esteem, not only for himself, but also brought honour upon the name of Jew everywhere." (8 Oct. 1909, 12, 43)

ROSENTHAL, Edward Aaron, son of Mr. and Mrs. Sam Rosenthal, of Ottawa, age five months, died on Nov. 2, 1911 (17 Nov. 1911, 15, 1)

ROSENTHAL, Frieda, beloved wife of Maurice Rosenthal, of Iberville, Que., died in the Royal Victoria Hospital, Montreal, Dec. 20, 1913, age 22. "May her soul rest in peace." (2 Jan. 1914, 17, 4)

ROSENTHAL, Hiram, who died Feb. 1, 1910, is mourned by his wife, 186 Laval Ave., Montreal, and children (31 Jan. 1913, 16, 8)

ROTHSCHILD, Mrs. J., formerly of Sault Ste. Marie, Ont., met with a fatal accident Sat. Nov. 1, 1913, at about 7 p.m. in Montreal. "The tragic event occurred as she was stepping off a street car." She leaves six children to mourn her loss (7 Nov. 1913, 16, 48)

RUDOLPH, Robert, son of Mr. and Mrs. A. Rudolph, 33 Laval Ave., Montreal, died after a brief illness with typhoid fever, age 17. "The deceased was a very popular and well liked young man, of sterling character and ability." (26 April 1912, 15, 23)

RYAN, Carrol, age 71, former editor of the Jewish Times and champion of the rights of Canadian Jewry, died Thurs. evening in Montreal last week. "Mr. Ryan, although not a co-religionist, was well known to our people, and more especially so to the readers of the Jewish Times. Since its inception, thirteen years ago, until the early part of last year, he practically edited the Jewish Times, primed, of course, occasionally by its proprietors. His extensive knowledge of the Jewish people, and their history, made the task a comparatively easy one for him, and during the period he was connected with it, betrayed a deep and abiding interest in all matters which concerned the people he caterd to." The funeral took place from the Masonic Temple, Dorchester St. W. Among those paying their last respects were:- S.W. Jacobs, K.C., Maxwell Goldstein, K.C., Lyon Cohen, Rabbi Nathan Gordon, Z. Fineberg, D.S. Friedman, M. Albert, Robert Jacobs, Samuel Goltman and Hyman P. Nerwich. Mr. Ryan is survived by three sons and one daughter (1 April 1910, 13, 20)

SAMUEL, Jacob, a partner in the firm of M. and R. Samuel, Benjamin & Co., of Toronto, and Samuel, Sons & Benjamin, of London, England, died recently in London. Jacob Samuel was born in Montreal on Nov. 27, 1851 and moved to Toronto with his parents while still a child. He was educated at Mrs. How's school and the old Collegiate Institute. In 1882 he moved to England where he helped his father manage the English branch of the business. Shortly after his arrival there he met and later married Miss Myers. Mr. Samuel is survived by his wife, two daughters and two sons, Harry and Cecil Samuel. Only the latter reside in Toronto (19 July 1912, 15, 32)

SAMUEL, Jacob Leo, age 80, died Tues. morn. Oct. 1, 1912 in the Montreal General Hospital after a brief illness. He was one of the oldest and most active members of the Montreal Jewish community. Born in London, England, he came to Canada at age thirteen. He was a trustee of the Spanish and Portuguese Congregation for over fifty years. He was elected its president last year. Mr. Samuel "...was in good health until about three weeks ago, just before Rosh Hashonah, when he was taken ill. He was removed to the General Hospital, where the physicians thought it advisable to operate on him, in the hope of saving his life. His advanced age, however, militated against his recovery, and on Tuesday morning he passed away." The funeral took place Tues. aft. to the Spanish and Portuguese Cemetery, Rabbi Meldola de Sola officiating. "May his soul rest in peace." (2 Oct. 1912, 15, 43)

SAMUELS, Louis, 71 Sullivan St., Toronto, a young person, who suffered an accident, died last Fri. (7 June 1912, 15, 26)

SAXE, William, of Montreal, eldest son of the late Michael Saxe, died on Wed. June 28, 1911. "The deceased was in his 58th year and was well known in this city as an authority on the Hebrew language, as well as on Jewish matters in general." The funeral took place from his residence to the Shaar Hashomayim Cemetery, Rev. I. de la Penha officiating. Mr. Saxe is survived by his wife, four sons and six daughters (7 July 1911, 14, 34)

SCHALEK, Marcus, age 63, died last Fri. at his residence, 1529 Park Ave., Montreal. "It has been fifteen years since Mr. Schalek came to Montreal, and his business career has been full of honor." Mr. Schalek is survived by his wife, a daughter and two sons, Arthur and Leo Schalek. The funeral took place last Mon., Rabbi Nathan Gordon officiating (19 May 1911, 14, 27)

SCHERMAN, Julius, one of the "grand old men" of the Montreal Jewish community, died after a short illness in the Homeopathic Hospital, McGill College Ave., on Aug. 31, 1913. Mr. Scherman came to Montreal as a young man fifty-seven years ago and made his home for the first twenty years with the late Mrs. Roman, and for the past thirty-seven years with Mr. and Mrs. Jacob Hirsch, 10 Bishop St. "Mr. Hirsch and Mr. Scherman met originally in London, England, on their way from their respective homes to the new world, and the friendship then formed lasted for considerably over a half century. At the celebration of Mr. and Mrs. Hirsch's golden wedding, in May last, Mr. Scherman was one of the few survivors who had attended the original ceremony, fifty years before." He was an active member of the Young Men's Hebrew Benevolent Society in the early days. "With such men as Mr. Harris Vineberg, Mr. D.A. Ansell, Mr. D.S. Friedman, and others, he stood for all that was great and noble in Jewish philanthropy, giving of himself to the good work, and reckoning neither personal convenience nor bodily comfort." He was also actively involved on behalf of the Montreal General Hospital and the Protestant Hospital for the Insane as a life governor. Mr. Scherman was a life-long member of the Shaar Hashomayim Synagogue and was one of its founders over fifty years ago. A pioneer in the jewellery business, he retired many years ago to devote himself to philanthropic work. He was one of the oldest members of the Dominion Commercial Travellers' Association. "The world is better for the lives of such men, and his scrupulous honesty, integrity, warm friendship, and absolutely blameless life will long remain as a sweet fond memory to countless men and women, whose privilege it was to know and appreciate the late lamented Julius Scherman." (5 Sept. 1913, 16, 39)

SCHEUER, Mrs. Edmund, wife of the superintendent of the Zionist Hebrew Free School of Toronto, died after an illness of three months on Sun. Nov. 6, 1913. Mrs. Scheuer was born in Neunkirchen, Germany and was married forty years ago. She came to Canada with her husband who became a member of the firm of Levy Bros. & Scheuer, in Hamilton. They lived there for thirteen years before moving to Toronto where she became a leader in the Jewish community (21 Nov. 1913, 16, 50-51)

SEGAL, Mrs. Clara, age 68, died on Sun. June 25, 1911 at her son's residence in Levis, Que. She is survived by her three surviving sons, William, Moses and Billy Reuben. "May her soul rest in peace." (7 July 1911, 14, 34)

SHAPIRO, Joseph, age 68, formerly of Montreal, died at his residence near Jerusalem. Mr. Shapiro arrived in Montreal in 1885 and carried on business there for nearly twenty years. "Some six years ago he, together with his wife, left this country to spend their remaining days in the ancient city. There he occupied himself with the study of the Talmud and in doing benevolent acts." In Montreal, he was a member of the Chevra Kadisha Congregation and the Sons of Benjamin. He is survived by his wife, two sons, Moses Shapiro, of Chicago, and David Shapiro, of Montreal, and two daughters, Mrs. A. Howard, of New York, and Mrs. N. Sloves, of Montreal (30 Sept. 1910, 13, 46)

SHAPIRO, Joshua, oldest member of his family, died on April 12, 1909 - the seventh day of Passover - in Montreal, age 72. A resident of Montreal for about twenty years, he had been an invalid for the past three years. He was "...born in Russia, and from childhood he was regarded as full of promise; bright and intelligent, having received an excellent Hebrew and Talmudical education, considerably more advanced than was usual at that period. His keen intellect and his ability to deal successfully with difficult problems - both social and commercial - soon earned him the title of "Joshua, the Diplomat."" He came to the United States in 1873 and assisted by his family built up an important business within five years. "However, finding that the difficulties of observing the orthodox rites of Judaism were increasing in America, and being anxious to follow the cherished ideas of his religion, he resolved to return to the Old Country. This he did, and after residing both in England and Scotland, eventually landed in Montreal. His observance of the Jewish principles was strict to a degree; he was of the old school, claiming to be a descendant of the celebrated family of Great Rabbis and Commentators. His house was always open, and he was always willing to extend a helping hand and offer of friendly advice." He is survived by his wife and six children: three sons - M. Shapiro, now living in New York; J. Shapiro, of Chicago; and D.H. Shapiro, of Montreal; three daughters - Mrs. L. Teplitsky, Mrs. D. Shapiro and Mrs. M. Rafelovitch, all of Montreal (23 April 1909, 12, 19)

SIMON, Jacob M., in loving memory of my dear father who died May 27, 1912. By his daughter, Mrs. S.M. Ogulnik, Montreal. "Though gone from sight to memory ever dear." (30 May 1913, 16, 25)

SLOVES, Bertha, wife of R. Jacobson, of Montreal, in loving memory of our dear mother who departed this life Cheshvan 6, 1918 (Nov. 5). "Gone but not forgotten." (7 Nov. 1913, 16, 48)

SOMMER, Kalman, age 25, died on Feb. 14, 1909, at his mother's home, 25 St. Dominque St., Montreal. He was "stricken with pneumonia, and although hopes of his recovery were entertained at first, yet the illness proved fatal. The deceased had a bright future before him and was considered an excellent talmudist." (26 Feb. 1909, 12, 11)

SOROSKY, Mrs. Sals (née Miss Nellie Feldheim), niece of Mrs. A. Rosenthal, Sr., of Ottawa, died Feb. 21, 1912, in Berlin, Germany (1 March 1912, 15, 16)

STEINBERG, Joseph, son of Wolf Lion Steinberg, the first rabbi of Shaar Hashomayim Congregation of Montreal, died in Chicago last month. He is survived by his wife and three children:- Natalie C., Julia Evelyn and Lionel Montefiore Steinberg. He was a brother to Mrs. Isaac Levy, of New York, and Mrs. Amelia Wilkinson, of Montreal, and the late Moses and Henry Steinberg (3 Nov. 1911, 14, 51)

STERN, Henry, formerly of Montreal, has died suddenly in New York, on Sun. March 28, 1909 (2 April 1909, 12, 16)

STERN, Mrs. A., of Cleveland, Ohio, died after lingering illness on April 1, 1911. Mrs. Stern and her daughters were former residents of Montreal who left several years ago to live in Cleveland (7 April 1911, 14, 21)

TANNENBAUM, Abraham, age 79, died last Sun. at his residence 235 St. Catherine St. W., Montreal. Although he had been ailing for quite some time death was unexpected. Mr. Tannenbaum arrived in New York from Poland about fifty years ago where he settled and carried on business for twenty-seven years before moving to Montreal where he resided until his death. "The deceased gentleman was of an extreme orthodox disposition and was a member of the McGill College Avenue Synagogue." He was active supporter of the Talmud Torah. He is survived by eight children:- Morris Tannenbaum, of Montreal; Benjamin, Harry and Michael Tannenbaum, of New York; Mrs. Myers, East London, South Africa; Mrs. Cohen, of Brooklyn, N.Y.; and Mesdames Roston and Abinovitz, both of Montreal. Rabbi Herman Abramowitz officiated at the funeral which took place Mon. aft. to the Shaar Hashomayim Cemetery (24 June 1910, 13, 32)

TASTICK, Florence, age 25, wife of Samuel Sabbath, of Montreal, died suddenly Tues. morn., Feb. 16, 1911. Toronto and New York papers copy (24 Feb. 1911, 14, 15)

TEPLITZKY, Lazarus D., in loving memory of our husband and father who died June 10, 1911. "May his soul rest in peace." (13 June 1913, 16, 27)

TEPLITZKY, Lazarus David, of Montreal, age 44, died suddenly last Sat. evening from an attack of spinal meningitis which lasted three days. Mr. Teplitzky was born in Russia and at age fifteen immigrated to Scotland where he stayed for almost nine years before coming to Montreal. During his twenty years in Montreal he very active in the Jewish community. He was a trustee of the Talmud Torah of Montreal, a director of the Baron de Hirsch Institute, the first president of the local board of Kashruth, a member of the Agudath Zion Society and up till two years ago an active member and former trustee of the Chevra Kadisha Congregation. "Charitable in the extreme he never refused a helping hand when needed; yet all this was done in an unostentatious manner. Many are the good deeds and numerous are the donations to the credit of the deceased gentleman, but which only the beneficiaries are aware of." Mr. Teplitzky is survived by his wife, three daughters and one son. The funeral took place Mon. aft. from his late residence, 477 St. Denis Blvd., to the Shaar Hashomayim Cemetery, Rabbi Herman Abramowitz officiating. The funeral was one of the largest ever attended in Montreal with a thousand people following the bier to the cemetery (16 June 1911, 14, 31)

VENDER, Joseph, age 48, died in Montreal of Thurs. Nov. 9, 1911. He was the father of Samuel, William, Rubin, Lazarus and Sarah Vender (17 Nov. 1911, 15, 1)

VINEBERG, Elias, age 89, retired merchant, died at his residence, 204 Bishop St., Montreal. A native of Russian Poland, Mr. Vineberg has resided in Montreal for forty-five years. He was an uncle of Moses Vineberg, furrier, St. Paul St. After he retired eighteen years ago, he devoted much time to the McGill College Avenue Synagogue, of which he was one of the oldest members. He is survived by four sons and five daughters. They are:- Solomon, Louis, Abraham and Simon Vineberg, and Mesdames M.J.

Glickman, S.M. Glickman, W. Rosenbloom, H. Vineberg and Sigler, all of Montreal (15 Dec. 1911, 15, 5)

VINEBERG, Marcus, age 59, died on Mon. Aug. 22, 1910, at 57 Argyle Ave., Montreal, after a lingering illness (26 Aug. 1910, 13, 41)

VINEBERG, Mrs. Joseph, died in Detroit, Mich. in Nov. and was buried in Montreal. She is survived by her children:- Louis Vineberg and Mrs. Adelson, of Detroit; and Albert, Abe and Sol Vineberg, of Montreal (21 Nov. 1913, 16, 50-51)

VINEBERG, Mrs. Mary, died at her home, 517 St. Urbain St., Montreal, last Sun., after a short illness. She is survived by her son and two daughters: Mrs. Rachel Horwitz and Miss Sadie Vineberg. Mrs. Vineberg was buried in the Back River Cemetery, Rabbi Herman Abramowitz officiating (10 Sept. 1909, 12, 39)

WARTELSKY, Mrs. Annie, died at her residence, 86 Colonial Ave., Montreal last Sun. "The deceased lady was eighty years of age and had resided in this country about forty years." She is survived by her husband and three children:- Hiram Silverstone, of Perth, Ont.; Mrs. L. Wartelsky, of Montreal; and Miss Sadie Wartelsky. Mrs. Wartelsky was buried on Tues. in the Shaar Hashomayim Cemetery (6 Jan. 1911, 14, 8)

WAXLER, Abraham, age approximately 35, was found dead in his room at 61 William St., Toronto. "Little is known about him, except that he was a labouring man. It was the fumes of gas that led to his discovery, and when the door was forced in it was found that the jet had been left half open." (10 Dec. 1909, 13, 4)

WEICHERT, Sigmund, age 81, secretary to the German Consulate in Toronto, died of a heart attack, at the home of his son, Louis Weichert, 129 Gore Vale Ave., Toronto. Born in Austria, he came to Canada to become secretary of the consulate. He is survived by his son and two daughters, Miss Clarice Weichert and Mrs. D.J. Van Dusen (5 Nov. 1909, 12, 47)

WEINFELD, Israel, a well-known and respected member of the Montreal Jewish community, died Tues. Sept. 2, 1913. He was a member of the Shaar Hashomayim Synagogue, the HSBA and other societies. Age 54, he died after an operation which was performed upon him at the Royal Victoria Hospital. He is survived by his wife and eight children, of which three are druggists and one an advocate. The funeral took place yesterday (Thurs.) (5 Sept. 1913, 16, 39)

WEINSTEIN, Saul, age 19, son of Mr. and Mrs. B. Weinstein, 832 Colonial Ave., Montreal, died last Tues. "The deceased was ailing for the past eight years, but was at all times of a bright and cheerful disposition." He was buried in the Roumanian Congregation's Cemetery (1 April 1910, 13, 20)

WEISBURGH, Nathan, age 79, father of H. Weisburgh, of Montreal, died on Nov. 1, 1909 in Albany, N.Y. Mr. Weisburgh will sit shiva at the home of his brother, Abraham Weisburgh, 440 Hudson Ave., Albany (5 Nov. 1909, 12, 47)

WEISS, Rabbi Louis, formerly rabbi of Anshe Shalom Synagogue in Hamilton, died on July 30, 1909, at the Olean, N.Y. General Hospital, as a result of formaldehyde poisoning. "He had suffered much loss of sleep, and took about two ounces of the drug as a sedative and stimulant." Rabbi Weiss was born and educated in Hungary in 1848. He came to the United States thirty years ago. Suffering from throat problems, he moved to Hamilton for its climate. Two years ago, he moved to Bradford Pa. to serve at Beth Seam Congregation (6 Aug. 1909, 12, 34)

WITTENBERG, N., age 34, was found dead in the Queen's Hotel, Montreal yesterday from a dose of carbolic acid. "Letters were found on him which stated his intentions to perform the rash act. He made the request that his body be sent to Winnipeg, and that a telegram and his photograph be forwarded to the Winnipeg "Free Press". As the letters were written in Yiddish, the Baron de Hirsch Institute was immediately notified. It at once wired the paper in question. A reply was received that the unfortunate man was known there. If arrangements do not miscarry, the deceased will be interred in the cemetery of the Baron de Hirsch Institute. He leaves a wife and two children in Winnipeg." (14 Jan. 1910, 13, 9)

Holidaying, Picnicing, Change of Food, Water, and Climate, often cause **Constipation.**

One to Two Daily will keep you in best of condition.

10c and 25c Boxes, at all Drug Stores, and at

John Weinfeld

458 St. Lawrence Blvd.
Phone East 1077

197 Bleury St.
Phone Main 1377

WOLFE, Max, well-known Ottawa furrier, died last Wed. morn., at his residence, 35 Stewart St., age 52. He had been ill for two weeks but his death was unexpected. "Mr. Wolfe had just eaten a hearty breakfast and was suddenly attacked with heart failure." Born in Germany, Mr. Wolfe came to New York thirty-two years ago and later moved to Toronto where he established a business on Yonge St. He came to Ottawa fifteen years ago opening a branch store at 200 Sparks St. The funeral took place Thurs. Jan. 4, 1912 at 1 p.m. He was buried in the Ottawa Jewish cemetery. He is survived by his wife, two sons, A. Harry and Jay Wolfe, and nine daughters, Mrs. Max B. Margosches (Ottawa), Mrs. Joel Pullan (Winnipeg), the Misses Nadie E., Esther, Dorothy, Adele, Violet and Gladys Wolfe, all of Ottawa, and Teresa Frances Wolfe, at present in Winnipeg (12 Jan. 1912, 15, 9)

WOLSEY, Samuel, age 40, who had been ill for some time, died in Monrovia, California, on July 8, 1909. A resident of Montreal for the past twenty-five years, he started out as a manufacturer under the name of Bernstein & Wolsey and then went into the real estate business. He is survived by his wife. The funeral took place Fri. at 2 p.m. from 290 Mountain St., Montreal, with Rabbi Meldola de Sola conducting the service. He was buried in the Spanish and Portuguese Cemetery (23 July 1909, 12, 32)

WORKMAN, Abraham, age 56, died at his residence, 19 Seymour Ave., Montreal, last Mon. evening, after a short illness. Born in Buffalo, N.Y., he came to Montreal 35 years ago and entered the clothing business. He eventually joined his brothers in the firm of Mark Workman Ltd., 326 Notre Dame St, W. He is survived by his wife; one daughter; three brothers, Charles A. Workman, Levi Workman and Mark Workman, all of Montreal; his sisters, Mrs. M. Cochenthaler, of Montreal, and Mrs. James Fresco, of Chicago; and his father, Isaac Workman. The funeral took place Wed. aft. at 2.30 p.m. Rabbi Herman Abramowitz officiated at the Shaar Hashomayim Cemetery (June 1909, 12, 25)

WORKMAN, I., age 85, died at his home, 10 Stanley St., Montreal, on Sun. His death came after six days of illness. Mr. Workman was born in Russia and came to Canada as a boy. He was in the clothing industry in Montreal for fifty years. He retired from business three years ago and spent his time at home. He is survived by his wife, four sons, Mark Workman (president of the Mount Sinai Sanatarium), Charles Workman, Lee Workman and Master E. Workman, and two daughters, Mrs. Cochenthaler, and Mrs. Fresco, of Chicago. The funeral was held Mon., Rabbi Herman Abramowitz officiating (14 March 1913, 16, 14)

YAPHE, Florence Ruth, beloved wife of Samuel Yaphe, Lachine Rapids Rd., Montreal, and only daughter of Mrs. E.R. Price, 852 Cadieux St., Montreal, died Thurs. Jan. 15, 1914, age 28 (13 Feb. 1914, 17, 7)

YOUNGHEART, Edward Opoczynski, age 48, head of a cigar manufacturing firm of that name, died at his residence, 152 Durocher St., Montreal on Wed. this week from a heart illness of five month's duration. Mr. Youngheart was born in Lenszyca, Poland. His father was a cavalry general in the Czar's army. Mr. Youngheart came to Montreal twenty-six years ago. He immediately joined the Canadian militia and became a lieutenant in the Duke of Connaught's Royal Canadian Hussars. He resigned his commission in 1905 when his regiment was transferred to St. Johns. He married Miss Adele Strauss, of Toronto. Mr. Youngheart was a prominent Jewish citizen and member of Temple Emanu-El. He is survived by his two brothers in Canada, Joseph Youngheart, of Montreal, and Felix Youngheart, of Toronto, and two sisters in Poland. The funeral takes place this Fri. aft. (3 March 1911, 14, 16)

ENGAGEMENTS AND MARRIAGES

ABRAHAMS, Alfred A., of London, Eng., and Miss Rose Berman, third daughter of Mr. and Mrs. S. Berman, of Westmount, Que., are engaged (18 Oct. 1912, 15, 45)

ABRAMOWICH, Morris, son of Mr. and Mrs. Abramowich, and Miss Fannie Shenker were married by Rev. S. Pechet on Sun. Dec. 22, 1912 at the home of the groom's parents in Saskatoon, Sask. The bride was given away by Mr. and Mrs. Leon Goldman. The bride was attended by Miss Minnie Abramowich, the groom's sister, and the Misses Marian Vogel, Jeannette Vigdur and Vera Jampolsky. Little Miss Rachel Abramowich was the flower girl. The best men were A. Bonder, Max Gordon, A. Hugo and Fred Schuman. Out-of-town guests included:- Mr. and Mrs. A. Abramowich (Bladsworth), Mrs. M. and Miss Arva Jampolsky (Lipton), Mr. and Mrs. S. Pechet (Southy), L. Pechet (Cupar), Mrs. M. Baratz (Cupar), Jack Baratz (Dysart), Miss Jeannette Vigdur (Lipton) and Miss R. Blauss (Vancouver). The groom is a young Saskatoon businessman. For several years he was in the general merchandise business in Davidson, Sask. The bride is a recent arrival from New York. By coincidence, the bride's brother, Maurice Shenker, and Miss Anna Ast, were married the same day in New York (24 Jan. 1913, 16, 7)

ABRAMOWITZ, Rabbi Herman, of Montreal, and Miss Theresa Bockar, daughter of Mr. and Mrs. I. Bockar, 231 East, 72nd St., New York, are engaged. Reception, Vienna Hall, New York, Sun. Jan. 22, 1911, 3 to 6 p.m. (6 Jan. 1911, 14, 8)

ABRAMOWITZ, Rabbi Herman, of Shaar Hashomayim Synagogue, Montreal, and Miss Theresa Bockar, daughter of Mr. and Mrs. I. Bockar, 231 East 72nd St., New York City, were married Thurs. evening, June 22, 1911, in the Shearith Israel Synagogue, 70th St. and Central Park West. Prof. Solomon Schecter, president of the Jewish Theological Seminary officiated, assisted by Rev. Dr. De Sola Pool and Rev. Dr. Elias Solomon. Sol. Kellert was best man and the ushers were Dr. B.J. Beck, Edward Levi, E.W. Jacobs, David Levy, Louis Levine and Harry Rotkowitz. The bridegroom was escorted by his mother. Lazarus Cohen, president of Shaar Hashomayim in Montreal, escorted the bride's mother. Miss Pauline Aisenstein was maid of honor. The reception and dinner were held in Vienna Hall. Rabbi and Mrs. Abramowitz will spend their honeymoon in the Adirondacks and the Thousand Islands. They will reside in Montreal (30 June 1911, 14, 33)

ABRAMS, Samuel and Miss Fannie Ghingold, were married in the Auditorium Hall, Montreal, last Sun. aft. The bride was given away by her brother, S. Ghingold. The bridesmaids were the groom's sister, Miss K. Abrams, and his niece, Miss K. Robitaille, of Sudbury (3 Sept. 1909, 12, 39)

ABRAMSKY, M.M., of Toronto, and Miss Freda Solomon, daughter of Mr. and Mrs. M. Solomon, of Montreal, are engaged (25 Oct. 1910, 13, 50)

ACKER, I., of Fort William, Ont., and Miss Rebecca Korn, daughter of Mr. and Mrs. S. Korn, were married on Tues. Jan. 3, 1911 at the home of the bride's parents in Toronto. The bride was led to the chuppa by her mother and her sister, Mrs. Kling. Miss Anna Korn was the bridesmaid. Mr. and Mrs. Acker will honeymoon in Detroit, Chicago, Minneapolis and St. Paul before taking up their residence in Winnipeg (13 Jan. 1911, 14, 9)

ACKER, Isidore, of Fort William, Ont., and Miss Rebecca Korn, third daughter of Mr. and Mrs. S. Korn, of Toronto, are engaged and will be married in Jan. 1911 (9 Dec. 1910, 14, 4)

ADLER, Samuel, of Hull, England, and Miss Rebecca Laterman, daughter of Mr. and Mrs. A. Laterman, of Montreal, are engaged (29 Oct. 1909, 12, 46)

AGOOS, S.L., of Boston, and Miss Rebecca Albert, daughter of Mr. and Mrs. H. Albert, were married at the residence of the bride's parents, 184 St. Catherine St. W., Montreal with only the immediate relatives present. Mrs. L. Lehrer, the bride's sister, was matron of honor. After a honeymoon to Quebec City and other cities, Mr. and Mrs. Agoos will reside in Boston (22 July 1910, 13, 36)

AGOOS, S.L., of Boston, Mass., and Miss Beccie Albert, of Montreal, daughter of Mr. and Mrs. H. Albert, are engaged (10 Dec. 1909, 13, 4)

ALBERT, Abraham, of Montreal, and Miss Esther Solomon, daughter of Mr. and Mrs. D. Solomon, are engaged (1 June 1911, 14, 29)

ALBERT, Moses, of Montreal, and Miss Lottie Hershberg will be married in Rochester, N.Y., June 12, 1912 (7 June 1912, 15, 26)

ALBERT, Moses, son of Mr. and Mrs. H. Albert, of Montreal, and Miss Lottie Hershberg, daughter of Mr. and Mrs. Isaac Hershberg, 31 North Goodman St., Rochester, N.Y., were married by Rabbi Herman Abramowitz, of Montreal, Wed. evening, June 12, 1912 in the Powers Hotel banquet hall, Rochester. Her sister, Mrs. H. Silverman was matron of honor and Miss Dorothy Silverman, the bride's niece, was flower girl. Charles Albert, of Montreal, the groom's brother, was best man. The ushers were Sol. M. Hershberg and Haskel I. Hershberg, the brides's brothers; Jack Albert, of Montreal, the groom's cousin; Harry Silverman and Sol. L. Levy, of Rochester; and Samuel Goldberg, of New York. After their honeymoon, Mr. and Mrs. Albert will reside in Montreal as of Sept. 1, 1912. Out-of-town guests included:- Mr. and Mrs. W. Albert, Mr. and Mrs. A. Kellnor, L. Lehrer, M. Goldberg, E. Albert, and Mr. and Mrs. Samuelson, all of Montreal; Mrs. N. Goodkowsky and L. Polakewitch, of Biddeford, Me.; Mrs. S.L. Agoos, of Boston, the groom's sister; Mrs. S. Simonsky and Mrs. A. Freedman, of Toronto; and J. Yanover and Miss Hattie Chopack, of New York (2 Aug. 1912, 15, 34)

ALBERT, Moses, the well-known Montreal druggist, and Miss Lottie Hershberg, daughter of Mr. and Mrs. I. Hershberg, of Rochester, N.Y., are engaged (12 Jan. 1912, 15, 9)

ALBERT, Samuel and Miss Celia Rutenberg, daughter of Mr. and Mrs. David Rutenberg, were married by Rabbi Herman Abramowitz, assisted by Rev. S. Goldstein, on Tues. night in the Auditorium Hall, Montreal. The bridesmaids were the bride's sisters, the Misses Lena and Fannie Rutenberg. Mrs. Celia Goglenug was matron of honor. J. Albert, the groom's brother, was best man. Mr. and Mrs. Albert honeymooned in the eastern U.S. and will reside on Park Ave., Montreal upon their return (1 April 1910, 13, 20)

ALBERT, Samuel and Miss Sarah Rutenberg, daughter of Mr. and Mrs. D. Rutenberg, all of Montreal, are engaged (26 Nov. 1909, 13, 2)

ALEXANDER, Solomon, a Vancouver lawyer, and Miss Esther Robinson, daughter of Louis Robinson, formerly of Montreal, are engaged (21 June 1912, 15, 28)

ALLAN, Harry, son of Mr. and Mrs. P. Allan, of Bradford, Pa., and Miss Cecilia Sereth, daughter of Mr. and Mrs. H.N. Sereth, of Montreal, are engaged (16 Jan. 1914, 17, 6)

ALLMAN, Joseph and Miss Gertrude Tobin, niece of Mr. and Mrs. S. Silverstone, of Montreal, are engaged (17 Nov. 1911, 15, 1)

ANKER, L.W. and Miss I. Friedman, both of Montreal, will be married on Jan. 10, 1912 in the Auditorium Hall, Montreal, followed by a reception (29 Dec. 1911, 15, 7)

ANKER, Leonard, son of Mr. and Mrs. Anker, of New York, and Miss Ida Friedman, daughter of Mr. and Mrs. A. Friedman, of Montreal, were married by Rabbi Herman Abramowitz on Wed. Jan 10, 1912 in the McGill College Avenue Synagogue, Montreal. Miss Nellie Rosenthal was maid of honor. Miss Annie Friedman, the bride's sister was bridesmaid. W. Karp was best man and Joe Friedman, the bride's brother, was usher. Following the ceremony a reception was held in the Auditorium Hall. Mr. and Mrs. Anker will reside in Montreal (12 Jan. 1912, 15, 9)

ARNOW, M. and Miss Fannie Kolber, of Chicago, who is well-known in Montreal circles, will be married in Chicago on Sun. (4 Feb. 1910, 13, 12)

ASTROFSKY, William, of Montreal, and Miss F. Miller, daughter of Mr. and Mrs. N. Miller, of Cornwall, Ont., are engaged (16 July 1909, 12, 31)

BALINSKY, Louis and Miss Rose Margaret Feldstein, eldest daughter of Mr. and Mrs. M. Feldstein, were married by Rabbi Hirsch Cohen, assisted by Rev. Judelsohn on Thurs. March 5, 1913. The bride was given away by her father and was attended by her sister, Miss Ida Feldstein and the Misses Rose and Toba Balinsky and Miss Jennie Jacobson. Mr. and Mrs. Balinsky left for New York, Atlantic City, Philadelphia and other cities on their honeymoon (13 March 1914, 17, 11)

BALINSKY, Louis and Miss Rose Margaret Feldstein, daughter of Mr. and Mrs. M. Feldstein,

1561 Park Ave., Montreal, are engaged and will be married in early March (27 Feb. 1914, 17, 9)

BALINSKY, M., of Grand Mere, Que., and Miss Bella Elbaum, of Montreal, are engaged (18 Nov. 1910, 14, 1)

BASKEWITZ, Jacob and Miss Annie Abramson, daughter of Mr. and Mrs. A. Abramson, Annex, were married by Rabbi Hirsch Cohen, on Sun. Aug. 29, 1909, in Standard Hall, Montreal (10 Sept. 1909, 12, 39)

BAULKIND, Samuel and Miss Fannie Fish, daughter of Mr. and Mrs. A. Fish, will be married Wed. Sept. 8, 1909, at 5 p.m., in the McGill College Ave. Synagogue, Montreal (3 Sept. 1909, 12, 38)

BAULKIND, Samuel, of Montreal, and Miss Fannie Fish, daughter of Mr. and Mrs. Abraham Fish, of Quebec City, were married by Rabbi Herman Abramowitz, assisted by Rev. S. Goldstein, on Wed. Sept. 8, 1909, in the Shaar Hashomayim Synagogue, Montreal (10 Sept. 1909, 12, 39)

BAXT, Harry G., of New York, and Miss Annie Sugarman, daughter of Mr. and Mrs. A. Sugarman, of Ottawa, are engaged (31 Dec. 1909, 13, 7)

BECKER, Harry I., of Montreal, and Miss Helen Greenberg, daughter of Mr. and Mrs. A. Greenberg, of Rochester, N.Y., are engaged (7 April 1911, 14, 21)

BENJAMIN, Morris and Miss Sarah Iseman, daughter of Mr. and Mrs. W. Iseman, will be married in the McCaul Street Synagogue, Toronto, on Sun. Jan 1. 1910. The reception will be held at 21 Draper St. (2 Dec. 1910, 14, 3)

BERG, Benjamin, of Hamilton, Ont., and Miss Rose Cadisky, daughter of Mr. and Mrs. J. Cadisky, 101 Augusta Ave., Toronto, are engaged (11 March 1910, 13, 17)

BERGER, A. and Mrs. J. Friedman, formerly of Montreal, were married in Cleveland, Ohio, on April 9, 1911 (28 April 1911, 14, 24)

BERGER, Julius, son of Rabbi and Mrs. J. Berger, of Ottawa, and Miss Rebecca Fitch, daughter of Mr. and Mrs. O. Fitch, of Quebec City, are engaged (9 Jan. 1914, 17, 5)

BERK, Louis, formerly of Montreal, and Miss Ida B. Kaplan, daughter of Rev. and Mrs. J. Kaplan, of Toronto, are engaged (9 Aug. 1912, 15, 35)

BERMAN, Martin, of Ottawa, and Miss Susan Silverman were married on Aug. 31, 1913 (5 Sept. 1913, 16, 39)

BERMAN, Martin, of Ottawa, formerly of New York, and Miss Susan Silverman, daughter of Mr. and Mrs. S. Silverman, of Quebec City, are engaged (5 July 1912, 15, 30)

BERNSTEIN, Harry, of Montreal, formerly of London, England, son of Mr. and Mrs. J. Bernstein, and Miss Florence Lauterman, daughter of Mr. and Mrs. M. Lauterman, of Montreal, are engaged. English and American papers please copy (11 April 1913, 16, 18)

BERNSTEIN, Isidore, son of Mr. and Mrs. H. Bernstein, and Miss Sophie Jacobson, daughter of Mr. and Mrs. S. Jacobson, all of Montreal, are engaged (7 Feb. 1913, 16, 9)

BERNSTEIN, William and Miss Annie Friedman, daughter of Mr. and Mrs. A. Friedman, were married by Rabbi Hirsch Cohen, assisted by Rev. Bloomfield, on Feb. 18, 1913 in Auditorium Hall, Montreal. Miss Ethel Kaufmann was maid of honor (7 March 1913, 16, 13)

BERNSTEIN, William and Miss Annie Friedman, daughter of Mr. and Mrs. A. Friedman, all of Montreal, are engaged (18 Oct. 1912, 15, 45)

BISHINSKY, Benjamin and Miss Molly Apple, both of Montreal, were married by Rev. Judelson, Sun. July 28, 1912 at 5 p.m., at the Universal Private Dancing Academy, Montreal (2 Aug. 1912, 15, 34)

BLANKSTEIN, Max and Miss Ida Crown, of Montreal, were recently married (16 April 1909, 12, 18)

BLOOMFIELD, S. and Miss Hannah May Brown, daughter of Mrs. A.J. Brown, of Nashville, Tenn., will be married March 5, 1912, in Nashville (1 March 1912, 15, 16)

BLOOMFIELD, Samuel, of Montreal, and Miss Hannah May Brown, of Nashville, Tenn., are engaged (19 May 1911, 14, 27)

BLUMENTHAL, B.Sc., Samuel and Miss Rose Kaplansky, both of Montreal, were married by Rabbi Nathan Gordon, on Tues. June 8, 1909, at 76 Park Ave., Montreal (11 June 1909, 12, 26)

BLUMENTHAL, Samuel, son of Mr. and Mrs. A. Blumenthal, and Miss Rose Kaplansky, daughter of Mr. and Mrs. A.L. Kaplansky, all of Montreal, will be married Tues. June 8, 1909 (23 April 1909, 12, 19)

BLUMENTHAL, Samuel, son of Mr. and Mrs. A. Blumenthal, and Miss Rose Kaplansky, daughter of Mr. and Mrs. A.L. Kaplansky, all of Montreal, are engaged (12 March 1909, 12, 13)

BLUMER, L., of Montreal, and Miss Rosie Vineberg, eldest daughter of Mr. and Mrs. Elias Vineberg, of Toronto, are engaged (1 Oct. 1909, 12, 42)

BLUMER, Lazar, of Montreal, and Miss Rose Vineberg, daughter of Mr. and Mrs. E. Vineberg, of Toronto, will be married in the University Avenue Synagogue, Toronto, on Sun. Feb. 27, 1910 at 6 p.m. (28 Jan. 1910, 13, 11)

BLUMER, Lazar, of Montreal, and Miss Rose Vineberg, daughter of prominent Zionist, E. Vineberg, 42 Spadina Road, Toronto, were married on Sun. Feb. 27, 1910 in the University Avenue Synagogue, Toronto. A reception followed at the home of the bride's parents. Among those present from Toronto were:- Mr. and Mrs. L. Gelber, Mr. and Mrs. M. Gelber, Mr. and Mrs. M.M. Levy, Mr. and Mrs. and Miss Espar and Mr. and Mrs. Garfinkel. Out-of-town guests included:- Miss Abramsky, of Kingston, Ont.; Mr. and Mrs. A. Blumer, Mr. and Mrs. D. Blumer, A. Rudolph, W. Gradenger, S. Popliger, and S. and M. Bernstein, all of Montreal. A. Harris, chairman of the National Committee, who was also present, had the names of the couple inscribed in the JNF Golden Book. The couple are on their honeymoon in New York and Atlantic City (4 March 1910, 13, 16)

BOLD, I., of Montreal, and Miss Ethel Horowitz, recently of New York, are engaged (19 July 1912, 15, 32)

BORONOW, Robert, eldest son of Mr. and Mrs. Richard Boronow, 79 St. Matthew St., Montreal, and Miss Pansy Fleishman, daughter of J. Fleishman, 1039 Barclay St., Vancouver, are engaged. The marriage will take place in early Aug. (8 July 1910, 13, 34)

BORONOW, Robert, eldest son of Mr. and Mrs. Richard Boronow, St. Matthew St., Montreal, and Miss Pansy Fleishman, daughter of J. Fleishman, will be married in Vancouver on Thurs. Aug. 4, 1910 (5 Aug. 1910, 13, 38)

BORTS, A., of Ottawa, and Miss Ida Greenspon, second eldest daughter of Mr. and Mrs. M. Greenspon, of Montreal, are engaged (16 Sept. 1910, 13, 44)

BOTTLER, Myer and Miss Sonny Nayov, daughter of Mr. and Mrs. Z. Nayov, were married by Rabbi Hirsch Cohen, at 204 St. Lawrence Blvd., Montreal (10 Sept. 1909, 12, 39)

BOULKIND, Samuel, of Montreal, and Miss Fannie Fish, daughter of Mr. and Mrs. A. Fish, of Quebec City, are engaged (25 June 1909, 12, 28)

BRAGER, J.N., of Halifax, and Miss Rose Gordon, daughter of Mr. and Mrs. Moses Gordon, of Toronto, will be married Jan. 29, 1913. Reception at 374 Markham St., Toronto (24 Jan. 1913, 16, 7)

BRAGER, J.N., of Halifax, N.S., and Miss Rose Gordon, daughter of Mr. and Mrs. M. Gordon, of Toronto, are engaged (15 March 1912, 15, 18)

BRAGER, J.N., of Halifax, N.S., and Miss Rose Gordon, second daughter of Mr. and Mrs. M. Gordon, of Toronto, were married by Rev. M. Kaplan in the McCaul Street Synagogue, Toronto on Wed. Jan. 29, 1913 at 5 p.m. The bride was given away by her father. Mrs. I. Lande, the bride's sister, was matron of honor. The Misses Annie and Hester Gordon, the bride's other sisters, were bridesmaids. Master Harold Lande was the page and Miss Rhoda Lande the flower girl. I. Lande was the best man and the groomsmen were J.L. Brager, the groom's brother, and Harry Gordon, of Montreal. After the ceremony dinner was served at the home of the bride's parents, 374 Markham St. Out-of-town guests included:- Mr. and Mrs. C. Brager, L. Brager, and Max Brager (Halifax), S. Gordon, J.C. Gordon, Harry Gordon, Mr. and Mrs. D. Gordon, Mr. and Mrs. J. Lande, and Mr. and Mrs. A.Z. Cohen (Montreal) (7 Feb.

1913, 16, 9)

BREITENBACH, Richard Weimann, of Munich, Germany, and Miss Zerlina M. Blout, daughter of Mr. and Mrs. Emanuel Blout, of Montreal, are engaged (12 Nov. 1909, 12, 48)

BRESLIN, Dr. L.J., eldest son of Mr. and Mrs. S. Breslin, and Miss Reva Nathanson, second daughter of Mr. and Mrs. B. Nathanson, were married by the Rev. J. Gordon on New Year's Day at the residence of the groom's parents, 54 Cecil St., Toronto. The bride's attendants were Miss Lena Breslin, the groom's eldest sister, and Miss Anna Nathanson, the bride's sister (16 Jan. 1914, 17, 6)

BRESLIN, Joseph, of Toronto, and Miss Rose Goldberg, of New York, will be married Sun. May 25, 1913 in the University Avenue Synagogue, Toronto (16 May 1913, 16, 23)

BRESLIN, Joseph, of Toronto, and Miss Rose Goldberg, of New York, are engaged (14 March 1913, 16, 14)

BRODIE, J., of Montreal, and Miss Tilly Miller, daughter of Mr. and Mrs. S. Miller, are engaged (28 May 1909, 12, 24)

BRODSKY, Samuel and Miss Pauline Charles, of Montreal, are engaged (7 March 1913, 16, 13)

BROWMAN, Saul and Miss Harriet E. Schwartz, of New York, will be married by Rabbi Herman Abramowitz on Sun. at 5 p.m. at the McGill College Ave. Synagogue, Montreal (Dec. 22, 1911, 15, 6)

BROWN, A., of Toronto, and Miss Martha Pullan, daughter of Mr. and Mrs. Elias Pullan, 80 D'Arcy St., Toronto, are engaged (25 Oct. 1912, 15, 46)

BROWN, Abraham and Miss Martha Pullan, eldest daughter of Mr. and Mrs. Elias Pullan, were married by Rabbi S. Jacobs, of Toronto, assisted by Rabbi J. Berger, of Ottawa, and Rev. Wladofsky, in the University Avenue Synagogue, Toronto on Thurs. Feb. 20, 1913. Harry Pullan was the best man. Miss Dora Pullan, the bride's sister, was maid of honor. A reception for 450 guests followed in the Temple building. Out-of-town guests included:- the bride's grandfather, B. Pullan, Rabbi J. Berger, Miss Berger, Charles Horwitz, Mr. and Mrs. A. Caplin, Mr. and Mrs. A.L. Florence, and Mr. and Mrs. Thomas Sachs, of Ottawa; G. Kramer, the Misses E. Kramer and E. Marcus, of Boston; and Miss Celia Helman, of Hamilton (28 Feb. 1913, 16, 12)

BRUSER, Michael, son of Mr. and Mrs. H. Bruser, of Winnipeg, and Miss Annie Wolochow, daughter of Mr. and Mrs. A. Wolochow, of Saskatoon, are engaged (15 Oct. 1913, 16, 45)

BURROWS, S., of Detroit, and Miss Mollie Nurrick, daughter of Mrs. L. Nurrick, of Toronto, will be married on March 16, 1911 (10 Feb. 1911, 14, 13)

CARSLEY, Israel and Miss Gertrude Herman were married by Rabbi Simon Glazer on Sun. Jan. 14, 1912 in the New Modern Hall, Montreal (19 Jan. 1912, 15, 10)

CHACHAMOWITZ, Abraham and Miss Tillie Wisenfield were married by Rabbi Simon Glazer on Jan. 8, 1912 in the Auditorium Hall, Montreal (19 Jan. 1912, 15, 10)

CHAWKIN, K. and Miss L. Goldman, both of Montreal, are engaged. An engagement party was held at the home of Mrs. I. Goldman, 2092 St. Lawrence Blvd., Montreal. Guests included H. Vosberg and Mr. and Mrs. S. Slotkoff (21 June 1912, 15, 28)

CHESSLER, B., of Belleville, Ont., and Miss Rose Klein, daughter of Mrs. Klein, of Kingston, Ont., are engaged (7 July 1911, 14, 34)

CLAMAN, I., of Vancouver, and Miss Maud Lazarus were married by Rabbi Nathan Gordon last Tues. aft. in the Windsor Hotel, Montreal. The bride was given away by her father. The bridesmaids were the bride's cousins, the Misses Gladys Blumenthal and Estella Abrahams. B. Gardner was best man and the ushers were Leonard Abrahams and Alex. Silverstone (9 June 1911, 14, 30)

CLAMAN, I., of Vancouver, B.C., and Miss Maude Lazarus, daughter of Mr. and Mrs. Henry Lazarus, Oliver St., Westmount, Que., are engaged (13 Jan. 1911, 14, 9)

COHEN, Abraham and Miss Gertrude Lehrer, daughter of Mr. and Mrs. H. Lehrer, were married by Rabbi Herman Abramowitz and Rev. S. Goldstein, on Wed. Jan. 5, 1910 in the McGill College Ave. Synagogue, Montreal. A reception and dinner followed in the Auditorium Hall (7 Jan. 1910, 13, 8)

COHEN, Arthur, of Toronto, and Miss Essie Wolfe, of San Francisco, were married in New York, on Tues. Nov. 15, 1910. Mr. and Mrs. Cohen will be "at home" at their residence, 165 Lowther Ave. Toronto, on Sun. Nov. 27, 1910 (25 Dec. 1910, 14, 2)

COHEN, David and Miss Eva Shearman, daughter of Mr. and Mrs. Lyon Shearman, were married by Rabbi Hirsch Cohen, on June 18, 1909, at 199 St. Lawrence Blvd., Montreal (25 June 1909, 12, 28)

COHEN, Frank and Miss Olga Rabinovitch, both of Montreal, were married by Rabbi Herman Abramowitz, assisted by Rev. Cohen on Sun. March 29, 1914 in the McGill College Avenue Synagogue, Montreal. The bride was given away by her father. Miss Bessie Cohen, the groom's sister, was maid of honor. The best man was Horace Cohen. The matrons of honor were Mesdames I. Goldwater, H. Rabinovitch, A. Cohen, the groom's mother, and A. Derosa, the bride's mother. After the ceremony dinner for 150 guests was served in Auditorium Hall (3 April 1914, 17, 14)

COHEN, Frank and Miss Olga Sandbrand-Rabinovitch, will be married on Sun. March 29, 1914 at 4.50 p.m., in the McGill College Avenue Synagogue, Montreal (27 Feb. 1914, 17, 9)

COHEN, Frank, youngest son of Mr. and Mrs. A. Cohen, of Montreal, and Miss Olga Rabinovitch, only daughter of Mr. and Mrs. A. Derosa, of Outremont, Que., are engaged (1 Oct. 1913, 16, 42-43)

COHEN, Harold, of St. Albans, Vt., and Miss Nellie Vineberg, daughter of Mr. and Mrs. J.L. Vineberg, of Montreal (formerly of Sherbrooke, Que.), are engaged (5 Jan. 1912, 15, 8)

COHEN, Harry and Miss Doris Simon, both staunch Zionists, were married in the University Street Synagogue, Toronto, last Wed. aft. (4 June 1909, 12, 25)

COHEN, Harry and Miss Sara Rapholovitch were married by Rabbi Herman Abramowitz, assisted by Rev. D. Epstein in the Auditorium Hall, Montreal, on Tues. Feb. 11, 1913. The bride was given away by her father. Mrs. A. Weiner, the groom's sister, was matron of honor. Miss Dorothy Halperin, the groom's niece, was maid of honor, and the Misses Jessie Halperin, Becky Cohen and Becky Blumberg were bridesmaids. Harry Bessner was best man and Max Bloomberg, Max Bernstein and Isidore Blumberg were groomsmen. Out-of-town guests included:- the groom's brother, Charles H. Cohen, of Chicago, Ill.; Mrs. M. Pollack, of Quebec City; and Mr. Levin and S.M. Hansher, of Toronto. The Young People's Hachnosis Orchim Society presented the couple with a silver tea service. Mr. and Mrs. Cohen went to New York for their honeymoon (21 Feb. 1913, 16, 11)

COHEN, Harry and Miss Sara Rapholovitch, daughter of Mr. and Mrs. R. Rapholovitch, 1515 Esplanade Ave., Montreal, will be married Feb. 11, 1913 (17 Jan. 1913, 16, 6)

COHEN, Harry, of Hamilton, Ont., and Miss Ettie Halpern, daughter of Rev. I. Halpern, of Toronto, are engaged (10 March 1911, 14, 17)

COHEN, Joseph and Miss Ada Bella Gross will be married Sun. May 25, 1913 in Montreal (2 May 1913, 16, 21)

COHEN, Julius A. and Miss Fanny Lurie, niece of Mr. and Mrs. Lewis Levy, 74 Laval Ave., Montreal, are engaged (1 April 1910, 13, 20)

COHEN, Mark, son of Mr. and Mrs. Moe Cohen, of Toronto, and Miss Evelyn Levy, of Rochester, N.Y., sister of Mrs. (Dr.) Levine, are engaged (2 Oct. 1912, 15, 42)

COHEN, Mitchell, of New York, and Miss Lena Lubinsky, daughter of Mr. and Mrs. J. Lubinsky, 248 Simcoe St., Toronto, are engaged (3 Jan. 1913, 16, 4)

COHEN, Samuel and Miss Rebecca Wexler, daughter of Mr. and Mrs. A. Wexler, will be married in the Chevra Kadisha Synagogue, St. Urbain St., Montreal, on Sun. July 2, 1911 (9 June 1911, 14, 30)

COHEN, William and Miss Sadie Vineberg, daughter of Mr. and Mrs. Maxwell Vineberg, of Montreal, were married by Rabbi Herman Abramowitz last Tues. aft. in the Auditorium Hall, Berthelet St., Montreal (12 Feb. 1909, 12, 9)

COOPER, Julius, of Montreal, and Miss Leba Ginsberg, daughter of Mr. and Mrs. M. Ginsberg, Drolet St., Montreal, are engaged (23 Feb. 1912, 15, 15)

COPPER, S.M., of Malden, Mass., and Miss Ruby Kaplan, daughter of Mr. and Mrs. I. Kaplan, of Yarmouth are engaged (30 Sept. 1910, 13, 46)

COPPER, Samuel F. and Miss Ruby Kaplan, daughter of Mr. and Mrs. Kaplan, of Yarmouth, N.S., are engaged (23 Sept. 1910, 13, 45)

CORNFELD, Jack and Miss Becky Samuel, daughter of Mr. and Mrs. M. Samuel, will be married in the McCaul Street Synagogue, Toronto, on Tues. Jan. 3, 1911. The reception will be held in the Cosmopolitan Club (2 Dec. 1910, 14, 3)

COSSMAN, Jack and Miss Rose Kert, daughter of Mrs. N. Sperber, are engaged (16 April 1909, 12, 18)

COTZEN, M.D. and Miss Alice Pinsler, daughter of Mr. and Mrs. Paul Pinsler, all of Montreal, are engaged (24 Jan. 1913, 16, 7)

COWEN, Jack, of Montreal, and Miss Rose Yampolsky, daughter of Mr. and Mrs. C. Yampolsky, of Montreal, are engaged and will be married shortly (3 April 1914, 17, 14)

DAVID, Jacob, of Ottawa, and Miss Gertrude Rubin, daughter of Mr. and Mrs. J. Rubin, of Montreal, were married by Rabbi Herman Abramowitz, assisted by Rev. S. Goldstein, on Sun. Sept. 5, 1909, in the Auditorium Hall, Montreal (10 Sept. 1909, 12, 39)

DAVIS, S., of Ottawa, and Miss Gertie Rubin, daughter of Mr. and Mrs. J. Rubin, of Montreal, are engaged (29 Jan. 1909, 12, 7)

DAVIS, Walter and Miss Mamie Woolfson were married on Sun. Sept. 28, 1913, in the Austro-Hungarian Synagogue, Milton St., Montreal. $8.00 was collected for the Herzl Wald (15 Oct. 1913, 16, 45)

DEUTSCH, Solomon, E.E., B.Sc., (France), of Montreal, and Miss Tillie Newman, daughter of Mr. and Mrs. D. Newman, of New York City, are engaged (23 April 1909, 12, 19)

DIAMOND, Samuel, of Ottawa, Ont., and Miss Sebina Rubin, daughter of Mr. and Mrs. J. Rubin, of Montreal, were married by Rabbi M.A. Lauterman, assisted by Rev. Judelson, last Sun. in the Auditorium Hall, Montreal. The Misses S. Hilf and S. Rubin were bridesmaids and N. Rubin was the best man. Lazarus Teplitzky was toastmaster. Rabbi Lauterman, Mr. Margolese, M.A. Levine and Isidore Friedman made speeches and E. Gordon made a presentation on behalf of Victoria Lodge, IOSB. Mr. Rubin is a longtime member of the IOSB. Out-of-town guests were:- Mr. and Mrs. L. Davis, Mr. and Mrs. J. Davis, Mr. and Mrs. A.J. Freiman, Mr. and Mrs. F. Diamond, I. Slonemsky (Ottawa), Mr. and Mrs. Freeman and daughters (Hamilton), and Charles and I. Kert (3 Feb. 1911, 14, 12)

DIAMONDSTEIN, William Benjamin and Miss Mamie Beatrice Ballon, eldest daughter of Mr. and Mrs. Samuel Ballon, Crescent St., Montreal, were married in New York on Sept. 21, 1913 (5 Sept. 1913, 16, 39)

DIAMONDSTEIN, William Benjamin, son of Rev. and Mrs. P.H. Diamondstein, of New York, and Miss Mamie Beatrice Ballon, eldest daughter of Mr. and Mrs. Samuel Ballon, Crescent St., Montreal, are engaged (21 March 1913, 16, 15)

DOLGORF, Samuel, of Toronto, and Miss Dora Kauffman, daughter of Mr. and Mrs. Jacob Kauffman, 286 Hess St. S., Hamilton, were married by Rabbi Jacob S. Minkin in Hamilton. Miss Bessie Kauffman, the bride's sister, was maid of honor and the bridesmaid was Miss Emma Kauffman. Saul Kauffman, the bride's brother, was best man. The bride received a gift from the Anshe Sholem Synagogue choir and congregation. Guests included Mrs. Dolgorf, the groom's mother, Jack Dolgorf (Montreal), Mrs. Unger and Abe Meyer, (Rochester), and Miss Anna Kauffman (Buffalo) (7 June 1912, 15, 26)

DRAIMIN, Charles, of Toronto, and Miss Bertha King, of Whitby, Ont., are engaged (18 March 1910, 13, 18)

DRAPKIN, A., of Fort William, Ont., and Miss Rose Fine, eldest daughter of Mr. and Mrs. M. Fine, of Ottawa, will be married April 15, 1913 in Ottawa (4 April 1913, 16, 17)

DRAPKIN, A., of Fort William, Ont., and Miss Rose Fine, eldest daughter of Mr. and Mrs. M. Fine, of Ottawa, were married by Rabbi S. Fyne, assisted by Rev. J. Berger and Rev. Mirsky on Tues. April 15, 1913, in the Racquet Court, Ottawa. The bride was given away by her parents. Miss Jennie Greenspon, of Montreal, was maid of honor and the bridesmaids were the Misses Becky Fine, the bride's sister, and Miss Essie Smith, her cousin. Miss Fanny Smith was the flower girl. Mrs. Maurice Fine was matron of honor. Ben Goldfield was best man and the ushers were C. Horwitz and I. Hyman. Out-of-town guests were Mr. and Mrs. M. Fine, of Toronto; and Mesdames Black and Spittel, of Fort William. Mr. and Mrs. Drapkin went to Montreal, Toronto and Fort William for their honeymoon (25 April 1913, 16, 20)

DUCOFFE, M.A., of Bridgewater, N.S., and Miss Ida E. Hoffman, daughter of Mr. and Mrs. Charles Hoffman, are engaged (7 June 1912, 15, 26)

DUNKLEMAN, David and Miss Rose Miller, eldest daughter of Mr. and Mrs. Miller, Yonge St., Toronto, were married Thurs. by Rabbi W. Gordon, and the Revs. M. Caplan and F. Cohen, in the University Avenue Synagogue, Toronto. Miss Adeline Miller, the bride's little sister led the bridal procession. After the ceremony Mrs. Miller received three hundred guests at the Cosmopolitan Club. Mr. and Mrs. Dunkleman spent their honeymoon in New York (28 Jan. 1910, 13, 11)

DWORKIN, Edward S. and Miss Annie Mendes will be married next Sun. evening, Jan. 2, 1910 at 6 p.m., at 269 Spadina Ave., Toronto (31 Dec. 1909, 13, 7)

DWORKIN, Henry S., manager of Dworkin's Advertising Bureau, Toronto, and Miss Dorothy Goldstick, 36 Division St., Toronto, are engaged (18 March 1910, 13, 18)

EDELSTEIN, Harry, second son of Mr. and Mrs. A.M. Edelstein, 315 Bay St., and Miss Mildred Hollander, eldest daughter of Mr. and Mrs. S. Hollander, 234 Slater St., all of Ottawa, are engaged (23 Aug. 1912, 15, 37)

EDELSTEIN, Harry, second son of Mr. and Mrs. A.M. Edelstein, of Dublin and Ottawa, and Miss Mildred Hollander, eldest daughter of Mr. and Mrs. S. Hollander, of Ottawa, were married by Rabbi S. Fyne in the King Edward Street Synagogue last Sun. The bride was given away by her parents. The bridesmaids were the Misses Sadie and Fanny Miller (Cornwall, Ont.), Sarah Dubinsky (Montreal), and Ray Edelstein. The groom was given away by his parents. J. Salter was best man. At the dinner, J. Holzman proposed the toast and Rabbi Fyne spoke on Jewish Orthodoxy, "...and hoped that true Jewish sentiment would always be manifested from the couple whom he had joined in holy matrimony." Out-of-town guests included:- L. Millar and Mesdames L. Lefkovitz and D.A. Millar. Harry Edelstein is The Canadian Jewish Times correspondent in Ottawa (21 March 1913, 16, 15)

EISEN, Ike and Miss Celia Glasser, daughter of Mr. and Mrs. David Glasser, all of Montreal, were married recently in Montreal (12 Sept. 1913, 16, 40)

EISENSTADT, S.M. and Miss Sadie Rudolph, eldest daughter of Mr. and Mrs. A. Rudolph, all of Montreal, are engaged (19 July 1912, 15, 32)

EISENSTADT, Solomon M., second son of Mr. and Mrs. Ch. Eisenstadt, of Georgenburg, Russia, and Miss Sadie Rudolph, eldest daughter of Mr. and Mrs. A. Rudolph, 33 Laval Ave., Montreal, will be married on Jan. 28, 1913 in the Majestic Hall, Guy St., Montreal (24 Jan. 1913, 16, 7)

EISENSTADT, Solomon M., son of Mr. and Mrs. Ch. Eisenstadt, of Georgenburg, Russia, and Miss Sadie Rudolph, eldest daughter of Mr. and Mrs. A. Rudolph, Laval Ave., Montreal, were married by Rabbi Herman Abramowitz on Tues. in Montreal. Miss Helena Eisenstadt was the bridesmaid and Miss B. Rudolph the maid of honor. A reception was held that evening in the Majestic Hall, Guy St. for 350 guests. Guests included:- Mr. and Mrs. Eisenstadt (Georgenburg, Russia), J.J. Eisenstadt (Prince Rupert, B.C.), L. Rubinowitch (Fort William, Ont.), Mr. Ness (Ivry, Ont.), Lazarus Cohen, Lyon Cohen, Lionel Coviensky, David Dainow, Louis Fitch, S. Hyams, Myer Isaacs, Sidney Isaacs, Mr. and Mrs. A.I. Rubinowitch, Mr. and Mrs. J.B. Rubinowitch, and the Misses Ethel Kaufman, B. Willinsky, E. Bernstein and M. Bernstein. Mr. and Mrs. Eisenstadt went to New York for their honeymoon (31 Jan. 1913, 16, 8)

EISMAN, Julius, of Toronto, and Miss Kathleen Isaacs, daughter of Mr. and Mrs. Joel D. Isaacs, of Chicago, Ill., are engaged (21 April 1911, 14, 23)

ELKIN, J., of Montreal, and Miss Esther Ogulnik, daughter of Mr. and Mrs. Paul Ogulnik, of Montreal, are engaged (4 March 1910, 13, 16)

ELKIN, Jacob, son of Mr. and Mrs. A. Elkin, and Miss Esther Ogulnik, sister of Paul Ogulnik, were married by Rabbi Herman Abramowitz, assisted by the Revs. Judelson and S. Goldstein, last Thurs. evening, June 9, 1910 in the Stanley Hall, Stanley St., Montreal. Miss Rose Elkin, the bridegroom's sister, was maid of honor. Misses Bessie Elkin and Edythe Ogulnik were bridesmaids. Miss Blanche Ogulnik, the bride's niece, was flower girl. Louis Ogulnik, the bride's brother, acted as best man. Max and Samuel Elkin were the ushers. Mr. and Mrs. Ogulnik left for the West on a honeymoon. On their return they will reside at 61 Esplanade Ave., Montreal (17 June 1910, 13, 31)

ENGEL, N.L. (B.Sc.), and Miss Sarah Lesser, daughter of Mr. and Mrs. M. Lesser, Mance St., all of Montreal, are engaged (7 Nov. 1913, 16, 48)

EPSTEIN, Harry, of Vancouver, and Miss Hirschfield, of New York, were married at the residence of William Diamond, of Edmonton, president of the Edmonton Hebrew Association. J. Berkman, the Association's treasurer, acted as toastmaster and Mr. Cooper, of Calgary, also spoke. J. Goodman, president of the local Hebrew Literary Institute made an appeal on behalf of the Herzl Wald. Mr. and Mrs. Epstein left that evening for Vancouver where they will reside (11 Aug. 1911, 14, 39)

ERDILEFSKY, A. and Miss Rosie Fineberg, daughter of Mr. and Mrs. A. Fineberg, all of Montreal, are engaged (12 Dec. 1913, 17, 1)

FEICZWEICZ, J., of Quebec City, and Miss Clara Mintz, of Montreal, are engaged (3 Jan. 1913, 16, 4)

FEINBERG, Harry and Miss Leah Crown, eldest daughter of Mr. and Mrs. Moses Crown, were married by Rabbi Herman Abramowitz, assisted by Rev. S. Goldstein, Tues. aft. in the Auditorium Hall, Montreal. The bride was given away by her father. Miss Mary Crown, the bride's sister was bridesmaid and her brother, Meyer Crown, acted as best man. Mr. and Mrs. Feinberg left on a honeymoon through the Thousand Islands. After visiting Toronto, Buffalo and Niagara Falls, they will reside in Sudbury, Ont. (24 June 1910, 13, 32)

FEINBERG, Harry, of Sudbury, Ont., and Miss Leah Crown, daughter of Mr. and Mrs. M. Crown, of Montreal, are engaged (1 April 1910, 13, 20)

FEINBERG, Harry, of Sudbury, Ont., and Miss Leah Crown, daughter of Mr. and Mrs. Moses Crown, of Montreal, will be married on Tues. June 21, 1910 in the Auditorium Hall, Montreal (17 June 1910, 13, 31)

FENSTER, Issie, 82 Laval Ave., and Miss Mary Flanders, daughter of Mr. and Mrs. M. Flanders, 915 Cadieux St., all of Montreal, are engaged (25 Sept. 1912, 15, 42)

FINE, Elias, 171 University Ave., Toronto, and Miss Sheindel Brimm, of Rochester, N.Y., were married by Rabbi W. Gordon and Rev. I. Cohen, in Goel Zedek Synagogue, Toronto (4 March 1910, 13, 16)

FINEBERG, H.S., son of Mr. and Mrs. A. Fineberg, 27 Craig St., and Miss Sadie Serchuck, daughter of Mr. and Mrs. H. Serchuck, 996 St. Lawrence Blvd., all of Montreal, were engaged Jan. 5, 1913 (10 Jan. 1913, 16, 5)

FINESTEIN, Harry and Miss Gertrude Levy, both of Toronto, are engaged (17 Feb. 1911, 14, 14)

FINESTONE, Ted. and Miss Brina Fox, daughter of Mrs. Fox, all of Montreal, are engaged (2 Jan. 1914, 17, 4)

FINK, Morris and Miss Rae Holzberg, both of Montreal, are engaged (11 June 1909, 12, 26)

FINKELSTEIN, Nathan and Miss Annie Greenberg, and Samuel Solomon and Miss Rose Finkelstein, were married in a double wedding ceremony on Nov. 4, 1913, at 229 Ontario St., Montreal. Nathan Finkelstein and Miss Rose Finkelstein are the grandchildren of Mrs. H. Holdengraber, of Sherbrooke, Que. Guests present included:- Mr. and Mrs. M.B. Echenberg, Mr. and Mrs. M. Smith, Mrs. M. Echenberg and her two daughters, of Sherbrooke, Que.; Mr. and Mrs. S. Holdengraber, of Bathurst, N.B.; Mr. and Mrs. O.L. Kerner, Mr. and Mrs. A. Holdengraber, Mr. and Mrs. L. Pozner, Mr. and Mrs. B. Finkelstein, Mr. and Mrs. Gould, Mrs. D. Fels, the Misses Clara Echenberg and Gould, Messrs. S. Kerner, G. Laxer and E. Segal (14 Nov. 1913, 16, 49)

FISHER, S., of Rimouski, Que., and Miss Annie Sorkis, daughter of Mr. I. Sorkis, 435 St. Urbain St., Montreal, are engaged (29 Jan. 1909, 12, 7)

FISHMAN, Philip and Miss Edith Wener, were married by Rabbi Herman Abramowitz, on Tues. March 2, 1909, at 3 p.m. in the Shaar Hashomayim Synagogue, Montreal (12 March 1909, 12, 13)

FITCH, Charles, of Montreal, and Miss Rebekah Feiczewicz, eldest daughter of Mr. and Mrs. D. Feiczewicz, of Quebec City, are engaged (20 Dec. 1912, 16, 2)

FLORENCE, Philip M., eldest son of Mr. and Mrs. A. Florence, Duluth Ave. W., and Miss Sarah Weinstein, eldest daughter of Mr. and Mrs. A. Weinstein, Clarke Ave., all of Montreal, are engaged (28 March 1913, 16, 16)

FREED, Harry, of Montreal, and Miss Flossie Goldstein, daughter of Mr. and Mrs. B. Goldstein, were married by Rabbi Nathan Gordon last Tues. evening in Auditorium Hall, Montreal (7 Jan. 1910, 13, 8)

FREEDMAN, Albert and Miss Mabel Hart, daughter of Mr. and Mrs. Lewis A. Hart, of Montreal, will be married on Oct. 14, 1909 (1 Oct. 1909, 12, 42)

FREEDMAN, Albert, of Montreal, son of Mr. and Mrs. Freedman, of Antwerp, Belgium, and Miss Mabel Hart, daughter of Mr. and Mrs. Lewis A. Hart, 236 Elm Ave., Westmount, Que., were married by Rabbi Meldola de Sola, on Oct. 14, 1909, at 8 p.m., at the home of the bride's parents. The bride's attendant was her sister, Miss Gladys Hart. Philip Hart acted as best man. "The honeymoon will be spent in Western Canada, and later Mr. and Mrs. Freedman will leave for Australia." (22 Oct. 1909, 12, 45)

FREEDMAN, Albert, son of Mr. and Mrs. S. Freedman, of Antwerp, Belgium, and Miss Mabel Hart, daughter of Mr. and Mrs. Lewis A. Hart, 236 Elm Ave., Westmount, Que., are engaged (18 June 1909, 12, 27)

FRIEDMAN, Benjamin, of Montreal, and Miss Mary Cohen, daughter of Mr. and Mrs. R. Cohen, will be married in June, 1909 (19 March 1909, 12, 14)

FRIEDMAN, Jack, of Montreal, and Miss Minnie Signer, daughter of Mr. and Mrs. A.J. Signer, of Montreal are engaged (1 April 1910, 13, 20)

FRIEDMAN, Jacob and Miss Minnie Signer, daughter of Mr. and Mrs. A.J. Signer, were married by Rabbis Hirsch Cohen and Herman Abramowitz last Tues. in the Shaar Hashomayim Synagogue, Montreal. That evening a reception was held in Auditorium Hall. Miss Gertie Signer was the bridesmaid and Maurice Schonfeld, of Minneapolis, was the best man (19 May 1911, 14, 27)

FRIEDMAN, Max, of Montreal, and Miss Anna Krawatz, daughter of Jake Krawatz, of New York, were engaged Sun. Sept. 15, 1912. The wedding will take place in Montreal in about three months (25 Sept. 1912, 15, 42)

FRIEZE, Jack, son of Mr. and Mrs. Frieze, of Montreal, and Miss Lily Denis, daughter of Mrs. Denis, are engaged (5 Dec. 1913, 16, 52)

GARBER, Ellie, son of Rabbi and Mrs. S. Garber, of Montreal, and Miss Sarah Shevell, daughter of Rev. and Mrs. I. Shevell, of New York, are engaged (11 July 1913, 16, 31)

GART, Max, of Chicago, and Miss Riva Rittenberg, of Montreal, were married by Rabbi Meldola de Sola on Sun. Dec. 7, 1913 in the Spanish and Portuguese Synagogue, Stanley St., Montreal. Mrs. B. Silver was the matron of honor. A reception was held at the home of Mr. and Mrs. B. Silver, 381 Elm Ave. Mr. and Mrs. Gart left for Chicago where they will reside (12 Dec. 1913, 17, 1)

GART, Ralph, of Chicago, and Miss Riva Rittenberg, niece of Mr. and Mrs. B. Silver, Elm Ave., Westmount, Que., are engaged (5 Dec. 1913, 16, 52)

GELBER, G., of Toronto, and Miss Sarah Katz, of Detroit, Mich., are engaged and will be married in May (13 Feb. 1914, 17, 7)

GETZBUN, Carl and Miss Fanny Goldbar, daugher of Mr. and Mrs. M. Goldbar, will be married in the McCaul Street Synagogue, Toronto, on Feb. 21, 1911 (10 Feb. 1911, 14, 13)

GILLMAN, Harry, of La Tuque, Que., and Miss Goldie Rutenberg, daughter of Mr. and Mrs. C. Rutenberg, of Montreal, are engaged (21 April 1911, 14, 23)

GLASSMAN, Thomas and Miss Sarah Sterling, both of Toronto, were married recently by Rabbi S. Jacobs in the Zionist Institute, Simcoe St., Toronto. Guests included the groom's mother, Mrs. Joseph Glassman (who had come specially from Liverpool, England to be present), Mr. and Mrs. Nathan Brenner, Mr. and Mrs. Joseph Cohn, Miss Landsberg and Barnett Stone (15 April 1910, 13, 22)

GLENN, Samuel and Miss Rosie Manuel were married by Rabbi I. Kahanovitch in Winnipeg. The couple left for New York and upon their return will reside in Winnipeg (10 Oct. 1913, 16, 44)

GLICKMAN, I. and Miss Lena Mirsky, daughter of Mr. and Mrs. H. Mirsky, all of Glace Bay, N.S., will be married on Thurs. March 7, 1911 (24 Feb. 1911, 14, 15)

GLUCK, Samuel, of Budapest, New York and Ottawa, and Miss Becca Edelstein, daughter of Mr. and Mrs. A.M. Edelstein, of Dublin and Ottawa, were married by Rev. Eighler, assisted by Samuel Engler, J.P., on Jan. 16, 1913 in Hoboken, N.J. (24 Jan. 1913, 16, 7)

GLUCKMAN, David and Miss Pearl Katz, daughter of Mrs. Miriam Katz, were married in the University Avenue Synagogue, Toronto last Sun. (28 Jan. 1910, 13, 11)

GOLD, Maurice, second son of Mr. and Mrs. I. Gold, and Miss Annie Solomon, daughter of Mrs. G. Solomon, all of Montreal, are engaged (31 Oct. 1913, 16, 47)

GOLDBERG, Avigdor, third son of Mr. and Mrs. I.L. Goldberg, of London, England, and Miss Ray Turner, eldest daughter of Mr. and Mrs. J.B. Turner, 627 St. Lawrence Blvd., Montreal, are engaged (14 Feb. 1913, 16, 10)

GOLDBERG, Moe and Miss Hattie Bernstein, daughter of Mr. and Mrs. H. Bernstein, were married on Sun. May 25, 1913 in the Chevra Kadisha Synagogue, St. Urbain St., Montreal. Miss Violet Bernstein, the bride's sister, was maid of honour and Miss Sophie Jacobson was the bridesmaid. Max Bernstein, the bride's brother acted as best man and Isidore Bernstein as groomsman. The matrons of honor were Mesdames C. Bernstein and M.B. Levitt. Dinner for the immediate family was held in Prince Arthur Hall, followed by a reception that evening (30 May 1913, 16, 25)

GOLDBERG, Saul and Miss Rebecca Diamond, daughter of Mr. and Mrs. S. Diamond, of Sault Ste. Marie, Ont., will be married on Jan. 2, 1910, at the home of the bride's parents (31 Dec. 1909, 13, 7)

GOLDBERG, Saul, of Chicago, and Miss Rhoda Diamond, daughter of Mr. and Mrs. S. Diamond, of Sault Ste. Marie, Ont., were married by Rev. J. Zimmerman, assisted by Rev. Broudie, both of the Soo, Mich., at the home of the bride's parents on Sun. evening, Jan. 2, 1910. Miss Miriam Diamond, the bride's sister, was maid of honor. The bridesmaids were the Misses Leah Diamond and Sarah Kozlow, of Soo Mich. Abraham Goldberg, of Chicago, the groom's brother, was best man. The ushers were Isaac Cohen, Abraham Cohen and Joel Diamond. About sixty guests attended. The couple left for Chicago (14 Jan. 1910, 13, 9)

GOLDEN, Abraham, a Boston merchant, and Miss Sarah Goldstein, vocalist, second daughter of Rev. S. Goldstein, formerly of Montreal and now of Boston, Mass., are engaged (1 March 1912, 15, 16)

GOLDENBERG, Bernard, of Three Rivers, Que., and Miss Rose Silverstone, daughter of Mr. and Mrs. J. Silverstone, 152 St. Joseph Blvd. W., Montreal, are engaged (18 April 1913, 16, 19)

GOLDENBERG, Bernard, of Three Rivers, Que., and Miss Rose Silverstone were married by Rabbi Simon Glazer on Sun. June 29, 1913, at the home of the bride's parents, 152 St. Joseph Blvd. W., Montreal. The bride was given away by her father. The bridesmaids were Mrs. Crystal, the bride's sister (New York), and the groom's sisters, Mrs. Parness, and the Misses Minnie and Marion Goldenberg. The flower girl was the bride's niece, Miss Rosaline Crystal. The groom was attended by his brother, Boyer Goldenberg and Charles Silverstone. Mr. and Mrs. Goldenberg went on a honeymoon out west and on their return will reside in Three Rivers (18 July 1913, 16, 32)

GOLDENBERG, Boyer, son of Mr. and Mrs. P. Goldenberg, of Three Rivers, Que., and Miss Ida Diamond, daughter of Mr. and Mrs. M. Diamond, are engaged (9 Jan. 1914, 17, 5)

GOLDENBERG, I., of Dalhousie, N.B., and Miss F. Kriger, daughter of Mr. and Mrs. S. Kriger, of Ottawa, are engaged (11 Oct. 1910, 13, 47)

GOLDENBERG, J., of Campbellton, N.B., and Miss Rose Lax, of Quebec City, were married by Rev. Eliasoph in the Beth Israel Synagogue, Quebec City. The bride was given away by Mr. and Mrs. H. Lax and the groom by Mr. and Mrs. E. Glassbourg. A reception followed in the Auditorium Hall (7 Feb. 1913, 16, 9)

GOLDENBERG, Joseph, of Campbellton, N.B., and Miss Rosie Lax, youngest daughter of Mr. and Mrs. J. Lax, of Quebec City, are engaged (1 Nov. 1912, 15, 47)

GOLDENSTEIN, Louis and Miss Rose Goldner, daughter of Mr. and Mrs. A. Goldner, of Montreal, are engaged and will be married in Feb. 1914 (2 Jan. 1914, 17, 4)

GOLDFINE, L., son of Mr. and Mrs. E. Goldfine, of Montreal, and Miss Ida Levy, daughter of Rabbi and Mrs. M.A. Levy, of Toronto, will be married in Toronto, on March 19, 1912 (12 Jan. 1912, 15, 9)

GOLDMAN, Jack, of Montreal, and Miss May Liverman, daughter of Mr. and Mrs. Liverman, 69 St. Famille St., Montreal, are engaged (29 Nov. 1912, 15, 51)

GOLDMAN, Jacob and Miss May Liverman, both of Montreal, will be married March 20, 1913 in Stanley Hall, Montreal (7 March 1913, 16, 13)

GOLDMAN, S.H., of Chicago, and Miss S. Bauet, of Toronto, are engaged (19 July 1912, 15, 32)

GOLDSMITH, Samuel and Miss Martha Davis, daughter of the late William Davis and Mrs. Rappaport, were married recently in the Holy Blossom Synagogue, Bond St., Toronto. Miss Anna Rosenberg acted as bridesmaid. The couple were members of the synagogue choir which is where they met (9 July 1909, 12, 30)

GOLDSTEIN, D. and Miss Jennie Frohman, both of Hamilton, Ont., are engaged (15 Oct. 1909, 12, 44)

GOLDSTEIN, E., of New Haven, Conn., and Miss Anna Adelson, of Winnipeg, will be married by Rabbi J.K. Levin, in the Shaarey Shomayim Synagogue, Winnipeg, on June 8, 1909 (28 May 1909, 12, 24)

GOLDSTEIN, Emmanuel and Miss Anna Adilman were married by Rabbi J.K. Levin, in Winnipeg, on June 8, 1909. The couple are spending their honeymoon in New Haven, Conn., the home of the bridegroom's parents (18 June 1909, 12, 27)

GOLDSTEIN, F. and Miss Ray Ackman, youngest daughter of Mrs. Anna Ackman, all of Montreal, are engaged (1 Sept. 1911, 14, 42)

GOLDSTEIN, I., formerly of Montreal, and Miss Clara Jonas, were married by Rabbi R. Farber, of Temple Emanu-El, on Thurs. Nov. 30, 1911 at the home of Mr. and Mrs. A.D. Goldstein, 1724 Pendrell St., Vancouver. The bride was given away by her brother-in-law, A.D. Goldstein. Mrs. D.A. Goldstein was matron of honor. Miss Sylvia Goldstein was the flower girl and Master Cyril Goldstein was the page. Meyer Goldstein acted as groomsman. Mr. and Mrs. Goldstein went to Seattle and other cities for their honeymoon. On their return they will reside in Vancouver (15 Dec. 1911, 15, 5)

GOLDSTEIN, Max, of Montreal, and Miss Leah Clayman, daughter of Mr. and Mrs. Wolf Clayman, were married by Rabbi Hirsch Cohen at the home of the bride's parents, 199 St. Lawrence Blvd., Montreal, on Thurs. June 3, 1909 (11 June 1909, 12, 26)

GOLDSTEIN, Reuben and Miss Minnie Tobias, daughter of Mrs. L. Tobias, of Winnipeg, are engaged (19 Feb. 1909, 12, 10)

GOLDWATER, Ralph and Miss Rebecca Miller, daughter of Lewis Miller, all of Lachine, Que., are engaged (18 Nov. 1910, 14, 1)

GOLT, David L., of Montreal, and Miss Bessie Godel, daughter of Mr. and Mrs. M. Godel, are engaged (18 Oct. 1910, 13, 48)

GOODMAN, J. and Miss Sabloff, both of Montreal, were married by Rabbi Hirsch Cohen on Thurs. June 28, 1912 in the Austro-Hungarian Synagogue, Milton St., Montreal. The bride was given away by her brother, H. Sabloff. After the ceremony a reception was held at the home of the bride's parents, 247 Craig St. W. Guests included Mr. and Mrs. J. Slovinsky, of Ottawa (5 July 1912, 15, 30)

GOODMAN, Michael, of Montreal, and Miss Fannie Phillips, daughter of Mr. and Mrs. F. Phillips, St. Lawrence Blvd., Montreal, are engaged (2 April 1909, 12, 16)

GOODMAN, Samuel, formerly of Rochester, N.Y., and Miss Ruby Jacobson, daughter of Mr. and Mrs. S. Bloom, Beatrice St., Toronto, are engaged (11 March 1910, 13, 17)

GOODWIN, Michael and Miss Fannie Phillips were married by Rabbi Hirsch Cohen in the Auditorium Hall, Montreal, last Tues. Jan. 18, 1910. The bridesmaids were the Misses Anna and Rebecca Phillips. Julius Cooper and A. Bavitz were the groomsmen (21 Jan. 1910, 13, 10)

GORDON, Rabbi Nathan and Miss Gertrude Workman, daughter of Mr. and Mrs. Mark Workman, all of Montreal, are engaged (12 May 1911, 14, 26)

GORDON, Rabbi Nathan and Miss Gertrude Workman, daughter of Mr. and Mrs. Mark Workman, all of Montreal, will be married Tues. Dec. 19, 1911 (15 Dec. 1911, 15, 5)

GORDON, Rabbi Nathan, son of Mr. and Mrs. F. Gordon, and Miss Gertrude Workman, daughter of Mr. and Mrs. Mark Workman, were married by Rabbi Isaac Landman, of Philadelphia, on Tues. at 5 p.m., at the home of the bride's parents, Sherbrooke St. W., Montreal. Miss Nina Workman, the bride's sister, was maid of honor. B. Gardiner was best man. The bride's brother, Philip Gordon, of New York, played the wedding music. Rabbi and Mrs. Gordon went to Washington and points south for their honeymoon. They will reside in Montreal on their return (22 Dec. 1911, 15, 6)

GREEN, N.L., of Regina, and Miss Dorothy Weidman, daughter of Mr. and Mrs. H.L. Weidman, of Winnipeg, are engaged (25 June 1909, 12, 28)

GREEN, N.L., of Regina, Sask., formerly of St. John, N.B., and Miss Dorothy Weldman, daughter of Mr. and Mrs. H. Weldman, of Montreal, are engaged (12 Feb. 1909, 12, 9)

GREENBAUM, Ed., of Chicago, and Miss Ena Vyse, of Toronto, are engaged (19 Sept. 1913, 16, 41)

GREENBERG, B., of Toronto, and Miss Esther Greenberg, daughter of Mr. and Mrs. Greenberg, 300 Richmond St., Toronto, are engaged (7 Feb. 1913, 16, 9)

GREENBERG, Benjamin and Miss Esther Greenberg, daughter of Mr. and Mrs. Greenberg were married by Rev. M. Kaplan, on Sun. Nov. 10, 1913 at the home of the bride's parents, Grace St., Toronto. Miss Tilley Greenberg, the bride's sister was bridesmaid. Others present included the bride's sister, Mrs. H. Palter (14 Nov. 1913, 16, 49)

GREENBERG, C., son of Mr. and Mrs. H. Greenberg, and Miss Bertha Leibovitch, daughter of Mr. and Mrs. P. Leibovitch, all of Ottawa, were married by Rabbi S. Fyne, assisted by Rev. Mirsky last Sun. in the Auditorium Hall, Ottawa. L. Goldberg was best man and the bridesmaids were the Misses L. and A. Steinberg and A. Althaus. Max Margosches sang "The Pink Lady". Guests included A.H. Wolfe and N. Goldberg, of Montreal and the Misses Fisher, of New York (27 Dec. 1912, 16, 3)

GREENBERG, Charles and Miss Bertha Leibovitch are engaged. The announcement was made on Sun. Dec. 17, 1911 at the home of Miss Leibovitch's parents, 375 Dalhousie St., Ottawa (22 Dec. 1911, 15, 6)

GREENBERG, Morris and Miss Annie Feinman, 141 York St., Toronto, will be married in the University Avenue Synagogue, Toronto, on Sun. Aug. 21, 1910 (12 Aug. 1910, 13, 39)

GREENBOW, Bert, of Syracuse, N.Y., and Miss Dora E. Goldberg, eldest daughter of Z. Goldberg, 296 West Notre Dame St., Montreal, are engaged (25 Nov. 1910, 14, 2)

GREENFARB, Solomon and Miss Mary Landsberg, daughter of Mr. and Mrs. A. Landsberg, 195 College St., Toronto, are engaged (16 Aug. 1912, 15, 36)

GREENSPOON, A. and Miss Fannie Kofsky, will be married Sun. Nov. 16, 1910 in the McCaul Street Synagogue, Toronto (11 Nov. 1910, 13, 52)

GREENWOOD, Harry, of Laurier Ave. W., and Miss Ida Shapiro, Mount Royal Ave. W., Montreal, niece of Mr. and Mrs. D.H. Shapiro, are engaged (11 July 1913, 16, 31)

GROFFER, Charles and Miss Ray Lerner, daughter of Mr. and Mrs. J. Lerner, all of Montreal, are engaged (14 July 1911, 14, 35)

GROSS, Hyman, son of Mr. and Mrs. A. Gross, of Montreal, and Miss Marie Weitzer, daughter of Mr. and Mrs. Hyman Weitzer, 85 Mitcheson St., Montreal, are engaged. An engagement party was held Tues. May 28, 1912 at home of the bride's parents (7 June 1912, 15, 26)

GROSS, Hyman, son of Mr. and Mrs. A. Gross, of Gross & Weiner, Montreal, and Miss Mary Weitzer, daughter of Mr. and Mrs. K. Weitzer, were married Tues. Feb. 4, 1913 at 7 p.m. in the Auditorium Hall, Montreal (31 Jan. 1913, 16, 8)

GROSSMAN, Harry, eldest son of Mr. and Mrs. Grossman, of Vancouver, and Miss Hilda Florence Claman, daughter of Mr. and Mrs. M. Claman, 110 St. Matthew St., Montreal, were married by Rabbi Nathan Gordon of Temple Emanu-El, Montreal, at the residence of the bride's parents on Mon. Nov. 1, 1910 at 5 p.m. Out-of-town guests were Mr. and Mrs. Grossman and daughter; A.D. Goldstein, the bride's uncle; Mr. and Mrs. William Goldstein; and Mr. Lepitzky, of Toronto. Mr. and Mrs. Grossman have gone on a four week honeymoon to the southern U.S. and on their return will reside in Vancouver, B.C. (4 Nov. 1910, 13, 51)

GROSSMAN, Harry, of Vancouver, B.C., and Miss Florence Claman, eldest daughter of Mr. and Mrs. M. Claman, of Montreal, are engaged. At Home, Sun. Oct. 24, 1909, 110 St. Matthew St. (22 Oct. 1909, 12, 45)

GROSSMAN, M., of Vancouver, and Miss Flossie Claman, daughter of Mr. and Mrs. M. Claman, St. Matthew St., Montreal, are engaged. Mr. and Mrs. Claman gave an "at home" Sun. Oct. 24, 1909 (29 Oct. 1909, 12, 46)

GRUPAR, Moses, son of Mrs. H. Grupar, 26 Power St., Toronto, and Miss Minnie Singer, daughter of Mr. and Mrs. P. Singer, 517 Queen St. E., Toronto, were married by Rev. Kaplan and Rabbi W. Gordon in the McCaul Street Synagogue, Toronto, last Sun. evening. A. Singer, Joseph Pinkus and Messrs. Lewis, Morris and Stein attended Mr. Grupar. Miss Harder was maid of honor and the bridesmaids were the Misses Goldie Singer and Pearl Pinkus. Among the guests present at the reception afterwards were:- Jacob Cohen, J.P., A.H. Birmingham, S. Levinter, M. Simon, Mr. and Mrs. K.L. Saphira, Mr. and Mrs. Henry Moses, Mr. and Mrs. Pinkus, Mr. and Mrs. Morris, Mr. and Mrs. Muscovitz, Mr. and Mrs. Himovitz, Mr. and Mrs. Davis, Mr. and Mrs. Lavoi, Mr. and Mrs. Solomon, of New York, Mr. and Mrs. Brengelmann and Lewis Rincovar. Mr. and Mrs. Grupar spent their honeymoon in Niagara Falls and Detroit and on their return will reside at 517 Queen St. E. (22 July 1910, 13, 36)

GUTTMAN, J.A., of Calgary, and Miss Leontina Ghitter, eldest daughter of Mr. and Mrs. M. Ghitter, were married by Rev. M. Bloomfield, assisted by a choir, on Sun. Sept. 21, 1913 in the Austrian-Hungarian Synagogue, Milton St., Montreal. Over five hundred guests were present. A a sit-down dinner for one hundred followed at the Cleveland Restaurant. The Calgary Zionist Society sent a telegram of congratulations. Mr. and Mrs. Guttman are spending their honeymoon in Toronto, Chicago, St. Paul and other cities (1 Oct. 1913, 16, 42-43)

GUTTMAN, Joseph A., of Calgary, and Miss L. Ghitter, daughter of Mr. and Mrs. M. Ghitter, Drolet St., Montreal, will be married on Sun. in the Austrian-Hungarian Synagogue, Milton St., Montreal (19 Sept. 1913, 16, 41)

HALPERN, Bernard and Miss Leah Levinson, daughter of Mr. and Mrs. N. Levinson, 63 Church St., Montreal, were married by Rabbi Herman Abramowitz, assisted by Rev. S. Goldstein, on Wed. aft. June 29, 1910, at the home of the bride's parents. The bride's attendant was Miss Annie Levinson. Louis Halpern, the groom's brother, acted as best man. Mr. and Mrs. Halpern left on a trip down the Saguenay River. Out-of-town guests were:- L.M. Kreinson, of Bradford, Pa.; Jack Kreinson, of Buffalo, N.Y.; Mrs. M.J. Rosenberg and Master Nathan Rosenberg, of Detroit (8 July 1910, 13, 34)

HALPERN, Bernard, of Montreal, and Miss Leah Levinson, eldest daughter of Mr. and Mrs. N. Levinson, Cherrier St., Montreal, are engaged (21

Jan. 1910, 13, 10)

HALPERN, S., 139 Commissioners St., and Miss M. Lerman, niece of Mr. and Mrs. S. Talpis, 34 St. Louis Square, all of Montreal, are engaged (24 Jan. 1913, 16, 7)

HANSHER, Charles and Miss Rose Kert, daughter of Mr. and Mrs. I. Kert, all of Montreal, are engaged (11 April 1913, 16, 18)

HANSHER, Harry and Miss Jennie Miller, both of Montreal, will be married on Tues. Jan. 9, 1911 in the Auditorium Hall, Montreal (Dec. 29, 1911, 15, 7)

HART, Roslyn E., son of Dr. and Mrs. Hart, of Montreal, and Miss Doris Goodwin, of New York, are engaged (15 Dec. 1911, 15, 5)

HART, Rufus E., son of Dr. and Mrs. David A. Hart, of Montreal, and Miss Doris Goodwin, of New York, were married in New York, on Thurs. June 6, 1912 (7 June 1912, 15, 26)

HARTMAN, Wiliam A., of Winnipeg, and Miss Lily Bernstein, of London, England, were married by Rabbi J.K. Levin, in Winnipeg, on June 1, 1909 (4 June 1909, 12, 25)

HECHT, Harry and Miss Goldia Goldberg were married Tues. evening by Rabbi Simon Glazer, assisted by Rev. M.J. Judelson, at the home of the bride's mother, 188 Cherrier St., Montreal. Mr. and Mrs. Hecht will reside in Montreal (5 Jan. 1912, 15, 8)

HECHT, Nathan, of Montreal, and Miss Goldia Augusta Goldberg, second daughter of the late Julius Goldberg and Mrs. J. Goldberg, 45 Drolet St., Montreal, are engaged (28 April 1911, 14, 24)

HEILLIG, M. and Miss Lillian Kellert, daughter of Mr. and Mrs. H. Kellert, Sherbrooke St. West, Montreal, will be married Nov. 3, 1909, at the home of the bride's parents (22 Oct. 1909, 12, 45)

HEILLIG, M. and Miss Lily Kellert, daughter of Mr. and Mrs. H. Kellert, of Montreal, are engaged (19 Feb. 1909, 12, 10)

HEILLIG, M., of Montreal, and Miss Lillian Kellert, daughter of Mr. and Mrs. H. Kellert, Sherbrooke St. W., Montreal, were married by Rabbi Herman Abramowitz, assisted by Rev. S. Goldstein, last Wed., at the home of the bride's parents. Miss Bessie Kellert, the bride's sister was maid of honor and Miss Rae Heillig, the bridegroom's sister was bridesmaid. The bride's two little nieces, Dorothy Kellert and Beatrice Fraid were flowergirls. L. Heillig, the bridegroom's brother, was the best man and the bride's brother, Solomon Kellert, was the usher (5 Nov. 1909, 12, 47)

HELLER, David and Miss Yanower were married by Rabbi Gordon on Feb. 1, 1911 in the Cosmopolitan Club, Toronto (10 Feb. 1911, 14, 13)

HELLER, I.E. and Miss Minnie Handleman, of Montreal, are engaged (29 Aug. 1913, 16, 38)

HERBERT, Samuel and Miss Vera Levy were married at the residence of the bride's sister, Mrs. A. Goodman, in Toronto (9 Aug. 1912, 15, 35)

HERMANT, Percy, general manager of the Imperial Optical Co. of Toronto, and Miss Dorothy Morris, daughter of Mr. and Mrs. N.L. Morris, of Montreal, are engaged (11 March 1910, 13, 17)

HERMANT, Percy, of Toronto, and Miss Dorothy Morris, daughter of Mr. and Mrs. M.L. Morris, of Montreal, are engaged (25 Feb. 1910, 13, 15)

HERR, B., of Syracuse, N.Y., and Miss Lessie Caplan, cousin of Mr. and Mrs. J. Merson, 1947 Mance St., Montreal, are engaged (19 Sept. 1913, 16, 41)

HERSCOVITCH, J. and Miss Annie Viner, daughter of Mrs. F. Viner, of Montreal, are engaged (23 May 1913, 16, 24)

HERZOG, Benjamin and Miss Eva Gold, daughter of Mr. and Mrs. I. Gold, of Montreal, will be married April 5, 1911 (24 March 1911, 14, 19)

HERZOG, Bennie and Miss Eva Gold, only daughter of Mr. and Mrs. I. Gold, all of Montreal, are engaged (25 Oct. 1910, 13, 50)

HIRSCHBERG, Sol, formerly of Toronto, and Miss Gertrude Beber, of Vancouver, were married Sun. Dec. 15, 1912 at the bride's home in Vancouver. Mr. and Mrs. Hirschberg went to Toronto for their honeymoon (20 Dec. 1912, 16, 2)

HIRSCHENBEIN, Moses, of St. Johns, P.Q., and Miss Annie Weiner, daughter of Mr. and Mrs. Isidore Weiner, of Montreal, were married by Rabbi Herman Abramowitz on Tues. at 6 p.m., in the Auditorium Hall, Berthelet St., Montreal (12 March 1909, 12, 13)

HIRSENHORN, Benny and Miss Annie Rosenfeld, daughter of Mr. and Mrs. I. Rosenfeld, will be married in the McCaul Street Synagogue, Toronto, on Wed. Sept. 14, 1910 (26 Aug. 1910, 13, 41)

HIRSKOVITCH, Hyman, eldest son of Mrs. Hirskovitch, 278 Murray St., Ottawa, and Miss Ettie Ferguson, eldest daughter of Mrs. Eva Ferguson, of Manchester, England, are engaged (6 Sept. 1912, 15, 39)

HOFFER, Charles and Miss Minnie Balcover, both of Montreal, were married last Sun. in Modern Hall, Montreal. The bride was given away by Mr. and Mrs. Simons and the groom by his parents. Benjamin Hoffer was master of ceremonies. Out-of-town guests were:- Mr. and Mrs. H. Lewis, Mr. and Mrs. H. Finklestein, Miss Gertrude Slover and F. Slover, of Ottawa (21 Feb. 1913, 16, 11)

HOFFMAN, Jack, of Amherst, N.S., and Miss Ray Schalek, daughter of Mr. and Mrs. M. Schalek, 427 St. Denis St., Montreal, are engaged (19 Feb. 1909, 12, 10)

HOLDENGRABER, Simon, of Bathurst, N.B., and Miss Annie Weinstein, daughter of L. Weinstein, of Montreal, are engaged (7 May 1909, 12, 21)

HOLDENGRABER, Simon, of Bathurst, N.B., and Miss Annie Weinstein, daughter of L. Weinstein, of Montreal, were married at the home of the bride's father. The bride was attended by her sister, Miss Celia Weinstein and one bridesmaid, Miss Rose Feldman. Miss Libbie Feldman was the flowergirl. Maxwell Weinstein was the best man (29 Oct. 1909, 12, 46)

HORCHOVER, Theodor and Miss Ida Freda Apotheker were married by Rabbi Nathan Gordon in Temple Emanu-El, Montreal last Mon. (16 Dec. 1910, 14, 5)

HORWITZ, Joseph and Miss Elsie Miller, youngest daughter of Mr. and Mrs. J.F. Miller, will be married June 4, 1913 in Temple Emanuel, Westmount, Que. (16 May 1913, 16, 23)

HYAMS, Harry and Miss Bessie Simons, of Toronto, were married by Rabbi S. Jacobs on Wed. A reception for friends and relatives was held at 313 Gerrard St. E., Toronto after which the couple left for Montreal (1 July 1910, 13, 33)

HYMAN, Harry B., of Montreal, and Miss Lillian Naurm, daughter of Mr. and Mrs. Samuel Naurm, of New York, are engaged (10 March 1911, 14, 17)

ISAACS, Ben and Miss May Bercovitch, youngest daughter of Mr. and Mrs. H. Bercovitch, of Montreal, are engaged (10 Oct. 1913, 16, 44)

ISAACS, Charles Lopez, son of Walter B. Isaacs, collector of customs and medical health officer at Port Antonio, Jamaica, B.W.I., and Miss Augusta Rose Weeksler, daughter of Mr. and Mrs. Charles Weeksler, Avenue Road, Toronto, were married by Rabbi S. Jacobs on Sept. 5, 1912 at the home of the bride's parents in the drawing room. Mrs. Levy, of Hamilton, played the wedding marches. The bride was given away by her father. The bridesmaids were the bride's sisters, Misses Fanny and Annie Weeksler. L. Lightstone, of Montreal, was best man. Mr. and Mrs. Isaacs left on the 7:10 train for New York, en route to their home, Green Castle, Jamaica (20 Sept. 1912, 15, 41)

ISAACS, Charles, of Jamaica, W.I., and Miss Gus Weeksler, of Toronto, will be married Sept. 5, 1912 (9 Aug. 1912, 15, 35)

ISAACS, Myer, of Montreal, and Miss Sybil Judel, of South Norwalk, Conn., are engaged (11 July 1913, 16, 31)

ISAACSON, William, son of Mr. and Mrs. W. Isaacson, of Denver, Col., formerly of Montreal, and Miss Leanore Moses were married in Denver on Wed. Jan. 22, 1913 (24 Jan. 1913, 16, 7)

ISBITZ, Harry, formerly of Rochester, N.Y., now of Toronto, and Miss Sarah Spector, daughter of Mr. and Mrs. N. Spector, 28 Kensington Ave., Toronto, are engaged (13 May 1910, 13, 26)

ISSEN, Jack, eldest son of Mrs. Mark Issen, and Miss Mabyl Berson, eldest daughter of Mr. and Mrs. I. Berson, were married in the Austrian-

From The Canadian Jewish Times   *Engagements and Marriages*

Hungarian Synagogue, Milton St., Montreal. Miss B. Issen was the maid of honor and the Misses E.L. Issen and J. Berson were bridesmaids. The Misses Sarah Abrahams and Annette Philips were flower girls. M. Berson was the best man and the ushers were B. Issen and D. Goodwin. H. Gould was master of ceremonies at the supper and dance held in Auditorium Hall after the wedding. The following day, Mr. and Mrs. Issen left on their honeymoon for Edmonton and other western cities (26 Dec. 1913, 17, 3)

ISSEN, Jack, eldest son of Mrs. Max Issen, and Miss Mabel Berson, eldest daughter of Mr. and Mrs. Berson, all of Montreal, are engaged (1 Oct. 1913, 16, 42-43)

JACOBS, Lyon W. (B.C.L.), a Montreal advocate, and Miss Sarah Florin, only daughter of Mr. and Mrs. B. Florin, of Montreal, were married by Rabbi Simon Glazer on Tues. Sept. 3, 1912, at the home of the bride's parents. Out-of-town guests were Phillip Florin and Mrs. J. Florin, both of New York City (11 Sept. 1912, 15, 40)

JACOBS, Lyon W., a Montreal lawyer, and Miss Sarah Florin, only daughter of Mr. and Mrs. B. Florin, formerly of New York, are engaged. Wedding early this fall (26 July 1912, 15, 33)

JACOBS, Lysle, son of Mr. and Mrs. Alfred Isaacs, of St. John, N.B., and Miss Lottie Jacob, of Brooklyn, N.Y., will be married in New York on June 18, 1913 (13 June 1913, 16, 27)

JASSBY, A.H. and Miss Bessie Pashin, daughter of Mr. and Mrs. J. Pashin, all of Montreal, are engaged (24 May 1912, 15, 24,)

JOSEFS, Julius, of Montreal, and Miss Annie Kendenstein, of Quebec City, are engaged (10 Sept. 1909, 12, 39)

JOSEPH, A. Pinto, eldest son of Mr. and Mrs. Montefiore Joseph, of Quebec City, and Miss Hortense Ury, of Schenectady, N.Y., were married at the home of the bride's parents on Wed. Oct. 27, 1909. Edward Joseph, the bridegroom's brother was best man and Miss Irene Ury was bridesmaid. Montreal guests included: Mrs. A. Sandeman, Miss M. Joseph and Miss S. Joseph. The couple will reside in Schenectady (5 Nov. 1909, 12, 47)

KAHN, Charles and Miss Rae Brodski, both of Montreal, are engaged (10 March 1911, 14, 17)

KAHN, Chas. and Miss Ray Brodsky, daughter of Mrs. A. Brodsky, will be married in the Auditorium Hall, Montreal, on Wed. June 28, 1911 (9 June 1911, 14, 30)

KAHN, J.J., only son of Mr. and Mrs. S. Kahn, of Montreal, and Miss Mildred Friefeld, daughter of Mr. and Mrs. I. Friefeld, of Newark, N.J., are engaged (27 March 1914, 17, 13)

KAHN, Samuel and Miss Alta Rhoda Goldblatt, only daughter of Mr. and Mrs. Philip Goldblatt, of Montreal, were married by Rabbi Simon Glazer at the home of the bride's parents on Thurs. Oct. 24, 1912. Out-of-town guests were Harry Morris, of Buffalo, N.Y., and Miss Esther Sugarman, of Ottawa (8 Nov. 1912, 15, 48)

KAHN, Samuel, of Buffalo, N.Y., and Miss Alta Goldblatt, daughter of Mr. and Mrs. P. Goldblatt, of Montreal, are engaged (5 Aug. 1910, 13, 38)

KAMMAN, Maurice, of Rochester, N.Y., and Miss Ida Willinsky, daughter of Mr. and Mrs. S.R. Willinsky, of Toronto, were married by Rabbi M. Kaplan in the Queen's Park Synagogue, on Thurs. July 1, 1909. The bride's attendants were her sister, Lila Willinsky and her cousin, Lillian Vise. Matthew Vise, A. Draiman, S. Kronick and S. Granatstein acted as ushers. L. Kamman, the bridegroom's brother was the best man. Out-of-town guests included: Mr. and Mrs. Kamman, the groom's parents; his sister, Miss Clara Kamman, and his brothers, Julius and Isidore Kamman; the groom's sister, Mrs. Levine and Mr. Goldstein, all of Rochester; and Mr. Melon, of Buffalo (16 July 1909, 12, 31)

KANDER, Meier, son of Mr. and Mrs. Isaac Kander, Aqueduct St., and Miss Anna Gold, daughter of Mr. and Mrs. S. Gold, St. Urbain St., all of Montreal, are engaged (2 May 1913, 16, 21)

KANDESTIN, Charles H., of Montreal, and Miss Augusta Wechsler, daughter of Mr. and Mrs. Wechsler, of New York, are engaged (17 Jan. 1913, 16, 6)

KAPLAN, Abraham, son of Mr. and Mrs. I. Kaplan, of Yarmouth, and Miss Lena Necktovitch, of South Boston, Mass., are engaged (30 Sept. 1910, 13, 46)

KAPLAN, S.M. and Miss Rose Strausberg were married in Chicago, Ill., on Sun. Oct. 29, 1911 (17 Nov. 1911, 15, 1)

KAPLANSKY, R., of Vancouver, son of R.L. Kaplansky, of Montreal, and Miss Bertha Forcimer, only child of Mr. and Mrs. B. Forcimmer, of Nanaimo, B.C., were married by Rabbi Goldberg, at the home of Mr. and Mrs. Goldbloom, 540 Burrard St., Vancouver. Miss Sadie Franks was bridesmaid and M. Kaplansky was best man. The couple spent their honeymoon in Harrison, Portland, Seattle, Spokane and other cities. Out-of-town guests included Felix Lewis and Mr. Breitenbach, both of Montreal (8 July 1910, 13, 34)

KAPLANSKY, Ruby, son of Mr. and Mrs. A.L. Kaplansky, 68 Park Ave., Montreal, and Miss Birdie Forcimer, only daughter of Mr. and Mrs. B. Forcimer, of Vancouver, formerly of Montreal, will be married on June 23, 1910 in Vancouver (17 June 1910, 13, 31)

KAPSTEIN, Edward M., formerly of Fall River, Mass., and Miss Sadie Sybil Myres, daughter of J. Myres, were married by Rev. Cashdan, assisted by Rabbi J.K. Levin, in the Shaarey Zedek Synagogue, Winnipeg, last week. Mrs. J.L. Rill was matron of honor and Miss Rosetta Myres was the maid of honor. The bridesmaids were the Misses B. Narovlansky, of Montreal, and M. Simon, of Alexandria, Ont. The groomsman were S. Hart Green, M.P.P., W. Zimmerman and M. Greenblot. The ushers were W. Myres and N. Weidman. The wedding breakfast was held at the home of I. Myres, 242 Spence St. Mr. and Mrs. Kapstein left on the Soo Line for New York and Virginia (30 Sept. 1910, 13, 46)

KARNOW, Solomon, of Brantford, Ont., and Miss Hettie Rubenstein, of Hamilton, Ont., were married at the home of the bride's brother, B. Rubenstein, on Thurs. aft. (16 July 1909, 12, 31)

KATZ, Dr. H., and Miss Lillie Caplan, both of Toronto, are engaged (19 July 1912, 15, 32)

KATZ, Dr. M. and Miss Lily Caplan were married by Rabbi Nathan Gordon, assisted by Cantor Wladofsky and the choir, last Wed. in the University Avenue Synagogue, Toronto. Miss Sarah Caplan, the bride's sister, was maid of honor. A reception for two hundred guests was held at the home of the bride's parents, Markham St. The couple left on their honeymoon to the U.S. (25 July 1913, 16, 33)

KAUFMAN, David, eldest son of Mr. and Mrs. I. Kaufman, 643 Henri Julien St., Montreal, and Miss Annie Bendarsky, eldest daughter of Mr. and Mrs. Bendarsky, 645 Henri Julien St., Montreal, are engaged. Mr. and Mrs. Kaufman gave an engagement party in the garden of their home (25 July 1913, 16, 33)

KAUFMAN, Philip and Miss Tessie Kaplan, and Louis Berk and Miss Ida Kaplan, were married in a double wedding ceremony last Thurs. evening in the McCaul Street Synagogue, Toronto. Miss Ida Kaplan was given away by her father, Rev. M. Kaplan, cantor of the McCaul Street Synagogue, who performed both ceremonies, assisted by Rabbi S. Jacobs and Rev. M. Gordon. Miss Tessie Kaplan was given away by Samuel Kaufman, of Chicago, the groom's brother. Miss Evelyn Kaplan, the brides' sister, was maid of honor and the best men were Samuel and Sol Kaplan. Guests included Mrs. Rose (Ottawa), Mrs. S. Strausberg (Chicago), Mesdames H. Kauffman and Weinberg (Rochester), Mrs. R. Berson (Chicago), Mrs. S. Berk (Montreal), Mrs. S. Wolfson (Worcester, Mass.), Meyer Cohen (Milwaukee), Harry Kauffman (Montreal), and S. Kaplan (Chicago) (16 May 1913, 16, 23)

KAUFMAN, Philip and Miss Tessie Kaplan, and Louis Berk and Miss Ida Kaplan, will be married in a double wedding ceremony Thurs. May 7, 1913, in the McCaul Street Synagogue, Toronto (2 May 1913, 16, 21)

KAUFMAN, Philip, formerly of Rochester, N.Y., and Miss Tessie Kaplan, daughter of Rev. and Mrs. J. Kaplan, of Toronto, are engaged (9 Aug. 1912, 15, 35)

KAUFMAN, R., of Manchester, England, and Miss Rose Vineberg, daughter of Mr. and Mrs. A.M. Vineberg, 233 Esplanade Ave., Montreal, are engaged (16 Aug. 1912, 15, 36)

KEEZEL, Jacob, of Killaloe, Ont., and Miss Esther Dover, of Eganville, Ont., eldest daughter of Mr. and Mrs. Harry Dover, will be married on Thurs. at 5.30 p.m., Aug. 23, 1910 in the King Edward Avenue Synagogue, Ottawa, followed by a reception in the Racquet Court, Metcalfe St. (29 July 1910, 13, 37)

KERT, Joseph and Miss Sarah Miller, daughter of Mr. and Mrs. S. Miller, of Montreal, are engaged (3 April 1914, 17, 14)

KERT, Max and Miss Stone, are engaged (19 Feb. 1909, 12, 10)

KEYFITZ, Arthur, of Montreal, and Miss Anna Gerstein, of New York, will be married shortly. The **Montreal Gazette** advertising staff gave a dinner in Mr. Keyfitz's honor (15 Oct. 1909, 12, 44)

KILLER, Lipe and Miss Sarah Sauplok, daughter of Mr. and Mrs. Jacob Sauplok, were married by Rabbi Hirsch Cohen on Mon. June 14, 1909, at 199 St. Lawrence Blvd., Montreal (18 June 1909, 12, 27)

KINDESTIN, Harry and Miss Ettie Josefo, were married by Rev. S. Goldstein, assisted by Rev. S. Herman, in the Auditorium Hall, Montreal last Sun. The bridesmaids were: the Misses Annie and Ida Kindestin, of Ste. Agathe, and the Misses Gertie and Bertie Josefo (24 Dec. 1909, 13, 6)

KING, Herman Samuel and Miss Esther Steiner, both of Toronto, were married June 27, 1912 at the bride's home, Roxborough St. (5 July 1912, 15, 30)

KIRSCH, Dr. Simon and Miss Malca Cossman, both of Montreal, were married by Rev. S. Goldstein on July 19, 1910 in the Shaar Hashomayim Synagogue, Montreal. Mrs. M. Mendelson, the bride's sister, was matron of honor and Miss S. Kirsch, the groom's sister, was bridesmaid. The groom's brother was best man. After the ceremony a family dinner was given at the residence of Mrs. M. Mendelson, Esplanade Ave. The Misses Nellie, Malca, Rose and Sadie Vineberg, the bride's cousins, and Miss Dorothy Sidel, of Chicago, were in charge of the dining room at the reception in the evening. Dr. and Mrs. Kirsch will reside in Madison, Wisc. after spending their honeymoon in the Western States (29 July 1910, 13, 37)

KIRSCH, Simon, son of Mr. and Mrs. Abraham Kirsch, and Miss Malca Cossman, sister of Mrs. M. Mendelsohn, all of Montreal, are engaged (23 April 1909, 12, 19)

KIZZEL, Jacob and Miss Esther Dover, daughter of Harry Dover, were married by Rabbi Joseph Berger, assisted by Revs. J. Mirsky and L. Doctor, on Tues. evening, Aug. 23, 1910, in the King Edward Street Synagogue, Ottawa. The bride was given away by her father. Miss Hattie Dover was maid of honor and the flower girls were the Misses Fanny Dover and Jennie Sayman. Mr. Gittelson acted as toastmaster at the supper for a hundred and fifty held after the ceremony at the Racquet Club. Speeches were made Rabbi Berger, Mr. Gorfinkel, John Dover, Harry Dover, Rev. L. Doctor and Julius Berger. After their honeymoon in the eastern U.S., Mr. and Mrs. Kizzel will settle in Killaloe, Ont. (9 Sept. 1910, 13, 43)

KLEIN, Abe M. and Miss Hannah Garmaise, niece of Mrs. Lazarus Cohen, will be married in Stanley Hall, Montreal, on Feb. 2, 1911. "The wedding will be a quiet one, only immediate relatives being invited." (13 Jan. 1911, 14, 9)

KLEIN, Abe M. and Miss Hannah Garmaise are to be married on Feb. 2, 1911, at 228 Bishop St., Montreal instead of in Stanley Hall because of a bereavement in the family of Miss Garmaise's uncle, Lazarus Cohen (27 Jan. 1911, 14, 11)

KLEIN, Abraham, of Montreal, and Miss Hannah Garmaize, niece of Mr. and Mrs. Lazarus Cohen, of Montreal, are engaged (15 July 1910, 13, 35)

KLEIN, Moe and Miss Rebecca Yaphe, eldest daughter of Mr. and Mrs. N. Yaphe, all of Montreal, are engaged (26 Dec. 1913, 17, 3)

KLEIN, Morris, of Montreal, and Miss Esther Sugarman, daughter of Mr. and Mrs. A.J. Sugarman, of Ottawa, are engaged. At an "at home" S. Talpis collected $6.50 for the Zionist National Fund (8 Sept. 1911, 14, 43)

KLING, Oscar and Miss Annie Shapiro, daughter of Mr. and Mrs. Shapiro, all of Toronto, are engaged (19 July 1912, 15, 32)

KOHNSTAMM, Jacob and Miss Annie Goldstick, daughter of Mr. and Mrs. William Goldstick, will be married Sun. July 3, 1910 at 26 Division St., Toronto (1 July 1910, 13, 33)

KORNBERG, Mr., of New York, and Miss Fannie Drucker, formerly of Montreal, now of New York, are engaged (2 July 1909, 12, 29)

KORNREICH, Abraham, formerly of New York, and Miss Dolly Cohen, daughter of Mrs. D. Cohen, Cathcart St., Hamilton, were married by Rabbi M. Kaplan, of Toronto, assisted by Rabbi Levine, of Hamilton, at the home of the bride's mother (16 July 1909, 12, 31)

KRAUS, B., of Montreal, and Miss Rose Davidson, daughter of M. Davidson, of Ottawa, are engaged (12 Dec. 1913, 17, 1)

KRAUS, Bernard, of Montreal, and Miss Rose Davidson, eldest daughter of M. Davidson, of Ottawa, were married by Rabbi S. Fyne, assisted by Rabbis Mirsky and J. Berger in the King Edward Street Synagogue. After the ceremony a dinner was served in the Racquet Court. Mrs. A.J. Freiman, president of the Synagogue's Ladies' Auxiliary, presented the bride with a beautiful silver candelabra (20 Feb. 1914, 17, 8)

KRONICK, Sam and Miss Gertrude Willinsky, and Arthur Jacobs and Miss Minnie Willinsky, Homewood Ave., Toronto, were married in a double wedding ceremony by Rabbi S. Jacobs, assisted by Rev. Kaplan in the Holy Blossom Synagogue, Bond St., Toronto, on Wed. Dec. 25, 1912. Mrs. Kronick was the matron of honor for Miss Gertrude and Mrs. Kamman for Miss Minnie Willinsky. The best men were Joseph Kronick and J. Kamman (3 Jan. 1913, 16, 4)

KRONICK, Samuel and Miss Gertrude Willinsky, daughter of Mr. and Mrs. L. Willinsky, all of Toronto, will be married by Rabbi S. Jacobs on Thurs. Dec. 27, 1912 in Holy Blossom Synagogue, Bond St., Toronto. A reception will follow at 70 Homewood Ave. Mr. Kronick is a well-known Zionist leader and member of the Zionist Federation council (13 Dec. 1912, 16, 1)

KRONICK, Samuel, of Toronto, and Miss Gertrude Willinsky, daughter of Mr. and Mrs. S.R. Willinsky, 70 Homewood Ave., are engaged (24 May 1912, 15, 25)

KUBELIK, F. Max and Miss Ethel Hyman, daughter of Mr. and Mrs. I.E. Hyman, of Montreal, will be married on Wed. Dec. 20, 1911 and "...owing to the illness of the bride's brother, only immediate relatives will be present (8 Dec. 1911, 15, 4)

KUBELIK, Max, of Toronto, and Miss Ethel Hyman, daughter of Mr. and Mrs. I.E. Hyman, of Montreal, are engaged (28 Jan. 1910, 13, 11)

LANDMAN, Rabbi Isaac, formerly of Temple Emanu-El, of Montreal, who is assistant rabbi of Dr. Kauskoff's Temple in Philadelphia, will be married to Miss Beatrice Eschner, of the same city, on Wed. Sept. 3, 1913 in the Temple, Philadelphia. Miss Eschner is a Cornell graduate and a well-known social worker in the Jewish community (29 Aug. 1913, 16, 38)

LAVUT, Mr., and Miss Simkewitz, of Cornwall, Ont., are engaged (21 May 1909, 12, 23)

LAZARUS, Charles and Miss Pauline Schwartz were married by Rabbi Herman Abramowitz and Rev. S. Goldstein last Sun. evening in Auditorium Hall, Montreal (7 Jan. 1910, 13, 8)

LEOPOLD, Samuel, of Montreal, and Miss Rhoda Atkins, of New York, were married June 6, 1912. Guests included his brother, Felix Leopold, of the Canadian Hat Mfg. Co., and his fiancé, Miss Netty Lewis, both of Montreal. After spending their honeymoon in Chicago, Washington, Buffalo and Niagara Falls, they will return to Montreal July 6. They will spend the summer at the Philadelphia Hotel, Ste. Agathe des Monts (14 June 1912, 15, 27)

LESSES, I., of Edmonton, Alta., and Miss Gussie Abramson, daughter of Mr. and Mrs. Joseph Abramson, formerly of Kingston, Ont., and now of Saskatoon, Sask., are engaged (25 July 1913, 16, 33)

LESSES, I., of Edmonton, and Miss Gussie Abramson, and I. Soskin and Miss Anngene Abramson were married in a double wedding ceremony by Rev. M. Zelchinhaw on Sun. Nov. 9, 1913 at 3 p.m. in Saskatoon. The Misses Abramson are the daughters of Mr. and Mrs. Joseph Abramson, formerly of Kingston, Ont. "Miss. J.J. Gallen, of the brides, and her little son, Master Raymond, of Calgary, Alta., were present." Mr. and Mrs. Lesses will reside in Edmonton and Mr. and Mrs. Soskin in Regina after their return from honeymoon trips (21 Nov. 1913, 16, 50-51)

LEVI, Michael, of Hamilton, and Miss Jennie Lyons, of Utica, N.Y., are engaged (18 June 1909, 12, 27)

LEVI, William, of St. John, N.B., and Miss Sadie Vineberg, daughter of Mr. and Mrs. Hyman

Vineberg, were married by Rabbi Herman Abramowitz, assisted by Rev. S. Goldstein on Wed. evening, Nov. 2, 1910 in the Majestic Hall, Guy St., Montreal. The bride was given away by her father. Miss Bluma Levi, of Chicago, the bridegroom's sister was maid of honor. Miss Nellie Vineberg, the bride's cousin, acted as bridesmaid. A.H. Vineberg, the bride's brother, was best man. The bride's other brother, Malcolm Vineberg, acted as groomsman. The couple left on a honeymoon to New York and Boston after which they will reside in St. John, N.B. (4 Nov. 1910, 13, 51)

LEVIN, Max L. and Miss Anna Coviensky, daughter of Mr. and Mrs. M. Coviensky, were married by Rabbi Herman Abramowitz, assisted by Rabbi Hirsch Cohen and Rev. S. Goldstein last Wed. evening in Majestic Hall, Montreal. Miss Ray Coviensky, the bride's sister, was maid of honor and the bride's brother, Lyon Coviensky, was best man. After the ceremony over 150 guests sat down to dinner and Rabbi Abramowitz acted as toastmaster. Those who spoke were Lazarus Cohen, Jacob Cohen, Lyon Cohen, A. Levin, Rabbi Hirsch Cohen and Clarence I. de Sola. "Mr. de Sola in his speech announced that admirers of the happy couple had decided to inscribe the name of Mr. and Mrs. Max L. Levin in the Golden Book." The couple went on their honeymoon to Atlantic City (16 Sept. 1910, 13, 44)

LEVIN, Max L. and Miss Anna Coviensky, daughter of Mr. and Mrs. M. Coviensky, Berri St., Montreal, will be married on Wed. Sept. 14, 1910 in the Majestic Hall, Guy St., Montreal (26 Aug. 1910, 13, 41)

LEVIN, Philip, of Montreal and Miss Sadie Jackson, daughter of Mr. and Mrs. A.H. Jackson, Grosvenor Ave., Montreal, were married by Rabbi Herman Abramowitz, assisted by Rev. S. Goldstein, on Tues. evening, March 9, 1909, at the home of the bride's parents. The bride's sister was maid of honor. Also present was the bride's brother, A.H. Jackson. The Misses Bernstein, Freeman and Cohen were in charge of the tea-room (12 March 1909, 12, 13)

LEVINE, Harry L., of Montreal, eldest son of Myer D. Levine, of Belfast, Ireland, and Miss Ethel Rothschild, daughter of Mr. and Mrs. Max Rothschild, of Sudbury, Ont., are engaged (2 May 1913, 16, 21)

LEVINE, J., of Montreal, and Miss Ethel Cohen, daughter of H. Cohen, are engaged (23 April 1909, 12, 19)

LEVINE, Louis D. and Miss Mary Shakofsky, second daughter of Mr. and Mrs. J. Shakofsky, all of Montreal, are engaged (9 Sept. 1910, 13, 43)

LEVINE, S. and Miss Gertrude Goldfine, both of Montreal, are engaged (1 Oct. 1909, 12, 42)

LEVINE, S., of London, England, and Miss Libbie Feinberg, daughter of Mr. and Mrs. B. Feinberg, of Toronto, were married by Rev. Caplan last Tues. in the University Avenue Synagogue, Toronto (25 Dec. 1910, 14, 2)

LEVINSON, Benjamin G., son of the late S. Levinson and Mrs. Levinson, of New York, and Miss Bessie Rudolfe, second daughter of Mr. and Mrs. A. Rudolfe, Laval Ave., Montreal, were married by Rabbi Herman Abramowitz, assisted by Rev. Cohen on March 19, 1914 at the home of the bride's parents. Maxwell Levinson, the groom's brother, was best man. After the ceremony, supper was served in the dining room. Mr. and Mrs. Levinson went to New York and other cities on their honeymoon. On their return they will reside at 1926 Mance St. (20 March 1914, 17, 12)

LEVINSON, E.R., a young and popular Winnipeg barrister, and Miss Sarah Horwitz, of Minneapolis, will be married in mid-March (24 Feb. 1911, 14, 15)

LEVINSON, E.R., of Winnipeg, and Miss Sarah Horwitz, were married by Rabbi Deinard at the home of the bride in Minneapolis on March 22, 1911. Mr. Levinson was given a party at the Royal Alexandra Hotel by his bachelor friends prior to leaving for Minneapolis (31 March 1911, 14, 20)

LEVITT, M., of Montreal, and Miss Bella Levine, daughter of Mr. and Mrs. A. Levine, were married on Nov. 21, 1909, in the New Modern Hall, Notre Dame St., Montreal, by Rabbi Herman Abramowitz, assisted by Rev. S. Goldstein. Miss A. Lipsin was the maid of honor and the Misses Ray Levitt, Dora Bernstein, Clara Samit and Hattie Bernstein were bridesmaids. Louis Levine, the bride's brother, was the best man and the ushers were M. Bernstein, H. Swartzman, P. Tarantur and M. Goldberg (26 Nov. 1909, 13, 2)

LEVY, Gabriel, of Hamilton, Ont., and Miss Blanche Sheurer, of Chicago, are engaged (29 Jan. 1909, 12, 7)

LEVY, Louis, eldest son of M. Levy, of Hamilton, Ont., and Miss Rose Takefman, eldest daughter of Mr. and Mrs. Louis Takefman, were married by Rev. M. Kaplan, of Toronto, on June 8, 1909, at Bas Jacob Synagogue, Hamilton (18 June 1909, 12, 27)

LEVY, M., of Hamilton, and Miss Minnie Steinert, of Boston, Mass., are engaged (18 June 1909, 12, 27)

LEVY, William, of St. John, N.B., and Miss Sadie Vineberg, daughter of Mr. and Mrs. Simon Vineberg, City Hall Ave., Montreal, are engaged (23 Sept. 1910, 13, 45)

LEWIS, A.P., of Toronto, and Miss Celia Friedman, of Albany, N.Y., will be married March 30, 1913 in Albany. "Mr. Lewis is a prominent Jewish citizen, and has been well known for his activity in club circles." (14 March 1913, 16, 14)

LEWIS, F.L. and Miss Nina Orkin, were married by Rabbi Nathan Gordon Tues. evening at the residence of the bride's sister, Mrs. J.M. Orkin, Clarke Ave., Montreal. Only the relatives of the bride and groom were present. Mr. and Mrs. Lewis left for San Francisco to spend the winter. They will reside in Montreal (19 Jan. 1912, 15, 10)

LEWITON, Louis, of Manchester, England, and Miss Ray Meyers, of Montreal, are engaged and will be married in Aug. (6 May 1910, 13, 25)

LEXIER, Samuel and Miss Estelle Milmet, daughter of Mr. and Mrs. A. Milmet, all of Montreal, are engaged (3 March 1911, 14, 16)

LIGHTSTONE, Harry and Miss Eva Shiller, daughter of Mr. and Mrs. Carl Shiller, all of Montreal, are engaged (9 Sept. 1910, 13, 43)

LIGHTSTONE, Harry and Miss May Freedman, both of Montreal, are engaged (24 Nov. 1911, 15, 2)

LIGHTSTONE, Harry, son of Mr. and Mrs. Michael Lightstone, McKay St., Montreal, and Miss Eva Schiller, daughter of Mr. and Mrs. Carl Schiller, are engaged (23 Sept. 1910, 13, 45)

LIGHTSTONE, John Jacob and Miss Jennie Engelberg, both of Montreal, are engaged (22 July 1910, 13, 36)

LIGHTSTONE, John Jacob, son of S. Lightstone, of Sherbrooke, Que., and Miss Jennie Engleberg, daughter of Mr. and Mrs. S. Engleberg, of Montreal, were married on Sun. Feb. 26, 1911 in Montreal. The reception was held at the home of the bride's brother, 999 St. Lawrence Blvd. (3 March 1911, 14, 16)

LIGHTSTONE, Max, of Montreal, and Miss Ethel Rosenbloom, of Toronto, are engaged (8 Oct. 1909, 12, 43)

LITWIN, Samuel, of Montreal, and Miss Jennie Dubrofsky, daughter of Mr. and Mrs. P. Dubrofsky, of Montreal, are engaged (6 May 1910, 13, 25)

LIVERAVET, Jacob and Miss Annie Aronovich were married by Rabbi Hirsch Cohen, on Sun. Sept. 5, 1909, in Montreal (10 Sept. 1909, 12, 39)

LIVERMAN, Max and Miss Annie Crystal, daughter of Mr. and Mrs. L. Crystal, all of Montreal, are engaged (5 Dec. 1913, 16, 52)

LONN, David, of Montreal, and Miss Dorothy Cooperman, of England, are engaged (17 June 1910, 13, 31)

LONN, David, of Montreal, and Miss Dorothy Cooperman, of Europe, niece of Harris Lonn, were married on Thurs. June 23, 1910 in the Modern Hall, Montreal. The bride was given away by her uncle. Mrs. J.S. Lonn, the bride's cousin, acted as matron of honor. Miss Marguerite Balacan acted as bridesmaid. Miss Frances Lonn was flower girl. Also present was Mrs. A. Silverman, of Yamaska, Que. (1 July 1910, 13, 33)

LUBICH, L., of Chicago, and Miss Rosie Vineberg, daughter of Mr. and Mrs. I. Vineberg, of Montreal, were married by Rabbi Herman Abramowitz, last Sun. evening, in the Auditorium Hall, Berthelet St., Montreal. I. Goldstein was the best man and Miss Flossie Goldstein was the bridesmaid. The couple will reside in Montreal (29 Oct. 1909, 12, 46)

LUBICH, Lawrence and Miss Rose Vineberg,

daughter of Mr. and Mrs. I. Vineberg, Ontario St. E., Montreal, will be married Oct. 24, 1909, in the Auditorium Hall, Montreal (8 Oct. 1909, 12, 43)

LURIE, Max, of Edmonton, Alta., and Miss G. Wallman, of Toronto, will be married Thurs. evening, Aug. 15, 1912, in the Musician's Temple, Toronto (9 Aug. 1912, 15, 35)

MALDAVER, Oscar and Miss Fanny Fineberg, both of Toronto, will be married March 23, next (31 Jan. 1913, 16, 8)

MALLENS, Max and Miss Annie Viner, both of Montreal, are engaged (8 Dec. 1911, 15, 4)

MARCUSE, Feodor, son of Mr. and Mrs. Berthold Marcuse, and Miss Ethel Grossman, second daughter of Mr. and Mrs. Israel Grossman, all of Montreal, are engaged (8 April 1910, 13, 21)

MARCUSE, Feodor, son of Mr. and Mrs. Bertholde Marcuse, of Westmount, Que., and Miss Ethel Grossman, daughter of Mr. and Mrs. Israel Grossman, were married by Rev. Isaac de la Penha on Mon. in the Spanish and Portuguese Synagogue, Stanley St., Montreal. The bride was given away by her father. After a wedding breakfast in the Windsor Hotel, the couple left on their honeymoon to New York and Atlantic City. On their return they will reside at 780 Sherbrooke St. E. (23 Sept. 1910, 13, 45)

MARGOLESE, Dr. O., and Miss Rosenblat, of Winnipeg, are engaged (15 Jan. 1909, 12, 5)

MARGOLESE, Dr. Oscar, formerly of Montreal, now of Winnipeg, and Miss Pearl Rosenblat, of Montreal, were married by Rabbi J.K. Levin, last Wed. aft. in the vice-regal suite of the Royal Alexandra Hotel, Winnipeg (5 March 1909, 12, 12)

MARGOSCHES, Max B. and Miss Anna Wolfe, eldest daughter of Mr. and Mrs. Max Wolfe, Stewart St., Ottawa, were married by Rev. M. Mirsky last week at the home of the bride's parents. The bride's sisters, the Misses Teresa Frances and Sadie Elenore Wolfe and Mrs. Joel Pullan were present. A. Harry Wolfe, the brides's brother, was best man. Mr. and Mrs. Margosches will spend their honeymoon in Borough Park, Brooklyn, N.Y., the guests of Mr. and Mrs. Moritz Silberhertz, relatives of the groom (7 July 1911, 14, 34)

MARGOSCHES, Max B., formerly of New York City, son of the late Herr Salo Margosches and Frau Dorothee Margosches, of Vienna, Austria and brother of Dr. Jacques Margosches, also of Vienna, will be married to Miss Anna Wolfe, eldest daughter of Mr. and Mrs. Max Wolfe, of Ottawa, on June 28, 1911. They will be married at the home of the bride's parents, 35 Stewart St., Ottawa (16 June 1911, 14, 31)

MARGOSCHES, Max B., of Ottawa, formerly of Brooklyn, N.Y., and Miss Anna Wolfe, daughter of Mr. and Mrs. Max Wolfe, of Ottawa are engaged. The engagement was announced at the wedding of her sister, Miss Phoebe Wolfe to Joel Pullan in Ottawa on June 7, 1910 (15 July 1910, 13, 35)

MARKS, A., of Montreal, and Miss Esther Sabloff, sister of E. Sabloff, are engaged (13 Feb. 1914, 17, 7)

MARKS, J.J. and Miss Nellie Golul, daughter of Mr. and Mrs. J. Golul, all of Ottawa, are engaged (18 Nov. 1910, 14, 1)

MEDNICK, Louis, second son of Mr. and Mrs. J. Mednick, 744 City Hall Ave., Montreal, and Miss Sophie Grew, eldest daughter of Mr. and Mrs. I. Balos, née Mrs. Grew, 101 Laurier Ave. W., are engaged. English and American papers please copy (3 April 1914, 17, 14)

MENDELS, Bernard and Miss Alice McClean were married in New York by Rabbi M. Krauskopf, on Jan. 3, 1911 (13 Jan. 1911, 14, 9)

MENDELSON, Max, of Calgary, and Miss May Bloomfield, daughter of Rev. and Mrs. M. Bloomfield, of Montreal, were married by the bride's father in the Austro-Hungarian Synagogue, Milton St., Montreal, on Feb. 9, 1913. After the ceremony a reception was held in the Universal Hall. Out-of-town guests included:- I. Cohen and Mr. and Mrs. S. Bercuson, of Calgary, and B. Segall, of Edmonton (14 Feb. 1913, 16, 10)

MENDELSON, S.M. and Miss Eva Booth, were married by Rev. M. Kaplan, assisted by Rabbi Gordon at the residence of Mr. and Mrs. K.L. Sapera, 31 St. Patrick St., Toronto. The bride was given away by Mr. Sapera. Mesdames Grossman and Sapera were matrons of honor. The wedding march was played by Miss T. Kaplan at the piano and N. Phillips, of Cornwall, Ont., on the violin. The Misses I. Kaplan and A. Sapera were vocal soloists at the supper. Among those present were:- Mr. and Mrs. Grossman, of Vancouver; Mr. and Mrs. J. Mehr, Mr. and Mrs. M. Mehr, Mr. and Mrs. S. Mendelson, Mr. and Mrs. Antipetsky, the Misses E. Rosenblatt and J. Davis (7 Oct. 1910, 13, 47)

MENDELSSOHN, Joseph and Miss Becky Nathanson, both of Montreal, are engaged (6 Jan. 1911, 14, 8)

MENDELSSOHN, Joseph and Miss Rebecca Nathanson, daughter of S.L. Nathanson, all of Montreal, will be married Sun. Aug. 27, 1911 (25 Aug. 1911, 14, 41)

MESHY, David, of Ottawa, and Miss Sadie Vineberg, niece of Mr. and Mrs. J. Rubin and daughter of the late Mrs. M. Vineberg, of Montreal, will be married in Nov. 1910 (5 Aug. 1910, 13, 38)

MEYERS, S.F. and Miss Sarah Bloom, daughter of Mr. and Mrs. Bloom, all of Edmonton, will be married Sun. June 15, 1913 (20 June 1913, 16, 28)

MICHAELS, Alfred Edward, of Montreal, and Miss Rebecca Freedman, of Antwerp, Belgium, were married on March 9, 1909, in Antwerp. The couple will reside in Montreal. "The bride's father is the largest diamond cutter in Europe, and is also well known in the United States and Canada. The bridegroom is the son of Mr. John Michaels, proprietor of the "Stonewall Cigar" factory of this city." (2 April 1909, 12, 16)

MICHAELS, Clarence and Miss Frankie Phillips, daughter of Mr. and Mrs. Nathan Phillips, of Cornwall, Ont., are engaged. Mr. and Mrs. Phillips will receive at the residence of Mrs. Harris Vineberg, 598 Argyle Ave., Westmount, Que., next Sun. (22 Jan. 1909, 12, 6)

MICHAELS, Clarence, of Montreal, and Miss Frances Phillips, daughter of Mr. and Mrs. Nathan Phillips, of Cornwall, Ont., were married by Rabbi Meldola de Sola, assisted by Rabbi Herman Abramowitz, last Tues. evening, at the residence of the bride's aunt, Mr. and Mrs. Harris Vineberg, 598 Argyle Ave., Westmount. The bridesmaid was the bridegroom's sister, Miss Violet Michaels and Gordon Phillips, the bride's brother, was best man. Mr. and Mrs. Michaels left on a honeymoon to New York and Atlantic City. Gifts included a cabinet of silver from the bride's sister, Mrs. A. Rosenthal, of Toronto (15 April 1910, 13, 22)

MICHAELS, Michael A., of Montreal and Miss Muriel Hart, Elm Ave., Westmount, daughter of Mr. and Mrs. Lewis Hart, were married by Rabbi Meldola de Sola, assisted by Rabbi Isaac de la Penha, at the home of the bride's parents, last Tues. aft. Miss Mabel Hart, the bride's sister attended. Arthur Hart, the bride's brother was best man. The couple will reside on Elm Ave. (4 June 1909, 12, 25)

MICHAELS, Michael and Miss Muriel Hart, eldest daughter of Mr. and Mrs. Lewis A. Hart, Elm Ave., Westmount, Que., will be married in June in Montreal (26 March 1909, 12, 15)

MICHALSON, Israel, of Montreal, and Miss Evelyn K. Hart, daughter of Mr. and Mrs. John Hart, of London, England, are engaged (16 Feb. 1912, 15, 14)

MIDDELSTADT, Lionel and Miss Leah Schwartz, daughter of Mr. and Mrs. M. Schwartz, will be married in the McCaul Street Synagogue, Toronto, on Sun. Dec. 25, 1910 (9 Dec. 1910, 14, 4)

MILLER, G., of Kingston, Ont., and Miss Anna Levy, Laval Ave., Montreal, are engaged (4 March 1910, 13, 16)

MILLER, Samuel David, of Cornwall, Ont., and Miss Fannie Frank, daughter of Mr. and Mrs. Khos. Frank, of Montreal, were married on Sun. Sept. 14, 1913 in the Chevra Kadisha Synagogue, St. Urbain St., Montreal (5 Sept. 1913, 16, 39)

MILLER, Samuel David, son of Alderman and Mrs. Jacob Miller, of Cornwall, Ont., and Miss Fannie Frank, youngest daughter of Mr. and Mrs. Khos. Frank, of Montreal, are engaged (25 Oct. 1912, 15, 46)

MILLMAN, Aaron and Miss Rose Getz, daughter of Mr. and Mrs. L. Getz, all of Montreal, are engaged (28 March 1913, 16, 16)

MILLMAN, Saul, of Montreal, and Miss Tony Getz, of Quebec City, are engaged (17 Dec. 1909, 13, 5)

MIRSKY, David, son of Rev. J. Mirsky, of Ottawa, and Miss Sadie Vineberg, daughter of the late Mrs. M. Vineberg (formerly of Montreal), were married by Rabbi J. Berger, assisted by Revs. L. Doctor and Wershof, on Sun. Nov. 13, 1910, at Hotel Maus, Ottawa. Out-of-town guests included:- the bride's aunt and uncle, Mr. and Mrs. J. Rubin, of Montreal; the bride's grandfather, C. Hilf, of Montreal; Miss Sadie Rubin and N. Rubin, of Montreal; Miss Sadie Hilf, St. Louis; Philip Glazer, of Montreal; Myer Mirsky, of California; the groom's sister, Mrs. M. Pearlman, of Port Arthur, Ont.; A. Harris, Montreal; and Max and Abe Sloves, of Montreal. A. Harris, chairman of the Jewish National Fund, suggested that guests contribute trees in the Herzl Wald in memory of the young couple's departed mothers (18 Nov. 1910, 14, 1)

MITNICK, Isaac, son of Mr. and Mrs. L. Mitnick, and Miss Mollie Jaslow, daughter of Mr. and Mrs. M. Jaslow, all of Montreal, are engaged. A reception for nearly two hundred guests was held in Auditorium Hall last Sun. evening (27 Jan. 1911, 14, 11)

MITNICK, Isaac, son of Mr. and Mrs. L. Mitnick, and Miss Mollie Jaslow, daughter of Mr. and Mrs. C. Rutenberg, were married Wed. evening, Feb. 21, 1912, in Auditorium Hall, Montreal. The bride was given away by her uncle, M. Jaslow (1 March 1912, 15, 16)

MORRIS, Leonard Henry, son of Mr. and Mrs. A.I. Morris, of London, Eng., and Miss Celia Levy, daughter of Mr. and Mrs. H.S. Levy, St. Dominique St., Montreal, were married by Rev. Cohen, assisted by his choir, last Sun. in Prince Arthur Hall, Montreal (22 Aug. 1913, 16, 37)

MYERS, Alfred and Miss Amelia Corper, both of London, England, were married by Rev. S. Goldstein, on Sun. aft. July 4, 1909, at the home of Mrs. Rose Jacobs, "Rosemary", Westmount, Que. No relatives from either side were present. Mrs. Jacobs, Mr. and Mrs. L.S. Margolese and Jack Levi gave away the bride and groom. Little Miss Margery Adele Freedman was the bridesmaid. The couple will reside in Montreal (16 July 1909, 12, 31)

MYERS, B., of Montreal, and Miss Daisy Bernstein, of Detroit, are engaged (7 May 1909, 12, 21)

MYERS, Benjamin, of Montreal, and Miss Daisy Bernstein, of Detroit, will be married in Detroit, on Sept. 7, 1909 (3 Sept. 1909, 12, 38)

MYERS, Ralph, formerly of Montreal, and Miss Rose Franks, daughter of Z. Franks, of Vancouver, are engaged (26 Nov. 1909, 13, 2)

MYERSON, J.W., of Montreal, and Miss Dora Miller, daughter of Mr. and Mrs. D. Miller, are engaged (28 May 1909, 12, 24)

MYERSON, William and Miss Dorothy Miller were married Wed. evening, Dec. 29, 1909 in Auditorium Hall, Montreal. The bride was given away by her brother, Harry Miller, of Sackville, N.B. Gerson Miller, of Kingston, Ont., was best man. Miss Etta Miller, the bride's sister, was bridesmaid and the Misses Irene Bouzensky and Winnie Miller, the flowergirls. The bridegroom's gift to the bride was a pearl necklace. Out-of-town guests were:- Mr. and Mrs. Harry Miller and son, of Sackville; Mr. and Mrs. Max Lithwick, of Ottawa; Gerson and Nathan Miller, of Kingston; Mrs. A. Ryan, of Ottawa; Mrs. R. Levy, of New York; and B. Ellison, of Kingston (7 Jan. 1910, 13, 8)

NADLER, H. and Miss B. Bell, both of Montreal, are engaged (25 Aug. 1911, 14, 41)

NEPSKY, Isaac and Madame Leah Frank were married by Rabbi Hirsch Cohen, on Tues. June 15, 1909, at 125 Colonial Ave., Montreal (18 June 1909, 12, 27)

NEUMANN, Arthur, of Montreal, and Miss Ray Josephson, daughter of Mr. and Mrs. Frank Josephson, 22 Knox St., Ogdensburg, N.Y., were married by Rabbi Brodie, of Syracuse, N.Y., Tues. evening, March 12, 1912, at the home of the bride's parents. Miss Sophie Mendels, of Montreal, was the bridesmaid and Louis Salomon, of Montreal, was best man. Guests from Montreal included:- Mr. and Mrs. Neumann, Ald. and Mrs. A. Blumenthal, Dr. and Mrs. J. Rubin, Mr. and Mrs. J. Gittleson, Joseph Adelsteine, Fischel Ship, H. and M. Blumenthal, and Mrs. A. Salomon. After their honeymoon in New York Mr. and Mrs. Neumann will reside in Montreal (22 March 1912, 15, 19)

NITKIN, Samuel and Miss Annie Wachman were married by Rabbi Simon Glazer Sat. night, Jan. 13, 1912 in the New Modern Hall, Montreal. See Skolnick-Wachman wedding (19 Jan. 1912, 15, 10)

OBER, Louis, of Montreal, and Miss Dora Goldstein, youngest daughter of Rev. and Mrs. S. Goldstein, formerly of Montreal and now of Boston, Mass., are engaged (12 April 1912, 15, 22)

ORENSTEIN, Harry and Miss Hattie Kert, daughter of Mr. and Mrs. I. Kert, of Montreal, are engaged (1 Nov. 1912, 15, 47)

ORTENBERG, Dr. Samuel and Miss Miriam Brainin, eldest daughter of Mr. and Mrs. Reuben Brainin, were married by Rabbi Herman Abramowitz on Sun. May 25, 1913 in the McGill College Avenue Synagogue, Montreal. The bridesmaids were the Misses Elizabeth Bernstein, Minnie Bernstein, Bertha Brainin and Dorothy Leo. The ushers were N.S. Fineberg, Dr. A. Glickman, Dr. Levine and Ed. Solomon. The Misses Ruth Bernstein and Raya Goldman were the flowergirls. The train-bearers were Master Theodore Harris and Miss Diana Wolofsky. A reception was held at the home of the bride's parents, Park Ave. Dr. and Mrs. Ortenberg went to New York, Atlantic City and Washington for their honeymoon (30 May 1913, 16, 25)

ORTENBERG, Dr. Samuel, son of Mr. and Mrs. D. Ortenberg, of Quebec City, and Miss Miriam Brainin, daughter of Mr. and Mrs. Reuben Brainin, of Montreal, are engaged. Mr. and Mrs. R. Brainin will be "at home" Sun. Feb. 9, 1913 at 2588 Park Ave. (31 Jan. 1913, 16, 8)

PAPERNICK, Harris and Miss Sarah Greisman, were married by Rabbi Weinreb last Tues. evening in the Terauley Street Synagogue, Toronto. The bride was given away by her mother and the groom was given away by his parents. The bridesmaids were the Misses Sarah Papernick, Copeman and Goodman. The groomsman were H. Segal, D. Froman, J. Goodman and H. Steinberg. Miss Gertie Breslin, the groom's niece, and Miss Pearl Greisman, the bride's sister, were flower girls. After the ceremony supper was served in the Sons of England parlors. Mr. and Mrs. Papernick will reside at 99 McCaul St., Toronto after spending their honeymoon in Detroit, Cleveland and New York (29 July 1910, 13, 37)

PAPERNICK, Harris and Miss Sarah Greisman will be married in the Machzike Hadas Synagogue, Toronto on Wed. July 20, 1910 at 6 p.m. (8 July 1910, 13, 34)

PARNASS, B., of Montreal, and Miss Lillie Goldenburg, eldest daughter of Mr. and Mrs. P. Goldenburg, of Three Rivers, Que., are engaged (27 Jan. 1911, 14, 11)

PARNASS, Mr., of Montreal, and Miss Sara Herzberg, of Quebec City, are engaged (26 Feb. 1909, 12, 11)

PESNER, Mr., eldest son of Mr. and Mrs. Pesner, of Montreal, and Miss Leah Soskin, eldest daughter of Mr. and Mrs. A. Soskin, Sanguinet St., Montreal, are engaged (11 Feb. 1910, 13, 13)

PETEGORSKY, Leon, of Ottawa, and Miss R. Wolinsky, daughter of Mr. and Mrs. M. Wolinsky, of East View, Ont., are engaged (15 March 1912, 15, 18)

PETEGORSKY, Leon, president of the Ottawa YMHA, and Miss Rebecca Volinsky, of Ottawa, were married by Rabbi Joseph D. Berger and Rev. S. Doctor in the King Edward Institute, Ottawa. At the reception following, Mr. Gittleson was toastmaster and short speeches were made by Rabbi Berger, A.L. Florence, Mr. Volinsky, Julius Berger and the groom's brother (2 Aug. 1912, 15, 34)

PIONICK, Dr. Maurice and Miss Esther Keyfitz, daughter of the late Nathan Keyfitz and Mrs. Rebecca Keyfitz, were married by Rabbi Nathan Gordon, assisted by Cantor Wladofsky, last week in the Cosmopolitan Club, Toronto. "The wedding was somewhat quiet, owing to the death of the bride's father, which occurred about nine months ago." Mrs. D. Levine, the bride's sister, was matron of honor. Out-of-town guests included the bride's brothers, Arthur Keyfitz, of the **Montreal Gazette** and Samuel Keyfitz, of Port McNicholl. After the wedding the couple went on a short honeymoon to the U.S. (4 July 1913, 16, 30)

PIVNIK, B.A., Maurice and Miss Esther A. Keyfitz, both of Toronto, are engaged (8 Oct. 1909, 12, 43)

PLISKOW, Myer, of Montreal, and Miss Florence Blumenthal, daughter of Mr. and Mrs. I. Blumenthal, of Hamilton, Ont., are engaged (26 July 1912, 15, 33)

PLISKOW, Myer, of Montreal, and Miss Florence Dinah Blumenthal, daughter of Mr. and Mrs. Isaac Blumenthal, 149 North James St., Hamilton, were married by Rabbi Jacob S. Minkin in Hamilton. Miss Annie Blumenthal was maid of honor and Misses Annie Frank and Cecilia Levy were bridesmaids. Maxwell Blumenthal, the bride's brother, was best man. Lou and Joe Blumenthal were groomsmen and little Leon Goldberg was the page. The ushers were Moe Levy, Leo and Maurice Kauffman. Saul Lyons was master of ceremonies. Guests included:- Charles Pliskow and Miss Florence Wolfe, of Detroit; Miss Nellie Freeman and Abe and Miss Eva Morris, of Toronto; Mr. and Mrs. T. Fox, of Brantford; Arthur Levy, James Cohen, Mr. and Mrs. Sam Goldberg, Mr. and Mrs. Moe Simons, Misses Mary Franks and Fannie Wexler. Mr. and Mrs. Pliskow went to New York for their honeymoon. They will return to Hamilton for the Israelitish Benevolent Society ball, before going to Montreal where they will reside (10 Jan. 1913, 16, 5)

POLLAK, Max, of Quebec City, and Miss Rebecca Tarantur, eldest daughter of Mr. and Mrs. Tarantur, of Montreal, were married this week in Standard Hall, Montreal. The bridegroom's sister, Miss Tillie Pollak, was maid of honor and his brother, Frank Pollak, was best man (3 Sept. 1909, 12, 38)

POLLOCK, Frank, of Quebec City, and Miss Lily Rosenberg, eldest daughter of Mr. and Mrs. E. Rosenberg, of Montreal, are engaged (28 Jan. 1910, 13, 11)

POMERANTZ, Joseph, and Miss Jenny Brown, daughter of Mr. and Mrs. B. Brown, 481 Queen St., Toronto, will be married in the University Avenue Synagogue, Toronto, on Aug. 30, 1910 (12 Aug. 1910, 13, 39)

POYANER, Meyer, of Montreal, and Miss Dorothy Moscovitz, of Edmundston, N.B., are engaged (25 June 1909, 12, 28)

POYANER, Myer, of Montreal, and Miss Dora Moscovicz, of Edmundston, N.B., were married in Edmundston by Rabbi B.L. Amdur, of St. John, N.B. The bride's attendants were the groom's sister, Miss Esther Poyaner and Miss Miriam Ross, of St. John. Little Miss Sarah Moscovicz, the bride's sister, acted as flower girl while Harry Poyaner, of Montreal, was best man. The couple left for Montreal where they will reside (18 Feb. 1910, 13, 14)

PRESNER, J. and Miss Anna Cohen, daughter of Rabbi Hirsch Cohen, all of Montreal, will be married at the residence of Rabbi Cohen, 187 Dorchester St. E., on Tues. May 16, 1911 (12 May 1911, 14, 26)

PRESNER, J. and Miss Anna Cohen, daughter of Rabbi Hirsch and the late Sarah Cohen, were married by Rabbis Cohen and Herman Abramowitz last Tues. at the residence of the bride's father, 187 Dorchester St. E., Montreal. The bride's sisters, the Misses Mary and Etta Cohen were bridesmaids. Harry Fuerst, the bride's uncle, was best man (19 May 1911, 14, 27)

PULLAN, Joel, of Winnipeg, and Miss Phoebe Wolfe, daughter of Mr. and Mrs. Max Wolfe, of Ottawa, are engaged (7 Jan. 1910, 13, 8)

PULLAN, Joel, of Winnipeg, only son of Mr. and Mrs. H. Pullan, of Ottawa, and Miss Phoebe Wolfe, second daughter of Mr. and Mrs. Max Wolfe, 35 Stewart St., Ottawa, were married at the home of the bride's parents on June 7, 1910 (15 July 1910, 13, 35)

PULLAN, Louis I., of Toronto, and Miss Rosetta Myers, of Winnipeg, will be married Tues. Dec. 30, 1913 at 5 p.m., in the Holy Blossom Synagogue, Bond St., Toronto (19 Dec. 1913, 17, 2)

PULLAN, Louis I., son of Mr. and Mrs. M. Pullan, of Toronto, and Miss Rosetta Myers, of Winnipeg, daughter of I. Myers and the late Mrs. Myers, were married by Rabbi S. Jacobs, assisted by Rev. M. Kaplan, in the Holy Blossom Synagogue, Bond St., Toronto. The bride was given away by her father. Miss Bessie Rosenburg, the bride's niece, was maid of honor. Harry Pullan, the groom's brother, was best man. Mrs. Philip Rosenburg, the bride's sister, was matron of honor. After the ceremony a reception was held in the Parkdale Assembly Hall, where the groom's mother received the guests. Among those present were:- Mesdames Granatstein, J.N. Manaseveth, L. Neveren, J.M. Pullan, N. Rosenburg (the groom's sister), and L. M. Singer. Out-of-town guests included:- A.W. Myers (Winnipeg); S.P. Myers (Montreal); B. Pullan, the groom's grandfather (Ottawa); Mrs. J.L. Rill (Winnipeg); Mr. and Mrs. Coplan (Ottawa); and Mr. and Mrs. N. Swartz. Mr. and Mrs. Pullan went to the eastern U.S. on their honeymoon and stayed at the Windsor Hotel while in Montreal. On their return they will reside at 101 Kendall Ave., Toronto (16 Jan. 1914, 17, 6)

PULLAN, Louis L., of Toronto, son of Mr. and Mrs. M. Pullan, and Miss Rosetta Myers, daughter of I. Myers, of Winnipeg, are engaged (8 Aug. 1913, 16, 35)

PYES, David L., of Grand Forks, N.D. and Winnipeg, and Miss Isabelle Naiman, second daughter of Mr. and Mrs. I. Naiman, were married on Sun. July 10, 1910 at the bride's home, 121 Pacific Ave., Winnipeg (29 July 1910, 13, 37)

RABIN, Harry and Miss Annie Reine, both of Montreal, are engaged (23 July 1909, 12, 32)

RABIN, Louis and Miss Annie Reim were married at the Roumanian Synagogue, Montreal, last Tues. aft. The bride was given away by her father. Misses Jennie Rabin and Rosie Goldner were bridesmaids. The couple will reside in Cobalt, Ont. (29 Oct. 1909, 12, 46)

RABINOVITCH, Dr. Max and Miss Annie Feigleson, daughter of Mr. and Mrs. Hyman Feigleson, Colonial Ave., Montreal, were married by Rabbi Simon Glazer at the home of the bride's parents on Tues. Miss Bessie Rabinovitch, the bridegroom's sister, attended the bride. Mr. Feigleson gave his daughter away and David Feigleson, the bride's brother, was the best man. The couple left that evening on their honeymoon and on their return will reside at 792 City Hall Ave. (13 May 1910, 13, 26)

RABINOVITCH, Dr. Max and Miss Annie Feigleson, daughter of Mr. and Mrs. H. Feigleson, will be married on Tues. May 10, 1910, at the home of the bride's parents, 224 Colonial Ave., Montreal (6 May 1910, 13, 25)

RABINOVITCH, Dr. Max, of Montreal, and Miss Annie Feigelson, daughter of Mr. and Mrs. H. Feigelson, 224 Colonial Ave., Montreal, are engaged (11 June 1909, 12, 26)

RABINOVITCH, Harry and Miss Lillie Rabinovitch, both of Montreal, were married yesterday by Rabbi Hirsch Cohen, in the Auditorium Hall, Berthelet St. (19 March 1909, 12, 14)

RAICH, David and Miss Sophie Jacobson, daughter of Mr. and Mrs. S. Jacobson, were married by Rev. S. Goldstein, on Sun. Jan. 11, 1914 at 2214 Clarke St., Montreal (16 Jan. 1914, 17, 6)

RAM, Samuel, son of Mr. and Mrs. B. Ram, and Miss Leah Bernstein, daughter of Mr. and Mrs. M. Bernstein, all of Montreal, are engaged (30 June 1911, 14, 33)

RAM, Samuel, son of Mr. and Mrs. B. Ram, and Miss Leah Bernstein, daughter of Mr. and Mrs. M. Bernstein, have broken off their engagement by mutual consent (14 July 1911, 14, 35)

RAMM, Harold, of Toronto, and Miss Gertrude Griesman, eldest daughter of Mr. and Mrs. Israel Griesman, 149 St. Patrick St., Toronto, are engaged (13 May 1910, 13, 26)

RAPPELBAUM, Leon and Miss Marguerite Balacan, fifth daughter and twelveth child of Mr. and Mrs. W. Balacan, all of Montreal, are engaged and will be married in June, 1911 (24 Feb. 1911, 14, 15)

RILL, Abraham and Miss Jenny Johnson, both of Montreal, were married by Rabbi J.K. Levin of Shaarey Shomayim Congregation, Winnipeg, on Tues. July 26, 1910. Miss Johnson was received into the Congregation of Israel earlier that day. The wedding was private and only the immediate relatives and personal friends of the bridegroom were present. They included Mr. and Mrs. J.L. Rill, Mr. and Mrs. A. Lewinson, Mrs. M. Lauer and Ed. Capstein (29 July 1910, 13, 37)

ROGGEN, Selig, of New York, and Miss Etta Wener, of Montreal, will be married Thurs. June 16, 1910 (10 June 1910, 13, 30)

ROGGEN, Selig, of New York, and Miss Etta Wener, daughter of H. Wener, 85 St. Famille St., Montreal, were married by Rabbi Herman Abramowitz, assisted by Rev. S. Goldstein, last Thurs. aft. The matron of honor was Mrs. Harry Wener. The bridesmaids were Miss Myrtle Levinson and Miss Florence Wener, the bride's sister. The ushers were Larry Goldberg and Mrs. Jack Wener. Mr. and Mrs. Roggen will spend some months in Europe (24 June 1910, 13, 32)

ROGGEN, Z., of New York, and Miss Etta

Wener, daughter of H. Wener, of Montreal, are engaged (15 April 1910, 13, 22)

ROME, Nathan and Miss Minnie Bernstein, will be married on Tues. Aug. 23, 1910 (5 Aug. 1910, 13, 38)

ROME, Nathan, son of Mr. and Mrs. I. Rome, of Worcester, Mass., and Miss Miriam Bernstein, daughter of Mr. and Mrs. H. Bernstein, were married by Rabbi Herman Abramowitz, assisted by Rev. S. Goldstein last Tues. aft., at the home of the bride's parents, 65 Hutchison St., Montreal. Miss Elizabeth Bernstein was maid of honor and the bridesmaids were the Misses Jeannette and Edythe Rome. Hyman Rome, of Gardner, Mass., was best man. Out-of-town guests included:- Mr. and Mrs. Maggid, Morton Rosenthal, of New York; J.L. Rome, of Gardner, Mass.; Mr. and Mrs. A.I. Rome, of Fitchburg; Harry, the Misses Jeannette, Edythe and Sophie Rome and Hyman, Philip and Mr. and Mrs. I. Rome, of Worcester, Mass.; Mr. and Mrs. C. Bernstein, of Maywood, N.J.; Dr. and Mrs. S. Richter, of New York; and Miss Mary Povitch, of Bath, Me. (26 Aug. 1910, 13, 41)

ROSCOM, David, of New York, and Miss Mabel Constance Goldstein, daughter of Mr. and Mrs. B. Goldstein, Bishop St., Montreal, are engaged (1 April 1910, 13, 20)

ROSE, Bernard, of Montreal, and Miss Ray Goodman, of Toronto, will be married at 29 Vanauley St., Toronto, on Sun. Dec. 11, 1910 (25 Nov. 1910, 14, 2)

ROSENAS, Harry, son of Mrs. N. Lesser, and Miss Leah Davidson, daughter of Mr. and Mrs. W.M. Davidson, all of Montreal, were married on March 23, 1909. Mrs. I. Vineberg was the matron of honor and Miss F. Rosenas was the bridesmaid (2 April 1909, 12, 16)

ROSENBERG, Arthur H., of New York, and Miss Bertha Rubin, daughter of Mrs. J. Rubin, of Rochester, N.Y., formerly of Hamilton, were married by Rabbi Jacob S. Minkin at his home, Catherine St. S., Hamilton, Sun. morn., June 2, 1912 (21 June 1912, 15, 28)

ROSENBERG, I., son of Mr. and Mrs. W. Rosenberg, and Miss Dora Rosenthal, daughter of Mr. and Mrs. J. Rosenthal, of Montreal, are engaged (20 Sept. 1911, 14, 45)

ROSENBERG, J. and Miss Esther Poyaner, daughter of Mr. and Mrs. A. Poyaner, all of Montreal, are engaged (11 Oct. 1910, 13, 47)

ROSENBLAT, Charles B., of Winnipeg, and the daughter of Mr. and Mrs. Ressman, of Chicago, Ill., were engaged Feb. 4, 1912 (9 Feb. 1912, 15, 13)

ROSENSTEIN, Jacob and Miss Rae Levine, daughter of Mr. and Mrs. S. Levine, all of Montreal, are engaged (30 Sept. 1910, 13, 46)

ROSENTHAL, Alderman Samuel, of Ottawa, and Miss Augusta Posnanzki, daughter of the late Samuel Posnanzki, former mayor of Chippewa Falls, Wisconsin, were married by Rev. Samuel Hirschberg, of Temple Emanu-El, at the Pfister Hotel, Milwaukee, on Mon. June 21, 1909, at noon. The bride's wreath was worn by the bridegroom's mother at her wedding forty-one years ago. The bride was given away by her brother, Maurice Posnanzki. Miss Pearl Evelyn Levy was the maid of honor and Arthur Rosenthal was the best man. Guests included: Mrs. A.S. Rosenthal and Mr. and Mrs. A. Rosenthal, of Ottawa; Julius Lesser, of Chicago; Mr. and Mrs. F. Kreider, of New York; Mrs. H.L. Levy and Miss Pearl Levy, of Eau Claire; Mr. and Mrs. J. Edward Posnanzki and Maurice A. Posnanzki, of Chippewa Falls; Rabbi and Mrs. Samuel Hirschberg, Mr. and Mrs. Emanuel Phillips, Mr. and Mrs. I.P. Kahn, Mr. and Mrs. Harry Glicksman, Mr. and Mrs. Nathan Glicksman, Mrs. F. Docter, Mrs. R. Silber, J. Docter, Miss Ray Muller, Miss Belle Heller, S.L. Stein, Miss M. Stein, Miss Dorothy Phillips, all of Milwaukee. The couple will reside in Ottawa (2 July 1909, 12, 29)

ROSENZVEIG, Jake, of Montreal, and Miss Lily Simkevitz, of Cornwall, Ont., are engaged (5 Nov. 1909, 12, 47)

ROSKAM, David, of Montreal, and Miss Mabel Goldstein, daughter of Mr. and Mrs. B. Goldstein, 267 Bishop St., Montreal, were married by Rabbi Nathan Gordon on Wed. in the Windsor Hotel, Montreal. Miss Sylvia Goldstein, the bride's sister, was her only attendant. Felix Lewis was the best man. Mr. and Mrs. Roskam will honeymoon in Bermuda (23 Dec. 1910, 14, 6)

ROSNER, David and Miss Rosie Greenberg, youngest daughter of Mrs. S. Greenberg, all of Montreal, are engaged (15 Sept. 1909, 12, 40)

ROST, Julius and Miss Fannie Gross, both of Montreal, are engaged (24 June 1910, 13, 32)

ROST, Julius and Miss Fannie Gross, daughter of Mr. and Mrs. Martin B. Gross, were married Sun. aft., July 11, 1911 in the Austrian Synagogue, Montreal. The bride's attendant was the bridegroom's sister, Miss Jane B. Rost. A reception was held at 133 Elgin St. Mr. and Mrs. Rost went to New York, Boston and surroundings on their honeymoon (16 June 1911, 14, 31)

ROTHER, Harry and Miss Fanny Shapiro, both of Montreal, are engaged (30 Dec. 1910, 14, 7)

ROUTTENBERG, Israel and Miss Rebecca Ornstein, both of Montreal, are engaged (10 Feb. 1911, 14, 13)

ROVIN, Maurice L., of Detroit, and Miss Annie Cohen, of Toronto, will be married on Sun. Oct. 30, 1910 at 103 D'arcy St., Toronto (11 Oct. 1910, 13, 48)

RUBENSTEIN, Samuel, of Hawksbury, Ont., and Miss Sadie Berkman, daughter of Mr. A. and the late Mrs. Berkman, of Montreal, were married by Rabbi Hirsch Cohen, in the Auditorium Hall, Montreal, last Sun. at 6 p.m. (4 June 1909, 12, 25)

RUBIN, Jas. and Miss B. Robinson were married recently in Hamilton, Ont. Rabbi S. Jacobs, of the Holy Blossom Synagogue, Bond St., in Toronto, officiated (25 Nov. 1910, 14, 2)

RUBIN, Joseph D., of Boston, Mass., and Miss Rose Rosenberg, daughter of Mr. and Mrs. A. Rosenberg, of Montreal, are engaged (31 Oct. 1913, 16, 47)

RUBIN, Maurice, son of Mr. and Mrs. J. Rubin, and Miss Rebecca Ellison, daughter of Mr. and Mrs. H. Ellison, all of Montreal, are engaged (3 Jan. 1913, 16, 4)

RUBIN, Maurice, son of Mr. and Mrs. J. Rubin, and Miss Rebecca Ellison, daughter of Mr. and Mrs. H. Ellison, were married by Rabbi Herman Abramowitz, on Wed. April 2, 1913, in Montreal. The bride was attended by her two sisters, the Misses Annie and Hilda Ellison. Speeches were made by Rabbi Herman Abramowitz, S. Fromson, Rev. S. Goldstein, H. Lang, Rev. J. Margolese, L. Margolese, Dr. O. Margolese (Winnipeg), E. Rubenstein, M. Rubin and L. Yellin. "The young couple waited over for Sheva Brochus and then left for a trip to New York." (11 April 1913, 16, 18)

RUBIN, Miss Gertie - her marriage which was to take place on July 4, 1909, has been postponed until Sept. 5 due to the illness of her father, J. Rubin (18 June 1909, 12, 27)

RUBINOFF, Israel and Miss Emma Nathanson, eldest daughter of Mr. and Mrs. B. Nathanson, of Toronto, are engaged (30 Aug. 1912, 15, 38)

RUBINOVICH, I.M., of Montreal, and Miss Mildred Isaacs, youngest daughter of Mrs. A. Isaacs, of St. John, N.B., are engaged (21 Jan. 1910, 13, 10)

SABBATH, J.L. and Miss Rose Kert, eldest daughter of Mrs. N. Sperber, all of Montreal, are engaged (18 Oct. 1910, 13, 48)

SABBATH, S. and Miss Florence Tartick, both of Montreal, are engaged (12 March 1909, 12, 13)

SACK, M.L. and Miss Hannah Witzling, both of Montreal, are engaged (23 Dec. 1910, 14, 6)

SAKS, Lucien Paul, son of Mr. and Mrs. Charles Saks, of London, England, and Miss Eva Goldstein, daughter of Mr. and Mrs. William Goldstein, Dorchester St., Westmount, Que., are engaged (20 June 1913, 16, 28)

SALOMON, Moses, of Montreal, and Miss Helen Rosenberg, of Winnipeg, were married by Rev. I. Cohen on Aug. 22, 1911, at the home of Mrs. Salomon, 451 St. Denis St., Montreal. Mr. and Mrs. Salomon went to New York on their honeymoon and on their return will reside in Montreal (1 Sept. 1911, 14, 42)

SAMUEL, Abe and Miss Martha Levine, daughter of Mr. and Mrs. M. Levine, of Toronto, were engaged June 18, 1913 (20 June 1913, 16, 28)

SAMUEL, Harry and Miss Irene Goldstein, daughter of Mr. and Mrs. William Goldstein, all of Toronto, are engaged (14 March 1913, 16, 14)

SAMUELS, Harold, of Vancouver, son of Mr. and

Mrs. M. Samuels, 1023 St. Urbain St., Montreal, and Miss Rose Dobrofsky, daughter of Mr. and Mrs. P. Dobrofsky, St. Urbain St., are engaged (9 Jan. 1914, 17, 5)

SANDPERL, Max and Miss Mary Gavrilowitz, daughter of Mr. and Mrs. Joseph Mendel Gavrilowitz, will be married on Sun. evening, March 12, 1911, in the Polish Synagogue, Elm St., Toronto (17 Feb. 1911, 14, 14)

SAXE, Henry and Miss Bessie Levinson, daughter of Mr. and Mrs. S. Levinson, 107 Drummond St., Montreal, were married by Rabbi Herman Abramowitz, assisted by Rev. S. Goldstein, Wed. aft., at the home of the bride's parents. The bride's attendant was Miss Sarah Levinson. William Levine was best man. The couple left on a honeymoon to New York and Atlantic City (24 June 1910, 13, 32)

SAXE, Henry and Miss Bessie Levinson, daughter of Mr. and Mrs. S. Levinson, Drummond St., all of Montreal, are engaged (15 Oct. 1909, 12, 44)

SCHACHTER, Max and Miss Sarah Cooper, daughter of Mr. and Mrs. K. Cooper, all of Montreal, are engaged. A party was held Sun. Dec. 1, 1912. The Misses Leba Ginsberg and Jessie Phillips assisted in receiving the guests. Speeches were made by Rabbi Hirsch Cohen, Lazarus Cohen, H. Lande and Lazarus Phillips (6 Dec. 1912, 15, 52)

SCHACHTER, Mr. and Miss Eva Weisberg, daughter of Mrs. Weisberg, all of Montreal, are engaged (27 Jan. 1911, 14, 11)

SCHACHTER, S., the well-known artist photographer, St. Lawrence Blvd., Montreal, and Miss Celia Bloomfield, of New York, were married by Rabbi Herman Abramowitz on Sun. in the Shaar Hashomayim Synagogue, Stanley St., Montreal. The bride's parents and sister came from New York for the wedding (20 June 1913, 16, 28)

SCHACHTER, Sol, photographer, 435 St. Lawrence Blvd., Montreal, and Miss Celia Bloomfield, of Brooklyn, N.Y., are engaged (17 Jan. 1913, 16, 6)

SCHACTER, Louis and Miss Claire Genser will be married on Tues. June 27, 1911, at 197 Notre Dame St. E., Montreal (16 June 1911, 14, 31)

SCHAPIRO, Aaron, of Montreal, and Miss Roselyn Shayne, eldest daughter of Dr. and Mrs. John Shayne, are engaged (2 Jan. 1914, 17, 4)

SCHEFFER, Isidor and Miss Rae Morris will be married Tues. Sept. 3, 1912, in the McGill College Avenue Synagogue, Montreal (23 Aug. 1912, 15, 37)

SCHEFFER, Isidor, of Valleyfield, Que., and Miss Rae Morris, daughter of Mrs. Gertrude Morris, of Montreal, were married by Rabbi Herman Abramowitz, assisted by Cantor I. Cohen in Shaar Hashomayim Synagogue, Montreal. The bride was given away by her uncle, Mr. Simonson, of Boston. Miss Sophie Klineberg, the groom's niece, was maid of honor and Max Scheffer, the groom's brother was best man. Guests included the bride's aunts, Mesdames W.B. Jones, Goldstone and Shapera and her uncle, Mr. Shapera, of Boston, Miss May Morris, of Buffalo, and Edward Morris, of Chicago. A reception was held afterwards at Patton's Parlors. Mr. and Mrs. Scheffer went to New York and Boston for their honeymoon (6 Sept. 1912, 15, 39)

SCHIFTAN, John and Miss Eva Heppner were married in the Shaarey Zedek Synagogue, Winnipeg, on Dec. 31, 1912 at 2 p.m. A reception followed in the Eureka Hall. Mr. and Mrs. Schiftan took the 5 p.m. train from the C.P.R. station to the U.S. (10 Jan. 1913, 16, 5)

SCHLESINGER, Edward and Miss Violet Ascher, daughter of H.S.G. Ascher, were married Thurs. evening, Sept. 15, 1910 at 8 p.m. at the summer residence of the bride's aunt and uncle, Mr. and Mrs. Clarence I. de Sola. The bride was given away by her father. The bridesmaids were cousins, the Misses Florence Mendes, of New York, and Jessica de Sola. Dr. Otto Schlesinger, the groom's brother, was best man. Mr. and Mrs. Schlesinger sailed for Europe on the steamer Victorian (23 Sept. 1910, 13, 45)

SCHLOSSBERG, S. and Miss Clara Dictar, both of Montreal, are engaged (13 June 1913, 16, 27)

SCHNAER, Joe, son of Mr. and Mrs. A. Schnaer, of Montreal, and Miss Gertie Press, daughter of Mrs. A.S. Press, 872 City Hall Ave., Montreal, are engaged (13 Dec. 1912; 16, 1)

SCHNAPP, Abe and Miss Bessie Sabbath, daughter of Mrs. N.S. Sabbath, all of Montreal, are engaged (26 July 1912, 15, 33)

SCHNEYER, Charles and Miss Bertha Lavut, daughter of M. Lavut, will be married on Tues. June 27, 1911, at the bride's residence, 995 St. Urbain St., Montreal (16 June 1911, 14, 31)

SCHOENROD, Nathan, of Chicago, Ill., and Miss Frances Merker, daughter of Mr. and Mrs. Merker, 309 Indian Road, Toronto, are engaged (18 July 1913, 16, 32)

SCHWARTZ, A., of Boston, Mass., and Miss Edith Ogulnik, daughter of Mr. and Mrs. Paul Ogulnik, of Montreal, are engaged (1 Oct. 1913, 16, 42-43)

SCHWARTZ, Joseph and Miss Lizzie Trager, daughter of Mr. and Mrs. L. Trager, will be married in the Chevra Kadisha Synagogue, St. Urbain St., Montreal, on Sun. June 25, 1911 (9 June 1911, 14, 30)

SCHWARZBARD, J., of La Tuque, Que., and Miss Rose Ortenberg, of Quebec City, are engaged (1 Oct. 1909, 12, 42)

SCHWARZBARD, Jacob, of La Tuque, Que., and Miss Rose Ortenberg, youngest daughter of Mr. and Mrs. D. Ortenberg, of Quebec City, were married by Rabbi S. Glazer, assisted by Rev. M.I. Eliasoph, of Quebec City, last Fri. in the Beth Israel Synagogue, Quebec City. Miss Sarah Herzberg was maid of honor and the bride's two little nieces, the Misses Annie and Rhoda Lerner were flower girls. Dr. S. Ortenberg, the bride's brother, gave her away and Ben Ortenberg, the bride's other brother, acted as best man. Mrs. L. Lerner, the bride's sister was also present. The reception was held on Sat. at the home of the bride's parents. Mr. and Mrs. Schwarzbard will reside in La Tuque (4 March 1910, 13, 16)

SEGAL, J. and Miss Fanny Barenblatt, daughter of Mr. and Mrs. I. Barenblatt, are engaged (23 Sept. 1910, 13, 45)

SEGAL, Z., nephew of B. Ram, and Miss Bessie Gordon, all of Montreal, are engaged (9 July 1909, 12, 30)

SEIDLER, I.M. and Miss Annie Sommer, daughter of Mrs. D. Sommer, all of Toronto, are engaged (8 April 1910, 13, 21)

SERCHUK, Harry and Miss Dorothea (Dolly) Serchuk, grand-daughter of Mr. and Mrs. M. Serchuk, of Montreal, are engaged. "The wedding will take place quietly in the middle of July." (6 March 1914, 17, 10)

SHANIKMAN, M. and Miss Ida Haberman, daughter of Mrs. H. Haberman, will be married at 135 Peter St., Toronto, on Mon. Sept. 5, 1910 (26 Aug. 1910, 13, 41)

SHAPIRO, Abe, youngest son of M. Shapiro, of Montreal, and Miss G. Liebling, eldest daughter of Mr. and Mrs. D. Liebling, of Quebec City, were married by Rev. I. Eliasoph on Dec. 31, 1911, in the Auditorium Hall, Quebec City. Miss Gelber, of Windsor, Ont., the bride's cousin, was maid of honor. Aron Shapiro, of Montreal, the groom's cousin was best man. About seventy-five guests from Montreal attended the wedding. After spending their honeymoon in New York, Mr. and Mrs. Shapiro will reside in Montreal (5 Jan. 1912, 15, 8)

SHAPIRO, Dave, of Montreal, and Miss Bessie Levy, youngest daughter of Mr. and Mrs. Louis Levy, of Moncton, N.B., are engaged (13 Jan. 1911, 14, 9)

SHAPIRO, Dave, youngest son of Mr. and Mrs. G. Shapiro, of Montreal, and Miss Bessie Levy, youngest daughter of Mr. and Mrs. Levy, of Moncton, N.B., were married by Rabbi Herman Abramowitz on Jan. 2, 1912 in the Auditorium Hall, Montreal. Miss R.S. Superior, the groom's niece, was maid of honor. A. Fencer was best man. Mr. and Mrs. Shapiro left for New York en route to Bermuda for their honeymoon. They will reside in Halifax, N.S. on their return (5 Jan. 1912, 15, 8)

SHAPIRO, George J. and Miss Eliza Marcuse, daughter of Mr. and Mrs. B. Marcuse, will be married Thurs. Dec. 5, 1912 at 6 p.m. in the Chevra Kadisha Synagogue, St. Urbain St., Montreal (29 Nov. 1912, 15, 51)

SHAPIRO, George J. and Miss Eliza Marcuse were married Thurs. Dec. 5, 1912 in the Chevra Kadisha Synagogue, St. Urbain St., Montreal. Out-of-town guests were:- Mesdames H. Mishkind, I. Mishkind, J. Mishkind, S.D. Friedman, Miss Luba Stein, and Master Leo Mishkind, of New York. Mr. and Mrs. Shapiro went to New York for the honeymoon and on their return will reside on Durocher St. (13 Dec. 1912, 16, 1)

SHAPIRO, George J., son of Mr. and Mrs. A. Shapiro, of Montreal, and Miss Eliza Marcuse, second daughter of Mr. and Mrs. B. Marcuse, are engaged (14 July 1911, 14, 35)

SHAPIRO, Samuel and Miss Ida Kandestin, both of Montreal, are engaged (12 Jan. 1912, 15, 9)

SHAPIRO, Wilford, of Kincardine, Ont., and Miss Sadie Rosen, of Toronto, are engaged and will be married in Feb., 1911 (9 Dec. 1910, 14, 4)

SHAPIRO, Wilfred, of Kincardine, Ont., and Miss Sadye Rosen, second daughter of Mrs. R. Rosen, were married by Rev. Caplan on Feb. 14, 1911 in the McCaul Street Synagogue, Toronto. Miss Ida Rosen, the bride's sister was maid of honor and the bridesmaids were the Misses Ethel Cohen and Doris Finmark. B. Rosen, the bride's brother, and S. Herbert were groomsmen. After the ceremony a reception was held in the Cosmopolitan Club, 174 Beverley St. (24 Feb. 1911, 14, 15)

SHERWIN, A., of New York, and Miss Irene Levi, daughter of Mr. and Mrs. D. Levi, Dorchester St., Montreal, were married by Rev. Dr. de Sola Mendes, on March March 17, 1909, in the rose room of the Hotel Majestic, New York. Mrs. Aarons, sister of the bridegroom, was matron of honor. The bridesmaids were Misses Sherwin, Hilda Levi and Blanche Sherwin, of New York, and Blanche Levi, the bride's sister. A.H. Sherwin, the bridegroom's brother, was best man. The ushers were: Dr. Agatson and Messrs. Cassil Levi, A. Schwernki and Monroe Schwernki. Mr. and Mrs. Sherwin will reside in New York (26 March 1909, 12, 15)

SHERWIN, A., of New York, and Miss Irene Levi, daughter of Mr. and Mrs. D. Levi, Dorchester St. West, Montreal, are engaged (12 Feb. 1909, 12, 9)

SHIEFF, Edward I., of West Fort William, Ont., and Miss Jennie Ness, daughter of Mr. and Mrs. A. Ness, 27 Park Ave., Montreal, are engaged (16 July 1909, 12, 31)

SHIP, Dr. A.P. and Miss Leah Sessenwein were married by Rabbi Herman Abramowitz, assisted by Cantor Cohen in Stanley Hall, Montreal. The bride's uncle was best man and her sister was maid of honor. Dr. and Mrs. Ship sail on the S.S. Megantic on Oct. 14, 1911 for an extended trip through Europe (13 Oct. 1911, 14, 48)

SHORE, Harry, real estate agent, York St., and Miss Fanny Kriger, eldest daughter of Mr. and Mrs. Samuel Kriger, 547 Rideau St., all of Ottawa, were married in the Rideau Street Synagogue by Rabbi J. Berger and the Rev. Doctor and Mirsky. Miss Leah Kriger, the bride's sister, was bridesmaid. The wedding was one of the largest to have taken place in some time. A cortage of 52 cabs went from the home of the bride to the synagogue. A reception and banquet for 250 guests followed in St. Patrick's Hall. The couple went to Montreal and Quebec City for their honeymoon (27 June 1913, 16, 29)

SILVER, Lazarus and Miss Maud Samuel, youngest daughter of Mrs. and the late Harris Samuel, of Montreal, are engaged (12 Feb. 1909, 12, 9)

SILVER, Lazarus P. and Miss Maude Samuel were married quietly at the home of the bride's mother, 103 Drummond St., Montreal, on Tues. March 16, 1909 at 4 p.m. with Rabbi Meldola de Sola and Rev. Isaac de la Penha officiating. The bride was given away by her brother, Charles Samuel. Her sister, Miss Gertrude Samuel was her only attendant. The bridegroom's brother, S. Samuel, was best man (19 March 1909, 12, 14)

SILVER, Lazarus P., son of Mr. and Mrs. B. Silver, Elm Ave., Westmount, and Miss Maude Samuel, daughter of the late Harris Samuel and Mrs. H. Samuel, Drummond St., Montreal, will be married "very quietly" on March 16, 1909 (5 March 1909, 12, 12)

SILVER, Moe, son of Mr. and Mrs. B. Silver, of Montreal, and Miss Elsie B. Silverman, daughter of Mrs. Lyon Silverman, Tupper St., Westmount, Que., are engaged (11 Sept. 1912, 15, 40)

SILVER, Moe, son of Mr. and Mrs. B. Silver, and Miss Elsie Rose Silverman, daughter of Mrs. Lyon Silverman, Tupper St., Westmount, Que., were married by Rabbi Nathan Gordon, of Temple Emanu-El, on Wed. June 18, 1913 in the Windsor Hotel, Montreal. The bride was given away by her brother, E. Silverman. Miss Louise Silverman was maid of honor. The bridesmaids were the Misses May Silver and Gertrude Silverman. Miss Annette Jacobs, the bride's niece, was flower girl. Sam Silver was the best man and the ushers were Leonard Abrahams, Sydney Goldstein and S.A. Jacobs. Miss Suzanne Kahn, of Brooklyn, N.Y., Mr. Silver, and Miss Edith Silver were out-of-town guests. After their honeymoon in the U.S. Mr. and Mrs. Silver will reside on Greene Ave., Westmount (20 June 1913, 16, 28)

SILVERMAN, Louis, of Cincinnati, Ohio, and Miss Elizabeth Lechtzier, daughter of Mr. and Mrs. Moses Lechtzier, 192 Langside St., Winnipeg, are engaged (21 Feb. 1913, 16, 11)

SILVERMAN, S.J., of Minneapolis, and Miss Sara Constance Ripstein, of Winnipeg, daughter of Mr. and Mrs. J. Ripstein, were married on Tues. Dec. 7, 1909 in Shaarey Zedek Synagogue, Winnipeg (10 Dec. 1909, 13, 4)

SILVERSTONE, Solomon, of Montreal, and Miss Rebecca Mendelsohn, of Toronto, were married by Rabbi Levy in Toronto last Sun. (31 Jan. 1913, 16, 8)

SIMCOVER, Sam and Miss Clara Brownstein, daughter of Mr. and Mrs. N. Brownstein, all of Montreal, are engaged (4 April 1913, 16, 17)

SIMON, Abraham and Miss Eva Bookman, daughter of Mr. and Mrs. M. Bookman, will be married on June 11, 1911, in Coronation Hall, 204 St. Lawrence Blvd., Montreal (9 June 1911, 14, 30)

SIMON, Arthur, son of Mr. and Mrs. H. Simon, of Montreal and Miss Frank, of Chicago, were married last Sat. night. They are expected shortly in Montreal (8 Jan. 1909, 12, 4)

SIMON, Harry and Miss Sarah Lefkowitz, daughter of Mr. and Mrs. Meyer Lefkowitz, are engaged. A reception will be held at 773 City Hall Ave., Montreal, on Sun. March 1, 1914, at 6 p.m. (27 Feb. 1914, 17, 9)

SIMON, Isaac and Miss Lizzie Schwersenski, daughter of Mr. Schwersenski, of Montreal, will be married in Vancouver on Jan. 6, 1914 (26 Dec. 1913, 17, 3)

SIMON, William and Miss Edith Goldberg, daughter of Mr. and Mrs. Isidore Goldberg, of Montreal, will be married by Rabbi Meldola de Sola, assisted by Rev. Isaac de la Penha, next Sun. aft., in the Shearith Israel Synagogue, Stanley St., Montreal (21 May 1909, 12, 23)

SIMON, William, of Montreal, formerly of Ottawa, and Miss Edythe Goldberg, daughter of Mr. and Mrs. Isidore Goldberg, of Montreal, are engaged (15 Jan. 1909, 12, 5)

SIMON, William, son of Mr. and Mrs. B. Simon, of Vancouver, B.C., and Miss Edythe Goldberg, second daughter of Mr. and Mrs. Isidore Goldberg, of Montreal, were married by Rabbi Meldola de Sola, assisted by Rev. Isaac de la Penha, last Sun., in the Spanish and Portuguese Synagogue, Stanley St., Montreal. Miss Dora Rosenthal, the bride's cousin, was maid of honor. Miss Anna Wolfe, of Ottawa, was bridesmaid. Miss Rose Goldberg was the flower girl. Harry Goldberg was the best man and Harry Rosenthal, the groomsman. The couple will reside in Seattle, Washington (28 May 1909, 12, 24)

SINGER, D.S., second son of Mr. and Mrs. J. Singer, and Miss Ella Lorie, eldest daughter of Mr. and Mrs. S. Lorie, were married by Rabbi S. Jacobs at the home of the bride's parents, Clarendon Ave., Toronto, Wed. April 6, 1910. The bride was given away by her father. The bridesmaids were Miss Zelna Lorie and Miss Fannie Singer. Mrs. I. Singer was matron of honor while Max Singer was best man. After the reception the couple left on the 7 p.m. train for California. On their return to Toronto in five weeks they will reside at 95 Kendall Ave. Out-of-town guests included Mrs. S. Vineberg, the groom's sister, of Montreal and Mrs. F.B. Goldreich, the bride's aunt, of Cleveland, Ohio (8 April 1910, 13, 21)

SINGER, Dr. and Miss Ella Lorie, daughter of Mr. and Mrs. S. Lorie, 48 Clarendon Ave., Toronto, will be married in Toronto, on Wed. April 6, 1910 (4 March 1910, 13, 16)

SINGER, Dr. and Miss Ella Lorie, both of Toronto, will be married on April 10, 1910. They will honeymoon in the Canadian North West. Dr. Singer is a prominent Freemason. St. John's Lodge No. 75 will present him with a dinner service (18 March 1910, 13, 18)

SINGER, Louis and Dr. Bessie Thelma Pullan, daughter of Mr. and Mrs. M. Pullan, were married on July 6, 1911 in the McCaul Street Synagogue, Toronto (30 June 1911, 14, 33)

SINGER, Louis, barrister, and Dr. Bessie Thelma Pullan, daughter of Mr. and Mrs. Pullan, all of Toronto, are engaged (12 Aug. 1910, 13, 39)

SINGER, William and Miss Regina Pinsler, daughter of Mr. and Mrs. Paul Pinsler, were married by Rabbi Herman Abramowitz on Sun. Oct. 29, 1911 in the McGill College Avenue Synagogue, Montreal. The bride was given away by her father. The bride was attended by her sister, Miss Alice Pinsler. The bride's brother, Jack Pinsler was best man. Afterwards a reception was held in Auditorium Hall (3 Nov. 1911, 14, 51)

SINGER, William, treasurer of the YMHA in Montreal, and Miss Regina Pinsler, daughter of Mr. and Mrs. P. Pinsler, are engaged. Mr. and Mrs. Pinsler, 333 Bleury St., Montreal will hold a reception next Sun. (16 Sept. 1910, 13, 44)

SKOLNICK, Abraham and Miss Rosie Wachman were married by Rabbi Simon Glazer Sat. night, Jan. 13, 1912 in the New Modern Hall, Montreal. See Nitkin-Wachman wedding (19 Jan. 1912, 15, 10)

SLOMOWITZ, Joseph and Miss Ida Mirewitz, both of London, England, were married by Rabbi Hirsch Cohen, at his home in Montreal, on Thurs. May 27, 1909 (11 June 1909, 12, 26)

SLOVES, A., of Montreal, and Miss Bessie Lavine, daughter of Mr. and Mrs. D. Lavine, of Trenton, N.J., are engaged (9 Feb. 1912, 15, 13)

SLOVES, A., son of Mr. and Mrs. N. Sloves, Park Ave., Montreal, and Miss Bessie Lavine, daughter of Mr. and Mrs. D. Lavine, of Trenton, N.J., were married recently (24 Jan. 1913, 16, 7)

SMITH, Wolf, of Ste. Agathe, and Miss Rebecca Stone, were married by Rabbi Hirsch Cohen, on Tues. Sept. 7, 1909, in Montreal (10 Sept. 1909, 12, 39)

SOLIN, Maxwell, of Montreal, and Miss Bertha Goldberg, daughter of Mr. and Mrs. L. Goldberg, of Quebec City, are engaged (23 April 1909, 12, 19)

SOLOMON, Avner, of Montreal, and Miss Sarah Colle, daughter of Mr. and Mrs. M. Colle, Laval Ave., Montreal, are engaged (9 Feb. 1912, 15, 13)

SOLOMON, H. and Miss Ella Segal, both of Montreal, are engaged (4 Nov. 1910, 13, 51)

SOLOMON, J. and Miss Jennie Gross, daughter of M. Gross, were married on Tues. Dec. 14, 1909 in the Auditorium Hall, Berthelet St., Montreal. The Misses Freida Solomon and Fannie Gross were bridesmaids (17 Dec. 1909, 13, 5)

SOLOWEIZIG, Myer and Miss Annie Axlar were married by Rabbi Hirsch Cohen, in the Auditorium Hall, Montreal, on Sun. June 27, 1909 (9 July 1909, 12, 30)

SOSKIN, I., of Regina, Sask., and Miss Aunyene Abramson, daughter of Mr. and Mrs. Joseph Abramson, formerly of Kingston, Ont., and now of Saskatoon, Sask., are engaged (25 July 1913, 16, 33)

SPANER, Jack and Miss Anna Kline were married at the home of the bride's parents in Edmonton. William Diamond, president of Beth Israel Congregation of Edmonton, was toastmaster. J. Goodman, president of the local Hebrew Literary Institute congratulated the couple and "...made an impassioned plea for Zionism, incidentally referring to the anti-Jewish riots in liberty-loving England as another evidence of Jewish insecurity even in so-called free countries..." (15 Sept. 1911, 14, 44)

SQUIRES, Abe, of Winnipeg, second son of Mr. and Mrs. J. Squires, of Youngstown, Ohio, and Miss Minnie Fishkin, eldest daughter of Mr. and Mrs. J. Fishkin, of Toronto, formerly of Owen Sound, Ont., are engaged (1 Aug. 1913, 16, 34)

STARK, Robert and Miss Jennie Gross, both of Montreal, are engaged (6 May 1910, 13, 25)

STEIN, Herman and Miss Ida Kaplan, daughter of Mr. and Mrs. I. Kaplan, of Yarmouth, N.S., are engaged and will be married in late Aug. (9 Aug. 1912, 15, 35)

STEINBERG, Max and Miss Jennie Solomon, daughter of Mr. and Mrs. E. Solomon, Dorchester St. West, Montreal, are engaged (1 Oct. 1909, 12, 42)

STEINBERG, Max, only son of Mr. and Mrs. H.I. Steinberg, of Montreal, and Miss Minnie Jurist, daughter of Mrs. D. Jurist, of New York, are engaged (3 April 1914, 17, 14)

STEINBERG, Peter, son of Mr. and Mrs. Victor Steinberg, and Miss Anna Steinberg, daughter of Mr. and Mrs. Peter Steinberg, all of Montreal, are engaged (14 Feb. 1913, 16, 10)

STEINER, Herbert M., manager of the Northern Crown Bank, Agnes St., and Miss Gertrude Tewsley, both of Toronto, were married Mon. Nov. 15, 1909. They are on their honeymoon in the eastern U.S. (19 Nov. 1909, 13, 1)

STEINKOPF, Max, a Winnipeg barrister, and Miss Hedwig Mayer, a cousin of the Hon. Oscar S. Strauss, were married Wed. Nov. 24, 1909, at the home of the bridegroom, 336 River Ave., Winnipeg with Rev. J.K. Levin and Rev. A. Cashden officiating (10 Dec. 1909, 13, 4)

STEINKOPF, Max, barrister-at-law, of Winnipeg, and Miss Hedwig Mayer are engaged. Miss Mayer is a cousin of the Hon. Oscar S. Strauss, U.S. Ambassador to Turkey. She is staying in Winnipeg with her sister, Mrs. Michael Ert (29 Oct. 1909, 12, 46)

STRAITHER, David and Miss Annie Bercson were married by Rabbi Hirsch Cohen, on June 27, 1909, at 7 Eden St., Montreal. $6.65 was collected for the Talmud Torah (9 July 1909, 12, 30)

STRAUSS, Leo, a former well-known Toronto boy now living in New York, and Miss May Brown, of New York, are engaged (14 March 1913, 16, 14)

STROBER, Louis, son of J. Strober, of Montreal, and Miss Minnie Frankle, daughter of Mr. and Mrs. Frankle, are engaged (30 May 1913, 16, 25)

SUGSONITSKY, I., of Montreal, and Miss Sarah Herzberg, daughter of Mr. and Mrs. Herzberg, of Quebec City, are engaged (29 March 1912, 15, 20)

TAFFERT, Harold and Miss Leah Vinegust, daughter of Mr. and Mrs. A. Vinegust, were married by Rev. Simon Glazer, on Tues. Aug. 31, 1909, in the Auditorium Hall, Montreal (10 Sept. 1909, 12, 39)

TAKEFMAN, Nathan, eldest son of Mrs. H. Takefman, and Miss Eva Harris, daughter of Mr. and Mrs. C. Harris, of Montreal, are engaged (14 Nov. 1913, 16, 49)

TANNENBAUM, Dr. David, of Montreal, son of Mr. and Mrs. M. Tannenbaum, and Miss Hannah Rosenberg, eldest daughter of Mr. and Mrs. C. Rosenberg, were married by Rev. I. de la Penha at the home of Mr. Rosenberg, Sherbrooke St. The bride was given away by her father. Only the immediate relatives were present. Dr. and Mrs. Tannenbaum will spend their honeymoon in Europe (23 June 1911, 14, 32)

TEREN, Miss Rosa, daughter of Mr. and Mrs. Joseph Teren, was married on June 19, 1909, by Rabbi Hirsch Cohen, at 199 St. Lawrence Blvd., Montreal (25 June 1909, 12, 28)

TOBIAS, Nathan and Miss Rebecca Pierce, eldest daughter of Mr. and Mrs. Charles Pierce, all of Montreal, are engaged (15 Oct. 1909, 12, 44)

TREFNER, Joseph and Miss Anna Cohen, daughter of Rabbi Hirsch Cohen, all of Montreal, are engaged (20 May 1910, 13, 27)

TRITT, Samuel Gerald and Miss Sarah Gross, daughter of Mr. and Mrs. B. Gross, were married at the residence of the bride, Elgin st., Montreal. Miss Jennie Tritt, the groom's sister, was maid of honor and Dr. C.J. Gross, the bride's brother was best man. Out-of-town guests were:- M. Goldner, of Winnipeg; Mr. and Mrs. Gardner, of Quebec City; Mr. Barash, Mrs. Genzer, Mrs. Goldie, of New York (1 July 1910, 13, 33)

TUROFSKY, Dr. Harry Alfred, (B.A.) eldest son of Mr. and Mrs. I. Turofsky, 21 Murray St., and Miss Etta Clara (Ettie) Levinter, eldest daughter of Mr. and Mrs. S. Levinter, 22 Cecil St., all of Toronto, are engaged (19 July 1912, 15, 32)

TUROFSKY, Dr. Harry Alfred, of Toronto, and Miss Hilda Pullan, daughter of Mr. and Mrs. Henry Pullan, of Ottawa, were married by Rabbis J. Berger and S. Fyne in the new Rideau Street Synagogue this week. This was the first wedding to be celebrated in the new synagogue. Guests included Mrs. Sachs, Mrs. Turofsky, the groom's mother, and Mrs. Wolff, of Toronto, the bride's sister. After the ceremony, the guests were taken in cabs to the Racquet Court for the banquet. The bride received a solid silver candle bar, engraved by H.L. Gittleson, master of ceremonies. It read "Presented to Miss Hilda Pullan by the congregation of Rideau Street Synagogue of Ottawa, in commemoration of first marriage in the synagogue." Dr. and Mrs. Turofsky left for New York and Atlantic City, and will reside at Scarboro Beach, Toronto (27 June 1913, 16, 29)

VAN RAALTE, Phineas, second son of Rev. Mr. and Mrs. S. Van Raalte, of Portsmouth, England, and Miss Rose Schorr, eldest daughter of Rev. Mr. and Mrs. Schorr, of Winnipeg, were married by Rabbi J.K. Levin, assisted by Rabbis Kahanovitch and E. Cashdan, on July 17, 1910. The bride was given away by her mother. Miss Schorr was assisted by the Misses Bertha Levin and Esther Milmet. R.S. Robinson presided over the banquet that evening. Among those present were:- Rabbi and Mrs. Kahanovitch, Rabbi J.K. Levin, Rabbi and Mrs. E. Cashdan, Mr. Cohen, barrister, Mr. and Mrs. Hide, Mr. and Mrs. Fred, Mr. and Mrs. I. Portigal, Mr. and Mrs. S. Levin, Mr. and Mrs. Milmen and daughters, Mr. and Mrs. Isaacs, Mr. and Mrs. Abramovitch, Mr. and Mrs. Bronfman and daughter, Mrs. Heitner, Mr. and Mrs. Moscovitz, Mr. and Mrs. Tapper, Mr. and Mrs. Levinson and J. Genser (29 July 1910, 13, 37)

VENIS, S., of Ottawa, and Miss E. Resch, daughter of Mr. and Mrs. B. Resch, of Montreal, were married by Rabbi Hirsch Cohen on Jan. 12, 1913 in the Auditorium Hall, Montreal. Ushers for the bride were Mr. and Mrs. J. Presner and for the groom Mr. and Mrs. S. Fishman, of Ottawa. The Misses E. Engle, R. Engle and Nellie Vineberg were bridesmaids and the best men were M. Venis, a brother of the groom, Mr. Finckle, of Ottawa, and M. Resch, a brother of the bride. Out-of-town guests were Mrs. Rosenthal (Hamilton), Mrs. M. Vineberg and daughter, Miss P. Vineberg and Sam Druckman (Winnipeg). Mr. and Mrs. Venis went to New York for their honeymoon. They will reside in Ottawa on their return (17 Jan. 1913, 16, 6)

VICTOR, J.A., of New York, and Miss Esther Ellenson, daughter of M. Ellenson, 211 McCaul St., Toronto, were engaged at the home of the bride's father, on Wed. evening, Jan. 1, 1913 (10 Jan. 1913, 16, 5)

VINEBERG, Louis and Miss Beccie Holstein, only daughter of Mr. and Mrs. Louis Holstein, 85 Shuter St., Montreal, are engaged (5 Nov. 1909, 12, 47)

VINEBERG, Louis and Miss Beckie Holstein, daughter of Mr. and Mrs. Louis Holstein, Shuter St., Montreal, were married by Rabbi Herman Abramowitz, assisted by Rev. S. Goldstein, last Wed. aft., in Stanley Hall, Montreal. Over six hundred guests attended. Miss Leah Lesser was the maid of honor and Miss Sarah Lesser, the bridesmaid. The bride was given away by her father and the best man was S.L. Holstein, the bride's brother. The couple left Wed. evening on their honeymoon in the U.S. They will reside in Montreal upon their return (11 Feb. 1910, 13, 13)

VINEBERG, Louis and Miss Beckie Holstein, daughter of Mr. and Mrs. Louis Holstein, 85 Shuter St., Montreal, are engaged (28 Jan. 1910, 13, 11)

VINEBERG, Malcolm, of Mattawa, Ont., and Miss Rebecca Phillips, daughter of Fischel Phillips, of Montreal, are engaged (3 Nov. 1911, 14, 51)

VINEBERG, Malcolm, of Mattawa, Ont., son of Mr. and Mrs. H. Vineberg, and Miss Rebecca Phillips, daughter of Mr. and Mrs. Fischel Phillips, of Montreal, were married by Rabbis Herman Abramowitz and Hirsch Cohen on Wed. evening in the Auditorium Hall, Montreal. Miss Jessie Phillips, the bride's sister was maid of honor and Joseph Vineberg, the groom's brother, was best man. Out-of-town guests included:- Mr. and Mrs. W. Levi (St. John, N.B.), Mr. and Mrs. H. Vineberg, Harry Vineberg and Master Lawrence Vineberg (Mattawa, Ont.), Mrs. R. Rosin (Ottawa), and Harold Cohen (St. Albans, Vt.). Mr. and Mrs. Vineberg will reside in Mattawa (26 Jan. 1912, 15, 11)

VINEBERG, Mr. and Mrs. S., of Montreal, were married in early Jan. in New York (22 Jan. 1909, 12, 6)

VINEBERG, Simon, son of Elias Vineberg, of Montreal, and Miss Gertrude Berman, daughter of Mr. and Mrs. L. Berman, formerly of Germany, are engaged (1 June 1911, 14, 29)

VINEBERG, Sol. S., son of Mr. and Mrs. Louis Vineberg, of Montreal, and Miss Rose Lachman, daughter of Mr. and Mrs. S. Lachman, of Detroit, Mich., will be married Feb. 15, 1912 (16 Feb. 1912, 15, 14)

VOGEL, Isidore and Miss Rebecca Serkan, second daughter of Mr. and Mrs. A. Serkan, 92 Selkirk Ave., Winnipeg were married by Rabbi J.K. Levin in a private ceremony at the home of the bride. Mr. and Mrs. Vogel left Winnipeg that evening for Vienna, the groom's birthplace. On their return they will reside in Oak Point, Man. (24 Feb. 1911, 14, 15)

WATSON, Josef K. and Miss Annie Taub, daughter of Mr. and Mrs. Samuel Taub, of Toronto, are engaged (25 March 1910, 13, 19)

WEIDMAN, Neiman J., of Winnipeg, and Miss Pearl Vineberg, daughter of Mrs. M. Vineberg, 421 Wardlaw Ave., Winnipeg, are engaged (29 Aug. 1913, 16, 38)

WEINBERG, Hillel, of Toronto, and Miss Edith Abramsky, of Kingston, Ont., will be married by Rabbi I. Kahanovitch, of Winnipeg, at the home of the bride's parents, Princess St., next Tues. (6 Jan. 1911, 14, 8)

WEINBERG, Jack, eldest son of Mr. and Mrs. P. Weinberg, 54 Stocks St., Cheltham, England, and Miss Becky Fink, second daughter of Mr. and Mrs. L. Fink, 46 Elizabeth St., Cheltham were married (20 May 1910, 13, 27)

WEINFELD, Louis, of Montreal, and Miss Daisy Symonds, daughter of Mrs. R. Symonds, of New York, are engaged. "The marriage will take place very quietly on Tuesday, Feb. 24th, in New York." (13 Feb. 1914, 17, 7)

WEINFIELD, John J., of Montreal, and Miss Sophie Sereth, daughter of Mr. and Mrs. N.H. Sereth, of Calgary, are engaged (13 Jan. 1911, 14, 9)

WEINFIELD, John J., of Montreal, and Miss Sophia Sereth, daughter of Mr. and Mrs. B.N. Sereth, of Calgary, Alta., will be married in Calgary on Tues. Aug. 15, 1911 (4 Aug. 1911, 14, 38)

WEINFIELD, John J., of Montreal, and Miss Sophia Sereth, daughter of Mr. and Mrs. H.N. Sereth, of Calgary, were married by Rabbi A.L. Cotersen on Aug. 15, 1911, at the home of the bride's parents. The bride's sister, Miss Cecilia Sereth was maid of honor. The bride's attendants were the Misses Emily Sereth; Mildred Casner (Chicago), Bessie Crystal (Edmonton), and Mrs. J.J. Alan (Calgary). The Misses Ruby and Clara Sereth, and Angie Bell (Edmonton) were flower girls. The groom's attendants were John Sternberg, Morris Kleiner, I.J. Barsky (New York), and F. LeVine. Mr. and Mrs. Weinfield spent their honeymoon in Vancouver (1 Sept. 1911, 14, 42)

WEINGARDEN, A.A., and Miss Muriel R. Shragge, daughter of Mr. and Mrs. B. Shragge, of Winnipeg, will be married in that city on Tues. June 22, 1909 (18 June 1909, 12, 27)

WEINGARDEN, A.A., of Detroit, and Miss Muriel Shragge, second daughter of Mr. and Mrs. B. Shragge, of Winnipeg, are engaged (7 May 1909, 12, 21)

WEINSTEIN, Barnett and Miss Miriam Bessner, will be married in the Auditorium Hall, Montreal, on Sept. 18, 1910 (19 Aug. 1910, 13, 40)

WEINSTEIN, Philip and Miss Molly Bloomfield, daughter of Rev. and Mrs. M. Bloomfield, will be married on Thurs. July 4, 1911, in the New Modern Hall, Notre Dame E., Montreal (9 June 1911, 14, 30)

WEINSTEIN, Philip and Miss Molly Bloomfield, daughter of the Rev. and Mrs. M. Bloomfield, were married Tues. July 4, 1911 in the New Modern Hall, Montreal. The bride was attended by her sister, Miss Ray Bloomfield. Mr. and Mrs. Weinstein leave next Sun. for Ottawa (7 July 1911, 14, 34)

WEINTRAUB, Milton, of New York, and Miss Dora Z. Fraid, daughter of Mrs. J.B. Fraid, of Cornwall, Ont., were married by Rabbi Herman Abramowitz, of Montreal, on Wed. evening, Dec. 8, 1909, at the home of the bride's brother, N.J. Fraid, Second Ave., Cornwall. The bride was given away by her eldest brother, L. Fraid, of Gananoque, Ont. Miss Mollie Fraid, the bride's sister, was bridesmaid. The bride's brother, Joseph Fraid, was best man. The couple left the same evening on a honeymoon out west after which they will reside in New York. Among the out-of-town guests were:- Mr. and Mrs. Lyon Cohen, Ralph Friedman, Jack Samuel, A. Fraid, Mesdames D.S. Friedman and Joseph Kellert and the Misses Kellert, all of Montreal and Mrs. L. Fraid, of Gananoque (17 Dec. 1909, 13, 5)

WEINTRAUB, Milton, of New York, and Miss Dora Fraid, of Cornwall, Ont., are engaged (29 Oct. 1909, 12, 46)

WEISMAN, J. and Miss Ray Fine, niece of Mr. and Mrs. L. Marcus, are engaged. A reception will be held at 740a De Lepee Ave., Outremont, Que., on Sun. March 1, 1914 (27 Feb. 1914, 17, 9)

From The Canadian Jewish Times — *Engagements and Marriages*

WEISSMAN, E., of Fort William, Ont., and Miss Rebecca Isaacson, of Toronto, will be married Feb. 11, 1913 (31 Jan. 1913, 16, 8)

WEXLER, Louis and Miss Esther Poyaner, both of Montreal, will be married Wed. Aug. 21, 1912 (2 Aug. 1912, 15, 34)

WHITE, Abraham and Miss Esther Esper, both of Toronto, were recently married (16 April 1909, 12, 18)

WHITE, Bernard C., of Montreal, and Miss Rose Harris, daughter of Mr. and Mrs. Maxwell Harris, were married by Rabbi Herman Abramowitz on Tues. Jan. 7, 1913 at the home of the bride's parents, 959 Dorchester St. W., Montreal. The bride was given away by her father. Mrs. M. Jacques Ornstein, of Fredericton, N.B., the bride's sister, was matron of honor. The bride's sister, Miss Anna Harris, was bridesmaid. The bride's little niece, Miss Thelma Simon, of Halifax, N.S., was the flower girl. Assisting at the reception were the Misses Edith, Eva and Lottie Harris. Mr. and Mrs. White went to New York and Washington, D.C., on their honeymoon. Out-of-town guests included:- Mr. and Mrs. John Simon (Halifax), Miss Charlotte Harris (New York), L. Harris and A. Harris (Boston), and Mrs. H. Simonsky and sons (Troy, N.Y.) (17 Jan. 1913, 16, 6)

WHITE, Bernard L. and Miss Rose Harris, daughter of Mr. and Mrs. M. Harris, all of Montreal, are engaged. Mr. and Mrs. Harris will be "at home" Sun. Nov. 10, 1912 at 959 Dorchester St. W. (8 Nov. 1912, 15, 48)

WHITE, E. and Miss Annie Solomon, daughter of Mr. and Mrs. S. Solomon, all of Montreal, are engaged (12 May 1911, 14, 26)

WHITE, Louis and Miss Gertrude Kronick, both of Toronto, were married in the McCaul Street Synagogue by the Rev. Caplan. A reception was tendered afterwards in the Zionist Institute Building, Simcoe St. (19 Nov. 1909, 13, 1)

WIGDOR, Joseph S., of Montreal, and Miss Annie Rabinovich were married on Feb. 10, 1912 in New York (1 March 1912, 15, 16)

WINEBERG, Hal, of Toronto, and Miss Edith Abramsky, daughter of Mr. and Mrs. J. Abramsky, of Kingston, Ont., are engaged (16 Dec. 1910, 14, 5)

WINSBERG, Paul, of Montreal, and Miss Hetty Adler, daughter of Mr. and Mrs. H. Adler, of Hull, England, are engaged (9 Jan. 1914, 17, 5)

WISEMAN, A., of Smith's Falls, Ont., and Miss Malca Vineberg, daughter of Mr. and Mrs. J.L. Vineberg, of Montreal, will be married on March 9, 1913 at 233 Esplanade Ave., Montreal (7 March 1913, 16, 13)

WISEMAN, Jacob, of Germany, now a Montreal resident, and Miss Rose Feldman, daughter of Mr. and Mrs. A. Feldman, 1126 St. Urbain St., Montreal, are engaged (18 July 1913, 16, 32)

WOLFE, A. Harry and Miss Anna Bald, both of Montreal, will be married on Aug. 17, 1913 (1 Aug. 1913, 16, 34)

WOLFE, A.H., formerly of Ottawa, and now of Montreal, son of the late Max and Mrs. Wolfe, of Ottawa, and Miss Anna Bald, daughter of Mr. and Mrs. Herman Bald, of Montreal, are engaged (6 June 1913, 16, 26)

WOLFE, Martin, of London, England, and Miss Irene Joseph, of Quebec City, will be married March 25, 1909 (12 March 1909, 12, 13)

WOLFF, Martin, and Miss Irene Joseph, eldest daughter of Mr. and Mrs. Montefiore Joseph, of Quebec City, were married by Rabbi Meldola de Sola, of Montreal, last Thurs., at the home of the bride's father, 113 Grand Allee. The bridesmaids were: Miss Rosetta Joseph, the bride's sister and Miss Rachel Wolff, the bridegroom's sister. At 4 p.m., Mr. and Mrs. Wolff left for England, via Halifax (2 April 1909, 12, 16)

WOLFSON, Samuel and Miss Edna Dell were married at 125 Burrows Ave., Winnipeg. The Misses Bertha and Violet Jacobson were bridesmaids (1 Oct. 1913, 16, 42-43)

WOLPAW, David, of Cleveland, and Miss Chiae Abramson, daughter of Mr. and Mrs. Joseph Abramson, of Kingston, Ont., were married by Rabbi Herman Abramowitz, of Montreal, on Tues. evening, at the home of the bride's parents, 185 Queen St. She was attended by her sister, Miss Rae Abramson. The groomsman was Max Teitelbaum (20 Aug. 1909, 12, 36)

WOLPAW, David, of Cleveland, Ohio, and Miss Chiae Abramson, daughter of Mr. and Mrs. Joseph Abramson, of Kingston, Ont., will be married Tues. Aug. 17, 1909 (13 Aug. 1909, 12, 35)

WOLPAW, David, of Cleveland, Ohio, and Miss Chiae Abramson, daughter of Mr. and Mrs. Joseph Abramson, of Kingston, Ont., are engaged (29 Jan. 1909, 12, 7)

YELKIN, Isaac, of Minneapolis, Minn., and Miss Jennie Levin, of Montreal, were married by Rabbi Simon Glazer at his residence, Montreal, on Jan. 13, 1912 (19 Jan. 1912, 15, 10)

ZALZMAN, Israel and Miss Hannah Berger, daughter of Mr. and Mrs. S. Berger, will be married at 2273 Waverley St., Montreal, on Sun. Jan. 1, 1911 (23 Dec. 1910, 14, 6)

ZAVILANSKY, David and Miss Rachel Thisber, daughter of Mr. and Mrs. S. Thisber, were married by Rabbi Hirsch Cohen, on Tues. Aug. 31, 1909, at 199 St. Lawrence Blvd., Montreal (10 Sept. 1909, 12, 39)

ZEMAN, Burnhardt, and Miss Saxe, of Montreal, will be married on April 21, 1909, at the home of Mr. and Mrs. L. Sapery, Durocher St., Montreal (9 April 1909, 12, 17)

ZIWITZ, Nachman, son of Rabbi and Mrs. Ziwitz, of Pittsburgh, and Miss Rachel Schwartz, daughter of Mr. and Mrs. Samuel Schwartz, of Toronto, will be married in the University Avenue Synagogue, Toronto, March 2, 1910 (18 Feb. 1910, 13, 14)

ZUCKER, Max and Miss Malca Goldenberg, both of Montreal, are engaged (23 Dec. 1910, 14, 6)

ZUSMAN, Abraham, of Jonquieres, Que., and Miss Sarah Greenspoon, eldest daughter of Mr. and Mrs. H. Greenspoon, of Montreal, will be married on March 21, 1912 in the New Modern Hall, Montreal (15 March 1912, 15, 18)

ZWIEG, Harry, of Toronto, and Miss Fanny Wolofsky, daughter of Mr. and Mrs. Aron Wolofsky, of Montreal, were married by Rabbi Hirsch Cohen, and Rev. Blumenthal with his choir, on Sun. July 6, 1913 in the Prince Arthur Hall, Montreal. The bride was given away by her uncle. L. Wolofsky, the bride's cousin, was best man and the ushers were M. Wolofsky and Harry Goldberg, of Toronto. Miss Mildred Wolofsky was maid of honor and the flower girls were the Misses Rosie Wolofsky and Sarah Wolofsky. The trail bearers were the bride's brother and sister, Philip and Sophie Wolofsky. Tables were set for 500 guests. Out-of-town guests were:- J. Garfinkle, I. Gold, L. Goldstein, L. Wolofsky and J. Goldenberg, all of Toronto. Mr. Goldenberg, representing the Toronto YMHA, presented the couple with a silver fruit dish. E. Marshall, general manager of the Excelsior Life Insurance Co. of Toronto, presented them with a sterling silver and gold tea set and silver tray. The Russian-Polish-Hebrew Sick Benefit Association of Montreal presented Aron Wolofsky with a sterling silver cup in honor of his good work and his first child's wedding. The couple left for Toronto and the U.S. to spend their honeymoon (18 July 1913, 16, 32)

MONUMENT NATIONAL THEATRE		**The Penalty of Pride** A Four Act Drama
THURSDAY JANUARY 29		Tickets sold by all Members, Phone E. 1829 for reservations. Box office will open Jan. 22nd, at 7 p.m. and following evenings.
CURTAIN RISES AT 8.15 P.M. SHARP		Tickets: $1.50, $1.00, 75c., 50c., 25c.

GENERAL NEWS ITEMS

ABERSON, D. and M. Lazarson, of Montreal, are the editors in charge of the new Zionist Yiddish weekly, **Das Yidische Volk**, to be published by the Zion Press Association. The first issue will appear on Feb. 25, 1909 (5 Feb. 1909, 12, 8)

ABRAMOWITZ, Rabbi Herman, 17 Hutchison St., Montreal, wrote a letter to the editor asking to hear from families willing to adopt a girl, age 4, now in a Protestant foster home in Ottawa. "Two elder brothers of her's have already been farmed out with Christian families, and have thus been lost to our faith. There is still a possibility of saving this little girl as the authorities would be very glad, in fact are anxious, to place her with a Jewish family, who would adopt her as their own child...It is hardly necessary for me to say that the adoption of such a child, and the saving of her to Judaism, would be a most meritorious act." (25 Nov. 1910, 14, 20)

ABRAMOWITZ, Rabbi Herman, an extract of his sermon "Proclaim Liberty Throughout The Land Unto All The Inhabitants Thereof", delivered in the Shaar Hashomayim Synagogue, Montreal on the first day of Passover, 1909, was reprinted (9 April 1909, 12, 17)

ABRAMOWITZ, Rabbi Herman, reprint of his lecture "The Contribution of the Jew to Modern Civilization" delivered before the Young People's Society of Shaar Hashomayim, Montreal (27 Dec. 1912, 16, 3)

ABRAMOWITZ, Rabbi Herman, was cross-examined during the Quebec libel case. In the printed transcript he stated that he was an Orthodox Jew, an American and came to Montreal from New York (6 June 1913, 16, 26)

ABRAMOWITZ, Rabbi Herman, was examined by S.W. Jacobs, K.C. during the Quebec libel case on Mon. May 19, 1913 in the Superior Court, Quebec City. In the printed transcript Rabbi Abramowitz states he is 33 years old, a graduate of the Jewish Theological Seminary and has been rabbi of the Corporation of English, German and Polish Jews, in Montreal for ten years (30 May 1913, 16, 25)

ABRAMOWITZ, Rabbi Herman, wrote an article "Judaism in the New and Old Worlds", based on his recent trip to Europe where he attended the Zionist Congress in Vienna as a Montreal Agudath Zion Society delegate (15 Oct. 1913, 16, 45)

ABRAMOWITZ, Rabbi Herman, wrote an article "Our Modern Emancipation" for the Passover issue (18 April 1913, 16, 19)

ABRAMOWITZ, Rabbi Herman; his interview on Canadian Jewry which appeared in last week's issue of the "Hebrew Student", New York (1 April 1910, 13, 20)

ABRAMOWITZ, Rabbis Herman and Meldola de Sola, of Montreal; Rabbi S. Fyne, of Ottawa; Rabbis Solomon Jacobs and Nathan Gordon, of Toronto; Reuben Brainin, Lazarus Cohen, and Clarence I. de Sola, of Montreal, have spoke out against the commercializing of Jewish liturgical music. Cantor Wladofsky, of the University Avenue Synagogue in Toronto, plans to give a public concert in the Montreal Armory Drill Hall (3 Jan. 1913, 16, 4)

ACKERMAN, L., 962 St. Urbain St., Montreal, wrote a letter to the editor commenting on Dr. Joseph Stern's letter to the editor about the S.W. Jacobs-Henri Bourassa correspondence exchange (18 Oct. 1912, 15, 45)

ACKERMAN, L., 962 St. Urbain St., Montreal, wrote a letter to the editor expressing support for the organization of a Kehilah in Montreal (20 Sept. 1912, 15, 41)

ADELSTEIN, Harry, Max W. Bloomberg, Clarence J. Cohen, Horace R. Cohen, Jacob Cohen, Harry Davidovitch, Minnie Feldman, Moses Fineberg, Louis Feingold, Harry Fishman, Edith Forman, Nathan Freedman, Fanny Freedman, Jennie Ginsberg, Sarah Gittelson, Louis Gross, Moses Gross, Benjamin Grossman, Hyman Halperin, L.E. Herscovitch, N. Hershfield, E. Miriam Isaacs, Annie Jacobs, Louis Jacobs, Leah Jacobson, Rosetta Joseph, Helen Kelsch, Lily Klein, Sophie Klineberg, Max Krigle, Jacob Leavitt, Lyon Levine, Cella Levine, Lazar Miller, Edward Orkin, Annie Potashner, Siegfried L. Rohr, Moses Sackner, Joseph Sanders, Rudolph Schafheitlin, Annie Sigler, Moses Sloves, Leah Sperber, Edward Workman, Elsie Workman, Maitland L. Leo, Moses Philip Finkelstein, Philip Brais, Isidore Boltuch and Rudolph Gaetz are the fifty-three Jewish students who passed the McGill University preliminary examinations (16 July 1909, 12, 31)

ADELSTEIN, Libbie, of Montreal, is a new member of the Young Israel Children's League (9 May 1913, 16, 22)

ADELSTEIN, Max, age 13, son of Mr. and Mrs. P. Adelstein, of Montreal, rescued a young woman from drowning last week at Cartierville, Que. "It appears that the girl, whilst bathing, was caught by a current. The young hero, hearing her cries for help, was coolheaded enough to rush for the boat and paddled along to the spot where he saw the girl, and as she appeared for the last time he caught her and brought her to shore, where she remained unconscious for about half an hour. This act of bravery is deserving of investigation by the Royal Humane Society" (5 Aug. 1910, 13, 38)

ALEXANDER, Maurice, Law' 10, has won the McGill University Gold Medal for public speaking. His subject was "South Africa After the War" (5 March 1909, 12, 12)

AMERICAN, Miss Sadie, noted "Settlement" worker in New York and secretary of the National Council of Women, gave two lectures in Montreal at the Royal Victoria College on Tues. and at the Baron de Hirsch Institute on Wed. aft. She advocated the establishment of a local council to work for the protection of Jewish immigrant girls. She recalled that fifteen years ago Montreal had a section of the Jewish Council of Women which died. Among those at the Baron de Hirsch lecture were: Mrs. C.A. Workman, Lyon Cohen, Louis Vineberg, Rabbi Nathan Gordon and Mrs. Max Goldstein. Mrs. I.S. Goldstein, Clark Ave., held a reception in Miss American's honor on Tues. aft. (11 Feb. 1910, 13, 13)

BALLON, Ellen, "the youthful little Canadian pianiste who only a few years ago, when hardly out of her infancy, made a notable success bordering on the sensation, at the Royal Victoria College and gave promise of great things in the future-has been engaged as soloist to appear with the New York Symphony Orchestra under the direction of Mr. Walter Damrosch, Monday, March 7. The young lady, who is well known to the Montreal musical public, after having studied under the able guidance and tuition of Miss Clara Lichtenstein, made such a wonderful and astonishing progress, has, with her sister, resided in New York for the last three years..." (14 Jan. 1910, 13, 9)

BALLON, Miss Ellen, daughter of Mr. and Mrs. Samuel Ballon, Crescent St., Montreal, received a gift of seven volumes on the "History of Music" from the Prime Minister of Canada, Sir Wilfrid Laurier, during the Premier's recent visit to New York, where Miss Ballon is studying piano under Raphael Joseffy (29 Jan. 1909, 12, 7)

BAMBERG, Lillian, wrote a story "Mr. Myerstein's Maneuver" for the special women's issue (21 Nov. 1913, 16, 50-51)

BAUM, Harry A. (Montreal), Nessie Segal (Levis, Que.), and David Rothschild (Westmount) are winners in Uncle Jacob's Map of Palestine Contest (10 Jan. 1913, 16, 5)

BEHR, A., wrote an article "Seasons Thoughts" (25 Sept. 1912, 15, 42)

BENJAMIN, E.A., 504 W. 111th St., New York, wrote a letter to the editor Dec. 13, 1912 about the article "The History of the Jews in Toronto" by S.J. Birnbaum, which was sent to him by Lewis A. Hart, of Montreal. Mr. Benjamin claims that his father was the first Jewish resident of Toronto, and not Judah G. Joseph as stated in the article. "...my father, Mr. Goodman Benjamin and his brother Mr. Samuel Benjamin went to Toronto in 1836 and were established in the clothing and dry goods business on King Street East, and during the rebellion, 1837, they received a government contract for the army clothing. They removed to Montreal in 1842 and there went into the wholesale dry goods business, my father married a Miss Julia Bedlier, of London, England, and was sister-in-law to Joseph Samuda, M.P., a large shipbuilder." (20 Dec. 1912, 16, 2)

BENNETT, Archie B., a former Queen's University student in Kingston, wrote an article "The Queen's University Bill Its Significance to the Jews of Canada" (7 June 1912, 15, 26)

BENNETT, Archie B., is the new editor of **The Canadian Jewish Times** (26 April 1912, 15, 24)

BENNETT, Archie B., will no longer edit **The Canadian Jewish Times** after this issue (1 Nov. 1912, 15, 47)

BENNETT, Archie B., wrote an article "Jewish Problems" for the Passover issue (18 April 1913, 16, 19)

BERCOVICI, Konrad, of Montreal, wrote an article "What the Jews have Contributed to the World's Music" (10 Oct. 1913, 16, 44)

BERMAN, Harold, wrote an article "A New Book of Esther" (6 Sept. 1912, 15, 39)

BERMAN, Miss Hannah, wrote a story "The Veil" (21 Feb. 1913, 16, 11)

BERMAN, Miss Hannah, wrote an article "Nahum Sokolow and his Place in Hebrew Literature" (14 March 1913, 16, 14)

BERNFELD, Dr. S., wrote an article "The Jewish Parliament of 1806" (25 Sept. 1912, 15, 42)

BERNSTEIN, H., of Montreal, translated "Statesman's and Pettycitizen Utopias" from the German for the paper (9 Aug. 1912, 15, 35)

BERNSTEIN, H., translated "Good News of Great Importance from Palestine" from the Haolam for the paper (20 Sept. 1912, 15, 41)

BERNSTEIN, Minnie, wrote a paper "The Jewish Wife" which was read before the Young People's Society of Shaar Hashomayim, Montreal and reprinted (26 Dec. 1913, 17, 3)

BERNSTEIN, Minnie, wrote an article "Zu Vos?" (13 Dec. 1912, 16, 1)

BERNSTEIN, Miss Minnie, who is in her sophomore year at the Royal Victoria College, Montreal, has won the Delta Sigma Society silver cup for public speaking. Her subject was "Judaism and Hellenism" (26 Feb. 1909, 12, 11)

BERO, Stanley, wrote a letter to the editor expressing pleasure that Montreal is to have a Child Welfare Exhibit and that Jewish leaders like Lyon Cohen are identified with it (18 Oct. 1912, 15, 45)

BERO, Stanley, wrote an article "A Ghetto Rose" (2 Oct. 1912, 15, 43)

BERO, Stanley, wrote an article "From Dock to the Farm" (4 April 1913, 16, 17)

BIRNBAUM, S.J. (B.A.), in his series "History of the Jews in Toronto" writes in detail about the dedication of the Holy Blossom Synagogue, Bond St., on Sept. 15, 1897. Miss Gertie Wolf, age 8, granddaughter of Marx Kassel, now living in New York, presented the golden key to the synagogue to Alfred D. Benjamin, the synagogue's president. Today Miss Wolf is private secretary to Rabbi Stephen Wise, in New York. The four Torahs were carried into the synagogue by Mark Cohen, Abraham Franklin, Barnett Laurence and Charles Stern, headed by Mr. Benjamin. During the ceremony solos were performed by J. Mahimove, A. Mansfield and Mrs. Edward Youngheart, under the direction of Cantor M. Solomon. Rabbi Lazarus preached the dedicatory sermon (14 March 1913, 16, 14)

BIRNBAUM, S.J. (B.A.), in his series "History of the Jews in Toronto" writes about Alfred D. Benjamin, who was born in Melbourne, Australia on Aug. 9, 1848. In 1854, his family returned to England where he was educated. Mr. Benjamin matriculated with honors from the University of London in 1865 and in 1866 received his B.A. degree with honors in Latin, French and German. In 1873, he came to Canada and settled in Montreal for five years. He went to England for one year, before returning to Toronto, Canada in 1879. Mr. Benjamin became president of Holy Blossom Synagogue in 1885. "He was a Jew of the finest mettle, was full of love for everything and everyone Jewish, and always did his utmost to enhance and win respect for the Jewish name. He was orthodox, but his orthodoxy was of that cultivated type that is bound to win respect among all classes of people, both Jew and Gentile." He and his brother, Frank D. Benjamin, each donated $5,000. towards construction of the Bond Street Synagogue which was dedicated Sept. 15, 1897. "He said that, on the deathbed of their father, David Benjamin, in 1893, they had conceived the idea of contributing sufficient money to form a nucleus for a fund to build such an edifice as this, in sacred memory of their father." Extremely generous, Mr. Benjamin never turned away any Jew in need. He served on the boards of many Jewish institutions including the Anglo-Jewish Association, Toronto Branch, the Talmud Torah Association, and the Hebrew Benevolent Society. In 1886, he married Miss Rosette Levy, the daughter of Jacob Levy, of London, England, who was closely identified with the major Jewish institutions of that city. Mr. Benjamin died suddenly in Toronto, on Jan. 8, 1900. His tombstone reads "Rest peacefully in thy last tomb, and may thy soul repose with God in eternity". "Mr. Benjamin set a remarkable example to the Jews of Toronto of true unselfish beneficience and nobility of character." (14 March 1913, 16, 14)

BIRNBAUM, S.J. (B.A.), in part five of his series "The History of the Jews in Toronto" writes about Egmund Gunther, who was born in Saxony, Germany, on Dec. 1, 1830. Gunther received his early education in Weimar and at age fifteen he became a watchmaker in that city. In 1856, he came to America and lived the first year in New York and Hamilton. In 1857, he settled in Toronto and entered the jewellery business with his brother at 9 King St. E. He moved to the corner of Melinda and Jordan in 1870 where he stayed for many years before moving to his own store at 10 Wellington St. E. Gunther joined the Board of Trade in 1886 and has been a member of King Solomon's Lodge, A.F. and A.M. (10 Jan. 1913, 16, 5)

BIRNBAUM, S.J. (B.A.), in part five of his series "The History of the Jews in Toronto" writes about Newman Leopold Steiner who was born in Bohemia, Austria, on Dec. 10, 1829, the eleventh child of Wolfgang Steiner. Educated in Vienna, he joined the Hungarian revolutionists in the revolt against Austria in 1848. He was on active service for eight months and received several wounds. Steiner and others followed Kossuth, the Hungarian revolutionary leader, to America in 1851. For about three years he lived in Buffalo where he became a sculptor. He settled in Toronto about 1856 and was a marble cutter on Parliament St., before removing to King St. In 1880, he set up business at the corner of Wilton and Victoria Sts., where he stayed until his retirement in 1886. On a visit to New York in 1876, he met and married Miss Bertha Sternberger, the daughter of Rabbi Leon Sternberger. Active in local politics as a reformer, Steiner was alderman for St. James Ward between 1880-1881 and 1883-1885 and for Ward Three, 1897-1899. He was president of the German Benevolent Society in Toronto for over twent-five years. Steiner was appointed a Justice of the Peace in the 1870s, the first Jew to receive this honor in Ontario. He died in 1902 and was survived by his wife, two daughters and three sons (10 Jan. 1913, 16, 5)

BIRNBAUM, S.J. (B.A.), in part four of his series "The History of the Jews in Toronto" writes about Jacob G. and Albert G. Ascher. Natives of Plymouth, England, they came to Canada with their parents in the 1840s and settled in Montreal where they became wealthy jewellers. About 1851, they opened a branch in Toronto and later moved there. They were both active in the Jewish community. It was at the suggestion of their son, Albert, that G.I. Ascher and his wife (who lived in Montreal), presented the Toronto Hebrew Congregation with its first Sepher Torah on April 8, 1857. A resolution of thanks, dated April 24, 1857 and signed by A. Behrends and A.S. Aarons, is still in the possession of Jacob Ascher, of New York. The Torah is in the Ark of Holy Blossom Synagogue and is recognized by a silver band on each handle with a Hebrew inscription. In the 1870s, Albert G. Ascher moved to Australia where he is still living. Jacob G. Ascher left Toronto for other North American cities. For a few years he lived in Montreal where he was co-edited the Montreal Star. He served as president and vice-president of the Young Men's Hebrew Benevolent Society. He later moved to New York (3 Jan. 1913, 16, 4)

BIRNBAUM, S.J. (B.A.), in part four of his series "The History of the Jews in Toronto" writes about A.D. Benjamin, who came to Toronto in 1879 and became a business partner of Lewis Samuel. The company, M. & L. Samuel, Benjamin & Co., is a member of the London Metal Exchange. After Lewis Samuel's death, A.D. Benjamin headed the firm. When he died in 1900, Sigmund Samuel became head of the firm. In 1909, the company built its headquarters at the southwest corner of Spadina and King Sts. (3 Jan. 1913, 16, 4)

BIRNBAUM, S.J. (B.A.), in part four of his series "The History of the Jews in Toronto" continues his essay on Lewis Samuel. "While on his return, in 1887, from a visit to his daughter, Mrs. Abraham Goodman, at San Francisco, Lewis Samuel was suddenly taken ill on board the steamer and when Victoria, B.C., was reached he was beyond all medical aid." He died in May and was buried in the Pape Avenue Cemetery with thousands attending. Engraved in Hebrew on his tombstone are the words "A good name is better than precious ointment." Lewis Samuel was survived by his wife, Kate Samuel, five daughters, Mrs. A. Goodman (San Francisco), Mrs. J.H. Rosenbaum (New York), Mrs. George R. Joseph (England), Misses Matilda and Henrietta Samuel, and one son, Sigmund Samuel. Kate Samuel died April 18, 1904 (3 Jan. 1913, 16, 4)

BIRNBAUM, S.J. (B.A.), in part one of his series "The History of the Jews in Toronto", writes about the first Jews, Judah George Joseph and Henry Abraham Joseph, who settled there in 1838. "They were both descended from an Anglo-Jewish family, which had originally come from the Netherlands." Born in London, England in 1798, Judah Joseph came to America with his family in 1830. An optician, he settled in Cincinnati before coming to Toronto where he developed a large jewellery business. He died May 17, 1857 and was buried in the Holy Blossom Congregation Cemetery on Pape Ave., south of Gerrard St. He was survived by two daughters and a son. He was predeceased by his youngest son, Edward. His eldest daughter, Louisa, married Hyman J. Altman, of Montreal, a traveller for J.G. Ascher, in 1858. After J.G. Joseph's death, Mr. Altman and his Christian partner, Thomas H. Lee, bought the business from Joseph's executor, Marcus Rosin. Mr. Altman was the buyer for J.G. Joseph & Co., living in Birmingham, Eng. After the business dissolved, he and his wife moved to New York, where she died. "Mr. Altman, to the best of the writer's knowledge, is still living in that city." Judah Joseph's second daughter married Mr. Kortosk, a

Montreal fur manufacturer. "In the sixties they left for Liverpool, England, with Mrs. J.G. Joseph, where all have died." Mr. Joseph's son, George Joseph, moved to Montreal shortly after his father's death and then to England where he recently died (29 Nov. 1912, 15, 51)

BIRNBAUM, S.J. (B.A.), in part one of his series "The History of the Jews in Toronto", writes about Henry Abraham Joseph, one of the first Jews to settle there. Mr. Joseph was born in Sorel, Que. and moved to Toronto in 1838 where he entered the fur business at 70 Yonge St. He had several business careers. In the fifties he became a hat and cap manufacturer at 60 Yonge St. and in 1860 he became a money-scrivener. "Mr. Joseph, like several others of his co-religionists, had the misfortune of being unmarried when he settled in Toronto and, there being no Jewesses in the city at the time, he married an English Church lady. This was the cause of his subsequent drifting away from Judaism, which does not, of course, imply towards Christianity. His children are still living in Toronto, and are strict adherents of the English Church. His daughters are at present members of St. Paul's Cathedral, Bloor St. East, Toronto." (29 Nov. 1912, 15, 51)

BIRNBAUM, S.J. (B.A.), in part six of his series "The History of the Jews in Toronto" writes about Joseph Simpson and his family who settled in Toronto in 1863. An American, Mr. Simpson was born in Charleston, S.C. in 1825. His father was Wilhelm Simpson, of Germany, and his mother was a daughter of William Cohen, of Nova Scotia. His parents died while he was still a child. He attended school in South Carolina until age 13, when he became a junior clerk with Howard & Co., Fancy Dry Goods, Charleston for three years. With nothing to lose, he joined the California Gold Rush in 1848. He was a miner, hotel-keeper and finally a merchant. Two years after the outbreak of the Civil War, Simpson, his wife and two sons, Ernest A., age two, and Rupert M., an infant, emigrated to Canada. He started out as a wholesale produce and grain merchant at 55 Front St. E. In 1864 he entered the carding and spinning business which has grown into a major concern stretching from Halifax to Vancouver. In 1872 he built his plant at the corner of Front and Berkeley Sts. Joseph Simpson was very active in the Jewish community and was a member of the National and Athletic Clubs and the Board of Trade (24 Jan. 1913, 16, 7)

BIRNBAUM, S.J. (B.A.), in part six of his series "The History of the Jews in Toronto" writes about Hyman Miller, eldest son of Alexander Miller, who was born in Birmingham, England in 1856. He came to New York with his parents in 1857 and to Toronto in 1861. In the 1870s, he joined M & L. Samuel & Co. In 1879, he was sent to Winnipeg as a travelling salesman where he saw a future in the wholesale hardware business. In 1882, he formed a partnership with Fred W. Morse. Their business grew into one of the largest hardware concerns in the Canadian West. They obtained a Dominion charter in 1904 and on Jan. 1, 1905 the Miller-Morse Hardware Co. was incorporated. Hyman Miller was president until his death. He was a member of the Winnipeg Board of Trade and a director of several companies including the Beaver Lumber Co. Socially prominent, he was a member of the St. Charles Country Club and the Carleton Club. An active member of the Jewish community, he was one of the trustees of the Russo-Jewish Committee and served as advisor to the Mansion House Committee concerning their land in the West. When his health began to fail, he travelled through England and the southern U.S., accompanied by his sister, Mrs. J.B. Cross. He died in Los Angeles on Jan. 3, 1913 and was buried in the Pape Avenue Cemetery, Toronto on Fri. aft., Jan. 10, Rabbi S. Jacobs officiating. Mr. Miller is survived by one son, C.A. Morell Miller, who is studying at Cambridge, England (14 Feb. 1913, 16, 10)

BIRNBAUM, S.J. (B.A.), in part six of his series "The History of the Jews in Toronto" writes about Samuel Stern, who was born in Cracow, Galicia in 1831. At age 17, Stern joined the Hungarian revolt against Austria and fought with the insurgent forces under Kossuth. With the cause lost by 1849, he came with Kossuth to New York in 1851. He stayed there for ten years in the mercantile trade. When the Civil War broke out, he joined the Union forces and was in the field for one year. He came to Toronto in the spring of 1862 and became a cigar maker. In 1866, he started a fancy goods import business at 11 King St. W. Stern grew wealthy and in 1873 he built the Stern Bldgs. at 38-40 Front St. E., now occupied by P.W. Ellis & Co. He lost them during the recession of 1877 but continued in his former business. He never regained his former position as a result of the '77 reverses. He stayed in Toronto until Aug. 1910 when he left to join his children in New York. He became a Freemason in 1854. In 1875, Stern founded the Toronto Hebrew Benevolent Society and was its first president (24 Jan. 1913, 16, 7)

BIRNBAUM, S.J. (B.A.), in part six of his series "The History of the Jews in Toronto" writes about Marx Kassel, who was born in Schroda, Russia, near the Posen boundary in 1830. Educated in his native town, Kassel left for England and settled in Hull. In 1856, he came to New York with his wife, the former Miss Minna Wolf, of Hull. A year later they moved to Toronto where he started out as a merchant tailor. He then entered the dry goods trade. As his business prospered, he opened a department store on Queen St. W., below Spadina in 1886. He retired from business a year later due to his wife's serious illness and subsequent death. Mr. Kassel was an active communal worker with the Toronto Hebrew Benevolent Society and served as president of Holy Blossom Congregation. He played a prominent role in the construction of the old Richmond Street Synagogue. Mr. Kassel's daughter, Ettie, died in Detroit in 1886 and her husband, Alexander Bernstein, died a few days later. Their remains were brought to Toronto and buried the same day in the Pape Avenue Cemetery. Mrs. Marx Kassel died in Toronto in 1887 and a few years later his daughter, Harriet passed away. His only remaining daughter, Deborah, married Bernard Wolf, who died in 1891, in Toronto. In 1899, she and her children moved to New York where she was appointed superintendent of the Women's Dept., of the Educational Alliance. Shortly after, Mr. Kassel moved to New York to make his home with his daughter (14 Feb. 1913, 16, 10)

BIRNBAUM, S.J. (B.A.), in part six of his series "The History of the Jews in Toronto" writes about Alexander Miller, who was born in Coblentz, Germany on March 28, 1823. At age eight, he became an orphan and went to live with his relatives in Birmingham, England. In 1857, he, his wife (the former Miss Rachel Joel), and his son, Hyman, went to New York. They settled in Toronto in 1861 where Mr. Miller was in the clothing business and later became a hammock manufacturer. A very active member of the Jewish community, Mr. Miller joined the Hebrew Congregation on April 24, 1864. He was president of Holy Blossom Synagogue as well as the Toronto Hebrew Benevolent Society. He was responsible for ensuring that Kosher meat was available to the community after Rev. Hyman Goldberg was no longer in Toronto to supervise. Mr. Miller joined the Masons in England in 1848 and was a member of B'nai Brith. He died Oct. 17, 1893, survived by his wife, who is still living in Toronto, four of his six sons and one daughter. They are Coleman and Isidore Miller, of Toronto; Joel Miller, of Chicago; Lawrence Miller, of New York; and Mrs. J.B. Cross, of Toronto (14 Feb. 1913, 16, 10)

BIRNBAUM, S.J. (B.A.), in part three of his series "The History of the Jews in Toronto" writes about Lewis Samuel who came to Toronto in 1856. Born in Hull, England in 1828, Mr. Samuel and his wife, a native of Sulzbach, Bavaria, came to New York in 1849 and then moved to Montreal. He moved to Toronto for better business opportunities and was soon followed by his brother, Mark Samuel. In 1857, they founded M. and L. Samuel & Co., metal dealers and importers at 115 Yonge St. The firm opened a branch in Montreal headed by Emmanuel Samuel. In 1860 Mark Samuel established a buying house at 28 Castle St., Liverpool, England, where he purchased supplies for the Canadian branches of the business. When they first settled in Toronto, Mrs. Lewis Samuel, who was strictly Orthodox, agreed to remain there on condition that a congregation be formed. Lewis Samuel agreed and played a major role in the creation of the first congregation, the forerunner of Holy Blossom Congregation, which met for the first time in June 1856. Rev. Hyman Goldberg, of New York, was the first rabbi, cantor and schochet in Toronto. Rev. Goldberg was the father of Mrs. Harris Vineberg, of Montreal. Lewis Samuel raised funds for the first synagogue in Toronto which opened in 1876 on Richmond St. south side, east of Victoria St. (20 Dec. 1912, 16, 2)

BIRNBAUM, S.J. (B.A.), in part three of his series "The History of the Jews in Toronto" writes about Isaac Davis who came to Toronto with his family in 1854. Mr. Davis was born in Moscow, Russia in 1806 during the Napoleonic wars. To avoid military conscription he fled to England in 1821. For this act his inheritance was confiscated by the Russian authorities. He stayed in England about thirteen years engaged in mercantile trade. In 1834, he came to Canada moving to Quebec City before settling in Montreal. After building a successful dry goods business in Montreal, he went to England in 1847 and married Miss Harriet Henry, the daughter of a wealthy and prominent Anglo-Jewish merchant. He and his wife returned to Montreal where they remained until 1854 when they moved to Toronto. He opened his first import and dry goods business at 28 Yonge St. and his second at 89 Yonge St. His stores were never open on the Sabbath or Jewish holidays. For many years Mr. Davis was the first naturalized Jew in Toronto, having become a Canadian citizen in

1837. After he retired in 1880, he was gabbai in the Richmond Street Synagogue for several years. He died Jan. 24, 1888 and was survived by his wife and three children, Henry Davis, manager of the Crochet and Knitting Specialty, David Davis and Mrs. Miller. Lionel Davis, of the law firm Davis & Mehr, is a grandson (20 Dec. 1912, 16, 2)

BIRNBAUM, S.J. (B.A.), in part three of his series "The History of the Jews in Toronto" writes about the Lumley family which came to Toronto from England in 1848. That year Morris Lumley, the head of the family, opened his first clothing store at 108 Yonge St., followed by a second one in 1858 at 644 Yonge St. His brother, Isaac Lumley, settled in Toronto in 1849 and also opened a clothing store at 161 King St. E. After amassing considerable wealth the brothers returned to England in 1863, where the family still exists (20 Dec. 1912, 16, 2)

BIRNBAUM, S.J. (B.A.), in part two of his series "The History of the Jews in Toronto", writes about Julius, Marcus and Samuel Rossin, natives of Germany who settled in Toronto shortly after the arrival of the Braham family. They established a jewellery business at 32 King St. E. which was nearly ruined by fire on several occasions. In 1855 Marcus and Samuel Rossin purchased some land at the corner of King and York Sts. and built the famous Rossin House, a five story combination hotel-store complex. In 1860, the Prince of Wales stayed there and it was home to many American visitors accustomed to the great hotels of New York and Chicago. After a disastrous fire on Fri. Nov. 14, 1862 which completely destroyed the hotel, the brothers opened a wholesale tobacco shop at 10 Wellington St. W. in addition to their jewellery store on 55 Front St. E. Discouraged by their misfortune of '62, they left Toronto three years later. Marcus, the eldest brother, returned to Germany while Samuel went to the United States. Both have since died (6 Dec. 1912, 15, 52)

BIRNBAUM, S.J. (B.A.), in part two of his series "The History of the Jews in Toronto", writes about Alfred Braham, the head of an Anglo-Jewish family, who settled in Toronto in 1844. He started out as a clothier at 70 King St. E., 8 Victoria Row, opposite St. James Cathedral. A successful businessman he made a great fortune which he invested in real estate. His wife Catharine Braham, died in 1859, age 34, perhaps a victim of the Asiatic cholera then raging in Canada. She was buried in the Pape Ave. cemetery. "Hers is the earliest Jewish grave in Toronto marked by a tombstone." For several years Alfred Braham lived in his own home at 26 St. Joseph St., Claverhill. He retired from business in 1868 and two years later moved to England where he lived in City Road, east of Euston Road, London, until his death in the nineties (6 Dec. 1912, 15, 52)

BIRNBAUM, S.J. (B.A.), in part two of his series "The History of the Jews in Toronto", writes about Abraham and Samuel Nordheimer, two brothers of a family of eight from Memelsdorf, Bavaria, Germany, who settled in Kingston, Ont., in 1839, where they opened a music store, A. & S. Nordheimer. Piano-makers, they moved to Toronto in 1842 where they established a flourishing business. In 1849, Abraham Nordheimer together with Judah George Joseph, deeded the Pape Avenue Cemetery to the Jewish community which was purchased from Sir John Beverley Robinson for $100. A. and S. Nordheimer contributed towards the erection of the first synagogue in 1876 as well as King Solomon's Lodge. Abraham Nordheimer and his wife returned to Germany in the sixties. He died in Baumberg in 1869. Samuel Nordheimer remained in Toronto where he became president of the Philharmonic Society and vice-president of the Canada Permanent Loan Co. He was appointed the German and Austrian consul for Ontario in March, 1899. He died on June 29, 1912 after a brief illness and left $2,500 out of a million dollar estate to charity. One of the five beneficiaries was the Toronto Jewish Benevolent Society (6 Dec. 1912, 15, 52)

BLOCK, Miss Mamie, of Charlottetown, P.E.I., had her letter to "Uncle Jacob" reprinted. She writes "I would like to join as a member in some league or society for I am proud I am a Jewess, and never hesitate to say I am, which means I belong to a great and well-known nation. I am the only girl of my age, who is fifteen years old, in the place I reside. I would like to show I am a Jewess and proud of it." (1 Aug. 1913, 16, 34)

BLOOM, Harry, merchant, defendant, of Montreal, and Dame Esther Breska, alias Hyams, of Montreal, plaintiff, wife of Harry Bloom, an action for separation of property in the Quebec Superior Court, District of Montreal. Henry Weinfield, attorney for the plaintiff, dated Aug. 22, 1910 (2 Sept. 1910, 13, 42)

BLOOM, Ida, plaintiff, of Montreal, wife common as to property of Harry Hyams, merchant, of Montreal, has instituted an action for separation of property against Harry Hyams, June 8, 1912 (21 June 1912, 15, 28)

BLOOMFIELD, Sam, of Montreal, served as presiding officer of the Ancient Order of Foresters, No. 7673, for the past year (22 Jan. 1909, 12, 6)

BLUMENTHAL, A., the Montreal alderman, was successful in getting approval for A. Valosky to open a wood yard (5 April 1912, 15, 21)

BLUMENTHAL, Abraham, is a candidate for alderman in the coming Montreal civic elections in the St. Louis Division under the Reform banner. "A business man of good reputation, he is well able to carry much needed business methods into our city administration. His integrity and honesty of purpose are recognized in all quarters, and he will, when elected, carry honour with him as a City Father." (28 Jan. 1910, 13, 11)

BLUMENTHAL, Abraham, was unsuccessful in his bid for election to Montreal City Council (4 Feb. 1910, 13, 12)

BRAININ, Joseph, of Montreal, wrote a letter to the editor about Rabbi J.S. Minkin's article on Heinrich Heine (8 Aug. 1913, 16, 35)

BRAININ, Reuben, wrote a short story "The Red Violet" (6 Dec. 1912, 15, 52)

BRAININ, Rubin, noted Hebrew scholar, who recently lectured in Montreal, gave an interview "Hebrew A Living Tongue; Yiddish Has No Future" (28 Jan. 1910, 13, 11)

BRAININ, Rubin, one of the world's greatest Hebrew writers, is touring the country for the purpose of promoting the Hebrew language. "Although, his lectures are delivered in Yiddish, he is not a believer in the jargon as having any future; but his use of this language is one of necessity, as many of his audience in any city, are not sufficiently acquainted with Hebrew for practical purposes." Mr. Brainin delivered two lectures in Montreal, "The Condition of the Jews in Many Lands" and "Dr. Herzl". A banquet was tendered Mr. and Mrs. Brainin on Mon. evening. Rabbi Nathan Gordon was the toast-master. Among the guests present were:- Mesdames A. Levin, Hiram Levy, M. Gelbman, M.P. Darwin, Z. Fineberg, A. Lozinsky, Felix Harris, I. Mishkin, the Misses Miriam Bernstein and Rose Harris, Messrs. Clarence I. de Sola, Hiram Levy, A. Levin, Leon Goldman, Z. Fineberg, M. Gelbman, M.P. Darwin, A. Harris, H. Lang, A. Lozinsky, Talpis, David Levy, S. Sanders, N.H. Godinsky, I. Mishkin, Pierce, Chas. Fisher, Michelin and Chodesh. At the suggestion of A. Harris, $50.00 was raised to inscribe the name of Mr. and Mrs. Brainin in the Golden Book (21 Jan. 1910, 13, 10)

BUDYK, Dr. J.C., of Montreal, wrote an article "The Cause and Treatment of Summer Diarrhoeas in Infants" (14 June 1912, 15, 27)

BUDYK, J.A. (B.A.) wrote a lengthy article "Canadian Anti-Semitism" (29 Nov. 1912, 15, 51)

CASH, Alexander, of Toronto, wrote a letter to the editor stating that contrary to what was reported in the July 4th edition, he will attend the Zionist Congress in Vienna at his own expense (11 July 1913, 16, 31)

COHEN, A., a member of the Young Men's Hebrew Association in Portland, Me., who has lived in Montreal only a short time, wrote a letter to the editor urging support for the YMHA in Montreal (31 Jan. 1912, 15, 12)

COHEN, A.I., of Clark's Harbor, N.S., wrote a letter to the editor, March 2, 1909, about his plans to emigrate to Palestine and requesting information (12 March 1909, 12, 13)

COHEN, Lyon, BdeHI president, while in London, England, gave an interview to the Jewish Chronicle. He said in part, "I should like to impress upon my friends in Europe that they should not be led into the idea that wholesale emigration to Canada is feasible or desirable. Both in the interests of the country and of the emigrants themselves it is necessary that the utmost caution should be observed. The country is able to absorb large numbers of immigrants, provided they come gradually, in such numbers as to enable us to deal with them systematically in order to do justice to individual requirements. We are very anxious to avoid the creation of ghettos with all the concomitant problems which congested Jewish districts involve." (3 Sept. 1909, 12, 38)

COHEN, Lyon, president of the Baron de Hirsch Institute, Montreal, gave an interview on "Jewish Charitable Institutions in New York" (4 Feb. 1910, 13, 12)

COHEN, Lyon, wrote an article "The Birth of the Jewish Times" in response to a request from Leon Goldman and Max Sanders, the publishers of The Canadian Jewish Times for the fifteenth anniversary issue (13 Dec. 1912, 16, 1)

COHEN, Lyon, wrote an article "The Material Future of the Jews in Canada" for the Passover issue (18 April 1913, 16, 19)

COHEN, Minnie, her sisters Ethel and Mabel and

her brother Walter Cohen, of Birmingham, England, are new members of the Young Israel Children's League. "Uncle Jacob" of the Home Page writes, "You are our first members in the British Empire, outside of Canada to join our League. I must congratulate you on this distinction." (9 May 1913, 16, 22)

COHEN, Miss Minnie and her brothers and sisters, Ethel Cohen (age 12), Mabel Cohen (age 11), and Walter Cohen (age 9), of Birmingham, England, have an uncle in Montreal, who sends them issues of **The Canadian Jewish Times**. They would like to join the Young Israel Children's League (30 May 1913, 16, 25)

COHEN, Mrs. Lyon, wrote an article "Jewish Endeavor Sewing School" for the special women's issue (21 Nov. 1913, 16, 50-51)

COHEN, Rabbi Montague N.A., now of San Francisco, wrote an article on "The Jew in Canada" for the San Francisco **Emanu-El**. Commenting on the article which it found offensive, **The Canadian Jewish Times** wrote, "The older families of Canadian Jews, long settled in the country, are indistinguishable from other people. They are held in the highest respect and have given to the public service ever since the conquest, men whose names are honoured in Canadian history. Those of a later generation have aided notably in the development of the country. Many have risen to affluence, and many more are lawyers, physicians and merchants, whose success and the positions they occupy are proofs of the freedom and amplitude of opportunities enjoyed by Jews in Canada. This Dominion at present is in a state of sudden expansion. Conditions are heterogenous. Jews, like other people, must fit themselves into their new environment. In the effort they need sympathy and encouragement, not ill-natured criticism and fault-finding. There are sensible men in Canadian Jewry who are doing nobly, as they have done in the past, for their immigrating co-religionists. They are content to do their work quietly, and their success is proved by the fact that many thousands of Jewish refugees from Europe have been so directed that they have been absorbed into the industrial life of the Dominion without causing the slightest disturbance, while aiding greatly in its development and progress "(24 Sept. 1909, 12, 41)

DAINOW, David, Louis Fitch, A.J. Levinson, of Montreal, and Rabbi Jacob S. Minkin are on the staff of **The Canadian Jewish Times**. Occasional contributors are Miss Hannah Berman and Rabbis Herman Abramowitz, S. Fyne and Meldola de Sola (10 Jan. 1913, 16, 5)

DAINOW, David, wrote a short story "The Lightweight - An Anglo-Jewish Story" (31 Jan. 1913, 8)

DAINOW, David, wrote a story "The Seder Meeting" for the Passover issue (18 April 1913, 16, 19)

DAINOW, David, wrote an article "The Anti-Semitism of Mr. Hillaire Belloc" (10 Jan. 1913, 16, 5)

DARWIN, Robert A., Harry Bessner, Master Philip Pressner, Mrs. R.A. Darwin, and the Misses Bella Gross, Mary Tritt, Clara Schwartz, Bessie Elkin, Frances Sigmund and Ida F. Apotheker, all of Montreal, had trees purchased in their names in the Herzl Wald (15 April 1910, 13, 22)

DAVIS, Mortimer B., of Montreal, was named by **The Canadian Jewish Times** in its editorial as a possible candidate for the Senate vacancy caused by the death of Quebec senator, Sir William MacDonald (11 Feb. 1910, 13, 13)

DAVIS, Mortimer B., of the Imperial Tobacco Company, deserves credit for his important contributions to the Canadian tobacco-growing industry, according to the Toronto News. "His experts have backed up the Ontario Department of Agriculture in its efforts to teach the Western Ontario farmer how to grow a good leaf." (19 Nov. 1909, 13, 1)

DE SOLA, Clarence I., wrote a letter to the editor on the progress of Canadian Zionism (18 April 1913, 16, 19)

DE SOLA, Mrs. Belle Maud, wrote an article "The Jew - Real and Imaginary" for the special women's issue (21 Nov. 1913, 16, 50-51)

DE SOLA, Rabbi Meldola, - his reply to Bishop Farthing in the **Montreal Gazette** was reprinted (5 Dec. 1913, 16, 52)

DE SOLA, Rabbi Meldola, preached on the desecration of the Sabbath and Festivals by attending theatrical performances. "He referred in scathing terms to performances given by a Jewish troupe on Simchath Torah and Friday nights, "in honour of the last days of Tabernacles," as stated in the hand bills issued." (15 Oct. 1909, 12, 42)

DE SOLA, Rabbi Meldola, wrote a letter to the editor denouncing Dr. Emil G. Hirsch "the high priest of Reform Judaism in Chicago" for his attacks on Orthodox Judaism (22 Nov. 1912, 15, 50)

DE SOLA, Rabbi Meldola, wrote an article "Chanukah Reflections" (6 Dec. 1912, 15, 52)

DE SOLA, Rabbi Meldola: reprint of his sermon "Anti-Semitism Powerless" (23 April 1909, 12, 19)

DESROSES, Alfred, age 33, formerly of Nice, France and now of Montreal, was converted to Judaism by the Rev. S. Goldstein, on Fri. Jan 29, 1909. His father was a Free-Thinker and his mother was Jewish. "Several months ago, he visited Rabbi Hirsch Cohen, of this city, and informed him of his intention of embracing Judaism. The Rabbi pointed out the many difficulties which lay before him, and the numerous obligations to which he would have to submit as a Jew, both before and after, if he were to be admitted as a member of the race." (12 Feb. 1909, 12, 9)

DROBKIN, Messrs., Popliger and Steinberg are proprietors of a new Kosher meat market in Montreal to be located at Prince Arthur, corner St. Dominique St. Rabbi Simon Glazer will supervise the Kashruth of the market (15 March 1912, 15, 18)

EDELSTEIN, H., wrote an article "The Jews of Dublin" (20 Dec. 1912, 16, 2)

EDELSTEIN, Hyman, wrote a poem "A Purim Ballad" (13 Feb. 1914, 17, 7)

EDELSTEIN, Hyman, wrote a sonnet "Passover" for the Passover issue (18 April 1913, 16, 19)

EDELSTEIN, Hyman, wrote an article "Ancient Hebrew Sports" (22 Oct. 1913, 16, 46)

EDLSTEIN, Hyman, wrote a poem "Baron and Lady de Hirsch" on the occasion of the fiftieth anniversary of the Baron de Hirsch Institute, Montreal (21 Nov. 1913, 16, 50-51)

EDLSTEIN, Joseph, wrote an article "The Jew in South Africa - His Contribution to the Building of the Empire of South Africa" (1 Oct. 1913, 16, 42-43)

ENGLEMAN, Miss Pauline, daughter of Solomon Engleman, formerly of Montreal, now of Des Moines, Iowa, has been appointed teacher of violin and piano at Tabor College, Ia. Mr. Engleman and his family left Montreal twenty years ago to establish a business in Des Moines. "At an early age, Miss Engleman showed remarkable talents as a musician, and her father gave the young lady every opportunity to cultivate her art." She graduated from Highland Park Conservatory and studied at the Chicago Musical College (26 March 1909, 12, 15)

ETTENBERG, Bernard, grade one, vocal dept., and Mrs. M.J. Heller, of Providence, R.I., grade two, received awards at the Montreal Conservatory of Music closing examinations (9 July 1909, 12, 30)

FARBER, R., of Vancouver, B.C., wrote a letter to the editor, Feb. 15, 1911, about Rabbi J.K. Levin's membership in the Protestant Ministerial Association in Winnipeg. "...I wish to inform the Winnipeg Star that it may publish that already ten years ago, during my first incumbency of the pulpit of Congregation Emanu-El of this city I was a member of the Ministerial Association of this city, comprised of all denominations, and on my return here to resume charge of the congregation the same body of clergymen immediately extended me the invitation to come to their meetings and participate in their deliberations, and, of course, elected me a member of their organization..." (24 Feb. 1911, 14, 15)

FINEBERG, Joe, 62 St. James St., Montreal, president of the Montreal Agudath Zion Society, cabled the **Jewish Chronicle** to find out if Sir Rufus Isaacs was sworn upon the Old Testament at his swearing-in as Lord Chief Justice of England (31 Oct. 1913, 16, 47)

FINEBERG, M., 185 Esplanade Ave.; M. Ravitch, 1427 Clarke St.; and M. Rittenberg, 228 St. Joseph Blvd. W., all of Montreal, circulated a letter, Nov. 7, 1912 (reprinted) concerning the need for a synagogue with a modern Hebrew school for the north end (15 Nov. 1912, 15, 49)

FINEBERG, Miss Lena, wrote an article "Montreal Hebrew Ladies' Aid Society" for the special women's issue (21 Nov. 1913, 16, 50-51)

FINKELSTEIN, M.J., of Winnipeg, wrote a letter to the editor, informing the readers the government now requires that immigrants produce passports before being allowed to enter Canada and the serious impact order this will have on Russian Jewish immigrants. Referring to the Order-in-Council of March 9, 1914, he wrote "This simply means that hereafter entry to Canada will be refused to Russian immigrants who cannot produce what is known as a "Governor's Passport," that is, a document issued by the governor of a Russian province or gubernia, authorizing the holder of the passport to emigrate from Russia to a foreign country for a short period of time. It must be remembered that such a document is never issued to anyone who wishes to leave the country permanently, nor is it issued to anyone who has committed any crime, misdemeanor or transgression against the laws of Russia, or even a police regulation." (13 Feb. 1914, 17, 7)

FITCH, Louis, B.A., received first rank honors in first year law at McGill University. Others who passed were: Third Year Arts - Bram C. de Sola, first rank honors; Miss H. Rosenberg and E. Solomon. Second Year Arts - Miss M. Bernstein, L. Tannenbaum, H. Herschorn and A.J. Levinson. Third Year - M. Goldblatt, J. Gronin, first rank honors; M. Kert, K. de S. Joseph, M. Budyk, A. Roback, E. Youngheart, A. Muhlstock and M. Grossman. Second Year Law - J.A. Goodstone, M. Alexander and L. Jacobs. First Year Law - Louis Fitch, B.A., first rank honors, prize of $75.00; B. Goldenberg, second place. First Year Science - N.B. Cohen and M. Hyman. Second Year Science - M. Lipsey. Third Year Science - A.S. Goodstone (civil); E. Mauer, (civil); R. Stark, (civil); and D. Hart (civil). Third Year Dentistry - Mr. Aronson. Pharmacy minor exams - C. Albert (30 April 1909, 12, 24)

FITCH, Louis, Law '11, has won the McGill University Silver Medal for public speaking. His subject was on "Zionism" (5 March 1909, 12, 12)

FITCH, Louis, reprint of his address for the plaintiff in the Quebec anti-semitic libel case (11 July 1913, 16, 31)

FITCH, Louis, was one of the authors of the Quebec Tercentenary Commemorative History published by the Quebec City Daily Telegraph (12 Feb. 1909, 12, 9)

FRANKEL, Mrs. Maurice, wrote an article "The Work Being Done by Jewish Women of Toronto" for the special women's issue (21 Nov. 1913, 16, 50-51)

FRANKEL, Mrs. Maurice, wrote an article "The Toronto Section of the Council of Jewish Women" for the Passover issue (18 April 1913, 16, 19)

FRIDMANN, S.M., a Montreal resident who lived in Norway for many years "...has informed us that in a letter he has just received from his father in Christiana, he is told that a law for the prohibiting of Schechita in Norway was discussed at a sitting of the Storthing, but the matter was ultimately left in obeyance (sic.)." (28 March 1913, 16, 16)

FRIEDLANDER, Rabbi J., of Congregation Anshe Shalom, Hamilton: the rabbi's correspondence exchange with the Anglican Bishop of Toronto in which he protests the operation of missions to the Jews (21 May 1909, 12, 22)

FRIEDLANDER, Rev. Elias., of Victoria, B.C., wrote a letter to the editor, Jan. 30, 1913 wishing The Canadian Jewish Times congratulations on its fifteenth anniversary (7 Feb. 1913, 16, 9)

FRIEDLANDER, Rev. J., former minister of Shaar Hashomayim Synagogue in Montreal, has written an article "Canada for a larger Jewish Colonization" which first appeared in The American Hebrew and was reprinted in The Canadian Jewish Times (16 Sept. 1910, 13, 44)

FROOMAN, L.E., passed third year medicine at McGill University (4 June 1909, 12, 25)

FYNE, Rabbi S., delivered an address "Death renders the truly great Greater" at the Herzl Memorial Service last Sun. which was reprinted (12 July 1912, 15, 31)

FYNE, Rabbi S., of Ottawa, wrote an article "The Jewish New Year" (11 Sept. 1912, 15, 40)

FYNE, Rabbi S., of Ottawa, wrote an article "Anti-Semitism" (7 June 1912, 15, 26)

FYNE, Rabbi S., of Ottawa, wrote an article "A Square Deal - Supposed Scene at the Protestant Mission House, Bethnal Green, London" (23 Aug. 1912, 15, 37)

FYNE, Rabbi S., wrote an article "Pentecost and its Inheritance" (6 June 1913, 16, 26)

GARBER, M., wrote a letter to the editor urging the formation of a Zionist Council in Montreal (25 Sept. 1912, 15, 42)

GARFINKLE, Miss Annie M., wrote an article "Woman's Position among the Jews - The Women of Israel have demonstrated that they can rise to the heights of fame in every field of endeavor" (11 Sept. 1912, 15, 40)

GELBMAN, Max, has sold his interest in The Canadian Jewish Times to Leon Goldman, of Montreal. "The journal is now the property of Messrs. Leon Goldman and Max Sanders. The policy of the paper will be the same as outlined several months ago on the occasion of the assumption of the active management by Mr. Sanders." (9 Aug. 1912, 15, 35)

GLAZER, Rabbi Simon, instituted a libel suit for $20,000.00 against the Keneder Adler which was to have been heard last Tues. The suit was settled out of court. "The action arose out of the general disputes between the butchers and "Schochtim," in which the reverend gentleman made himself somewhat conspicuous. The "Eagle" entered the lists, and during the controversy, made certain alleged derogatory statements against Mr. Glazer, which roused his ire, and as a consequence, the action for damages was entered. A few days before the trial, the applicant, we understand, made overtures to the defendants, with a result that the action was dropped, each party paying their own costs." (23 April 1909, 12, 19)

GLAZER, Rabbi Simon, of Montreal, who brought suit against The Jewish Eagle and its manager, H. Wolofsky for libel several months ago, is continuing with his lawsuit. Mr. Wolofsky is represented by S.W. Jacobs, K.C. and Rabbi Glazer by Mr. Sperber. An account of the examination for discovery is provided (23 June 1911, 14, 32)

GLAZER, Rabbi Simon, was re-elected rabbi of Chevra Kadisha Synagogue, St. Urbain St., Montreal. As well, Rabbi Glazer is chief rabbi of the following Montreal and Quebec City congregations: Austria-Hungarian Synagogue, Milton St.; Romanian Synagogue, Chenneville St.; Beth Judah Synagogue, Lagauchetiere St.; Kehal Yeshurun, Galician Synagogue, Colonial Ave., near Sherbrooke St; Kal. Israel Chaverim, Papineau.; Tifereth Israel, Mile End; Shomrim Laboker, Cadieux St.; Beth Solomon, St. Charles Borrommée St.; and Beth Israel, Quebec City (16 Feb. 1912, 15, 14)

GLAZER, Rabbi Simon, wrote a letter to the editor, March 29, 1910, concerning his alleged status as Chief Rabbi of Montreal. "Certainly not; and I defy any one who will prove that I have laid claim to such office or title. Am I the Chief rabbi of the United Orthodox congregations? Yes. And I would be misrepresenting my office, to which I am elected by ten congregations, here and in Quebec, if I should renounce the title." (1 April 1910, 13, 20)

GLAZER, Rabbi Simon: in a previous edition it was reported that his libel action "...against the "Keneder Adler" had been settled out of court, and that each party were to pay their own costs. The first part of the statement is correct, but with regard to the costs of the action we were misinformed, inasmuch as all costs, including fees for lawyers on both sides, and the costs of the court, etc., are to be borne by the defendants." (30 April 1909, 12, 20)

GLICKMAN, Marcus, of Westmount, Que.; Bessie Schlein, of Montreal; and Naomi Miller, of Lachine Locks, Que., are new members of the Young Israel Children's League (14 Feb. 1913, 16, 10)

GOLD, M., M.Z. Krolik, E.C. Levine and J. Segal passed their first year physics in the McGill University medical program. Other first year graduates in practical chemistry and botany were: S. Astrofsky, M.Z. Krolik, E.C. Levine and J. Segal. Second Year, organic chemistry - Joseph Kolber, J.J. Rosenbaum and W.R. Stone. histology - J.J. Rosenbaum and W.R. Stone. Third Year, bacteriology - A.M. Aronson and A. Glickman. Other graduating Arts at McGill inadvertently omitted were: First Year - J. Budyk. Second Year - J. Levinson (29 Jan. 1909, 12, 7)

GOLDBLATT, A., Gronin, Kert, E. Youngheart, A. Muhlstock, K. Joseph and A. Roback passed their first year in Arts at McGill University, Montreal. Others who passed were: Second Year Arts - Miss Minnie Bernstein, H. Hirsborn, L. Tannenbaum. Third Year Arts - Miss H. Rosenberg and E. Solmon. Science, First Year - N. Cohen and Hyman. Third Year Science - E. Mauer, S. Goodstone and A. Starke. Law (legal history) - L. Fitch and B. Goldberg. (Roman law) - L. Fitch (first in class) (15 Jan. 1909, 12, 5)

GOLDHAMER, Charlie and Sollie, of Toronto; and Sydney Neuman, of New York, are new members of the Young Israel Children's League. Sydney Neuman is the first American to join the League according to "Uncle Jacob" (21 Feb. 1913, 16, 11)

GOLDMAN, Henry, of Montreal, is a new member of the Young Israel Children's League (9 May 1913, 16, 22)

GOLDMAN, Leon, 17 Esplanade Ave., Montreal, wrote a letter June 9, 1912, to Max Sanders, the new manager of The Canadian Jewish Times wishing him success "...in the remodelling of the only Jewish weekly in Canada." (14 June 1912, 15, 27)

GOLDMAN, Leon, of Montreal, wrote an article "Isaiah and the Jewish Nation" (9 Aug. 1912, 15, 35)

GOLDMAN, Samuel, of Montreal, and Jacob Lachovetiz, of Ottawa sent some of their poems to "Uncle Jacob" of the Home Page who writes, "Both are interesting, but why not take as your theme some aspect drawn from Jewish historic lore? In contributing original work to our page Hebraism should be your guiding star." (16 May 1913, 16, 23)

GOLDSTEIN, B., the Montreal Baron de Hirsch Institute first vice-president, gave a report of his visit to the Dominion Detention Hospital for immigrants at Sans Bruit, outside Quebec City (20 Aug. 1909, 12, 36)

GOLDSTEIN, Ed., Lyon Levinson, Marvie Workman, Sam Jacobs, Noel Friedman, George Blumenthal and Leo Livingstone are members of the Primrose team (Jewish hockey champions), Montreal (22 Jan. 1909, 12, 6)

GOLDSTEIN, J., 998 Dorchester St. W., Montreal, wrote a letter to the editor against the idea of establishing a Kehilah in Montreal, but in favor of "...a "United Charities" so (sic.) soon as the community has settled down, and has proved its communal wants." (30 Aug. 1912, 15, 38)

GOLDSTEIN, Maxwell, in an interview with the London Jewish Chronicle on "Jewish Affairs in Canada" which was reported in The Jewish Times said... " "The cause of many of our troubles is the vast influx of foreign Jews into the Dominion. They form ghettos among themselves and create a great deal of prejudice. Certain of the French Press are very antipathetic to the Jews. One Roman Catholic priest exhorted his flock not to sell landed property to the Jews, who, he said, would become their masters if they were allowed to become property owners. The new-comers have not only formed congregations of their own, but they have even appointed a foreign Chief Rabbi for themselves. At one time he styled himself the Chief Rabbi of Canada, but now he is recognized by the foreign section as the Chief Rabbi of the United Hebrew Congregations. The difficulty with us is how to co-operate with these people. They must not be ignored. The only thing to do is take them by the hand, and lead them by persuasive methods to recognize their duties to the community. Recently, owing to the stringency of our immigration laws, and owing also to the fact that our means of assistance have become exhausted, the tide of immigration has greatly lessened in volume. If it could be restrained for a few years longer I have no doubt but what we should be able to assimilate and consolidate all sections of the community." "What are the relations between the Orthodox congregations and the Reform section?" he was asked. "Socially they mingle and intermarry, but communally the Orthodox congregations fail to appreciate the importance of the Reform movement, and show an unwillingness to recognize our ministers." "Are the Jews of Canada prosperous on the whole?" "Yes. Canada is prospering, and our people are sharing in the general prosperity. Jews are great buyers of real estate, and they hold their own in the commercial world. As manufacturers they are chiefly engaged in the clothing, tobacco, jewellery and rubber-goods trades. Canada is not a place for loiterers, but there is any amount of scope for hard-workers, and particularly for people who will settle on the land and are ready to go to the great North West Territories. The city of the future is Winnipeg."" (30 July 1909, 12, 33)

GOLDSTEIN, Mrs. J., wrote an article "The Friendly League of Jewish Women of Canada" for the special women's issue (21 Nov. 1913, 16, 50-51)

GOLDSTICK, I., of Toronto, wrote an article " A Blind Guide" (11 Sept. 1912, 15, 40)

GOLDSTICK, I., of Toronto, wrote an article "On the study of Jewish History" (19 July 1912, 15, 32)

GONIONDZER, A., has a column "Chips from many Blocks" in the paper. He comments on the Montreal garment workers' strike and hopes for an early settlement (28 June 1912, 15, 29)

GOODMAN, B., of Montreal, wrote a letter to the editor June 10, 1912, about his article titled the "Red Peril" which appeared in a recent issue of the Volks-Zeitung. J.J. Goodman, of Winnipeg, is greatly annoyed over the article "...and is trying by means of explanatory letters in the Jewish press in Canada to renounce the authorship of it. Just imagine a.man disclaiming what he never wrote! Mr. Goodman takes particular exception to the fact that the article in question bore "his" signature. As I am the real author of that unlucky article, therefore permit me to tell Mr. Goodman that it did not bear his signature, but my own, as it was through a typographical error that the initial letter "yod" had been substituted for a "beth."" (28 June 1912, 15, 29)

GORDON, Miss Annie, wrote an article "Baroness Clara de Hirsch" for the special women's issue (21 Nov. 1913, 16, 50-51)

GORDON, Rabbi Nathan, of Montreal, wrote a letter to the editor on the subject of intermarriage (11 Feb. 1910, 13, 13)

GORDON, Rabbi Nathan, wrote an article "Woman's Place in Communal Charities" for the special women's issue (21 Nov. 1913, 16, 50-51)

GORDON, Rabbi Nathan: part of a sermon "The Demands of the Twentieth Century", delivered on the first day of Passover, 1909 (16 April 1909, 12, 18)

GOTTLIEB, Saul, of Toronto, won first place in Uncle Jacob's Map of Palestine Contest, along with Harry A. Baum, of Montreal (17 Jan. 1913, 16, 6)

GRONIN, J. (B.A.), reviewed the play "Everywoman" - a modern symbolical play (18 Oct. 1912, 15, 45)

GRONIN, J. (B.A.), reviewed the play "Disraeli" by Louis N. Parker (11 Oct. 1912, 15, 44)

HAMBURG, B., sec. of the Glace Bay Zionist Society, wrote a letter to the editor stating that neither he nor the Society has any knowledge of J. Berman who claimed to have been present at the "at home" given Oct. 28, 1912. "All our Jewish people are known to us by name, therefore can it be possible for this so-styled false onlooker and sympathizer to give any criticism of our Hebrew young men as to the entertainment of our Jewish young ladies at the "At Home," so this proves how much truth and reliability can be attached to such communications, when the writer of them signs under a fictitious name and is ashamed to show his colors." (22 Nov. 1912, 15, 50)

HART, Mrs. Annette Lewis, wrote an article "Our Hebrew Orphans' Home" for the special women's issue (21 Nov. 1913, 16, 50-51)

HARTMANN, William A., of Winnipeg, a German Protestant, was converted to Judaism on May 14, 1909, in the presence of Rabbis A. Kahanovich, J.K. Levin and Rev. Saul Schaar (28 May 1909, 12, 24)

HASKELL, Mrs. Fredelle Wilner, reprint of her paper "Organized Communal Life Among the Jews", read before the Young People's Society of the Shaar Hashomayim Synagogue, Montreal (28 March 1913, 16, 16)

HEPPNER, Max, "the agent if the Ica, continues to visit regularly the three colonies of Hirsch, Oxbow and Qu'Appelle, while Rabbi Herman Abramowitz, of Montreal, inspected the schools and organized the religious services. Hirsch numbers 172 persons who cultivate 10, 240 acres of good land, which last year yielded crops valued at 22,000 dollars. A synagogue has been erected, and the teacher has arranged to visit the two schools of the colony, situated about six miles apart, twice a week, in order to give instruction in Hebrew and Biblical History. [sic] at Qu'Appelle, the largest of the Canadian colonies, there are 586 inhabitants spread over an area of 28,973 acres. The colony is not in a flourishing condition as a result of the ruin of their harvest in 1906. Education, too, is very backward, and the teacher sent out by the Ica has great difficulties to contend with. Oxbow and Bender have had a fairly satisfactory year and their condition is improving." This was reported in the JCA's annual report (10 Sept. 1909, 12, 39)

HEPPNER, Max, wrote a letter to the editor from Regina, Sask., Sept. 3, 1909, on the Sunday law in the west (1 Oct. 1909, 12, 42)

HOLDENGRABER, Jacob (Annex), Raya Goldman, Matie Schaffer (Esplanade Ave.), and Bella Segal, all of Montreal, are new members of the Young Israel Children's League (4 April 1913, 16, 17)

JACOBS, Alex. Claude, in a letter to the editor writes "As an Englishman and a member of the Jewish faith, I wish to protest against the way poor emigrants from Russia of our religion are grossly neglected by Jews of this city. I happened to be at the C.P. Rly. Station (in Montreal) this evening with a fellow Englishman and we were absolutely disgusted to witness a party of Russo-Jewish emigrants outside the station without a local member of our faith to give these birds of passage a word of advice or help. As you are aware these people can only speak Yiddish, and being ignorant of this language, I was unable to assist them...I believe this city boasts of many rich Jewish people who have made their money within the last few years and surely they support some institution to give these poor pilgrims a helping hand and advise them how to proceed on their weary way to various parts of this great country of Canada." The editor states the C.P.R. employs a Yiddish interpreter who directs immigrants and where necessary refers them to the Montreal Baron de Hirsch Institute (1 June 1911, 14, 29)

JACOBS, Rabbi S., of Holy Blossom Synagogue, Toronto, gave an interview to The Canadian Jewish Times about his recent trip to Europe and Jewish life there (30 Aug. 1912, 15, 38)

JACOBS, S.W., addressed the Young People's Society of the Shaar Hashomayim Synagogue Thurs. evening last week on "The Trail of the Jewish Emigrant". According to Mr. Jacobs there 1,408 Jewish farmers in various colonies sponsored by the Jewish Colonization Association. Miss

Leonore Freedman gave a reading and Miss Jennie Stanley performed several piano solos that evening (7 March 1913, 16, 13)

JACOBS, S.W. and Harry Gordon, both of Montreal, wrote letters to the editor in favor of establishing a Kehilah in Montreal (30 Aug. 1912, 15, 38)

JACOBS, S.W., in the Quebec Recorder's Court, successfully defended several Jewish bakers, Messrs. Richstone, Schachter and Jacobson, whose van drivers were charged with illegally delivering bread on Sun. Dec. 19, 1909. Rabbi Hirsch Cohen testified to the court about the inability of Jewish bakers to carry on business, if the right to deliver bread on Sun. was taken from them. "He stated that for many years Sunday delivery was the custom among Jews, and this was recognized by the authorities, who in no way interfered with the trade until recently (24 Dec. 1909, 13, 6)

JACOBS, S.W., of Montreal, encloses an exchange of correspondence he had with Henri Bourassa publisher of Le Devoir in which Mr. Jacobs rebuked M. Bourassa for the publication of an anti-Semitic article which appeared in that paper relating to the conviction of Max Adelson for selling spruce beer unfit for human consumption (2 Oct. 1912, 15, 43)

JACOBS, S.W., wrote an article "How the Jewish Times was Started" in response to a request from Leon Goldman and Max Sanders, the publishers of The Canadian Jewish Times for the fifteenth anniversary issue (13 Dec. 1912, 16, 1)

JASSKY, A.H., Harry Joseph (Vancouver), J.G. Eliasoph (Quebec City), Joseph Cohen, Rosa Klein, Hattie Lazarus, Joseph Leavitt, David Louis Mendel and Benjamin Silver have passed their matriculation examinations and will enter McGill University as undergraduates (16 July 1909, 12, 31)

JOSEPH, Montefiore, of Quebec City, was examined by S.W. Jacobs during the Quebec libel case on May 20, 1913 in the Superior Court, Quebec City. In the printed transcript Mr. Joseph stated that he was born and had lived in Quebec City all his life (13 June 1913, 16, 27)

JOSPE, J., secretary of the Zionist Bureau in Montreal, wrote a letter to the editor, 18 Ab, 5672 concerning the work of the organization in promoting Zionism across the country (9 Aug. 1912, 15, 35)

KAHANOVITCH, Fred, of Winnipeg; Lawrence Cossman, of North Sydney, N.S.; and Dora Mishkin, of Montreal, are new members of the Young Israel Children's League (14 March 1913, 16, 14)

KAHANOVITCH, Miss Sophie, of Winnipeg, is a new member of the Young Israel Children's League (4 July 1913, 16, 30)

KANOVITZ, Rabbi Joseph, Professor of Theology and head of the Jewish Theological Seminary of Safed, Palestine, is in Montreal on a fund-raising tour. Montrealers who have contributed are: Hiram Levy, J.W. Jacobs, B. Gardner, H. Wener, H. Kellert, Max Goldberg, M. Tannenbaum, J. Ettenberg, John J. Weinfeld, S. Miller, D. Pepon, J. Elkin, A. Levin, B. Rubin, I.S. Goldenstein, M. Michalson, Harry Freedman, H. Caplan, J. Roston, William Albert, A. Rudolph, P. Goldenberg, J. Cohen, Jacob Garmaise, A. Poyaner, F. Ship, Maurice Ryan, A.H. Jackson, M. Albert, L. Teplitzky, L. Lefkovitz, J. Diamond, S. Ballon, J. Finestone, L. Holstein, N. Silver, I. Workman, A.I. Rubinovich, S. Kolber, Jacob Manolson, L. Abinovitch, P. Goldstein, William Abinovitch, Harris Vineberg, T.H. Livingstone, Samuel Wener, Max Vineberg, M.L. Morris, A.L. Gittleson, M. Rapp, I. Grossman, H. Albert, D.S. Shapiro, J.L. Gittleson, L. Mazer, J. Usher, M. Diamond, Jacob Idder, Israel Goldberg, I.J. Levenhof, M. Lesser, H. Steinberg, S. Strean, L. Friedman, K. Goldberg, I. Berson, Mrs. Raphelowitz, Max Vineberg, S.L. Routten, I. Bowitch, I.N. Salaman, L. Taplitch, A. Garmaise, Solomon Greenspoon, M. Baile, M. Zakan, Elias Goldfine, N.H. Person, I. Brodsky, E.E. Cohen, M. Geffen, Moses Morris, B. Cooper, E. Brown, M. Shiner and Mrs. Cooper (26 March 1909, 12, 15)

KAPLAN, Miss Blanche Lillian, twelve year old daughter of Rabbi and Mrs. Bernard M. Kaplan (former rabbi of Montreal's Shaar Hashomayim Synagogue and now of San Francisco) is considered a musical protege (31 Dec. 1909, 13, 7)

KAUFFMAN, Officer, of the Montreal police force, is seeking Thomas Morris, a Jewish negro, charged with having committed a serious offence in New York. "The communication received states that Morris is a full-blooded negro...and that he speaks no other tongue except Yiddish. Officer Kauffman after ransacking the seventh and eighth wards has failed to find any trace of this black-faced Israelite." (8 Jan. 1909, 12, 4)

KELLERT, Raphael and his brothers Michael and Charles, of Montreal, have played as soloists and as trios in Paris. Their musical accomplishments have "...won for them the well-merited applause and appreciation of both Parisian music lovers and critics." (14 Jan. 1910, 13, 9)

LANDE, Isaac, of Montreal, wrote a letter to the editor expressing approval for the organization of a Kehilah in Montreal (6 Sept. 1912, 15, 39)

LANDMAN, Rabbi Isaac, formerly of Montreal, was re-elected assistant rabbi of Keneseth Israel Congregation, of Philadelphia (22 Jan. 1909, 12, 6)

LAVUT, Menasseh, merchant; Joseph Levinoff, butcher; Louis Glazer, tailor; Max Bessner, butcher; David Berlin, tailor; Max Margolis, tailor; Samuel Kabalotsky, watchmaker; Simon Albert, grocer; Hirsch Stern, teacher; and Isaac Lavut, merchant; all of Montreal, will apply to the Quebec Legislature to incorporate "Congregation Nusach Hoaari" (11 March 1910, 13, 17)

LEFSON, Mr., Leduc Lane, Montreal, was attacked last Sat. evening between 5 and 7, on St. Lawrence Blvd. between De Montigny and Ontario St. It was..."the scene of a sharp conflict between some of our people and a number of mis-guided French-Canadians. For some time, the conditions of the affair resembled those of a miniature riot; and, as usual, at first the policemen were conspicuous by their absence. According to the accounts of trustworthy witnesses, the trouble originated through the cowardly action of two French-Canadians, who went so far as to grossly insult one of our people by plucking his beard and throwing him on the pavement. Some friends who were passing went to the rescue of the injured party, named Lefson,...At this juncture, an Ontario street car passed and three more French-Canadians, seeing the fight between their friends, jumped out of the car and joined in the melee. The mob assumed such proportions that in the heat of the battle many innocent persons were struck. By the time the constables arrived, the crowd was unmanageable. One constable, to disperse the crowd, drew a revolver, but this had no effect. As a result of this, it is stated, a woman had two front teeth knocked out, and others also received blows. St. Lawrence street was packed with people from one side of the street to the other, blocking cars and vehicles completely...From beginning to end the trouble lasted almost two hours. It was some time before the police could reach the source of the fight, and by the time they did get there it is said that those responsible for the outbreak made good their escape. Order was not restored until seven o'clock. The police... were called out no less than three times to subdue several small combats that were waged between the Jews and their antagonists...We understand that an organization is contemplated, with the object, if possible, of preventing a recurrence of such an outbreak, and steps are being taken to have the understanding in working order at an early date." (27 Aug. 1909, 12, 37)

LEO, J.S., of Montreal, was elected president of the Canadian Chess Association. He is also president of the Westmount Club. Mr. Leo's father was also a noted chess player. J.S. Leo played with Steinitz at the Jewish Workingman's Club in London, England, in the late seventies (22 Jan. 1909, 12, 6)

LESSER, Bennie, Zave Levinson, Dave Fraid, Herman Cohen, Max Cohen Hessie Cohen and Lenard Abrams are members of the Montefiore hockey team, Montreal. They played against the Primrose team last Sat. night. Harry Levinson was the referee and Harry Vineberg was the judge of play (22 Jan. 1909, 12, 6)

LEVENSON, Dr. A., wrote an article "Achad Ha'am the Man" (2 Oct. 1912, 15, 43)

LEVENSON, Dr. A., wrote an article "Achad Ha'am and His Philosophy" for in two parts (6 Sept. 1912, 15, 39)

LEVERENZ, Otto, S. Holdengraber, David Rothschild, Morris Taylor and Peter Usher, all of Montreal, and Mamie Block, of Charlottetown, P.E.I., are new members of the Young Israel Children's League (20 June 1913, 16, 28)

LEVIN, Rabbi J.K., of Shaarey Shomayim Synagogue, Winnipeg: his article "Judaism and Work" (14 May 1909, 12, 22)

LEVITT, Rev., of Halifax, was acquitted of causing unnecessary cruelty to animals by slaughtering them according to Shechita (4 July 1913, 16, 30)

LEWIS, A.P., of Toronto, wrote an article "Is the Citizen of the Central District of Toronto an Intelligent Voter?" (28 March 1913, 16, 16)

LIGHTSTONE, B., passed first year practical dentistry with honors at McGill University School of Dentistry. Other McGill students that passed were: Maxwell Gold, physics and bacteriology; Second Year - A.M. Aronson, in all subjects; A. Glickman and B. Lightstone, in anatomy. Third

Year - A.M. Aronson, with honors on orthodontia, metallurgy and dental pathology; A. Glickman, bacteriology (4 June 1909, 12, 25)

LIPSEY, Joseph, Science II, McGill University, Montreal, obtained first class standing (22 Jan. 1909, 12, 6)

LIPSKY, Louis, wrote an article "The Jewish Year 5673 - A Review" (1 Oct. 1913, 16, 42-43)

LIPSKY, Louis, wrote an article "The Next Step in Zionism" for the Passover issue (18 April 1913, 16, 19)

LITNER, Myer, who was a resident of Montreal up till two weeks ago, has disappeared. In July 1909, he left his wife and seven children, the eldest being a boy, age 15, and the youngest a girl, age 2. "Previous to this, however, he was living with a woman in the city and it was discovered that he eloped with her. Shortly after that his whereabouts was found and on him being charged in court with non-support of his wife and children he was sentenced to contribute toward their support $25 per month. This, he did for some four or five months when he again eloped with the same woman. He is a furrier by trade and is posssesed of a little means. The photograph reproduced herewith is a good likeness of the man and any information of him through the office of the Jewish Times will be gratefully appreciated by the deserted wife. It is believed that he is either in Toronto or Hamilton." (29 July 1910, 13, 37)

LITTNER, Myer, was caught by the police in Toronto and is being held by the detective department. The Canadian Jewish Times was instrumental in bringing the wife-deserter to justice. The paper received the following telegram: "Have got Mr. Littner who you were looking for in your last paper, in detective department. Wants wife's address. Answer quick." (12 Aug. 1910, 13, 39)

LIVINGSTONE, Jennie F., wrote an article "Jewish Women's League for Cultural Work in Palestine" for the special women's issue (21 Nov. 1913, 16, 50-51)

MAGNES, J.L., chairman of the New York Kehillah, wrote a letter to the editor in answer to a request from The Canadian Jewish Times about the aims and objectives of the Kehillah movement in North America (17 Jan. 1913, 16, 6)

MARGOLESE, Louis S., of Montreal, in the absence of S.W. Jacobs, K.C., is representing H. Wolofsky and the proprietors of The Jewish Eagle, in connection with the rule for contempt of court applied for by Rabbi Simon Glazer (30 June 1911, 14, 33)

MATOFF, Michael, the Russian violinist, will be the soloist at the annual concert of the Cornwall Philharmonic Society, today (23 April 1909, 12, 19)

MATOFF, Michael, will give a recital in Windsor Hall under the patronage of the Mayor of Montreal on Jan. 26, 1910 (14 Jan. 1910, 13, 9)

MENDELS, J.H., heads the list of councillors at the recent municipal elections in Perth, Ont. Mr. Mendels is the son of the late M. Mendels, of Perth. Mr. Mendels had previously served on council. "He was avert to being a candidate again, but his requisition was so unanimously signed that it was difficult for him to refuse to accede to their wishes." (13 Jan. 1911, 14, 9)

MENDELSOHN, Mrs. R.M., wrote a letter to the Woman's Page supporting the Equal Suffrage platform. It "...stands for reform in every possible way, such as Abolition of Child Labor, Abolition of White Slavery, and urging every possible reform in the present system. I must say, in conclusion, that every sensible man and woman should uphold the great world wide movement, and advocate it in every possible [way] as one step in the advance of social betterment." (3 Jan. 1913, 16, 4)

MILLER, A. (grade two-Academy); W. Herman and Mert Jacobs (grade three-model A.); Mildred Blout (grade three model G.); Adolphe Mishkin (grade two-model B.) are students at Westmount Academy who passed the Quebec examination (27 Aug. 1909, 12, 37)

MINKIN, Fanny T., wrote an article "Arrested Development of the Jewish Woman" for the special women's issue (21 Nov. 1913, 16, 50-51)

MINKIN, Mrs. Jacob S., of Hamilton, will be in charge of the "Woman's page in The Canadian Jewish Times (16 May 1913, 16, 23)

MINKIN, Rabbi Jacob S. (M.A.), wrote an article "War" (5 July 1912, 15, 30)

MINKIN, Rabbi Jacob S., (M.A.) wrote an article "The Jew in Modern Literature" in three parts for the paper (23 Aug. 1912, 15, 37)

MINKIN, Rabbi Jacob S., gave an interview to the Hamilton Herald speaking out against the dangers of intermarriage (7 Feb. 1913, 16, 9)

MINKIN, Rabbi Jacob S., of Hamilton, Ont., wrote an article "The Aim of Judaism" (14 June 1912, 15, 27)

MINKIN, Rabbi Jacob S., wrote an article "Israel the Superman of History" (2 oct. 1912, 15, 43)

MINKIN, Rabbi Jacob S., wrote an article "The Vision of the Rainbow" (1 Nov. 1912, 15, 47)

MINKIN, Rabbi Jacob S., wrote an article "A Review of the Year 5672" (20 Sept. 1912, 15, 41)

MINKIN, Rabbi Jacob S., wrote an article "Problems of German Jewry" part one "The Social Problem" (15 Nov. 1912, 15, 49)

MINKIN, Rabbi Jacob S., wrote an article "Problems of German Jewry" part two "The Problem of Conversion" (13 Dec. 1912, 16, 1)

MINKIN, Rabbi Jacob S., wrote an article "Liberal Judaism" (6 Dec. 1912, 15, 52)

MINTZ, Moses, of Montreal, was the subject of an unflattering article in the Montreal Herald, Aug. 21, 1913. "While it is of no great importance, yet the spirit of the item is rather to ridicule than to give a fair account." The Canadian Jewish Times launched a campaign against the prejudiced treatment of Jews in the Canadian press (29 Aug. 1913, 16, 38)

MITNIK, L., manager of several Yiddish theatrical companies in Montreal, wants to establish a permanent Yiddish theatre there. "Mr. Mitnik has interested a member of our local coreligionists, and a lot of ground on St. Lawrence Boulevard, just above Ontario St. has been selected. If plans do not miscarry, building operations will commence at once, and Mr. Mitnik hopes that before long Montreal Jewry will have a theatre of its own which will accomodate 700 people." (21 May 1909, 12, 23)

MYERSON, Moses, Jacob Yaphe, Harry Silverman, Harry Budyk, William Mazur, Sarah K. Talpis, Jennie Weinstein, Sarah Valinsky and Beatrice Morris (Jan. graduates) have been awarded commissioner's scholarships for free tuition for four years in the Montreal Protestant high schools, based on final exams held in Jan. 1909 (9 July 1909, 12, 30)

NATHANSON, Joseph, of Sydney, N.S., wrote a letter to the editor, Nov. 12, 1912, denying the contents of "... a letter from a Mr. 'J. Berman' complaining that an 'At Home,' held under the auspices of the 'Glace Bay Zionist Society,' at which occasion the Jewish youth of that town danced with their 'Gentile Girls' and the Jewish girls were not noticed...". Referring to Mr. Berman's letter, he asks: "Is that right? Is this the way to uplift Zionism?" (22 Nov. 1912, 15, 50)

NERVICH, Hyman P., of Montreal, editor of The Canadian Jewish Tribune, has been appointed managing editor of The Canadian Jewish Times. The Tribune was in existence for seven months and published its last issue on Dec. 25, 1908 (8 Jan. 1909, 12, 4)

NEWMAN, Mrs. J.N., wrote an article "Hebrew Children's Fresh Air Fund" (21 Nov. 1913, 16, 50-51)

OBER, Louis, 193 Mance St., Montreal, wrote a letter to the editor, Feb. 2, 1911 about two children who were prevented from being reunited with their mother. The children were detained at the U.S. border and returned to Montreal. The mother, who was living in New York, had sent a messenger to take them across the border. "If your readers will consider that the "mother" referred to is an

---

Telephones: Main 7287 and East 5410

J. N. Neumann
General Insurance
Established 1898
Special Agent for
Mutual Life Ins. Co. of New York.
North British and Mercantile Ins. Co.

Room 512 Transportation Building

immoral woman, who has been arrested here in Montreal for keeping disorderly houses, that the "messenger" she sent to Montreal for the purpose of bringing her children to her is alleged to be one of that highly undesirable class of persons who live on the proceeds of the prostitution of the women under their control...I think there will be very little hard feeling against the Immigration officials for their action in returning the children to Montreal instead of allowing them to proceed to their destination." (3 Feb. 1911, 14, 12)

OSOWSKY, Miss Judith, is the first child from Winnipeg to join the Young Israel Children's League (17 Jan. 1913, 16, 6)

PHILLIPS, Lazarus, Solomon Rinkof, Mary Valinsky, Rachel Kishner and Esther Issen (June graduates) have been awarded commissioner's scholarships for free tuition for four years in the Montreal Protestant high schools, based on final exams held in June 1909 (9 July 1909, 12, 30)

PIERCE, Charles, merchant, Isaac Kremeor Pierce, accountant and Nathan Tobias, capitalist, incorporated C. Pierce & Company Ltd. (12 Nov. 1909, 12, 48)

RAM, B., a Montreal grocer, lost a case for damages against the Boston & Maine R.R. "The plaintiff, in the winter of 1910, ordered a quantity of Passover rum from a Boston firm which was intended for sale for the Passover season. Owing to the neglect of the Railway Company's officials, the car containing the rum was side-tracked on the line for many weeks and the goods did not arrive in Montreal until after the Pesach holidays. Mr. Ram claimed for the profit which he would have made on the sale of the rum...". In his judgment the judge remarked "...that the Boston & Maine R.R. could scarcely know that Moses commanded the children of Israel to drink rum on the Passover and that in the failure of the plaintiff to notify the company as to when the goods were intended for the company should not be held liable." (30 June 1911, 14, 33)

RASKIN, P.M., wrote a poem "The Feast of Weeks" (6 June 1913, 16, 26)

RASKIN, P.M., wrote a poem "Two Angels - A Talmudic Legend" (7 Feb. 1913, 16, 9)

RESSLER, Lillian, wrote an article "Men and Women" for the Woman's Column (7 Nov. 1913, 16, 48)

ROBACK, Abraham A., of Montreal, wrote an article "Orthodoxy - A Movement?" (28 June 1912, 15, 29)

ROBACK, Abraham A., of Montreal, wrote an article "Yiddish or Assimilation" (21 June 1912, 15, 28)

ROBACK, Abraham A., wrote an article "Is Montreal destined to be a Jewish Centre?" (2 Aug. 1912, 15, 34)

ROSE, Bernard, has passed his first and second year law exams at Laval University (4 June 1909, 12, 25)

ROSE, Miriam D., wrote a letter to the editor in favor of suffrage for women. "The majority of women are now forging to the front every day and making a place for themselves. Look about in every direction and you will observe women holding executive positions of responsibility." (17 Jan. 1913, 16, 6)

ROSENBAUM, J.J. and J. Segal passed first year medicine at McGill University (4 June 1909, 12, 25)

ROSENBERGER, M., of Montreal, wrote a letter to the editor, March 29, 1910, attacking the Yiddish language (1 April 1910, 13, 20)

ROSENBERGER, Mr., of Montreal, and his supporters have formed a Vigilance Committee in response to the assault of a Jew (Mr. Lefson) on St. Lawrence Blvd., in Montreal last Sat. night. Lyon Cohen, who was interviewed on the matter, said, "I would be very sorry to see any vigilance committee of any kind formed to look after Jewish interests in Montreal, where we are under the British flag, the symbol of Justice, Liberty and Freedom. The majority of responsible and influential Jews in this city will never countenance Mr. Rosenberger's move. I prefer to believe that the attacks on Jews do not indicate any feeling of hatred between the French population and ourselves, but are perpetrated by a few irresponsible rowdies. I consider the arrest of three Jews and no others on Saturday simply a coincidence, and I will have to be possessed of far more evidence than that before believing that there is any intention on the part of the police force to discriminate against our race. I am a believer in peaceful and sensible methods; and you will see that all the important Jewish organizations of the city will frown upon this attempt to form a vigilance committee, which would only serve to fan the slight trouble into fierce race riots." (27 Aug. 1909, 12, 37)

ROSENFELD, Morris, the well-known Yiddish poet, will give a reading in the Baron de Hirsch Auditorium, on Sun. evening March 7, 1909 (12 Feb. 1909, 12, 9)

ROTHSCHILD, David, and Geraldine Rothschild, of Westmount, Que., and Annie Klein, of Montreal have joined the Young Israel Children's League (10 Jan. 1913, 16, 5)

ROTHSCHILD, E. (Westmount, Que.), Bertha Segal (Levis, Que.), and Tessie Soskin (Toronto), are children who have written to "Uncle Jacob" of the "Home Page" (3 Jan. 1913, 16, 4)

RUBENSTEIN, Moses and Elias Mauer, both of Montreal, were inscribed in the JNF Golden Book (15 April 1910, 13, 22)

RUBIN, M., 333 St. Louis St., Montreal, wrote a letter to the editor about an article which appeared in The Canadian Eagle about the Baron de Hirsch Institute (18 Oct. 1910, 13, 49)

RYAN, Capt. Carrol, has retired as editor of The Jewish Times. He joined the paper from its inception eleven years ago. "His services to Canadian Jewry will never be forgotten." (15 Jan. 1909, 12, 5)

SABBATH, J.L., donor of the J.L. Sabbath trophy of the Montefiore Hockey Club, Montreal, presented the silver cup last week to the Primrose Club which won all of the six games played. Team members are:- Ed. Workman, captain; Harry Levinson, manager; "Doc" Jacobs, Samuel Jacobs, Lyon Levinson, Richard Michaelson, Leo Livingstone, Ed. Goldstein, Nat. Holstein and George Blumenthal (11 March 1910, 13, 17)

SABBATH, J.L., has donated a silver cup trophy for what is believed to be the first Jewish hockey league in' Canada. The League, located in Montreal, is composed of the following five clubs:- Young Men's Zionist and Literary Society; Beaconsfield Club, formerly the Boys' Athletic Club; Primrose Club; and the Eureka Club. League officers are:- J.L. Sabbath, hon. president; Harry Davidovitch (Beaconsfield), president; J. Cohen (Young Men's Zionist and Literary), 1st vice-president; L. Kert (Eureka), 2nd vice-president; S. Jacobs (Primrose), secretary; H. Levinson (Primrose), treasurer (24 Dec. 1909, 13, 6)

SALOMON, M., wrote a letter to the editor about the disqualification of Jewish voters in the Montreal St. Louis Ward (21 Feb. 1913, 16, 11)

SAMUELS, Rose, 80 Lilly St., Winnipeg, formerly of Montreal, wrote a letter to the editor about an offensive joke "...in reference to a Jewish rabbi and an Irishman..." directed against the Jewish people which was told in a local theatre (20 June 1913, 16, 28)

SANDERS, Max, is the new manager and publisher of The Canadian Jewish Times. "I realize that the publication of which I am taking charge is now at a very low ebb. It does not command the respect of the community such as the only Jewish English people (sic.) in this country, it should command. Mismanagement in the editorial as well as in the business department is responsible for this condition. However, I am confident that before very long this paper will be pulled out of the rut into which it had sunk, and will be converted into a journal worthy of reaching every Jewish home in the Dominion." (7 June 1912, 15, 26)

SCHALIT, A.L., Jewish Colonization Association representative, who spent seven months touring the Jewish farm colonies in Canada, gave an interview on "The Jewish Farmer" (21 Jan. 1910, 13, 10)

SCHEUER, Edmund, 88-90 Yonge St., Toronto, wrote a letter June 17, 1912, to Max Sanders wishing him success and stating "...that with a Jewish population of 100,000 in Canada to-day I do not see why your publication could not be made a paying venture." (21 June 1912, 15, 28)

SCHNAIER, S., presided at a memorial meeting on Sun. in the BdeHI, Montreal, for the playwright, Jacob Gordin, of New York. Others on the platform were: Leon Goldman, L. Landau and L. Elstein (18 June 1909, 12, 27)

SEGAL, Mendle, Billy Ram, and Moses Signer, of Montreal; and Bertha Boyaner, of St. John, N.B., are new members of the Young Israel Children's League (28 March 1913, 16, 16)

SHAFFET, Conan, 25 S. Prospect St., Akron, Ohio, wrote a letter to the editor about Rabbi Jacob S. Minkin's article "Colors of the Rainbow" (15 Nov. 1912, 15, 49)

SHANE, Mary, of Brookville Station, St. John, N.B., is a new member of the Young Israel Children's League (2 May 1913, 16, 21)

SHULMAN, J., of Toronto, wrote a letter to the editor Sept. 29, 1912 supporting the building of a gymansium for the Jewish youth of Toronto. "At present, if a Jew wishes to obtain the benefits of a gymnasium he must join a Christian Association, where half of his fees will be spent in carrying on missionary or other religious work. If the Jews of this city had a Y.M.H.A. somewhat on the lines of the Y.M.C.A. this energy would be spent in furthering Jewish causes instead of Christian ones. It is really a disgrace that a Jew, if he wishes to engage in athletics, should have to join an association one of whose main objectives is to further the Christian religion." (2 Oct. 1912, 15, 43)

SILVER, Benjamin (sixth on the list with 795 marks out of 900 possible), Rosa Klein, David Louis Mendel, Rebecca Echenberg, Joseph Leavitt, Joseph Cohen, Sheppard Shapiro, Annie Samuels, Hattie Lazarus and Abraham Weinfield have obtained their School Leaving Certificates issued by the Quebec Education Dept. (16 July 1909, 12, 31)

SILVER, Lazarus Pheneas, mining engineer, incorporated Silver & Lipman Import Company Ltd. (12 Nov. 1909, 12, 48)

SINGER, M.J., has graduated with honors from the University of Toronto School of Pharmacy. Other graduates were A.B. Hashmal, B.A., and M. Isaacs, of Montreal (4 June 1909, 12, 25)

SOLOMON, Hyman, of Montreal, sent his essay on "Don Isaac Abarbanel" written in Yiddish to "Uncle Jacob" of the Home Page (16 May 1913, 16, 23)

SOSKIN, Miss Tessie, of Toronto, wrote "Our Story: A Sea-side Adventure" for the Home Page (1 Nov. 1912, 15, 47)

SPERBER, Marcus M., announced a change in ownership and management of The Canadian Jewish Times in the editorial (10 Nov. 1911, 14, 52)

STARK, R. and E. Mauer, McGill science students, enrolled in a military course last year and have now obtained their commission in the Canadian militia. They will join the militia in Quebec City (2 July 1909, 12, 29)

STEINE, M.B. and M. Markus, two members of the Council of the Federation of Zionist Societies of Canada, recently visited the world Zionist movement headquarters in Cologne, Germany, where they were cordially received by Herr Wolffsohn, head of the Zionist movement. They had received letters of introduction from Clarence I. de Sola, president of the Canadian Federation. It was announced that Herr Wolffsohn will visit Canada next Oct. and will be the guest of Mr. de Sola while in Montreal (25 Feb. 1910, 13, 15)

STEINE, M.B., of Montreal, presently in Swift Current, Sask., wrote a letter to the editor, Aug. 24, 1912, urging The Canadian Jewish Times to increase its circulation to the Jewish community outside of Montreal (6 Sept. 1912, 15, 39)

STEINE, M.B., of Montreal, wrote a letter to the editor of The Canadian Jewish Times attacking the paper for not doing more in the Halifax Shechita case. "It was the solemn duty of your paper to know of the calibre, the size and the influence of the Halifax community. It was your duty to know what is to be done without waiting for a continuous invitation from the Baron de Hirsch Institute Legislative Committee. It is the duty of the "Jewish Times," the only English speaking Jewish paper in this great Dominion to know where we are attacked and to have us prepared to ward off the blow. We have no Kehillah, we have no institution whatever to unite us in time of peril, we are like a vessel broken in a thousand fragments, and open to be attacked by every vagabond, and it should be the duty of the Jewish press to give the warning. Your paper ought at all times to be the centre of our camp, the watchman in the tower, the bugle call, the means of bringing us together man to man, shoulder to shoulder to defend a common cause." (13 June 1913, 16, 27)

STEINE, M.B., wrote a letter to the editor asking the Montreal Jewish community to support the campaign for the Hebrew Sheltering Home on St. Urbain St at Evans St. Membership subscriptions can be sent to:- A. Berman, of Berman Bros., treasurer, Blumenthal Bldg.; Henry Bye, finance secretary, 30 Hospital St.; H. Sourkes c/o the Home, 16 Evans St.; or M.B. Steine, 502 St. Paul St. (2 Aug. 1912, 15, 34)

STEINE, M.B., wrote a letter to the editor, urging the formation of an independent federation of Jewish charities in Montreal with delegates from every society on its managing board. "A Kehillah can follow later on similar lines." He pointed out that the Baron de Hirsch Institute is just one of several charitable organizations doing good work in Montreal (17 Jan. 1913, 16, 6)

STERN, Dr. Joseph, of Montreal, chaired the Morris Rosenfeld poetry reading in the Baron de Hirsch Auditorium. Among those taking part in the program were: Miss M. Gorfinkle, pianoforte solo; Miss J. Blout, violin solo; Miss R. Bloch, recitation; and Miss B. Kellert, vocal solo. Harris Vineberg moved the vote of thanks, seconded by Maxwell Goldstein, K.C. (19 March 1909, 12, 14)

STERN, Dr., presided at the Sholom Aleichem benefit evening given in the BdeHI, Montreal, last Sun. About five hundred people attended and $50.00 was raised. Others participating were: Rabbis Herman Abramowitz and Hirsch Cohen and Messrs. Schnaier, Yampolsky, Leon Goldman and Goldstein (22 Jan. 1909, 12, 6)

STERN, Joseph, wrote a letter to the editor condemning S.W. Jacobs for his harsh treatment of M. Bourassa, publisher of Le Devoir over the publication of an anti-semitic article in that paper. "As it is, this unfortunate correspondence only aggravated matters and left relations in a worse state of hate than before." (11 Oct. 1912, 15, 44)

TALPIS, S., of Montreal, wrote a letter to the editor, Jan. 20, 1913, calling attention to the first literary concert of the local Hebrew Speaking Circle on Feb. 2, 1913 at 8.30 p.m. (24 Jan. 1913, 16, 7)

TALPIS, S., of Montreal, wrote a letter to the editor, March 18, 1913, expressing his surprise to learn that the notorious anti-Semite, Prof. Goldwin Smith, was a contributor to the Holy Blossom Synagogue building fund, according to S.J. Birnbaum's article "History of Jews in Toronto" (14 March 1913, 16, 15)

TALPIS, S., wrote a letter to the editor advising fellow Jews in Montreal to check their tax assessment record to ensure their taxes are being paid to the Protestant Board. "Recently I went to the City Hall to pay some real estate taxes, and looking over the assessment records of St. Louis Ward, I found myself, as well as a number of other co-religionists, classed as Catholics, whose school tax goes entirely to Panel No. 1, which is the Catholic School Board." (3 March 1911, 14, 16)

TALPIS, S., wrote an article "Passover Reflections" (10 April 1914, 17, 15)

TALPIS, S., wrote an article "The Season of Freedom" for the Passover issue (18 April 1913, 16, 19)

TANNENBAUM, David, of Montreal, has graduated in medicine from McGill University. He graduated high school and entered McGill six years ago. He received his B.A. degree four years ago (4 June 1909, 12, 25)

TAYLOR, Morris, of Toronto, and David Cecil Roth, of Montreal, are first prize winners in "Uncle Jacob's" essay contest. Second prizes were won by Solomon Holdengraber and Raya E. Goldman, both of Montreal. Peter Usher, of Montreal won third prize. Honorable mentions went to Cecil Usher, of Montreal, and Fred Kahanovitch, of Winnipeg (9 May 1913, 16, 22)

TAYLOR, Morris, of Toronto, sent his essay on Benjamin D'Israeli to "Uncle Jacob" of the Home Page, (2 May 1913, 16, 21)

TIPOGRAPH, M., is chairman of the committee organizing the Sholem Ash lecture in Montreal, on Sun. April 10, 1910 (1 April 1910, 13, 20)

TOLZERS, A.W., of Montreal, wrote a letter to the editor, Nov. 22, 1910, about the Jewish communities in Western Canada which he visited on a recent trip representing the Yeshivay "Torah Vodaath" (25 Nov. 1910, 14, 2)

VEXLER, Miss Fannie, of Fort Worth, Texas, is a new member of the Young Israel Children's League (29 Aug. 1913, 16, 38)

VINEBERG, Abel: his article "How the Toronto Jew regards his fellow Christian" (14 May 1909, 12, 22)

VINEBERG, Harris, 598 Argyle Ave., Montreal, has received much support for his letter to the editor of the Montreal Gazette which appeared on Feb. 6, 1909, in support of the Bickerdike Bill (19 Feb. 1909, 12, 10)

VINEBERG, Harris and Rabbi Hirsch Cohen wrote letters to the editor in favor of establishing a Kehilah in Montreal (16 Aug. 1912. 15, 36)

VINER, J., a McGill University student, wrote a letter to the editor complaining that young Jewish men who are not McGill students are attending student functions (22 Oct. 1913, 16, 46)

VOLANSKY, M., of Saskatoon, wrote a letter to the editor, Nov. 19, 1912, asking the paper to announce that a YMHA was established in the city. "At any time any of our Jewish friends from the East are passing our way we will be only to pleased to have them drop in." (29 Nov. 1912, 15, 51)

WALDMAN, Joseph Hugo, manufacturer, a notice of incorporation of Waldman Exploration and Development Company (Ltd.) (8 Oct. 1909, 12, 42)

WEBBER, Louis, president of the Baron de Hirsch Hebrew Benevolent Society in Halifax, wrote a letter to the editor, June 2, 1913 asking the Montreal community for help in explaining

Shechita to the local county court. The case against Rev. Levitt for killing cattle in accordance with Jewish law goes to trial before the judge on June 10 (6 June 1913, 16, 26)

WEINFIELD, Andrew, represented the Dominion Soda Water Company, 347-349 St. Dominique St., Montreal, in a test case on Sunday trading. "It was argued by the counsel for the defendants that as the concern was wholly composed of Jews, they did not do any business from Friday at sundown until Saturday evening. In the prosecution, two witnesses, constables, testified to having seen a large waggon of the accused company, delivering cylinders of soda water on the day mentioned. For the defendants, Mr. Samuel Cohen, secretary of the Dominion Soda Water Company, testified that as the majority of their customers were owners of small refreshment restaurants, and as they had only small soda water tanks, they could not buy and keep enough soda water to tide them over from Friday night until Monday. It was also shown that all their customers were Jews, and that though they could deliver some of their soda water cylinders on Saturday evening after sundown, it was impossible to supply all their customers in that short space of time, and therefore they had to continue their delivery of cylinders on Sunday. The president of the Dominion Soda Water Company, Mr. Abraham Reudner, said that his factory was situated off the main street and did not disturb the public peace, and that his delivery wagon did not make any more noise than a cab." (15 Sept. 1909, 12, 40)

WISEMAN and Pine, two Montreal Jewish boys pretending to be homeless orphans, were found out by The Canadian Jewish Times. They live with their parents at 42 Bronsbin Lane and 207 St. Charles Borromee, respectively. "The boys are two young scamps, and have got beyond the reach of parental influence. The gentlemen who took them in hand, and clothed and fed them, were, undoubtedly, imbued with the highest motives, but their generosity has been sadly misplaced in this instance." (31 Dec. 1909, 13, 7)

WOLFE, Miss Theresa Frances, of Ottawa, is another young Jewish Canadian singer who is making a name for herself. Barely out of her teens, she sang in Carnegie Hall, New York on the evening of March 29, 1910. "Miss Wolfe possesses a soprano voice of a beautiful dramatic-lyric quality, which has been spendidly trained. Her rendition of the difficult aria "Wie Nahte Mir der Schlummer" from "Der Freischutz," by Weber, was very fine and showed to advantage the beauty and range of her voice." (8 April 1910, 13, 21)

ZACKS, Samuel, and Celia Zacks, of Kingston, Ont.; and Gertrude Rodin, 390 Flora Ave., Winnipeg, are new members of the Young Israel Children's League (7 Feb. 1913, 16, 9)

For Your New Home.

You should buy New Table Utensils, such as Cutlery, Cut Glass, Silverware, Etc., Etc.

If you are ready to buy any of these articles, we are prepared to give you Value for your Money.

Every article purchased from us is of the

   HIGHEST QUALITY.

The success of our business is Reasonable Prices.

A call at our establishment will convince you.

BLOOMFIELD BROS.
17 Notre Dame Street, West, MONTREAL
We have no Branches

PART TWO — GEOGRAPHICAL ENTRIES

ST. JOHN, NEW BRUNSWICK AND ST. JOHN'S, NEWFOUNDLAND

AMDUR, Mrs. B.L., Mrs. Ashkins, Isaac Baab, L. Boyaner, Louis Brager, Mrs. E. Budowitch, J. Budowitch (janitor), Myer Budowitch, L. Cohen, M. Cohen, S.K. Cohen, Miss Sadie Cohen, A. Druker, H. Gilbert, Miss J. Goldman, Minnie Goldman, Mrs. Tillie Goldman, J. Gordon, L. Green, A. Haines, A.S. Hart, R.T. Hayes, N. Holtzman, L. Hoorvitch, I. Isaacs, Sidney Isaacs, L.A. Kaplan, Louis Kominsky, W. Levi, J. Marcus, N. Meltzer, A. Michalson, F. Michalson, Miss F. Michalson, Miss Minnie Michalson, J. Perchanok, Miss Jennie Perchanok, A. Poyas, H. Robinson, Max Ross, M. Satzman, M. Shechter, J. Stekolsky and William Webber, all of St. John, NB, donated funds to the Bezalel School in Jerusalem, Palestine (26 Jan. 1912, 15, 11)

BENMOSCHE, Rev. H., of the Hebrew Immigration Society of St. John, NB, visited the Detention House to investigate the incident where five strong young men and one woman were sent back to England because they lacked the $25.00 required by law of every immigrant (4 April 1913, 16, 17)

GITTELSON, E.G., of St. John's, Nfld., was in Montreal visiting his parents and friends. While in Montreal, he spoke to The Canadian Jewish Times about the Jewish community in St. John's. "He informed us that there were about seventy-five Jewish souls in the city and surroundings; from all appearances doing very well. During the Holy Days services are held in a hall, and as they have a schochet, he comes in very handy on those days, especially as the Jewish population is so small. They have neither a school question nor any Sunday observance trouble." (26 Aug. 1910, 13, 41)

LEWIS, Sam D. and Mrs. Lewis Green are in charge of the Hazen Avenue Synagogue Sabbath School, St. John, NB, which held its Purim party recently. Miss Yetta Tanzman, a post biblical student, delivered the welcoming address. School staff members are:- Mrs. S.D. Lewis and the Misses Green, Seleg, Belle Amdur, Bessie Gilbert, Bessie Marcus and Golde Williams (4 April 1913, 16, 17)

POYES, L., is president of the Hebrew Immigration Society of St. John, NB. "As its name implies it deals with the Jewish immigrant. On his arrival they take him in hand and see him safely on the way to his destination. When the immigrant has any trouble with the immigration officer, it is this society that does all in its power to get him out of it, and in many other respects renders valuable service to the new arrival." Others on the executive are:- Mrs. Louis Green, vice-pres.; Mr. Isaacs, sec.; Louis Green, treas.; and Mrs. Hart (16 Dec. 1910, 14, 5)

Palestine Products

FOR PASSOVER

Palestine Wines and Cognacs are known the world over for their beneficial qualities, and I take much pleasure to announce that I have secured the sole Canadian agency of the INDEPENDENT WINE GROWERS in the colony "PETACH TIKWAH," and will sell their products at the following low prices:—

Sweet Wines

	Per Bottle	Per Dozen
Sherry	$ .85	$ 9.00
Port	.90	10.00
Alicante	1.00	11.00
Tokay	1.40	13.50
Malaga	1.50	14.00

White Wine

Sauterne	.65	7.00

Claret Wine

Medoc	.70	7.50

Cognacs

Fine Old	1.25	13.50
Very Old	1.50	16.50

I have also a full line of Hungarian, Russian, and Californian Brandies and Wines, such as:

Hungarian Shlivovitz	$1.10	$10.50
California Grape Brandy	1.00	10.00
Vishnick (Cherry Brandy)	.95	9.50
Peach Brandy and Apricot Brandy	.95	9.50

Lipsky's or Yaffa's Russian Spirits.

60% Sykes 120 proof		$1.00
70% 120		1.10
80% 145		1.20
90% 160		1.40

NOTE.—The above goods are sold by the best dealers in Toronto, Winnipeg, Ottawa, Quebec, Calgary, Fort William, and Vancouver.

S·L·Nathanson

MAIN STORE:
1072 St. Lawrence Boulevard.

BRANCHES:
18 Ontario St. East.   21 Demontigny Wes
MONTREAL, Que.

NOVA SCOTIA

ABRAMOWITZ, Rev. J., the chazzan in Glace Bay, was elected president of the Glace Bay Zionist Society at the monthly meeting on Sun. April 13, 1913. Other officers elected were:- M. Mendelson, vice-pres.; Abe Schniderman, treas.; S. Goorovitz, rec. sec.; and B. Hamburg, fin. sec. (18 April 1913, 16, 19)

ADLER, Messrs. and Anchel, Abraham I. Cohen, Isidore Cohen, Nathan Cohen, Isaac Smofsky, Isaac Steinberg, and Mesdames Rachel Cohen and Lizzie Smofsky, all of Clark's Harbour, N.S., contributed funds to the Zionist Federation, Montreal (22 March 1912, 15, 19)

ALBERT, H., M. Carrell, J. Ein, A. Green, H. Greenberg, H. Hamburg, M. Lighter, S. Markus, W. Mendelson, H. Miller, A. Sidersky and B. Siegel, all of Glace Bay, remitted contributions for the Bezalel Fund to the Zionist Federation (22 March 1912, 15, 19)

BECKER, I., H. Brody (Victoria Rd.), Phil. Cohen, B. Feder, Luis Gallen, B. Mickal, I. Natenson, Joseph Natenson, M. Natenson, M. Spinner and Charles Wyman, all of Sydney, contributed to the Bezalel School for Arts and Crafts in Jerusalem, Palestine (23 Feb. 1912, 15, 15)

CHERRIN, William, B. Hamburg, Mr. Lurie, M. Mendelson, N. Michael, Abe Schniderman and S. Soorovitz were members of the Glace Bay Zionist Society responsible for organizing the "Simchas Baes Hasohovo" held in the Glace Bay Synagogue Hall, York St., Sun. evening Oct. 19, 1913. Assisting them were:- Mesdames Louis Cohen and H. Greenberg and the Misses Lilly Brody, Jennie Marcus and Fannie Shondling. Taking part in the musical entertainment were:- M. Jessell, Abe Rubin and the Misses Sadie Ehmann, Ray Hamburg and Emma Levin (31 Oct. 1913, 16, 47)

CHIPPEN, A., M. Jessel, E. Mendelson, N. Michael and H. Mirsky, all of Glace Bay, organized a "Simchas Bais Hashevo" at the local synagogue Sun. evening, Sept. 24, 1912 for the benefit of the National Fund and the local Hebrew schools. Speeches were made by Rev. Bachrach, Rev. Sakuto, of Sydney and Rev. J. Abramowitz. Master Michael Bachrach performed a musical solo. Communicated by Ben Hamburg (11 Oct. 1912, 15, 44)

CITRON, S.I., Sam Davidson, and Mrs. Myer David, all of Bridgewater, N.S., contributed funds to the Zionist Federation, Montreal (22 March 1912, 15, 19)

COHEN, L., E. Elman, M. Maganett, H. Mirsky and B. Myers, all of Glace Bay, remitted contributions for the Bezalel Fund to the Zionist Federation (23 Aug. 1912, 15, 37)

COHEN, Levi, president of the Glace Bay Zionist Society, presided at the society's concert and dance. Speakers were H. Mirsky and Rev. Bachrach (15 Oct. 1909, 12, 44)

COHEN, Louis, president of the Glace Bay Zionist Society, addressed the Society's fifth anniversary jubilee celebration on Sun. evening, March 16, 1913 in the Synagogue Hall, York St. Among those present were:- the chazzan, Rev. Abramowitz, the schochet, Rev. Levin, M. Jessel, Mrs. N. Goorovitz, and Mrs. Max Stockler, of Sydney (4 April 1913, 16, 17)

COHEN, Louis, president of the Glace Bay Zionist Society, was the principal speaker at the Chanukah Ball held Mon. Dec. 26, 1910. Members of the organizing committee in charge were:- A. Sniderman, William Mendelson, M. Green, M. Karrel, Mesdames L. Cohen and B. Seigal, and Miss H. Brown (6 Jan. 1911, 14, 8)

COHEN, Louis, was elected president of the Glace Bay Zionist Society last Sun. Other officers elected were:- H. Wolfson, vice-pres.; A. Siderski, treas.; Joseph Nathanson, rec. and corr. sec.; and Israel Hamburg, fin. sec. (5 March 1909, 12, 12)

COHEN, Louis, was re-elected by acclamation, president of the Glace Bay Zionist Society. Other officers elected were:- Mrs. B. Siegal, vice-pres.; Miss Sarah Magonett, treas.; I. Hamburg, fin. sec.; Joseph Nathanson, rec. & corr. sec. (11 Feb. 1910, 13, 13)

COHEN, Louis, was re-elected president of the Glace Bay Zionist Society on Sun. Nov. 9, 1913. Other officers elected were:- William Mendelson, vice-pres.; William Cherrin, rec. sec.; B. Hamburg, fin. sec.; Abe Schniderman, treas.; Mr. Lurie and N. Michael, exec. (21 Nov. 1913, 16, 50-51)

EHMANN, Mr. and Mrs. S.L., York St., Glace Bay, gave a dinner and reception on Sun. Dec. 21, 1914, in honor of their daughter, Miss Martha Ehmann, who will soon be married. Mrs. Ehmann received the guests assisted by her daughters Misses Martha and Sadie Ehmann and Miss Hilda Brown (2 Jan. 1914, 17, 4)

GREEN, Mr. and Mrs. H., of Sydney, gave a surprise birthday party in honor of Miss Edith I. Cohen, of Waterbury, Conn., last Sun. July 6, 1913 at the home of Mr. and Mrs. Isaac Green. Those present were:- H. Benjamin, Dave Epstein, Sam Epstein, I. Feinstein, Louis Gallen, I. Garber, Sam Gordon, Arthur Green, Solomon Green, I. Hamburg, M. Hamburg, A. Jacobson, H. Lighter, M. Myers, Jacob Nathanson, Joe Nathanson, N. Nathanson, H. Waterman, Mr. and Mrs. I. Glickman, Mr. and Mrs. I. Nathanson, the Misses Esther Brody, Lilly Brody, M. Fried, Fanny Gordon, Ray Hamburg, Celia Lubchansky, Annie Michael, Libbie Mirsky, Tillie Mirsky, Esther Nathanson and Bessie Sadofsky (18 July 1913, 16, 32)

HOFFMAN, C., of Amherst, N.S., purchased one tree in the Herzl Wald (12 March 1909, 12, 13)

JESSELL, Mr. and Mrs. M., of Glace Bay, gave a birthday party in honor of their daughter, Rebecca, on Sun. Dec. 15, 1912. Those taking part included Miss Susie Myers and Mr. Abramovitz (20 Dec. 1912, 16, 2)

LEVIN, Rev. P., who was until recently secretary of the Yarmouth Zionist Society, has accepted a position with the synagogue in Gardner, Mass., "...and it is felt by the Zionists of Yarmouth that Gardner's gain means Nova Scotia's loss, as Mr. Levin was an ardent and untiring worker for the Zionist cause. As a Hebrew scholar he did much to promote an interest in Hebrew learning in the Jewish community of Yarmouth. Despite, however, Mr. Levin's departure, the Zionists of Yarmouth continue to do good and efficient propaganda work under the able presidency of Mr. I. Citron, the head of the Zionist Society of Yarmouth, and as an evidence of their practical activity, they have recently remitted to the Canadian Federation, the sum of $25.50 to cover shekel and federation fees, and also for a share in the Anglo-Palestine Company, to be purchased in the name of Mr. Abraham I. Cohen, of Clark's Harbour, Shelburne County, N.S. The latter gentleman is an exceptionally active Zionist, and he is also assisting materially in forwarding Zionist propaganda in the far-off countries (sic.) of the Atlantic Coast." (23 July 1909, 12, 32)

LEVITT, Rev. Abraham, of Halifax, has been charged by the Halifax Society for the Prevention of Cruelty to Animals, "...claiming that the process of slaughtering animals by the Jewish method is cruel." (4 April 1913, 16, 17)

MENDELSON, E., who was a delegate to the Zionist Convention, gave a report at the regular meeting of the Glace Bay Zionist Society. Other speakers were Rev. Abramowitz, Rev. Levin and Louis Cohen. L. Bernstein, William Cherrin, S. Green, Sol. Green, B. Hamburg, M. Mendelson and A. Schniderman were appointed to the banquet and dance committee in honor of the former secretary, S. Goorovitz and Louis Cohen (13 Feb. 1914, 17, 7)

MIRSKY, H., president of the Glace Bay Zionist Society, conducted the memorial service to commemorate the seventh anniversary of the death of Theodor Herzl on July 7, 1912 in the Savoy Theatre. Rev. Zakuto, of Sydney, the guest lecturer for the evening, gave a lantern show presentation on the Zionists in Palestine. Miss Revoe, a recent arrival in Glace Bay, also spoke on the aims and ideals of the Zionist movement. Members of the arrangements committee were:- H. Mirsky, pres; H. Albert, vice-pres.; M. Jessel, treas.; and W. Mendelson (2 Aug. 1912, 15, 34)

MIRSKY, H., Rabbi J. Abramovitch and Mrs. Max Fried spoke at the bazaar given by the Hebrew Ladies' Aid Society, of Glace Bay, on Wed. Aug. 20, 1913, in the vestry rooms of the Sons of Israel Synagogue. The bazaar was held to raise funds for erecting a fence around the building. On the musical program were:- H. Mirsky and the Misses Esther Brody, Sophie Ein, Emma Levin, Rosy Sacks and Mrs. Nathan Jacobson. Organizers were the Society's president, Mrs. Max Fried, and Mesdames L. Cohen, P. Ein, J. Gittelson, N. Jacobson, J. Levin and S. Marcus (29 Aug. 1913, 16, 38)

MIRSKY, S., of the Glace Bay and Sydney Zionist Society, is responsible for the National Fund boxes committee (19 Feb. 1909, 12, 10)

NATHANSON, Israel and H. Green laid the cornerstone of the new synagogue in Sydney which is located on Mt. Pleasant St., at Whiney Pier. Speakers at the dedication ceremonies included Rabbi Abramovitch, of Glace Bay and Rabbi Bachrach, of Sydney. Speaking in Hebrew, Rabbi Abramovich "...asked the members of the Hebrew congregation to stand firmly by the faith of their forefathers, and be united in all their religious work." (1 Aug. 1913, 16, 34)

NATHANSON, Israel, of Sydney, purchased one tree in the Herzl Wald in celebration of the Brith Milah of his infant son, Yechiel Nathanson (30 July 1909, 12, 33)

NATHANSON, J., of Sydney, and H. Mirsky, of Glace Bay, are responsible for the National Fund boxes in those cities. They are assisted by M. Freed, A. Siderski and M. Spinner. The Glace Bay Zionist Society has seventy-five members (22 Jan. 1909, 12, 6)

NATHANSON, Joseph, of Sydney, ordered one share in the Anglo-Palestine Company from the Zionist Executive in Montreal (25 June 1909, 12, 28)

SAKUTO, G., minister of the Hebrew Educational Society of Sydney sent a cheque for $21.65 to the paper which was collected at the Bar Mitzvah of Master Cossman for the Salonika Jewish Relief Fund. Donors were:- M. Bonavitsky, I. Becker, Mr. Brody, P. Cohon, D. Cossman, Mrs. Druker, G. Ein, H. Green, M. Lubchansky, B. Michael, Rev. Sakuto, F. Sherman, W. Shlossberg, L. Silverman, M. Spinner and Ch. Wyman (3 Jan. 1913, 16, 4)

SIEGEL, Mrs. Dora, of Glace Bay, contributed to the Herzl Wald in the name of her late grandfather, Jacob Lieb (28 June 1912, 15, 29)

WHITEHOUSE, Joseph, of Lunenberg, N.S., contributed to the Jewish National Fund (22 March 1912, 15, 19)

WHITEHOUSE, Samuel, of Lunenberg, N.S., wrote a letter to the editor, April 28, 1913, enclosing a clipping from a Halifax newspaper about the Schechita trial and the conviction of Rev. Abraham Levitt "...for killing an animal according to the Jewish belief, namely by cutting its throat and letting it bleed to death." (2 May 1913, 16, 21)

WYMAN, C., David Epstein, Joseph Nathanson and Miss Lena Mirsky organized the library fund bazaar and dance held Nov. 28, 1909, on behalf of the Hebrew Youth of Sydney (3 Dec. 1909, 13, 3)

QUEBEC — OTHER CENTERS

COHEN, Nathan, Arthur Markus, D. Fels, Samuel Rittenberg, Miss Hannah Rosenberg, B.A., and others were Montreal visitors at St. Johns, Que., last Sat. for the regatta. "After the regatta a banquet was given by the local yacht club at which many of our co-religionists were present." (12 Aug. 1910, 13, 39)

COHEN, Rabbi Hirsch, was elected rabbi of the first synagogue in Lachine, known as Beth Israel, which was dedicated Sun. Oct. 3, 1909. Rabbi Herman Abramowitz performed the dedication service and Rabbi Meldola de Sola and Rabbi Cohen spoke a few words. At the conclusion of the service Lazarus Cohen "...speaking in the name of the officers of the synagogue, expressed his thanks to all those who took sufficient interest in Lachine Jewry, to be present." Officials of the synagogue are:- J. Mandelstam, pres.; S. Freedman, parnass; A. Goldwater, treas.; M. Miller, sec.; H. Caplan, J. Sochter and M. Maiser, trustees (8 Oct. 1909, 12, 43)

ECHENBERG, M., was elected president of the Sherbrooke Zionist society on Sun. Feb. 13, 1910. Other officers are:- S. Kuschner, vice-pres.; J. Rosenbloom, treas.; A. Echenberg, fin. sec.; and Miss R. Smith, rec. sec. (18 Feb. 1910, 13, 14)

FREEDMAN, S., who is soliciting funds for the erection of a synagogue in Lachine, reports that Montreal has contributed $390 and Lachine $347 towards the cost. Contributors to date have been:- LACHINE: S. Goldwater, Max Miller, J. Mandelstam, S. Freedman, S. Yaphe, T. Rosenthal, J. Schechter, S. Silver, M. Davis, L. Baskin (Pittsburgh), H. Freedman, T. Sechter, M. Levin, K. Lerman, B. Gameroff, M. Seligman, J. Greenbaum, H. Hurwitz, M. Mizur, H. Kusner, M. Powerin, Mr. Golowsky, T. Hindelman and Max Farber MONTREAL: Mortimer B. Davis, S.W. Jacobs, K.C., Mark Workman, J.A. Jacobs, Harris Vineberg, D.F. Friedman, Rabbi Herman Abramowitz, A. Jacobs, A. Levin, J.H. Blumenthal, Louis T. Margolese, E.W. Jacobs, S.A. Jacobs, H. Bernstein, M. Poverin, M. Tannenbaum, T. Konigsberg, S. Ballon, A. Fineberg, A. Poyanor, Z. Fineberg, D. Shapiro, Henry Weinfield, D. Miller, H. Caplan, L. Lapkovitz, P. Popliger, E. Bindman, J. Steinberg, C. Levin, S. Sigler and C. Mendelssohn (9 July 1909, 12, 30)

FREIDMAN, Samuel and Mr. Goldwater are chiefly responsible for building the synagogue in Lachine. "The number of coreligionists in that town has rapidly grown of late, and at present there is close upon a hundred Jewish families who make Lachine and its environments (sic.) their home. The majority of them are employees of the Canada Car Company, and other large manufacturing concerns located there; but there are also quite a few in active business in the town proper. It is, therefore, not surprising that their first spiritual thoughts should be of a place of worship of their own, as it has been felt that their numbers justified more than the holding of worship, during the festivals especially, in a hall (21 May 1909, 12, 23)

STEINE, Dr. S., Miss Blumberg, of Chicago, and Mr. Ellison, of Montreal, were weekend guests of Mr. and Mrs. Tannenbaum at Iberville (12 Aug. 1910, 13, 39)

TANNENBAUM, Miss Hattie, has returned to Iberville after spending two months visiting friends in Detroit, Chicago and other cities (12 August 1910, 13, 39)

The best souvenir that parents can give to their children and children to their parents, is undoubtedly their life size portrait finished by a First-class artist: - -

Mr. I. Ressler will guarantee that he is in a position to make a very natural portrait either, Pastel, Water Color or Crayon. Oil portraits a speciality.

Prices within reach of every purse.

The public is respectfully invited to visit Mr. Ressler's Studio

512 CITY HALL AVENUE

For further information, ring up Bell Telephone East, 391

MONTREAL

AARON, Simon and Adolph Aaron are at Ste. Agathe for a few weeks (28 July 1911, 14, 37)

AARONSON, J., returned from Seattle where he spent the past two months (2 May 1913, 16, 21)

AARONSON, Miss Rose, is spending her holidays in Ste. Agathe (1 Aug. 1913, 16, 34)

ABECOSIS, Gabriel M., of London, England, was in Montreal during the week (6 Aug. 1909, 12, 34)

ABINOVITCH, Mr. and Mrs. L., 4878 Sherbrooke St., wish their friends a happy New Year (1 Oct. 1913, 16, 42-43)

ABINOVITCH, Mrs., is in the hospital suffering from typhoid fever (17 Dec. 1909, 13, 5)

ABINOVITCH, Mrs. L., Sherbooke St., Westmount, is in New York to attend the wedding of her cousin, Miss Miriam Robinson. She is the guest of Mrs. S. Cohen, of Brooklyn (9 May 1913, 16, 22)

ABINOVITCH, Mrs., Sherbrooke St. W., is in New York for the Bar Mitzvah of her nephew (8 Nov. 1912, 15, 48)

ABINOVITCH, P., passed first year commerce, McGill University (16 May 1913, 16, 23)

ABINOVITZ, P., H. Cohen, N. Fineberg, M. Garber, L. Gross, Ch. Hershon, A.B. Illiewitz, H. and M. Jacobs, D. Lauer, M. Lightstone, L. Sessenwein and the Misses M. Goldenberg, R.Groner, S. Klineberg, L. Livingstone, M. Rosenberg, R. Ruttner, Ida and Freda Schwartz, R. Shara, I. Siegler, Y. and E. Silver, S. Solomon and M. Tannenbaum are teachers at the Baron de Hirsch School who attended a sleigh ride Sat. night (21 Feb. 1913, 16, 11)

ABRAHAMS, George, has returned from a trip to Vermont (8 Sept. 1911, 14, 43)

ABRAHAMS, George, is spending the week at Beaurepaire, the guest of Mrs. R.H. Blumenthal (23 July 1909, 12, 32)

ABRAHAMS, George, is visiting his sister, Mrs. H.B. Franklin in Allston, Mass. (12 April 1912, 15, 22)

ABRAHAMS, George, won four prizes in the Y.M.C.A. fields sports competitions (24 Sept. 1909, 12, 41)

ABRAHAMS, H.L., is in New York on a short visit (19 Jan. 1912, 15, 10)

ABRAHAMS, I., has gone to New York and Boston (7 July 1911, 14, 34)

ABRAHAMS, L., has returned from a short trip to New York (4 Feb, 1910, 13, 12)

ABRAHAMS, L., has returned from New York and Boston (13 Jan. 1911, 14, 9)

ABRAHAMS, L., is spending a few weeks at Rideau, Ont. (23 July 1909, 12, 32)

ABRAHAMS, Leonard, has gone on a short trip to New York (12 May 1911, 14, 26)

ABRAHAMS, Miss Estelle, has returned from Alexandria Bay (19 Aug. 1910, 13, 40)

ABRAHAMS, Miss Estelle, is the guest of her aunt, Mrs. M. Bernstein (11 July 1913, 16, 31)

ABRAHAMS, Miss Estelle, leaves for Old Orchard Beach (28 July 1911, 14, 37)

ABRAHAMS, Miss Estelle, left for Back Bay, Boston, where she will visit her sister, Mrs. Harry B. Franklin (15 Jan. 1909, 12, 5)

ABRAHAMS, Miss Estelle, spent the week at Beaurepaire, the guest of her aunt, Mrs. R.H. Blumenthal (7 July 1911, 14, 34)

ABRAHAMS, Miss Estelle, who has spent the past six months with her sister, Mrs. H.B. Frankel, of Boston, has returned home (9 July 1909, 12, 30)

ABRAHAMS, Miss Grace, Argyle Ave., left for Kennebunkport where she will meet her sister, Mrs. H.B. Franklin and daughter, of Allston, Mass. (25 July 1913, 16, 33)

ABRAHAMS, Miss Grace, has gone to Boston where she will spend the winter with her sister, Mrs. Harry B. Franklin (23 Dec. 1910, 14, 6)

ABRAHAMS, Miss Grace, has returned from Atlantic City and New York (12 March 1909, 12, 13)

ABRAHAMS, Miss Grace, has returned from New York and Atlantic City (18 March 1910, 13, 18)

ABRAHAMS, Miss Grace, left for Old Orchard Beach and Boston for a few weeks (6 Aug. 1909, 12, 34)

ABRAHAMS, Miss, Mt. Pleasant Ave., is visiting Mrs. M. Bernstein, of New York (28 May 1909, 12, 24)

ABRAHAMS, Miss Rosalind, of Brookline, Mass., is the guest of her aunt, Mrs. S. Abrahams, Argyle Ave., Westmount (27 Dec. 1912, 16, 3)

ABRAHAMS, Miss, spent the weekend in Beaurepaire, the guest of Mrs. R.H. Blumenthal (2 July 1909, 12, 29)

ABRAHAMS, Mr. and Mrs. I., Argyle Ave., Westmount, have gone to Boston and New York. Mrs. Abrahams will remain in Boston with her daughter, Mrs. H.M. Franklin for a few weeks (5 Jan. 1911, 15, 8)

ABRAHAMS, Mr. and Mrs., of New York, are visiting their daughter, Mrs. Benjamin Lesser (25 Oct. 1910, 13, 50)

ABRAHAMS, Mr. and Mrs. S. and family have moved out to Lakeside for the summer (6 May 1910, 13, 25)

ABRAHAMS, Mrs. A. and Miss Grace Abrahams have returned from vacation (30 Aug. 1912, 15, 38)

ABRAHAMS, Mrs. P., has returned from Allston, Mass. where she visited her daughter, Mrs. H.B. Franklin for three months (19 April 1912, 15, 23)

ABRAHAMS, Mrs. S., Argyle St., gave a party in honor of her grandchild, Miss Audrey Dorothy Franklin, of Boston. Those present included:- Master Rosenthal and the Misses Dorothy Blumenthal, Alice Goldstein, Elsie Heinsheimer, Annette Jacobs, Valerie Scherwin and Gertie Wener (7 June 1912, 15, 26)

ABRAHAMS, Mrs. S., gave a dance at her home, Argyle Ave., Westmount, Thurs. evening, Jan. 2, 1913, in honor of her niece, Miss Rosalind Abrahams, of Brookline, Mass. Assisting in receiving were the Misses Grace and Estelle Abrahams. Miss Freda Luxembourg, of New York sang. Guests included Alexander Blumenthal, Lyon and Harry Levinson, Sam and M. Silver and the Misses Annie Ballon, Gladys, Muriel and Irene Blumenthal, Eva Friedman, Jessie and Stella Goldstein, Muriel and Gladys Goldstein, Dorothy and Marjorie Goldstein, Sylvia Goldstein, Flossie and Effie Hyman, Myrtle Levinson, Tillie Levinson, Sara Levinson, Grace Lewis, Belle Myers (Syracuse, N.Y.), Jean Michaelson, Edythe Ogulnik, Bertha Phillips (Cornwall), Gertie, Theresa and Beatrice Samuels, Elsie Silverman, Cyril Stein (Cleveland), and Nina and Daisy Workman (10 Jan. 1913, 16, 5)

ABRAHAMS, Mrs. S., is spending two weeks with her daughter, Mrs. H.B. Franklin, in Boston (8 July 1910, 13, 34)

ABRAHAMS, Mrs. S., Mt. Pleasant Ave., has left for a months' stay in Boston (24 Sept. 1909, 12, 41)

ABRAHAMS, Mrs. Samuel, Mt. Pleasant Ave., has returned from a two months' visit with her daughter, Mrs. Franklin, of Boston (3 Dec. 1909, 13, 3)

ABRAHAMS, S., has returned from a short visit to New York (9 July 1909, 12, 30)

ABRAHAMS, S., Hutchison St., has returned from a short trip to New York (15 Jan. 1909, 12, 5)

ABRAHAMS, S., Lakeside, has left on a short trip (1 July 1910, 13, 33)

ABRAHAMS, Sam, left for Boston and New York (6 June 1913, 16, 26)

ABRAHAMS, Samuel, has returned from a business trip to Boston and New York (21 Jan. 1910, 13, 10)

ABRAMOWITZ, Dr. Herman, is in New York on a short trip (19 Feb. 1909, 12, 10)

ABRAMOWITZ, Rabbi and Mrs. Herman, 211 Stanley St. send New Year greetings (11 Sept. 1912, 15, 40)

ABRAMOWITZ, Rabbi and Mrs. Herman, 211 Stanley St., wish their friends a happy New Year (1 Oct. 1913, 16, 42-43)

ABRAMOWITZ, Rabbi and Mrs. Herman, sail for Europe on June 26, 1913 (20 June 1913, 16, 28)

ABRAMOWITZ, Rabbi Herman, acknowledges receipt of a cheque for $100 from Mrs. E. Holstein, of Fort Coulogne, Que. collected from her friends to be applied towards the Jewish Consumptive Hospital at Ste. Agathe (9 Dec. 1910, 14, 4)

ABRAMOWITZ, Rabbi Herman and family have returned from vacation in the Catskill Mountains (30 Aug. 1912, 15, 38)

ABRAMOWITZ, Rabbi Herman, and H.N. Friedman were visiting governors at the General Hospital the past week (5 March 1909, 12, 12)

ABRAMOWITZ, Rabbi Herman and his mother left for New York, Wed. night, for two months (25 June 1909, 12, 28)

ABRAMOWITZ, Rabbi Herman, delivered an address on the significance of Chanukah at the YMHA annual Chanukah party on Sun. Dec. 28, 1913. Lyon Cohen and J. Goldstein also spoke. On the program were the twenty voices of the Halevi Juvenile Choral Society and Miss Ida Bloom who charmed the audience with her beautiful voice. Also appearing were Horace Cohen and Phil Abinovitch in their sketch "Is he In?"; as well as L. Brodie, I. Goldberg, Charles Hershorn, I. Rabinovitch and L. Ram. S.B. Gordon was the toastmaster. Arrangements committee members were:- L. Brodie, J. Carrick, A. Cohen, H. Diner, I. Diner, N. Ginns, M. Goldberg, W. Gubbins, C. Lambert, E. Losinsky, A. Pesner, I. Snare, A. Winer and J. Winer (9 Jan. 1914, 17, 5)

ABRAMOWITZ, Rabbi Herman, expects to leave for New York next Wed., for a holiday. On Fri. June 18, 1909, he will officiate at the wedding of Miss Bella Bluestone, daughter of Dr. J. Bluestone, of New York, to Rabbi H. Kauvar, of Denver, Col. (18 June 1909, 12, 27)

ABRAMOWITZ, Rabbi Herman, gave an interview to the London Jewish Chronicle in the latest issue on the position of the Jews in Canada. He stayed over in London prior to his journey to Vienna to attend the Zionist Congress on Sept. 2, 1913 (15 Aug. 1913, 16, 36)

ABRAMOWITZ, Rabbi Herman, has returned from vacation in New York (20 Aug. 1909, 12, 36)

ABRAMOWITZ, Rabbi Herman, has returned from New York (11 March 1910, 13, 17)

ABRAMOWITZ, Rabbi Herman, is back in Montreal (9 Sept. 1910, 13, 43)

ABRAMOWITZ, Rabbi Herman, is leaving for New York at the end of the week. He was invited to occupy the pulpit of the late Professor Joseph M. Asher (18 Feb. 1910, 13, 14)

ABRAMOWITZ, Rabbi Herman, is spending the summer at Long Beach, N.J. (15 July 1910, 13, 35)

ABRAMOWITZ, Rabbi Herman, officiated at the tombstone dedication ceremony in memory of the late A. Rosenthal which took place in the Shaar Hashomayim Cemetery. Family members from Ottawa came for the ceremony (18 Oct. 1910, 13, 49)

ABRAMOWITZ, Rabbi Herman, spent the past week in New York (11 Nov. 1910, 13, 52)

ABRAMOWITZ, Rabbi Herman, was in Montreal on Tues. for the Rome-Bernstein wedding and soon expects to resume his holidays (26 Aug. 1910, 13, 41)

ABRAMOWITZ, Rabbi Herman, was in New York during the week (12 May 1911, 14, 26)

ABRAMOWITZ, Rabbi Herman, was in Ottawa on Tues. to officiate at the marriage of Miss Phoebe Wolfe to Joel Pullan, of Winnipeg (10 June 1910, 13, 30)

ABRAMOWITZ, Rabbi Herman, was present at the sleigh-drive held Sat. night, Feb. 21, 1914 by the religious school teachers and friends of the Baron de Hirsch Institute and the Shaar Hashomayim Synagogue. Among those present were:- P. Abinovitch, H. Cohen, N. Fineberg, M. Garber, H. Goldblatt, L.M. Gross, B. Illwitz, Archie Jacobs and son, I. Kert, D. Lauer, A. Milstock, N. Silver, L.M. Tannenbaum, Mr. and Mrs. H. Bloomfield, Mr. and Mrs. Lyon Cohen, Mr. and Mrs. E.M. Gordon, Mr. and Mrs. J. Levinson, Mr. and Mrs. L.N. Sack, and the Misses H. Gordon, J. Heillig, S. Klineberg, G. Lande, R. Ratner, M. Rosenberg, R. Shara, E. Stein and A. and D. Vineberg (27 Feb. 1914, 17, 9)

ABRAMOWITZ, Rabbi Herman, will inspect the Jewish farm colony at Macaza, Que., and while there will officiate at a wedding (8 Oct. 1909, 12, 43)

ABRAMSKY, Miss K., of Kingston, Ont., is visiting friends in Montreal (5 Aug. 1910, 13, 38)

ABRAMSON, Joseph, of Kingston, Ont., was in Montreal during the week (25 Aug. 1911, 14, 41)

ACKERMAN, Hyman, Milton Ackerman, Bennie Aaronson, Jacob Arbess, H. Besman, M. Bessner, Dora Bernfield, J. Birnbaum, Julius Block, A. Cohen, Bessie Cohen, S. Ginsberg, M. Greenberg, M. Hornstein, Sarah Issen, Esther Kellnor, R. Levin, Esther Levitt, L. Lightstone, R. Mendelson, Elsie Osmiensky, Clara Paskal, Bessie Richman, B. Rosen, S. Rosenberg, M. Scherzer, A. Schneider, E. Schwartz, R. Schwartz, Ethel Shoster, S. Silverman, A. Solomon, Pearl Squire, R. Tannenbaum, P. Tetchell and R. Wagner graduated from Mount Royal School (3 March 1911, 14, 16)

ACKERMAN, Hyman, who won a scholarship at Mount Royal School, was disqualified from receiving it because he lived outside the school district boundary (3 March 1911, 14, 16)

Bell Telephone Main 3695.　　　MRS. S. ADELSON, Prop.

UP-TO-DATE

NEW YORK כשר DELICATESSEN STORE

246 ST. CATHERINE ST. WEST.

Latest Assortment of Smoked Meats, All sorts of Ballogna, Canned goods, Fresh Importations every day, Sauer Kraut, Salads and Pickles.

All Telephone orders promptly attended to,　　　Delivery Twice Daily

---

ADDELSON, A., was elected president of the Victoria Social and Literary Club last Sun. aft. Other officers elected were:- S. Katz, vice-pres.; H. Firestone, treas.; Maxwell Bercusson, corr. and rec. sec.; and S. Althouse, fin. sec. (17 March 1911, 14, 18)

ADELMAN, Mr. and Mrs., of Winnipeg, are visiting their mother, Mrs. Joseph Vineberg (23 June 1911, 14, 32)

ADELMAN, Mrs. L., of Winnipeg, is visiting her mother, Mrs. J. Vineberg, Elgin Ave., Westmount (21 Feb. 1913, 16, 11)

ADELSON, Mesdames, G. Asner, Charles Cohen, Pascal and Rosenbloom, on behalf of the Ladies' Society, were mainly responsible for presenting a Sepher Torah to the Talmud Torah, Montreal Hebrew Free School. The Torah will be used by the boys on the Sabbath and Holy Days (31 Jan. 1913, 16, 8)

ADELSTEIN, Mr. and Mrs. J.L., 281 St. Joseph Blvd., wish their friends a happy New Year (1 Oct. 1913, 16, 42-43)

ADELSTEIN, P. and daughter, Sarah, sail on the S.S. Royal George, on July 1, 1913 for Europe where they will stay for four months (27 June 1913, 16, 29)

ADELSTEIN, Peter and daughter Sara, returned from an extended trip through Europe (10 Oct. 1913, 16, 44)

ADILMAN, Mrs. H., of Winnipeg, hosted an "evening", on Aug. 11, 1909, in honor of her guest, Miss Sadie Vineberg, of Montreal (20 Aug. 1909, 12, 36)

ADLER, Jacob P., will present "The Stranger" and "Solomon the Wise" at the Monument National, Oct. 7-8, 1909 (24 Sept. 1909, 12, 41)

ADLER, L., 375 St. James St.; Joseph Binder, 567 Notre Dame W.; R.A. Bloom, 561 Notre Dame W.; Jacob Cohen, 321 Notre Dame W.; Julius Cohen, 425 Notre Dame W.; Max Gelbman, 337a Notre Dame W.; Max Harris, 446 St. James St.; Isaac Hirsch, 21 Pea Lane; Michael and Robert Hirsch, 611 St. James; Jacob A. Jacobs, 309 St. James St.; Harris and Jacob Kellert, 351 St. James St.; Francis W. Leon, 148 St. Antoine, William F. Levi, 148a St. Antoine; Joseph and Solomon Levinson, 311 Notre Dame W.; Julius B. Miller, 439 St. James St.; Henry Moses, 13 Taillifer; Joseph Morris, 5 Dufferin; Solomon M. Shapiro, 359 Notre Dame W.; Morris Switzman, 300 St. James St.; and Mark Workman, 122 St. Antoine, all of St. Joseph Ward, are persons on the Parliamentary Voters' revision list (3 Feb. 1911, 14, 12)

ADLER, Mrs. M.J., is in New York on holiday (18 March 1910, 13, 18)

AFTEL, Miss Stephanie, of Toledo, Ohio, is the guest of Mrs. Louis Lewis (26 July 1912, 15, 33)

AFTEL, Mrs. and daughter, of Toledo, Ohio, were guests of Mr. and Mrs. Louis Lewis, Sherbrooke St. W. (30 June 1911, 14, 33)

AFTELL, Miss, has returned to her home in Toledo, Ohio (22 Jan. 1909, 12, 6)

ALBERT, C., of New York, is registered at the Carslake Hotel (19 Nov. 1909, 13, 1)

ALBERT, Charles, is spending his vacation at Old Orchard Beach (13 Aug. 1909, 12, 35)

ALBERT, F., Park Ave., has left for Cowansville (8 April 1910, 13, 21)

ALBERT, J., has gone to New York, Boston, and Old Orchard Beach for two weeks (20 Aug. 1909,

ALBERT, M., has again been re-elected to the Board of the Montreal College of Pharmacy (1 June 1911, 14, 29)

ALBERT, M., has been re-elected to the Council of the Pharmaceutical Association of Quebec (13 Aug. 1909, 12, 35)

ALBERT, M., has returned from a two months' trip abroad (30 July 1909, 12, 33)

ALBERT, M., has returned from a trip to the Lakes (25 July 1911, 14, 36)

ALBERT, M., has returned from visiting his mother and sisters at their summer cottage, "Pleasantview", Old Orchard Beach (13 Aug. 1909, 12, 35)

ALBERT, Moe, who served on the board of directors of the Montreal College of Pharmacy for twelve years, was elected its vice-president at a recent meeting. J.J. Weinfeld was elected to the board at the same meeting (13 June 1913, 16, 27)

ALBERT, Morris, J. Albert, Harry Bloomfield, Bernard Rose and Drs. Sperber and Budyk attended a meeting last Sun. aft. to discuss the formation of a Young Men's Hebrew Association (12 March 1909, 12, 13)

ALBERT, Moses, A.Z. Cohen, David Levi and Dr. Norman Viner took part in a symposium "Should there be a Jewish Vote?" at the Young People's Society of Shaar Hashomayim meeting on Mon. evening, Jan. 11, 1909. Performers were Miss Leba Livingstone (pianoforte solo), and Mr. Broder (vocal solo) (15 Jan. 1909, 12, 5)

ALBERT, Mr. and Mrs. M., are living at 5 Prince Arthur Apts., 709 St. Urbain St., for the winter (29 Nov. 1912, 15, 51)

ALBERT, Mr. and Mrs. Samuel, have returned to Montreal from Kentville, Ont. (15 April 1910, 13, 22)

ALBERT, Mr. and Mrs. Samuel, have returned from New York and are living at 1710 Park Ave. (22 April 1910, 13, 23)

ALBERT, Mrs. Joseph, of Cleveland, is visiting his sister, Mrs. J.G. Perlson (10 Sept. 1909, 12, 39)

ALBERT, Samuel, is leaving next week on a short trip to Kalamazoo, Mich. (22 Oct. 1909, 12, 45)

ALBERT, Samuel, is on holiday at Old Orchard Beach (6 Aug. 1909, 12, 34)

ALBERT, W., leaves for a two months' trip abroad (21 May 1909, 12, 23)

ALEXANDER, J., of New York, is staying at the Corona Hotel (15 Jan. 1909, 12, 5)

ALEXANDER, Lewis, a well known solicitor in Cape Town, passed through Montreal last Fri., en route for Vancouver, where he will visit his sister (27 Aug. 1909, 12, 37)

ALEXANDER, M., returned from Old Orchard and Kennebunk Beach (15 Aug. 1913, 16, 36)

ALEXANDER, Maurice, has been appointed a life member of the McGill University Literary and Debating Society (25 March 1910, 13, 19)

ALEXANDER, Maurice, will spend the summer at Lake St. Joseph, Que., and Old Orchard Beach (16 July 1909, 12, 31)

ALEXANDER, Morris, J.A. Goodman, Lyon Jacobs and L. Millman passed their B.C.L. examinations at McGill University, Faculty of Law (13 May 1910, 13, 26)

ALEXANDER, Mrs. A.J. and family are at Tadoussac for the summer (12 July 1912, 15, 31)

ALEXANDOR, A.J., Lazarus Cohen, Lyon Cohen, Mortimer B. Davis, Clarence I. de Sola, Isaac Friedman, Moses J. Glickman, Tobias Glickman, E.W. Jacobs, Jacob J. Jacobs, S.W. Jacobs, M. Jaslow, A. Lessor, A. Levine, Felix Lewis, M. Margolick, Paul Ogulnik, Ascher Pierce, J. Samenhof, A.M. Vineberg, Moses A. Vineberg, J.H. Waldman and I. Weinberg responded to the Baron de Hirsch Institute financial appeal. "...some three hundred families are at the present time solely dependent upon the Institute for the bare needs to keep body and soul together." (5 Feb. 1909, 12, 8)

ALEXANDOR, A.J., was in New York for a few days on business (26 Nov. 1909, 13, 2)

ALEXANDOR, Miss Ada, of Higher Broughton, Manchester, England, has arrived in Montreal aboard the S.S. Victorian, to visit her brother, A.J. Alexandor (20 Aug. 1909, 12, 36)

ALTMAN, Samuel and S.A. Jacobs, have sailed for Europe aboard the S.S. Empress of India via Halifax (11 March 1910, 13, 17)

ALTMAN, Samuel, of Austria, spent the past week in Montreal (25 Feb. 1910, 13, 15)

ALTMAN, Samuel, of Vienna, is in Montreal for a short stay (26 Feb. 1909, 12, 11)

ANDREES, J., of New York, was a guest at St. Lawrence Hall (4 June 1909, 12, 25)

ANSELL, D.A., Consul-General for Mexico, has returned from his short holiday at Ste. Irenee (13 Aug. 1909, 12, 35)

ANSELL, D.A., Mexican Consul, and Clarence I. de Sola, Belgian Consul "...attended the requiem mass in this city for the repose of the soul of King Leopold of Belgium, and were accomodated with seats in the Chancel with the rest of the Consular body." (7 Jan. 1910, 13, 8)

ANSELL, David A., Consul-General for Mexico, left last Fri. for New York. He sailed this week for the Mediterranean and will be away three months (3 Feb. 1911, 14, 12)

ANSELL, David A., Consul-General of Mexico, has returned to Montreal after an extended visit to Mexico on affairs of state (12 March 1909, 12, 13)

ANSELL, David A., has returned from Murray Bay and St. Irenee des Bains (2 Sept. 1910, 13, 42)

ANSELL, David A., Mexican Consul, has returned from Italy, Paris and England (8 April 1910, 13, 21)

ANSELL, David A., sails from New York on the S.S. Berlin on June 20, 1912 for Gibralter and Mediterranean ports (19 Jan. 1912, 15, 10)

ANSELL, Miss Daisy, of Baltimore, stayed at the Windsor Hotel for a couple of days (2 July 1909, 12, 29)

ANTIPETSKY, H., of Toronto, is in Montreal (4 Nov. 1910, 13, 51)

ARNOVITZ, S., sailed on Aug. 15, 1913, on the S.S. Megantic, for London, Eng., where he will meet his brother, J. Arnovitz, from Calcutta, India. He will return to Montreal in two months' time (22 Aug. 1913, 16, 37)

ARNOWITZ, J., a well known and prominent attorney in Calcutta, India, is the guest of his sister, Mrs. J.B. Ellison, Church St. (18 June 1909, 12, 27)

ARNOWITZ, J., of Calcutta, India, who was in Montreal for the last two months, sailed for England aboard the S.S. Laurentic, en route for India (30 July 1909, 12, 33)

ARON, Adolph, has been appointed District Deputy Grand Master of the IOSB (9 June 1911, 14, 30)

ARON, Adolph, has returned from Rochester, N.Y., where he visited his sister, Mrs. M.I. Rose, formerly of Montreal (23 July 1909, 12, 32)

ARON, Adolph, has returned from Ste. Agathe des Monts (14 July 1911, 14, 35)

ARON, Adolph, has returned from two weeks in New York and Rochester (25 March 1910, 13, 19)

ARON, Adolph, was installed as president of Franz Joseph Lodge, IOSB on Jan. 3, 1909. Other officers installed were:- S. Popliger, vice-pres.; Isidore Friedman, sec.; S. Goldner, treas.; A.M. Freidlich, M. Hirshorn and L. Rabin, trustees (15 Jan. 1909, 12, 5)

ARON, H., was the guest of D. Waiser and family at Magog, Que. (20 May 1910, 13, 27)

ARON, Milton, has returned from a week in Quebec City (20 Aug. 1909, 12, 36)

ARON, Mr. and Mrs. Adolph and family, 106 St. Lawrence Blvd., wish their friends a happy New Year (1 Oct. 1913, 16, 42-43)

ARONBERG, Albert, of Chicago, was the guest of his aunt Mrs. M. Ginsberg, 149 Drolet St., for a few days (12 Aug. 1910, 13, 39)

ARONSON, A. and J. Glickman graduated dentistry from McGill University (12 May 1911, 14, 26)

ARONSON, Joseph, 115 Craig St. W., tel. Main 4374, of the Dorval baseball team, would like to arrange games with other teams (7 July 1911, 14, 34)

ARONSON, Mrs. A., Pacific Ave., San Francisco will host a card party at her home, next Wed. where guests will meet her niece, Miss Libbie Jacobs, of Montreal - San Francisco Emanu-el (4 March 1910, 13, 16)

ASCHER, D.D., H. Lande, A. Cohen and R.G. Davis are Montrealers who were in New York last week (25 July 1911, 14, 36)

ASHER, H.S., was a passenger on the S.S. Hesperian which sailed from Glasgow last Tues. (12 March 1909, 12, 13)

ASHER, Isidore, gave a party in honor of his guest, Miss Annie Levy, of Toronto, on Sun. Dec. 7, 1913. Among those present were A.K. Viner and Miss Sara Friedman (12 Dec. 1913, 17, 1)

ASHER, J., of Boston, is a guest at the Bath Hotel (13 Aug. 1909, 12, 35)

ASNER, S., was elected treasurer of the Montreal Hebrew Sheltering Home in place of I. Goldberg who resigned (24 Feb. 1911, 14, 15)

ASTROFSKY, H., has returned from a trip to Kingston (12 Aug. 1910, 13, 39)

ASTROFSKY, S. (Med. '12) and B. Silver (Arts '13) spoke in the affirmative and W. Hyman (Sci. '12) and B. Ilevitch (Med. '14) in the negative at a Maccabean Literary Circle debate held last Sat. aft. "Resolved: That the establishment of a Jewish hospital at present would be beneficial to the community". Dr. Max Rabinovitch also spoke on the subject (12 Nov. 1909, 12, 48)

ASTROFSKY, Samuel and J. de Hart, two Jewish McGill University students were among those chosen to play for McGill in the water polo tournament against the C.P.R. (5 Nov. 1909, 12, 47)

AUDRUS, C., of Philadelphia, was registered at the Place Viger Hotel (5 Feb. 1909, 12, 8)

AUDRUS, J., of New York, was registered at the St. Lawrence Hall (18 March 1910, 13, 18)

AUERBACH, Fischel, of Toronto, was in town for a short stay (8 Jan. 1909, 12, 4)

AUERBACH, M., S. Fenster, and Mr. Cohen were in New York last week (15 Sept. 1909, 12, 40)

AUERBACH, Marcus, has left for New York and Boston (13 May 1910, 13, 26)

AUERBACH, Marcus, has returned from a short stay in New York (21 Jan. 1910, 13, 10)

AUERBACH, Marcus, has spent the past week in Providence and New York (10 Sept. 1909, 12, 39)

AUERBACH, Marcus, is at Old Orchard, Me., for a few weeks (11 Aug. 1911, 14, 39)

AUERBACH, Mr. and Mrs. Marcus, have returned to Montreal and are residing on Prince Arthur Ave. (24 May 1912, 15, 25)

AUGUST, Jack, 20 Sherbrooke St. E., is on a business trip throughout Ontario (10 Jan. 1913, 16, 5)

AUGUST, Mr. and Mrs. Joseph, 20 Sherbrooke St. E., will attend the wedding of Mr. August's nephew in New York and will be guests of his uncle in Boston (10 Jan. 1913, 16, 5)

AZEFF, L., R.A. Darwin, D. Feldman, W. Finkelstein, M. Held, Maxwell Lightstone, Mr. McKinley and B.M. Speyer were elected Bnai Zion Kadimah delegates to the Zionist Convention in Montreal on Dec. 25, 1913 (12 Dec. 1913, 17, 1)

BACAL, A., of Montgomery, Que., was in Montreal this week en route to Cornwall, Ont., to visit his father-in-law (11 Aug. 1911, 14, 39)

BACAL, Mr. and Mrs. A., of Montmagny, Que., spent a month in Montreal visiting friends and relatives (21 Feb. 1913, 16, 11)

BACAL, Mr. and Mrs. A., of Montmagny, Que., who were in Montreal for a month, left for Cornwall, Ont., to visit Mrs. Bacal's parents, Mr. and Mrs. G. Goldstein (27 Feb. 1914, 17, 9)

BACAL, Mr. and Mrs. A., will visit Mrs. Bacal's parents in Cornwall, Ont. (28 Feb. 1913, 16, 12)

BACAL, Mrs. A., of Montmagny, Que., is in Montreal for a month, the guest of Mr. and Mrs. H. Bazar (31 Oct. 1913, 16, 47)

BACHARACH, J., of Toronto, was in Montreal on a short trip (11 Oct. 1910, 13, 48)

BACHRACK, B., of Toronto, is in Montreal (24 June 1910, 13, 32)

BAERE, Miss, of New Brunswick, N.J., who is the guest of Mrs. H. May, Mount Royal Ave., will stay for the Carnival (29 Jan. 1909, 12, 7)

BALINSKY, Miss Rose, gave a china shower last Sun. in honor of the approaching marriage of Miss Rose Feldstein (27 Feb. 1914, 17, 9)

BALLIN, B., has returned to New York (26 March 1909, 12, 15)

BALLON, Dr. David (B.A.), has been appointed house surgeon at the Royal Victoria Hospital (11 June 1909, 12, 26)

BALLON, Dr. and the Misses Ballon are vacationing in Shawbridge (22 July 1910, 13, 36)

BALLON, Dr. D.H., has returned from Europe (9 Jan. 1914, 17, 5)

BALLON, Dr. David H., house surgeon, has been appointed assistant to Dr. Hackett at the Royal Victoria Hospital (22 July 1910, 13, 36)

BALLON, Dr. David H., of the Royal Victoria Hospital, has gone on a trip to Europe (4 Aug. 1911, 14, 38)

BALLON, Dr. David H., who left Montreal in Jan. to spend a year in Europe, is in Berlin, Germany after having spent a month in Giessen (21 March 1913, 16, 15)

BALLON, Dr. David H., who spent the past year in Vienna, Berlin, Geissen and Paris doing specialized surgical work, sails for home Dec. 12, 1913, aboard the S.S. America from Cherbourg (12 Dec. 1913, 17, 1)

BALLON, Florence, age seven, performed on the cello at a concert last Tues. night (11 June 1909, 12, 26)

BALLON, Isidor (B.A., B.C.L.), has passed the Quebec Bar examination (9 July 1909, 12, 30)

BALLON, Isidore (B.A., B.C.L.), left Paris last Sat. for New York, en route for Montreal (11 June 1909, 12, 26)

BALLON, Isidore, spent the weekend at Ste. Agathe (9 Sept. 1910, 13, 43)

BALLON, Isidore, was a passenger on La Savoie, arriving home on Tues. from New York (18 June 1909, 12, 27)

BALLON, Miss and Miss Ellen Ballon, of New York, are visiting their parents on Crescent St. for a few weeks (6 Aug. 1909, 12, 34)

BALLON, Miss Annie, left for New York where she will visit her sisters (20 Feb. 1914, 17, 8)

BALLON, Miss Ellen, will give a piano recital in Montreal at the New Windsor Hall by the end of March following her New York debut with the New York Symphony (21 Jan. 1910, 13, 10)

BALLON, Misses, Crescent St., have returned to New York to resume their musical studies (24 Sept. 1909, 12, 41)

BALLON, Misses Mamie and Ellen, have returned to New York (29 April 1910, 13, 24)

BALLON, Misses Mamie B. and Ellen, will stay with their parents, Mr. and Mrs. S. Ballon, 82 Crescent St. for another ten days before returning to New York (8 April 1910, 13, 21)

BALLON, Mr. and Mrs. and family are at their summer cottage at Dorval for the rest of the summer (13 Aug. 1909, 12, 35)

BALLON, Mr. and Mrs. S. and family are at Pointe Claire for the summer (14 July 1911, 14, 35)

BANKS, N. and daughter, Carrie Banks, are spending their summer vacation at Old Orchard, Me. (1 Aug. 1913, 16, 34)

BANKS, S., S. Blaustein, Charles Eisenstadt, L.O. Kalmanovitz, J. Kling, M. Rubin, S. Shlossberg and H. Shuster were appointed proxy-delegates to the Zionist Convention in Montreal on Dec. 25, 1913 (19 Dec. 1913, 17, 2)

BARNETT, J. and the Misses Barnett, accompanied by Sydney Kempler, of New York, were in Montreal for a short visit (27 Aug. 1909, 12, 37)

BARON, G., has sailed on the S.S. Mauretania for London, Eng. (6 May 1910, 13, 25)

BARON, G., of Antwerp, stayed at Freeman's while in Montreal (26 April 1912, 15, 24)

BARON, George, was in Montreal for the past week (1 April 1910, 13, 20)

BARRON, G., who was in Montreal for a few months, has left for Australia (26 March 1909, 12, 15)

BARTLE, Miss, who has been visiting friends, returned home to New Brunswick, N.J. (19 Feb. 1909, 12, 10)

BASHEIN, Jacob, of New York, was the guest of Mr. and Mrs. D. Shapiro, 216 Park Ave., last week (5 March 1909, 12, 12)

BASHEIN, Jacob, of the Hebrew Sheltering Orphan Asylum of New York, visited the Baron de Hirsch Institute (5 March 1909, 12, 12)

BATSON, Mr. and Mrs. J. and family, of London, England, arrived in Montreal and are residing with their relatives, Mr. and Mrs. A.

My personal attention given to all orders entrusted to me. I have had the experience as Cutter and Designer with the best Tailors in Montreal, New York, etc.
SATISFACTION GUARANTEED.
My Dress Suits are of the best to be had in or out of this city
A Trial once given ensures future patronage

L. AZEF,
187 Dorchester Street West   Tel. Main 6491

Goodson, Durocher St. (20 June 1913, 16, 28)

BAUER, S., of Lynn, Mass., was a guest at the Place Viger Hotel (30 July 1909, 12, 33)

BAUM, Abe A., is in Toronto on business and will be back about Jan. 12, 1914 (2 Jan. 1914, 17, 4)

BAUM, B., J. Diamond, A.J. Livinson and the Misses A. Goldblatt, E. Jacobson, A. Ressler and R. Hoffman are teachers at the Chevra Kadisha Synagogue Sunday School for 1910-1911 (30 Dec. 1910, 14, 7)

BAUM, H., A.J. Livinson and the Misses A.R. Goldblatt, E. Jacobson and L. Ressler are teachers at the Chevra Kadisha Sunday School. The school's closing exercises were held June 7, 1911. L. Shapiro spoke on behalf of the congregation (9 June 1911, 14, 30)

BAUM, H.A., wrote a poem "Ode to Israel" (29 Nov. 1912, 15, 51)

BAUM, Lieut. H., who is stationed with the Royal Canadian Dragoons at St. John, Que., was in Montreal on weekend leave visiting his parents (3 April 1914, 17, 14)

BAZAR, S., M. Flanders, G. Rabinovitch, M. Rabinovitch, S. Rabinovitch, Mesdames L. Abinovitch, S. Cohen, M.S. Enzer, J. Dinovitzer, C.B. Fainer, G. Fischel, A.L. Gittleson, A.J. Godner, M. Groner, M. Harris, A. Higger, S. Hirsch, A. Jacobs, R.E. Lesser, H.M. Levinoff, T. Loebel, A. Neumann, P. Ogulnik, I. Ornstein, A. Rabinovitch, G. Rabinovitch, S. Rabinovitch, D. Rasminsky, M. Schalek, M. Usher, S. and E. Vosberg, the Misses G. Crown, M. Crown, F. Flanders, A. Harris, E. Harris, P. Hoffman, R. Klein, Paltiel, L. Ressler, R. Schalek, A. Schleifer, F. Schwartz, C. Solomon, E. Solomon and B. Viner were visitors at the provision party of the Hebrew Children's Fresh Air Camp (20 June 1913, 16, 28)

BECKER, H., is spending some time in Cobalt, Ont. (7 Oct. 1910, 13, 47)

BECKER, H.L., has gone to Dublin, Ireland for two months to visit his parents (31 Dec. 1909, 13, 7)

BECKER, J., has returned from Ireland where he visited his parents (22 April 1910, 13, 23)

BECKER, Miss, of Dublin, Ireland, who spent the past few weeks with her brother, H.J. Becker, left for Chicago to visit Mr. and Mrs. Becker (3 April 1914, 17, 14)

BECKER, T., of Philadelphia, is visiting his brother, H. Becker (2 Oct. 1912, 15, 43)

BEECHER, H., was installed as president of the Regal Club on Sun. March 15, 1913. Other officers installed were:- B. Gold, vice-pres.; M. Sigler, sec.; and P. Witzling, treas. (21 March 1913, 16, 15)

BEERMAN, M., has returned from a business trip to New York, Boston and Portland (4 Feb. 1910, 13, 12)

BEHRER, Joseph, of Philadelphia, was in Montreal during the week (29 Oct. 1909, 12, 46)

BELASCO, Mr., of England, formerly of Montreal, was here visiting friends and relatives (30 June 1911, 14, 33)

BELKIN, G., is in New York (26 July 1912, 15, 33)

G. BELKIN
408 ST. LAWRENCE ST. - - - Tel. E. 4864
Just Received a Stock of New Year Cards and Festival Prayer Books — LOWEST PRICES.
Country Orders Promptly Attended To.

BELL, Miss, of Edmonton, pupil of Miss Sophie Myers, passed her examinations and received her Licentiate in Music degree from the London College of Music, England (6 June 1913, 16, 26)

BEMAK, Miss Bella, of Brooklyn, N.Y., is visiting her sister, Mrs. L. Aron, 419 St. Lawrence Blvd. (12 Aug. 1910, 13, 39)

וויין פאר פסח

STRICTLY KOSHER

Best Domestic Wine for Pesach and throughout the year, can be obtained from—

Rev. B. BECKER
668 St. Dominique Street, Montreal

BENDER, Emanuel, Joseph Fineberg, Dr. Norman Viner and the Misses Hattie Matts, Fanny Ratner and Ida Seigler participated in the Agudath Zion Society program last Sun. evening, March 10, 1912 (15 March 1912, 15, 18)

BENJAMIN, L., read a paper "Anti-Semitism" to the Progressive Club last Sun. at the Baron de Hirsch Institute (7 May 1909, 12, 21)

BENJAMIN, L., was captain of the seniors at the first outing of the Young Men's Social and Athletic Club which took place during the weekend on St. Helen's Island. J. Clare was captain of the juniors. The 100 yard race was won by C. Cohen and the sack race by D. Yudelmark. W. Finkelstein won the 220 yard race and J. Borshow the long jump. In the two mile race A. Benjamin came first and C. Cohen second. The swimming race was won by C. Cohen with D. Yudelmark second. Miss Fanny Myers awarded the prizes (22 Aug. 1913, 16, 37)

BENJAMIN, Miss Dina, has returned after visiting friends in St. Louis, Chicago and Detroit (13 Oct. 1911, 14, 48)

BENJAMIN, Miss Dina, was the guest of Mrs. G. Geller, at Highlands, Que. (29 Aug. 1913, 16, 38)

BENJAMIN, Miss Dina, was the guest of Mrs. J. Rubin, at Beaconsfield, Que. (5 Sept. 1913, 16, 39)

BENJAMIN, Miss Dora and her little sister Evelyn, have returned home after spending the past two months at St. Gabriel de Brandon (27 Aug. 1909, 12, 37)

BENJAMIN, Moe, of New York, was the guest of his aunt, Mrs. A. Jacobs, Dorchester St. W. (21 June 1912, 15, 28)

BENJAMIN, Mr., of New York, is the guest of his aunt, Mrs. A. Jacobs, Mansfield St., for a week (2 July 1909, 12, 29)

BENJAMIN, Mrs. T., of New York, is in Montreal for a few weeks (27 Oct. 1911, 14, 50)

BENJAMIN, S., was registered at the Breslin Hotel while in New York (9 Dec. 1910, 14, 4)

BENJIMAN, Mrs. C.A. and Miss Benjiman, of New York, and Arthur Benjiman, of Kansas City, and Mr. and Mrs. S.D. Benjiman, of Kansas City, were in Montreal for the Michaels-Hart wedding on Tues. (4 June 1909, 12, 25)

BENNETT, A., sends New Years greetings (11 Sept. 1912, 15, 40)

BENOWICK, Miss Sylvia, Esplanade Ave., is visiting her grandmother, Mrs. Isaacs, in Syracuse, N.Y., and will visit Albany and New York with relatives (11 July 1913, 16, 31)

BENSWANGER, Mrs., of New York, is the guest of her parents, Mr. and Mrs. Boas, the "Sherbrooke" (8 Jan. 1909, 12, 4)

BERCOVITCH, Mr. and Mrs. Peter, have gone to New York and Atlantic City on a short holiday (31 Dec. 1909, 13, 7)

BERCOVITCH, Mr. and Mrs. Peter, returned from a short visit to New York (27 Feb. 1914, 17, 9)

BERCOVITCH, Mrs. Peter and her sister, Miss Etta Levine, are in Atlantic City for a few weeks (16 May 1913, 16, 23)

BERCOVITCH, Peter, pres. of the Laurier Liberal Club, was elected chairman of the United Hebrew Citizens' Association at a meeting held under the auspices of the Independent Citizens' League, last Sun., in the Labor Temple. "The object of the meeting was to unite in the choice of a Jewish candidate at the forthcoming elections...Eventually, it was resolved that a United Hebrew Citizens' Association be formed consisting of three members from every political club in the city, and the object of which shall be to make strenuous efforts to naturalize every Jew who is eligible for citizenship." Other UHCA officers elected were:- H. Bloomfield, pres. of the Disraeli Political Club, treas.; Max Schechter, sec. Committee members are:- A. Blumenthal, pres. of the Independent

Citizens' League, Jos. Miller, B. Rose, H. Shriberg, M. Aronson, J. Albert, M. Jacobs, H. Steinman, J. Makinoff and S. Levinsky (19 May 1911, 14, 27)

BERCOWITZ, Mrs. Joseph, of Porcupine, Ont., is the guest of her parents, Mr. and Mrs. Z. Paltiel, St. Urbain St. (13 June 1913, 16, 27)

BERCUSSON, Maxwell, H. Arbess, William Etcovitch, L.J. Kofman and Miss E. Mendel will be on the program of the Victoria Social and Literary Club annual concert and ball, Sun. Feb. 26, 1911 (17 Feb. 1911, 14, 14)

BERGER, E., of Boston, passed through Montreal en route for Chicago (8 Jan. 1909, 12, 4)

BERGER, E., of Boston, was in Montreal for a few days, the guest of Mr. and Mrs. Gus. Fischel (27 Aug. 1909, 12, 37)

BERGER, Emil, of Boston, was in Montreal on a short visit (10 Dec. 1909, 13, 4)

BERGER, Julius, son of Rabbi Joseph D. Berger, of Ottawa, has returned home after attending the Jacob Lang Bar Mitzvah in Montreal (25 March 1910, 13, 19)

BERGER, Julius, son of Rabbi Joseph D. Berger, of Ottawa, is expected back from holidays at Westboro on Sept. 1, 1910 (26 Aug. 1910, 13, 41)

BERGER, Miss Sarah, daughter of Rabbi and Mrs. Joseph D. Berger, of Ottawa, was the guest of Mr. and Mrs. H. Lang, St. Urbain St., for a few weeks (17 Feb. 1911, 14, 14)

BERGER, Mrs. Emil, of Boston, Mass., is visiting her sister, Mrs. Gus Fischel (8 Dec. 1911, 15, 4)

BERGER, Mrs. J.D. and Master Eli Berger, of Ottawa, are visiting Rabbi and Mrs. Banon in Boston (27 Dec. 1912, 16, 3)

BERGER, Mrs. L. and Mrs. M. Dubrofsky are visiting New York (22 March 1912, 15, 19)

BERGMAN, Barnet, after six months' stay in Montreal, is returning home to England (15 Oct. 1913, 16, 45)

BERGMAN, Barnet, of London, England, has arrived in Montreal (11 July 1913, 16, 31)

BERLIN, Felix, sends New Year greetings (11 Sept. 1912, 15, 40)

BERLIN, Mr., M. Albert, Myer Crown, Clarence I. de Sola, J. Eidelberg, Charles Fisher, H. Freiman, Lyon Heillig, I. Kirschberg, A. Levin, S. Levinson, H. Levy, S. Litner, Joseph Miller, S.L. Nathanson, A.D. Paltiel, A. Rabin, Z. Ruttenberg, O. Shiller, D. Sperber, Adolphe Stark and J.J. Weinfield contributed to the Zionist Central Fund (11 July 1913, 16, 31)

BERLIN, Mrs. S. and daughter, Pauline, Elm Ave., are visiting friends and relatives in New York and Philadelphia for a few weeks (27 Dec. 1912, 16, 3)

BERLIND, Mr. and Mrs. H. and family are at their cottage at Boucherville (30 July 1909, 12, 33)

BERLINER, E., of Washington D.C., stayed at the Corona Hotel while in Montreal (12 March 1909, 12, 13)

BERLINER, E.M., of Washington, D.C., is a guest at the Corona Hotel (22 Oct. 1909, 12, 45)

BERLINER, Mr. and Mrs. E., are spending the summer at Strathmore (25 June 1909, 12, 28)

BERLINER, Mr. and Mrs. E., have left for New York, en route for Europe (8 March 1912, 15, 17)

BERLINER, Mr. and Mrs. Edgar, have settled down for the summer at Strathmore (11 June 1909, 12, 26)

BERLINER, Samuel, secretary, Grand Lodge, District No. 1, IOBB, of New York, was in Montreal on B'nai B'rith business (13 May 1910, 13, 26)

BERMAN, A., has returned from two months at Hot Springs, Ark. (27 Jan. 1911, 14, 11)

BERMAN, Archie, has gone to Mount Clemens on holiday (24 Nov. 1911, 15, 2)

BERMAN, Miss A., 70 St. Famille St., and Miss G. Litner, 694b City Hall Ave., secretaries of the Young People's Hachnosis Orchim Society are organizing the membership campaign for another five hundred members (27 Feb. 1914, 17, 9)

BERMAN, Miss E., Greene Ave., Westmount, is spending a few weeks in New York (10 April 1914, 17, 15)

BERMAN, Miss Esther and Miss Dora Rothschild, of Westmount, are visiting the Thousand Islands (19 July 1912, 15, 32)

BERMAN, Miss Esther, Greene Ave., is at Averne, N.Y. for a few weeks (8 Aug. 1913, 16, 35)

BERMAN, Miss R., Greene Ave., is in New York for several weeks (15 Nov. 1912, 15, 49)

BERMAN, Miss Rose, chaired the Young People's Hachnosis Orchim Society social and popcorn party last Sun. Participating in the musical program were:- L. Brazer, Mr. Rinder, Max Kolber, I. Mendelsohn and Miss B. Brazer (20 Feb. 1914, 17, 8)

BERMAN, Misses Rose and Esther Berman have left for Bar Harbor, Me. (6 Aug. 1909, 12, 34)

BERMAN, Mr. and Mrs. J., are visiting Mesdames I. Weinberg and A.M. Weinberg, Elm Ave. (26 April 1912, 15, 24)

BERMAN, Mrs. L.J., St. Mark St., left for Arverne, N.Y. (1 Aug. 1913, 16, 34)

BERNFIELD, M., M. Garber, J. Viner, H. Warshawsky and the Misses Goldwater and Goldstein passed third year arts, McGill University. B. Bernstein, C. Goldwater and Miss S. Sperber passed second year arts. Misses R. Weinfield and S. Talpis passed first year arts (16 May 1913, 16, 23)

BERNSTEIN, Bessie, Esther Weisberg, Rebecca Rosenzweig, G. Sigler, Fanny Cohen, Leah Friedman, M. Zimmerman, Z. Weisberg, R. Valinsky, H. Bravstein, Celia Superior, R. Kibrick, S. Geller, L. Helfand and S. Chaskelson graduated from Dufferin School (3 March 1911, 14, 16)

BERNSTEIN, D.L. and H.S. Fineberg were judges at the Young People's Hachnosis Orchim Society debate "Is Capital Punishment Justifiable", last Sun. I. Popliger and H. Sourkes spoke in favor of capital punishment while Maurice Hart, S. Schachter, Maurice Wechsler and the Misses A. Navarich and Rose Samuels spoke in favor of its abolition (31 Jan. 1913, 16, 8)

BERNSTEIN, Dr. D.H., was elected president of the Hebrew Children's Fresh Air Fund at the last meeting. Other officers elected were:- Adolph Aron, H. Schleifer and Mrs. J.L. Gittleson, vice-pres.; Mrs. J.N. Neumann, gen. sec.; Mesdames J. Cohen and H. Schleifer, asst. secs.; M. Zelicowitch, treas.; M. Flanders and G. Bazar, trustees; Joseph Bessner, Reuben Brainin, Dr. S. Ortenberg, George and S. Rabbinowich, and S. Skibelsky, board of directors. Mrs. J.N. Neumann, 3 Laval Ave., the energetic secretary, is accepting donations to the Fund which has purchased a home in Shawbridge, Que. "...for the benefit of the poverty-stricken Jewish mothers and their poorly fed children, who, during the hot summer months, had no opportunity of spending a little while in the open country air..." (16 May 1913, 16, 23)

BERNSTEIN, Dr. L., is president of the Young People's Society of Hachnosis Orchim which organized a successful concert and ball (4 March 1910, 13, 16)

BERNSTEIN, Dr. Ludwig B., superintendent of the Sheltering Guardian Society of New York, is registered at the Windsor Hotel (4 Feb. 1910, 13, 12)

BERNSTEIN, E.G., of Messrs. H. Bernstein & Sons, has left for England aboard the S.S. Victorian (19 Nov. 1909, 13, 1)

BERNSTEIN, H. and family will leave shortly for Chateauguay for the summer (18 June 1909, 12, 27)

BERNSTEIN, M., 30a Duluth W.; Mrs. Benjamin, 62 Drolet; Mr. Bloom, 40 Drolet; Mr. Braides, 1086 Clarke; R. Cohen, 9b Drolet; M. Colle, 190 Laval Ave.; Mrs. Eschenbaum, 58 Drolet; Mr. Feldman, 1126 St. Urbain; Mr. Goldberg, 1159 Clarke; Mr. Goldfine, 1161 Clarke; Mr. Greenberg, 317 Laval Ave.; Mrs. Herman, 462 Sanguinet; S. Klein, 512 Sanguinet; Mrs. Kosawatski, 44 Bagg; J. Levitt, 657 City Hall; M. Levitt, 1100 Clarke; B. Mendel, 1131 St. Urbain; Miss Millman, 415 Sanguinet; H. Nathanson, 1072 St. Lawrence; Mr. Rosenfeldt, 25 Drolet; Mrs. Rosenthal, 186 Laval Ave.; M. Sassemer, 60 Drolet; Mrs. Schliefer, 41 Drolet; Mr. Sherman, 34 Bagg; Mr. Speyer, 1122 St. Urbain; J. Steinhouse, 3b Drolet; S. Tritt, 1098 Clarke; Mr. Vineberg, 41 Bagg; J. Winer, 73 Sherbrooke E.; and J.C. Zacks 910 St. Lawrence Blvd., made donations to the Young Men's Zionist and Literary Society (10 Jan. 1913, 16, 5)

BERNSTEIN, M., Hutchison St., went on a business trip to Europe (15 Aug. 1913, 16, 36)

BERNSTEIN, M. Montefiore, and Miss Minnie Bernstein, Hutchison St., have gone to Ste. Agathe for a fortnight (12 March 1909, 12, 13)

BERNSTEIN, M. Montefiore, returned from his trip abroad (12 Sept. 1913, 16, 40)

BERNSTEIN, Max and Miss Pauline Bernstein, of Louisville, Kentucky, are in Montreal on a visit (18 April 1913, 16, 19)

BERNSTEIN, Miss Clara V., of New York, will be the guest of her aunt, Mrs. R.H. Blumenthal at Beaurepaire for the summer (8 July 1910, 13, 34)

BERNSTEIN, Miss Clara V., of New York, was the guest of Miss Maud Lazarus, Kingston Ave.,

From The Canadian Jewish Times   Montreal

Westmount (26 Aug. 1910, 13, 41)

BERNSTEIN, Miss Clara V., of New York, was the guest of her cousins, the Misses Silverman, Tupper St, Westmount (25 July 1911, 14, 36)

BERNSTEIN, Miss Clara V., who was the guest of her aunt, Mrs. B.H. Bernstein, Beaurepaire, has returned home to New York (9 Sept. 1910, 13, 43)

BERNSTEIN, Miss E., of Detroit, is the guest of Mrs. L.B. McFarlane (28 July 1911, 14, 37)

BERNSTEIN, Miss Edna, who is visiting her sister, Mrs. Blout in Ottawa, was in Toronto to attend the charity ball (9 Jan. 1914, 17, 5)

BERNSTEIN, Miss Elizabeth, has gone to Worcester, New York and Boston (11 Nov. 1910, 13, 52)

BERNSTEIN, Miss Elizabeth, is in New York visiting friends (14 Feb. 1913, 16, 10)

BERNSTEIN, Miss, entertained her Sunday School class at a snowshoe tramp last Sun. (19 Feb. 1909, 12, 10)

BERNSTEIN, Miss Lizzie, returned from a visit to her sister, Mrs. Rome, in Worcester, Mass. (20 Feb. 1914, 17, 8)

BERNSTEIN, Miss Minnie, Hutchison St., has returned from Worcester (26 Jan. 1912, 15, 11)

BERNSTEIN, Miss Minnie, is spending the summer at Woodlands, the guest of Mrs. E.G. Bernstein (22 July 1910, 13, 36)

BERNSTEIN, Miss Minnie, returned from Toronto where she was the guest of Mrs. Percy Hermant, Sussex Court (20 March 1914, 17, 12)

BERNSTEIN, Miss Miriam, president of the Daughters of Zion, opened the annual dance which took place in Stanley Hall, on March 30, 1910. Others participating were:- the Misses Hattie Matts, Ray Heillig, Ida Siegler, Minnie Bernstein, Rose Harris, Jane Rost, Sarah Lesser, Lillian Wetstein, Singer and Kaufman and Messrs. Henry Bye, Leon Goldman, Joe Frueberg, Jack Aronson, Arthur Ginsberg, Nathaniel S. Fineberg and Max Cohen, Mesdames Levy, E.G. Bernstein, Leon Goldman and Felix Harris (8 April 1910, 13, 21)

BERNSTEIN, Miss Miriam, spent the weekend at Ste. Agathe (16 July 1909, 12, 31)

BERNSTEIN, Miss, of Detroit, was the guest of Mrs. J. Hirsch, Bishop St. (30 June 1911, 14, 33)

BERNSTEIN, Miss, of New York, is the guest of her aunt, Mrs. R.H. Blumenthal, Beaurepaire (7 July 1911, 14, 34)

BERNSTEIN, Miss Reba, who was the guest of her cousins, the Misses Jacobs, Sherbrooke St. W., over the winter has returned home to Chicago (10 April 1914, 17, 15)

BERNSTEIN, Misses, have gone to Worcester to visit their sister, Mrs. Nathan Rome. They will the spend the rest of the summer at Old Orchard (14 July 1911, 14, 35)

BERNSTEIN, Mr. and Mrs. C., left last Wed. evening for Englehart, Ont., for the winter (14 Jan. 1910, 13, 9)

BERNSTEIN, Mr. and Mrs. C., of New York, are here for the Carnival and are visiting Mr. and Mrs. H. Bernstein, Hutchison St. (19 Feb. 1909, 12, 10)

BERNSTEIN, Mr. and Mrs. E., have taken a cottage at Chateauguay for the summer (9 July 1909, 12, 30)

BERNSTEIN, Mr. and Mrs. E.G., are occupying a cottage in Woodlands (22 July 1910, 13, 36)

BERNSTEIN, Mr. and Mrs. H. and family, 65 Hutchison St., wish their friends and relatives a happy New Year (1 Oct. 1913, 16, 42-43)

BERNSTEIN, Mr. and Mrs. H., Hutchison St., gave a reception in honor of the engagement, well-known local Zionist leader Miss Miriam Bernstein to Nathan Rome, of Worcester, Mass. Mesdames Henry Weinfield and E.G. Bernstein assisted in receiving. Misses Rae Heillig, Rae Tannenbaum, Dorothy Leo, Beccie Pierce, Elizabeth and Minnie Bernstein were in charge of the dining room (10 June 1910, 13, 30)

BERNSTEIN, Mr. and Mrs., of Cleveland, were guests of Mrs. G.E. Goldstein, Beaurepaire (4 Aug. 1911, 14, 38)

BERNSTEIN, Mr. and Mrs., St. Lawrence Blvd., were honored at a party given by the family on Sun. evening, Jan. 12, 1913. Guests included:- Lew Bernstein, V. Goldberg, Jack and Joe Harris, J. Springer and the Misses K. Atkins, Milly Soskin and Ray Turner (17 Jan. 1913, 16, 6)

BERNSTEIN, Mrs. A. and her two children, of New York, are guests of Mrs. M. Dobrofsky, Esplanade Ave., for a month (30 May 1913, 16, 25)

BERNSTEIN, Mrs., has returned home to Fargo, N.D., after visiting her daughter, Mrs. H.L. Blout, of Westmount (4 Nov. 1910, 13, 51)

BERNSTEIN, Mrs. M. and Miss Clara V. Bernstein, of New York, will remain here for the summer (7 July 1911, 14, 34)

BERNSTEIN, Mrs. M., has returned home to New York after spending the summer in Montreal, the guest of Mrs. I.A. Abrahams (10 Sept. 1909, 12, 39)

BERNSTEIN, Mrs. M., of New York, is spending the summer with her sister, Mrs. Blumenthal at Beaurepaire (9 July 1909, 12, 30)

BERNSTEIN, Mrs. M., of New York, was the guest of Mrs. Samuel Abrahams, of Montreal (16 July 1909, 12, 31)

BERNSTEIN, Mrs. M., of New York, and Miss Grace Abrahams were guests of Mrs. Silverman, at Boucherville for the weekend (30 July 1909, 12, 33)

BERNSTEIN, Mrs., will be the guest of her sister, Mrs. I. Abrahams, Argyle Ave., Westmount (7 July 1911, 14, 34)

BERNSTEIN, P., Lucy Goodstone and Sarah Somer received scholarships at Dufferin School (3 March 1911, 14, 16)

BERNSTEIN, S. and Miss Elizabeth Bernstein returned from Tannersville, Catskills (23 Aug. 1912, 15, 37)

BERO, Stanley, Baron de Hirsch Institute manager, is leaving to take a similar position in a large American city. Among those present at a farewell dinner at the Montefiore Club last Tues. evening were:- Lyon Cohen, Max Heppner, H. Horsfall, H. Rosenblatt and Louis Vineberg (7 May 1909, 12, 21)

BERO, Stanley, left for New York last Tues. evening (7 May 1909, 12, 21)

BERO, Stanley, Louis Fitch, H.E. Hirshorn, J. Levine, M. Lightstone, A. Muhlstock and G.S. Tritt took part in a debate "Resolved: That it would be in the best interests of the Jewish community of Montreal to adopt a federated system of charities" at the Maccabean Literary Circle meeting last Sun. aft. (26 Feb. 1909, 12, 11)

BERO, Stanley, national organizer for the Hebrew Sheltering and Immigrant Aid Society, is touring the mid-west on behalf of his organization (6 Oct. 1911, 14, 47)

BERSON, Miss Mabel, was given a kitchen shower by members of the YWHA in honor of her approaching marriage to J. Issen. Those present included:- the Misses J. Berson, R. Brotman, J. Goldstein, R. Harle, B. Issen, E.L. Issen, A. Pinsler, J. Schulich, B. Silver and B. Singer (5 Dec. 1913, 16, 52)

BERSON, Myer, Sol. Cohen, M. Frank, Moe Garfinkle, Teddy Garfinkle, Morris Goldberg, Charles Lambert, Jack Livinson and Sam H. Shalinsky are members of the YMHA picnic committee. The picnic will be held Sun. July 20, 1913 at Otterburn Park, St. Hilaire. Mr. Shalinsky is chairman. Other members assisting are:- L.H. Bernstein, Harry Cohen, D. Goldstein, J. Goldstein, Solomon Kellert, D. Livinson and Louis Rubenstein (18 July 1913, 16, 32)

BESNER, M., has returned from Moncton, N.B. (25 June 1909, 12, 28)

BESSNER, H., C. Bindman, H. Ressler, J. Tapperberg, M. Bessner, S.E. Manolson, H. Adelstein, P. Vineberg, H. Schwartz, P. Merson, H. Orenstein and J. Moskovitch were members of the organizing committee of the Eureka A.A.A. first annual concert and ball. Those taking part in the program were:- Edward Vineberg, Hyman Orenstein, Bernard Corber and the Misses Sarah Gittelson, Eva Gittelson, Sadie Solomon, Lily Vineberg, Hyalie Freeman, M. Marcuse and F. Bloomberg (27 Jan. 1911, 14, 11)

BESSNER, H., was elected president of the Young People's Society of Hachnosis Orchim at the semi-annual meeting on Sun. April 9, 1910. Other officers elected were:- I. Dovico and Miss F. Gross, vice-pres.; J. Harris, treas.; H.S. Fineberg, corres. sec.; Miss H. Hirsch, fin. sec. On the Board of Directors are: A. Sourkes, sergeant-at-arms; S. Bessler, J. Pinsler, A.P. Shoster, F. Cohen, I. Sourkes and Misses B. Gross, F. Golt, A. Gold, R. Cohen and B. Schachter; ex-offico, D.L. Bernstein (15 April 1910, 13, 22)

BESSNER, H., was elected president of the Young People's Hachnosis Orchim Society last Sun. aft. in the Baron de Hirsch Institute. Other officers elected were:- H.A. Fineberg, vice-pres.; Miss R. Echenberg, 2nd vice-pres.; M.M. Kolber, treas.; Miss B. Volinsky, fin. sec., Miss J. Goldberg, corr.- sec.; A. Sourkes, sergeant-at-arms; D.L. Bernstein, I. Dovia, H. Hurt, A. Issenman, H. Sourkes and the Misses V. Bernstein, R. Cohen, F. Frank, F. Golt and E. Steinsberg (7 April 1911, 14, 21)

BESSNER, H., was elected president of the Young People's Hachnosis Orchim Society on Oct. 20, 1912 in the Baron de Hirsch Institute. Other officers elected were:- H. Sourkes and Miss R. Samuels, vice-pres.; W. Goldman, fin. sec.; Miss A. Naravich, rec. sec.; M. Kolber, treas.; M. Bernstein, sergeant-at-arms; D.L. Bernstein, I. Bernstein, M. Hart, M. Wechsler and the Misses V. Bernstein, R. Burman, S. Raphalovitch, A. Silverman and E. Turner, board of directors. Others participating at the meeting were W. Wexler and Miss Vilensky (25 Oct. 1912, 15, 46)

BESSNER, Harry, was elected president of the Young People's Hachnosis Orchim Society last Sun. Other officers elected were:- A.L. Shoster, 1st vice-pres.; Miss R. Cohen, 2nd vice-pres.; I. Caplan, fin. sec.; H.S. Fineberg, corr. sec.; M. Kolber, treas.; I. Sourkes, sergeant-at-arms; H. Sourkes, L. Goldberg, S. Bessler, A. Sourkes, M. Shuleman and the Misses F. Frank, F. Golt, E. Steinberg, S. Greenshon and S. Raefaelovitch, executive (18 Nov. 1910, 14, 1)

BIEBER, Mr. and Mrs. A. and daughter have left for Quebec City (30 July 1909, 12, 33)

BIEBER, Mr. and Mrs. A. and daughter are spending a few weeks in Atlantic City (16 May 1913, 16, 23)

BIEBER, Mr. and Mrs. A. and family have left Old Orchard, Me., for Ste. Agathe where they will spend the rest of the summer (1 Aug. 1913, 16, 34)

BIERMAN, F., of Shawinigan Falls, is in Montreal (27 Aug. 1909, 12, 37)

BILSKY, Alec, of Toronto, was in Montreal the past week (1 Aug. 1913, 16, 34)

BILSKY, Miss E., of Ottawa, was in Montreal (16 Sept. 1910, 13, 44)

BILSKY, Miss Etta, of Ottawa, is the guest of Mrs. Alec. Bilsky, Dorchester St. W. (4 Nov. 1910, 13, 51)

BILSKY, Miss Eva, of Ottawa, was in Montreal for a few days (1 Dec. 1911, 15, 3)

BILSKY, Miss, has returned to Ottawa after visiting Mrs. N. Silver, 9 Souvenir Ave. (24 Dec. 1909, 13, 6)

BILSKY, Miss, of Ottawa, is the guest of Mrs. N. Silver, Souvenir St. (5 Nov. 1909, 12, 47)

BILSKY, Mr. and Mrs. A.M. and daughter have returned from Caledonia Springs (5 Nov. 1909, 12, 47)

BILSKY, Mr. and Mrs. A.M. and daughter have returned to Cobalt after spending some time in Montreal (17 Dec. 1909, 13, 5)

BILSKY, Mr. and Mrs. A.M. and family have moved to Toronto (29 Nov. 1912, 15, 51)

BILSKY, Mr. and Mrs. A.M., stayed at the Knickerbocker Hotel in New York (19 April 1912, 15, 23)

BILSKY, Mrs. A., of Cobalt, Ont., is in Montreal (21 May 1909, 12, 23)

BILSKY, Mrs. A.M. and daughter are spending the holidays in Montreal, guests of her sister, Mrs. D.S. Friedman, Colonial Apts. (24 Sept. 1909, 12, 41)

BILSKY, Mrs. A.M. and daughter have gone to Ottawa for a week (1 Oct. 1909, 12, 42)

BILSKY, Mrs. A.M. and daughter, of Cobalt, Ont., were in Montreal the past week (25 Feb. 1910, 13, 15)

BILSKY, Mrs. A.M., gave a children's party in honor of her daughter Annie's birthday. Prize winners were:- Sydney Pierce, Solly Jacobs, Norman Friedman, Ed. and Tom Wing and Miss Annette Jacobs (9 Aug. 1912, 15, 35)

BILSKY, Mrs. Alec and daughter, of Cobalt, Ont., are guests of Mrs. D.S. Friedman, Colonial Apts. (12 March 1909, 12, 13)

BILSKY, Mrs. Alec and Mrs. A. Pierce have left for Boston on a short visit (3 March 1911, 14, 16)

BILSKY, Mrs. Alec., family and maid are at Old Orchard for the summer (14 July 1911, 14, 35)

BILSKY, Mrs. Alexander and daughter left for Cobalt, Ont. They were guests of Mrs. D.S. Friedman (11 June 1909, 12, 26)

BILSKY, Mrs. Alexander, of Cobalt, Ont., who was in Montreal visiting her sister, Mrs. D.S. Friedman, left for New York Tues. evening where she will meet her husband (19 March 1909, 12, 14)

BILSKY, Mrs. and daughter have returned to Cobalt, Ont. (2 April 1909, 12, 16)

BILSKY, Mrs. and her daughter, Mrs. I. Freedman, of Ottawa, visited Mrs. Alec Bilsky, Dorchester St. W., this week (3 March 1911, 14, 16)

BILSKY, Samuel, of Ottawa, spent a few days in Montreal (8 Oct. 1909, 12, 43)

BILSKY, Samuel, of Ottawa, was in Montreal on a visit (19 Nov. 1909, 13, 1)

BINDMAN, C., chaired the Eureka A.A.A. theatre party and banquet on Sun. evening, March 15, 1913 held in honor of its victorious bowling team. Mr. Bindman is leaving Montreal. The trophy was donated by Peter H. Merson and B.H. Schwartz to the Montefiore Bowling League. Louis Rubenstein made a presentation to I. Caplan (28 March 1913, 16, 16)

BINDMAN, C., chaired the evening of the Eureka A.A.A. annual sleigh drive on Sun. evening, Feb. 19, 1911. The sleigh ride took place from the residence of A. Bessner, 34 Guildbault St. (24 Feb. 1911, 14, 15)

BINSWANGER, Mrs. H., of New York, spent the past week with her parents, Mr. and Mrs. B.A. Boas, at the New Sherbrooke Apts. (24 Sept. 1909, 12, 41)

BIRKENTHAL, Miss Camille, of Toronto, was the guest of Miss Ruth Goldstein (30 July 1909, 12, 33)

BISHINSKY, W., of Bishinsky Bros. Mfgs. Ladies' Coats and Suits, Montreal, returned from a successful trip out east (13 June 1913, 16, 27)

BISMARCK, Bernard, who underwent a serious operation at Dr. Piche's hospital, has completely recovered and is back home (1 April 1910, 13, 20)

BLAUSTEIN, H. and family will soon leave for Chateauguay for the summer (11 June 1909, 12, 26)

BLAUSTEIN, S., J.B. Ellis, Joseph Fineberg, Charles Fisher, L. Frankel, M. Fromson, M. Ryan, S. Siegler, M. Slobodsky and S. Sternklar received their Land Fund certificates at the fifteenth annual meeting of the Agudath Zion Society of Montreal on Sun. June 22, 1913, in the Baron de Hirsch Institute. Golden Book certificates were presented to David Kirschberg and Master Philip Wolofsky. Albums containing Golden Book and Land Fund certificates were presented to Master Ben Zion Steine, son of M.B. Steine in honor of his recent Bar Mitzvah and to Clarence I. de Sola in appreciation of his work on behalf of the Zionist cause in Canada (27 June 1913, 16, 29)

BLAUSTEIN, S., Messrs. N. Simonson, C.W. Davis, A.S. Morris, A. Rosenberg, H. Schloman, C.L. Morris, L. Rubenstein, M. Goldberg and A. Goldner were in New York last week (4 June 1909, 12, 25)

BLEEKMAN, Miss, of Cleveland, and Mrs. Joseph Stein are guests of Mrs. George Goldstein, Elgin Ave. (23 Dec. 1910, 14, 6)

BLOCH, Miss Edna, of Toronto, is the guest of Mrs. M. Goldstein, Westmount Ave. (24 May 1912, 15, 25)

BLOCH, Miss Jennie, a pupil of Miss Sophie Myers, was the solo pianist at the YMCA on Mon. Feb. 23, 1914. "Miss Bloch though only ten years old gave an excellent rendition of some difficult pieces and received great applause." (27 Feb. 1914, 17, 9)

BLOCH, Misses Mabel and Edna, of Toronto, will spend the summer at Beaconsfield, Que. (7 June 1912, 15, 26)

BLOCH, Mr., of Chicago, was in Montreal the past week (3 Dec. 1909, 13, 3)

BLOCH, Mrs. and Miss Edna Bloch are spending the summer at Val Morin, Que. (18 July 1913, 16, 32)

BLOCK, Aron, of Kansas City, is visiting his parents, Mount Royal Ave. West (21 June 1912, 15, 28)

BLOCK, Aron, of Kansas City, Kansas, is visiting his parents, Mr. and Mrs. M. Block, 141 Mount Royal Ave., Westmount (14 July 1911, 14, 35)

BLOCK, Aron, of Kansas City, Kansas, is visiting his parents, Mr. and Mrs. M. Block (11 April 1913, 16, 18)

BLOCK, M., was re-elected president of Aberdeen Lodge, No. 159, IOSB, on Sun. Dec. 26, 1909. Other officers elected were:- P. Dubrofsky, vice-pres.; H. Hart, sec.; H. Bercovitch, treas.; A. Rubinovitch, H. Bercovitch and P. Dubrofsky, trustees; Joseph Gold, outside guardian; Dr. S.F. Stein, physician. The Lodge commemorates its sixteenth anniversary at the annual ball to be held Jan. 12, 1910 (31 Dec. 1909, 13, 7)

BLOCK, Miss Jennie, of Montreal, is a ten year old child prodigy who will be performing a piano solo at the YMHA Symphony concert in Windsor Hall on April 24, 1913 (18 April 1913, 16, 19)

BLOCK, Miss Katie and Miss A. Finkelstein are vacationing at Shawbridge (6 Aug. 1909, 12, 34)

BLOCK, Miss Rhoda, has returned from abroad (3 Sept. 1909, 12, 38)

BLOOMER, M., H. Lang, S. Margolese, C. Mower, I. McKinley, S. Schlosberg, A. Zuckes and the Misses Nellie and Clara Mintz, Sara Rosenthal and Clara Schwartz helped organize the B'nai U' Bnoth Zion Kadimah eighth annual dance

B'nai U' Bnoth Zion Kadimah eighth annual dance last Sun. in Auditorium Hall (23 Feb. 1912, 15, 15)

BLOOMFIELD, David, leaves next week on a business trip to England, Germany, France, Switzerland and Italy (14 Jan. 1910, 13, 9)

BLOOMFIELD, H., is in Ontario on a business trip (1 June 1911, 14, 29)

BLOOMFIELD, Harry and M. Albert have been elected delegates by their respective lodges of the Ancient Order of Foresters, to the High Court Convention in Sarnia, Ont., on Aug. 20 , 1909 (6 Aug. 1909, 12, 34)

BLOOMFIELD, Harry, has been elected District Chief Ranger of the Ancient Order of Foresters, for Hochelaga, at the High Court Convention, held in Sarnia, Ont. (10 Sept. 1909 12, 39)

BLOOMFIELD, Harry, has left on a business trip to Ontario (24 Feb. 1911, 14, 15)

BLOOMFIELD, Harry, has returned from a business trip to Toronto (18 March 1910, 13, 18)

BLOOMFIELD, Harry, has returned from a buying trip to Boston, New York and Providence (22 July 1910, 13, 36)

BLOOMFIELD, Harry, has returned from a business trip to the eastern U.S. (9 Dec. 1910, 14, 4)

BLOOMFIELD, Harry, is on a business trip to Ottawa, and is expected to return to-day (11 June 1909, 12, 26)

BLOOMFIELD, Harry, is president of the Disraeli Club (formerly the Disraeli Conservative Club) which has turned independent. "Its leanings will still, however, be towards Conservatism; but it recognizes that it is by far a better policy to vote for an honest Liberal, than a doubtful Conservative, and vice versa. The Club will also now take in hand a spirited manner the naturalization of all those eligible for citizenship." (12 March 1909, 12, 13)

BLOOMFIELD, Harry, leaves tomorrow night for a ten day trip to Boston, Providence and New York (18 June 1909, 12, 27)

BLOOMFIELD, Harry, president of the Disraeli Conservative Club, chaired the first meeting of the season last week. He stated that prospects for the Conservative Party were very bright. Officers elected were:- Samuel Slatkoff, 1st vice-pres.; Henry Kronenberg, 2nd vice-pres.; Samuel Bloomfield, sec.; L. Birk, treas.; S. Lang, B. Shapiro, H. Shapiro, H. Ernstein, M. Singer and A. Albert (23 Sept. 1910, 13, 45)

BLOOMFIELD, Harry, was installed as president of the Disraeli Conservative Club last Wed. evening. Other officers installed were:- Samuel Slapcoff, Samuel Bloomfield, J. Albert, H. Ernstein, L. Birke, M. Singer, M. Goldberg, S. Lang, M. Cohen and A. Shapiro (6 Jan. 1911, 14, 8)

BLOOMFIELD, Harry, who is on a business trip in the eastern U.S., is expected back next week (16 July 1909, 12, 31)

BLOOMFIELD, Harry, who left for an extended trip of the southern U.S., was presented with an engraved gold-mounted walking cane, by members of the Disraeli Club of which he is president (25 June 1909, 12, 28)

BLOOMFIELD, Mr. and Mrs. H. and family have taken up their summer cottage at Dorval (26 May 1911, 14, 28)

BLOOMFIELD, Mr. and Mrs. Harry, 4019 Dorchester St. W., will be "at home" Sun. March 8, 1914 to celebrate their tenth wedding anniversary (6 March 1914, 17, 10)

BLOOMFIELD, Mr. and Mrs. Sam, have returned from a visit to New York (22 Nov. 1912, 15, 50)

BLOOMFIELD, Mr. and Mrs. Sam, Plaza Apts., celebrated the Pidyan Ha Ben of their new born son, on Wed. June 18, 1913 (27 June 1913, 16, 29)

BLOOMFIELD, S., of Cornwall, was a guest at the Bath Hotel (11 June 1909, 12, 26)

BLOOMFIELD, Samuel (secretary); M. Solomon (referee of games); Samuel Albert (time-keeper); and H. Jacobs (on the games committee) are organizing a picnic at Ste. Rose, under the auspices of the Ancient Order of Foresters (16 July 1909, 12, 31)

BLOOMFIELD, Samuel, has gone on a trip through the southern states to Memphis, New Orleans and New Mexico (2 April 1909, 12, 16)

BLOOMFIELD, Samuel, has left for Florida and Cuba (24 Feb. 1911, 14, 15)

BLOOMFIELD, Samuel, has recovered from his recent indisposition (13 Aug. 1909, 12, 35)

BLOOMFIELD, Samuel, has returned from a short visit to New York (28 May 1909, 12, 24)

BLOOMFIELD, Samuel, has returned from a holiday in New York (19 Aug. 1910, 13, 40)

BLOOMFIELD, Samuel, has returned from his trip south (23 April 1909, 12, 19)

BLOOMFIELD, Samuel, has returned from New York (6 Jan. 1911, 14, 8)

BLOOMFIELD, Samuel, is spending a few weeks in Atlantic City (1 Oct. 1909, 12, 42)

BLOOMFIELD, Samuel, left last Wed. for Ottawa (10 Feb. 1911, 14, 13)

BLOOMFIELD, Samuel, was in Ottawa during the week (16.Sept. 1910, 13, 44)

BLOOMFIELD, Samuel, was in Ottawa this week on a business trip (24 Sept. 1909, 12, 41)

BLOOMFIELD, Samuel, was in Quebec City during the week on business (27 May 1910, 13, 28)

BLOOMSTONE, Mr. and Mrs. H., 51 St. Famille St., wish their friends and relatives a happy New Year (10 Oct. 1913, 16, 44)

BLOOMSTONE, Mrs. Harold and little daughter are spending the summer at Lancaster, Ont. (9 July 1909, 12, 30)

BLOOMSTONE, Mrs. Harry, 51 St. Famille St., entertained last Sun. evening at cards. Winners were M. Crown, and the Misses Mary Crown and J. Greenspon (21 March 1913, 16, 15)

BLOUT, Miss, is visiting friends in New York and Washington (25 Feb. 1910, 13, 15)

BLOUT, Miss Lena, is in Washington on a visit (8 Jan. 1909, 12, 4)

BLOUT, Mr. and Mrs. E., have returned from Atlantic City (30 July 1909, 12, 33)

BLOUT, Mr. and Mrs. Emanuel, are spending the summer at Ste. Agathe (2 July 1909, 12, 29)

BLOUT, Mr. and Mrs., have taken up their summer residence at Cartierville (25 June 1909, 12, 28)

BLOUT, Mrs., of Ottawa was in Montreal for a few days (22 Dec. 1911, 15, 6)

BLOUT, Mrs., of Ottawa, was in Montreal for a brief stay (13 Dec. 1912, 16, 1)

BLUCHER, Miss Marie, a talented mezzo-soprano and Messrs. P. Presner and M. Gralik, two excellent violinists, will perform with the YMHA Symphony Orchestra in Windsor Hall, Thurs. evening, April 24, 1913 (4 April 1913, 16, 17)

BLUCHER, Miss Mary, a former McGill music student who went abroad last Aug. to continue her musical studies, made her first appearance in Berlin, early in Jan. in the opera "La Boheme" as Mimi. Miss Blucher is studying under Madame Kahn, a teacher of the Berlin Opera Conservatory (27 Feb. 1914, 17, 9)

BLUCHER, Misses Marie, Eva Goldstein and Rose Koffman were awarded scholarships for the 1912-1913 session at the McGill University Conservatory of Music (25 Oct. 1912, 15, 46)

BLUM, Mrs. J. and Miss O.L. Leavitt sailed from Liverpool for Montreal on the Allan Liner 'Virginian' last Fri. (4 June 1909, 12, 25)

BLUM, Mrs., of Waverley, N.Y., was in Montreal visiting her father, A. Tchwrenski (10 March 1911, 14, 17)

BLUMBERG, Messrs. and Jacobs have opened a business "The Rochester Tailors", at 263 Notre Dame St. W. (15 April 1910, 13, 22)

BLUMBERG, Miss H., of Dorval, Que., gave a shower at her home in honor of Miss Hattie Tannenbaum on Sun. May 25, 1913 (30 May 1913, 16, 25)

BLUMBERG, Miss Sara, of Annapolis, Md., is the guest of her cousin, Mrs. Wolf Shankman, of Ottawa (20 Aug. 1909, 12, 36)

BLUMBERG, Mr. and Mrs. and family who spent the summer at Dorval, have taken up their residence at 7 St. Mark St. (22 Oct. 1909, 12, 45)

BLUMENTHAL, A., is president of the newly formed Jewish Citizens' Association which held its first meeting in the Labour Temple last Sun. "The object of the formation is to instruct all those eligible on the duties of of citizenship and to assist them in obtaining naturalization papers." (11 Feb. 1910, 13, 13)

BLUMENTHAL, Abraham, was re-elected alderman for St. Louis Ward in the municipal elections. L. Rubenstein was elected alderman for St. Lawrence Ward. "We are informed that while the majority of voters in the two Wards are co-religionists, a not inconsiderable number of non-Jews cast their votes for both victorious candidates - a fact which makes their election all the more pleasing." (10 April 1914, 17, 15)

BLUMENTHAL, Ald. and Mrs. A., sailed on the Royal Edward for Europe (8 Aug. 1913, 16, 35)

BLUMENTHAL, Ald. and Mrs. Abraham., 90a

St. Famille St., wish their friends a happy New Year (1 Oct. 1913, 16, 42-43)

BLUMENTHAL, Alderman Abraham, is going out west Sun. Dec. 8, 1912, to study the high cost of living in other Canadian cities. His first stop will be in Winnipeg on Dec. 11, 1912 (6 Dec. 1912, 15, 52)

BLUMENTHAL, George, delivered an address on "Sir Wilfrid Laurier" to the fortnightly meeting of the Primrose Club (17 Dec. 1909, 13, 5)

BLUMENTHAL, George, has gone to Old Orchard, Me., for two weeks (12 Aug. 1910, 13, 39)

BLUMENTHAL, George, son of Mr. and Mrs. R.H. Blumenthal, has recovered from his recent illness. The family will go to their summer residence at Beaurepaire this week (18 June 1909, 12, 27)

BLUMENTHAL, Israel and family are now located at Beaurepaire (11 June 1909, 12, 26)

BLUMENTHAL, Israel, chaired the Shearith Israel School closing exercises on Sun. aft. Prize and testimonal winners were:- Max Blumberg, Philip de la Penha, Jesse Ginsberg, Daniel Goldstein, Willie Kaplansky, Gordon Lightstone, Julius Miller, David Saink, Solly Samuel, Louis Shanker and the Misses Rose Ginsberg, Dorothy Hart, Dolly Kirschberg and Ruth Miller (4 June 1909, 12, 25)

BLUMENTHAL, Israel, left on a trip to Palestine. Mr. Blumenthal is treasurer of the Spanish and Portuguese Synagogue. He will visit Jerusalem, Jaffa, Hebron and the agricultural colonies and will meet with Messrs. Ruppin, D. Levontin and Boris Schatz (5 March 1909, 12, 12)

BLUMENTHAL, Israel, met with Dr. Boris Schatz founder of the Bezalel Arts and Crafts School while in Palestine. Dr. Schatz, "assured him that what they required was not orders, but more capital to enable them to expand their business, and he hoped that the Canadian Jews would bear this in mind and send larger contributions for support of the work being done by the Anglo-Palestine Bank, - the Palestinian branch of the Zionist Jewish Colonial Trust. Mr. Blumenthal also said "... that some of the prominent men in Palestine said to him that Canadian Jews ought to organize parties to visit Palestine and become acquainted with the land. They complained that this idea was not sufficiently understood in Canada." (30 April 1909, 12, 20)

BLUMENTHAL, Israel, now visiting Palestine, had his correspondence with Clarence I. de Sola reprinted (16 April 1909, 12, 18)

BLUMENTHAL, Israel, reported on his trip to Palestine. "He was particularly surprised to find the Jews living there under such favourable conditions and many having such comfortable homes. Where he had expected to find much squalour and want, he was agreeably surprised to find people living under conditions which would be envied by many living in Western lands. He was astonished at the wonderful orange groves which he saw in the neighbourhood of Jaffa, and still more astonished at the splendid specimens of handicraft which he witnessed being manufactured by the artisans of the Bezalel School. Mr. Blumenthal brought back with him a couple of specimens of their silverwork of extremely beautiful design and exquisite workmanship. He states that the silk woven rugs and carpets which he saw being produced were simply superb, and Mr. Guggenheim, of California, who was there at the same time, placed orders for them amounting to a large sum, to be exported to California." (30 April 1909, 12, 20)

BLUMENTHAL, J. Leo, has gone to Atlantic City and New York (11 March 1910, 13, 17)

BLUMENTHAL, Jr., A., has left for Winnipeg (21 Jan. 1910, 13, 10)

BLUMENTHAL, Miss Gladys, arrived from Toronto to spend the holiday with her parents, Mr. and Mrs. I. Blumenthal, Elm Ave. (29 Oct. 1909, 12, 46)

BLUMENTHAL, Miss Irene, Elm Ave., is visiting Miss Edith Ogulnik at Lake Manitou (23 Aug. 1912, 15, 37)

BLUMENTHAL, Miss Irene, has returned from Ottawa (8 Nov. 1912, 15, 48)

BLUMENTHAL, Miss Irene, left for Lake Placid, N.Y. (22 Aug. 1913, 16, 37)

BLUMENTHAL, Miss R.H., accompanied by her niece, Miss Grace Abrahams, has left for Atlantic City to spend a few weeks (11 Feb. 1910, 13, 13)

BLUMENTHAL, Mr. and Mrs. I. and family have gone to Beaurepaire for the summer (16 June 1911, 14, 31)

BLUMENTHAL, Mr. and Mrs. I., Elm Ave., Westmount, have gone to New York and Atlantic City for two weeks (10 March 1911, 14, 17)

BLUMENTHAL, Mr. and Mrs. I., have returned from Toronto. Their daughter, Miss Gladys Blumenthal will be studying at Branksmere Hall (1 Oct. 1909, 12, 42)

BLUMENTHAL, Mr. and Mrs. R.H. and family, Elm Ave., have taken up their summer residence at Beaurepaire (10 June 1910, 13, 30)

BLUMENTHAL, Mr. and Mrs. R.H., are guests at the Chateau Frontenac, Quebec City (25 Nov. 1910, 14, 2)

BLUMENTHAL, Mr. and Mrs. R.H., Elm Ave., have returned from New York and Atlantic City (11 March 1910, 13, 17)

BLUMENTHAL, Mr. and Mrs. R.H., have returned from the Thousand Islands and Alexandria Bay (19 Aug. 1910, 13, 40)

BLUMENTHAL, Mr. and Mrs. S., will be "At Home" Sept. 5, 1909, at 1630 Mance St. (3 Sept. 1909, 12, 38)

BLUMENTHAL, Mr. and Mrs. Sam, are guests of Ald. and Mrs. A. Blumenthal at Bondville, Que. (19 July 1912, 15, 32)

BLUMENTHAL, Mr. and Mrs. Samuel, have returned from their honeymoon and will make their home at 540 Mance St., Mile End (18 June 1909, 12, 27)

BLUMENTHAL, Mrs. George, Elm Ave., entertained the Primrose Club Tues. evening, Feb. 15, 1910 (18 Feb. 1910, 13, 14)

BLUMENTHAL, Mrs. I., is in New York for a week (26 Nov. 1909, 13, 2)

BLUMENTHAL, Mrs. R.H., has gone to New York to visit her sister (30 Sept. 1910, 13, 46)

BLUMENTHAL, Mrs. R.W., Beaurepaire, gave a hay cart ride on Aug. 7, 1911 in honor of her daughter Irene's birthday (11 Aug. 1911, 14, 39)

BLUMENTHAL, Mrs. Robert, and Miss Grace Abrahams left for a few weeks' stay in Atlantic City (12 Feb. 1909, 12, 9)

BLUMENTHAL, Mrs. Robert, leaves for New York where she will meet Mr. Blumenthal on his return from the southern states (5 Feb. 1909, 12, 8)

BLUMENTHAL, Mrs. S., has moved to Toronto (12 May 1911, 14, 26)

BLUMENTHAL, Phillip and Charlie Goldstein are attending Upper Canada College, Toronto (1 Oct. 1909, 12, 42)

BLUMENTHAL, Phillip and Ed. Goldstein are holidaying at Weir, Que. (16 Aug. 1912, 15, 36)

BLUMENTHAL, Phillip, is in New York for two weeks (8 March 1912, 15, 17)

BLUMENTHAL, R. and daughter and Mr. and Mrs. I. Blumenthal have gone on an automobile trip to Plattsburg, N.Y. (25 July 1911, 14, 36)

BLUMENTHAL, R.H. and H.N. Friedman have gone to New Orleans, La. (13 Jan. 1911, 14, 9)

BLUMENTHAL, R.H. has gone to New York and will return with his wife and daughter who have been there the past two weeks (11 Oct. 1910, 13, 48)

BLUMENTHAL, R.H., has returned after a month's absence (21 Jan. 1910, 13, 10)

BLUMENTHAL, R.H., has returned from Atlantic City (5 March 1909, 12, 12)

BLUMENTHAL, R.H., has returned from Toronto (15 Oct. 1909, 12, 44)

BLUMENTHAL, R.H., spent the weekend at Caledonia Springs, Ont. (7 April 1911, 14, 21)

BLUMENTHAL, R.H., was at Caledonia Springs for a short visit (19 Nov. 1909, 13, 1)

BLUMENTHAL, R.H., was unanimously elected a director of the Board of the Hebrew Free Loan Association at its last meeting (24 Nov. 1911, 15, 2)

BLUMENTHAL, R.H., will leave shortly for a four week's trip to Hot Springs (8 Jan. 1909, 12, 4)

BLUMENTHAL, R.N. and family have gone to Plattsburgh for a few days by automobile (13 Aug. 1909, 12, 35)

BLUMENTHAL, S., civil engineer, has accepted a position as engineer of bridges with the city of Toronto (5 May 1911, 14, 25)

BLUMER, D. and his mother went to New York and Atlantic City on holiday (3 Nov. 1911, 14, 51)

BLUMER, D. and N.H. Godinsky contributed to the Zionist Land Fund (19 May 1911, 14, 27)

BLUMER, Lazare and his mother have left for Mount Clemens for the summer (16 July 1909, 12, 31)

BLUMER, Mr. and Mrs. D. and family will spend the summer at Summerlea (2 July 1909, 12, 29)

BOAS, A.B., spent a few days at Lake Placid, N.Y. (28 July 1911, 14, 37)

BOAS, Bendix A., 288 Sherbrooke W.; Moses Book, 556 Dorchester; Joseph Cochenthaler, 136 Peel St.; Copel Engelberg, 27 St. Monique; H. Goldberg, 579 St. Catherine W.; Jacob A. Jacobs, 280 St. Catherine; Sam. E. Lichtenhein, 204 Peel St.; Benny Leibovitch, 169 Stanley; Morris Michaels, 100 Windsor; R.C. Miller, 335 Craig St.; G.V. Samuel, 173 Mansfield; Harris Samuel, 103 Drummond; David H. Shapiro, 8 Victoria St.; Abraham Vineberg, Albert Vineberg, 512 St. Catherine; and Jacob Workman, 81 Latour, all of St. George's Ward, are persons on the Parliamentary Voters' revision list (3 Feb. 1911, 14, 12)

BOAS, Bendix A., 670 Sherbrooke W.; P.R. Diamond, 802 Dorchester W.; Albert Greenberg, 802 Dorchester W.; Nathan Lewis, 802 Dorchester St. W.; Marcus Vineberg, 57 Argyle Ave.; Joseph Wakiman, 920 St. Catherine W.; and Abraham S. Workman, 19 Seignieur, all of St. Andrew Ward, are persons on the Parliamentary Voters' revision list (3 Feb. 1911, 14, 12)

BOAS, Benjamin, is spending a few weeks in Atlantic City (30 Dec. 1910, 14, 7)

BOAS, Bernard, is in Chicago for a few weeks (18 Aug. 1911, 14, 41)

BOAS, Mr. and Mrs. B.A., "Sherbrooke", left for Atlantic City (12 Feb. 1909, 12, 9)

BOAS, Mr. and Mrs. B.A., are in Chicago visiting their daughter, Mrs. Oppenheimer (2 April 1909, 12, 16)

BOAS, Mr. and Mrs. B.A., leave shortly for Atlantic City where they will spend the summer (9 July 1909, 12, 30)

BOAS, Mrs. B.A., is spending the summer at Knowlton, Que. (18 July 1913, 16, 32)

BOLTOUCH, I.W., is president of the Disraeli Literary and Debating Club, a society for young boys, which will hold its first concert on Sun. evening, May 22, 1910 in the Baron de Hirsch Institute auditorium (13 May 1910, 13, 26)

BOLTUCK, I.W., organized the mock parliament held last Sun. in the Baron de Hirsch Institute assembly hall. Those taking part in the debate were:- L. Phillips and H. Halperin for the Liberals, H. Budyk and A. Viner for the Conservatives and A. Zoodick and Mr. Lazar for the Socialists (8 March 1912, 15, 17)

BOLTUCK, Master J.W., is president of the Disraeli Club for boys attending high school. Those taking part in the program were:- Charles M. Colle, M.H. Myerson, D. Boltuck, Philip Presner and the Misses Sarah Sperber, B. Gross, Lillian Wetstein and Bessie D. Boltuck (27 May 1910, 13, 28)

BOLTUCK, Miss Bessie, City Hall Ave., is spending her vacation at Old Orchard, Me. (1 Aug. 1913, 16, 34)

BOOKMAN, Miss R., gave a party at her residence on Sun. Jan. 4, 1914. Among those present were:- I. Bendarsky, D. Bloomberg, M. Bookman, N. Bookman, E. Ellis, J. Feldman, the Misses R. Bendarsky, L. Bletcher and R. Bookman (9 Jan. 1914, 17, 5)

The Most Talked of Store in Montreal.

Every body is asking how we manage to give such big values in Fine Diamonds and High-Class Jewellery at such low prices, when poorer goods are sold elsewhere for the same price. If you study your own interest you will certainly call and see for yourself that what we say is correct, your Jeweller buys his Diamonds from us.

HOW ABOUT YOU.

ALL GOODS SOLD BY US ARE GUARANTEED.

Vineberg & Bloomstone,
Diamond Jewellers, 105 Craig St. West
"THE STORE OF OPPORTUNITIES"

Coaches for Weddings.   Tel. Uptown 2667

William Wray
UNDERTAKER

113 University Street.   Montreal

X. Zionistenkongreß in Basel!

Der ausführliche Bericht über die Verhandlungen des X. Zionistenkongresses in Basel (9. bis 15. Aug. a. c.) wird ausschließlich durch **die tägliche Kongreßausgabe der „Welt", des** Zentralorgans der Zionistischen Weltorganisation, veröffentlicht. Wer über den X. Zionistenkongreß genau unterrichtet sein will, abonniere die Kongreßausgabe der „Welt". Der Bezugspreis beträgt: für Deutschland M 1.70, für Österreich-Ungarn Kr. 2.—, für Rußland Ro. 1.—, für Großbritannien u. die Kolonien Sh. 2/2, für Holland Hfl. 1.20, Vereinigte Staaten u. Canada Doll. 0.50, für alle übrigen Länder Frs. 2.50. Bestellungen gegen Voreinsendung des Betrages (auch in Briefmarken) richte man an den

Verlag „Die Welt" Köln a. Rh., Karolingerring 31.

> # NAHUM SOKOLOW Will address a Mass Meeting at the **MONUMENT NATIONAL**
>
>  (Montreal) on Monday, May 19th, at 8.30 p.m. sharp. Reserved Seats, **$1.00, 50c., & 25c.,** to be obtained by phoning Main 7114, or at the Box Office on the evening of the meeting.
>
> ## Come and Hear One of our Greatest Living Orators.

BORONOW, Mr. and Mrs. Robert and child, of Vancouver, are in Montreal for a few weeks (13 Feb. 1914, 17, 7)

BORONOW, R., is spending a few weeks in Ste. Agathe des Monts (3 Dec. 1909, 13, 3)

BOULKIND, Mr. and Mrs., City Hall Ave., gave a Purim dinner in honor of their friends (28 March 1913, 16, 16)

BOULKIND, Mr. and Mrs. S., City Hall Ave., gave an "at home" Tues. evening in honor of Miss Ratner, of New York, who is on a visit. Mrs. Boulkind was assisted by her sister, Mrs. (Dr.) Wiseman. Guests included:- A.J. Livinson, B.A., Dr. H. Bernstein, Dr. C.J. Gross, Mr. and Mrs. S.G. Tritt and Mr. and Mrs. J. Ettenberg (1 Dec. 1911, 15, 3)

BOULKIND, Mr. and Mrs. S., have returned from a long trip to Europe and Palestine. Mr. Boulkind intends to practice as a druggist in Montreal (6 May 1910, 13, 25)

BOYANER, Mrs. D., of Edmonton, Alta., is the guest of her sister, Mrs. I. Levinoff, Mance St. (25 July 1911, 14, 36)

BRAGER, Mrs. J.M., of Halifax, N.S., is visiting Mrs. I. Lande, Grosvenor Ave. (29 Aug. 1913, 16, 38)

BRAININ, Mr. and Mrs. Reuben, 2588 Park Ave., wish their friends a happy New Year (1 Oct. 1913, 16, 42-43)

BRAININ, Mr. and Mrs. Reuben, gave a reception at their home in honor of their daughter, Miriam's engagement to Dr. Samuel Ortenberg, on Sun. Feb. 7, 1913. Assisting in receiving the guests were:- Mesdames L. Goldman and Mrs. Dr. Bernstein. Assisting at the table were:- Mrs. Dr. Tannenbaum, Mrs. E.G. Bernstein and the Misses Minnie Bernstein and Bertha Brainin. Rabbis Hirsch Cohen and Herman Abramowitz addressed the couple (14 Feb. 1913, 16, 10)

BRAININ, Mr. and Mrs. Rubin, who are arriving in Montreal this aft., were the guests of Mr. and Mrs. Roddin, 427E Kalamazoo Ave., Kalamazoo, Mich. (14 Jan. 1910, 13, 9)

BRAININ, Mrs. Reuben and daughter, Park Ave., returned from six weeks in New York and Long Branch, N.Y. (1 Oct. 1913, 16, 42-43)

BRAININ, Reuben, is chairman of the committee organizing the "Kunst Abend" (evening of Jewish Art) to be held Sun. Dec. 22, 1912 in the Baron de Hirsch Institute. Master Fredie Cohen, the child pianist of Toronto, age 14, is on the program (20 Dec. 1912, 16, 2)

BRAININ, Reuben, is chairman of the committee organizing the banquet in honor of Nahum Sokolow, the Zionist leader, on Tues. May 20, 1913 at 9.30 p.m., in the Auditorium Hall. Other members are:- J. Jampolsky, H. Lang, J. Skibelsky, S. Talpis, B. Weiner and Mrs. B.M. Speyer. Mr. Sokolow will deliver an address in English in the Monument National Theatre Mon. night. He was brought to Canada by the Canadian Zionist Federation and will lecture in Toronto (16 May 1913, 16, 23)

BRAININ, Reuben, left Tues. evening for New York, en route for Europe where he will attend the Zionist Congress in Vienna as a delegate of the Agudoth Zion Society of Montreal (8 Aug. 1913, 16, 35)

BRAININ, Reuben, returned home from an extended trip to Europe. While there he attended the Zionist Congress as an Agudath Zion Society delegate. "He was met at the station by his family and a large number of intimate friends and admirers." (12 Dec. 1913, 17, 1)

BRAININ, Reuben, spoke in Yiddish on the topic "Das Befraiung: From Bondage to Liberty" at the YMHA Friday Night Talk, April 25, 1913 (9 May 1913, 16, 22)

BRAININ, Ruben, acknowledges receipt of $100 from A. Levin. The money is for subscriptions to Mr. Brainin's new Hebrew paper, the **Hadoar** which will be published shortly (3 Feb. 1911, 14, 12)

BRAININ, Ruben, editor of **The Jewish Eagle** will speak at the next B'nai U' Bnoth Zion Kadimah regular meeting Sun. May 5, 1912 at 8 p.m. (26 April 1912, 15, 24)

BRAININ, Rubin and Mr. Schalit, of the ICA, were present at the reception in honor of the engagement of Miss Theresa Bockart to Rabbi Herman Abramowitz, which was held in Vienna Hall, New York last Sun. (27 Jan. 1911, 14, 11)

BREITMAN, Master Reuben, age 12, won a free scholarship and medal at the Alexander School, Sanguinet St. (27 June 1913, 16, 29)

BROCK, H.H., of Buffalo, was in Montreal this week (18 Oct. 1910, 13, 49)

BRODIE, Mrs. and Miss Brodie are occupying "Pine Grove" this season at Leggat's Point, Little Metis (2 July 1909, 12, 29)

BROIDY, J.I., of New Glasgow, N.S., stayed at the Windsor Hotel last week (31 Jan. 1913, 16, 8)

BROIDY, Mr. and Mrs. S., and daughter, of Springhill, N.S., are in Montreal for the wedding of their niece, Miss Edith Wener and are the guests of Mrs. B. Wener. Afterwards Mr. and Mrs. Broidy will visit New York and Boston (5 March 1909, 12, 12)

BRONDER, Miss, returned home to Sault Ste. Marie after a month's visit, the guest of Miss Dora Rothschild, Grosvenor Ave. (27 March 1914, 17, 13)

BROTMAN, M. and L. Morosnick, of Winnipeg, are in Montreal until the end of Jan. (16 Jan. 1914, 17, 6)

BROUDY, Jack W., of Toronto, and Maurice Levy, of Montreal, who is attending the University of Toronto, are spending the vacation with Mr. and Mrs. Levy, 143 Villeneuve St., Montreal (30 Dec. 1910, 14, 7)

BROWN, E.A., general representative of the Globe Feature Film Co., left Montreal Feb. 26, 1912 to open offices in Toronto and Winnipeg (28 Feb. 1913, 16, 12)

BROWN, Mrs. J. and Master Jerome Brown, of New York, are guests of Mr. and Mrs. Max Harris, Dorchester St. W. (5 March 1914, 17, 10)

BROWNE, Miss, of Nashville, Tenn., is visiting her sister, Mrs. Greenblatt, Bellevue Flats (9 Dec. 1910, 14, 4)

BROWNE, Mrs., of Nashville, Tenn., is visiting her daughter, Mrs. Greenbaum, Tupper St. W. (11 Aug. 1911, 14, 39)

BROWNSTEIN, Mr. and Mrs., of Calgary, Alta., were in Montreal to attend the Aronson-Rosenberg wedding (14 June 1912, 15, 27)

BUCHAN, Mrs., of Winnipeg, and Mrs. Goltman, of New York, are in Ottawa, the guests of their mother, Mrs. N. Marks, Sparks St. (30 July 1909, 12, 33)

BUCKEY, D.L., of Chicago, stayed at the Place Viger Hotel (11 Oct. 1910, 13, 48)

BUCKEY, Dan. L., of Chicago, was registered at the Place Viger Hotel (1 April 1910, 13, 20)

BUDYK, Dr. J., medical officer of the King Edward Benefit Association, received a presentation for his services rendered over the past three years. "The testimonial stated that the members extremely regret that he was compelled to resign and they tendered him their good wishes for the future." P. Katz, J.P., made the presentation (2 Dec. 1910, 14, 3)

BUDYK, Dr. J.F., has returned from Tadoussac (3 Sept. 1909, 12, 38)

BUDYK, H., of the Montreal High School, headed the list in both sciences and letters at the preliminary examinations for admission to first year law at Laval University (17 Jan. 1913, 16, 6)

BUDYK, Harry and Miss D. Budyk, Main St., are spending the summer with Mrs. M. Segal, of Levis, Que., at Cacouna (12 July 1912, 15, 31)

BUDYK, J.H., Mrs. M. Budyk and Miss Nessie Segal, who were on holiday at Cacouna, have returned to Dr. Budyk's home, St. Famille St. (15 Aug. 1913, 16, 36)

BUDYK, Mrs. M., of Montreal, and her daughter, Mrs. M. Segal, of Levis, Que., are on holiday at Cacouna, Que. (25 Aug. 1911, 14, 41)

BUEGELERSEN, H.P., of New York, is in Montreal on business (1 June 1911, 14, 29)

BURMAN, Miss Rose, Bleury St., has returned from Boston (20 Sept. 1912, 15, 41)

BURMAN, Miss Rose, Bleury St., is in New York and Boston for a few weeks (21 March 1913, 16, 15)

BURMAN, Miss Rose, has left to spend the winter in Boston with her sister, Mrs. D.H. Epstein (22 Jan. 1909, 12, 6)

BURMAN, William, St. Famille St., is in Ste. Agathe on holiday (4 July 1913, 16, 30)

BURNSTEIN, Harry and Miss Fanny Burnstein returned from vacation in New York (31 Jan. 1913, 16, 8)

BURROWS, Misses, of New York, are guests of their cousin, Rabbi and Mrs. Herman Abramowitz, Stanley St., for a few weeks (6 March 1914, 17, 10)

BYE, Henry, 30 St. John St., is accepting applications for janitor of the Hebrew Sheltering Home (15 March 15, 18)

BYE, Henry, has gone to England on business (26 April 1912, 15, 24)

BYE, Henry, has returned from a lengthy stay in England (21 June 1912, 15, 28)

BYE, Henry, left for England on Wed. He will be away eight weeks (9 May 1913, 16, 22)

BYE, Henry V., is sailing for England on the S.S. Victorian, Fri. June 24, 1910 to visit his parents (24 June 1910, 13, 32)

BYE, Henry, won the gold watch donated by M. Vineberg, jeweller, Notre Dame St., to the Montreal Hebrew Sheltering Home (3 March 1911, 14, 16)

CAFFENBERG, J., of Boston, is registered at the Windsor Hotel (7 May 1909, 12, 21)

CAFFENBURG, A., of Boston, was registered at the Windsor Hotel this week (4 March 1910, 13, 16)

CAFFENBUY, R., of Boston, stayed at the Windsor Hotel (15 Jan. 1909, 12, 5)

CANU, Mrs. E., of Newark, N.J., is the guest of her cousin, Mrs. H.E. Meyers, Prince Arthur St. W. (23 Dec. 1910, 14, 6)

CAPLAN, H., of St. John, N.B., is visiting Montreal (21 June 1912, 15, 28)

CAPLAN, Miss, has returned home to Yarmouth, N.S. with her brother after spending some time in Montreal (26 March 1909, 12, 15)

CAPLAN, R., of St. John, N.B., was in Montreal briefly (9 Feb. 1912, 15, 13)

CAPLAN, R., was elected president of the Zeire Zion Society at the semi-annual meeting on Sun. March 8, 1914. Other officers elected were:- I. Schwisberg, vice-pres.; H.G. Friefeld, sec.; M.L. Levitsky, Hebrew sec.; J. Levinthal, corr. sec.; J. Birnbaum, treas.; M. Flanders and B. Joseph, sec.; I. Pevsner, librarian; S. Nissenholtz, publicity. J. Sohmer read a paper on the "History of the Society" (20 March 1914, 17, 12)

CAROUSKY, S.R., of Kingston, Ont., is a guest at the Turkish Bath Hotel (22 Oct. 1909, 12, 45)

CARSLEY, M. and Miss Charlotte Carsley, Common St., spent last Sun. in Ste. Agathe (13 June 1913, 16, 27)

CARSLEY, Miss Charlotte, Common St., is in Boston and Woonsocket, R.I., for a few weeks (10 April 1914, 17, 15)

CARSLEY, Miss Charlotte, Common St., left last Sun. for Ste. Agathe and will not return till Sept. (4 July 1913, 16, 30)

CARSLEY, Mrs. Charlotte, Common St., returned from Ste. Agathe where she spent the summer (29 Aug. 1913, 16, 38)

CASSILS, Miss Irene, of New York, is visiting the Misses Tannenbaum, Metcalfe St. (29 Dec. 1911, 15, 7)

CASSILS, Miss, of New York, who has been visiting her aunt, Mrs. Tannenbaum, Metcalfe St., has returned home, accompanied by her cousin, Mrs. Lil Tannenbaum (4 March 1910, 13, 16)

CHASKELSON, Miss S., 81 Dorchester St. W., will provide information on the club which is for Jewish ladies age sixteen years up (15 March 1912, 15, 18)

CHAZANOVITCH, Mr., who is from Europe, will edit a new newspaper for the workers Folks Zeiting (8 March 1912, 15, 17)

CHERTCOFF, Y., is clerk to the board of the Mount Sinai Sanatorium (6 Dec. 1912, 15, 52)

CHORLTON, D.M., has gone to New York and Philadelphia on a visit (27 Aug. 1909, 12, 37)

CHORLTON, Mr. and Mrs. David M., 119 Union St., wish their friends and relatives a happy New Year (1 Oct. 1913, 16, 42-43)

CLAMAN, I., of Vancouver, stayed at the Windsor Hotel (20 Sept. 1912, 15, 41)

CLAMAN, Misses Flossie and Eva Claman, St. Matthew St., have left for Vancouver where they will spend a few months with their uncle, Abraham Goldstein (30 April 1909, 12, 20)

CLAMAN, Morris, St. Matthew St., is in New York (11 Nov. 1910, 13, 52)

CLAMAN, Mr. and Mrs. I., have returned from their honeymoon and will spend the summer at Beaurepaire, the guests of Mr. and Mrs. H. Lazarus (23 June 1911, 14, 32)

CLAMAN, Mr., spent a short time in Beaconsfield (25 June, 1909, 12, 28)

CLAMAN, Mrs. M. and family are at Shawbridge for a few weeks (28 July 1911, 14, 37)

CLAMAN, Mrs. M. and family have moved to Vancouver (6 Oct. 1911, 14, 47)

CLARK, Mr. and Mrs., of Ottawa, were guests of Mrs. J.A. Jacobs, Greene Ave. (16 Sept. 1910, 13, 44)

COCHENTHALER, M., has returned from a short trip to New York (1 Oct. 1909, 12, 42)

COCHENTHALER, M., is spending Passover in New York and Atlantic City (5 April 1912, 15, 21)

COCHENTHALER, Miss Carrie, Bishop St., has left for New York, where she will spend several months visiting her brother (5 March 1909, 12, 12)

COCHENTHALER, Miss Carrie, is visiting Mrs. N. Marks, of Ottawa (15 Oct. 1909, 12, 44)

COCHENTHALER, Mrs. M., is spending a few weeks in New York (17 March 1911, 14, 18)

COCHENTHALER, Rebecca, Miriam Glickman, Etta Jacobovitch, P. Kalmon, N. Silver, I. Rosenberg, A. Ram, S. Nissinholz, H. Mendelsohn, P. Vrenstein, J. Cohen, T. Bloomfield, Bessie Singer, Lillian Lasker, S. Landskroner, G. Littner, Clara Jacobs, B. Herman, Sadie Heillig, R. Klezmer and Rebecca Hohenstein graduated from Aberdeen School (3 March 1911, 14, 16)

COHEN, A., of New York, was a guest at the Windsor Hotel (1 Oct. 1913, 16, 42-43)

COHEN, A.J., has gone to New York on a visit (23 Sept. 1910, 13, 45)

COHEN, A.Z., has returned to Montreal after spending a few days at Stanhope, P.E.I. (16 July 1909, 12, 31)

COHEN, B., of Sherbrooke, Que., is in Montreal (9 July 1909, 12, 30)

COHEN, G., of New York, was a guest at the

Windsor Hotel (30 July 1909, 12, 33)

COHEN, H., well-known in the real estate and wholesale business, and S. Schachter, the successful photographer, will join L. Miller, a leading insurance agent with Metropolitan Insurance Co., as partners in their newly established insurance business, the National Assurance Agency, 435 St. Lawrence Blvd. Mr. Cohen will be the manager and S. Schachter, the assistant manager (12 Sept. 1913, 16, 40)

COHEN, Harry B., delivered a lecture on "Music as an Art" to a recent meeting of the Progressive Literary and Debating Society. "He pointed out how Jews, when given the opportunity, are specially gifted in this art, and contrasted Russia, the country of oppression, with other European centres." (14 Jan. 1910, 13, 9)

COHEN, Horace and Nathan, Lyon and Harry Levinson and Joe Horowitz spent the weekend at Shawbridge, Que. (9 Aug. 1912, 15, 35)

COHEN, Horace, received his diploma in commerce, McGill University, Department of Commerce. "Mr. Cohen has the distinction of being the first and only Jewish graduate of the Department of Commerce - a recent addition to the University course." (16 May 1913, 16, 23)

COHEN, Horace, was elected manager of the Eureka baseball team and Eddie Kert, this year's captain. A new face on the team is I. Kert (9 May 1913, 16, 22)

COHEN, I. and J. Abramson, both of Kingston, Ont., were in Montreal soliciting funds for the construction of a synagogue in Kingston (16 Sept. 1910, 13, 44)

COHEN, I. and J. Abramson, of Kingston, were in Montreal during the week (16 Sept. 1910, 13, 44)

COHEN, J., Clarence I. de Sola, E.D. Jacobs and V. Michaelis were recent visitors to New York (4 Feb. 1910, 13, 12)

COHEN, J., was elected president of the Young Men's Zionist & Literary Society on Sun. Oct. 8, 1910. Other officers elected were:- J.C. Zacks, vice-pres.; H. Nathanson, fin. sec.; J. Leavitt, corr. sec.; J. Levy, treas.; J. Gronin and J. Viner, council (11 Oct. 1910, 13, 48)

COHEN, Joseph (president), J. Levy (treasurer), J.C. Zacks, A. Marks, J. Viner and W. Harris were responsible for organizing the Young Men's Zionist and Literary Society gala night at the Orpheum (22 April 1910, 13, 23)

COHEN, Joseph, has gone to Kingston on vacation (22 July 1910, 13, 36)

COHEN, L., of Boston, is visiting his brother, H.L. Cohen. Mr. Cohen is an old resident of Montreal (2 April 1909, 12, 16)

COHEN, L.H., spent the weekend at Lakeside (15 July 1910, 13, 35)

COHEN, Lazarus, was elected president of the Shaar Hashomayim Synagogue Other officers elected were:- F. Ship, parnass; N. Silver, treasurer; Myer Crown, hon. secretary; J. Levinson, A.H. Jackson, Samuel Bloomfield and Ph. Glickman, trustees. Marcus Hirsch and B. Jacobs were scrutineers (11 Nov. 1910, 13, 52)

COHEN, Lazarus, was unanimously re-elected president of the Shaar Hashomayim Congregation (7 Nov. 1913, 16, 48)

COHEN, Lyon and family are at Shawbridge for the summer (4 Aug. 1911, 14, 38)

COHEN, Lyon and sons have returned from Old Orchard Beach (27 Aug. 1909, 12, 37)

COHEN, Lyon, is expected home today after a week in New York (28 Jan. 1910, 13, 11)

COHEN, Lyon, is on a trip to New York (13 Jan. 1911, 14, 9)

COHEN, Lyon, returned from Europe last night aboard the R.M.S. Empress of Ireland (20 Aug. 1909, 12, 36)

COHEN, Lyon, was elected hon. president of the Progressive Literary Circle last Sun. aft. in the Baron de Hirsch Institute. Other officers elected were:- Marcel Marcus, pres.; B.R. Segal, 1st vice-pres.; Miss J. Phillips, 2nd vice-pres.; Miss R. Rosenthal, sec.; C.M. Mendel, treas.; H.L. Colle, J. Cohen, J.I. Myerson and the Misses R. Dobrofsky and E. Mendel, council members (28 April 1911, 14, 24)

COHEN, Lyon, was nominated hon. president of the YMHA at the annual meeting. Others nominated were:- J. Goldstein, pres.; Sol. Kellert, vice-pres.; Max Singer, 2nd. vice-pres.; Sol. Cohen, treas.; Samuel Shalasky, fin. sec.; E. Soloman, rec. sec.; Jack Sigman, corr. sec.; M. Goldberg, sgt.-at-arms; S. Belanstein, Harry Gordon, Nathan Lande, J. Levi, M.L. Levine, Dave Livinson, J. Livinson, J. Neumann and G. Rabinovitch, directors (19 Dec. 1913, 17, 2)

COHEN, Lyon, was re-elected to the Council of the Montreal Reform Club (21 May 1909, 12, 23)

COHEN, Mark, editor of the Dunedin Star of New Zealand, who is one of the delegates to the Imperial Press Conference to be held in London next month, passed through Montreal yesterday. While in town he visited the Montefiore Club (21 May 1909, 12, 23)

COHEN, Mark, editor of the Dunedin Star, who passed through Montreal last month, en route for England, has been interviewed by the London Jewish World (25 June 1909, 12, 28)

COHEN, Mark, one of the New Zealand delegates to the Imperial Press Conference, passed through Montreal this week en route for home. He and Mrs. Cohen are visiting Niagara Falls en route to the coast (30 July 1909, 12, 33)

COHEN, Mark, who was one of the representatives at the Imperial Press Conference in London, had his gold watch, chain and sovereign purse, valued at 70 pounds sterling, stolen during his return journey (10 Dec. 1909, 13, 4)

COHEN, Max and Esther Brandess received scholarships at Mount Royal School (3 March 1911, 14, 16)

COHEN, Miss Anna, has returned home from New York where she spent the past few months visiting her grandmother (22 Oct. 1909, 12, 45)

COHEN, Miss Beckie, 663 City Hall Ave., gave a surprise party in honor of her cousin, Miss Dorothy Halperin at her home, Sun. evening, Nov. 8, 1912. The Misses Jessie Halperin and Violet Bernstein received the guests. Those assisting at the table were:- the Misses Halperin, Bernstein and Bessie Simon (13 Dec. 1912, 16, 1)

COHEN, Miss Bessie, gave a surprise party on Jan. 10, 1914 in honor of Miss Olga Rabinovitch (16 Jan. 1914, 17, 6)

COHEN, Miss Hattie, spent the last weekend at Woodlands, the guest of Mr. and Mrs. Jackson (23 July 1909, 12, 32)

COHEN, Miss Libbie, is rapidly recovering from an appendicitis operation in the Royal Victoria Hospital (22 Jan. 1909, 12, 6)

COHEN, Miss M., of New York, is visiting her sister, Mrs. Max Lipman (27 June 1913, 16, 29)

COHEN, Miss Mildred, of Buffalo, has returned home after visiting Mrs. Asher Pierce, Westmount (18 March 1910, 13, 18)

COHEN, Miss Mildred, of Buffalo, N.Y., is the guest of Mrs. Ascher Pierce, Western Ave. (14 Feb. 1913, 16, 10)

COHEN, Miss Mildred, returned home to Buffalo (7 March 1913, 16, 13)

COHEN, Miss Miriam and her cousin, Miss Lillian Levy, of New York City, will spend a week at Woodlands, the guests of Mr. and Mrs. Joseph Pressner (4 Aug. 1911, 14, 38)

COHEN, Miss, of Buffalo, is the guest of Mrs. Ascher Pierce, Mount Pleasant Ave. (26 March 1909, 12, 15)

COHEN, Miss, of Buffalo, is the guest of Mrs. C.A. Workman, Kensington Ave. (31 Dec. 1909, 13, 7)

COHEN, Miss R., gave a skating party in honor of Miss Sadie Vineberg, who will be married shortly (29 Jan. 1909, 12, 7)

COHEN, Miss Rose, has returned from a three months' visit to her sister, Mrs. W.M. Cohen, at Lanark, Ont. (30 July 1909, 12, 33)

COHEN, Miss Rose, has returned from a long stay in New York (15 Oct. 1909, 12, 44)

COHEN, Miss Rose, of Chicago, is the guest of Mrs. H. Hart, Mt. Stephen Ave., Westmount (16 Feb. 1912, 15, 14)

COHEN, Mr. and Mrs. Charles, are spending a few days with their aunt, Mrs. Robitaille, Lake Megantic (22 July 1910, 13, 36)

COHEN, Mr. and Mrs. Charles, of Chicago, are visiting their grandparents, Mr. and Mrs. S. Singer (22 July 1910, 13, 36)

COHEN, Mr. and Mrs. H., 76 Mance St., wish their friends and relatives a happy New Year (10 Oct. 1913, 16, 44)

COHEN, Mr. and Mrs. J. and family, Buckingham Ave., have gone to Ste. Agathe for the summer (25 June 1909, 12, 28)

COHEN, Mr. and Mrs. Jacob and family are spending the summer at Ste. Agathe des Monts (16 July 1909, 12, 31)

COHEN, Mr. and Mrs. Julian A., Laval Ave., gave a social last Sun. evening at their home in honor of the visit of Mrs. Cohen's mother, Mrs. R. Bulfowitch, of Guelph, Ont. Those assisting were:- the Misses Ray Coviensky, Olga Guilaroff, Winnie Monblatt (Hamilton), Jessie Phillips, I. Shapiro, Sophie Singer and Mrs. Beckie Cohen.

Guests included:- I. Cohen, L. Cohen, J. Cooper, M. Levitt, L. Levy, Mr. and Mrs. H. Cohen, and Mr. and Mrs. Nathan Lande (3 Jan. 1913, 16, 4)

COHEN, Mr. and Mrs. Lazarus, leave Sat. evening for New York to attend the wedding of their nephew, Ruben Harris, to Miss Flossie Haft, of that city (21 Jan. 1910, 13, 10)

COHEN, Mr. and Mrs. Lyon, 25 Rosemount Ave., Montreal, wish their friends a happy New Year (1 Oct. 1913, 16, 42-43)

COHEN, Mr. and Mrs. Lyon, attended the Conference of Charities and Correction this week in Buffalo, N.Y. (18 June 1909, 12, 27)

COHEN, Mr. and Mrs. Lyon, left on a short trip to Buffalo and Detroit (11 June 1909, 12, 26)

COHEN, Mr. and Mrs. M., Notre Dame St., gave a Purim party on Sun. March 23, 1913. Guests included:- M. Crown, S. Feldman, I. Segal and the Misses M. Davis (Toronto), Rose Feldman and E. Weinstein (Black Lake) (4 April 1913, 16, 17)

COHEN, Mr. and Mrs. Perry (formerly Miss Mae Genser) of New York, are in Montreal visiting friends (14 March 1913, 16, 14)

COHEN, Mr., was elected president of the YMHA Literary and Debating Circle at the clubrooms, 52 Ontario St. W., Mon. night, Oct. 31, 1910. Other officers elected were:- J. Goldman, vice-pres.; and L. Ober, sec. W.C. Munn, M.A., is the literary instructor and critic. Those intending to take part in the debates this season are:- B. Isson, W. Singer, J. Malkinson, I. Bald, J. Pinsler, S.B. Gordon, A.M. Goldstein, M. Gupin and I. Mitnick (4 Nov. 1910, 13, 51)

COHEN, Mrs. A., St. Mark St., gave a shower Wed. aft. Dec. 4, 1912 in honor of her sister, Miss Rose Berman, who will be married shortly. Those assisting were:- Mrs. L. Berman and the Misses Esther Berman, Ethel Rothschild (Sudbury), Dora Rothschild, Eva Goldstein, Elsie Workman and Ruth Endelman. Mesdames N.H. Godinsky and A. Levine wished Miss Berman well (13 Dec. 1912, 16, 1)

COHEN, Mrs. A.Z. and Master Arthur E. Cohen are spending the summer at Cliff House, Stanhope, P.E.I. (16 July 1909, 12, 31)

COHEN, Mrs. A.Z., has returned from Stanhope, P.E.I. (27 Aug. 1909, 12, 37)

COHEN, Mrs. A.Z., is spending the summer at Little Metis, Que. (15 July 1910, 13, 35)

COHEN, Mrs. and son, of Indianapolis, are visiting Mr. and Mrs. N. Fraid, in Cornwall, Ont. (9 July 1909, 12, 30)

COHEN, Mrs. I. and family, Western Ave., left for Stanhope, P.E.I., where they will spend the summer (16 July 1909, 12, 31)

COHEN, Mrs. J., left for New York, prior to returning home to Detroit (22 Aug. 1913, 16, 37)

COHEN, Mrs. L.H., is at Old Orchard for two weeks (4 Aug. 1911, 14, 38)

COHEN, Mrs. Laurie, of Toronto, spent a few weeks in Montreal (15 Jan. 1909, 12, 5)

COHEN, Mrs. Lazarus and Miss Garmaise, have left for Ste. Agathe for the summer (9 July 1909, 12, 30)

COHEN, Mrs. Lazarus, who spent the past two months at Ste. Agathe, is now at Caledonia Springs (27 Aug. 1909, 12, 37)

COHEN, Mrs. Lyon and sons Horace and Lawrence have gone to Shawbridge to spend the summer (8 July 1910, 13, 34)

COHEN, Mrs. Lyon and sons, who were at Shawbridge, have left for Old Orchard Beach where they will remain until the end of August (23 July 1909, 12, 32)

COHEN, Mrs. Lyon, who met with a serious accident last week, is doing well and is expected to be up in a day or two (1 June 1911, 14, 29)

COHEN, Mrs. R., Miss Ettie Cohen and Dr. J. Cohen, of Buffalo, N.Y., are visiting Mr. and Mrs. N. Silver, 9 Souvenir Ave. (31 Dec. 1909, 13, 7)

COHEN, Mrs. R., of Buffalo, is the guest of Mrs. N. Silver, Souvenir Ave. (16 Sept. 1910, 13, 44)

COHEN, Mrs. R., of Carbondale, Penn., is the guest of Mrs. D. Levy (22 Jan. 1909, 12, 6)

COHEN, Mrs. William, entertained in honor of her sister, Miss Francis Vineberg, of New York. Guests included Miss G. Crown and Messrs. Harris and Crown (13 Oct. 1911, 14, 48)

COHEN, Rabbi Hirsch, conducted the memorial service in the Adas Yeshuran Synagogue last Sun. for Rabbi Rabinowitz, who died recently in Kovno (18 Feb. 1910, 13, 14)

COHEN, Rabbi Hirsch, is in New York attending the convention of Orthodox Rabbis (25 July 1911, 14, 36)

COHEN, Rabbi Hirsch, who attended the Philadelphia Convention of Orthodox Rabbis, will deliver an address on the proceedings to the Synagogue, 416 City Hall Ave., Sat aft., Dec. 18, 1909 (17 Dec. 1909, 13, 5)

COHEN, Rabbi Hirsch, will preach at the Musach Ari Synagogue, 416 City Hall Ave., Sat. aft., and at the Adath Jeshurun Synagogue on Tues. aft. (2 April 1909, 12, 16)

COHEN, Rabbi Hirsch, will preach in the City Hall Ave. Synagogue, Sat. at 4 p.m. on "The Old and New Generation". (7 April 1911, 14, 21)

COHEN, Rabbi I., of Brooklyn, N.Y., was the guest of Miss and the Messrs. Rubenstein, St. Urbain St. (12 Sept. 1913, 16, 40)

COHEN, Rev. Montague N.A., of Victoria B.C., has been elected rabbi of Temple Bnai Israel, Butte, Montana (27 Aug. 1909, 12, 37)

COHEN, Richard, Grand Master of the IOSB, attended the Blumenthal-Kaplansky wedding, Tues. June 8, 1909 (11 June 1909, 12, 26)

COHEN, S., of Cobalt, Ont., is in Montreal (17 June 1910, 13, 31)

COHEN, S., of South Bend, Ind., is the guest of Mr. and Mrs. Lazarus Cohen, 228 Bishop St. (18 June 1909, 12, 27)

COHEN, S.W., of Cobalt, Ont., is at the Windsor Hotel (2 July 1909, 12, 29)

COHEN, Sam, of Cobalt, Ont., was in Montreal for the holidays (22 Oct. 1913, 16, 46)

COHEN, Samuel, tailor; R. Abraham Bros., store; and Samuel Bercovitsky, store; suffered heavy losses as a result of a fire in Cobalt (9 July 1909, 12, 30)

COHEN, Samuel W., of Cobalt, Ont., is staying at the Ritz Carlton Hotel (18 July 1913, 16, 32)

COHEN, Sarah, wife common as to property of Eli Bagan, of Montreal, has instituted an action for separation of property, No. 2099 in the Quebec Superior Court, District of Montreal, on Jan. 28, 1914 (13 Feb. 1914, 17, 7)

COHEN, William, of New York, is visiting his sister, Mrs. M. Vineberg, Bishop St. (5 Feb. 1909, 12, 8)

COHN, Harry, of New York, is the guest of his sister, Mrs. M.A. Vineberg, Tupper St. (13 Jan. 1911, 14, 9)

COHN, Harry, of New York, is visiting his sister, Mrs. M. Vineberg, Tupper St., Westmount (5 April 1912, 15, 21)

COHN, Harry, of New York, is visiting his sister, Mrs. M.A. Vineberg, Tupper St. (20 Sept. 1912, 15, 41)

COHN, Henry L., who was in Winnipeg for three weeks, will be back in Montreal by the end of Jan., by way of Chicago (19 Jan. 1912, 15, 10)

COHN, Louis, has returned from two weeks in the Adirondacks (16 Aug. 1912, 15, 36)

COHN, Louis, left for Old Orchard Beach for two weeks (23 July 1909, 12, 32)

COHN, Willie and Harry Cohn, of New York, were guests of their sister, Mrs. M. Vineberg during the holiday week (29 Sept. 1911, 14, 46)

COLLE, H.L., was chairman of the Progressive Literary & Debating Circle concert and ball held last Wed. in Stanley Hall. Lyon W. Jacobs, founder and past president of the Circle, gave an address. The Misses Sophie and Esther Mendels provided entertainment (7 April 1911, 14, 21)

COLLE, M., was elected president of the Hebrew Sick Benefit Association of Montreal at the annual meeting. Other officers elected were:- M. Coopersmith, 1st vice-pres.; C. Waghelstein, 2nd vice-pres.; M. Levitt, treas.; H. Feigelson, fin. sec.; C. Kalmanovitch, rec. sec.; P. Dobrofsky, M. Rapp and L. Axelrod, trustees. The Association secured the services of Drs. M. Rabinovitch and N. Shacher for the coming year (4 March 1910, 13, 16)

COOPER, Mrs. H., of Calgary, Alta., is visiting her sister, Mrs. Charles Greenman, 74 Laval Ave. (27 Jan. 1911, 14, 11)

COOPERSMITH, M., was elected president of the Hebrew Sick Benefit Association of Montreal on Dec. 14, 1913 in St. Joseph Hall. Other officers elected were:- I. Axelrod, 1st vice-pres.; L. Wollman, 2nd vice-pres.; M. Levitt, treas.; H. Feigelson, fin. sec.; C. Kalmanovitch, rec. sec.; M. Jacobson, H. Schwartz and J. Temmer, trustees (16 Jan. 1914, 17, 6)

COPPER, Mrs. R., of Malden, Mass., is visiting her sister, Mrs. T. Hoffman, 198 St. Joseph Blvd. (28 April 1911, 14, 24)

CORBER, B., Harry Kaufman and the Misses Minnie Kalin and Sarah Sperber performed at the YMHA entertainment last Sun. evening (30 April

1909, 12, 20)

COSSMAN, J., has gone to New York and Atlantic City (12 July 1912, 15, 31)

COSSMAN, J., is in New York for three weeks (17 Jan. 1913, 16, 6)

COSSMAN, Jack and Dave Kirsch are in New York on business (18 Oct. 1912, 15, 45)

COSSMAN, Miss L., of North Sydney, N.S., is visiting her aunt, Mrs. M. Mendelsohn, 211 Esplanade Ave. (2 Jan. 1914, 17, 4)

COSSMAN, Miss Leah, of North Sydney, made her debut at the Young Ladies' Hebrew Sewing Society ball at the Ritz-Carlton Hotel on Dec. 29, 1913. She was chaperoned by her aunt and uncle, Dr. and Mrs. S. Kirsch (9 Jan. 1914, 17, 5)

COSSMAN, Miss Malca, who was at Ste. Agathe, is now the guest of Mr. and Mrs. David Cossman at North Sydney, N.S., for the rest of the summer (13 Aug. 1909, 12, 35)

COSSMAN, Mrs. Dave, of North Sydney, C.B., is visiting Mr. and Mrs. Mendelsohn, 181 Esplanade Ave. (18 Oct. 1912, 15, 45)

COSTINO, Miss Annie and Miss Sarah Wittal left for Old Orchard, Me. (18 July 1913, 16, 32)

COVIENSKY, Lionel, is secretary of the North End Synagogue which will hold a meeting on Sun. June 15, 1913 at 2.30 p.m. in the Baron de Hirsch Institute (13 June 1913, 16, 27)

COVIENSKY, Mr. and Mrs., 433 Berri St., were "at home" last Tues. evening in honor of the engagement of their daughter, Miss Annie Coviensky to Max L. Levin. Guests included:- Mr. and Mrs. Lazarus Cohen, Mr. and Mrs. Hiram Freedman, Mr. and Mrs. A. Levin, Mr. and Mrs. Lyon Cohen, Rabbi Hirsch Cohen, Mr. and Mrs. Phillips, Mr. and Mrs. N. Lande, Leon Goldman, H. Lang, Mr. and Mrs. G. Margolis, Mr. and Mrs. D. Jackell, Mr. and Mrs. Fischel Cohen, Mr. and Mrs. S. Levin, S. Levy, Mr. and Mrs. H. Bernstein and Mr. and Mrs. Max Fineberg (10 June 1910, 13, 30)

COVNER, Dina, wife common as to property of Bernard Bertzovsky, merchant, of Montreal, has instituted an action for separation of property, No. 48 in the Quebec Superior Court, District of Montreal, on Jan. 13, 1914 (20 Feb. 1914, 17, 8)

COWAN, Harry, of New York, is visiting his sister, Mrs. M.A. Vineberg, Bishop St. (9 April 1909, 12, 17)

COWAN, Harry, of New York, is visiting his sister, Mrs. M.A. Vineberg, Tupper St., Westmount (7 Oct. 1910, 13, 47)

COWAN, Miss Miriam, of London, England, arrived in Montreal (27 June 1913, 16, 29)

COWAN, Mrs., of London, Eng., and her son, Leslie Cowan have arrived in Montreal (5 Sept. 1913, 16, 39)

COWAN, Willie, of New York, was the guest of his sister, Mrs. W.L.A. Vineberg, Tupper St. W. (19 Jan. 1912, 15, 10)

CROSSMAN, Miss Malca, accompanied by Jack Crossman, have gone to New York to attend the wedding of her brother, Hiram Crossman to Miss Fannie Braderman (17 June 1910, 13, 31)

CROWDER, Mrs., of New York, is the guest of Mr. and Mrs. Gus Fischel (6 Oct. 1911, 14, 47)

CRYSTAL, Dr. E., 248 Sherbrooke St. E., has returned home from the Women's Hospital, Mountain St., where she underwent an operation. She has recovered from her recent illness and will receive at her home next Sat. and Sun. (2 Dec. 1910, 14, 3)

CRYSTAL, Dr. E., has returned from New York where she spent a month (1 Nov. 1912, 15, 47)

CRYSTAL, L. and Miss Annie Crystal, have gone to Old Orchard, New York and Philadelphia (26 July 1912, 15, 33)

CRYSTAL, M. and B. Crystal, of New York, spent a few days in Montreal renewing acquaintances (7 May 1909, 12, 21)

CRYSTAL, Miss A., 248 Sherbrooke St., was given a surprise party at her home, Wed. evening, Nov. 13, 1912, by Miss May Liverman and several other friends (22 Nov. 1912, 15, 50)

CRYSTAL, Miss A., left on an extended summer trip to the U.S. Northeast (1 Aug. 1913, 16, 34)

CRYSTAL, Miss Annie, Sherbrooke St. E., and Miss Bertha Willensky, Albina St., leave shortly for a holiday at Old Orchard, Me. (4 Aug. 1911, 14, 38)

CRYSTAL, Miss Annie, who visited her uncle in New York, has returned to Bordeaux for the summer (6 Aug. 1909, 12, 34)

CRYSTAL, Mr. and daughter, Miss Annie Crystal, have gone to Burlington and New York for the summer (1 July 1910, 13, 33)

CRYSTAL, Mrs. E., lady doctor, has moved her office from 33 Ontario St. E., to 248 Sherbrooke St. E., between Sanguinet St. and St. Denis Blvd. (13 May 1910, 13, 26)

CRYSTAL, Mrs. M.J. and family, of New York, are visiting Mrs. Crystal's parents, Mr. and Mrs. J. Silverstone, 130 Pine Ave. (29 July 1910, 13, 37)

CURTIS, Mrs. J.B. and daughters, returned home to New York after two weeks in Montreal, the guests of Mrs. R. Lemlein, St. Catherine St. W. (19 Dec. 1913, 17, 2)

DAINOW, David, 1032 St. Urbain St., wishes his friends a happy New Year (1 Oct. 1913, 16, 42-43)

DAINOW, David, a staff member of The Canadian Jewish Times, spoke on the Jewish communities of New York, London and Montreal, at the YMHA Friday Night Talk (14 Feb. 1913, 16, 10)

DAINOW, David, is spending the weekend in Toronto (29 Aug. 1913, 16, 38)

DAINOW, David, of London, England, has arrived in Montreal (3 Jan. 1913, 16, 4)

DANIEL, Mrs. L., of Sherbrooke, Que., was in the Montreal the past week (6 March 1914, 17, 10)

DARWIN, J.A., of Kingston, is in Montreal on a visit (26 Nov. 1909, 13, 2)

DARWIN, Mr. and Mrs. Maurice P., are at "Darwinia Villa", St. Lambert, for the summer (25 June 1909, 12, 28)

DARWIN, N.P., is on a short visit to New York (21 Jan. 1910, 13, 10)

DARWIN, R.A., B'nai Zion Kadimah treasurer, purchased seven Jewish Colonial Trust shares in his own name from the Zionist Federation (30 July 1909, 12, 33)

DARWIN, R.A., was elected president of the B'nai Zion Kadimah last Sun., Nov. 2, 1913, in the Baron de Hirsch Institute. Other officers elected were:- Bernard M. Weiner, vice-pres.; S. McKinley, treas.; H. Lang, fin. sec.; and B.M. Speyer, corr. sec. (7 Nov. 1913, 16, 48)

DARWIN, Robert A., of millinery fame and prominent Canadian Zionist, has created the Forum Summer Garden for summer attractions at this magnificent building on St. Catherine St. W. which takes up the whole city block. "The idea of an open-air place of amusement at the Forum was suggested by Mr. Theo. Horchover who was retained as manager, and is at present busily engaged with capenters, painters, gardeners, and electricians getting the open air court laid out in the form of a garden." (15 April 1910, 13, 22)

DAVID, Major R.S., of St. Lambert, Que., has gone on a trip to New York (12 Nov. 1909, 12, 48)

DAVID, Miss Rosalie and Miss Marguerite Mendes, of New York, are guests of Dr. and Mrs. Hart (29 Dec. 1911, 15, 7)

DAVIDOVITCH, H., was elected president of the Boys' Athletic Club at the annual meeting on Sun. Oct. 24, 1909. Other officers elected were:- M. Kaplansky, sec., and S. Elkin, Treas. The Association's new name is the Beaconsfield Club (29 Oct. 1909, 12, 46)

DAVIDSON, Mr. and Mrs., 653 City Hall Ave., send New Year greetings (11 Sept. 1912, 15, 40)

DAVIDSON, Mr. and Mrs. H.M., 653 City Hall Ave., wish their friends and relatives a happy New Year (10 Oct. 1913, 16, 44)

DAVIS, C.L., of Toronto, is in Montreal for a few days (12 Nov. 1909, 12, 48)

DAVIS, Dave, of New York City, who was the guest of his sister, Mrs. M.F. Wolfe, has gone to Ottawa and Toronto (17 June 1910, 13, 31)

BELL TEL. EAST 4417

MRS. E CRYSTAL,

LADIES' DOCTOR

248 SHERBROOKE EAST
Bet. Sanguinet & St. Denis Sts.

OFFICE HOURS
10 TO 11 A.M.
2 TO 4 P.M.
7 TO 9 P.M.

MONTREAL

DAVIS, E.R. and family are at their cottage at Ahuntsic for the summer (4 June 1909, 12, 25)

DAVIS, Eugene, of Troy, N.Y., is the guest of his aunt, Mrs. M. Harris, Dorchester St. W. (2 Aug. 1912, 15, 34)

DAVIS, Harry E., sails for England on the S.S. Corsican today (30 June 1911, 14, 33)

DAVIS, Harry, has gone abroad for a few weeks (17 Dec. 1909, 13, 5)

DAVIS, Harry, has gone abroad for two months (15 July 1910, 13, 35)

DAVIS, Harry, has returned from a business trip abroad (5 Feb. 1909, 12, 8)

DAVIS, Harry, has returned from abroad, accompanied by his brother (26 Aug. 1910, 13, 41)

DAVIS, Harry, sailed for England via New York and will be away for two months (15 Dec. 1911, 15, 5)

DAVIS, Maurice E. and family are holidaying at St. Andrews-by-the-Sea (30 July 1909, 12, 33)

DAVIS, Maurice, has returned from New York (17 March 1911, 14, 18)

DAVIS, Maurice, left last evening for New York en route for Cuba (27 Jan. 1911, 14, 11)

DAVIS, Miss Gladys, Mackay St., has returned from New York (29 Oct. 1909, 12, 46)

DAVIS, Miss Gladys, MacKay St., has returned from New York (22 Oct. 1909, 12, 45)

DAVIS, Miss Hazel, of New York City, will spend the summer in Ottawa with her aunt, Mrs. Max Wolfe (17 June 1910, 13, 31)

DAVIS, Miss Mabel, of Montreal, is visiting friends in North Hatley, Que. (22 July 1910, 13, 36)

DAVIS, Miss Rae, of Worcester, Mass., is a guest of Mr. and Mrs. N. Levinson, Church St. (15 Dec. 1911, 15, 5)

DAVIS, Mortimer B., has returned to Montreal (26 March 1909, 12, 15)

DAVIS, Mortimer B., is among the exhibitors at the Horse Show to be held in Montreal next week (7 May 1909, 12, 21)

DAVIS, Mortimer B., left for Europe this week where he will join Mrs. Davis (18 April 1913, 16, 19)

DAVIS, Mr. and Mrs., and Miss Nellie Davis, Drummond St., have returned from their trip south (2 April 1909, 12, 16)

DAVIS, Mr. and Mrs. H. Lawrence, Selkirk Ave., will spend the summer at Beaconsfield (14 May 1909, 12, 22)

DAVIS, Mr. and Mrs. H.E., Melville Ave., Westmount, spent a few days at Caledonia Springs (13 March 1914, 17, 11)

DAVIS, Mr. and Mrs. Harry and son left for Kingston by boat (30 July 1909, 12, 33)

DAVIS, Mr. and Mrs. Harry and family are at Shawbridge. Mr. Davis has recovered from his recent illness (23 June 1911, 14, 32)

DAVIS, Mr. and Mrs. Lawrence and family will soon be at cottage no. 1, Beaconsfield (11 June 1909, 12, 26)

DAVIS, Mr. and Mrs. Lawrence and family, Selkirk Ave., closed their country residence at Beaconsfield on Mon. and returned to town (15 Sept. 1909, 12, 40)

DAVIS, Mr. and Mrs. M. and family will spend the summer at St. Andrews-by-the-Sea, N.B. (16 July 1909, 12, 31)

DAVIS, Mr. and Mrs. M.B., have returned from a short vist to Quebec City (24 Dec. 1909, 13, 6)

DAVIS, Mr. and Mrs. M.E. and family have left for Old Orchard Beach (16 July 1909, 12, 31)

DAVIS, Mr. and Mrs. Mortimer B., were in Ste. Agathe on Sun. to inspect their new summer home which is being built (10 June 1910, 13, 30)

DAVIS, Mr. and Mrs. Mortimer B., sailed last Fri. for Europe (15 July 1910, 13, 35)

DAVIS, Mr. and Mrs. Mortimer B., Pine Ave., are expected back from Europe on Sept. 26, 1910 (23 Sept. 1910, 13, 45)

DAVIS, Mr. and Mrs. Mortimer, hosted a dinner Wed. evening before taking their friends to the Horse Show (14 May 1909, 12, 22)

DAVIS, Mr. and Mrs. Mortimer, left Tues. evening for New York (30 April 1909, 12, 20)

DAVIS, Mr. and Mrs. Mortimer, spent the weekend at Ste. Agathe (11 June 1909, 12, 26)

DAVIS, Mr. and Mrs. Mortimer, were guests of the Governor General in Ottawa this weekend (24 May 1912, 15, 25)

DAVIS, Mrs. A. and her daughter, of Detroit, are visiting Mrs. A.J. Vineberg, Prince Arthur Apts. (15 Sept. 1909, 12, 40)

DAVIS, Mrs. A., who stayed at the Welland, has recovered from her recent illness and has returned home to Detroit (29 April 1910, 13, 24)

DAVIS, Mrs. B., 124 Huron St., Toronto, is visiting her daughter, Mrs. L. Caplan in Montreal (2 Jan. 1914, 17, 4)

DAVIS, Mrs. Harry and son, Elm Ave., will spend the summer at Weir, Ont. (16 July 1909, 12, 31)

DAVIS, Mrs. Horace, has returned home from Old Orchard Beach (3 Sept. 1909, 12, 38)

DAVIS, Mrs. M., Bishop St., is visiting friends in New Haven, Conn. (2 April 1909, 12, 16)

DAVIS, Mrs. Maurice and Miss Gladys Davis, Mackay St., have left on a trip to New York (23 April 1909, 12, 19)

DAVIS, Mrs. Maurice and Miss Gladys Davis, Mackay St., have returned from New York (7 May 1909, 12, 21)

DAVIS, Mrs. Maurice and Miss Gladys Davis, Mackay St., have returned from St. Andrew's, N.B. (10 Sept. 1909, 12, 39)

DAVIS, Mrs. Maurice, entertained at bridge on Sat. evening (5 Feb. 1909, 12, 8)

DAVIS, Mrs. Maurice, entertained at luncheon Thurs. May 6, 1909 (14 May 1909, 12, 22)

DAVIS, Mrs. Melvin, Sherbrooke St., entertained at "Bridge" Tues. aft. (26 Feb. 1909, 12, 11)

DAVIS, Mrs. Melvin, Sherbrooke St., has left to visit her sister, Mrs. Oppenheimer, of Chicago (22 Jan. 1909, 12, 6)

DAVIS, Mrs. Melvin, Sherbrooke St., has returned from Chicago where she was the guest of her sister, Mrs. Oppenheimer (5 Feb. 1909, 12, 8)

DAVIS, Mrs. Melvin, Sherbrooke St., has returned from a trip to New York (7 May 1909, 12, 21)

DAVIS, Mrs. Melvin, Sherbrooke St., has returned from Old Orchard Beach (15 Sept. 1909, 12, 40)

DAVIS, Mrs. Melvin, Sherbrooke St., has gone to Chicago to spend some time with her sister, Mrs. Oppenheimer (22 Oct. 1909, 12, 45)

DAVIS, Mrs. Melvin, who was the guest of her parents, Mr. and Mrs. B.A. Boas, "The Sherbrooke", has left for New York and Atlantic City (6 May 1910, 13, 25)

DAVIS, Mrs. Mortimer B., sailed from New York on the S.S. Mauritania (7 March 1913, 16, 13)

DAVIS, Mrs. Mortimer B., will be a patroness of the Charity Ball to be held in the Windsor Hotel on Jan. 5, 1910 (24 Dec. 1909, 13, 6)

DAVIS, Mrs. Mortimer, gave a debutante's dance last Mon. evening, at her residence, Pine Ave., in honor of her niece, Miss Gladys Davis (26 Feb. 1909, 12, 11)

DAVIS, Mrs. Mortimer, Pine Ave., has issued invitations for a home dance, Wed. evening, Jan. 27, 1909, in honor of her niece, Miss Gladys Davis (22 Jan. 1909, 12, 6)

DAVIS, Mrs. Mortimer, Pine Ave., has issued invitations to a house dance for Mon. evening, Feb. 22, 1909, in honor of her niece, Miss Gladys Davis (12 Feb. 1909, 12, 9)

DAVIS, Mrs. Mortimer, Pine Ave., spent the weekend at the Laurentide Inn, Ste. Agathe (23 April 1909, 12, 19)

DAVIS, R., of Troy, N.Y., has returned home after visiting his cousin, Mrs. M. Harris, Crescent St. (3 Sept. 1909, 12, 38)

DAVIS, William and M.B. Davis are visiting governors at the Western Hospital for the ensuing week (12 Aug. 1910, 13, 39)

DE LA PENHA, Miss S. and Miss Annie Solomon are in Carlsbad, Ont. for two weeks' holiday (5 Aug. 1910, 13, 38)

DE LA PENHA, Miss Sarah, has returned from New York where she spent several months (15 Oct. 1909, 12, 44)

DE LA PENHA, Miss Sarah, has returned from two weeks in Caledonia Springs, Ont. (19 Aug. 1910, 13, 40)

DE LA PENHA, Mrs. Isaac, left last night for a ten days' trip to New York (21 May 1909, 12, 23)

DE LA PENHA, Rev. and Mrs. I., were in charge of the Shearith Israel Sunday School outing for the bigger children to Longueuil last Sun. Those present were:- the Misses Sarah, Rose and Bella Narovlansky, Edith Ogulnik, Annie Samuel and Masters Max Blumberg, David Frank, Joe Rose, "Dollie" Kirschberg, Solly Samuel, Philip de la Penha and Max Erdrich (10 June 1910, 13, 30)

From The Canadian Jewish Times   *Montreal*

DE LA PENHA, Rev. and Mrs. I., have moved from 45 Sussex Ave. to 32 Prince Arthur West (1 Dec. 1911, 15, 3)

DE LA PENHA, Rev. I., is expected to return from New York this morn. (24 March 1911, 14, 19)

DE PASS, J., formerly of London, England, has moved to Montreal where he has opened an office as an electrical engineer (6 Aug. 1909, 12, 34)

DE SOLA, Bram C. (B.A.), S. Tritt, L. Tannenbaum (B.A.), H.E. Hershorn (B.A.), S. Eliasoph, and A.J. Livinson (B.A.) passed second year law, McGill University. I. Kert (B.A.), A.W. Muhlstock (B.A.), J. Budyk (B.A.), and L. Lavat passed first year law (16 May 1913, 16, 23)

DE SOLA, Bram, had article on the Jewish School Question appear in the current issue of the "University Magazine" (10 Dec. 1909, 13, 4)

DE SOLA, Bram, has returned from New York, where he was the guest of his aunt, Mrs. L.P. Mendes (11 June 1909, 12, 26)

DE SOLA, Clarence I., has recovered from his recent indisposition (14 Jan. 1910, 13, 9)

DE SOLA, Clarence I., has returned from a week in Ottawa (12 May 1911, 14, 26)

DE SOLA, Clarence I., is in Ottawa (14 May 1909, 12, 22)

DE SOLA, Clarence I., was in Ottawa during the week (18 March 1910, 13, 18)

DE SOLA, Clarence I., was in New York during the week (16 June 1911, 14, 31)

DE SOLA, Clarence I., who after the Zionist Convention in Toronto, left for New York, has returned home (6 Jan. 1911, 14, 8)

DE SOLA, Mr. and Mrs. Clarence and family have moved into their summer residence at Quixano, on the Peak (9 July 1909, 12, 30)

DE SOLA, Mr. and Mrs. Clarence I., have taken up their residence at 450 Clarke Ave., for the summer (24 June 1910, 13, 32)

DE SOLA, Mr. and Mrs. Clarence I. and party are on an automobile tour in the Adirondacks (14 July 1911, 14, 35)

DE SOLA, Mr. and Mrs. Clarence I. and family are at the Belmont, Lake Placid, N.Y. (4 Aug. 1911, 14, 38)

DE SOLA, Mr. and Mrs. Clarence, 594 Pine Ave. W., wish their friends a happy New Year (1 Oct. 1913, 16, 42-43)

DE SOLA, Mrs. Clarence and children are spending a few weeks in Cleveland, the guests of Mrs. de Sola's parents (26 Feb. 1909, 12, 11)

DE SOLA, Mrs. Clarence and children, have returned from Cleveland where they visited Mrs. de Sola's parents (2 April 1909, 12, 16)

DE SOLA, Mrs. Clarence I., organized the J.L. Samuel testimonial at the Spanish and Portuguese Congregation, assisted by Mesdames Isaac Rose, Meldola de Sola, Joseph Kirschberg, David Levy, L.P. Silver and the Misses S. Rubenstein and K. Morris (17 Dec. 1909, 13, 5)

DE SOLA, Mrs. Clarence I., organized and directed the Jewish ladies' committee for the Rose and Violet Day in aid of the Royal Edward Institute and the Children's Memorial Hospital. Some of the chaperones assisting her were:- Mesdames William Albert, J.L. Adelstein, S. Bloomfield, I.S. Goldenstein, Leon Goldman, Robert Goltman, Nathan Gordon, B. Groner, H. Hart, Lyon Hoffman, S.M. Holofcener, Archie Jacobs, N. Jurist, Jacob Kellert, A. Lesser, H. Livingstone, H. Lonn, Jacob Manolson, A.E. Morris, Paul Ogulnik, Sam Ogulnik, S. Rabinovitch, Martin Simon, Sidney Stern, I. Weinberg, H. Wener and M. Zelecovitz (22 Oct. 1913, 16, 46)

DE SOLA, Mrs. Clarence I., organized and directed the Jewish ladies' committee for the Rose and Violet Day in aid of the Royal Edward Institute and the Children's Memorial Hospital. Some of the assistants were:- the Misses Alice Abinovitch, Estelle Abrahams, Sara Adelstein, Anna Aronson, A. Ballon, E. Berman, E. Bernstein, A. Block, Annie Brodie, Leah Brown, R. Dubrofsky, Bessie Elkin, R. Elkin, Beckie Engel, Sarah Engel, Ida Feldstein, Rose Feldstein, Fanny Flanders, Eva Friedman, Eva Gittleson, Sara Gittleson, D. Goldenberg, Mirry Goldenberg, Rose Goldner, Estelle Goldstein, Mildred Gorfinkle, Bella Greenspoon, May Greenspoon, J. Greenspoon, Tilly Hart, Emily Hecht, Florence Hecht, Bessie Herman, Mollie Herman, Bessie Hoffman, Polly Hoffman, K.E. Hornstein, Etta Jacobson, Dorothy Kellert, Rose Klein, Sophie Kleinberg, Lily Lasker, Rose Lepine, Leah Lesser, Sarah Lesser, Etta Levine, Eva Levinson, Mabel Levinson, Tillie Levinson, Blanche Levy, Gladys Livingstone, Leba Livingstone, Ruby Livingstone, Ruth Livingstone, Eva Lustgarten, Lena Markson, Bessie Matts, E. Morris, Rosalie Morris, Edith Ogulnik, Pauline Rabinovitch, Madge Rosenberg, Rose Rosenberg, Fanny Rutenberg, L. Rutenberg, Anna Ruttenberg, Ray Ruttenberg, Rae Salomon, Sadie Salomon, Teresa Samuel, Annie Samuels, Fanny Samuels, Gertrude Samuels, J.L. Schafer, Annie Schleifer, Bella Schleifer, Freda Schwartz, Yetta and Etta Silver, Sophie Singer, Miriam Tannenbaum, Becky Tichler, Mary Tritt, Lilly Vineberg, Rae Vineberg, Rose Vineberg, Sara Waldman, Rose Wener, Ruth Workman, Sybil Youngheart, Fanny Zelicovitch (22 Oct. 1913, 16, 46)

DE SOLA, Mrs. Clarence I., was elected president of the newly organized, Friendly League of Jewish Women of Canada, on Thurs. aft., Feb. 27, 1913. Other officers elected were:- Mrs. J. Goldstein, 1st vice-pres.; Mrs. D. Levy, 2nd vice-pres.; Mrs. J.A. Jacobs, 3rd vice-pres.; Miss Minnie Bernstein, rec. sec.; Miss Annie Kirschberg, fin. sec.; Mrs. A.E. Morris, corr. sec.; Mrs. Nathan Gordon, treas.; Mesdames E. Berliner, D.H. Bernstein, Charles Friedman, B. Groner, S. Hart, Jacob Kellert, J.S. Leo, A. Lesser, J. Manolson, Alfred Michaels, Paul Ogulnick, M. Rabinovitch, David Tannenbaum, Harris Vineberg and H. Wener, board of directors (14 March 1913, 16, 14)

DE SOLA, Mrs. Clarence, McGill College Ave., gave a young girls' luncheon in honor of her niece, Miss Louise de Sola, who is a debutante (8 Nov. 1912, 15, 48)

DE SOLA, Mrs. M., Sherbrooke St., entertained at "Bridge" on Tues. aft. (12 Nov. 1909, 12, 48)

DE SOLA, Mrs. Meldola, attended the Wolfe-Joseph wedding in Quebec City last Thurs. (2 April 1909, 12, 16)

DE SOLA, Mrs. Meldola, will entertain at Bridge on Mon. aft. Jan. 11, 1909 (8 Jan. 1909, 12, 4)

DE SOLA, Rabbi Abraham, former rabbi of the Spanish and Portuguese Congregation of Montreal, is descended from Don Bartolome, of Navarre, also known as Baruch ben Ishak ibn Daud (28 Feb. 1913, 16, 12)

DE SOLA, Rabbi and Mrs. Meldola and family are at Rivière du Loup for the summer (9 July 1909, 12, 30)

DE SOLA, Rabbi and Mrs. Meldola, have returned from Europe where they spent the summer (15 Sept. 1911, 14, 44)

DE SOLA, Rabbi and Mrs. Meldola, who are in London, England, on a visit, have recently celebrated their silver wedding anniversary (16 Aug. 1912, 15, 36)

DE SOLA, Rabbi Meldola and family, who were in Europe, sail for Montreal from Liverpool on Sept. 8, 1910. His son, Bram de Sola, who graduated with first class honors from McGill this year, will enter Oxford University for post-graduate studies (2 Sept. 81910, 13, 42)

DE SOLA, Rabbi Meldola, is on a visit to New York (31 Dec. 1909, 13, 7)

DE SOLA, Rabbi Meldola, leaves today for a few months stay in England (6 Jan. 1911, 14, 8)

DE SOLA, Rabbi Meldola, who left Sat. night for New York to attend the memorial service for the late Rabbi J. Mayer Asher, has returned home (26 Nov. 1909, 13, 2)

DE SOLA, Rabbis Meldola, Herman Abramowitz, and Nathan Gordon, met with the Principal of McGill University, last Tues., to have the examinations which are to be held during Passover postponed (5 March 1909, 12, 12)

DE SOLA, Rev. Meldola, and Mr. and Mrs. D.S. Friedman and Master Norman Friedman sail on the S.S. Virginian, on June 18, 1913 (20 June 1913, 16, 28)

DE WALTOFF, Miss F., and Dr. de Waltoff, of New York, are guests of Mrs. H. Bernstein, Dixie (27 June 1913, 16, 29)

DE YOUNG, Miss Anna, of Roxbury, Mass., is visiting Miss Gertrude Hart, Shuter St. (15 Aug. 1913, 16, 36)

DEN BOW, N., has returned from the southern U.S. where he visited his family (1 June 1911, 14, 29)

DENBOW, N., has returned from New York where he spent a week with his sister, Mrs. J. Gordon, formerly of Montreal (10 June 1910, 13, 30)

DENENBERG, M. and daughter left for Old Orchard, Me. (11 July 1913, 16, 31)

DENENBERG, M., was re-elected president of the Montreal Hebrew Free School on Sun. aft. Jan. 19, 1913. Other officers elected were:- H. Levy, vice-pres.; Lionel Coviensky, hon. sec.; Lazarus Cohen, chrmn., fin. comm.; Rabbi Hirsch Cohen, chrmn., board of education; S. Fox, bldg. superintendent; H. Lozinski, principal; S. Boulkind, Reuben Brainin, R.A. Darwin, M.J.

Glickman, H. Lande, H. Lehrer, A. Levin, M. Ravitch, L. Rosenbloom, G. Shapira, J. Tannenbaum, B. Wiener, L. Yellin and Rabbi Herman Abramowitz, directors (24 Jan. 1913, 16, 7)

DENENBERG, Moses, is president of the Montreal Talmud Torah, Hebrew Free School. Serving on various committees are:- Reuben Brainin, Lazarus Cohen, Lionel Coviensky, R.A. Darwin, S. Fox, M.J. Glickman, T. Glickman, L. Goldberg, H. Lande, H. Lang, H. Lehrer, A. Levin, Hiram Levy, M. Ravitch, Laz. Rosenbloom, G. Shapiro, B. Wiener, L. Yellin, and Rabbis Herman Abramowitz and Hirsch Cohen (31 Jan. 1913, 16, 8)

DENNENBERG, M. and M. Margolick are visiting governors at the Montreal General Hospital this week (31 March 1911, 14, 20)

DENNENBERG, M., president of the Hebrew Free School (Talmud Torah) of Montreal, St. Urbain St., and Lazarus Cohen, the financial secretary, are conducting a fund-raising campaign for the expansion of the building which is nearing completion. Other board members are:- G. Shapiro, H. Lang, Rev. S. Goldstein, L. Rosenbloom, H. Lande, F. Holzberg, M. Sessenwein, D. Berlin, M. Lavut, David Levy, J. Astrofsky, H. Levy and S.P. Persky (9 Sept. 1910, 13, 43)

DEROSA, A., steamship agent, 65 St. Antoine St., was appointed Commissioner of the Superior Court (2 Jan. 1914, 17, 4)

DEROSA, Mr. and Mrs. A., Edward Charles Apts., Outremont, gave a reception in honor of their daughter (10 Oct. 1913, 16, 44)

DEROSA, Mr. and Mrs. A., Edward Charles Apts., Outremont, gave a reception in honor of the engagement of their daughter, Miss Olga Rabinovitch to I. Cohen (15 Oct. 1913, 16, 45)

DEROSA, Mr. and Mrs. A., gave a dance in honor of their debutante daughter, Olga Rabinovitch on Thurs. in Victoria Hall (31 Jan. 1913, 16, 8)

DEROSA, Mrs. A., is giving a dance in Victoria Hall, Westmount, on Jan. 16, 1913, in honor of her debutante daughter, Miss Olga Rabinovitch (3 Jan. 1913, 16, 4)

DEUTSCH, S., leaves tomorrow for a short trip to New York (2 April 1909, 12, 16)

DEUTSCH, S., secretary of the Chevra Kadisha Sunday School, gave a progress report of the school's activities. The school was founded six years ago (26 Dec. 1913, 17, 3)

DIAMOND, G., 582 St. Denis Blvd., sailed for England aboard the S.S. Laurentic on Aug. 6, 1910 on a business trip (12 Aug. 1910, 13, 39)

DIAMOND, J., of Boston, was a guest at the Silverman-Silver wedding (20 June 1913, 16, 28)

DIAMOND, J., was elected president of the Chevra Kadisha Congregation of Montreal at the annual meeting last Sun. Other officers elected were:- R. Jacobson, vice-pres. (Parnass); J. Rosenbloome, treas.; H. Feigelson, sec.; I. Friedman, superintendent; I. Goodman, gabei rishon; S. Frank, gabei sheni; S. Moscovitch, A. Fineberg and A. Cronstein, trustees (25 Oct. 1910, 13, 50)

DIAMOND, Miss Fanny and Miss Bessie Berson are vacationing at Kingston, Toronto and Niagara Falls (22 Aug. 1913, 16, 37)

DIAMOND, Miss Hilda, St. Paul St., returned from vacation at Ste. Agathe (8 Aug. 1913, 16, 35)

DIAMOND, Miss Lena, 582 St. Denis St., has left on a visit to Kingston, Ont. (2 Sept. 1910, 13, 42)

DIAMOND, Miss Lena, St. Denis St., has returned from Kingston, Ont. where she spent the past five weeks with Mrs. Susman and and Mrs. Cohen (30 Sept. 1910, 13, 46)

DIAMOND, Miss Ray, St. Urbain St., is spending two weeks in Ottawa (18 July 1913, 16, 32)

DIAMOND, Misses R. and I., are in New York on an extended trip (21 March 1913, 16, 15)

DIAMOND, Mr. and Mrs. B. and son, of Chicago, are visiting her parents, Mr. and Mrs. J. Diamond, St. Denis St. (8 Aug. 1913, 16, 35)

DIAMOND, Mr. and Mrs. J. and family, 582 St. Denis St., have taken up their summer residence at Cartierville (24 June 1910, 13, 32)

DIAMOND, Mr. and Mrs. J., St. Denis St., are in Chicago visiting their daughter, Mrs. B. Diamond (6 June 1913, 16, 26)

DIAMOND, Mrs. S., of Ottawa, is visiting her parents, Mr. and Mrs. Rubin (10 March 1911, 14, 17)

DINOVITZER, Mr. and Mrs. Joseph, of Chicoutimi, Que., have gone on a month's trip to Quebec City, Montreal and New York (28 Jan. 1910, 13, 11)

DIRECTOR, Mrs. I. and her little daughter Rosalie, have returned to Sault Ste. Marie, Ont. (19 March 1909, 12, 14)

DOBROFSKY, Joseph A., left Fri. for New York on a business trip (29 March 1912, 15, 20)

DOBROFSKY, Joseph and his sister, Miss Rose, left Thurs. on holiday for New York, Atlantic City and Washington (21 June 1912, 15, 28)

DOBROFSKY, M., Esplanade Ave., received a surprise birthday party (16 Feb. 1912, 15, 14)

DOBROFSKY, Mesdames M., C.B. Fainer and D. Shapiro, gave Mrs. J.H. Vineberg a surprise party in honor of her 25th birthday on Mon. (6 March 1914, 17, 10)

DOBROFSKY, Mr. and Mrs., Esplanade Ave., gave a reception at their home on Sun. evening in honor of the engagement of their sister, Miss Rose Dobrofsky to Harold Samuels, of Vancouver. Mrs. M. Dobrofsky received the guests, assisted by the Misses Rose and E. Dobrofsky and D. and R. Samuels (9 Jan. 1914, 17, 5)

DOBROFSKY, Mr. and Mrs. P., are in New York visiting their daughters (5 Dec. 1913, 16, 52)

DOBROFSKY, Mrs. M. and daughter Edith, accompanied by Mrs. M. Wiseman, went to Mt. Clemens for three weeks (11 July 1913, 16, 31)

DOBROFSKY, Mrs. M. and Mrs. M. Wiseman are staying at the Belmont Hotel, New York (10 Jan. 1913, 16, 5)

DOBROFSKY, Mrs. M., is on vacation in New York, the guest of Dr. and Mrs. Bernstein (5 Dec. 1913, 16, 52)

DOBROFSKY, Mrs. Myer, hosted an aft. tea at her home, 227 Esplanade Ave., Dec. 11, 1912 in honor of Mrs. M. Albert. Receiving the guests were Mesdames Astrof and S. Levy. Assisting in serving were Mesdames Goldner and P. Ogulnick (20 Dec. 1912, 16, 2)

DOVER, Harry, of Aylwin, Que., has enrolled in the McGill Medical Faculty. His brother, Joseph Dover, is taking his place as postmaster of Aylwin (15 Oct. 1909, 12, 44)

DOVER, Harry, third year medicine, McGill, won the Sutherland gold medal for clinical chemistry. Mr. Dover is an excellent student having won several certificates and a medal from the Ottawa Collegiate Institute (14 June 1912, 15, 27)

DOVER, Miss Hattie, of Aylwin, Que., and Miss Esther Dover, of Eganville, Ont., were visiting their friends in Ottawa, last week (11 Feb. 1910, 13, 13)

DRAIMAN, Archie, "...has returned from his western trip. The Toronto boys will be glad to have him back." (2 Oct. 1912, 15, 43)

C. J. DRESSER

MERCHANT TAILOR

Your Patronage Solicited   89 NOTRE DAME WEST

DREYFUS, Miss F., of Boston, is the guest of Mrs. Samuel Abrahams, Mt. Pleasant Ave., for a few weeks (11 Feb. 1910, 13, 13)

DREYFUS, Mr. and Mrs. Isaac and Miss Theresa Dreyfus, of Delphis, Ind., passed through Montreal last week en route for Europe aboard the S.S. Lake Manitoban, which sailed for Liverpool on Sat. (13 Aug. 1909, 12, 35)

DREYFUS, Mr. and Mrs. Theo. and family, of New York, stayed at the Windsor Hotel, en route for Nova Scotia leaving by boat, Aug. 13, 1912 (16 Aug. 1912, 15, 36)

DRUCKER, Mrs. P., of New York, is in Montreal visiting her parents, Mr. and Mrs. S. Waxman (8 Oct. 1909, 12, 43)

DUKAS, J., president of the Hebrew Free Loan Association in New York, and Mr. Neuhouse, spent a few days in Montreal this week (30 April 1909, 12, 20)

DUKAS, Julius J., of New York, was in Montreal last week (17 June 1910, 13, 31)

ECHENBERG, Miss Bertha and sister, of Sherbrooke, Que., are guests of Miss F. Golt (28 June 1912, 15, 29)

ECHENBERG, Miss R., of Sherbrooke, Que., is spending a few weeks visiting Miss I. Golt, St. Antoine St. (6 May 1910, 13, 25)

ECHENBERG, Miss R., of Sherbrooke, Que., has returned home (27 May 1910, 12, 28)

ECHENBERG, Miss Rebecca, gave a tea and china shower on Thurs., in honor of Miss Fanny Golt who is soon to be married (15 Aug. 1913, 16, 36)

EDELSTEIN, Mr. and Mrs., of New York, are honeymooning in Montreal and are guests of Mr. and Mrs. I. Shapiro, Clarke St. (15 Oct. 1913, 16, 45)

EDLOW, Dr. S., 1020 St. Lawrence Blvd., who made a good name for himself while practicing in New York, is physician to the Hebrew Ladies' Sick Benefit Association of Montreal (15 Aug. 1913, 16, 36)

EIDLOW, Samuel, physician, is applying to the Quebec Legislature for a Bill authorizing the Quebec College of Physicians and Surgeons to admit him to membership in the College and to practice medicine (10 Oct. 1913, 16, 44)

EISENSKIN, Mr. and Mrs. J., of Vienna and Berlin, stayed at the Windsor Hotel during a recent visit (26 April 1912, 15, 24)

EISENSTADT, J.J., of Prince Rupert, B.C., is in Montreal for his brother's wedding (24 Jan. 1913, 16, 7)

EISENSTAT, C., T. Garfinkle, L. Gittleson, W. Orenstein and B. Silverman are members of the YMHA bowling team (27 Dec. 1912, 16, 3)

EISENSTAT, Charles, is on holiday at Ste. Agathe (28 July 1911, 14, 37)

ELBAUM, Miss Bella, of New York, who is a guest of Mr. and Mrs. B. Ram, will remain for several months (28 may 1909, 12, 24)

ELIASOPH, I., received his degree in civil engineering, McGill University, Faculty of Science (16 May 1913, 16, 23)

ELIASOPH, Mrs. M.B., has gone to New York to spend the holidays with her parents (14 April 1911, 14, 22)

ELIASOPH, Rev. and Mrs. M.I., of Quebec City, are in Montreal for the Miller-Frank wedding and are guests of Mr. and Mrs. Thos. Frank (12 Sept. 1913, 16, 40)

ELKAN, M., has returned from a short trip to New York (30 Sept. 1910, 13, 46)

ELKHAN, Mr., leaves shortly on a trip to Cuba (29 Jan. 1909, 12, 7)

Elkin, Mrs. A. and the Misses Rose and Bessie Elkin, have gone on a long trip to Old Orchard, Me., Boston and New York (16 July 1909, 12, 31)

ELKIN, E.M., has left for Old Orchard Beach (13 Aug. 1909, 12, 35)

ELKIN, Miss Rose, has returned from Old Orchard Beach and Boston (3 Sept. 1909, 12, 38)

ELKIN, Miss Rose, has returned from New York (26 April 1912, 15, 24)

ELKIN, Miss Rose, returned to Woodlands from Lake Manitou where she visited Mrs. P. Ogulnik (16 Aug. 1912, 15, 36)

ELKIN, Mr. and Mrs. A. and family are at Beloeil for the summer (14 July 1911, 14, 35)

ELKIN, Mr. and Mrs. A. and family have returned from Woodlands, Que. (30 Aug. 1912, 15, 38)

ELKIN, Mr. and Mrs. J. and son, Mr. and Mrs. A. Elkin and the Misses Elkin are at Woodlands for the summer (13 June 1913, 16, 27)

ELKIN, Mr. and Mrs. J., Esplanade Ave., left for Atlantic City for two weeks (28 March 1913, 16, 16)

ELKIN, Mrs. A., has returned home after visiting her son, Isidore Elkin, of Brooklyn, N.Y. (17 Dec. 1909, 13, 5)

ELKIN, Mrs. A., Mrs. S. Diamond and Miss Bessie Elkin have returned from a trip to Old Orchard Beach and Boston (27 Aug. 1909, 12, 37)

ELKIN, Mrs. J., 61 Esplanade Ave.; Mrs. H. Hart, 426 Mt. Stephen Ave.; Mr. and Mrs. A. Lesser, Prince Arthur Apts.; Mrs. H.H. Livingstone, 959 Tupper St.; Mr. and Mrs. M. Rittenberg, 228 St. Joseph Blvd.; and Dr. and Mrs. Rubin, Prince Arthur Apts., are selling tickets to the play "Joseph and His Brethren" for the benefit of the Hebrew Orphans' Home (31 Oct. 1913, 16, 47)

ELLENSON, Miss Ethel, of Kingston, Ont., has gone to Toronto, Hamilton and Brantford to visit friends (5 Aug. 1910, 13, 38)

ELLIS, J.B., M. Fromson, and S. Sigler contributed to the Zionist Land Fund (28 March 1913, 16, 16)

ELLISON, A. and Miss Kate Ellison have returned from Dorval where they spent the summer (22 Oct. 1909, 12, 45)

ELLISON, E., of A. Ellison & Son Ltd., has gone on business to Portland, Boston and New York (16 Dec. 1910, 14, 5)

ELLISON, M., of New York, is visiting relatives in Montreal (24 Sept. 1909, 12, 41)

ELLISON, Messrs. A. and T. Ellison and Miss Ellison are spending the summer at Dorval (11 June 1909, 12, 26)

ELLISON, W., of Waterloo, Ont., is staying at the St. James Hotel (26 March 1909, 12, 15)

ELMAN, Mischa, the famous young Russian Jewish violinist, will appear tonight in Montreal (6 March 1914, 17, 10)

ELMAN, Mischa, the great Russian violinist, met his friend Michael Matoff while in town. They had dinner together at the Windsor Hotel (2 April 1909, 12, 16)

ENDELMAN, Miss Ruth, 427 Elm Ave., gave a masquerade party on Sat. March 16, 1912. Best costume prizes were awarded to Philip Abinovitch and Miss Rose Rosenberg. Louis Sessenwein and Miss Esther Stein won the guessing contest (22 March 1912, 15, 19)

ENGEL, A., B. Goldenberg and M. Marcus were the Senior Bar successes at Laval University, Faculty of Law (17 Jan. 1913, 16, 6)

ENGEL, Adam, of New York, stayed at the Windsor Hotel (10 Dec. 1909, 13, 4)

ENGLEMAN, Miss Pauline and her father were guests of Mr. and Mrs. M. Coviensky. Miss Engleman will remain a few weeks longer, the guest of Mrs. M. Fineberg, Esplanade Ave. (15 Oct. 1909, 12, 44)

ENGLEMAN, Miss Pauline, of Des Moines, Iowa, who was on an extended visit in Montreal, has gone to New York to visit relatives and friends, prior to her return home (31 Dec. 1909, 13, 7)

ENGLEMAN, S., of Des Moines, Iowa, was the guest of Mr. and Mrs. M. Coviensky, Berri St. (15 Oct. 1909, 12, 44)

ENRICH, S.M., of New York, is a guest at the Place Viger Hotel (7 May 1909, 12, 21)

ENUSHEVSKY, I., of Toronto, is in Montreal on business (3 April 1914, 17, 14)

ENUSHEVSKY, JR. I., of Toronto, is staying at the Windsor Hotel for two weeks, en route to points east (31 Oct. 1913, 16, 47)

ENZER, Mr., of Fort William, Ont., was in Montreal for a few days this week (19 March 1909, 12, 14)

EPPENSTEIN, Mr. and Mrs., of Chicago, were the guests of Mrs. G. Fischel (5 Feb. 1909, 12, 8

EPSTEIN, H., of Calgary, who was registered at the Windsor Hotel, has returned home (8 Oct. 1909, 12, 43)

EPSTEIN, Max, of Hamilton, Ont., spent some time in Montreal (21 May 1909, 12, 23)

EPSTEIN, Miss, is the guest of Mrs. William Rosenbloom (9 Dec. 1910, 14, 4)

EPSTEIN, Miss Kate, of New York, is visiting her sister, Mrs. N. Schleifer, 63 Mount Royal Ave. (25 Aug. 1911, 14, 41)

EPSTEIN, Miss Sophie, of Toronto, has gone to Barrie for a few weeks. Miss Epstein's name will be familiar to Jewish social life in Montreal because she was here a year ago with her younger sister, Libbie Epstein (20 Aug. 1909, 12, 36)

EPSTEIN, Mr. and Mrs. D.H., of Boston, are staying with their mother, Mrs. G. Burman, St. Famille St., where they intend to make their permanent home (4 July 1913, 16, 30)

EPSTEIN, Mr. and Mrs. Max, of Hamilton, are visiting their parents, Mr. and Mrs. Freiman, Woods Ave. (6 Sept. 1912, 15, 39)

EPSTEIN, Mrs. M., of Hamilton, who spent two weeks with her sister, Mrs. N. Lawe, at Ahuntsic, has left for Ottawa where she will be the guest of Mrs. H. Freeman (13 Aug. 1909, 12, 35)

EPSTEIN, Mrs. R., of New York, formerly of Montreal, is visiting her daughter, Mrs. H. Schleifer for a few months (23 Dec. 1910, 14, 6)

EPSTEIN, Mrs. W., sails on the S.S. Teutonic on July 1, 1911 (30 June 1911, 14, 33)

ERDILEFSKY, Miss Molly and Miss Goldie Flanders gave a surprise party on Sun. March 22, 1914 in honor of Miss Bess Fineberg. Miss Rose Fineberg presented the surprise package (3 April 1914, 17, 14)

ERDRICH, Mr. and Mrs., and Mrs. Holofcener and son have a cottage at Dorval, Que., for the summer (18 July 1913, 16, 32)

ERKHEIMER, A., of London, England, was a guest at the Place Viger Hotel this past week (19 Nov. 1909, 13, 1)

ERKSHEIMER, A., of London, England, was a guest at the Windsor Hotel (8 Oct. 1909, 12, 43)

ERXSHEIMER, A., of London, England, is a guest at the Windsor Hotel (19 May 1911, 14, 27)

ERXSHEIMER, A., of Vienna, Austria, was a guest at the Place Viger Hotel (7 April 1911, 14, 21)

ETTENBERG, Joseph, a well-known Montreal real estate broker, has opened up a stock broker's office at 92 Notre Dame St. W. "If we are well informed, this is the first business of its kind in Montreal operated by a co-religionist." (18 July 1913, 16, 32)

ETTENBERG, Mr. and Mrs. J. and family, who were at Shawbridge, left last Wed. for Old Orchard Beach for the rest of the season (6 Aug. 1909, 12, 34)

ETTENBERG, Mr. and Mrs. J., and Mr. and Mrs. A.W. Myers, of Winnipeg, who were in Boston and New York for two weeks, have returned to Montreal (28 Jan. 1910, 13, 11)

ETTENBERG, Mr. and Mrs. J. and family are at Old Orchard Beach (23 Aug. 1912, 15, 37)

ETTENBERG, Mr. and Mrs. J., are spending a holiday in New York (25 March 1910, 13, 19)

Telephones: Main 5240, 5244

J. Ettenberg & Co.
Stock Brokers
Stocks, Bonds, Grains, Provisions and Cotton

92 Notre Dame Street West
Montreal

EZEKIEL, Mr. and Mrs. Bert., of Syracuse, N.Y., will take up their residence in Montreal (3 April 1914, 17, 14)

FAIRBANK, Miss, held a social evening at her home, 430a Colonial Ave., on Sun. Jan. 4, 1914 (9 Jan. 1914, 17, 5)

FEEN, Miss Sarah, assisted by Miss P.S. Hoffman, directed a playet, "The King's Choice", at the Chevra Kadisha Sunday School Purim celebration held in the Baron de Hirsch Institute on Sun. aft. Members of the cast were:- Harry A. Baum, Abe Usher, and the Misses Frances August, Marguerite Bloom, Jennie Boyaner, Margaret Cohen, Rachel Gerson, Anna Ginsberg, Ray Ginsberg, Anna Klein, Rosie Klein, Sarah Kurtz, Sadie Lerner, Annie Marks, Jennie Robinson and Sarah Schleifer. Costumes were designed and made by the Misses Sarah Sloves and Rosa Klein. M. Garfinkle led the YMHA Symphony Orchestra and Miss Lillian Klein conducted the Halevi Juvenile Choral Society. Alex Goldberg performed a cello solo, accompanied by Miss Anne Ginsberg. Miss Lillian Ressler recited a poem "The Legend of Rabbi Ben Levi" by Longfellow. Others who assisted were:- M. Block, S. Deutsch, M. Frank, T. Garfinkle, J. Klein, A.J. Livinson, B. Marks and the Misses F. Flanders, R. Gallay, E. Jacobson, C. Livinson, P. Marks and Maude Moskovitch (28 March 1913, 16, 16)

FEINBERG, Bernard, of Paris, France, is visiting Mr. and Mrs. A.I. Rubinovich, 4462 Sherbrooke St., Westmount (12 April 1912, 15, 22)

FEINBERG, Mrs. H., and her young daughter, of Sudbury, are visiting Mrs. Feinberg's parents, Mr. and Mrs. M. Crown (19 Dec. 1913, 17, 2)

FEINBERG, Mrs. Harry, of Sudbury, Ont., is visiting her parents, Mr. and Mrs. Myer Crown (13 Jan. 1911, 14, 9)

FEINBERG, Mrs. Harry, of Sudbury, Ont., is visiting her parents, Mr. and Mrs. Moses Crown, Anderson St. (5 Jan. 1912, 15, 8)

FEINBERG, Mrs. Harry, of Sudbury, Ont., is visiting her parents, Mr. and Mrs. M. Crown, Anderson St. (24 Jan. 1913, 16, 7)

FEINER, P., was the toastmaster at the Rothchild Social Club banquet held in the Commercial Dining Rooms on Thurs. Dec. 25, 1913. Speakers included the club president, I. Seigel, Isidor Bernstein and Mendelsohn. Miss B. Rosen and Miss B. Siegler gave vocal solos and Miss Gertie Signer a recitation (2 Jan. 1914, 17, 4)

FELDMAN, I.J. and family are spending the summer at Beloeil (23 June 1911, 14, 32)

FELDMAN, I.J. and family, Holton Ave., Westmount, returned from St. Bazile where they spent the summer (12 Sept. 1913, 16, 40)

FELDMAN, M., experienced Hebrew teacher, has returned from vacation and will be resuming lessons at 1121 St. Dominique St. (19 Sept. 1913, 16, 41)

FELDMAN, Miss Ida, has returned from New York where she spent several months with friends and relatives (12 Nov. 1909, 12, 48)

FELDMAN, Miss Sophie, returned from Old Orchard, Boston and New York (6 Sept. 1912, 15, 39)

FELDMAN, Mrs. S., Prince Arthur St. E., has returned from visiting relatives (2 Aug. 1912, 15, 34)

FELDMAN, S.J. and family are spending the summer at Beloeil (1 July 1910, 13, 33)

FELDMAN, Samuel H., who spent the last three years at Black Lake, has moved back to Montreal to live (22 Nov. 1912, 15, 50)

FELS, Miss Minnie, leaves for New York on Dec. 31, 1909 to visit her mother, Mrs. A. Fels (24 Dec. 1909, 13, 6)

FELS, Mr. and Mrs. and family are spending the summer at St. Johns, Que. (8 July 1910, 13, 34)

FENSTER, Miss Carrie, has returned from a trip to New York (22 April 1910, 13, 23)

FENSTER, Miss Carrie, Laval Ave., gave a linen shower and tea Sun. aft., in honor of Miss Mary Flanders' approaching marriage. Assisting at the table were:- Mesdames Hyman Schleifer and H.M. Levinoff and the Misses Fanny Flanders and Jennie Tritt. Mrs. H. Lefkovitz, of Sturgeon Fall, Ont., was also present (28 Feb. 1913, 16, 12)

FENSTER, Mr. and Mrs. H., Mr. and Mrs. Harry Bloomfield, Mr. and Mrs. Newman and Mr. and Mrs. Paul Ogulnik are among those spending the summer at Dorval, Que. (27 May 1910, 13, 28)

FIDERSKI, Miss Ray, of Glace Bay, N.S., is visiting her cousin, Miss Anna Levy, 74 Laval Ave. (7 Jan. 1910, 13, 8)

FIERST, Harry, of New York, is the guest of Rabbi Hirsch Cohen (13 June 1913, 16, 27)

FINBURGH, Alfred A., of Leicester, England, is the guest of his uncle and aunt, Mr. and Mrs. Z. Fineberg, Shuter St. (26 May 1911, 14, 28)

FINBURGH, Alfred, of Leicester, England, is visiting his uncle and aunt, Mr. and Mrs. Z. Fineberg, of Montreal (27 May 1910, 13, 28)

FINE, Miss Rose, is the guest of Mr. and Mrs. Blankstein, 1130 St. Urbain St. (30 Aug. 1912, 15, 38)

FINE, Miss Rose, of Ottawa, entertained on Sun. evening Sept. 19, 1909, in honor of Miss Esther Dover, of Eganville, Ont. (24 Sept. 1909, 12, 41)

FINE, Morris, of Montreal, spent the two days of Rosh Hashana with his parents in Ottawa. He returned home Sun. (24 Sept. 1909, 12, 41)

FINEBERG, Alfred, of Leicester, Eng., is the guest of his uncle and aunt, Mr. and Mrs. Z. Fineberg, Shuter St. (25 June 1909, 12, 28)

FINEBERG, Harry and Moe, are spending the summer at Old Orchard Beach (5 Aug. 1910, 13, 38)

FINEBERG, J., 14 Craig St. W., or Leon Goldman, 23 Esplanade Ave., are asking Agudath Zion Society members to notify them about their

---

S. FEIGELMAN
Stationery and Book Store

Also a great assortment of all English and American publications, and sheet music of all descriptions. :: :: :: :: ::

421 St. Lawrence Blvd.   MONTREAL

change of addresses (7 May 1909, 12, 21)

FINEBERG, Joseph, is at Old Orchard on vacation (14 July 1911. 14, 35)

FINEBERG, Joseph, left last night for a short holiday at Old Orchard Beach (19 Aug. 1910, 13, 40)

FINEBERG, Joseph, president of the Agudath Zion Society of Montreal, chaired the semi-annual meeting on Sun. Dec. 7, 1913. The following delegates were elected to represent the Society at the Zionist Convention in Montreal on Dec. 25:- M. Berkowitz, H. Bloomstone, A. Cohen, H. Cohen, Joseph Eidelberg, A.H. Fineberg, Charles Fisher, Louis Fitch, M. Fromson, T. Glickman, D. Gordon, J. Jospe, S. Kahn, I. Kirschberg, I. Lande, H. Lehrer, Jacob Leiter, M. Levitt, Hiram Levy, H. Lozinsky, Dr. S. Ortenberg, A.D. Paltiel, A. Rabin, Z. Ratner, L. Shara, I.C. Skiebelski, Max Usher, B.M. Weiner and H. Wolofsky (12 Dec. 1913, 17, 1)

FINEBERG, Joseph, sailed on the S.S. Empress of Ireland on June 26, 1913, for a pleasure trip to Europe. He will attend the Zionist Congress in Vienna on Sept. 2, 1913 (27 June 1913, 16, 29)

FINEBERG, Joseph, was elected president of the Montreal Agudath Zion Society at the annual meeting last Sun. evening in the Baron de Hirsch Institute. Other officers elected were:- L. Goldman, A. Levine, I. Lande, A. Harris, H.P. Nerwich, H. Cohen, Clarence I. de Sola, D. Levy, S. Haskell, O. Bercusson, M. Fromson, A. Morris, L. Heillig, D. Feldman, H. Lozinsky, C. Fisher, L. Ackerman, M.L. Levin, D. Blumer, H. Lang, Z. Ratner, D. Zarakin, and N. H. Godinsky (12 May 1911, 14, 26)

FINEBERG, Joseph, was in New York this week (10 June 1910, 13, 30)

FINEBERG, M.A., N.S., is spending the summer at Ste. Agathe (16 July 1909, 12, 31)

FINEBERG, Master Max, age 13, son of Z. Fineberg, 722 Shuter St., received the gold medal and scholarship for general proficiency at the Berthelet Street School closing (27 June 1913, 16, 29)

FINEBERG, Miss Rose, is at home recovering from an appendicitis operation at the Royal Victoria Hospital (20 Dec. 1912, 16, 2)

FINEBERG, Mr. and Mrs. A. and Miss Rose Fineberg left for Rochester, N.Y., where they will attend the Gordon-Gordon wedding (18 July 1913, 16, 32)

FINEBERG, Mr. and Mrs. A., gave a birthday party in honor of their daughter, Rose, on Wed. Feb. 19, 1913. Guests included:- S. Althouse, A. Chernoff, M. Crown, H. Feldstein, A.J. Fineberg, H.S. Fineberg, F. Wilson and the Misses J. Cooperman, F. Fineberg and S. Shaw (28 Feb. 1913, 16, 12)

FINEBERG, Mr. and Mrs. Max, 185 Esplanade Ave., wish their friends a happy New Year (1 Oct. 1913, 16, 42-43)

FINEBERG, Mr. and Mrs. Max, Esplanade Ave., sail on the S.S. Royal George, on July 1, 1913 for Europe (27 June 1913, 16, 29)

FINEBERG, Mr. and Mrs. Max, gave a housewarming at their new home, 185 Esplanade Ave. Those assisting were the Misses Beccie Cohen, Miriam Cohen, Ray Coviensky and Jessie Phillips (27 Dec. 1912, 16, 3)

FINEBERG, Mr. and Mrs. Z., 722 Shuter St., wish their friends and relatives a happy New Year (1 Oct. 1913, 16, 42-43)

FINEBERG, Mr. and Mrs. Z., accompanied by Miss Agnes and Master Maxie Fineberg, are expected to return on the S.S. Megantic today after a three months' stay in Europe (8 Oct. 1909, 12, 43)

FINEBERG, Mr. and Mrs. Z., will leave for England and the Continent, on Fri. July 2, 1909, aboard the S.S. Megantic (25 June 1909, 12, 28)

FINEBERG, Mrs., Esplanade Ave., gave a dinner Sun. evening in honor of her cousin, Miss Cooper who will soon be married to Mr. Schnaer (27 Dec. 1912, 16, 3)

FINEBERG, Mrs. M. and family, 16 Sherbrooke St. E., are in St. Bruno, Que., for the summer (28 June 1912, 15, 29)

FINEBERG, Mrs. Z. and daughter, Agnes Fineberg and Master Max Fineberg are on vacation (14 July 1911, 14, 35)

FINEBERG, Mrs. Z., left last night for Old Orchard Beach (12 Aug. 1910, 13, 39)

FINEBERG, Nathan S. (M.A.), first year law, McGill University, came first and won the $100.00 prize (12 May 1911, 14, 26)

FINEBERG, Z., has joined his family for two weeks at Ferndale, Catskills (11 Aug. 1911, 14, 39)

FINEBERG, Zigmond, believes he has done his share in organizing the Hebrew Free Loan Association "Gemiluth Chessodim" and a new Board will shortly be formed. Some of the subscribers to date are:- B. Goldstein, vice-pres. of the Baron de Hirsch Institute; M. Michalson, Joseph A. Bessner, J. Rubin, Joseph Kahne, D. Sternklar, J. Roston, George Rabinovitch, John J. Weinfield, D. Steinberg, A. Lessor, P. Popliger, M. Albert, Saul Rainblatt, R. Jacobson, M. Dobrofsky, J. Albert, Jack Levy, L. Alder, M.S. Superior, E. Jacobs, M. Adelstein, B. Ram, C. Spector, W. Gredinger, M. Feldman, Moses Levitt, H. Caplan, Bernard Fox, J. Shalinsky, L. Azef, S. Sigler, M. Meld, L. Nathanson, M. Zelicovitz, A. Victor, Leon Green, S. Kolber, A. Schachter, A.M. Levy, H. Vosberg, Nathan Liekler, H. Hart, M. Fenster, L. Teplitzky, M. Mendelsohn, A. Bieber, H. Fenster, L. Frischling, J.H. Victor, S.L. Ruttenberg and N. Stern (17 March 1911, 14, 18)

FINEBERG, Zigmond, collected donations for the Hebrew Free Loan Association from the following subscribers:- S. Levinson, A.H. Jackson, Sam Bloomfield, H.M. Levinoff, Joseph Stern and B.J. Hayes (31 March 1911, 14, 20)

FINEBERG, Zigmond, who has been the chief organizer of the Hebrew Free Loan Association, is canvassing the community for donations. Some of the subscribers to date are:- Lazarus Cohen, Lyon Cohen, S.W. Jacobs, K.C., Isaac Kert, A. Levin, H.M. Levine, Louis S. Margolese, Thomas M. Morgan, Carl Rosenberg, Harris Vineberg and A. Wollenberg (10 March 1911, 14, 17)

FINKELSTEIN, Mr. and Mrs. Max and son left Ottawa and are visiting Mr. and Mrs. Kahn, St. Urbain St. (16 May 1913, 16, 23)

FINN, Miss Libbie, of Ottawa, is the guest of her friend, Miss Rose Harris (2 Jan. 1914, 17, 4)

FIRTH, Mr. and Mrs. John S., of Cleveland, Ohio, are visiting Mr. and Mrs. Clarence de Sola at their summer residence (29 July 1910, 13, 37)

FISCHBEIN, Miss Rose, of Brooklyn, N.Y., is visiting Mr. and Mrs. L. Ressler, Park Ave. (7 Nov. 1913, 16, 48)

FISCHEL, G., is in the Maritimes on a business trip (22 Oct. 1909, 12, 45)

FISCHEL, Mr. and Mrs. Gustav, have moved from 1 Winchester Ave. to 420 Prince Albert Ave., Westmount (31 March 1911, 14, 20)

FISCHEL, Mr. and Mrs. S., are spending a few days at Caledonia Springs (10 Sept. 1909, 12, 39)

FISCHEL, Mrs. G., entertained at "Bridge" in honor of her niece, Miss Frank, of Chicago (15 Jan. 1909, 12, 5)

FISCHEL, Mrs. G., has fully recovered from the slight accident she sustained a short time ago (5 Nov. 1909, 12, 47)

FISCHEL, Mrs. G., hosted a bridge game in honor of Mrs. Schradsky, of New York. Mrs. Bert Levine won the first prize (3 Dec. 1909, 13, 3)

FISCHEL, Mrs. Gus and Master Leon and Victor Fischel will spend the summer at Lake Champlain (11 July 1913, 16, 31)

FISCHEL, Mrs. Gus., Winchester ave., will host the first "Bridge" of the season (15 Oct. 1909, 12, 44)

FISCHEL, Mrs. S., is staying at the Caledonia Springs Hotel (18 July 1913, 16, 32)

FISCHEL, Mrs. S., left Tues. morn. for New York where she will take up permanent residence. Mrs. Fischel was a Montreal resident for many years. She was on the board of the Ladies' Hebrew Benevolent Society for over thirty-five years and was a past president and treasurer (19 Sept. 1913, 16, 41)

FISCHEL, Rudolph and George Blumenthal have returned from two weeks at Weir, Que. (2 Aug. 1912, 15, 34)

FISCHEL, Rudolph, of Westmount, is in Chicago for a few weeks visiting relatives (1 Oct. 1913, 16, 42-43)

FISCHEL, S., was a guest at the Hotel Astor, New York (13 Jan. 1911, 14, 9)

FISCHEL, Sarah, is hon. secretary of the Ladies' Hebrew Benevolent Society which holds its thirty-fifth annual meeting Sun. Dec. 1, 1912 at 1 p.m. (29 Nov. 1912, 15, 51)

FISCHMAN, Mrs. S. and Master Norman Fischman, of Ottawa, are visiting her parents, Mr. and Mrs. Finkelstein, of Toronto (2 Jan. 1914, 17, 4)

FISCHMAN, S., of Ottawa, is visiting friends in Toronto and Kingston (7 July 1911, 14, 34)

FISH, Dr. J.B., resigned as superintendent of the Mount Sinai Sanatorium (27 Feb. 1914, 17, 9)

FISHER, J., of Smith's Falls, is registered at the Grand Union (24 Dec. 1909, 13, 6)

FISHER, Miss, of Brooklyn, N.Y., is the guest of Mrs. A. Goldstein, St. Catherine St. E. (26 Feb. 1909, 12, 11)

FISHER, Mr. and Mrs., have returned to New York after visiting Mrs. Fisher's brothers, Saul and Maurice Tipograph, of Montreal (9 Sept. 1910, 13, 43)

FISHER, Mrs. K. and daughter have gone to New Glasgow, Que., for the summer (22 July 1910, 13, 36)

FISHER, Mrs. S., 21 Esplanade Ave., gave a tea and linen shower in honor of Miss R. Goodman, of New York. Assisting at the table were Mesdames A. Drainow and F. Marcuse and Miss Jennie Greenspon (20 Dec. 1912, 16, 2)

FISHERMAN, Mrs. and Master Norman Fisherman, of Ottawa, are guests of her parents, Mr. and Mrs. Finkelstein, of Toronto (27 Dec. 1912, 16, 3)

FISHMAN, M., of New York, is registered at the Russell Hotel (26 Nov. 1909, 13, 2)

FISHMAN, Mr. and Mrs. P. and family are at Old Orchard Beach, Me. They will motor to Atlantic City before returning to Montreal (8 Aug. 1913, 16, 35)

FISHMAN, Mrs. P. and baby are spending the summer at New Glasgow (22 July 1910, 13, 36)

FISHMAN, Mrs. P. and Mrs K. Fisher and her little daughter are spending the summer at Ste. Agathe des Monts (23 July 1909, 12, 32)

FISHMAN, Mrs. P., is visiting relatives in New York (6 June 1913, 16, 26)

FISHMAN, P., has returned from a business trip to New York (20 Oct. 1911, 14, 49)

FISHMAN, P., is on holiday in Atlantic City (25 Aug. 1911, 14, 41)

FISHMAN, P., returned from an important business trip to New York (16 May 1913, 16, 23)

FISHMAN, P., the well-known real estate broker, returned from an extensive tour across Europe. "He left on Thursday for New York to complete a real estate transaction of great magnitude." (2 May 1913, 16, 21)

FITCH, Louis, (B.A.) in the final year of law at McGill University, won the Gold Medal and the Macdonald Scholarship of $750.00 (12 May 1911, 14, 26)

FITCH, Louis, addressed the Junior Maccabean Concert held last Sun. Members of the cast were:- Masters Joseph Orenstein, M. Schweisberg, J. Solomon, Louis Zwibel and the Misses B. Sloves and A. Teplitzky. R. Caplan trained the youngsters (3 April 1914, 17, 14)

FITCH, Louis, has gone to Quebec City to visit his parents (26 May 1911, 14, 28)

FITCH, Louis, has returned after visiting his parents in Quebec City (7 Jan. 1910, 13, 8)

FITCH, Louis, has returned to Montreal after a stay in Quebec City and Indian Lorette, Que. (24 Sept. 1909, 12, 41)

FITCH, Louis, is on holiday visiting his parents in Quebec City (19 Aug. 1910, 13, 40)

FITCH, Louis, is one of the two students who have been chosen to represent McGill against Ottawa in the Inter-University Debating Championship, to be held in Montreal, Dec. 3, 1909 (12 Nov. 1909, 12, 48)

FITCH, Louis, is spending a few weeks in Quebec City visiting his parents (24 Dec. 1909, 13, 6)

FITCH, Louis, of McGill University, spent the weekend in Quebec City with his parents (12 March 1909, 12, 13)

FITCH, Louis, spoke on Jewish Nationalism to the Young People's Society of Shaar Hashomayim Synagogue last Wed. evening. Others present were:- David Dainow, Alton Goldbloom, J. Viner, Rabbi Herman Abramowitz and Miss Leba Livingstone (4 April 1913, 16, 17)

FLANDERS, A.H., was engaged as collector for the Mount Sinai Sanatorium (31 Jan. 1913, 16, 8)

FLANDERS, A.H., was re-engaged as collector of outstanding membership dues for the Hebrew Free Loan Association (20 Feb. 1914, 17, 8)

FLANDERS, M., was elected vice-president of the Young Men's Hebrew Debating Society on Thurs. Dec. 12, 1913. J. Laing and J. Rosenberg were elected executive members. H.G. Friefeld gave a talk followed by a debate between H. Lehrer (affirm.) and R. Docks (neg.) " Resolved that Women Have a Right to the Suffrage" (19 Dec. 1913, 17, 2)

FLEISCHMAN, William, Simon Franklin, A. Isaacs, W. Isaacs, A. Pierce, Mr. and Mrs. E. Youngheart and Miss R. Goldstein arrived on the S.S. Laurentic from Liverpool yesterday (20 Aug. 1909, 12, 36)

FLEISIG, David and J. Wechsler, of London, England, arrived in Montreal (27 June 1913, 16, 29)

FLEISIG, Miss Rae, 1032 St. Urbain St., is accepting memberships in the Welcome Club For Jewish Working Girls which was recently inaugurated by the Friendly League of Jewish Women under the presidency of Mrs. Clarence I. de Sola. "The Club work is being organized by Miss Fleisig of London, England, who has spent three years in that city in similar work...The aim of the Club is to gain the co-operation of the Montreal working girls in befriending and providing wholesome evening amusement for strangers from the day they enter our city. The Club meets every evening, except Friday, at the Baron de Hirsch Institute in a cosy tastefully decorated room." Those wishing to volunteer their time should contact Mrs. de Sola, 594 Pine Ave. (8 Aug. 1913, 16, 35)

FLEISIG, Miss Ray, a staff member of the Jews' Free School, London, England, has just moved to Montreal (13 Dec. 1912, 16, 1)

FLEISIG, Samuel, of Halifax, N.S., is visiting his sister, Miss Rae Fleisig, St. Urbain St. (29 Aug. 1913, 16, 38)

FLORENCE, A., of Calgary, is in Montreal to attend his daughter Sophie's wedding which takes place March 30, 1913 (28 March 1913, 16, 16)

FLORENCE, Miss, Duluth Ave., was given a surprise party in honor of her approaching marriage, by the Misses L. Weiss and S. Weinstein, at the home of the Misses S. and F. Hart, City Hall Ave., Sun. evening, Jan. 26, 1913. Guests included P. Florence, T. Wilson, and the Misses J. Breitshatz, C. Rosenbaum, S. Shaw and P. Weinstein (31 Jan. 1913, 16, 8)

FORCIMER, Mr. and Mrs. E., of Nanaimo, B.C., were in Montreal for a short stay (14 March 1913, 16, 14)

FOSS, Mr. and Mrs. L. and A. Foss, of Boston, came by automobile to Montreal and were guests of Mrs. E. Lichtenhein, Peel St., for a few days (9 July 1909, 12, 30)

FOX, Bernard, returned from his Mediterranean cruise (1 Aug. 1913, 16, 34)

FOX, Mr. and Mrs., of New York, were in Montreal (1 Sept. 1911, 14, 42)

FRAID, Joseph, of Cornwall, was in Montreal for the Holy Days (20 Sept. 1912, 15, 41)

FRAID, Louis and Nathan, of Cornwall, Ont., attended the funeral of their young nephew, only son of Mr. and Mrs. J. Weintraub, who died after a short illness (19 April 1912, 15, 23)

FRAID, Louis, of Gananoque, Ont., spent a few days in Montreal (12 Feb. 1909, 12, 9)

FRAID, Miss Dora, is visiting her sister, Mrs. J. Weintraub, in New York (18 July 1913, 16, 32)

FRAID, Miss Mollie, has returned home to Cornwall, Ont. (5 Feb. 1909, 12, 8)

FRAID, Mr. and Mrs. L., of Gananoque, Ont., have taken up their residence in Montreal (6 May 1910, 13, 25)

FRAID, Mr. and Mrs. Lou, Tupper St., Westmount, were guests of Mr. and Mrs. Fraid in Cornwall (3 Jan. 1913, 16, 4)

FRAID, Mr. and Mrs. Nathan, of Alexandria,

DONALDA
MY SPECIAL PERFUME
AN EXQUISITE ODOR MADE FROM FLOWERS FRAGRANT AND LASTING.
Sold only by
BERNARD FOX,
Pharmaceutical and Dispensing Chemist
238 St. Catherine St. West
BELL TEL. MAIN 4389   A few doors west of Bleury St

Ont., were in Montreal to attend the Bar Mitzvah of Mrs. Fraid's nephew, Master Lawrence Cohen (1 Oct. 1913, 16, 42-43)

FRAID, Mrs. Louis, accompanied by her son, has returned home to Gananoque, Ont., after spending a few weeks with her parents, Mr. and Mrs. H. Kellert, Sherbrooke St. W. (11 June 1909, 12, 26)

FRAID, Mrs. Louis and family are at the "Inn", Gananoque, Ont. for the balance of the summer (12 Aug. 1910, 13, 39)

FRAID, Mrs. Louis, Miss Beatrice and Master Bertram Fraid are at Gananoque, Ont. for the summer (14 July 1911, 14, 35)

FRAID, Mrs. Louis, Miss Beatrice and Master Bertram Fraid, Tupper St., are at Old Orchard, Me., for a month (18 July 1913, 16, 32)

FRAID, Mrs. Louis, of Gananoque, Ont., is visiting her mother, Mrs. H. Kellert, Sherbrooke St. (28 May 1909, 12, 24)

FRAID, Mrs. Louis, of Gananoque, Ont., is the guest of her parents, Mr. and Mrs. J. Kellert, Sherbrooke St. (24 Sept. 1909, 12, 41)

FRAID, Mrs. N.J., of Cornwall, Ont., is visiting her mother, Mrs. Friedman, Bishop St. (12 Feb. 1909, 12, 9)

FRAID, Mrs. N.J., of Cornwall, Ont., spent a few days here last week (21 May 1909, 12, 23)

FRAID, Mrs. Nathan and daughters, of Cornwall, are visiting Mrs. N. Friedman, Bishop St. (25 Oct. 1910, 13, 50)

FRAID, Mrs. Nathan and her daughter, of Cornwall, were guests of her mother, Mrs. N. Friedman, Bishop St. (13 Jan. 1911, 14, 9)

FRAID, Mrs. Nathan and little daughter are visiting Mrs. N. Friedman, Bishop St. (29 Oct. 1909, 12, 46)

FRAID, Mrs. Nathan, of Cornwall, is spending a few weeks with her mother, Mrs. N. Friedman, Bishop St. (10 Sept. 1909, 12, 39)

FRAID, Mrs., of Cornwall has returned home after spending the past ten days with Mr. and Mrs. Louis Fraid (24 June 1910, 13, 32)

FRAID, Mrs., of Cornwall, was the guest of Mr. and Mrs. Louis Fraid while in Montreal en route for New York to visit her daughter (12 May 1911, 14, 26)

FRAID, Mrs., of Cornwall, was the guest of Mr. and Mrs. Louis Fraid, Tupper St. Mrs. Fraid spent several weeks in New York visiting her daughter, Miss Wintraub (16 June 1911, 14, 31)

FRAID, Nathan, of Cornwall, Ont., was in Montreal for a few days (23 June 1911, 14, 32)

FRANK, Louis, of Chicago, was a guest at the Welland (8 Oct. 1909, 12, 43)

FRANK, Miss, of Chicago, is visiting her sister, Mrs. Arthur Simon, Grosvenor Ave., Westmount (10 Nov. 1911, 14, 52)

FRANK, Miss Rose, St. Lawrence Blvd., left Tues. for Lake Placid where she will spend the summer (9 May 1913, 16, 22)

FRANK, Mr. and Mrs., are at Valois, Que., for the summer (9 July 1909, 12, 30)

FRANK, Mr. and Mrs. Khos., left on a trip to New York on Sun. (15 Oct. 1913, 16, 45)

FRANK, Mrs. L., has left for Philadelphia to attend her mother's funeral (4 June 1909, 12, 25)

FRANK, Mrs. S., is visiting her daughter, Mrs. M. Goldenberg in Three Rivers, Que. (15 March 1912, 15, 18)

FRANKEL, Mrs. H.B., accompanied by her daughter, of Boston, will spend the rest of the summer with her parents, Mr. and Mrs. S. Abrahams, at Apple Hill Cottage, Lakeside, Que. (5 Aug. 1910, 13, 38)

FRANKLIN, H., of Dayton, is staying at the Albion Hotel (9 July 1909, 12, 30)

FRANKLIN, J.A., sailed on the S.S. Laurentic on July 8, 1913 for two months' vacation in Europe (11 July 1913, 16, 31)

FRANKLIN, J.L., was elected president of the B'nai U' Bnoth Zion Kadimah Society Sun. Nov. 12, 1911 in the Baron de Hirsch Institute. Other officers elected were:- M. Gelbman, vice-pres.; H. Lang, treas.; S. Schlossberg, fin. sec.; Miss Clara Mintz, rec. sec.; E. Mauer, M. McKinley, S. Margolies, Maxwell Lightstone and the Misses Sarah Rosenthal and Mary Tritt, executive (17 Nov. 1911, 15, 1)

FRANKLIN, Mr., of New York, was the guest of Mr. and Mrs. A. Jacobs, Dorchester St. W. (3 March 1911, 14, 16)

FRANKLIN, Mr., of Pittsburgh, Pa., is visiting his sister, Mrs. Fraid, St. Charles Apts., Armsbury Ave. (4 July 1913, 16, 30)

FRANKLIN, Mr., of Toronto, was in Montreal for a few days (16 July 1909, 12, 31)

FREDIN, Dame Fanny, wife of John Rudnikoff, merchant, instituted an action, no. 2665, on July 23, 1913 for separation of property in the Quebec Superior Court, District of Montreal (12 Sept. 1913, 16, 40)

FREEDMAN, Albert, has returned from Antwerp on the S.S. Empress of Ireland (30 July 1909, 12, 33)

FREEDMAN, B., was registered at the Victoria Hotel while in Quebec City the past week (6 May 1910, 13, 25)

FREEDMAN, D., returned from a trip to New York (13 Feb. 1914, 17, 7)

FREEDMAN, D.S., left for Cobalt, the guest of Mr. and Mrs. R.M. Bilsky (16 July 1909, 12, 31)

FREEDMAN, Dr. A., who has spent the past few years at the Royal Victoria, Alexandria and Women's Hospitals, has opened his consulting rooms at 257 Sherbrooke St. E. (3 Sept. 1909, 12, 38)

FREEDMAN, Dr. A., who is on the staff of the Royal Victoria Hospital, will read a paper at the Canadian Medical Association meeting in Winnipeg, on Aug 23-24, 1909 (20 Aug. 1909, 12, 36)

FREEDMAN, Dr. A.O., lectured on "The Present Conditions of the Jews of Montreal" at the YMHA Friday Night Talks (7 March 1913, 16, 13)

FREEDMAN, Dr. Seymour, has gone south for a few weeks (7 April 1911, 14, 21)

FREEDMAN, I., has returned from two weeks at Old Orchard, Me. (2 Aug. 1912, 15, 34)

FREEDMAN, Isidore amd Mrs. Freedman have just returned from several months in Europe (21 Jan. 1910, 13, 10)

FREEDMAN, M., has gone to Ste. Agathe des Monts for the summer (24 June 1910, 13, 32)

FREEDMAN, M., is in Atlantic City for a month. He will visit Philadelphia and New York before returning home (10 March 1911, 14, 17)

FREEDMAN, Max and Lyon Coviensky are spending a holiday at Ste. Agathe in the Laurentian Mountains (23 July 1909, 12, 32)

FREEDMAN, Max, has returned from a two weeks' holiday in New York (4 Feb. 1910, 13, 12)

FREEDMAN, Miss Eva, has returned home after spending the winter in Cobalt, Ont., the guest of Mrs. Alexander Bilsky (12 March 1909, 12, 13)

FREEDMAN, Moe, has opened a new drug store at the corner of St. Lawrence and St. Cuthbert St. "It is being stocked with all the necessary chemical and drug supplies, and every care and attention will be given to patrons. Doctor's prescriptions will be carefully made up." (6 June 1913, 16, 26)

FREEDMAN, Mr. and Mrs. B., 86 Park Ave., received last Sun. in honor of the Bar Mitzvah of their son, Lewis. Mrs. Freedman was assisted by her two sisters, Mesdames Joseph Levinson and Ralph Wetstein. Young ladies assisting were:- the Misses Lily and Annie Samuels, Myrtle Levinson, Hattie and Rebecca Kellert, and Hannah Brown (Nashville, Tenn.) (23 Dec. 1910, 14, 6)

FREEDMAN, Mr. and Mrs. Harry and family have returned from Woodlands where they spent the summer and have moved to their new residence at 124 Clandeboye Ave. (20 Sept. 1911, 14, 45)

FREEDMAN, Mr. and Mrs. Harry, are at their summer residence at Woodlands (15 July 1910, 13, 35)

FREEDMAN, Mr. and Mrs. Isidore and daughter, Western Ave., have left for a few weeks at Old Orchard Beach (23 July 1909, 12, 32)

FREEDMAN, Mr. and Mrs. Isidore, have left on a trip to Europe (3 Dec. 1909, 13, 3)

FREEDMAN, Mrs. A.L. and daughter are spending the summer at Shawbridge (30 June 1911, 14, 33)

FREEDMAN, Mrs. B. and young sons, Park Ave., are spending the summer in the Laurentian Mountains (9 July 1909, 12, 30)

FREEDMAN, Mrs. H.W., 764 St. Joseph Blvd., will spend the remainder of the summer in Ste. Agathe (30 July 1909, 12, 33)

FREEDMAN, Mrs. H.W., has fully recovered from her attack of typhoid fever (4 Feb. 1910, 13, 12)

FREEDMAN, Mrs. T. and family returned from Coteau du Lac (2 Aug. 1912, 15, 34)

FREEDMAN, Rachel, hon. secretary of the Ladies' Chevra Kadisha, requests members to attend a meeting on Sun. at 3 p.m., in the vestry rooms, McGill College Ave. (16 Jan. 1914, 17, 6)

FREEDMAN, Sam, of New York, is the guest of his cousins, Mr. and Mrs. M. Feldstein (17 Jan. 1913, 16, 6)

FREEMAN, H.D., of Ottawa, spent a few days in Montreal (9 July 1909, 12, 30)

FREEMAN, K., has been appointed Relief Officer of the Baron de Hirsch Institute (12 Nov. 1909, 12, 48)

FREEMAN, Miss Hyalie, gave an informal tea last week for officers of the Primrose Club (25 Nov. 1910, 14, 2)

FREEMAN, Miss Hyalie, is in Worcester, Mass., visiting relatives (13 Feb. 1914, 17, 7)

FREEMAN, Miss Hyalie, judged the YWHA debate "Should a Woman Marry for Love or Money?" Misses D. Ratner and R. Samuels took the affirmative and Misses J. Schulich and J. Garfinkle the negative. The affirmative was judged the winner (10 April 1914, 17, 15)

FREEMAN, Miss Hyallie, is at Shawbridge, Que., for a few weeks (25 July 1911, 14, 36)

FREEMAN, Miss Hyallie, Tupper St., is in New York for a few weeks (7 March 1913, 16, 13)

FREEMAN, Miss Pearl, of Ottawa, is visiting her sister, Mrs. N. Lande, 27 Sherbrooke St. E. (19 Nov. 1909, 13, 1)

FREEMAN, Miss Pearl, of Ottawa, Ont., is visiting her sister, Mrs. N. Lande, 27 Sherbrooke St. (26 Feb. 1909, 12, 11)

FREEMAN, Miss Sadie, was given a surprise party at her residence, 460 Guy St., on Sun. Jan. 11, 1914. Among those present were:- John Schepes and the Misses B. and L. Fedderman, Annie Freeman, Fannie Mitnick and Mesdames J. Freeman and Myer Freeman. "Would the lady who by mistake took a pair of carriage boots belonging to Miss Flossie Hyman kindly return same to 4044 Tupper St. Westmount and receive hers in exchange." (16 Jan. 1914, 17, 6)

FREEMAN, Mrs. K. and family thank their friends for their expressions of sympathy on their recent bereavement (15 Nov. 1912, 15, 49)

FREEMAN, Mrs. K. and Miss Hyallie Freeman, Tupper St., returned from Old Orchard, Me. (29 Aug. 1913, 16, 38)

FREEMAN, S., has returned home to Vancouver, B.C., after two weeks in Montreal (3 March 1911, 14, 16)

FREEMAN, Sim., of Edmonton, Alta., who sails for Europe April 7, 1911, was the guest of Mr. and Mrs. J.S. Gabriel in Ottawa on the weekend (7 April 1911, 14, 21)

FREIDLANDER, Rev. Elias, of Vancouver, B.C., who was in Montreal for a week, left for New York where he expects to remain for several months (8 Jan. 1909, 12, 4)

FREIDMAN, Louis, Alexander Silver and the Misses Annie Kleinberg, Gertrude Lande and Sarah Weiner graduated from Shaarey Shomayim Sunday School last Sun. morn. (7 June 1912, 15, 26)

FREIDMAN, Mr. and Mrs. I. and Miss Eva Freidman have left for the Gaspé (2 Aug. 1912, 15, 34)

FREIDMAN, Mrs. N., her son Hesse Friedman and Miss Lily Samuels have returned from the Saguenay trip (23 Aug. 1912, 15, 37)

FREIDMAN, Nolan, is the guest of Phil Blumenthal, at Beaurepaire, Que. (1 Aug. 1913, 16, 34)

FREIDMAN, Ralph, spent the weekend at Wing's Hotel, Foster, Que. (2 Aug. 1912, 15, 34)

FREIMAN, A.J., of Ottawa, Miss Lily Vineberg, of Detroit, Miss Bilsky, of Ottawa and Mrs. R. Cohen, of Buffalo, N.Y., were out-of-town guests who attended the reception given by Mr. and Mrs. N. Silver, Souvenir Ave., in honor of the Bar Mitzvah of their son, Alexander (16 Sept. 1910, 13, 44)

FREIMAN, A.J., of Ottawa, was in Montreal on Tues. and left the same evening for New York (7 Jan. 1910, 13, 8)

FREIMAN, A.J., of Ottawa, was in Montreal this week (4 March 1910, 13, 16)

FREIMAN, A.J., of Ottawa, was in Montreal this week (1 June 1911, 14, 29)

FREIMAN, A.J., spent Sun. in Montreal (16 Sept. 1910, 13, 44)

FREIMAN, Miss Pearl, of Ottawa, has returned home after visit with her sister, Mrs. Nathan Lande, Sherbrooke St. (11 Feb. 1910, 13, 13)

FREIMAN, Mr. and Mrs. H., Woods Ave., have returned from Old Orchard, Me. (6 Sept. 1912, 15, 39)

FREIMAN, Mrs. A.J. and Mrs. R. Weinberg, of Ottawa, have returned home after visiting Mr. and Mrs. N. Silver, Souvenir Ave. (26 Aug. 1910, 13, 41)

FREIMAN, Mrs. Archibald and family and Miss Lucy Bilsky, all of Ottawa, left last Mon. for Hillcrest, for the summer (2 July 1909, 12, 29)

FREUND, Emil, of New York, was in Montreal the past week (19 Sept. 1913, 16, 41)

Friedlander, Dr. Israel, S. Haskell and Mrs. Wolsey contributed to the Zionist Land Fund (14 April 1911, 14, 22)

FRIEDLANDER, Professor J. Israel, returned to New York last Wed. (24 Feb. 1911, 14, 15)

FRIEDMAN, D.S. and R.H. Blumenthal have left for New York en route for Nassau, Bahama Islands, where they will spend six weeks on holiday (17 Dec. 1909, 13, 5)

FRIEDMAN, D.S., attended the Shearman-Levi wedding in New York (19 March 1909, 12, 14)

FRIEDMAN, D.S., was one of the visiting governors at the Western Hospital this week (7 May 1909, 12, 21)

FRIEDMAN, David, 802 Dorchester St. W., is accepting donations to help the Baron de Hirsch Legislative Committee appeal the verdict in the Quebec City libel case. Members of the fund-raising committee are:- Joseph Levinson (chairman), David Friedman (treas.), Z. Fineberg, Sol Kellert, Max Sanders and H. Wolofsky. "This question of taking the Quebec Libel Case to the High Court is of great importance to all Jewish communities of Canada. It is not a Quebec or a Montreal case, as it affects the entire Jewish population of the Dominion, and it is up to all our co-religionists that they should contribute to the funds necessary to fight the case." (7 Nov. 1913, 16, 48)

FRIEDMAN, H., J. Samenhof and M. Hirsch, spent the past week at Lake Placid, N.Y. (15 July 1910, 13, 35)

FRIEDMAN, H., was in New York last week (14 Jan. 1910, 13, 9)

FRIEDMAN, Hess. N. and his nephew, Noel D. (Friedman?) are in the States (15 Dec. 1911, 15, 5)

FRIEDMAN, Isidore and A. Aron are delegates to the IOSB annual convention next week in New York (4 March 1910, 13, 16)

FRIEDMAN, Isidore and Adolph Aron left last night for New York where they will meet the IOSB Grand Master to discuss the status of the Order in Montreal (22 Oct. 1909, 12, 45)

FRIEDMAN, Isidore, has gone on a holiday to New York (20 Oct. 1911, 14, 49)

FRIEDMAN, Isidore, has gone to Old Orchard Beach for a two weeks' holiday (22 July 1910, 13, 36)

FRIEDMAN, Isidore, has returned from New York (29 Nov. 1912, 15, 51)

FRIEDMAN, Isidore, is leaving tomorrow for New York, where he will represent the Montreal IOSB branches at the annual convention. He will also visit Albany and Philadelphia (12 Feb. 1909, 12, 9)

FRIEDMAN, Isidore, was appointed District Deputy Grand Master of the IOSB in Montreal. There are four lodges in Montreal with hundreds of members. Mr. Friedman has lived in Montreal for the past fifteen years and is an active member of the Austro-Hungarian Synagogue (19 March 1909, 12, 14)

FRIEDMAN, Isidore, was elected president of the Shaarei Tefila, Austro-Hungarian Synagogue, Milton St., at a special meeting last Sun., after the resignation of Joseph A. Besner who "...found his engagements too numerous to devote any of his time to the office..." (29 Dec. 1911, 15, 7)

FRIEDMAN, Isidore, will spend his vacation at Old Orchard (25 July 1913, 16, 33)

FRIEDMAN, Jack, has gone to Old Orchard Beach on holiday (5 Aug. 1910, 13, 38)

FRIEDMAN, Max, has gone to New York, Boston and Philadelphia (1 July 1910, 13, 33)

FRIEDMAN, Max, is on vacation (28 June 1912, 15, 29)

FRIEDMAN, Max, St. Lawrence Blvd., has returned from New York, Boston and Philadelphia (29 July 1910, 13, 37)

FRIEDMAN, Miss Eva, Elm Ave., will be the guest of Mrs. Alexander Bilsky in Cobalt, Ont., for a month (22 Jan. 1909, 12, 6)

FRIEDMAN, Miss Eva, is spending a few weeks at Weir, Ont. (10 June 1910, 13, 30)

FRIEDMAN, Miss Eva, is the guest of her aunt, Mrs. L. Friedman, Lakeside (15 July 1910, 13, 35)

FRIEDMAN, Mr. and Mrs. C., Elm Ave., have gone to the coast for two months (16 Sept. 1910, 13, 44)

FRIEDMAN, Mr. and Mrs. C.L. and family will

spend a few weeks at the Chateau St. Louis, Valois, Que. (9 July 1909, 12, 30)

FRIEDMAN, Mr. and Mrs. C.L., are spending a few weeks in New York and Atlantic City (16 April 1909, 12, 18)

FRIEDMAN, Mr. and Mrs. C.L., who vacationed in Atlantic City, New York and Philadelphia, are home again (30 April 1909, 12, 20)

FRIEDMAN, Mr. and Mrs. D.S. and son are at Old Orchard Beach (23 July 1909, 12, 32)

FRIEDMAN, Mr. and Mrs. D.S. and family and Mr. and Mrs. A.M. Bilsky and daughter are spending the summer at Vaudreuil (8 July 1910, 13, 34)

FRIEDMAN, Mr. and Mrs. I. and family are at their summer cottage, Pointe Claire (16 June 1911, 14, 31)

FRIEDMAN, Mr. and Mrs. Isaac and their son, Walter, left for Boston last Sun. morn. (7 May 1909, 12, 21)

FRIEDMAN, Mr. and Mrs. Isaac, have gone to Cleveland, Ohio, by boat, for a few weeks (30 July 1909, 12, 33)

FRIEDMAN, Mr. and Mrs. S.D., are in Chicago for a few days (27 Dec. 1912, 16, 3)

FRIEDMAN, Mrs. B. and sons, 86 Park Ave., are spending the summer in Winchester, Ont. (12 Aug. 1910, 13, 39)

FRIEDMAN, Mrs. C.L., Elm Ave., gave a dinner for twelve last Sun. evening (31 Dec. 1909, 13, 7)

FRIEDMAN, Mrs. D.S. and her son are visiting her sister, Mrs. Bilsky, in Cobalt (9 July 1909, 12, 30)

FRIEDMAN, Mrs. D.S. and Master Norman Friedman are at Caledonia Springs, Ont. (14 July 1911, 14, 35)

FRIEDMAN, Mrs. D.S. and Master Norman have returned from Caledonia (28 July 1911, 14, 37)

FRIEDMAN, Mrs. D.S. and son left for New York to meet Mr. Friedman who is returning from the West Indies (21 Jan. 1910, 13, 10)

FRIEDMAN, Mrs. D.S., Dorchester St. W., is visiting her sister, Mrs. A.M. Bilsky in Toronto (29 Aug. 1913, 16, 38)

FRIEDMAN, Mrs. H. and Miss Elsie Cohen, of Woodlands Que., were guests of Mrs. R. Rabinovich, Sherbrooke St., Westmount (15 July 1910, 13, 35)

FRIEDMAN, Mrs. Isidore has gone to New York to visit her mother, Mrs. Engleman, who is seriously ill (5 Nov. 1909, 12, 47)

THE ST. DENIS GAS AND ELECTRIC Co.
Wholesale and Retail Dealers.
914 ST. DENIS STREET.
Prop. G. FRIEDMAN :: :: Phone St. L. 5497.

FRIEDMAN, Mrs. N., is visiting her daughter, Mrs. N. Fraid, of Cornwall, Ont. (9 July 1909, 12, 30)

FRIEDMAN, Mrs. N., is visiting her daughter, Mrs. N. Fraid, Cornwall, Ont. (22 July 1910, 13, 36)

FRIEDMAN, N. and Herbert Vineberg have returned from two weeks in New York (15 July 1910, 13, 35)

FRIEDMAN, Ralph, is spending a few weeks in Bermuda (30 Dec. 1910, 14, 7)

FRISCHLING, Mr. and Mrs. L., City Hall Ave., gave a birthday party at their home in honor of their niece, Miss Bertha Zulauf, of New York. Miss Hattie Frischling received the guests. Louis Gross and the Misses Hattie Frischling and Sophie Slatkoff performed a comical sketch (18 July 1913, 16, 32)

FRITZ, J., of Boston, Mass., stayed at the Windsor Hotel while in Montreal (22 Aug. 1913, 16, 37)

FROMSON, M., has gone to New York and Philadelphia on a business trip (27 Aug. 1909, 12, 37)

FROMSON, Master Abraham, age 13, son of M. Fromson, the well-known Zionist leader, won a free scholarship at the Aberdeen Street School examinations (27 June 1913, 16, 29)

FROMSON, Mr. and Mrs. M., 64 Colonial Ave., send New Year greetings (11 Sept. 1912, 15, 40)

FROMSON, Mr. and Mrs. M., wish their friends and relatives a happy New Year (1 Oct. 1913, 16, 42-43)

FUERST, Isidor, the Jewish Publication Society of Philadelphia representative, is in Montreal on business (25 Sept. 1912, 15, 42)

GABRIEL, Mrs. J.S. and daughter, of Ottawa, is visiting her parents, Mr. and Mrs. I. Livinson (4 Aug. 1911, 14, 38)

GALITZKI, Mr. and Mrs., of Chicago; Miss S. Blumberg, of Annapolis; and W. Jacobs, of Rock Valley; and G. Nathan, of South Dakota, were in Montreal for "Old Home Week" (24 Sept. 1909, 12, 41)

GALLET, Mrs. Joseph, of New York, is the guest of Mrs. E. Blout, Cote St. Antoine Road (26 Feb. 1909, 12, 11)

GALLOP, Miss, of Ottawa, is in Montreal visiting friends (14 Jan. 1910, 13, 9)

GALLY, Miss Rose and Miss Pauline Marks are holidaying at Ste. Agathe, Que. (16 Aug. 1912, 15, 36)

GAMSU, Miss Lena, is visiting Mr. and Mrs. Harry Freedman (31 Jan. 1913, 16, 8)

GARAFE, Samuel, was in Quebec City this week (31 Dec. 1909, 13, 7)

GARBER, L.E., son of Rabbi Garber, left for Europe aboard the S.S. Empress of Ireland. He will spend three months touring the major cities of England, France and Germany (19 April 1912, 15, 23)

GARBER, Mr. and Mrs. E., who were married in New York on Dec. 9, 1913, returned to Montreal and will reside at 380 Park Lafontaine Apts. (19 Dec. 1913, 17, 2)

GARBER, Rabbi S., returned from New York, where he officiated at the wedding of his son Ellie and Miss Sarah Schevel on Tues. Dec. 9, 1913 (19 Dec. 1913, 17, 2)

PHONE MAIN 5903

M. FROMSON

Practical Shop and Office Fitter, Carpenter, Cabinet Maker and General Contractor.

40 ANDERSON ST., - MONTREAL

All kinds of Counters, Show Cases, Office Partitions, Shelvings, Desks, etc., made to order. Hardwood Floorings, Store Fronts and Dumb Waiters in Dining Rooms and all kinds of Repairs to property, inside and out.

Highest satisfaction guaranteed and most reasonable prices.

As for references you may refer to some of the following firms that I have contracted considerable amount of work, such as the Montreal Light, Heat and Power Co., W. H. Scroggie, Ltd., John A. Barry and Co., John D. Ivy and Co., Ltd., Wholesale Milliners, Notre Dame St., John Fisher Son and Co., Wholesale Woollen Merchants, E. F. Walter and Co. Importers, McGill St., John Murphy Co., G. Orban, Wholesale Furriers, St. Paul Street, Landau and Cormack, Ltd, Cigarette Manufacturers, Darwin's High Class Milllnery Parlors, 297 St. Catherine West. and many other leading firms in this city that are too numerous to mention.

GARDNER, Adolph, Arts '16, passed his McGill University examinations (13 June 1913, 16, 27)

GARDNER, Miss Yetta, has returned from two weeks at Ste. Agathe (30 Aug. 1912, 15, 38)

GARDNER, N., was the guest of Mr. and Mrs. I. Claman, Beaurepaire (4 Aug. 1911, 14, 38)

GARFINKLE, M., C. Isaacs, L. Rosenberg, B. Silverman and W. Wolman are new faces on the YMHA baseball team this year. Hy. Gold will pilot the team this year. "Hans Wagner, the pot-sided pitcher, and Johnny Jacobs, the hard hitting third baseman of last year's team, have deserted the amateur game, and are now playing in the City League with the Villeray team." Other players are H. Fishman, P. Garfinkle, Ted Garfinkle and Feldstein (9 May 1913, 16, 22)

GARFINKLE, M., was elected president of the Young Men's Hebrew Amateur Orchestra at the YMHA rooms Sun. evening. Other officers elected were:- L. Ober, treas.; L. Gittelson, sec.; and P. Presner, librarian (7 April 1911, 14, 21)

GARFINKLE, Ted, N. Miller, Myer Kander, M. Latsky, Abe and Sam Shalinsky, Myer Mochkowsky, Nathan Takefman, Mrs. Etta Cohen and the Misses Frances Blumberg, Leah Shapiro, Rose Gallay, Annie, Fanny and Lillie Gold, and Pauline and Mary Marks arrived from Ste. Agathe des Monts, Sun. evening, Aug. 18, 1912 (23 Aug. 1912, 15, 37)

GEFFEN, E., of Calgary, who attended the Zionist Convention in Toronto, was in Montreal (30 Dec. 1910, 14, 7)

GELBER, M., of Toronto, is here on business (5 March 1909, 12, 12)

GELBER, Mrs. George and her daughter, of Providence, R.I., are guests of Mrs. Gelber's mother, Mrs. M. Vineberg (17 June 1910, 13, 31)

GELBMAN, M., 118 St. James St., chairman of the Zionist National Fund committee, will supply boxes to those societies requesting them (5 March 1909, 12, 12)

GELBMAN, M., has returned from New York (10 March 1911, 14, 17)

GELBMAN, Max, is organizing the Jewish Consumptives Aid Association concert to be held next Sun. evening in the Baron de Hirsch Institute (16 April, 1909, 12, 18)

GELBMAN, Mr. and Mrs. M., gave a dinner for ten last Thurs. evening (21 Jan. 1910, 13, 10)

GELBMAN, Mrs. M., fell after getting off a street car and sustained serious injuries (29 Sept. 1911, 14, 46)

GELBMAN, Mrs. M., has gone to Philadelphia to visit her daughter, Mrs. F. Steinberg and will then spend the rest of the summer in Atlantic City (14 July 1911, 14, 35)

GELBMAN, Mrs. M., has returned home after spending a holiday with her daughter, Mrs. Sternberg, in Atlantic City and Philadelphia (9 Sept. 1910, 13, 43)

GELLER, Miss Rhoda, age 7, passed the sixth grade violin examination at the McGill Conservatorium. Youngest in her class, she was the only one to pass with distinction (27 June 1913, 16, 29)

GELLER, Mr. and Mrs. George and daughter, of Winnipeg, are in Montreal visiting Mrs. Geller's parents, Mr. and Mrs. Maxwell Vineberg, en route to New York, where they will reside (9 April 1909, 12, 17)

GELLER, Mrs. George and daughter, of New York, will spend the summer with Mr. and Mrs. M. Vineberg, Notre Dame St. (18 June 1909, 12, 27)

GELLER, Mrs. George M., entertained Sun. evening in honor of her sister, Miss Francis Vineberg, of New York (13 Oct. 1911, 14, 48)

GELLER, Mrs. George, of New York, and her little daughter, left to spend the summer at Lancaster, Ont. (9 July 1909, 12, 30)

GENSER, Mr. and Mrs. E., Mr. and Mrs. J. Brodie, Mr. and Mrs. J.L. Sabbath, and Mr. and Mrs. L. Vineberg gave a party for twenty-seven children at Messrs. Gensers' summer resort at Joliette, Que., Sun. Aug. 11, 1912. Master J. Segal won the 400 yard race in very good time (23 Aug. 1912, 15, 37)

GETZ, M., has returned from a visit to his parents in Quebec City (12 Aug. 1910, 13, 39)

GINSBERG, J., visited Quebec City during the week (19 Feb. 1909, 12, 10)

GINSBERG, Louis, left for Europe aboard the S.S. Victorian (24 May 1912, 15, 25)

GINSBERG, Miss Belle, St. Urbain St., has gone to Boston for two weeks (16 April 1909, 12, 18)

GINSBERG, Miss Helen, Drolet St., has gone to Winnipeg where she will spend two months with her sister, Mrs. B. Lauer (29 July 1910, 13, 37)

GINSBERG, Miss Helen, has returned from Winnipeg where she spent three months with her sister, Mrs. B. Lauer (18 Oct. 1910, 13, 49)

GINSBERG, Miss Helen, St. Urbain St., left for Edmonton to visit her sister, Mrs. B. Lauer (4 July 1913, 16, 30)

GINSBERG, Miss Leta, Drolet St., has left for Winnipeg where she will visit her sister, Mrs. B. Lauer (2 July 1909, 12, 29)

GINSBERG, Miss Libbie, has returned home from Winnipeg (15 Sept. 1909, 12, 40)

GINSBERG, Miss Selma A., returns home to New York, Sat. Aug. 13, 1911, after being a guest of Mr. and Mrs. Rubin, St. Urbain St. (11 Aug. 1911, 14, 39)

GINSBERG, Mrs. J., has left on an extended trip to Europe (24 Dec. 1909, 13, 6)

GINSBERG, Mrs. M., Drolet St., has gone to Winnipeg to visit her daughter, Mrs. B. Lauer (1 Sept. 1911, 14, 42)

GITTELSON, Mrs. Julius L. and family have returned from Lake Manitou (27 Aug. 1909, 12, 37)

GITTELSON, Mr. and Mrs. A.L., 913 St. Denis St., have gone on holiday to Murray Bay (25 Aug. 1911, 14, 41)

GITTELSON, Mr. and Mrs. Julius L., report that their son, Lawrence, has fully recovered from his recent severe accident (27 Aug. 1909, 12, 37)

GITTLESON, Miss B., gave a snowshoe tramp (11 Feb. 1910, 13, 13)

GITTLESON, Miss Eva, hosted a pink ribbon luncheon, Sat. Dec. 5, 1909 for eighteen. Prize winners were:- the Misses S. Rosenberg and R. Salomon and Messrs. M. Levinson and L. Levinson (10 Dec. 1909, 13, 4)

GITTLESON, Mr. and Mrs. A.L., have left for the Thousand Islands, Niagara Falls, Toronto, Detroit and Chicago (9 Sept. 1910, 13, 43)

GITTLESON, Mr. and Mrs. A.L., left for a short trip to Washington and New York (15 Jan. 1909, 12, 5)

GITTLESON, Mr. and Mrs. Abe L., have returned from ten days in New York, Philadelphia and Atlantic City (3 Nov. 1911, 14, 51)

GITTLESON, Mrs. A. and daughter Eva have returned from Old Orchard, Me. (9 Aug. 1912, 15, 35)

GITTLESON, Mrs. J.L. and family are guests of Mr. and Mrs. I. Cohen, in Smith's Falls, Ont. (31 Dec. 1909, 13, 7)

GITTLESON, Mrs. Julius, is spending a few weeks in New York (9 Dec. 1910, 14, 4)

GLASER, Lewis, of Montreal, has returned home after a two months' visit with his daughter, Mrs. Harry Evans (22 April 1910, 13, 23)

GLASER, Rabbi Simon, was re-elected minister of the Austro-Hungarian Congregation for the next three years at an annual salary of $300.00, at a meeting held last Sun. in the synagogue, Milton St. (8 Oct. 1909, 12, 43)

GLAZER, Rabbi S., addressed the Chevra Kadisha Sunday School closing exercises on May 18, 1913 in the synagogue, St. Urbain St. On the program, Master Heller read an original poem "Our Hope" by H. Baum. Peter Usher, C. Asslie, B. Marks and the Misses M. Cohen and Marks sang the "Song of Moses". The teaching staff presented A.J. Livinson, B.A., with a diamond stick pin on the occasion of his fifth year as school principal. Staff members are:- Mr. Livinson, Harry Baum, Myer Block, Sender Deutsch and the Misses Fanny Flanders, Rose Gallay, Annie Ginsberg, Rachel Ginsberg, Polly Hoffman, Lillian Klein, Rosa Klein, Sadie Lerner, Cecillia Levinson, Polly Marks, Maude Moskovitch and Sarah Sloves (30 May 1913, 16, 25)

GLAZER, Rabbi Simon, delivered the keynote address "Judas Maccabeus and the Perpetuation of Judaism" at the Chevra Kadisha Sunday School Chanukah Festival, Dec. 28, 1913, in the Synagogue, 292 St. Urbain St. N. Sloves spoke on behalf of the executive board. On the program were the Halevi Juvenile Choral Society under the direction of Miss L. Klein and the Misses Sarah Levin and Annie Ginsberg who recited poems. Miss Ida Bloom, "a little prima dona in the bud" sang "Die Yiddishe Blume". Members of the teaching staff are:- A.H. Baum, Julius Block, Myer Block, Sender Deutsch, A.J. Livinson and the Misses Marguerite Cohen, Sarah Feen, Rose Frank, Annie Ginsberg, Rachel Ginsberg, Rhoda Goldblatt, Lilian Klein, Rosa Klein, Sadie Lerner, Cecilia Levinson and Sarah Steinberg (2 Jan. 1914, 17, 4)

GLAZER, Rabbi Simon, spoke on "The Significance of Purim" at the YMHA Friday Night

Talk (28 March 1913, 16, 16)

GLAZER, Rabbi Simon, will be getting a home. His friends are raising funds for purchasing a home and presenting it to the rabbi. "Rabbi Glazer has been in Montreal for the last five years, and because of being the head of the majority of synagogues in this city, questions arose which has called forth strong opposition to the Rabbi from quarters which have never been overly friendly to any of Rabbi Glazer's predecessors. Among the labouring classes he is known as the peace-maker, for he never grants a "get" unless the case be a real deserted woman." (1 March 1912, 15, 16)

GLICKMAN, D., has left on an extended business trip to the western provinces (29 Jan. 1909, 12, 7)

GLICKMAN, M.J., has left for Europe on a business trip (5 March 1909, 12, 12)

GLICKMAN, Miss D., is president of the Young Ladies' Hebrew Orphans and Protection Association. The aim of the Association is to provide poor Jewish orphans with clothing. Since its founding in Oct. 1906 it has distributed clothing each fall and spring. Other officers are:- Miss Annie Cohen, vice-pres.; Miss B. Camisher, treas.; Miss M. Goldberg, trustee; and Miss M. Hermann, fin. sec. Miss A.L. Schleifer, 41 Drolet St., is the secretary (16 Dec. 1910, 14, 5)

GLICKMAN, Miss Mabel, is visiting Mr. and Mrs. Tolzess, Besserer St., Ottawa (12 July 1912, 15, 31)

GLICKMAN, Miss Mabel, left Beloeil to spend several weeks at Old Orchard, Me. (25 July 1913, 16, 33)

GLICKMAN, Mr. and Mrs. P. and Mr. and Mrs. T. Glickman left Beloeil to spend several weeks at Old Orchard (25 July 1911, 14, 36)

GLICKMAN, Mr. and Mrs. M.J., 4047 Dorchester St. W., wish their friends a happy New Year (1 Oct. 1913, 16, 42-43)

GLICKMAN, Mr. and Mrs. P. and family, and Mr. and Mrs. P.B. Glickman and family have gone to Beloeil for the summer (25 June 1909, 12, 28)

GLICKMAN, Mr. and Mrs. P. and family are spending the summer at Beloeil (2 July 1909, 12, 29)

GLICKMAN, Mr. and Mrs. P.B. and Mrs. T. Glickman have left Beloeil to spend two weeks at the Caledonia Springs Hotel (12 Aug. 1910, 13, 39)

GLICKMAN, Mr. and Mrs. P.B. and family are at Beloeil for the summer (16 June 1911, 14, 31)

GLICKMAN, Mr. and Mrs. P.B. and family returned to Montreal after closing their summer cottage at Beloeil. They have taken up their new residence at 320 Elm Ave., Westmount (29 Sept. 1911, 14, 46)

GLICKMAN, Mr. and Mrs. P.B., have opened their new summer residence which has just been completed at Beloeil. Mr. and Mrs. S. Fox will be their guest for the summer (8 July 1910, 13, 34)

GLICKMAN, Mr. and Mrs. Phillip, 24 Victoria St., held a reception for four hundred guests on Mon. Feb. 2, 1914, in Majestic Hall in honor of their son's Bar Mitzvah (13 Feb. 1914, 17, 7)

GLICKMAN, Mr. and Mrs. S., 997 St. Hubert St., wish their friends a happy New Year (10 Oct. 1913, 16, 44)

GLICKMAN, Mr. and Mrs. T., 785 Shuter St., were "at home" Sat. and Sun., Jan. 25, 1913, in honor of their son, Lawrence's Bar Mitzvah, which took place in the Shaar Hashomayim Synagogue. Assisting in receiving were Mesdames P. Glickman and P.B. Glickman. Assisting at the table were Mrs. W. Rosenbloom and the Misses Lillie Glickman, Sara and Jennie Samuels, and Miss Yetta Silver (31 Jan. 1913, 16, 8)

GLICKMAN, Mr. and Mrs. T., 795 Shuter St., wish their friends a happy New Year (1 Oct. 1913, 16, 42-43)

GLICKMAN, Mr. and Mrs. T. and family, Shuter St., have left for their summer residence at Beloeil (24 June 1910, 13, 32)

GLICKMAN, Mr. and Mrs. T. and family, Shuter St., are at their summer cottage at Beloeil for the summer (16 June 1911, 14, 31)

GLICKMAN, Mr. and Mrs. T., Nathan Glickman and young daughter, accompanied by Miss Ida B. Sushelsky, of Boston, have left Beloeil for Old Orchard Beach (26 July 1912, 15, 33)

GLICKMAN, Mr. and Mrs. T.B. and family have left Beloeil for West Baden Springs (2 July 1909, 12, 29)

GLICKMAN, Mrs. B., St. Dominique St., has gone to Mt. Clemens for a month (30 June 1911, 14, 33)

GLICKMAN, Mrs. B., St. Urbain St., left for Mt. Clemens for a month (11 July 1913, 16, 31)

GLICKMAN, P., 40 St. Louis Square, has gone to Europe on business (8 Dec. 1911, 15, 4)

GLICKMAN, P., of Montreal, was the guest of Mr. and Mrs. Hansher, 9 Rosebery Ave., Toronto, this week (25 June 1909, 12, 28)

GLICKMAN, S.M., Messrs. Tobias and Philip sailed from New York on the S.S. Prinz Frederick Wilhelm for England and the continent, to visit relatives (10 Dec. 1909, 13, 4)

GLICKMAN, T., is chairman of a newly formed society for the study of Talmud and related subjects. The "Chevra Shaas" is organized under the auspices of the Shaar Hashomayim Congregation. A.T. Cohen is treasurer and S. Talpis, secretary. Rabbi Hirsch Cohen has agreed to serve as reader. "Of the different resolutions brought forward and passed upon by those present, one was to the effect that the ancient Hebrew tongue shall be the official language of the society, and all correspondence, proceedings, etc., are to be conducted only in that language." (10 Nov. 1911, 14, 52)

GODINSKY, Nathan H. and Moses Albert have been called to His Majesty's Commission of the Peace for the City and District of Montreal (2 Dec. 1910, 14, 3)

GOLD, H., was elected president of the Young Men's Hebrew Association which is located at 54 Ontario St. W. Other officers elected were:- Max Singer, vice-pres.; M. Soskin, sec.; M. Goldstein, asst.-sec.; W. Singer, treas.; L. Golland, sergeant-at-arms; W. Sweedler, D. Spector, M. Goldberg and S. Goldfield, exec. committee. Samuel Bloomfield was elected hon. pres. (7 Jan. 1910, 13, 8)

GOLD, Maxwell, Harry Gross and Sam Solomon received their D.D.S. degrees, McGill University, Faculty of Dentistry (16 May 1913, 16, 23)

GOLD, Miss Dora, gave a little birthday party at her parents' home, 1101 St. Lawrence Blvd., Sun. evening, Nov. 3, 1912 (15 Nov. 1912, 15, 49)

GOLD, Miss Katie, St. Urbain St., gave a party last Thurs. evening. H. Lipman, Lawrence Ram and Miss Minnie Shuster entertained during the evening (15 Aug. 1913, 16, 36)

GOLD, Miss Lina, returned home to New York, after visiting her sister, Mrs. S. Midownik, 372a Park Lafontaine (6 March 1914, 17, 10)

GOLD, Misses Fannie and Hillie, St. Urbain St., returned from a weekend in Ottawa where they were guests of Mr. and Mrs. L. Green (30 May 1913, 16, 25)

GOLD, Mr. and Mrs. J., 1101 St. Lawrence Blvd., hosted a social evening after a sleigh ride for Montefiore Club members Sun. Feb. 4, 1912. Among those present were:- Lyon Bercovitch, Isidore Popliger, M.P. Finkelstein, W. Bernfeld and the Misses Lily Ressler and Dora Ratner (9 Feb. 1912, 15, 13)

GOLD, Mr., president of the YMHA, leaves shortly to take up residence in Brandon, Man. Max Singer was elected president to replace him. Other officers elected were:- S. Rawson, 1st vice-pres.; Jack Pinsler, 2nd vice-pres.; A.H. Goldstein and H. Cohen, council (15 July 1910, 13, 35)

GOLD, S., 1044 St. Urbain St., gave a supper and social at his home in honor of his brother, A. Gold, of Brandon, Man. Entertainment was provided by Louis Blumberg and Miss Bertha Lax, violin; and Miss Anna Gold, piano solo (31 Jan. 1913, 16, 8)

GOLDBERG, , S.I., has gone to New York to spend a holiday with his children (22 April 1910, 12, 23)

Tel. Main 6161

Z. Goldberg & E. Zuckerman

Caterers for

Weddings, Parties, Entertainments

ETC.

80 & 84 St. Catherine St. West, Montreal

Apply ZUCKERMAN'S RESTAURANT   Prices according to Bill of Fare

GOLDBERG, Dame Sarah, wife of Israel Capolovitch, trader, instituted an action, no. 437, for separation of property in the Quebec Superior Court, District of Montreal (12 Sept. 1913, 16, 40)

GOLDBERG, H., of Toronto, was the guest of Mr. and Mrs. L.H. Jacobs (14 Feb. 1913, 16, 10)

GOLDBERG, Max, Lyon Cohen, S.W. Jacobs, K.C., and E. Freedman, of Antwerp, were passengers on the R.M.S. Empress of Ireland which sails from Quebec City this aft. (2 July 1909, 12, 29)

GOLDBERG, Miss Bertha, of Quebec City, is visiting Mr. and Mrs. J. Solin, City Hall Ave. (18 June 1909, 12, 27)

GOLDBERG, Miss J., has resigned as sec. of the Young People's Hachnosis Orchim Society. Miss S. Rafelovitch was elected in her place (9 June 1911, 14, 30)

GOLDBERG, Miss Julia, Cherrier St., has returned home from Cartierville where she was the guest of Miss Hilda Diamond (18 Aug. 1911, 14, 40)

GOLDBERG, Mr. and Mrs. J.L. and daughter, Dora, are in New York for their niece's wedding, Miss Anna Miller (22 Nov. 1912, 15, 50)

GOLDBERG, Mr. and Mrs. R., Miss Lizzie Goldberg and Master Ben Goldberg, 528 Homer St., Vancouver, are at the Windsor Hotel, Montreal on their return from a trip through Europe (24 Nov. 1911, 15, 2)

GOLDBERG, Mrs. H., has returned from Ste. Agathe (15 Sept. 1909, 12, 40)

GOLDBERG, Mrs. L. and Miss M. Goldberg, of Quebec City, are visiting Mrs. M. Solin, St. Urbain St. (28 Feb. 1913, 16, 12)

GOLDBERG, Mrs. P., of Pointe Claire, Que., will spend the rest of the summer at Mt. Clemens (16 Aug. 1912, 15, 36)

GOLDBERG, Rose and Gertrude Signer obtained a high standing in the McGill matriculation results (23 July 1909, 12, 32)

GOLDBERG, Z., J. Rosenthal and M. Elkin were in New York last week (11 June 1909, 12, 26)

GOLDBLATT, H. (B.A., Med '16) was elected president of the Maccabean Circle at the last meeting of the session, Sun. March 22, 1914. Other officers elected for the coming term were:- M. Garber (Arts '14), vice-pres.; B.L. Silver (B.A. Sci. '16), treas.; Adolph Gardner (Arts '16), sec.; Eli M. Friedman (Arts '17), asst. sec.; Max Bernfeld (Arts '14), Horace R. Cohen (Arts '15) and Charles A. Goldstein (Arts '16), committee (27 March 1914, 17, 13)

GOLDBLATT, Harry (B.A., Med. '16), was elected president of the Maccabean Circle at the annual elections on March 30, 1913 in the Royal Arcanum Chambers. Other executive members elected were:- Jack Viner, Arts '14, vice-pres.; Charles A. Goldstein, Arts '15, treas.; Philip Abinovitch, Comm. '14, sec.; Lyon Levine, Arts '15, asst. sec.; M. Garber, Arts '14, W. Muhlstock, Law '15, A.J. Livinson, B.A., Law '14 (ex-officio), committee (4 April 1913, 16, 17)

GOLDBLATT, Harry and N.S. Fineberg left for Cleveland to attend the Zeta Beta Tau Fraternity annual convention. They are representing the Upsilon Chapter of McGill University. Mr. Fineberg is one of the speakers at the banquet (26 Dec. 1913, 17, 3)

GOLDBLATT, Miss A., read a paper on "Shekolim" written by Mrs. Felix Harris at the Montreal Daughters of Zion meeting, Jan. 7, 1912 (19 Jan. 1912, 15, 10)

GOLDBLATT, Miss A., will read a paper at the Daughters of Zion meeting, Sun. aft. Feb. 12, 1911 in the Baron de Hirsch Institute (10 Feb. 1911, 14, 13)

GOLDBLOOM, Alton, who is studying arts and medicine at McGill University, has gone to Winnipeg for the summer 96 May 1910, 13, 25)

GOLDENBERG, B., (B.C.L.) has returned to Toronto (16 Aug. 1912, 15, 36)

GOLDENBERG, B., graduated law from McGill University (12 May 1911, 14, 26)

GOLDENBERG, B., of Toronto, was in Montreal, the guest of his father (5 Jan. 1912, 15, 8)

GOLDENBERG, B., wishes his friends and relatives a happy New Year (10 Oct. 1913, 16, 44)

GOLDENBERG, Miss Dorothy, daughter of Mr. and Mrs. P. Goldenberg, was tendered a surprise party by her friends at her home, 1551 Mance St., on Sun. evening, Dec. 24, 1910 (30 Dec. 1910, 14, 7)

GOLDENBERG, Mr. and Mrs. P. and family, 1551 Mance St., have returned Pointe Claire, Que., where they spent the summer (8 Sept. 1911, 14, 43)

GOLDENBERG, Mr. and Mrs. P. and family, 1551 Mance St., are summering at Pointe Claire. Mrs. S. Ryan, of Montreal spent a week with Mrs. Goldenberg (21 June 1912, 15, 28)

GOLDENBERG, Mrs. M., of Three Rivers, Que., was in Montreal for a few days (31 Oct. 1913, 16, 47)

GOLDENBERG, Mrs. Moe and the Misses Ruthie and Dorothy Goldenberg, of Three Rivers, Que., are in Montreal to attend the Miller-Frank wedding (5 Sept. 1913, 16, 39)

GOLDENSTEIN, I.S., has left on a trip to England and the Continent (23 April, 1909, 12, 19)

GOLDENSTEIN, I.S., who left Thurs. evening for New York, en route for Europe had a narrow escape. "The train he was on met with disaster in collision, many people being killed and injured. Fortunately his coach was one of the two that kept the rails, and he escaped injury. Friends who were aware of the fact that he was on the train, were uneasy as to his fate, all being greatly relieved to hear that he has escaped, and were loud in their congratulations of the fact to Mrs. Goldenstein." (7 Jan. 1910, 13, 8)

GOLDENSTEIN, Mr. and Mrs. I.S., 225 Clarke Ave., sail for Europe aboard the S.S. Royal George (8 July 1910, 13, 34)

GOLDENSTEIN, Mr. and Mrs. I.S., Clarke Ave., have returned from several months in Europe (3 March 1911, 14, 16)

GOLDENSTEIN, Mr. and Mrs. I.S., have returned from a two months' tour in Europe (2 Sept. 1910, 13, 42)

GOLDENSTEIN, Mr. and Mrs. I.S. sailed for Europe last week from New York aboard the S.S. Amerika (13 Jan. 1911, 14, 9)

GOLDENSTEIN, Mrs. I.S. and the Misses Michalson, have left for Alexandria Bay and other points (13 Aug. 1909, 12, 35)

GOLDENSTEIN, Mrs. I.S., will entertain Mrs. S. Simon, of England, who arrives today on the R.M.S. Empress of Britain. Mrs. Simon is en route for Toronto where she is a delegate to the International Congress of Women which begins next week (11 June 1909, 12, 26)

GOLDMAN, Dr. I., left for New York and Atlantic City (1 Aug. 1913, 16, 34)

GOLDMAN, J., is chairman of the Young People's Hachnosis Orchim Sixth Annual Ball committee which will be held at the Ritz-Carlton Hotel on Thurs. Feb. 5, 1913. Committee members are:- W. Goldman, Max Kolber, Mrs. S.H. Cohen, and Miss Rose Burman (2 Jan. 1914, 17, 4)

GOLDMAN, J., was chairman of the Hebrew Sheltering and Orphan Home annual picnic held last week in Dominion Park. Credit is due to the Young People's Hachnosis Orchim Society which organized the function for the past four years running. Miss A. Burman was treasurer of dancing and Miss R. Burman, chairlady of dancing. Those assisting were:- W. Goldman, J. Golt, H. Mills; Masters J. Becker, M. Cohen, S. and M. Goldman, N. Vineberg; the Misses S. Becker, M. Berson, S. and F. Blitz, A. Bernstein, B. Bernstein, O. Bernstein, V. Bernstein, B. and M. Cohen, B. Cumisher, A. and K. Deskin, A. Disk, M. Frank, M. Freeman, E. Goldberg, R. Goldenberg, A. Graefsky, B. Greenspan, B. and R. Levitt, M. Levitt, Landon, R. Leibovitz, D. Levy, S. Lefkovitch, M. and C. Margolick, R. Mendelson, S. Osman, P. and L. Pearson, D. Simon, M. Spiegel, M. Stone, A. Steinhouse, C. Turner, F. Vineberg, L. Weiner and Woolf (15 Aug. 1913, 16, 36)

GOLDMAN, Leon, 17 Esplanade Ave., is in New York on business (17 Jan. 1913, 16, 6)

GOLDMAN, Leon and A. Levin visited the Sanatorium in Ste. Agathe on Victoria Day (26 May 1911, 14, 28)

GOLDMAN, Leon, has returned from a business trip to Toronto (9 Sept. 1910, 13, 43)

GOLDMAN, Leon, has returned from a business trip to Toronto (20 Oct. 1911, 14, 49)

GOLDMAN, Leon, has returned from New York (26 March 1909, 12, 15)

GOLDMAN, Leon, has returned from New York (14 Jan. 1910, 13, 9)

GOLDMAN, Leon, leaves for New York tomorrow night (11 March 1910, 13, 17)

GOLDMAN, Leon, leaves for Toronto tomorrow night on a business trip (8 April 1910, 13, 21)

GOLDMAN, Leon, leaves Sat. on a business trip to New York and the eastern U.S. for a fortnight (5 March 1909, 12, 12)

GOLDMAN, Leon, leaves tomorrow for New York, Philadelphia and Boston on business (24 March 1911, 14, 19)

GOLDMAN, Leon left for New York on a short business trip on Wed. evening (7 Jan. 1910, 13, 8)

GOLDMAN, Leon, left Wed. night for London, Ont. and Toronto on business (7 Oct. 1910, 13, 47)

GOLDMAN, Leon, presided at the Agudath Zion Society semi-annual meeting last Sun. evening. Delegates elected to the Tenth Zionist Federation Convention were:- H. Bloomstone, Henry Bye, J. Fineberg, D. Jackel, N. Lande, H. Levinsky, M. Levitt, Hiram Levy, H.P. Nervich and M.N. Sperber (5 Nov. 1909, 12, 47)

GOLDMAN, Leon, will be the principal speaker at the Montreal Daughters of Zion monthly meeting next Sun. Others on the program are Mrs. Judah Bernstein, reading and Miss Eva Morris, violin solo (28 April 1911, 14, 24)

GOLDMAN, Master Moe, son of Dr. Alex Goldman, of New York, is visiting his uncle, Leon Goldman, Esplanade Ave. (8 Aug. 1913, 16, 35)

GOLDMAN, Mr. and Mrs. I. and family are at Brome Lake, Que., for the summer (11 July 1913, 16, 31)

GOLDMAN, Mr. and Mrs. Leon, 17 Esplanade Ave., send New Year greetings (11 Sept. 1912, 15, 40)

GOLDMAN, Mr. and Mrs. Leon, 17 Esplanade Ave., wish their friends a happy New Year (1 Oct. 1913, 16, 42-43)

GOLDMAN, Mr. and Mrs. Leon, were at home Sun. June, 1912 on the occasion of their son Arthur's Bar Mitzvah. The Misses Miriam Brainin and Bernstein assisted in receiving the guests. The Misses Dorothy Leo, Bertha Brainin, Minnie Bernstein, and Wertheimer were in charge of the dining room while Mrs. E.G. Bernstein cut the ices. Guests included:- Mr. and Mrs. Clarence I. de Sola, Mr. and Mrs. Reuben Brainin, Rabbi Herman Abramowitz, Dr. Joseph Fish, Mr. and Mrs. Lyon Cohen and Gregory Sanders (14 June 1912, 15, 27)

GOLDMAN, Mrs. H., of Glace Bay, N.S., is visiting her parents, Mr. and Mrs. B. Glickman (18 Aug. 1911, 14, 40)

GOLDMAN, Mrs. H., of Glace Bay, N.S., is visiting her parents, Mr. and Mrs. B. Glickman, St. Urbain St. (5 Sept. 1913, 16, 39)

GOLDMAN, Mrs. L., is spending the summer in the Laurentians (6 Aug. 1909, 12, 34)

GOLDMAN, Mrs. Leon and children are spending the rest of the summer at St. Agathe (2 Sept. 1910, 13, 42)

GOLDMAN, Mrs. Leon and children, Esplanade Ave., have returned from Ste. Agathe (9 Sept. 1910, 13, 43)

GOLDMAN, Mrs. Leon and children returned from New York where they spent a few weeks visiting her parents (21 Jan. 1910, 13, 10)

GOLDMAN, Mrs. Leon and family are at Chateauguay Basin for the summer (9 July 1909, 12, 30)

GOLDMAN, Mrs. Leon and family have returned to town from Ste. Agathe where they spent the summer (10 Sept. 1909, 12, 39)

GOLDMAN, Mrs. Leon and her little children left for New York to attend the golden wedding anniversary of her parents, Mr. and Mrs. N. Pollin (24 Dec. 1909, 13, 6)

GOLDNER, Mr. and Mrs. A.J., Berri St., returned from their trip to Toronto, Niagara Falls and Buffalo (19 Sept. 1913, 16, 41)

GOLDNER, Mr. and Mrs. S., Mr. and Mrs. N. Wolf and Mr. and Mrs. S. Joseph, all of Montreal, were in New York last week (2 July 1909, 12, 29)

GOLDSMITH, Mesdames Leo and J. and family, of Cincinnati, are visiting their parents, Mr. and Mrs. Ed. Lichtenhein, Peel St. (24 June 1901, 13, 32)

GOLDSMITH, Mr. and Mrs. Leopold, of Cleveland, Ohio, are visiting their daughter, Mrs. Clarence de Sola, at Quixano (30 July 1909, 12, 33)

GOLDSMITH, Mrs. J., son and maid, have returned home to Cincinnati after visiting Mrs. Goldsmith's parents, Mr. and Mrs. Ed. Lichtenhein, Peel St. (30 Sept. 1910, 13, 46)

GOLDSMITH, Mrs. Laura and grandson have left for Cleveland, Ohio (30 May 1913, 16, 25)

GOLDSMITH, Mrs. Leon and son, and Mrs. Jack Goldsmith and son, of Cincinnati, have arrived and are guests of their parents, Mr. and Mrs. E. Lichtenhein, Peel St. (18 June 1909, 12, 27)

GOLDSTEIN, A.D., was in Montreal briefly, en route to his home in Vancouver (24 Jan. 1913, 16, 7)

GOLDSTEIN, A.M., 2nd vice-pres. of the YMHA is ill in the Royal Victoria Hospital (26 May 1911, 14, 28)

GOLDSTEIN, Abraham, of Vancouver, B.C., is visiting his sister, Mrs. M. Claman, St. Matthew St. (9 April 1909, 12, 17)

GOLDSTEIN, C.A., read an article on Jewish university life at Cambridge at the first meeting of the Maccabean Circle (12 Jan. 1912, 15, 9)

GOLDSTEIN, Edward, Bishop St., is in Atlantic City for two weeks (2 May 1913, 16, 21)

GOLDSTEIN, H. and son, of New York, were guest of his sister, Mrs. Joseph Kruger, Mance St. (16 Feb. 1912, 15, 14)

GOLDSTEIN, Herbert, formerly of Toronto, has moved back to Montreal (16 Aug. 1912, 15, 36)

GOLDSTEIN, Herbert, of Toronto, passed through Montreal en route for Old Orchard Beach (6 Aug. 1909, 12, 34)

GOLDSTEIN, Herbert, of Toronto, spent the past two weeks visiting his mother, Mrs. S.J. Goldstein and family, St. Luke St. (25 Oct. 1910, 13, 50)

GOLDSTEIN, Herbert, of Toronto, spent the holidays with his mother, Mrs. S.J. Goldstein, St. Luke St. (6 Oct. 1911, 14, 47)

GOLDSTEIN, Herbert, of Toronto, was in Montreal the past week visiting his mother, Mrs. B.J. Goldstein (18 Feb. 1910, 13, 14)

GOLDSTEIN, Herbert, of Toronto, were in Montreal for the holidays (3 Jan. 1913, 16, 4)

GOLDSTEIN, J., a leading Montreal businessman, was elected president of the Young Men's Hebrew Association at the annual meeting last Sun. in the club room, 495 St. Charles Borromee St. Other officers elected were:- N.U. Godinsky, 1st vice-pres.; Dr. J. Rubin, 2nd vice-pres.; S. Cohen, treas.; M. Goldberg, fin. sec.; M. Goldstein, rec. sec.; Louis Ober, corr. sec.; S. Blaustein, M. Finestone, H. Gold, M. Gorfinkle, C. Lambert, S. Rawson, B. Rose and M. Singer, board of directors (12 Jan. 1912, 15, 9)

GOLDSTEIN, J., president of the YMHA, installed the following officers of the YMHA Snowshoe Club for 1912-1913:- Davis Livinson, pres.; A. Harry Wolfe, vice-pres.; F. Berlin, sec. & treas.; J. Sigman, corr. sec.; H. Rawson, captain; S. Rawson, scout; and Charles Herman, whipper-in (11 Oct. 1912, 15, 44)

GOLDSTEIN, J., was elected president of the YMHA at the annual meeting on Sun. Jan. 5, 1913. Other officers elected were:- Lyon Cohen, hon. pres.; N.H. Godinsky, 1st vice-pres.; Dr. J. Rubin, 2nd vice-pres.; E.W. Jacobs, treas.; M. Goldberg, fin. sec.; E. Solomon, rec. sec.; D. Livinson, sergeant-at-arms; S. Blaustein, J.A. Jacobs, S. Kellert, J. Levi, A. Levine and B. Rose, directors (10 Jan. 1913, 16, 5)

GOLDSTEIN, L., of Rochester, N.Y., was in Montreal the past week (29 Aug. 1913, 16, 38)

GOLDSTEIN, Master Charlie, and Phil Blumenthal have returned from Toronto, to spend the holidays with their parents (8 Jan. 1909, 12, 4)

GOLDSTEIN, Master Charlie, had a party celebrating his Bar Mitzvah on Sat. Jan. 9, 1909 (22 Jan. 1909, 12, 6)

GOLDSTEIN, Master Harry, is recovering from a recent operation for appendicitis at the Royal Victoria Hospital (22 Jan. 1909, 12, 6)

GOLDSTEIN, Max, spent the weekend in Sherbrooke, Que. (7 Jan. 1910, 13, 8)

GOLDSTEIN, Maxwell (K.C.) and his wife sail on the S.S. Laurentic tomorrow for a two months' trip to England and the continent (18 June 1909, 12, 27)

GOLDSTEIN, Maxwell (K.C.) and Mrs. Goldstein and S.W. Jacobs, K.C., have returned from an extended tour in Europe (3 Sept. 1909, 12, 38)

GOLDSTEIN, Maxwell, has been elected a member of the Laws Committee of the Royal Arcanum (15 April 1910, 13, 22)

GOLDSTEIN, Maxwell, has been president of Temple Emanu-El since 1907. Past presidents of the temple have been:- B.A. Boas (1882-1887), B. Kortosk (1887-1888), S. Davis (1888-1895), B.A. Boas (1895-1898), E. Lichtenhein (1898-1900), Sigmund Fischel (1900-1901) and B.A. Boas (1901-1907). Other current-serving officers are:- Mortimer B. Davis, vice-pres.; Mark Workman, treas.; Sigmund Fischel, hon. sec.; S.L. Herman, hon. asst. treas.; L.H. Cohen, hon. asst. sec.; B. Kortosk, H. Frankel, A. Goldstein, Louis Lewis and A. Sommer, Board of Trustees. The dedication of the new temple on Sherbrooke St. W. took place Sun. Sept. 17, 1911 (20 Sept. 1911, 14, 45)

GOLDSTEIN, Maxwell, was re-elected president of Temple Emanu-El, Sherbrooke St., last Sun. aft. Other officers elected were:- Mark Workman, vice-pres.; A. Sommer, hon. treas.; S.L. Herman, hon. sec.; M.B. Davis, Louis Lewis, B. Goldstein, J.M. Orkin and H. Frankel, board of trustees (3 Nov. 1911, 14, 51)

GOLDSTEIN, Maxwell, will lecture on "The Educational Problems of Montreal" before the Oriental Society of McGill University, Tues. Feb. 21, 1991 at 8 p.m. (17 Feb. 1911, 14, 14)

GOLDSTEIN, Miss Amy, is visiting the Misses Goldstein at Lachine, Que. (16 Aug. 1912, 15, 36)

GOLDSTEIN, Miss, Bishop St., has returned from Ottawa (19 May 1911, 14, 27)

GOLDSTEIN, Miss Eva, Dorchester St. W., gave a 5 p.m. tea at Robinson's on Mon. Dec. 23, 1912 (27 Dec. 1912, 16, 3)

GOLDSTEIN, Miss Eva, passed the final examination for licentiates (Performer's Class) at the McGill local examination in music, and will receive the diploma of L.Mus. (27 June 1913, 16, 29)

GOLDSTEIN, Miss Gladys, Beaurepaire, had a birthday party. "Marshmallows were toasted over a bon fire at the shore and corn was popped." (1 Sept. 1911, 14, 42)

GOLDSTEIN, Miss Irene, of Toronto, is in Montreal, en route for Europe (26 April 1912, 15, 24)

GOLDSTEIN, Miss Mabel, Bishop St., is in New York for several weeks (11 Nov. 1910, 13, 52)

GOLDSTEIN, Miss Mabel, has gone to New York on a visit for a few weeks (31 Dec. 1909, 13, 7)

GOLDSTEIN, Miss Mabel, has returned from New York where she spent the past six weeks (11 Feb. 1910, 13, 13)

GOLDSTEIN, Miss Mabel, has returned from a short stay in New York (9 Dec. 1910, 14, 4)

GOLDSTEIN, Miss Mabel, Pointe Claire, is at Old Orchard Beach for a few weeks (6 Aug. 1909, 12, 34)

GOLDSTEIN, Miss Mabelle, arrived home from Lakeside last week (3 Sept. 1909, 12, 38)

GOLDSTEIN, Miss Marjorie, won a third year scholarship in modern languages at McGill University (8 Nov. 1912, 15, 48)

GOLDSTEIN, Miss Muriel and Gladys Goldstein have returned from Ottawa Ladies' College and will spend the summer with their parents at Beaurepaire (23 June 1911, 14, 32)

GOLDSTEIN, Miss Muriel and Miss Gladys Goldstein, have left for Ottawa to take up a college course for young ladies (9 Sept. 1910, 13, 43)

GOLDSTEIN, Miss, of Rochester, N.Y., is the guest of her sister, Mrs. J. Danielson, Mount Royal Ave. (12 Sept. 1913, 16, 40)

GOLDSTEIN, Miss Ruth, is in Toronto, the guest of her aunt, Mrs. William Goldstein (30 Dec. 1910, 14, 7)

GOLDSTEIN, Miss Ruth, is visiting Mrs. J. Blout, in Ottawa (6 Sept. 1912, 15, 39)

GOLDSTEIN, Miss Sarah, has returned from New York (16 July 1909, 12, 31)

GOLDSTEIN, Miss Sarah, of Montreal, plans to sail from New York aboard the S.S. Princess Irene, on Aug. 28, 1909, for Milan Italy, to continue her vocal studies (20 Aug. 1909, 12, 36)

GOLDSTEIN, Miss Sylvia, Bishop St., gave a linen shower on Thurs. May 22, 1913, in honor of her cousin, Miss Elsie Silverman who will be married to M. Silver in June (23 May 1913, 16, 24)

GOLDSTEIN, Miss Sylvia, Bishop St., is the guest of Mrs. S. Roskam and family in New York for a few weeks (21 Feb. 1913, 16, 11)

GOLDSTEIN, Miss, who is studying voice in New York, spent a few days in Montreal, visiting her parents, Rev. and Mrs. Goldstein (26 March 1909, 12, 15)

GOLDSTEIN, Misses, are at Phillipsburg, Ont. for a few weeks (25 July 1911, 14, 36)

GOLDSTEIN, Misses Muriel and Gladys, who are attending Ottawa Ladies' College are spending the holiday with their parents, Mr. and Mrs. B. Goldstein, Bishop St. (30 Dec. 1910, 14, 7)

GOLDSTEIN, Misses Ruth and Jessie Goldstein are spending a couple of weeks at Old Orchard Beach, Me. (6 Aug. 1909, 12, 34)

GOLDSTEIN, Misses Ruth and Jessie Goldstein

are leaving for Valois, Que. (30 June 1911, 14, 33)

GOLDSTEIN, Misses Ruth and Jessie, leave for Old Orchard Beach where they will spend two weeks (30 July 1909, 12, 33)

GOLDSTEIN, Misses Ruth and Stella, are at Valois for the summer (15 July 1910, 13, 35)

GOLDSTEIN, Mr. and Mrs. A., St. Matthew St., and their daughter, Mrs. I.J. Goldstein, are at Caledonia Springs for a few weeks (30 July 1909, 12, 33)

GOLDSTEIN, Mr. and Mrs. A.D., accompanied by Mrs. S.J. Goldstein, have left for Old Orchard Beach (1 July 1910, 13, 33)

GOLDSTEIN, Mr. and Mrs. B. and family have returned from their country residence, Clairemont Villa, Lakeside (10 Sept. 1909, 12, 39)

GOLDSTEIN, Mr. and Mrs. B., were in Ottawa to attend their daughter's graduation from the Ottawa Ladies' College (27 June 1913, 16, 29)

GOLDSTEIN, Mr. and Mrs. Bernard and family, Mr. and Mrs. George Goldstein, Mr. and Mrs. Isaac Friedman and family, and Mr. and Mrs. A.M. Vineberg and family are at Lakeside for the season (11 June 1909, 12, 26)

GOLDSTEIN, Mr. and Mrs. George E. and daughter leave for Cleveland to attend the wedding in early Dec. of Mrs. Goldstein's sister, Miss Stein (1 Dec. 1911, 15, 3)

GOLDSTEIN, Mr. and Mrs. George, Elgin Ave., are guests of Mr. and Mrs. B. Goldstein, Pointe Claire (11 June 1909, 12, 26)

GOLDSTEIN, Mr. and Mrs. George, have gone on the Saguenay trip for a few weeks (15 July 1910, 13, 35)

GOLDSTEIN, Mr. and Mrs. J. and family, Dorchester St., are at the "Chateau", Valois (15 July 1910, 13, 35)

GOLDSTEIN, Mr. and Mrs. J., Dorchester St., have returned from Atlantic City (30 April 1909, 12, 20)

GOLDSTEIN, Mr. and Mrs. M., of Ottawa, have moved to Montreal (17 June 1910, 13, 31)

GOLDSTEIN, Mr. and Mrs. Max, Master Charles and Miss Amy Goldstein are at Little Métis, Que. for several weeks (28 July 1911, 14, 37)

GOLDSTEIN, Mr. and Mrs. William, have returned home to Toronto (29 Oct. 1909, 12, 46)

GOLDSTEIN, Mrs. and daughters, Luke St., are at Chateauguay for the summer (12 July 1912, 15, 31)

GOLDSTEIN, Mrs. B., Bishop St., is in New York, the guest of her sister, Mrs. M. Bernstein (14 Nov. 1913, 16, 49)

GOLDSTEIN, Mrs. Ethel, of Toronto, is visiting her cousins, Mr. and Mrs. David Roskam, Tupper St. (16 Feb. 1912, 15, 14)

GOLDSTEIN, Mrs. George, Clairemont Villa, Pointe Claire, entertained the whist club on Aug. 18, 1909 (27 Aug. 1909, 12, 37)

GOLDSTEIN, Mrs. George E., gave a tea on Mon. Dec. 30, 1912 at the Windsor Hotel in honor of her sister, Miss Cyril Stein, of Cleveland, Ohio. Guests included:- Mesdames Max Goldstein, William Goldstein (Toronto), Hellie Hart, M. Heillig, and the Misses Grace Abrahams and Hilda Levi (New York) (3 Jan. 1913, 16, 4)

GOLDSTEIN, Mrs. George E., has gone to spend several weeks with her mother, Mrs. Stein, in Cleveland (12 March 1909, 12, 13)

GOLDSTEIN, Mrs. George, hosted an aft. tea last Tues. in honor of her mother, Mrs. Stein, who is visiting her. Those present were:- Mesdames I. Goldstein, Max Goldstein, S.J. Goldstein, H. Lazarus, Silverman, Abrahams, Blumenthal, Friedman and Heyman (3 Dec. 1909, 13, 3)

GOLDSTEIN, Mrs. I., is visiting in Newark, N.J. (22 April 1910, 13, 23)

GOLDSTEIN, Mrs. J. and daughters are in the Adirondack Mountains (12 Aug. 1910, 13, 39)

GOLDSTEIN, Mrs. J. and family are at Lake Champlain for the summer (9 July 1909, 12, 30)

GOLDSTEIN, Mrs. J., has returned with her sister after visiting friends in the States for the past five weeks (7 May 1909, 12, 21)

GOLDSTEIN, Mrs. J., is in New York and Atlantic City for several weeks (16 Feb. 1912, 15, 14)

GOLDSTEIN, Mrs. J., is spending a few weeks in Atlantic City (2 April 1909, 12, 16)

GOLDSTEIN, Mrs. M., accompanied by her daughter, Miss Eva Goldstein, has returned from Ottawa where they visited her parents, Mr. and Mrs. F. Phillips (6 Jan. 1911, 14, 8)

GOLDSTEIN, Mrs. M. and daughter, Eva, returned from home Ottawa where they visited her parents, Mr. and Mrs. F. Phillips (3 Jan. 1913, 16, 4)

GOLDSTEIN, Mrs. Maxwell, has gone to Toronto to visit her parents, Mr. and Mrs. C. Stern (17 March 1911, 14, 18)

GOLDSTEIN, Mrs. Maxwell, has returned from a visit with her parents, Mr. and Mrs. Stern, in Toronto (18 March 1910, 13, 18)

GOLDSTEIN, Mrs. Maxwell, St. Matthew St., is visiting her parents, Mr. and Mrs. C. Stern, in Toronto (22 Oct. 1909, 12, 45)

GOLDSTEIN, Mrs., of New York, is visiting her parents, Mr. and Mrs. Sigmund (10 March 1911, 14, 17)

GOLDSTEIN, Mrs., of Sherbrooke, Que., spent a week in Montreal with relatives (2 July 1909, 12, 29)

GOLDSTEIN, Mrs. S. and son, of New York, have returned home having spent the summer at Val Morin with Mrs. Goldstein's parents, Mr. and Mrs. A. Sigmund (15 Sept. 1911, 14, 44)

GOLDSTEIN, Mrs. S., of New York, is in town for several months visiting her parents, Mr. and Mrs. A. Sigmund (4 June 1909, 12, 25)

GOLDSTEIN, Mrs. S.J. and Miss Stella Goldstein spent two weeks at Weir, Ont. (10 June 1910, 13, 30)

GOLDSTEIN, Mrs. S.J., has returned from Old Orchard Beach (5 Aug. 1910, 13, 38)

GOLDSTEIN, Mrs. Sam and sons, of New York, are guests of Mr. and Mrs. Joseph Stringer, Mance St. (2 Oct. 1912, 15, 43)

GOLDSTEIN, Mrs. W. and Miss Eva Goldstein, Dorchester St. W., have gone abroad for two months (30 June 1911, 14, 33)

GOLDSTEIN, Mrs. William and Miss Eva Goldstein, Dorchester St., are in New York (30 Aug. 1912. 15, 38)

GOLDSTEIN, Mrs. William, of Toronto, is the guest of her sister, Mrs. Joseph Youngheart (22 Oct. 1909, 12, 45)

GOLDSTEIN, Mrs. William, of Toronto, is visiting her sister, Mrs. Joseph Youngheart, Bishop St. (1 July 1910, 13, 33)

GOLDSTEIN, Mrs. William, of Toronto, is the guest of her sister, Mrs. Joseph Youngheart, Bishop St. (25 Oct. 1910, 13, 50)

GOLDSTEIN, Mrs. William, of Toronto, is visiting Mrs. Joseph Youngheart, Bishop St. (27 Oct. 1911, 14, 50)

GOLDSTEIN, Mrs. William, of Toronto, was in Montreal (10 March 1911, 14, 17)

GOLDSTEIN, N.W., was in charge of arrangements for the annual YMHA Snowshoe Club dance held last Thurs. in Auditorium Hall. Those assisting were:- M. Bald, M. Berson, S. Brody, Joseph Bernard Ellison, M. Frank, E.T. Garfinkle, M. Garfinkle, P. Garfinkle, J. Garrick, S. Gold, M. Goldberg, L. Goldfarb, W. Gubbins, Charles Herman, David Livinson, E. Lozinsky, J. Margolius, M. Margolius, A. Pesner, H. Rawson, S. Rawson, J. Sigman, D. Stone and A.H. Wolfe (7 Nov. 1913, 16, 48)

GOLDSTEIN, Rev. S., has been elected Cantor of the Congregation Beth Jacob, of Boston, Mass. (15 Sept. 1911, 14, 44)

GOLDSTEIN, the Rev. Salo H., of Vienna, is a guest of Rabbi Gunsberg, of Montreal. He is touring Canada and hopes to visit all the main cities before returning to Europe (15 Jan. 1909, 12, 5)

GOLDSTEIN, Walter, of Toronto, was in Montreal this week (7 Feb. 1913, 16, 9)

GOLDSTEIN, William, of Toronto, has joined Mrs. Goldstein, who is the guest of Mrs. Joseph Youngheart, Bishop St. (4 Nov. 1910, 13, 51)

GOLDSTONE, Mrs. F., of Spokane, is visiting her sister, Mrs. F. Kolber (24 March 1911, 14, 19)

GOLDVOGEL, Louis, was in Montreal for a short visit (26 Nov. 1909, 13, 2)

GOLSTEIN, E., of New York, was registered at the Carslake Hotel (30 July 1909, 12, 33)

GOLT, Joseph and Miss Frances Golt are spending

a holiday in New York (15 Oct. 1909, 12, 44)

GOLT, Miss Fannie, celebrated her birthday last Tues. evening. Among those present were:-the Misses B. Schachter, A. Gold, A. Solomon, J. Rost, R. Echenberg, S. Smith, M. Wilson and E. Rost, and Messrs. I. Sourkes, D. Bernstein, H. Cohen, A. Schachter, S. Fineberg and S. Golt (6 May 1910, 13, 25)

GOLT, Misses Fannie and Rebecca, will spend the summer with friends in Sherbrooke, Que. (22 July 1910, 13, 36)

GOLT, Moses and Miss Faiga Golt have left on a visit to Sherbrooke, Que. (1 July 1910, 13, 33)

GOLT, S. and daughter, Fannie, left for New York and the Northeast (4 July 1913, 16, 30)

GOLTMAN, A.S., of New York, stayed at the Carslake Hotel (25 June 1909, 12, 28)

GOLTMAN, Dr. M. and wife, of Memphis, Tenn., were in Montreal for the unveiling of a headstone in memory of his late father, Solomon Goltman, in the Spanish & Portuguese Cemetery (25 Nov. 1910, 14, 2)

GOLTMAN, Dr. Max, of Memphis, Tenn., stayed at the Windsor Hotel while in Montreal (1 Aug. 1913, 16, 34)

GOLTMAN, Miss Frances, is visiting her aunt, Miss Michalson, 709 Sherbrooke St. W. (25 Feb. 1910, 13, 15)

GOLTMAN, Miss Stephanie, has returned home to New York after spending the summer the guest of Miss Theresa Wolfe (23 Sept. 1910, 13, 45)

GOLTMAN, Mr. and Mrs. Robert and family have left for Cacouna for several weeks (9 July 1909, 12, 30)

GOLTMAN, Mr. and Mrs. Robert and family have returned from Cacouna where they spent the past few weeks (6 Aug. 1909, 12, 34)

GOLTMAN, Mrs. A., of Ottawa, is visiting Mr. and Mrs. S. Goltman, St. Catherine St. W. (1 Oct. 1913, 16, 42-43)

GOLTMAN, Mrs. A.M., left for Ottawa after visiting Mr. and Mrs. S. Goltman, St. Catherine St. W. (11 Oct. 1912, 15, 44)

GOLTMAN, Mrs. C.E., has recovered from an appendicitis operation (12 July 1912, 15, 31)

GOLTMAN, Mrs. Robert and the Misses Michaelson, have returned from New York and Atlantic City (4 Feb. 1910, 13, 12)

GOLTMAN, Robert, has once again taken charge of Goltman's Business College, Karn Hall, 591 St. Catherine St. W. (16 Sept. 1910, 13, 44)

GOLTMAN, Robert, principal, Goltman's Business College (est. 15 years), 725 St. Catherine St. W., near Mackay St., has issued a school calender and prospectus (9 Dec. 1910, 14, 4)

GOLTMAN, Robert, was re-appointed lecturer in shorthand at McGill University for the next session (16 May 1913, 16, 23)

GOODKOWSKY, Mr. and Mrs. and daughter, of Biddeford, Me., returned home last Sat. evening (23 April 1909, 12, 19)

GOODKOWSKY, Mr. and Mrs. N. and their two daughters, of Biddeford, Me., are guests of Mrs. Goodkowsky's parents, Mr. and Mrs. H. Albert (16 April 1909, 12, 18)

GOODMAN, J.J., the well-known author who is connected with the Immigration Department in Winnipeg, and R.L. Richardson, the owner of the Winnipeg Tribune, called on Richard Pierce while in Montreal (24 Nov. 1911, 15, 2)

GOODMAN, Mrs., of Toronto, has returned home (11 March 1910, 13, 17)

GOODMAN, R., of New York, is in Montreal on a business trip (12 Nov. 1909, 12, 48)

GOODSON, Joe, of Goodson Bros., Montreal, left for London, England on a two months' trip (16 Jan. 1914, 17, 6)

GOODSON, Joesph, is extending his visit to London, England due to his mother's serious illness (27 March 1914, 17, 13)

GOODSTONE, A.S., R.S. Stark, and E. Mauer (supplememtary) passed their B.S.c. examinations at McGill University, Faculty of Science (13 May 1910, 13, 26)

GORDON, David, was elected president of the Hebrew Immigrant Aid Society which held its first general meeting in Prince Arthur Hall last Thurs. Dec. 4, 1913. Other officers elected were:- Gedaliah Rabinovitch, 1st vice-pres.; Albert Vechsler, 2nd vice-pres.; M.L. Brown, sec.; W. Myerson, fin. sec.; M. Levitt, treas.; Mr. Goldenberg, chairman of the members' committee (12 Dec. 1913, 17, 1)

GORDON, H., has gone by boat to Alexandria Bay and Toronto via the Thousand Islands (2 Aug. 1912, 15, 34)

GORDON, Harry, donated a bookcase to the Mount Sinai Sanatorium (1 Aug. 1913, 16, 34)

GORDON, Harry, former proprietor and manager of the City House Furnishing Co., left Sun. Jan. 5, 1913, on a business trip and will visit the furniture manufacturing towns in Ontario and the U.S. (10 Jan. 1913, 16, 5)

GORDON, Harry, general manager of the City House Furnishing Co., is giving away bronze busts of Sir Wilfrid Laurier to all customers who call this month. The company is celebrating the anniversary of its move into a new five-story building (15 Nov. 1912, 15, 49)

GORDON, Harry, has returned from a trip through western Ontario, Buffalo, Chicago and Detroit (4 Feb. 1910, 13, 12)

GORDON, Harry, has returned from a business trip to the Maritimes (6 Jan. 1911, 14, 8)

GORDON, Harry, has returned from Caledonia Springs (18 Aug. 1911, 14, 40)

GORDON, Harry, has returned to Montreal (24 Feb. 1911, 14, 15)

GORDON, Harry, is in Toronto for the wedding of his sister, Miss Rose Gordon (31 Jan. 1913, 16, 8)

GORDON, Harry, of the City House Furnishing Co. sends New Year greetings (11 Sept. 1912, 15, 40)

GORDON, Harry, of the City House Furnishing Co., returned from an extensive motor tour to the Catskills, Atlantic City and other places of interest (25 July 1913, 16, 33)

GORDON, Harry, wishes his friends a happy New Year (1 Oct. 1913, 16, 42-43)

GORDON, J., is visiting his mother in Ottawa (2 Aug. 1912, 15, 34)

GORDON, M.A., Rabbi Nathan, who spent the summer in New York, is expected to return to Montreal next Wed. (27 Aug. 1909, 12, 37)

GORDON, Miss Bessie, Metcalfe St., entertained at bridge on Mon. aft. (25 Feb. 1910, 13, 15)

GORDON, Miss Hester, of Toronto, is visiting her sister, Mrs. I. Lande (28 June 1912, 15, 29)

GORDON, Miss Hilda, Clarke Ave., was given a surprise party on the occasion of her fifteenth birthday (21 March 1913, 16, 15)

GORDON, Miss Hilda, daughter of Mr. and Mrs. E.M. Gordon, 139 Elgin Ave., who was dangerously ill in the Royal Victoria Hospital, is convalescing at home (22 March 1912, 15, 19)

GORDON, Miss, of Kingston, Ont., is the guest of Mrs. Markey, Dorchester St. (19 Feb. 1909, 12, 10)

GORDON, Miss Rose and her sister, Mrs. I. Lande have gone to Miss Gordon's home in Toronto by boat through the Thousand Islands (2 Aug. 1912, 15, 34)

GORDON, Miss Rose, has returned to Toronto (13 Jan. 1911, 14, 9)

GORDON, Miss Sara, read a paper "Intellectual Qualities of the Jew" at the Young People's Society of Shaar Hashomayim meeting last Tues. (12 Feb. 1909, 12, 9)

GORDON, Moses, of Toronto, has returned home after visiting his daughter, Mrs. I. Lande, Westmount. Mr. Gordon was present at the marriage of his son, S.E. Gordon to Miss S. Rutenberg (5 Aug. 1910, 13, 38)

GORDON, Moses, of Toronto, is staying with his daughter, Mrs. I. Lande (11 Oct. 1912, 15, 44)

GORDON, Mrs., accompanied by Mrs. Baer, who was visiting her daughter, Mrs. L. Goldner, has returned to Troy, N.Y. (3 Dec. 1909, 13, 3)

GORDON, Mrs. D., Esplanade Ave., gave a birthday party in honor of her five-year old daughter, Malca (12 Sept. 1913, 16, 40)

GORDON, Mrs. David, Esplanade Ave., gave a farewell dinner party on Jan. 12, 1911, in honor of Miss Rose Gordon who returned to Toronto (27 Jan. 1911, 14, 11)

GORDON, Mrs. David, gave a party in honor of Miss Annie Gordon, prior to her return to Toronto (25 Feb. 1910, 13, 15)

GORDON, Mrs. F., of New York, mother of Rabbi Nathan Gordon, is the guest of Mr. and Mrs. Mark Workman (15 Dec. 1911, 15, 5)

GORDON, Mrs. Moses, of Toronto, is spending a few weeks at Hotel Vermont, Ste. Agathe des Monts (28 July 1911, 14, 37)

GORDON, Mrs. Nathan, is visiting her sister, Mrs. M. Rosenthal in Ottawa (3 Jan. 1913, 16, 4)

GORDON, Mrs. Rose, of Toronto, is visiting her sister, Mrs. I. Lande, Grosvenor Ave., Westmount (2 Dec. 1910, 14, 3)

GORDON, Mrs. S.E., 71 Hutchison St., gave a small dinner party Dec. 14, 1910, in honor of Miss Rose Gordon, of Toronto, prior to the opera (30 Dec. 1910, 14, 7)

GORDON, Rabbi Nathan came from New York to officiate at the funeral of Miss Fannie Harris last Thurs. and returns to that city Sat. evening (24 June 1910, 13, 32)

GORDON, Rabbi Nathan, chaired the meeting called to organize a B'nai Brith Lodge in Montreal. Rabbi Joseph S. Kornfeld, of Columbus, Ohio, (formerly of Montreal), Rabbi Israel Klein, of Chicago, and A.B. Seelenfreund, Grand Secretary of the Order, spoke in favor of the formation of a new lodge. Peter Bercovitch was elected first president of Mount Royal Lodge, No. 729. Other officers elected were:- J. Levinson, Sr., vice-pres.; Dr. Simon Kirsch, sec.; Charles Redlich, treas.; J. Becker, asst. monitor; A.S. Levine, warden; I. Popliger, outdoor guard; Rabbi Nathan Gordon, monitor; M. Block, H. Gordon and M. Lightstone, trustees (14 Feb. 1913, 16, 10)

GORDON, Rabbi Nathan, has been rabbi of Temple Emanu-El since 1906. Previous rabbis who served the temple have been:- Samuel Marks (1882-1889), S. Eisenberg (1889-1890), A.M. Bloch (1890-1891), H. Veld (1891-1899), E. Friedlander (1899-1901), Isaac Landman (1901-1904), and Joseph Kornfeld (1904-1906) (20 Sept. 1911, 14, 45)

GORDON, Rabbi Nathan, has returned from New York where he spent the summer (9 Sept. 1910, 13, 43)

GORDON, Rabbi Nathan, intends leaving on vacation next Tues. evening for New York (10 June 1910, 13, 30)

GORDON, Rabbi Nathan, is back from New York where he had been visiting his parents (26 Feb. 1909, 12, 11)

GORDON, Rabbi Nathan, is leaving for Toronto on Sat. night, where he will deliver an address Sun. evening to the United Zionists, at a monster meeting to be held in the University Street Synagogue (15 Jan. 1909, 12, 5)

GORDON, Rabbi Nathan, leaves next Tues. evening for New York to visit his parents. On Fri. night, Feb. 19, 1909, he will deliver an address in Clinton Hall, the downtown branch of the Free Synagogue, at the invitation of Dr. Stephen S. Wise. He returns Feb. 21 (12 Feb. 1909, 12, 9)

GORDON, Rabbi Nathan, leaves Sat. night for Kingston, Ont., where he will address the local Zionist society (25 March 1910, 13, 19)

GORDON, Rabbi Nathan, leaves tomorrow night for New York for two months. He will officiate at the wedding of his cousin, Dr. Nathan Broder to Miss Tessie Kresner, both of New York, on June 22, 1909 (18 June 1909, 12, 27)

GORDON, Rabbi Nathan, leaves tomorrow night for New York to visit his parents (16 June 1911, 14, 31)

GORDON, Rabbi Nathan, returned from New York where he visited his parents. He left yesterday for Portland, Ont., to visit Mr. and Mrs. Mark Workman (25 July 1911, 14, 36)

GORDON, Rabbi Nathan, was in Ottawa this week (20 Oct. 1911, 14, 49)

GORDON, Rabbi Nathan, will address the Zionists in Ottawa, on Sun. Dec. 19, 1909 (17 Dec. 1909, 13, 5)

GORDON, Rabbi Nathan, will chair the "Evening with Sholem Ash" concert on Sun. April 10, 1910 at 8 p.m. Those taking part in the concert are:- the Misses Hyalie Freiman, Jackson and Olga and Dolly Guilaroff, and Master Kaufman (8 April 1910, 13, 21)

GORDON, Rabbi Nathan, will receive his M.A. degree at the McGill University Convocation, this aft. (30 April 1909, 12, 20)

GORDON, Rabbi Nathan, will speak before the Free Speech Society, on Sun. Dec. 12, 1909, on "Priest and Prophet in the Bible" (10 Dec. 1909, 13, 4)

GORDON, S., of Troy, N.Y., is visiting his daughter, Mrs. L. Goldner (8 April 1910, 13, 21)

GORFINKEL, Mrs. Max and children, 76 Berkley St., Toronto, have returned from a two months' holiday at Charlton, Ont. (2 Sept. 1910, 13, 42)

GORFINKLE, Miss M., has returned from a holiday in New York (8 Dec. 1911, 15, 4)

GORFINKLE, Mrs., is rapidly recovering from her recent illness (21 May 1909, 12, 23)

COLLECTIONS AND VALUATIONS.

LOANS ON 1st, 2nd and 3rd MORTGAGES.

A. GORN
REAL ESTATE BR_KER

EAGLE BLDG.
516 ST. LAWRENCE BVD.
phone East 1263.

Residence:
1221 ST. URBAIN

GOROSH, S., has gone to New York on business (23 Sept, 1910, 13, 45)

GRAFF, Mr. and Mrs. J.B. and son, will return home to Syracuse, N.Y., Sat. night, after being the guests of Mr. and Mrs. J. Merson, Mance St. (11 July 1913, 16, 31)

GRANKLIN, J.L., formerly of Thetford Mines, Que., has moved to Chicoutimi, Que. (4 April 1913, 16, 17)

GREEN, Clifford, returned home to Ottawa after spending the weekend in Montreal (16 May 1913, 16, 23)

GREEN, Harry, of St. John, N.B., is visiting his cousin, Mrs. Gustav Fischel, Prince Albert Ave., Westmount (2 Oct. 1912, 15, 43)

GREEN, J., of Chicago, is visiting his daughter, Mrs. Gustav Fischel, Prince Albert Ave., Westmount (22 Aug. 1913, 16, 37)

GREEN, J., of Chicago, who visited his daughter, Mrs. Gustave Fischel, Prince Albert Ave., has gone to St. John, N.B., via Boston, to visit his daughter, Mrs. Emil Berger (2 Aug. 1912, 15, 34)

GREEN, Miss Helen, of Ottawa, is the guest of Miss T. Gold, 1044 St. Urbain St., for a few weeks (31 Oct. 1913, 16, 47)

GREEN, Miss Helen, of Ottawa, was the guest of Miss Tillie Gold, St. Urbain St., over the weekend (16 May 1913, 16, 23)

GREEN, Miss, of St. John, N.B., is the guest of Mrs. Arthur Simon, Grosvenor Ave. (8 Dec. 1911, 15, 4)

GREEN, Misses Adela and Lily, of Adamsville, Mass., were guests of Mr. and Mrs. Max Harris, Dorchester St. W. (7 Nov. 1913, 16, 48)

GREEN, Mr. and Mrs. Louis, of Ottawa, left Thurs. last week for two weeks on the Great Lakes (28 July 1911, 14, 37)

GREEN, Mr. and Mrs. Nathan, of Vancouver, B.C., passed through Montreal, en route for St. John, N.B. In town they were guests of Mrs. Gus. Fischel, Westmount (16 July 1909, 12, 31)

GREEN, Mrs., of Ottawa, is the guest of her sister, Mrs. Fred Markey, Dorchester St. (11 Feb. 1910, 13, 13)

GREEN, S. Hart, M.P.P. of Winnipeg, attended the Goldstein-Roskom wedding in Montreal (30 Dec. 1910, 14, 7)

GREENBERG, Dave and Abe, went fishing for a week (2 Aug. 1912, 15, 34)

GREENBERG, I., is staying at the Chateau Laurier, Ottawa (21 June 1912, 15, 28)

GREENBERG, Lionel, of Boston, spent a few days visiting his parents, Mance St. (26 Feb. 1909, 12, 11)

GREENBERG, Miss Essie H., of New York, is visiting Mrs. A. Kirsch (28 March 1913, 16, 16)

GREENBERG, Miss H., gave a linen shower in honor of Miss Lily Tannenbaum who will be married shortly (11 Oct. 1912, 15, 44)

GREENBERG, Miss Helen and Mrs. Greenberg, of Rochester, N.Y. have moved back to Montreal (25 July 1911, 14, 36)

GREENBERG, Miss Helen, has gone to New York for several weeks to visit relatives (23 Feb. 1912, 15, 15)

GREENBERG, Miss Helen, is visiting the Misses Tannenbaum at Iberville, Que. (2 Aug. 1912, 15, 34)

GREENBERG, Miss Helen, St. Charles Rd., Outremont, is in Buffalo, N.Y. for a few weeks visiting relatives (16 May 1913, 16, 23)

GREENBERG, Miss, of Boston, is visiting relatives in Montreal (27 Dec. 1912, 16, 3)

GREENBERG, Miss, of Rochester, N.Y., is visiting Mrs. Albert Wener (23 Dec. 1910, 14, 6)

GREENBERG, Mr. and Mrs., of Chicago, were

From The Canadian Jewish Times — Montreal

Uptown 2879 & 2815   Montreal

When you are ready to buy a hat remember the

Well-Known Millinery

Old England

532 St. Catherine W.

Under the Supervision of MR. ISIDOR GREENBERG

---

guests of Mrs. G. Fischel (15 Sept. 1909, 12, 40)

GREENBERG, Mrs. A., 37 St. Catherine Road, is selling The Jewish Encyclopaedia on easy terms (25 Sept. 1912, 15, 42)

GREENBERG, Mrs. M., Mance St., Annex, is host to her sister, of Rochester, N.Y. (14 Feb. 1913, 16, 10)

GREENBERG, Mrs., Mance St., has returned from Boston (16 April 1909, 12, 18)

GREENBERG, Mrs. S. and Miss Soth Greenberg, of New York, are guests of Mrs. P. Myers, Crescent St. (6 Aug. 1909, 12, 34)

GREENBLATT, M., has left on a visit (23 Dec. 1910, 14, 6)

GREENFORD, Sam, leaves Sun. for Michigan where he is a delegate for the Equitable Life Assurance Society convention. Afterwards he will attend the wedding of Saul Greenfarb in Toronto (4 July 1913, 16, 30)

GREENHOOD, J., of New York, stayed at the Windsor Hotel (20 Sept. 1912, 15, 41)

GREENHOOD, Joseph, of New York, was registered at the St. Lawrence Hall (25 Oct. 1910, 13, 50)

GREENHOOD, W., of New York, was a guest at the St. Lawrence Hall (21 May 1909, 12, 23)

GREENSPAN, Miss Jennie, was the guest of her sister, Mrs. A. Borts, in Ottawa (5 Jan. 1912, 15, 8)

GREENSPON, Miss Fannie, has returned from New York where she spent the holidays with friends Mrs. James Goldie and Miss Mary Gensor (17 June 1910, 13, 31)

GREENSPON, Miss Jennie, gave a linen shower at 63 Esplanade Ave., on Sun., in honor of the approaching marriage of Miss Rose Goldner. Assisting at the table were:- the Misses B. Asner, Sarah and Rose Greenspon, Florence Hecht, Milly Hecht, Reba Singer and Mrs. Perry Cohen (20 Feb. 1914, 17, 8)

GREENSPON, Miss Jennie, returned from Ottawa where she spent the weekend (7 Nov. 1913, 16, 48)

GREENSPON, Mrs. M., has returned from Ottawa where she visited her daughter, Mrs. A. Borts (10 Feb. 1911, 14, 13)

GREENSPOON, J., gave a dinner Sun. evening. Guests included:- H. Bessner, M. Greenspoon, M. Singer, A. Sourkes, S. G. Greenspoon, H. Singer, H. Wilensky, I. Sourkes and J. Dovin. At the suggestion of Mr. Bessner, $10.00 was collected for the Jewish National Fund (25 March 1910, 13, 19)

GREENSTEIN, Mrs. M., Miss H. Greenstein, and Masters C. and M. Greenstein were passengers on the S.S. Sicilian which arrived from London, via Le Harve, last Mon. (30 July 1909, 12, 33)

GREENSTON, Miss, has returned from Ottawa (2 Sept. 1910, 13, 42)

GREISMAN, Miss Francis H., of New York, is the new superintendent of the Hebrew Sheltering Home and Orphanage Asylum of Montreal and is the guest of the president, M.B. Steine (9 Aug. 1912, 15, 35)

GRINON, M.J., of Philadelphia, stayed at the Windsor Hotel (8 March 1912, 15, 17)

GRONER, Miss Ruth, arranged and supervised the dramatic numbers at the Purim entertainment under the auspices of the Young Men's Club of the Spanish and Portuguese Synagogue, Stanley St. (31 March 1911, 14, 20)

GRONER, Miss Ruth, Elm Ave., sailed on the Empress of India and will spend the summer abroad with relatives (16 May 1913, 16, 23)

GRONER, Mr. and Mrs. B., Elm Ave., Westmount, spent the week at Rouses Point, N.Y. (5 Sept. 1913, 16, 39)

GRONER, Mrs. B., Elm Ave., has returned home after several months abroad (8 Oct. 1909, 12, 43)

GRONER, Mrs. B., Elm Ave., leaves on the S.S. Corsican which sails for England on July 2, 1909 (2 July 1909, 12, 29)

GRONIN, J. and J. Myerson have gone to Melocheville, Que., for a few days (2 Sept. 1910, 12, 42)

GRONIN, J., McGill Arts '12, son of Mr. and Mrs. M. Gronin and B. Silver, McGill Arts '13, son of Mr. and Mrs. M. Silver, 121 Park Ave., were prize winners this year. Mr. Gronin received a $150.00 scholarship for two years in French and German and Mr. Silver received $150.00, major in mathematics and physics and minor Latin (18 Oct. 1910, 13, 49)

GROSS, Bernard and daughters, the Misses Rose and Mary Gross and son Moses Gross, left last Sat. morn. for California where they will take up their permanent residence (7 April 1911, 14, 21)

GROSS, Dr. C.J., 11A Sherbrooke St., has returned to the city (3 Sept. 1909, 12, 38)

GROSS, Dr. C.J., has returned to Montreal and will resume practice (7 July 1911, 14, 34)

GROSS, Dr., has gone to Southern California for a month (9 June 1911, 14, 30)

GROSS, Dr., has moved his office to 1st floor, 512 St. Lawrence Blvd. (19 May 1911, 14, 27)

GROSS, Miss, 146 Milton St., is selling tickets for the First Grand Annual Ball of the Hebrew Ladies' Relief Society to be held in Auditorium Hall, Berthelet St., on Wed. Feb. 10, 1909 (5 Feb. 1909, 12, 8)

GROSS, Miss J., is in New York on a short visit (19 Feb. 1909, 12, 10)

GROSS, Miss Sara, who spent two weeks at Caledonia Springs, has returned to Montreal (16 July 1909, 12, 31)

GROSS, Misses Rose and Bella, have returned from New York where they were guests of Miss May Genzer, formerly of Montreal (15 July 1910, 13, 35)

GROSS, Mr. and Mrs. and Mr. and Mrs. Weiner and families are spending the summer at Iberville (8 July 1910, 13, 34)

GROSS, Mrs. B., 133 Elgin St., left last Sat., on the S.S. Laurentic, for Liverpool. Mrs. Gross intends to spend two months at Karlsbad, Germany, after which she will visit relatives in Austria (25 June 1909, 12, 28)

GROSSMAN, H., of Vancouver, is a guest at the Corona Hotel (15 Oct. 1909, 12, 44)

GROSSMAN, Maxwell, Arts '12, McGill University, has returned home to Vancouver (30 April 1909, 12, 20)

GROSSMAN, Mr. and Mrs. A., of Vancouver, are staying at the Windsor Hotel (30 Sept. 1910, 13, 46)

GROSSMAN, Mr. and Mrs. Harry, of Vancouver, who were abroad for the past three months, stayed at the Ritz-Carlton Hotel before returning home. Mrs. Grossman presented a Sefer Torah mantle to Temple Emanu-El in memory of her late father, Morris Claman (22 Oct. 1913, 16, 46)

GROSSMAN, Mr. and Mrs. Harry, of Vancouver, stayed at the Ritz Carlton Hotel while in Montreal, en route for Europe where they will spend six months (23 May 1913, 16, 24)

GROSSMAN, Mrs. Harry, of Vancouver, was in Montreal to attend the funeral of her father, Mr. Claman (28 July 1911, 14, 37)

GROSSMAN, Mrs. S.M., of Toronto, is visiting Mr. and Mrs. Rittenberg, Mance St. (4 Feb. 1910, 13, 12)

GRUDGINSKY, Mr. and Mrs. Nathan, recently celebrated their wedding anniversary (3 Jan. 1913, 16, 4)

GRUMBACHER, L., of New York, was a guest at the Windsor Hotel (15 Sept, 1909, 12, 40)

GUILAROFF, Miss O.. performed a pianoforte solo at the Young People's Hachnosis Orchim Society, Wed. evening, Nov. 20, 1912 in the Auditorium Hall. Others appearing on the program were:- Miss P. Hoffman, recitation; Miss A. Kert, violin solo, accompanied by Miss R. Kert; Miss Rosen and Mr. Waxler, vocal solo; Mr. Dalton, comic songs. H. Sourkes moved a vote of thanks, seconded by Miss A. Navarich (29 Nov. 1912, 15, 51)

GUILAROFF, Mrs. Eugene and children, of London, arrived aboard the S.S. Victorian and are staying at 997 St. Urbain St. (15 Sept. 1909, 12, 40)

GUROFSKY, Louis, of Toronto, was in Montreal for a few days (13 May 1910, 13, 26)

GUROFSKY, Louis, of Toronto, was in Montreal for a few days (26 May 1911, 14, 28)

GUTSTEIN, Mr. and Mrs., of Prince Rupert, B.C., are in Montreal visiting friends (20 Dec. 1912, 16, 2)

HAAS, George and Max, of Toronto, sailed for Europe aboard the S.S. Hesperian (24 Sept. 1909, 12, 41)

HAAS, Miss, of Buffalo, N.Y., is visiting her sister, Mrs. C.A. Workman, Kensington Ave., Westmount (4 Aug. 1911, 14, 38)

HAAS, Miss, of Buffalo, N.Y., will spend the coming Holy Days with her sister, Mrs. C.A. Workman, Kensington Ave. (30 Sept. 1910, 13, 46)

HAAS, Miss, returned home to Syracuse, N.Y., after spending the summer with her sister, Mrs. Charles A. Workman (30 Aug. 1912, 15, 38)

HALPERIN, Miss Jessie E., City Hall Ave., is recovering from a recent attack of scarlet fever (13 June 1913, 16, 27)

HALPERN, Mrs. B., has gone on a trip to Buffalo, N.Y., and Bradford, Pa. (11 Aug. 1911, 14, 39)

HALPERN, Mrs. Bernard, Crescent St., is in New York for a few weeks (16 May 1913, 16, 23)

HALPERN, Rev. I., of Toronto, accompanied by his youngest daughter, Miss Mollie Halpern, has gone to Austria to visit his mother (8 July 1910, 13, 34)

HALPIN, J., of Kingston, Ont., is registered at the Corona Hotel (12 Nov. 1909, 12, 48)

HAMILTON, Mr. and Mrs. John, of Toronto, are visiting the Misses Harris, Tupper St. (29 Dec. 1911, 15, 7)

HAMILTON, Mr. and Mrs. John, of Toronto, are guests of the Misses Harris, Tupper St. (27 Dec. 1912, 16, 3)

HAMILTON, Mr. and Mrs. John, of Toronto, are spending the holiday season with the Misses Harris, Tupper St. (26 Dec. 1913, 17, 3)

HANDLEMAN, Miss, has recovered from her recent attack of pneumonia (15 March 1912, 14, 18)

HANSHER, Mr. and Mrs. S.M., of Toronto, are guests of Mr. and Mrs. M. Slabosky, 1959 Mance St. (9 Jan. 1914, 17, 5)

HANSHER, Mrs. A. and daughter, of Milwaukee, are visiting Mr. and Mrs. M. Slabotsky (7 March 1913, 16, 13)

HANSHER, Mrs. M. and her daughter, Mrs. M. Slabosky and child, have left for Chicago and Milwaukee (29 Nov. 1912, 15, 51)

HARRIS, A. and daughter left last night for Toronto to attend the Zionist convention (23 Dec. 1910, 14, 6)

HARRIS, A. and Miss R. Harris have left for Old Orchard Beach (22 July 1910, 13, 36)

HARRIS, A. and the Misses Rosie and Dora Harris, left last night for New York. The Misses Harris will spend a short holiday at Rockaway Beach (2 July 1909, 12, 29)

HARRIS, A., chairman of the Jewish National Fund for Canada, has returned from a quick trip to Winnipeg, Port Arthur and Toronto (8 April 1910, 13, 21)

HARRIS, A., has returned from a business trip to Toronto (16 June 1911, 14, 31)

HARRIS, A., has returned from his trip to Ontario (10 June 1910, 13, 30)

HARRIS, A., is in Toronto on business (20 Oct. 1911, 14, 49)

HARRIS, A., is on a business trip to Ontario (25 Feb. 1910, 13, 15)

HARRIS, A., Jewish National Fund chairman has gone to Winnipeg, Port Arthur and Fort William (16 Aug. 1912, 15, 36)

HARRIS, A., leaves tomorrow night for Ottawa and Toronto (3 March 1911, 14, 16)

HARRIS, A., left on Tues. night for Ottawa, Toronto and points west. He expects to return Nov. 18, 1909 (5 Nov. 1909, 12, 47)

HARRIS, A., of New York, is visiting his sisters, the Misses Harris, Tupper St. (31 Dec. 1909, 13, 7)

HARRIS, Aaron, has returned home to New York after spending the past month with his sisters, the Misses Harris, Tupper St., Westmount (4 Feb. 1910, 13, 12)

HARRIS, Aaron, of New York, has returned home after visiting his sisters for a few weeks (8 July 1910, 13, 34)

HARRIS, C.A., has returned from New York (5 Jan. 1912, 15, 8)

HARRIS, Julius, returned from Halifax where he was the guest of his sister, Mrs. John Simon (25 April 1913, 16, 20)

HARRIS, M., has returned from a week in New York (16 April 1909, 12, 18)

HARRIS, M., is in Boston for the funeral of his sister who died suddenly last week (22 Nov. 1912, 15, 50)

HARRIS, Major and Mrs. S., of Vancouver, were in Montreal, en route for a two months' trip to Europe (15 Oct. 1909, 12, 44)

HARRIS, Major and Mrs. S., passed through Montreal this week on their return from Europe, en route home to Vancouver (10 Dec. 1909, 13, 4)

HARRIS, Master David, of the Aberdeen School, son of Mr. and Mrs. A. Harris, has won a Commissioner's scholarship (8 July 1910, 13, 34)

HARRIS, Maxwell, Crescent St., has returned home after a week in New York (23 April 1909, 12, 19)

HARRIS, Miss Bessie, left for Chicago on Sun. Dec. 21, 1913 where she will visit her sister for several months (26 Dec. 1913, 17, 3)

HARRIS, Miss Esther, Frontenac Apts., is the guest of her sister, Mrs. H.M. Freedman in Atlantic City (14 March 1913, 16, 14)

HARRIS, Miss Lottie, of New York, is visiting her aunt, Mrs. Max Harris, Dorchester St. W. (3 Jan. 1913, 16, 4)

HARRIS, Miss M., of New York, is visiting her aunt, Mrs. M. Harris, Crescent St. (17 June 1910, 13, 31)

HARRIS, Miss Rose and Master David Harris have returned from Old Orchard, Me. (25 Aug. 1911, 14, 41)

HARRIS, Miss Rose, Crescent St., is in Halifax vsiting her sisters for a month or so (12 Aug. 1910, 13, 39)

HARRIS, Miss Rose, daughter of Mr. and Mrs. A. Harris, is recovering nicely after her operation this week in the Royal Victoria Hospital (20 Sept. 1912, 15, 41)

HARRIS, Miss Rose, has gone to Halifax to visit her sister, Mrs. J. Simon (29 Sept. 1911, 14, 46)

HARRIS, Miss Rose, has returned from Old Orchard (26 Aug. 1910, 13, 41)

HARRIS, Miss Rose, has returned from Toronto (13 Jan. 1911, 14, 9)

HARRIS, Miss Rose, is suffering from appendicitis. She will be moved to the Royal Victoria Hospital for an operation after she recovers her strength (16 Aug. 1912, 15, 36)

HARRIS, Miss Rose, read an article on Zionism at the Montreal Daughters of Zion meeting last Sun. aft., March 21, 1909. Leon Goldman spoke on "Zionist Propaganda Work in New York City". (26 March 1909, 12, 15)

HARRIS, Miss Sarah, won the first prize for Bridge and Mrs. Jacobs for Euchre at the Bridge-Euchre given by the Temple Sisterhood (19 Nov. 1909, 13, 1)

HARRIS, Misses Max and Stella, are visiting Mr. and Mrs. Simon, in Halifax (16 June 1911, 14, 31)

HARRIS, Misses, Tupper St., have gone to Lake Placid, N.Y., for a month (22 July 1910, 13, 36)

HARRIS, Misses, Tupper St., have returned from Lake Placid, N.Y. (26 Aug. 1910, 13, 41)

HARRIS, Misses, Tupper St., left for St. John and Digby, N.S., where they will spend the next four weeks (16 July 1909, 12, 31)

HARRIS, Misses, Tupper St., were the guests of Mrs. Harkness, St. Rose, for a few days (9 July 1909, 12, 30)

HARRIS, Mr. and Mrs. A., 633 City Hall Ave., send New Year greetings (11 Sept. 1912, 15, 40)

HARRIS, Mr. and Mrs. A. and family are spending the summer at Chateauguay (8 July 1910, 13, 34)

HARRIS, Mr. and Mrs. A. and family have returned from Chateauguay where they spent the summer (9 Sept. 1910, 13, 43)

HARRIS, Mr. and Mrs. Max and family, Crescent St., are at Vaudreuil for the summer (7 July 1911, 14, 34)

HARRIS, Mr. and Mrs. Max, left for Boston to attend his niece's wedding (18 Feb. 1910, 13, 14)

HARRIS, Mr. and Mrs. Maxwell, 959 Dorchester St. W., will be "At Home" on Nov. 10, 1912 (8 Nov. 1912, 15, 48)

HARRIS, Mrs. A., has returned from a holiday at New Glasgow, Que. (25 Aug. 1911, 14, 41)

HARRIS, Mrs. Felix, has lost her father who died early this month in Manchester, England (27 Oct. 1911, 14, 50)

HARRIS, Mrs. Felix, is on holiday at Rockaway Beach, N.Y. (7 July 1911, 14, 34)

HARRIS, Mrs. M. and Miss Rose Harris, Crescent St., are in New York (21 Jan. 1910, 13, 10)

HARRIS, Mrs. M.L., has recovered from her recent illness (9 July 1909, 12, 30)

HARRIS, Mrs. M.L., left for New York to attend the funeral of her brother, Mr. Levinne, who passed away after a long illness in Ashville (28 May 1909, 12, 24)

HARRIS, Mrs. Max, has returned from visiting her daughter, Mrs. John Simon in Halifax (28 July 1911, 14, 37)

HARRIS, Mrs., of New York, is visiting her daughter, Mrs. J. Berman, St. Mark St. (6 Sept. 1912, 15, 39)

HARRIS, S., will be in Caledonia Springs, Ont. (22 July 1910, 13, 36)

HARRIS, S.J., of Halifax, is registered at the St. Lawrence Hall (1 Oct. 1909, 12, 42)

HARRIS, Samuel, spent a few days at Caledonia Springs, Ont. (9 July 1909, 12, 30)

HARRIS, Samuel, Tupper St., is convalescing from his recent illness (22 Jan. 1909, 12, 6)

HARRIS, Theodor, son of Mr. and Mrs. Felix Harris, is seriously ill with an attack of scarlet fever (27 Jan. 1911, 14, 11)

HARRIS, Theodor, young son of Mr. and Mrs. Felix Harris, has completely recovered from his recent serious illness (10 March 1911, 14, 17)

HART, Mrs. Claude and son are visiting Mrs. Philip Myers, of Quebec City (9 July 1909, 12, 30)

HART, Claude, has recovered from his attack of typhoid fever (19 Aug. 1910, 13, 40)

HART, Dr. and Mrs. D.A., celebrated their thirty-fifth wedding anniversary last week with a large family gathering (31 March 1911, 14, 20)

HART, Dr. and Mrs. David A., returned from New York. Their guests are Mr. and Mrs. Roslyn E. Hart who were married Wed. June 5, 1912 at the home of Mr. and Mrs. P.L. Mendes in New York (21 June 1912, 15, 28)

HART, Dr. and Mrs., gave a dinner in honor of M. Michaels and Miss Muriel Hart and Miss Ascher and Mr. Schlissinger, on Wed. evening (7 May 1909, 12, 21)

HART, Dr. and Mrs., Sherbrooke St., have left for Elizabethtown, N.Y. (13 Aug. 1909, 12, 35)

HART, Dr. and Mrs., Sherbrooke St., Westmount, have gone to New York (10 Feb. 1911, 14, 13)

HART, Dr. and Mrs., Sherbrooke St. W., have returned from New York (3 March 1911, 14, 16)

HART, Dr. David A., Mrs. V.S. Hart and family, and Reginald Hart leave on holiday next Sun. for Elizabeth, N.Y. (7 July 1911, 14, 34)

HART, Dr., Sherbrooke St. W., returned from New York on Wed. (12 Nov. 1909, 12, 48)

HART, H., has returned from a few days in New York (4 Feb. 1910, 13, 12)

HART, L.M., of Chicago, is staying at the Corona Hotel (15 Jan. 1909, 12, 5)

HART, Miss M., has returned home, after spending a few weeks in New York (15 Jan. 1909, 12, 5)

HART, Miss Tillie, is on vacation in Sudbury, Ont. (9 Aug. 1912, 15, 35)

HART, Mr. and Mrs. Alan and family sailed for Scotland (26 July 1912, 15, 33)

HART, Mr. and Mrs. Alan J., have returned from Hamilton where Mr. Hart attended the Merchants' Convention (24 Sept. 1909, 12, 41)

HART, Mr. and Mrs. Claude and son have moved to New York to take up residence (17 Dec. 1909, 13, 5)

HART, Mr. and Mrs. Claude and son are at St. Jovite, Que. for the summer (14 July 1911, 14, 35)

HART, Mr. and Mrs. Claude B., are not permanently residing in New York and will return to Montreal in a few months. Mr. Hart will frequently be in Montreal to attend to his local business (24 Dec. 1909, 13, 6)

HART, Mr. and Mrs. Louis A., Elm Ave., are at Caledonia Springs for a few weeks (2 Aug. 1912, 15, 34)

HART, Mr. and Mrs. Sam, are at Caledonia Springs for a few weeks (27 June 1913, 16, 29)

HART, Mr. and Mrs. Samuel, are at Manoir Richelieu, Murray Bay (4 Aug. 1911, 14, 38)

HART, Mr. and Mrs. William, spent a few days at Caledonia Springs (2 July 1909, 12, 29)

HART, Mrs. Alan and family and Mrs. I. Cohen and family are at Little Metis, Que. for the summer (14 July 1911, 14, 35)

HART, Mrs. Allan, gave a linen shower last Tues. aft., in honor of the impending marriage of Miss Muriel Hart (28 May 1909, 12, 24)

HART, Mrs. and Rosyln Hart have returned home from Elizabethtown and Saratoga Springs, accompanied by Mr. and Mrs. Ruben, of New York. Roslyn Hart's health has improved (20 Aug. 1909, 12, 36)

HART, Mrs. Claude and son are in Montreal on a visit (18 March 1910, 13, 18)

HART, Mrs. D., Sherbrooke St., entertained at Bridge on Tues. aft. (16 April 1909, 12, 18)

HART, Mrs. D.A. and Mrs. L.M. Ruben have returned from three weeks in New York (12 Nov. 1909, 12, 48)

HART, Mrs. D.A., Sherbrooke St. W., gave a "kitchen shower" for Miss Muriel Hart, who will be married shortly (14 May 1909, 12, 22)

HART, Mrs. D.A., Sherbrooke St. W., entertained last Tues. evening, in celebration of the seventh birthday of her grandson, Master Cyril Hart (7 May 1909, 12, 21)

HART, Mrs. D.A., Sherbrooke St. W., and her son Roslyn E. Hart, have gone to New York and Atlantic City for ten days (31 Dec. 1909, 13, 7)

HART, Mrs. David A. and her sister, Mrs. L. Ruben are in New York to attend the Graff-Brandon wedding and are registered at the St. Regis Hotel (22 Oct. 1909, 12, 45)

HART, Mrs. David A., Sherbrooke St., and her son, R. Hart have gone to Knowlton for a couple of weeks for the benefit of R. Hart's health (10 Sept. 1909, 12, 39)

HART, Mrs. H., has to Atlantic City for a few weeks (14 July 1911, 14, 35)

HART, Mrs. Samuel and daughter have returned home after a few weeks at Mount Clemens (16 July 1909, 12, 31)

HART, Mrs. Samuel and daughter, Ruth Hart, have returned from several weeks' holiday in Chicago and Milwaukee (4 Feb. 1910, 13, 12)

HART, R.E., has returned home from four weeks in Germany (7 July 1911, 14, 34)

HART, Reginald, Sherbrooke St., is confined to the house by illness (20 Aug. 1909, 12, 36)

HART, Rosyln, is recovering from his attack of typhoid fever (9 July 1909, 12, 30)

HASKELL, Mrs. and Miss Haskell have left for Boston, where they stayed with Mrs. Prime (7 May 1909, 12, 21)

HASKELL, S., was in New York during the week (17 Nov. 1911, 15, 1)

HAYES, B.J., is back after a two weeks' vacation at Ste. Agathe (18 June 1909, 12, 27)

HAYES, Mr. and Mrs. B.J. and family returned to their new home, 8 and 9 Mount Royal Ave., from l'Assomption, where they spent the summer (24 Sept. 1909, 12, 41)

HAYES, Mr. and Mrs. B.J. and family are summering at St. Faustin, Que. (25 July 1913, 16, 33)

HECHT, Mr. and Mrs. Nathan, are at Murray Bay for a few weeks (16 Aug. 1912, 15, 36)

HEFT, Mr. and Mrs. S., City Hall Ave., gave a party in honor of Miss L. Rinkoff and I. Bell, of New York. Miss S. Heft received the guests, assisted by the Misses Fanny Heft and S. Wetstein. Out-of-town guests present were:- Miss H. Birke, of New York; M. Rubin, and H. Solomon, of Boston; and Mr. Katzman, of Washington (25 July 1913, 16, 33)

HEILLIG, I., Messrs. M. Albert, Harry Wener and Samuel Vineberg left for Europe last week (28 May 1909, 12, 24)

HEILLIG, Lyon, sailed for Europe on the S.S. Megantic for a two months' business trip (16 June 1911, 14, 31)

HEILLIG, Miss Ray, is the guest of Dr. and Mrs. Zeman, in Hartford, Conn. (18 Nov. 1910, 14, 1)

HEILLIG, Mr. and Mrs. M., Tupper St., have returned from Caledonia Springs (14 July 1911, 14, 35)

HEILLIG, Mr. and Mrs. R.E. and family returned from their summer holiday at Woodlands (12 Sept. 1913, 16, 40)

HEILLIG, Mrs. M., has left for Old Orchard Beach (22 July 1910, 13, 36)

HEILLIG, Mrs. M., Tupper St., Westmount, has returned from a month in Old Orchard, Me. (19 Aug. 1910, 13, 40)

HEIM, J., of Berlin, Germany, is a guest at the Place Viger Hotel (17 June 1910, 13, 31)

HEIMERDINGER, Mr. and Mrs. Harry, of New York, were in Montreal for a short stay (14 July 1911, 14, 35)

HEIMERDINGER, Mrs. Harry and daughters were guests of Mrs. Charles Redlich during their stay (28 July 1911, 14, 37)

HEINSHEIMER, E., of London, England, is staying at the Place Viger Hotel (16 April 1909, 12, 18)

HEINSHEIMER, Mr. and Mrs. Art, of Buffalo, are spending a couple of weeks with Mr. and Mrs. Hillie Hart (8 Jan. 1909, 12, 4)

HEINSHEIMER, Mr. and Mrs. Arthur, have returned from two weeks' stay at Val Morin (1 July 1910, 13, 33)

HEISLER, H., of New York, stayed at the Queen's Hotel (19 Jan. 1912, 15, 10)

HELLER, Mr. and Mrs. M.J., have returned from a long trip to New York and the southern U.S. They will spend the rest of the summer at Bordeaux, Que., with Mr. and Mrs. Sherman, Mrs. Heller's parents (30 July 1909, 12, 33)

HENNESSY, Mrs. S., of Winnipeg, accompanied by her son, is visiting her parents, Mr. and Mrs. Joseph Miller, Roseberry Apts., Sherbrooke St. W. (23 Sept. 1910, 13, 45)

HEPPNER, Max, is in Montreal for a few months (6 Jan. 1911, 14, 8)

HEPPNER, Max, manager of the Hirsch and Qu'Appelle colonies in the North West, left for Winnipeg, accompanied by H. Horsefall, clerk of the BdeHI Board. They will visit the colonies shortly (5 March 1909, 12, 12)

HEPPNER, Max, of Winnipeg, was in Montreal this week and left last night for Old Orchard Beach for a few weeks (29 July 1910, 13, 37)

HERDT, Joseph and son, of Detroit, Mich., stayed at the Windsor Hotel while in Montreal (15 Aug. 1913, 16, 36)

HERMAN, H.L., has gone to New York to attend his mother's funeral. She died after a short illness (23 Dec. 1910, 14, 6)

HERMAN, Miss Ray, is spending a holiday in Toronto (27 May 1910, 13, 28)

HERMAN, Mrs. R., of Toronto, is visiting her cousins, and is staying with Mrs. Diamond, 582 St. Denis (27 March 1914, 17, 13)

HERMAN, S.K., left for New Orleans, La. (20 Feb. 1914, 17, 8)

HERMAN, S.L., has returned from a short stay in New York (7 Oct. 1910, 13, 47)

HERMAN, S.L., stayed at Hotel Navarre while in New York (22 March 1912, 15, 19)

HERMAN, S.L., stayed at the Royal Palace Hotel, Atlantic City, the past week (30 Aug. 1912, 15, 38)

HERSCHEL, J., of New York, is at the Queen's Hotel (5 March 1909, 12, 12)

HERSCHMAN, Rev. and Mrs., have returned to Detroit after spending a holiday in Ste. Agathe (6 Aug. 1909, 12, 34)

HERSHBERG, Mr. and Mrs. I., of Rochester, N.Y., are visiting their daughter, Mrs. M. Albert, Prince Arthur Apts. (13 Dec. 1912, 16, 1)

HERSHBERG, Mrs. I., of Rochester, N.Y., is visiting her daughter, Mrs. M. Albert, Prince Arthur Apts. (12 Sept. 1913, 16, 40)

HERSHBERG, Mrs. Sam. and Master Bertram Hershberg, of Rochester, N.Y., are visiting Mrs. M. Albert, Victoria Ave., Westmount (2 Jan. 1914, 17, 4)

HERSHORN, Mr. and Mrs. and family are spending the summer at Woodlands (5 Aug. 1910, 13, 38)

HERTZ, Miss Elizabeth, of Quebec City, gave a linen shower on Aug. 27, 1913, in honor of Miss Susan Silverman who was married to Martin Berman, of Ottawa, on Aug. 31, 1913 (5 Sept. 1913, 16, 39)

HERTZBERG, Mr. and Mrs., of New York, are guests of Mr. and Mrs. Jacob Hirsch, Bishop St. (17 June 1901, 13, 31)

HEYMAN, Mr. and Mrs. Isaac, Elm Ave., have returned from their summer residence in Gaspé, Que. (25 Oct. 1910, 13, 50)

HEYMAN, Mrs., has returned home after visiting her daughter Mrs. W. Goldstein (25 Oct. 1910, 13, 50)

HILF, Mr. and Mrs. William, of Johnston City, Ill., are visiting Mrs. Hilf's sister, Mrs. J. Rubin, Craig St. (28 July 1911, 14, 37)

HILLMAN, Miss Gertrude, of Worcester, Mass., is the guest of Mrs. H.H. Livingstone, Tupper St. (23 Feb. 1912, 15, 15)

HIMMELRICH, Mr. and Mrs. I., of Providence, R.I., are guests of Mr. and Mrs. Jacobs, Laval Ave. for a few weeks (8 July 1910, 13, 34)

HIMMELRICH, Mrs. I., of Providence, R.I., and M.J. Rosenberg were guests of their sister, Mrs. Max Jacobs, Laval Ave. (6 Oct. 1911, 14, 47)

HIRSCH, Arthur, has returned from a short stay in New York (8 July 1910, 13, 34)

HIRSCH, Arthur, has returned from a short stay in New York (15 July 1910, 13, 35)

HIRSCH, Arthur, is in New York (29 Dec. 1911, 15, 7)

HIRSCH, Arthur, is spending a week in Chicago (31 Dec. 1909, 13, 7)

HIRSCH, Arthur, L.H. Cohen and Dr. H. Lightstone were in charge of arrangements for the Bachelor's Ball held at the Windsor Hotel, on Mon. Feb. 8, 1909 (12 Feb. 1909, 12, 9)

HIRSCH, Arthur, returned from a short stay in New York (19 Sept. 1913, 16, 41)

HIRSCH, Arthur, was in New York (20 Oct. 1911, 14, 49)

HIRSCH, Elias, left for New York and the South where he has taken up residence (16 Jan. 1914, 17, 6)

HIRSCH, Essie, president of the Hebrew Young Ladies' Sewing Society of Montreal, issued an appeal for used clothing for the coming winter (4 Nov. 1910, 13, 51)

HIRSCH, J.A., has left on a short trip to Chicago (31 Dec. 1909, 13, 7)

HIRSCH, Jacob and Lizzie Levine celebrated their golden wedding anniversary Wed. evening, May 7, 1913 at the Montefiore Club, Guy St. Rabbi Herman Abramowitz officiated at the religious ceremony. They were presented with a Kiddush cup from the Shaar Hashomayim Congregation and a flower vase from the Ladies' Chevra Kadisha Society. Mr. and Mrs. Hirsch were married on May 7, 1863 in the English, German and Polish Synagogue, St. Constant St., Montreal. They have been Canadian citizens for the past sixty years, having lived in Richmond, Que. for a lengthy period before and after their marriage where Mr. Hirsch was a businessman. The late Marcus Levine, Mrs. Hirsch's father, was also in business in Richmond, previously having lived in St. Andrew's, Que. In 1875, Mr. and Mrs. Hirsch moved to Montreal for the benefit of their growing family. Mr. Hirsch is president of J. Hirsch & Sons, Ltd., in which his sons are associated. Mr. Hirsch is one of the founders of the Shaar Hashomayim Congregation and was on the Board of Trustees for many years. He was on the building committee when the new synagogue was built on McGill College Ave. Mrs. Hirsch has been president of the Ladies' Chevra Kadisha for many years. Immediate family members present were:- Mr. and Mrs. Michael Hirsch and their sons, J. Arthur Hirsch, T. Percy Hirsch and Robert Hirsch; Mr. and Mrs. Archie Jacobs and their children, Melvyn G. Jacobs and Miss Ernestina F. Jacobs; Marcus J. Hirsch and the Misses Sophia and Essie Hirsch. Out-of-town guests were:- Mrs. Hirsch's only brother, William M. Levine, of New York, and his daughters, Miss Rhea Levine and Mrs. Stella Koenigsberger, and his sons and daughter-in-law, Marcus A. Levine and Mr. and Mrs. Samuel W. Levine. Others present were:- Sydney Koenigsberger, Mrs. Paul Kunz, Mr. and Mrs. Joseph Mendels and family, Perth, Ont.; Mr. and Mrs. Adam Klopot and family, of Boston; A.M. Finlayson, Dr. Hugo Kunz, the Misses Beccie and Rosalie Sussman, Mr. and Mrs. Samuel Fein and son and Mrs. L.H. Peavy, all of New York (9 May 1913, 16, 22)

HIRSCH, Jacob and Miss Sophie Hirsch are at Caledonia Springs, Ont. (14 July 1911, 14, 35)

HIRSCH, Jacob, is rapidly recovering from his illness (7 Oct. 1910, 13, 47)

HIRSCH, Jacob L., of New York, who lived in Montreal until 1902 and A. Goldbloom, of Winnipeg, who left Montreal in 1899, are visiting the city (15 Sept. 1909, 12, 40)

HIRSCH, M., is on a trip to Cuba (20 Oct. 1911, 14, 49)

HIRSCH, Marcus and Miss Essie Hirsch, Bishop St., have gone to New York for a few days (25 March 1910, 13, 19)

HIRSCH, Marcus, Bishop St., is in New York (26 March 1909, 12, 15)

HIRSCH, Marcus, spent the past week in New York (10 Feb. 1911, 14, 13)

HIRSCH, Michael, was elected hon. pres. of the Montefiore Bowling League at the annual meeting. Other officers elected were:- Louis Rubenstein, hon. vice-pres.; William Bernfeld, pres.; Marvin Jacobs, vice-pres.; Ed. Kert, sec. treas.; Max Bernfeld, P. Fischel, committee (12 Dec. 1913, 17, 1)

HIRSCH, Michael, was elected president of the Montefiore Club at the thirty-first annual meeting. J. Levi, the president gave the annual report at the meeting. Other officers elected were:- I. Friedman, vice-pres.; M.J. Hirsch, hon. treas.; J. Levin, hon. sec.; L.H. Cohen, L.H. Jacobs, D. Kirsch, D. Roskam and J. Samenhoff, council (29 Sept. 1911, 14, 46)

HIRSCH, Michael, was elected president of the Montefiore Club by acclamation at the thirty-second annual meeting held in the club room on Guy St., on Sept. 16, 1912. Other officers elected were:- Isaac Friedman, vice-pres.; Marcus J. Hirsch, treas.; Jack Levi, hon. sec.; A.A. Abrahams, L.H. Cohen, C.L. Friedman, G.E. Goldstein and D. Kirsch, council members. Maxwell Goldstein, K.C., was reappointed hon. counsel (20 Sept. 1912, 15, 41)

HIRSCH, Michael, was elected president of the Montefiore Club at the club house this week. Other officers elected were:- Isaac Friedman, vice-pres.; M.J. Hirsch, hon. treas.; Jack Levi, hon. sec.; Maxwell Goldstein, K.C.; A.A. Abrahams, Lewis H. Cohen, C.L. Friedman, G.E. Goldstein and D. Kirsch, council (19 Sept. 1913, 16, 41)

HIRSCH, Miss, Bishop St., is the guest of Mr. and Mrs. Kuntz in New York for a few weeks (19 April 1912, 15, 23)

HIRSCH, Miss Essie, Mrs. Henry Saxe, Mrs. J. Levinson and the Misses I. and Lillian Levinson are summering at Lake Placid, N.Y. (18 July 1913, 16, 32)

HIRSCH, Miss Essie, thanks the following who assisted her in the recent house-to-house canvass in aid of the Victorian Order of Nurses:- Mrs. Tannenbaum and the Misses Estelle Abrahams, Annie Ballon, Ray and Sadie Cohen, H. Freeman, Eva Gittleson, Sylvia Goldstein, Flossie Hyman, Lena Jacobs, B. Kellnor, Etta Levine, Lily Levinson, Myrtie Levinson, Rosalind Lewis, Miss Pierce (Timmins, Ont.), Rose Rosenberger, Gertie and Lily Samuels, Yetta Silver, G. Silverman, Ray Tannenbaum and Rose Vineberg (20 Feb. 1914, 17, 8)

HIRSCH, Miss Essie, was elected president of the Hebrew Young Ladies' Sewing Society at the annual meeting held in the Baron de Hirsch Institute on Sun. Nov. 6., 1910. Other officers elected were:- Miss Gertrude Silverman, vice-pres.; Miss Lillie Tannenbaum, treas.; Miss Rosalind Lewis, sec.; Mesdames Henry Saxe and David Chorlton and the Misses Beccie Samuel and Sara Michaelson, council (11 Nov. 1910, 13, 52)

HIRSCH, Miss Essie, was elected president of the Hebrew Young Ladies' Sewing Society at the seventeenth annual meeting on Sun. Oct. 29, 1911 in the Baron de Hirsch Institute. Other officers elected were:- the Misses Gertrude Silverman, vice-pres.; Lillian Tannenbaum, treas.; Rosalind Lewis, hon. sec.; the Misses Bessie Saxe, Fannie Charlton, Annie Samuel, Beccie Samuel, Myrtie Levinson and Sara Michaelson (3 Nov. 1911, 14, 51)

HIRSCH, Miss Essie, was elected president of the Montreal Hebrew Sheltering and Orphans' Home Ladies' Auxiliary on Sun. Feb. 2, 1913. Other officers elected were:- Mrs. J. Jacobs, 1st vice-pres.; Mrs. Ascher Pierce, 2nd vice-pres.; Mrs. H. Hart, 3rd vice-pres.; Mrs. H.H. Livingstone, treas.; Mrs. J. Elkin, sec.; Mesdames L. Abinovitch, A.Z. Cohen, I. Cohen, A. Goldner, A. Harris, M.J. Heillig, H. Levy, J. Manolson, Ch. Michaels, P. Ogulnick, D. Shapiro, I. Sourkes, H. Vineberg, M. Vineberg and A. Zigmond (7 Feb. 1913, 16, 9)

HIRSCH, Miss Essie, was elected president of the Hebrew Young Ladies' Sewing Society at the nineteenth annual meeting on Sun. Nov. 2, 1913. Other officers elected were:- Miss Gertie Silverman, vice-pres.; Miss Rae Tannebaum, treas.; Mrs. Hannah Tannebaum, sec.; Mesdames M.J. Heillig, Henry Saxe, and the Misses B. Kellert, Etta Levine, A. Levinson and Annie Samuel, committee (7 Nov. 1913, 16, 48)

HIRSCH, Miss, is the guest of Mrs. Archie Jacobs, at Val Morin (6 Aug. 1909, 12, 34)

HIRSCH, Miss Sophie, has returned from five weeks in New York (15 July 1910, 13, 35)

HIRSCH, Mr. and Mrs J., Miss Hirsch, Mrs. I. Levinson, Miss Sara Levinson, J. Levinson, Jr., Benjamin W. Jacobs, Miss Roslyn Lewis, Louis Lewis, J. Felix Mendelssohn, G.W. Jacobs, B. Gardner, Mr. and Mrs. M. Michaelson, Mr. and Mrs. G. Lewis, J.N. Jacobs, Miss Sara Michaelson, B. Kortosk are spending the week-end at the hotel in Caledonia Springs (23 July 1909, 12, 32)

HIRSCH, Mr. and Mrs. I., Bishop St., are at Caledonia Springs for a few weeks (2 July 1909, 12, 29)

HIRSCH, Mr. and Mrs. Jacob, Bishop St., have gone to Caledonia Springs, Ont., for a week (1 July 1910, 13, 33)

HIRSCH, Mr. and Mrs. M., "Sherbrooke", are in New York (12 March 1909, 12, 13)

HIRSCH, Mr. and Mrs. M. and Master Percy Hirsch are at Old Orchard Beach (22 July 1910, 13, 36)

HIRSCH, Mr. and Mrs. M., have gone to New York en route to Cuba (3 March 1911, 14, 16)

HIRSCH, Mr. and Mrs. Michael, "The Sherbrooke", have gone to Cuba via New York (23 Sept. 1910, 13, 45)

HIRSCH, Mr. and Mrs. Michael, are spending the week in New York (4 Feb. 1910, 13, 12)

HIRSCH, Mr. and Mrs. Michael, gave a supper Thurs. evening, March 27, 1912. Guests included Leon Kofman, Arthur Hirsch and the Misses Ernestine Jacobs and Miriam Tannenbaum (5 April 1912, 15, 21)

HIRSCH, Mr. and Mrs. Michael, returned from four weeks vacation in Cuba (14 Nov. 1913, 16, 49)

HIRSCH, Mrs. J. and Miss Essie Hirsch, have left for Old Orchard (14 July 1911, 14, 35)

HIRSCH, Mrs. M., "The Sherbrooke", has returned from New York, accompanied by Mrs. Cohen who will be her guest (11 Nov. 1910, 13, 52)

HIRSCH, Mrs. M.J., is spending a month in New York (7 March 1913, 16, 13)

HIRSCH, Mrs. Michael, is spending a few weeks in New York (22 Oct. 1909, 12, 45)

HIRSCH, Mrs. W., has returned from New York and Atlantic City (16 April 1909, 12, 18)

HIRSCH, Robert, has been appointed a Justice of the Peace by the provincial government, for the city and district of Montreal (5 March 1909, 12, 12)

HIRSCH, the Misses, Bishop St., gave a "kitchen shower" for Miss Lily Kellert who will be married next week. Miss Z. Blout won a prize. Out-of-town guests present were:- Mrs. B. Zeamen, Hartford; Mrs. Bilsky, Cobalt; and Miss Myers, Syracuse (29 Oct. 1909, 12, 46)

HIRSCHFELDER, Miss Maude, has returned to Toronto after spending six months in New York and Philadelphia (24 Sept. 1909, 12, 41)

HIRSCHMAN, Rev. and Mrs. A.N., of Detroit, spent a day in Montreal, the guests of Mr. and Mrs. Leon Goldman, Esplanade Ave., en route for Ste. Agathe (9 July 1909, 12, 30)

HIRSCOVITCH, Mr. and Mrs., gave a birthday party in honor of their daughter, Fannie, on Sun. March 2, 1913. Refreshments were served by Mrs. A. Higger and Miss L. Hirscovitch. Piano selections were played by H. Pinsler and Miss E. Harris. Out-of-town guests were Miss Goldie David, of Boston and F. Lewis, of Winnipeg (14 March 1913, 16, 14)

HIRSHBERG, J.B., presented H.J. Livinson with the William S. Hyman Memorial Tablet at the unveiling held Sun. Nov. 12, 1911 in the Maccabean Circle room in the Royal Arcanium Chambers (17 Nov. 1911, 15, 1)

HIRSHBERG, Mrs. H. and Miss Lottie Hirshberg, of Rochester, N.Y., are guests of Mrs. M. Lehrer and H. Albert, 446 Mt. Stephen Ave. (23 Feb. 1912, 15, 15)

HIRSHFIELD, S.E., of New York, was a guest at the St. Lawrence Hall (9 July 1909, 12, 30)

HOFFMAN, I. has returned home to Amherst after visiting his sons in the city (24 Nov. 1911, 15, 2)

HOFFMAN, I., of Amherst, N.S., is the guest of Mr. and Mrs. T. Hoffman, St. Joseph Blvd., for a week (10 Nov. 1911, 14, 52)

HOFFMAN, Jack, of Charlottetown, P.E.I., is in Montreal for a few days (4 Aug. 1911, 14, 38)

HOFFMAN, Jack, of Charlottetown, was in Montreal the past week (5 Sept. 1913, 16, 39)

HOFFMAN, Jack, returned home to Charlottetown, P.E.I., after visiting Mr. and Mrs. M. Hoffman, St. Joseph Blvd. (2 Aug. 1912, 15, 34)

HOFFMAN, M.B., of Amherst, N.S., was in Montreal this week (8 March 1912, 15, 17)

HOFFMAN, Master Nathan and Miss Hazel Hoffman are spending the summer with their grandparents, Mr. and Mrs. Kaplan, Yarmouth, N.S. (4 July 1913, 16, 30)

HOFFMAN, Miss Bessie, has returned home to Amherst after visiting Mr. and Mrs. Hoffman, St. Joseph Blvd. (16 June 1911, 14, 31)

HOFFMAN, Miss Bessie, of Amherst, is visiting Mrs. Ginsberg, St. Joseph Blvd. for a few weeks (24 Feb. 1911, 14, 15)

HOFFMAN, Miss Bessie, of Amherst, is the guest of her brother, M. Hoffman, St. Joseph Blvd. (10 March 1911, 14, 17)

HOFFMAN, Miss Ida, of Amherst, N.S., is visiting her sister-in-law, Mrs. T. Hoffman, St. Joseph Blvd. (5 Jan. 1912, 15, 8)

HOFFMAN, Miss P., was elected president of the newly formed Young Ladies' Zionist Society last Sun. aft. in the Baron de Hirsch Institute. Other officers elected were:- Miss L. Ressler, vice-pres.; Miss B. Rosenthal, sec.; and Miss C. Fenster, treas. (1 June 1911, 14, 29)

HOFFMAN, Miss P.B., is principal of the Chevra Kadisha Sunday School. Other staff members are:- A.J. Livinson (superintendent), M. Block, H. Baum, S. Deutsch and the Misses F. Flanders, R. Gallay, A. Ginsberg, L. Klein, R. Klein, P. Marks, M. Moshovitch (secretary) and S. Sloves (13 Dec. 1912, 16, 1)

HOFFMAN, Miss Pauline, is at Lake Placid, N.Y., for a few weeks (8 Aug. 1913, 16, 35)

HOFFMAN, Miss R., of Chicago, is visiting friends in Toronto and Kingston (5 Aug. 1910, 13, 38)

HOFFMAN, Miss, who has been visiting her brother in Winnipeg, passed through Montreal en route to her home in Amherst, N.S. (15 Jan. 1909, 12, 5)

HOFFMAN, Mr. and Mrs. Morris and sons, St. Joseph Blvd., left on a two months' trip to Saskatoon and will stop over in Winnipeg to visit relatives (18 July 1913, 16, 32)

HOFFMAN, Mr. and Mrs. T., St. Joseph Blvd., celebrated their crystal wedding anniversary at a party Sun. evening, Sept. 22, 1912 (2 Oct. 1912, 15, 43)

HOFFMAN, Mrs. M. and family, St. Joseph Blvd., are visiting her parents, Mr. and Mrs. I. Caplan (4 Aug. 1911, 14, 38)

HOFFMAN, Mrs. S., is visiting her parents, Mr. and Mrs. J. Kaplan, in Yarmouth, N.S. (18 July 1913, 16, 32)

HOFFMAN, Mrs. S., St. Joseph Blvd. E., has recovered from her recent operation (14 June 1912, 15, 27)

HOFFMAN, Mrs. T. and children have returned from Boston where Mrs. Hoffman attended her brother's wedding (17 March 1911, 14, 18)

HOFFMAN, Mrs. T., St. Joseph Blvd., was in Boston (8 Dec. 1911, 15, 4)

HOFFMAN, Mrs. T., St. Joseph Blvd., entertained in honor of her sister, Miss Fannie Kaplan, of Yarmouth, N.S. (7 March 1913, 16, 13)

HOFFMAN, Oscar, little son of Mr. and Mrs. Morris Hoffman, St. Joseph Blvd., has recovered from his recent appendicitis operation (19 April 1912, 15, 23)

HOFFMAN, T. and son have returned from a visit to their parents in Amherst (12 May 1911, 14, 26)

Tel. Uptown 431

H. Hoichberg & Co.

STOCK BROKERS

Stocks, Bonds, Grains, Provisions and Cotton.

BLUMENTHAL BLDG.

HOLDENGRABER, Mr. and Mrs. Adolph, 1690a St. Urbain St., gave a Bar Mitzvah party on Sun. evening, Nov. 9, 1913, in honor of their son Sol. Those assisting were:- S. Kerner, Mrs. D. Fels, Master Gittleson and the Bar Mitzvah boy (14 Nov. 1913, 16, 49)

HOLDENGRABER, Mrs. S. and daughter, Miss Millie Hubert, of Bathurst, N.B., are visiting Montreal (1 Oct. 1913, 16, 42-43)

HOLOFCENER, I.D., of Ottawa, is in the Montreal General Hospital (2 April 1909, 12, 16)

HOLOFCENER, I.D., of Ottawa, was in Montreal during the week (19 Aug. 1910, 13, 40)

HOLOFCENER, Mrs., 5 Mark St., gave a linen shower Wed. Dec. 25, 1912 in honor of Miss Rose Harris who will be married to B. White on Tues. Jan. 7, 1913 (27 Dec. 1912, 16, 3)

HOLSTEIN, Louis, is president of a new organization founded for the purpose of establishing a Jewish orphanage in Montreal (8 April 1910, 13, 21)

HOLSTEIN, Louis, was in Ottawa for a few days this week (18 March 1910, 13, 18)

HONSBERGER, G., of Toronto, is in Montreal (20 Aug. 1909, 12, 36)

HORNSTEIN, Miss K.E., president of the Montreal Hebrew Day Nursery Auxiliary, chaired the first general meeting on Thurs. Sept. 18, 1913 at 8 p.m. Other officers are:- Miss J. Sheifer, vice-pres.; Miss S.A. Ressler, rec. and corr. sec.; Miss M.D. Brotman, fin. sec.; Miss R.C. Brotman, treas.; Misses A. Pinsler and F. Yaphe, trustees; Misses R. Harris and M. Jurist, finance comm. The package party will be held at the home of Mrs. H. Lonn, 237 Esplanade Ave. on Oct. 12 at 8 p.m. Miss S.A. Ressler, Esplanade Ave., is accepting membership applications (1 Oct. 1913, 16, 42-43)

HORNSTEIN, Misses K.E., M. Jurist, A. Pinsler and J. Sheifer were in charge of arrangements for the Hebrew Sheltering and Orphan Home picnic on Sun. (22 Aug. 1913, 16, 37)

HORSFALL, H., resigned his position as manager of the Baron de Hirsch Institute and is now manager of the Canadian Commitee of the Jewish Colonization Association. "It may interest our readers to know that Mr. Horsfall is one of those to whom has not belonged the 'good fortune' (which would also have been ours) of being born Jews. For by his complete identification with all our interests, his profound sympathy with the poor and oppressed Jewish immigrants, in handling whom he has shown the utmost tact and fellow-feeling, he has created among our community an abiding impression that he is one of those few 'Goyim' who possess a real Jewish heart." (16 Jan. 1914, 17, 6)

HORWITZ, Mrs. I., returned home to Toronto(after spending five weeks with her sister, Mrs. David Rasminsky, Mance St. (21 Feb. 1913, 16, 11)

HYAMS, H., is in Quebec City on business (25 Nov. 1910, 14, 2)

HYAMS, Joseph, of Boston, was in Montreal for a short visit (1 April 1910, 13, 20)

HYAMS, Mr. and Mrs. S., Hutchison St., have left for Europe aboard the S.S. Laurentic (12 Aug. 1910, 13, 39)

HYAMS, Mr. and Mrs. Samuel, 95 Hutchison St., have returned from New York (7 May 1909, 12, 21)

HYMAN, H., conducted the High Holy Day services at the Mount Sinai Sanatorium (22 Oct. 1913, 16, 46)

HYMAN, H., of Gaspé, is spending the Passover holidays with his family in Montreal (5 April 1912, 15, 21)

HYMAN, H.B., of Montreal, was in Quebec City during the week and stayed at the Chateau Frontenac (21 May 1909, 12, 23)

HYMAN, Isaac and Horatio, of Gaspé, Que., are in Montreal (3 April 1914, 17, 14)

HYMAN, Louis, of the Ottawa YMHA was a guest of the Montreal YMHA last weekend (20 Sept. 1912, 15, 41)

HYMAN, Miss Muriel, of Cleveland, is visiting her aunt, Mrs. M.A. Vineberg, Tupper St. (1 April 1910, 13, 20)

HYMAN, Miss, of St. Matthews, South Carolina, is visiting her grandmother, Mrs. Levine, St. Joseph Blvd. (22 July 1910, 13, 36)

HYMAN, Misses Florence and Effie, have returned from Gaspé (4 Nov. 1910, 13, 51)

HYMAN, Mr. and Mrs. and family, Mansfield St., will leave next week for Gaspé where they will spend the summer (25 June 1909, 12, 28)

HYMAN, Mr. and Mrs. and the Misses Hyman, of Cleveland, are spending Passover with Mrs. Hyman's sister, Mrs. M.A. Vineberg (9 April 1909, 12, 17)

HYMAN, Mr. and Mrs. H. and family, Tupper

St., sailed on the S.S. Cascapedia for Gaspé where they will spend the summer (23 June 1911, 14, 32)

HYMAN, Mr. and Mrs. Isaac and family are at their summer residence in Gaspé, Que. (23 June 1911, 14, 32)

HYMAN, Mrs. Isaac and family, Elm Ave., left for Gaspé where they will spend the summer (2 July 1909, 12, 29)

HYMAN, Mrs., Bishop St., is visiting her daughter, Mrs. William Goldstein, in Toronto (12 May 1911, 14, 26)

HYMAN, Mrs. H. and family, accompanied by Miss Jessie Goldstein, leave June 20, 1910 to spend the summer at Gaspé (17 June 1910, 13, 31)

HYMAN, Mrs. H., was at Lakeside the past week (10 June 1910, 13, 30)

HYMAN, Mrs. H.J. and Miss Margery Hyman, Tupper St., Westmount, are in New York for a brief visit (22 Oct. 1913, 1913, 16, 46)

HYMAN, Mrs. Horatio and family sailed on June 29, 1909 for their summer residence at Gaspé (2 July 1909, 12, 29)

HYMAN, Mrs. I.E. and Miss Hyman, accompanied by her daughter, Mrs. Max Kubelik and son, will spend the summer at Fox River, Que. (4 July 1913, 16, 30)

HYMAN, Mrs. I.E., Elm Ave., entertained the Primrose Club at a party, last Wed. (19 Feb. 1909, 12, 10)

HYMAN, Mrs. Isaac and family, Elm Ave., have gone to the Gaspé for the summer (24 June 1910, 13, 32)

HYMAN, Mrs. Isaac, Elm Ave., has gone to London, England for two months (4 Nov. 1910, 13, 51)

HYMAN, Mrs. J. and daughter, Tupper St., are in New York (15 Dec. 1911, 15, 5)

HYMAN, Nathan, who was in Montreal for a few days has returned to Gaspé (22 Jan. 1909, 12, 6)

HYMAN, Willie, has gone to the Gaspé for the summer (10 June 1910, 13, 30)

HYMANS, Mr. and Mrs. S., Hutchison St., have gone to Europe for three months (22 Aug. 1913, 16, 37)

ISAACS, B., stayed at the Breslin Hotel, while in New York (9 Feb. 1912, 15, 13)

ISAACS, Benjamin, sails tomorrow on the S.S. Megantic on a business trip to Europe (22 July 1910, 13, 36)

ISAACS, Henry, of New York, is visiting his aunt, Mrs. Joseph Kellert, Union Ave. (25 April 1913, 16, 20)

ISAACS, John, is spending the week in Montreal (11 July 1913, 16, 31)

ISAACS, M., of Philadelphia, was in Montreal, en route for the Provinces (25 Oct. 1910, 13, 50)

ISAACS, M.R., of Philadelphia, Pa., was a guest at the Windsor Hotel (16 June 1911, 14, 31)

ISAACS, M.R., of Philadelphia, stayed at the Windsor Hotel while in Montreal (14 March 1913, 16, 14)

ISAACS, M.R., of Philadelphia, was a guest at the Windsor Hotel (11 June 1909, 12, 26)

ISAACS, M.R., of Philadelphia, was a guest at the Windsor Hotel (26 Nov. 1909, 13, 2)

ISAACS, Miss R. Irene, of St. John, N.B., left for New York, where she will visit her brother, Lyle Isaacs, 2415 Clarendon Rd., Brooklyn (9 Jan. 1914, 17, 5)

ISAACS, Miss Ruby, of St. John, N.B., is the guest of Mrs. Z. Davis for a few weeks (31 Dec. 1909, 13, 7)

ISAACS, Miss Ruby, of St. John, N.B., has returned home after spending the past two months here (25 Feb. 1910, 13, 15)

ISAACS, Mr. and Mrs. M.R., of Philadelphia, were registered at the Windsor Hotel while in Montreal (17 Feb. 1911, 14, 14)

ISAACS, Mrs. A., of St. John, N.B., is the guest of her daughter, Mrs. I.M. Rubinovich, Sherbrooke St., Westmount (3 Feb. 1911, 14, 12)

ISAACS, Mrs., accompanied by her niece, Miss Estelle Heller, of Syracuse, is visiting Mrs. J. Benowick, Esplanade Ave. (9 July 1909, 12, 30)

ISAACS, Mrs. J., who visited her daughter, Mrs. I. Rubinovitch, 4480 Sherbrooke St. W., left for Chicago en route to California where she will spend the winter (5 Dec. 1913, 16, 52)

ISAACS, Mrs. L., is the guest of her sister, Mrs. Rubinovitch, Sherbrooke St. W., Westmount (8 Dec. 1911, 15, 4)

ISADORE, J. and Dr. Sol. Rosengarten, of Detroit, Mich., stayed at the Ritz-Carlton Hotel while in Montreal (15 Aug. 1913, 16, 36)

ISRAEL, Mrs. and family, of Charleston, S.C., are visiting her sister, Mrs. S.E. Lichtenhein, at Beaurepaire, Que. (4 July 1913, 16, 30)

ISRAEL, Mrs., of Charleston, S.C., is visiting her sister, Mrs. S.E. Lichtenhein, Peel St. (10 Nov. 1911, 14, 52)

ISRAEL, Mrs., who was the guest of her sister, Mrs. S.E. Lichtenhein, has returned home to Charleston, accompanied by Miss Emma Levine, who will spend a few months with her (1 Dec. 1911, 15, 3)

ISSENMAN, A., has been hired as the YMHA physical instructor (16 April 1909, 12, 18)

ISSENSTADT, C., S. and M. Rubinowitz contributed to the Zionist Land Fund. Other contributions were made in honor of the Misses Belle Ginsburg, Jane Rost, Ida Siegler and Rose Vineberg (11 July 1913, 16, 31)

ISSENSTEIN, Miss Pauline, of New York, is the guest of Rabbi and Mrs. Herman Abramowitz, Stanley St. (8 Dec. 1911, 15, 4)

JACKSON, Mr. and Mrs. A.E., leave shortly to spend the summer in Belgium (1 June 1911, 14, 29)

JACKSON, Mr. and Mrs. A.H. and family took up their summer residence at Woodlands yesterday (11 June 1909, 12, 26)

JACKSON, Mr. and Mrs. A.H., are spending the summer at Woodlands (8 July 1910, 13, 34)

JACKSON, Mrs. A.H., sailed on the S.S. Victorian for Europe (28 July 1911, 14, 37)

JACKSON, Mrs. A.H., writing from Bellevue, Que., sent in eight dollars to the Hebrew Children's Fresh Air Fund. Five dollars was donated by Mrs. H. Solomon, Richmond Square, Montreal, and three dollars by Masters Philip and Harold Jackson, of Bellevue (1 Aug. 1913, 16, 34)

JACOBI, Mrs. and children, of Chicago, are spending the summer with Mrs. Samuel Myers, in Ottawa (2 July 1909, 12, 29)

JACOBS, Jack and his sisters, the Misses Jacobs left for Peaks Island, Maine, for a few weeks (16 July 1909, 12, 31)

JACOBS, A.W., won first prize in the Harness Horse Class, with "Grand Duke" at the Horse Show last night. Mortimer B. Davis was also a prize winner (14 May 1909, 12, 22)

JACOBS, B.W. and the Misses Jacobs, McGill College Ave., have gone by boat to Cleveland for a few weeks (25 July 1911, 14, 36)

JACOBS, Ben W., has returned from Val Morin, Que. (23 Aug. 1912, 15, 37)

JACOBS, Benjamin, went to New York last night for a ten days' holiday (22 Oct. 1909, 12, 45)

JACOBS, D., of New York, was in Montreal the past week (30 Dec. 1910, 14, 7)

JACOBS, E.J., of Jamaica, is on a business trip and is registered at the Queen's Hotel (1 Oct. 1909, 12, 42)

JACOBS, E.W. and Miss Sarah Jacobs have returned from Atlantic City (5 May 1911, 14, 25)

JACOBS, E.W., has gone on a trip to New York (2 Sept. 1910, 13, 42)

JACOBS, E.W., has gone on a short trip to New York (18 Nov. 1910, 14, 1)

M. ITCOVECI,

Carpenter, Joiner and Cabinet Maker, Builder and Contractor.

Store Fixtures, Office Partitions put up.   Cutting Tables made to order.
All kinds of Jobs and Repairing Neatly Done.

615-617 ST. JAMES ST. WEST, MONTREAL

ESTIMATES GIVEN AT LOWEST PRICES

JACOBS, E.W., is on a visit to Toronto (21 May, 1909, 12, 23)

JACOBS, E.W., left for New York on Wed. night (25 June 1909, 12, 28)

JACOBS, Eli and Miss Libbie Jacobs are in New York (27 Dec. 1912, 16, 3)

JACOBS, Harry, has returned from ten days in New York (29 Dec. 1911, 15, 7)

JACOBS, Henry, and Mesdames M. Cohen, M. Dobrofsky and Finestone gave a bouquet of flowers to Mr. and Mrs. M.A. Silverman, Mount Royal Ave., on the occasion of the Brith Milah of their infant son. Among those present were:- S. Bernstein, M. Fox, A. Slatkin, L. Wener, Mr. Blumberg, Mr. Holdengraber, Mr. and Mrs. L. Kleinberg, and Mr. and Mrs. D. Rasminsky (14 March 1913, 16, 14)

JACOBS, I., has left for the Porcupine district (7 July 1911, 14, 34)

JACOBS, I.W., of the Bibliophile Press, London Eng., passed through Montreal on Mon., en route to Winnipeg to visit his daughter, Mrs. Arakie Cohen and Edmonton to visit his son (31 Dec. 1909, 13, 7)

JACOBS, J.A., has returned from New York (31 March 1911, 14, 20)

JACOBS, J.A., has returned from New York (20 March 1914, 17, 12)

JACOBS, J.A., spent a few days in Quebec City this week (19 Feb. 1909, 12, 10)

JACOBS, J.H., sailed on the S.S. Adriatic. He will be abroad for several months (16 Jan. 1914, 17, 6)

JACOBS, J.L., is back in town from his trip to England (8 Jan. 1909, 12, 4)

JACOBS, J.W. and A.W. Jacobs are in Toronto for a week (29 Aug. 1913, 16, 38)

JACOBS, J.W., has recovered from his recent illness (7 Oct. 1910, 13, 47)

JACOBS, J.W., of London, England, who has been visiting his daughter, Mrs. Arakie Cohen, in Winnipeg, is in Montreal. He leaves for New York on Mon., en route home (4 Feb. 1910, 13, 12)

JACOBS, Jacob A., chaired the presentation ceremony for Lyon Cohen, past president of the Baron de Hirsch Institute, on Sun. aft. Dec. 22, 1912 (27 Dec. 1912, 16, 3)

JACOBS, Joseph H. and R.H. Blumenthal, have gone on a trip to the southern U.S. (29 Dec. 1911, 15, 7)

JACOBS, L., Jacob Metten, and Mr. and Mrs. A. Morris were among the passengers on the S.S. Sicilian which arrived in Montreal last Tues. (7 May 1909, 12, 21)

JACOBS, Lionel, Law '10, was elected president of the Progressive Literary and Debating Circle at its first meeting last Sun. Other officers elected were:- N. Mendelsohn, Science '13, vice-pres.; L. Marcuse, Law '13, sec. treas.; L. Benjamin and B.R. Seigel, committee (30 April 1909, 12, 20)

JACOBS, Lyon, has returned from holidays in Ste. Agathe (9 Sept. 1910, 13, 43)

JACOBS, Lyon W. and Maurice Tetreau, McGill University law graduates, have formed a law partnership with offices in the Eagle Bldg., St. Lawrence Blvd. (17 Jan. 1913, 16, 6)

JACOBS, Lyon W., was elected president of the Progressive Literary and Debating Circle at a meeting on Sun. March 17, 1910. Other officers elected were:- Lyon Cohen, hon. pres.; H.L. Colle, 1st vice-pres.; Miss R. Aronson, 2nd vice-pres.; N. Mendelsohn, sec.; Miss S. De La Penha, treas.; Miss S. Solomon, B.R. Segal, Dr. C.J. Gross, Dr. S.F. Stein, council; Maxwell Lightstone, sergeant-at-arms (6 May 1910, 13, 25)

JACOBS, Miss, Dorchester St. W., gave a linen shower in honor of Miss Ray Silverston who will be married to Mr. Marks, of Winnipeg, in April, 1914 (13 March 1914, 17, 11)

JACOBS, Miss Ernestine, Crescent St., has gone to visit her relatives, Mr. and Mrs. Dave Jacobs, in New York for several weeks (10 Feb. 1911, 14, 13)

JACOBS, Miss I., has gone to New York to spend Passover with her aunt, Mrs. Silverstein (14 April 1911, 14, 22)

JACOBS, Miss Lena, Crescent St., left for Toronto where she will be the guest of Rabbi and Mrs. S. Jacobs (2 Jan. 1914, 17, 4)

JACOBS, Miss Lena, has returned from Brantford, Ont., where she spent a few weeks (14 Jan. 1910, 13, 9)

JACOBS, Miss Lena, is visiting her aunt, Mrs. Joseph Mendels, in Perth, Ont. (15 July 1910, 13, 35)

JACOBS, Miss Lena, is visiting her aunt, Mrs. Joseph Mendels, in Perth, Ont. for a few weeks (11 Aug. 1911, 14, 39)

JACOBS, Miss Libbie leaves shortly for San Francisco where she will spend several months with her uncle, A. Aronson (24 Dec. 1909, 13, 6)

JACOBS, Miss Libbie, left for San Francisco last Mon. evening where she will stay with her uncle and aunt for several months. Miss Miriam Jacobs, who accompanied her sister to Chicago, has returned home (14 Jan. 1910, 13, 9)

JACOBS, Miss Lillian, of Detroit, is the guest of her cousins, Mr. and Mrs. J.A. Jacobs, at Rougemont, Que. (29 Aug. 1913, 16, 38)

JACOBS, Miss, of New York, is visiting her aunt, Mrs. N. Michaels, Luke St. Apts. (25 July 1913, 16, 33)

JACOBS, Miss P. and Mr. and Mrs. J. Foss, of New York, are guests of Mrs. R. Lemlein, St. Catherine St. W. (19 Sept. 1913, 16, 41)

JACOBS, Miss Sarah, has returned from a week's visit to New York (8 Jan. 1909, 12, 4)

JACOBS, Miss Tina and Miss Sophie Hirsch are at Val Morin for a few weeks (8 Aug. 1913, 16, 35)

JACOBS, Misses Fanny and Miriam, Dorchester St., left for the U.S. Northeast (18 July 1913, 16, 32)

JACOBS, Misses Mary and Libbie, are in Atlantic City for a month (18 July 1913, 16, 32)

JACOBS, Misses, McGill College Ave., have gone to Peak's Island, Maine, for the summer (15 July 1910, 13, 35)

JACOBS, Misses, McGill College Ave., have returned from Peak's Island, Me., where they spent the summer (19 Aug. 1910, 13, 40)

JACOBS, Mr. and Mrs. A., Dorchester St. W., were guests of Mrs. S.A. Jacobs, St. Dorothee, Que. (28 July 1911, 14, 37)

JACOBS, Mr. and Mrs. Eli, have returned from New York where they attended their cousin's wedding (23 Dec. 1910, 14, 6)

JACOBS, Mr. and Mrs. Harry, hosted a Progress Club meeting Thurs. evening, Feb. 22, 1912 (8 March 1912, 14, 17)

JACOBS, Mr. and Mrs. J.A., and J. Samenhof have gone to New York (26 Feb. 1909, 12, 11)

JACOBS, Mr. and Mrs. J.A., and Messrs. B. Kortosk, S.W. Jacobs, E.W. Jacobs, L. Lewis and J. Samenhoff were at Caledonia Springs over the weekend (11 June 1909, 12, 26)

JACOBS, Mr. and Mrs. J.A. and family and maid, are visiting New York and Atlantic City (16 Sept. 1910, 13, 44)

JACOBS, Mr. and Mrs. J.A., are at their summer home in Beaurepaire for the season (11 June 1909, 12, 26)

JACOBS, Mr. and Mrs. J.A. are among the visiting governors at the General Hospital this week (11 June 1909, 12, 26)

JACOBS, Mr. and Mrs. J.A., escaped severe injury as a result of an automobile collision last Sun. evening. Apart from some damage to the car, no one was hurt (15 Sept. 1909, 12, 40)

JACOBS, Mr. and Mrs. J.A., have gone to New York and Atlanic City on a short trip (22 Oct. 1909, 12, 45)

JACOBS, Mr. and Mrs. J.A., have returned from New York and Atlantic City (5 Nov. 1909, 12, 47)

JACOBS, Mr. and Mrs. J.A., left for Cobalt for a few days (16 July 1909, 12, 31)

JACOBS, Mr. and Mrs. L.H. and family are guests at the Hotel Grand, Chambly (9 July 1909, 12, 30)

JACOBS, Mr. and Mrs. L.H. and family are spending the summer at Baker's Hotel, Gaspé Basin, Que. (23 June 1911, 14, 32)

JACOBS, Mr. and Mrs. Lyon W., Henri Julien Ave., were tendered a surprise party at their home on Sun. evening to mark their recent marriage. Maxwell Lightstone was one of the toastmasters (15 Nov. 1912, 15, 49)

JACOBS, Mr. and Mrs. Lyon W., Henri Julien Ave., and Mrs. Jacobs' mother, Mrs. Florin, have gone to New York to attend the engagement reception of Mrs. Jacobs' uncle, Phil Florin (27 Dec. 1912, 16, 3)

JACOBS, Mr. and Mrs. Max and Master Arthur Jacobs, Laval Ave., have returned from Caledonia Springs, Ont. (9 Sept. 1910, 13, 43)

JACOBS, Mr. and Mrs. Max and Master Arthur, Parc Lafontaine Ave., are spending the holidays in Providence, R.I. (25 April 1913, 16, 20)

JACOBS, Mr., of Detroit, is visiting his daughter, Mrs. L. Vineberg, Mansfield St. (5 Aug. 1910, 13, 38)

JACOBS, Mrs. A., has returned from visiting her daughter, Mrs. Joseph Rosenthal, in Toronto (18 March 1910, 13, 18)

JACOBS, Mrs. A., Mansfield St., is visiting her daughter, Mrs. Rosenthal, in Toronto (18 Feb. 1910, 13, 14)

JACOBS, Mrs. Abraham, Dorchester St. W., returned from Toronto where she visited her daughter, Mrs. Rosenthal (7 Feb. 1913, 16, 9)

JACOBS, Mrs. Abraham, has presented a torah to

the Montreal Hebrew Free School (Talmud Torah) (14 April 1911, 14, 22)

JACOBS, Mrs. Al. and Master Bernard Jacobs, Labelle St., returned from St. Gabriel de Brandon (22 Aug. 1913, 16, 37)

JACOBS, Mrs. Archie and daughter have returned from Perth, Ont. where they were guests of Mrs. Joseph Mendels (2 Sept. 1910, 13, 42)

JACOBS, Mrs. Archie, Miss Tena Jacobs and Master Melvin Jacobs are spending the summer at Val Morin, Que. (9 July 1909, 12, 30)

JACOBS, Mrs. Archie, spent the past week in Perth, the guest of Mrs. J.H. Mendels (14 Jan. 1910, 13, 9)

JACOBS, Mrs. H. and her daughter, Mrs. L.S. Margolese were passengers on the S.S. Megantic which sailed June 7, 1912 (14 June 1912, 15, 27)

JACOBS, Mrs. J.A. and family have left for Bluff Point, Lake Champlain, N.Y. (30 June 1911, 14, 33)

JACOBS, Mrs. J.A. and Mrs. D.S. Friedman have returned home from New York and Atlantic City. Mr. Jacobs had to remain in New York on business (30 April 1909, 12, 20)

JACOBS, Mrs. Joseph and Master Sol Jacobs, Lincoln Ave., spent the week at Caledonia Springs, Ont. (14 July 1911, 14, 35)

JACOBS, Mrs. Joseph and Master Sollie Jacobs, Lincoln Ave., sail aboard the S.S. Lake Megantic on June 24, 1910 for London where they will be the guests of Mrs. Jacobs' mother (10 June 1910, 13, 30)

JACOBS, Mrs. Joseph and Master Solly Jacobs, Lincoln Ave., have returned from abroad. Miss Lederer, Mrs. Jacobs' sister, accompanied her and will spend a few months in Montreal (16 Sept. 1910, 13, 44)

JACOBS, Mrs. L.N. and family, Wood Ave., will spend the summer at Portland, Ont. (1 July 1910, 13, 33)

JACOBS, Mrs. M., of Boston, is the guest of Mrs. Anna Rost (17 June 1910, 13, 31)

JACOBS, Mrs. Max, 206 Laval Ave., has gone to Boston for a month (7 July 1911, 14, 34)

JACOBS, Mrs. Max and Master Arthur Jacobs, Parc Lafontaine, are visiting Mrs. Rosenberg in Providence, R.I. (26 Dec. 1913, 17, 3)

JACOBS, Mrs. Max and son, 206 Laval Ave., are in Boston for two weeks (29 Dec. 1911, 15, 7)

JACOBS, Mrs. Max and son, Arthur S. Jacobs, are in Boston and Providence for two weeks (27 Dec. 1912, 16, 3)

JACOBS, Mrs. Max, has gone to North Attleboro, Mass. for a few weeks to visit relatives (22 April, 1910, 13, 23)

JACOBS, Mrs. Max, is spending a few weeks with her parents, Mr. and Mrs. Rosenberg, in North Attleboro, Mass. (14 Jan. 1910, 13, 9)

JACOBS, Mrs. Morris, of New York, is spending the summer with her daughter, Mrs. N. Michaels, Elm Ave. (2 July 1909, 12, 29)

JACOBS, Mrs., of New York, is visiting her daughter, Mrs. A.E. Morris, Westmount Ave. (6 Aug. 1909, 12 34)

JACOBS, Mrs. Rose and Jack Levi were registered at the Chateau Frontenac, Quebec City, last week, arriving from there on the S.S. Corsican with Miss Amelia Cooper, who was being chaparoned by Mrs. Jacobs, until her marriage to Alfred Myers, on July 4, 1909 (16 July 1909, 12, 31)

JACOBS, Mrs. Rose, was the guest of honor at her eighty-fifth birthday celebration, on Mon. Jan. 17, 1910, held at the Montefiore Club. The party for sixty-two was given by her sons, Morris, John and Abraham Michaels and her son-in-law, L.S. Margolese. J. Michaels acted as toastmaster and the speakers included Morris, Abraham and Victor Michaels, Rabbi Herman Abramowitz, C.L. Friedman, Jack Levi, Michael Hirsch, M. Goldstein, K.C., A.E. Myers, J. Goldstein and B. Marcus. "Mrs. Rose Jacobs, replied to the many speeches laudatory of herself in a very feeling and able manner, which proved that she was fully entitled to the name given to her in the toast-list, "Ye Younge Ladye of ye Evente"." (21 Jan. 1910, 13, 10)

JACOBS, Mrs. Rose, Westmount Ave., gave a dinner Wed. evening, Feb. 10, 1909, to celebrate the birthday of Jack Levi (12 Feb. 1909, 12, 9)

JACOBS, Mrs. S.A. and daughter, accompanied by Miss Louise Silverman, have gone to Quebec City to meet Mr. Jacobs, who is returning from a three months' stay abroad (10 June 1910, 13, 30)

JACOBS, Mrs. S.A. and little daughter are at Boucherville, Que. for a few weeks (16 July 1909, 12, 31)

JACOBS, Mrs. S.A., Greene Ave., gave an aft. tea, Tues. Dec. 31, 1912 in honor of her guest, Miss Bertha Phillips, of Cornwall, Ont. Guests included:- the Misses Irene Blumenthal, Eva and Edith Harris, May Oliver, Yetta and Edith Silver and Ruth Workman (3 Jan. 1913, 16, 4)

JACOBS, Mrs. Solomon, is recovering from her illness (30 April 1909, 12, 20)

JACOBS, R., is in New York (11 Oct. 1912, 15, 44)

JACOBS, R.A., has returned from a three months' trip abroad (7 April 1911, 14, 21)

JACOBS, R.F., of New York, stayed at the Corona Hotel (5 March 1909, 12, 12)

JACOBS, Rabbi S., of Toronto, is in England on holiday and is expected to attend the Zionist Congress in Basle next month (28 July 1911, 14, 37)

JACOBS, Robert A., is spending a few weeks in New York (20 March 1914, 17, 12)

JACOBS, Robert, has left for a three months' trip abroad (30 Dec. 1910, 14, 7)

JACOBS, Robert, is back in Montreal from the Porcupine gold fields (24 June 1910, 13, 32)

JACOBS, Robert, is in Atlantic City (5 April 1912, 15, 21)

JACOBS, Robert, is in New York on a short trip (27 Oct. 1911, 14, 50)

JACOBS, S.W. (K.C.), was appointed a member of the Bar of Montreal Library Committee and Maxwell Goldstein, K.C., was placed on the Reception Committee by the Bar's Council (18 June 1909, 12, 27)

JACOBS, S.W. (K.C.), has been appointed commissioner by the Attorney General's dept., to go to Ireland to examine witnesses in the Dillon murder case. The trial will take place on Sept. 2. Mr. Jacobs sails on July 2, 1909, aboard the Empress of Ireland (25 June 1909, 12, 28)

JACOBS, S.W., chaired the meeting of the Young People's Society of Shaar Hashomayim on Wed. March 18, 1914. M. Garber read a paper on "Jewish National Pride" and Rabbi Herman Abramowitz lectured on the Jewish communities he visited on his recent trip to Europe. On the musical program were the Misses Ruth Groner and Hortense Markus (20 March 1914, 17, 12)

JACOBS, S.W., gave an interview on his meeting with the Rt. Hon. Herbert Samuel, the British Postmaster General in London, England. Mr. Samuel told him that he will sail for Canada on Aug. 22, 1913 on the Empress of Britain which is due to arrive here on Aug. 28. Mr. Samuel will first go to Ottawa for discussions with the Dominion government and then head west to tour the Jewish farm colonies. He will return east in Oct. and will probably spend Yom Kippur in Montreal. Mr. Samuel's father, Edwin Samuel established the great private banking firm of Samuel Montagu & Co. in partnership with the late Ellis Franklin, and Samuel Montagu, later Lord Swaythling (22 Aug. 1913, 16, 37)

JACOBS, S.W., leaves next Fri. for two months in Europe. He will attend the Zionist Congress in Basle (23 June 1911, 14, 32)

JACOBS, S.W., lectured on "The Jew in England before and after Emancipation", at the Young People's Society of Shaar Hashomayim, in honor of the jubilee of Jewish emancipation in England which is now being celebrated in London. Miss Minnie Bernstein read a paper "The Jewish Old Maid" (8 Jan. 1909, 12, 4)

JACOBS, S.W., of Cornwall, Ont., was in Montreal on a visit this week (15 Jan. 1909, 12, 5)

JACOBS, S.W., of Cornwall, Ont., was in Montreal for a short visit (5 Sept. 1913, 16, 39)

JACOBS, S.W., pleaded a case before the Supreme Court of Canada in Ottawa this week (19 Nov. 1909, 13, 1)

JACOBS, S.W., spent Tues. in Ottawa (3 Dec. 1909, 13, 3)

JACOBS, S.W., was elected vice-president of the Jewish Publication Society of America (6 June 1913, 16, 26)

JACOBS, S.W., was in Chicago on business (22 July 1910, 13, 36)

JACOBS, S.W., was in Ottawa this week to argue an appeal before the Supreme Court of Canada (4 March 1910, 13, 16)

JACOBS, S.W., was named to the Library Committee and Maxwell Goldstein, K.C., to the Legislative Committee of the Montreal Bar Council (10 June 1910, 13, 30)

JACOBS, S.W., will spend the weekend at the Philadelphia Hotel in Ste. Agathe (1 June 1911, 14, 29)

JACOBS, W., of Newark, is registered at the

Grand Union Hotel (5 Nov. 1909, 12, 47)

JACOBSOHN, Misses, of New York, are guests of the Misses Silverman, Tupper St., Westmount (18 Aug. 1911, 14, 40)

JACOBSOHN, Mrs. Landau and family are visiting their aunt, Mrs. G. Lewis, Sherbrooke St. W. (26 July 1912, 15, 33)

JACOBSON, Alfred and E.J. Jacobson were passengers on the S.S. Ottawa, which arrived from Liverpool last Fri. (9 July 1909, 12, 30)

JACOBSON, Joseph, J., of New York, stayed at the Windsor Hotel while in town (14 June 1912, 15, 27)

JACOBSON, Morisce, 471 St. Dominique, of St. Louis Ward, is on the Parliamentary Voters' revision list (3 Feb. 1911, 14, 12)

JACOBSON, Mr. and Mrs. S., Clarke Ave., gave a party at their home, Sun. Feb. 2, 1913, in honor of their daughter, Sophie's engagement to Isidore Bernstein. S.Z. Fels was toastmaster. Speeches were made by H. Bernstein, L. Cohen, S. Jacobson and Harris Vineberg (7 Feb. 1913, 16, 9)

JACOBSON, Mrs. J.J., has returned home to St. Louis, Mo., after visiting her brother, M. Rubinsky (18 Aug. 1911, 14, 40)

JACOBSON, Peter, of Victoria Lodge, IOSB, received a presentation for his service to the Lodge on Sun. morn. (26 March 1909, 12, 15)

JASLOW, H., L.M. Leo, Elias Mauer and R.S. Stark took part in a debate on "whether Poali Zionism is desirable at the present time" at the B'nai Zion Kadimah meeting, Sun. evening, May 2, 1909 (7 May 1909, 12, 21)

JASSBY, Miss Eva, has gone to Los Angeles to visit friends (24 Nov. 1911, 15, 2)

JASSBY, N.A., was a guest at the Montreal House, Old Orchard, Me. (1 Aug. 1913, 16, 34)

JOEL, Miss Minnie E., of Boston, Mass., is the guest of Miss Jane B. Rost (25 July 1911, 14, 36)

JONAS, Misses Freda and Meta, of New York, were guests of the Misses Silverman, Elm Ave. (13 Aug. 1909, 12, 35)

JONES, Thomas and Mr. and Mrs. Herbert Lubin have gone to New York, Philadelphia and Washington by automobile (2 Aug. 1912, 15, 34)

JOSEFFY, Mr. and Mrs. Raphael, have returned to New York after visiting Mr. and Mrs. S. Ballon, Crescent St. Miss Joseffy, who accompanied her parents will return to New York about Aug. 20, 1910 with Miss Ellen Ballon (9 Sept. 1910, 13, 43)

JOSEFO, Miss Gertie, Milton St., went to New York, Long Branch and Centerville (25 July 1913, 16, 33)

JOSEFO, Mr. and Mrs. Julius, were guests of Mr. and Mrs. Harry Silberman, Bridge St., Quebec City (4 Nov. 1910, 13, 51)

JOSEFO, Mr. and Mrs. Julius, were guests of Mr. and Mrs. S. Shapiro while in Bedford, Que. (25 July 1913, 16, 33)

JOSEFO, Mrs. John, of New York, is visiting her parents, Mr. and Mrs. Josefo, 369 Sanguinet St. (19 July 1912, 15, 32)

JOSEFO, Mrs. Julius, 144 Elgin St., has gone to Quebec City for two weeks to visit her sister, Mrs. Harry Silberman (27 May 1910, 13, 28)

JOSEFO, Mrs. Julius, gave a tea Mon. in honor of Miss Augusta Wechsler, of New York. Assisting at the table were Mesdames Jack Brodie, Sam Shapiro and Miss Rose Miller (24 Jan. 1913, 16, 7)

JOSEFS, Mr. and Mrs. Julius, are in New York for two weeks, the guests of Mr. and Mrs. Sidney W. Lyman (26 Dec. 1913, 17, 3)

JOSEPH, A. Pinto, of Quebec City, was high on the list in the essay competition "The Government of Empire" conducted by the London Standard (29 April 1910, 13, 24)

JOSEPH, Henry and Maxwell Goldstein, K.C. are visiting governors to the Montreal General Hospital (7 April 1911, 14, 21)

JOSEPH, Henry, was criticized by the pro-Liberal Canadian Jewish Times in an editorial for urging the Jewish community to vote Conservative because the Liberal Party is annexationist and pro-reciprocity with the United States. Joseph was also criticized for thinking Jews would have greater political opportunitiy within the Conservative Party because Disraeli and Lord Herschell attained great heights in the British Conservative Party. "We venture to think that no more silly argument has ever appeared than this put up by Mr. Joseph. As is well-known, that gentleman is little associated or allied with the Jewish community of Montreal, either directly or indirectly. With the exception of perhaps one or two personal friends, the Jewish community, as a body, is a perfect stranger to him." (20 Sept. 1911, 14, 45)

JOSEPH, Jack, of London, England, will soon pay Montreal another visit (8 Jan. 1909, 12, 4)

JOSEPH, Miss Fanny and Miss Rachel Joseph, of Villa Cotta, Nice, France, are visiting their relatives in Canada, and are guests of Mrs. Joseph's sister, Mrs. Arthur A. Sandeman, of Montreal (2 Sept. 1910, 13, 42)

JOSEPH, Miss L., of London, England, who is touring Canada, is the guest of Mrs. B. Wetstein, 61 Church St. (19 Aug. 1910, 13, 40)

JOSEPH, Miss Muriel, of Quebec City, is the guest of Mrs. A.A. Sandeman, Crescent St. (14 May 1909, 12, 22)

JOSEPH, Miss Phyllis, of London, England, is the guest of her grandmother, Mrs. S. Stevenson, Cote St. Antoine Road (22 oct. 1909, 12, 45)

JOSEPH, Miss Rachel, of Nice, France, is the guest of Mrs. A.A. Sandeman for the summer (26 July 1912, 15, 33)

JOSEPH, Misses, Mansfield St., have returned from New York (24 Dec. 1909, 13, 6)

JOSEPH, Mr. and Mrs. Andrew C. and family, of Quebec City, were guests of Mr. and Mrs. Horace Joseph (11 June 1909, 12, 26)

JOSEPH, Mr. and Mrs. G.A. and family have returned from Pointe Claire (10 Sept. 1909, 12, 39)

JOSEPH, Mr. and Mrs. Henry, Dorchester St., are at the Royal Poinciana Hotel, Palm Beach (5 Feb. 1909, 12, 8)

JOSEPH, Mr. and Mrs. Henry, Dorchester St., have returned from Florida (26 Feb. 1909, 12, 11)

JOSEPH, Mr. and Mrs. Henry, Dorchester St., have returned from Atlantic City (6 May 1910, 13, 25)

JOSEPH, Mr. and Mrs. Henry, have returned home from Toronto (4 June 1909, 12, 25)

JOSEPH, Mr. and Mrs. Horace and family have taken up their residence at Pointe Claire (11 June 1909, 12, 26)

JOSEPH, Mr. and Mrs. Horace and the Misses Joseph, Mansfield St., have closed their country residence in Pointe Claire and returned to Montreal (10 Sept. 1909, 12, 39)

JOSEPH, Mr. and Mrs. Horace, have left on a short trip to New York (9 April 1909, 12, 17)

JOSEPH, Mrs. Henry, Dorchester St., entertained at dinner Sat. evening (25 June 1909, 12, 28)

JOSEPH, Mrs. Henry, Dorchester St., gave a musicale Tues. aft. (19 Nov. 1909, 13, 1)

JOSEPH, Mrs. Henry, Dorchester St., gave a dinner party Wed. evening for twelve (24 Dec. 1909, 13, 6)

JOSEPH, Mrs. Horace, and the Misses Joseph, Mansfield St., have gone south (12 March 1909, 12, 13)

JOSEPH, Mrs. Horace and the Misses Joseph, Mansfield St., have returned from their trip south (23 April 1909, 12, 19)

JOSEPH, Mrs. Horace, entertained last Mon. (7 May 1909, 12, 21)

JOSEPH, Mrs. Horace, Mansfield St., entertained at tea on Tues. aft. (12 Nov. 1909, 12, 48)

JOSEPH, Mrs. Montefiore, has returned from New York where she attended her son's wedding (19 Nov. 1909, 13, 1)

JOSEPH, Mrs. Muriel, of Quebec City, who was the guest of Mrs. A.A. Sandeman, Crescent St., has gone to New York to visit her aunt (18 March 1910, 13, 18)

JOSEPH, Rabbi Theodore F., secretary of the New York Committee of the Jewish Theological Seminary of America, is in Montreal on business (18 Aug. 1911, 14, 40)

JOSEPHSON, Mrs. R., Roy St., is in New York for a week (28 June 1912, 15, 29)

JOSPE, J., sends New Year greetings (11 Sept. 1912, 15, 40)

JOSPE, J., wishes his friends and relatives wishes his friends and relatives a happy New Year (1 Oct. 1913, 16, 42-43)

JOSPE, Mr., secretary of the Hebrew Sheltering and Orphan's Home, received a fifty dollar donation from The Busy Bee Club which was recently organized by young children. Club officers are:- Miss Leonore Freedman, pres.; Miss Naomi Cohen, treas.; Miss L. Cohen, sec.; Misses Roslyn Caplan, Celia Freedman and Sadie Freedman, members (22 Oct. 1913, 16, 46)

JUDAH, Mr. and Mrs. H.H., have gone to Ste. Agathe for a few days (2 April 1909, 12, 16)

JUDEL, Miss Sybil, of South Norwalk, Conn., is visiting Mrs. J. Ettenberg, Shuter St. (20 June

1913, 16, 28)

JUDELSON, Rev. M.J., was re-elected chazan of Congregation Chevra Kadisha, Thurs. evening, Feb. 8, 1911 for another two year term (16 Feb. 1912, 15, 14)

JURIST, Gustav, celebrated his fifth birthday Sat. aft., Dec. 6, 1913. The Misses Carolyne Jurist and Rebecca Baunbiger entertained the children at the party (12 Dec. 1913, 17, 1)

JURIST, Maurice, of New York, and David Jurist, of Toronto, are guests of their sister, Mrs. N. Jurist, Roy St., over the holidays (1 Oct. 1913, 16, 42-43)

JURIST, Mrs. G., of New York, and Mrs. M. Jurist accompanied by Mrs. T.H. Lonn, of Montreal, are spending a few weeks at the Rosenberg Hotel, Sharon Springs, N.Y. (29 Aug. 1913, 16, 38)

KAFFENBURG, Al, of Boston, Mass. stayed at the Windsor Hotel (22 Dec. 1911, 15, 6)

KAHN, Miss Suzanne, of Brooklyn, N.Y., is visiting the Misses Silverman, Tupper St. (13 June 1913, 16, 27)

KAISER, Miss Annie, of New York, is spending the summer with Rev. and Mrs. S. Goldstein, Pine ave. (16 July 1909, 12, 31)

KALISH, Miss Rose, of Boston, has returned home after visiting her aunt, Miss M. Harris, Crescent St. (12 Aug. 1910, 13, 39)

KALMANOVITCH, Mr. and Mrs. S. and family are spending the summer at St. Lin, Que. (25 July 1913, 16, 33)

KANDESTIN, Charles H. and Miss Augusta Wechsler are in Quebec City for the weekend visiting Mr. Kandestin's sister, Mrs. Harry Lieberman (24 Jan. 1913, 16, 7)

KANDESTIN, Charles H., has gone to the Maritimes on business after spending the summer in Ste. Agathe (9 Sept. 1910, 13, 43)

KANDESTIN, Charles H., is the guest of Mr. and Mrs. Paul Wechsler in Corona, Long Island (20 Dec. 1912, 16, 2)

KANDESTIN, Charles H., will stay at the McAlpine Hotel in New York for the next few weeks (26 Dec. 1913, 17, 3)

KAPLAN, F.R., of McKeesport, is a guest at the Corona Hotel (3 Sept. 1909, 12, 38)

KAPLAN, H., of Ottawa, was in New York last week (5 Nov. 1909, 12, 47)

KAPLAN, J., of Yarmouth, N.S., was in Montreal en route to New York (12 March 1909, 12, 13)

KAPLAN, J.H., of Toronto, is registered at the St. Lawrence Hall (3 Sept. 1909, 12, 38)

KAPLAN, Miss Blanche, the twelve year old daughter of Rabbi and Mrs. Bernard M. Kaplan, made her musical debut before a thousand people in San Francisco (11 Feb. 1910, 13, 13)

KAPLAN, Miss Fannie, of Yarmouth, N.S., is the guest of her sister, Mrs. Hoffman, 198 St. Joseph Blvd. W., Annex (10 Jan. 1913, 16, 5)

KAPLAN, Miss Ida and Mrs. Hoffman have gone to Boston to attend their brother's wedding which takes place early this month (3 March 1911, 14, 16)

KAPLAN, Miss Ida, of Yarmouth, N.S., is the guest of Mr. and Mrs. S. Lagowitz, 118 Clark St., Annex (19 Feb. 1909, 12, 10)

KAPLAN, Miss Ida, of Yarmouth, N.S., is visiting her sister, Mrs. Hoffman, St. Joseph Blvd., prior to going to Boston to attend her brother's wedding (17 Feb. 1911, 14, 14)

KAPLAN, Mr. and Mrs. A., of Yarmouth, N.S., arrived on Thurs, from Boston where they visited Mrs. Kaplan's sister, Mrs. T. Hoffman (17 March 1911, 14, 18)

KAPLAN, Mr. and Mrs. I.H., 1944 Mance St., wish their friends and relatives a happy New Year (1 Oct. 1913, 16, 42-43)

KAPLAN, Mr. and Mrs. Wolfe and Miss Sylvia Simons, of Detroit, Mich., were in Montreal for a few days, the guests of Mr. and Mrs. Kaplan, Arlington St. (29 Aug. 1913, 16, 38)

KAPLANSKY, A.L., was appointed collector for the Baron de Hirsch Institute (24 Sept. 1909, 12, 41)

KAPLANSKY, J., was in Montreal for a few days (21 April 1911, 14, 23)

KAPLANSKY, J.A., of Toronto, was in Montreal the past week (9 Sept. 1910, 13, 43)

KAPLANSKY, J.A., was in Montreal visiting his parents, Mr. and Mrs. A.L. Kaplansky, Mance St. (12 Sept. 1913, 16, 40)

KAPLANSKY, Julius A., has gone on a business trip out east (14 Jan. 1910, 13, 9)

KAPLANSKY, Julius A., is expected to return from his business trip to Ontario (25 March 1910, 13, 19)

KAPLANSKY, Julius A., was in Montreal visiting his parents (8 July 1910, 13, 34)

KAPLANSKY, Julius, has returned from New York and Bermuda (29 Dec. 1911, 15, 7)

KAPLANSKY, Julius, is visiting his parents, Mr. and Mrs. A. Kaplansky, 68 Park Ave. (17 Dec. 1909, 13, 5)

KAPLANSKY, Michael, has left for Vancouver where he will join his brother in business (15 April 1910, 13, 22)

KAPLANSKY, Michael, visited his parents, Mr. and Mrs. A. Kaplansky, Mance St., during the Holy Days (15 Oct. 1913, 16, 45)

KAPLANSKY, Mr. and Mrs. J.A., spent the weekend with their daughter, Mrs. B.S. Hayes and family, at Dixie, Que. (25 July 1913, 16, 33)

KASKY, Louis, of New York, is spending a week in Montreal (1 Oct. 1909, 12, 42)

KASSELS, Miss Irene, of New York, is the guest of her aunt, Mrs. Tannenbaum, Metcalfe St. (31 Dec. 1909, 13, 7)

KATZ, Mrs. P. and Miss F. Rost, of the King Edward Ladies' Mutual Benefit Association made a motion to donate $25 to the Montreal Maternity Hospital. Mrs. Bloomberg, president; Mrs. I. Brooker, vice-president; and P. Katz, trustee, made the donation (3 March 1911, 14, 16)

KATZ, Oskar, of London, England, is a passenger on the S.S. Virginian, which sails for Liverpool today (11 June 1909, 12, 26)

KATZ, P., president of the King Edward Benefit Association, was toastmaster at a banquet given in honor of Bernard Rose last Sun. evening in the Auditorium Hall. Among the speakers were:-

Smart Ideals in Tailoring

Your Fall and Winter Clothing Should be Ordered at

WM. N. KARP
39 St. Lawrence Boulevard

FOR MANY YEARS IN NEW YORK I HAVE MADE THE BEST FIFTH AVENUE WORK. MY AIM IS TO GIVE MONTREAL THE BENEFIT OF MY EXPERIENCE

Large Range of Cloths and Patterns

Tel. Main 6553

Henry Kronenberg, S. Slatkoff, Louis Berke, L. Mitnick, N. Ashkiloonay and H. Heft (5 Aug. 1910, 13, 38)

KAUFFMAN, Miss Bessie, of Hamilton, Ont., is the guest of Mrs. I. Shapiro, Esplanade Ave. (17 Feb. 1911, 14, 14)

KAUFFMAN, Miss, of Hamilton, Ont., is visiting Mrs. D. Shapiro (3 March 1911, 14, 16)

KAY, Miss, of Manchester, England, is visiting her sister, Mrs. Felix Harris, Esplanade Ave. (17 Jan. 1913, 16, 6)

KAY, Miss, of Manchester, England, who was the guest of her sister, Mrs. Felix Harris, Esplanade Ave., left for New York, en route for England (21 March 1913, 16, 15)

KAY, Mrs. Asna, of Manchester, England, who is on an extended visit with her sister, Mrs. Felix Harris, St. Joseph Blvd., has returned from a trip to New York (26 Nov. 1909, 13, 2)

KAY, Mrs. William, of Brooklyn, N.Y., is visiting her sister-in-law, Mrs. Felix Harris (22 July 1910, 13, 36)

KECES, S., is spending his summer vacation at New Glasgow and Ste. Agathe des Monts, Que. (1 Aug. 1913, 16, 34)

KEEN, M., of the Carmel Wine Co., New York, is in Montreal on business (23 Aug. 1912, 15, 37)

KEISER, Miss, of Boston, is the guest of her aunt, Mrs. M. Harris, Crescent St. (15 July 1910, 13, 35)

KELF, Alexander, who has sailed for England, will spend some time abroad (20 Aug. 1909, 12, 36)

KELLERT, B., is visiting his cousin J. Isaacs, in Far Rockaway, L.I. (27 June 1913, 16, 29)

KELLERT, Ernest, has gone to New York and Chicago (30 Sept. 1910, 13, 46)

KELLERT, J. and Miss Kellert spent the week at Caledonia Springs, Ont. (7 July 1911, 14, 34)

KELLERT, Jacob and Miss Kellert have returned from Caledonia Springs (14 July 1911, 14, 35)

KELLERT, Jake, accompanied by Miss Beccie Kellert, left for Old Orchard Beach to join his wife and family (6 Aug. 1909, 12, 34)

KELLERT, Miss Hattie, is visiting her sister Mrs. L. Fraid, in Gananoque, Ont. (6 Aug. 1909, 12, 34)

KELLERT, Misses, Sherbrooke St. W., gave a party at their residence in honor of their cousin, Miss Matts, of London, England, on Thurs. Feb. 5, 1914. Guests included:- the Misses Annie Levinson, Beck Samuels, Louise Silverman and Nina Workman (13 Feb. 1914, 17, 7)

KELLERT, Mr. and Mrs. H., were "At Home" last Sun. in honor of the engagement of their daughter, Miss Lillie Kellert to M.J. Heilig. Those assisting were:- the Misses Essie Hirsch, Hattie Matts, Myrtie Levinson, Ray Heilig, Annie Saxe, Mrs. N.J. Fraid and Mrs. Jacob Kellert (5 March 1909, 12, 12)

KELLERT, Mr. and Mrs. Jacob accompanied by Miss Beccie Kellert, left by car yesterday for Philadelphia where they will visit their daughter who is attending school there (16 June 1911, 14, 31)

KELLERT, Mr. and Mrs. Jacob and family are at Old Orchard, Me. for the summer (25 July 1911, 14, 36)

KELLERT, Mr. and Mrs. Jake, have left on a three weeks' trip to Florida and New York (15 Jan. 1909, 12, 5)

KELLERT, Mr. and Mrs. Joseph, have left for New York, where they will take up their residence (9 July 1909, 12, 30)

KELLERT, Mr. and Mrs. Joseph, Park Ave., have returned from a trip to New York (24 Nov. 1911. 15, 2)

KELLERT, Mr. and Mrs., will receive at their home, 77 Mackay St., on Sun. Feb. 28, 1909 (19 Feb. 1909, 12, 10)

KELLERT, Mrs. H. and the Misses Kellert, Sherbrooke St. W., have returned from two months' stay abroad (2 Sept. 1910, 13, 42)

KELLERT, Mrs. I., Bishop St., has returned from New Orleans (11 March 1910, 13, 17)

KELLERT, Mrs. J. and daughter are spending the summer at Old Orchard Beach (9 July 1909, 12, 30)

KELLERT, Mrs. J. and family, Bishop St., are at Old Orchard Beach (22 July 1910, 13, 36)

KELLERT, Mrs. J., has returned from her holiday (4 March 1910, 13, 16)

KELLERT, Mrs. Jacob, has left for a short stay in New Orleans, La. (4 Feb. 1910, 13, 12)

KELLERT, Mrs. Jake and daughter, Miss Frances Kellert, have returned from Philadelphia (30 Dec. 1910, 14, 7)

KELLERT, Sol, returned from a short stay at Long Branch, N.Y. (18 July 1913, 16, 32)

KELLERT, Sol. and his sisters, the Misses Hattie and Beck Kellert, are spending a few weeks at Lakewood, N.Y. (30 Dec. 1910, 14, 7)

KELLERT, Sol., is back from Europe. He returned to New York on the incoming Oceanic (8 Jan. 1909, 12, 4)

KELLERT, Solomon and Miss Beccie Kellert, left for New York Wed. night for a short visit (21 Jan. 1910, 13, 10)

KELLNOR, A., has left for a trip to Europe (17 June 1910, 13, 31)

KELLNOR, Miss Etta, Elm Ave., gave a party Sat. evening, Feb. 22, 1913 (28 Feb. 1913, 16, 12)

KELLNOR, Mr. and Mrs., St. Denis St., entertained their friends Sun. evening, in honor of their fifteenth wedding anniversary (26 March 1909, 12, 15)

KEMPNER, Mr. and Mrs. J., of Plattsburgh, N.Y., were guests of Mrs. Walther, while in Montreal (7 Oct. 1910, 13, 47)

KER, Mrs. John, of Brantford, Ont., is visiting her sister, Miss S. Rubenstein. Mrs. Ker is a delegate to the Child's Welfare Exhibition being held in Montreal (18 Oct. 1912, 15, 45)

KERNER, B., of Fredericton, N.B., is the guest of Mr. and Mrs. O. Kerner (6 Oct. 1911, 14, 47)

KERNER, H., of Fredericton, N.B., was in Montreal the past week (9 Dec. 1910, 14, 4)

KERNER, Mr., of Fredericton, N.B., is in Montreal visiting friends on City Hall Ave. (26 Feb. 1909, 12, 11)

KERNER, Mrs. O.L. and family are summering at Bathurst, N.B. (4 July 1913, 16, 30)

KERNER, S., of Fredericton, N.B., passed through Montreal this week, en route to the Toronto Exhibition (3 Sept. 1909, 12, 38)

KERR, Mr. and Mrs. J., of Brantford, Ont., are guests of Miss Rubenstein (29 Dec. 1911, 15, 7)

KERT, Charles, of Ottawa, was in Montreal this week on a business trip (18 June 1909, 12, 27)

KERT, Edward, Peter H. Merson, B.H. Schwartz and Joe. Tupper were appointed to interview all the Jewish athletic clubs in Montreal with a view to forming a Jewish baseball league here (14 March 1913, 16, 14)

KERT, L., M. Lerner, S. Merson and L. Millar, a quartette, sang at a dance given by the young members of the Merson Social Club last Sun. night (24 Jan. 1913, 16, 7)

KERT, L., was in Ottawa for a few days this week (18 June 1909, 12, 27)

KERT, L., will attend the IOSB convention in Boston on March 17, 1912. He will also visit relatives in Boston (15 March 1912, 15, 18)

KERT, Levi, IOSB delegate, has left for New York to attend the annual convention (11 March 1910, 13, 17)

KERT, Max, has gone to Quebec City on business for two weeks (22 Oct. 1909, 12, 45)

KERT, Miss Rose, gave an "at home" on April 18, 1909, at her residence, 330 Laval Ave. (23 April 1909, 12, 19)

KERT, Mr. and Mrs. A. and daughter, of Ottawa, have gone to Winnipeg to attend the wedding of Miss Beamolt (6 Jan. 1911, 14, 8)

KERT, Mrs. A. and daughter, of Ottawa, are guests of Mesdames M. and S. Ryan at their Mountain View Cottage, Ivry (5 Aug. 1910, 13, 38)

KERT, Mrs. A. and Miss P. Beamolt, of Winnipeg, who were guests of Mr. and Mrs. S. Ryan, Wood Ave., left for Ottawa (6 Sept. 1912, 15, 39)

KERT, Mrs. H.I., of Englehart, Ont., after visiting relatives in Montreal, hosted a musicale on July 20, 1909, given in honor of her guests, the Misses Nellie and Sadie Vineberg, of Montreal (30 July 1909, 12, 33)

KERT, Mrs. H.I., returned home to Englehart, Ont., after a few months in Montreal, the guest of her sister, Mrs. J.L. Vineberg (21 March 1913, 16, 15)

KEYFITZ, Arthur of the Montreal Gazette and his wife have gone to Toronto to spend Passover week with their mother and father "...-their parents' fiftieth Passover since marriage." (29 March 1912, 15, 20)

KEYFITZ, Miss, of Toronto, is visiting her sister, Mrs. Woolman, Dorchester St. W. (18 Oct. 1912, 15, 45)

KIER, Mrs. J., of Brantford, is visiting her sister, Miss Rubenstein (24 Sept. 1909, 12, 41)

KING, Mr. and Mrs. Joseph, of Toronto, were in Montreal at the Windsor Hotel, en route for Quebec City (9 Sept. 1910, 13, 43)

KING, S., of Whitby, Ont., stayed at the Windsor Hotel (22 July 1910, 13, 36)

KING, S., of Whitby, Ont., was a guest at the Windsor Hotel (11 Aug. 1911, 14, 39)

KING, Theo., of Toronto, stayed at the Windsor Hotel (5 April 1912, 15, 21)

KING, Theo., of Toronto, stayed at the Windsor Hotel (11 July 1913, 16, 31)

KING, Theo., of Toronto, was a guest at the Windsor Hotel (3 March 1911, 14, 16)

KING, Theo., of Toronto, was in Montreal for a few days (18 Feb. 1910, 13, 14)

KING, Theo., of Whitby, Ont., stayed at the Windsor Hotel (11 Oct. 1910, 13, 48)

KING, Theo., of Whitby, Ont., was a guest at the Windsor Hotel (7 July 1911, 14, 34)

KING, Theodore, of Whitby, Ont., was at the Windsor Hotel (29 Jan. 1909, 12, 7)

KINSKY, I., who was in Montreal for several years, has returned to his home in Detroit (13 Aug. 1909, 12, 35)

KIRSCH, Dr. and Mrs. S., of Madison, Wis., are visiting Mr. and Mrs. M. Mendelson, 181 Esplanade Ave. (31 March 1911, 14, 20)

KIRSCH, Dr. Simon, spoke on the topic "The Jew and Socialism, with some reflections upon Jewish Nationalism" at the YMHA Friday Night Talk, April 11, 1913 (9 May 1913, 16, 22)

KIRSCH, Mrs. A., eldest daughter of Mr. and Mrs. L. Goldberg, gave a dinner in honor of her parents' fiftieth wedding anniversary on Sun. March 23, 1913. "The couple were presented with numerous gifts, among which was a well-filled purse of gold." The purse was presented by one of their great-grandchildren, Master Edward, the eldest son of Dr. and Mrs. S. Kirsch (28 March 1913, 16, 16)

KIRSHBERG, Misses Miriam and Annie, are at Ferndale, Catskills for the summer (14 July 1911, 14, 35)

KISHNER, Miss Ettie, was elected president of the newly formed Herzl Girls' Zionist Society composed of young girls attending high school. Maxwell Lightstone was the organizer. Other officers are:- Miss Annie Pottashner, vice-pres.; Miss Edith Rost, corr. sec.; Miss Sarah Dovia, treas.; the Misses Minnie Lightstone, Rachel Kishner and Bessie Silver (29 April 1910, 13, 24)

KLEIN, I., of Hamburg, Germany, was registered at the Queen's Hotel the past week (25 Oct. 1910, 13, 50)

KLEIN, J., has returned home from New York (29 Nov. 1912, 15, 51)

KLEIN, Jacob, Bennie Marks, Sam Moskovitch, Sydney Schleifer, Jacob Steinberg, and the Misses Polly Epstein, Sarah Epstein, Rachel Gerson, Dorothy Marks, Bella Payne, Sadie Rosenberg, Molly Rubin and Sarah Schleifer were promoted at the Chevra Kadisha Sunday School semi-annual promotion day, March 2, 1913 (7 March 1913, 16, 13)

KLEIN, Miss R., secretary of the Young Ladies' Zionist and Literary Society, is selling tickets for the dance Wed. March 20, 1912 (8 March 1912, 15, 17)

KLEIN, Miss Rosa, was elected president of the Young Ladies' Zionist and Literary Society at a meeting held last Sun. in the Baron de Hirsch Institute. Other officers elected were:- Miss Pauline Hoffman, vice-pres.; Miss Sophie Klineberg, sec.; and Miss Mary Tritt, treas. (1 Nov. 1912, 15, 47)

KLEIN, Misses Rose and Lillian, are spending two weeks in Cleveland visiting relatives (15 Aug. 1913, 16, 36)

KLEIN, Mrs. A., has returned to Montreal after spending a few weeks at Chateauguay (3 Sept. 1909, 12, 38)

KLEINBERG, N., a former special agent in the Quebec City branch office of the Manufacturers Life Insurance Co., was promoted to general agent for the Montreal local office last Jan. He and his family moved to Montreal and are now living at 1657 Hutchison St. (13 June 1913, 16, 27)

Office—Main 1708   Residence—St. Louis 8294

N. Kleinberg
. . Montreal . .

General Agent,

**Manufacturers' Life Insurance Coy.
260 St. James Street**

REPRESENTING :

Alliance Fire Insurance Company.   Dominion of Canada Guarantee and Accident Insurance Company

---

KLEINBERG, Otto, is president of the Young Judeans Society, which was recently established by some pupils of the St. Urbain St. Talmud Torah. "The purpose of the new society is to propagate national ideals and to establish a special library for Jewish youths." Other officers are:- I. Pevner, sec.; and Leon Levin, son of A. Levin, treas. (27 June 1913, 16, 29)

KLINE, Miss Lille, is in Cleveland visiting friends (30 Aug. 1912, 15, 38)

KLINE, M., of New York, was a guest at the Windsor Hotel (17 March 1911, 14, 18)

KLINEBERG, Miss Sophie, received the Bloomfield Memorial Gold Medal at the Shaar Hashomayim Religious and Hebrew Day School at the closing and graduating exercises on Sun. June 5, 1910. Other graduates this year were:- Miss Malca Friedman (Edward Moss Silver Medal); David Lauer (William and Hannah Jacobs Memorial Silver Medal); Miss Beccie Toplitski (Mr. and Mrs. Lyon Cohen Memorial Medal); the Misses Florence Wener, Edith Matts, Ruby Livingstone, Beatrice Morris, Ruth Cohen, Libbie Abinovitch, Madge Rosenberg and Lyon Levine (17 June 1910, 13, 31)

KLINEBERG, O., was re-elected president of the Young Judeans at the semi-annual meeting on Sun. evening, Nov. 9, 1913 in the Talmud Torah bldg., St. Urbain St. Other officers elected were:- A. Goldman, vice-pres.; M. Fineberg, sec.; D. Stein, treas.; B. Glickman, L. Glickman, J. Harris, J. Klein, L. Levin and J. Magid, exec. (14 Nov. 1913, 16, 49)

KLOPOT, Mrs. Adam and daughter, of Boston, are visiting Mrs. C. Redlich, Park Ave., Annex (16 June 1911, 14, 31)

KLOPOT, Mrs. Adam and son, of Boston, are the guests of Samuel Roman (15 Sept. 1909, 12, 40)

KOCHMAN, Mrs. B., and her daughters, of Schenectady, N.Y., have returned home after visiting Mrs. Kochman's sisters, Mesdames Isidore Friedman and K. Zacharia (18 Aug. 1911, 14, 40)

KOLBER, Dr. J., has been appointed house physician in the New York City Nursery and Child's Hospital (28 June 1912, 15, 28)

KOLBER, Dr. Joseph, went to New York and Atlantic City (21 June 1912, 15, 28)

KOLBER, Dr. Joseph, who visited his parents the past week, has returned to New York (20 Sept. 1912, 15, 41)

KOLBER, Max, has gone to Toronto, Detroit and Chicago for a two weeks' visit (4 Feb. 1910, 13, 12)

KOLBER, Miss Esther, is at Shawbridge, Que. on vacation (9 Aug. 1912, 15, 35)

KOLBER, Misses Etta and Fanny, returned from two weeks in Shawbridge, Que. (23 Aug. 1912, 15, 37)

KOLLNER, J., of New York, was in Montreal during Carnival week (26 Feb. 1909, 12, 11)

KOPEL, Miss Esther, of Leeds, England, is in Montreal to attend her brother's marriage to Miss Sophie Florence which takes place Sun. March 30, 1913 (28 March 1913, 16, 16)

KORNFELD, Rabbi J., of Columbus, Ohio, stayed at the Windsor Hotel while in Montreal (14 Feb. 1913, 16, 10)

KORTOSK, B., has recovered from his recent illness (26 March 1909, 12, 15)

KORTOSK, E.H., S. Hart, A. Wener, M. Vineberg, H. Singer, H. Kellert & Son, P. Adelstein, A.J. Alexander, M. Fenster, M. Sessenwein, L. Adelstein, J.L. Adelstein, M. Liverman, M. Block, O. Orenstein, S. Zulauf, H. Shertzer, S. Rubin, M. Asher, J. Ellenberg, A.E. Pierce, S.W. Jacobs, T. Brown, J. Wener, M.L. Levin and M. Rothchild contributed funds to the Montreal Hebrew Sheltering Home (12 Aug. 1910, 13, 39)

KRAMER, Mrs. and two sons, of New York, are visiting Mrs. Joseph Kellert, "Belleview" (16 Sept. 1910, 13, 44)

KREDENCER, S., was elected president of the Hebrew Consumptive Aid Association. Other officers are:- I. Kessler, vice-pres.; Miss M. Ratner, treas.; P. Sklover, fin. sec.; and A. Axebrad, rec. sec. M. Rubin, who had been financial secretary for three years, declined to accept office for another year (27 Jan. 1911, 14, 11)

KREINSON, L.M., of Bradford, Pa.; Mrs. M.J. Rosenberg and Master Nathan Rosenberg, of Detroit, Mich., who visited Mr. and Mrs. N. Levinson, Church St., have returned home (29 July 1910, 13, 37)

KREINSON, Louis, of Bradford, Pa., was the guest of his sister, Mrs. N. Levinson, last week (20 Sept. 1912, 15, 41)

KRONICK, S., of Toronto, is in Montreal on business (4 Aug. 1911, 14, 38)

KRONICK, S., of Toronto was in Montreal on Mon. (14 Jan. 1910, 13, 9)

KRONICK, S., of Toronto, was in Montreal on business (8 Sept. 1911, 14, 43)

KRONICK, S., of Toronto, was registerd at the St. Lawrence Hall this week (13 May 1910, 13, 26)

KRONICK, S., who was in Montreal during the week, returned to Toronto last night (14 May 1909, 12, 22)

KRUGER, Jean, Mance St., is visiting his grandparents, Mr. and Mrs. L. Samuelson, in Rochester N.Y. (25 July 1913, 16, 33)

KRUGER, Joseph, was in New York, a guest of his brother-in-law, Mr. Goldstein (16 April 1909, 12, 18)

KRUGER, Joseph, was in Toronto for a few days (19 Nov. 1909, 13, 1)

KRUGER, Mr. and Mrs. J. and family, Mance St., Annex, have returned from St. Marguerite, Lake Charlebois (24 Sept. 1909, 12, 41)

KRUGER, Mr. and Mrs. Jos. and family, Mance St., Annex, will spend the summer at Pointe Claire (16 June 1911, 14, 31)

KRUGER, Mrs. Joseph and family are spending the summer at Lake Charlebois (23 July 1909, 12, 32)

KRUGER, Mrs. Joseph and family are spending the summer at Shawbridge, Que. (12 Aug. 1910, 13, 39)

KRUGER, Mrs. Joseph and family will spend the summer at Weir, Ont. (15 July 1910, 13, 35)

KRUGER, Mrs. Joseph, Mance St., Annex, entertained a few friends in honor of her mother, Mrs. Samuelson, of Rochester, N.Y. (22 Oct. 1909, 12, 45)

KRUGER, Mrs. Joseph, Mance St., Annex, gave a thimble party for fifteen young ladies Wed. aft. in honor of Miss Kassels, of New York, and Miss Rittenberg, of Toronto (21 Jan. 1910, 13, 10)

KRUGER, Mrs. Joseph, Mance St. Annex, hosted a euchre on Wed. Nov. 9, 1910 (11 Nov. 1910, 13, 52)

KRUSS, Dr. and Mrs. M., of New York, who have been visiting Miss Reba Goltman, of Montreal, have left for Toronto and Niagara Falls (13 Aug. 1909, 12, 35)

KUBELIK, M., of Toronto, was in Montreal the past week (14 Jan. 1910, 13, 9)

KUBELIK, Max, has gone on a short trip to New York and Boston (18 Nov. 1910, 14, 1)

KUBELIK, Max, is the guest of his sister, Mrs. Ralph Raphael, King Edward Apts. (14 Jan. 1910, 13, 9)

KUBELIK, Max, of Toronto, was in Montreal for a few days (30 July 1909, 12, 33)

KUBELIK, Max, of Toronto, was in Montreal the past week (15 April 1910, 13, 22)

KUBELIK, Max, of Toronto, was in Montreal the past week (4 Aug. 1911, 14, 38)

KUBELIK, Max, of Toronto, was in Montreal this week (8 Sept. 1911, 14, 43)

KUBELIK, Max, of Toronto, was the guest of his sister, Mrs. Ralph Raphael (14 May 1909, 12, 22)

KUBELIK, Max, of Toronto, was the guest of her sister, Mrs. R. Raphael (12 Nov. 1909, 12, 48)

KUPPENHEIMER, J.D., has gone on a short visit to the Adirondack Mountains (27 Aug. 1909, 12, 37)

KUPPENHEIMER, J.D., of Toronto, stayed at the Queen's Hotel (20 Sept. 1912, 15, 41)

KUPPENHEIMER, J.D., of Toronto, stayed at the Ritz Hotel while in Montreal (19 Dec. 1913, 17, 2)

KUPPENHEIMER, Joseph, of New York, was in Montreal visiting his mother, Mrs. Kuppenheimer, Mance St. (9 April 1909, 12, 17)

KUPPENHEIMER, Mr. and Mrs. J.D., were guests of Mrs. Paul Ogulnik, in Shawbridge, Que. (26 Aug. 1910, 13, 41)

LALIN, Mrs. J., has returned from four weeks' stay at New Glasgow (4 Aug. 1911, 14, 38)

LAMBERT, C., was elected hon. president of the YMHA junior dept. on Sun. evening, Nov. 12, 1911. Other officers elected were:- M. Lazarus, pres.; I. Hoffer, vice-pres.; A. Presner, sec.; I. Asner, corr. sec.; I. Cohen, sergeant-at-arms; M. Herman, H. Levinson, D. Stone and A. Viner, directors (17 Nov. 1911, 15, 1)

LAMBERT, Mr. and Mrs., of New York, were guests of Mr. and Mrs. I. Abrahams, at Lakeside (26 Aug. 1910, 13, 41)

LANDAU, Charles and Michael, were in Montreal this week (9 Aug. 1912, 15, 35)

LANDAU, L., editor of the Jewish Eagle, left last night for a four or five days trip to New York (19 March 1909, 12, 14)

LANDAU, L., who recently left the Canadian Jewish Eagle has joined a Jewish paper in New York (8 Oct. 1909, 12, 43)

LANDAU, Michael, is a guest at the Corona Hotel (25 June 1909, 12, 28)

LANDE, I., has returned from two weeks in New York, Buffalo and Toronto (11 March 1910, 13, 17)

LANDE, I., school committee chairman, presided at the Baron de Hirsch Free School closing exercises. E.M. Gordon, the principal, submitted his annual report. Miss Ida Rosenberg delivered the address and Miss Celia Goldenblatt read an essay on Spinoza. Isidore Blumenthal, Edward Blumenfield, J. Hornstein, Issie Matloff and the Misses Bertha Friedman and Adela Klineberg gave recitations in Hebrew and English. Speeches were made by Lyon Cohen and Reuben Brainin. Graduating students who were awarded prizes were:- Ida Rosenberg (Bloomfield Memorial Medal), Rose Solomon (N. Sloves Silver Medal), J. Hornstein, Isidore Schaefer, Annie Friedman, Adela Klineberg Miriam Lankofsky and Alice Schaefer. Voluntary teachers are:- Louis Gross, Harry Jacobs, David Lauer, Dr. E.C. Levine, Louis Sissenwain, Lawrence Tannenbaum, B.A., and the Misses Jennie Heillig, Hattie Lazarus, M. Rosenberg, Esther Stein and Miriam Tannenbaum (11 July 1913, 16, 31)

LANDE, I., was elected president of the Liberal-Conservative Club of St. Lawrence this week. Other officers elected were:- D. Friedman, hon. vice-pres.; N. Denberg, vice-pres.; M. Bernstein, sec.; Bernard Rose, S. Slatken, H. Gordon, P. Popliger and D. Blumer, executive committee (25 Aug. 1911, 14, 41)

LANDE, Misses Gertrude and Aida Cohen gave a surprise party Sun. night for Miss Florence Poyaner. M. Myerson delivered the toast. A. Viner was in charge of the program (19 April 1912, 15, 23)

LANDE, Mr. and Mrs. H., spent a holiday in New York (29 July 1910, 13, 37)

LANDE, Mr. and Mrs. I. and family have left for Toronto, en route to New York to attend the wedding of Miss Francis Lande (25 Feb. 1910, 13, 15)

LANDE, Mr. and Mrs. I. and family, Grosvenor Ave., Westmount, will spend a few months at Hotel Vermont in Ste. Agathe (28 July 1911, 14, 37)

LANDE, Mr. and Mrs. I. and family, Grosvenor Ave., Westmount have gone to Toronto via the Thousand Islands (2 Aug. 1912, 15, 34)

LANDE, Mr. and Mrs. I., Grosvenor Ave., Miss Annie Gordon and Moses Gordon, of Toronto, are spending a few weeks at Old Orchard Beach (22 Aug. 1913, 16, 37)

LANDE, Mr. and Mrs. N., 484 Strathcona Ave., returned from two weeks in New York (27 Dec. 1912, 16, 3)

LANDE, Mr. and Mrs. Nathan and family, 484 Strathcona Ave., have returned from Old Orchard, Me. (6 Sept. 1912, 15, 39)

LANDE, Mr. and Mrs. Nathan, are spending their holidays in Ottawa, the guests of Mr. and Mrs. H. Frieman, McLaren St. (15 Sept. 1909, 12, 40)

LANDE, Mrs. I. and family, Grosvenor Ave., have gone to Toronto to visit her parents, Mr. and Mrs. Moses Gordon, Markham St. (8 Sept. 1911, 14, 43)

LANDE, Mrs. I. and family, Westmount, have returned home after a holiday with her parents, Mr. and Mrs. M. Gordon, in Toronto (27 May 1910, 13, 28)

LANDE, Mrs. I., Grosvenor Ave., Westmount,

gave a social evening in honor of her sister, Miss Rose Gordon, of Toronto. Prof. L. Koffman played the violin (6 Jan. 1911, 14, 8)

LANDE, Mrs. I., is spending a few weeks with her parents, Mr. and Mrs. M. Gordon, in Toronto (11 March 1910, 13, 17)

LANDMAN, Rabbi Isaac, who a few years ago occupied the Temple Emanu-El of Montreal pulpit, is now a playwright. He is in Toronto supervising the first production of his play "A Man of Honour", which will open in the Toronto Opera House (18 June 1909, 12, 27)

LANG, H., 677 St. Urbain St., is chairman of the B'nai U' Bnoth Zion Kadimah Society ball and tombola committee (9 Feb. 1912, 15, 13)

LANG, H., Bleury St., hosted a B'nai Zion Kadimah council meeting at his home on Jan. 19, 1909 (22 Jan. 1909, 12, 6)

LANG, Mr. and Mrs. H., 677 St. Urbain St., send New Year greetings (20 Sept. 1912, 15, 41)

LANG, Mr. and Mrs. H., St. Urbain St., gave a farewell dinner last Mon. in honor of S. Gorosh, who has moved to Winnipeg where he will represent The Canadian Jewish Times. Among those present were:- Mr. and Mrs. M. Gelbman, E. Mauer, Maxwell Lightstone and Mr. Schlosberg (19 May 1911, 14, 27)

LANGEBERG, H.F., of St. Louis, is a guest at the Windsor Hotel (27 Aug. 1909, 12, 37)

LAREDO, A., of London, Eng., is a guest at the Windsor Hotel (30 Sept. 1910, 13, 46)

LAREDO, A.M., has sailed home for England but is expected to return in five or six weeks. "Mr. Laredo has been so well impressed with Canada that he has extended a branch of his large mercantile affairs here and a number of his associates will accompany him on his return." Mr. Laredo is a member of the Spanish and Portuguese Congregation in London and has joined the Spanish and Portuguese Congregation in Montreal (18 Nov. 1910, 14, 1)

LASKER, Miss Lillian, of Woodlands, and Miss Mollie Wicks, are guests of Miss Sadie A. Ressler, at the Pinewood Villa, Morin Heights, Que. (15 Aug. 1913, 16, 36)

LASKER, Mr. and Mrs., chaperoned the Dolly Dimple Social Club snowshoe tramp on Sat. March 9, 1912. Later a tramp supper was served at the home of Mrs. I. Ressler (15 March 1912, 15, 18)

LAUCHMAN, Mr. and Mrs. J., of Detroit, are visiting their daughter, Mrs. Sol Vineberg, St. Catherine St. W. (31 Jan. 1913, 16, 8)

LAUCHMAN, Mrs. J., of Detroit, is visiting her daughter, Mrs. S.L. Vineberg, St. Catherine St. W. (20 Feb. 1914, 17, 8)

LAUDERMAN, Mr. and Mrs. A.A., have returned from the South (4 Nov. 1910, 13, 51)

LAUER, B., of Winnipeg, was in Montreal for a few days (12 Feb. 1909, 12 9)

LAUER, Mr. and Mrs. B., have returned to Winnipeg after visiting Mrs. Lauer's parents, Mr. and Mrs. M. Ginsberg (26 Feb. 1909, 12, 11)

LAURIE, A.J., of Guelph, Ont., is visiting his uncle, L. Levy, 74 Laval Ave., en route for Ottawa (26 Feb. 1909, 12, 11)

LAURIE, Dr., has left town for a couple of weeks (11 June 1909, 12, 26)

LAUTERMAN, Dr. Max and S. Strauss are expected to return from Europe tomorrow (6 May 1910, 13, 25)

LAUTERMAN, Dr. Max, has been appointed a member of the King Edward Institute for Tuberculosis Medical Board (29 Oct. 1909, 12, 46)

LAUTERMAN, Dr. Max, is in good health in Naples (25 Feb. 1910, 13, 15)

LAUTERMAN, Dr. Maxwell, who holds a commission of Major in the Duke of York's Hussars, presided at a luncheon at the Military Institute last week for Frederic Villiers, the famous war correspondent, who has moved to Montreal (18 Oct. 1910, 13, 49)

LAUTERMAN, Misses Dinah, Sylvia Goldstein, Gertie Samuels and Hannah Rosenberg were debutantes at the Hebrew Young Ladies' Sewing Society fifteenth annual dance on Nov. 29, 1910. Miss Tannebaum was the convenor and the Misses Essie Hirsch and Gertrude Sherman received the guests. Charles Samuels, L.H. Cohen, M.J. and J.A. Hirsch were responsible for floor management (9 Dec. 1910, 14, 4)

LAVINE, Miss Bessie, of Trenton, N.J., who is engaged to A. Sloves, of Montreal, was the guest of his parents, Mr. and Mrs. N. Sloves, 104 Park Ave. (16 Aug. 1912, 15, 36)

LAX, M., has opened an exclusive ladies' tailoring and millinery store, "The Fashion Novelty" at 120 Sherbrooke St. W., corner Bleury (27 March 1914, 17, 13)

LAZAROVICZ, Mr. and Mrs. L. and family, of Quebec City, are passing the summer at Tadousac (6 Aug. 1909, 12, 34)

LAZAROVITZ, Master D., of Quebec City, was the guest of his grandmother, Mrs. W. Serchuk (25 July 1913, 16, 33)

LAZAROWITZ, Louis and David Ortenberg, both of Quebec City, sued the anti-Semite Plamandon two years ago for libel. The trial takes place Wed. May 10, 1913. The Quebec Minister of Public Works and S.W. Jacobs, Q.C., will appear for the prosecution (9 May 1913, 16, 22)

LAZARUS, Mesdames Henry, C.L. Friedman, J. Goldstein and Michael Hirsch were patronesses of the Maccabean Circle second annual dance held last Tues. evening in Stanley Hall (3 Feb. 1911, 14, 12)

LAZARUS, Miss Maude, is the guest of her aunt, Mrs. I. Blumenthal in Beaurepaire (9 July 1909, 12, 30)

LAZARUS, H., returned home to Vancouver, Fri. evening after winding up the estate of his late mother, Mrs. D. Lazarus. Mr. Lazarus will visit New York and Philadelphia before returning home (18 Oct. 1912, 15, 45)

LAZARUS, Miss Hattie S., left for a few weeks in New York and Atlantic City (20 June 1913, 16, 28)

LAZARUS, Mr. and Mrs. Henry, have moved to Vancouver where they will reside (15 March 1912, 14, 18)

LAZARUS, Mr. and Mrs., of Hamilton, stayed at the Windsor Hotel during their visit (27 Dec. 1912, 16, 3)

LAZARUS, Mrs. H. and Miss Maude Lazarus, Oliver St., Westmount, are in New York (17 March 1911, 14, 18)

LAZARUS, Mrs. H. and Mrs. Maude Lazarus have gone to Val Morin for several weeks (1 July 1910, 13, 33)

LAZARUS, Mrs. H., Hutchison St., acknowledges the sympathy of her friends on the death of her mother in New York recently (18 March 1910, 13, 18)

LAZARUS, Mrs. Henry and daughter are guests of Mrs. Philip Myers, of Quebec City (29 Oct. 1909, 12, 46)

LAZARUS, Mrs., is dangerously ill at the home of her daughter, Mrs. S. Abrahams, Argyle Ave., Westmount (25 Aug. 1911, 14, 41)

LEAN, Abraham W., formerly William Lean, was converted to Judaism on Sun. May 25, 1913. Mr. Lean, age 22, was born in Glasgow, Scotland of Protestant parents. The ceremony took place in Mr. Lean's home, 1203 St. Urbain St., Montreal. "Rev. S. Goldstein performed the ceremony of initiating the convert, assisted by Dr. Rabinovitch. The formal conversion was made by Rabbi Hirsch Cohen, who prior to the ceremony admonished Mr. Lean regarding the principles of the Jewish belief, and informed him that if there was any doubt in his mind as to the propriety of the action he was about to take, it was not yet too late for him to withdraw. Mr. Lean declared that he was satisfied that the step he was about to take was correct, and that he was sincerely desirous of becoming a Jew." Mr. Lean received instruction in Hebrew and religion from Rev. Goldstein for several months (30 May 1913, 16, 25)

LEAVITT, B. and Hiram Freedman have returned from their business trip to New York (30 July 1909, 12, 33)

LEAVITT, E., leaves shortly for New York (25 Feb. 1910, 13, 15)

LEAVITT, Joseph, Moses Sacksner, Benjamin Silver and Miss Amelia Hecht received their B.A. degrees, McGill University, Faculty of Arts (16 May 1913, 16, 23)

LEDERER, Miss, has presented a set of ladies' underwear (four pieces, handiwork) to be raffled for the benefit of the Ladies' Hebrew Benevolent Society. Tickets may be purchased from Mrs. Joseph Jacobs, 30 Lincoln Ave., where the garments may be seen (31 March 1911, 14 20)

LEDERER, Miss Theresa, who was the guest of her sister, Mrs. Joseph Jacobs, Lincoln Ave., for the past few months, sailed on June 22, 1911 aboard the S.S. Laurentic for her home in London, England. (23 June 1911, 14, 32)

LEE, J., was elected president of the Spalding Junior Montefiore Baseball League at a meeting on April 17, 1913. Other officers elected were:- F. Berlin, vice-pres.; H. Geller, sec.; Thos. Wall, treas. (16 May 1913, 16, 23)

LEEB, Irving, of Philadelphia, was registered at the Windsor Hotel (17 Feb. 1911, 14, 14)

LEESER, Mrs. Al., Prince Arthur Apts., will give a tea Thurs. aft. Jan. 21, 1909, in honor of her sister, Miss Ida Wohl, of Cleveland, Ohio (15 Jan. 1909, 12, 5)

LEFKOWITZ, Mr. and Mrs. Meyer, 773 City Hall Ave., gave a birthday party for their nine year old twin daughters, Ruth and Dorothy Lefkowitz, on Sat. Feb. 14, 1914 (27 Feb. 1914, 17, 9)

LEFKOWITZ, Mr. and Mrs. Meyer, City Hall Ave., gave a reception on the occasion of the engagement of their daughter Sarah to Harry Simon. Guests included:- D. Florin, Mr. and Mrs. L. Adler, Mr. and Mrs. J. Barnett, Mr. and Mrs. L. Frischling, Mr. and Mrs. Lyon W. Jacobs, Mr. and Mrs. I. Lavut, Mr. and Mrs. R. Marks, Mr. and Mrs. Miller, Mr. and Mrs. Simon, and Mr. and Mrs. S. Slatkoff (6 March 1914, 17, 10)

LEITER, Mrs., Hutchison St., is spending a fortnight in Sydney, N.S. (8 Aug. 1913, 16, 35)

LEMLEIN, Bert, of Brooklyn, N.Y., visited his mother, Mrs. R. Lemlein, St. Catherine St. W. (8 March 1912, 15, 17)

LEO, J.S., has left for a trip west (26 Aug. 1910, 13, 41)

LEO, J.S., the Zionist Federation corresponding secretary, has just returned from a trip out west. "While there, he had conferences and meetings with a number of the leaders of the Jewish communities in various cities of the Northwest provinces, and it is anticipated that much good will result from his work in promoting more active propaganda and improved organization of the societies already existing, and the founding of new ones...Mr. Leo believes that a visit from the other leaders of the Movement to the West would produce very excellent results, and for this reason he strongly favours the holding of the next Convention of the Federation in one of the Far Western cities, - in Victoria, Calgary, or Winnipeg. He believes that the East should do this much to help the growth of the Movement in the West, and that such a gathering would be very largely attended." (16 April 1909, 12, 18)

LEO, Mrs., 437 Argyle Ave., Westmount, is accepting applications for the kindergarten class in Hebrew to be started under the auspices of the Montreal Daughters of Zion Society (8 Nov. 1912, 15, 48)

LEO, Mrs. J.S., met the Countess of Aberdeen at the home of Lady Drummond on Sun. (17 Jan. 1913, 16, 6)

LEO, Mrs. J.S., was elected president (for a third term) of the Montreal Daughters of Zion Society on Sun. aft., Nov. 9, 1913. Other officers elected were:- Mrs. Clarence I. de Soia, 1st vice-pres.; Mrs. Leon Goldman, 2nd vice-pres.; Mrs. Reuben Brainin, 3rd vice-pres.; Mrs. J. Rose, treas.; Mrs. Felix Harris, rec. sec.; Miss Brainin, corr. sec.; Mesdames A.J. Alexander, F. Kirschberg, J. Kirschberg, A. Levine, H. Levy, A. Rost, R. Simand, M. Sanders, and the Misses E. Bernstein, M. Bernstein, B. Glinzburg, J. Schwartz, S. Singer and J. Wertheimer, council members (14 Nov. 1913, 16, 49)

LEPITZKY, J., of Toronto, was in Montreal the past week (4 Nov. 1910, 13, 51)

LERNER, Mrs. L., is at Ste. Agathe for a few weeks (25 July 1911, 14, 36)

LERNER, Mrs. L., of Quebec City, spent four weeks at Ste. Agathe des Monts and then went to La Tuque, Que. (11 Aug. 1911, 14, 39)

LESSER, A., R.H. Blumenthal and Z. Auerbach were in Quebec City last week (19 March 1909, 12, 14)

LESSER, Miss Bertha, is in Halifax visiting her mother (20 Dec. 1912, 16, 2)

LESSER, Mr. and Mrs. A., Prince Arthur Apts., have as their guests, Mrs. Lesser's mother and sister, Mrs. L. Wohl and Miss Ida Wohl, of Cleveland (17 Feb. 1911, 14, 14)

LESSER, Mr. and Mrs. and family are spending the summer at Chateauguay Basin (25 June 1909, 12, 28)

LESSER, Mr. and Mrs. Ben, have gone to New York (9 Dec. 1910, 14, 4)

LESSER, Mr. and Mrs. Moses and family, of Pittsburgh, Pa., were guests at the Windsor Hotel (23 June 1911, 14, 32)

LESSER, Mrs. A., Prince Arthur Apts., assisted by Mrs. I. Weinberg, gave a tea Thurs. aft., in honor of her sister, Miss Ida Wohl, of Cleveland, Ohio. Mrs. S.M. Ogulnik, was in charge of the tea table, assisted by the Misses Leah and Sarah Lesser, Annie Aronson and Beckie Holstein (29 Jan. 1909, 12, 7)

LESSER, Mrs. H., of Nairn Centre, Ont., is in Montreal (22 Oct. 1909, 12, 45)

LESSER, Mrs., of Halifax, N.S., is the guest of Mrs. Nathan Silver, Souvenir Ave. (13 June 1913, 16, 27)

LEVENSTEIN, Miss Ray and Miss Sadie Ram are at the Castel des Monts Hotel in Ste. Agathe for a few weeks (18 July 1913, 16, 32)

LEVENSTEIN, Miss Ray, has returned from a holiday in St. Laurent (19 Aug. 1910, 13, 40)

LEVENSTEIN, Miss Ray, will spend several weeks in Ste. Agathe (19 July 1912, 15, 32)

LEVETUS, Mrs. H. and the Misses Birkenthal, of Toronto, have suffered the loss of their mother who died last week (1 Oct. 1909, 12, 42)

LEVI, Jack and Maurice, have gone to England to attend their parents' golden wedding anniversary (14 June 1912, 15, 27)

LEVI, Jack, was elected president of the Montefiore Club Thurs. evening last week. Other officers elected were:- M.J. Hirsch, vice-pres.; Lewis H. Cohen, hon. treas.; L.H. Jacobs, hon. sec.; Michael Hirsch, Isaac Friedman, E. Blout, Jack Samenhof, Charles L. Friedman, council; and Maxwell Cohen, K.C. (23 Sept. 1910, 13, 45)

LEVI, Lester, is in Atlantic City for a few weeks (27 Dec. 1912, 16, 3)

LEVI, Lyon, is in New York on a short visit (21 Jan. 1910, 13, 10)

LEVI, Lyon, of Toronto, was in Montreal the past week (14 March 1913, 16, 14)

LEVI, Maurice, returned from a short stay in New York (22 Aug. 1913, 16, 37)

LEVI, Miss Bluma, who visited Mrs. William Levi in St. John, N.B., has returned to Ottawa (28 July 1911, 14, 37)

LEVI, Miss Hilda, of New York, is visiting her aunt, Mrs. David Levi, Mount Stephen Ave. for a few weeks (24 Dec. 1909, 13, 6)

LEVI, Miss Hilda, of New York, is the guest of the Misses Samuels, Drummond St. (27 Dec. 1912, 16, 3)

LEVI, Miss Irene, Dorchester St., has returned to Montreal for a short visit, prior to her marriage which takes place in New York, on March 17, 1909 (12 March 1909, 12, 13)

LEVI, Miss, of London, England, is the guest of Mrs. Henry Saxe, Western Ave. (27 Dec. 1912, 16, 3)

LEVI, Mr. and Mrs. D., and Miss Blanche Levi left Sun. night for New York to attend the wedding of Miss Irene Levi to H.P. Shearman which took place on Wed. March 17, 1909 (19 March 1909, 12, 14)

LEVI, Mr. and Mrs. David, Dorchester St. West, will receive in New York City, on Feb. 28, 1909, in honor of the engagement of their daughter, Irene, to A. Sherwin, of New York (19 Feb. 1909, 12, 10)

LEVI, Mr. and Mrs. David, Westmount, are visiting their daughter, Mrs. Schwerin, in New York (4 Feb. 1910, 13, 12)

LEVI, Mrs. D., Dorchester St., gave a luncheon in honor of Mr. Lhevinne (5 Feb. 1909, 12, 8)

LEVI, Mrs. D., Dorchester St., will hold a reception, Feb. 28, 1909 at the Majestic Hotel, New York, in honor of her daughter's engagement to Mr. Sherwin (26 Feb. 1909, 12, 11)

LEVI, Mrs. D., Mount Stephen Ave., was "At Home" Wed. aft. in honor of her daughter, Mrs. Sherwin, of New York, who is visiting her. Mesdames J.S. Leo and I.G. Goldenstein poured tea and coffee (22 April 1910, 13, 23)

LEVI, Mrs. Maurice, St. Catherine St. W., returned from a trip abroad (18 July 1913, 16, 32)

LEVI, Mrs. Maurice, Wood Ave., Westmount, is at Old Orchard, Me., for a few weeks (9 Aug. 1912, 15, 35)

LEVI, Mrs. Raphael, of New York, is visiting Mrs. D. Levi, St. Luke St. (14 Nov. 1913, 16, 49)

LEVI, Mrs. William, has returned home to St. John, N.B., after visiting relatives in Mattawa, Toronto and Montreal (27 Oct. 1911, 14, 50)

LEVI, Mrs. William, of St. John, N.B. (née Sadie Vineberg, of Montreal) received Tues. aft. Jan. 31, 1911, at her home 2 Exmouth St., St. John. She was assisted in receiving by her sister-in-law, Mrs. Paul Levi. Mrs. Alfred Isaacs and Miss Mattie Levi assisted in the tea room (10 Feb. 1911, 14, 13)

LEVI, Percy, has left for Toronto where he will reside (22 Jan. 1909, 12, 6)

LEVIN, A., 81 Durocher St., is in New York for a few days on business (14 Jan. 1910, 13, 9)

LEVIN, A., has returned from a business trip to New York (11 Nov. 1910, 13, 52)

LEVIN, A., Shuter St., returned from a week at Old Orchard (15 Aug. 1913, 16, 36)

LEVIN, A., was in Toronto on Mon. on business (19 Nov. 1909, 13, 1)

LEVIN, A., was in Toronto on Sun. and Mon. (25

Feb. 1910, 13, 15)

LEVIN, A., was on a business trip to Toronto (9 Sept. 1910, 13, 43)

LEVIN, A., went to Boston Wed. night to attend his nephew's birthday and will then proceed to Old Orchard Beach (22 July 1910, 13, 36)

LEVIN, Abraham, (J.P.), gave an interview to The Canadian Jewish Times about his seven weeks' trip to Europe. There he met Prof. Otto Warburg in Berlin. Mr. Levin has lived in Montreal for twenty years and has built up a large business, the Dominion Cord and Tassel Co. He is a justice of the peace in Montreal and was recently elected vice-president of the Federation of Zionist Societies of Canada (15 Jan. 1909, 12, 5)

LEVIN, E.C., Lawrence Tannenbaum and Horace Cohen were some of the teachers at the Baron de Hirsch Free School which held its closing exercises on Sun. May 28, 1911. Essays were read by David Mendel, Philip Myervitz and Miss Ida Rosen (1 June 1911, 14, 29)

LEVIN, J., left for a few weeks at Mount Clemens (14 Nov. 1913, 16, 49)

LEVIN, Mr. and Mrs. A., 14 Durocher St., send New Year greetings (11 Sept. 1912, 15, 40)

LEVIN, Mr. and Mrs. A., 81 Durocher St., gave a dinner last Sat. in honor of the approaching marriage of Mr. Levin's brother, Max L. Levin to Miss Anna Coviensky. Those present were:- Rabbi Herman Abramowitz, Lazarus Cohen, Mr. and Mrs. M. Coviensky, Mr. and Mrs. Max Fineberg, M. Brown, of Boston, Mrs. Margolius, Mrs. Abramowitz and Mr. Phillips (16 Sept. 1910, 13, 44)

LEVIN, Mr. and Mrs. A. and son, and A. Harris left Tues. night for New York. Messrs. Levin and Harris sail for Europe tomorrow where they will attend the Zionist Congress in Basle. Mrs. Levin and son will spend the summer at Old Orchard (23 June 1911, 14, 32)

LEVIN, Mr. and Mrs. A., are on holiday in New York (25 March 1910, 13, 19)

LEVIN, Mr. and Mrs. A.A. and Master Leon Levin have returned from Old Orchard, Me. (30 Aug. 1912, 15, 38)

LEVIN, Mr. and Mrs. S., 991 St. Urbain St., have issued invitations for a "Siyyum Torah" which will take place on Rosh Hashana evening (Oct. 5, 1909) 7 to 12 p.m., at Congregation Adath Eshovran, 841 St. Lawrence Blvd. Rabbis Herman Abramowitz, Hirsch Cohen, M.A. Levin and S. Goldstein and choir will officiate at the ceremony (1 Oct. 1909, 12, 42)

LEVIN, Mrs. A. and son, 81 Durocher St., have returned from two months at Old Orchard Beach (26 Aug. 1910, 13, 41)

LEVIN, Mrs. A. and son are spending the summer at Old Orchard Beach. Mr. Levin spent a few days there before going to New York and then returning to Montreal (8 July 1910, 13, 34)

LEVIN, Mrs. A. and son Leon Levin have returned home from Old Orchard, Me. (25 Aug. 1911, 14, 41)

LEVIN, Mrs. H., Hutchison St., has gone to Hartford, Conn., visit her niece, Mrs. B. Zeeman (19 Jan. 1912, 15, 10)

LEVIN, Mrs. H.M., has recovered from her recent illness (6 May 1910, 13, 25)

LEVIN, Rev. M.A., a Ziere Zion Society member, remitted $1.50 for the purchase of an olive tree in the Herzl Wald in memory of David Zemmleman, a member who died Jan. 12, 1909. Members of the society are Talmud Torah students who are learning Hebrew (19 Feb. 1909, 12, 10)

LEVINE, A., was in New York on a business trip during the week (15 Oct. 1909, 12, 44)

LEVINE, A.A., won $100 in gold in the Ladies' Hebrew Benevolent Society raffle which he then donated to the Hebrew Free Loan Association and the LHBS (6 June 1913, 16, 26)

LEVINE, B., of Depencer & Levine, returned from Britannia-on-the-Bay (5 Sept. 1913, 16, 39)

LEVINE, B., of the Star Realty Co., is on vacation at Britannia-on-the-Bay (22 Aug. 1913, 16, 37)

LEVINE, E. and J. Segal graduated McGill University, Faculty of Medicine and received their M.D. degrees. Harry Dover, of Ottawa, fourth year medicine, won a prize (13 June 1913, 16, 27)

Are you interested in the Moral and Educational upbringing of your Children?

...... IF SO, READ ......

"Pedagogy among the Jews"

An Historical Enquiry

By REV. M. A. LEVINE,

Principal of the Montreal Hebrew Free School, 410 Bleury Street,

Deals exclusively with education among the Jews. Replete with Proverbs and Expressions from Talmud and Midrash and descriptions of the systems of teaching in ancient and modern times.

Highest encomiums from press and scholars.   A book you should not do without.

LEVINE, H.E.M., is ill at home (2 April 1909, 12, 16)

LEVINE, H.E.M., St. Joseph Blvd., is in the course of complete recovery from his lengthy illness and painful operation (21 May 1909, 12, 23)

LEVINE, H.M., managing-director of the Montreal Shirt and Overall Co., was nominated for president of the Dominion Commercial Travellers Association (14 Nov. 1913, 16, 49)

LEVINE, M.I., is on a pleasure tour of Toronto, Boston and Niagara Falls (10 Sept. 1909, 12, 39)

LEVINE, Miss Etta, is the guest of Miss Sylvia Goldstein at Dixie, Que. (22 Aug. 1913, 16, 37)

LEVINE, Miss Etta, was convenor of the Young Ladies' Hebrew Sewing Society eighteenth annual charity dance at the Ritz-Carlton Hotel on Mon. Dec. 29, 1913. The debutantes were:- the Misses Eva Gittleson, Fanny Heillig, Effie Hyman, Mamie Lightstone, Leba Livingstone, Edith Ogulnik, M. Rosenberg, Rose and Sadie Solomon, Florence Wener and Ruth Workman (2 Jan. 1914, 17, 4)

LEVINE, Miss Ettie, although still seriously ill, is reported showing improvement (31 Dec. 1909, 13, 7)

LEVINE, Miss Martha, of Midland, Ont., has gone on a month's trip to Toronto and Hamilton (11 Feb. 1910, 13, 13)

LEVINE, Miss Minnie, of London, England, sister of Rev. Walter Levine, of that city, stayed over in Montreal the past weekend, en route to Calgary to visit her brother (25 July 1913, 16, 33)

LEVINE, Miss Rae, is visiting her sister, Mrs. W. Shenkman, of Ottawa (16 April, 1909, 12, 18)

LEVINE, Miss Ray, St. Urbain St., has returned from a visit to her sister, Mrs. W. Shankman, in Ottawa (6 May 1910, 13, 25)

LEVINE, Miss Ruth, daughter of Mrs. Herbert Levine, unfurled the Union Jack at the official opening of the Mount Sinai Sanatorium in Ste. Agathe on Sun. June 29, 1913. Louis Vineberg was chairman of the excursion committee. Speakers included Michael Hirsch, chairman of the executive committee; Mark Workman, pres. of the Sanatorium; Ascher Pierce; J.A. Jacobs; treas.; Maxwell Goldstein, K.C., hon. counsel; Lyon Cohen; Alderman A. Blumenthal; Rabbi Nathan Gordon; Reuben Brainin; Dr. J.B. Fish, superintendent; and M. Rubin (4 July 1913, 16, 30)

LEVINE, Miss Ruth, was the guest of Miss Dorothy Cookson at Longueil on Sat. (5 July 1912, 15, 30)

LEVINE, Mr. and Mrs. A., 81 Durocher St., convey their thanks for the kind enquiries during their son's illness (10 Sept. 1909, 12, 39)

LEVINE, Mr. and Mrs. A.S., of Westmount, are going south for a couple weeks (27 Feb. 1914, 17, 9)

LEVINE, Mr. and Mrs. H.M. and Miss Ruth Levine sailed by the Tunisian, June 16, 1911 for a short stay abroad (16 June 1911, 14, 31)

LEVINE, Mr. and Mrs. H.M., St. Joseph Blvd., Annex, are spending the week in New York (12 May 1911, 14, 26)

LEVINE, Mr. and Mrs. H.M., St. Joseph Blvd., left for Charleston and Norfolk, Va., and will be away several weeks (16 May 1913, 16, 23)

LEVINE, Mr. and Mrs. Herbert, are in Atlantic City for a few weeks (1 Oct. 1909, 12, 42)

LEVINE, Mr. and Mrs. Solomon, will soon occupy their summer cottage at Cartierville (18 June 1909, 12, 27)

LEVINE, Mrs. A. and children are spending a couple of weeks at Ste. Agathe (16 July 1909, 12, 31)

LEVINE, Mrs. and Miss Mina Levine, have gone to Charleston, S.C., for a few months (12 Nov. 1909, 12, 48)

LEVINE, Mrs. H.M. and daughter, Mrs. M. Hirsch and Miss Bertha Raphael are in New York for a week (3 Nov. 1911, 14, 51)

LEVINE, Mrs. H.M., and Miss Ruth Levine are in New York visiting their brother, A. Raphael (26 April 1912, 15, 24)

LEVINE, Mrs. Herbert, is in Norfolk, Va., visiting her sister, Mrs. Caton (8 Nov. 1912, 15, 48)

LEVINE, Mrs. J., of Brooklyn, N.Y., is the guest of her daughter, Mrs. Maxwell Harris, Crescent St. (23 April 1909, 12, 19)

LEVINE, Mrs. P. and Miss Minnie Jackson are spending two weeks in Pont Viau (5 Aug. 1910, 13, 38)

LEVINE, Mrs. R. and Miss Mina Levine are visiting Mrs. Joseph Mendels, in Perth, Ont. (5 Sept. 1913, 16, 39)

LEVINE, Mrs. R.H. and daughter sailed on the S.S. Campania for Charlottetown, P.E.I. and will be away for a few weeks (8 July 1910, 13, 34)

LEVINE, Rev. M.A., principal of the Montreal Talmud Torah, has returned from Ottawa, Toronto and Hamilton. In Hamilton he delivered a sermon during Yom Kippur (18 Oct. 1910, 13, 49)

LEVINE, S., was in Ottawa visiting his daughter, Mrs. W. Shankman (15 July 1910, 13, 35)

LEVINE, William and Mark Levine, of New York, were in Montreal (4 Feb. 1910, 13, 12)

LEVINE, Willie, is visiting his sister, Mrs. Louis Sapery, in New York (20 March 1914, 17, 12)

Levinne, William, is spending a few days in Boston (21 May 1909, 12, 23)

LEVINOFF, Mr. and Mrs. H.M., Pine Ave. W., left for a week in New York and Atlantic City (27 March 1914, 17, 13)

LEVINOFF, Mr. and Mrs. R. and children, of Cochrane, Ont., who visited Mr. Levinoff's brother, H.M. Levinoff, Pine Ave., have gone to Toronto to visit Mrs. Levinoff's parents, Mr. and Mrs. Rittenberg, Grange Ave. (17 March 1911, 14, 18)

LEVINOFF, Mrs. H.M., donated $25.00 to the Hebrew Ladies' Aid Society which will "...assist the society in carrying out its good work amongst poor Jewish families." (15 Oct. 1913, 16, 45)

LEVINOFF, Mrs. I., called the newspaper's attention to the picture show "The Fire Bug". "This picture shows how two Jews, desirous of securing their insurance money, set fire to their property, etc." The insult has aroused a great deal of indignation and we have been asked to call attention to the matter." (5 Sept. 1913, 16, 39)

Levinson, Misses Myrtie and Bessie, are spending a holiday in New York (11 March 1910, 13, 17)

LEVINSON, A.H., spent the weekend with his sister, Mrs. J.S. Gabriel (5 Jan. 1912, 15, 8)

LEVINSON, A.H., who is in Ottawa on business, was the guest of his sister, Mrs. J.S. Gabriel. He, Mrs. Gabriel and her daughter will return to Montreal for Passover (7 April 1911, 14, 21)

LEVINSON, A.J., 189 Craig St., wishes the past and present members of the Maccabean Circle and his many relatives and friends a happy New Year (1 Oct. 1913, 16, 42-43)

LEVINSON, A.J., Arts '11, was elected president of the Maccabean Circle for 1911-1912. Other officers elected were:- J.B. Hirschberg, Med. '14, vice-pres.; Harry Dover, Med. '14, sec.; J. Segal, Med. '13, treas.; N. Fineberg, M.A., Law '13 and H. Goldblatt, Arts '11, executive; E.C. Levine, Med. '13, ex-officio. Louis Fitch, B.A., who is about to graduate law, was elected an hon. life member (14 April 1911, 14, 22)

LEVINSON, Ben, local manager of S. Weisglass Ltd., has returned from holidays in New York (20 Sept. 1912, 15, 41)

LEVINSON, Harry and Miss Myrtie Levinson have returned from New York (13 Jan. 1911, 14, 9)

LEVINSON, Harry, has returned from the Porcupine district (28 July 1911, 14, 37)

LEVINSON, Joseph, has returned from Old Orchard Beach (13 Aug. 1909, 12, 35)

LEVINSON, Joseph, Stanley St., returned Tues., from an extended trip out west (19 Feb. 1909, 12, 10)

LEVINSON, Jr., J., has returned from his trip to the West (26 Feb. 1909, 12, 11)

LEVINSON, Jr. Joseph, is in California (8 Jan. 1909, 12, 4)

LEVINSON, Lyon and the Misses Levinson, Church St., have returned from Old Orchard (2 Sept. 1910, 13, 42)

LEVINSON, Lyon, Church St., has gone to Old Orchard Beach for his summer holidays (29 July 1910, 13, 37)

LEVINSON, Lyon, Elm Ave., left for Chicago, Winnipeg and Vancouver and other points west (13 June 1913, 16, 27)

LEVINSON, Lyon, is captain of the Primrose hockey team (5 March 1909, 12, 12)

LEVINSON, Lyon was elected president of the Tanglewood Club annual meeting on Wed. Dec. 8, 1909 at 8 p.m. Other officers elected were:- Florence Wener, vice-pres.; and Flossie Claman, sec.-treas. (10 Dec. 1909, 13, 4)

LEVINSON, Miss Annie, Church St., returned from six weeks in New York where she visited relatives (29 March 1912, 15, 20)

LEVINSON, Miss Bessie, leaves next Tues. evening for Old Orchard Beach for the summer (23 July 1909, 12, 32)

LEVINSON, Miss Cecila, Craig St. E., is on the road to complete recovery from her recent illness (23 May 1913, 16, 23)

LEVINSON, Miss Cecilia, is visiting her sister, Mrs. J.S. Gabriel, Church St., Ottawa (29 Dec. 1911, 15, 7)

LEVINSON, Miss, Drummond St., has gone to New York for a few weeks (4 March 1910, 13, 16)

LEVINSON, Miss Ethel, of Toronto, was a passenger on the S.S. Victorian bound for Europe last Fri. (4 June 1909, 12, 25)

LEVINSON, Miss Leah, of Bradford, Pa., is the guest of her parents, Mr. and Mrs. N. Levinson, Cherrier St. (20 Aug. 1909, 12, 36)

LEVINSON, Miss Leah, of Chicago, is staying with Mr. and Mrs. J.L. Sabbath (14 March 1913, 16, 14)

LEVINSON, Miss Lily, spent a short holiday at Hudson-on-the-Lake (3 Sept. 1909, 12, 38)

LEVINSON, Miss M., Bishop St., leaves for New York where she will spend a few weeks (25 Feb. 1910, 13, 15)

LEVINSON, Miss Mabyl, Church St., has returned home after spending the weekend with Miss Simon, in Alexandria, Ont. (4 Nov. 1910, 13, 51)

LEVINSON, Miss Mabyl, has left for Old Orchard Beach where she will spend a few weeks (12 Aug. 1910, 13, 39)

LEVINSON, Miss Mabyl, has left for Old Orchard Beach (11 Aug. 1911, 14, 39)

LEVINSON, Miss Myrtie, Bishop St., has gone to New York for a few weeks (30 Dec. 1910, 14, 7)

LEVINSON, Miss Mystie and Harry Levinson have returned from their holiday at Old Orchard, Me. (19 Aug. 1910, 13, 40)

LEVINSON, Miss Sara, Drummond St., has returned from New York where she was visiting relatives (2 April 1909, 12, 17)

LEVINSON, Miss Sarah, leaves for New York for an extended visit (22 Jan. 1909, 12, 6)

LEVINSON, Miss Tilly and Lyon Levinson are spending a few days in Ste. Agathe (8 July 1910, 13, 34)

LEVINSON, Miss Tilly, Cherrier St., is in New York for a few weeks (25 March 1910, 13, 19)

LEVINSON, Miss Tilly, Elm Ave., is visiting Miss Simon, Alexandria, Ont. (28 March 1913, 16, 16)

LEVINSON, Miss Tilly, has returned from New York, Worcester and Boston (22 April 1910, 13, 23)

LEVINSON, Misses Mabyl and Tilly Levinson are at Old Orchard Beach (30 July 1909, 12, 33)

LEVINSON, Misses Tilly and Annie, are spending a few weeks at Old Orchard Beach (12 Aug. 1910, 13, 39)

LEVINSON, Mr. and Mrs. S., 107 Drummond St., will be "at home" on Sun. Oct. 31, 1909 (29 Oct. 1909, 12, 46)

LEVINSON, Mr. and Mrs. S., Drummond St., were "at home" to their friends on Sun. Oct. 31, 1909, in honor of their daughter, Miss Sarah Levinson. Guests included Mesdames S. Wener, W. Levin and Zeaman (5 Nov. 1909, 12, 47)

LEVINSON, Mrs. B., who has been visiting her parents, has returned to Winnipeg, accompanied by Miss Hattie and Master I. Levinson (26 Feb. 1909, 12, 11)

LEVINSON, Mrs. I. and her daughter, Cecilia, returned from Ottawa where they visited Mr. and Mrs. J.S. Gabriel (30 Aug. 1912, 15, 38)

LEVINSON, Mrs. I., is visiting her daughter in Ottawa (19 April 1912, 15, 23)

LEVINSON, Mrs. Joseph and family left on Wed. for Old Orchard Beach (23 July 1909, 12, 32)

LEVINSON, Mrs. S., 107 Drummond St., donated ten dollars to the Montreal Hebrew Free School (5 Dec. 1913, 16, 52)

LEVINSON, Mrs. S. and Miss Lily Levinson, Drummond St., have returned from Caledonia Springs (26 Aug. 1910, 13, 41)

LEVINSON, Mrs. S. and Miss Sarah Levinson have returned from Caledonia Springs (13 Aug. 1909, 12, 35)

LEVINSON, N., Cherrier St., is in New York on business (11 Feb. 1910, 13, 13)

LEVINSON, N., Church St., is in New York on business (5 May 1911, 14, 25)

LEVINSON, the Misses Mabyl and Tilly, have returned from Old Orchard Beach (20 Aug. 1909, 12, 36)

LEVINSON, W., Church St., has gone to Winnipeg for several weeks on business (4 Nov. 1910, 13, 51)

LEVINSON, Zave and E.G. Silverman, returned from Lake Ouimet, St. Jovite, Que., where they were guests at Gray's Rock Inn (22 Nov. 1912, 15, 50)

LEVINSON, Zave and Mrs. Levinson, are at Caledonia Springs, Ont. for a few weeks (25 July 1911, 14, 36)

LEVINSON, Zave, has returned from New York (19 Jan. 1912, 15, 10)

LEVITT, Joseph, of New York, is visiting his parents, Mr. and Mrs. B. Levitt, City Hall Ave. (29 Aug. 1913, 16, 38)

LEVITT, M., has returned to Montreal from his business trip to New York (22 Oct. 1909, 12, 45)

LEVITT, Mr. and Mrs. Sam and family are summering at Ste. Agathe (25 July 1913, 16, 33)

LEVY, A., of Hamilton, Ont., was registered at the Windsor Hotel (5 March 1909, 12, 12)

LEVY, B., 153 Laval Ave., who was in the General Hospital for six weeks with an attack of typhoid fever, has returned home (6 May 1910, 13, 25)

LEVY, C.J., of Pittsburgh, Pa., is at the St. James Hotel (11 June 1909, 12, 26)

LEVY, David, left on Mon. for a few weeks in New York (23 June 1911, 14, 32)

LEVY, David, returned home last Sat. on the S.S. Virginian (14 May 1909, 12, 22)

LEVY, David, returned on Mon. from a five months stay in Europe (21 Jan. 1910, 13, 10)

LEVY, David, was elected president of the Agudoth Zion Society of Montreal at the annual meeting last Sun. Other officers elected were:- Leon Goldman, 1st vice-pres.; A. Levin, 2nd vice-pres.; M.B. Steine, treas.; Joseph Fine, corr. sec.; S. Haskell, rec. sec.; A. Harris, fin. sec.; Lyon Heillig, L. Ackerman, Charles Fisher, Manuel Levitt, Max Levine, O. Bercuson, Z. Ratner, S. Willinsky, Hiram Levy, Harry Bloomstein, Rev. A. Levin, Principal I. Skibelski, David Blumer, Isaac Lande, Max Gelbman, H. Lozinsky, H. Lang, M. Fromson and S. Talpis, council members. A. Ellison won the raffle for a Jewish Colonial Bank share. (13 May 1910, 13, 26)

LEVY, Herbert, of Toronto, was in Montreal the past week (13 Jan. 1911, 14, 9)

LEVY, J., G.A. Goldstein, B. Jacobs, E. Goldstein and K. Leishman are among the boys who were at Camp Agaming, St. Donat de Montcalm, Que. (3 Sept. 1909, 12, 38)

LEVY, J., was registered at the Chateau Frontenac while in Quebec City (9 Dec. 1910, 14, 4)

LEVY, Jos. C.E., 219 St. Urbain; Louis Ressler, 80 Dufferin Square; Maud Sanderman, 29 Cote; Joseph Steinberg, 197 Elgin; Esther White, 74 St. Lawrence; John J. Weinfield, 458 St. Lawrence; and Mark Workman, 156 Bleury, all of St. Lawrence Ward, are persons on the Parliamentary Voters' revision list (3 Feb. 1911, 14, 12)

LEVY, Maurice, Samuel Ram and Marcel Marcus leave for Toronto and the Muskoka Lakes Mon. night (12 Aug. 1910, 13, 39)

LEVY, Miss Berthe, of Pittsburgh, Pa., wrote a letter to The Canadian Jewish Times, about her brother Rene J. Levy who went down with the Titanic. He possessed "...all the good traits of a Jew, having been raised as a Jew by good and religious parents." (24 May 1912, 15, 25)

LEVY, Miss Bessie, returned home to Moncton, N.B., last night after visiting Mr. and Mrs. D. Shapiro, Park Ave. (10 Feb. 1911, 14, 13)

LEVY, Miss Ida, daughter of Rabbi M.I. Levy, of Toronto, is visiting Mr. and Mrs. E. Goldfine, Ontario St. (29 Dec. 1911, 15, 7)

LEVY, Miss Lily Lois, of New York, is visiting friends and relatives and is the guest of Miss Miriam Cohen (25 July 1911, 14, 36)

LEVY, Miss Lily, of New York, is the guest of her cousins, Rabbi H. Cohen and family (6 Oct. 1911, 14, 47)

LEVY, Miss, of New York, is visiting Mrs. Hiram Vineberg (9 Dec. 1910, 14, 4)

LEVY, Mr. and Mrs. S.L., of Buffalo, N.Y., are guests of Mrs. Moe Albert, Prince Arthur Apts. (31 Jan. 1913, 16, 8)

LEVY, Mr. and Mrs. W., are spending the summer at Bluff Point, Lake Champlain, N.Y. (30 June 1911, 14, 33)

LEVY, Mrs. D., is directress of the YWHA, which held a general meeting on Sun. Jan. 26, 1913. Elected to various committees were:- the Misses E. Benjamin, B. Cohen, S. Dovia, M. Frank, G. Gordon, F. Hirschfield, E.L. Issen, E. Jacobs, D. Ratner, L. Saxe, J. Schulich, B. Silver,

F. Silverman, A. Strassburg and C. Wagner (7 Feb. 1913, 16, 9)

LEVY, Mrs. D., was elected directress of the YWHA. Other officers are:- Mrs. J. Goldstein, hon. pres.; Miss Pinsler, pres.; Miss B. Cohen, vice-pres.; Miss R. Brotman, treas.; Miss R. Turner, fin. sec.; and Miss W.F. Presser, corr. sec. (31 Jan. 1913, 16, 8)

LEVY, Mrs. V., of Pittsburgh, Pa., has returned home after visiting her son, B. Levy, 153 Laval Ave. (17 June 1910, 13, 31)

LEVY, Rev. Dr. J. Leonard, speaks in Temple Emanu-El, on Sun. May 15, 1910 at 11 a.m. on "The Meaning and Message of Modern Judaism". He will be the guest of Rabbi Nathan Gordon (13 May 1910, 13, 26)

LEWIN, Mark, of Philadelphia, visited his sister, Mrs. S.E. Lichtenhein, Dorchester St. W. (5 March 1909, 12, 12)

LEWIN, Miss, Dorchester St., entertained Mon. aft. at cards (5 Feb. 1909, 12, 8)

LEWIN, Miss, have gone to Philadelphia and the South for a visit for a few weeks (7 May 1909, 12, 21)

LEWIN, Mrs. and family, of Philadelphia, are guests of their sister, Mrs. S.E. Lichtenhein, at Beaurepaire for a few weeks (2 July 1909, 12, 29)

LEWIN, Mrs. and Miss Lewin who been travelling abroad the past two years, have returned to Montreal and will spend the winter with S.E. Lichtenhein (30 Sept. 1910, 13, 46)

LEWIN, Mrs., has gone to New York to join her daughter, Miss Eina Lewin, where they will leave for an extended trip abroad (14 Jan. 1910, 13, 9)

LEWINSON, Mrs. Jerome and son, and Mrs. Herman Frankel and family are at Abenakis Springs (22 Aug. 1913, 16, 37)

LEWIS, Felix, has returned from Ste. Agathe, Que. (27 Aug. 1909, 12, 37)

LEWIS, Felix, leaves shortly for Europe (19 March 1909, 12, 14)

LEWIS, Joseph, of Ottawa, is registered at the Carslake Hotel (19 Nov. 1909, 13, 1)

LEWIS, Louis and Miss Lewis have returned from a short visit to Atlantic City (1 Oct. 1909, 12, 42)

LEWIS, Louis, donated $1.50 for an olive tree to be planted in the Herzl Wald in his name (19 Feb. 1909, 12, 10)

LEWIS, Louis, is in Toronto on business and will return Tues. (13 Jan. 1911, 14, 9)

LEWIS, Miss Grace, Mount Stephen Ave., is the guest of Mr. and Mrs. S.L. Vineberg in Brockville, Ont. (29 Aug. 1913, 16, 38)

LEWIS, Miss Grace, Sherbrooke St. W., has gone to Toledo, Ohio for a few weeks (3 March 1911, 14, 16)

LEWIS, Miss Grace, Sherbrooke St. W., has returned from Toledo, Ohio where she visited her aunt (16 June 1911, 14, 31)

LEWIS, Miss Margaret, Sherbrooke St., will spend a short holiday in New York (24 Dec. 1909, 13, 6)

LEWIS, Miss R. and Mrs. A. Heinsheimer were guests of Mrs. E. Berliner at Dorval, Que. (12 July 1912, 15, 31)

LEWIS, Miss Rosalind, is spending a few weeks in the Mountains (1 Sept. 1911, 14, 42)

LEWIS, Miss Rosalind, left for Vancouver where she will spend a few weeks with Mr. and Mrs. Felix Lewis (6 June 1913, 16, 26)

LEWIS, Miss Rosalind, returned home after spending the past three months in Vancouver, Seattle and Chicago (14 Nov. 1913, 16, 49)

LEWIS, Miss Rosalind, will spend a few weeks in New York with friends (9 April 1909, 12, 17)

LEWIS, Miss Roslyn, who was on holiday at Caledonia Springs, is now at Ste. Agathe (23 July 1909, 12, 32)

LEWIS, Mr. and Mrs. Felix and Mr. and Mrs. S. Stern, are spending a few weeks in Atlantic City and New York (19 Sept. 1913, 16, 41)

LEWIS, Mr. and Mrs. Louis, are registered at the Knickerbocker Hotel, New York, for a few days (19 Feb. 1909, 12, 10)

LEWIS, Mrs. and Miss Lewis are spending a few weeks at Ste. Agathe (2 July 1909, 12, 29)

LEWIS, Mrs. Felix, has returned from a short visit to New York (10 Sept. 1909, 12, 39)

LEWIS, Mrs. Felix, left for Chicago to attend the wedding of her brother, Mr. Simcoe to Miss Frank (8 Jan. 1909, 12, 4)

LEWIS, Mrs. Felix, of Vancouver, is in Montreal visiting her sister, Mrs. M.J. Orkin. Mr. and Mrs. Orkin sail for Europe on June 16, 1912 (24 May 1912, 15, 25)

LEWIS, Mrs. George, has left for a visit to Toledo, Ohio (30 Dec. 1910, 14, 7)

LEWIS, Mrs. Louis, has returned home and is recovering after undergoing a serious operation in the hospital (1 June 1911, 14, 29)

LEWIS, Mrs. N. and Miss Lewis are visiting Mrs. J.A. Jacobs, at Pine Bluffs, N.Y. (8 Sept. 1911, 14, 43)

LEWIS, Mrs. Nathan and daughter, Miss Helen Lewis, have returned from a long trip to Toledo and Mount Clemens. They will join Mrs. J.A. Jacobs in St. Anne's for the summer (18 June 1909, 12, 27)

LEWIS, Mrs. Nathan, Miss Helen Lewis, Jacob A. Jacobs, D.S. Friedman, Eli W. Jacobs, Jack Samenhof and Benjamin W. Jacobs were weekend visitors at Caledonia Springs (13 Aug. 1909, 12, 35)

LEWIS, Mrs. S., of St. John, N.B., is the guest of Mrs. I. Rubinovitch, Sherbrooke St. W. (24 May 1912, 15, 25)

LEWIS, Mrs. S.B., is the guest of her sister, Mrs. I.M. Rubinovich, Sherbrooke St., Westmount (3 Feb. 1911, 14, 12)

LEWIS, Samuel D., of St. John, N.B., was in Montreal on a short visit (10 Sept. 1909, 12, 39)

LICHTENHEIN, L., of Boston, spent a few days in Montreal visiting his parents (24 Sept. 1909, 12, 41)

LICHTENHEIN, Louis, of Boston, is in Montreal for a few days (18 June 1909, 12, 27)

LICHTENHEIN, Louis, of Boston, stayed at the Windsor Hotel (11 July 1913, 16, 31)

LICHTENHEIN, Louis, of Boston, was in Montreal for a few days (31 Dec. 1909, 13, 7)

LICHTENHEIN, Louis, of Boston, was in Montreal visiting his parents who are guests at the Windsor Hotel (30 June 1911, 14, 33)

LICHTENHEIN, Mr. and Mrs. E. and Mr. and Mrs. J. Goldsmith and family, Cincinnati, have gone to Atlantic City (22 July 1910, 13, 36)

LICHTENHEIN, Mr. and Mrs. E., have returned from Cincinnati and Atlantic City (2 April 1909, 12, 17)

LICHTENHEIN, Mr. and Mrs. E., have gone to Atlantic City for a few weeks (16 July 1909, 12, 31)

LICHTENHEIN, Mr. and Mrs. E., have left for Cincinnati to visit their daughter, Mrs. L. Goldsmith (31 Dec. 1909, 13, 7)

LICHTENHEIN, Mr. and Mrs. E., have given up their residence on Peel St. and are now residing in the Windsor Hotel (4 Nov. 1910, 13, 51)

LICHTENHEIN, Mr. and Mrs. E., left for New York, to attend the funeral of their nephew, Alfred Foss, of Boston, who died Sat. Oct. 18, 1909, after a short illness (29 Oct. 1909, 12, 46)

LICHTENHEIN, Mr. and Mrs. Ed., are guests at the Windsor Hotel for several months (19 May 1911, 14, 27)

LICHTENHEIN, Mr. and Mrs. Ed., are spending the summer in Atlantic City (7 July 1911, 14, 34)

LICHTENHEIN, Mr. and Mrs. Ed., Peel St., leave for Cincinnati where they will visit their daughters (15 Jan. 1909, 12, 5)

LICHTENHEIN, Mr. and Mrs. Ed., who were guests at the Windsor Hotel for the past two months, have gone to Cincinnati to spend the winter (20 Oct. 1911, 14, 49)

LICHTENHEIN, Mr. and Mrs. S.E. and family, accompanied by Mrs. Lewin, have left for Beaurepaire where they will spend the summer (11 June 1909, 12, 26)

LICHTENHEIN, Mr. and Mrs. S.E. and son, accompanied by Mrs. Lewin and Miss Anna Lewin are spending the summer at Beaurepaire (16 June 1911, 14, 31)

LICHTENHEIN, Mr. and Mrs. S.E. and son opened their summer cottage at Beaurepaire (30 May 1913, 16, 25)

LICHTENHEIN, Mr. and Mrs. S.E., are spending a few days at Caledonia Springs (10 Sept. 1909, 12, 39)

LICHTENHEIN, Mrs. Edward and Mrs. I.E. Lichtenhein left Mon. night for Boston to attend the funeral of Louis Foss, of Brookline, Mass., who died suddenly in New York on Sun. Nov. 8, 1913 (14 Nov. 1913, 16, 49)

LICHTENHEIN, Mrs. S.E. and Master Philip Lichtenhein, Peel St., are spending a few weeks in Atlantic City (7 April 1911, 14, 21)

LICHTENHEIN, Mrs. S.E. and Master Phillip, Peel St., left for Atlantic City (14 March 1913, 16, 14)

LICHTENHEIN, Mrs. S.E. and son have returned from their trip south (16 April 1909, 12, 18)

LICHTENHEIN, Mrs. S.E. and son leave on an extended trip to Charleston and the southern U.S. (5 March 1909, 12, 12)

LICHTENHEIN, Mrs. S.E., Peel St., is having an "At Home", Mon. Dec. 20, 1909 from 4 to 7 p.m. (17 Dec. 1909, 13, 5)

LICHTENHEIN, Mrs. Samuel E., is president of the Temple Emanuel Sisterhood (13 Dec. 1912, 16, 1)

LICHTENHEIN, S.E., has moved from 951 Dorchester St. W., to 304 Peel St. (7 May 1909, 12, 21)

LICHTENHEIN, S.E., has returned from a trip to Winnipeg (4 June 1909, 12, 25)

LICHTENHEIN, S.E., has returned from a short visit to New York (17 Dec. 1909, 13, 5)

LICHTENHEIN, S.E., will be in New York this week (12 Feb. 1909, 12, 9)

LICHTENSTEIN, Miss Clara, of the Royal Victoria College, is on a vacation tour through the U.S. (22 Oct. 1909, 12, 45)

LIGHTSTONE, Bernard, who received his Doctor of Dental Surgery degree at McGill, has opened an office at 116 St. Catherine St. W. "Here is hoping that he will pull well with the local community" (14 June 1912, 15, 27)

LIGHTSTONE, Dr., 130 Crescent St., has returned from Europe (10 Sept. 1909, 12, 39)

LIGHTSTONE, Dr. H. and his sister will sail for London and Paris, where they will spend a few weeks (21 May 1909, 12, 23)

LIGHTSTONE, Dr. H., has returned from a short trip to New York (5 Feb. 1909, 12, 8)

LIGHTSTONE, Dr. H., leaves for London on May 14, 1910, per S.S. Laurentic where he intends to settle permanently. In recognition of his services, the staff of Bishop's College (which has since amalgamated with McGill) will confer the degree of "ad eundem in absentia" at its June convocation in the medical faculty (6 May 1910, 13, 25)

LIGHTSTONE, Dr. H., Mr. and Mrs. Asher Pierce and Master Sidney Pierce were some of the Montrealers who registered at the High Commissioner's office in London, during the week ending June 29, 1909 (16 July 1909, 12, 31)

LIGHTSTONE, Dr. Hyman, formerly of Montreal, is practising in London, England. An ear, nose and throat specialist, he was appointed to the staff of the London Hospital (26 Dec. 1913, 17, 3)

LIGHTSTONE, Dr. Hyman, of London, England, is visiting his parents, after a four years' absence from home (27 Dec. 1912, 16, 3)

LIGHTSTONE, M., sails June 10, 1913 on the S.S. Laurentic for England where he will lecture in the major cities. He will also attend the Zionist Congress in Vienna on Sept. 2 (6 June 1913, 16, 26)

LIGHTSTONE, M., was elected president of Victoria Lodge, IOSB on Sun. Dec. 26, 1909. Other officers elected were:- M. Fromson, vice-pres.; I. Sourkes, treas.; L. Kert, rec.-sec.; M.A. Lauterman, fin.-sec.; F. Lewis, inside guardian; P. Jacobson, L. Shapiro and M. Lessor, trustees (31 Dec. 1909, 13, 7)

LIGHTSTONE, Maxwell, left Wed. for a weeks' holiday in Toronto (20 May 1910, 13, 27)

LIGHTSTONE, Maxwell, spoke on "The Four Attitudes of Zionism" at the Sun. April 27, 1913 meeting of the Zeire Zion Society (2 May 1913, 16, 21)

LIGHTSTONE, Maxwell, went to Sherbrooke Fri. to spend the weekend with his parents (29 Dec. 1911, 15, 7)

LIGHTSTONE, Maxwell, will deliver an illustrated lecture on "Jewish Activities in Canada" under the auspices of the B'nai U'Bnoth Zion Kadima, on Sun. April 6, 1913 in the Baron de Hirsch Institute. Tickets may be obtained from H. Lang, 677 St. Urbain St. Committee members in charge of the event are:- Reuben Brainin (chairman), Lyon Cohen, D. Feldman, Louis Fitch, Leon Goldman, J.S. Leo, E. Mauer, S. McKinley, M. Rubin, B.M. Speyer and M.B. Weiner (28 March 1913, 16, 16)

LIGHTSTONE, Michael, leaves on the S.S. Tunisian on Jan. 17, 1914 for London and Paris, where he will visit his children and family (16 Jan. 1914, 17, 6)

LIGHTSTONE, Michael, McKay St., is rapidly recovering from his recent illness (30 July 1909, 12, 33)

LIGHTSTONE, Miss Minnie, of Montreal, is visiting Mr. and Mrs. T. Vineberg, Sherbrooke, Que. for several weeks (7 Jan. 1910, 13, 8)

LIGHTSTONE, Miss Minnie, spent the weekend with her parents in Sherbrooke, Que. (29 Dec. 1911, 15, 7)

LIPMAN, Arthur (B.A.), has received his M.D. degree from Queen's University, Kingston (9 June 1911, 14, 30)

LIPMAN, B., has gone to New York for a short stay (25 Nov. 1910, 14, 2)

LIPMAN, Mr. and Mrs. Harris, of New York, are visiting their parents, Mr. and Mrs. B. Lipman, Brock St. (26 April 1912, 15, 24)

LIPSEY, Miss Fannie, Argyle Ave., has left for Chicago where she will visit relatives for a few weeks (5 March 1909, 12, 12)

LITOWITZ, Israel, president of the Hebrew Consumptive Aid Association, chaired the general meeting last Sun. evening. Mr. Blumberg was elected vice-president to replace Mr. Rudolph who resigned (2 April 1909, 12, 16)

LIVERMAN, Louis, 69 St. Famille St., gave a snowshoe party at his residence, Sat. evening, Feb. 4, 1912. Guests included:- J.D. Asner, N. Beecher, M. Brodie, Barney Cohen, Louis Cohen, Joseph Dobrofsky, Harry Feldstein, M. Liverman, Dave Livinson, Louis and I. Rosenbloom, L. Rubenstein, A. and M. Sloves, S. Sweedler and the Misses L. and B. Asner, M. Beecher, A. and R. Burman, M. Cohen, A. Crystal, Rose and Ray Dubrofsky, I. Feldstein, A. Goldberg, E. and R. Jacobson, S. Krulewitch, May Liverman, S. Miller, E. and R. Rosenbloom, Rose Shapira, R.L. Shapiro and S. Sloves (16 Feb. 1912, 15, 14)

LIVINGSTON, Mrs. H., Park Ave., has returned from Ottawa where she spent the past week (3 Dec. 1909, 13, 3)

LIVINGSTONE, Mrs. H.H., is president of the Jewish Women's League for Cultural Work in Palestine, Montreal Branch, which held their second quarterly meeting on Thurs. May 8, 1913 in the Baron de Hirsch Institute (23 May 1913, 16, 24)

LIVINGSTONE, Mrs. H.H., 959 Tupper St., is holding a special meeting of the Jewish Women's League for Cultural Work in Palestine at her home on Sun. Oct. 26, 1913 (22 Oct. 1913, 16, 46)

LIVINGSTONE, Mrs. H.H., was re-elected president of the Jewish Women's League for Cultural Work in Palestine at the annual meeting on March 15, 1914 in the Baron de Hirsch Institute. Mrs. I. Harris resigned as vice-president because she is soon leaving the city. She was presented with life membership. Other officers elected were:- Mrs. J. Rose, 1st. vice-pres.; Mrs. R. Brainin, 2nd vice-pres.; Mrs. L. Goldman, treas.; Mrs. J. Elkin, rec. sec.; Mrs. S. Ortenberg, corr. sec.; Mrs. Cohen, chrmn. membership comm. (27 March 1914, 17, 13)

LIVINSON, A. Jacob, is visiting Toronto, Hamilton and Buffalo (29, Aug. 1913, 16, 38)

LIVINSON, A.J., chaired the YMHA Friday Night Talk on Jan. 9, 1914. Mr. Livinson introduced the topic which was Jewish immigration to America before and since 1881. Also taking part in the symposium were Messrs. Hyman Edelstein, Gordon, Herman and Reisner. Bernard Rose, B.C.L., "...ably described the mechanism and raison d'etre of the various clauses of the Canadian Immigration Act." (16 Jan. 1914, 17, 6)

LIVINSON, A.J., left for an extended stay in Ottawa where he will assist the registrar of the Exchequer Court (18 July 1913, 16, 32)

LIVINSON, A.J., was elected hon. president of the Young Men's Hebrew Debating Society. Other officers elected were:- G.H. Friefeld, pres.; H.M. Lehrer, sec.-treas.; R. Dachs and H.A. Shapiro, exec. council (5 Dec. 1913, 16, 52)

LIVINSON, A.J., was granted a first class academy diploma by the Protestant Committee of the Council of Public Instruction, Quebec (25 July 1911, 14, 36)

LIVINSON, A.J., YMHA librarian received book donations from:- Philip Abinovitch, Horace R. Cohen, David Dainow, Bram de Sola, S. Eliasoph, H.E. Herschorn, Dr. E.C. Levine, A.H. Livinson, D.J. Segal and Saul Tritt (20 June 1913, 16, 28)

LIVINSON, D., was in charge of the YMHA fourth annual reception held Sat. evening in the Auditorium Hall. Assisting him were:- I. Bald, M. Bald, B. Benjamin, F. Berlin, L. Bernstein, J. Cohen, S. Cohen, M. Frank, P. Garfinkle, T. Garfinkle, H. Gold, M. Goldberg, N.W. Goldstein, H. Gubbins, C. Herman, P. Ironstone, S. Kaufman, J. Kozinsky, A.H. Livinson, J. Livinson, J. Margolius, J. Merson, M. Merson, J. Ostro, H. Rawson, S. Rawson, C. Schnaer, A. Solomon, E.S. Solomon, J. Strusser, S.R. Vineberg and W.H. Wynne (10 Jan. 1913, 16, 5)

LIVINSON, Dave, was director and chief organizer of the YMHA Snowhoe Club first annual dance held last Sun. in the Auditorium Hall.

Others involved in organizing the dance were:- F. Berlin, L. Bernstein, H.J. Carsley, J. Daniels, M. Frank, M. Garfinkle, T. Garfinkle, N.W. Goldstein, C. Herman, H. Herman, D. Krukin, A.H. Livinson, J. Margolius, I. Miller, H. Rawson, S. Rawson, J. Sigman, B. Silverman, J. Soloman, N. Takefman, W. Wisse and A. Harry Wolfe (11 Oct. 1912, 15, 44)

LIVINSON, David, was elected president by acclamation of the YMHA Snowshoe Club. Other officers elected by acclamation were:- Sol Kellert, hon. patron; J. Goldstein, hon. pres.; N.W. Goldstein, sec.-treas.; S. Rawson, captain; N. Rawson, 1st lieut.; and Charles Herman, 2nd lieut. J. Sigman and F. Berlin were nominated for vice-pres. (5 Sept. 1913, 16, 39)

LIVINSON, Davis, is president of the YMHA Snowshoe Club, Montreal (19 Jan. 1912, 15, 10)

LIVINSON, I., has returned from Ottawa where he visited his daughter, Mrs. J.S. Gabriel (24 March 1911, 14, 19)

LIVINSON, Miss Myrtie, Sherbrooke St., will spend several weeks visiting relatives in New York (19 April 1912, 14, 23)

LIVINSON, Mrs. I., 189 Craig St. E., gave a tea party in honor of Mrs. A. Borts, of Ottawa. Miss Cecilia Livinson poured tea. Guests included Mrs. H. Singer, and Mrs. J.S. Gabriel, of Ottawa (7 Feb. 1913, 16, 9)

LOBITZ, Miss, has returned home to Syracuse, N.Y., after visiting Mrs. Gus Fischel, Prince Albert Ave. (12 May 1911, 14, 26)

LOBITZ, Mr., of Boston, was in Montreal the past week (25 Feb. 1910, 13, 15)

LOBSCHUTZ, Miss, has returned home to Syracuse after visiting Mrs. G. Fischel, Winchester Ave. (31 Dec. 1909, 13, 7)

LOEB, A., of Vienna, Austria, stayed at the Windsor Hotel while in Montreal this week (22 Aug. 1913, 16, 37)

LONN, Mrs. H., 658 City Hall Ave., won a raffle held for the benefit of a poor family, Sun. aft., April 6, 1913 (11 April 1913, 16, 18)

LONN, Mrs. H., was elected president of the Hebrew Ladies' Relief Society at its sixth annual meeting on Sun. Feb. 22, 1914 in the Baron de Hirsch Institute with Mrs. J. Sourkes presiding. Other officers elected were:- Mrs. M. Gold, vice-pres.; Mrs. J. Steinsberg, treas.; Miss R. Steinsberg, rec. sec.; H. Rappaport, fin sec.; Mesdames Anna Rost and H. Levinoff, fin. comm.; Mesdames Joe Merson and M. Usher, investigating comm.; Mesdames M. Gold and Hoishberg, grocery comm.; Mesdames Axferad, Dora Lonn, Anna Rost, S. Serbin, M. Slabotsky, J. Sourkes and J. Usher (20 March 1914, 17, 12)

LOPSITZ, Miss, returns to Syracuse, N.Y. Sat. night, after her visit with Mrs. Gustave Fischel, Westmount (7 Jan. 1910, 13, 8)

LORADO, M.D., returned from Europe where he spent several months (30 Aug. 1912, 15, 38)

LOUIS, Felix, is spending the holidays in New York (24 Dec. 1909, 13, 6)

LOUIS, Miss Grace, is the guest of her aunt, Mrs. I. Blumenthal, Beaurepaire (5 Aug. 1910, 13, 38)

LOUIS, Miss Grace, will spend a few months at Ste. Agathe des Monts (13 Aug. 1909, 12, 35)

LOUIS, Miss Minnie D., read a paper "Mission Work Among the Unenlightened Jews" at the last Friday Night Talk of the YMHA, held in the Association rooms, St. Urbain St. J. Goldstein "...contrasted present communal life in Montreal with that of a generation or two ago, and maintained that we have no reason to be otherwise than optimistic about the continuous progress we have made." (3 Jan. 1913, 16, 4)

LOUIS, Mr. and Mrs. L. and Mrs. N. Louis are spending a few weeks at Caledonia Springs, Ont. (22 July 1910, 13, 36)

LOUIS, Mrs. Nathan and Miss Louis are at Cacouna, Que. for the summer (25 July 1911, 14, 36)

LOWENTHAL, Mrs. C. and Miss F. Lowenthal, of New York, stayed at the Windsor Hotel while in Montreal (25 July 1913, 16, 33)

LOZINSKI, H., is principal of the Montreal Hebrew Free School, 141-143 St. Urbain St., which held its seventeenth annual meeting, Jan. 19, 1913 at 2.30 p.m. Mr. Lozinski recently attended the first Hebrew Teachers' Congress in New York (17 Jan. 1913, 16, 6)

LOZINSKI, H., principal of the Montreal Hebrew Free School, collected donations from the following persons for the annual picnic which took place on Aug. 14, 1913 on St. Helen's Island:- Rabbi Herman Abramowitz, M. Adelstein, M. Bavitz, D. Bloomfield, Henry Bye, Lazarus Cohen, L. Coviensky, R.A. Darwin, M. Denenberg, V. Edelberg, H. Fineberg, Z. Fineberg, Max Heppner, L. Holstein, J.H. Inclor, E. Kussner, H. Lang, A. Levin, M.L. Levin, B. Miller, M.L. Morris, Carl Rosenberg, G. Sanders, B. Shaffer, J. Tanenbaum, Benjamin Weiner and L. Zealin (22 Aug. 1913, 16, 37)

LOZINSKY, H., principal of the Hebrew Free School, St. Urbain St., delivered an address on "Jewish Education in Montreal" on March 28, 1913, in the YMHA Hall (4 April 1913, 16, 17)

LOZINSKY, Mr. and Mrs. H., 831 St. Urbain St., send New Year greetings (11 Sept. 1912, 15, 40)

LUBELSKY, S., of Toronto, has returned home after spending several weeks in Europe (5 Nov. 1909, 12, 47)

LUBELSKY, S., of Toronto, who was in Montreal this week, left for Atlantic City to visit friends (8 April 1910, 13, 21)

LUBIN, Herbert, is president of Messrs. H. Lubin & Co., 87 Notre Dame St. W. "Though a very young man to hold the position he does at the head of this firm of financial and real estate agents, Mr. Lubin has won his way to distinction through his ability in the calling he has chosen." (9 May 1913, 16, 22)

LURIE, Miss Emma, of Cincinnati, is the guest of Miss B. Asch, Park Ave., Annex (22 Aug. 1913, 16, 37)

LURIE, Miss Fanny, Laval Ave., has left for Ottawa where she will be the guest of Mrs. H. Freeman for two weeks. She will then holiday in Toronto (13 Aug. 1909, 12, 35)

LUSHER, Harry, is spending July at Greenberg's Hotel in Ste. Agathe (4 July 1913, 16, 30)

LUSTGARTEN, Mrs. S., who was the guest of Mrs. Mortimer B. Davis, has returned home to New York (24 Sept. 1909, 12, 41)

LUXEMBOURG, Miss Freda, of Brooklyn, N.Y., is a guest of Mrs. N. Levinson, Elm Ave. (10 Jan. 1913, 16, 5)

LUXEMBOURG, Miss Freda, returned home to Brooklyn (21 Feb. 1913, 16, 11)

LYON, W.S., of London, England, is in Montreal to attend the wedding of his son, Alfred E. Lyon to Miss Beta S. Michaels, Dorchester St. W. Mr. Lyon is "...renewing a lot of old friendships that were founded during a previous visit to Canada, about forty years ago, at which time he was engaged in a mineralogical survey of the Dominion and the United States." He will visit the U.S. before returning to England (10 June 1910, 13, 30)

LYONS, Alfred, has returned from London, England where he visited his parents (8 Jan. 1909, 12, 4)

LYONS, Mr. and Mrs. S., of Ottawa, are the guests of Mr. and Mrs. M. Lyons, 5 Laval Ave., Montreal (1 April 1910, 13, 20)

MAIER, Max, of New York, who will be married to Miss Mae Blumenthal, on June 24, 1909, at Pine Bluff, Ark., stayed at the Windsor Hotel (18 June 1909, 12, 27)

MALAMUTH, J.L., the young Yiddish author, recently wrote a play "The Golden Chain" which was produced at the People's Theatre, Montreal (26 Dec. 1913, 17, 3)

MALKINSON, J. and J. Goldman took the affirmative position on the topic "Resolved; That the right of Suffrage be extended to women" at the YMHA Literary & Debating Circle debate, Mon. Nov. 7, 1910, at 8.30 p.m. Sol Cohen and S.B. Gordon for the negative. W.C. Munn challenged Bernard Rose to a political debate (11 Nov. 1910, 13, 52)

MALKINSON, J., is the YMHA's comedian (15 Dec. 1911, 15, 5)

MALKINSON, Jack, St. Urbain St., gave a party in honor of Maurice Winevoope who has just returned from a trip out west. Guests included Miss N. Ross and I. Boyaner, of St. John, N.B. (11 Oct. 1912, 15, 44)

MALKINSON, Miss Jean, 1333 St. Urbain St., is visiting her cousins in and around New York for a few weeks (3 April 1914, 17, 14)

MANIS, M., has recovered from his recent operation (25 July 1911, 14, 36)

MANOLSON, J., is recovering from his recent illness. His wife and son acknowledge the kind inquiries of their friends (20 Oct. 1911, 14, 49)

MANOLSON, S.E., president of the Eureka A.A.A., and Miss Fanny Jacobson, president of the Amaranth Club, spoke at a social held Wed. evening, Feb. 1, 1911, at the Amaranth Club, 189 Mount Royal Ave. W. (3 Feb. 1911, 14, 12)

MANOLSON, S.E., was elected president of the Eureka A.A.A. on Thurs. Oct. 12, 1911 at the first meeting of the season. Other officers elected were:- P. Abinovitch, vice-pres.; I. Kaplan, sec.;

and E. Kert, treas. (20 Oct. 1911, 14, 49)

MANOLSON, S.E., was elected president of the Eureka Club of Montreal last Sun. Other officers elected were:- J. Tapperburg, vice-pres.; E. Kert, treas.; and H. Schwartz, sec. (15 Sept. 1909, 12, 40)

MARCUS, M., of St. John, N.B., stayed at the Windsor Hotel last week (31 Jan. 1913, 16, 8)

MARCUSE, Miss Eliza, daughter of Mr. and Mrs. B. Marcuse, will be married Thurs. Dec. 5, 1912 at 6 p.m., in the Chevra Kadisha Synagogue (22 Nov. 1912, 15, 50)

MARCUSE, Otto, who was surgeon to the Nova Scotia Steel and Coal Company at Belle Island, Nfld., has returned to Montreal and has opened his consulting room at 2542 Park Ave. (20 Oct. 1911, 14, 49)

MARGOLESE, Dr. O., of Winnipeg, is in Montreal visiting his parents (12 Jan. 1912, 15, 9)

MARGOLESE, Dr. Oscar, of Winnipeg, left for New York for a month (4 April 1913, 16, 17)

MARGOLESE, L.S. (B.C.L.), was in New York last week (8 Jan. 1909, 12, 4)

MARGOLESE, L.S., has returned from Los Angeles (2 Aug. 1912, 15, 34)

MARGOLESE, Mr. and Mrs. S.L., returned from a two months' trip to the Pacific coast (29 Aug. 1913, 16, 38)

MARGOLESE, Mrs. O. and children, of Winnipeg, accompanied by her sister, Miss Mary Rosenblat, are guests of Mr. and Mrs. J. Margolese, of Montreal, now at their summer cottage in St. Bruno, Que. (12 July 1912, 15, 31)

MARGOLICK, Mr. and Mrs. G., have returned from Fort William, Ont., by boat (25 July 1913, 16, 33)

MARGOLIES, Miss Rosalind, has returned home to New York, after visiting Mr. and Mrs. M. Feldstein (20 Sept. 1912, 15, 41)

MARKS, Alexander, recently deceased, was inscribed in the JNF Golden Book by the Young Men's Zionist and Literary Society of Montreal (22 July 1910, 13, 36)

MARKS, F., of Boston, is a guest at the St. Lawrence Hall (4 June 1909, 12, 25)

MARKS, Jack, of New York, is in Montreal (29 Dec. 1911, 15, 7)

MARKS, Miss Mira, gave a picnic for her friends last Sun. aft. at the Pines (7 June 1912, 15, 26)

MARKS, Mrs. A. and daughters, of New York, are guests of Mr. and Mrs. S. Goltman, St. Catherine St. (6 Oct. 1911, 14, 47)

MARKS, Mrs. I.H., Miss Phoebe Marks and Master David M. Marks, of New York City, have arrived in Ottawa and will spend a few weeks with Mrs. Marks' sister, Mrs. Max Wolfe, at Villa L'Ete, Britannia-on-the-Bay (1 July 1910, 13, 33)

MARKS, Mrs. N., and daughter, and Mrs. L. Preston, of Ottawa, stayed at the Windsor Hotel (24 May 1912, 15, 25)

MARKS, Mrs. N., of Ottawa, is the guest of Miss Cochenthaler, Bishop St. (15 Jan. 1909, 12, 5)

MARKS, Mrs. N., of Ottawa, is the guest of Mrs. Cochenthaler, Bishop St. (24 Dec. 1909, 13, 6)

MARKS, Mrs. N., of Ottawa, is the guest of Miss Cochenthaler, Bishop St. (9 Sept. 1910, 13, 43)

MARKS, Mrs. N., of Ottawa, is the guest of the Misses Cochenthaler, Bishop St. (20 June 1913, 16, 28)

MARKSON, Mrs. H., of Albany, N.Y., is the guest of her sister, Mrs. Julius Benowick, Esplanade Ave. (15 July 1910, 13, 35)

MARKUS, Arthur A., leaves this evening for Toronto and the west (12 April 1912, 15, 22)

MARKUS, Arthur A., spent the weekend at St. Johns, Que. (28 July 1911, 14, 37)

MARKUS, M., 198 Mance St., leaves on Sun. night for London, Ont., to attend the Canadian Order of Foresters Convention. He is the only Jewish member to be elected a delegate (4 June 1909, 12, 25)

MARKUS, M., has gone to Ottawa on business (19 Aug. 1910, 13, 40)

MARKUS, M., has left for a trip west (10 Feb. 1911, 14, 13)

MARKUS, M., has returned from a business trip to Toronto and other Ontario cities (10 June 1910, 13, 30)

MARKUS, M., has returned from a trip out west (25 Nov. 1910, 14, 2)

MARKUS, M., has returned from an extended business trip to Europe (18 March 1910, 13, 18)

MARKUS, M., has returned home after several weeks in the West (26 Nov. 1909, 13, 2)

MARKUS, M., is a delegate at the Canadian Order of Foresters convention in Toronto (16 June 1911, 14, 31)

MARKUS, M., is away for a fortnight out west (20 May 1910, 13, 27)

MARKUS, M., leaves for Europe on a short business trip next Wed. (7 Jan. 1910, 13, 8)

MARKUS, M., leaves next Mon. on a business trip out west (6 May 1910, 13, 25)

MARKUS, M., leaves shortly for the west on business (13 Jan. 1911, 14, 9)

MARKUS, M., left last Mon. evening for New York (10 March 1911, 14, 17)

MARKUS, M., left Tues. night for Toronto and points west on a business trip (29 Oct. 1909, 12, 46)

MARKUS, M., was in Kingston, Ont. during the week on business (1 April 1910, 13, 20)

MARKUS, Mr. and Mrs. M. and family, 198 Mance St., are spending the summer at Vaudreuil (6 Aug. 1909, 12, 34)

MARKUS, Mr. and Mrs. M. and family are at their cottage "Villanova", Senneville, St. Anne de Bellevue (28 July 1911, 14, 37)

MARKUS, Mr. and Mrs. M., Mance St., were "at home" Sun. Dec. 4, 1910, in honor of the Bar Mitzvah of their son Arthur Marcus. Mrs. Marcus received, assisted by her daughter Hortense Markus (9 Dec. 1910, 14, 4)

MARKUS, Mr. and Mrs. M., will spend the rest of the summer at St. Anne de Bellevue (12 Aug. 1910, 13, 39)

MARKUS, Richard, has returned from a short trip to New York and Philadelphia (29 Oct. 1909, 12, 46)

MARSHALL, L., of Glace Bay, N.S., is in Montreal on business (9 April 1909, 12, 17)

MARTIN, Abe, of Buffalo, N.Y., was in Montreal the past week (24 May 1912, 15, 25)

MATOFF, Professor Michael, has moved from 44 St. Louis Square to 136 Laval Ave. (7 May 1909, 12, 21)

MATTS, B., returned from London, England where he attended the funeral of his father (10 Oct. 1913, 16, 44)

MATTS, B.J., has gone abroad for two months (29 Aug. 1913, 16, 38)

MATTS, Benjamin, of Manchester, England, is in Montreal (20 Oct. 1911, 14, 49)

MATTS, Miss Edythe, hosted the Progress Club's first social evening of the season on Thurs. Nov. 23, 1911 (1 Dec. 1911, 15, 3)

MATTS, Miss Rose, St. Matthew St., is in Buckingham for a few weeks (16 July 1909, 12, 31)

MATTS, Miss, St. Matthew St., is in Boston for a few weeks (3 March 1911, 14, 16)

MATTS, Miss, St. Matthew St., is at Old Orchard for a few weeks (28 July 1911, 14, 37)

MATTS, Misses, Olivier Ave., entertained their cousin Miss Emily Matts, of London, England (10 April 1914, 17, 15)

MATTS, Mr. and Mrs. L.J. and family are at their summer residence, Ferme Neuve, Mattsville, Que. (1 Aug. 1913, 16, 34)

MAUER, E., has returned from a short stay in New York (6 Jan. 1911, 14, 8)

MAUER, Elias and Maxwell Lightstone leave tomorrow for Sherbrooke, Que. to address the local Zionist Society (3 March 1911, 14, 16)

MAUER, Elias, lectured on "The Resources and Recent Developments in Palestine" at the B'nai Zion Kadimah meeting last Sun. evening. Sender Deutsch chaired the meeting. (12 Feb. 1909, 12, 9)

MAY, Mr. and Mrs. Barney, of Pittsburgh, Pa., stayed at the Ritz-Carlton Hotel while in Montreal, and have left for the Saguenay (8 Aug. 1913, 16, 35)

MAY, Mrs., gave a bridge party in honor of Miss Baere. Mrs. Mark Roman won the first prize while the second prize went to Miss Hannah Harris (5 feb. 1909, 12, 8)

MAYER, Julius M., many years a resident of Canada, was appointed a United States District Court judge in New York (23 Feb. 1912, 15, 15)

MAYER, Mr. and Mrs. Max, were guests at the Windsor Hotel (30 July 1909, 12, 33)

MAYER, Mrs. Max, is the guest of Mrs. H. Simon, Sherbooke St. W. (3 Dec. 1909, 13, 3)

MAYERS, Mrs. and Miss, of New York, were at the St. Lawrence Hall, Montreal, en route for

Quebec City (26 Aug. 1910, 13, 41)

MCFARLANE, Mr. and Mrs. L.B., Dorchester St. W., have gone abroad for a few months (8 Sept. 1911, 14, 43)

MCFARLANE, Mr. and Mrs. L.B., Dorchester St. W., sail for Europe on Sept. 3, 1912 (6 Sept. 1912, 15, 39)

MCFARLANE, Mr. and Mrs. L.B., left for Detroit to attend the Myers-Bernstein wedding which took place Sept. 7, 1909 (10 Sept. 1909, 12, 39)

MCKINLEY, S., was elected president of the B'nai U' Bnoth Zion Kadimah at the annual meeting on Sun. Oct. 27, 1912 in the Baron de Hirsch Institute. Other officers elected were:- J. Goldman, vice-pres.; H. Lang, treas.; M. Rubin, fin. sec.; and B. English, corr. sec. (1 Nov. 1912, 15, 47)

MEISELS, Rev. S., the famous cantor of Ohabei Sholem Synagogue, Chicago, Ill., will conduct services in the Auditorium Hall, Jan. 5 and 6, 1912 (5 Jan. 1911, 15, 8)

MELKMAN, Solomon, of New York, a former resident of Montreal, is a guest at the Windsor Hotel (16 July 1909, 12, 31)

MENDEL, G.F., of Wyoming, is registered at the Place Viger Hotel (13 Aug. 1909, 12, 35)

MENDEL, Joseph, of Perth, Ont., was in Montreal for a few days (4 June 1909, 12, 25)

MENDELOWITZ, Mrs., St. Urbain St., is on an extended visit to her parents in St. Louis (1 Aug. 1913, 16, 34)

MENDELS, I., has returned from Vaudreuil, where he spent the summer with his wife and family, because of illness (27 Aug. 1909, 12, 37)

MENDELS, Misses, of Perth, Ont., are visiting their aunt, Mrs. C. Redlich (16 April 1909, 12, 18)

MENDELS, Mr. and Mrs. Joseph, of Perth, Ont., were in Montreal the past week (10 Nov. 1911, 14, 52)

MENDELS, Mrs. Joseph and son are in town for the Holy Days visiting Mr. and Mrs. Redlich (11 Oct. 1910, 13, 48)

MENDELS, Mrs. Joseph, of Perth, Ont., visited her sister, Mrs. C. Redlich, St. Joseph Blvd. (5 March 1909, 12, 12)

MENDELS, Mrs. Joseph, of Perth, Ont., has returned home after several weeks' visit, to her father, Samuel Roman (1 Oct. 1909, 12, 42)

MENDELS, Mrs. Joseph, of Perth, Ont., was in Montreal for a few days prior to her departure for Boston, where she will visit her sister, Mrs. Adam Klopot (14 Jan. 1910, 13, 9)

MENDELS, Mrs. Joseph, of Perth, was in Montreal on a short visit (16 June 1911, 14, 31)

MENDELSOHN, J. Felix, is leaving Sat. on the S.S. Tunisian from Halifax for a six weeks' trip to the Old Country (24 Dec. 1909, 13, 6)

MENDELSOHN, M., Esplanade Ave., was given a surprise birthday party last Sun. evening, Dec. 15, 1912. Dr. A. Freedman presented the gift on behalf of the thirty couples present. Assisting at the table were:- the Misses Annie Mendelsohn, Ray Mendelsohn, Jessie Phillips, Malca Vineberg and Mrs. S. Ryan (20 Dec. 1912, 16, 2)

MENDELSOHN, M., left last Sat. to join his wife and family at Old Orchard, Me. (18 July 1913, 16, 32)

MENDELSOHN, Miss Dolly, sailed for England and the continent aboard the Empress of Ireland (11 Oct. 1911, 15, 44)

MENDELSOHN, Miss Dolly, who was abroad for three months, returned on the S.S. Empress of Ireland (7 March 1913, 16, 13)

MENDELSOHN, Mr. and Mrs. M., 211 Esplanade Ave., wish their friends and relatives a happy New Year (10 Oct. 1913, 16, 44)

MENDELSOHN, Mrs. M., 918 St. Denis St., will receive on Sun. evening in honor of her sister, Miss Malcah Cossman (30 April 1909, 12, 20)

MENDELSOHN, Mrs. M., Esplanade Ave., gave a bridge party for twenty-five couples in honor of her niece Miss Leah Cossman. Those present included:- H.L. Vineberg, the Misses Rae Kirsch, Rae and Annie Mendelsohn, Nellie and Jennie Vineberg, Lilly Vineberg, Mesdames H. Adelman (Winnipeg) and S. Kirsch (27 Feb. 1914, 17, 9)

MENDELSON, Miss Ray, of Calgary, is in Montreal for a few weeks, the guest of her father, Rev. Bloomfield (19 Dec. 1913, 17, 2)

MENDELSSHON, J. Felix, entertained a party of lady friends at Bennetts, on Wed. aft. (8 Jan. 1909, 12, 4)

MENDELSSOHN, A. gave $2,000 and Mrs. Wolsey $1,000 to the Ste. Agathe Sanatorium building fund (15 April 1910, 13, 22)

MENDELSSOHN, Felix, of Toronto, is staying the Windsor Hotel (11 June 1909, 12, 26)

MENDELSSOHN, J. Felix, has again located in Montreal. Sometime ago it was announced that he would settle in Toronto (5 Feb. 1909, 12, 8)

MENDELSSOHN, J. Felix, is at the Windsor Hotel (10 Sept. 1909, 12, 39)

MENDELSSOHN, J. Felix, is staying at the Windsor Hotel (9 April 1909, 12, 17)

MENDELSSOHN, J. Felix, sails today for Europe and thanks his friends for the expressions of sympathy on the death of his father (17 June 1910, 13, 31)

MENDELSSOHN, Miss D., Tupper St., Westmount, is the guest of Miss Nina Workman, Rideau, Ont. (12 Sept. 1913, 16, 40)

MENDELSSOHN, Mrs. and Miss Dolly Mendelssohn, Durocher St., have gone abroad for the summer (4 Aug. 1911, 14, 38)

MENDELSSOHN, Mrs. C. and Miss Dolly Mendelssohn sailed last night on the S.S. Royal George for three months in Europe (28 July 1911, 14, 37)

MENDES, Bram P. and the Misses Marguerite and Florence Mendes, of New York, have accompanied their parents on a visit to Montreal (2 Sept. 1910, 13, 42)

MENDES, Mr. and Mrs. Leonard Pereira, of New York, are in Montreal to visit Mrs. Mendes' brother, Clarence I. de Sola and his wife (2 Sept. 1910, 13, 42)

MERSON, Julius, returned from a visit to Plattsburgh, N.Y. (10 Jan. 1913, 16, 5)

MERSON, Mr. and Mrs. Joseph, 1947 Mance St., wish their friends a happy New Year (10 Oct. 1913, 16, 44)

MERSON, Mrs. Joseph, is the guest of her parents, Mr. and Mrs. A. Herr, in Syracuse, N.Y. (31 Jan. 1913, 16, 8)

MERSON, Peter, 656 City Hall Ave., gave a party at his home, Sun. Jan. 19, 1913 (31 Jan. 1913, 16, 8)

MERSON, Peter, has returned from Toronto where he was the guest of his cousin, Mrs. D. Levinsky (10 Jan. 1913, 16, 5)

MERSON, S. and H. Millar, gave the use of their spacious hall for the Sons of Israel Society first annual concert and ball to be held Sun. Feb. 2, 1913 (24 Jan. 1913, 16, 7)

MEYER, M., of New York, is staying at the Place Viger Hotel (20 Aug. 1909, 12, 36)

MEYER, Miss Gertrude, who was the guest of Miss Berman, Greene Ave., left for New York, en route for her home in Tyler, Texas (7 March 1913, 16, 13)

MEYER, Mr. and Mrs. Max, of St. Louis, Mo., passed through Montreal en route for England (4 June 1909, 12, 25)

MEYER, Mrs. Hans, accompanied Mrs. Jake Goldstein to New York. Mrs. Goldstein leaves for Germany and will be away for several months (16 May 1913, 16, 23)

MEYERS, E.P., of Winnipeg, was in Montreal, the past week (25 June 1909, 12, 28)

MEYERS, Mr. and Mrs., of Geneva, N.Y., are guests of Mr. and Mrs. Abe Greenberg, St. Charles Rd., Outremont (13 Feb. 1914, 17, 7)

MEYERS, Mrs., is visiting her son, H. Meyers, Prince Arthur St. W. (20 Sept. 1912, 15, 41)

MICHAELS, Abraham, chaired the semi-annual meeting of the Spanish and Portuguese

---

Superior Tailoring Company

High-Class Gentlemen's Tailors.

An air of distinction is shown on the men who wear our CLOTHES.

S. MENDELSOHN,

Tel. E. 5996   828 St. Lawrence Blvd.

Congregation on Thurs. evening, Nov. 10, 1910. Israel Blumenthal was appointed chairman of the school committee. Albert Friedman, Ascher Pierce, J.L. Samuel and M. Lightstone were appointed to a committee charged with increasing the choir's membership (18 Nov. 1910, 14, 1)

MICHAELS, Alfred, accompanied by Mr. and Mrs. Isidore Freedman and daughter, left for New York, en route for Antwerp, to attend the wedding of A. Michaels (22 Jan. 1909, 12, 6)

MICHAELS, Clarence, Messrs. B. Rubin, J. Ginsberg, A. Levinson and R. Raphael were in Quebec City last week (4 June 1909, 12, 25)

MICHAELS, Miss Violet, has returned from Weir, Ont., where she spent two weeks (24 June 1910, 13, 32)

MICHAELS, Morris and Harris Kellert are visiting governors at the Montreal General Hospital (9 July 1909, 12, 30)

MICHAELS, Morris, is spending a few weeks in Atlantic City (15 Oct. 1909, 12, 44)

MICHAELS, Mr. and Mrs. Abe, are at Old Orchard Beach (15 July 1910, 13, 35)

MICHAELS, Mr. and Mrs. Abraham, have returned from New York. Mrs. Michaels spent the past six weeks in California visiting her parents (29 Oct. 1909, 12, 46)

MICHAELS, Mr. and Mrs. Alfred, are at Old Orchard, Me. (19 Aug. 1910, 13, 40)

MICHAELS, Mr. and Mrs. Clarence, are in Toronto (1 July 1910, 13, 33)

MICHAELS, Mr. and Mrs. John and Mr. and Mrs. Alfred Michaels leave shortly for Europe (16 June 1911, 14, 31)

MICHAELS, Mr. and Mrs. M., are spending a few weeks in Atlantic City (11 June 1909, 12, 26)

MICHAELS, Mr. and Mrs. Michael, have returned from their honeymoon and moved into their home on Elm Ave., Westmount (25 June 1909, 12, 28)

MICHAELS, Mrs. Abe., has returned from New York where she visited her parents (29 Dec. 1911, 15, 7)

MICHAELS, Mrs. Abraham, has gone to Atlantic City for a month (16 June 1911, 14, 31)

MICHAELS, Mrs. Alfred, presented prizes to students at the closing exercises of the Spanish and Portuguese Synagogue Sunday School last Sun. Percy Jacobson, chairman of the school committee presided. Others on the platform were:- Alfred Michaels, Jacob L. Samuel, the congregation's president, Clarence I. de Sola and Rev. I. de la Penha. Student prize winners were:- Sollie Samuels, David Frank, Rosie Ginzberg, Jessie Ginzberg, Maurice Bruker, Jennie Erdrich, Regina Seiden, Dolly Kirschberg, Nellie Cohen, David Kirschberg, Esther Frank, Charles Bruker, Philip de la Penha, Ernest Bruker, Harry Bruker, Sadie Rutenberg, Gordon Lightstone, Abraham Crown, Maurice Katz, I. Kirschberg and Antonio Seiden (1 June 1911, 14, 29)

MICHAELS, Mrs. Clarence, accompanied by her son, is visiting her parents, Mr. and Mrs. S. Phillips, Cornwall, Ont. (3 March 1911, 14, 16)

MICHAELS, Mrs. John, gave a dinner and house dance at her home "Omnavista" on Tues. evening in honor of Clarence I. Michaels and his fiancée, Miss Phillips, of Cornwall, Ont. (12 Feb. 1909, 12, 9)

MICHAELS, N. and daughter are spending the summer at Old Orchard Beach, Maine (15 July 1910, 13, 35)

MICHAELS, V., is spending a few weeks at Weir, Que. (6 Aug. 1909, 12, 34)

MICHAELS, Victor, of Vancouver, B.C., is visiting his mother on Elm Ave. (30 Dec. 1910, 14, 7)

MICHAELSON, Harris, president of I. Michaelson & Sons Ltd., sailed for Europe last Fri., aboard the S.S. Laurentic (25 June 1909, 12, 28)

MICHAELSON, M., was in Quebec City recently (2 July 1909, 12, 29)

MICHAELSON, Miss Jennie, has returned from New York (22 Jan. 1909, 12, 6)

MICHAELSON, Miss Jennie, Sherbrooke St. W., is visiting Miss Mendes, in New York (9 Dec. 1910, 14, 4)

MICHAELSON, Miss Sarah, Sherbrooke St., W., is at Saranac Lake for a few weeks (20 Sept. 1912, 15, 41)

MICHAELSON, Miss, Sherbrooke St. W., entertained Thurs. aft. in honor of Miss Mendes (26 Nov. 1909, 13, 2)

MICHAELSON, Mr. and Mrs., are guests at the Caledonia Springs Hotel, Caledonia, Ont. (19 Aug. 1910, 13, 40)

MICHAELSON, Mr. and Mrs. M., have returned from New York (22 Jan. 1909, 12, 6)

MICHALSON, Harris, Sidney Moss, A. Pierce, Mrs. Pierce and Master Sidney Pierce were passengers on the S.S. Laurentic which sailed last Sat. (25 June 1909, 12, 28)

MICHALSON, I. and the Misses Michalson, 709 Sherbrooke St. W., have gone on an extended trip to Europe (13 May 1910, 13, 26)

MICHALSON, Israel and the Misses Michalson, are in St. Johns, en route for Europe aboard the S.S. Empress of Britain. Harris Michalson will join his brother and sister in June (24 May 1912, 15, 25)

MICHALSON, J., spent a few days in Quebec City this week (11 June 1909, 12, 26)

MICHALSON, Miss, Sherbrooke St. W., who has been ill for several weeks, has recovered and is leaving for Lakewood, Atlantic City and New York (10 Feb. 1911, 14, 13)

MICHALSON, Misses, 709 Sherbrooke St. W., have returned to Montreal after spending four months touring the principal cities of Europe (12 Aug. 1910, 13, 39)

MICHALSON, Misses, 709 Sherbrooke St. W., have returned after seven weeks in the eastern U.S. (21 April 1911, 14, 23)

MICHALSON, Mrs. M., has left for Old Point Comfort, Va., where she will spend a few weeks (3 Dec. 1909, 13, 3)

MICHEL, J.F., of New York, was registered at the Place Viger Hotel (8 Oct. 1909, 12, 43)

MICHLIN, Dr. and Mrs. S., have returned home to New York (27 Jan. 1911, 14, 11)

MICHLIN, Isidore, has left on an extended business trip out west (27 Jan. 1911, 14, 11)

MICHLIN, Mr. and Mrs. Isidore, have taken temporary residence at the Chesterfield Apts. (15 Aug. 1913, 16, 36)

MILLER, B., of Toronto, was in Montreal for a few days (5 Nov. 1909, 12, 47)

MILLER, I., returned home from a weekend in Ottawa where he was the guest of Mr. and Mrs. L. Green (30 May 1913, 16, 25)

MILLER, Isidore, of Toronto, was in Montreal for a few days (18 March 1910, 13, 18)

MILLER, J., of Buffalo, is a guest at the Carslake Hotel (12 Nov. 1909, 12, 48)

MILLER, J.B., presented an etrog, lulov and wine for Succoth to the patients in the Mount Sinai Sanatorium (15 Oct. 1913, 16, 45)

MILLER, Miss Elsie, Greene Ave., is at Weir, Que., for the summer (6 Aug. 1909, 12, 34)

MILLER, Miss Fanny, of Cornwall, Ont., is the guest of Miss Fanny Frank (20 Oct. 1911, 14, 49)

MILLER, Miss Sara, is summering in Toronto, the guest of her aunt, Mrs. S. Hansher (9 Aug. 1912, 15, 35)

MILLER, Mr. and Mrs. Max and family, of Lachine, Que., are spending the summer on their farm "Oxyden" (30 July 1909, 12, 33)

MILLER, Mr. and Mrs. S., held a reception on Sun. Feb. 23, 1913, in honor of Mrs. A. Hansher, of Milwaukee (7 March 1913, 16, 13)

MILLER, Mr. and Mrs. S.D., left Montreal to take up residence in Cornwall, Ont. (31 Oct. 1913, 16, 47)

MILLER, Mrs., has returned home after visiting her sister, Mrs. A.E. Morris, Westmount Blvd. (28 July 1911, 14, 37)

MILLER, Mrs. J.B., is in Atlantic City for three weeks (15 Aug. 1913, 16, 36)

MILLER, Mrs. Jacob and Miss Beckie Miller, of Cornwall, Ont., were the guests of Mrs. Khos. Frank in Montreal for a few days (5 Sept. 1913, 16, 39)

MILLER, Mrs. John and daughter, Sherbrooke St. W., have returned from Toronto (25 Oct. 1910, 13, 50)

MILLER, Mrs. John and Miss Miller, are spending a few weeks at Weir, Ont. (16 July 1909, 12, 31)

MILLER, Nathan, of New York, is on a business trip through Canada. While in Ottawa, Mr. Miller was the guest of his cousin, Samuel B. Miller (6 Aug. 1909, 12, 34)

MILLER, Samuel B., of Ottawa, and Nathan Miller, of New York, were guests at the Windsor Hotel this week (6 Aug. 1909, 12, 34)

MILLER, Samuel B., of Ottawa, is going to New York on a short trip (9 April 1909, 12, 17)

MILLIMAN, Miss B., is visiting the Misses Getz, in Quebec City (12 Aug. 1910, 13, 39)

MILLMAN, Miss B., 286 Sherbrooke St. W., gave an "at home" Tues. Sept. 14, 1909, in honor of Miss Hattie Swartz, of New York. Miss Ida F. Apotheker assisted in receiving the guests and Mrs. A. Grundler acted as chaperon. Among those present were:- Miss Jeanette Swartz, New York; the Misses Miriam, Elizabeth and Minnie Bernstein; Miss Mary Goldstein and George Alexander, of Valparaiso, Ind.; Maurice Alexander, John J. Weinfeld, Simon Bernstein and Emanuel Leavitt (24 Sept. 1909, 12, 41)

MILLMAN, Miss Bena, has returned from Fraserville, Que., where she visited her brother, Saul Millman. While there she was joined by the Misses Getz and Max Getz. The entire party left for Quebec City to attend the Werzburg-Arenovitz wedding (27 Aug, 1909, 12, 37)

MINTZ, H., of Boston, was the guest of B. Silver, Elm Ave. (8 July 1910, 13, 34)

MIRSKY, Rabbi and son, Solomon Mirsky, are guests of Mr. and Mrs. A. Harris (24 Feb. 1911, 14, 15)

MISHKIN, Mrs. Edward, of New York, is the guest of Mrs. A. Shapiro (4 June 1909, 12, 25)

MISHKIN, Mrs. I., 1897 Esplanade Ave., has taken over the Darwin Millinery Store at 308 St. Lawrence Blvd. under the new name "The Fashion" (6 Dec. 1912, 15, 52)

MITNICK, Miss Fannie, returned from New York where she was the guest of Mrs. Schneider (5 Sept. 1913, 16, 39)

MOHL, William, of Cleveland, Ohio, is visiting his sister, Mrs. Al. Lesser, Prince Arthur Apts. (18 April 1913, 16, 19)

MONASON, Miss, of New York, is the guest of Mrs. Ornstein, 21 Esplanade Ave. (14 July 1911, 14, 35)

MONASSON, Miss F., who was the guest of Mrs. O. Ornstein, 21 Esplanade Ave., has returned home (25 Aug. 1911, 14, 41)

MONBLATT, Miss Winnie, of Hamilton, Ont., is visiting her cousin, Mrs. J.A. Cohen, 290 Laval Ave. (27 Jan. 1911, 14, 11)

MOND, Sir Alfred, M.P. for Swansea, Wales in the British House of Commons who has been touring Canada, delivered an address on free trade to the Canadian Club (18 Oct. 1910, 13, 49)

MOORE, Miss Kathleen, Clarke Ave., entertained this week at a girls' luncheon (26 Nov. 1909, 13, 2)

MOORE, Mrs. W., has returned from a short stay in New York (18 March 1910, 13, 18)

MORRIS, A.S., Messrs. M. Lehcovitz, S. Rosenseen, A. Simon and R. Adelson, all of Montreal, were in New York recently (5 Nov. 1909, 12, 47)

MORRIS, E., of Calgary, Alta., is staying at the St. James Hotel (24 Dec. 1909, 13, 6)

MORRIS, L., a clothier at 360 Notre Dame St. W., was in a serious auto accident last Fri. morn. "...when a wheel of a Lachine bound car rode over a foot of the unfortunate gentleman. He was taken by ambulance in a serious condition to the General Hospital, where his condition gradually improved. Mr. Morris had to have his foot amputated." (18 July 1913, 16, 32)

MORRIS, M.L. and A.J. Alexander, have gone on a trip to Toronto (23 Dec. 1910, 14, 6)

MORRIS, M.L. and A.J. Alexander have sailed on the Lusitania for Europe (15 Jan. 1909, 12, 5)

MORRIS, Miss Dora, 64 Mance St., gave a party for forty guests last Mon. evening (6 May 1910, 13, 25)

MORRIS, Miss Dora, has left for Shawbridge where she will spend the summer (11 June 1909, 12, 26)

MORRIS, Miss Dore, Mance St., gave a house party last Sat. evening in honor of her sister, Mrs. Gelber, of Toronto (7 May 1909, 12, 21)

MORRIS, Miss Dorothy, Mance St., is visiting her sister Mrs. L. Gelber, in Toronto (6 Aug. 1909, 12, 34)

MORRIS, Miss K., Westmount Blvd., is visiting Mr. and Mrs. C. Miller in Toronto (27 March 1914, 17, 13)

MORRIS, Mr. and Mrs. A.E. and Miss Morris are in Atlantic City (22 April 1910, 13, 23)

MORRIS, Mrs. A.E., Belvedere Lodge, Westmount Ave., gave a dinner last Sun. evening in honor of Miss Frankie Phillips, of Cornwall, Ont., and Clarence Michaels (12 Feb. 1909, 12, 9)

MORRIS, Mrs. A.E., is visiting her sister in Chicago (30 Dec. 1910, 14, 7)

MORRIS, Mrs. G., Laval Ave., returned from Valleyfield, Que., where she visited her daughter, Mrs. Isidore Schaeffer (14 March 1913, 16, 14)

MOSCOVITCH, Miss Esther, who is in New York visiting friends and relatives, is expected back Tues. (20 Sept. 1911, 14, 45)

MOSCOVITZ, Mrs. J. and her daughter, Miss Dora Moscovitz, of Edmundston, N.B., have returned home after a three weeks' visit with Mr. and Mrs. S. Poyaner (28 Jan. 1910, 13, 11)

MOSES, Mr. and Mrs., of Chicago, have left for Hamilton and Toronto (27 Aug. 1909, 12, 37)

MOSHER, A., is a guest at the Place Viger Hotel (12 Aug. 1910, 13, 39)

MOSHER, Joseph, of London, England, was registered at the Windsor Hotel (1 July 1910, 13, 33)

MOSKOVICH, Joe and Miss Tanna Moskovich, 11 Sherbrooke St. E., are at Old Orchard, Me., for a few weeks (9 Aug. 1912, 15, 35)

MOSKOVITCH, Joe, McNicoll Ave., returned from Old Orchard, Me. (8 Aug. 1913, 16, 35)

MOSKOVITCH, Miss Esther, celebrated her birthday with a party last Sun., given in her honor by her parents, Mr. and Mrs. F. Moscovitch. Covers were laid for thirty five (1 Dec. 1911, 15, 3)

MOSKOVITCH, Miss Tanna and Miss Esther Moskovitch have gone on holiday to New York (23 Sept. 1910, 13, 45)

MOSKOVITCH, Mr. and Mrs. S., 15 McNicoll Ave., wish their friends and relatives a happy New Year (1 Oct. 1913, 16, 42-43)

MOSKOVITCH, Mr. and Mrs. S. and family are moving from 11 Sherbrooke St. E., to 15 McNicoll Ave. Telephone, Uptown 7261 (9 May 1913, 16, 22)

MOSKOVITCH, Mrs. F. and son Joseph Moskovitch, have for a few weeks in New York (23 Sept. 1910, 13, 45)

MOSKOVITCH, S., McNicoll Ave., left on a business trip to Boston and New York (31 Oct. 1913, 16, 47)

MOSKOVITCH, S., Sherbrooke St. E., is in Boston and New York on business (20 Dec. 1912, 16, 2)

MOUER, E. and his mother, Mrs. Tannenbaum, have gone to New York on holidays (23 Dec. 1910, 14, 6)

MULSTOCK, A.W., M. Herzberg, E. Heishorn and M. Grossman took part in a debate on "Racial Prejudice" at the Maccabaean Literary Circle, Jan. 30, 1910. J. Levinson read a paper on "The Role of the Press in the Jewish Community" (4 Feb. 1910, 13, 12)

MUSCAT, B., is visiting his aunt, Mrs. L. Sapery, Durocher St. (19 Feb. 1909, 12, 10)

MUSCOVITZ, Miss R., of Montreal, is visiting Mr. and Mrs. A. Bacal, at Montmagny (15 Aug. 1913, 16, 36)

MUSKOVITCH, Mr. and Mrs. S. and daughter Tanna, returned from Old Orchard (15 Aug. 1913, 16, 36)

MUSKOVITZ, Miss Maude, has returned from two weeks at Ste. Agathe (16 Aug. 1912, 15, 36)

MYER, Max, of New York, was in Montreal the past week (11 March 1910, 13, 17)

MYER, Miss S., of Glace Bay, N.S., is visiting her sister, Mrs. D. Gordon, Esplanade Ave. (7 Nov. 1913, 16, 48)

MYER, Mr. and Mrs. Max, are at the Windsor Hotel for a few days (19 Nov. 1909, 13, 1)

MYERS, A.E., thanks his many friends for their remembrance and sympathy in his late bereavement (6 June 1913, 16, 26)

MYERS, A.W., of Winnipeg, returns home tonight via New York and Chicago (28 Jan. 1910, 13, 11)

MYERS, B., of Hamilton, and Samuel Myers, of Ottawa, and their wives, are visiting their parents, Mr. and Mrs. Myers, Crescent St. (31 Dec. 1909, 13, 7)

MYERS, Isidore, has returned to Toronto after a few weeks in Montreal (16 Dec. 1910, 14, 5)

MYERS, J.F., of Toronto, is staying at the Windsor Hotel (4 Nov. 1910, 13, 51)

MYERS, L.A., of Birmingham, England, is at the Corona Hotel (12 March 1909, 12, 13)

MYERS, Master Philip, president, formed the "Success Club" on Sun. Oct. 24, 1910 assisted by Miss Ruth Kellert, vice-president, Master Irwin Rubinovich, secretary and Clarence Goldstein, treasurer (25 Oct. 1910, 13, 50)

MYERS, Meyer and daughter, Miss Eva Myers

have returned home to Syracuse (29 Oct. 1909, 12, 46)

MYERS, Miss, Crescent St., gave an "at home" on Sun. Feb. 8, 1914 in honor of her nieces, Miss Eva Myers, of Syracuse, and Miss Marion Myers, of Ottawa (20 Feb. 1914, 17, 8)

MYERS, Miss Eva, of Syracuse, is visiting her aunt, Miss Myers, Crescent St. (15 Sept. 1909, 12, 40)

MYERS, Miss Eva, of Syracuse, N.Y., is visiting her aunt, Miss Sophie Myers, Crescent St. (29 Dec. 1911, 15, 7)

MYERS, Miss Eva, who has been spending the past few months with her aunt, Miss Sophia Myers, Crescent St., has returned to Syracuse (19 Feb. 1909, 12, 10)

MYERS, Miss Marion, of Ottawa, is visiting her grandparents, Mr. and Mrs. Myers, Crescent St. (6 Sept. 1912, 15, 39)

MYERS, Miss, of Syracuse, N.Y., and brother are visiting their grandparents, Mr. and Mrs. P. Myers, Crescent St. (22 April 1910, 13, 23)

MYERS, Miss Rosetta, of Winnipeg, is the guest of Mr. and Mrs. J. Ettenberg, Shuter St. (11 April 1913, 16, 18)

MYERS, Miss Sophie, has left for Detroit to attend her brother's wedding (3 Sept. 1909, 12, 38)

MYERS, Miss Sophie, has returned from Detroit (24 Sept. 1909, 12, 41)

MYERS, Mr. and Mrs. A.W., of Winnipeg, who spent the past four months in Europe, were in Montreal this week. Mr. Myers left for Winnipeg and Mrs. Myers for Alexandria, Ont. where she will spend the Holy Days with her parents, Mr. and Mrs. I. Simons (15 Sept. 1911, 14, 44)

MYERS, Mr. and Mrs. Ben and son, of Hamilton, Ont., are visiting their parents, Mr. and Mrs. P. Myers, Crescent St. (29 Dec. 1911, 15, 7)

MYERS, Mr. and Mrs. Ben, of Hamilton, Ont., are guests of their parents, Mr. and Mrs. P. Myers, Crescent St. (7 Oct. 1910, 13, 47)

MYERS, Mr. and Mrs. Benjamin, have moved to Hamilton (1 Oct. 1909, 12, 42)

MYERS, Mr. and Mrs. Benjamin, of St. John's, Nfld., are the guests of Mr. and Mrs. J.L. Gittleson (14 Jan. 1910, 13, 9)

MYERS, Mr. and Mrs. Benjamin, of Hamilton, have returned home after a few days in Montreal (1 April 1910, 13, 20)

MYERS, Mr. and Mrs. Benjamin, of Hamilton, Ont., were guests of their parents, Mr. and Mrs. P. Myers, Crescent St., during the holidays (30 Dec. 1910, 14, 7)

MYERS, Mr. and Mrs. Benjamin, will be "at home" Sun. Sept. 19, 1909, at their parents' residence, 172 Crescent St. (15 Sept. 1909, 12, 40)

MYERS, Mr. and Mrs. Phillip, of Quebec City, were in Montreal, en route for New York where they will spend a few weeks (26 Nov. 1909, 13, 2)

MYERS, Mr. and Mrs. S.P., 192 Bishop St., entertained thirty-five couples in honor of their son, Phillip, Sat. evening, Feb. 1, 1913 (7 Feb. 1913, 16, 9)

MYERS, Mr. and Mrs. Samuel and son, of Ottawa, visited their parents, Crescent St. (25 March 1910, 13, 19)

MYERS, Mr. and Mrs. Samuel, of Ottawa, were in Montreal to attend the "At Home" given Sept. 18, 1909, in honor of the newly married couple, Mr. and Mrs. Benjamin Myers (24 Sept. 1909, 12, 41)

MYERS, Mr. and Mrs. Samuel, of Ottawa, were in Montreal for a few days (16 Sept. 1910, 13, 44)

MYERS, Mrs. A.W., of Winnipeg, who was in Montreal for the past few weeks, left last night for Alexandria, Ont., on a month's holiday to her parents, Mr. and Mrs. Isaac Simon (28 Jan. 1910, 13, 11)

MYERS, Mrs. J., of East London, South Africa, returned from an extended tour. She was accompanied by her sister, Mrs. Roston. While in Montreal she will stay with her sister, Mrs. L. Abinovitch (1 Oct. 1913, 16, 42-43)

MYERS, Mrs. P. and Miss Sophie Myers have returned from Hamilton and Toronto (6 Aug. 1909, 12, 34)

MYERS, Mrs. P. and Miss Sophie Myers are guests at the Caledonia Springs Hotel, Caledonia, Ont. (5 Aug. 1910, 13, 38)

MYERS, Mrs. P. and Miss Sophie Myers were guests of Mr. and Mrs. Ben Myers, in Hamilton, Ont. (4 Aug. 1911, 14, 38)

MYERS, Mrs. Philip, of Quebec City, is visiting her mother, Mrs. Silverstone, Elm St. (30 April 1909, 12, 20)

MYERS, Mrs. Philip, of Quebec City, is in Montreal for a few weeks (19 Nov. 1909, 13, 1)

MYERS, Mrs. S.P., accompanied by Miss Levy (who has been visiting friends in Toronto), have left for New York (19 Feb. 1909, 12, 10)

MYERS, Mrs. S.P., has returned from New York (1 Dec. 1911, 15, 3)

MYERS, Myer, of Syracuse, N.Y., and Ben Myers, of Hamilton, were in town for the funeral of their sister-in-law, wife of Sam Myers, Ottawa, who died after a short illness. The funeral was held Fri. morn. (27 Dec. 1912, 16, 3)

MYERS, Myer, of Syracuse, N.Y., is in Montreal for a few weeks (15 Oct. 1909, 12, 44)

MYERS, Myer, of Syracuse, N.Y., is the guest of his parents, Mr. and Mrs. P. Myers, Crescent St. (21 June 1912, 15, 28)

MYERS, O.P., of Detroit, stayed at the Turkish Bath Hotel (5 March 1909, 12, 12)

MYERS, Philip and Mrs. S.P. Myers are in Toronto for a week, the guests of Mr. and Mrs. J. Vise (28 Feb. 1913, 16, 12)

MYERS, Philip, of Quebec City, was in Montreal for a few days (24 Dec. 1909, 13, 6)

MYERS, S.P. and Hiram Levy are among the visiting governors at the Montreal General Hospital this week (27 Aug. 1909, 12, 37)

Phone Main 6621.   Box 185, Montreal
SPECIAL DEPARTMENT FOR COBALT STOCKS.
S. P. Myers Stock Broker
All New York Stocks Bought and Sold on Commission for Cash or on Margins.
ROOM 15, 132 ST. JAMES STREET.

MYERS, Samuel, of Ottawa, was in Montreal for a few days (26 Feb. 1909, 12, 11)

MYERSON, J.J., of Sudbury, Ont., a well-known former Montreal businessman, is in town on business (21 June 1912, 15, 28)

MYERSON, M.H., was elected president of the Disraeli Club on Sun. July 16, 1911. Other officers elected were:- J. Cohen, vice-pres.; S.H. Shalinsky, treas.; M. Frank, sec.; W.H. Wisse, corr. sec.; L. Bernstein, sergeant-at-arms; M. Shulman, B. Shulman, T. Garfinkle, S. Beecher, J. Sommer, M. Gross, C.M. Colle and N. Jacobs, executive (28 July 1911, 14, 37)

NAROVLANSKY, J., has left for Winnipeg (3 Dec. 1909, 13, 3)

NAROVLANSKY, Miss B., of Montreal, who is visiting the Misses Ripstein in Winnipeg, is spending a few weeks with Mrs. L. Abremovich at her summer home at Winnipeg Beach (2 Sept. 1910, 13, 42)

NAROVLANSKY, Miss Rebecca, has gone to visit friends in Minneapolis and Winnipeg (19 Aug. 1910, 13, 40)

NAROVLANSKY, Mr. and Mrs. and family, of Winnipeg, are moving to Montreal (15 Oct. 1909, 12, 44)

NAROVLANSKY, Mrs. S.H. and family have moved to Winnipeg (24 Feb. 1911, 14, 15)

NATHANSON, Henry and Mr. and Mrs. S.L. Nathanson are booked to sail on the S.S. Royal Edward on June 17, 1913 for a trip to Palestine and Europe (6 June 1913, 16, 26)

NATHANSON, S.L., 1072 St. Lawrence Blvd., is donating five gallons of the best port wine to the Mount Sinai Sanatorium "...to give the patients of the institution an opportunity of celebrating the Seder in the old-fashioned and orthodox way..." B. Ramm, proprietor of the St. Lawrence Grocery, 414 St. Lawrence Blvd., is donating one dozen bottles of the best imported wines (4 April 1913, 16, 17)

NERWICH, Hyman P., read a paper on the Jews of South Africa at the Young People's Society of Shaar Hashomayim meeting last Tues. evening (10 Feb. 1911, 14, 13)

NESS, Mr. and Mrs., 27 Park Ave., have returned home after spending the summer at Britannia Bay (15 Sept. 1909, 12, 40)

NESS, Mrs. H., has left for Melocheville, Que. (2 Sept. 1910, 13, 42)

NESS, Mrs. R., was elected a delegate to the IOSB convention in New York, at a Princess of Wales Lodge meeting (10 Feb. 1911, 14, 13)

NESS, R., subscribed for two trees in the Herzl Wald in the name of Mr. and Mrs. William

Myerson (14 Jan. 1910, 13, 9)

NESS, Robert, chaired the B'nai Zion Kadimah Society of Montreal annual meeting on Sun. evening, April 18, 1909. Officers elected were:- R. Stark, pres.; H. Jaslow, vice-pres.; R.A. Darwin, treas.; H. Lang, fin. sec.; S. Gorosh, rec. sec.; Sender Deutsch, J. Gross, S. Lesenoff, H. Markus, Elias Mauer and M. Rubenstein (23 April 1909, 12, 19)

NESS, Robert, of Howick, is at the Queen's Hotel (19 Feb. 1909, 12, 10)

NEUMANN, Mrs. J.N., hosted a tea and shower last Thurs. in honor of Miss Rose Harris. Assisting Mrs. Neumann were Mesdames I. Cohen and H. Schleifer. Out-of-town guests were:- Misses L. Harris and R. Rosenzwaig (New York) and Mrs. Simon (Halifax). Others present were:- Mesdames H. Astrof, A. Derose, J. Elkin, J.L. Gittleson, R. Heillig, C. Loebel, A. Neumann, S. Rosenveesen, and Miss A. Harris (10 Jan. 1913, 16, 5)

NEWMAN, Mesdames J.N., J.L. Gittelson, D. Fels, I. Kussner and David Gordon were in charge of a dance held July 29, 1911 at the Philadelphia Hotel, Ste. Agathe de Monts. H. Goldberg is the proprietor of the hotel (11 Aug. 1911, 14, 39)

NIMEROF, Miss Annie, is spending a holiday at Ste. Agathe (28 July 1911, 14, 37)

OBENDORFFER, H. and Miss Obendorffer, of Kingston, Ont., were in Montreal for a few days (12 Nov. 1909, 12, 48)

OBENDORFFER, H., of Kingston, Ont., was in Montreal for a few days (14 Jan. 1910, 13, 9)

OBENDORFFER, Miss H., of Kingston, was in Montreal, en route to Quebec City (1 Aug. 1913, 16, 34)

OBENDORFFER, Mrs. S., of Kingston, Ont., was in Montreal, the guest of Mrs. L. Silverman, en route for Halifax, where she is a delegate to the Woman's Council (1 July 1910, 13, 33)

OBER, Louis, has from Boston where he visited his parents (20 Sept. 1911, 14, 45)

OBER, Louis, has returned from Boston where he spent Passover with his parents (28 April 1911, 14, 24)

OBER, Louis, of the Montreal YMHA, leaves Sat. for Boston to spend the Passover week with his parents (29 March 1912, 15, 20)

OBERNDORFFER, Herman, of Kingston, was in Montreal the past week (18 March 1910, 13, 18)

OGULNIK, Miss E., has left for Macdonald College (4 April 1913, 16, 17)

OGULNIK, Miss Edith, is visiting Miss Irene Blumenthal at Beaurepaire (16 Aug. 1912, 15, 36)

OGULNIK, Mr. and Mrs. Paul, 432 Claremont Ave., will receive on Sun. March 13, 1910, in honor of their daughter's engagement, Miss Esther Ogulnik to J. Elkin (11 March 1910, 13, 17)

OGULNIK, Mr., has left for New York to visit relatives and Miss Esther Ogulnik has made her residence with her brother, S.M. Ogulnik, 438 Claremont Ave. (26 March 1909, 12, 15)

OGULNIK, Mrs. P., Victoria Ave., gave a shower in honor of Miss Lily Tannenbaum, Wed. Oct. 9, 1912 (18 Oct. 1912, 15, 45)

OLLENDORF, Clarence, of New York, was in Montreal for a few days (12 Feb. 1909, 12, 9)

OPPENHEIMER, Mr. and Mrs., of Chicago, who were guests of Mrs. Oppenheimer's parents, Mr. and Mrs. Boas, have returned home (24 Sept. 1909, 12, 41)

OPPENHEIMER, Mr. and Mrs., of Chicago, have returned from England and are the guests of Mrs. Oppenheimer's parents, Mr. and Mrs. B.A. Boas, "The New Sherbrooke" (10 Sept. 1909, 12, 39)

OPPENHEIMER, Mrs., of Chicago, is visiting her mother, Mrs. B.A. Boas, "The Sherbrooke" (24 Nov. 1911, 15, 2)

OPPENHEIMER, Mrs., of Chicago, who was the guest of her sister, Mrs. Melvin Davis, Sherbrooke St., has sailed for England (25 June 1909, 12, 28)

ORKEN, H.B., of Winnipeg, was in New York on business (30 July 1909, 12, 33)

ORNSTEIN, David, of Paris, France, is in Montreal visiting his brother, Jacques Ornstein (8 Sept. 1911, 14, 43)

ORNSTEIN, J., of Fredericton, N.B., was in Montreal for a few days (5 Sept. 1913, 16, 39)

ORNSTEIN, Mr. and Mrs. Jacques, are spending the summer with their parents at Vaudreuil (7 July 1911, 14, 34)

ORNSTEIN, Mr. and Mrs. M., has moved to Fredericton, N.B., where they will reside (5 April 1912, 15, 21)

ORNSTEIN, Mr. and Mrs. M., have been in Huntingdon, Que. for several weeks (29 Dec. 1911, 15, 7)

ORNSTEIN, Mrs. Jacques, has returned home to Moncton after spending a few weeks visiting her parents, Mr. and Mrs. M. Harris, Crescent St. (16 Sept. 1910, 13, 44)

ORNSTEIN, Mrs. M. Jacques, of Halifax, N.S., who has been the guest of Mr. and Mrs. Maxwell Harris for the past three months has returned home (5 March 1909, 12, 12)

ORNSTEIN, Mrs. Max, of Moncton, N.B., is visiting her parents, Mr. and Mrs. M.L. Harris, Crescent St. (17 Feb. 1911, 14, 14)

ORTENBERG, Dr. and Mrs. Samuel, 124 Pine Ave. E., wish their friends and relatives a happy New Year (1 Oct. 1913, 16, 42-43)

ORTENBERG, Dr. and Mrs. Samuel, returned from their honeymoon and are residing at 124 Pine Ave. E. (4 July 1913, 16, 30)

ORTENBERG, Dr. S., has been appointed assistant physician to the Montreal Protestant Infants' Home and Hospital. He has opened a consulting room in St. Urbain St., just above Prince Arthur (15 April 1910, 13, 22)

ORTENBERG, Dr. S., has returned to Montreal from his medical studies in Berlin and London (28 Jan. 1910, 13, 11)

ORTENBERG, Dr. S., spent the weekend at Ste. Agathe (25 July 1911, 14, 36)

ORTENBERG, Dr. S., was a passenger on the S.S. Megantic, which sailed for England last Sat. (9 July 1909, 12, 30)

ORTENBERG, Dr. S., was appointed physician to the King Edward Benefit Association (14 April 1911, 14, 22)

ORTENBERG, Dr. S., who has resigned from the medical staff of the Western Hospital, will sail shortly for a six months' trip to Europe. First, he will spend a short time with his parents in Quebec City. He plans to visit the main hospitals in Berlin, London, Vienna and Paris (4 June 1909, 12, 25)

ORTENBERG, Dr. Samuel, read a paper "The Jew in Intellectual Pursuits" at the Shearith Israel Circle opening meeting on Tues. Jan. 5, 1909. Miss Jeanette Blout performed a violin solo (15 Jan. 1909, 12, 5)

ORTENBERG, Dr. Samuel, returns in Feb. from Europe where he has studied in the London and Berlin hospitals (14 Jan. 1910, 13, 9)

ORTENBERG, Dr. Samuel, will read a paper at the next Progressive Literary and Debating Circle meeting, Sun. Nov. 13, 1910 (11 Nov. 1910, 13, 52)

ORTENBERG, Miss Rose, has returned to Quebec City after spending the past month in Montreal (26 Feb. 1909, 12, 11)

PAPPENHEIM, Miss Bertha, of Frankfort-on-the-Main, was a delegate to the International Womens' Conference held in Toronto (23 July 1909, 12, 32)

PARENT, Mrs., of Chatham, N.B., en route for Vancouver, was a guest of the Misses Harris, Tupper St. (16 July 1909, 12, 31)

PASHOVSKY, Mrs. and Miss, of New York, are guests of Mrs. Wetstein, 61 Church St. (26 Jan. 1912, 15, 11)

PAWLOSWKA, Madame, leaves Aug. 6, 1913 for Europe where she will pursue her medical studies (8 Aug. 1913, 16, 35)

PAYNE, Chester, is spending a few weeks at Shawbridge, Que. (20 June 1913, 16, 28)

PAYNE, Mrs. S., Bishop St., is spending the summer at Burlington Beach (6 Aug. 1909, 12, 34)

PAYNE, Mrs. S., Bishop St., is visiting friends in Pennington, Vt. (11 Oct. 1912, 15, 44)

PEARLMAN, Mrs. and son, of Regina, Sask., are guests of her sister, Mrs. M. Hoffman, St. Joseph Blvd. (9 Feb. 1912, 15, 13)

PEARLMAN, Mrs. R., of Port Arthur, Ont., is visiting her parents in Ottawa for a few weeks (26 Aug. 1910, 13, 41)

PEARSON, Mrs. Samuel, has gone to Albany, N.Y., where she will be the guest of her cousin, Mrs. Simon Pearson. She will then visit New York, Washington and Boston (20 Aug. 1909, 12, 36)

PEDLOW, Isaac F. and Miss Pedlow, of Renfrew, Ont., are at the Corona Hotel (28 May 1909, 12, 24)

PERGAMENT, Miss, has returned to New York after visiting Miss Aronson (3 March 1911, 14, 16)

PERGAMENT, Mrs. J., has returned home to New York, after visiting her daughter, Mrs. B. Mendels (14 June 1912, 15, 27)

PHILLIPS, Lazarus, chaired the YMHA Literary Circle's first meeting of the season (26 Dec. 1913,

17, 3)

PHILLIPS, Master Lazarus, won the bronze medal and scholarship at the Aberdeen School (25 June 1909, 12, 28)

PHILLIPS, Miss Bertha, of Cornwall, is visiting Mrs. S.A. Jacobs (27 Dec. 1912, 16, 3)

PHILLIPS, Miss Frankie, of Cornwall, is spending a few weeks with Mrs. Harris Vineberg (24 Dec. 1909, 13, 6)

PHILLIPS, Mr. and Mrs. Henry and daughter, Clarke St., left for Boston, Old Orchard, Atlantic City and New York (4 July 1913, 16, 30)

PHILLIPS, Mr. and Mrs. N., of Cornwall, Ont., were "At Home" at their sister's residence, 598 Argyle Ave., Westmount, on the occasion of their daughter's engagement (29 Jan. 1909, 12,7)

PHILLIPS, Mrs. N., of Cornwall, is visiting her daughter, Mrs. Clarence Michaels (8 March 1912, 15, 17)

PHILLIPS, Mrs. S., of Cornwall, Ont., is visiting her daughter, Mrs. V. Michaels (25 Nov. 1910, 14, 2)

PHILLIPS, W., of Chicago, is staying at the Grand Union (20 Aug. 1909, 12, 36)

PICKELMAN, L., of New York, is in Montreal for a few days (25 June 1909, 12, 28)

PIERCE, A. and Eli Jacobs are back from New York (10 Dec. 1909, 13, 4)

PIERCE, Ascher, E.W. Jacobs, B. Isaacs, and N. Silver were among the Montrealers in New York last week (8 Jan. 1909, 12, 4)

PIERCE, Ascher, purchased one tree in the Herzl Wald in the name of his son, Master Sydney D. Pierce (15 Jan. 1909, 12, 5)

PIERCE, Ascher was Chosan Torah and Albert Freidman Chosan Beresheth on Simchat Torah at the Spanish and Portuguese Synagogue. At the Shaar Hashomayim Synagogue these honors were given to Mo. Heillig and M.L. Levin, respectively (25 Oct. 1910, 13, 50)

PIERCE, Charles, has gone to Toronto on a short visit (15 Oct. 1909, 12, 44)

PIERCE, M., has joined the Alliance Insurance Company (13 Jan. 1911, 14, 9)

PIERCE, M.A., of New York, is the guest of Henry H. Rose, Vercheres Ave., for several days after which he will leave for Ottawa, Toronto and Winnipeg (12 Aug. 1910, 13, 39)

PIERCE, Miss B., of Timmins, Ont., is the guest of Mr. and Mrs. Ascher Pierce (16 Jan. 1914, 17, 6)

PIERCE, Mr. and Mrs. Ascher, are in Atlantic City (25 March 1910, 13, 19)

PIERCE, Mr. and Mrs. Ascher, have returned from Atlantic City and New York (15 April 1910, 13, 22)

PIERCE, Mr. and Mrs. J., of Winnipeg, are visiting their son, A. Pierce and their family, Mt. Pleasant Ave. (22 Oct. 1909, 12, 45)

PIERCE, Mrs. Ascher and Miss Yetta Silver are in Buffalo visiting friends (19 Jan. 1912, 15, 10)

PIERCE, Mrs. Ascher and son are at Nargansett Pier for the summer (15 July 1910, 13, 35)

PIERCE, Mrs. Ascher, left for Ottawa to attend the Bar Mitzvah of her nephew, Master L. Bilsky (20 Feb. 1914, 17, 8)

PIERCE, R., who was away for an extended period, has returned to Montreal (26 March 1909, 12, 15)

PIERCE, Richard, Max Fineberg, M.L. Levin and Nathan Lande contributed to the Zionist Land Fund (26 May 1911, 14, 28)

PIERCE, Richard, of Winnipeg, is in Montreal (5 March 1909, 12, 12)

PINCKES, Jack, of Chicago, is spending the weekend with Mr. and Mrs. I. Sugarman at the summer cottage, Kirk's Ferry, Que. (18 July 1913, 16, 32)

PINSLER, Jack, chairman of the YMHA entertainment committee, was responsible for organizing the picnic at Otterburn Park last Sun. Others involved in the event were:- A.M. Goldstein, treas.; L. Ober, sec.; and Samuel Bloomfield, William Singer, L. Rosenburg, B. Lazarus and S. Brodsky (15 July 1910, 13, 35)

PINSLER, Miss A., was re-elected president (by acclamation) of the YWHA of Montreal at its headquarters, 667 St. Urbain St. Other officers elected were:- Miss J. Goldstein, vice-pres.; Miss J. Garfinkle, treas.; Miss J. Schulich, corr. sec.; Miss B. Silver, fin. sec.; Mrs. Jack Issen, and the Misses R. Berman, R. Brotman, E.L. Issen, W.F. Presser, D. Ratner, F. Silverberg and C. Wagner, board of committee (13 Feb. 1914, 17, 7)

PINSLER, Miss Alice and Miss Dora Schachter spent a few weeks at Shawbridge, Que. (2 Aug. 1912, 15, 34)

PINSLER, Miss Alice, recently returned from New York where she was the guest of Mrs. Julia Rothman (1 Oct. 1913, 16, 42-43)

POLEKSWICH, Miss Dora, of Biddeford, Me., is visiting Mrs. H. Levy, 86 Shuter St. (23 Feb. 1912, 15, 15)

POLIN, Mr. and Mrs. N., of New York, are visiting their daughter and son-in-law, Mr. and Mrs. Leon Goldman, Esplanade Ave. (7 June 1912, 15, 26)

POLLACK, J., of Allston, Mass., was in Montreal for a short stay (7 Nov. 1913, 16, 48)

POLLACK, Mr. and Mrs. B.J., 1433 Cadieux St., send New Year greetings (11 Sept. 1912, 15, 40)

POLLIN, Moe, of New York, is visiting his aunt, Mrs. Leon Goldman (1 March 1912, 15, 16)

POLLIN, N., of New York, is visiting his sister, Mrs. L. Goldman, Esplanade Ave. (5 March 1909, 12, 12)

POLONSKY, Miss Fanny, celebrated her nineteenth birthday with a party at her sister's home on Sun. Nov. 19, 1911 (24 Nov. 1911, 15, 2)

POPLIGER, I. and M. Lightstone, spoke at the banquet in the Auditorium Hall following the Montefiore Club's annual sleigh ride on Sun. Feb. 16, 1913. On the musical program were the Misses Sadie Ressler and Bessie Seigler (21 Feb. 1913, 16, 11)

POPLIGER, I., is in Toronto for a week (3 Jan. 1913, 16, 4)

POPLIGER, I., was elected president of the Montefiore Circle for young Jewish men, at the semi-annual meeting. Other officers elected were:- P. Garfinkle, vice-pres.; Chas. M. Colle, sec.; H. Gold, treas.; M. Bernfeld, W. Bernfeld, S. Hyams, Theo. Jacobs and S. Resch, committee members (11 Oct. 1912, 15, 44)

POPLIGER, Isidore, is president of the Hebrew National Society, a society organized to oppose Jewish missionaries preaching Christianity in the street. It obtained a permit from the mayor to hold meetings in the street and the first one was held July 2, 1911. Other officers are:- M. Hart, vice-pres.; and I. Goldberg, sec. (25 July 1911, 14, 36)

POPLIGER, Isidore, N.S. Fineberg, M.A., and Nathan Solomon received their B.C.L. degrees, McGill University, Faculty of Law (16 May 1913, 16, 23)

POPLIGER, Isidore, Nathan Fineberg and Nathan Solomon passed the recent Bar examination in Quebec City and have been admitted to the Bar. Messrs. Popliger and Solomon entered McGill University in 1910 and graduated in 1913, Mr. Solomon taking first rank honors (11 July 1913, 16, 31)

POPLIGER, Isidore, who was operated on a few days ago for appendicitis, is now completely recovered and will resume his law practice on Mon. (9 Jan. 1914, 17, 5)

POPLIGER, S., Franz Joseph Lodge delegate, is at the IOBB Convention in New York (31 Jan. 1913, 16, 8)

POPLIGER, S., was elected president of the Franz Joseph Lodge, IOSB last Sun. Other officers elected were:- Max Levin, vice-pres.; Isidore Friedman, fin. and rec. sec.; S. Goldner, treas.; P. Kamisher, sergeant-at-arms; D. Blumer, S. Kalmanowitz and A.M. Friedlieb. Isidore Friedman was elected delegate to the IOSB annual convention in New York on March 13, 1910 and Adolph Aron as the alternate (24 Dec. 1909, 13, 6)

POPLINGER, Mrs., of New York,

M. PIERCE
INSURANCE AGENT.

Special Agent for the Alliance Assurance Co
*Fire, Accident, Plate Glass,
Rent and Life Insurance.*
608 EASTERN TOWNSHIP BANK BLDG.
TEL. MAIN 2178.

is the guest of the Misses Lauterman (20 June 1913, 16, 28)

PORTEOUS, Dr. and Mrs., of Chicago, were "at home" to their friends on Aug. 24, 1910 in the Windsor Hotel (2 Sept. 1910, 13, 42)

PORTEOUS, J., of Chicago, Ill., was in Montreal, en route for the Porcupine District (20 Oct. 1911, 14, 49)

PORTEOUS, Miss, of Chicago, is the guest of Mrs. Ascher Pierce, Mt. Pleasant Ave. (24 Dec. 1909, 13, 6)

PORTIS, Miss Carrie, of Chicago, returned home Mon. evening after visiting her cousin, Mrs. Asher Pierce (14 Jan. 1910, 13, 9)

POYANER, Miss, has returned from New Glasgow where she spent a few weeks' holiday with Mr. and Mrs. Segall (9 Sept. 1910, 13, 43)

POYANER, Misses, are back from Ivry, Lake Manitou (3 Sept. 1909, 12, 38)

POYANER, Mr. and Mrs. M., have gone to Edmundston, N.B., where they will be guests of Mr. and Mrs. J. Moscovitz (24 June 1910, 13, 32)

POYANER, Mrs. A. and daughter, Miss Florence Poyaner, have gone on a trip to Pittsburgh (5 Nov. 1909, 12, 47)

POYANER, Mrs. A. and daughter, Mrs. H.M. Sevinoff have returned from a three months' trip abroad (30 Sept. 1910, 13, 46)

POYANER, Mrs. A. and her daughter, Mrs. H.M. Levinoff, have left on the Empress of Ireland for a three months' trip abroad. They will visit Paris, Karlsbad and Vienna (24 June 1910, 13, 32)

POYANER, Myer, has returned from Edmundston, N.B. (3 Sept. 1909, 12, 38)

POZNER, Mr. and Mrs. L., are visiting Mr. and Mrs. A. Pozner, in New York (24 Dec. 1909, 13, 6)

PRESNER, Louis, of Winnipeg, returned home to visit his mother, Mrs. I. Presner, St. Urbain St. (1 Aug. 1913, 16, 34)

PRESNER, Mrs. I., St. Urbain St., left for Winnipeg to visit her daughter, Mrs. B.Z. Levinson (13 June 1913, 16, 27)

PRESSER, Miss W.F., 32 Clark St., secretary of the YWHA, is accepting membership applications. Members will be pleased to learn that Miss Jean Rost will again lead the gym class and basketball team (7 Nov. 1913, 16, 48)

PRESSER, Miss W.F., 410 Bleury St., is secretary of the YWHA which is accepting applications for membership (16 May 1913, 16, 23)

PRESSER, Miss Winnie F., celebrated her birthday with a skating party given by in her honor by the D.D.S.C., on Sun. Jan. 14, 1912 (19 Jan. 1912, 15, 10)

PRESSMAN, Mr. and Mrs., of New York, were the guests of Mrs. Joseph Kruger, while in Montreal (6 May 1910, 13, 25)

PRESSMAN, Tonnie, of New York, is visiting his uncle, Meyer Lefkowitz, City Hall Ave. (8 Aug. 1913, 16, 35)

PRESSNER, M., who was abroad for six months, has returned (23 Feb. 1912, 15, 15)

PRESTON, Mrs. J., of Ottawa, was the guest of Miss Cochenthaler, Bishop St. (4 Nov. 1910, 13, 51)

PRUZANSKY, Jacob and M.L. Zach, were elected Montreal delegates to the Fifth Poali Zion Convention to be held in Montreal on Oct. 19, 1910. A. Kamanoff, J. Poshertnick and Max Blackman hold proxies (11 Oct. 1910, 13, 48)

PULASKI, J., returned home to Philadelphia to attend the wedding of her sister who was married on Dec. 27, 1913, to L. Glaser (2 Jan. 1914, 17, 4)

PULLAN, L.J., of M. Pullan & Sons, Toronto, stayed at the Windsor Hotel while in Montreal on business. He left for New York and Atlantic City (28 March 1913, 16, 16)

PURITZMAN, Miss Bessie, went to New York for several weeks to visit relatives (15 Dec. 1911, 15, 5)

PURITZMAN, Miss Sophie and her sister Sarah are at New Glasgow, Que., for the summer (12 July 1912, 15, 31)

RABINOVITCH, Dr. Max, has moved his office from 221 Bleury St. to 791 City Hall Ave., corner of Pine Ave. (6 May 1910, 13, 25)

RABINOVITCH, George and Samuel, have paid off their $14,000 in liabilities incurred through the failure of their dry goods business ten years ago. Last Mon., the brothers paid off all thirty-six creditors at their office in the Royal Trust Building, St.James St. "As the last debt was payed off Mr. George Rabinovitch stepped forward, and taking his brother by the hand, said: 'Well, Samuel, we have been true to our promise, our name is now clear, we do not owe a cent in the world.'". The brothers are now properous real estate businessmen (19 Dec. 1913, 17, 2)

RABINOVITCH, George, the well-known and popular real estate dealer, was interviewed by the real estate dept. editor of The Canadian Jewish Times. The young broker's favorite locality is St. Lawrence Blvd. and St. Catherine St. (18 April 1913, 16, 19)

RABINOVITCH, George, wishes his friends a happy New Year (1 Oct. 1913, 16, 42-43)

RABINOVITCH, Miss Annie, Esplanade Ave., leaves for New York tomorrow night (13 Jan. 1911, 14, 9)

RABINOVITCH, Miss Olga, has recovered from her recent illness (5 Sept. 1913, 16, 39)

RABINOVITCH, Mr. and Mrs. Max, 163 Esplanade Ave. wish their friends and relatives a happy New Year (1 Oct. 1913, 16 42-43)

RABINOVITCH, Mr. and Mrs. S., 225 Esplanade Ave., wish their friends and relatives a happy New Year (1 Oct. 1913, 16, 42-43)

RABINOVITCH, Mrs. Aaron, has gone out west for two months (13 Jan. 1911, 14, 9)

RABINOWITZ, Aron, has returned from a successful trip out west (1 Sept. 1911, 14, 42)

RABINOWITZ, Dr. Max, read a paper "Jews in Medicine, during and prior to the Middle Ages" at the Shaar Hashomayim Young People's Society meeting Tues. evening, Jan. 25. 1909 in the Baron de Hirsch Institute. Professor Stephen Leacock, M.A., also read a paper "Benjamin Disraeli: His Political Ideas" (29 Jan. 1909, 12, 7)

RACHOFSKY, Miss, is visiting her cousin, Miss M. Rittenberg, Mance St., Annex (25 Nov. 1910, 14, 2)

RACHOFSKY, Miss Minnie, has returned home to Denver after spending a month visiting her cousin, Mrs. M. Rittenberg (23 Dec. 1910, 14, 6)

RAFOLOVITCH, Miss Lena, of New York, is a guest of Mr. and Mrs. Rafolovitch, Cartierville (16 July 1909, 12, 31)

RAFOLOVITCH, Mr. and Mrs. M., are at their summer residence in Cartierville (16 July 1909, 12, 31)

RAFOLOVITCH, Mr. and Mrs., Park Ave., gave a champagne dinner at their home last Sun., in honor of their niece, Miss Sara Rafolovitch's approaching marriage to Harry Cohen. The Misses Rose and Becky Teplitzky, nieces of Mrs. Rafolovitch, performed vocal and piano solos. Present was Jacob Shopira, of Chicago, Mrs. Rafolovitch's brother (7 Feb. 1913, 16, 9)

RAGINSKY, A. and daughter, Miss Pauline Raginsky, are in New York on a short trip (21 June 1912, 15, 28)

RAISCUBARG, I., manager of the Chicago branch of the Jewish Consumptive Relief Society of Denver, is in Montreal to recruit membership (25 March 1910, 13, 19)

RAM, Samuel, general manager of the Globe Feature Film Co., was the guest of the president of the International Feature Film Co., last week in New York at the Astor Hotel (28 Feb. 1913, 16, 12)

RAM, Samuel, returned last Tues. from a short trip to Toronto (26 Feb. 1909, 12, 11)

RAM, Samuel, son of B. Ram, left on a business trip to New York, Chicago and Winnipeg. He was appointed general sales manager for the Globe Specialty Co., of Chicago for all Canada and will live in Winnipeg (15 Oct. 1913, 16, 45)

RAMSAY, Miss, is the guest of Miss Joseph, at Lake St. Joseph (6 Aug. 1909, 12, 34)

RAPHAEL, Miss Beatrice, of New York, is visiting her grandparents, Mr. and Mrs. William Raphael, Shuter St., for the summer (19 July 1912, 15, 32)

RAPHAEL, Miss Bertha and Miss Annie Silverstone have returned from the Laurentians (28 July 1911, 14, 37)

RAPHAEL, Miss Bertha, Durocher St., is spending a few weeks at Val Morin (14 July 1911, 14, 35)

RAPHAEL, Miss Bertha, Durocher St., leaves for New York where she will spend the winter (15 Nov. 1912, 15, 49)

RAPHAEL, Miss Bertha, is spending a few weeks at Dixie, Que. (22 Aug. 1913, 16, 37)

RAPHAEL, Miss Bertha left for New York Sat. evening. She will visit her sister in Norfolk, Va., for several months (14 Jan. 1910, 13, 9)

RAPHAEL, Miss Claire, of New York, is visiting

her aunt, Mrs. A.A. Sandeman (30 Sept. 1910, 13, 46)

RAPHAEL, Miss Clare, of New York, is the guest of her aunt, Mrs. A.A. Sandeman (29 April 1910, 13, 24)

RAPHAEL, Miss Louise, has returned from a few weeks visit to friends in Toronto (11 Feb. 1910. 13, 13)

RAPHAEL, Miss, of New York, is visiting her grandmother, Mrs. Raphael, Victoria St., for a few weeks (9 July 1909, 12, 30)

RAPHAEL, Mr. and Mrs. and daughter, King Edward Apts., leave for Hanlon's Point, and will be guests of Mrs. I. Kubelik for the summer (2 July 1909, 12, 29)

RAPHAEL, Mr. and Mrs. R. and daughter are visiting Mrs. Kubelick, in Toronto (24 Dec. 1909, 13, 6)

RAPHAEL, Mr. and Mrs. Ralph and daughter, have moved to Toronto (25 Feb.1910, 13, 15)

RAPHAEL, R., Sussex Ave., returned from Toronto, after a short stay (15 Jan. 1909, 12, 5)

RAPHAEL, Ralph, of New York, attended the golden wedding anniversary of his parents, Mr. and Mrs. William Raphael (1 Nov. 1912, 15, 47)

RAPHAEL, Ralph, of Toronto, was in Montreal the past few days (15 April 1910, 13, 22)

RAPHAEL, Ralph, of Toronto, was in Montreal for a few days (12 Aug. 1910, 13, 39)

RAPHAEL, Ralph, of Toronto, was in Montreal the past week (25 Nov. 1910, 14, 2)

RAPHAEL, Ralph, of Toronto, was in Montreal for the week (20 Oct. 1911, 14, 49)

RAPHAEL, Ralph, of Toronto, was in Montreal, en route for Halifax (1 Aug. 1913, 16, 34)

RAPHAEL, Rudolph, of New York, was in Montreal visiting his parents, Mr. and Mrs. William Raphael, Durocher St. (2 Jan. 1914, 17, 4)

RAPP, M., is registered at the St. Louis Hotel, Quebec City (7 Jan. 1910, 13, 8)

RAPPOPORT, Mrs., Esplanade Ave., accompanied by her daughter and her sister, Miss Beerman, leave April 9, 1911 for Los Angeles (7 April 1911, 14, 21)

RAPPORT, Mr., has returned home to Sherbrooke, Que. (3 March 1911, 14, 16)

RATNER, Mr. and Mrs. Z., wish their friends a happy New Year (1 Oct. 1913, 16, 42-43)

RATNER, Z. and family, 1603 Cadieux St., send New Year greetings (11 Sept. 1912, 15, 40)

RAWSON, S., was master of ceremonies at a social held at the YMHA, 52 Ontario St., last Sun. Others participating were:- J. Pinsler, I. Mitnick, G. Heller, Louis Ober, S.B. Gordon, J. Malkinson and B. Rose (11 Nov. 1910, 13, 52)

REDLICH, Charles and Master Frank Redlich have returned from a trip to the Coast (3 Dec. 1909, 13, 3)

REDLICH, Frank and the Misses Eva Goldstein and Ruth Levine have returned from Perth, Ont., where they visited the Misses Mendels (6 Jan. 1911, 14, 8)

REDLICH, Frank, Arthur King and the Misses Eva Goldstein and Mary Blucher will take part in the Young-People's Shaar Hashomayim meeting next Tues. (9 Dec. 1910, 14, 4)

REDLICH, Joseph, of Ottawa, was in Montreal briefly (22 July 1910, 13, 36)

REDLICH, Mr. and Mrs. Charles and daughter are in Boston this week, the guests of Mr. and Mrs. Adam Klopot (29 Sept. 1911, 14, 46)

REDLICH, Mrs. C. and daughters are spending a few weeks at St. Anns, Que. (22 Aug. 1913, 16, 37)

REDLICH, Mrs. Charles, has returned from New York (22 Dec. 1911, 15, 6)

REDLICH, Mrs. J., has returned from Schenectady, N.Y., where she attended the golden wedding anniversary of relatives (15 July 1910, 13, 35)

REINHARZ, David, of New York, accepted the position of superintendent of the Commercial Travellers Ltd. (11 Oct. 1912, 15, 44)

REMACH, G.K., of New York, is the guest of Mr. and Mrs. S.P. Myers, Bishop St. (30 Aug. 1912, 15, 38)

RESSLER, Miss Twinnie S., Esplanade Ave., gave a snow-shoe tramp Sat. aft. (8 March 1912, 15, 17)

RESSLER, Mrs. L. and her son, Mr. Hyman Ressler, are spending several days in New York (23 April 1909, 12, 19)

RICHENBURG, Miss Annie, has gone to New York to visit relatives (6 Oct. 1911, 14, 47)

GOOD BREAD
Richstone's Pure Rye Bread. Pure Black Bread. White Bread. Cakes Best in City.
BEST FLOUR ONLY USED
EXPERIENCED BAKERS EMPLOYED
Head Office: 523 Cadieux Street, Tel. East 6535
Branches all Over the Cit

RICHSTONE, A.S., has moved to Vancouver, B.C. (10 Feb. 1911, 14, 13)

RICHTER, Dr. and Mrs. S., of New York, have returned home after visiting Mrs. Richter's sister, Mrs. Leon Goldman, Esplanade Ave. (26 Aug. 1910, 13, 41)

RICHTER, Miss Frances E., of New York, is the guest of Mrs. Leon Goldman, Esplanade Ave. (5 March 1909, 12, 12)

RICHTER, Miss Francis, who was the guest of Mrs. Leon Goldman, has returned to New York (26 March 1909, 12, 15)

RICHTER, Mrs. S., of New York, is visiting her sister, Mrs. Leon Goldman, Esplanade Ave. (29 July 1910, 13, 37)

RIFFENSTEIN, Miss, is spending a holiday at Tadousac (23 July 1909, 12, 32)

RIGLER, Miss Jennie, gave a social evening in honor of her brother's fiancée, Miss Grace B. Thaler, of Brooklyn, N.Y. Those present were:- the Misses M. Kolber, M. Rigler, R.E. Rigler, Rose Samuels and F. Schliefer (5 Dec. 1913, 16, 52)

RILL, J.L., of Winnipeg, is visiting his sister, Mrs. Ettenberg, 75 Shuter St. (11 Oct. 1912, 15, 44)

RITTENBERG, M., has donated $10.00 to the Baron de Hirsch Institute for the consumptives relief fund (14 Jan. 1910, 13, 9)

RITTENBERG, M., has left for Ashville, N.C. (7 April 1911, 14, 21)

RITTENBERG, M., is in Toronto for the funeral of his brother, Sam Rittenberg, who died Nov. 22, 1912, at the home of his parents after a long illness (29 Nov. 1912, 15, 51)

RITTENBERG, M., Mance St., Annex, is visiting his parents in Toronto (15 Oct. 1909, 12, 44)

RITTENBERG, M., Mance St., has recovered from a recent illness (22 Jan. 1909, 12, 6)

RITTENBERG, M., was in Toronto for a few days (1 April 1910, 13, 20)

RITTENBERG, Miss Belle, has returned home to Toronto after an enjoyable stay (25 Feb. 1910, 13, 15)

RITTENBERG, Miss Belle, of Toronto, is visiting Mrs. M. Rittenberg, Mance St. (21 Jan. 1910, 13, 10)

RITTENBERG, Miss Belle, of Toronto, is visiting her sister, Mrs. I. Levinhoff (9 Aug. 1912, 15, 35)

RITTENBERG, Miss Belle, of Toronto, is visiting her sister, Mrs. I. Levinoff, 1523 Park Ave. (5 Dec. 1913, 16, 52)

RITTENBERG, Mr. and Mrs. M. and family have returned from Ste. Agathe (27 Aug. 1909, 12, 37)

RITTENBERG, Mr. and Mrs. M., are summering at Beaconsfield, Que. (2 Aug. 1912, 15, 34)

RITTENBERG, Mr. and Mrs. M., gave a reception in honor of their son Alfred's Bar Mitzvah on Sun. Feb. 13, 1910. Those assisting in receiving were her sister-in-law, Mrs. Grossman, of Toronto, and Miss Belle Rittenberg. The Misses Tannenbaum, Cassil, Mendel and Mrs. Joseph Kruger assisted at the table. The grandparents, Mr. and Mrs. Rittenberg, of Toronto attended and will remain for a week (18 Feb. 1910, 13, 14)

RITTENBERG, Mr. and Mrs. Moe, are at Manoir Richelieu, Murray Bay (4 Aug. 1911, 14, 38)

RITTENBERG, Mr. and Mrs., of Toronto, are in

Montreal. Their son, Sam Rittenberg is recovering from his recent operation (12 July 1912, 15, 31)

RITTENBERG, Mrs. M., Mance St., is visiting her parents in New York (5 March 1909, 12, 12)

RITTENBERG, Mrs. Moe, St. Joseph Blvd., is in Toronto for a few weeks (4 July 1913, 16, 30)

RITTENBERG, Samuel, has returned from Toronto where he visited his parents (15 July 1910, 13, 35)

RIVENOVITCH, Miss Susie and Miss Jennie Covecy gave a surprise party in honor of Miss Annie Rivenovitch at her residence, 1055 St. Catherine St. E., on Sun. evening, Nov. 30, 1913. Susie Rivenovitch received the guests and presented her sister, Annie with a wrist-watch (12 Dec. 1913, 17, 1)

ROBACK, A.A., is leaving shortly for Harvard University. His friends are arranging an evening in his honor on Sun. Sept. 21, 1913, in the Baron de Hirsch Institute. Mr. Roback, who has his M.A., is returning for his Ph.D. (12 Sept. 1913, 16, 40)

ROBACK, Abraham A., the brilliant young philosopher, who last spring won the highest honors in philosophy at McGill University, will lecture on "The Philosophy of Life", Sun. evening, Sept. 15, 1912 at 8 p.m., in the Baron de Hirsch Institute. Mr. Roback plans on leaving shortly for Harvard for post-graduate work in philosophy (11 Sept. 1912, 15, 40)

ROBINSON, J., of Winnipeg, was in Montreal (21 June 1912, 15, 28)

ROBINSON, Mrs., of New York, who visited her son in Winnipeg, is spending a couple of weeks with her sister, Mrs. A. Jacobs, Mansfield St. (27 Aug. 1909, 12, 37)

ROCKSTEIN, Jacob, Mr. and Mrs. John Michaels, Mrs. Maurice Levi, Mr. and Mrs. A.E. Morris and Miss K. Morris, Mr. and Mrs. I. Blumenthal and the Misses Gladys and Muriel Blumenthal were among those sailing on the S.S. Lake Megantic, Tues. May 27, 1913 (30 May 1913, 16, 25)

ROESNER, Miss Hilda, St. Urbain St., is the guest of Mr. and Mrs. Sam Karakofsky, Lippincott Apts., Toronto (11 July 1913, 16, 31)

ROGGEN, Mr. and Mrs. Selig and Rabbi Meldola de Sola sailed for Europe aboard the S.S. Megantic last Sat. (1 July 1910, 13, 33)

ROMAN, Mr. and Mrs. Marcus and daughter returned from a trip to New York (11 Oct. 1910, 13, 48)

ROMAN, Mr. and Mrs. Marcus and daughter are in Atlantic City (27 Oct. 1911, 14, 50)

ROMAN, Samuel, is in Boston visiting his daughter, Mrs. A. Klopot (8 July 1910, 13, 34)

ROME, H.J., of Gardner, Mass., was the guest of Mr. and Mrs. H. Bernstein while in Montreal (10 June 1910, 13, 30)

ROME, Mr. and Mrs. I., of Worcester, Mass., were the guests of Mr. and Mrs. H. Bernstein while in Montreal (10 June 1910, 13, 30)

ROME, Mr. and Mrs. Nathan, have returned to Worcester, Mass. after visiting Mrs. Rome's parents, Mr. and Mrs. H. Bernstein (27 Jan. 1911, 14, 11)

ROME, Mr. and Mrs. Nathan, of Worcester, Mass., are guests of Mrs. Rome's parents, Mr. and Mrs. H. Bernstein, Hutchison St. (13 Jan. 1911, 14, 9)

ROME, Mrs. Nathan, Worcester, Mass., is spending a holiday with her parents, Mr. and Mrs. H. Bernstein, Hutchison St. (20 Oct. 1911, 14, 49)

ROME, Nathan, of Worcester, is a guest at the Windsor Hotel (11 Feb. 1910, 13, 13)

ROOS, Miss, of Boston, is the guest of Mrs. I. Simon, Sherbrooke St., Westmount (15 Jan. 1909, 12, 5)

ROOS, Miss, of Boston, who has been visiting Mrs. H. Simon, returns home Fri. (5 Feb. 1909, 12, 8)

ROSCOM, D., is in New York for the holidays visiting his parents (24 Dec. 1909, 13, 6)

ROSCOM, D., left on a short trip to New York (6 Aug. 1909, 12, 34)

ROSCOM, Miss Fannie has returned after spending the past two weeks as the guest of Miss Goldstein, Pointe Claire (19 Aug. 1910, 13, 40)

ROSCOM, Miss Fannie, is the guest of Miss Goldstein, Pointe Claire, for a few weeks (5 Aug. 1910, 13, 38)

ROSCOM, Misses, of New York, are guests of Mrs. B. Goldstein, Pointe Claire (24 June 1910, 13, 32)

ROSCON, L., is spending the holidays in New York with his parents (8 Jan. 1909, 12, 4)

ROSCOW, J., left on a trip to Toronto and the West (12 March 1909, 12, 13)

ROSE, B., of Montreal, has received his Master of Laws degree from Laval University (17 June 1910, 13, 31)

ROSE, Bernard, is president of the St. Lawrence Conservative Association. Other officers are:- Harry Gordon, 1st vice-pres.; Dr. Norman Viner, 2nd vice-pres.; Manuel Levitt, hon. sec.; and Nathan Lande, treas. (7 Feb. 1913, 16, 9)

ROSE, Bernard, Maurice Alexander and Isidore Goodstone were successful candidates at the recent Bar examinations (15 July 1910, 13, 35)

ROSE, I., spent a few days in Quebec City last week (11 June 1909, 12, 26)

ROSE, Miss, of St. Joseph, Mo., is the guest of Miss Hattie Blumberg, St. Mark St. (26 Dec. 1913, 17, 3)

ROSE, Mr. and Mrs. M.L., 146 St. Joseph Blvd., wish their friends and relatives a happy New Year (1 Oct. 1913, 16, 42-43)

ROSE, Mrs. B.A., and Miss Miller are spending the summer at Lake Placid, N.Y. (7 July 1911, 14, 34)

ROSE, Mrs. M.L., is president of the Hebrew Day Nursery which held its inaugural meeting on July 16, 1913 in the Baron de Hirsch Institute. The society has four hundred members. The society's object "...will be to establish a nursery where children may be properly looked after during the day, when their mothers are busy working." Other officers are:- Mrs. M.J. Adler, treas.; Miss Lillian Wetstein, rec. sec.; Miss J.L. Schleifer, fin. sec.; and Lyon Jacobs, hon. solicitor. Miss Wetstein writes "It has been a well-known fact for many years to the Jewish social worker, that many Jewish women would be glad to work, house work, factory work, and some of them even being capable of doing office work, if it were not for the fact that their children cannot be left alone during the day." (1 Aug. 1913, 16, 34)

ROSE, Mrs. M.L., of Rochester, N.Y., is visiting her parents, Mr. and Mrs. Simon Aron, 419 St. Lawrence Blvd. (23 July 1909, 12, 32)

ROSE, S., of Detroit, has been visiting his uncle, A.H. Jackson, St. Urbain St. (5 March 1909, 12, 12)

ROSE, Samuel, of Detroit, is the guest of Mr. and Mrs. A.H. Jackson (12 March 1909, 12, 13)

ROSEN, J., passed the preliminary examinations for admission to first year law at Laval University (17 Jan. 1913, 16, 6)

ROSEN, Mr. and Mrs. and family, who are residing in Ste. Agathe, were in Montreal for a few days (29 Oct. 1909, 12, 46)

ROSEN, Mrs. H., was in Montreal for a few days (26 Feb. 1909, 12, 11)

ROSEN, Mrs. N. and family, of Ste. Agathe, were visiting their mother, Mrs. H. Samuels, Drummond St. (9 Dec. 1910, 14, 4)

ROSENBAUM, Dr. J., is in Waterloo on vacation. He will assume his duties at the Royal Victoria Hospital on his return (21 June 1912, 15, 28)

ROSENBAUM, Dr. J., of the Royal Victoria Hospital, left on vacation for England (15 Oct. 1913, 16, 45)

ROSENBAUM, J., has returned from two weeks' vacation in Boston (8 Sept. 1911, 14, 43)

ROSENBAUM, Joseph, of Richmond, is registered at the Place Viger Hotel (15 Oct. 1909, 12, 44)

ROSENBAUM, Mrs. L., of Boston, is the guest of J. and B. Rosenbaum, 1736 Mance St. (16 Aug. 1912, 15, 36)

ROSENBERG, A., stayed at the Broadway Central Hotel while in New York (22 March 1912, 15, 19)

ROSENBERG, A.G., Joseph Levinson and Mr. and Mrs. J.M. Orkin were returning passengers on the S.S. Laurentic (26 July 1912, 15, 33)

ROSENBERG, Gabriel, of Dublin, Ireland, has been performing with the orchestra of the Quinlan Opera Company while in Montreal (20 March 1914, 17, 12)

ROSENBERG, Miss Hannah, gave a snow-shoe tramp, Mon. evening, Feb. 14, 1910 at the home of her parents, ?60 Sherbrooke St. W. (18 Feb. 1910, 13, 14)

ROSENBERG, Miss Ida, a Baron de Hirsch Hebrew School pupil, addressed the Rt. Hon. Herbert Samuel in Hebrew on his visit to the Baron de Hirsch Institute. She "...welcomed him to Canada in the name of all the Jewish children, and declared that Canadian Jewish children were proud that one of their race should have been appointed to a position in the British cabinet." (15 Oct. 1913, 16, 45)

ROSENBERG, Miss Rose and Miss Schleider returned from their holidays at Joliette, Que. (1 Aug. 1913, 16, 34)

ROSENBERG, Mr. and Mrs. C. and family have opened their summer cottage at Chateauguay (25 June 1909, 12, 28)

ROSENBERG, Mrs. and Miss R. Rosenberg, of New York, are guests at the Manor Richelieu, Murray Bay (23 July 1909, 12, 32)

ROSENBERG, Mrs. J., of Westmount, has returned from Mystic (20 Sept. 1911, 14, 45)

ROSENBERG, Mrs., of Providence, R.I., is visiting her daughter, Mrs. Max Jacobs at Lafontaine Park for a few weeks (23 Aug. 1912, 15, 37)

ROSENBERGER, M., a former resident of South Africa for seventeen years, lectured on that country to the Progressive Literary and Debating Club last Sun. (4 June 1909, 12, 25)

ROSENBERGER, M., gave an address on the Franco-German war at the open meeting of the Progressive Literary Circle last sun. evening in the Baron de Hirsch Institute (12 May 1911, 14, 26)

ROSENBLAT, Charles B., has gone to Chicago, en route for California where he will remain for some time (12 Jan. 1912, 15, 9)

ROSENBLAT, Charles B., of Winnipeg, gave a theatre party at His Majesty's Theatre, Wed. evening, and a late supper at the Windsor Hotel, Fri. evening, Feb. 11, 1910. Guests were:- Mr. and Mrs. Louis Margolese, Mrs. Rose Jacobs, Jack Levi and Mr. and Mrs. A. Michaels (18 Feb. 1910, 13, 14)

ROSENBLAT, Charles B., of Winnipeg, who was recently in Montreal while en route to New York, has returned here to arrange matters in connection with his approaching marriage (11 Feb. 1910, 13, 13)

ROSENBLAT, Charles B., of Winnipeg, who spent the past five weeks in Montreal, has returned home (4 March 1910, 13, 16)

ROSENBLAT, Chas. D., of Winnipeg, is visiting relatives and staying at the Carslake Hotel (21 Jan. 1910, 13, 10)

ROSENBLATT, C.B., will visit his home in Montreal and will attend the wedding of Miss Rebecca Ellison (4 April 1913, 16, 17)

ROSENBLATT, H., has returned to Montreal from his extended trip out west (17 Dec. 1909, 13, 5)

ROSENBLATT, H., is in Montreal for a few months before returning to the West (23 Dec. 1910, 14, 6)

ROSENBLATT, Mr., left for Vancouver where he will remain for some time (24 Sept. 1909, 12, 41)

ROSENBLATT, Mrs. H. and her sister, Miss Lavine have returned to Trenton, Ont. (16 Aug. 1912, 15, 36)

ROSENBLOOM, Joseph, of Sherbrooke, was in Montreal for a few days (22 Jan. 1909, 12, 6)

ROSENBLOOM, Max, returned home to Edmonton, after a two months' visit with his parents, Mr. and Mrs. L. Rosenbloom (6 March 1914, 17, 10)

ROSENBLOOM, Mr. and Mrs. Joseph, of Sherbrooke, Que., were in Montreal the past week (25 Nov. 1910, 14, 2)

ROSENBLOOM, Mrs. Joseph and Miss Dorothy Rosenbloom, of Sherbrooke, Que., are visiting Mr. and Mrs. J.L. Vineberg (29 Nov. 1912, 15, 51)

ROSENBLOOM, Mrs. Joseph, of Sherbrooke, Que., was in Montreal on a short visit (4 March 1910, 13, 16)

ROSENBLOOM, Mrs. Joseph, of Sherbrooke, was in Montreal for a few days (23 Sept. 1910, 13, 45)

ROSENES, Mr. and Mrs. H., of Notre Dame de Grace, wish their friends and relatives a happy New Year (10 Oct. 1913, 16, 44)

ROSENSVEIG, L., returned to Vancouver after visiting his parents, City Hall Ave. (8 Aug. 1913, 16, 35)

ROSENSVEIG, Miss Dora, City Hall Ave., left for Vancouver where she will be the guest of her brother, L. Rosensveig (8 Aug. 1913, 16, 35)

ROSENSVIEG, Miss Dora, who returned from Vancouver last week, was the guest of honor at a tea given by her friends at the Ritz-Carlton Hotel, on Sun. aft. (1 Oct. 1913, 16, 42-43)

ROSENTHAL, A., Colonial Ave., celebrated his birthday with a party on Sun. July 6, 1913. Guests were received by J. Rosenthal and ices were cut by Mrs. G. Norman (11 July 1913, 16, 31)

ROSENTHAL, Adolph and his mother, Mrs. A. Rosenthal, Sr., have gone to Germany. Mr. Rosenthal is there on business and Mrs. Rosenthal will visit her relatives in Berlin (10 March 1911, 14, 17)

ROSENTHAL, Alderman S., of Ottawa, is staying at the Windsor Hotel (11 June 1909, 12, 26)

ROSENTHAL, J., of New York, was the guest of his aunt, Mrs. H. Samuels, Drummond St. (26 Feb. 1909, 12, 11)

ROSENTHAL, J., of New York, was at the Queen's Hotel during the week (11 Oct. 1910, 13, 48)

ROSENTHAL, J., was elected president of the Royal Social Club on Sun. Oct. 26, 1913, at 363 Colonial Ave. Other officers elected were:- F.S. Lauria, sec. treas.; E. Ruttenberg, I. Sandarsky and A. Schwartz, exec. E. Ruttenberg presented the club with a pennant and performed a violin solo (31 Oct. 1913, 16, 47)

ROSENTHAL, Jack, of Toronto, is the guest of Mr. and Mrs. Abraham Jacobs (8 Aug. 1913, 16, 35)

ROSENTHAL, Jake, of Toronto, is visiting Mr. and Mrs. A. Jacobs, Dorchester St. W. (13 Jan. 1911, 14, 9)

ROSENTHAL, Joseph, of Toronto, was the guest of her mother, Mr. and Mrs. A. Jacobs, Dorchester St. W. the past week (24 Feb. 1911, 14, 15)

ROSENTHAL, Miss Bella, has returned from Richelieu, Que., where she was the guest of Miss Bessie Viner (27 Aug. 1909, 12, 37)

ROSENTHAL, Miss Bella, is the guest of her uncle, Mr. Levy, in New York (23 Sept. 1910, 13, 45)

ROSENTHAL, Miss Belle, has gone to New York to visit her uncle, L. Levy (30 Sept. 1910, 13, 46)

ROSENTHAL, Miss Dollie, of New York, is visiting Mrs. A.M. Vineberg, 233 Esplanade Ave., for a few weeks (19 July 1912, 15, 32)

ROSENTHAL, Miss, of New York, is the guest of Mrs. Samuels, Drummond St. (24 Feb. 1911, 14, 15)

ROSENTHAL, Miss Sarah, has gone to Chicago to visit relatives (15 Sept. 1911, 14, 44)

ROSENTHAL, Mr. and Mrs. H. and son, of Ottawa, were guests of Mrs. M. Workman (16 Sept. 1910, 13, 44)

ROSENTHAL, Mr. and Mrs. Harry and Master Robert Rosenthal, of Ottawa, were guests of Mr. and Mrs. Mark Workman, Sherbrooke St. W. (27 Feb. 1914, 17, 9)

ROSENTHAL, Mr. and Mrs. Harry, of Ottawa, were in Montreal during the past week (22 Jan. 1909, 12, 6)

ROSENTHAL, Mr. and Mrs. Samuel, of Ottawa, will spend the summer at Britannia (2 July 1909, 12, 29)

ROSENTHAL, Mr., of Providence, R.I., is visiting his sister, Mrs. Max Jacobs, Laval Ave. (24 Feb. 1911, 14, 15)

ROSENTHAL, Mrs. A. and family, of Toronto, are guests of Mr. and Mrs. A. Jacobs, Dorchester St. W. (13 Jan. 1911, 14, 9)

ROSENTHAL, Mrs. A., of Ottawa, was in Montreal for a short stay (24 June 1910, 13, 32)

ROSENTHAL, Mrs. B. and Mr. and Mrs. Arthur Rosenthal, of Ottawa, are guests at the Windsor Hotel (24 Nov. 1911, 15, 2)

ROSENTHAL, Mrs. M. and Master Robert Rosenthal, of Ottawa, are visiting Mr. and Mrs. Mark Workman, Sherbrooke St. W. (7 March 1913, 16, 13)

ROSENTHAL, Sr., Mrs. and Mr. and Mrs. A. Rosenthal, who attended the Rosenthal-Posnanzki wedding in Milwaukee, have returned to Ottawa after a visit to Chicago and Toronto. Mr. and Mrs. Rosenthal Sr., have left for their summer home at Britannia (2 July 1909, 12, 29)

ROSENTZVIEG, Mr. and Mrs. I., City Hall Ave., are at Mt. Clemens for a month (27 June 1913, 16, 29)

ROSKAM, D., is spending a few days in New York (15 Dec. 1911, 15, 5)

ROSKAM, Edward, of New York, was the guest of Mr. and Mrs. Dave Roskam (26 July 1912, 15, 33)

ROSKAM, L., is spending a week with his parents in New York (27 Oct. 1911, 14, 50)

ROSKAM, Mr. and Mrs. Dave, are spending the holidays in New York (29 Sept. 1911, 14, 46)

ROSKAM, Mr. and Mrs. Dave, Tupper St., returned from a four months' trip to the coast (29 Aug. 1913, 16, 38)

ROSKAM, Mr. and Mrs. David, have returned from a trip to the Saguenay (18 Aug. 1911, 14, 40)

ROSKOM, Mr. and Mrs. Dave, are at their summer cottage at Beaurepaire (16 June 1911, 14, 31)

ROSS, Miss Miriam D., of St. John, N.B., has moved to Montreal (18 Oct. 1912, 15, 45)

ROST, Julius, has gone on a business trip to the Maritimes (9 Sept. 1910, 13, 43)

ROST, Julius, has returned from a business trip to the Maritimes (15 April 1910, 13, 22)

ROST, Miss Anna, is visiting friends in Chicago (4 July 1913, 16, 30)

ROST, Miss Edith, is spending a month's holiday at Lake Champlain (17 June 1910, 13, 31)

ROST, Miss Jane B., has returned from a visit to Boston (30 Sept. 1910, 13, 46)

ROST, Miss Jane B., left for Boston, Providence and the South. She will return by the end of Jan. (29 Dec. 1911, 15, 7)

ROST, Miss Jean, will instruct the YWHA gymnastic class, owing to Mrs. Dr. Tannebaum's leaving town. Members wishing to join the class should inform Miss E. Jacobs (4 April 1913, 16, 17)

ROST, Mrs. A. and Mrs. J. Adler have returned from New York (1 April 1910, 13, 20)

ROST, Mrs. A., was installed as president of the Hebrew Ladies' Relief Society at a general meeting held in the Baron de Hirsch Institute, March 12, 1911. Other officers installed were:- Mesdames H. Merson, I. Sourkes, I. Astrofsky, J. Steinburg and S. Press (17 March 1911, 14, 18)

ROST, Mrs. Anna, is in Boston to attend the wedding of her nephew, Robert H. Spira, formerly of Vienna, Austria, to Miss Evelyn B. Webber, of Dorchester, Mass. She was accompanied to Boston by Mrs. Julius Rost (18 Oct. 1912, 15, 45)

ROTH, I., of New York, is visiting his daughter, Mrs. I. Vineberg, 887 Mount Royal Ave. (20 Aug. 1909, 12, 36)

ROTHBART, I. and B. Schulman fought a four-round boxing bout at the YMHA's smoking concert last Thurs. night. The other bout was between Rothbart and Kid Shear (23 Dec. 1910, 14, 6)

ROTHSCHILD, Ben, of Cochrane, Ont., is in Montreal (29 Dec. 1911, 15, 7)

ROTHSCHILD, Benjamin, has been appointed postmaster at Cochrane, Ont. (14 May 1909, 12, 22)

ROTHSCHILD, J., Grosvenor Ave., is recovering from his illness at home (22 Oct. 1913, 16, 46)

ROTHSCHILD, J., Western Ave., is recovering from his operation at the Montreal General Hospital (18 Oct. 1912, 15, 45)

ROTHSCHILD, Miss D., Western Ave., gave a party in honor of Miss Ada Silverberg, of Toronto, who is visiting Miss Ruth Groner, Elm Ave. Guests included:- P. Saks, H. Engleman, B. Isaacs, M. Levy, H. List, M. Robitaille, A. Abrahams and the Misses E. and R. Berman and P. Robitaille (12 July 1912, 15, 31)

ROTHSCHILD, Mr. and Mrs. Ben, of Cochrane, Ont., are spending the Holy Days with her parents, Mr. and Mrs. P. Silverstone, Lorne Ave. (20 Sept. 1912, 15, 41)

ROTHSCHILD, Mr. and Mrs. Ben, of Cochrane, Ont., stayed at the Ritz-Carlton Hotel while in Montreal (14 Feb. 1913, 16, 10)

ROTHSCHILD, Mr. and Mrs. J., of Sudbury, Ont., have moved to Montreal and are living on Western Ave. (8 Sept. 1911, 14, 43)

ROTHSCHILD, Mr. and Mrs. M. and family are at St. Faustine, Que., accompanied by Sol. Silverstone and sister (19 Aug. 1910, 13, 40)

ROTHSCHILD, Mr. and Mrs. Max and family have moved from Sudbury to Montreal and are living on Lansdowne Ave. (22 Oct. 1913, 16, 46)

ROTHSCHILD, Mrs. Ben, returned home to Cochrane, Ont., after visiting her parents, Mr. and Mrs. P. Silverstone, Lorne Ave. (4 July 1913, 16, 30)

ROTHSCHILD, Mrs. J. and family left for Averne, Long Island (11 July 1913, 16, 31)

ROTHSCHILD, Mrs. J. and family returned from New York and Averne, L.I. (22 Aug. 1913, 16, 37)

ROTHSCHILD, Mrs. M. and daughters, of Sudbury, Ont., are guests of Mr. and Mrs. M. Rothschild, Tupper St. (11 Nov. 1910, 13, 52)

ROWAN, Mrs. M. and daughter have returned from a visit to New York (24 May 1912, 15, 25)

RUBEN, J.H., of Pittsburgh, is registered at the Windsor Hotel (13 Aug. 1909, 12, 35)

RUBEN, L.M., was registered at the Latham Hotel while in New York (9 Dec. 1910, 14, 4)

RUBEN, Mr. and Mrs. L.M., are now residing in Montreal at the "Murray", 81 McKay St. (10 Sept. 1909, 12, 39)

RUBEN, Mr. and Mrs. L.M., are registered at the Windsor and will sail for Europe aboard the Laurentic on May 14, 1910 (6 May 1910, 13, 25)

RUBEN, Mr. and Mrs. L.M., are at the Windsor Hotel for the winter months (11 Oct. 1912, 15, 44)

RUBEN, Mr. and Mrs. L.M., of New York, will spend the remainder of the summer in Montreal (30 July 1909, 12, 33)

RUBEN, Mr. and Mrs. L.M., were in Quebec City this week (26 May 1911, 14, 28)

RUBEN, Mr. and Mrs. L.M., who spent two weeks at the Ritz-Carlton Hotel, returned home to New York (22 Oct. 1913, 16, 46)

RUBEN, Mr. and Mrs. Ludovie, have returned home from four months in Europe (2 Sept. 1910, 12, 42)

RUBEN, Mr. and Mrs. Ludwig, of New York, are guests of Dr. and Mrs. D.A. Hart, Sherbrooke St. (16 April 1909, 12, 18)

RUBEN, Mrs. L.M., has returned from New York and gave a tea this week in honor of Miss Pauline Lightstone (Madame Donalda) (8 April 1910, 13, 21)

RUBEN, Mrs. L.M., who has returned to Montreal to reside, entertained at the Windsor Hotel last Wed. (15 Oct. 1909, 12, 44)

RUBENSTEIN, I., 699 Upper St. Urbain St., has won the Montreal Horticultural Society's first prize for the best kept city garden (23 Sept. 1910, 13, 45)

RUBENSTEIN, L., has returned from a short trip to New York (7 May 1909, 12, 21)

RUBENSTEIN, L., stayed at the Chateau Frontenac in Quebec City last week (16 April 1909, 12, 18)

RUBENSTEIN, Lazarus, is visiting his sister, Mrs. J. Keir, of Brantford, Ont. (12 July 1912, 15, 31)

RUBENSTEIN, Louis, is a visiting governor at the Montreal General Hospital this week (16 June 1911, 14, 31)

RUBENSTEIN, Louis, was elected president of the Montreal Amateur Athletic Association at the annual meeting on Mon. evening (30 May 1913, 16, 25)

RUBENSTEIN, Miss Hattie, returned home to Sault St. Marie, after visiting Miss Rothschild, Western Ave. (7 March 1913, 16, 13)

RUBENSTEIN, Miss is leaving to visit her sister, Mrs. Cohen, in Fort Wayne, Ind. (15 Oct. 1909, 12, 44)

RUBENSTEIN, Miss, is visiting her sister, Mrs. J. Kerr, in Brantford, Ont. (19 Sept. 1913, 16, 41)

RUBIN, B., is in New York for a short stay (28 June 1912, 15, 29)

RUBIN, Dr. J., was elected president of the Montreal YMHA hockey club on Sun. Dec. 21, 1913. Management committee members are:- H. Gold, business manager; I. Tannenbaum, hon. coach, M. Goldberg, hockey committee; Dave Livinson, sec. The following submitted their names to the secretary:- Phil. Abinovitch, G. Abrahams, H. Adelstein, H. Beecher, L. Cohen, I. Goldberg, Samuel Elkin, Edgar H. Goldstein, Samuel Jacobs, B. Joseph, E. Kert, David Kirsch, Lyon Levinson, A. Sourkes, I. Tannenbaum, H. Vineberg and A.K. Viner. The best players will be chosen for the team which will play its first game on Jan. 6, 1914 against the Italian Hockey Club (26 Dec. 1913, 17, 3)

RUBIN, H., has returned from Ivry, where he was the guest of Mr. and Mrs. J.L. Gittleson (3 Sept. 1909, 12, 38)

RUBIN, M., fin. sec. of the Montreal Hebrew Consumptive Aid Society, has moved from 333 St. Louis St. to 305 Sanguinet St. (12 May 1911, 14, 26)

RUBIN, Miss Sophie, of Montreal, gave a surprise party last Sun. in honor of Miss Bella Pearl at the home of Mr. and Mrs. Pearl, 479 Wellington St., Ottawa. R. Edelstein was master of ceremonies. B. Bercovitch, R. Edelstein, S. Mirsky and the Misses B. Mirsky and Sophie Rubin provided entertainment (15 Dec. 1911, 15, 5)

RUBIN, Mr. and Mrs. J. and family are visiting their daughters in Ottawa, Mr. and Mrs. J. Diamond and Mr. and Mrs. J. Davis (2 Aug. 1912, 15, 34)

RUBIN, Mr. and Mrs. J., have gone to Ottawa to attend the Brith Milah of their first grandchild, the son of Mr. and Mrs. Davis (27 Oct. 1911, 14, 50)

RUBIN, Mr. and Mrs. L.M., have returned from New York (6 Jan. 1911, 14, 8)

RUBIN, Mr. and Mrs. L.M., of New York, are visiting Dr. and Mrs. D.A. Hart, Sherbrooke St. W. (2 July 1909, 12, 29)

RUBIN, Mrs. C.S. and son, Mrs. S. Cohen, Mr.

and Mrs. Harry Vineberg and son, Mrs. I. Goldstein, Miss Ray Heillig, Miss Jennie Heillig, Master Willie Heillig, Mrs. Barney Freedman and sons, Mrs. A.L. Friedman and daughter, Mrs. S. Wener and daughter, Miss Lillian Levinson, Mrs. J. Roston son and daughter, Mrs. I. Weinberg and son, Miss Lillian Samuel, Mrs. Lyon Cohen and sons, Mr. and Mrs. M.L. Morris and the Misses Morris and Miss Ida Sigler are holidaying at Shawbridge. Late arrivals are Mr. and Mrs. Berman, of Cleveland; Mrs. M. Fineberg; and Miss Annie Feigelson (23 July 1909, 12, 32)

RUBIN, Mrs. J., and her youngest son, Abraham Rubin, have gone to Ottawa to visit her children, Mesdames J. Davis and J. Diamond (24 Feb. 1911, 14, 15)

RUBIN, Mrs. J., has gone to Ottawa to visit her daughters, Mesdames J. Davis and S. Diamond (25 July 1911, 14, 36)

RUBIN, S., is spending a holiday at Ste. Agathe (13 Aug. 1909, 12, 35)

RUBINOVICH, Erwin, 448 Argyle Ave., Westmount, secretary of the Success Club, is taking membership applications (25 Nov. 1910, 14, 2)

RUBINOVICH, J.B., has gone to New York (10 Feb. 1911, 14, 13)

RUBINOVICH, Misses Sylvia and Frieda, Sherbrooke St., were guests of the Misses Rudolph at Vaudreuil for a few weeks (30 Aug. 1912, 15, 38)

RUBINOVICH, Mr. and Mrs. A.I., celebrated their twentieth wedding anniversary Sun. evening at 4462 Sherbrooke St., Westmount with their relatives and friends. The table was in charge of the Misses Hattie and Libbie Cohen and the Misses Sylvia and Frieda Rubinovich (21 Jan. 1910, 13, 10)

RUBINOVICH, Mr. and Mrs. J.B., 448 Argyle Ave., Westmount, wish their friends and relatives a happy New Year (1 Oct. 1913, 16, 42-43)

RUBINOVICH, Mr., has returned from a business trip to New York (27 Jan. 1911, 14, 11)

RUBINOVICH, Mrs. I.M. (née Mildred Isaacs, of St. John, N.B.) received this week for the first time since her marriage at her home, 4480 Sherbrooke St. W., Westmount. She was assisted by her mother, Mrs. A. Isaacs and her sister, Mrs. S.D. Lewis, of St. John. In the tea room was Mrs. Gustave Fischel, assisted by the Misses Rosalind Lewis, Beccie Kellert, Annie Samuels and Hattie Cohen (10 Feb. 1911, 14, 13)

RUBINOVICH, Mrs. I.M., 4480 Sherbrooke St., Westmount, will receive on Feb. 5, 1911 from 4 to 6 p.m. for the first time since her marriage (3 Feb. 1911, 14, 12)

RUBINOVICH, Mrs. J.B., 448 Argyle Ave., Westmount, was "At Home" Sun. aft. She was assisted by Mesdames J. Cohen, A.I. Rubinovich, H. Freedman, and H.H. Livingstone and the Misses Hyallie Freeman, Hattie Cohen, Libbie Cohen, Leba Livingstone and Sylvia Rubinovich (20 May 1910, 13, 27)

RUBINOVITCH, J.B., was registered at the Chateau Frontenac, Quebec City, last Sat. (22 Jan. 1909, 12, 6)

RUBINOVITCH, Mr. and Mrs. I., Sherbrooke St. W., have returned from a trip to the Lower Provinces (19 May 1911, 14, 27)

RUBINOVITCH, Mr. and Mrs. J., have endowed a bed in the Hebrew Sheltering and Orphans' Home in memory of their beloved daughter, Leona. They donated $100 for the bed and will contribute $10 year for its upkeep (25 July 1913, 16, 33)

RUBINOVITCH, Mrs. A.I. and the Misses Sylvia and Frieda Rubinovitch, Sherbrooke St. W., left for Arverne, Long Island (4 July 1913, 16, 30)

RUBINOVITCH, Mrs. A.I., Sherbrooke St., Westmount, served luncheon last Sun. in honor of her nephew, Hillel Eisenstadt and her niece, Miss Helena Eisenstadt, both from Georgenburg, Russia. Guests included her cousin, Dr. Ch. Zhitlovsky, Miss Sadie Rudolph and S.M. Eisenstadt (24 Jan. 1913, 16, 7)

RUBINOVITCH, Mrs. F., of New York, is the guest of Mr. and Mrs. M. Slabosky, 1959 Mance St. (9 Jan. 1914, 17, 5)

RUBINOVITCH, Mrs. Israel and daughter and maid are summering at Gananoque, Ont. (2 Aug. 1912, 15, 34)

RUBINSKY, Miss Belle and Miss Sophie Mendel have returned from a holiday at Longueuil (11 Aug. 1911, 14, 39)

RUBINSKY, Miss Belle, has left on an extended trip to Chicago, Cleveland and Minneapolis (2 April 1909, 12, 16)

RUBINSKY, Miss Belle, is at home with a fractured ankle (27 Dec. 1912, 16, 3)

RUBINSKY, Miss Ethel, of Chicago, is visiting her sister, Mrs. H. Wener, St. Famille St. (10 March 1911, 14, 17)

RUBINSKY, Miss Ethel, of Chicago, is the guest of her cousin, Mrs. H. Wener, St. Famille St. (20 Sept. 1912, 15, 41)

RUBINSKY, Miss Ethel, of Chicago, was the guest of honor at a bridge and formal dance given by Mr. and Mrs. Harry Wener, on Wed. Feb. 8, 1911. Prize winners were:- J. Cossman, Louis Cohen and the Misses Jeanette Blout and Hattie Kellert (10 Feb. 1911, 14, 13)

RUBINSKY, Miss Ethel, who visited Mrs. S. Roggen in New York for a few weeks, is now the guest of her sister, Mrs. Harry Wener, in Montreal (3 Feb. 1911, 14, 12)

RUBINSKY, Miss M., of Chicago, is the guest of her aunt, Mrs. H. Wener, St. Famille St. (22 Nov. 1912, 15, 50)

RUBNER, J.A., of Toronto, is registered at the Queen's Hotel (27 Aug. 1909, 12, 37)

RUDOLPH, A. and daughter are spending the summer at Ste. Agathe (13 Aug. 1909, 12, 35)

RUDOLPH, A., sails tomorrow morn. on the S.S. Megantic for a two months' stay in Europe. He will be in London for the Coronation (9 June 1911, 14, 30)

RUDOLPH, M., Drolet St., has gone to Chicago for a few weeks to attend his cousin's wedding, Miss Jessie Rudolph (30 Aug. 1912, 15, 38)

RUDOLPH, M., Drolet St., is in Richmond, Que., for two months (1 Aug. 1913, 16, 34)

RUDOLPH, Miss Sadie, has returned to Vaudreuil after spending a few weeks visiting friends in Ogdensberg and Watertown, N.Y. (12 Aug. 1910, 13, 39)

RUDOLPH, Misses Sadie and Bessie, have returned from a holiday in Ste. Agathe (20 Aug. 1909, 12, 36)

RUDOLPH, Mr. and Mrs. A. and family have taken a cottage at Vaudreuil for the summer (8 July 1910, 13, 34)

RUDOLPH, Mr. and Mrs. A. and Miss Bessie Rudolph, Laval Ave., returned home after spending the summer abroad (12 Sept. 1913, 16, 40)

RUDOLPH, Mr. and Mrs. A., Laval Ave., have gone to Caledonia Springs for two weeks (23 July 1909, 12, 32)

RUDOLPH, Mrs. A. and daughter, Laval Ave., are visiting friends in New York (24 Nov. 1911, 15, 2)

RUDOLPH, Mrs. A. and the Misses Sadie and Bessie Rudolph went to Quebec City to meet Mr. Rudolph who is a passenger on the "Empress of Britain" (11 Aug. 1911, 14, 39)

RUTENBERG, Mr. and Mrs. D., 991 St. Urbain St., celebrated their silver wedding anniversary on Sun. Dec. 14, 1914. Among those present were their children, grand-children, relatives and friends (2 Jan. 1914, 17, 4)

RUTENBERG, Mr. and Mrs. D. and family, 40 St. Louis St., have returned to town after spending the summer at Chambly Canton (3 Sept. 1909, 12, 38)

RUTENBERG, Mr. and Mrs., have returned to Toronto. They spent a few weeks with their daughter, Mrs. J. Leonstroff and Ian M. Rutenberg, Mance St., Annex (15 March 1912, 15, 18)

RYAN, Mr. and Mrs. F., of Ottawa, have taken up their residence in Montreal with Mr. and Mrs. M. Ryan, 5 Laval Ave. (15 April 1910, 13, 22)

RYAN, Mr. and Mrs. M. and daughter and Mr. and Mrs. S. Ryan are spending the summer in the Laurentians at their Mountain View Cottage (1 July 1910, 13, 33)

RYAN, Mr. and Mrs. M. and family are at their summer cottage, Ivry, Lake Manitou (5 May 1911, 14, 25)

RYAN, Mr. and Mrs. Morris and daughter Ivry, have returned to Montreal and are residing at 231 Mance St. (8 Nov. 1912, 15, 48)

RYAN, Mr. and Mrs. S., are in Ottawa spending the Passover holidays with Mrs. Ryan's parents (5 April 1912, 15, 21)

RYAN, Mr. and Mrs. S., Wood Ave., Westmount, gave a skating party, Wed. evening, Feb. 21, 1912. Guests included Miss Sophie and Minnie Feldman (23 Feb. 1912, 15, 15)

SABBATH, J.L., is on a business trip in Ottawa (12 Aug. 1910, 13, 39)

SABBATH, J.L., leaves shortly on business for Quebec City (3 March 1911, 14, 16)

SABBATH, Mr. and Mrs. J.L., have returned

SPECIAL for LADIES

The Fall Season is now at hand and we have imported the latest patterns and designs from New York and Paris. We have a magnificent stock of materials for Costumes and Skirts. A trial order will convince you of our ability to produce perfect fitting garments. Prompt attention and reasonable prices are our specialities.

A. SABBATH,
High-Class Ladies' Tailoring,
912 ST. LAWRENCE BLVD.

---

from their honeymoon (27 Jan. 1911, 14, 11)

SABLOFF, H., was given a surprise party on his return trip from New York at his home, Craig St. W., by his sisters, Mrs. A. Goodman and Miss E. Sabloff, on Sun. March 2, 1913 (7 March 1913, 16, 13)

SACKS, Paul, sailed on the S.S. King Edward on Sept. 5, 1913 and will be abroad for two months (12 Sept. 1913, 16, 40)

SACKSNER, G., L. Tannenbaum and S. Eliasoph took part in the symposium "What should the Jew do to assure the maintenance of his faith among his posterity into the lands into which he immigrates?" at a Maccabean Circle meeting, held Sun. Nov. 26, 1911. I. Hirshberg read a paper "The Jew in the Medical World" (8 Dec. 1911, 15, 4)

SALINSKI, Mr. and Mrs. A., of Geneva, N.Y., were guests of Mrs. Greenberg, St. Joseph Blvd. (23 Feb. 1912, 15, 15)

SALINSKY, Frank, of Boston, was in Montreal for a few days (7 March 1913, 16, 13)

SALOMON, Louis, of Malone, N.Y., is in Montreal for a few days (6 Jan. 1911, 14, 8)

SALOMON, Louis, of Malone, N.Y., was in Montreal on a short visit (2 Jan. 1914, 17, 4)

SALOMON, M., has returned from a business trip out West (24 June 1910, 13, 32)

SALOMON, M., is leaving shortly for a long trip out west (6 Aug. 1909, 12, 34)

SALOMON, M., is on a business trip in the Maritimes (22 April 1910, 13, 23)

SALOMON, M., left Sat. evening for New York to attend the funeral of his grandfather, S. Krischok, who died Sat. Jan. 6, 1910 (14 Jan. 1910, 13, 9)

SAMENHOF, Jack, is spending a few weeks at Caledonia Springs (13 June 1913, 16, 27)

SAMIT, Miss Bella, gave a surprise party in honor of Miss Fanny Diamond at Miss Diamond's residence, 582 St. Denis St., on Sat. evening, Dec. 6, 1913. Refreshments were served by Mrs. B. Diamond and Miss Hilda Diamond (12 Dec. 1913, 17, 1)

SAMIT, Mr. and Mrs. Charles and family, Pine Ave. W., returned from Old Orchard, Me., where they summered (29 Aug. 1913, 16, 38)

SAMMETT, Mrs. H., 76 Benoit St., wishes her friends and relatives a happy New Year (1 Oct. 1913, 16, 42-43)

SAMMIT, Mr. and Mrs. C. and three children sailed on the S.S. Laurentic on June 23, 1911 (30 June 1911, 14, 33)

SAMMIT, Mr. and Mrs. Charles and family have gone on a trip to Boston (17 Feb. 1911, 14, 14)

SAMMIT, Mr. and Mrs. Charles and family sailed on the S.S. Royal George. They toured England and the Continent and will visit Mr. Sammit's sister in Carlsbad, Germany (28 July 1911, 14, 37)

SAMMIT, Mrs. Charles and family, 298 Pine Ave. W., have returned from Boston (10 March 1911, 14, 17)

SAMUEL, J.L., leaves shortly for Philadelphia where he will spend the winter (14 Jan. 1910, 13, 9)

SAMUEL, Miss Georgie V., sailed aboard the S.S. Lake Manitoba bound for England where she will spend the summer (2 July 1909, 12, 29)

SAMUEL, Miss, of Charleston, is the guest of Mrs. Meldola de Sola, Sherbrooke St. (19 Nov. 1909, 13, 1)

SAMUEL, Mr. and Mrs. R.R., Summerhill Ave., leave shortly for their summer home at Val Morin (14 May 1909, 12, 22)

SAMUEL, Mrs. and daughter were in Ste. Agathe visiting Mr. and Mrs. N. Rosen and family (16 July 1909, 12, 31)

SAMUEL, Stuart, M.P. for Tower Hamlets, London, Eng., who is touring Canada and the United States, is registered at the Windsor Hotel (27 Jan. 1911, 14, 11)

SAMUELS, Charles and Emile Mendelsohn left for New York and will sail on the Baltic for Europe on March 12, 1914 (13 March 1914, 17, 11)

SAMUELS, Jack, has returned from a three months' visit to Baltimore and Philadelphia (26 Aug. 1910, 13, 41)

SAMUELS, Jack, is the guest of Mr. and Mrs. Rose at Beloeil, Que. (16 Aug. 1912, 15, 36)

SAMUELS, Jacob, is visiting friends in Baltimore for a couple of months (29 Jan. 1909, 12, 7)

SAMUELS, Miss Annie left for New York last Sat. night where she will stay for a few weeks (21 Jan. 1910, 13, 10)

SAMUELS, Miss B., is the guest of Miss M. Myers in Ottawa (3 Jan. 1913, 16, 4)

SAMUELS, Miss B., Shuter St., who attended her uncle's wedding in New York, has returned home accompanied by her sister, Miss Samuels, of New York (23 Sept. 1910, 13, 45)

SAMUELS, Miss D. and Miss R. Guttman are holidaying at Weir, Que. (15 Aug. 1913, 16, 36)

SAMUELS, Miss, Drummond St., has returned from New York (11 March 1910, 13, 17)

SAMUELS, Miss, Durocher St., has returned from New York where she spent a few weeks with relatives (22 Jan. 1909, 12, 6)

SAMUELS, Miss Gertie, is in New York, the guest of Miss Mendes (23 Dec. 1910, 14, 6)

SAMUELS, Miss I., has returned from Ste. Agathe where she was visiting her sister (12 Aug. 1910, 13, 39)

SAMUELS, Miss Lil, is spending a few weeks at Shawbridge, Que. (9 July 1909, 12, 30)

SAMUELS, Miss Lily and Mrs. Abe Friedman and daughter are in Atlantic City for a few weeks (18 July 1913, 16, 32)

SAMUELS, Miss Lily, is in Gananoque, Ont. for the summer (14 July 1911, 14, 35)

SAMUELS, Miss Lily, is the guest of Miss Goldstein, Clairemont Villa, Point Claire (22 July 1910, 13, 36)

SAMUELS, Miss R., of New York, is visiting her sisters, the Misses Samuels, Shuter St. (8 Nov. 1912, 15, 48)

SAMUELS, Miss Ray, has returned from a visit to New York (31 Dec. 1909, 13, 7)

SAMUELS, Miss Ray, has returned to New York (14 Jan. 1910, 13, 9)

SAMUELS, Miss Rose, St. Urbain St., leaves for Winnipeg on Sun. March 9, 1913 (7 March 1913, 16, 13)

SAMUELS, Miss Sara, has returned to New York after visiting her sisters, the Misses Samuel, Shuter St. (21 Jan. 1910, 13, 10)

SAMUELS, Miss Sara, Shuter St., is the guest of her aunt, Mrs. Samuels, in Boston, for a few weeks (18 Nov. 1910, 14, 1)

SAMUELS, Misses Annie and Lily, are in New York for a few weeks (19 April 1912, 15, 23)

SAMUELS, Mr. and Mrs. Jack, of New York, were guests at the Windsor Hotel (30 Sept. 1910, 13, 46)

SAMUELSOHN, B., of Rochester, N.Y., is the guest of Mr. and Mrs. J. Kruger (16 Aug. 1912, 15, 36)

SAMUELSOHN, Mrs. J., of Rochester, N.Y., is visiting her daughter Mrs. Joseph Kruger, Mance St. (10 April 1914, 17, 15)

SAMUELSON, Mr. and Mrs. J., of Rochester, N.Y., are guests of their daughter, Mrs. Joseph Kreiger, Mance St., Annex (19 April 1912, 15, 23)

SAMUELSON, Mr. and Mrs., of Rochester, N.Y., were guests of their daughter, Mrs. Joseph Kruger, Mance St., this week (2 Sept. 1910, 13,

SAMUELSON, Mrs. J., returned home to Rochester, N.Y., after visiting her daughter, Mrs. Joseph Kruger, Mance St., Annex (27 Dec. 1912, 16, 3)

SAMUELSON, Mrs., of Rochester, N.Y., is visiting her daughter, Mrs. Joseph Konyer, Mance St., for a few weeks (8 Oct. 1909, 12, 43)

SANDELSON, Mrs. and little daughter, returned home to New York after visiting her sister, Mrs. S. Haskell (28 March 1913, 16, 16)

SANDEMAN, A., Crescent St., has returned from a short trip to Winnipeg (21 Jan. 1910, 13, 10)

SANDEMAN, A.A., Crescent St., has returned from a trip to New York (9 April 1909, 12, 17)

SANDEMAN, Mr. and Mrs. A., are spending a few days in Atantic City and New York (26 Nov. 1909, 13, 2)

SANDEMAN, Mr. and Mrs. A., Crescent St., left for Quebec City to attend the Wolff-Joseph wedding (26 March 1909, 12, 15)

SANDEMAN, Mr. and Mrs. A.A., Crescent St., returned home from England this week aboard the S.S. Victorian (25 July 1911, 14, 36)

SANDEMAN, Mr. and Mrs. A.A., Crescent St., are in New York attending the marriage of Mrs. Sandeman's niece, Miss Raphael (16 Feb. 1912, 15, 14)

SANDEMAN, Mrs. A.A., Crescent St., entertained Thurs. aft., for Mrs. Montefiore Joseph, of Quebec City. The Misses Marguerite and Sybil Joseph were in charge of the tea room. Guests included Mesdames Mortimer Davis, Clarence de Sola and Meldola de Sola (12 Nov. 1909, 12, 48)

SANDEMAN, Mrs. A.A., Crescent St., gave a shower and tea on Wed. aft. (7 May 1909, 12, 21)

SANDEMAN, Mrs. A.A., Crescent St., gave a luncheon on Tues., in honor of Miss Phyllis Joseph, of London, England (22 Oct. 1909, 12, 45)

SANDEMAN, Mrs. A.A., Crescent St., has left for New York from where she sails for Europe to visit relatives for a few weeks (28 May 1909, 12, 24)

SANDEMAN, Mrs. A.A., gave a girls' tea this week in honor of her guest, Miss Clare Raphael, of New York (6 May 1910, 13, 25)

SANDEMAN, Mrs. A.A., has returned from New York (1 April 1910, 13, 20)

SANDEMAN, Mrs. A.A., has returned home from Quebec City (2 April 1909, 12, 16)

SANDEMAN, Mrs. A.A., is a passenger on the incoming C.P.R. liner, Empress of Britain (9 July 1909, 12, 30)

SANDEMAN, Mrs. A.A., was slowly regaining consciousness last night and the doctors say her condition is much more favorable than the day before (8 Nov. 1912, 15, 48)

SANDEMAN, Mrs. A.A., who was abroad for the past two months, returned on the S.S. Victorian (23 July 1909, 12, 32)

SANDERS, G., has gone to Toronto on business (31 March 1911, 14, 20)

SANDERS, Max, manager of The Canadian Jewish Times, was in a railroad accident. He "...was unfortunate enough to be travelling to Ottawa in the train which ran over a portion of track weakened by the washing away of ballast by the recent bad weather. The engine plunged off the metals when rounding a corner, pulling with it the tender, baggage car, two passenger coaches and the Pullman parlor car. Mr. Sanders, who received some bruises and was badly shaken up, after resting for a night and a day at the Chateau Laurier, Ottawa, where he received medical attendance, returned to Montreal, and is now recuperating in his home, under the care of Dr. David Hart, the eminent physician." (4 April 1913, 16, 17)

SANDERS, Mr. and Mrs. M., 205 Esplanade Ave., send New Year greetings (11 Sept. 1912, 15, 40)

SANDERS, Mr. and Mrs. M., 6 Plaza Apts. wish their friends and relatives a happy New Year (1 Oct. 1913, 16, 42-43)

SANDERS, Mrs. M. and children are spending the summer with Mrs. I. Ressler and family, at their summer cottage in the Laurentians (25 July 1913, 16, 33)

SANDLER, Miss Libbie, of Benton Harbor, Mich., who visited her aunts here, Mesdames M. Carsley and Sandy, left for Kingston, en route to her home (19 Sept. 1913, 16, 41)

SANELSON, L., of Rochester, N.Y., is a guest at Freeman's Hotel (29 Sept. 1911, 14, 46)

SANFT, Mr. and Mrs. A.A., spent a few days at Knowlton, Que. (22 July 1910, 13, 36)

SANFT, Mrs. A.A., has returned from a short visit to New York (10 Sept. 1909, 12, 39)

SAPERY, Abraham, returned home to New York after visiting his relatives in the city (22 Oct. 1913, 16, 46)

SAPERY, H., of New York, stayed at the Windsor Hotel while in Montreal (7 March 1913, 16, 13)

SAPERY, L., has returned from a trip abroad (9 April 1909, 12, 17)

SAPERY, Mrs. Louis and sons, of New York, who spent the summer with her sister, Mrs. C. Weinfield, have returned home (23 Sept. 1910, 13, 45)

SAPERY, Mrs. Louis, of New York, is visiting her sister, Mrs. H. Weinfield, Durocher St. (5 Nov. 1909, 12, 47)

SAPERY, Mrs., of New York, and her son, have returned home after spending a few weeks with her sister, Mrs. Weinfield (18 Feb. 1910, 13, 14)

SAUNDERS, Mr. and Mrs. M.H., of Winnipeg, are staying at the Windsor Hotel (24 Jan. 1913, 16, 7)

SAUNDERS, R., left for England to visit his parents (25 June 1909, 12, 28)

SAXE, E., stayed at the Turkish Bath Hotel (5 Jan. 1912, 15, 8)

SAXE, Henry, has returned from a short visit to New York (18 March 1910, 13, 18)

SAXE, Henry, left on a short trip to New York (27 June 1913, 16, 29)

SAXE, J.B., has returned from a holiday in Virginia and New York (11 Oct. 1910, 13, 48)

SAXE, J.B., read a paper on "Territorialism" at the last meeting of the Shaar Hashomayim Young People's Society (2 April 1909, 12, 16)

SAXE, Joel B., resident secretary of the Canadian section of the Society of Chemical Industry, Montreal Branch, sent a resolution of condolence to Mrs. Eda K. Loeb, wife of Dr. Morris Loeb, of New York, who died Oct. 8, 1912 (27 Dec. 1912, 16, 3)

SAXE, Joel B., secretary of the Montreal Chemical Society, spoke on the topic "Israel Zangwill, Itoland and the Jewish Territorial Movement" at the YMHA Friday Night Talk, April 18, 1913 (9 May 1913, 16, 22)

SAXE, Miss, and Mrs. F. Kahn left for New York and Hartford where they will spend a few weeks (5 March 1909, 12, 12)

SAXE, Mr. and Mrs. H., are spending a few days at Caledonia Springs, Ont. (12 Aug. 1910, 13, 39)

SAXE, Mr. and Mrs. Harry, have returned from New York (23 Feb. 1912, 15, 15)

SAXE, Mrs. Henry, 4280 Western Ave., will be "at home" Thurs. aft. March 2, 1911 (24 Feb. 1911, 14, 15)

SAXE, Mrs. Henry, has returned from Old Orchard (28 July 1911, 14, 37)

SCHACHTER, D., R. Silverman, F. Filatreault, Julius Wener, E. Kert, H. Gold, N. Jacobs, M. Frank, J.D. Asner, H. Gittleson, J. Merson, L. Wineman, W. Wisse, T. Garfinkle, J. Jacobs, A. Shalinsky and S. Shalinsky were winners in field sports at the YMHA annual picnic at Otterburn Park (19 July 1912, 15, 32)

SCHACHTER, S., art photographer, is taking sittings at his photo-studio, 435 St. Lawrence Blvd. (18 April 1913, 16, 19)

SCHACHTER, S., is vacationing at St. Agathe, Que. (26 July 1912, 15, 33)

SCHACHTER, S., photographer, is going to New York on business for several days (27 Dec. 1912, 16, 3)

SCHAEFFER, Mr. and Mrs. A., of Valleyfield, Que., were guests of their mother, Mrs. G. Morris, Laval Ave., over the holidays (22 Oct. 1913, 16, 46)

SCHAFFER, B., M. Rittenberg and J. Vineberg are visitors at Ste. Agathe (23 July 1909, 12, 32)

SCHAFFER, E.A., of New York, is a guest at the Place Viger Hotel (27 Aug. 1909, 12, 37)

SCHALEK, L. and A., spent a few days at St. Faustin, Que. (25 July 1913, 16, 33)

SCHALEK, M., 427 St. Denis St., is in the General Hospital with a broken leg (12 Feb. 1909, 12, 9)

SCHALEK, M., St. Denis St., has left for New York (2 July 1909, 12, 29)

From The Canadian Jewish Times

Are You Going Abroad?

We are agents for all the Best Ocean Lines ⚓ ⚓ Ring Main 1448 and one of our staff will call with all information. ⚓ ⚓

SCHAFER & WALL
14 Craig Street W., MONTREAL

SCHALEK, Miss Rae and Mrs. Schalek, Park Ave., will spend a few weeks in New York (20 Dec. 1912, 16, 2)

SCHALEK, Mr. and Mrs. D. Levi each donated one ton of coal to the Hebrew Sheltering and Orphans' Home (9 Jan. 1914, 17, 5)

SCHALEK, Mrs. M. and Miss Ray Schalek, Park Ave., are staying at the Square Lake House, St. Faustin, Que. (25 July 1913, 16, 33)

SCHEFFER, Mr. and Mrs. Isador, of Vallyfield, spent the Holy Days visiting Mrs. Y. Morris, Laval Ave. (2 Oct. 1912, 15, 43)

SCHER, Misses Sarah and Eva, 20 Mayor St., gave a linen shower at their residence in honor of Miss Rose Shayne who will soon be married. Those present included:- the Misses Dorothy Arent, Sarah Caplan, Lily Davis, Nancy Freedman, Charlotte Scher, Tilly Shayne, A. Silverberg, Lillian and Kate Steinberg, and Molly Vise (6 March 1914, 17, 10)

SCHEUER, Miss, of Toronto, is the guest of Mrs. Ed. Youngheart, Durocher St. (24 Feb. 1911, 14, 15)

SCHILLER, J., of New York, was in Montreal the past week (4 Aug. 1911, 14, 38)

SCHILLER, Mrs. Charles, of Loretteville, Que., returned home after spending the weekend with her parents, Mr. and Mrs. W. Serchuk (6 March 1914, 17, 10)

SCHIVERIN, Mr. and Mrs., of New York, are visiting their parents, Mr. and Mrs. David Levi, Mt. Stephen Ave., Westmount (15 April 1910, 13, 22)

SCHLEIFER, H., the well-known real estate and financial agent, of 561 St. Lawrence Blvd., was written up in the **Canadian Real Estate News**. "It rightly asks why people still go to Porcupine to seek their fortune, and starve and freeze, when there is so much money made right in the heart of our city." Mr. Schleifer does a brisk business in the St. Lawrence and St. Louis wards. He transacted the sale of the St. Lawrence and Ontario St. corner for Carl Rosenberg to the Rabbinowitz brothers (18 April 1913, 16, 19)

SCHLEIFER, Hyman, held a fund-raising meeting at his office 516 St. Lawrence Blvd., for the purpose of purchasing property at Shawbridge for the Fresh Air Society of Montreal. Subscribers were:- J.A. Besner 238 Elm Ave.; M. Flanders, 516 St. Lawrence Blvd.; A. Goldsmidt, 41 Arcade St.; A. Gorn, 1221 St. Urbain St.; Max Rabinovitch, 163 Esplanade Ave.; Sam Rabinovitch, 516 St. Lawrence Blvd.; S. Rosenveesen, 1008 St. Urbain St.; S. Schraiber, 1119 Clarke St.; I. Weinfield, 170 Laval Ave.; H. Wolofsky, manager of **The Eagle**; and Moses Zelicovitch, 1234 St. Urbain St. (29 Nov. 1912, 15, 51)

SCHLEIFER, Miss A.L., is secretary of the Young Ladies' Hebrew Orphans' Protective Association (27 May 1910, 13, 28)

SCHLEIFER, Miss B., was elected president of the Minerva Girls on March 17, 1912. Other officers elected were:- Miss J. Rigler, vice-pres.; Miss F. Shleifer, sec.; Miss F. Rosentsveig, treas.; and Miss S. Hershorn, trustee (29 March 1912, 15, 20)

SCHLEIFER, Miss F., 41 Drolet St., is secretary of the Minerva Girls club (8 March 1912, 15, 17)

SCHLEIFER, Mr. and Mrs. H. and family returned from New York where they spent Passover with their parents (12 April 1912, 15, 22)

SCHLEIFER, Mr. and Mrs. H., are in New York for the wedding of Mrs. Schleifer's sister, Miss Hilda Epstein (21 March 1913, 16, 15)

SCHLEIFER, Mr. and Mrs. H., returned home from six weeks' vacation at Ste. Agathe (15 Aug. 1913, 16, 36)

SCHLEIFER, Mrs. Charles and Master Jack Schleifer, of Cobalt, Ont., are guests of Mr. and Mrs. I.A. Kaufman (22 Aug. 1913, 16, 37)

SCHLIEFER, H., returned home from a business trip to New York (12 Dec. 1913, 17, 1)

SCHLOMAN, D., has returned from a trip to New York (28 May 1909, 12, 24)

SCHLOMAN, H., has gone to New York on business (3 March 1911, 14, 16)

SCHLOMAN, M.L., went to New York on business this week (15 Dec. 1911, 15, 5)

SCHNAIER, B., will speak in Yiddish at the first public lecture of the Baron de Hirsch Educational Committee, tomorrow Sat. at 8 p.m. (11 Feb. 1910, 13, 13)

SCHNAIER, Charles H., Louis Shuker, H. Novak, J. Prusansky, J. Cohen, T. Geller, L. Melzer and B. Lachovitzky are convention committee members organizing the Poali Zionist annual convention to be held in Montreal (19 Aug. 1910, 13, 40)

SCHNITZER, Mr., of New York, is visiting his sister, Mrs. M. Vineberg, Bishop St. (15 Jan. 1909, 12, 5)

SCHOENHAUSS, Otto, was a guest at the St. Lawrence Hall (26 Feb. 1909, 12, 11)

SCHRADSKY, Mrs. and daughter, have returned home to New York after visiting Mrs. Marcus Roman (3 Dec. 1909, 13, 3)

SCHULHOFF, Miss, of New York, is the guest of her aunt, Mrs. A. Sommers, Westmount Ave. (2 Oct. 1912, 15, 43)

SCHUMANN, Mrs. J., of New York, has returned home after visiting her sister, Mrs. Ralph Raphael (19 Nov. 1909, 13, 1)

SCHWAB, Ludwig, is visiting his aunt, Mrs. S. Oberndorffer, in Kingston (26 Dec. 1913, 17, 3)

SCHWAB, Ludwig, of New York, is visiting his brother, W. Schwab, Dorchester St. W. (1 Aug. 1913, 16, 34)

SCHWAB, Max and Ludwig, have left for Detroit. Ludwig Schwab expects to take up his residence in Cuba (13 March 1914, 17, 11)

SCHWAB, Max, of Chicago, Ill., is a guest at the Windsor Hotel (29 Dec. 1911, 15, 7)

SCHWAB, Max, of Chicago, Ill., was registered at the Queen's Hotel during the past week (29 Sept. 1911, 14, 46)

SCHWAB, Max, of Chicago, stayed at the Windsor Hotel (23 Feb. 1912, 15, 15)

SCHWAB, Max, of Kingston, Ont., is spending time in Montreal (7 May 1909, 12, 21)

SCHWAB, Max, who has been residing in Montreal for the past year has left for Farnham, Que. (14 Jan. 1910, 13, 9)

SCHWAB, Max, who visited his parents in Germany, stayed at the Windsor Hotel while in Montreal (20 Sept. 1912, 15, 41)

SCHWAB, Max, who was in Farnham, Que. the past few months, has returned to Montreal (1 April 1910, 13, 20)

SCHWARTZ, A., returned home to Boston (1 Oct. 1913, 16, 42-43)

SCHWARTZ, F.W., of New York, is staying at the Corona Hotel (4 June, 1909, 12, 25)

SCHWARTZ, J., of New York, is registered at

the Grand Union Hotel (22 Oct. 1909, 12, 45)

SCHWARTZ, J., of Savannah, is in Montreal on a visit (3 Sept. 1909, 12, 38)

SCHWARTZ, Louis, of Philadelphia, wishes his cousin, Mason Silverman, wife and family, and also Joe Balcon, wife and family a happy New Year (1 Oct. 1913, 16, 42-43)

SCHWARTZ, Louis, of Philadelphia, wishes his cousin, H. Lonn, his wife and family, and also uncle, W. Balcon and auntie, Anna Balcon, a happy New Year (1 Oct. 1913, 16, 42-43)

SCHWARTZ, M., stayed at the Broadway Central while in New York (29 Nov. 1912, 15, 51)

SCHWARTZ, M.B., 1910 Mance St., wishes his friends a happy New (10 Oct. 1913, 16, 44)

SCHWARTZ, Miss Clara, is in New York until the end of next week (28 Feb. 1913, 16, 12)

SCHWARTZ, Miss Clara, left for Old Orchard, Boston, Portland and New York (29 Aug. 1913, 16, 38)

SCHWARTZ, Mrs., dressmaker, has returned to Montreal after five years sojurn in New York, and is re-opening her business at 2475 Hutchison St. "All the latest New York afternoon and evening gowns a specialty." (1 Oct. 1913, 16, 42-43)

SCHWARTZ, Mrs. S. and daughter, Miss Ettie Schwartz have moved back to Montreal after living five years in New York (1 Oct. 1913, 16, 42-43)

SCHWARTZ, Samuel, of Montreal, returned from a trip to Toronto and Ottawa (14 Nov. 1913, 16, 49)

SCHWARZBARD, Mrs. J., has returned from La Tuque where she spent a fortnight with her parents, Mr. and Mrs. D. Ortenberg (8 July 1910, 13, 34)

SCHWEIZBERG, Samuel, a St. Urbain St. Talmud Torah pupil, welcomed the Rt. Hon. Herbert Samuel to the Baron de Hirsch Institute on Thurs. Oct. 9, 1913. "He said that he and his fellow-students were to be congratulated at being given the opportunity of seeing among them one of their race who had become so famous. He was glad to see that the traditions of the race had not proved a bar against Jews in holding high office to which His Majesty the King had appointed him. The students of the Hebrew schools were, as Canadian Jewish children, most loyal subjects of His Majesty. At the conclusion of his address, Master Schweizberg cried 'Long Live the King; Long Live the Empire!' and this was taken up by the audience and loudly applauded." (15 Oct. 1913, 16, 45)

SCHWERSENSKI, Mr., leaves for Vancouver to attend the wedding of his daughter, Lizzie to Isaac Simon which takes place Jan. 6, 1914 (26 Dec. 1913, 17, 3)

SCHWERSENSKI, Mrs. A.D., has gone to Boston to attend the unveiling of her late father's headstone, M. Nathan Jacobs (14 June 1912, 15, 27)

SCHWISBERG, Samuel, Barney Usher, Horace Phillips, Sam Shulman, Carl Rabinovitch, Joseph Dubinitsky, Nathan Segal, Hyman Lipsey, H. Claman, Sophie Gittleson, Jacob Cohen, Abram Shulemson, Felix Bernstein, Max Cohen, Laura Kalmanovitch, Hilda Talpis, Sarah Torontow, Lucy Goodstone, Sarah Somer, Annie Rivenovitch and Esther Brandes were awarded Protestant school commissioners' scholarships at the final examinations in Jan. and June, 1911 (7 July 1911, 14, 34)

SEBAG-MONTEFIORE, Mrs. Arthur and Miss Sebag-Montefiore, of London, England, are staying at the Ritz-Carlton Hotel in Montreal (19 Sept. 1913, 16, 41)

SEGAL, Bernard R., the only Jewish graduate optometrist in Montreal, opened his office and factory at 508 St. Lawrence Blvd. not quite two years ago. He has now opened a branch at 27 St. Catherine St. W. due to his growing business (18 April 1913, 16, 19)

ARE YOU IN DOUBT?

 If you need a Pair of Glasses call to see me  I will give you an Honest Advice

BERNARD R. SEGAL
Graduate Optometrist & Manufacturing Optician
508 St. Lawrence Blvd. - MONTREAL

SEGAL, J., 54 Roy St., and L. Tannenbaum, B.A., 111 Metcalfe St., are selling tickets for the annual Maccabean Circle dance to be held Jan. 30, 1912 (10 Nov. 1911, 14, 52)

SEIDEN, Henry, was in New York on business this week (17 Nov. 1911, 15, 1)

SEIDMAN, M., was initiated into the Franz Joseph Lodge, IOSB last Sun. (7 May 1909, 12, 21)

SEIFERT, Mr. and Mrs. C.E., have left Montreal to move to New York (16 July 1909, 12, 31)

SEIFERT, W., of Quebec City, is visiting Lake St. Joseph (13 Aug. 1909, 12, 35)

SEIGLER, Miss Ida, has returned from Macdonald College, St. Anne de Bellevue, where she studied French (26 July 1912, 15, 33)

SEIGLER, Miss Ida, read a paper "The Value of French Conversation in This Province" at the Bannantyne Avenue School (12 May 1911, 14, 26)

SEIGLER, Miss Ida, St. Famille St., returned from a short trip to Toronto (12 Jan. 1912, 15, 9)

SEIGLER, Miss Ida, was elected chairman of the Zion Circle at its first members' meeting on Sept. 4, 1913. Other officers elected were:- Miss Jane B. Rost, sec. treas.; Messrs. Groner, Jaffe, Linder, Marcus, Rozine, Misses R. Goldner, M. Hecht, L. Wetstein and Mrs. S. Kahn, exec. council (12 Sept. 1913, 16, 40)

SEIGLER, Miss Ida, will give a report on the Zionist convention in Toronto to the Montreal Daughters of Zion (13 Jan. 1911, 14, 9)

SEIGLER, Mrs. M. and Miss Bessie Seigler are spending a few weeks at Abenakis Springs (26 July 1912, 15, 33)

SELENGER, Mr. and Mrs., have returned from abroad where they spent the past few months (26 Feb. 1909, 12, 11)

SELIG, Mrs. Rosie, a widow, whose husband died six months ago in Winnipeg, is looking for someone to care for her three boys, ages six, eight and ten. "Mrs. Selig, who now has a room at 1348 St. Urbain Street, is not well enough nor able enough to take care of the boys. She would gladly give them to some respectable family, for she fears that her inablity to give them proper care will eventually lead them astray, and, at least, the older one will land in a reformatory." (16 Feb. 1912, 15, 14)

SELLINGER, Mr. and Mrs. I., has returned from St. Agathe (27 Aug. 1909, 12, 37)

SEMPLINER, Mr. and Mrs. J., Bay City, were in Montreal for a few days (8 Sept. 1911, 14, 43)

SERCHUK, Charles and L. Lazarovitz, of Quebec City, returned home after a short stay in Montreal (6 March 1914, 17, 10)

SERCHUK, H., of Montreal, left for Quebec City, where he will join a party on a hunting trip in northern Quebec (18 Oct. 1912, 15, 45)

SERCHUK, W. and daughter, Mrs. J. Sternleib, will be guests of Mrs. L. Lazarovitz, in Quebec City, and then leave for La Tuque (25 July 1913, 16, 33)

SERETH, Miss Cecilia, of Calgary, is visiting her sister, Mrs. John J. Weinfield, 254 Sherbrooke St. E. (15 Dec. 1911, 15, 5)

SERETH, Mrs. H.N. and daughter, Miss Sophie Sereth, are in Montreal, the guests of Mr. and Mrs. I. Weinfield, 170 Laval Ave. (30 Dec. 1910, 14, 7)

SESSENWEIN, Isaac, Dorchester St. W., has left for California for an extended period (12 March 1909, 12, 13)

SESSENWEIN, L., was at the Chateau Frontenac while in Quebec City (12 March, 1909, 12, 13)

SESSENWEIN, Miss Belle, is spending a few weeks in Detroit and Mt. Clements (30 July 1909, 12, 33)

SESSENWEIN, Mr. and Mrs. C. and family, Bishop St., have returned from Old Orchard Beach, accompanied by Mrs. S.P. Myers and son (12 Aug. 1910, 13, 39)

SESSENWEIN, Mr. and Mrs. M., 822 Dorchester St. W., will be "at home" Sun. Aug. 20, 1911 (18 Aug. 1911, 14, 40)

SESSENWEIN, Mrs. L. and family are at Watch Hill, R.I. for the month (25 July 1913, 16, 33)

SHAER, D., is vacationing at Ste. Agathe des Monts (8 Aug. 1913, 16, 35)

SHALEK, Mrs. and Miss Ray Shalek are spending

the summer at Shawbridge (23 June 1911, 14, 32)

SHALINSKY, J., Dorchester St. W., left last Sun. for Boston and Old Orchard (1 Aug. 1913, 16, 34)

SHALINSKY, S.H., 121 Dorchester St. W.; is accepting applications from those men over age sixteen for membership in the Disraeli Club (17 Nov. 1911, 15, 1)

SHALIT, A.L., of Paris, France, who was in Canada last year on behalf of the Jewish Colonization Association, is back (24 June 1910, 13, 32)

SHANFIELD, Mrs., has returned to New York after spending the summer with her parents (15 Oct. 1909, 12, 44)

SHANFIELD, Mrs. Joseph and Miss Beckie Shanfield, of New York, are guests of Mrs. I. Vineberg, Mount Royal Ave. (13 Aug. 1909, 12, 35)

SHANFIELD, Mrs., of New York, is visiting her parents (5 Feb. 1909, 12, 8)

SHANKMAN, Mrs. W., of Ottawa, who was in New York, Philadelphia and Boston, has returned home (8 April 1910, 13, 21)

SHANKMAN, Mrs. Wolf and children, of Ottawa, are spending a few weeks at New Glasgow, Que. (25 June 1909, 12, 28)

SHANKMAN, Mrs. Wolf, of Ottawa, has returned home after a visit with her parents, Mr. and Mrs. S. Levine (12 Nov. 1909, 12, 48)

SHANKMAN, Mrs. Wolf, of Ottawa, is visiting her parents, Mr. and Mrs. S. Levine (18 June 1909, 12, 27)

SHANKMAN, Mrs. Wolf, of Ottawa, is visiting her parents, Mr. and Mrs. Levine (4 Feb. 1910, 13, 12)

SHAPERA, Mr. and Mrs. Charles, of Boston, were guests of Mrs. G. Morris, Laval Ave. (16 Sept. 1910, 13, 44)

SHAPIRO, D.H., and H. and L. Wener were recent Montreal visitors to New York (31 Dec. 1909, 13, 7)

SHAPIRO, Miss Leah, St. Louis Square, is in Chicago for a month visiting relatives (15 Aug. 1913, 16, 36)

SHAPIRO, Mr. and Mrs. A. and family, Esplanade Ave., are at Old Orchard, Me. (18 July 1913, 16, 32)

SHAPIRO, Mr. and Mrs. Charles, of Boston, Mass., were in Montreal for the Morris-Schaeffer wedding (6 Sept. 1912, 15, 39)

SHAPIRO, Mr. and Mrs. D., 216 Park Ave. wish their friends and relatives a happy New Year (1 Oct. 1913, 16, 42-43)

SHAPIRO, Mr. and Mrs. D. and daughter are holidaying in New York, the guests of Mr. and Mrs. J. Bashien (18 June 1909, 12, 27)

SHAPIRO, Mr. and Mrs. Gershon, left last Sat. evening on the S.S. La Houraine for Jaffa, Palestine, where they will make their home. Friends and relatives gathered at the pier to wish them bon voyage. Prior to their departure, Mr. Shapiro was honored at a banquet at the home of their youngest son, David Shapiro, Hutchison St., given by the Montreal Talmud Torah of which he had served as treasurer. Lazarus Cohen, M. Denenberg, Hiram Levy, M.J. Glickman and Rabbi Hirsch Cohen made speeches (6 June 1913, 16, 26)

SHAPIRO, Mr. and Mrs. H., have taken up their summer residence at Cartierville (18 June 1909, 12, 27)

SHAPIRO, Mr. and Mrs. S., 927 Mount Royal Ave., have left for Beaurepaire for the summer (18 June 1909, 12, 27)

SHAPIRO, Mrs. A. and Mrs. R. Eliasoph were called to New York to attend the funeral of their father, J. Mishkin (1 Sept. 1911, 14, 42)

SHAPIRO, Mrs. L. and family, 125 St. Lawrence Blvd., are spending the summer at Ste. Agathe des Monts (7 July 1911, 14, 34)

ANTWERP DIAMOND Co.

L. SHAPIRO, Prop.

Direct importers of

DIAMONDS and PRECIOUS STONES

THE TRADE SUPPLIED ONLY

125 St. Lawrence Boulevard, Montreal

TELEPHONE EAST 5320.

SHAPIRO, Sam, of Bedford, Que., is visiting his sister, Mrs Harry Lieberman, in Quebec City (24 Jan. 1913, 16, 7)

SHAPIRO, Sam, of Montreal, and Miss Ida Kandestin have returned from Quebec City where they visited their sister, Mrs. H. Silverman (19 Jan. 1912, 15, 10)

SHARKAFSKI, Miss Rose, has returned home from a visit to her sister, Mrs. A. Silverman in Toronto (12 March 1909, 12, 13)

SHAW, Miss Sarah, Waverley St., gave a social evening at her home on Thurs. April 24, 1913. Guests included:- the Misses Ida and Rebecca Nadler, A. Ram, Serchuk and Veingust (2 May 1913, 16, 21)

SHAYNE, Dr. and Mrs. John, of Toronto, send New Year greetings (11 Sept. 1912, 15, 40)

SHAYNE, Dr. John, of Toronto, has left for the Zionist Congress in Basle, via New York (28 July 1911, 14, 37)

SHAYNE, Dr. John, of Toronto, was in Montreal. Dr. Shayne was one of Canada's representatives at the Tenth Zionist Congress in Basle. He took a prominent and active part in the proceedings (15 Sept. 1911, 14, 44)

SHAYNE, Dr. John, president of the B'nai Zion Society of Toronto, will speak on "Our Inheritance", on Sun. March 30, 1913 at 8 p.m. sharp in the Baron de Hirsch Institute. Dave Kadishewitz, of Quebec City, will address the meeting in Yiddish (28 March 1913, 16, 16)

SHAYNE, Dr. John, the well-known Zionist leader from Toronto, who was in Montreal recently to address the Agudath Zion Society, returned home to accept the government position of immigration inspector for Toronto (11 April 1913, 16, 18)

SHEIFER, Miss J.L., was elected president of the Montreal Hebrew Day Nursery Auxiliary on Wed. evening. Jan. 7, 1914 at the Baron de Hirsch Institute. Other officers elected were:- Miss F. Yaphe, vice-pres.; Miss S.A. Ressler, rec. sec.; Miss K.E. Hornstein, fin. sec.; J. Illivitch, treas.; Misses M. Jasper and M. Jurist, trustees. Miss Ressler, 1642 Esplanade Ave., is accepting applications for membership (16 Jan. 1914, 17, 6)

SHENKMAN, Mr. and Mrs. Wolf, were in Montreal this weekend. They attended the Lazar-Levine wedding (15 Nov. 1912, 15, 49)

SHENKMAN, Mrs. W. and daughter are visiting their parents, Mr. and Mrs. S. Levine, in Ottawa (31 Jan. 1913, 16, 8)

SHENKMAN, Mrs. Wolf and children, of Ottawa, are visiting her parents, Mr. and Mrs. S. Levine (23 Feb. 1912, 15, 15)

SHENKMAN, Mrs. Wolf and son, of Ottawa, have gone on a two weeks' holiday to New York and Philadelphia (25 March 1910, 13, 19)

SHENKMAN, Wolf, of Ottawa, has left on an extended trip to New York and Philadelphia (16 April 1909, 12, 18)

SHERWIN, Mr. and Mrs. J., of New York (formerly Miss Irene Levi) was in Montreal for a few days visiting her parents, Mr. and Mrs. D. Levi, Dorchester St. W. (4 June 1909, 12, 25)

SHEVELL, Miss Sarah, of New York, is the guest of Rabbi and Mrs. S. Garber, Clarke St. (11 July 1913, 16, 31)

SHILDKRAUT, Rudolph, the great Hebrew actor of Vienna, Austria, is visiting his cousin, Mr. and Mrs. Hornesteine, 70 St. Charles Borrommee St. (16 Feb. 1912, 15, 14)

SHILLER, Miss Eva, has returned home after spending several weeks in Ste. Agathe (6 Aug. 1909, 12, 34)

SHIP, Dr. A.P., who is in Europe, took at short course at the London Hospital. On Nov. 22, 1911, he will study at an important hospital in Paris (17 Nov. 1911, 15, 1)

SHIP, Dr. and Mrs. A.P., are at Old Orchard, Me., for a few weeks (23 Aug. 1912, 15, 37)

SHIP, Dr. and Mrs. A.P., have returned from their honeymoon in Europe. While in Europe, Dr. Ship spent most of his time attending the Royal Charity Hospital in Berlin (26 Jan. 1912, 15, 11)

SHIP, Dr. M.L., delivered a lecture in Yiddish on child care at the Child Welfare Exhibition. Afterwards he held a clinic. Mrs. Leo, on behalf of the Victorian Order of Nurses, was in charge of the event and was assisted by Mesdames Leon Goldman and J.B. Rubinovich (25 Oct. 1912, 15, 46)

SHIP, Dr. M.L., is at Lake Placid, N.Y., for a month (11 Aug. 1911, 14, 39)

SHIP, N., Mrs. Sarah Kaiserman, B. Goldin, B. Goldberg, I. Herschkovitz, W. Signer, I.M. Levitt, G. Zudick, S. Malis, Mrs. Ethel Herkovitz, I. Taylor, Mrs. K. Herskovitz, Mrs. G. Malis, Mrs. Levitt, Mrs. R. Signer, Mrs. M. Gilled, Mrs. A. Undelman, Mrs. I. Raboo, Mrs. N. Johnson and I. Koffman contributed donations to the Bessarabia Hebrew Sick Benefit Society Cemetery (26 Aug. 1910, 13, 41)

SHLIEFER, F., Drolet St., hosted the banquet of the Young Men's Hebrew Dramatic Society Inner-circle, Sun. evening, March 22, 1914. Hostesses were Mrs. F. Shliefer and Miss A. Shliefer. M. Flanders chaired the evening. Speeches were made by R. Docks, G.H. Friefeld, H.M. Lehrer, J. Levy and S. Rendon (27 March 1914, 17, 13)

SHLUKER & CHODAS LUMBER CO.

The only Jewish Lumber Yard in Canada.

CHERRY and HARDWOOD, DRESSED LUMBER
and MOULDINGS at lowest Prices.

ALSO DEALERS IN WOOD AND COAL

Mail Orders promptly attended to.

302-306 Cadieux St., Montreal

SHNEYER, K., was elected president of the newly formed musical society, "the Musical and Dramatical Circle" (Hazomir), on Jan. 7, 1914. "The purpose of the above circle is mainly to introduce Jewish National Songs, under the direction of K. Bercovici, the well-known music teacher. It will also be the object of this organization to give a dramatical and literary education to its members." Other officers elected were:- M. Dickstein, corr. sec.; Mrs. Rose Rubenstein, fin. sec.; A. Komaroff, treas., K. Bercovici, J. Malamuth and E. Rubenstein, exec. comm. (16 Jan. 1914, 17, 6)

SHULICH, Miss J., was elected vice-president of the YWHA at the Sun. May 4, 1913 meeting, owing to the resignation of Miss B. Cohen. Miss A. Pinsler, president, chaired the meeting (16 May 1913, 16, 23)

SHUSHELSKY, Miss Ida, of Salem, Mass., is visiting her cousins, Mr. and Mrs. T. Glickman, at Beloeil, Que. (19 July 1912, 15, 32)

SIDEL, Miss Dorothy M., of Chicago, is visiting her sister, Mrs. S. Stern, St. Urbain St. (13 Aug. 1909, 12, 35)

SIDERSKI, A., of Glace Bay, N.S., was a visitor in Montreal (21 May 1909, 12, 23)

SIDERSKI, A., of Glace Bay, N.S., has returned home after a three weeks' visit with friends and relatives (4 March 1910, 13, 16)

SIDERSKI, Archie, of Glace Bay, N.S., is a guest at the Carslake Hotel (11 Feb. 1910, 13, 13)

SIDERSKI, Miss, is the guest of Mrs. Lande, Strathcona Ave., Westmount (17 June 1910, 13, 31)

SIEGEL, Miss Anna, of Brooklyn, N.Y., is visiting her aunt, Mrs. A. Elkin (20 Sept. 1912, 15, 41)

SIEGLER, Miss Ida, is on holiday at Old Orchard Beach, Me. (11 Aug. 1911, 14, 39)

SIEGLER, Miss Ida, read a paper "Preparations for Zionism" at the Montreal Daughters of Zion meeting last Sun. evening in the Baron de Hirsch Institute. Rabbi Herman Abramowitz lectured on "The Jewish Woman and Her Possible Influence on Zionism". Others taking part in the program were:- Clarence I. de Sola and the Misses Miriam Bernstein, Dorothy Morris, Sadie Vineberg and Lily Wetstein (15 Jan. 1909, 12, 5)

SIGLER, Miss Ida, St. Famille St., has left for Old Orchard Beach (20 Aug. 1909, 12, 36)

SIGMUND, Miss Frances, has returned from New York, where she was visiting her sister, Mrs. S. Goldstein (22 Jan. 1909, 12, 6)

SIGMUND, Miss Frances, has returned from New York where she visited her sister, Mrs. S. Goldstein, for the past month (4 Feb. 1910, 13, 12)

SIGMUND, Miss Frances, is in New York visiting her sister, Mrs. S.H. Goldstein (12 Sept. 1913, 16, 40)

SIGMUND, Miss Martha, was given a surprise party by her friends last Sun. (26 April 1912, 15, 24)

SIGMUND, Misses Frances and Martha, returned from Lac des Isles, St. Margaret, Que. where they summered (29 Aug. 1913, 16, 38)

SIGMUND, Mrs. A. and the Misses F. and M. Sigmund have returned from Val Morin where they spent the summer (15 Sept. 1911, 14, 44)

SIGMUND, Mrs. A., returned from Prefontaine, Que. where she spent a month (29 Aug. 1913, 16, 38)

SIGMUND, Mrs. and daughter, have returned to Montreal from Ste. Agathe (6 Aug. 1909, 12, 34)

SILBERMAN, Miss Susan, of Quebec City, has left for Macdonald College, St. Anne de Bellevue, where she is studying for her teacher's certificate (10 Sept. 1909, 12, 39)

SILBERSTEIN, L., has returned home to Chelsea, Mass., after a two weeks' visit with Rev. S. Goldstein, 94 Pine Ave. W. (13 Jan. 1911, 14, 9)

SILVA, J., of Portland, Me., is staying at the Windsor Hotel (16 April 1909, 12, 18)

SILVER, B., chaired the Spanish and Portuguese Synagogue closing exercises last Sun. Willie Kaplansky won the Ross Levi Memorial Medal and Miss Rosie Ginsberg received the Sarah de la Penha Memorial Medal, which was donated by Rev. Isaac de la Penha. Mrs. Robert Goltman presented prizes to the following pupils:- Max Cohen, Raphael de Sola, Paul Darwin, Eliot Goldwater, Gerald Goldwater, Donald Goltman, Stanley Hart, Eli Hayes, Solomon Hayes, David Kaplansky, David Kirschberg, Bernard Lehberg, Lionel Rose, Leo Rosenweesen, Moses Silverstein, Shea Silverstein and the Misses Adela Cohen, Jennie Erdrich, Annie Frank, Jessie Ginsberg, Ethel Goldwater, Gladys Lehberg, Bessie Shanker and Jennie Shanker (30 May 1913, 16, 25)

SILVER, B., stayed at the Broadway Central Hotel while in New York (21 Jan. 1910, 13, 10)

SILVER, B., was elected president of the Spanish and Portuguese Synagogue at the annual general meeting on May 28, 1913. Officers elected were:- Clarence I. de Sola, parnass; Michael Michaels, treas.; Percy Jacobson, sec.; S. Haskell, I.S. Goldstein, J.S. Leo, M. Lightstone, M.L. Rose, trustees; cemetery committee, B.J. Hayes (Gabbai Beth Haim), S. Blaustein; seating committee, S. Erdrich, Charles Fisher, M. Lightstone, M.L. Rose; choir committee, Albert Freedman, Isaac Kirschberg, M. Lightstone; and Rabbi Meldola de Sola, school committee (6 June 1913, 16, 26)

SILVER, Benjamin, was elected president of the Spanish and Portuguese Congregation "Shearith Israel" at a special general meeting held last Sun. to replace the late Jacob L. Samuel (8 Nov. 1912, 15, 48)

SILVER, H.J., returned to Montreal on Mon. from his vacation in the Laurentians (13 Aug. 1909, 12, 35)

SILVER, J.H., has returned from the Laurentian Mountains where he spent a few days (16 July 1909, 12, 31)

SILVER, Joseph, of Merrickville, Ont., was in Montreal for a few days (6 Sept. 1912, 15, 39)

SILVER, L., Sherbrooke, is a guest at the Stanley Hall (7 May 1909, 12, 21)

SILVER, Lazarus, has gone to the Cobalt district for a few months (9 July 1909, 12, 30)

SILVER, M., 121 Park Ave., is in New York on business (7 Jan. 1910, 13, 8)

SILVER, M. and Lucky Gordon are at Sixteen Island Lake for a few days (9 Aug. 1912, 15, 35)

SILVER, M., has gone to the Maritimes for a few weeks (17 Feb. 1911, 14, 14)

SILVER, M., has returned from a two weeks' vacation in Newport and Boston (25 June 1909, 12, 28)

SILVER, M., has returned from Boston (19 Feb. 1909, 12, 10)

SILVER, M., is an elected governor of the Baron de Hirsch Institute (25 Nov. 1910, 14, 2)

SILVER, Master Benjamin, has been awarded a McGill $100 exhibition on the basis of his matriculation examination held recently for entrance to the Faculty of Arts (30 July 1909, 12, 33)

SILVER, Miss Edith, daughter of Mr. and Mrs. M. Silver, 121 Park Ave., celebrated her eleventh birthday last Tues. with a party (18 Feb. 1910, 13, 14)

SILVER, Miss Mae, has returned from Shawbridge where she was the guest of Mr. and Mrs. Lazarus Silver (14 July 1911, 14, 35)

SILVER, Miss May, is president of the Rose Sewing Circle, named in honor of Mrs. Rose Jacobs. The Circle is made up of young women who make clothing articles for poor children. Miss Violet Michaels is the secretary and Miss Dorothy Hart, treasurer (4 Feb. 1910, 13, 12)

SILVER, Miss Yetta, Souvenir Ave., was given a theatre party by her friends on Mon. to mark her birthday (14 Feb. 1913, 16, 10)

SILVER, Moe, left for a two months' stay in Boston (15 Jan. 1909, 12, 5)

SILVER, Mr. and Mrs. Joseph, of Kingston, Ont., were in Montreal to attend the wedding of Mrs. Silver's sister, Miss Jackson (12 March 1909, 12, 13)

SILVER, Mr. and Mrs. Lazarus, have returned from a three months' trip abroad (18 June 1909, 12, 27)

SILVER, Mr. and Mrs. M. and daughter, Miss Edith Silver, Park Ave., have returned from Russia where they visited Mrs. Silver's mother (9 Sept. 1910, 13, 43)

SILVER, Mr. and Mrs. N., Messrs. M. Auerbach, A.M. Ruttenberg, J. Samuel, A. Levine and D.H. Shapiro were in New York last week (28 May 1909, 12, 24)

SILVER, Mr. and Mrs. Nahum, Souvenir Ave., has returned from a week in New York (27 May 1910, 13, 28)

SILVER, Mrs. and daughter, Elm Ave., have returned home after spending the past two months abroad (11 June 1909, 12, 26)

SILVER, Mrs. and daughter have returned from Toronto and Hamilton (10 Sept. 1909, 12, 39)

SILVER, Mrs. M., 121 Park Ave., accompanied by her daughter, sails today on the S.S. Megantic for Europe to visit her parents in Russia. They will be away for two months (24 June 1910, 13, 32)

SILVER, Mrs. Moe, 1100 Greene Ave., Westmount, will be at home to her friends every second and fourth Thurs. of each month (7 Nov. 1913, 16, 48)

SILVER, Mrs. N., is in Buffalo, N.Y., visiting relatives (7 March 1913, 16, 13)

SILVER, Mrs. N. and Mrs. Asher Pierce are in Halifax where they attended the wedding of their niece, Miss Yetta Lesser to Mr. Katz (21 Jan. 1910, 13, 10)

SILVER, Mrs. Nathan and daughters are spending the summer at Ivry, Que. (25 July 1913, 16, 33)

SILVER, Mrs. Nathan, her daughters and son Master Alexander Silver are at Shawbridge, Que. for a few weeks (9 Aug. 1912, 15, 35)

SILVER, N., has returned from a week in St. Louis, Mo. (6 Jan. 1911, 14, 8)

SILVER, N., Souvenir Ave., has left for an extended trip to St. Louis and the midwestern U.S. (22 Jan. 1909, 12, 6)

SILVER, Nathan, returned from a short trip to Detroit (31 Jan. 1913, 16, 8)

SILVERBERG, Miss Ada, of Toronto, attended the Zionist Convention in Montreal and was a guest of Miss Ruth Groner, Elm Ave. (2 Jan. 1914, 17, 4)

SILVERBERG, Miss Ada, of Toronto, is the guest of Miss Ruth Groner, of Westmount, Que. (12 July 1912, 15, 31)

SILVERBERG, Miss Eva, of Toronto, will be the guest of Miss Rose Samuels, while attending the Zionist Convention in Montreal (26 Dec. 1913, 17, 3)

SILVERBERG, Miss Rose, of Toronto, is the guest of Miss Ray Vineberg, Esplanade Ave. (2 Jan. 1914, 17, 4)

SILVERMAN, Dr. A.H., of Lowell, Mass., is visiting his parents, Mr. and Mrs. S. Silverman, in Quebec City (7 Jan. 1910, 13, 8)

SILVERMAN, Edwin L. and Miss Elsie Silverman, are at Ste. Agathe des Monts (25 Nov. 1910, 14, 2)

SILVERMAN, Miss Elsie, has returned from visiting her sister, Mrs. S.A. Jacobs, Rapides L'Allemands, St. Dorothee (4 Aug. 1911, 14, 38)

SILVERMAN, Miss Elsie, is the guest of Miss L. Woods at Lake St. Joseph (13 Aug. 1909, 12, 35)

SILVERMAN, Miss Elsie, Tupper St., is the guest of Miss Sylvia Goldstein (19 July 1912, 15, 32)

SILVERMAN, Miss Elsie, was the guest of her cousins, the Misses Abrahams at Lakeside on the weekend (8 July 1910, 13, 34)

SILVERMAN, Miss Gertie, spent the weekend at Brome Lake, Que. (9 Aug. 1912, 15, 35)

SILVERMAN, Miss Gertie, was a guest of Mrs. R.H. Blumenthal at Beaurepaire for the week (22 July 1910, 13, 36)

SILVERMAN, Miss Hattie, is back from a ten days' holiday in New York (11 June 1909, 12, 26)

SILVERMAN, Miss Hattie, left last night for New York where she expects to visit friends for several weeks (21 May 1909, 12, 23)

SILVERMAN, Miss Hattie, was the guest of her aunt, Mrs. R.H. Blumenthal, Beaurepaire, for a few days (10 Sept. 1909, 12, 39)

SILVERMAN, Miss Hattie, wrote an article "The Business Girl" for the paper (15 Sept. 1911, 14, 44)

SILVERMAN, Miss J.S., was the guest of the Misses Harris, Vaudreuil for the weekend (28 July 1911, 14, 37)

SILVERMAN, Miss, of New York, was a guest at the Windsor Hotel (12 May 1911, 14, 26)

SILVERMAN, Miss Susan, Macdonald College, is in Quebec City visiting her parents, Mr. and Mrs. S. Silverman (31 Dec. 1909, 13, 7)

SILVERMAN, Miss Susan, of Quebec City, has been appointed principal of the Marbleton Model School, Marbleton, Que. (19 Aug. 1910, 13, 40)

SILVERMAN, Misses and the Misses Blout were guests of Mrs. Goldstein, Lakeside, on Dominion Day (9 July 1909, 12, 30)

SILVERMAN, Misses, Elm Ave., have gone on a short trip to Toronto and Hamilton (27 Aug. 1909, 12, 37)

SILVERMAN, Misses, Elm Ave., were guests of Mrs. Abrahams for the weekend at Lakeside (23 Sept. 1910, 13, 45)

SILVERMAN, Misses Frankie and Annie, are visiting their parents in Cornwall, Ont. (3 Jan. 1913, 16, 4)

SILVERMAN, Mr. and Mrs., have returned home from Bradford (27 Aug. 1909, 12, 37)

SILVERMAN, Mr. and Mrs. S., Prince Arthur West, have returned home from a short visit to Mrs. Silverman's parents at "Maplehurst", Bedford, Que. (24 Feb. 1911, 14, 15)

SILVERMAN, Mr. and Mrs. S., Prince Arthur St. W., have returned from Bedford (26 May 1911, 14, 28)

SILVERMAN, Mr. and Mrs. S., were recent guests of Mrs. E.W. Jones (11 June 1909, 12, 26)

SILVERMAN, Mrs. and Miss Silverman are at the Charion Hotel, Boucherville, Que. (16 July 1909, 12, 31)

SILVERMAN, Mrs., Elm Ave., is the guest of Mrs. Abrahams at Lakeside (8 July 1910, 13, 34)

SILVERMAN, Mrs. J., of Perth, Ont., is visiting Mrs. Schloman, Sussex St. (22 Oct. 1913, 16, 46)

SILVERMAN, Mrs. L., entertained last Sun. in honor of Mr. and Mrs. B. I. Cohen. The Misses Jennie Greenspon and Rose Cohen assisted in receiving (20 Oct. 1911, 14, 49)

SILVERMAN, Mrs. Lyon and family, 4056 Tupper St., wish their friends and relatives a happy New Year (1 Oct. 1913, 16, 42-43)

SILVERMAN, Mrs. Lyon and family, Tupper St., send New Year greetings (11 Sept. 1912, 15, 40)

SILVERMAN, Mrs. Lyon and Miss Silverman were guests of Mrs. S.A. Jacobs at Rapides L'Allemand, St. Dorothee, Que. (23 June 1911, 14, 32)

SILVERMAN, Mrs. S. and sons Harry and Arthur Silverman, Mance St., Annex, have returned from Boston where they were guests of Mr. and Mrs. Baker (8 Sept. 1911, 14, 43)

SILVERSTONE, Alexander, spent Labour Day at Beaurepaire, the guest of his sister, Mrs. L.H. Blumenthal (10 Sept. 1909, 12, 39)

SILVERSTONE, M., has moved to Cochrane, Ont. (20 Oct. 1911, 14, 49)

SILVERSTONE, Miss R., is at Wing's Hotel, Brome Lake, Que. (12 July 1912, 15, 31)

SILVERSTONE, Mrs. S. and daughter have left for New York, Pittsburgh and Scranton for the summer (17 June 1910, 13, 31)

SILVERSTONE, Mrs. W., was a guest of her daughter, Mrs. I. Blumenthal at Beaurepaire (2 Aug. 1912, 15, 34)

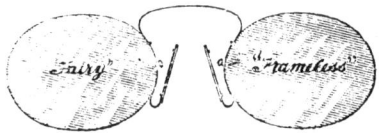

```
Tel. Up 3376

I. SILVERSTONE
Teacher of Violin
37 HUTCHISON STREET - - - MONTREAL
```

SILVERSTONE, Mrs. William, has returned home from Quebec City where she spent the past month with her daughter, Mrs. Phillip Myers (10 Sept. 1909, 12, 39)

SILVERSTONE, Mrs. William, is spending a few weeks at Beaurepaire, with her daughter, Mrs. I. Blumenthal (9 July 1909, 12, 30)

SILVERSTONE, Mrs. William, is summering St. Jovite, Que. (11 Aug. 1911, 14, 39)

SILVERSTONE, Mrs. William, is visiting her daughter, Mrs. Blumenthal, at Beaurepaire (9 Sept. 1910, 13, 43)

SILVERSTONE, Samuel and B. Levy have left for Carbondale, Pa. (26 Aug. 1910, 13, 41)

SILVERSTONE, Sol., is in the Western Hospital (26 March 1909, 12, 15)

SIMON, George and I. Simon, of Alexandria, stayed at the Queen's Hotel (20 Sept. 1912, 15, 41)

SIMON, George, of Alexandria, Ont., stayed at the Queen's Hotel while in Montreal (7 Feb. 1913, 16, 9)

SIMON, Herman and Mr. and Mrs. Sydney Stern are in New York and Atlantic City (19 April 1912, 15, 23)

SIMON, J., of Chicago, was a guest at the Windsor Hotel (19 May 1911, 14, 27)

SIMON, J., of Hamilton, was in Montreal this week en route for Ottawa (20 March 1914, 17, 12)

SIMON, J., of Philadelphia, stayed at the Windsor Hotel during his visit (27 Dec. 1912, 16, 3)

SIMON, John, of Halifax, was in Montreal during the week (1 April 1910, 13, 20)

SIMON, John, of Halifax, was the guest of Mr. and Mrs. M. Harris, Crescent St. (30 Dec. 1910, 14, 7)

SIMON, L., of New York, was in Montreal to attend the Bar Mitzvah of his grandson, Master Jake Simon, eldest son of Mr. and Mrs. M. Simon (20 Feb. 1914, 17, 8)

SIMON, M., of Hamilton, was in Montreal briefly (2 Oct. 1912, 15, 43)

SIMON, Miss M., of Alexandria, Ont., has returned home after spending several weeks in Montreal (15 April 1910, 13, 22)

SIMON, Miss M., of Alexandria, Ont., is in Montreal for a few weeks (29 Sept. 1911, 14, 46)

SIMON, Miss M., of Alexandria, Ont., is in Montreal for a few weeks (7 Feb. 1913, 16, 9)

SIMON, Miss Mollie, of Alexandria, Ont., was in Montreal for a few days. She visited her sister, Mrs. S.W. Jacobs, in Cornwall (19 May 1911, 14, 27)

SIMON, Miss Mollie, of Alexandria, Ont., is the guest of her cousins, Mr. and Mrs. A. Simon, Euclid St., Toronto (13 March 1914, 17, 11)

SIMON, Miss Molly, of Alexandria, Ont., is the guest of the Misses Levinson, Elm Ave., for a few days (20 June 1913, 16, 28)

SIMON, Miss, of Alexandria, is the guest of Mrs. Jacobs, Greene Ave. (1 Oct. 1909, 12, 42)

SIMON, Miss, of Alexandria, Ont., and her sister, Mrs. Myers, of Winnipeg, were in Montreal for a few days (11 March 1910, 13, 17)

SIMON, Miss, of Alexandria, was in town (13 Jan. 1911, 14, 9)

SIMON, Misses Rosa and Freda, of New York, are visiting their cousin, Mrs. F.M. Ogulnik, 438 Claremont Ave., Westmount (25 Aug. 1911, 14, 41)

SIMON, Mr. and Mrs. Arthur, of Chicago are spending their honeymoon in Montreal and will remain here for a few weeks (22 Jan. 1909, 12, 6)

SIMON, Mr. and Mrs. H., Victoria Ave., Westmount, are in Los Angeles (14 Feb. 1913, 16, 10)

SIMON, Mr. and Mrs. H., Victoria Ave., are spending a few weeks in Cuba (13 Feb. 1914, 17, 7)

SIMON, Mr. and Mrs. J., of Halifax, and R. Davis, of Troy, N.Y., are guests of Mr. and Mrs. Maxwell Harris, Crescent St. (13 Aug. 1909, 12, 35)

SIMON, Mr. and Mrs. John, of Halifax, are visiting Mrs. Simon's parents, Mr. and Mrs. M. Harris, Crescent St. (6 Aug. 1909, 12, 34)

SIMON, Mr. and Mrs. Sol., of Philadelphia, Pa., are guests at the Windsor Hotel (5 Jan. 1911, 15, 8)

SIMON, Mr., Miss M. Simon and brother, of Alexandria, Ont., were guests at the Queen's Hotel (11 Oct. 1910, 13, 48)

SIMON, Mrs. A. and baby are guests of Mr. and Mrs. Green in St. John, N.B. (14 July 1911, 14, 35)

SIMON, Mrs. A., Grosvenor Ave., is spending a few weeks in New York (14 Nov. 1913, 16, 49)

SIMON, Mrs. Arthur and baby are visiting Mrs. Frank in Chicago (8 Sept. 1911, 14, 43)

SIMON, Mrs. H., leaves shortly for San Francisco where she will visit her sister (19 March 1909, 12, 14)

SIMON, Mrs. J., of Halifax, N.S., who visited her parents, Mr. and Mrs. Maxwell Harris, Crescent St., has returned home, accompanied by her sister, Miss Edythe Harris (3 Sept. 1909, 12, 38)

SIMON, Mrs. John and family, of Halifax, N.S., are in Montreal (27 Dec. 1912, 16, 3)

SIMON, Mrs. Martin, will leave shortly on a visit to Cleveland (5 March 1909, 12, 12)

SIMON, Mrs. S., gave an "at home" in honor of her guests, Mrs. Arthur Simon, Mrs. Frank, of Chicago, and Miss Roos, of Boston. Mrs. Arthur Simon wore her wedding dress. Guests included:- Mrs. Sydney Stein, of New York and Mrs. F. Lewis. The Misses Lewis, Levinson and Workman presided over the tables (29 Jan. 1909, 12, 7)

SIMON, Mrs. William (née Miss Edythe Goldberg), of Vancouver, B.C., is in Montreal visiting her parents (5 Aug. 1910, 13, 38)

SIMON, Sol, of Philadelphia, Pa., stayed at the Windsor Hotel (27 Oct. 1911, 14, 50)

SIMON, Sol, of Philadelphia, stayed at the Windsor Hotel while in Montreal (20 June 1913, 16, 28)

SIMON, William, who was in the U.S. on business, has returned to Montreal, and will live with his parents, Mr. and Mrs. B. Simon, St. Urbain St. (18 Nov. 1910, 14, 1)

SIMON-BURNSCHBURG, R., of Paris, is on a business trip and is staying at the Place Viger Hotel (30 July 1909, 12, 33)

SIMONSKI, Mr. and Mrs. A., of Toronto, were guests of Mr. and Mrs. Harry Vineberg while in Montreal (20 Oct. 1911, 14, 49)

SIMONSON, S., of Boston, Mass., was the guest of Mrs. G. Morris, Laval Ave. (6 Oct. 1911, 14, 47)

SIMSON, S., of Boston, was the guest of Mrs. C. Morris while in Montreal (24 Sept. 1909, 12, 41)

SINGER, E., of Toronto, spent the New Year here (8 Jan. 1909, 12, 4)

SINGER, Fred., of New York, was registered at the St. Lawrence Hall (18 Feb. 1910, 13, 14)

SINGER, Frederick, of New York, is registered at the St. Lawrence Hall (26 Feb. 1909, 12, 11)

SINGER, Frederick, of New York, was a guest at the St. Lawrence Hall (15 Oct. 1909, 12, 44)

SINGER, Max, has returned from Boston and New York (26 Jan. 1912, 15, 11)

SINGER, Max, was chairman of the first annual dance organized by the Young Men's Hebrew Association last Sun. evening in the Auditorium Hall. Other committee members were:- W. Swedler, sec.; J. Shapiro, J. Marcovitch, M. Goldberg, L. Golland, S. Goldfield, C. Schnaer, A. Albert, A.N. Goldstein, M. Soskin, L. Ober, H. Firestone and H. Cohen. During the evening brief speeches were made by Samuel Bloomfield, the hon. pres.; A.H. Munn, Bernard Rose and W. Swedler (4 March 1910, 13, 16)

SINGER, Miss Reba, returned home from New York where she was the guest of her uncle and aunt, Mr. and Mrs. F. Singer (13 Feb. 1914, 17, 7)

SINGER, Miss Sophie, 427 St. Denis St., Montreal, secretary of the Montreal Daughters of Zion Society, is receiving contest entries for the best original Jewish playet or sketch written in English. The prize is five shares in the Jewish Colonial Trust, value $25.00 (22 Nov. 1912, 15, 50)

SINGER, Misses Riba and Sophie, have returned from Old Orchard, Me. (2 Sept. 1910, 13, 42)

SINGER, Mr. and Mrs. Frank, have returned from Buffalo, Niagara Falls and the Thousand Islands (26 Aug. 1910, 13, 41)

SINGER, Mr. and Mrs. Frank, have returned from their trip (2 Sept. 1910, 13, 42)

SINGER, Mr. and Mrs. Fred, of New York, are guests at the Windsor Hotel (20 Oct. 1911, 14, 49)

SINGER, Mr. and Mrs. H., 198 Park Ave., gave a tea party for their daughter, Miss Freda Singer, on Dec. 22, 1912. Misses Jennie Greenspon and R. Goldner poured tea for forty of her little friends (27 Dec. 1912, 16, 3)

SINGER, Mr. and Mrs. H., 63 Esplanade Ave., gave a party Sun. evening, March 22, 1914 to celebrate their tenth wedding anniversary. Mrs. Singer was assisted by Miss Reba Singer in receiving the guests. In charge of the table were Mesdames Louis Goldenstein, Lyon Hoffman and Miss Jennie Greenspon (27 March 1914, 17, 13)

SINGER, Mr. and Mrs. Herman and daughter will spend the summer at Caledonia Springs (16 July 1909, 12, 31)

SINGER, Mr. and Mrs. Herman and daughter Freda are at Caledonia Springs for the rest of the summer (25 July 1911, 14, 36)

SINGER, Mr. and Mrs. William, left for Toronto, Niagara, New York, Boston and Philadelphia (11 July 1913, 16, 31)

SINGER, Mrs. Aaron, of New York, is visiting her cousins, Mr. and Mrs. Herman Singer (4 July 1913, 16, 30)

SINGER, Mrs. F., of Romania, is visiting Mr. and Mrs. S. Singer (14 Jan. 1910, 13, 9)

SINGER, Mrs. H. and daughter, of Toronto, were in Montreal visiting her daughter, Mrs. Solomon Vineberg, Mt. Pleasant Ave. (16 July 1909, 12, 31)

SINGER, Mrs. M. and I. Singer have returned to Toronto after visiting Mrs. J. Mendels, St. Famille St. (13 Jan. 1911, 14, 9)

SINGER, Mrs. M., of Toronto, is visiting her mother, Mrs. Mendels, Bishop St. (15 Dec. 1911, 15, 5)

SINGER, Mrs. M., of Toronto, was in Montreal to attend the Goldstein-Jacks wedding which took place at the Ritz-Carlton Hotel on Thurs. Jan. 8, 1914 (16 Jan. 1914, 17, 6)

SINGER, William, was elected president of the YMHA at the annual meeting last Sun. aft. Other officers elected were:- I. Mitnick, 1st vice-pres.; S.B. Gordon, 2nd vice-pres.; Sol. Cohen, treas.; A.M. Goldstein, fin. sec.; Louis Ober, corr. sec.; Aaron Aronson, rec. sec.; and J. Pinsler, sergeant-at-arms. Trustees include I. Bald, N. Beecher, S. Brodsky, W. Burman, J. Goldman, N. Goldstein and S. Rawson (13 Jan. 1911, 14, 9)

SLABOTSKY, Mr. and Mrs. M., gave a birthday party in honor of their little daughter, Esther, on Sun. aft., March 2, 1913 (7 March 1913, 16, 13)

SLATKOF, S., J. Lozof, Mr. and Mrs. P. Katz, Mr. and Mrs. Brotman and Mr. and Mrs. H. Ehrenstein presented a golden locket set with diamonds to Dr. J.S. Budyk on Sun. evening at Mr. Brotman's home (31 March 1911, 14, 20)

SLOBOSKY, Mr. and Mrs. M., 623 City Hall Ave., celebrated their wooden wedding anniversary last Sat. night (12 Jan. 1912, 15, 9)

SLOMENSKY, I. and A., were in Montreal this week on business (15 April 1910, 13, 22)

SLOMENSKY, Mr., of Ottawa, was in Montreal during the week (1 April 1910, 13, 20)

SLOMINSKY, I., of Ottawa, is in Montreal for a few days (14 Jan. 1910, 13, 9)

SLOVER, Miss Gertrude, returned home to Ottawa after visiting relatives in Montreal (6 Dec. 1912, 15, 52)

SLOVES, A., has left on an extended trip out west (27 Jan. 1911, 14, 11)

SLOVES, Miss Sara, Park Ave., returned from five weeks in New York, Trenton and Philadelphia (24 Jan. 1913, 16, 7)

SLOVES, Mr. and Mrs. N., Park Ave., celebrated their twenty-fifth wedding anniversary with a family dinner on Sun. June 15, 1913. Their children presented them with a silver tea service (20 June 1913, 16, 28)

SMELZER, Mrs. J.H. and family are guests at Leggatt House, Little Metis (3 Sept. 1909, 12, 38)

EVERYTHING

In the line of Jewellery made and Repaired.
Diamond Setting our Specialty.

N. SLOVES & CO.,
17 BLEURY STREET,   **2nd Floor.**

SMITH, Miss E., of Ottawa, is visiting Mr. and Mrs. M. Blankstein, St. Urbain St. (14 Feb. 1913, 16, 10)

SMITH, Mrs. and daughter Rachel Smith, of Sherbrooke, Que., were in Montreal and attended the Daughters of Zion dance on Wed. evening (1 April 1910, 13, 20)

SOHMER, J., 990 St. Dominique St., was re-elected president by acclamation of the Zeire Zion Society on Sun. Sept. 7, 1913. Other officers elected were:- R. Caplan, vice-pres.; H. Neamton, gen. sec.; S. Shweisberg, corr. sec.; M.L. Levitsky, Hebrew sec.; J. Birnbaum, treas.; J.M. Levinthal and H. Tolshinsky, librarians; B. Laxer, sergeant-at-arms; B. Joseph, M.L. Levitsky and S. Nissenholtz, exec. council (12 Sept. 1913, 16, 40)

SOHMER, J., J. Birnbaum, R. Caplan and L. Levitsky, of the Zeire Zion Society, were chosen delegates at a general meeting on Sun. Nov. 30, 1913, to the annual Zionist convention to be held in Montreal on Dec. 25 (5 Dec. 1913, 16, 52)

SOHMER, J., was re-elected president of the Zeire Zion Society at the semi-annual elections on Sun. March 9, 1913. Other officers elected were:- H. Neamton, vice-pres.; S. Nissenholtz, gen. sec.; H. Philips, corr. sec.; M.L. Levitsky, Hebrew sec.; J. Birnbaum, treas.; L. Becker, R. Caplan, S. Rosenberg and S. Swisberg, exec. council; B. Joseph and J. Levinthal, librarians; M.L. Levitsky, Hebrew librarian; and I. Vosberg, sergeant-at-arms (14 March 1913, 16, 14)

SOLBERGER, J., arrived last Sat. from Liverpool on the S.S. Ottawa (28 May 1909, 12, 24)

SOLIN, J., has gone to New York on business (5 May 1911, 14, 25)

SOLIN, Mr. and Mrs. J., 661 St. Urbain St., with their relatives and friends a happy New Year (10 Oct. 1913, 16, 44)

SOLIN, Mr. and Mrs. J. and daughter, send New Year greetings (20 Sept. 1912, 15, 41)

SOLIN, Mr. and Mrs. J. and daughter are at Old Orchard, Me. (15 Aug. 1913, 16, 36)

SOLIN, Mr. and Mrs. M., have gone to New York for ten days (11 April 1913, 16, 18)

SOLIN, Mrs. J. and daughter have returned from Burkes' Falls and Toronto (6 Sept. 1912, 15, 39)

SOLIN, Mrs. J., entertained at tea on Tues. Feb. 25, 1913 (28 Feb. 1913, 16, 12)

SOLIN, Mrs. J., has returned from Quebec City (1 Sept. 1911, 14, 42)

SOLIN, Mrs. M. and son are visiting her mother, Mrs. L. Goldberg in Quebec City (21 June 1912, 15, 28)

SOLOMON, D. (chairman), D. Blumer, M. Colle, B. Glass, J. Goodman, L. Kalmonovitz, J. Manolson, P. Popliger, S. Popliger, L. Solomon, D. Sperber, J. Steinberg, M.B. Steine and M. Zelicovetz are members of the fund-raising committee for a Jewish orphanage in Montreal (23 Sept. 1909, 12, 41)

SOLOMON, Ed., was elected president of the Montefiore Baseball League for the season. Other officers elected were:- Louis Rubenstein, hon. pres.; Peter Merson, vice-pres.; H. Swartz, sec.; and P. Garfinkle, treas. (9 May 1913, 16, 22)

SOLOMON, Edward, Miss Hannah Rosenberg and Bram C. de Sola passed their Arts, B.A. examinations at McGill University. Mr. de Sola took double first rank honors in most of his subjects (13 May 1910, 13, 26)

SOLOMON, H. and family will soon leave for their residence at Woodlands for the summer (11 June 1909, 12, 26)

SOLOMON, L., is president of Talmud Torah Anshe Sephard, 154 Elgin St., which held a concert in the Baron de Hirsch Institute last Sun. Those participating included:- Cantor M.J. Judelson and choir, Mr. Yampolsky, the Misses Bessie Elkin, Bella Gross and Sarah Sperber (piano) and Masters J. Baker, B. Figler, M. Skiebelsky, J. Blumenfeld (piano) and P. Pressner (violin) (2 Sept. 1910, 13, 42)

SOLOMON, M., has returned from his extended business trip out west (31 Dec. 1909, 13, 7)

SOLOMON, M., leaves tomorrow for the Maritimes on business (19 Aug. 1910, 13, 40)

SOLOMON, M., of Malone, N.Y., was in Montreal for a few days (6 Oct. 1911, 14, 47)

SOLOMON, Miss Clara, is spending a holiday at Weir, Ont. (29 July 1910, 13, 37)

SOLOMON, Miss Clara, visited her brother, Mr. and Mrs. Louis Solomon, at Shawbridge, Que. (9 Aug. 1912, 15, 35)

SOLOMON, Miss Eva, returned home to Boston after visiting her sister, Mrs. H. Vosberg, Mance St. (15 Aug. 1913, 16, 36)

SOLOMON, Miss Evelyn, of Boston, Mass., is visiting her sister, Mrs. H. Vosberg, Mance St. (7 March 1913, 16, 13)

SOLOMON, Miss Freda and her brother attended the Abramsky-Weinberg wedding in Kingston, Ont. last Tues. (13 Jan. 1911, 14, 9)

SOLOMON, Miss Julia, of Boston, Mass., is visiting her sister, Mrs. Harry Vosberg, at Dorval for the summer (6 Aug. 1909, 12, 34)

SOLOMON, Miss Ray, has returned from Chateauguay, where she was the guest of Miss Sarah Rosenberg (16 July 1909, 12, 31)

SOLOMON, Miss Sadie, is spending her vacation in Ste. Agathe des Monts (5 Aug. 1910, 13, 38)

SOLOMON, Mr. and Mrs. H. and family, Mr. and Mrs. A.H. Jackson and family, Mr. and Mrs. H. Friedman and family and Mr. and Mrs. Alexander are spending the summer at Woodlands (23 July 1909, 12, 32)

SOLOMON, Mr., returned home to Russia after visiting his sons, H. Steinman, Rivard St., and I. Steinman, Duluth St. (21 Feb. 1913, 16, 11)

SOLOMON, Mrs. A., accompanied by her father, M. Blumenthal, is visiting her sister, Mrs. I. Josephson, in Malone N.Y. (5 Aug. 1910, 13, 38)

SOLOMON, S., of Toronto, was a guest at the Corona Hotel (22 Oct. 1909, 12, 45)

SOLOMON, W.B., of Boston, was registered at the Windsor Hotel (11 March 1910, 13, 17)

SOLOMONS, Mrs. Louis, hosted a formal dance on Wed. at Patton's Hall in honor of her sister, Miss Adela McKinley. Among those present were:- H. McKinley, Louis Solomons and the Misses R. and L. Feldman, B. and E. Issen, L. Jacobson, Pauline McKinley, and E. and D. Rothschild (20 Feb. 1914, 17, 8)

SOLVEY, Miss Dora, collected $3.00 at the Lazarus-Gordon wedding for the Hebrew Consumptive Aid Association (8 July 1910, 13, 34)

SOMER, Mrs. A., is ill (26 March 1909, 12, 15)

SOMMER, A., is in New York (26 Feb. 1909, 12, 11)

SOMMER, Mr. and Mrs. B. and family are summering at Fabyan House, Lake Champlain (5 Sept. 1913, 16, 39)

SOMMER, Mrs. A., is at Ste. Agathe (11 June 1909, 12, 26)

SOSKIN, M., one of the original founders and secretary of the YMHA, leaves shortly to take up permanent residence in Prince Rupert, B.C. He was presented with a silver cigarette case at a reception chaired by Samuel Bloomfield. Speeches were made by W.C. Munn, W. Sweedler, H. Bloomfield and Dr. S. Steine (22 April 1910, 13, 23)

SOURKES, H.L., 435 St. Urbain St., sec. of the Montreal Hebrew Shelter and Home for the Aged, asks the public to notify him of any aged or homeless persons deserving the consideration of the Society. The applications of Mrs. R. Cohen and D. Dascal for admission to the Home for the Aged were approved at a special meeting (19 May 1911, 14, 27)

SOURKES, Harry, I. Rothbart, I. Bald and S.B. Gordon took part in a debate "Resolved, That capital punishment be abolished" at a YMHA meeting Tues. night (9 Dec. 1910, 14, 4)

SPERBER, Marcus, chaired a meeting last Sun. for the purpose of making final arrangements for the establishment of the YMHA. "About twenty-five young men handed in their names for enrollment, and as the membership fee is only fifty cents a month, the organization, it is expected, will be a large one. Until the constitution is drawn up and accepted, it is intended to hold weekly meeting, after which the meeting will be monthly." Provisional officers are:- Harry Bloomfield, hon. pres.; Maxwell Sperber, pres.; D. Shapiro, 1st vice-pres.; W. Sweedler, 2nd vice-pres.; and J. Albert, treas. (19 March 1909, 12, 14)

SPERBER, Marcus M., was re-elected president of the Independent Citizens League at the annual meeting held Sun. aft., Dec. 10, 1911 in the Labor Temple. Other officers elected were:- H. Steinman, 1st vice-pres.; Samuel Cliff, 2nd vice-pres.; Morris Lipshitz, fin. sec.; M. Silverman, rec. sec.; S. Moscovitch, treas.; Messrs. Benihasker and Wexler, board of trustees. "The society has been instrumental in making some two thousand Jews as citizens, was always in the fore in looking after Jewish immigrants who, through some technicality, were debarred from landing, in looking after the cases of Jews who were assaulted on the streets and last, but certainly not least in seeing that Jewish names on voters lists should not be effaced." (15 Dec. 1911, 15, 5)

SPERBER, Marcus, was elected president of the YMHA last Sun. Other officers elected were:- P. Kahn, 1st vice-pres.; W.W. Sweedler, 2nd vice-pres.; Morris Goldberg, sec.; J. Albert, treas.; A. Albert, S. Rawson, W. Singer, M. Soskin and D. Spector, advisory board (23 April 1913, 12, 19)

SPERBER, Miss Sarah, won an exhibition open to second year students at McGill University (8 Nov. 1912, 15, 48)

SPEYER, B.M., 140 Nelson St., Ottawa, sends New Year greetings (11 Sept. 1912, 15, 40)

SPEYER, B.M., 625 St. Urbain St. (temporarily of 28-30 Wellington St. W., Toronto), wishes his friends and relatives a happy New Year (10 Oct. 1913, 16, 44)

SPEYER, B.M., of Montreal, will be in Ottawa on business during the Passover week and will be the guest of Mr. and Mrs. K. Cohen, Nelson St. (18 April 1913, 16, 19)

SPEYER, B.M., of Ottawa, will be in Montreal for the wedding of Miss Fanny Hoichberg and Sam Cohen, of Osgoode Station (9 Aug. 1912, 15, 35)

SPEYER, B.M., St. Urbain St., left for Toronto, where he will be the temporary sales manager for Heillig, Joseph & Co., 28-30 Wellington St., W. (19 Sept. 1913, 16, 41)

SPEYER, B.M., St. Urbain St., returned from a week at Ste. Agathe (25 July 1913, 16, 33)

SPIGLER, Miss Dorothy, of Philadelphia, is the guest of the Friedman and Weisman families for the better part of the summer (4 July 1913, 16, 30)

SPITZER, Dr. V. and wife stayed at the Windsor Hotel (27 Aug. 1909, 12, 37)

STAN, Miss Nancy, of New York, is visiting her cousin, Dr. E. Crystal, Sherbrooke St. E. (1 Nov. 1912, 15, 47)

STAPLES, Miss, of Fredericton, N.B., was the guest of the Misses Harris, Tupper St., Westmount (16 April 1909, 12, 18)

STARK, R., chaired the Montreal B'nai Zion Kadimah meeting on Sun. evening, May 16, 1909. Mr. Schneier lectured on "Modern Ideas and Nationalism" (21 May 1909, 12, 23)

STARK, R., has returned from a business trip to the Porcupine (11 March 1910, 13, 17)

STARK, R.S., was elected president of the B'nai u' B'noth Zion Kadimah Society last Sun aft. in the Baron de Hirsch Institute. Other officers elected were:- H. Lang and Miss J. Gross, vice-pres.; Robert A. Darwin, treas.; S. Gorosh, fin. sec.; Miss Ida F. Apotheker, corr. and rec. sec.; Miss R. Echenberg, of Sherbrooke, Que., the Misses M. Tritt, and B. Gross, Messrs. M. Rubenstein, E. Mauer, M. Gelbman, M. Gorofe and Charles Waghelstein, members of the council (13 May 1910, 13, 26)

STEIN, Dr. S.F., 26 St. Famille St., has been appointed physician to the Aberdeen Lodge, IOSB (8 Oct. 1909, 12, 43)

STEIN, Dr. Seymour F., has left on an extended trip to the southern U.S. (31 March 1911, 14, 20)

STEIN, Dr. Seymour F., medical superintendent of the Western Hospital, has resigned his position. He will spend a month or six weeks at his home in Kemptville, Ont., before opening an office in the city (15 Jan. 1909, 12, 5)

STEIN, Dr. Seymour F., St. Famille St., has returned to town (12 May 1911, 14, 26)

STEIN, Dr. Seymour F., who several weeks ago resigned his position as medical superintendent at the Western Hospital, is private practice. His office is at 88 Ste. Famille St., the residence of Mr. and Mrs. D. Stein (14 May 1909, 12, 22)

STEIN, Dr. Seymour, has gone south for a few weeks (27 March 1914, 17, 13)

STEIN, Dr. Seymour T., is attending the Congress of North American Surgeons (15 Nov. 1912, 15, 49)

STEIN, Master J., of Cleveland, is visiting his sister, Mrs. George Goldstein (24 June 1910, 13, 32)

STEIN, Master Morrie and Miss Helen Stein, who were visiting their grandparents, Mr. and Mrs. Kutner, have returned to New York (15 Sept. 1909, 12, 40)

STEIN, Master Reginald, of Cleveland, Ohio, was the guest of his sister, Mrs. George Goldstein at Beaurepaire for a few days (30 June 1911, 14, 33)

STEIN, Miss Cyrille, was in Toronto, the guest of

Mr. and Mrs. William Goldstein, en route to her home in Cleveland. In Montreal, Miss Stein was the guest of her sister, Mrs. George E. Goldstein, Elgin Ave., Westmount (9 April 1909, 12, 17)

STEIN, Miss E., of Cleveland, is the guest of her sister, Mrs. G.E. Goldstein (13 Dec. 1912, 16, 1)

STEIN, Miss Elsie, has returned home to Cleveland after a visit with her sister, Mrs. George Goldstein (9 Dec. 1910, 14, 4)

STEIN, Miss Elsie, of Cleveland, is visiting her sister, Mrs. George Goldstein, Elgin Ave., Westmount (23 Sept. 1910, 13, 45)

STEIN, Mr. and Mrs. H. (née Miss Ida Kaplan), Yarmouth, N.S., are honeymooning in Boston. They will spend the Holy Days, the guests of their sister, Mrs. T.H. Hoffman, 198 St. Joseph Blvd. (20 Sept. 1912, 15, 41)

STEIN, Mr. and Mrs. Sydney and Mrs. Felix Lewis, Sherbrooke St. W. (1 Dec. 1911, 15, 3)

STEIN, Mrs. I., of Cleveland, who spent the winter with her daughter, Mrs. G. Goldstein, Elgin Ave., has returned home (18 March 1910, 13, 18)

STEIN, Mrs. M., of New York, is visiting Mr. and Mrs. A. Shapiro, 1236 St. Urbain St. (19 May 1911, 14, 27)

STEIN, Mrs., of Cleveland, is visiting her daughter, Mrs. George Goldstein, Elgin Ave., Westmount (5 Nov. 1909, 12, 47)

STEIN, Mrs., of Cleveland, is visiting her daughter, Mrs. Leo E. Goldstein at Beaconsfield (30 Aug. 1912, 15, 38)

STEIN, Mrs. S. and daughter Helen, have returned home after visiting Mrs. Stein's sister, Mrs. M.J. Vineberg (18 Aug. 1911, 14, 40)

STEIN, Mrs. Sydney, of New York, is visiting her parents, Mr. and Mrs. H. Simon, Westmount (5 Feb. 1909, 12, 8)

STEIN, Mrs. Sydney, of New York, is visiting her parents, Mr. and Mrs. I. Simon, Westmount (22 Jan. 1909, 12, 6)

STEINBERG, J. and Philip Popliger sailed on July 14, 1910 aboard the S.S. Empress of Ireland for England, France, Austria, Germany, Italy and Romania (22 July 1910, 13, 36)

STEINBERG, J. and sister, Miss Rose Steinberg, are spending two weeks in Portland, Old Orchard Beach, Me., and Boston (13 Aug. 1909, 12, 35)

STEINBERG, Joseph, president of the Beth David, better known as the Romanian Synagogue, will preside at the mortgage burning ceremony. "The Beth David purchased their synagogue from the Shearith Israel Congregation, when the latter erected their present magnificent structure. The Beth David synagogue is located in Chenneville street, and was built nearly a century ago." Past presidents of Beth David since the synagogue was purchased are:- David Blumer, I. Litner, B. Lerner, P. Popliger, B. Rosenberg, Meyer Selicovitch, and I. Singer and M. Yeruslawitz (29 Dec. 1911, 15, 7)

STEINBERG, Miss Sarah, president of the Jewish Girls' Sewing Circle, gave a short address at the Chanukah festival held at the home of Miss Sylvia Cohen. Other speakers were:- the Misses Sarah Feen, Jennie Greenspoon and Ruth Miller (2 Jan. 1914, 17, 4)

STEINBERG, Mr. and Mrs. J., are at Ste. Agathe for the summer (12 July 1912, 15, 31)

STEINDLER, J., of New York, stayed at the Windsor Hotel (4 June 1909, 12, 25)

STEINDLER, J., of New York, stayed at the Windsor Hotel (25 Oct. 1912, 15, 46)

STEINE, M.B., 819 University St., is sailing for Europe on Nov. 29, 1912 aboard the S.S. Empress of Ireland (29 Nov. 1912, 15, 51)

STEINE, M.B., has gone on a business trip to Europe (6 Jan. 1911, 14, 8)

STEINE, M.B., has returned from Europe (25 Feb. 1910, 13, 15)

STEINE, M.B., was elected president of the Montreal Hebrew Sheltering Home last Sun. evening. J. Steinberg, president, chaired the meeting. Other officers elected were:- L. Holstein, 1st vice-pres.; Charles Fisher, 2nd vice-pres.; I. Goldberg, treas.; Henry Bye, cor.-sec.; J. Goldman, rec. sec.; M. Vineberg, H. Vineberg, D. Sperber, M. Steinhouse, J. Dovia, J. Diamond, M. Joseph, M. Hoffman, J. Harris, M. Feldstein, I. Sourkes, H. Sourkes, M. Saltzman, H. Bessner, S.G. Franks, and Mesdames Asner, Rosen, Greenberg, Bronstein, Fineberg, M. Feldstein, A. Sigmund, I. Goldberg, H. Goldman and Miss F. Gold (18 Nov. 1910, 14, 1)

STEINE, Mr. and Mrs. M.B., 819 University St., were "at home" Sun. Nov. 24, 1912 in honor of the Bar Mitzvah of their son, Ben Zion Steine. Mrs. Al. Lesser assisted in receiving and the Misses L. Lesser, S. Lesser, B. Goldstein, A. Aronson, B. Pierce and Rutenberg assisted in serving. Speeches were made by Clarence I. de Sola, J. Fineberg, M.B. Steine and Mrs. J. Manolson (29 Nov. 1912, 15, 51)

STEINE, Mr. and Mrs. M.B., 819 University St., wish their friends a happy New Year (1 Oct. 1913, 16, 42-43)

STEINHOUSE, B., of Montreal, is in Portland, Me., visiting his sister, Mrs. J. Rosen, for a fortnight (16 Aug. 1912, 15, 36)

STEINHOUSE, Miss Annie, gave a surprise party in honor of Miss Rose Bernstein, at 3B Drolet St., Sun. evening, Dec. 22, 1912. Miss Annie Steinhouse and Joe Steinhouse received the guests. Sam Cohen gave the toast. Assisting at the table were:- Harry Goldstein, Joe Bernstein, Charles Steinhouse and Miss Bertha Dubin (27 Dec. 1912, 16, 3)

STEINMAN, H., 1st vice-pres. of the Independent Citizens' League of Montreal, has been appointed Commissioner of the Superior Court for Montreal and legal commissioner of the League. "Mr. Steinman is prepared to make out citizen's papers for any one who has been in this country three or more years." (12 May 1911, 14, 26)

STEINSBURG, Miss Bessie, of Cleveland, was the guest at a theatre party given by Misses Eva Steinsburg and Rose Cohen at the Princess, Wed. evening, Jan. 10, 1912 (19 Jan. 1912, 15, 10)

STERN, Dr. Joseph, has moved from 102 St. Lawrence Blvd. to 304 St. Catherine W. (14 May 1909, 12, 22)

STERN, Dr. Joseph, spent the holidays in Atlantic City (21 April 1911, 14, 23)

STERN, Dr. Seymour, Miss Hannah Rosenberg, B.A. and Samuel Ostrofsky were guests of Mr. and Mrs. Tannenbaum at Iberville on the weekend (8 July 1910, 13, 34)

STERN, I., of Pittsburg, N.Y., attended the Lazarus-Claman wedding in Montreal (16 June 1911, 14, 31)

STERN, J.B., of Winnipeg, was a guest at the Stanley Hotel (25 June 1909, 12, 28)

STERN, Miss Addie, of Cleveland, who was the guest of Mrs. Maxwell Goldstein for the past few months has returned home (5 March 1909, 12, 12)

STERN, Miss Addie, was the guest of Mr. and Mrs. I. Freedman at Lakeside (30 June 1911, 14, 33)

STERN, Miss, of Cleveland, is the guest of Mr. and Mrs. M. Goldstein, St. Matthew St. (12 May 1911, 14, 26)

STERN, Mr. and Mrs. Charles, of Toronto, are guests of their daughter, Mrs. W. Goldstein, Pointe Claire (22 July 1910, 13, 36)

STERN, Mr. and Mrs. Charles, returned home to Toronto by boat after visiting their daughter, Mrs. M. Goldstein (26 Aug. 1910, 13, 41)

STERN, Mr. and Mrs. L., of New York, were guests at the Queen's Hotel (7 Oct. 1910, 13, 47)

STERN, Mr. and Mrs. Sydney, are spending a few weeks in Montreal with Mrs. Stern's parents, Mr. and Mrs. H. Simon (17 Dec. 1909, 13, 5)

STERN, Mr., of Toronto, is visiting his daughter, Mrs. Maxwell Goldstein, 82 St. Matthew St. (7 May 1909, 12, 21)

STERN, Mrs. Charles, has gone to New York and Atlantic City (29 Dec. 1911, 15, 7)

STERN, Mrs. Charles, has returned home from a visit to Toronto (25 July 1913, 16, 33)

STERN, Mrs. Sydney, is a member of the Temple Emanuel Sisterhood purchasing committee (13 Dec. 1912, 16, 1)

STERN, Mrs. Sydney, of New York, is visiting her parents, Mr. and Mrs. H. Simon, Western Ave. (10 Sept. 1909, 12, 39)

STERN, Sir Edward and Lady, were in Montreal at the Place Viger Hotel en route to the West. Lyon Cohen, J.A. Jacobs, S.W. Jacobs, K.C., and Harris Vineberg called on Sir Edward to discuss Jewish colonization matters. Max Heppner has been placed at his disposal (2 Sept. 1910, 13, 42)

STERN, Sir Edward D. and Lady Stern, have returned to Montreal from the coast. Sir Edward is a major in the British Yeomanry and has twenty years service. On Sun. they visited the Baron de Hirsch Institute where they met the president and the board (25 Oct. 1910, 13, 50)

STERNBERG, Mr. and Mrs. Wolff, of Toronto, stayed at the Corona Hotel for a few days (18 July 1913, 16, 32)

STERNBERG, Mr. and Mrs. Woolf, of Toronto, spent a few days in Montreal, the guests of Mrs. H. Wilkinson, McGill College Ave. (19 Feb. 1909, 12, 10)

STERNE, Mr. and Mrs. M.B. and family and Mr. and Mrs. Louis Holstein and family are at Chateauguay for the summer (8 July 1910, 13, 34)

STONE, Barnett, and his niece, Miss Smith, both of Toronto, arrived in Montreal by boat via Quebec City (28 July 1911, 14, 37)

STONE, Miss Annie, of Wilkesbarre, Pa., is the guest of Miss Katie Stone, 153 Laval Ave. (1 Oct. 1909, 12, 42)

STONE, Miss Kate, has left to take up her residence with her people in Wilkesbarre, Pa. (29 Sept. 1911, 14, 46)

STONE, Miss Katie, is visiting relatives and friends in Montreal (19 Aug. 1910, 13, 40)

STONE, Miss Katie, of Carbondale, Pa., leaves Tues. for Boston prior to returning home (28 Jan. 1910, 13, 11)

STONE, Miss Katie, who was away in Carbondale, Pa., for the past six months, has returned to Montreal and is staying with her sister, Mrs. Levay, Laval Ave. (20 Aug. 1909, 12, 36)

STONE, Mr. and Mrs. Samuel, of Wilkes Barre, Pa., who were guests of Mrs. Levay, have returned home (20 Aug. 1909, 12, 36)

STRAUSS, H., of London, England, who is on a business trip, is staying at the Windsor Hotel (27 May 1910, 13, 28)

STRAUSS, Miss, of Toronto, was in Montreal on holiday (5 Aug. 1910, 13, 38)

STRAUSS, Mr. and Mrs. J., of London, Eng., stayed at the Windsor Hotel (26 April 1912, 15, 24)

STRAUSS, Mr. and Mrs., were in Montreal, en route for Toronto (11 Nov. 1910, 13, 52)

STRAUSS, Mr. and Mrs., were in Montreal the past week (10 Feb. 1911, 14, 13)

STUART, Miss, of Boston, Mass., is visiting her sister, Mrs. Joseph Stuart for a few weeks (27 Feb. 1914, 17, 9)

STUTCHINSKY, Samuel, of Gananoque, Ont., was in Montreal on business for a few days (26 Jan. 1912, 15, 11)

SUGARMAN, Miss Esther, of Ottawa, who was in Montreal for the Kalin-Goldblatt wedding, is in Quebec City, the guest of her sister, Mrs. L. Silverman, 64 Desfosses St. (8 Nov. 1912, 15, 48)

SUGARMAN, Miss Esther, returned home to Ottawa after visiting her sister, Mrs. C. Silverman, in Quebec City (31 Jan. 1913, 16, 8)

SUGARMAN, Mr. and Mrs. A.J. and family are summering at Kirk's Ferry, Que. (18 July 1913, 16, 32)

SUGARMAN, William, of Edmonton, was in Montreal on business (16 Sept. 1910, 13, 44)

SUPERIOR, J.H., has recently opened an optical shop at 27 St. Catherine St. W. (20 Aug. 1909, 12, 36)

SUPERIOR, Mr. and Mrs. M.S., 1664 Park Ave., wish their friends and relatives a happy New Year (1 Oct. 1913, 16, 42-43)

SYMONSKI, Mrs. D. and family, of Troy, N.Y., are guests of Mr. and Mrs. Max Harris, Dorchester St. W. (17 Jan. 1913, 16, 6)

TAILLEFER, Miss Dora, of Sault Ste. Marie, Ont., is in Montreal for a month visiting friends (28 Jan. 1910, 13, 11)

"A Happy New Year to All"
Why not look fashionable for the HIGH FESTIVALS?

We have the latest novelties of Parisian and American models. We cater to the exclusive set of Montreal and know we can please you. Our Ten Dollar Dress or Opera Coat will make you look smart. Call or Phone us and be convinced.

Madames Taitleman and Givner
... HIGH-CLASS DRESSMAKING ...

Phone Uptown 1044 - 141 Stanley St., Montreal

TALPIS, Hilda, A. Schulemson, J. Cohen, Sarah Toronto and Laura Kalmanovitch received scholarships and medals at Aberdeen School (3 March 1911, 14, 16)

TALPIS, J.H., of El Paso, Texas, is visiting his brother, S. Talpis, of Montreal, at his summer residence in Cartierville (15 July 1910, 13, 35)

TALPIS, Mr. and Mrs. S., 34 St. Louis Square, wish their friends a happy New Year (1 Oct. 1913, 16, 42-43)

TALPIS, Mr. and Mrs. S., gave a party at Cartierville in honor of A. Klein, of Montreal and Miss Anna Garmaise, niece of Mrs. Lazarus Cohen. $7.50 was collected for the Talmud Torah, St. Urbain St. (15 July 1910, 13, 35)

TALPIS, Mr. and Mrs. S., have taken up their summer residence in Cartierville (6 May 1910, 13, 25)

TALPIS, Mrs. J.H., of El Paso, Texas, is the guest of Mr. and Mrs. I. Talpis, St. Louis Square (11 July 1913, 16, 31)

TANNEBAUM, Mr. and Mrs. M., and Miss Rae Tannebaum have returned from New York (26 Feb. 1909, 12, 11)

TANNENBAUM, David, of Mt. Sinai Hospital, New York, is spending the summer with his parents at Iberville, Que. (8 July 1910, 13, 34)

TANNENBAUM, Dr. and Mrs. D., have left for Europe (14 July 1911, 14, 35)

TANNENBAUM, Dr. David, has been appointed House Surgeon at Mount Sinai Hospital, New York. He will assume his duties July 1, 1909 (25 June 1909, 12, 28)

TANNENBAUM, Dr. David, has returned to New York after spending two weeks with his parents (15 Oct. 1909, 12, 44)

TANNENBAUM, Isidore, was in Longueuil for the weekend (18 Aug. 1911, 14, 40)

TANNENBAUM, Lawrence (first rank honors in economics and political science), J. Levison, H.E. Herschorn and Miss Lena Letomoff graduated from McGill University (12 May 1911, 14, 26)

TANNENBAUM, Lawrence, will take charge of the Baron de Hirsch Sunday School post-graduate course (15 Oct. 1913, 16, 45)

TANNENBAUM, M. and family, Metcalfe St., are at the "Villa Richelieu", Iberville, for the summer (9 July 1909, 12, 30)

TANNENBAUM, Miss Hattie, has gone to New York for several weeks (20 Oct. 1911, 14, 49)

TANNENBAUM, Miss Hattie, is in Portland, Me., for a few weeks (2 Aug. 1912, 15, 34)

TANNENBAUM, Miss, Metcalfe St., has gone to Boston to attend her cousin's wedding (24 Feb. 1911, 14, 15)

TANNENBAUM, Miss Miriam, will visit her aunt, Mrs. D. Israel, in Far Rockaway, Long Island (18 July 1913, 16, 32)

TANNENBAUM, Miss Rae, has gone to New York for two months (12 Nov. 1909, 12, 48)

TANNENBAUM, Miss Ray, is the guest of the Misses Greenberg, Rochester, N.Y. (4 July 1913, 16, 30)

TANNENBAUM, Mr. and Mrs. and family, Metcalfe St., have returned from Iberville where they spent the summer (2 Sept. 1910, 13, 42)

TANNENBAUM, Mr. and Mrs., Metcalfe St., leave for New York and Washington (4 Feb. 1910, 13, 12)

TANNENBAUM, Mrs. I., returned from New York where she attended her mother's funeral this week (25 Oct. 1910, 13, 50)

TAPPERBERG, J., 25 Esplanade Ave., has left for Boston and Revere Beach (7 July 1911, 14, 34)

TASHANSKOFSKY, Mr., has returned to New York after visiting Mrs. Ralph Wetstein (23 Dec. 1910, 14, 6)

TAUB, Sydney, of Toronto, was in Montreal for a few days (2 Sept. 1910, 13, 42)

TEITELBAUM, H., is chairman of the concert in aid of a local family in distress, to be held in the Baron de Hirsch Institute, Sun. evening, March 6, 1910 at 7.30 p.m. (4 March 1910, 13, 16)

TEITELBAUM, Max, is leaving next week for Saskatoon (26 April 1912, 15, 24)

TEITLEBAUM, Max, has returned from Saskatchewan where he has been fortunate in making good real estate investments (26 Jan. 1912, 15, 11)

TEPLITZKY, Miss Rose, returned from her vacation in New York (15 Oct. 1913, 16, 45)

TEPLITZKY, Mr. and Mrs. L. and their daughter, Rose Teplitzky, accompanied by Miss Sarah de la Penha, left for a two weeks' trip to New York, last Tues. (25 June 1909, 12, 28)

THALER, A. and Miss Grace Thaler, of Brooklyn, N.Y., are guests of Mr. and Mrs. B. Rigler (5 Dec. 1913, 16, 52)

THAW, Master Sonny, left for Quebec City, where he is the guest of his aunt, Mrs. Charles Schiller, of Indian Lorette (25 July 1913, 16, 33)

TIPOGRAPH, Maurice, is in Ste. Agathe on holiday (5 Aug. 1910, 13, 38)

TIPOGRAPH, Mr. and Mrs. Carl M., are in Montreal on their honeymoon and are staying with their brother on St. Catherine St. (7 March 1913, 16, 13)

TOLZES, A.W., is authorized to collect donations for the Montreal Hebrew Sheltering Home. Some of the contributors are:- Mrs. A. Kirschberg in memory of her late daughter, Bella; Max Stein; and D. Sperber (29 July 1910, 13, 37)

TOLZESS, A.W., of Ottawa, is in Montreal (3 March 1911, 14, 16)

TOLZESS, W.H., who is representing Rabbi Rhemes Yeshibah, passed through Montreal en route to his home in Ottawa (5 May 1911, 14, 25)

TOPP, I., of Meaford, Ont., is in Montreal on a business trip (6 Aug. 1909, 12, 34)

TRITT, Jr., Saul, was elected president of the Young Men's Zionist and Literary Society at the semi-annual meeting on Sun. Sept. 17, 1911. Other officers elected were:- Lyon Bercovitch, vice-pres.; Max Bernfeld, corr. sec.; Henry Nathanson, fin. sec.; William Bernfeld, Samuel Hyams, J.C. Zacks and Maxwell Bercusson, council (29 Sept. 1911, 14, 46)

TRITT, Mesdames S.G., M. Greenberg, I. Lande, E.J. Hayes, R. Heillig and A.L. Gittleson were the committee in charge of organizing a benefit for the sick and poor of Ste. Agathe (15 Sept. 1911, 14, 44)

TRITT, Miss Jennie, 11 Ernest St., gave a linen shower on April 6, 1913, in honor of the approaching marriage of Miss Bella Gross. Miss Minnie Shapiro gave a musical recitation. Mrs. Percy Cohen and Miss Jennie Greenspon assisted at the table (11 April 1913, 16, 18)

TRITT, Mrs. J., has gone to Winnipeg for a few weeks to visit her son (4 Nov. 1910, 13, 51)

TUCKER, M.H., of Kansas City, Kansas, is visiting his uncle and aunt, Mr. and Mrs. J. Merson, 656 City Hall Ave. (14 July 1911, 14, 35)

TUCKER, Miss Etta, of Kansas City, Kan., is the guest of her sister, Mrs. Joseph Merson, City Hall Ave. (10 Jan. 1913, 16, 5)

TURNER, Mr. and Mrs. J.B., St. Lawrence Blvd., gave an engagement party on Sun. evening, March 23, 1913, in honor of the forthcoming marriage of their daughter, Miss Ray Turner to Avigdor Goldberg, of London, England. Paul Katz, J.P., was toastmaster. Speeches were made by:- David Dainow, Jack Harris, M. Rubenstein, Alexander Schachter, J.B. Turner, Rabbi Simon Glazer and the Misses Mary Berson and Fanny Bernstein (28 March 1913, 16, 16)

TURNER, Mrs., of Toronto, is spending the holidays with her parents, Mr. and Mrs. Jacobs, Dorchester St. W. (2 April 1909, 12, 17)

UDITSKY, Max, a Montreal butcher, laid a charge of criminal libel and a suit for $1,000. damages against Rabbi Hirsch Cohen on Wed. "Early in June, Rabbis Hirsch Cohen, Blitz and Garber issued a circular instructing Jewish people to purchase of those butchers who only sold meet that had been passed by the Schochetim." Mr. Uditsky complained he had lost business as a result of the circular. Joseph Cohen and S.W. Jacobs, K.C., represented Rabbi Cohen. The case was carried over for trial in Sept. (20 June 1913, 16, 28)

UDOW, J. and his children, Gertrude and David Udow, have returned home to Winnipeg. They were guests of Mesdames C. Pierce and H. Wolsey (8 Sept. 1911, 14, 43)

UHRY, Paul, 68 Park Ave., has returned home after spending a week's holiday in New York (19 Nov. 1909, 13, 1)

USHER, M., St. Louis Square, is in Old Orchard for a few weeks (1 Aug. 1913, 16, 34)

VENDER, S., 411 St. James St., has the lady's gold watch which was raffled last night for the benefit of a distressed family. The winner should contact Mr. Vender (24 Feb. 1911, 14, 15)

VENDER, Samuel, sends New Year greetings (11 Sept. 1912, 15, 40)

VICTOR, J., of La Tuque, Que., is in Montreal on business for two weeks (1 Aug. 1913, 16, 34)

VICTOR, Jack, of La Tuque, Que., returned from Europe aboard the S.S. Mauritania. He visited the major cities and spent much time with his family in Romania (10 April 1914, 17, 15)

VINEBERG, A.H., left Tues. night on a short trip to Cobalt, Ont. (18 June 1909, 12, 27)

VINEBERG, A.H., Montreal barrister, has moved to Porcupine Lake where he intends to practice law and become a mining agent and broker. "Mr. Vineberg's new location is the scene of the recent remarkable gold discoveries in that country, and is situate some two hundred miles north of Cobalt. He is well known to the Jewish community of Montreal, having lived here practically all of his life, and has taken an active interest in the communal, social and professional life of the city." (1 April 1910, 13, 20)

VINEBERG, A.J., was the guest of Mr. and Mrs. M. Glickman at Ste. Agathe on the weekend (25 Aug. 1911, 14, 41)

VINEBERG, A.M. and J. Michaelson have returned from a few weeks in the South (17 Feb. 1911, 14, 14)

VINEBERG, Abe, is in New York on a short stay (6 May 1910, 13, 25)

VINEBERG, Abel, of Toronto, is visiting his parents, Mr. and Mrs. A.M. Vineberg, St. Urbain St., for a week (6 Aug. 1909, 12, 34)

VINEBERG, Abraham, has returned from a short trip to New York (25 June 1909, 12, 28)

VINEBERG, Abraham M. and R.H. Blumenthal are vacationing in Hot Springs, Va. (22 Jan. 1909, 12, 6)

VINEBERG, Dr. and Mrs. H., of New York, were registered at the Windsor Hotel (8 Sept. 1911, 14, 43)

VINEBERG, Harris E., actuary of the Security Life and Annuity Company, Greensboro, N.C., is visiting his parents in Montreal for two weeks (13 Aug. 1909, 12, 35)

VINEBERG, Harris, leaves today for a six weeks' business trip to Europe (21 May 1909, 12, 23)

Come to Our Concerts

Every Sunday between 6 and 9.30 pm.

We serve the highest class Kosher meals in Montreal.

In bright and home-like surroundings

PAY US A VISIT

Commercial Dining Room

(*M. THUNA.—Proprietor*)

318 St. Lawrence Blvd., MONTREAL.

TABLES RESERVED FOR PARTIES.   PHONE MAIN 5156

PORCUPINE GOLD FIELDS

A. H. VINEBERG, B.A., B.C.L.
BARRISTER, MINING AGENT & BROKER

High-grade Gold and Silver properties dealt in. Good engineering and mining staff in connection. Exploration trips conducted.

PORCUPINE LAKE, - - ONT.

VINEBERG, Harris, returned from a short business trip to England last Fri. (2 July 1909, 12, 29)

VINEBERG, J.H., of Halifax, is staying at the St. Lawrence Hall (27 Aug. 1909, 12, 37)

VINEBERG, Jack (Akron), Max Cohen and Miss Lily Jacobs (Detroit), were in Montreal this past week for the unveiling of their mother's headstone, the late Mrs. L. Vineberg. They were guests of the Misses M. and R. Vineberg, Dorchester St. W. (15 Aug. 1913, 16, 36)

VINEBERG, Jack, of Indianapolis, was in Montreal for a few days (16 April 1909, 12, 18)

VINEBERG, Jake, of Minneapolis, and Miss Lily Vineberg, of Detroit, were in Montreal for their mother's funeral. Mrs. Vineberg died July 13, 1912 "...after a long illness borne with much fortitude." (19 July 1912, 15, 32)

VINEBERG, Joseph, is the guest of his sister, Mrs. William Levi in St. John, N.B. (28 July 1911, 14, 37)

VINEBERG, JR., Solomon S. and Benjamin W. Jacobs spent the weekend in Quebec City (9 July 1909, 12, 30)

VINEBERG, L., Mansfield St., has returned from holiday at Tadousac, Que. (25 Aug. 1911, 14, 41)

VINEBERG, Louis and family thank their friends for their condolences on the loss of their mother (26 July 1912, 15, 33)

VINEBERG, Louis, has returned from Detroit, Chicago and Indianapolis where he visited relatives (14 Jan. 1910, 13, 9)

VINEBERG, Louis, has returned from New York (10 Sept. 1909, 12, 39)

VINEBERG, Louis, left on a short visit to Saranac Lake, N.Y. (21 May 1909, 12, 23)

VINEBERG, Louis, of New York, was the guest of his brother, A. Vineberg, Dorchester St. W. (8 Dec. 1911, 15, 4)

VINEBERG, Louis, was in Ste. Agathe at the new sanatorium being erected there (10 June 1910, 13, 30)

VINEBERG, M.A., spent a few days in Toronto this week (26 March 1909, 12, 15)

VINEBERG, M.A., stayed at the St. Denis Hotel while in New York (21 Jan. 1910, 13, 10)

VINEBERG, Miss B., of Ottawa, is visiting her sister, Mrs. A. Pierce, Mt. Pleasant Ave. (13 Jan. 1911, 14, 9)

VINEBERG, Miss Eva, has returned home from a visit to her sister, Mrs. Joseph Shanfield, in New York (17 Feb. 1911, 14, 14)

VINEBERG, Miss Frances, entertained at whist last Sun. evening. Prize-winners were Myer Guinsberg and Miss Nellie Vineberg (30 Dec. 1910, 14, 7)

VINEBERG, Miss Frances, has left for New York (13 Jan. 1911, 14, 9)

VINEBERG, Miss Frances, has returned from a three weeks' holiday in Winchester, Chesterville and Morrisburg, Ont. (20 Aug. 1909, 12, 36)

VINEBERG, Miss Francis, who has been in New York for sometime, is visiting her parents for a few weeks (29 Sept. 1911, 14, 46)

VINEBERG, Miss Gertrude, has returned from Williamsburg where she was the guest of Miss Vaughan Casselman (20 Aug. 1909, 12, 36)

VINEBERG, Miss Lilly, of Detroit, spent a few days in Montreal visiting her parents (8 Jan. 1909, 12, 4)

VINEBERG, Miss Lily, of Detroit, is visiting her parents, Mr. and Mrs. L. Vineberg, Mansfield St. (9 Sept. 1910, 13, 43)

VINEBERG, Miss Lily, of Detroit, Mich., was in Montreal visiting her parents (5 Jan. 1912, 15, 8)

VINEBERG, Miss Lily, of Detroit, returned home last Tues. (16 Sept. 1910, 13, 44)

VINEBERG, Miss Lily, of Detroit, spent the past week in Montreal with her parents, Mr. and Mrs. L. Vineberg, Mansfield St. (15 Sept. 1909, 12, 40)

VINEBERG, Miss Lily, of Detroit, visited her parents, Mansfield St. (16 June 1911, 14, 31)

VINEBERG, Miss M., has returned from Ste. Agathe des Monts (25 Nov. 1910, 14, 2)

VINEBERG, Miss Malca, has returned from a short visit to Sherbrooke (13 Aug. 1909, 12, 35)

VINEBERG, Miss Malca, has returned from the Thousand Islands (16 Aug. 1912, 15, 36)

VINEBERG, Miss Malca, of Montreal, is visiting Mrs. J. Rosenbloom, Portland Ave. (6 Aug. 1909, 12, 34)

VINEBERG, Miss Mary, has returned from Lake Placid, N.Y. (14 July 1911, 14, 35)

VINEBERG, Miss Mary, has returned home after an extended visit away (9 April 1909, 12, 17)

VINEBERG, Miss Mary, won the ladies' underwear which was raffled last Tues. for the benefit of the Ladies' Hebrew Benevolent Society. Miss Lederer thanks all the ladies who sold tickets (9 June 1911, 14, 30)

VINEBERG, Miss Nellie, of Ottawa, is visiting her sister, Mrs. Ascher Pierce, Mt. Pleasant Ave. (12 Nov. 1909, 12, 48)

VINEBERG, Miss Rose, has gone to visit her brother in Minneapolis and will stop over in Detroit to visit her aunt (23 Dec. 1910, 14, 6)

VINEBERG, Miss Rose, has returned from Peak's Island, Me. (6 Aug. 1909, 12, 34)

VINEBERG, Miss Rose, Mansfield St., has returned from Detroit and Indianapolis (3 March 1911, 14, 16)

VINEBERG, Miss Rose, was at Tadousac House, Little Metis for a few weeks (4 Aug. 1911, 14, 38)

VINEBERG, Miss Sadie and Joseph Vineberg are spending two weeks in Mattawa and Temiscaming (29 July 1910, 13, 37)

VINEBERG, Miss Sadie, chaired the Montreal Daughters of Zion meeting Sun. aft., Feb. 7, 1909 in the Baron de Hirsch Institute. Mrs. Felix Harris, formerly of Manchester, Eng., now of Montreal, gave an address "Reminiscences of Congresses I Have Attended". Miss Rae Heillig read an article "The Cultural Side of Palestine". Miss Rose Harris, 633 City Hall Ave., is selling tickets to the society's annual Purim dance to be held Mon. evening, March 8, 1909 in Auditorium Hall, 17 Berthelet St. (12 Feb. 1909, 12, 9)

VINEBERG, Miss Sadie, gave a linen shower in honor of her cousin, Miss Gertie Rubin (18 June 1909, 12, 27)

VINEBERG, Miss Sadie, has returned from New York, where she was visiting Mrs. S. Goldstein (22 Jan. 1909, 12, 6)

VINEBERG, Miss Sadie, has returned home from visiting friends in Chicago and Winnipeg for the past few months (17 Dec. 1909, 13, 5)

VINEBERG, Miss Sadie, is a guest of Mrs. H.I. Kert in Englehart, Ont. (16 July 1909, 12, 31)

VINEBERG, Miss Sadie, who spent the last few weeks at the King Edward Hotel, Englehart, Ont., is visiting her cousin, Mrs. H. Adilman, St. Mary's Place, Winnipeg (20 Aug. 1909, 12, 36)

VINEBERG, Misses Mary and Rose, are visiting their sister, Miss L. Vineberg, of Detroit (20 Sept. 1912, 15, 41)

VINEBERG, Mr. and Miss Rose Vineberg, Mansfield Ave., will vacation in Portland, Maine (16 July 1909, 12, 31)

VINEBERG, Mr. and Mrs. Abraham, Elm Ave., are spending a few weeks in New York (26 Nov. 1909, 13, 2)

VINEBERG, Mr. and Mrs. Albert, are at Old Orchard, Me. (14 July 1911, 14, 35)

VINEBERG, Mr. and Mrs. Albert, have returned from New York (29 Dec. 1911, 15, 7)

VINEBERG, Mr. and Mrs. Harris, 598 Argyle Ave., Westmount, wish their friends a happy New Year (1 Oct. 1913, 16, 42-43)

VINEBERG, Mr. and Mrs. Hyman and family are spending the summer at Mattawa, Ont. (1 July 1910, 13, 33)

VINEBERG, Mr. and Mrs. M., of Montreal, sailed Tues. Nov. 14, 1911 from New York, aboard the S.S. Kronprinzessin Cecilie of the North German Lloyd Line (17 Nov. 1911, 15, 1)

VINEBERG, Mr. and Mrs. M., sail for Europe aboard the Virginian which leaves Montreal today (11 June 1909, 12, 26)

VINEBERG, Mr. and Mrs. M., Tupper St., have returned from a four months' trip abroad (30 Sept.

1910, 13, 46)

VINEBERG, Mr. and Mrs. M.A., have moved to Tupper St., Westmount (29 Oct. 1909, 12, 46)

VINEBERG, Mr. and Mrs. M.A., Tupper St., have gone on a two months' trip abroad (18 Nov. 1910, 14, 1)

VINEBERG, Mr. and Mrs. M.A., Tupper St., sailed for England on June 10, 1911 (16 June 1911, 14, 31)

VINEBERG, Mr. and Mrs. Max, were "at home" last Sun. March 23, 1913, in honor of the Bar Mitzvah of their youngest son, Norman. Assisting at the table were Mrs. Jacob Kellert and the Misses Dora Benjamin and S. Samuels. Assisting the hostess in receiving were Mesdames Harry Bloomstone, William Cohen, George Geller and William Rosenbloom. Young ladies who served the guests were the Misses Gertie and Olive Vineberg, Ruth and Dorothy Kellert, Dina Benjamin and Tillie Glickman (28 March 1913, 16, 16)

VINEBERG, Mr. and Mrs. Moses, have returned from New York and Cleveland (4 March 1910, 13, 16)

VINEBERG, Mr. and Mrs. Moses, sail on the S.S. Laurentic tomorrow morn. from Montreal on a European holiday (18 June 1909, 12, 27)

VINEBERG, Mr. and Mrs. S., were "at home" at the Corona Hotel, Sun. Jan. 17, 1909, to receive their friends' congratulations on their marriage in early Jan. (22 Jan. 1909, 12, 6)

VINEBERG, Mr. and Mrs. S.L. and family, are visiting Mrs. Vineberg, St. Urbain St. (12 Feb. 1909, 12, 9)

VINEBERG, Mrs., 298 Pine Ave. W., has left on a trip to the U.S. and then to Winnipeg to visit her daughter, Mrs. Adilman (31 Dec. 1909, 13, 7)

VINEBERG, Mrs. A., Crescent St., left on vacation for Atlantic City (23 July 1909, 12, 31)

VINEBERG, Mrs. A.B. and Master Joseph Vineberg have left for Old Orchard Beach (23 July 1909, 12, 32)

VINEBERG, Mrs. A.B., and son, Stayner Ave., have left for Old Orchard Beach where they will spend a month (23 July 1909, 12, 32)

VINEBERG, Mrs. A.J. and Mrs. A. Davis, of Detroit, are in New York for several weeks (17 Nov. 1911, 15, 1)

VINEBERG, Mrs. A.M. and family will occupy "Tuxedo" in Pointe Claire for the summer (4 June 1909, 12, 25)

VINEBERG, Mrs. A.M., Elm Ave., spent some time in New York (24 Nov. 1911, 15, 2)

VINEBERG, Mrs. A.M., who has been in the Royal Victoria Hospital for some weeks, is convalescent (5 March 1909, 12, 12)

VINEBERG, Mrs. Abe and Master Joseph Vineberg spent the weekend at Dorval, the guest of Mrs. Alf. Vineberg (26 Aug. 1910, 13, 41)

VINEBERG, Mrs. E., of Toronto, is visiting her daughter, Mrs. L. Blumer (31 March 1911, 14, 20)

VINEBERG, Mrs. Ellis, of Toronto, is visiting her daughter, Mrs. David Bloomer, Sanguinet St. (8 July 1910, 13, 34)

VINEBERG, Mrs. Harry, has returned from a month in Boston (10 March 1911, 14, 17)

VINEBERG, Mrs. Henry and family have returned home from Lake Manitou (27 Aug. 1909, 12, 37)

VINEBERG, Mrs. I., who spent the past two months in New York with her daughter, Mrs. Shanfield, has returned home (1 April 1910, 13, 20)

VINEBERG, Mrs. J., of Cornwall, Ont., was in Montreal during the week (4 Nov. 1910, 13, 51)

VINEBERG, Mrs. J.L., has returned from Sherbrooke where she was the guest of Mr. and Mrs. Joseph Rosenbloom (20 Sept. 1911, 14, 45)

VINEBERG, Mrs. J.L., is in Sherbrooke, Que. (5 Aug. 1910, 13, 38)

VINEBERG, Mrs. M.A., is visiting her sister, Mrs. Heyman, in Cleveland (25 Nov. 1910, 14, 2)

VINEBERG, Mrs. S., 298 Pine Ave. W., has returned from a four months' visit to her daughter, Mrs. H. Adilman, in Winnipeg (29 April 1910, 13, 24)

VINEBERG, Mrs. S., of Brockville, Ont., is the guest of her cousin, Mrs. Hillie Hart, Mt. Stephen Ave. (5 Dec. 1913, 16, 52)

VINEBERG, Mrs. S.L., of Brockville, Ont., was a guest of Mrs. J.A. Jacobs, 1014 Dorchester St. W. (16 Feb. 1912, 15, 14)

VINEBERG, Mrs. Sol and her daughter, Miss Goldie Vineberg, are in Detroit for a few weeks visiting Mrs. Vineberg's parents, Mr. and Mrs. Lauchmann (13 June 1913, 16, 27)

VINEBERG, N., 1518 Mance St., is accepting membership applications from boys wishing to join a newly organized society to help the Hebrew Sheltering Home. A meeting will be held at the home, 16018 Evans St., on Sun. Oct. 26, 1913, at 2.30 p.m. (22 Oct. 1913, 16, 46)

VINEBERG, N., 1518 Mance St., was elected president of the Junior Maccabeans on Sun. Oct. 26, 1913. Other officers elected were:- S. Holdengraber, vice-pres.; J. Freedman, treas.; and J. Ornstein, sec. (14 Nov. 1913, 16, 49)

VINEBERG, Simon, has accepted a challenge for the Marathon Dance issued by S.A. La Salle, of Quebec City for the championship of Canada. The dance is expected to last from four to five hours without stopping. Mr. Vineberg's manager and trainer says that he is in the best of condition (9 April 1909, 12, 17)

VINEBERG, Simon, who is competing in the Marathon Dance to be held in Stanley Hall next Thurs. evening, is in excellent condition and expects to win first prize (30 April 1909, 12, 20)

VINEBERG, Sol. and Joseph Levinson, Jr. are visiting governors to the Montreal General Hospital this week (25 July 1911, 14, 36)

VINEBERG, Sol. and sister, Miss Rose Vineberg are spending a few weeks at Peak's Island, Maine (5 Aug. 1910, 13, 38)

VINEBERG, Sydney, Mansfield St., has gone to Detroit for a few weeks (11 Aug. 1911, 14, 39)

VINEBERG, T., of Sherbrooke, Que., was in Montreal during the week on business (1 April 1910, 13, 20)

VINEBERG, Thomas, of Sherbrooke, Que., was in Montreal for a few days (21 June 1912, 15, 28)

VINER, Dr. H., has left for the Laurentian Mountains for a few weeks (23 July 1909, 12, 32)

VINER, Dr., has gone to the Adirondacks for a holiday (29 July 1910, 13, 37)

VINER, Dr. Norman, has been appointed Clinical Assistant of the Neurological Dept., Montreal General Hospital (16 April 1909, 12, 18)

VINER, Dr. Norman, has returned from his holiday in the Laurentians (13 Aug. 1909, 12, 35)

VINER, Dr. Norman, has suffered face and head injuries in an accident (5 March 1909, 12, 12)

VINER, Dr. Norman, is spending a few weeks at Lake Placid, N.Y. (18 Aug. 1911, 14, 40)

VINER, J., spent the weekend at Chateauguay (3 Sept. 1909, 12, 38)

VINER, J., won the Mackenzie scholarship in third year economics at McGill University (8 Nov. 1912, 15, 48)

VINER, M.B., of the Federal Tobacco Co., donated five dollars to the Montreal Talmud Torah (22 Oct. 1913, 16, 46)

VINER, Miss Annie, is in Ste. Agathe des Monts on vacation (28 July 1911, 14, 37)

VINER, Mrs., daughter Miss Bessie and son Jacob Viner are on holiday at Weir, Que. (28 July 1911, 14, 37)

VOEGLER, Benjamin, of Toronto, was in Montreal the past week (25 Oct. 1910, 13, 50)

VOGEL, H., of Toronto, is a guest at the Albion Hotel (26 Nov. 1909, 13, 2)

VOLMAN, L., was elected president of the Hebrew Sick Benefit Association of Montreal at the annual meeting last week. M. Colle chaired the meeting. Other officers elected were:- A. Falick, 1st vice-pres.; I. Axbrod, 2nd vice-pres.; M. Levitt, treas.; H. Feigelson, fin. sec.; S. Kalmanovitch, rec. sec.; M. Colle, P. Dalerofsky and J. Temmer, trustees (13 Jan. 1911, 14, 9)

VOSBERG, Mr. and Mrs. and sons are spending two weeks in New York and Boston (25 Sept. 1912, 15, 42)

WAGHELSTEIN, C., is president of the Malbish Arumim Society which was founded three years ago to distribute clothing to orphans and other poor children. Other officers are:- S. Cohen, vice-pres., and D. Aronovitch, sec. treas. (12 Nov. 1909, 12, 48)

WALDMAN, J.H., has returned from Porcupine Camp where he spent several weeks looking after his interests (31 March 1911, 14, 20)

WALDMAN, J.H., Mortimer B. Davis, J.A. Jacobs, Moses Vineberg, Ascher Pierce and Mark Workman each contributed $5,000.00 towards the establishment of a tuberculosis sanatorium in Ste. Agathe (8 April 1910, 13, 21)

WALDMAN, J.H., Samuel Hart, Solomon Kellert,

Israel Blumenthal, Albert M. Wener, and Mesdames Mark Workman and Charles L. Friedman became Life Governors of the Montreal General Hospital this year (11 Nov. 1910, 13, 52)

WALDMAN, Mrs., of Ottawa, was in Montreal the past week (27 Oct. 1911, 14, 50)

WALKEM, Mrs. R.T., who is in town visiting Mrs. Henry Joseph, will later go to Halifax (4 June 1909, 12, 25)

WALOVICH, Mr. and Mrs. V., former Montreal residents, have moved back to Montreal from New York (25 Aug. 1911, 14, 41)

WARNECKE, J., of New York, was registered at the Windsor Hotel (18 Feb. 1910, 13, 14)

WARTELL, H.B., of Manchester, N.H., formerly of Kingston, Ont., is in Montreal on business (26 Jan. 1912, 15, 11)

WARTELL, Mr. and Mrs. H.B. and son Lewis, are visiting Mrs. Wartell's sister, Mrs. M. Carsley, Common St. (11 April 1913, 16, 18)

WASSERMAN, Miss, of St. Louis, Mo., is the guest of her sister, Mrs. Berliner, and will spend the summer with her at Strathmore (9 July 1909, 12, 30)

WASSERMAN, Mrs., Miss Wasserman and brother are guests of Mrs. E. Berliner, Dorval, Que. (26 Aug. 1910, 13, 41)

WEBBER, Maurice, St. Urbain St., is in Quebec City for the week (25 Oct. 1912, 15, 46)

WECHSLER, Maurice, St. Urbain St., is in Toronto this week (29 Nov. 1912, 15, 51)

WECHSLER, Miss Augusta, of New York, is the guest of Mr. and Mrs. M. Josefo, Bagg Ave. (17 Jan. 1913, 16, 6)

WECKSLER, Miss Fannie, Winchester St., Toronto, gave a linen shower Tues., in honor of the impending marriage of Miss Byrde Sugarman. Among those present were:- the Misses Rose Ripstein, of Winnipeg, Bettie Strauss, Berthe Streamer, Rhoda Scheuer, Mildred Marks, Bertha King, Etta Vise, Therese Strauss, Adele Strauss, Gertie Wolfe, of New York and Mesdames Julius Lazarus and Benjamin Myers, of Hamilton (26 Nov. 1909, 13, 2)

WEESBERG, Mrs. H., donated fifty dollars to the Montreal Talmud Torah, on the recovery of her son, Joseph, from his recent illness (22 Oct. 1913, 16, 46)

WEIL, J., of Magog, Que., leaves today aboard the S.S. Empress of Britain on a business trip to Germany and France (17 June 1910, 13, 31)

WEIL, Miss Della A., of New York, is the guest of Mrs. Al. Lesser, Prince Arthur Apts. (14 Feb. 1913, 16, 10)

WEINBERG, Miss J. and Miss Eva Levy, of Cleveland, are guests of Mr. and Mrs. David Martin, 894b City Hall Ave. (19 July 1912, 15, 32)

WEINBERG, Mr. and Mrs. I. and Master Marvin Weinberg are at Square Lake Inn, St. Faustin, Que. (1 Aug. 1913, 16, 34)

WEINBERG, Mrs. I. and son will spend the summer at Shawbridge (4 June 1909, 12, 25)

WEINBERG, Mrs. Ike and son have returned from Shawbridge and have gone to Cleveland to visit Mrs. Weinberg's mother, Mrs. Berman (26 Aug. 1910, 13, 41)

WEINBURG, Isaac and son will spend the summer at Shawbridge (11 June 1909, 12, 26)

WEINER, Mr. and Mrs. H.L., are spending a holiday at Montfort (3 Sept. 1909, 12, 38)

WEINER, Mrs. A. and family will spend the summer at St. Jerome, Que. (12 July 1912, 15, 31)

WEINFELD, John J., druggist, wishes his friends and customers a happy New Year (1 Oct. 1913, 16, 42-43)

WEINFELD, Mr. and Mrs. H. and family are at Chateauguay Basin for the summer (25 June 1909, 12, 28)

WEINFELD, Mrs. Harry and Miss Vera Weinfeld, Durocher St., left for Altantic City and New York, where they will be guests of Mr. and Mrs. Sapery (22 Oct. 1913, 16, 46)

WEINFELD, Otto, of Boston, was registered at the Windsor Hotel (25 March 1910, 13, 19)

WEINFIELD, Mr. and Mrs. H. and daughter are spending the summer at Chateauguay (23 July 1909, 12, 32)

WEINFIELD, Mr. and Mrs. H., are at Strathmore, Que., for the summer (27 June 1913, 16, 29)

WEINFIELD, Mr. and Mrs. Harry and family are summering at Lakeside, Que. (16 Aug. 1912, 15, 36)

WEINFIELD, Mr. and Mrs. John J., are in Calgary on vacation (18 April 1913, 16, 19)

WEINFIELD, Mrs. H., has gone to Hartford and New York for a few weeks (6 May 1910, 13, 25)

WEINFIELD, Otto, of Philadelphia, was guest at the St. Lawrence Hall (29 Oct. 1909, 12, 46)

WEINPOHL, O., of Boston, was a guest at the Windsor Hotel (16 July 1909, 12, 31)

WEINPOHL, O., of New York, stayed at the St. Lawrence Hall (2 April 1909, 12, 16)

WEINPOHL, O., of New York, was registered at the Windsor Hotel (26 Aug. 1910, 13, 41)

WEINPOHL, O., of New York, was registered at the Queen's Hotel (10 Feb. 1911, 14, 13)

WEINPOHL, O., of Philadelphia, stayed at the Windsor Hotel (24 Nov. 1911, 15, 2)

WEINPOHL, Otto, of New York, is at the Queen's Hotel (19 Feb. 1909, 12, 10)

WEINPOHL, Otto, of New York, stayed at the Place Viger Hotel (10 Dec. 1909, 13, 4)

WEINPOHL, Otto, of New York, was a guest at the Place Viger Hotel (10 Sept. 1909, 12, 39)

WEINTRAUB, J., of New York, was the guest of Mr. and Mrs. Louis Fraid, Tupper St. (24 May 1912, 15, 25)

WEISS, Adolph, 1128 St. Urbain St., is leaving for Europe on Tues. aboard the S.S. Kaiser Wilhelm (9 Feb. 1912, 15, 13)

WEISS, Adolph and Adolph Aron have gone to Old Orchard, Me., for ten days (18 Aug. 1911, 14, 40)

WEISS, Adolph, has left on an extended business trip to Europe (24 Feb. 1911, 14, 15)

WEISS, Adolph, has returned from a business trip to Europe (8 April 1910, 13, 21)

WEISS, Adolph, leaves shortly on a business trip to England, France, Germany, Austria and Switzerland (4 Feb. 1910, 13, 12)

WEISS, Adolphe, 2161 Mance St., is on a business trip to Europe, France and Germany (27 Feb. 1914, 17, 9)

WEISS, Mrs. A. and family are summering at Hotel Vermont, Ste. Agathe des Monts (4 July 1913, 16, 30)

WEISS, Mrs. A. and son, 1128 St. Urbain St., are at Ste. Agathe for the summer (14 July 1911, 14, 35)

WEISS, Mrs. Adolph and son are spending the summer in New Glasgow, Que. (15 July 1910, 13, 35)

WEISS, Mrs. Adolphe, is visiting her sister, Mrs. Wolf Shankman, of Ottawa for a few weeks (12 Nov. 1909, 12, 48)

WEISS, Mrs. Adolphe, St. Urbain St., will attend her cousin's wedding in Baltimore, Md. (14 Feb. 1913, 16, 10)

WELMERTZ, A., of New York, is in Montreal (15 Oct. 1909, 12, 44)

WENDES, Misses, of New York, are visiting Mrs. D. Hart, Sherbrooke St. W. (19 Jan. 1912, 15, 10)

WENER, Albert, has left for a two months' trip to Europe (19 March 1909, 12, 14)

WENER, Albert, leaves shortly for abroad (23 Sept. 1910, 13, 45)

WENER, D., is holidaying at Sixteen Island Lake (13 Aug. 1909, 12, 35)

WENER, Jack, has gone on a business trip to New York (17 Dec. 1909, 13, 5)

WENER, Jack, Lyon Levinson and Samuel Elkin have returned from Ste. Agathe, Que. (20 Aug. 1909, 12, 36)

WENER, Louis, was a passenger aboard the S.S. Empress of Ireland which sailed from Quebec City for Liverpool, last Fri. (10 Sept. 1909, 12, 39)

WENER, Miss Etta, has gone on holiday to New York (6 May 1910, 13, 25)

STYLE, FIT AND FINISH — ALL GARMENTS GUARANTEED

H. WEISBURGH
Fine Custom Tailoring

117 BLEURY STREET — MONTREAL

WENER, Miss Etta, has returned from Old Orchard Beach (3 Sept. 1909, 12, 38)

WENER, Miss Etta, is spending a few weeks in New York (29 Oct. 1909, 12, 46)

WENER, Miss Fannie, left for Inverness, Cape Breton, to visit her parents (27 March 1914, 17, 13)

WENER, Mr. and Mrs. Albert, are at Manoir Richelieu, Murray Bay (4 Aug. 1911, 14, 38)

WENER, Mr. and Mrs. I., Guy St., have gone on a short trip to New York (1 Dec. 1911, 15, 3)

WENER, Mr. and Mrs. Jacob and daughter were guests at the Windsor Hotel for a few days (8 Dec. 1911, 15, 4)

WENER, Mr. and Mrs. M. and family are in a cottage in Ste. Agathe (6 Aug. 1909, 12, 34)

WENER, Mrs. B., of New York, has returned home (9 Sept. 1910, 13, 43)

WENER, Mrs. H., 85 St. Famille St., is convalescent after her recent illness (27 May 1910, 13, 28)

WENER, Mrs. H. and family are back from Ste. Agathe (3 Sept. 1909, 12, 38)

WENER, Mrs. Harry, accompanied by Mrs. Samuel Hart, has gone to Chicago to visit her parents (17 Dec. 1909, 13, 5)

WENER, Mrs. Sam and family are at Caledonia Springs (25 July 1911, 14, 36)

WENER, Mrs. Samuel and baby daughter have left for Shawbridge, Que. to spend the summer (9 July 1909, 12, 30)

WENER, Mrs. Samuel has left for New York to join her husband who is returning from abroad (8 Oct. 1909, 12, 43)

WENER, Mrs. Z., Sherbrooke St., has returned from Mount Clemens, Mich. (16 July 1909, 12, 31)

WENER, S., returned from England Sun. on the S.S. Empress of Ireland (8 Jan. 1909, 12, 4)

WENER, Samuel, has gone to New York en route for Europe (3 sept. 1909, 12, 38)

WENER, Samuel, has returned from abroad, via New York (1 April 1910, 13, 20)

WENER, Samuel, has returned from Old Orchard Beach (13 Aug. 1909, 12, 35)

WETSTEIN, Louise, daughter of Mrs. R. Wetstein, 61 Church St., is sick with typhoid fever (29 Oct. 1909, 12, 46)

WETSTEIN, Miss Lillian, directed the play "The Dream of Bath Zion" by Leon Zolotkoff, which was performed at Montreal Daughters of Zion annual ball on Tues. evening in Stanley Hall. Miss Ruth Groner played Bath Zion. Other performers were:- J. Aronson, Harry Fineberg, Ralph Groner, Jacob Silverberg and the Misses Miriam Goldenberg, Jennie Greenspon, Jane B. Rost and Bessie Siegler (28 Feb. 1913, 16, 12)

WETSTEIN, Miss Lillian, St. Urbain St., has left on a ten days' holiday in New York (16 April 1909, 12, 18)

WETSTEIN, Miss Louise, 61 Church St., was a guest of Mr. and Mrs. M. Markus, Ste. Anne de Bellevue (4 Aug. 1911, 14, 38)

WEXLER, Mr. and Mrs. and Miss Lillian Wexler, Bagg St., are at Old Orchard for several weeks (25 July 1913, 16, 33)

Special Millinery Announcement

The latest fall millinery creations, of Paris, London and New York, such as

BEAUTIFULLY TRIMMED HATS

Untrimmed Shapes in Plush, Velvet, Velour, Beaver and Felt, also Plumes, Fancy Feathers, Paradise, Ospreys, etc., etc.

Are now being shown by the well known milliner.

ALBERT WEXLER
66 ST. CATHERINE ST. EAST
AND 2016 ST. LAWRENCE BOULEVARD
ALSO BY
ALBERT WEXLER AND COHEN
563 ST. CATHERINE EAST
NEAR AMHERST

The largest, only exclusive millinery departmental store of Montreal.

WEXLER, O., is in New York (15 March 1912, 15, 18)

WHITE, Mrs. W., of Hamilton, Ont., is visiting her mother, Mrs. S. Solomon, 71 Arcade (1 Dec. 1911, 15, 3)

WILKINSON, H.N., is the guest of Mrs. S. Abrahams, Mt. Pleasant Ave. (15 April 1910, 13, 22)

WILKINSON, Mrs. A., is visiting Mrs. Sternberg in Toronto (20 Dec. 1912, 16, 2)

WILKINSON, Mrs. A., returned home to Montreal after two months' away in Ottawa and Toronto (7 March 1913, 16, 13)

WILKINSON, Mrs. H., who travelled abroad for the past two years, has returned to Montreal, en route for New York and Rockaway, L.I., where she will spend the summer with her sister (14 June 1912, 15, 27)

WILKINSON, Mrs. H.M. and Miss Minnie Meyers, of New York, were guests of Mr. and Mrs. B. Goldstein, at Dixie, Que., on Sun. (25 July 1913, 16, 33)

WILKINSON, Mrs. H.M., has returned from three months in New York (11 Oct. 1912, 15, 44)

WILKINSON, Mrs. H.N., has returned from a few months' trip, and has left again for a short stay in New York (25 March 1910, 13, 19)

WILKINSON, Mrs. H.N., has returned to Montreal after spending the winter in the western States and Canada. She will stay at 41 McGill College Ave. She sails for Europe on June 3, 1910, per S.S. Corsican to visit her aunt, Mrs. Leo, in London, Eng. (27 May 1910, 13, 28)

WILLENSKY, S. and A. Harris worked at the raffle held after the Siyum Hatorah at the Montreal Hebrew Sheltering Home last Sun. (30 Sept. 1910, 13, 46)

WILSON, Frank, of the firm of Wilson & Waldman, of Toronto, was in Montreal on business this week (7 June 1912, 15, 26)

WINSTOCK, J., of New York, is registered at the St. Lawrence Hall (22 April 1910, 13, 23)

WINSTOCK, Miss, of Ottawa, is the guest of Mrs. F. Switzman, 174 St. Joseph Blvd. W. (26 Dec. 1913, 17, 3)

WINSTOCK, S., of New York, stayed at the Windsor Hotel for a few days (7 May 1909, 12, 21)

WINTERS, Mrs. and daughter, of Toronto, are visiting her parents, Mr. and Mrs. L.B. McFarlane, Dorchester St. W. (3 Jan. 1913, 16, 4)

WISE, Mrs. Adolph, leaves shortly for New Glasgow for the summer (18 June 1909, 12, 27)

WISEMAN, Dr. M., has resumed practice after his recent indisposition (1 Oct. 1909, 12, 42)

WITTES, S., returned on the S.S. Royal George from a trip abroad (22 Aug. 1913, 16, 37)

WITZLING, Phil, will manage the Regal baseball team again this year (9 May 1913, 16, 22)

WIZNITZER, Miss Anna, of Quebec City, is the guest of the Misses Gross, Elgin St. (16 July 1909, 12, 31)

WOHL, I.P., of Cleveland, Ohio, is staying with his sister, Mrs. A. Lesser, Prince Arthur Apts. (3 Dec. 1909, 13, 3)

WOHL, I.T., of Cleveland, Ohio, is visiting his sister, Mrs. R. Lesser, Prince Arthur Apts. (12 Feb. 1909, 12, 9)

WOHL, Miss Ida, of Cleveland, Ohio, returned home last Thurs. evening after visiting her sister, Mrs. A. Lesser, Prince Arthur Apts. (23 April

1909, 12, 19)

WOHL, Mrs. and Miss Wohl, return to Cleveland Sun. March 19, 1911 after visiting Mrs. C. Lesser (17 March 1911, 14, 18)

WOLF, David, collected $7.51 for the Hebrew Consumptive Aid Association at the Brith Milah of the infant son of Mr. and Mrs. J. Fox, Viger Ave. (15 July 1910, 13, 35)

WOLF, F.W., of Indianapolis, is a guest at the Corona Hotel (13 Aug. 1909, 12, 35)

WOLF, Frank, of Philadelphia, is in Montreal (24 Dec. 1909, 13, 6)

WOLFE, A. Harry, of Ottawa, Ont., leaves early next week to attend a class in gun laying at Petawawa, in connection with the annual C.F.A. training course there. Mr. Wolfe is a member of the 23rd Battery (30 July 1909, 12, 33)

WOLFE, A. Harry, who went to Ottawa for his sister's wedding, has returned to Toronto (17 June 1910, 13, 31)

WOLFE, A., of Murphy Ltd., was in New York on business this week (13 May 1910, 13, 26)

WOLFE, H., read a paper on the "Jewish Outlook in Palestine" at the YMHA Friday Night Talk. The chairman, A.J. Livinson, "...traced the causes which called forth the Young Israel Movement, with its great task of stirring up a revival of Judaism amidst the Jewish youth of America." (24 Jan. 1913, 16, 7)

WOLFE, Max, of Ottawa, is on a business trip to Toronto (1 July 1910, 13, 33)

WOLFE, Max, of Ottawa, was in Montreal for two days on business (11 Feb. 1910, 13, 13)

WOLFE, Miss, of Ottawa, is spending a couple of days with Mrs. J. Rubin, prior to leaving for New York (19 Feb. 1909, 12, 10)

WOLFE, Miss Sadie E., is the guest of Miss Florence Danson, Parkdale, in Toronto (30 Dec. 1910, 14, 7)

WOLFE, Miss Teresa Frances, of Ottawa, will give a recital there under the patronage of the Governor General of Canada and Lady Grey (11 Nov. 1910, 13, 52)

WOLFE, Miss Theresa, of Ottawa, was invited by the Lieutenant-Governor of Ontario to meet the Governor General at Government House, Toronto, on April 7, 1910 (8 April 1910, 13, 21)

WOLFE, Misses Anna and Theresa, of Ottawa, stayed at the Windsor Hotel prior to leaving for New York where they will resume their musical studies (11 Feb. 1910, 13, 13)

WOLFE, Mr. and Mrs. L., who spent the summer at Stoneypoint, Que., left for New York and Boston (1 Oct. 1913, 16, 42-43)

WOLFE, Mr. and Mrs. Max and Miss Wolfe, of Ottawa, returned home on Wed. after attending the Simon-Goldberg wedding. They stayed at the Windsor Hotel (28 May 1909, 12, 24)

WOLFE, Mr. and Mrs. Max and family, and Miss A. Wolfe, of Ottawa, have moved to their summer home, "L'Ete Villa", at Britannia-on-the-Bay (7 May 1909, 12, 21)

WOLFE, Mr. and Mrs. Max and family, of Ottawa, have returned to the city from their summer home and will occupy their new residence on Cathcart St. (15 Oct. 1909, 12, 44)

WOLFE, Mr. and Mrs. Max and family have returned to Ottawa from Britannia-on-the-Bay where they spent the summer (23 Sept. 1910, 13, 45)

WOLFE, Mrs. Max, and her little daughter Dorothy Wolfe, of Ottawa, are in New York visiting relatives (24 March 1911, 14, 19)

WOLFE, Mrs. Max and little Miss Adele Wolfe, of Ottawa, have returned to "Villa L'ete", Britannia-on-the-Bay, after a trip to New York and Brighton Beach, L.I. Mrs. Wolfe was accompanied by Miss Stephanie Guttman. Miss Guttman is the sister of Mme. Melanie Guttman-Rice, the famous teacher and former director of the Conried Metropolitan Opera School, of New York (30 July 1909, 12, 33)

WOLFE, the Misses, of Ottawa, were registered at the Windsor Hotel while in Montreal for the Zionist Convention (26 Nov. 1909, 13, 2)

WOLFF, Mr. and Mrs. Martin, were passengers on the S.S. Laurentic, which arrived from Liverpool on Fri. May 7, 1909 (14 May 1909, 12, 22)

WOLFF, Mrs. and Herbert Wolff, of Ottawa, spent the weekend in Montreal (25 June 1909, 12, 28)

WOLFF, Mrs., of Detroit, is visiting Mr. and Mrs. Maurice Wolff, King George Apts. (1 Aug. 1913, 16, 34)

WOLLENBERG, Mr. and Mrs., of Wollenberg's Market send New Year greetings (11 Sept. 1912, 15, 40)

WOLSEY, Mrs. H., has gone on a visit to Winnipeg (8 Sept. 1911, 14, 43)

WOLSEY, Mrs. Hannah, returned home to Winnipeg after spending a few weeks in Montreal visiting friends (11 April 1913, 16, 18)

WOLSEY, Mrs. S. and her niece, Miss Pierce, are in Atlantic City for a few weeks (14 April 1911, 14, 22)

WOLSLEY, Mrs. B., is spending a few weeks at St. Faustin, Que. (27 Aug. 1909, 12, 37)

WOOLMAN, Mrs. L. and Miss Irene Woolman, Dorchester St. W., are in Toronto for the wedding of Miss Keyfitz (13 June 1913, 16, 27)

WORKMAN, C.A., left Sun. aft. on an extended trip to California (21 Jan. 1910, 13, 10)

WORKMAN, C.A., returned this week from California and the coast (25 Feb. 1910, 13, 15)

WORKMAN, Chas. A., has returned from a six weeks' trip to California (4 March 1910, 13, 16)

WORKMAN, Mark and Miss Nina Workman have returned from a short trip to Boston (4 Nov. 1910, 13, 51)

WORKMAN, Mark and party are expected home tomorrow on the R.M.S. Empress of Britain (14 May 1909, 12, 22)

WORKMAN, Mark, chaired the Sun. Oct. 6, 1912 meeting of the Herzl Dispensary Campaign. Appointed team captains were:- A. Aaron, Paul Katz, A. Levin, Maxwell Lightstone, J. Merson, H. Mills, I. Popliger, Mesdames Adler, Blow, Firestein, Press, Wagner and Miss S. Raphalovitch (11 Oct. 1912, 15, 44)

WORKMAN, Mark, is president of the Herzl Dispensary Campaign which seeks to raise $10,000. The Dispensary opened June 2, 1912 and has treated over two thousand patients. Other campaign officers are:- J.A. Jacobs, 1st vice-pres.; A. Levin, 2nd vice-pres.; A.M. Vineberg, treas.; C.J. Gross, sec.; Z. Fineberg, J. Goldstein, Carl Rosenberg, governors; Maxwell Lightstone and Drs. J.G. Budyk and D. Tannenbaum, organizers (16 Aug. 1912, 15, 36)

WORKMAN, Mark, was elected president of the Mount Sinai Sanatorium. Other officers elected were:- Mortimer B. Davis, 1st vice-pres.; Moses Vineberg, 2nd vice-pres.; Ascher Pierce, 3rd vice-pres.; J.A. Jacobs, hon. treas.; and A.Z. Cohen, hon. sec. (7 March 1913, 16, 13)

WORKMAN, Miss Daisy, was the guest of Miss Blumenthal at Beaurepaire the past week (26 Aug. 1910, 13, 41)

WORKMAN, Miss Gertrude, read a paper on Ibsen's "The Master Builder" at the Temple Emanu-El Sisterhood Literary Circle meeting Sun. Dec. 4, 1910 at 3 p.m. Miss Nina Workman read a paper on "Reciprocity" (9 Dec. 1910, 14, 4)

WORKMAN, Miss, is the guest of her sister, Mrs. Harry Rosenthal, in Ottawa (29 Oct. 1909, 12, 46)

WORKMAN, Miss Nina, is visiting her sister, Mrs. M. Rosenthal, in Ottawa (7 April 1911, 14, 21)

WORKMAN, Miss Ruth, Kensington Ave., returned from a visit to Toronto (10 Oct. 1913, 16, 44)

WORKMAN, Miss Winnifred, has returned to Ottawa after spending a week in Montreal (8 Oct. 1909, 12, 43)

WORKMAN, Mr. and Mrs. C.A., have gone to New York and Atlantic City (20 Oct. 1911, 14, 49)

WORKMAN, Mr. and Mrs. Charles, have returned from Toronto (1 April 1910, 13, 20)

WORKMAN, Mr. and Mrs. M. and family are at their summer cottage "Rideau" for the summer at Rideau, Ont. (9 July 1909, 12, 30)

WORKMAN, Mr. and Mrs. Mark, 585 Sherbrooke St. W., and their daughters the Misses Gertie and Nina Workman, are spending the Passover holidays in New York and Atlantic City (14 April 1911, 14, 22)

WORKMAN, Mr. and Mrs. Mark and family leave shortly for their summer cottage in Portland, Rideau Lakes, Ont. (23 June 1911, 14, 32)

WORKMAN, Mr. and Mrs. Mark, Hutchison St., accompanied by the Misses Workman, leave shortly on a Mediterranean trip. Mr. and Mrs. H. Rosenthal, of Ottawa, are joining them (22 Jan. 1909, 12, 6)

WORKMAN, Mr. and Mrs. Mark, were in Ottawa this week, the guests of Mr. and Mrs. Harry Rosenthal (4 June 1909, 12, 25)

WORKMAN, Mrs. C.A., is president of the Ladies' Hebrew Benevolent Society. Other officers are:- Miss Rubenstein, hon. pres.; Mrs. D.S. Friedman, vice-pres.; Mrs. S. Fischel, treas.; Mrs.

G. Fischel, hon. sec.; Mesdames L. Abinovitch, A.L. Gittleson, Jos. Jacobs, Paul Ogulnick, Ascher Pierce and Miss S. Hirsch, board of trustees. The Society is thirty-eight years old. It held its last bazaar five years ago (13 June 1913, 16, 27)

WORKMAN, Mrs. Charles A., has returned from Buffalo where she was visting her sister (10 June 1910, 13, 30)

WORKMAN, Mrs. Charles A., has returned from visiting her sister, Miss Haas, in Buffalo, N.Y. (17 Feb. 1911, 14, 14)

WORKMAN, Mrs. Charles A., Kensington Ave., is going to Buffalo, N.Y., to visit her sister (19 Jan. 1912, 15, 10)

WORKMAN, Mrs. Chas., and daughter have returned from a visit with relatives in Syracuse (15 Jan. 1909, 12, 5)

WORKMAN, Mrs. Flora and Miss Elsa Workman have returned from Boston where they spent the summer, accompanied by Mrs. Shear and daughter, of Malden, Mass. (30 Sept. 1910, 13, 46)

WORKMAN, Mrs. I. and Miss Elsie Workman, Seymour Ave., are visiting relatives in Utica, N.Y. (22 March 1912, 15, 19)

WORKMAN, Mrs. M., St. Famille St., has returned from Syracuse, N.Y., where she visited her mother (22 Jan. 1909, 12, 6)

WORKMAN, Mrs. Mark and daughters have been spending the past week in New York (29 Oct. 1909, 12, 46)

WORKMAN, Mrs. Mark, has returned from Ottawa where she was visiting her daughter, Mrs. Harry Rosenthal (3 Dec. 1909, 13, 3)

WORMSER, Mrs., is visiting her daughter, Mrs. Marcus Roman, for a few weeks (17 Feb. 1911, 14, 14)

WORMSER, Mrs. M., of New York, has returned home accompanied by her mother, Mrs. S. Goltman (12 Nov. 1909, 12, 48)

WYSE, Miss, is visiting Mrs. Ruben (15 Sept. 1909, 12, 40)

YOUNGHEART, Joseph, left for a short stay in New York (12 Feb. 1909, 12, 9)

YOUNGHEART, Mr. and Mrs. Edward and Miss Rhoda Block left for Europe on the S.S. Virginian (11 June 1909, 12, 26)

YOUNGHEART, Mr. and Mrs. Edward, have returned from a short trip to Toronto (5 Feb. 1909, 12, 8)

YOUNGHEART, Mr. and Mrs. Edward, left Wed. for a short stay in Toronto (22 Jan. 1909, 12, 6)

YOUNGHEART, Mr. and Mrs. Edward, Mrs. Meldola de Sola, son and daughter, Dr. H. Lightstone, Isidore Michaelson and the Misses Michaelson are sailing for Europe aboard the S.S. Laurentic on May 14, 1910 (6 May 1910, 13, 25)

YOUNGHEART, Mr. and Mrs. Joseph and Miss Sybil Youngheart are spending the summer at Ste. Agathe des Monts (23 June 1911, 14, 32)

YOUNGHEART, Mrs. E., of Toronto, is visiting friends in Montreal (21 April 1911, 14, 23)

YOUNGHEART, Mrs. Ed., who has been abroad, has returned to Montreal and is residing on Bishop St. (25 Oct. 1912, 15, 46)

YOUNGHEART, Mrs. Edward, entertained last Tues. evening at tea in honor of her guest, Miss Strauss, of London, England (8 Jan. 1909, 12, 4)

YOUNGHEART, Mrs. Edward, has left Europe via New York, where she will spend the summer (5 May 1911, 14, 25)

YOUNGHEART, Mrs. Joseph and daughter have gone to the Gaspé for the summer (8 July 1910, 13, 34)

YOUNGHEART, Mrs. Joseph, left for Toronto to attend the marriage of her niece, Miss Irene Goldstein to H.M. Samuels, which takes place Wed. June 18, 1913 (13 June 1913, 16, 27)

YUDELL, Misses, of Kentucky, N.Y., are guests of their aunt, Mrs. Joseph Ettenberg (7 March 1913, 16, 13)

ZACKS, I., was in Kingston visiting his parents (6 Jan. 1911, 14, 8)

ZACKS, J., purchased one tree in the Herzl Wald in celebration of Samuel Hirsch Yancovitch (16 April 1909, 12, 18)

ZACKS, J.C., has gone to Kingston, Ont., to spend a week with his parents (22 July 1910, 13, 36)

ZACKS, J.C., visited his parents in Kingston, Ont., last week (3 March 1911, 14, 16)

ZAMENHOFF, Dr. Ludwig, is the guest of his aunt, Mrs. Nathan Lewis, Colonial Apts. During his stay Dr. Zamenhoff will spend a few days with Mr. and Mrs. J.A. Jacobs, at Beaurepaire (26 Aug. 1910, 13, 41)

ZEAMEN, Mrs. Bernhardt, of Hartford, is the guest of Mrs. H. Weinfield for two weeks (29 Oct. 1909, 12, 46)

ZEEMAN, Mrs. B. and son, of Hartford, Conn., were guests of Mrs. Harry Weinfeld, while in Montreal (24 June 1910, 13, 32)

ZEEMAN, Mrs. Bernhardt and child, of Hartford, Conn., were guests of Mrs. Harry Weinfield at Lakeside, Que. and will be guests of Mrs. Heillig, Hutchison St., while in Montreal (6 Sept. 1912, 15, 39)

ZELICOVITCH, Mr. and Mrs. Myer, leave for five months in Europe on June 17, 1913 by the S.S. Royal Edward (13 June 1913, 16, 27)

ZEMAN, Dr. and Mrs., of Hartford, Conn., entertained last Sun. in honor of their guests, the Misses Ray Heillig and Elizabeth Bernstein, of Montreal (25 Nov. 1910, 14, 2)

ZEMAN, Mrs. B. and son have returned home to Hartford after spending the summer at St. Anne de Bellevue (19 Aug. 1910, 13, 40)

ZIMMERMAN, Mr., spent a few days in Kingston (19 Feb. 1909, 12, 10)

ZUCKER, Mrs. M. and daughter, have gone to Campbellton, N.B., for two months (1 Aug. 1913, 16, 34)

ZUCKERMAN, Mr., is no longer authorized to receive donations or make collections at weddings and Brith Milahs on behalf of the Montreal Hebrew Sheltering Home (30 June 1911, 14, 33)

OTTAWA REGION

ABELSON, Jesse H., president of the Ottawa Young Men's Zionist Society, chaired a general meeting last Sun. Jan. 22, 1911 at 2.20 p.m. in the King Edward Hebrew Institute. Jesse H. Abelson, Joe Kert and Max Katz are members of the Bible class committee. Leon Petegorsky, Charles Horwitz and Jesse Abelson are members of the liaison with other Zionist societies committee. I.D. Holofcener, FZSC vice-pres. and L. Epstein, a new FZSC council member spoke about the Zionist movement (27 Jan. 1911, 14, 11)

ABELSON, Miss M., is hon. sec. of the Adath Yeshurun Congregation Hebrew Girls' School. Teachers are the Misses B. Abelson and L. Finn. Rabbi S. Fyne is in charge of the school which has sixty students, ages six to sixteen (31 Jan. 1913, 16, 8)

BERGER, Julius, son of Rabbi Joseph D. Berger, of Ottawa, has returned from New York where he spent the year at the Jewish Theological Seminary of America and the College of the City of New York. He will spend the summer with his parents and return to New York in Sept. to resume his studies (12 July 1912, 15, 31)

BERGER, Rabbi Joseph D., is attending the convention of Orthodox Rabbis in Malden, Mass. He is staying with his father-in-law, Rabbi J. Ch. Baron (12 July 1912, 15, 31)

BERGER, Rabbi Joseph, delivered a Hadron at the Siyum of Sisha Sidrei Mishna given under the auspices of the Chevra Mishnaes, at the Rideau Street Synagogue on Sun. evening, Aug. 21, 1910. Those present at the dinner following the ceremony included:- Rev. Lyon Doctor, Mrs. Maurice Grimberg, and Messrs. Held, Roodman, Gorfinkel, Gittelson, Draisin, Slonimsky, Glatt and Friendly. "An exceptionally eloquent speech was made by Mr. Julius Berger, who explained how the Torah binds up and unites all the Jews." (9 Sept. 1910, 13, 43)

BERGER, Rabbi Joseph, delivered the memorial service in the Rideau Street Synagogue, on Sun. aft. Feb. 27, 1910, for the "Great Goanim", Rabbi Eleazer of Telsh, Rabbi Hirsch of Kovno, the Rabbi of Wilkomir, Rabbi Moshe Chariff, of Slabodky and Rabbi Shmayai, of Schavell, all of Russia. "The synagogue was crowded, and many wept bitterly at the mention of the late rabbis. Rabbi Joseph Berger eulogized them at great length with deep pathos and enthusiasm." (11 March 1910, 13, 17)

BETCHERMAN, M. is captain of the Sons of Israel hockey team which played the YMHA Juniors, captained by Dave Millar on Sun. at the association rink (21 Feb. 1913, 16, 11)

BILSKY, Samuel and Joseph Edelstein organized a meeting of Jewish residents to protest the showing of the film the "Fire Bug" at the Casino and National theatres. The Chief of Police ordered the film not be shown. "Great indignation is being felt here that a picture of this kind, which gives the impression that the Jewish people are professional fire-bugs and set fires regularly for financial gain, should have been passed by the Ontario and Quebec Boards of Censor." (12 Sept. 1913, 16, 40)

BILSKY, Samuel, was elected Chief Ranger of the King Solomon Court of the Ancient Order of Foresters which was formed last week. Other officers elected were:- H. Merson, Sub-Chief Ranger; S. Horwitz, sec.; L. Green, treas.; Albert Horwitz, Senior Woodward; M. Fine, Junior Woodward; A. Rafel, Senior Beedle; S. Diamond, Junior Beedle. There are forty charter members (9 July 1909, 12, 30)

BLANKSTEIN, Mr. and Mrs. and son, Israel Blankstein, of Montreal, were guests of Mr. and Mrs. M. Fine and Mr. and Mrs. Smith (9 Sept. 1910, 13, 43)

BOMBERG, Mrs. M., returned home to Toronto after visiting relatives here (23 Aug. 1912, 15, 37)

BRAININ, Reuben, editor of the **Jewish Eagle**, lectured on Zionism under the auspices of the Men's Zionist Society of Ottawa last Sun. night in the Auditorium Hall. Other speakers were:- M. Gittleson, E. Held and I. Slonemsky. M. Lechovitz, chairman of the event, and Rabbis J. Berger and S. Fyne all spoke in Yiddish (13 Dec. 1912, 16, 1)

CONCERT and DANCE

will be held under
the auspices of the

Ottawa Men's Zionist Society,
SUNDAY, MAY 4th, at 8 p.m.
In the HEBREW INSTITUTE.

❉ *A Splendid Programme Arranged* ❉

TICKETS - 50 cents each

may be obtained from
J. Holzman, Esq., 53 Daly Av.   H. Edelstein, Esq., 315 Bay St.
A. Ash, Esq., 192 Rideau St.   (*Secy. of Concert Committee*)

CAPLAN, Miss B., chaired the mass meeting of the Young Men's Zionist Association and the Daughters of Zion propaganda committees this week. Committee members are:- Mr. Dworkin, M. Frank, S. Horn, Samuel Horwith, Samuel B. Miller, A. Harry Wolfe and the Misses B. Caplan, Rose Fine, Hilda Pullan, Anna Wolfe and Phoebe Wolfe. A debate took place on Zionism vs. Territorialism (25 June 1909, 12, 28)

CAPLIN, Miss Bessie, and the Misses Phoebe Wolfe, Anna Wolfe, Hilda Pullan, Rose Fine and E. Wolfe and Messrs. B. Goldfield, H.S. Merson, A. Harry Wolfe, J. Slonemsky, W. Cohen and Kert were in charge of arrangements for the annual Ottawa Hebrew Young People's Zion Society concert and dance, held in St. George's Hall, on Tues. evening, Jan. 19, 1909 (29 Jan. 1909, 12, 7)

COHEN, S., of Toronto, was in Ottawa last week (19 Aug. 1910, 13, 40)

COHEN, William, chaired a joint meeting of the Ottawa Young Men's Zionist Association and the Ottawa Daughters of Zion Society, held recently in Robert Allan Hall (16 April 1909, 12, 18)

DAVIDSON, Miss Rose, gave a "Pink Tea" and surprise linen shower in honor of Miss Teresa Wolfe. Serving at the table were Mesdames Archie Coplan, Max Lithwick and Max Wolfe. Assisting were:- the Misses Lillian Davidson, Amy and Bernice Mendels (Montreal), and Esther and Dorothy Wolfe (14 Nov. 1913, 16, 49)

DAVIS, Miss Jennie, of Montreal, is visiting Mrs. A. Kert and friends (11 April 1913, 16, 18)

DOVER, Joseph, read a letter of appeal sent to the community leaders asking for their support for the Jewish Literary, Debating and Dramatic Society. Other speakers at the opening meeting were:- W. Bernett, H. Dover, Hyman Edelstein, B. Goldfield and the Misses B. Abelson, B. Guitess and B. Sugarman (15 Oct. 1913, 16, 45)

EDELSTEIN, Hyman, president of the Jewish Literary, Debating and Dramatic Society, will read a paper "Shakespeare's Treatment of the Jew" at the season's opening meeting on Sun. Sept. 28, 1913 at 8 p.m. Sir Wilfred Laurier hopes to be present (12 Sept. 1913, 16, 40)

EDELSTEIN, Hyman, was elected president of the Jewish Literary, Debating and Dramatic Society on Sun. in the Hebrew Institute, King Edward Ave. Other officers elected were:- Julius Berger, registrar; Miss Annie Holzman, librarian; H. Dover, council; Rabbi S. Fyne, Dr. Glashan and J.D. Berger, council (4 July 1913, 16, 30)

EDELSTEIN, Joseph, will address the next meeting of the Jewish Literary and Debating Society on Sun. July 13, 1913, at 8 p.m. He is well-known in the Old Country as an orator and is connected to several leading Irish newspapers. He arrived last week in Ottawa from Dublin (11 July 1913, 16, 31)

EDELSTEIN, Mr. and Mrs. H., were honored by the Ottawa Men's Zionist Society on the occasion of their marriage by a contribution to the Zionist Land Fund (11 July 1913, 16, 31)

EPSTEIN, Miss Libbie, of Toronto, is visiting Miss Sadie Wolfe (21 Feb. 1913, 16, 11)

ETTENSON, Miss Esther, of Toronto, visited Ottawa for a few days (5 July 1912, 15, 30)

FERGUSON, Miss Miriam, of Manchester, England, is in Ottawa and will reside with her sister, Mrs. J. Herscovitch (28 March 1913, 16, 16)

FINE, M., was elected president of the newly

organized Ohave Zion Society on July 7, 1912 in the Machzikie Hadas Synagogue. Other officers elected were:- E. Lechovitz, 1st vice-pres.; B. Shore, 2nd vice-pres.; O. Petegorsky, treas.; A. Caplan, rec. sec.; Rev. Baker, fin. sec.; M. Jacobson, M. Korn and H. Shore, propaganda comm. "Following the election a brief but warm address was delivered by Mr. J. Berger, son of Rabbi J. Berger, of Ottawa, in which he explained the functions of Zionism and the duties of the officers." The society has forty-five members (26 July 1912, 15, 32)

FINE, Maurice, has just returned to Toronto aftter visiting his relatives in Ottawa (14 Jan. 1910, 13, 9)

FINE, Maurice, of Toronto, was in Ottawa visiting his parents, Mr. and Mrs. M. Fine. He attended the Kizzel-Dover wedding while in town (9 Sept. 1910, 13, 43)

FINE, Miss B. and Mrs. M. Fine, 123 Daly Ave., returned from a vacation at Vars, Ont. (30 Aug. 1912, 15, 38)

FINE, Miss Rose, gave a tea at the Chateau Laurier on Jan. 2, 1913 in honor of her guests, Mr. and Mrs. Maurice Fine, of Toronto; Miss Jennie Greenspon, of Montreal; and A. Drapkin, of Fort William, Ont. (10 Jan. 1913, 16, 5)

FINE, Miss Rose, was honored with a linen shower on Sun. by the Ottawa Ladies' Aid Society. Present were the Misses Caroline Moscovitz, Becky Fine, and Esther and Dorothy Wolfe (11 April 1913, 16, 18)

FINE, Mr. and Mrs. Maurice, of Toronto, are visiting Mr. and Mrs. M. Fine, Cumberland St. (3 Jan. 1913, 16, 4)

FINKELSTEIN, H., was elected president of Agudath Achim Congregation on Oct. 22, 1913. Other officers elected were:- S. Cohen, vice-pres.; H. Berlin, 1st trustee; Mr. Betcherman, 2nd trustee; Mr. Kronick, 3rd trustee; W. Friedman, 4th trustee; H.L. Sadinski, 5th trustee; Mr. Brahinski, treas.; and K. Cohen, sec. (31 Oct. 1913, 16, 47)

FINKELSTEIN, Harry and Miss Rose Finkelstein, of Toronto, are guests of Mr. and Mrs. S. Fischman, Florence St., on an extended visit (8 Aug. 1913, 16, 35)

FINKELSTEIN, S., of Boston, and Mrs. M. Finkelstein, of Toronto, returned home after spending a week with Mr. and Mrs. S. Fishman, Gladstone St. (23 Aug. 1912, 15, 37)

FINN, Miss Libbie, gave a party Wed. July 31, 1912, in honor of her out-of-town guests, Miss Nellie Raphael, of Hamilton, and Miss Edith Kaplan, of Chicago (9 Aug. 1912, 15, 35)

FISHMAN, S., of the Globe Furnishing Co., returned from a trip to Boston and New York (29 Aug. 1913, 16, 38)

FOGLE, Mr. and Mrs. J.R., and Miss N. Fogle returned from New York, Boston and Philadelphia (24 Jan. 1913, 16, 7)

FORMAN, Miss E., of Montreal, is visiting Mrs. Sarah Weinstock (28 Feb. 1913, 16, 12)

FRANK, A., A.J. Freiman, Mr. Gittleson, I.D. Holofcener, Samuel Horwith, Mr. Sidenberg and the Misses H. Pullan, A. Wolfe, Dorothy Wolfe, Esther Wolfe were present at a combined social of the Ottawa Daughters of Zion Society and the Young Men's Zionist Association. Miss Pullan read a paper "The Duty of Zionists and Zionism towards the Jewess" (14 May, 1909, 12, 22)

FREIMAN, A.J., chaired a meeting of the Ottawa Men's Zionist Society, last Thurs. (22 Jan. 1909, 12, 6)

FREIMAN, A.J., presided at the Purim festival given by the King Edward Street Synagogue Ladies Auxilliary for over six hundred children. Children participating in the program were:- B. Muscovitz, J. Levine, B. Myers, David Bilsky and the Misses Clara Kert, Eva Bilsky, Sara Cooper, Annie Futrel, Rachel and Gertrude Hollander, Clara Kaminsky, Jennie Levin and Pearl Slonemsky (22 March 1912, 15, 19)

FREIMAN, A.J., president of the King Edward Street Synagogue, formally opened the King Edward Hebrew Institute, of Ottawa, last Mon. evening. I.D. Holofcener, building committee chairman chaired the event. Speakers were Rabbi Herman Abramowitz, of Montreal; Rabbi Joseph Berger, of Ottawa; Rev. Marschoff, superintendent of the Hebrew School; and M. Bilsky, parnass of the synagogue. Other members of the building committee are:- C. Kaplan, treas.; M. Fine, Talmud Torah chairman; L. Green; M. Slominsky; and A.J. Freiman. "The Institute is a beautiful building and will be to Ottawa what the Baron de Hirsch is to Montreal, and the Zionist Institute to Toronto - a truly Jewish centre of communal activity, for different societies and religious classes. It is adjunct to the King Edward Street Synagogue and will to a great extent be supported by them." The Jewish community numbers 1,500 and has three congregations and several benevolent and Zionist societies (25 Nov. 1910, 14, 2)

FREIMAN, A.J., was elected president (by acclamation) of Adath Yeshurun Congregation, King Edward Ave., on Sun. Oct. 15, 1913. Other officers elected by acclamation were:- W. Abelson, vice-pres.; A. Ash, treas.; I.L. Tolzess, sec.; C. Caplan, M. Goldfield, S. Katz, S. Richter, I. Slonemsky, and A.W. Tolzess, trustees; C. Caplan, C.F. Finn, A. Myers, B. Pearl, B. Pelof, I. Slonemsky and A.W. Tolzess, board of education (7 Nov. 1913, 16, 48)

FREIMAN, A.J., was honored at a banquet tendered by the Adath Jeshurun Congregation, King Edward Ave., in recognition of his tenth anniversary as president of the synagogue (13 Feb. 1914, 17, 7)

FREIMAN, Lawrence, little son of Mr. and Mrs. A.J. Freiman, has completely recovered from his recent illness (18 Feb. 1910, 13, 14)

FREIMAN, Mrs. A.J. is president of the King Edward Street Synagogue Ladies' Auxilliary Society. Other officers are:- Mrs. C.I. Finn, 1st vice-pres.; Mrs. E. Beiber, 2nd vice-pres.; Mrs. A.H. Caplan, 3rd vice-pres.; Miss B. Vineberg, treas.; Mrs. A. Ash, sec.; Mesdames A. Kert, M. Bilsky and C. Caplan, advisory board (22 March 1912, 15, 19)

FREIMAN, Mrs. A.J., is president of the Ladies' Herzl Society. Other officers are:- Mrs. Leikin, vice-pres.; Miss Abelson, sec.; and Mrs. W. Shenkman, treas. (18 April 1913, 16, 19)

FREIMAN, Mrs. A.J., wife of the president of the King Edward Street Synagogue, was given a surprise party by the congregation last Sun. in the Hebrew Institute to mark her return to health and to honor her for her work on behalf of the local poor and other charitable causes. Mrs. Freiman recently underwent a severe internal operation. On behalf of the Ladies Auxilliary, Mesdames W. Abelson, J. Freedman and J. Holzman presented her with an inscribed loving cup (23 Aug. 1912, 15, 37)

FREIMAN, Mrs. Archie J. and Mrs. A. Kert were honored by the Ottawa Ladies' Hebrew Benevolent Society last Thurs. evening, Dec. 11, 1913 in the King Edward Avenue Institute. The president, Mrs. A. Rosenthal, Sr., read the addresses. Mrs. J. Holzman made a presentation to Miss Beck Vineberg (19 Dec. 1913, 17, 2)

FRIEDMAN, Jacob, contributed $25.00 to the Zionist National Land Fund (23 Aug. 1912, 15, 37)

FYNE, Rabbi S., delivered a sermon devoted to the sinking of the Titanic at a memorial service last Sat. in the King Edward Avenue Street Synagogue (26 April 1912, 15, 24)

FYNE, Rabbi S., of Philadelphia, Pa., has accepted the call to B'nai Jeshuran Congregation, Ottawa (31 Jan. 1912, 15, 12)

FYNE, Rabbi S., superintendent of the Adath Yeshurun Hebrew School, awarded prizes to the following students at the recent examinations held in Dec.:- Harold Pearl, Isidore Abelson, Moses Kaminsky, Albert Benjamin, Cecil Slonimsky, Gordon Caplan, Emanuel Caplin, Reuben Hansher, David Coplan, Jacob Cooper and Willie Greenberg (28 Feb. 1913, 16, 12)

GABRIEL, Mrs. J.S., gave an "at home" last Wed., in honor of her sister, Miss Cecilia Levinson, of Ottawa. Miss Finn poured the chocolate. Those present included:- F. Holzman, A. Holzman, J. Louis, B. Mirsky and the Misses L. Davidson and Englsen (New York) (5 Jan. 1912, 15, 8)

GITTLESON, H.L., a wholesale druggist, is one of the old residents of Ottawa, according to an article "The Ottawa Jewish Community" written for The Canadian Jewish Times. Some of the early Jewish inhabitants were L. Solomon (a former lumber merchant, now retired), Mr. Michelson (a diamond merchant no longer resident in Ottawa), the Dovers (wholesale produce store), J. Freedman (wholesale produce merchant), Mr. de Silberg (optician), and Mr. Bilsky (jeweller) (18 April 1913, 16, 19)

GITTLESON, H.L., presided at the Rideau Street Synagogue Hebrew School annual picnic and awarded prizes for sports to the following boys:- A. Brill, M. Goldberg, A. Held, A. Lifshitz, F. Merson, Z. Roodman and J. Sadinsky. Miss Millie Sadinsky won a gold ring donated by Mr. Lightstone, jeweller, Rideau St. The second girls' prize was won by Miss Sara Horwitch. Master M. Cohen won the medal for highest scholastic marks, presented by Mrs. A.L. Florence. A. Lifshitz won the consolation prize, presented by Mrs. Harry Shore. J. Roodman won the prize for second class, donated by S. Myers. Master H. Toronto and Miss Kriger won the third class medal (4 July 1913, 16, 30)

GLATT, Mr. and Mrs. Myer, are expected to

return from their summer vacation on Sept. 14, 1910 (9 Sept. 1910, 13, 43)

GLICKMAN, Miss Mabel, of Montreal, is visiting friends, Mr. and Mrs. Gould and Mr. and Mrs. L. Davis (5 July 1912, 15, 30)

GLUCK, Mr. and Mrs. Samuel, celebrated their recent marriage by hosting a party last Sun. (31 Jan. 1913, 16, 8)

GLUCK, S., is on a short vacation to New York and Philadelphia (10 Jan. 1913, 16, 5)

GOLDFIELD, B. and William Cohen are fund-raising for the family of a young man, age 27, who died recently (29 Jan. 1909, 12, 7)

GOLDFIELD, B., was elected president of the Young Men's Zion Association of Ottawa last Sun. at a general meeting in the King Edward Hebrew Institute. Other officers elected were:- L. Epstein, hon. member; L. Petegorsky, vice-pres.; E. Barnett, treas.; Charles H. Horwitz, sec.; and J. Kert, sergeant-at-arms (31 March 1911, 14, 20)

GOLUB, Miss Nellie, hosted a party recently. Guests included:- the Misses Pearl Freeman, Libbie Finn, Birdie Abelson, Rose Davidson, Beamolt, Pearl and Claire Beamolt, Messrs. L. Epstein, J. Marks, Wm. Holtzman, Samuel Millar, Alex. Slonemsky, Charles and Hyman Kert, Harry Wolfe and Jesse Slonemsky (28 May 1909, 12, 24)

GOLUB, Mrs. J., a well-known communal worker, is leaving Ottawa (11 April 1913, 16, 19)

GREEN, Mr. and Mrs. L., Miss Helen and Master Jena, of Ottawa, went on a trip down the Great Lakes (19 July 1912, 15, 32)

GUTTMAN, Miss Stephanie, is expected shortly from New York and will be the guest of the Misses Wolfe at "L'ete Villa", Britannia-on-the-Bay for a few weeks (9 July 1909, 12, 30)

HELD, Joe, was the guest of his uncle, M. Held over the weekend (24 Jan. 1913, 16, 7)

HOLOFCENER, I.D., A.J. Freiman and Messrs. Wershof, Fine and Pearl delivered speeches at the grand Purim Festival organized by the Ladies' Herzl Zion Society for the Talmud Torah children. Mr. Wershof, teacher of the King Edward Avenue Synagogue Talmud Torah received a gift. Organizers were:- Mesdames I.D. Holofcener, A.J. Freiman, L. Davis, Pearl, Green, Levine, Fogle, Ross, Litwick and the Misses S. Vineberg, E. Bilsky, M. Markson, Finn, Davidson, Ableson, Fitzger and Golub (8 April 1910, 13, 21)

HOLOFCENER, I.D., is the "...'the old war-horse,' as he is popularly referred to..." of the Zionist movement in Ottawa and is the current president of the Ottawa Men's Zionist Society. His predecessor was J. Holzman, "...a most conscientious and assiduous worker in the noble cause." (18 April 1913, 16, 19)

HOLOFCENER, I.D., is the new president of the Ottawa Men's Zionist Society, replacing J. Holzman who would not accept re-election. Other officers elected were:- W. Abelson and A.W. Tolzes, vice-pres.; L. Green, treas.; A. Ash, rec. sec.; and Rabbi S. Fyne, fin. sec. (7 Feb. 1913, 16, 9)

OTTAWA MEN'S ZIONIST SOCIETY

The Jewish public of Ottawa is hereby cordially invited to attend

A MASS MEETING

to be held at the

HEBREW INSTITUTE, KING EDWARD AVE.,

on

Sunday Next, Feb. 16th,

AT 8 P.M.

The Meeting will be addressed by well-known speakers.

HOLOFCENER, Mrs. I.D., was elected president of the new Ladies' Zionist Society on Sun. March 20, 1910 in the King Edward Street Synagogue. Other officers elected were:- Mesdames Slonemsky, Fogle and L. Davis, vice-pres.; Miss M. Markson, sec.; Miss E. Bilsky, treas.; Mesdames Ross, Davis and A.J. Freiman, advisory council (25 March 1910, 13, 19)

HOLZMAN, Miss Annie, passed her Collegiate exams with highest honors (5 July 1912, 15, 30)

HOLZMAN, Misses F. and A., of Ottawa, are spending a few weeks at Beaconsfield, Que. (4 Aug. 1911, 14, 38)

HOLZMAN, Mr. and Mrs. J., gave a surprise-whist at their home on Nov. 30, 1913 in honor of I.W. Holzman's birthday. Ladies present were:- F. and A. Holzman, Mesdames I. Sugarman, H.A. Wolfe, and the Misses B. and H. Abelson, L. Finn, B. Phillips, E.H. and B. Sugarman, M. Slonemsky, and E.and S. Wolfe (12 Dec. 1913, 17, 1)

HORWITZ, C., leaves for Toronto for a few days and will visit several American cities (27 Dec. 1912, 16, 3)

HORWITZ, Charles, is in Toronto to attend the wedding of Miss Martha Pullan to A. Brown (21 Feb. 1913, 16, 11)

HORWITZ, Charles, of Ottawa, leaves in a few days to visit friends in Toronto and Detroit (19 Aug. 1910, 13, 40)

HORWITZ, Charles, returned to Ottawa from a lengthy trip through western Ontario and Illinois (24 Jan. 1913, 16, 7)

HORWITZ, Charles, secretary of the Ottawa Young Men's Zionist Association, is in Toronto, visiting friends (9 Sept. 1910, 13, 43)

HORWITZ, Chas. and Benjamin Goldfield, Form 2A; Miss Ethel Kaminsky, Form 2E; Josie Horwitz and Eli Wershof, Form 1B; Miss Rose Lapine, Form 1E; Miss Julia Golub, Junior Com., received honor certificates from the Ottawa Collegiate Institute for passing their exams in 1908. Among those promoted to higher forms are:- Miss Rebecca Sugarman from Form 3 to 4; Benjamin Goldfield, Charles Horwitz and Miss Ethel Kaminsky from Form 2 to 3; Julius Berger, Lewis Cohen, Miss Jennie Freedman, Miss Julia Golub, Josie Horwitz, Miss Rose Lapine, Willie Millar, Eli Wershof and Miss Esther Wolfe from Form 1 to 2 (2 July 1909, 12, 29)

HYMAN, L., S. Schwarz, and the Misses Blanche Millar and S. Weinstock returned from Montreal where they attended the YMHA Ball (10 Jan. 1913, 16, 5)

KAUFMAN, L. (Montreal), M. Gould and Miss S. Gould (Baltimore), are guests of Mr. and Mrs. A. Futeral, Nelson St. (10 Jan. 1913, 16, 5)

KERT, Miss Clara, gave a theatre party (11 April 1913, 16, 18)

KERT, Miss Clarabel, of Ottawa, will spend two weeks in Ivry on the Lake, the guest of Miss Becca Ryan (9 Aug. 1912, 15, 35)

LEPINE, Miss R., is spending the holidays with Miss Esther Wolfe, 34 Stewart St. (3 Jan. 1913, 16, 4)

LEVIN, Miss Anna, entertained her friends at her summer cottage last Wed. (9 Sept. 1910, 13, 43)

LEVIN, Miss, of Ottawa, is visiting her friends and relatives, Mr. and Mrs. J. Roston, Park Ave., Montreal (28 Feb. 1913, 16, 12)

LEVIN, Mr. and Mrs. Moses E., have returned from Westboro where they spent their summer vacation (9 Sept. 1910, 13, 43)

LEVINE, Miss Annie, Somerset St. E., gave an "at home" last Wed. (10 Jan. 1913, 16, 5)

LEVINE, Miss Reba, of Baltimore, is visiting her cousin, Mr. and Mrs. W. Shenkman, at Britannia-on-the-Bay (8 Aug. 1913, 16, 35)

LIEBERMAN, Miss B., who was the guest of the Ottawa Ladies' Aid at their annual charity ball, returned to Toronto (28 March 1913, 16, 16)

LITHWICK, Mrs. Max, gave a tea and linen shower last Sun. in honor of the forthcoming marriage of Miss Fanny Kriger who will be married June 22, 1913. Assisting at the table were:- Mesdames J. Freedman, E.M. Lesner and Max B. Margosches and the Misses Rose Davidson, Libbie Finn, Jennie Freedman and Leah Kriger (13 June 1913, 16, 27)

MARGOSCHES, Mr. and Mrs. Max B., have returned from Britannia-on-the-Bay. They will be guests of Mrs. Margosches' parents, Mr. and Mrs.

Max Wolfe for two weeks before moving into their apartment, at 508 Besserer St. (29 Sept. 1911, 14, 46)

MARGOSCHES, Mrs. Max B., convenor of the Hebrew Ladies' Aid Society, thanked the following ladies for their donations:- Mesdames Baxt, Benjamin (Rideau St.), I. Benjamin, Martin Berman, W. Bernett, A. Cohen, Cooper, A.H. Coplan, Sam Diamond, S. Epstein, L. Frank, J. Freedman, S. Fyne, A. Gould, R. Kaminsky, Leiken, E.M. Lerner, Max Lithwick, J.J. Marks, M. Max, L. Petegorsky, W. Shenkman, I. Slonemsky, B. Smith, I. Sugarman, A. Topless and M. Wolfe and the Misses S. Berger, Cooper, Davidson, P. Friendly, L. Kriger, Miller, E. Sugarman and Sadie E. Wolfe. Monies raised were baskets of fresh fruit and jars of preserves which were distributed to the five city hospitals in honor of the Jewish New Year (10 Oct. 1913, 16, 44)

MARGOSCHES, Mrs. Max B., gave a dinner last Tues. evening in honor of Isadore Bald and Miss Anna Bald (13 June 1913, 16, 27)

MARGOSCHES, Mrs. Max B., was elected president (by acclamation) of the Ottawa Ladies' Aid Society at its inaugural meeting held in the YMHA clubrooms, Sparks St., on Dec. 7, 1911. Other officers elected were:- Miss Bessie Guitess, 1st. vice-pres.; Misses Sara Weinstock and Mildred Hollander, 2nd and 3rd vice-pres.; Miss Esther Sugarman, 480 St. Patrick St., corr. sec.; Miss Silverman, rec. sec.; Miss Leah Kriger, treas.; Miss Rose Fine, auditor; Misses Hilda Pullan and Hattie Sugarman, investigating comm.; Misses B. Edelstein and Cooper, sick comm.; Misses Sadie E. Wolfe and S. Weinstock, membership comm.; and Misses M. Hollander and Cooper, entertain. comm. Membership is open to any Jewish woman over fifteen years (15 March 1912, 15, 18)

MARGOSCHES, Mrs. Max B., was re-elected president by acclamation of the Ottawa Ladies' Aid Society. Other officers elected were:- Mrs. Max Wolfe, hon. pres.; Miss Esther Sugarman, corr. sec.; Miss Leah Weinstock, rec. sec.; Miss Leah C. Kriger, treas.; Misses Bessie Miller, Jennie Cooper and Carolyn Moscovitch, 1st, 2nd, and 3rd vice-pres,; and Mrs. Samuel Gluck, auditor. Miss Rose Fine, who was married and moved to Fort William, Ont., resigned and was made an hon. member (23 May 1913, 16, 24)

MENDELS, B., of Montreal, was in Ottawa on a business trip (19 Aug. 1910, 13, 40)

METRICK, N., returned from Toronto (10 Jan. 1913, 16, 5)

MILLAR, L., who lived in Winnipeg for the past year, has returned to Ottawa. Mr. Millar has always been active in the YMHA movement (10 Jan. 1913, 16, 5)

MILLAR, R.H., was elected president of the Ottawa Hebrew Benevolent Association at the fifteenth annual meeting held last Sun. in the King Edward Institute. Other officers elected were:- S. Caplin, V. Petegorsky and W. Shenkman, vice-pres.; L. Green, treas.; and A. Slomensky, sec. Communicated by R. Edelstein (27 Dec. 1912, 16, 3)

MILLER, Herman, the popular YMHA athlete, lectured on "The Social Disposition of the Jewish People" last Sun. evening. The Misses J. Golub, E. Kaminsky, Blanche Millar and May Slonemsky took part in the following discussion (17 Jan. 1913, 16, 6)

It is Good Taste to Link Old Passover with the Land of its Glorious Past

Do so by welcoming it with the **Pure and Delicious Carmel Wines and Cognacs,** grown in the Jewish Vineyards of Palestine, made and matured in the famous Grandes Caves de Rishon-le-Zion.

MANY GOLD MEDALS AND DIPLOMAS.

USE THE CARMEL OLIVE OIL A FOOD AND A MEDICINE

כשר לפסח

Beware of Imitations.

NONE GENUINE WITHOUT "CARMEL WINE CO., NEW YORK," ON LABEL.

SOLE AGENTS FOR U.S. AND CANADA:

CARMEL WINE CO., NEW YORK

OUR CANADIAN REPRESENTATIVES:

FRASERS, LTD., MONTREAL

THE CARMEL PRODUCTS CAN ALSO BE OBTAINED AT:

MONTREAL:—Fraser's, Ltd.; Fraser, Viger & Co.; R. Jacobson; B. Ram & Co.; St. Lawrence Grocery.
TORONTO:—Swan Bros.; Mochie & Co., Ltd.; R. H. Howard & Co.
HAMILTON:—James Osborne & Son.
OTTAWA:—Bate & Co.; S. J. Major, Ltd,
QUEBEC:—A. Grenier; Eudore Patry.

MILLER, Hermann, is directing the YMHA entertainment program at the next meeting on Sun. April 13, 1913 (4 April 1913, 16, 17)

MILLER, Samuel B., was elected president of the Young Men's Zionist Association. Other officers elected were:- B. Goldstein, vice-pres.; William Cohen, treas.; H.M. Kert, rec. sec.; Charles Hurwitz, corr. sec.; Leon Petegorsky and Louis Sadinsky, trustees; D. Gorfinkel, sergeant-at-arms (28 May 1909, 12, 24)

MIRSKY, David, was elected president of the Young Men's Zion Association of Ottawa at the general meeting held Sun. April 10, 1910 in the King Edward Avenue Synagogue. Other officers elected were:- Benjamin Goldfield, vice-pres.; Leon Petergorsky, treas.; Charles Horwitz, sec.; Max Katz, sergeant-at-arms; David Gorfinkel and Clifford Green, trustees (15 April 1910, 13, 22)

MIRSKY, Mrs. S.D., has undergone a successful serious operation (21 Feb. 1913, 16, 11)

MITTELL, Master Harold, of Kingston, is visiting Mr. and Mrs. S. Fischman, Florence St. (8 Aug. 1913, 16, 35)

ORNSTEIN, Miss Beckie, of Montreal, is visiting Mr. and Mrs. J. Holzman (19 Aug. 1910, 13, 40)

PEARL, Master Harold, eldest son of Mr. and Mrs. B. Pearl, 754 Albert St., received the gold medal for efficiency at the recent examinations held by the Agudath Yeshurun Congregation Hebrew School (21 Feb. 1913, 16, 11)

PEARL, Mr. and Mrs. B., gave a party on Purim (28 March 1913, 16, 16)

PETEGORSKY, L., is hon. president of the Ottawa YMHA which has two fine club rooms on Sparks St. in downtown Ottawa. Other officers are:- Charles Horwitz, pres.; H. Wolfe, vice-pres.; S. Korn, treas.; and Ben Rose, sec. (23 Feb. 1912, 15, 15)

PETEGORSKY, Sam, of Ottawa, visited his friend, M. Averbuck, in Montreal (28 Feb. 1913, 16, 12)

PINCO, A., has gone to New York for two weeks (31 Jan. 1913, 16, 8)

PULLAN, Miss Hilda, has returned to Ottawa, after spending a week at her home in Toronto. Her mother, Mrs. H. Pullan, is dangerously ill in the Lynhurst Hospital (2 Aug. 1912, 15, 34)

RAFFALOVITCH, Rev. I., rabbi of the Hope Place Synagogue, Liverpool, England, visited his old friend and colleague, Rabbi S. Fyne, with whom he stayed while in Ottawa. He preached at Adath Yeshurun Congregation and attended two Brith Milahs while in Ottawa. He left Sun. evening for Toronto (1 Nov. 1912, 15, 47)

RAPHAEL, Miss Nettie, returned home to Hamilton Sat. after spending the past three weeks with Miss Sadie E. Wolfe. Miss Wolfe left Sun. for New York and Brighton Beach to visit relatives (23 Aug. 1912, 15, 37)

RAYHEAD, Miss Nettie, of Hamilton, Ont., is the guest of Miss Sadie Wolfe for a few days (2 Aug. 1912, 15, 34)

ROSENSTEIN, Mrs. J. and baby are visiting her sister Mrs. Wolf Shenkman in Ottawa and will attend the Zionist convention (5 July 1912, 15, 30)

ROSENTHAL, Mrs. A., is hon. president of the newly formed Ottawa Hebrew Ladies Sewing Circle which met last Sun. aft. in the King Edward Avenue Synagogue. Other officers elected were:- Mrs. I.D. Holofcener, president; Mrs. L. Green and Miss B. Vineberg, vice-pres.; Miss Rose Fine, sec.; Mrs. M. Finklestein, treas.; Mesdames A. Rosenthal and A.J. Freiman, purchasing committee; Mesdames Ross and R. Leikan, relief committee (25 March 1910, 13, 19)

ROSENTHAL, Mrs. A., was re-elected president of the Ottawa Hebrew Ladies' Benevolent Society. Other officers elected were:- Mrs. H. Freiman, 1st vice-pres.; Mrs. Max Wolfe, 2nd vice-pres.; Mrs. Davis, 3rd vice-pres.; Miss Beccie Vineberg, sec.; Mrs. A.J. Freiman, treas.; Mesdames Golub and Smith, investigation committee; Mrs. Fine, sick committee (24 Dec. 1909, 13, 6)

ROSENTHAL, S., a former alderman, was elected about nine years ago and served for four successive years. "Mr. Rosenthal was not closely identified with the activities of the Jewish community; but his mother is the President of the Ottawa Jewish Ladies' Benevolent Society." (18 April 1913, 16, 19)

ROSENTHAL, Sr., Mrs. A., was elected president of the Ottawa Hebrew Ladies' Benevolent Society for the tenth consecutive year. Other officers elected were:- Mrs. M. Wolfe, 1st vice-pres.; Mrs. A. Kert, 2nd vice-pres.; Mrs. M. Fine, 3rd vice-pres.; Miss Beck Vineberg, sec.; Mrs. A.J. Freiman, treas. (25 Oct. 1910, 13, 50)

ROSENTHAL, Sr., Mrs. A., who has been abroad for nine months, has returned home. Frau Oberneek and Sol Lehman, of Berlin, Germany, are visiting Mrs. Rosenthal, 388 Elgin St. (17 Nov. 1911, 15, 1)

ROSENTHAL, SR., Mrs. A., president of the Ottawa Ladies Benevolent Society and Mrs. A. Freeman, treas., gave a report on the concert in aid of the Jewish poor on Wed. evening, Feb. 2, 1910, in St. Patrick's Hall. Those assisting were Miss Beck Vineberg, Martin Feldheim and H. de Silberg (18 Feb. 1910, 13, 14)

RUBIN, E., of New York, is in Ottawa on business (28 Feb. 1913, 16, 12)

RUBIN, Miss S., of Montreal, is visiting her sisters, Mrs. J. Davis and Mrs. S. Diamond (13 Dec. 1912, 16, 1)

RUBIN, Miss Sophie, returned to Montreal after spending the last two weeks with her sisters, Mesdames S. Diamond and J. Davis (28 March 1913, 16, 16)

RUBIN, Mr. and Mrs. J., are visiting their daughters, Mesdames S. Diamond and J. Davis (24 Jan. 1913, 16, 7)

SABBATH, J.L., was in Ottawa on a business trip last week (19 Aug. 1910, 13, 40)

SEGAL, D., of Montreal, spent the weekend in Montreal (7 Feb. 1913, 16, 9)

SIMON, Alderman George, will organize a branch of the Canadian Zionist Federation in Alexandria, Ont. A. Markson will assist him (25 March 1910, 13, 19)

SIMONSKY, L.I., moved, and Jess Abelson seconded, "That a vote of condolence be forwarded to Mr. Joseph Dover, our Registrar, and Miss Dover on account of the recent death of their mother" at the Ottawa Jewish Literary and Dramatic Circle meeting on Wed. March 18, 1914. Miss Becca Sugarman read a paper on "Passover" (27 March 1914, 17, 13)

SLOMINSKY, I., was elected president of the Ottawa Hebrew Benevolent Society at the annual meeting on Sun. Other officers elected were:- L. Green A. Kert and H. Finkelstein, vice-pres.; J. Holzman, treas.; M. Finkelstein, sec. H.J. Freiman was appointed chairman of the fund-raising committee. "The president, in his report, drew attention to the distress prevailing in the city, and pointed out the necessity for more funds. The Society, he said, were hard put to meet the calls made upon it, especially during this part of the year..." (14 Jan. 1910, 13, 9)

SLONEMSKY, Miss May, daughter of Mr. and Mrs. I. Slonemsky, gave a party last Sat. night in honor of her cousin, Miss Pauline Marks, of Montreal. Guests included J. Abelson, M. Cooper, R. Edelstein, W. Holyman, L. Hyman, H. Millar, W. Millar, S. Schwarz, I. Simonsky, J. Slonemsky, I. Tolzes and the Misses J. Golub, A. Holyman, H. Holzman, E. Kaminsky, R. Lepine, A. Levin, R. Lewis, Blanche Millar, R. Mirsky, Dorothy Wolfe and E. Wolfe (3 Jan. 1913, 16, 4)

SLOVER, F. and Miss G. Slover returned from Montreal where they attended the wedding of Charles Hoffer (28 Feb. 1913, 16, 12)

SOLOMON, Miss Annie, of Montreal, has returned home after spending a week in Ottawa, the guest of Mr. and Mrs. M. Fine (9 Sept. 1910, 13, 43)

SPEYER, B.M., returned from a short visit to Montreal (23 Aug. 1912, 15, 37)

SUGARMAN, I., chaired the consecration ceremony of the Agudath Achim Synagogue. He transferred the key of the synagogue to the president, A.L. Florence. Rabbis Joseph Berger, S. Fyne, and Simon Glazer, of Montreal spoke at the ceremony. In his address, Rabbi Berger said that the occasion was a holy one for Jews in Ottawa and that consecrating synagogues was at the behest of G-d. "The Rabbi reminded the assembly that it was the Synagogue which acted as a stronghold to the Jews who fled from their persecutors during the Spanish Inquisition. The scrolls of the Law was found in the hands of our co-religionists, who have been massacred in the past because of their religious beliefs." H. Finkelstein, the past president, was presented with an inscribed gold medal for devotion and efforts to see the synagogue built (24 Jan. 1913, 16, 7)

SUGARMAN, Isidore, is chairman of the building committee for the new Agudath Achim Congregation synagogue. The cornerstone was laid by Mr. Sugarman, Mon. aft. at 417 Rideau St. Rabbi Joseph Berger, of Agudath Achim and Rabbi S. Fyne, of the King Edward Street Synagogue conducted the service. The new synagogue which will be completed in a few months, will seat four hundred people and will be fifty by seventy feet in size. The congregation was founded with about sixty members eight years ago and first met in a private house. Other building committee members are:- M. Roodman, treas.; K. Cohen, sec.; A. Sugarman, A. Levison, S. Cohen and H. Segalowitz. H. Finkelstein is the president of the synagogue (5 July 1912, 15, 30)

SUGARMAN, Miss E., corr. secretary of the Ottawa Daughters of Zion Society, remitted $36. to the Zionist National Executive in Montreal (5 March 1909, 12, 12)

SUGARMAN, Miss Esther, 480 St. Patrick St., is secretary of the committee in charge of the Purim Charity Ball to be held at the Chateau Laurier, Wed. evening, March 19, 1913 (7 March 1913, 16, 13)

SUGARMAN, Mr. and Mrs. A.J., 17 Sweetland Ave., hosted a Purim party given by the Ottawa Ladies' Aid Society (13 March 1914, 17, 11)

SUGARMAN, Mr. and Mrs. A.J. and family returned from Kirk's Ferry where they spent the summer and are residing at 17 Sweetland Ave. (12 Sept. 1913, 16, 40)

WEINSTOCK, Miss Sarah, gave a party last Sun. Guests included M. Lerner, D. Segal, I. Tolzes, J. Wolfe and the Misses B. Miller, D. Miller, C. Moskovitz and B. Smith (7 Feb. 1913, 16, 9)

WEINSTOCK, Mrs. J., is the guest of Mrs. J. Ornstein, in Montreal (31 Jan. 1913, 16, 8)

WOLFE, A. Harry, of Montreal, was in Ottawa for a few days visiting his mother, Mrs. M. Wolfe (2 Aug. 1912, 15, 34)

WOLFE, Corporal A.H., Corporal W.C. Miller and Privates C. Gallin, J. Kert, J. Korn, H. Miller and M. Moscovitch, all of 23rd Battery, Canadian Field Artillery, of Ottawa, are the young Jewish men of Ottawa who left for the Petawawa military camp for two weeks (16 June 1911, 14, 31)

WOLFE, Jay, is recovering from his recent operation and is likely to leave Water St. Hospital by week's end (21 June 1912, 15, 28)

WOLFE, Miss Anna, the newly elected president of the Ottawa Daughters of Zion, gave a tea last Sat. aft. The Misses Hilda Pullan and Sadie Wolfe presided over the tea-table (7 Jan. 1910, 13, 8)

WOLFE, Miss Esther, 15 year old president of the Junior Branch of the Ottawa Daughters of Zion, was responsible for arranging the Purim entertainment, Tues. evening, March 29, 1911. The young people who performed were:- Louis Saidenberg, drum solo; Ben Moscovitch, recitation of "Ode to Purim"; Maurice Cohen, piano solo; Miss Anna Wolfe, who arranged for quartette the song "Fair Palestine"; Sam Mirsky, Jack Levine, Leonard Walstein and Maurice Brahinsky sang "Fair Palestine"; Carolyn Moscovitch and Jay Wolfe in a duet of "Charming Weather"; Annie Holzmann, reading; Beckie Fine, rendition of "Cowboy"; Louis Caplin, reading; Sam Caplan, reading of "Queen Esther"; Beccie Fine, who sang "Supposin"; Adele Wolfe, rendition of "The Kaiser's Questions"; Charles Shapiro and Ben Moscovitch and Adele Wolfe in "Jimmie Valentine"; Ruth Levy, her production of the allegorical sketch "The Festival of Feasts" starring Jay Wolfe as Rosh Hashanah, Annie Futtrell as Yom Kippur, Mollie Saidenberg as Succoth, Josie Horwitz as Chanukah, Hyman Steinberg as Pesach, Louis Cohen as Shavouth, Helen Green as Purim, Annie Holzmann as Vashti, Jack Levin as Haman, Maurice Moscovitch as Ahasuerus, and Esther Wolfe as Queen Esther (7 April 1911, 14, 21)

WOLFE, Miss Esther, has returned from Montreal where she visited Mrs. Joseph Adelstein and Miss Rose Lepine (2 Aug. 1912, 15, 34)

WOLFE, Miss Sadie E., entertained at whist Sun. evening in honor of her brother, A. Harry Wolfe and his fiancée, Miss Anna Bald, of Montreal (13 June 1913, 16, 27)

WOLFE, Miss Sadie Elinore, first president of the Ottawa Daughters of Zion Society, was inscribed in the JNF Golden Book (6 May 1910, 13, 25)

WOLFE, Miss Sadie, is in Toronto for the holidays, the guest of Miss Florence Danson, Jameson Ave., Parkdale (27 Dec. 1912, 16, 3)

WOLFE, Miss Teresa F., organized the Japanese Tea given by the Ottawa Ladies' Aid Society, Tues. evening, May 28, 1912 at the "Sifton". Those taking part in the program were:- Jack Levine, Bernard Myers, Sammie Mirsky, Leonard Walstein, Julius and Kalman Smith, Jack Goldsmith, Louis Hyman, J. Wolfe, Charles Horwitz, and the Misses Pearl Friendly, Esther and Hattie Sugarman, Dorothy and Adele Wolfe, Dora Millar, Bessie Millar, Blanche Millar, Sara Weinstock, Carolyn Moscowitz and Becca Fine (7 June 1912, 15, 26)

WOLFE, Miss Teresa Frances, the young Canadian Prima Donna, gave recitals in Pittsburgh, Baltimore and Philadelphia and will soon give one in New York (31 Jan. 1913, 16, 8)

WOLFE, Misses Sadie E., Bessie Caplan, Rose Fine, Hilda Pullan and Anna Wolfe were elected Ottawa Daughters of Zion delegates to the Tenth Zionist Convention, at a meeting, Oct. 31, 1909 (12 Nov. 1909, 12, 48)

WOLFE, Mrs. Max, entertained about 35 children at a lawn party, Mon. aft. in honor of her little daughter Adele's birthday. Miss Leslie Caplan won first prize and Miss Annie Golub the booby prize (3 Sept. 1909, 12, 38)

WOLFE, Mrs. Max, is recovering after undergoing a serious operation at the General Memorial Hospital in New York City (21 April 1911, 14, 23)

WOLFE, Mrs. Max, of Ottawa, accompanied by her little daughter, Adele, left for New York on Mon. where she will visit her relatives before going to Brighton Beach, L.I. for two weeks (9 July 1909, 12, 30)

WOLFE, the Misses, directed the Chanukah evening organized by the Ottawa Daughters of Zion in St. John's Hall, on Wed. evening, Dec. 8, 1909. About fifty children participated including Louis Caplin, Beccie Millar, Henrietta Myers, Violet Wolfe, Regina Hollow, Sam Mirsky, Mamie Lapine, Helen Abelson, Louis Saidenberg, John Saidenberg, Beccie Fine, Dorothy Wolfe, David Goldstein, Annie Holtzman, Jay Wolfe, Edith Hollow, Maurice Moscovitch, Leonard Wolstein and Bennie Moscovitch (17 Dec. 1909, 13, 5)

WOLFE, the Misses, entertained several friends at "L'ete Villa", Britannia-on-the-Bay on July 4, in honor of Independence Day (9 July 1909, 12, 30)

WOLFE, the Misses, of Ottawa, entertained at a "Pop Corn Dance" Mon. night, Aug. 23, 1909 at "Villa L'ete', Britannia, in honor of Miss Stephanie Guttman who returned home to New York City on Thurs. Miss Anna Wolfe, who accompanied her, will be the guest of Miss Melanie Guttman during her stay. (3 Sept. 1909, 12, 38)

WOOLFSON, Miss Rosa, of New York, is in Ottawa, the guest of Mr. and Mrs. Davis and family (22 Oct. 1913, 16, 46)

VULCAN is the Latest Style in SUMMER COLLARS

Your only Safeguard is our

TRADE MARK

The CANADIAN UNDERWEAR CO.,
309 Notre Dame Street West, - MONTREAL.

TORONTO

AARONS, Mrs., Parkdale, hosted a Whist Club meeting on Wed. night. Mrs. S.M. Grosman won the prize. The next meeting will be held at the home of Mrs. L. Gelber, 293 Huron St. (29 Oct. 1909, 12, 46)

ABRAMSKY, Miss Katie, of Kingston, Ont., who was the guest of Mrs. Daniels in Montreal, has returned home (12 Aug. 1910, 13, 39)

ALEXANDER, B., M. and L. Gelber, M. Goldsmith, P. Herman, J. Hillelson, H. Kaplan, A. Marcus, E. Pullan, S. Rogul, D. Seigel, H. Shulman, Louis M. Singer, and the Misses L. Close, L. Goldstick, M. Solway, Y. and J. Wilson contributed funds to the Bezalel School for Arts and Crafts in Jerusalem, Palestine (23 Feb. 1912, 15, 15)

ALKOVITZKY, Miss Dr. Liza, is visiting friends in the city from Los Angeles (16 Aug. 1912, 15, 36)

ASTOR, Misses, of Rochester, N.Y., were in Toronto (20 Sept. 1912, 15, 41)

ASTOWSKI, Miss Amelia, spent the weekend in Toronto (30 Aug. 1912, 15, 38)

AUERBACH, Mrs., who was in St. John's Hospital for several weeks, is now convalescent (2 Oct. 1912, 15, 43)

AUSTIN, Mrs. B., is visiting her sister in the city (30 Aug. 1912, 15, 38)

BACKRACK, Miss Sadie, 327 Sherborne St., hosted a meeting at her home to discuss the formation of a Jewish girls' sewing school to counteract the missionary activities of the Presbyterian Mission to the Jews, on Terauly St. Other volunteer workers at the meeting included:- Mesdames I.H. Siegel, convenor; D. Levin, assistant; and S. Lewis, cutter (30 June 1911, 14, 33)

BEIBER, Miss Kate, is visiting friends in New York (16 Aug. 1912, 15, 36)

BERGER, Julius, of Ottawa, was the guest of Elias Pullan (6 Sept. 1912, 15, 39)

BERGER, Mr. and Mrs. and Mr. Lempert left last Tues. on a visit to Europe (21 April 1911, 14, 23)

BERGER, Mrs., alias Rebecca Cooper, was shot by an unknown man while standing on the doorstep of her cottage on Chestnut St. "Witnesses testified that the man and woman had been talking together for some time (proving that they were on familiar terms), when the former suddenly drew his revolver and fired a bullet into her mouth, which travelled to her brain and caused almost instant death, and the man disappeared. At first the suspicion fell on a man by the name of Abel Berger, or Abel Cohen, who made his appearance at the scene of the murder soon after the shooting, and on whom a revolver was found. As yet the mystery has not been quite disentangled." (7 June 1912, 15, 26)

BIRKENTHAL, Miss Helen, of New York, was in Toronto to attend her sister's funeral which took place a week ago (28 Feb. 1913, 16, 12)

BIRNBAUM, J., left for Preston, Ont. (23 Aug. 1912, 15, 37)

BIRNBAUM, S.J., A. Brown, Benjamin Brown, Abraham Singer, Louis M. Singer, Joseph Singer, A. Willinsky, the Misses Julia and Henrietta Gottlieb, Susan Halpern, Lily Kaplan, Augusta Kenen, Ray Landsberg, Martha Lavine, Martha and Dora Pullan, and Mesdames J. Mehr, Louis M. Singer and A. Willinsky were some of the guests present at the Judean Literary and Debating Club annual ball held Jan. 16, 1913 in the Knights of Columbus Hall (24 Jan. 1913, 16, 7)

LYRIC THEATRE TORONTO
Cor. Agnes & Terauley

WEISSMAN, AUERBACH AND LITMAN
STOCK COMPANY

are now playing at the Lyric every Wednesday, Friday and Saturday Evenings with a first class company. The best Yiddish plays.

The Theatre has been newly decorated and the plays are beautifully staged.

RAM & RROWN, Managers.

BLACK, Charles and Samuel Factor, came first and second respectively in first year law at the Christmas examinations at Osgoode Hall. Of the 300 to 400 students at Osgoode Hall, only eight or ten are Jewish (7 Feb. 1913, 16, 9)

BLACK, Misses Rose, Rose Birnbaum, Nellie Broudy, Florence Danson, Rose Gekdzaeler, Esther Gitson, Fannie Goodman, Susan Halpern, Fanny Korn, Fanny Lepofsky, Mollie Levinter, Eva Morris (Montreal), Pearlstein (Hamilton), Albina Simonski, Gussie Sundell and Annie Ziegler (Montreal) were some of the ladies present at the second annual ball of the Mosaic Alumni held Wed. Feb. 19, 1913 in the Metropolitan Assembly Rooms (28 Feb. 1913, 16, 12)

BLACK, Mrs. Hugo and daughter are summering at Beaconsfield, Que. (19 July 1912, 15, 32)

BLANKSTEIN, M.I., of New York, is in Toronto and will stay with the Symphony Orchestra for the season (6 Sept. 1912, 15, 39)

BLAUSTEIN, Mr., of Montreal, is visiting friends in Toronto (12 Aug. 1910, 13, 39)

BLOOMFIELD, Harry, president of the Disraeli Conservative Club of Montreal, delivered the keynote address on the subject of the importance of Jewish immigration to Canada, to the Central and South Toronto Conservative Club last mon. evening. "Mr. Bernard Rose of Montreal, delivered an address in which he claimed that the more protective scheme of administration as set forth by the Conservative leader was especially favorable to Jewish industry, and would result in the rapid advancement of Canada." (9 Sept. 1910, 13, 43)

BLUMER, Mr. and Mrs. D., of Montreal were in Toronto for a few days (4 March 1910, 13, 16)

BOCHENCK, Joseph, is president of the Toronto Hebrew Sick Benefit Society. Other officers are:- I.K. Lewin, vice-pres.; D. Pullan, fin. sec.; D. Maroff, rec. sec.; and M. Neidenberg, treas. (27 Jan. 1911, 14, 11)

BOCHENEK, Mr. and Mrs. Joseph, have returned from visiting friends in New York and Montreal (8 April 1910, 13, 21)

BOCHENEK, Mrs. Joseph, has gone to Mount Clemens for a month (8 July 1910, 13, 34)

BOGATSKY, Mrs., is on a holiday trip to New York (25 Feb. 1910, 13, 15)

BOGORAD, S., of Rochester, N.Y., was in Toronto (20 Sept. 1912, 15, 41)

BRAND, Miss Millie, is the guest of the Misses Solway (19 July 1912, 15, 32)

BRANDT, Miss Millie gave a recitation and Miss Ida Webber performed a piano solo at the Nordau Zion Club literary meeting held Sun. (17 Jan. 1913, 16, 6)

BRESLIN, Dr. L.J., is taking a post-graduate course in medicine in New York (9 Aug. 1912, 15, 35)

BRESLIN, Dr. L.J., of the Guelph General Hospital, is on a short visit in Toronto en route for New York (26 July 1912, 15, 33)

BRESLIN, Dr. L.J., who took a postgraduate course in medicine in New York, is returning to Toronto to practice. Dr. Breslin graduated from the University of Toronto Faculty of Medicine with a silver medal (28 Feb. 1913, 16, 12)

BRESLIN, Dr. Louis, spoke on the "Effects of Congestion on the Female Sex" at a literary meeting of the Hebrew Ladies' Sewing Circle, on Tues. evening. Rabbi S. Jacobs spoke on "Jewish Women" (28 March 1913, 16, 16)

BRESLIN, J. and H., have returned from a short stay in Quebec City (16 Aug. 1912, 15, 36)

BRESLIN, Miss Gertie, is the newly-installed president of the Nordau Girl's Club. Other officers are:- Miss Elsie Papernick, vice-pres.; Miss Bessie Silver, fin. sec.; Miss Sadie Harbor, corr. sec.; Miss Sadie Weingarten, treas.; and Miss Gertie Samuels, curator. Miss Selina Swiss chaired the evening (16 May 1913, 16, 23)

BRESLIN, Miss Gertie, is visiting Oshawa, Ont. (9 Aug. 1912, 15, 35)

BRESLIN, Miss Rose, returned home from Kingston where she visited friends (23 Aug. 1912, 15, 37)

BRESLIN, Mr. and Mrs. M., gave a supper in honor of their eighth wedding anniversary. Joseph Abramsky, of Kingston, was toastmaster (28 March 1913, 16, 16)

BRESLOVE, David, a third year classics student at University College, (and the only Jewish student in classics) was elected president of the Classical Association of the University of Toronto. "Before coming to the University Mr. Breslove always took high standing in the various institutions which he attended, and during the three years of his present course has taken scholarships in every year." (21 March 1913, 16, 15)

BRESLOVE, L., in the honor matriculation examination ranked fifth in general proficiency in Ontario and was awarded a Edward Blake scholarship for free tuition in the University of Toronto (9 June 1911, 14, 30)

BRODEY, I., hon. pres. of the Ladies' Hebrew Aid Society, and Mrs. S. Lewis, the financial secretary, were honored at a recent meeting last Sun. evening. Mr. Brodey was president of the society for fifteen years and Mrs. Lewis for a similar length of time. Mrs. A.A. Simonsky made the presentation to Mr. Broudy and Mrs. M. Mehr to Mrs. Lewis. Present officers of the society are:- Mrs. D. Lavine, pres.; Mrs. M. Smith, treas.; Mrs. A. Lewis, fin. sec.; Mrs. M. Rosenberg, rec. sec.; Mesdames S. Isaacson, A. Landsberg and M. Lieberman, relief comm. (25 April 1913, 16, 20)

BRODEY, I., is hon. president of the Toronto Hebrew Ladies' Aid Society which held its fourteenth annual ball on Nov. 18, 1913. The debutantes were:- the Misses Rebecca Cohen, Esther Goodman, Lieberman, Narol and Temes. Officers of the society are:- Mrs. D. Lavine, pres.; Mrs. M. Cohen, vice-pres.; Mrs. S. Lewis, sec.; Mrs. N. Rosenberg, rec. sec.; Mrs. N. Smith, treas.; and Mesdames Landsberg, Lieberman and Narol, trustees (19 Dec. 1913, 17, 2)

BRODIE, J.B., D. Brody, C. Cohn, A. Gitson, M.C. Gold, W.H. Goodman, A.R. Gordon, E.C. Gordon, M. Gordon, A. Kelz, D. Perlman, J. Rashofsky and M. Samuel were successful Junior matriculants in Group A., passing all subjects (16 Aug. 1912, 15, 36)

BRODSKY, Miss R., daughter of Rabbi Brodsky, of Newark, N.J., is visiting in Toronto (5 July 1912, 15, 30)

BROIDY, A., (B.A.) obtained first class honors in biology and physics from the University of Toronto. This year he was a Fellow in Biology (9 June 1911, 14, 30)

BROOKSTEIN, Miss Hannah, Misses Jennie Draimin, Rose Tugendhaft, Mary Landsberg, Violet Davis and Messrs. Julius Ramm, Max Lurie, Arthur Fleishman and Prof. Dushman are voluntary teachers at the Zionist Jewish School which held its annual closing exercises in the McCaul Street Synagogue on Sun. June 26, 1910 at 3.30 p.m. The school, which has 157 female students ages seven and up, is under the direction of its superintendent, Edmund Scheuer. It operates out of the Zionist Institute, Simcoe St. (17 June 1910, 13, 31)

BROUDY, Miss Helen, was given a surprise party on Sun. evening by the B'noth Zion Kadimah, at McGee St., in honor of her approaching marriage (21 March 1913, 16, 15)

BROWN, Miss May and Miss Gertie Wormser were guests of Miss Bettie Straus in Toronto, en route for Muskoka (16 Aug. 1912, 15, 36)

BROWN, Miss R., returned from Newtonville, Ont. (23 Aug. 1912, 15, 37)

CAPLAN, Zusman, a young violinist, gave a recital in Association Hall, assisted by Master Frederick Cohen, age 10. Cohen is the son of a poor tailor in the Bronx, N.Y., "...and when his exceptional musical ability was discovered the family was stinted for several years in order to give the child a musical education." Mr. Caplan is a member of the Toronto Symphony Orchestra. He comes from the same district in Russia as the great Mischa Elman (22 April 1910, 13, 23)

CASH, Alexander, Barnett Stone and Messrs. Ram and Korotkin, of the United Zionists, were responsible for producing the play "The Stranger" at Massey Hall, Wed. night. Over 2,000 people attended (29 Oct. 1909, 12, 46)

CASH, Alexander, Barnett Stone and Rabbi J. Gordon, of Toronto, organized the B'nai and B'not Zion Society in Brantford, Ont. There are thirty-six members. The first meeting was held Sun. Dec. 20, 1908. Mr. Moldever received a supply of Shekel books for the Zionist Federation for Shekel Day (8 Jan. 1909, 12, 4)

CASH, Alexander, chaired the closing exercises of the Zionist Jewish School for Jewish girls held in the McCaul Street Synagogue. Over five hundred people were present. Prizes were awarded to the Misses Sylvia Singer, Rose Beer, Hilda Ginsberg, Bessie Pullan, Sarah Roth, Bella Friedman, Lily Singer and Rose Rosenblum (1 July 1910, 13, 33)

CASH, Alexander, chaired the Theodor Herzl memorial meeting and service held by the B'nai Zion Association of Toronto, on Sun. July 11, 1909 (23 July 1909, 12, 32)

CASH, Alexander, has returned from a few weeks' stay in Preston, Ont. (22 July 1910, 13, 36)

CASH, Alexander, L. Gurofsky, Emanuel I. Kenen, Elias Pullan, Mr. Rider and Dr. John Shayne were nominated as delegates to the Zionist Congress in Vienna. Dr. Shayne and Mr. Cash were elected and "A subscription was taken up to help pay the expenses of sending the delegates, and about $150 was collected." (4 July 1913, 16, 30)

CASH, Alexander, was elected president (by acclamation) of the Toronto Zionist Council last Thurs. Other officers elected were:- Mrs. Selick, vice-pres.; Mr. Rose, treas.; and Mr. Glosberg, sec. (18 July 1913, 16, 32)

CHARMINSKY, A., was appointed president of a newly-formed English-speaking congregation. Other officers elected were:- H. Stanley, sec.; R. Greenberg, treas.; J. Feather, rec. sec.; I. Jacobson and L. Abrahams, directors; S. Nieman, L. Paul and L. Silverman, trustees (29 Oct. 1909, 12, 46)

COHAN, Morris, returned from a four months' trip to Panama (21 March 1913, 16, 15)

COHEN, David, was elected president of the Judean Athletic Club last week. Other officers elected were:- Reuben Hazzan, vice-pres.; Harry Simonsky, sec.; Mr. Havelock, treas.; C. Owens, sergeant-at-arms; D. Friedman, L.J. Gurofsky, William Samuels, Percy Stein and J. Teich, executive (17 Jan. 1913, 16, 6)

COHEN, Dr. Henry, of Galveston, Texas, a frequent visitor to the Toronto Zionist Sabbath School, sent six dozen textbooks to the princpal (28 Feb. 1913, 16, 12)

COHEN, I., Alexander Cash, Samuel Kronick, C. Lurie, C. Pasternack, Elias Pullan, J. Ram and Barnett Stone were elected directors of the Zionist Institute at a shareholders' meeting on Wed. Jan. 15, 1913. The directors agreed to purchase a site for a new Zionist building on St. Patrick St., near Bathurst St. (24 Jan. 1913, 16, 7)

COHEN, Jacob, has been appointed a magistrate of the Toronto Police Court. "For many years Mr. Cohen has figured in the history of the Toronto Police Court, earning the good wishes of the magistrates by his assistance, rendered free, as interpreter and general assistant in any Jewish cases that might have come up for trial. But where Mr. Cohen's aid has proved most efficient has been in helping his less fortunate brethren in their trials, and settling the majority of the cases out of court, at the express desire of the presiding magistrate, who recognizing that circumstances are different to the ordinary case, hands the offending parties over to Mr. Cohen to be reasoned with privately, and in such instances Mr. Cohen is generally successful." (3 Sept. 1909, 12, 38)

COHEN, Jacob, president of the Cosmopolitan Club, welcomed the guests to a garden party given at the Club garden, Beverly St., last Wed. (8 July 1910, 13, 34)

COHEN, Jacob, president of the Cosmopolitan Club, held at "at home" Wed. evening, Jan. 26, 1910 for about 250 guests (4 Feb. 1910, 13, 13)

COHEN, Jacob, was elected president of the Cosmopolitan Club at the annual elections held Wed. Sept. 21, 1910. Other officers elected were:- M.G. Greenberg, vice-pres.; L. Hartman, treas.; H.A. Harris, sec.; S. Lubelsky and Joseph Harris, directors (30 Sept. 1910, 13, 46)

COHEN, Magistrate Jacob, replies to his critics for fining the socialist orator, Matthew Weyman for holding an open-air meeting. He said "I have nothing to fear. The honor of Magistrate was conferred upon me in recognition of my services as Jewish interpreter in the Police Court for many years. While I am a foreigner, generally speaking, I have no hesitation in declaring that my residence in Canada has taught me that I should not overlook the fact that, like many others, I am duty bound as a naturalized citizen to appreciate the responsibilities of Canadian citizenhood." "In this connection I might say that I show no preference to any creed or nationality. My aim and whole purpose is to administer justice as I think right, and this policy will always be adhered to while I am permitted to occupy my present position. Jews and Gentiles alike get the same square treatment, and if they are not satisfied with my method of dispensing justice they have the right to appeal." (29 Aug. 1913, 16, 38)

COHEN, Miss Mamie, was elected president of the newly-formed B'noth Zion Juniors. Other officers elected were:- Miss Annie Berman, vice-pres.; Miss Fanny Brandwan, sec.; and Miss Bella Weintraub (13 June 1913, 16, 27)

COHEN, Mr. and Mrs. Arthur, are on a fishing trip at Bobcayageon (5 July 1912, 15, 30)

COHEN, Mrs. J.S. and her daughter, Miss Cecile Cohen, returned from Pointe-aux-Caril (29 Aug. 1913, 16, 38)

COHEN, Mrs. Joseph, has recovered from her recent illness (29 Aug. 1913, 16, 38)

COHN, David, is the newly elected president of the Judean Athletic Club. Other officers are:- Rubin Hazzan, vice-pres.; Louis Prager, treas.; Harry Simonsky, sec.; Harry Freed, sergeant-at-arms; S. Eason, A. Isaacson, H. Krugel, S. Pearlman and L. Turofsky, counsellors (26 July 1912, 15, 33)

COHN, I., of Chicago, was in Toronto for a few days (6 Sept. 1913, 15, 39)

COHN, J., H. Cohn, E.C. Fetzer, W. Rohleder and P.T. Seibin were successful Junior matriculants in Group D., without partial matriculation (16 Aug. 1912, 15, 36)

COHN, Mark G., has returned from holidays in Muskoka (16 Aug. 1912, 15, 36)

COHN, Miss B., of Rochester, N.Y., is visiting her sister in Toronto (20 Sept. 1912, 15, 41)

COHN, Mr. and Mrs. W., are visiting in Toronto (19 July 1912, 15, 32)

COOPER, Mrs. I. was elected president of the newly formed Jewish Day Nursery at a meeting last Mon. Other officers elected were:- Mrs. Landsberg, vice-pres.; Mrs. Fremes, treas.; Mrs. Halpern, sec.; and Rev. Caplan, hon. pres. Rev. Caplan, president of the Jewish Free Dispensary, told the meeting that the Dispensary would provide five rooms free of charge to the nursery. The Home is located at 111 Elizabeth St. (16 June 1911, 14, 31)

COPMAN, Miss Mary, returned from Preston, Ont. (30 Aug. 1912, 15, 38)

CORMAN, Miss, of New York, is visiting Miss R. Eismer in the city (30 Aug. 1912, 15, 38)

CORN, Harry, is in Preston, Ont. (9 Aug. 1912, 15, 35)

CORN, Miss A., returned from Preston, Ont. (30 Aug. 1912, 15, 38)

COSTINSKY, Cantor A., of the Jewish Congregation "Men of England", conducted the service marking the completion of the Sepher Torah held in the Zionist Institute, Sun. Dec. 26, 1909, 5 p.m. Rabbi S. Jacobs delivered the address and Rev. Kaplan conducted the choir. Miss A. Brand, Messrs. Gostinsky, Jacobson and Rev. Cohen participated in the musical program. A. Charwinsky, president of the congregation, presented pictures to S. Newman and A. Silver. H. Stanley is hon.-secretary of the congregation (31 Dec. 1909, 13, 7)

CUTLER, Miss Tillie, returned from Olcott Beach where she spent a month (30 Aug. 1912, 15, 38)

DANIELS, Miss, gave a party Sun. evening, Aug. 4, 1912 at her home for young men and women. Guests included:- Ben Cohen, Harry Cohn, Mr. Finemark, Harry Lavine, Theodore Levy, Abraham Moldaver, Mr. Pauline, R. Rose, Percy Shulman and the Misses Rose Bochner (Guelph), Martha and Ray Lavine, Miss Pauline and Mrs. Pikus, née Annie Webber (New York) (9 Aug. 1912, 15, 35)

DANSON, Miss Florence, has gone to Hamilton for a few days to visit Miss Raphael (3 Feb. 1911, 14, 12)

DAVIES, Miss Rhoda, is spending a few weeks at her parents' cottage in Carling, Muskoka (16 Aug. 1912, 15, 36)

DAVIS, A., obtained a B.Sc. in mining engineering with first rank honors from the University of Toronto (9 June 1911, 14, 30)

DAVIS, Arthur, mining engineer, has returned from the Barrie District, where he was on a survey (9 Aug. 1912, 15, 35)

DAVIS, Lionel, barrister, is summering at Pine Lands, Muskoka (9 Aug. 1912, 15, 35)

DAVIS, Lionel, barrister, returned from vacation at Muskoka, Ont. (30 Aug. 1912, 15, 38)

DAVIS, M. and J. Birnbaum spoke at the last meeting of the Cadmus Literary Circle which was held at the home of ? Soskin, 16 Lansdowne Ave. Miss Sophie Epstein, one of the club's most active members is on a trip to Europe (28 June 1912, 15, 29)

DAVIS, M., Emanuel J. Kenen and P. Levine were judges and examiners in Hebrew proficiency at the Hebrew School, 154 St. Patrick St., which is run by M. Cohen. Children passing the test were:- D. Asher and Barnet Cohen, first class; Sidney Applebaum and Louis Finkelstein, second class; Louis Cohen, A.I. Kenen, L.L. Kenen, M. Lizenwitz, D. Petersky, Yetta Pullan and Sam Rosenblum, third class (11 April 1913, 16, 18)

DAVIS, Miss Violet, is visiting relatives in London, England (19 July 1912, 15, 32)

DAVIS, Mrs. Henry and her daughter, Miss Violet Davis, returned from the Adirondacks where they spent the summer (29 Aug. 1913, 16, 38)

DICKMAN, Adolf, has returned from Kingston, Ont. where he was the guest of Mr. and Mrs. Abramsky (19 July 1912, 15, 32)

DICKMAN, Mr., some time ago, brought an action against Rabbis Gordon and Weintraub, resulting from a quarrel over the regulation of Schechita in Toronto (14 March 1913, 16, 14)

DONNENFELD, J., is president of the Romanian Sick Benefit Society, Adas-Israel of Toronto, which held its first annual ball on Feb. 2, 1910 in St. George's Hall. Other officers of the Society are:- D. Haimowitz, treas.; and M. Cohen, sec. Among those present were:- J. Cohen, Miss Haimowitz, Mesdames J. Donnenfeld, Siegler, Shein, Cohen and Ziff (18 Feb. 1910, 13, 14)

DRAIMAN, Archie, returned from his trip out west (11 Oct. 1912, 15, 44)

DRAIMIN, M., presided at the second annual banquet of the Zion Literary Club of Toronto at William's Cafe on Jan. 16, 1909. Speakers included:- G.M. Cohen, S.W. Davis, B. Geldzaeler and I. Vise (26 Feb. 1909, 12, 11)

DRAIMIN, Mrs. Charles, is in New York visiting her sister, Mrs. Will Goodman (1 Oct. 1913, 16, 42-43)

DRAIMIN, Mrs. Charles, is the guest of Mrs. Joseph King, in Whitby (29 Aug. 1913, 16, 38)

DUNKELMAN, Mr. and Mr. Rosenthal, two junk dealers were lured to a house where they were attacked by an unknown assailant. "It appears that on arriving at the appointed place Rosenthal and Dunkelman were met by a man with an iron rod. They were both knocked down, robbed and even stripped of their clothes. Fortunately Dunkelman was only apparently dead, and on recovery had strength enough left to make his way home. He soon, however, fell back into a state of unconsciousness from which he has but lately recovered. Rosenthal was killed on the spot. The murderer, a certain Gibson, was afterwards discovered." (7 June 1912, 15, 26)

DUSHMAN, Dr. Saul, of Schenectady, N.Y., spent three days in Toronto (19 July 1912, 15, 32)

DUSHMAN, Saul, has obtained a Ph.D. degree from the University of Toronto (9 June 1911, 14, 30)

DWORKIN, Harry, has returned from a business trip to New York (12 Aug. 1910, 13, 39)

DWORKIN, Messrs., Elizabeth St., are The Canadian Jewish Times representatives in Toronto (21 June 1912, 15, 28)

DWORKIN, Mrs. E., has returned from three weeks in Port Dover, Ont. (16 Aug. 1912, 15, 36)

EISSENBERG, M., M. Gelber, J. Hillelson, Daniel Jacobs, Rev. M. Kaplan, Mr. and Mrs. Emanuel I. Kenen, Habokuk Lubetsky, L. Lubetsky, Mr. and Mrs. J. Magder, M. Pomerantz, Mr. and Mrs. Rubinoff, S. Samuels, Mrs. J. Selick, E.I. Wolfson and Master Murry Clavir contributed to the Zionist Land Fund.

DWORKIN BROS.
64 ELIZABETH ST., TORONTO.

The Hebrew and English Book Sellers

We have just received our stock of the latest artistic NEW YEAR GREETING CARDS. Our prices are moderate.

We will be pleased to send out New Year's cards and prayer books to any part of the country. Just write what you want and send remittance to . . .

DWORKIN BROS.
64 Elizabeth Street, Toronto.   M. 5556

Contributions were made in honor of the Misses Edith Clavir and Annie Tanzman. Trees in the Herzl Wald were purchased in the name of Samuel Most (11 July 1913, 16, 31)

ELKAN, M., of Ed. Youngheart & Co., Montreal, is in Toronto for a few days (14 March 1913, 16, 14)

ENUSHEVSKY, Miss Jennie, is in the U.S. for five months, and will visit New York and Philadelphia (31 Jan. 1913, 16, 8)

FACTOR, Sam, is at Sparrow Lake, Ont., for a few weeks (9 Aug. 1912, 15, 35)

FACTOR, Sam, returned from two weeks at Crystal Beach (30 Aug. 1912, 15, 38)

FEINBERG, L., Rabbi J. Gordon, Gabriel Kling and L. Pollack are members of the recently organized Talmud Torah campaign committee (6 Sept. 1912, 15, 39)

FERIERSTOCK, Miss, hon. president of the Pride of Zion Society, chaired the annual monthly meeting, Sun. March 22, 1914. Those present included:- the Misses Lillian Chasey, Sadie Greenspon, Rose Mercer, Mollie Wasserman, and Mesdames E. Goldstick and J. Selick (27 March 1914, 17, 13)

FINBERG, Isidor, second year law, University of Toronto, won a scholarship. Samuel Factor and Charles Black, both in first year law, won scholarships. Mr. Factor came first in the class and Mr. Black came in second (20 June 1913, 16, 28)

FINBERG, Isidore, came first in second year law at the Christmas examinations at Osgoode Hall (7 Feb. 1913, 16, 9)

FINE, Mrs. Maurice, Baldwin Apts., gave a dinner party in honor of her sister-in-law, Miss Rose Fine, of Ottawa. Guests included:- M. Diamond, M.C. Pink, Mr. and Mrs. D.G. Davidson, Mr. and Mrs. J. Hirschberg, Mr. and Mrs. H. Ross, Mrs. S. Nurick, and the Misses Kate Nurick and Lillian Steinberg (31 Jan. 1913, 16, 8)

FINKELSTEIN, H., chaired the Mosaic Alumni meeting on June 23, 1912. A. Dickman's membership application was approved (28 June 1912, 15, 29)

FINKELSTEIN, Harry, read a paper on politics at the last Mosaic Alumni Society meeting (21 Feb. 1913, 16, 11)

FITCH, Louis, the well-known Montreal lawyer, addressed seven hundred Zionists in the Lyric Theatre in Toronto last Sun. "In the course of his speech, Mr. Fitch referred to the fact that in Palestine Jewish children were being given a thorough Hebrew training, and spoke their own ancient tongue, Hebrew." That same night he spoke at the Orange Hall (6 March 1914, 17, 10)

FLEISHMAN, Arthur, Julius Ramm, Dr. S. Dushman, W. Webber and the Misses Jennie Draimin, Mary Landsberg, Violet Davis, Rose Tugendhaft and Lizzie Meinster are volunteer teachers at the Zionist Jewish Free School which meets twice a week in the Zionist Institute, 249 Simcoe St. The school has 250 Jewish female students, from age seven years up. Edmund Scheuer is the school superintendent (1 June 1911, 14, 29)

FOGLER, Ben, spent his holidays in the Thousand Islands (9 Aug. 1912, 15, 35)

FRAENKEL, Leo, was elected president of Holy Blossom Congregation (German Synagogue) last Sun. Oct. 23, 1910. Other officers elected were:- S. Samuel, vice-pres.; William Goldstine, treas.; Arthur Cohen, sec.; I.C. Levy, A. Levy, S. Lorie, and Messrs. Merker, Lubelsky and Loeser (25 Oct. 1910, 13, 50)

FRAENKEL, Mrs. Maurice, Isabella St., leaves shortly for England to visit friends (25 March 1910, 13, 19)

FRANK, Henry, has returned from his purchasing trip to New York (5 July 1912, 15, 30)

FRANK, Henry, is about again, recovering from six weeks of illness (23 Aug. 1912, 15, 37)

FRANKEL, Leo and his wife, are in Frankfurt-on-Main, Germany for the golden wedding anniversary celebration of his parents, Herr and Frau Gottschall Frankel which took place Tues. Jan. 21, 1913. In Toronto, the occasion was celebrated with a family reunion at a dinner given by Mr. and Mrs. Maurice Frankel at their home, 120 Isabella St. Guests present were:- Rabbi and Mrs. S. Jacobs, Miss Julia Mayer (New York), Jacob Levy (Toronto), Mr. and Mrs. Herman Frankel and son, Joseph (Montreal), Ike Frankel (Montreal), Miss Elsa Nickelsburg, Mr. and Mrs. Herman Loeser, Louis, Egmont, Carl and Ivan Frankel and Master Leo M. Frankel (31 Jan. 1913, 16, 8)

FRANKEL, Leo, president of Holy Blossom Synagogue and Rabbi S. Jacobs distributed prizes to the religious school students last Sun. aft. Benno Scheuer conducted the choir (25 June 1909, 12, 28)

FRANKEL, Leo, was re-elected president of the Bond Street Synagogue. Other officers re-elected were:- S. Samuel, vice-pres.; William Goldstein, treas.; Arthur Cohn, sec.; S. Lawry, S. Merker, A. Levy, J. Levy, H.N. Loeser and B. Sugarman, trustees (2 Oct. 1912, 15, 43)

FRANKEL, Louis, is spending two weeks at Lake Rousseau (29 Aug. 1913, 16, 38)

FRANKEL, Mr. and Mrs. Leo and their sons Carl and Roy were joined in Baden-Baden by Mr. Frankel's parents (22 Aug. 1913, 16, 37)

FRANKEL, Mr. and Mrs. Maurice and family are in the Adirondacks (19 July 1912, 15, 32)

FRANKEL, Mr. and Mrs. Maurice, gave a surprise party in honor of the sixteenth birthday of their son, Ivan (2 Oct. 1912, 15, 43)

FRANKEL, Mrs. Leo, 504 Jarvis St., gave a reception at her home last Mon. (18 Feb. 1910, 13, 14)

FRANKEL, Mrs. Maurice, presented the Helena Frankel gold medal to Miss Frances Sieman at the Holy Blossom Sunday School closing exercises. Mrs. H.G. Levetus, past president of the Council of Jewish Women, presented the silver medal to Miss Fanny Pronoffsky (20 June 1913, 16, 28)

FRANKEL, Mrs., principal of the Holy Blossom Synagogue Sabbath School, delivered an address which was reprinted (19 July 1912, 15, 32)

FREEMAN, H., of the Judean Athletic Club, won the one mile walk at a recent track and field meet. Other winners were:- M. Stein and D. Pearlman, 220 yard race and S. Samuels, standing broad jump (16 Aug. 1912, 15, 36)

FREMES, Mr. and Mrs. S., will soon move to their beautiful new residence on Palmerston Blvd. (29 Aug. 1913, 16, 38)

FRIEDMAN, Harry, M. Herzlich, Nathan Phillips and Ephraim Sugerman, B.A., passed their final examinations at Osgoode Hall Law School and were called to the Ontario Bar. Other University of Toronto graduates receiving their degrees were:- Abraham Brodey, B.A., his L.L.B.; Isidore Goldstick and Percy Shulman, their B.A.s'; Meyer H. Goodman, his B.A.Sc.; and Maurice Pionick, his D.D.S. David Breslove, third year arts, won the Moss Scholarship for Classics, and Harry Finklestein, third year arts, the first Alexander Mackenzie Scholarship in Political Science (13 June 1913, 16, 27)

GARBER, Frank, son of Mr. and Mrs. M. Garber, celebrated his birthday Fri. evening, Aug. 23, 1912 (30 Aug. 1912, 15, 38)

GARDINER, Jacob and N.F. Freedman are members of the Judean Athletic Club (28 June 1912, 15, 29)

GARFUNKEL, Mr. and Mrs. Charles and family are vacationing at Elgin House, Lake Joseph, Muskoka (2 Aug. 1912, 15, 34)

GEBURTIG, M., was elected president of the McCaul Street Synagogue. Other officers elected were:- D. Finkelstein, vice-pres.; I. Goodman, treas.; M. Brown, sec.; and A. Cohn, 1st trustee (11 Oct. 1912, 15, 44)

GELBER, Lipa, chaired the discussion "The Relation of Social Work to Judaism", at the Hebrew Literary Society meeting last Sun. evening (15 April 1910, 13, 22)

GELBER, Mr. and Mrs. Lipa, are spending Passover in Montreal with Mrs. Gelber's parents, Mr. and Mrs. J.L. Morris (29 April 1910, 13, 24)

GELDZAELER, Ben, was on a fishing trip at Bobcaygeon, Ont. (9 Aug. 1912, 15, 35)

GELDZAELER, L., leaves shortly for Austria to visit friends (29 April 1910, 13, 24)

GENESOV, M., A. Glassberg, E. Goldstick, I. Goldstick and P. Shulman, were elected delegates to the Toronto Zionist Council at the last meeting of the Nordau Zion Club (31 Jan. 1913, 16, 8)

GINSBERG, Miss I., of London, Ont., is visiting friends in Toronto (5 July 1912, 15, 30)

GINSBURG, Miss Annie, of London, Ont., was in Toronto visiting friends (6 Sept. 1912, 15, 39)

GLASSBERG, Aaron, 109 Elizabeth St., writes "There is being formed in the city a cadet corps for Jewish boys only, having the name of Queen Esther Cadets. Already there are enough to form a company but great difficulty is encountered in the matter of purchasing uniforms for the boys - the rest of the accoutrement is supplied by the Government. It is here that the Toronto Jews can show their appreciation, both morally and financially, of the spirit on the part of the boys who are prepared to prove to our Gentile brethren that the Jews of Canada will not shirk their share in her defence." (22 Aug. 1913, 16, 37)

GLICKMAN, M. Oser, is the temporary local

manager of the Jewish Theatre, located on Agnes, corner of Terauley Sts. A contract was closed in the office of Louis M. Singer between Messrs. Pasternak and Rabinowitz, and Edwin A. Relkins, of the first Yiddish Theatrical Exchange, of New York, for the lease of the Jewish Theatre in Toronto, for the 1910-1911 season. The theatre will now be known as Edwin A.Relkin's Lyric Theatre (12 Aug. 1910, 13, 39)

GOLD, I., was installed as president of the YMHA. Other officers installed were:- M. Siegel, vice-pres.; L. Banet, treas.; H. Kofsky, fin. sec.; M. Fein, rec. sec.; K. Cohen, 1st trustee; A. Goldberg, 2nd trustee; M. Hirschorn, 3rd trustee; and A. Rappaport, sergeant-at-arms. H. Zweig, YMHA past president, obtained a charter for the society (12 July 1912, 15, 31)

GOLDBERG, Miss Fanny, 535 Richmond St. W., and Miss Lily Herman, 61 Gerrard St., will supply information to those Jewish girls wishing to join the newly-formed Daughters of Israel Society which will open a Sunday School at the McCaul Street Synagogue (23 May 1913, 16, 24)

GOLDBERG, Mrs. David, held a reception in honor of her recently married daughter, Mrs. Robkin (19 Sept. 1913, 16, 41)

GOLDBERG, Mrs. Hyman, Bathurst St., received for the first time since her marriage on Thurs. Dec. 1, 1910 (2 Dec. 1910, 14, 3)

GOLDBERG, Samuel, Maurice Hans, Hyman Katz, Isidore Fink, Samuel Gleek were arrested and charged with being disorderly as a result of a riot at the corner of Agnes and Terauley Sts. Sun. night, sparked by a Jewish missionary, Dr. Soskin, of Louisville, Ky. "...who it is claimed, has been attacking the Jews at a series of meetings during the week...". Others arrested were Harry Pinchefsky for assaulting the police and Nathan Girdstone for obstructing the police. Rabbi S. Jacobs came down to the police station but could not arrange bail. Dr. John Shayne, president of the B'nai Zion Association, "...stated that Mrs. Lizzie Pinchefsky was sitting in front of her store at 91 Agnes street, when the policeman ordered her to go inside and when she questioned the order, struck her over the seventh rib with his club and when she threw up her hand, struck again and fractured one of her fingers." Others for whom Dr. Shayne had medical certificates were;- Harry Pinchefsky and Joseph Weiss, bruises on the head; Nathan Girdstone, swelling over the left shoulder; and Samuel Goldberg, swelling below right ear (23 June 1911, 14, 32)

GOLDENBERG, B. (B.C.L.), of Toronto,was in town for a few days visiting his father (16 Aug. 1912, 15, 36)

GOLDENBERG, S., was chairman at the dedication ceremony of new synagogue "Hebrew Men of England" which is situated on Simcoe St., next door to the Associated Hebrew Charities. Rabbi M. Levy is the spiritual leader (30 Aug. 1912, 15, 38)

GOLDSMITH, Mrs. Perry, Carlton St., gave a tea last Mon. (3 Feb. 1911, 14, 12)

GOLDSTEIN, Herbert, is leaving Toronto to accept a more lucrative position in Montreal (9 Aug. 1912, 15, 35)

GOLDSTEIN, Herbert, of Montreal, a former Toronto boy, is a guest in the city (5 Sept. 1913, 16, 39)

GOLDSTEIN, Milton and Miss Fannie Singer were awarded medals at the Holy Blossom Synagogue Sabbath School closing exercises, Sun. aft., June 16, 1912 by Leo Frankel, the synagogue president. Mrs. Maurice Frankel is the school principal (21 June 1912, 15, 28)

GOLDSTEIN, Miss I., is on a visit with Mrs. Frank D. Benjamin, in London, England (5 July 1912, 15, 30)

GOLDSTEIN, Miss Irene, returned from her four months' trip abroad (20 Sept. 1912, 15, 41)

GOLDSTEIN, Mr. and Mrs. William, are receiving congratulations on the engagement of their daughter, Irene, to Harry Samuel, of Toronto (14 March 1913, 16, 14)

GOLDSTEIN, Mrs. William, returned from her visit to Montreal (28 Feb. 1913, 16, 12)

GOLDSTEIN, Mrs. William, returned from Montreal with her aged mother who will spend the summer at the Goldstein residence (19 July 1912, 15, 32)

GOLDSTEIN, Samuel, attempted suicide at the United Hebrew Charities Bldg. Mr. Goldstein called at the building Sat. evening and asked to be allowed to see his children who were being kept there. "He was informed by the caretaker that no visitors were allowed in the building after nine o'clock and was told to come again. This seems to have upset Goldstein, and returning a few minutes later, he asked for a glass of water. On this being given him he was seen a few moments after to totter backwards, and it was soon discovered he had by some means taken poison. Medical aid and the police were immediately telephoned for, and Goldstein was removed to the hospital." (21 Feb. 1913, 16, 11)

GOLDSTICK, M., of Waltham, Mass., is spending his holidays with his parents, Mr. and Mrs. T. Goldstick in Toronto (5 July 1912, 15, 30)

GOLDSTICK, Miss Dorothy, has gone to Acton, Ont. for a few weeks (19 Aug. 1910, 13, 40)

GOLDSTUCK, Miss Betty, hosted a stag party at her home last Sat. evening given by the Herzl Girls Zionist Society for their members. Some of the girls present were:- the Misses Eva Goldhar, Betty and Jennie Goldstick, Raby Herman, Clara Israels, Esther and Augusta Kenen, Elizabeth and Rose Meinster, Florence Most, Anna Nathanson, Lillie Rosenfield, Esther Shulman, Minnie Silver, Henrietta Stein and Fanny Taylor (14 Nov. 1913, 16, 49)

GOODMAN, H.M. and W.N. Winkler read papers at the Mosaic Alumni meeting last Sun. (21 March 1913, 16, 15)

GOODMAN, H.M., was elected president of the Mosaic Alumni, a society founded by Jewish students at the University of Toronto. Other officers elected were:- A.E. Halpern, vice-pres.; E.F. Singer, treas.; J. Ross, fin. sec.; S. Factor (Osgoode, Ont.), rec. sec.; C. Temes, sergeant-at-arms; C. Black (Osgoode, Ont.), H. Friedman and H. Finkelstein, executive council (29 Dec. 1911, 15, 7)

GOODMAN, Mr. and Mrs. L. and Mrs. Feinstein, of New York, are visiting Toronto (26 July 1912, 15, 33)

GOODMAN, Mrs. L., was given a surprise party at her home Sun. evening, Aug. 25, 1912 at her home (30 Aug. 1912, 15, 38)

GOODMAN, Mrs., of New York, visited her parents, Mr. and Mrs. King, Lowther Ave. She was accompanied home by her sister Mrs. Charles Draiman (11 Oct. 1912, 15, 44)

GORDON, A. and P. Shulman are the Nordau Zion delegates to the Zionist convention in Ottawa (28 June 1912, 15, 29)

GORDON, Alexander, is moving to Montreal from Toronto, much to the great regret of the Nordau Zion Club (9 Aug. 1912, 15, 35)

GORDON, Alexander, raised the question of the influence of Toronto missionaries on Jewish children and advocated immediate steps be taken against the evil at a Nordau Zion Club meeting, July 4, 1912. Miss S. Swiss is a newly admitted member. A report was given on the outing held in honor of Max Lurie, formerly of Toronto and now of Edmonton, Alta. (9 Aug. 1912, 15, 35)

GORDON, J.M., was a successful Junior matriculant in Group B., passing nine subjects (16 Aug. 1912, 15, 36)

GORDON, Miss Hester, of Toronto, is visiting her sister, Mrs. I. Lande in Montreal (28 June 1912, 15, 29)

GORDON, Moses, returned home to Toronto from a visit to his daughter, Mrs. I. Lande, of Westmount, Que. (20 Sept. 1912, 15, 41)

GORDON, Mrs. M. and Miss Hester Gordon left for Ahmic Harbor for the summer (4 July 1913, 16, 30)

GORDON, Rabbi J., collected funds for the Relief of Jews in Salonika from:- G. Chiat, H. Cohen, H. Elisus, S. Ellinson, N. Fineman, A. Gold, M. Gold, S. Gold, M. Gordstein, M. Gotkin, A. Greenspaun, M. Gulcau, D. Kaufman, L. Kelman, E. Kellman, A. Levy, E. Levy, A. Mernick, D. Norwitsky, M. Rumm, E. Sackovitz, M. Saladinsky, Sam Saladinsky, E. Shube, B. Slotkin, F. Slotkin, H. Slotkin, Sam Slotkin, I. Sniderman and M. Snitsky (27 Dec. 1912, 16, 3)

GORDON, Rabbi J., originated the idea of an "Achusah" to be patterned along the lines of a similar society in St. Louis. The plan was submitted to the B'nai Zion Society. "A tract of land will be bought in Palestine amounting in value to 50 to 75 thousand dollars, which will be in the private possession of the shareholders of the company." Alexander Cash will purchase $5,000. worth of shares. Rabbi Gordon and Barnett Stone will purchase shares at $1,000 each (30 Aug. 1912, 15, 38)

GORDON, Rabbi Nathan, of Montreal, addressed a Zionist mass meeting of over 1200 people in the University Avenue Synagogue, Sun. night, Jan. 17, 1909. The meeting, which was chaired by Barnett Stone, was organized by the United Zionists of Toronto. Edmund Scheuer led the school choir. L. Miller, of Buffalo, spoke in Yiddish on the principles of Zionism (22 Jan. 1909, 12, 6)

GOTESKIND, Moses, a peddler, was brutally assaulted last week. "The peddler was invited to enter a house at 1349 Dundas Street Junction to show his goods. No sooner had he entered, however, into the Gentile's house, than a pail of water was thrown over him. On the peddler protesting, he was set upon by his assailant, and had two of his front teeth thrown out. The peddler on escaping from the house, went to the police station and issued a summons against his assailant." (1 Aug. 1913, 16, 34)

GOTTLIEB, Miss Julia and Miss Lillian Miller returned from their vacation in Rochester, N.Y. (23 Aug. 1912, 15, 37)

GRANATSTEIN, A., E.R. Sugarman, S.M. Maher. M.A. Pollock, A. Draimin, J. Singer, M. Swartz, S. Herzlich and I.R. Smith were on the reception committee at the eighth annual ball of the Judeans' Literary Club held last Wed. evening at McConkey's. There 250 guests and supper was served in the Palm Room (21 Jan. 1910, 13, 10)

GRANATSTEIN, I.M., 53 St. Patrick St., is visiting friends in New York (18 March 1910, 13, 18)

GRANATSTEIN, I.M., St. Patrick St., has returned home from England (10 March 1911, 14, 17)

GRANATSTEIN, I.M., Wellington St., has gone on a three months' business trip to Leeds, England (6 May 1910, 13, 25)

GRANATSTEIN, Mr. and Mrs. J.T. and their two children, 161 Beverley St., will sail from Halifax for England on Feb. 11, 1911 aboard the S.S. Empress of Ireland, en route for Leeds where Mr. Granatstein has a branch of his business. Mr. and Mrs. Mimshewitz, Bathurst St., tendered a reception for them at their home. A theatre party was given in their honor by Mr. and Mrs. Rosenberg (10 Feb. 1911, 14, 13)

GRANATSTEIN, Mr. and Mrs. S.J., 161 Beverly St., had a birthday party for their daughter, Lillie, on Sun. aft. with about thirty-five children attending (28 Jan. 1910, 13, 11)

GREENBLATT, Mr. is president of the K'neseth Yisrael Synagogue which was dedicated Sun. Sept. 8, 1912. Mr. Jacobs is the treasurer. Rabbis Levy and Gordon and B. Nathanson addressed the audience and Cantor Wladofsky conducted the choir (11 Sept. 1912, 15, 40)

GREISMAN, H., has returned from a business trip to Washington (15 April 1910, 13, 22)

GREISMAN, Mrs. H., was elected president of the Roumanian Benefit Society, Avas Achim. Other officers elected were:- Mrs. S. Shafer, vice-pres.; Mrs. Mayerbach, treas.; and Mrs. M. Hartman (6 Jan. 1911, 14, 8)

GROSSMAN, Mr., left last Fri. to visit friends in England and Austria (17 June 1910, 13, 31)

GROSSMAN, Mrs. S.M., gave a whist party Wed. aft. at her summer home, 42 Lake Front, Kew Beach, in honor of her sister, Mrs. I. Levinoff, of Montreal, who is visiting her parents, Mr. and Mrs. I. Rittenberg. Prizes were won by Mesdames I. Seigal and A.A. Simonski (21 June 1912, 15, 27)

GROSSVOGEL, Mr., has gone to Strassbourg, Germany, his native town, for three months (31 Jan. 1913, 16, 8)

GUROFSKY, Joseph chaired a meeting last Sat. evening which was held by Controller Geary who is candidate for mayor. Other speakers at the meeting were Jacob Cohen and Louis Gurofsky (31 Dec. 1909, 13, 7)

GUROFSKY, L.S., J. Mehr, J. Meyer, S. Schwartz, Mrs. Manheim, Rabbi Gordon and the relatives of the late W. Korotkin donated funds towards the Chesed Shel Emeth of Toronto (1 Nov. 1912, 15, 47)

GUROFSKY, Louis, has gone on a few weeks' business trip to England, Russia, Germany and Romania (17 June 1910, 13, 31)

GUROFSKY, Louis, has returned from a business trip to Montreal (1 June 1911, 14, 29)

GUROFSKY, Louis, wrote a letter to the editor, Feb. 19, 1910, soliciting support and funds for building the general hospital in Toronto (25 Feb. 1910, 13, 15)

Are you thinking of a trip to Europe either for business or pleasure?

We are agents for all the ocean liners.

Phone Adelaide 260 and one of our staff will call with all information.

Louis Gurofsky
113 Queen. West
TORONTO

White Label Ale

is chosen mostly for flavor—flavor that's produced by purity, cleanliness and experience.

GET IT AT DEALERS AND HOTELS

DOMINION BREWERY CO., LIMITED
TORONTO.

HALPERN, Mrs. Susie, was given a surprise party, Sat. evening, Dec. 2, 1911, by her friends at her home to mark her nineteenth birthday (8 Dec. 1911, 15, 4)

HANF, Miss, of New York, is the guest of Miss Gertrude Pasternak (26 July 1912, 15, 33)

HARRIS, Bud, of Buffalo, N.Y., was in Toronto (6 Sept. 1912, 15, 39)

HARRIS, Mrs. A. and her two daughters are visiting friends in Toronto (23 Aug. 1912, 15, 37)

HARRIS, Mrs. H., has returned from Montreal where she visited Mr. and Mrs. Shapiro (18 Feb. 1910, 13, 14)

HARRIS, S., 178 Queen St., has gone to Europe on business and will also visit his mother in Russia (21 April 1911, 14, 23)

HARRIS, S., 178 Queen St., has returned from a business trip to New York (26 Aug. 1910, 13, 41)

HARRIS, S., has returned from a weeks' holiday in Chicago (1 July 1910, 13, 33)

HARRIS, S., has returned from a business trip to Europe (30 June 1911, 14, 33)

HARRIS, S., has returned from a short stay in New York (11 Oct. 1910, 13, 48)

HART, Mr. and Mrs. Roslyn, of Montreal, were in Toronto (6 Sept. 1912, 15, 39)

HARTMAN, M., chaired the Hebrew Literay Society meeting last evening at which J. Bochenek spoke on "The Biography of Baruch D'Espinoza" (27 May 1910, 13, 28)

HARTMAN, Mr. and Mrs. Louis, have returned from New York where they visited friends (3 Feb. 1911, 14, 12)

HARTMAN, Mrs. Louis, Mesdames Berger, Maierbach, Goldstein, M. Hartman and the Misses Goldstein and Berger were in charge of the Austrian Ladies' Aid Society garden party and dance held last Wed. at the Cosmopolitan Club (12 Aug. 1910, 13, 39)

HEISER, Mrs. Ida, has gone to Buffalo, N.Y., to visit her brother, Mr. Snow (5 May 1911, 14, 25)

HELPERN, Miss Ettie; the Misses Korn; Miss Clara Teich; the Misses Kaplan; Miss Brodsky, of New York; Miss Pearl Levy, of Syracuse; the Misses Epstein; Mrs. Penturn, of Montreal; Miss Rebecca Soltz; the Misses Gordon; Miss Gray; Dr. Bessie Pullan; the Misses Breslau; Miss Fanny Goodman; Mrs. I.H. Siegel; Mr. and Miss Nathanson; Mr. and Mrs. S. Lewis and A.P. Lewis, convenor organized the fifth annual outing for Jewish children at the Centre Island picnic grounds, on Thurs. Sept. 2, 1909 (10 Sept. 1909, 12, 39)

HELPERT, Mrs. N., 52 D'Arcy St., secretary of

the Jewish Day Nursery and Children's Home, is accepting contributions for the home. "This institution combines the various functions of a children's creche, an orphan asylum and a relief organization." (21 March 1913, 16, 15)

HENSHER, Mrs. S.M., gave a party in honor of Mrs. Louis Vineberg, of Montreal. Among those present were:- Mr. and Mrs. L. Gelber, Mr. and Mrs. D. Levin, Dr. and Mrs. S. Levin, Mr. and Mrs. Geldzaler, Mr. and Mrs. P. Rosenberg and daughter, Mr. and Mrs. B. Roberts, B. Silberman, A. Rosenberg, E. Keyfitz, Messrs. A.P. Lewis, H. Selinjee and W. Hensher, of Montreal (28 May 1909, 12, 24)

HERBERT, Mr. and Mrs. Samuel (née V. Levy, of London, Eng.), returned from their honeymoon trip out east and are living in Toronto (30 Aug. 1912, 15, 38)

HERMAN, Miss R., is visiting friends in Ottawa (5 July 1912, 15, 30)

HERMANT, Mr. and Mrs. Percy, have just returned from a trip to the coast and California and are residing in the Sussex Court Apt., St. George St., Toronto (25 Oct. 1910, 13, 50)

HERMANT, Percy, is in Montreal, the guest of T.L. Morris (29 April 1910, 13, 24)

HERSHMAN, Mr., of Montreal, was in Toronto during the week (25 Nov. 1910, 14, 2)

HERTZ, Mrs. Emanuel (née Blanche Rosenthal), was in Toronto (6 Sept. 1912, 15, 39)

HESSER, S., was in Toronto (30 Aug. 1912, 15, 38)

HIRSCHBERG, Abraham, of New York, is visiting friends in Toronto (16 Aug. 1912, 15, 36)

HIRSCHBERG, Mr. and Mrs. J., 118 Grange Ave., gave a luncheon party at their home in honor of their son's birthday. Miss Millie Hirschberg and Miss Kate Murick provided the musical program and Miss Lillian Steinberg performed several vocal solos. Guests included:- Mr. and Mrs. G. Fainman and son, Mr. and Mrs. Maurice Fine, Mr. and Mrs. J. Freidman, Mrs. I. Helpert, Mr. and Mrs. Sam Hirschberg, Mr. and Mrs. Sol Hirschberg (Vancouver), Miss Ruth Misslow, Mrs. S. Nurick, Mr. and Mrs. H. Ross, and Mr. and Mrs. Schaeffer (17 Jan. 1913, 16, 6)

HIRSCHBERG, Mr. and Mrs. J., returned home after several weeks at Preston Springs (29 Aug. 1913, 16, 38)

HIRSCHFELDER, Miss Maud, is leaving for New York and Boston in May and will afterwards to abroad (15 April 1910, 13, 22)

HIRSHFELDER, Miss Maude, is visiting her sister in Ottawa (8 April 1910, 13, 21)

HOFER, Miss W., is visiting her sister in Toronto (19 July 1912, 15, 32)

HURWITZ, Mr. and Mrs. and son are spending three weeks in Pickering, Ont. (26 July 1912, 15, 33)

HYMOWITZ, B., is visiting friends in Toronto (5 July 1912, 15, 30)

ISAACS, Joel, of Chicago, a former Toronto resident, was in town visiting friends. A member of B'nai Brith, he is trying to establish a lodge in Toronto. "There should be no difficulty in enlisting the sympathy of the requisite number of members to form a branch of this Society in Toronto. The fraternity is well-known all over this Continent and Europe for its good work in behalf of the Jew and Judaism." (19 Sept. 1913, 16, 41)

JACOB, Rabbi S., returned from his trip to England and Europe (5 Sept. 1913, 16, 39)

JACOBS, Mrs. A., of Montreal, is in Toronto visiting her daughter, Mrs. Joseph Rosenthal (11 March 1910, 13, 17)

JACOBS, Mrs. A., of Montreal, is visiting her daughter, Mrs. I. Rosenthal, Carlton St. (4 March 1910, 13, 16)

JACOBS, Rabbi S., addressed a large gathering at Holy Blossom Synagogue during Chanukah. His text was taken from the dying words of Mattathias from the Book of Maccabees, "And ye, my children, be valiant and show yourselves men in behalf of the Law, for therein shall ye attain glory." (17 Dec. 1909, 13, 5)

JACOBS, Rabbi S., chaired the lecture given by the noted Hebrew scholar, Rubin Brainin on "The Life of Herzl" in the Agnes Street theatre, last Sun. night. Louis Singer moved the vote of thanks, seconded by B. Nathanson in Yiddish (25 Feb. 1910, 13, 15)

JACOBS, Rabbi S., criticized the notion that there is more wife desertion amongst the Jewish population in Toronto than other groups, at the Conference of Charities and Corrections held last week. He said "Why should the poor Jew be particularized as if to brand him as a monster practicing all the vices and crimes in the human calender?" (29 Oct. 1909, 12, 46)

JACOBS, Rabbi S., delivered a sermon "Next Year We Hope to be Free Men" on the first day of Passover in the Holy Blossom Synagogue (29 April 1910, 13, 24)

JACOBS, Rabbi S., has left for Kingston, Jamaica "...bearing with him Toronto's hearty good wishes for a safe and pleasant journey (9 July 1909, 12, 30)

JACOBS, Rabbi S., has left for Jamaica to visit friends (12 Aug. 1910, 13, 39)

JACOBS, Rabbi S., of Holy Blossom Synagogue, is on his annual trip to his native city, Sheffield, England (5 July 1912, 15, 30)

JACOBS, Rabbi S., of the Holy Blossom Synagogue, is also in charge of the Sunday School. "Official figures give the number of Jewish people in Toronto at about 15,000, which makes it the second largest Jewish centre in the Dominion. There are six principal synagogues in Toronto to meet the religious demand, and it is satisfactory to note that they are all orthodox." (7 May 1909, 12, 21)

JACOBS, Rabbi S., offered his personal support and that of the Bond Street Synagogue for the establishment of a YMHA in Toronto (25 Oct. 1912, 15, 46)

JACOBS, Rabbi S., preached a sermon about charity at the Succoth service (11 Oct. 1912, 15, 44)

JACOBS, Rabbi S., returned from his annual visit to his native city in England (23 Aug. 1912, 15, 37)

JACOBS, Rabbi S., spoke in favor of women's suffrage at City Hall on Jan. 24, 1913 declaring that "...no people in the world were more anxious to elevate womankind than the Jewish people." (31 Jan. 1913, 16, 8)

JACOBS, Rabbi S., was a member of the committee organized to petition the Minister of Justice in Ottawa to commute to life imprisonment the death sentence of a young man named Gibson who was found guilty of the murder of a Jewish peddler named Rosenthal (22 Oct. 1913, 16, 46)

JACOBS, Rabbi S., was elected hon. pres. of a new Zionist Society formed last Sun. evening in the Cosmopolitan Club. "The object of the formation of the new society was to attract more of the English speaking Jews to the movement." Other officers elected were:- Louis M. Singer, pres.; L. Levinsky, vice-pres.; Elias Pullan, treas.; A.P. Lewis, sec.; Barnett Stone, S. Fremes, C. Garfunkle, A. Goldberg and B. Laster, exec. comm. (20 June 1913, 16, 28)

JACOBS, Rabbi S., was elected vice-president of the Associated Charities of Toronto at its annual meeting on Tues. Feb. 8, 1910 (18 Feb. 1910, 13, 14)

JACOBS, Rabbi S., was present at a dinner given by the Lt. Governor of Ontario last week (24 March 1911, 14, 19)

JACOBS, Rabbi S., will sail for England on the S.S. Mauritania and will return to Toronto at the end of Aug. (27 June 1913, 16, 29)

JACOBS, S., of Buffalo, N.Y., was in Toronto (20 Sept. 1912, 15, 41)

JAFFE, K., Baldwin St., was in New York on business (3 Feb. 1911, 14, 12)

JOSEPH, J.N., of London, England, was in Toronto on business (20 Sept. 1912, 15, 41)

JOSEPHI, Miss K., is convenor of the Jewish Working Girls' Club which was organized by the Toronto Council of Jewish Women. Other committee members are:- Miss Adelaide Cohen, treas.; Mrs. Henry Frank, sec.; Mesdames Leo Frankel, S. Jacobs, H. Levetus, H. Marks, S. Samuel and the Misses M. King and Violet Davis (22 Nov. 1912, 15, 50)

JOSEPHI, Miss Kate, returned from a two months' trip to New York (22 Aug. 1913, 16, 37)

JOSEPHI, Miss, of New York, is visiting her aunt, Mrs. J.S. Cohen (29 Aug. 1913, 16, 38)

KAHN, F., is touring the North West on business (5 July 1912, 15, 30)

KAHN, Mrs. F., is visiting her sister, Mrs. Isaacs, in Chicago (5 July 1912, 15, 30)

KALLMEYER, Mrs. and daughters received Sun., prior to sailing for Europe where Miss Minnie will continue her art studies under the best masters in Berlin and Paris. They have rented their home in Rosedale to a professor from the University of Toronto (2 Oct. 1912, 15, 43)

KALLMEYER, Mrs. and her three daughters returned from Europe where they resided for one year. Miss Minnie Kallmeyer, a talented painter, studied at Munich and Paris art schools (5 Sept. 1913, 16, 39)

KAMMAN, Julius, read a paper on his visit to a

large steel works in the U.S. and the operation of a blast furnace at a Mosaic Alumni meeting on Feb. 2, 1913. I. Rabinovitch read a paper on the evolution of man (7 Feb. 1913, 16, 9)

KAPLAN, Miss Ida B., gave a masquerade dance at her residence, 166 John St., in honor of the marriage of her brother, S.M. Kaplan to Miss Rose Strausberg in Chicago on Sun. Oct. 29, 1911. B. Goldenberg, of Montreal proposed the toast. Miss M. Willinsky and B. Goldenberg won prizes for best costume while Miss S. Halpern and D. Vise took the waltz prizes (17 Nov. 1911, 15, 1)

KAPLAN, Miss L., 166 John St., Miss Geldzaeler, 115 Bond St., and Miss Keyfitz, 295 Simcoe St., of the Jewish Endeavor Sewing School are receiving contributions of books for a library to be opened which will help counteract the influence of missionaries (31 Jan. 1912, 15, 12)

KAPLAN, Miss Tessie, was given a surprise birthday party at her residence, 166 John St. The Misses Jennie Fremes, of New York, Ida Kaplan and Anna Sapera, assisted in receiving. Abe Singer proposed the toast. Among those present were:- the Misses Esther Rosenblatt, Rose Geldzaeler, Minnie Smith, Rose Fisher, of London, Susan Halpern, Elizabeth Epstein, Rose Smith, Lillian Epstein, of Detroit, Minnie Lieberman, Jennie Zivian, Gertrude Willinsky, Etta Levinter, Fanny Goodman, Mrs. M.R. Kawin, Max Fremes, Charlie Fremes, Moe Lieberman, Nathan Phillips, of Cornwall, Sol Kaplan, Lou Levy, Alex. Kohl, Theodore Levy, D. Vise and others (11 Nov. 1910, 13, 52)

KAPLAN, Mr. and Mrs. S.N., of Chicago, are guests of their parents, Rev. and Mrs. J. Kaplan, in Toronto (9 Aug. 1912, 15, 35)

REV. M. KAPLAN
:-: PRACTICAL :-:
מוהל ומסדר קדושין
166 JOHN ST.   **TORONTO**
PHONE MAIN 5906.

KAPLAN, Rabbi M., is chairman of the committee struck to establish a Jewish Shelter Home in Toronto, at a meeting held in the McCaul Avenue Synagogue last Sun. Other committee members are:- S. Levinter, L. Waldman and I. Bezvinik. Contributors are:- I. Singer, M. Bachrak, M. Gelber, I. Fremers, E. Pullan, S.S. Levinter, Louis Gelber, M. Lubinsky, J. Mayer, Rotstine Bros., and M. Antipetsky (13 May 1910, 13, 26)

KASEL, Gabe, of Chicago, visited the Scheuers and Strauses in Toronto (23 Aug. 1912, 15, 37)

KAUFFMAN, Mr. and Mrs. P., stayed at the Windsor Hotel while in Montreal (9 Jan. 1914, 17, 5)

KAUFMAN, Philip, lost control of the auto he was driving and ran down Miss Lillian Stein and another Jewish girl. Miss Stein died five hours later from injuries. Mr. Kaufman is under arrest and his trial is still pending (7 June 1912, 15, 26)

KENEN, I.E., Charles Pasternack and Rev. J. Waldman raised funds for the 2,000 children expected to be present at the Fresh Air Picnic organized by the Zionists on Tues. Aug. 13, 1912. Dr. John Shayne is Picnic committee chairman, Charles Pasternack, treasurer and J. Ram, secretary (9 Aug. 1912, 15, 35)

KING, Leo and son, Charles King, were in Toronto on a short visit (5 July 1912, 15, 30)

KING, Mr. and Mrs. Harry (née Steiner) are living in the Gloucester Apts. until spring when their new home on Walker Ave. will be ready (11 Oct. 1912, 15, 44)

KING, Mr. and Mrs. J.S., are staying at the Wolcott Hotel, in New York (6 May 1910, 13, 25)

KING, Mrs. Samuel, is touring Italy and Egypt (28 March 1913, 16, 16)

KING, Oscar and his brother-in-law, Maurice Cohen, are on a fishing trip (29 Aug. 1913, 16, 38)

KING, Oscar, Julius Ramm, Dr. S. Dushman and the Misses Jennie Draimin, Violet Davis, Jennie Goldstick, Mary Landsberg, Lizzie Meinster, Bessie Pullan, Jean Segal and Lily Singer are teachers at the Toronto Zionist Sabbath School. All are former pupils, with the exception of Dr. Dushman and Mr. Ramm (28 June 1912, 15, 29)

KLING, Mr. and Mrs., have returned from a short stay in Atlantic City (9 Aug. 1912, 15, 35)

KOFSKY, Mr., was elected president of the YMHA at the annual elections on Sun. Dec. 29, 1912. Other officers elected were:- M. Siegal, vice-pres.; H. Zweig, fin. sec.; Mr. Steinberg, rec. sec.; M. Levine, treas.; and Mr. Rappaport, sergeant-at-arms (10 Jan. 1913, 16, 5)

KOHL, Harry and Joseph Ross, are University of Toronto students who will be competing in the International Wrestling Tournament at the University of Pennsylvania in Philadelphia next week. Mr. Kohl won the Dominion wrestling championship several years ago and is studying analytical chemistry in the School of Science. Mr. Ross won several interfaculty and intercollegiate wrestling competitions and is studying mining engineering (14 Feb. 1913, 16, 10)

KRONICK, Samuel, has gone to Muskoka for a few days (2 Dec. 1910, 14, 3)

KRONICK, Samuel, has returned from a business trip to Montreal (8 April 1910, 13, 21)

KRONICK, Samuel, has returned from a business trip to Montreal (5 Aug. 1910, 13, 38)

KRONICK, Samuel, has returned from a business trip to Toronto (10 Feb. 1911, 14, 13)

KRONICK, Samuel, has returned from New York (29 April 1910, 13, 24)

KRONIK, S., has returned from a business trip to Montreal (18 March 1910, 13, 18)

LANDSBERG, J., was elected managing director of the Judean Athletic Club's rugby team which is being formed. It is anticipated the team will make its first appearance in the Intermediate City League. H. and D. Kohl are business managers (16 Aug. 1912, 15, 36)

LANDSBERG, Miss Mary, is president of the Toronto Daughters of Zion. Those participating at the first meeting of the season were:- Mrs. L. Cohen and the Misses Esther Gottlieb, Yetta Gottlieb, Annie Korn, Gertrude Nanniver, E. Landsberg, F. Lifchis, S. Rosen, D. Finemark and A. Brankstone (23 Sept. 1910, 13, 45)

LANDSBERG, Miss Mary, was re-elected president of the Toronto Daughters of Zion Society at the semi-annual meeting held recently. Other officers elected were:- Mrs. H. Cohen, vice-pres.; Miss Bertha Bernstein, treas.; and Miss Yetta Gotloeb, sec. (9 July 1909, 12, 30)

LANDSBERG, Miss Mary, will be inscribed in the Golden Book by members of Toronto Zionist Council on the occasion of her marriage which takes place on July 17, 1913 (11 July 1913, 16, 31)

LASTER, B. and H. Segal collected funds for the Relief of Jews in Salonika from :- B. Laster and family, G. Appel, E. Appelbaum, N. Baker, A. Berger, P. Blitstein, J. Breslin, A. Cash, A. Cohen, A. Crown, D. Davis, H. Davis, A. Dubin, J. Exler, H. Frankel, J. Garfunkel, G. Gelber, L. Goles, G. Goodman, H. Greisman, S. Greisman, N. Halpert, L. Hartman, E. Harris, J. Harris, H.E. Heller, A.C. Hirshman, A. Levine, S. Levinter, C. Lewis, S. Meyer, A. Midanik, J. Mehr, H. Papernek, N. Pchasias, Sam Peterboro, K. Pollock, D.E. Pullan, S. Rosen, B. Rosenthal, L. Rotenberg, A. Rotstein, M. Rubin, N. Rumm, E. Samuel, M. Segal, S. Schwartz, K.L. Shapiro, L. Shomer, P. Shore, Z. Shore, Eva Shulman, H. Shulman, P. Shulman, J. Singer, B. Stone, R. Tozman, M. Vineberg, S. Weber, C. Wilder, Frank Wilson, R. Wise and A. Zager (20 Dec. 1912, 16, 2)

LAVINE, Capt. Jack, commands the Queen Esther Cadets, which was founded a few months ago. "Besides military drill every Saturday night at the Armouries the Cadets are also instructed in physical drill by Serg't. Keith, Q.O.R., upon whose recommendation Captain Lavine and the following were elected by the cadets as commanders:- 1st. Lieut. Aaron Glassberg, 2nd Lieut. Pincus Yuskewitz and Sergeants H. Goldstein, H. Gordon, B. Kaminsky and C. Oielchaum. The Zionist Federation granted the QEC a charter "...so that now the only thing worrying the boys is how to induce the Jewish fathers to help them buy their uniforms, which is the only equipment the Government does not supply." (12 Dec. 1913, 17, 1)

LAVINE, D., was elected president of the University Avenue Synagogue. Other officers elected were:- S. Swartz, vice-pres.; J. Yanover, parnass; H. Vineberg, gabbai; M. Louis, sec.; M. Cohn, I. Cooper, I.F. Granatstein, S.M. Grosman, L. Levinsky and Z. Shor, trustees (11 Oct. 1912, 15, 44)

LAVINE, Misses Martha and Ray, have returned from Guelph where they were guests of Miss Rose Bochner (26 July 1912, 15, 33)

LAVINE, Mrs. (Dr.), Beverley St., gave a whist and tea Sun. aft. May 15, 1910, in honor of her seventh wedding anniversary. Guests included:- Mesdames J. Greenberg, S. Hansher, Arent, S.M. Grossman, and L. Bloom, of Rochester, N.Y., and the Misses Rittenberg (27 May 1910, 13, 28)

LEBOFSKY, Miss Annie, a student at Niagara Street Public School, received a book prize from the Imperial Daughters of the Empire for the best essay on "The British Empire" written by a Toronto school child (29 Dec. 1911, 15, 7)

LEO, Maitland, of Montreal, returned from Porcupine, Ont. (6 Sept.1912, 15, 39)

LEVETUS, Miss Lily B., is president of the Jewish Working Girls' Club which opened for the season at 36 Walton St., Sat. evening, Sept. 24, 1910. She is also president of the Council of Jewish Women of Toronto (30 Sept. 1910, 13, 46)

LEVI, E., has written a ritual book for the Zionist Jewish Free school. "The book is admirably adapted for the purpose, containing opening and closing prayers, hymns and grace after meals; the last named in both English and Hebrew (11 Oct. 1912, 15, 44)

LEVIN, Rev. M.A., of Montreal, was on a short visit to Toronto (11 Oct. 1910, 13, 48)

LEVINE, David, president of the University Avenue Synagogue, is summering with his family at Jackson's Point (22 Aug. 1913, 16, 37)

LEVINE, Jack, was elected president of the Queen Esther Cadets Corp at the election of club officers on Dec. 28, 1913. Other officers elected were:- Aaron Glassberg, vice-pres.; Sam Rosenthal, sec. (by acl.); Pincus Yuskovitz, treas.; Chas. Oelbaum, sergt.-at-arms; Simon Dickman, H. Goldstein, Abe Kaminsky, H. Lipschitz, A. Markowitz, Albert Naroll and Sam Sigal, exec. board (9 Jan. 1914, 17, 5)

LEVINE, Mr. and Mrs., 65 Sullivan St., gave a surprise party in honor of their daughter, Miss Martha Levine and her fiancé, A. Samuels (7 Nov. 1913, 16, 48)

LEVINNE, Mrs. D. and children, Shaw St., are on vacation at Jackson's Point (1 Aug. 1913, 16, 34)

LEVINSON, N., Church St., is in New York on business (17 Feb. 1911, 14, 14)

LEVY, A.S., has returned from Europe. His wife and sister remained behind with Mrs. Joseph Levy in Marienbad, Germany (19 July 1912, 15, 32)

LEVY, A.S., of Hamilton, was in Toronto for the day (30 Aug. 1912, 15, 38)

LEVY, Miss Blanche, returned from a stay in New York (30 Aug. 1912, 15, 38)

LEVY, Miss Evelyn, of Rochester, N.Y., is visiting her sister, Mrs. Dr. Levine (29 Aug. 1913, 16, 38)

LEVY, Mortimer, J. Landsberg, L. Marcus, S. Steinberg, J. Teich and C. Temes are members of the Judean Athletic Club hockey team which accepted an invitation to play the Montreal YMHA team. D. Cohen, pres., and L.J. Gurofsky, vice-pres., of the club will probably accompany the team to Montreal (14 March 1913, 16, 14)

LEWIN, Mrs. A., Beverley St., is spending the holidays at Muskoka (19 Aug. 1910, 13, 40)

LEWIS, A.P. chaired the Hebrew Literary Society last Sat. evening in the Zionist Institute. Louis M. Singer lectured on "The Jew and his Neighbor." (17 June 1910, 13, 31)

LEWIS, A.P., chaired the founding meeting of the Jewish Ratepayers' Association held Sun. Oct. 17, 1909 in the University Avenue Synagogue chambers. He stated "We all have different opinions on most subjects. The Jew is a plain-spoken, independent thinker, alive to the interests of his people. The question of increased taxes now agitating Ward 3 interests us in many ways. The Assessment Commissioner reports an increase of 18 millions above last year for Ward 3; the population in our section has decreased by 2,888. In the face of these figures, the Moral and Social Reform and Foreign Missions 'appeal for help to grapple with the 30,000 foreigners in Toronto, mostly Jews.'" Others at the meeting were Louis M. Singer, Mr. Goodman and Dr. John Shayne (22 Oct. 1909, 12, 45)

LEWIS, A.P., Rev. J. Waldman, Philip Shear, S. Rogul, Dr. John Shayne, B. Stone, Mr. and Mrs. Emanuel I. Kenen, Mr. and Mrs. Seilig, and the Misses J. Cohen, S. Smith, E. Goodman, E. Greenberg, S. Kaplan, M. Levin, E. Levinsky, L. Levinsky, A. Silverberg, E. White, Fundberg, Kenen and Landsberg worked hard to make the Zionist Fresh Air annual picnic a success. The picnic was held Tues. Aug. 13, 1913 on Central Island (16 Aug. 1912, 15, 36)

LEWIS, A.P., was elected president of the Hebrew Ratepayers Association at a meeting held last Sun. Other officers elected were:- Dr. John Shayne, 1st vice-pres.; J. Goodman, 2nd vice-pres.; Chas. Sher, 3rd vice-pres.; Chas. Pasternak, hon. treas.; Louis M. Singer, hon. corr. sec.; S. Goldenberg, hon. rec. sec. Naturalization Committee members are: Dr. Shayne, chairman; Jacob Cohen, J.P., L. Shumer, Messrs. Daniels, Fingerhoot and Gelber. Municipal Committee members are: Mr. Sher, chairman; S. Glickman, L. Gurofsky, Messrs. Lesser and Glickman. Propaganda Committee members are: J. Goodman, chairman; Z. Broody, A. Sher, J. Fine and Mr. Yoshkovitz. Press Committee members are: A.P. Lewis, Louis M. Singer and S. Goldenberg (19 Nov. 1909, 13, 1)

LEWIS, A.P., was elected president of the Judeans, Wed. evening, Dec. 14, 1910. Other officers elected were:- Arch. Draimin, vice-pres.; B. Brown, treas.; D. Cadesky, sec.; M. Levy, J. Singer, R. Smith, executive committee; M. Levy, J.W. Brody and M. Schwartz, membership committee (2 Dec. 1910, 14, 3)

LEWIS, Mr. and Mrs. S. and Mr. and Mrs. I.H. Siegel, 70 Leuty St., wish their relatives and friends a happy New Year (10 Oct. 1913, 16, 44)

LIEBERMAN, Miss Rebecca, was in Ottawa last Tues. for the grand ball at the Chateau Laurier (28 March 1913, 16, 16)

LORIE, Mr. and Mrs. A., have returned from the West Indies where they spent the winter (10 March 1911, 14, 17)

LORIE, Mr. and Mrs. S., are visiting their daughter Zelina Lorie, who is at school in Wiesbaden, Germany (19 July 1912, 15, 32)

LUBELSKY, S., has left on a business trip to Montreal and New York (21 Jan. 1910, 13, 10)

LUBELSKY, S., has returned from a short trip to Winnipeg (22 July 1910, 13, 36)

LUBELSKY, S., has returned from Atlantic City (15 April 1910, 13, 22)

LUBELSKY, S., manager of the Eaton Co. in Toronto, was in New York on a business trip (10 Dec. 1909, 13, 4)

LUBELSKY, S., returned from a business trip to Europe last Thurs. (5 May 1911, 14, 25)

LUBELSKY, Sigmund, has returned from a short visit to New York (18 March 1910, 13, 18)

LUBELSKY, Sigmund, left last night for Europe on business (6 May 1910, 13, 25)

LUBINSKY, J., has left on an extended trip to England, France, Germany and Austria (4 Feb. 1910, 13, 12)

LUBLESKY, Sigmund, left for Europe yesterday on business (10 March 1911, 14, 17)

LURIE, C., Barnett Stone, Alexander Cash and

Samuel Kronick have loaned $500 each towards the construction of the new $25,000 Zionist Assembly Hall to be built on the lawn of the Zionist Institute, facing University Ave. (16 Aug. 1912, 15, 36)

LURIE, Max, is one of the Nordau Zion club founders, who has made his home in Edmonton. He is visiting Toronto and will be honored with a banquet (14 June 1912, 15, 27)

LURIE, Max, of Edmonton, a former member of the Nordau Zion Club, forwarded ten dollars to the club (21 March 1913, 16, 15)

LYONS, Jake and family are in their new home on Kendall Ave. (30 Aug. 1912, 15, 38)

LYONS, Misses Pauline, Rose Jacobs, Ray Jacobs, Dora Franklin, Stella Miller, Minnie Willinsky, Jessie Bloom, Eva Rittenberg, Jessie Brown (Detroit), Sadie Aaron, Sactre Arent, M. Wolff (Ottawa), M. Pullan, L. Harris (Hamilton), Benjamin, Teich, Davis, Goldsmith, Scheuer, Levy, Bernbohm, Mintz (Hamilton), Taube, Stein (Cleveland), Draimin, Kaplan, Keyfitz, Broudey, Marks, Fremes (New York), Raphael (New York), Danson, Cadesky, Schwartz, Pullan (Ottawa), Mendelsohn, Ibson, Prager, Kaufman (Hamilton), Duefell (Hamilton) and Mesdames Sam Herbert, Sol. Herbert, I. Herbert, I. Horwitz, Arthur Simonsky, Palter, Mendelsohn and Dr. Bessie Pullan were among those present at the Judeans' ninth annual ball last Wed. night at McConkey's. Messrs. A.P. Lewis, Joseph Singer, M. Pollak, M. Smith, Cadesky, Wilson and Brody were members of the arrangements committee ((27 Jan. 1911, 14, 11)

MARGOLIS, J., a student at Schecter's Seminary, New York, is on vacation visiting his parents in Toronto (26 July 1912, 15, 33)

MAYER, Miss Emma, is the guest of Mr. and Mrs. Leo Fraenkel, Jarvis St. (5 May 1911, 14, 25)

MEHR, Jacob, William Waldman, Jacob Bezwinik, S.M. Grossman, D.Z. Singer, K.L. Shapira, A. Pullan and Messrs. Antipetsky, Lewinter, Frimes, Rotstein and Wilensky have formed a Matzo fund for the poor this coming Passover and have themselves subscribed $1,000.00. Rev. M. Kaplan is the chairman (1 April 1910, 13, 20)

MEHR, Mrs. M., 93 Nassau St., is receiving contributions for the Passover Shoe and Stocking Fund organized by the Hebrew Ladies' Sewing Circle (11 April 1913, 16, 18)

MERIN, Miss S., returned home to New York after a visit to Toronto (23 Aug. 1912, 15, 37)

MEYERS, Ben, has recovered from a severe illness (22 Aug. 1913, 16, 37)

MICHAEL, Mr. and Mrs., of Little Rock, Ark., are spending the summer with their daughter, Mrs. Edgar Weil in Burlington, Ont. (9 Aug. 1912, 15, 35)

MIDANIK, Miss Annette, returned from Havelock, Ont. (30 Aug. 1912, 15, 38)

MILLER, Mr. and Mrs. Coleman, were "at home" Sept. 7, 1912, in honor of their twenty-fifth wedding anniversary (2 Oct. 1912, 15, 43)

MILLER, Hyman, of Winnipeg, is in Toronto visiting his mother and grandmother (23 Aug. 1912, 15, 37)

The History of the .. Toronto Jews ..

¶ We wish to inform our readers that we will shortly print in the Jewish Times the History of the Toronto Jews

From the first Jew that settled in Toronto up-to-date

Our readers may expect something of real interest.

Management "Jewish Times."

MILLER, Mr. and Mrs. Isidore, purchased a home on Kendall St., where they will shortly move (2 Oct. 1912, 15, 43)

MILLER, Mr. and Mrs., of Rochester, N.Y., are guests of Mr. and Mrs. P. Sher, Major St. (17 Feb. 1911, 14, 14)

MILLER, Mrs. Isadore and daughter, Miss Stella Miller and Miss Ethel Goldstein returned from Point au Baril where they spent the summer (22 Aug. 1913, 16, 37)

MILLER, Mrs. L.E., and her niece, Miss Violet Davis, who are in Europe, will spend the Holy Days in London, England (30 Aug. 1912, 15, 38)

MILLER, Mrs. Lucille, is spending the winter in New York (21 March 1913, 16, 15)

MINKIN, Rabbi J.S., of Hamilton, spoke on "Women's Suffrage" from the Jewish standpoint, at the Hebrew Ladies' Sewing Circle meeting. "After dealing with the supposed 'inabilities' of women, which he said were really 'disabilities' imposed by men themselves, the Rabbi passed on to a comparison between the feminine ideals of the Christian and Jewish religions. Christianity, he said, puts women on a pedestal so high that mortal eyes cannot reach her. Judaism places her side by side with man, as his companion and his equal mentally, morally, physically, religiously, and intellectually." (16 Jan. 1914, 17, 6)

MINKIN, Rabbi, of Hamilton, addressed the B'nai Zion Society in Toronto on Sun. (1 June 1911, 14, 29)

MOSES, Henry, was elected the first president of the Hebrew Roumanian Sick Benefit Society at its founding meeting on Sun. Jan. 15, 1910 (21 Jan. 1910, 13, 10)

MOYER, Carl, returned home to Garret, Indiana after visiting his sister, Mrs. N. Halpert, D'Arcy St. (11 April 1913, 16, 18)

NAROLL, Master, is president of the Junior Zionist Literary Council. Other officers are:- Miss Jennie Firerstock, vice-pres.; Alexander Shayne, treas.; and Miss Freda Kenen, sec. (3 April 1914, 14)

NARROL, A.A., was elected president of the B'nai Zion Juniors for the next six months. Other officers elected were:- Alexander Shatz, vice-pres.; Burney Vise, treas.; Sam. Luxenberg, fin. sec.; Morris Lavine, rec. sec.; and Charles Egelnick, marshal (10 April 1914, 17, 15)

NATHANSON, B. and D. Shatz are Baale tefila for the newly created Yavneh congregation, a Zionist synagogue organized by the B'nai Zion in Toronto (23 Aug. 1912, 15, 37)

NATHANSON, B., chaired the Hebrew Literary Society meeting last Sat. evening. Mr. Perlstein led the discussion "The Evolution of Jewish History" (13 May 1910, 13, 26)

NATHANSON, B., Norman Ramm, Morris Genser, David Springman, David Siegel, and M. Slabodsky contributed to the Zionist Land Fund (28 June 1912, 15, 29)

NATHANSON, B., superintendent of the Toronto Talmud Torah spoke on "Jewish Women in Charity" at the Toronto Hebrew Ladies' Sewing Circle meeting, Tues. aft., Jan. 23, 1912, 218 Simcoe St. Those attending included:- Mesdames S. Harris, J. Hillelson, N. Rosenberg and I.H. Siegel (31 Jan. 1912, 15, 12)

NATHANSON, George M., a Detroit lawyer, spent two days in Toronto visiting his parents, Mr. and Mrs. B. Nathanson (20 Sept. 1912, 15, 41)

PAPERNICK, Miss Elsie, is president of the Nordau Girls club which will move its meeting to the Associated Charities building on Simcoe St. "The girls have decided to do some sewing for the poor who apply at that institution." Other officers are:- Miss Sophie Lester, vice-pres.; Miss B. Silver, treas.; and Miss May Weingarten, sec. (28 June 1912, 15, 29)

PASTERNAK, Mr. and Mrs. Charles, have gone to Mount Clemens for a month (8 July 1910, 13, 34)

PAUBE, Morris, of Calgary, formerly of Toronto, was in the city (20 Sept. 1912, 15, 41)

PEARLMAN, J., has returned from a trip to New York (26 July 1912, 15, 33)

PERRY, Miss Hannah, of Indianapolis, is visiting Mrs. N. Helpert, D'Arcy St. They left for two weeks at Jackson's Point (1 Aug. 1913, 16, 34)

PHILLIPS, L., B. Cohn, W. Harris and the Misses S. Caplan, Augusta Kenen, R. Cohn and C. Peuesh spent a day picniking at Olcott Beach (19 July 1912, 15, 32)

POLLOCK, Dr. M.A., 225 University Ave., moved his office to 149 Beverley St. (19 Dec. 1913, 17, 2)

POLLOCK, G. and H. Herschkowitz were successful Junior matriculants in Group C., who have partial matriculation, with more than three subjects still to write (16 Aug. 1912, 15, 36)

PRAGER, Miss E., is president of the Literdram, a young ladies club. Other members are:- Misses M. Livingstone, M. Lifchis, J. Zivian, M. Lieberman, S. Halpern, A. Sapera, F. Korn, Minnie Willoughby, Edith Espar, L. Solway, S. Ginsberg and M. Bernstein (15 April 1910, 13, 22)

PROSKY, Samuel, whose land abuts that of the Congregation Beth Hamedrash Chevrah Thilim, is being compelled to tear down part of a building which the congregation claims he erected on their land. "Mr. Prosky claims that the land is his according to a competent surveyor's plan made 30 years ago, and, in any event, would be his by a ten year's grant of possession." The court has reserved judgment in the case (7 March 1913, 16, 13)

PULLAN, A., was elected president of Goel Zedek Synagogue last Sun. (25 Oct. 1910, 13, 50)

PULLAN, Miss D., 80 d'Arcy St., is visting friends in Ottawa (5 July 1912, 15, 30)

PULLAN, Miss Dora, has returned from Hamilton and Paris, Ont. (9 Aug. 1912, 15, 35)

PULLAN, Mr. and Mrs. M., Sherbourne St., gave a dinner Sun. Feb. 23, 1913, for the out-of-town guests who attended the wedding of their niece, Miss Martha Pullan, eldest daughter of Mr. and Mrs. Elias Pullan on Thurs. Feb. 20. Mrs. Pullan was assisted in receiving by her daughters, Mrs. Norman Rosenberg and Mrs. Dr. Pullan-Singer (28 Feb. 1913, 16, 12)

PULLAN-SINGER, Dr. Bessie T., Master Bunnell and nurse, with her sister, Mrs. N. Rosenberg and little daughter, Merle, are in Atlantic City for the summer (25 July 1913, 16, 33)

RAFELMAN, Mr. and Mrs. A., returned from three weeks' vacation at Preston Springs (1 Aug. 1913, 16, 34)

RAFELMAN, Mrs. A., was elected president of the Jewish Day Nursery and Children's Home which takes care of about thirty-five children and has a membership of about four hundred. Other officers elected were:- Mrs. Landsberg, vice-pres.; Mrs. Fremes, treas.; Mrs. N. Helpert, fin. sec.; and Mrs. Mendelson, rec. sec. (1 Aug. 1913, 16, 34)

RAFFELMAN, Mrs. A., was elected president of the Day Nursery and Children's Home. Other officers elected were:- Mrs. A. Landsberg, vice-pres.; Mrs. A. Fremes, treas.; H. Halpert, fin sec.; M. Mendelsohn, rec. sec.; and Rev. M. Kaplan, hon. pres. (11 Oct. 1912, 15, 44)

RAUNER, Mr. and Mrs. A., are guests of Mr. and Mrs. W. Rauner in Toronto (26 July 1912, 15, 33)

RELKIN, Edwin A., owner of the only Yiddish Theatrical Exchange of New York, is on a business trip to Toronto (5 Aug. 1910, 13, 38)

RITTENBERG, Mr. and Mrs. I., 31 Grange Ave., gave a surprise party at their residence in honor of their daughter, Mrs. Boyaner, of Edmonton, Alta. who has recovered from a severe illness. The Misses Eva and Belle Rittenberg assisted. Among those present were:- Mesdames I. Cooper, B. Cooper, S. Fremes, S.M. Grossman, K.L. Sapera, Rafelman, Helpert, Granatstein, Keyfitz, Levinsky, Ticktin and D. Levine (7 July 1911, 14, 34)

ROCK, Jack, a former Toronto boy, from Chicago, is on a visit (30 Aug. 1912, 15, 38)

ROSE, Miss Della E., of New York, is spending a holiday with her aunt, Mrs. H. Cohen, 434 Palmerston Blvd. (12 Aug. 1910, 13, 39)

ROSEN, H., leaves shortly for England on a business and social trip. He will also spend a few weeks in Carlsbad, Bohemia (29 April 1910, 13, 24)

ROSEN, Harry, has returned to Toronto after a two months' visit in England, Russia and Austria (5 Aug. 1910, 13, 38)

ROSEN, M., Alexander Cash, S. Garfinkel, J. Cohen, J.P., L. Levinsky, B. Nathanson, M. Sheffer, L. Leiboosky and Miss Mary Landsberg contributed to the Zionist Land Fund (23 June 1911, 14, 32)

ROSEN, Miss Sadie, and the Misses Esther Gottlieb, Yetta Gottlieb, Judith Landsberg, Annie Samuels, Ida Rosen, Ethel Cohen, Racie Breeman, Bessie Breebawm, Nellie Freeman, Bessie Gottloeb, Annie Corn, Flora Danson, Sadie Wolfe (Ottawa) and Mesdames Halpert, Taube, J. Gevinsky and Dr. Shayne were among those present at the Toronto Daughters of Zion annual dance and ball, held last Wed. in the Temple building (10 Feb. 1911, 14, 13)

ROSEN, R., returned from Chicago (23 Aug. 1912, 15, 37)

ROSENBAUM, Miss Fanny, of Rochester, N.Y., is visiting friends in Toronto (23 Aug. 1912, 15, 37)

ROSENBERG, Fred, returned from a trip to Europe (21 March 1913, 16, 15)

ROSENBERG, Mrs. P., 408 Bathurst St., hosted a tea Tues. aft., in honor of her sister, Miss Rosetta Myers, of Winnipeg. Those assisting were:- Mrs. L.H. Wolfe, of Detroit, and the Misses Jennie Draiman, Sadie Arent, Pearl Broady and Francis Merker (14 Jan. 1910, 13, 9)

ROSENFELD, Morris, lectured in the Association Hall, Toronto on Fri. evening (1 June 1911, 14, 29)

ROSENTHAL, Miss Rose, of Rochester, N.Y., who was a guest of the Nathanson's, was given a farewell party at the home of Mr. and Mrs. S. Breslin, 54 Cecil St. (6 Sept. 1912, 15, 39)

ROSENTHAL, Mr. and Mrs. W. and family, Palmerston Ave., have gone to Kerr Beach for the summer (1 June 1911, 14, 29)

ROSENTHAL, Mrs. Joseph, received at tea last Wed. in honor of her mother, Mrs. A. Jacobs, of Montreal. Those assisting were:- the Misses Ella Lorie, Marks, Rhoda Scheur, Fannie Wecksler, Violet Davis and Mrs. H. Goldberg (18 March 1910, 13, 18)

ROSENTHAL, Mrs. M., Palmerston Blvd., leaves shortly for Cleveland where she will spend a month with her parents (8 July 1910, 13, 34)

ROSS, S.W., a Mosaic Alumni Society member, left for Montreal to take up a position with the Canadian Pacific Railway (2 May 1913, 16, 21)

ROTHSCHILD, Miss Rose, of Rochester, N.Y., is the guest of Miss Reva Nathanson (23 Aug. 1912, 15, 37)

ROUDA, Mrs. J., of Cincinnati, is visiting her parents, Mr. and Mrs. Philip Gottlieb in Toronto (23 Aug. 1912, 15, 37)

RUBENSTEIN, Miss, of Rochester, N.Y., is visiting Mr. and Mrs. Mehr, Carlton St. (28 March 1913, 16, 16)

RUBINSTEIN, Mrs., 239 Simcoe St., nearly lost her son, age five, to kidnapping last Wed. She sent him to the grocery store at about 9 p.m. but did he not return. The parents visited all the city hospitals and police stations with no success. "However, at 4 o'clock the next morning the little lad made his appearance. He informed his parents that he was met on the street by a man who promised to buy him candy. The little lad refusing to go with him, the stranger threatened him with a revolver. They reached an outlying district and entered a stable where the man put the boy to sleep. When he awoke the stranger had gone. He then found his way back home, after much inquiry. The police think that the man who has already taken two other children away in like manner, is insane, but have not yet been able to trace him." (18 July 1913, 16, 32)

RUTHENBERG, Louis, age 16, is a musical prodigy who arrived in Canada five years ago with his parents from Austria. A violinist, he will give a concert in the Association Hall on Tues. March 8, 1910 (4 March 1910, 13, 48)

SAMUEL, Mr. and Mrs. Sigmund, are in Atlantic City for a few days (28 March 1913, 16, 16)

SAMUEL, Mr. and Mrs. Sigmund, returned from their trip abroad (23 Aug. 1912, 15, 37)

SAMUEL, Mr. and Mrs. Sigmund, Walmer Road, received on Mon. (25 March 1910, 13, 19)

SAMUEL, Mr. and Mrs. Sigmund, entertained their friends in honor of the Bar Mitzvah of their son Lewis Samuel (1 Oct. 1913, 16, 42-43)

SAMUEL, Mrs. Sigmund, received the guests at the fifteenth annual Charity Ball of the Jewish Benevolent Societies held in the Temple on Thurs. evening, Dec. 30, 1909. Among those present were:- Mr. and Mrs. Maurice Frankel, Mr. and Mrs. S. Singer, Mr. and Mrs. A. Levy, Mr. and Mrs. C. Miller, Mr. and Mrs. S. Frankel, Mr. and Mrs. Joseph King, Rabbi and Mrs. S. Jacobs, Mr. and Mrs. Merkur, Mr. and Mrs. Lubelsky, Jacob Cohen, J.P., Albert Cohn, Samuel Levinson, Mark Cohen, Dr. Singer, Messrs. Draiman, Marks, Stone, Harris and Kronik, Mesdames H.S. Loeser, Leo Frankel, Abendorfer, Ahrens, Freedman, Vise, Jacob, Woolf, Rosenbaum, W. Rosenthal, A. Cohen, the Misses Blanche Levy, Willinsky, Draiman, Meeker, Woschsler, Steinburg, Van Houton, Merkin and Strauss (7 Jan. 1910, 13, 8)

SAMUEL, Mrs. Sim, 132 Springhurst Ave., South Parkdale, returned from several weeks spent at her mother's summer home (6 May 1910, 13, 25)

SAMUEL, Rt. Hon. Herbert, British Postmaster General, addressed the Canadian Club Sat. aft. On Sun. aft., he opened the new premises of the Jewish Working Girls' Club at 254 McCaul St. He was introduced by Rabbi S. Jacobs. The Toronto correspondent wrote, "The visit of Mr. Samuel to Canada cannot fail to be of benefit to Canadian Jews. In the first place it should inspire our youth to emulate the example set by a distinguished Jew, and next it should teach our non-Jewish fellow-citizens to form an estimate of the Jew, not by the shortcomings of the uncultured of us, but by the highest ideals our best representatives have attained." (10 Oct. 1913, 16, 44)

SAMUEL, Sigmund, vice-president of the Holy Blossom Synagogue, presided at the annual meeting last Sun. Three motions passed were: 1) that the president...may on regular Sabbath services call as few as three persons to the reading of the Torah 2) that men and women may occupy seats in any part of the synagogue at all services 3) the use of an organ and choir on Yom Kippur may be permitted (1 Oct. 1913, 16, 42-43)

SAMUEL, Stuart, a British M.P., and Mrs. Samuel, of London, stayed at the Queen's Hotel (3 Feb. 1911, 14, 12)

SAMUELS, Mr. and Mrs. S., are in London, England, Mrs. Samuels' old home (5 July 1912, 15, 30)

SAPERA, Mrs. K.L., St. Patrick St., hosted a successful whist last Tues. aft. for the Hebrew Ladies' Sewing Circle (23 May 1913, 16, 24)

SCHEINMAN, Mr. and Mrs. T.J. and family are vacationing at Elgin House, Lake Joseph, Muskoka (2 Aug. 1912, 15, 34)

SCHEINMAN, Mrs. L.J. and family returned home after a stay at Linberg and Welland, Ont. (29 Aug. 1913, 16, 38)

SCHEUER, E., superintendent of the Zion Hebrew School, organized the children's Chanukah party held last Sun. (8 Jan. 1909, 12, 4)

SCHEUER, Edmund, is president of the Toronto branch (est. 1880) of the Anglo-Jewish Association. Other committee members are:- W. Goldstein, vice-pres.; F.D. Benjamin, treas.; Samuel King, hon. sec.; and Jacob Cohen, Henry Davis, Leo Frankel, Rev. S. Jacobs and Sigmund Samuel. The Toronto branch has forty-one members. Headquartered in London, England, the AJA is an independent branch of the Alliance Israélite Universelle which was founded in Paris in 1860. Founded in 1871, the AJA unites the Jews of the British Empire and has branches throughout the United Kingdom and its colonies. "The object of the Association is to work everywhere for the emancipation and moral progress of the Jews, and to give effectual support to those Jews who are suffering persecution because they are Jews." (4 April 1913, 16, 17)

SCHEUER, Edmund, was robbed New Year's Eve when his jewellery store was broken into by thieves and about 100 diamond rings were stolen. "The thieves evaded the burglar alarm appliances by sawing a hole in the ceiling and entering through it, showing much ingenuity in accomplishing their deed and effecting their escape." (10 Jan. 1913, 16, 5)

SCHEUER, Jr., E.S., is in New York on a business trip (19 Sept. 1913, 16, 41)

SCHEUER, Miss Rhoda, was in Hamilton visiting her aunt, Mrs. H. Levy (5 July 1912, 15, 30)

SCHEUER, Mr. and Mrs. Edmund, observed Yom Kippur with Mrs. H. Levy, in Hamilton (2 Oct. 1912, 15, 43)

SCHEUER, Mr. and Mrs. Edmund, Rosedale, entertained the two hundred children of the Zionist Hebrew Free School to a picnic in the garden of their home on Wed. July 3, 1913. "All the children, who were neatly dressed, carried British and Zionist flags, and as they drove through the city attracted a great deal of interest, people stopping to watch them pass by." (11 July 1913, 16, 31)

SCHEUER, Mrs. Edmund, 32 Chestnut Park, received on Thurs. Feb. 24, 1910, with her sister, Mrs. Ed. Youngheart, of Montreal (4 March 1910, 13, 16)

SCHEZ, Abraham, has been appointed superintendent of the Thrift Dept., Sun Life Assurance Co. of Canada (15 April 1910, 13, 22)

SCHWARTZ, D., was elected vice-president of the Goel Tzedek Congregation at a meeting last Sun. P. Cohen and Mr. Lewinsky were elected trustees (11 Nov. 1910, 13, 52)

SCHWARTZ, L. and Miss Paula Weiss won the waltz prize at the Young Men's Zion Club concert and ball held on Wed. March 16, 1910 in St. George Hall (25 March 1910, 13, 19)

SCHWARTZ, Mrs. L.M. and children, and Miss Rose Schwartz, of Toronto, daughter of Samuel Schwartz, are on an extended trip in the U.S. They will return about Sept. 1, 1912 (26 July 1912, 15, 33)

SEILIG, Mrs. J., is president of the B'noth Zion Kadimah Society. Other officers are:- Miss Silverberg, vice-pres.; Mrs. Star, treas.; and Miss Black, sec. Mrs. Seilig and Mrs. Garfinkle are delegates to the Zionist convention in Ottawa (28 June 1912, 15, 29)

SELICK, Mrs., was elected president (by acclamation) of the B'noth Zion Kadimah at the annual election. Other officers elected were:- Miss Silverberg, vice-pres.; Miss Baskin, treas.; Miss Haskell, rec. sec.; and Miss Black, fin. sec. (11 July 1913, 16, 31)

SHAPIRO, Miss A.H., went to New York en route to Atlantic City with friends (9 Aug. 1912, 15, 35)

SHAPIRO, Miss Annie H., returned from New York and Atlantic City (30 Aug. 1912, 15, 38)

SHAPIRO, Mrs. Theresa, wife of K.L. Shapiro, tobacconist in Toronto, is in New York and will return home on Jan. 15, 1914 (9 Jan. 1914, 17, 5)

DIAMONDS BOUGHT AT SCHEUER'S

The Oldest Established Wholesale Diamond Importers in Canada

Are always a good investment. They are always worth their money.

Because—We will at any time allow the full price paid for any of our diamonds in exchange for more costly ones. We will refund the price paid less ten per cent. within one year from date of purchase for any of our diamonds $30 and over.

Highest Quality Lowest Price

If you think of buying any Diamond Jewelry, mail to my address the amount you wish to invest, with a description of the article required, and I will send you good value for your money. If not satisfied with the article sent, return it at my expense, and I will send your money back immediately.

EDMUND SCHEUER
90 Yonge Street,   -   TORONTO

SHAYNE, Alex., was elected president of the B'nai Zion Juniors, a club for boys between 12 and 16 years. The club received a charter from the Zionist Federation and has applied to join the Toronto Zionist Council. Other officers elected were:- William Steinwortzel, vice-pres.; Bernard Wise, treas.; Jacob Samuels, rec. sec.; Ben Kaufman, fin. sec.; Henry Ferber, sergeant-at-arms; Israel Gold, Maurice Geneson and Ben Webber, trustees; Ben Clavir, Aaron Cohen, Ben Feldman, Jack Lavine, Sam Lavine, Ab. Narrol and Israel Ross, executive (7 Feb. 1913, 16, 9)

SHAYNE, Alexander, is president of the newly formed Bnai Zion Juniors Society for boys between the ages of 11 and 15. Other officers are:- Master Steinworzel, vice-pres.; B. Vise, treas.; Benny Kaufman and H. Palter, marshal (16 Aug. 1912, 15, 36)

SHAYNE, Dr. John, chaired the mass meeting in Massey Hall on Oct. 19, 1913 which was organized to protest the ritual murder charge brought against Mendel Beillis, of Kieff, by the Russian authorities (22 Oct. 1913, 16, 46)

SHAYNE, Dr. John, has returned from a two weeks' holiday in New York (7 Oct. 1910, 13, 47)

SHAYNE, Dr. John, newly elected president of the B'nai Zion Sick Benefit Society, was installed last Sun. at the Zionist Institute (25 Nov. 1910, 14, 2)

SHAYNE, Dr. John, was elected president of the B'nai Zion Association of Toronto for 1913. Other officers elected were:- M. Rosen, vice-pres.; S. Rogul, treas.; I. Unterman, rec. sec.; M. Mirochnick, fin. sec.; M. Pomerantz, marshal; Emanuel I. Kenen, S. Samuels and A. White, trustees; Alexander Cash and H. Lubetzky, executive (17 Jan. 1913, 16, 6)

SHULMAN, Misses Esther and Elsie, are at Havelock, Ont. for a few weeks (9 Aug. 1912, 15, 35)

SHULMAN, Mr. and Mrs. P., have returned from their trip to the U.S. (26 July 1912, 15, 33)

SIEGAL, Mrs. I.H., was re-elected president of the Toronto Hebrew Ladies' Sewing Circle by acclamation at the annual meeting held in the Cosmopolitan Club. Other officers elected were:- Mrs. Cohen, vice-pres.; Mrs. Geldzaeler, treas.; and Mrs. J. Selick, sec. Donations were received from Mesdames Lunenfeld (Galt, Ont.), K.L. Sapera and L. Yolles (29 Dec. 1911, 15, 7)

SIEGEL, D., chaired the Nordau Zion club meeting on Sun. July 7, 1912. Other speakers were:- P. Shulman and M. Gordon who reported on the Twelfth Annual Zionist convention in Ottawa, and M. Genesov and W. Webber (12 July 1912, 15, 31)

SIEGEL, Mrs. I.H., president of the Toronto Hebrew Ladies' Sewing Circle, was head convenor of the bazaar held recently in the McCaul Street Synagogue assembly room. Funds realized from the bazaar are medical care of maternity cases. Convenors were:- Mesdames Geldzaeler, Rosenthal, Faube, Kaplan, Lewis, Keyfitz, King, Rosenthal, Spain, Sapera, Rafelman, Lavine, Melio, Greisman and Miss Libbie Epstein. Assistants were:- Misses Ettie Halpern, Rosa Geldzaeler, Annie Karn, Ray Geldzaeler, May Taube, Ida Kaplan, Lillie Kaplan, Annie Shapiro, S. Halpern, B. Karn, E. Polloker, Sarah Stein, Dora Pullen, Evelyn Kaplan, Jessie Kaplan, Fannie Taylor, Bettie Goldstick, Miriam Fin and Rose Ingentaft. Applications for membership can be made to Mrs. Hillelson, 529 Queen St. W. (18 March 1910, 13, 18)

SIEGEL, Mrs. I.H., was re-elected president of the Hebrew Ladies' Sewing Circle. Other officers elected were:- Mrs. A. Raffelman, vice-pres.; Mrs. K.L. Sapera, treas.; Mrs. Bertha Levine, sec.; Mesdames Lieberman, Pasternak, Helpert, Fremes and Hartman, relief committee; Mrs. M. Geldzaler, convenor and distibutor. "The hospital visitation committee reported results of its visits, endorsed the plan originated by Rev. M. Kaplan to provide Kosher food for the Jewish patients, and suggested financial assistance for so worthy a purpose." (13 Jan. 1911, 14, 9)

SIEGEL, Mrs., is president of the Hebrew Ladies' Sewing Circle which is holding a sale in the McCaul Street Synagogue vestry room, on Tues. Jan. 18, 1910 at 7 p.m. Other executive members are:- Mrs. Geldzaeler, vice-pres.; Mrs. Hillels, sec.; and Mrs. Rosenthal, treas. (7 Jan. 1910, 13, 8)

SILVERBERG, Miss Ada, led the singing of Hatikvah and Ein Keloheinu at the first annual Purim play and concert given by the B'noth Zion Juniors at the Lyric Theatre on March 17, 1914. Also performing were Miss Nellie Haskell, elocutionist, and Miss Ella Shatzky, pianist. Miss Jennie Ferstadt addressed the audience (20 March 1914, 17, 12)

SILVERMAN, F., has returned home to Rochester, N.Y. after a visit in Toronto (5 July 1912, 15, 30)

SIMON, Miss Doris, was elected president of the Daughters of Zion Society last week. Other officers elected were:- Miss Dora Finemark, vice-pres.; Miss Esther Keyfitz, treas.; and Miss Annie Korn, sec. (8 Jan. 1909, 12, 4)

SIMONSKI, Isidore, has returned to town after motoring through Michigan (30 Aug. 1912, 15, 38)

SIMONSKI, Mrs. Arthur, Glenoble Apts., gave a dance and card party in honor of Miss Lena Sadowski, of Massey, Ont., last Thurs. evening, Oct. 30, 1913. Among those present were:- Mr. Dalzorf, C. Fremes, H. Levy, M. Levy, I. Simonski and M. Simonski and the Misses Danson, Davis, Sadowksi, Scheuer, Simonski, B. Rittenberg, and E. Rittenberg (7 Nov. 1913, 16, 48)

SIMONSKY, Isidore, manager of National Sales Co., is summering with friends in Muskoka (9 Aug. 1912, 15, 35)

SIMONSKY, Mrs. S., 107 Queen St., is accepting donations for the Pesach Shoe Fund. The fund provides poor Jewish children with decent footwear (10 April 1914, 17, 15)

SINGER, A., will spend a few weeks at Crystal Beach (16 Aug. 1912, 15, 36)

SINGER, Abraham, returned from Crystal Beach (30 Aug. 1912, 15, 38)

SINGER, E.F. (B.A., L.L.B.), was elected president of the Mosaic Alumni, Jewish Students Society at the University of Toronto. Other officers elected were:- J. Kamman, vice-pres.; Samuel Factor, treas.; C.N. Temes, sec.; B.D. Goodman, fin. sec.; M. Rottenberg, sergeant-at-

---

Toronto Citizens

OF

WARD FOUR

Elect

SINGER

FOR

ALDERMAN

arms; H. Davidovitch, I. Finberg, J. Spring, councillors; and Edmund Scheuer, hon. pres. (1 Nov. 1912, 15, 47)

SINGER, E.F., (B.A., LL.B.) is president of the Mosaic Alumni, the Jewish Students' Society of Toronto, which was founded Dec. 3, 1911. Abraham Halpern was the founder and chief organizer of the Alumni along with J. Ross, Sam Factor and S. Corn. Other officers are:- H. Finkelstein, vice-pres.; Charles Black, treas.; S. Ross, fin. sec.; P. Shulman, rec. sec.; and D. Goodman, sergeant-at-arms (21 June 1912, 15, 28)

SINGER, E.F., returned from a trip to Albany and New York (28 Feb. 1913, 16, 12)

SINGER, Fred, Mark Cohen, Mrs. Joseph Cohen and Miss B. Geldzaeler are some of the teachers at the Holy Blossom Synagogue Sabbath School this year. Over one hundred children are enrolled (11 Oct. 1912, 15, 44)

SINGER, L., is chairman of the Associated Hebrew Charities membership campaign (22 Nov. 1912, 15, 50)

SINGER, Louis M., is treasurer of the Hebrew Literary Society whose object is the promotion of the Hebrew language. M. Oser Glickman is secretary, pro tem (4 March 1910, 13, 16)

SINGER, Louis M., was elected (by acclamation) president of McCaul Street Synagogue, the oldest Jewish congregation in Toronto, last Sun. (25 Oct. 1910, 13, 50)

SINGER, Louis, the well-known lawyer is running for the office of Alderman in Ward Four. "Mr. Singer is a young and respected member of the Toronto Jewish Community, and his many fine qualities and capabilities should make him fit to fulfil the responsibilities to which he aspires." (26 Dec. 1913, 16, 3)

SINGER, Max, E. Marks, H.B. Fogler, Arthur Cohen, Charles Draimin and Joseph Harris are in charge of the Hebrew Cosmopolitan Club Ball to be held Wed. evening, Nov. 17, 1909 (29 Oct. 1909, 12, 46)

SINGER, Miss Minnie, daughter of Mr. and Mrs. P. Singer, will be married on Sun. July 17, 1910 at 6 p.m. in the McCaul Street Synagogue (8 July 1910, 13, 34)

SINGER, Mrs. Louis M., Indian Rd., gave a tea in honor of Miss Minnie Bernstein, of Montreal (20 March 1914, 17, 12)

SINGER, Mrs. Mannie J., Kendall Ave., hosted a bridge and linen shower on Thurs. aft., March 31, 1910, in honor of Miss Ella Lorie who was married to Dr. Singer on April 6. Guests included:- the Misses Dinnick, Della Miller, Pauline Lyons, Fanny Singer, Adelaide Cohen, Lulu Levy, Irene and Ethel Goldstein, Bertha Steiner, Rita Laurence, Bertha King, Hilda Loeser, Elsie Micklesburt, Edna Block, Mildred Marks, Rea Jacobs and L. Fogler and Mesdames J. Singer, Herbert Steiner, A. Singer, Sternberg, Strauss, Winters and Goldreich (8 April 1910, 13, 21)

SINGER, Rev. Henry, the apostate superintendent of the Toronto Jewish Mission, who was conducting an open air service, Mon. night, July 14, 1913, in the area of St. Patrick St. and Kensington Ave., was mobbed by a group of Jewish men, women and children hurling insults. Five people were arrested. Some were charged with disorderly conduct and others with obstruction (25 July 1913, 16, 33)

SMITH, Mrs. Nathan, hosted the Hebrew Ladies' Sewing Circle annual meeting at her home, Simcoe St. Misses Louise Spad and Annie Smith provided entertainment (25 Oct. 1910, 13, 50)

SOKOLOW, Nahum, the great Hebrew patriot, arrived in Toronto at the train station on Thurs. morn., May 22, 1913. He was taken to the King Edward Hotel by Barnett Stone, Dr. John Shayne and Mr. Harris, of Montreal. Mr. Sokolow was presented the freedom of the city by the Mayor of Toronto. He then visited Queen's Park where he met the Premier of Ontario. A Kosher luncheon was given in his honor by the City Fathers at the Queen's Hotel. Thurs. evening, he spoke to 2,000 persons in Massey Hall. Rabbi S. Jacobs presided. On Fri. night, Mr. Sokolow spoke at a special service in the Holy Blossom Synagogue on the practical work of Zionism already accomplished in Palestine. He was welcomed by Leo Frankel, the president. On Sat. morn., he spoke on the relation between religion and Zionism in the University Avenue Synagogue. Samuel Kronick was toastmaster at the banquet for 200 that evening. Speakers included Rabbis Jacobs and Gordon, Edmund Scheuer, B. Nathanson, Dr. Shayne, Louis M. Singer and J. Cohen, J.P. On Sun. aft., Mr. Sokolow visited Toronto's communal institutions. That aft., he left for Hamilton in a special car reserved for him and the fifty people accompanying him. He returned to Toronto Mon. morn. and left for Winnipeg that evening (30 May 1913, 16, 25)

SOLOWAY, Dr. L.G., has opened a consulting room at 30 St. Patrick St. (24 March 1911, 14, 19)

SOLWAY, Miss Lena, has returned from her visit to the Bluffs (19 July 1912, 15, 32)

SOSKIN, Mr., of Hamilton, is visiting relatives in Toronto (5 July 1912, 15, 30)

SPRING, Joe, is at Mount Clemens, Mich. for a few weeks (9 Aug. 1912, 15, 35)

National Matzo & Biscuit Co., Limited.

95-105 ONTARIO STREET
TORONTO

Only MATZO FACTORY in Canada

Manufacturers of High Grade Matzos of all Kinds.

Egg Matzos, Berliner Tea Matzos, Social Tea Matzos Square and Round Matzos, and Macaroni.

The Kashruth of Matzos, manufactured by us is vouched for by Rabbi Meldola de Sola, of Montreal, Vice-President of the Union of Orthodox Congregations of the United States and Canada, also by the best known rabbis of the Dominion.

STEIN, Miss Lillie, has returned from New York (16 Aug. 1912, 15, 36)

STEINBERG, Miss Lily, the talented young vocalist performed some beautiful solos during the Holy Day services (11 Oct. 1912, 15, 44)

STEINBERG, Mr. and Mrs. B., have returned from their honeymoon in Atlantic City (5 July 1912, 15, 30)

STERN, Sam, a vaudeville singer, was threatened during the course of his act last week when he gave a gentle burlesque on Yiddish opera. "One afternoon a Jewish gentleman in the audience stood up and called Jerosh Stern a liar, adding a few adjectives as emphatic trimmings. Later on another well-known citizen called at the theatre and threatened to make trouble, saying he would have Stern prevented from doing his act." (11 March 1910, 13, 17)

STONE, Barnett, a prominent Toronto businessman and Zionist leader, was chiefly responsible for the sale of the old Zionist Institute and the purchase of the site for the new building. He has been president of the Toronto Zionist Council since its formation and an active member of the B'nai Zion Association. He has regularly attended the Canadian Zionist Federation's annual conventions in Montreal and Toronto, as well as American Zionist conventions (14 Feb. 1913, 16, 10)

STONE, Barnett and Alexander Cash, officers of the B'nai Zion Association, made a presentation to Edmund Scheuer, superintendent of the B'nai Zion Sabbath School. Rabbi J. Friedlander, of Hamilton, addressed the children (16 July 1909, 12, 31)

STONE, Barnett, has returned from a business trip to Cobalt, Ont. (3 Feb. 1911, 14, 12)

STONE, Barnett, Rabbi S. Jacobs, Miss Mary Landsberg, L. Gurofsky, Mr. Nathanson, principal of the Talmud Torah, Alexander Cash, Mr. Yaffe,

P. Levi, A.P. Lewis, Mr. Levetus, L. Singer and Mr. Schalet, of the Knights of Zion, Minneapolis, were present at the B'nai Zion Society Chanukah banquet, Sun. evening, Dec. 27, 1908, in the Zionist Assembly Hall (8 Jan. 1909, 12, 4)

STONE, Barnett, sails on the S.S. Imperator on Aug. 9, 1913 for Europe where he will attend the Zionist Congress in Vienna (8 Aug. 1913, 16, 34)

STONE, Barnett, was elected president of the B'nai Zion Society at a recent meeting. Other officers elected were:- I. Woolfson, vice-pres.; Mr. Freeman, treas.; Mr. Seigal, sec.; and Alexander Cash, fin. sec. (4 June 1909, 12, 25)

STONE, Valentine, age 27, who is of German extraction, was converted to Judaism on Sun. (21 March 1913, 16, 15)

STRAUS, E., of London, England, is visiting Edmund Scheuer who has returned from a two weeks' buying trip in New York (20 Sept. 1912, 15, 41)

STRAUS, Leo, an old Toronto boy now living in New York, is visiting relatives in the city (9 Aug. 1912, 15, 35)

STRAUS, Leo, is in Muskoka for a few weeks (16 Aug. 1912, 15, 36)

STRAUS, Miss Adele, is summering in Beaconsfield, Que. (9 Aug. 1912, 15, 35)

STRAUS, Miss Adele, spent the weekend in Hamilton with friends (5 July 1912, 15, 30)

STRAUSS, Miss Betty, returned from Grimsby Beach (22 Aug. 1913, 16, 37)

STRAUSS, Miss Betty, was in Buffalo on the weekend visiting friends (28 March 1913, 16, 16)

STRAUSS, Miss Edna, returned from New York where she visited her sister, Mrs. Joseph Rosenthal (28 Feb. 1913, 16, 12)

STRAUSS, Miss, has returned from a holiday in Montreal (12 Aug. 1910, 13, 39)

STRAUSS, Mr. and Mrs. Alfred (née Miss Rhoda Block), of London, England, are in Toronto (28 March 1913, 16, 16)

STRAUSS, Mr. and Mrs. Alfred (née Rhoda Block), of London, England, are in Toronto (1 Oct. 1913, 16, 42-43)

STREMER, Mrs., entertained her grand-daughter, Miss Cohen, who returned home to Philadelphia (2 Oct. 1912, 15, 43)

SUGARMAN, Ephy, spent the weekend in Whitby, the guest of his sister, Mrs. Joseph King (30 Aug. 1912, 15, 38)

SUGARMAN, Mr. and Mrs. William, of Edmonton, have rented a furnished residence at 480 Huron St., and intend to spend the winter in Toronto (19 Sept. 1913, 16, 41)

TAUBE, S., is on a business trip out west for two weeks (8 April 1910, 13, 21)

TAYLOR, Miss Fanny, was elected president of the Herzl Girls club. Other officers elected were:- Gertie Pasternack, vice-pres.; Florence Most, treas.; and Doris Ephraim, sec. (14 June 1912, 15, 27)

TAYLOR, Miss Ida, is visiting friends in Massey, Ont. (19 July 1912, 15, 32)

TAYLOR, Mr., has returned from his trip to Cochrane and Cobalt, Ont. (16 Aug. 1912, 15, 36)

TEICH, Joe, is manager of the Judean Athletic Club of Toronto's juvenile hockey team. M.J. Spergle is manager of the junior team. (29 Dec. 1911, 15, 7)

TUROFSKY, H.A., was elected president of the Judean Society at its last meeting. Other officers elected were:- M. Katz, vice-pres.; Mr. Herzlich, fin. sec.; Mr. Kadesky, rec. sec.; M.A. Pollock, B.A., A. Granatstein, B.A., A. Draimin, M. Swartz and Louis M. Singer, executive (4 March 1910, 13, 16)

UNTERMAN, I., C. Lurie, B. Nathanson, E. Pullan, Barnett Stone, Alexander Cash, Samuel Kronick, M. Ross, A. White, M. Wolfson, Dr. L.J. Breslin, Dr. John Shayne, Rev. J. Waldman, Rev. I. Levy, and Messrs. Gelber, Greenberg, Levit, Manson and Moldaver are Toronto delegates to the Federation of Zionist Societies of Canada convention (14 June 1912, 15, 27)

VIENER, Miss Freda, of Chicago, is visiting her sister in Toronto (26 July 1912, 15, 33)

VINEBERG, Mrs. Hillel, has returned home to Toronto after spending a few weeks with her parents, Mr. and Mrs. Joseph Abramsky, of Kingston (28 June 1912, 15, 29)

VINEGARDEN, Miss May, has returned from two weeks at Uxbridge, Ont. (9 Aug. 1912, 15, 35)

VISE, Miss Pearl, 351 Bathurst St., age 14, won first prize in the national writing competition at the Canadian National Exhibition (11 Sept. 1912, 15, 40)

WALDMAN, Louis, has gone to Mount Clemens for a few weeks (8 July 1910, 13, 34)

WALDMAN, Louis, has returned from a two weeks' stay in Mount Clemens (22 July 1910, 13, 36)

WALDMAN, Louis, has returned from a three weeks' stay at Mount Clemens (12 Aug. 1910, 13, 39)

WALDMAN, Louis, has returned from visiting friends in New York, Boston and Montreal (3 Feb. 1911, 14, 12)

WALDMAN, Louis, led the discussion on "Materialism and Ritual" at the Hebrew Literary Society meeting, Sat. evening, March 26, 1910. Rev. M. Kaplan chaired the meeting (1 April 1910, 13, 20)

WALDMAN, Mrs. Louis and daughters have left for a two months' visit to Europe (21 April 1911, 14, 23)

WEBBER, S., was elected hon. president of the Associated Hebrew Charities. Other officers elected were:- Rabbi Gordon and Rev. Kaplan, hon. vice-pres.; Louis M. Singer, pres.; M. Cohen, vice-pres.; Charles Pasternack, treas. (11 Oct. 1912, 15, 44)

WEBBER, W., was elected president of the Nordau Zion Society at the last meeting. Other officers elected were:- Ed Goldstein, vice-pres.; M. Geneson, treas.; J. Lavine, fin. sec.; and Miss S. Swiss, rec. sec. (18 Oct. 1912, 15, 45)

WEBER, Miss Gertrude and Miss Tessie Kaplan gave a surprise garden party in honor of Miss Anna Sapera, at her residence, 31 St. Patrick St. The Misses Lillian Mendelsohn and Katherine Weber assisted. Among those present were:- the Misses R. Fisher, S. Halpern, S. Ginsberg, D. Morris, R. Gekdzaeler, M. Livingstone, D. Pullan, M. Lieberman, J. Zivian and Messrs. W. Draiman, L. Simonski, I. Vise, D. Vise, A. Singer, H. Pullan, C. Fremes, M. Fremes, S. Kaplan, I. Fineberg and B. Geldsaler (1 July 1910, 13, 33)

WEBER, Mrs. and Miss Bessie Weber have gone to Dalhousie for a few weeks' holiday (8 July 1910, 13, 34)

WEBER, W., president of the Nordau Zion Club, chaired a literary evening at the Zionist Institute, Toronto, on Mon. April 25, 1910. Others participating were:- Miss Berkovitz, Mrs. Friedberg and Mr. Garbent (6 May 1910, 13, 25)

WEIL, Edgar, the popular manager of the Strand Theatre, and his wife, are summering at the Montieth Hotel, Muskoka (29 Aug. 1913, 16, 38)

WEIL, Henry, a well-known communal worker of Buffalo, spent a day in Toronto, en route to the Canadian Northwest (5 Sept. 1913, 16, 39)

WEIL, Mr. and Mrs. Willie, former well-known Toronto residents, are in the city calling on their friends (9 Aug. 1912, 15, 35)

WEKSLER, Charles, has gone on a business trip to Montreal and New York (5 Aug. 1910, 13, 38)

WEKSLER, Charles, has returned home from a week in New York (18 March 1910, 13, 18)

WEKSLER, Mr. and Mrs. Charles and family have to Atlantic City to spend the summer (8 July 1910, 13, 34)

WEKSLER, Mrs. Charles, has returned home from a holiday in Europe (17 June 1910, 13, 31)

WEKSLER, Mrs. Charles, Winchester St., is expected home next week from her two months' visit to Romania (6 May 1910, 13, 25)

WILLINSKY, Dr. A.I., who recently received a degree from Dublin University, has left for Vienna, and will return to Toronto in August (13 May 1910, 13, 26)

WILLINSKY, Dr. I.A., 70 Homewood Ave., who was abroad the past year taking a post-graduate course in Dublin, Berlin, Vienna and Paris, has returned home. Mrs. and Miss Sadie Willinsky met him in New York (12 Aug. 1910, 13, 39)

WLADOFSKY, Cantor B., chazan of the University Avenue Synagogue, agreed not to give a paid public concert in a Montreal hall because it has aroused so much opposition from leading rabbis and lay leaders there. Louis Gurofsky, a prominent member of the synagogue, said he would assume personal responsiblity for any damages in case of lawsuit as result of the cancellation. Gurofsky said that while these concerts of sacred music are tolerated in the U.S., they are not in Canada and England and that these feelings should be respected. Elias Pullan also endorsed the position of the Montreal rabbis and The Canadian Jewish Times (10 Jan. 1913, 16, 5)

WLADOFSKY, Cantor B., was appointed cantor of the University Avenue Synagogue. "As a result the attendance... has enormously increased, the synagogue being absolutely thronged on Friday nights and Saturday mornings. The membership of the congregation has also substantially grown since the arrival of Mr. Wladofsky." A previous attempt to hire him had failed (18 Oct. 1912, 15, 45)

WOLF, Miss Gertie, private secretary of Rabbi Dr. Stephen Wise, of New York, spent her holidays in Toronto, the guest of Mrs. Henry Davis (19 July 1912, 15, 32)

WOLFE, Miss Anna, of Ottawa, has returned home (10 March 1911, 14, 17)

WOLFE, Miss Teresa Frances, now recognized as one of the greatest Canadian lyric sopranos, will give a recital in Massey Hall on Mon. Feb. 27, 1911 (17 Feb. 1911, 14, 14)

WOLFE, Mrs., has returned to Ottawa (3 Feb. 1911, 14, 12)

YOOSPRICH, B., was elected president of K'neseth Yisrael Congregation, West Toronto. Other officers elected were:- D. Dubrofsky, vice-pres.; A. Viener, gabbai rishon; H. Starazumnik, gabbai sheni; H. Greenblat, treas.; S. Sloat, fin. sec.; and Ch. Naphtalin, rec. sec. (11 Oct. 1912, 15, 44)

YOUNGHEART, Mrs. E., returned from her trip abroad and is living with her sister, Mrs. Edmund Scheuer (20 Sept. 1912, 15, 41)

YOUNGHEART, Mrs. Joseph and her daughter, Sybil, are guests of Mrs. William Goldstein in Toronto (26 July 1912, 15, 33)

YOUNGHEART, Mrs., of Montreal, who visited her sister, Mrs. Edmund Scheuer, has gone to Lakewood with her niece, Miss Edna Strauss (31 Jan. 1913, 16, 8)

ZIWITZ, Mr. and Mrs. Nachem, are spending the Holy days in Pittsburgh with Rabbi and Mrs. Ziwitz (29 April 1910, 13, 24)

ZIWITZ, Rabbi, of Pittsburgh, was in Toronto visiting his son, A. Ziwitz, 34 Cecil St. He lectured before the Beth Jacob Synagogue on Sat. (11 Nov. 1910, 13, 52)

When in Toronto and if you want a first-class **Kosher** meal at reasonable prices

Call at The Vienna Cafe & Quick Lunch

85 Queen Street West.

Furnished Rooms by Day or Week.   L. TEICH, Prop

EVERY Alaska brass or steel bed is marked by an attractiveness of design and finish that will please the most critical purchaser.

And every bed bearing this trademark.

is positively guaranteed against all possible defects in material or workmanship.

The best furniture dealers everywhere sell and recommend Alaska beds.

Ask yours to show you the latest designs.

ALASKA FEATHER & DOWN COMPANY LIMITED
MONTREAL AND WINNIPEG.

We are also makers of Mattresses, Springs, Couches, Pillows and Bedding Specialties.

Have Something in the Bank :: ::   Fifty Dollars, a hundred, five hundred—always keep on hand some ready money.

It is granted that your money can be made to earn more than 3%, but this isn't the point. The point is to always have a little money at your immediate command in the custody of a good bank. Money in the bank will give you a most comfortable feeling—and it is ready whenever you want or need it.

THE BANK OF TORONTO

You can start a Savings account with the Bank of Toronto with a deposit of $1.00.

ST. LAWRENCE BLVD. BRANCH

C. L. PARKINSON, Manager.

M. DOBROFSKY,
Res. St. Louis 3894

S. BERNSTEIN,
Res. Uptown 2989

Bernstein Realty Co.

Real Estate Mortgage Loans, Collections and Valuations

Eagle Bldg.,
516 St Lawrence Boulevard.

Telephone
East 3786

NORTHERN ONTARIO

DIAMOND, Mr. and Mrs. S., James St., Sault Ste. Marie, gave a party at their home in honor of their guest, Dr. Leon J. Solway, of Toronto. Those present were:- Mr. and Mrs. Geo. E. Willus, the Misses Rebecca Miriam and Clara Diamond, Clara Cohen, Hattie and Esther Rubenstein; and from the Michigan "Soo":- Mrs. W. Kotzon and the Misses Lillian Newark, Sara Kotzon and Sara Sugar, of Brimley, Mich. (8 Oct. 1909, 12, 43)

ENZER, Joseph, is president of the Shaar Hashomayim Congregation in Fort William and M. Hoffer is treasurer. "It may be interesting to your readers to know that the community in this town is growing rapidly. There are about forty Jewish families, most of whom are in business and the others mechanics, all of whom are doing well. We are building a pretty little synagogue, funds for which were raised amongst ourselves and Jews in the neighborhood... We have also a schochet who takes the place of a Rabbi. We have had quite a number of weddings here recently, and two more are taking place next Sunday." (23 Sept. 1910, 13, 45)

ENZER, Joseph, president of the community, was chairman of a mass meeting called on Sun. Oct. 29, 1911 to organize a Talmud Torah in Fort William. Z. Weretnikow, E. Weissman, J. Enzer and A. Katzva are the prime movers largely responsible for the organization of the school. Executive committee members are:- Joseph Enzer, pres.; Z. Weretnikow, vice-pres..; J.W. Kasler, treas.; and J. Livinstein, sec.; Board of Education members are:- M. Pearlman, A. Dunne, E. Weissman, William Shaffer and J. Joseph. The former principal of the Ottawa Talmud Torah, A. Wershof, was appointed principal. Forty-one pupils are currently enrolled (24 Nov. 1911, 15, 2)

GILBERT, A., Charles Gurowicz, Joseph Enzer, H. Leff and Sam. Tritt, of Fort William, contributed funds to the Bezalel School of Arts and Crafts in Jerusalem, Palestine (23 Feb. 1912, 15, 15)

HOFFER, Max, is president of the Har Zion Society of Port Arthur and Fort William which held a meeting last Sun. in the Shaar Shomayim Synagogue of Fort William. J.S. Leo, of Montreal spoke on the aims of Zionism. J. Enzer moved a vote of thanks, seconded by E. Wiseman. I. Enzer moved and M. Pearlman seconded that $50 be remitted to the FZSC for the Canadian Zionist Land Fund. Other officers of the Society are:- I. Enzer, vice-pres.; B. Hollenburg, treas.; M. Pearlman, sec. Entertainment committee members are;- William Shaffer, E. Wiseman, S. Acker, N. Adelman, I. Goldstein, A. Heller and N. Fox (24 March 1911, 14, 19)

PEARLMAN, M., secretary of the Har Zion Society of Port Arthur, Ont., remitted $34.00 to the Zionist Federation executive in Montreal (12 Feb. 1909, 12, 9)

ROTHSCHILD, Max, A., M. Hoffer, A. Heller, I. Acker, J. Enzer, I. Enzer, A. Dunne, A. Heper and A. Broufman, of Fort William, were donors to the Zionist Land Fund (14 April 1911, 14, 22)

RUBENSTEIN, Miss Hattie, McDougall Ave., Sault Ste. Marie, gave a party for her friends in honor of her sister, Miss Esther Rubenstein, who is a pupil at Farrand School, Harper Hospital, Detroit, Mich. Out-of-town guests included:- Misses E. Berman and D. Rothschild, of Montreal, and Messrs. A. Gould, of Boston, Mass., and D. Lowrie, of Ann Arbor, Mich. (9 Aug. 1912, 15, 35)

SILVERMAN, I., is secretary of the Cobalt Zionist Society (11 Oct. 1912, 15, 44)

WILLIS, Mrs. George E., gave a linen shower at her home, Beverley St., Sault Ste. Marie, in honor of Miss Rhoda Diamond who will be married next month (24 Dec. 1909, 13, 6)

ONTARIO, OTHER CENTERS

HAMILTON

BLOCK, Mrs., accompanied by her daughter, Caroline Block, of Dallas, Texas, is the guest of her sister, Mrs. L. Strauss (16 July 1909, 12, 31)

BLOCK, Mrs., accompanied by her daughter, Caroline Block, of Dallas, Texas, is the guest of her sister, Mrs. L. Strauss (16 July 1909, 12, 31)

BLOOM, Harry, was elected president of the Hamilton Zionist Society. Other officers elected were:- Max Epstein, vice-pres.; David Sweet, sec.; and M. Simon, treas. (31 Jan. 1913, 16, 8)

BLUMENSTIEL, I., has just returned from a business trip to New York (21 May 1909, 12, 23)

BLUMENSTIEL, I., has returned home from a trip to Cuba (26 Feb. 1909, 12, 11)

BLUMENSTIEL, Mrs. C., of Rochester, N.Y., was the guest of Mr. and Mrs. D. Sweet (18 June 1909, 12, 27)

BLUMENTHAL, Mr. and Mrs. Samuel, of Montreal, were guests of Mr. and Mrs. J. Kauffman for the day (18 June 1909, 12, 27)

DALGORF, Samuel and Leslie Kauffman were in Toronto to watch the Marathon race (7 May 1909, 12, 21)

DAVIS, Mr., of Toronto, delivered a lecture on the "Jews of Spain" to the Young People's Society Anshe Sholem (19 March 1909, 12, 14)

DORMAN, Mr., of Montreal, was a visitor in town (26 Feb. 1909, 12, 11)

FINKELSTEIN, D.B., of Buffalo, is the guest of S. Taube (21 May 1909, 12, 23)

FISHBEIN, Mr. and Mrs., presented the Ohavei Zion Society with a beautiful silk banner of the National Colors at the first Chanukah concert and dance held Mon. evening, Dec. 29, 1913 (9 Jan. 1914, 17, 5)

FOX, Samuel, of Brantford, was a visitor in Hamilton (23 April 1909, 12, 19)

FRANK, Mrs. Abraham, has just returned from Toronto (7 May 1909, 12, 21)

FRIEDLANDER, Dr. Joseph, of Hamilton, will deliver a paper "Look into the Future" at the Federation of American Zionists 12th annual convention in New York, July 12-15, 1909 (11 June 1909, 12, 26)

FRIEDLANDER, Dr. Joseph, will lecture on "Zionism" to the United Zionists of Toronto at the Zionist Institute next Sun. (23 April 1909, 12, 19)

FRIEDLANDER, Rabbi J., addressed the post-graduate class of the Holy Blossom Synagogue in Toronto, last Sun. (26 Feb. 1909, 12, 11)

FRIEDLANDER, Rabbi J., addressed the Zionists in Toronto last Sun. (7 May 1909, 12, 21)

FRIEDLANDER, Rabbi J. and his assistants, the Misses Sarah Mintz, Gussie Morris, Etta Lyons, Rose Raphael and Rose Levy organized the children's Chanukah party, Sun. Dec. 20, 1908 at Anshe Sholem Congregation (8 Jan. 1909, 12, 4)

FRIEDLANDER, Rabbi J., chaired an open meeting of the Young People's Society of Temple Anshe Sholem, on Mon. night, Jan. 18, 1909. Rabbi Nathan Gordon, of Montreal, lectured on "Uriel Acosta". Others taking part in the program were Misses Mintz and Wolfe (22 Jan. 1909, 12, 6)

FRIEDLANDER, Rabbi J., lectured on the ideals of the Grand Order of Israel to the David Wolfsohn Lodge, on Sun. aft. (21 May 1909, 12, 23)

FRIEDLANDER, Rabbi J., of Anshe Sholem Congregation, is attending the Zionist Convention in New York (18 June 1909, 12, 27)

FRIEDLANDER, Rabbi J., was invited to speak at the Unitarian Church last Sun. (23 April 1909, 12, 19)

FRIEDLANDER, Rev. J., remitted $5.50 from the Hamilton Zionist Society to the Zionist Federation executive in Montreal (1 Oct. 1909, 12, 42)

FRIEDMAN, M., of Montreal, was in Hamilton for a few days (7 May 1909, 12, 21)

FRIEDMAN, Max, of Montreal, was in Hamilton for a few days (16 April 1909, 12, 18)

FRIEDMAN, Sidney, was elected president of the YMHA of Hamilton at the annual elections held in the Association's headquarters, King St. E., Sun. aft., Sept. 7, 1913. Other officers elected were:- Rabbi J.S. Minkin and Ph. Fuerst, ex-officios; Sidney H. Glass, vice-pres.; Harry Morris, publicity sec.; Louis Raphael, fin. sec.; Sam Cohen, treas.; T. Bernstein, M. Epstein, H. Goldstein, L. Harris, M. Levy, H. Lewis, S. Lyons, G. Ringel, H. Sherrin, H. Siderski, D. Sutton, H. Sutton, D. Sweet and M. Wolfe, exec. comm. (12 Sept. 1913, 16, 40)

GOLDBERG, M., of Niagara Falls, and N. Brenner, of Rochester, N.Y., were guests of Mrs. and Mrs. J. Kauffman (21 May 1909, 12, 23)

GOLDSTEIN, Mr. and Mrs. M., held a reception in honor of their son Joe's Bar Mitzvah (8 Jan. 1909, 12, 4)

HARRIS, A., presided at the Chevra-Kadisha annual dinner held in the Temple Sholem vestry, on Sun. Jan. 10, 1909. Speeches were given by Rabbi J. Friedlander and S.J. Shalett, of Minneapolis (22 Jan. 1909, 12, 6)

HARRIS, I., left on a trip to Buffalo, Rochester and New York (16 July 1909, 12, 31)

HARRIS, Miss Selina, hosted a party in honor of Miss Jennie Lyons, of Utica, N.Y. (22 Jan. 1909, 12, 6)

HARRIS, Miss Selina, was in Toronto visiting friends (12 Feb. 1909, 12, 9)

HARRIS, S., has gone to Fort William, Ont., where he intends to open a business (16 April 1909, 12, 18)

HAUMAN, Mrs., of Toronto, was visiting in Hamilton (26 Feb. 1909, 12, 11)

ISAACS, Prof., of New York, gave a lecture on the "Story of the Synagogue" at Anshe Sholem Temple (19 March 1909, 12, 14)

JACOBS, Louis, of New York, is in Hamilton for a few days (16 April 1909, 12, 18)

JACOBS, N., of Niagara Falls, was the guest of Mr. and Mrs. J. Kauffman for a few days, en route to Boston, where he intends to study music (7 May 1909, 12, 21)

JACOBS, Rabbi, of Holy Blossom Temple, Toronto, lectured on "Jesus of Nazareth" to the Young People's Society of Anshe Sholem, last Sun. (23 April 1909, 12, 19)

KAPLANSKY, J., of Montreal, was in Hamilton for a few days (18 June 1909, 12, 27)

KAPLANSKY, J., of Montreal, was in Hamilton for a few days (23 April 1909, 12, 19)

KAPLANSKY, Julius, of Montreal, was in Hamilton (26 Feb. 1909, 12, 11)

KAUFFMAN, the Misses Emma and Bessie, have returned from Toronto (21 May 1909, 12, 23)

KAUFFMAN, Miss Dora, is visiting Mrs. Hauman, Toronto (26 Feb. 1909, 12, 11)

KAUFFMAN, Mr. and Mrs. J. and the Misses Kauffman attended the Meyer-Shapiro wedding in Rochester (16 July 1909, 12, 31)

KAUFFMAN, Mrs. J., Misses Bessie and Emma Kauffman are visiting in Toronto (7 May 1909, 12, 21)

KUBELICK, M., of Toronto, spent a few days in Hamilton (23 april 1909, 12, 19)

LAZARUS, J., left for London, Ont., where he plans to open a branch store for Raphael & Co. (19 March 1909, 12, 14)

LAZARUS, Julius, left for New York and other points east (12 Feb. 1909, 12, 9)

LAZARUS, Mrs. J. and son, left for Utica, N.Y., to be present at her sister-in-law's wedding anniversary (8 Jan. 1909, 12, 4)

LAZARUS, Mrs. J., hosted a whist party at her home, 75 East Ave., on Wed. Feb. 3, 1909, in honor of Miss Jennie Lyons, of Utica, N.Y. Prize winners were the Misses Helen Morris and Selina Harris and Mesdames L. Strauss and M. Shacofsky (12 Feb. 1909, 12, 9)

LAZARUS, Mrs. J.L., is visiting in Toronto (2 April 1909, 12, 16)

LEVI, Rabbi Leonard, of Pittsburgh, was the guest of the Fireside Club. He lectured to Jews and Christians in the Centenary Church schoolroom (2 April 1909, 12, 14)

LEVISON, J., of Montreal, was in Hamilton for a few days (7 May 1909, 12, 21)

LEVY, Mr. and Mrs. Adolph and family will leave on an extended trip to Europe (16 April 1909, 12, 18)

LEVY, Benjamin, has returned from New York (16 April 1909, 12, 18)

LEVY, Dr. J. Leonard, of Pittsburgh, Pa., spoke to the YMHA on Tues. Dec. 9, 1913. Rabbi J.S. Minkin chaired the event. On the reception committee, besides Rabbi Minkin, was D. Sweet, a personal friend of Rabbi Levy (19 Dec. 1913, 17, 2)

LEVY, Miss Minnie, of Buffalo, N.Y., is visiting Miss Selina Harris, West Ave. N. (8 Jan. 1909, 12, 4)

LEVY, Miss Minnie, who was the guest of Miss

S. Harris, returned home to Buffalo (16 July 1909, 12, 31)

LEVY, Miss Rose and Gabriel Levy are visiting in Chicago (26 Feb. 1909, 12, 11)

LEVY, Miss Rose, was in Toronto where she met Mrs. Youngheart, of Montreal (26 Feb. 1909, 12, 11)

LEVY, Moe, left on a short trip to Boston (8 Jan. 1909, 12, 4)

LEVY, Mr. and Mrs. Joseph, are spending a few weeks in New York (22 Jan. 1909, 12, 6)

LEVY, Mrs. Adolph, has just returned from New York where she had gone to meet Mr. Levy on his return from Europe (8 Jan. 1909, 12, 4)

LEVY, Mrs. Herman, accompanied by Mr. and Mrs. Adolph Levy, left for Chicago, to attend the wedding of her son, Gabriel, to Miss Blanche Shire (2 April 1909, 12, 14)

LEVY, the Misses, South John St., hosted a party in honor of Miss Jennie Lyons, of Utica, N.Y. Pedro game winners were Miss Helen Morris and M. Levy (29 Jan. 1909, 12, 7)

LEVY, William, of New York, is visiting his sister, Mrs. S. Blustien (21 May 1909, 12, 23)

LEWIS, Jacob, was in Buffalo for a few days (12 Feb. 1909, 12, 9)

LYONS, J., was in St. Catherines, Windsor and Chatham on business (16 April 1909, 12, 18)

LYONS, Julius, spent a few days in Niagara Falls, Ont. (26 Feb. 1909, 12, 11)

LYONS, Miss Jennie, has returned home to Utica, N.Y. (2 April 1909, 12, 16)

LYONS, Miss Jennie, of Utica, N.Y., is the guest of her relatives, Mr. and Mrs. S. Lyons, Elgin St. (8 Jan. 1909, 12, 4)

LYONS, Mr. and Mrs. Saul, of Toronto, spent last Sun. with Mr. and Mrs. J. Morris, Duke St. (16 April 1909, 12, 18)

LYONS, Mr. and Mrs. Saul, of Amsterdam, N.Y., have moved to Hamilton intending to start a business (7 May 1909, 12, 21)

LYONS, Mrs. S., Victoria St. N., gave a pedro party in honor of her out-of-town guests:- Misses Ethel Warrinsky and Minnie Levy, of Buffalo, N.Y.; Miss Jennie Lyons, of Utica, N.Y.; and Miss I. Kaplan, of Toronto (22 Jan. 1909, 12, 6)

LYONS, S.H., of Toronto, is the guest of Mr. and Mrs. J. Morris (7 May 1909, 12, 21)

LYONS, Saul, of Amsterdam, N.Y., was in Hamilton for a few days (2 April 1909, 12, 14)

MACK, Lou, is visiting some of his relatives in New York, Boston and Montreal (8 Jan. 1909, 12, 4)

MARCUSE, F., of Montreal, was in Hamilton on a short visit (7 May 1909, 12, 21)

MINKIN, Rabbi and Mrs. Jacob S., were given a surprise party last evening by members of the Hughson Street Temple and their wives at the home of Mr. and Mrs. M. Levy, 18 Aikman Ave. "In a very able and impressive address David Sweet, who acted as toastmaster, dwelt at some length on the valuable services rendered by the rabbi and his wife to the congregation to which he has just been elected for a third term, with a considerable increase in salary." M. Levy and M. Silverman also made speeches (9 May 1913, 16, 22)

MINKIN, Rabbi Jacob S., of Hamilton, addressed a meeting of the newly organized Zionist Society "Ohave Zion", of London, Ont. The meeting was chaired by Mr. Gerson. While in London Rabbi Minkin was the guest of Mr. and Mrs. Fishbein (4 April 1913, 16, 17)

MINTZ, I., chaired a mass meeting, on Sun. Jan. 10, 1909, called to establish a Talmud Torah school in Hamilton. Others taking part in the meeting were:- Rabbis J. Friedlander and Levine; S. Shapiro, of Dundas, Ont.; M. Walters and S.J. Shalett, of Minneapolis; D. Sweet; and I. Davidovitz, of the Poale Zion Society (22 Jan. 1909, 12, 6)

MINTZ, Miss Sara, is spending a few days with Mrs. King, of Toronto (26 Feb. 1909, 12, 11)

MORRIS, J. and A. Samter, of Detroit, returned home after an long trip through the western and southern U.S. (19 March 1909, 12, 14)

MORRIS, J., of Hamilton and A. Samter, of Detroit, have gone on a trip to California (22 Jan. 1909, 12, 6)

MORRIS, Master Cecil, celebrated his fourth birthday at the home of his parents, 94 Duke St. Master Louis Lyons, of Toronto, was the guest of honor (18 June 1909, 12, 27)

MORRIS, Miss Helen, has returned from Toronto where she visted the Misses Wecksler (22 Jan. 1909, 12, 6)

MORRIS, Mr. and Mrs. J., are the guests of Mr. and Mrs. Saul Lyons, in Toronto (16 April 1909, 12, 18)

MORRIS, Mrs. J. and son are at the Welland House, St. Catherines, Ont. (16 July 1909, 12, 31)

MORRIS, Mrs. J. and son, Duke St., are the guests of Mrs. Cora Kauffman, of Detroit (22 Jan. 1909, 12, 6)

MORRIS, Mrs. J. and son, Duke St., returned home from Detroit (26 Feb. 1909, 12, 11)

MORRIS, the Misses and Selina Harris spent a few days in Buffalo, N.Y. (18 June 1909, 12, 27)

MYERS, Benjamin, of Montreal, spent a short time in Hamilton (26 Feb. 1909, 12, 11)

PEVSNER, Madame Bella, the well-known Zionist lecturer spent a week in Hamilton, the guest of Rabbi and Mrs. Jacob S. Minkin. She delivered several lectures on Zionism in the Crystal Palace and the Hughson Street Synagogue. She made an appeal on behalf of the Bezalel School of Art in Palestine. Donors included J. Blumenthal, W. Farrar, W. Goldberg, Moe Levy and D. Sweet (2 Oct. 1912, 15, 43)

PEVSNER, Madame Bella, the well-known Zionist lecturer spent a week in Hamilton, the guest of Rabbi and Mrs. Jacob S. Minkin. She delivered several lectures on Zionism in the Crystal Palace and the Hughson Street Synagogue. She made an appeal on behalf of the Bezalel School of Art in Palestine. Donors included J. Blumenthal, W. Farrar, W. Goldberg, Moe Levy and D. Sweet (2 Oct. 1912, 15, 43)

RABINOVITCH, A., of Montreal, spent last week in Hamilton (26 Feb. 109, 12, 11)

RAPHAEL, I. and his daughter Mabel, spent the holidays in Buffalo, N.Y. (16 April 1909, 12, 18)

RAPHAEL, I., was in Toronto for a short time (26 Feb. 1909, 12, 11)

RAPHAEL, Miss Rose, has returned home after spending the weekend in Toronto (2 April 1909, 12, 14)

ROSE, Miss Tylle, of Montague, Mich., and Miss Berde Steinburg, of Detroit, are guests of Miss Selina Harris, West Ave. (12 Feb. 1909, 12, 9)

ROSE, S., of Montreal, was in Hamilton on a short visit (23 April 1909, 12, 19)

ROSENSHADT, J., of New York, is spending a few days with his mother (7 May 1909, 12, 21)

ROSENSHADT, J., of Puerto Rico, is on a short trip visiting his mother (19 March 1909, 12, 14)

ROSENSHADT, Jacob, has returned to New York after a short visit with his mother (21 May 1909, 12, 23)

ROSENSHADT, Miss Bertha, of New York, is spending the holiday with her mother, Mrs. Rosenshadt, Robert St. (8 Jan. 1909, 12, 4)

ROSENSHADT, Mrs. T., has returned from a short visit to Rochester, N.Y. (18 June 1909, 12, 27)

SAMTER, A., of Detroit, Mich., is visiting his niece, Mrs. J. Morris, Duke St. (18 June 1909, 12, 27)

SCHLOMAN, H., of Montreal, spent last week in Hamilton (12 Feb. 1909, 12, 9)

SCHOFSKY, M., read a paper "Judas Maccabeeus" at the Young People's Society meeting, on Sun. Dec. 27, 1908 (8 Jan. 1909, 12, 4)

SHACOFSKY, Mrs. M. and Miss Etta Lyons, gave a whist party at their home, Wilson St., last Wed., in honor of Miss Jennie Lyons, of Utica, N.Y. Prize winners were Miss Gussie Morris, H. Morris, H. Bloom and Miss Lena Levy (26 Feb. 1909, 12, 11)

SHAIR, Mrs. Adolf, of Chicago, is visiting her daughter, Mrs. E.H. Levy (19 July 1912, 15, 32)

SHAIR, Mrs. Adolf, of Chicago, is visiting her daughter, Mrs. E.H. Levy (19 July 1912, 15, 32)

SHERRIN, H., presented the YMHA charter to the president, Sid. Freedman at the third annual banquet. Those present included:- Dave Fauman, of Toronto; H. Goldstein, the retiring president; and Rabbis Jacob S. Minkin and Ph. Furst. Sam Cohen, the treasurer, sang "From the Largess of My Heart" (31 Oct. 1913, 16, 47)

SHEUER, Edmund, of Toronto, addressed the Anshe Sholem Young People's Society on "Nathan the Wise". Miss Rose Levy played the organ prelude. There was a violin solo by M. Levy and a duet by Misses Mintz and Findlay (7 May 1909, 12, 21)

SIDERSKI, H., has left on an extended tour of Europe (19 March 1909, 12, 14)

SILVERMAN, Mrs. M. and son are summering at Sea Breeze, Rochester, N.Y. (16 July 1909, 12,

SILVERMAN, Mrs. Moe and son are visiting Mr. and Mrs. Silverman, in Rochester, N.Y. (8 Jan. 1909, 12, 4)

SILVERSTONE, Mr., of Montreal, was the guest of Mr. and Mrs. M. Simons, Bold St. (21 May 1909, 12, 23)

SIMONS, M., has gone on a business trip (23 April 1909, 12, 19)

SIMONS, Mr. and Mrs. M., of Montreal, are visiting in Hamilton (26 Feb. 1909, 12, 11)

STEINBERG, Miss, of Detroit and Miss Tylle Rose, of Montague, Mich., have returned home (19 March 1909, 12, 14)

STRAUS, Julius, was recently elected president of Anshe Sholom Congregation. A.S. Levy was elected vice-president. "Both these gentlemen are energetic workers and adherents of the Reform movement. It is therefore thought that they will strive to re-introduce the reform worship as it was practiced thirty years ago when the then quaint little temple was dedicated." (19 July 1912, 15, 32)

STRAUS, Julius, was recently elected president of Anshe Sholom Congregation. A.S. Levy was elected vice-president. "Both these gentlemen are energetic workers and adherents of the Reform movement. It is therefore thought that they will strive to re-introduce the reform worship as it was practiced thirty years ago when the then quaint little temple was dedicated." (19 July 1912, 15, 32)

STRAUSS, J., has gone on a business trip to the Old Country (7 May 1909, 12, 21)

STRAUSS, J., has returned from a trip to the Old Country (16 July 1909, 12, 31)

STRAUSS, J., spent the holidays in Rochester and Syracuse (16 april 1909, 12, 18)

STRAUSS, Julius, has returned from a trip to the Old Country (29 Jan. 1909, 12, 7)

STRAUSS, Miss Daly, of Toronto, spent the weekend with her cousin, Miss Rose Levy (7 May 1909, 12, 21)

STRAUSS, Mr. and Mrs. Louis, spent Sun. at Niagara Falls (18 June 1909, 12, 27)

STRAUSS, the Misses and Leo. Strauss, of Toronto, were in Hamilton for the day (16 July 1909, 12, 31)

SWEET, David, was re-elected president of the Young People's Society of Temple Anshe Sholom at a meeting last Sun. night. Other officers elected were:- Moe Silverman, vice-president; Julius Lazarus, secretary; Joe Levy, treasurer; M. Schafosky, H. Siderski, M. Levy and H. Morris, Board of Governors (29 Jan. 1909, 12, 7)

SWEET, Mr. and Mrs. D., have returned from Buffalo and Rochester (16 July 1909, 12, 31)

SWEET, Mr. and Mrs. D., Robert St., entertained the Anshe Sholom Temple choir, last Fri. evening. Prizes were won by Mrs. A. Levy and L. Levy (22 Jan. 1909, 12, 6)

TAUBE, Mrs. M., has just returned from Buffalo where she visited her parents, Mr. and Mrs. Gumbinsky (12 Feb. 1909, 12, 9)

VECHSLER, H., is president of the Zionist Society of London which has twenty-five members. Other officers are:- Miss R. Epstein, vice-pres.; A. Black, sec.; Miss E. Siskind, treas.; M. Epstein, J. Silberstein, Mrs. Zimmerman, and the Misses J. Engle and S. Taylor, exec. committee (4 June 1909, 12, 25)

VECHSLER, H., is president of the Young People's Zion Association of London (9 July 1909, 12, 30)

VINEBERG, M., left for London, Ont., where he has taken charge of the Raphael & Co. branch store (2 April 1909, 12, 14)

WARRINSKY, Miss Ethel, of Buffalo, N.Y., is visiting her aunt, Mrs. I. Levy, Victoria Ave. N. (8 Jan. 1909, 12, 4)

WECKSLER, Miss Fannie, who has returned from an extended trip through the eastern States, was the guest of Miss Byrde Morris for a few days, en route to Toronto (2 April 1909, 12, 14)

WECKSLER, Miss Fanny, of Toronto, en route for Boston, was the guest of Miss Byrde Morris, James St. N. (29 Jan. 1909, 12, 7)

WECKSLER, the Misses, of Toronto, spent the weekend with Miss Gussie Morris, Robert St. (16 July 1909, 12, 31)

WOLFE, Joseph R., of San Diego, Cal., has lost his wife, Rachel, who died May 31, 1909 (21 May 1909, 12, 23)

ZIMMERMAN, M., was in Hamilton for a few days (12 Feb. 1909, 12, 9)

KINGSTON

ABRAMSKY, Miss Katie, has returned from Toronto where she spent the winter visiting her sister, Mrs. M. Breslin (29 March 1912, 15, 20)

ABRAMSON, H., of Peterborough, visited Mr. and Mrs. L. Abramson in Kingston (30 Aug. 1912, 15, 38)

ABRAMSON, J., was elected president of the Kingston Zionist Society at a meeting last Sun. Other officers elected were:- K. Zacks, vice-pres.; A.B. Bennett, sec.; A. Circle, treas.; Cantor Rothblat, Charles Tomares, B. Zbar, Dave Bennett, William Susman and Ralph Suzberg, council. Speakers at the meeting were J.C. Zack, of Montreal, J. Abramson, Charles Tomares and A.B. Bennett (29 Dec. 1911, 15, 7)

ABRAMSON, Joseph, is one of the pioneer Jewish settlers in Kingston. He has lived there for over twenty years and has been during that time president of the Zionist society and the congregation. He is a well-known Zionist leader and is currently a vice-president of the Zionist Federation. He is leaving Kingston for Saskatoon where he intends to settle and go into business (26 April 1912, 15, 24)

ABRAMSON, L., is in Montreal for a week on business (23 May 1913, 16, 24)

ABRAMSON, L., president of the Kingston Zionist Society chaired a meeting on Sun. aft. C. Tomares delivered an address on Zionism in Yiddish and William Susman gave a lecture and accompanying slide show presentation. Cantor Rotblatt sang Hatikvah and other Zionist songs (9 Aug. 1912, 15, 35)

ABRAMSON, Louis, is president of the Jewish Congregation in Kingston which laid a foundation stone last Mon. aft. for the first synagogue in Kingston. Other officers are:- S. Bennett, secretary; I. Cohen, treasurer; and A. Shear, J. Tuck and K. Zacks, trustees. "The Kingston community dates back about twenty years when a congregation was formed, but owing to the paucity of numbers no attempt was made before to erect a place of worship. During the High Holidays services were held in a large hall. Ten years ago the Jewish population commenced to increase rapidly and now numbers about fifty families. The oldest Jewish citizen is Mr. S. Obendorffer, eighty-four years old, and who has resided in the town fifty-two years." (11 Oct. 1910, 13, 48)

ABRAMSON, Mr. and Mrs. J. and their daughter, Miss G. Abramson are in Cleveland visiting Mr. and Mrs. Wolpaw. From there they leave for the west where they will reside (30 Aug. 1912, 15, 38)

ALLAN, Mrs. J.J., daughter of Mr. and Mrs. J. Abramson, left Thurs. night for her home in Calgary. Her sister, Miss Annie Abramson, accompanied her as far as Toronto, where she will be the guest of Mr. and Mrs. Oberndorffer (6 Jan. 1911, 14, 8)

ALLEN, Mrs. Rachel, of Calgary, is visiting her parents, Mr. and Mrs. Joseph Abramson (26 April 1912, 15, 24)

BALD, Mr. and Mrs., of Montreal, are in Kingston visiting friends (12 Dec. 1913, 17, 1)

BENNETT, Archie, was in Peterborough visiting his cousins, Mr. and Mrs. Hyman Zacks (6 Jan. 1911, 14, 8)

BRESLER, Mrs., of Toronto, is visiting her parents, Mr. and Mrs. J. Abramsky (30 Aug. 1912, 15, 38)

CHANAINE, J. and his daughter, Ella Chanaine, were in Kingston visiting his brother-in-law and sister, Mr. and Mrs. Susman (10 Oct. 1913, 16, 44)

CHANAINE, Mr., of Montreal, and son Willie, are in Kingston on business. They are staying with Mr. Chanaine's brother-in-law and sister, Mr. and Mrs. Susman (9 Aug. 1912, 15, 35)

CHESSLER, Mrs. B., of Belleville, has returned home after spending a week visiting friends in Peterborough (2 Aug. 1912, 14, 34)

CIRCLE, A., has returned from New York where he received medical attention (30 Aug. 1912, 15, 38)

COHEN, I., president of the Kingston Zion Society, remitted twenty dollars to the Zionist Federation executive in Montreal for the Party Fund (3 Sept. 1909, 12, 38)

COHEN, I., vice-president of the local congregation, presided at the lecture on modern anti-semitism delivered by J. Sklower, a noted speaker and writer. "The speaker reviewed the condition of Jews in various parts of the world and showed that anti-Semitism was very much in evidence. Even in Canada some of this was evident (10 Oct. 1913, 16, 44)

DAVIS, Miss L., of New York, who visited Mr. and Mrs. J. Turk in Kingston, left for Montreal to visit relatives (30 Aug. 1912, 15, 38)

DAVIS, Miss, of New York City, is spending a few weeks visiting her relatives, Mr. and Mrs. J. Turk (9 Aug. 1912, 15, 35)

DAVIS, P., of Montreal, is visiting his friends, Mr. and Mrs. J. Turk (23 May 1913, 16, 24)

DAVIS, P., of Montreal, paid a short visit to his relatives, Mr. and Mrs. J. Turk (19 Aug. 1912, 15, 36)

DIAMOND, Mr. and Mrs. J., visited their relatives, Mr. and Mrs. M. Susman (30 Aug. 1912, 15, 38)

ELLENSON, Mordecai I., of Toronto, who is attending Queen's University, "... has been compelled to discontinue his studies temporarily, on account of overstraining eyes (26 Jan. 1912, 15, 11)

ELLENSON, Mr. and Mrs. Moses, Princess St., hosted a dance of the Kingston Social Club last Sat. evening. Most of the young Jewish men in Kingston belong to the club (3 March 1911, 14, 16)

GOTHER, A., a Roman Catholic, converted to Judaism on Nov. 24, 1912. The circumcision took place at the home of Mr. and Mrs. Wartelsky. "The operation was successfully performed by Rev. H. Rotblatt and the necessary benedictions were pronounced by Mr. C. Tomares, who also gave him his new name, Abraham. This conversion was not approved of very much by the local Jews and Mr. Gother had to get over many obstacles before he was converted." Mr. Gother comes from a respectable family in Germany. He has been in Canada several years and is an electrician. "This is the first case of its kind in Kingston and it was not gained by any zealous attempts of missionaries, only by the man's own convictions." (29 Nov. 1912, 15, 51)

GREEN, Joseph, 2 Princess St., lost his store and residence in a fire on Fri. Jan. 12, 1912. "The entire stock and furniture were destroyed by the fire, but the loss, which was very heavy, is partly covered by insurance." (26 Jan. 1912, 15, 11)

KATZ, M., of Kingston, is going to Montreal on business (23 May 1913, 16, 24)

KUTZ, Mrs. H. and her nephew, Master S. Hansman, have returned home to New York after visiting their relatives in Kingston (30 Aug. 1912, 15, 38)

KUTZ, Mrs., of New York, is visiting her brother and sister-in-law, Mr. and Mrs. Max Susman, Colborne St. (2 Aug. 1912, 14, 34)

LESSES, Dr. Max, has returned home to Salem, Mass., after visiting his parents, Mr. and Mrs. L. Lesses, Chatham St. (2 Aug. 1912, 14, 34)

LESSESS, Dr., of Salem, Mass., visited his parents, Mr. and Mrs. L. Lessess (6 Jan. 1911, 14, 8)

LIPMAN, B. and H. Salsberg organized the Kingston Hebrew School picnic at Kingston Mills on Wed. Aug. 7, 1912 (19 Aug. 1912, 15, 36)

LIPMAN, B., Brock St., is in New York for a short time prior to opening his new store here in Kingston (23 May 1913, 16, 24)

LIPMAN, Dr. A., has gone to Cochrane, Ont. to take a medical position there (19 Aug. 1912, 15, 36)

LIPMAN, Dr. A., is in town visiting his parents, Mr. and Mrs. B. Lipman (12 Dec. 1913, 17, 1)

MEDNEDOFF, Rev. M., of Richmond, Virginia, delivered an address on Zionism at the Herzl memorial meeting Sun. evening (1 Aug. 1913, 16, 34)

RUBIN, Miss, of Picton, Ont., visited Mr. and Mrs. K. Zacks, en route to Toronto (30 Aug. 1912, 15, 38)

SALSBERG, Miss A., is in Boston and Manchester visiting friends (29 Nov. 1912, 15, 51)

SALSBERG, Miss Dorothy, returned home after spending a few weeks in Orange, N.J. (10 Oct. 1913, 16, 44)

SUSSMAN, Mrs. H., of New York, visted her son, M. Sussman in Kingston. She left for Montreal to visit Mr. and Mrs. J. Diamond (30 Aug. 1912, 15, 38)

TURK, Miss L., was given a surprise party by the Jewish young people of Kingston on Sun. night, May 11, 1913, prior to her departure for Rochester, N.Y., where she will spend some time (23 May 1913, 16, 24)

WAITELSKY, Mr. and Mrs. and their son, Louis, of Manchester, N.J., (formerly of Verona, Ont.) are visiting their friends, Mr. and Mrs. H. Salsberg, Barrie St., "...and will probably make their permanent residence in this city." (23 May 1913, 16, 24)

WOLPAW, Mr. and Mrs. D. and child, of Cleveland, are visiting Mrs. Wolpaw's parents, Mr. and Mrs. Joseph Abramson, Queen St. (2 Aug. 1912, 14, 34)

ZACKS, Harry and Miss Fried, of Peterborough, who have been visiting Mr. and Mrs. D. Zacks, Barrie St., have returned to their home in Peterborough (2 Aug. 1912, 14, 34)

ZACKS, M., has gone to Peterborough to visit relatives (19 Aug. 1912, 15, 36)

ZACKS, Miss M., is in Toronto, visiting her relatives, Mr. and Mrs. S. Bennett (29 Nov. 1912, 15, 51)

ZIVIAN, I., of Gananoque, Ont., visited Mr. and Mrs. A. Circle in Kingston (30 Aug. 1912, 15, 38)

LONDON

SISKIN, Julius, Isaac Rushavensky and William Laff, all of London, Ont., were charged with contravening the Sunday Labor Law. "The two former were picking rags and cutting rubber on the 17th in Laff's warehouse, and both testified that their arrangement with Laff was to work six days a week, observing Saturday as the day of rest. Laff was fined $10 and costs." (29 Oct. 1909, 12, 46)

OWEN SOUND

FISHKIN, Miss Minnie, age 14, daughter of Mr. and Mrs. J. Fishkin, of Owen Sound, Ont., who is a pupil at the West Grey Teachers' Institute, won the medal for the highest number of marks obtained by any pupil in the district (29 Oct. 1909, 12, 46)

WINNIPEG, MANITOBA

ABRAHAMSON, Esther, Ethel Bere, Lena Calof, Gertrude Caminetsky, J.W. Cohen, Sophie Granovsky, Esther Lyons, Annie Miasnik, Ethel Meyers, Sarah Neiman, G. Shapera, H. Shinbane, Anna Shirroff, H.E. Schneider and N. Zimmerman were successful Arts candidates (part 1) in the matriculation examinations at the University of Manitoba (18 July 1913, 16, 32)

ABRAHAMSON, Mary, C. Abramovitch, J.C. Berg, Hilda Davis, Solomon Kobrinski, N.C. Levin, A. Levinson, H. Leverson, S. Portigal, G. Salamon, V. Schweizar, E.A. Skafel, E.A. Skaletar, H. Sokolofsky, P. Wald and H. Weidman were successful Arts candidates (part 2) in the matriculation examinations at the University of Manitoba (18 July 1913, 16, 32)

ABRAHAMSON, S., a Manitoba College graduate of 1913, was elected to represent the province in the annual triangle debates between Manitoba, Grand Forks and Fargo (7 Feb. 1913, 16, 9)

ABRAHAMSON, Simon, "gave a comprehensive account of Russian persecution of the Jews, denouncing the charge against Beillis as absurd" at a large protest meeting on Sun. aft., Oct. 12, 1913 in the Grand Theatre (22 Oct. 1913, 16, 46)

ABRAHAMSON, Simon (B.A.), was awarded $150.00 first prize at the recent LL.B. degree examination, University of Manitoba (22 Oct. 1913, 16, 46)

ABRAHAMSON, Simon, a University of Manitoba law student, was selected today, Jan. 13,, 1913, as the Manitoba Rhodes scholar for 1914. Age 22, he received his B.A. with high honors in 1912 and is ranked as one of the best debaters in the university. Mr. Abrahamson was born in Mile End, London, England and came to Canada as a boy (16 Jan. 1914, 17, 6)

ABRAHAMSON, Simon, son of the newly-elected school trustee, has won a Rhodes scholarship. The scholarship, which is worth $4,500., will take Mr. Abrahamson to Oxford University where he will study law and philosophy for three years. "Mr. Abrahamson's career has been a brilliant one, and a repetition of his success is confidently expected of him across the Atlantic." (13 Feb. 1914, 17, 7)

ABRAMOVITCH, S., P. Narovlansky, W. Tobias and J. Zimmerman sang with spirit at the "Persian Garden Tea", organized by the Young People's Hebrew Association at their headquarters in the Shaar Shomayim Synagogue. Those present included:- the Misses Sara Lyon, Hettie Rosen, Bella de Taube, Ethel Tobias, Eva Wodlinger, L.G. Wodlinger and Mesdames R. Goldstein and H. Isaacs, Jr. (11 April 1913, 16, 18)

ABRAMSON, M., was elected school trustee for Ward 5 (26 Dec. 1913, 17, 3)

ABREMOVICH, Miss Tess, returns home to St. Paul after visiting her cousin, Miss Ethel Abremovich (15 Sept. 1909, 12, 40)

ARONOVICH, Mrs. A.H. and family left Wed. June 9, 1909 for Grand Forks, N.D. to visit relatives (18 June 1909, 12, 27)

ARONOVITCH, A.H., president of B'nai Brith, Max Heppner, M. Haid, H. Weidman, R.S. Robinson, M. Steinman, D. Balkowsky, Moses Finkelstein, B. Shragge, H.E. Wilder, F. Cherniak, L. Rice, L. Berger, J. Cohn, I. Ripstein, M.W. Triller, J.A. Chmelnitski, S.A. Ripstein and A. Berg were members of a committee appointed to carry on the work of the newly formed Winnipeg United Hebrew Charities and canvass for subscriptions. Rabbis Kahanovitch and J.K. Levin spoke at the organizing meeting held in the Colonial Theatre last Sun. (3 March 1911, 14, 16)

ATRUBIN, Messrs., contributed to the Zionist Land Fund (28 June 1912, 15, 29)

ATRUBIN, N., of the Winnipeg B'nai Israel Zion Society, forwarded $25.00 to the Zionist Federation executive in Montreal (16 April 1909, 12, 18)

ATRUBIN, N., treasurer of the B'nai Israel Zion Society of Winnipeg, remitted contributions for National Fund stamps and the Herzl Wald in the names of Meyer Czetzic, Baruch Czernak, Nachman Grover, Idel Kaplan, Sheshet Kofsky and his brother, Jacob Weler and Rabbi Kahanovitch (3 Sept. 1909, 12, 38)

ATRUBIN, Nathan, Rabbi Israel J. Kahanovitch, Rev. M.A. Ashinsky (Pittsburgh), Mr. and Mrs. Abraham Millmutt, Mr. and Mrs. Jacob Heitner, Mr. and Mrs. Naphtali Teitelbaum, H. Kopelowich, and H.A. Ashofsky, Rev. Elias Cashdan, Rev. Pesach Schorr and David Atrubin were inscribed in the JNF Golden Book (22 July 1910, 13, 36)

BALCOVSKE, Dr. D., has returned from a trip out east (3 March 1911, 14, 16)

BARONDESS, Joseph, Commissioner of Education for the State of New York visited Winnipeg. He was the guest of Mr. and Mrs. H. Saltzman who held a reception in his honor. "Speaking at the Talmud Torah, Mr. Barondess protested against the placing of Hebrew as a secondary language in the gymnasium at Haifa in Palestine and urged the cultivation of the Hebrew language not only as the language of our race, but as the best means of preventing assimilation." Mr. Barondess later addressed members of the B'nai Brith (13 Feb. 1914, 17, 7)

BATEMAN, Mesdames A., S. Bryier, J. Kluner, A. Knelman, L. Marcus, M. Rosenblat, R. Steinman and E. Tapper were responsible for organizing the Hebrew Ladies' Aid Society annual dance held Thurs. evening in Minuk's Hall, Dufferin Ave. (2 May 1913, 16, 21)

BECKERMAN, H.M. and M.L. Frankenstein organized the first annual YMHA Field Day on Sun. July 27, 1913 in Riverside Park. The winners were:- W.V. Tobias, Syd Rosen, Jack London, A. Zimmerman, B. Fostovsky, A.E. Weidman, Dave Beckerman, S. Brownstone, D. Finkelstein, Buddy Weidman, A. Abramovich, M. Weidman, M. Polinsky, I. Moscovitz, Charles Cohen and the Misses Esther Vineberg, Annie Herman, Ida Finkelstein, E. Black and M. Narovlansky. Winners of the five men a side football tournament were:- A.E. Weidman, M.A. Marshall, L.D. Moroswky, M.H. Brotman and John Weidman. Official judges were:- Dr. Abramovitch, Frank Huffman and A. Abramovitch. The Misses Rose Ripstein, Pearl Vineberg and Annie Weidman presented the prizes (15 Aug. 1913, 16, 36)

BERCHANSKY, S., has just left for the east on a business trip (1 Oct. 1909, 12, 42)

BERCOVICH, Mrs. A., wife of Dr. Bercovich, formerly of Montreal, gave a matinée party followed by a luncheon at her residence, 360 Selkirk St., to mark her first wedding anniversary (26 March 1909, 12, 15)

BERCOVITCH, Dr. A., was appointed gynecologist to the Winnipeg General Hospital. "This hospital is the leading one in our city, and this appointment is evidence of Dr. Bercovitch's ability. Dr. Bercovitch came about six years ago from Montreal." (18 July 1913, 16, 32)

BERE, Miss May, read a paper "dealing with ideals and the ideal in ever-day life" at a Young People's Hebrew Association literary evening on Sun. night (22 Oct. 1913, 16, 46)

BERG, S. and J.P. Schnerch passed parts 1 and 2 in the matriculation examinations at the University of Manitoba (18 July 1913, 16, 32)

BERGER, A., was elected president of the House of Jacob Congregation at its annual meeting last Sun. Other officers elected were:- I. Jacobson, vice-pres.; and L. Berger, treas. Messrs. Chmelnitsky, Kovansky, Philips, Cherniak, Starkoff and Gakky. Rabbi Kahanovitch, Rev. Waldman and C. Todman delivered speeches (15 Oct. 1909, 12, 44)

BERMAK, Charles J., passed first year medicine at the University of Manitoba (20 June 1913, 16, 28)

BLOOMFIELD, A.J. and Max Steinkopf were responsible for founding Winnipeg Lodge No. 650, IOBB in 1909. At present there are 325 members and 75 applications for initiation. D. Beckerman is the president and A.J. Abramovich, secretary (11 April 1913, 16, 18)

BLOOMFIELD, Dolly, eldest daughter of Mr. and Mrs. A.J. Bloomfield, who underwent a throat operation on Jan. 5, 1909, is now convalescent (15 Jan. 1909, 12, 5)

BLOOMFIELD, Mrs. A.J., won the diamond ring presented by I.S. Goldenstein, of Montreal, raffled at Mrs. G. Frankfurter's charity whist Jan. 12, 1911. Mesdames Harry Saunders and Churchill distributed the proceeds (27 Jan. 1911, 14, 11)

BRAND, P., returned from a trip to the major cities in Canada and the U.S. "...for the purpose of further advancing the big building scheme which he has in hand at present, and for which a company will be floated shortly." (24 Jan. 1913, 16, 7)

BRAUNSTEIN, J., I. Abramovitch, M.S. Smith and A. Strachuran were the committee in charge responsible for organizing a ball in Minuk's Hall on Jan. 2, 1911 for the benefit of a mother and children in distress who want to return to their home in New York. C.B. Rosenblat and Miss A. Henner sold the tickets (27 Jan. 1911, 14, 11)

BRONFMAN, Allan, passed second year Arts at the University of Manitoba winning a scholarship in French and hon. mention in German. Others passing second year Arts were:- May Bere, who won a scholarship in German, Joseph Cherniack, William Diamond, Samuel Helman and Charles

Ripstein (20 June 1913, 16, 28)

BRONFMAN, Mr., and Messrs. Budnitsky, Raisky and Rosen conducted the Purim festival examination at the Rosh Pina Synagogue Hebrew School, corner of Martha and Henry Sts. Prize winners were:- Abie Rosenblat, Harry Moscovitch, Harry Levi, Aaron Genser, Louise, Willie and Dave Finkelstein, Leon Moscovitch, Jake Peerles, Teddie Liss, Frank Levi, Sam Smilovitch, Alex Koleski, Sam Vineberg and Hyman Husfeld. "The pupils, their parents and friends who were present, sat down to a banquet given by the principal, Mr. Nathan Rosenblat, who urged the parents to take more interest in the work carried on under his supervision and asked them for their co-operation." (24 March 1911, 14, 19)

BROTMAN, E.A., passed Part 1, Arts., University of Manitoba (22 Oct. 1913, 16, 46)

BROTMAN, M., and J. London were nominated for chairman of the Young People's Hebrew Association on June 8, 1913 at the semi-annual general meeting. Nominees for vice-chairman were F. Frankenstein, L. Morosnick and N.C. Tobias. The vote will be held Sun. June 15 (20 June 1913, 16, 28)

BROTMAN, M.H., is chairman of the Young People's Hebrew Association which has 185 members. Other executive members are:- J. Landau, vice-chrmn.; Miss L.G. Wodlinger, treas.; Miss A.D. Wodlinger, fin. sec.; Charles K. Ripstein, rec. sec. (18 April 1913, 16, 19)

BROWN, L. and brother, Albert Brown have moved to Vancouver, B.C., after living many years in Winnipeg (3 Feb. 1911, 14, 12)

BROWN, Phillip, president of Shaarey Shomayim Synagogue, and Mrs. Max Goldstein were responsible for convening a committee which organized the highly successful ten days' "Kermess" at the Synagogue (17 Dec. 1909, 13, 5)

BROWN, Phillip, was elected president of Shaarey Shomayim Congregation. Other officers elected were:- M. Haid, first vice-pres.; R.S. Robinson, parnass; B. Levinson, treas.; P. Presner, fin. sec.; S. Hart Green, rec. sec.; Messrs. I. Ripstein, J. Rosen, A.H. Aronovich, G. Frankurter, G. Harris and J.L. Lehberg, trustees (29 Oct. 1909, 12, 46)

CAMINTESKY, Ira, is the leader and pianist of a Jewish boys' orchestra which has recently been formed. Other members are:- N. Adelman, 1st violin; L. Goldbloom, 2nd violin; A. Covens, cornet; and Sam Warnick, drums (17 Dec. 1909, 13, 5)

CASHDAN, Hyman, third year engineering at the University of Manitoba, won a scholarship in civil engineering (20 June 1913, 16, 28)

CASHDAN, Rev. and Mr. Kowlson will serve as first and second chazan respectively in the new congregation created after the amalgamation of Shaarey Zedek and Shaarey Shomayim congregations. Aaron Cohen will act as shochet as well as chazan during the weekdays. "The last service in the Shaarey Zedek Synagogue took place on Sept. 6th, and after that all Divine Worship, for both congregations, will be held in the Dagmar Street Synagogue." The new congregation will probably be looking for a new rabbi (12 Sept. 1913, 16, 40)

CHMELNITSKY, J., president of the House of Jacob Synagogue, resigned over a disagreement about the election of a chief rabbi. After a hurried meeting the resignation was accepted and L. Berger, a former vice-president, was elected to succeed him (24 Jan. 1913, 16, 7)

CHMELNITSKY, Miss Goldie, was elected president of the Girl's Benevolent Loan Society at the annual elections on April 16, 1913. Other officers elected were:- Mrs. M. Finkelstein, hon. pres.; Miss R. Marshall, vice-pres.; Miss P. Beamolt, sec.; Miss L. Saper, corr. sec.; Miss M. Kanter, treas.; Misses G. Finkleman, S. Rosen, P. Vineberg, A. Weidman, B. Weidman and L. Wodlinger, trustees (6 June 1913, 16, 26)

CLAYMAN, I., passed through Winnipeg last week, en route to Montreal, on a buying trip for the B. Gardner Co. He has recovered from the very serious operation he underwent in Victoria, B.C. (18 June 1909, 12, 27)

CLAYMAN, Isidore, manager of the B. Gardner Co. Ltd., has recovered from his recent serious illness and leaves shortly for Montreal on a buying trip (15 Jan. 1909, 12, 5)

COBLENTZ, Miss R., left for Minneapolis on Sun. Jan. 16, 1910 to visit friends (28 Jan. 1910, 13, 11)

COBLENZ, Mr. and Mrs., formerly of Gretna, Man., now of Winnipeg, entertained on Sun. March 7, 1909, in celebration of their thirty-fourth wedding anniversary (26 March 1909, 12, 15)

CODDON, Miss Etta, entertained at bridge on Sun. Feb. 19, 1911. Winners were:- Misses S. Huffman (New York) and L. Schuman (Denver) (3 March 1911, 14, 16)

COHEN, E. Arakie, examined the students of the Shaarey Shomayim Congregation Hebrew School on March 12, 1911. Mr Cohen "... pointed out that Sha'arey Shomayim was the only synagogue affording the children a thorough Hebrew and religious education on modern lines in the city of Winnipeg." Miss Etta Levinson, on behalf of the children, presented Mrs. H.A. Isaacs with a bouquet. H.A. Isaacs, chairman of the school board (31 March 1911, 14, 20)

COHEN, E.A., addressed the Young People's Association last Sun., hoping there would be more lectures and debates. "He urged them not to allow the Association to become purely social, but to see more evenings were devoted to intellectual culture than there had been up to the present." (6 June 1913, 16, 26)

COHEN, E.A., delivered the address at the re-consecreation service last Sun. in the newly amalgamated synagogue. Mr. Cohen took for his text "Behold How Good and How Pleasant it is for Brethren to Dwell Together in Unity". He talked about problems facing the community and stressed religious education for the young. Rabbi Kahanovitch spoke in Yiddish and Rev. Warshaft, principal of the Talmud Torah, gave an address in English. Rev. Cashdan led the choir of boys and girls (10 Oct. 1913, 16, 44)

COHEN, E.A., was appointed patron of the newly formed University Club. The club is for the forty Jewish boys who have graduated university and decided to form a club (26 Dec. 1913, 17, 3)

COHEN, E.A., will deliver the address at the re-consecration service of the Shaarey Zedek and Shaarey Shomayim Amalgamated Synagogue on Sun. Sept. 21, 1913 at 2.30 p.m. (19 Sept. 1913, 16, 41)

COHEN, Miss, of Toronto, is visiting Mrs. Max Goldstine who gave a dance in honor of her sister (1 Oct. 1913, 16, 42-43)

COHEN, Miss S., of Toronto, is in Winnipeg visiting her sister, Mrs. Max Goldstein, Mayfair Ave. (31 Dec. 1909, 13, 7)

COHEN, Mr. and Mrs. E.A., will soon close their summer cottage at Sherington Park. Mrs. Cohen's mother, Mrs. I.W. Jacobs and her sister, Miss Dorothea Jacobs, who spent all summer with her, are returning to New York (12 Sept. 1913, 16, 40)

COHEN, Mr., of Prince Rupert, who was visiting Winnipeg, has left on an extended trip east (1 Oct. 1909, 12, 42)

DE TAUB, Miss Bella, has left for a long stay in Toronto (1 Oct. 1913, 16, 42-43)

DIRECTOR, Mrs. I., of Sault Ste. Marie, Ont., is the guest of Miss Fanny Camenetsky. She will leave shortly to visit the Seattle Exposition in Washington (2 July 1909, 12, 29)

DRUCKMAN, S., chairman of the Montefiore Club camp committee, and A. Barish, secretary, were thanked for their contributions to the successful summer camp of 1913. The club "...had procured an ideal spot for camping; land situated on a beautiful bend of the Red River, just above its junction with the Assiniboine. From this location, high, dry, clear and airy, the members had easy access to the river in which they bathed in the early morning. Seven wedged shaped tents were provided for sleeping accomodation...The Montefiore boys indulged in sports to their heart's content. Rowing, swimming, football, baseball, cricket, etc., were among their favorite sports." N. Weinstein and H. Rufus Isaacs provided the musical program at the formal opening of the camp in May (10 Oct. 1913, 16, 44)

EDELMAN, Norman, Harry Isaacs, Mrs. Roy Frankfurter and the Misses Rosie Ripstein, Fanny Robinson and Annie Weidman gave a musical performance at the last Young People's Hebrew Association meeting (1 Oct. 1913, 16, 42-43)

EFFINBINE, Miss Effie, of St. Paul, is the guest of her cousins, Miss F. Caminetski and Miss Annie Lyone (15 Sept. 1909, 12, 40)

ELMAN, Mischa, the world renowned violinist, performed in Winnipeg on May 5, 1911 before 3,000 people. Dr. Gaster's Benevolent Society, an old established charitable organization devoted to the care of Jewish immigrants, gave a banquet in honor of Mr. Elman in the Manitoba Hall after the performance. Mr. Elman was accompanied by his father, Saul Elman and his accompanist, Percy B. Kahn. M. Haid was the toastmaster. Other speakers were:- E. Arakie Cohen, M.A., B.C.L.; M. Steinkopf, B.A.; S. Hart Green, B.C.L., M.P.P.; Rabbi J.K. Levin, B.A.; M.J. Finkelstein, B.A., B.C.L.; and E.R. Levinson, B.C.L. Baruch Goldstein, editor of the local Yiddish newspaper, spoke in Yiddish (12 May 1911, 14, 26)

FELS, Joseph, millionaire soap manufacturer and "Single-taxer", spoke before Winnipeg Lodge, No. 650, IOBB on "Not a cent for charity, but millions to abolish the need of it." (27 Jan. 1911, 14, 11)

FINKELSTEIN, M., left for Europe (1 Oct. 1913, 16, 42-43)

FINKELSTEIN, Max, chaired the banquet given in honor of Nahum Sokolow on Sun. Speakers included:- Rabbi Kahanovitch, Jacob Smelinsky, Joseph Finkelstein and H. Vineberg. "At his first lecture, Herr Sokolow made a deep impression on our Winnipeg brethren. His message from suffering Jews in persecuted lands was listened to with close attention. Our South End brethren, who were present at this meeting, have just realized the real meaning of Zionism and the great hopes it holds out for the amelioration of the Jewish people." (13 June 1913, 16, 27)

FINKELSTEIN, Max J., represented Slava Federenko, the Russian political refugee before a Winnipeg court and obtained an acquittal for his client. The case attracted a great deal of attention throughout Canada and the U.S. Mr. Federenko had been arrested on the application of the Russian Consul for extradition on a charge of murder. The Russian Freedom League retained Mr. Finkelstein as counsel. "After weeks of strenuous work on the case, this large-hearted young barrister refused a fee of $1,500, this being part of the funds raised all over the Dominion for Federenko's defence." (13 Jan. 1911, 14, 9)

FINKELSTEIN, Mr. and Mrs. T., celebrated their golden wedding anniversary on Sept. 17, 1913, surrounded by their children, grandchildren and great-grandchildren. Mr. and Mrs. Finkelstein have lived in Winnipeg for thirty-one years (1 Oct. 1913, 16, 42-43)

FINKELSTEIN, Mrs. M., president of the Winnipeg Daughters of Zion Society, chaired a mass meeting recently (9 July 1909, 12, 30)

FINKELSTEIN, Mrs. T. and Mrs. S.A. Ripstein and Miss Gertrude Ripstein have gone on an extended trip to the east (3 March 1911, 14, 16)

FOGEL, Harry S., passed first year Arts at the University of Manitoba winning a scholarship in Latin and mathematics. Others passing first year Arts were:- Goldie L. Finesilver, Douglas Rosen, Herbert Tobias, William Tobias, Abe Vineberg and W. Harry Zimmerman (20 June 1913, 16, 28)

FRANKENSTEIN, M.L., is president of the newly formed Montefiore Club for young Jewish men which has at last become a reality. Other executive board officers are:- M.L. Goldstein, vice-pres.; S. Racko, sec.; Julius Adler, treas.; L. Chechik, Leon Elias, William Gunn, M. Racko and A.E. Wilder, trustees. The club members subscribed five hundred dollars for a sinking fund. "Mr. Julius Adler, formerly of Montreal, was highly instrumental in the subscription of this sum, he having donated One Hundred Dollars, on condition that Five Hundred Dollars be raised." (31 Jan. 1913, 16, 8)

FRANKFURTER, Mrs. G., gave a reception in honor of her new daughter-in-law, Mrs. Roy Frankfurter. Presiding over the tea table were:- Mesdames Edgar Frankfurter, R.S. Robinson, Shragge and Churchill. Assisting were:- the Misses Rachel Coblentz, Ida Cohen, Jessie Horwitz, Rose Ripstein, Fannie Robinson and Hattie Rosen (1 Oct. 1913, 16, 42-43)

FRANKFURTER, Mrs. G., has gone east on her annual business trip (3 Feb. 1911, 14, 12)

GARDNER, Mr. and Mrs. M., have returned from Montreal (7 May 1909, 12, 21)

GELLER, Mr. and Mrs. G. and daughter are leaving shortly to move to New York (26 March 1909, 12, 15)

GOLDENSTEIN, I.S., of Montreal, while in Winnipeg on business, donated a diamond ring to Mrs. M.H. Saunders for purposes of charity (13 Jan. 1911, 14, 9)

GOLDSTEIN, Cantor S.H., left Tues. June 22, 1909 for Philadelphia, where he will probably take up a position (2 July 1909, 12, 29)

GOLDSTEIN, Harry, was master of ceremonies at the Ladies' Aid Society of Rosh Pina Synagogue annual ball held last Tues. evening. The three debutantes who were present were the Misses Lilly Lechtzier, Gertrude Rosenblatt and Millie Springman (7 Feb. 1913, 16, 9)

GOLDSTEIN, Max, proprietor of the Manitoba Clothing Co. and Alderman M. Finklestein, J.P., of the North West Hide Co., are members of the World Fair Delegation touring through the West (7 May 1909, 12, 21)

GOLDSTEIN, Mrs. Max, accompanied by her daughter, Ruby, has returned home after spending the summer with her parents in Toronto (15 Sept. 1909, 12, 40)

GOLDSTEIN, Mrs. Max, was a team captain for the Ninette Sanatorium for Consumptives Manitoba Tag Campaign. Among her workers in Winnipeg were:- Mesdames E.A. Cohen, H. Isaacs, Hess, and the Misses R. Goldstein, L. Hermann, Zoe Isaacs, D. Levinson, T. Malabar, L. Moscovitz, Z. Moscovitz, H. Rosen and M. Rosenblat (20 June 1913, 16, 28)

GOLDSTEIN, Mrs. R., is convenor of section two of the Young People's Hebrew Association (11 April 1913, 16, 18)

GOLDSTEIN, Mrs. S. and children, relict of the late Siegfried Goldstein, of 2 Ripstein Block, are staying with Mr. and Mrs. C. Horwitz, in West Selkirk, Man. (28 May 1909, 12, 24)

GOLDSTEIN, S., formerly of New Haven, Conn., has recently opened up a new, modern theatre called "The Pastime" (1 Oct. 1909, 12, 42)

GOODMAN, Aaron David and his bride Shoshana had trees in the Herzl Wald purchased in their names. Trees were also purchased in the names of the following infants:- Jacob Tuviah Ben Bazalel Tedman, Isaac Ben Mordecai Rubish, Mordecai Ben Myer Tshetchick and Isaac Ben Naftali Gerlownin. Other purchasers were:- Benjamin Roshkovsky, M. Simowitz and Mr. and Mrs. Morris Kaplan (11 July 1913, 16, 31)

GREEN, S. Hart, chaired the formal opening of the Esther Robinson Jewish Orphanage on Nov. 23, 1913 in the Winnipeg Talmud Torah. Located at 73 Robinson St., the orphanage is the first of its kind in Winnipeg and Western Canada. Members of Mrs. Sarah Levi's family purchased the gold key to the institution for her at auction. Mrs. Rachel Diner purchased a ward for $200. in memory of her late husband, Simon Diner. Mrs. Heppner presented a new Sefer Torah for use in the synagogue, "...and the customary usage of completing the inscriptions in same was proceeded with for the benefit of the Orphanage and realized a handsome sum." That day the Orphanage realized $800. which will go towards supporting the forty-four inmates now being cared for. Rev. S. Wolff, of the House of Jacob Synagogue, with a young male choir supplied the music. M. Haid chaired the banquet (12 Dec. 1913, 17, 1)

GREEN, S. Hart, member for North Winnipeg in the Manitoba Legislature, gave his maiden speech. "Mr. Green held the close attention of the House for an hour and a quarter while he discussed the needs of labor in the province, and the principles of direct legislation...His maiden speech will be chiefly remembered for its masterly oratory, and more especially for the splendid way in which he defended the foreign-born element in Winnipeg..." (24 Feb. 1911, 14, 15)

GREEN, S. Hart, member-elect for North Winnipeg in the Manitoba Legislature, was guest of honor at a banquet in the Royal Alexandra Hotel Tues. night. Ex-Alderman M. Finklestein was chairman. Speakers included Arakie Cohen. The Winnipeg Free Press reports that Mr. Green, a Liberal, belongs to the younger school of advanced radicals who strongly favor the initiative and referendum. He is president of Winnipeg Lodge, IOBB. The Winnipeg North constituency contains the Jewish quarter. Although there are from four to seven thousand Jewish residents, there are only eleven hundred naturalized of them who have the franchise. Winnipeg North is the most cosmopolitan constituency in Canada (22 July 1910, 13, 36)

GREENBERG, Mr. and Mrs. Isaac, returned from their honeymoon and are guests of Mr. Greenberg's parents for a short time (19 Sept. 1913, 16, 41)

GUNN, W., president of the Montefiore Club, gave the welcoming address at opening of the new headquarters of the Montefiore Club on Sept. 14, 1913. Other speakers were:- M.J. Finkelstein, Messrs. Rice, Beckerman and Weinstein (1 Oct. 1913, 16, 42-43)

GUNN, William, is chairman of the Montefiore Club. Other officers are:- Julius Adler, L. Chechik, M. Rackow, S. Rackow, Charles Rosenfield, Charles Smithkin, Montague Stahl and Abraham E. Wilder. "For the next four months - or as long as the summer will last - every member of the Montefiore Club will be able to ride out to the camp every night (a distance of only 3 miles), located in the Windsor Park, on the banks of the Red River, and indulge in fresh air sports, apparatus for which is being furnished. If the weather will not permit outdoor sport, the members will find sufficient amusement and recreation in the large marquee - now being built - which will be equipped with a library, piano, gramophone, card games, billiard table, lounge chairs, etc. After which the members may retire for the night to their private tents; wake up in the morning to find their breakfast ready for them in the marquee, which is convertible into a dining room." Alex. Barish, S. Druckman, M. Goldstein, Montague Stahl and John I. Stein are in charge of the camp (16 May 1913, 16, 23)

GUNN, William, was elected president of the newly formed Hebrew Amateur Jewish Athletic Association at the first election of permanent officers, Sun. Dec. 11, 1910. Other officers elected were:- Norman Tebis, vice-pres.; J.L.

Stein, fin. sec.; A.E. Wilder, corr. and rec. sec.; S. Adelman, treas.; William Levin, W.H. Zimmerman, N. Zimmerman, executive board; Charles Ripstein, H. Bercovich, B. Druxerman, trustees; W. Trebeis, H. Finkelman and N. Adelman, auditors (13 Jan. 1911, 14, 9)

HAID, Miss Ray, the daughter of Mr. and Mrs. M. Haid, has recovered from her recent appendicitis operation (19 Sept. 1913, 16, 41)

HALTER, Samuel, 176 Logan Ave., is in England on an extended trip to his home (28 May 1909, 12, 24)

HEILIG, M., Benjamin Rattner, L. Segel, Pesach Selichowsky, Isaac Serebrin, Reubin Serebrin, David Shapiro, A.M. Solowsky, H. Tcherkow, the Misses Chaene Assofsky, Channah Rasin, Chaiya Rattner, Deborah Rattner and Frida Rattner contributed to the Herzl Wald Fund. Other donations were made by Charles Golding and Rebecca Ritberg. J. Jospe, of Montreal, donated $1.50 in memory of his beloved cousin, Leona Rubinovich (23 Aug. 1912, 15, 37)

HEIMAN, Miss J., of Morden, Man., has returned home after being the guest of Mrs. H. Steinkopf, River Ave. (31 Dec. 1909, 13, 7)

HESS, S.E., of St. Paul, spoke at a recent meeting of B'nai B'rith Winnipeg Lodge (12 Sept. 1913, 16, 40)

HORWITZ, Miss, of Minneapolis, is visiting relatives in Winnipeg (2 July 1909, 12, 29)

HYMAN, Marcus, has arrived in Winnipeg from London, England where he has been a barrister for over three years. He will open a practice here (10 Oct. 1913, 16, 44)

כשר WHEN TRAVELING WEST STOP AT כשר

European Commercial Restaurant

34 Martha St., Winnipeg, Man.

Large commodious and fully moderate rooms. Up-to-date and strictly Kosher

I. ISAACOVITCH, Prop.

KAHANOVITCH, Chief Rabbi I., who has held the position in Winnipeg for the past six years, is being challenged for the post. "He has always been respected, and up to this year there has been no dissenting voices raised against him. However, a short time ago he attempted to introduce a little more strictness into the Kosher meat question. To a good many congregations this seemed nothing but right, but a few small congregations objected to this and began to bring forward the question of a new chief rabbi." Rabbi Goretzky, of Pittsburgh was their candidate. J. Chelmnitsky, president of the House of Jacob Synagogue recently resigned because he supported Rabbi Goretzky against the wishes of the congregation. The struggle for leadership of the community continues (31 Jan. 1913, 16, 8)

KAPSTINE, Mrs. Edward, held her post nuptial reception at her apt., River-View Mansions, Jan. 10, 1911. She was assisted by her two sisters, Mrs. J.L. Rill and Miss Rosetta Myers, and the Misses S. Hoffman (New York), B. Narovlansky, Hattie Robinson and Ethel Abramovitch (27 Jan. 1911, 14, 11)

LABOVITCH, I., the Jewish dancing professor, was burnt out of his home last Wed, evening. "He and his family were sleeping when the blaze occurred. The two children were badly burnt, while Mrs. Labovitch was burnt badly about on the left arm." They were taken to the Winnipeg General Hospital where they were reported doing well and will be out in a few days. Last Sat. evening a benefit dance in aid of the family was held in Minuk's Hall and about $700. was raised (31 Jan. 1913, 16, 8)

LAUER, Master Louis, son of Mr. and Mrs. M. Lauer, Harriet St., suffered a broken ankle as a result of a skating accident. (17 Dec. 1909, 13, 5)

LECHTZIER, A., hosted a surprise party on Sun. Oct. 17,1909 in honor of Mrs. Samuel Halter (née Miss Isaacs of Cardiff, Wales). Among those present were:- Miss Mary Shapiro, of Duluth; the Misses Heppner; and Miss Sadie Vineberg, of Montreal (29 Oct. 1909, 12, 46)

LECHTZIER, Mr. and Mrs. Moses, 192 Langside Ave., gave a party in honor of their daughter Elizabeth's engagement to Louis Silverman, of Cincinnati. Guests present were:- H. Adilman, Rev. and Mrs. E. Cashdan, B. Druxerman, Samuel Halter, J.P., Charles Isman (Redvers, Sask.), Barney, Jack, Jacob and Samuel Lechtzier, Samuel Wolfson, Mr. and Mrs. A. Altman, Mr. and Mrs. Frank Druxerman, Mr. and Mrs. Phillip Glube, Mr. and Mrs. Emanuel Goldstein, Mr. and Mrs. L. Goldstein, Mr. and Mrs. J.I. Kline, Mr. and Mrs. A. Lechtzier, Mr. and Mrs. Ph. Lechtzier, Mr. and Mrs. Elias Leon, Mr. and Mrs. M.L. Ostfield, Mr. and Mrs. Ph. Presner, Mr. and Mrs. B. Rosenfeld, Mr. and Mrs. J. Shinbane, Mr. and Mrs. E. Tapper, Mesdames Maurice Halter (Rhein, Sask.) and Jake Tapper, and the Misses Daisy, Hattie and Lilly Lechtzier. A. Lechtzier was toastmaster "... and the usual toast for our King and Country was drunk." (21 Feb. 1913, 16, 11)

LEHBERG, Mrs. Paula and family leave Winnipeg on Thurs. for Montreal and thence to New York, en route to Germany. "Good wishes of all their friends go with her on the journey, and one and all hope she will find a happier life across the Atlantic than she has experienced in Winnipeg since the sad death of her husband 18 months ago." (2 May 1913, 16, 21)

LEHBERG, Mrs. Paula and family were wished "bon voyage" at the C.P.R. Station April 30, 1913. Among those present were:- Claude Jacob, Jack Lyon, Mrs. Max Goldstein and Mr. and Mrs. Cohen. "At Montreal Mrs. Lehberg was met by her brother-in-law, Mr. E. Lehberg, who accompanied her to New York. There she embarked on the "President Lincoln," and sailed for Hamburg." (16 May 1913, 16, 23)

LEVI, Mrs. L.H., entertained at tea in the white room of "The Grange" in honor of her sister, Miss Lillian Schumann, of Denver, Col. Those present included:- the Misses Nell Silverstein, Sarah Hoffman (Newark, N.J.), Beck Narovlansky, Rosetta Myers, Etta Codden, Flo. Valoshin, Sophie Margolese, Ripstein, Levi and Robinson (24 March 1911, 14, 19)

LEVIN, A.C., passed the Sept. supplemental in arithmetic, University of Manitoba. Others who passed the Sept. matriculation (part 1) are M.C. Levin in physics; N. Zimmerman in arithmetic and algebra; E.A. Skaleter in botany; R. Bergman in spelling. In part 2 (supplemental), D. Zimmerman passed in French authors; A.C. Levin in physics and H. Levinson in engineering geometry (22 Oct. 1913, 16, 46)

LEVIN, Rabbi and Mrs. J.K., leave shortly for Helena, Montana where they will make their home. Rabbi Levin was appointed rabbi of Temple Emanuel of Helena. Members of the Shaarey Shomayim congregation met July 14, 1912 in the synagogue chambers to bid Rabbi and Mrs. Levin farewell and godspeed. The Shaarey Shomayim Synagogue was consecrated in 1907 by Rabbi Levin, who has occupied the pulpit since that time (26 July 1912, 15, 33)

LEVIN, Rabbi J.K., has issued a plea for more YMHA's in Canada in an article. He reports that W. Gunn and J.I. Stein organized a YMHA in Winnipeg a few weeks ago which now has a membership of eighty-five (25 Nov. 1910, 14, 2)

LEVIN, Rabbi J.K., of Shaarey Shomayim Synagogue, was elected a member of the Winnipeg Ministerial Association at the regular monthly meeting, Jan. 23, 1911 (3 Feb. 1911, 14, 12)

LEVIN, Rabbi J.K., pays tribute to the late King Edward the Seventh who died May 6, 1910 (27 May 1910, 13, 28)

LEVIN, Rabbi J.K., reprint of his protest against missions to the Jewish people issued to the local press (22 April 1910, 13, 23)

LEVIN, Rabbi J.K., reprint of his article "Christian Prejudice Against the Jew" (4 Nov. 1910, 13, 51)

LEVINSON, E.R. (B.A., B.C.L.), was appointed Crown Prosecutor of the city of Winnipeg. "This the first time in the history of the Dominion of Canada that a Jew has become public prosecutor." Mr. Levinson comes from a well-known Australian family in Melbourne and has lived in Winnipeg for eight years (26 July 1912, 15, 33)

LEVINSON, E.R., has resigned his position as crown prosecutor (13 Feb. 1914, 17, 7)

LEVINSON, Mrs. A., 126 Rupert St., is rapidly recovering from a serious operation at the General Hospital, on May 12, 1909 (28 May 1909, 12, 24)

LEXIER, Miss Elizabeth, Miss Dorothy Levison and Miss Ada Haid were debutantes at the Eighth Annual Ball of the Ladies' Aid Society of Shaarey Shomayim Congregation held in the Manitoba Hall on March 15, 1911 (24 March 1911, 14, 19)

MARGOLESE, Dr. and Mrs. Oscar (née Pearl Rosenblatt), are on their honeymoon in the States (26 March 1909, 12, 15)

MARGOLIUS, George, is mourning the death of his mother which took place in Russia. The news reached him Nov. 12, 1910 (25 Nov. 1910, 14, 2)

MARGOLIUS, Mr. and Mrs. G. and baby have moved to Vancouver, B.C. (3 Feb. 1911, 14, 12)

MARGOLIUS, Mr. and Mrs. G., celebrated their first wedding anniversary, on Sun. Jan. 3, 1909. Guests included:- B.Z. Levinson, N. Levinson, Joe Youngheart and Dr. Margolese (15 Jan. 1909, 12, 5)

MARGOLIUS, Mrs. George and baby son are in Grand Forks, N.D. Mrs. Margolius, who has been ill for a while, will stay with her parents, Mr. and Mrs. Pyes during her convalescence (25 June 1909, 12, 28)

MILLER, Mrs. L.J. and son Myron, have gone to live at the home of her father-in-law in Calumet, Mich. (26 March 1909, 12, 15)

MOROSNICK, L.B., was elected chairman of the YPHA for 1914. Other officers elected were:- H.A. Wodlinger, vice-chrmn.; Miss Dora Robinson, treas.; Miss H. Rosen, fin. sec.; and L. Halter, rec. sec. C. Brotman, N. Weidman and Mrs. M. Abramovitch were elected trustees of the contingent fund (26 Dec. 1913, 17, 3)

MOROSNICK, Louis D., president of the Young People's Hebrew Association, chaired a debate "Resolved that the freedom of the Press should be limited", held March 1, 1914. "The negative was upheld by Mr. M. Lebarsky and Miss G. Berg, who were awarded the decision over Mr. Laurence Seipp and Miss G. Finesilver (affirmative)." One of the club's members, Miss Sara Romanovsky received the gold medal for oratory at United College. At a recent oration contest of the Jewish Student's Association winners were:- Miss Finesilver "The Influence of Women on Civilization", Miss Romanovsky "Tolstoy", and Miss May Bere "Faust thru' the Ages". (13 March 1914, 17, 11)

MOSCOVITCH, Ephraim, Elijah Mittler, David Atrubin and Abraham J. Atrubin, Solomon Shore, Mr. and Mrs. Isaac Portugal, Abraham Milmet and S.R. Robinson contributed to the Zionist Land Fund (4 Aug. 1911, 14, 38)

MYERS, Miss Rosetta, of Winnipeg, has gone on a pleasure trip to Toronto and Montreal for several months (14 Jan. 1910, 13, 9)

MYERS, Mr. and Mrs. A.W., have left for the east (14 Jan. 1910, 13, 9)

NAROVLANSKY, Mr. and Mrs. S.H. and daughter are moving to Montreal. A party was given Tues. evening, Sept. 7, 1909, in honor of Miss R. Narovlansky (15 Sept. 1909, 12, 40)

NAROVLANSKY, Mr. and Mrs. S.H. and family, who have resided in Winnipeg for the past twenty-five years, have moved to Montreal where they will make their new home (1 Oct. 1909, 12, 42)

NAROVLANSKY, S.H., purchased one tree in the Herzl Wald in the name of his daughter, Miss Sarah Leah Narovlansky (16 April 1909, 12, 18)

NAROVLANSKY, S.H., purchased one tree in the Herzl Wald in the name of his daughter, Miss Rebecca Narovlansky (12 March 1909, 12, 13)

NAROVLANSKY, S.H., purchased one tree in the Herzl Wald in the name of Miss Marguerita Narovlansky (25 June 1909, 12, 28)

NAROVLANSKY, S.H., purchased one tree in the Herzl Wald in the name of his daughter, Miss Bella Narovlansky (4 June 1909, 12, 25)

NAROVLANSKY, S.H., purchased one tree in the Herzl Wald in the name of his wife (15 Jan. 1909, 12, 5)

NEUFELD, Miss Elizabeth, it was reported, was the subject of a long article in the Winnipeg Free Press. Miss Neufeld was described as a "very remarkable and constructive young woman who knew something of the wide world before she took to wearing long dresses." (22 Oct. 1913, 16, 46)

NIEMAN, Mrs., of Winnipeg, has moved to Saskatoon to reside (1 Oct. 1913, 16, 42-43)

O'CONNOR, Michael, age 72, "...underwent an operation on July 12th last, and was received into the Covenant of Abraham in Winnipeg, Man. The operation was performed by Rev. Saul Schor, and witnessed by A. Bercovich, M.D., C.M., Rabbi Kahanovich, and Rev. J.K. Levin, B.A. Mr. O'Connor's mother was a Jewess, who married out of the faith, and his father, an Irish Catholic, was killed in the war of 1837, one week before his son was born. The nearest town (Montreal) being about 60 miles from his birthplace, the widowed mother was unable to have the Abrahamic rite performed. Throughout his long and chequered life Mr. O'Connor has lived up to Judaism. He is now all alone in the world, and being a man of considerable wealth, his ambition is to adopt a Jewish boy to comfort his old age." (16 July 1909, 12, 31)

PIERCE, Mr. and Mrs. Jacob and Mr. and Mrs. Leon Abramovitch will shortly close their summer cottages at Oak Point and return to Winnipeg (12 Sept. 1913, 16, 40)

PIUS, Mrs. D., hosted a bridge game Sun. Feb. 19, 1911 (3 March 1911, 14, 16)

PULLAN, J., a young Jewish businessman from Ottawa, now of Winnipeg, and proprietor of the Pullan Paper Stock Co., suffered a $3,500. loss when his warehouse was burned down Sat. evening, May 29, 1909. "He had succeeded in working up a most lucrative business in waste paper...the only one of its kind in Winnipeg. Unfortunately, it was impossible to get insurance except at preposterous rates, owing to the inflammable nature of the product. It is strongly suspected that the holocaust was due to incendiarism." (4 June 1909, 12, 25)

PULLAN, Joel, of the Pullan Paper Stock Co., has returned from his business trip to the States (29 Oct. 1909, 12, 46)

PULLAN, Mrs. Joel, 5 Shipman Court, gave a "parcel shower" Wed. aft. in aid of the Children's Hospital Bazaar. She was assisted by her sister, Miss Tess Wolfe who is visiting her (10 Nov. 1911, 14, 52)

PULLAN, Mrs. Joel, gave a tea in honor of Miss Nell Silverstein who will be married in June. Those assisting were:- Mesdames M. Shragge and Dave Pyes and the Misses Annie Lyone, Hattie Robinson, Bee Narovlansky and Goldye Ripstein (24 May 1912, 15, 25)

PULLAN, Mrs. Joel, is convenor general of the Grand Bazaar and Dance to be held in the Talmud Torah Hall, March 8-11, 1914, in aid of the United Hebrew Charities of Winnipeg. Assisting her are:- Miss Rose E. Ripstein, sec., and Mrs. B. Levinson, treas. Working at the different booths are:- Mesdames M. Abramovitch, A. Berg, S.H. Birch, Bryer, H. Finesilver, George Frankfurter, Roy Frankfurter, J. Finkleman, George Harris, I. Korn, J. Kronson, B. Levinson, I. Portigal, William Plumm, P. Presner, F. Rosenblat, Sanford, M.A. Studner, and the Misses Ethel Abramovitch, Tessie Abramovitch, Ida Cohen, Etta Coddon, Jean de Taube, Anna Levi, Sara Lyone, Flora Levi, Irene Shragge, Flo Volushin, Cynthia Weidman and Lizzie Wodlinger (27 Feb. 1912, 17, 9)

RILL, Mr. and Mrs. J.L., 151 Kennedy St., celebrated their third wedding anniversary on Jan. 2, 1910 which is also the birthday of their twin babies, a boy and girl (14 Jan. 1910, 13, 9)

RILL, Mrs. Julius L. and twin children left this week for an extended trip east. She will visit Mrs. J. Ettenberg in Montreal (10 Oct. 1913, 16, 44)

RIPSTEIN, D., is president of the new Shaarey Zedek Synagogue which is to be built on the east side of Lizzie St. in the heart of the Jewish quarter at a cost of $65,000. The decision to build was taken at a meeting held in the old building on Tues. Jan. 14, 1913. The new synagogue will be ready by Aug. 3, 1913. S. Bere is vice-pres. and A.J. Abramovitch, sec. Building committee members are:- J. Ripstein (chairman), K. Finkelstein, M. Finkelstein, L. Seipp, B. Shragge, Ald. A. Skaleter and H. Weidman. Shaarey Zedek was founded in 1888 with about thirty members. Today it numbers six hundred and includes some of the wealthiest Jews in the city. The new synagogue will seat two thousand and will have a ladies' gallery (24 Jan. 1913, 16, 7)

RIPSTEIN, Isaac, is president of Winnipeg Lodge, No. 650, IOBB. The lodge has two hundred and thirty members. Sig. Livingstone, a prominent lawyer from Bloomington, Ill., will lecture to the lodge on Nov. 2, 1911 (3 Nov. 1911, 14, 51)

RIPSTEIN, Isaac, was elected president of Congregation Shaarey Shomayim at the annual general meeting. Other officers elected were:- A. Levinson, vice-pres.; M. Haid, parnass; Ed. Frankfurter, treas.; and H.A. Isaacs, sec.; Hiram Adelman, A.H. Aronovitch, L. Elias, G. Frankfurter, J. Freeman, and G.B. Harris, trustees (3 Nov. 1911, 14, 51)

RIPSTEIN, Miss Claire, gave a Valentine party, Tues. Feb. 14, 1911. Prize winners were:- Will Tobias and the Misses Sophie Margolius and Irene Shragge (3 March 1911, 14, 16)

RIPSTEIN, Miss Goldye, gave a theatre party on May 22, 1909 in honor of Miss Dorothy Robinson (28 May 1909, 12, 24)

RIPSTEIN, Miss Rose E., leaves shortly for Toronto to attend the wedding of Miss Byrde Sugerman of that city to J. King (22 Oct. 1909, 12, 45)

RIPSTEIN, Mrs. I., gave large reception in her new home, 27 Kennedy St., Wed. aft., Nov. 16,

1910. She was assisted in receiving by Mesdames T. Finkelstein and S.A. Ripstein. Miss Rose E. Ripstein presided over the tea table and Mrs. Frank Huffman cut the ices. The Misses Bee Narovlansky (Montreal), Goldye and Claire Ripstein assisted (25 Nov. 1910, 14, 2)

ROBINSON, Miss Hattie, Rupert St., gave a "whist" on Mon. aft., Dec. 20, 1909. Prizewinners were:- the Misses S. Huffman, of New York, Ethel Abremovich and S. Margolius (31 Dec. 1909, 13, 7)

ROBINSON, R.S. and son Nathan have returned from New York. Mr. Robinson's mother has returned with him and will spend the summer in Winnipeg. She will be present at her son's twentieth wedding anniversary, which coincides with the Bar Mitzvah, on June 19, 1909, of Sydney, eldest son of R.S. Robinson (28 May 1909, 12, 24)

ROBINSON, R.S., president of the board of management, presided at the cornerstone laying of the Winnipeg Hebrew Public School at the corner of Flora Ave. and Charles St. on Sun. aft. July 28, 1912. Others on the platform were:- A. Berg, vice-pres.; A. Milmet, treas.; L. Cherniak, sec.; S. Budnitsky, collector; A. Asofsky, L. Berger, A. Cherniak, I. Chmelnitsky, M. Finkelstein, T. Finkelstein, I. Jacobson, P. Lechtzier, H. Portigal, S.A. Ripstein, L. Seipp, S. Shore, A. Skaletar, M. Steinkopf and H. Weidman. Chief Rabbi I. Kahanovitch delivered a stirring address in Hebrew, "...in which he reviewed briefly the history of the struggles and persecutions through which the Hebrew people had passed during the past 2,000 years." "Following the Jewish custom at the laying of foundation stones, bids were called for, and the person subscribing the largest sum will have his name engraved upon the corner stone." Those honored were:- M. Milmet, Herman Steinkopf, H. Glesby, A. Shragge and B. Wilence. The building is expected to open next Jan. debt-free and will cost approximately $60,000. The school will be the only educational institution for Jews and replaces a building built five years ago at Dufferin and Atkins which is now too small (9 Aug. 1912, 15, 35)

ROSENBLAT, Mrs. Nathan and her committee were responsible for the successful charity ball of the Winnipeg Hebrew Ladies' Aid Society on Jan. 18, 1914. Committee members were:- Mesdames A. Charach, Forgan, H. Huskolovitch, J. Kluner, Levi, Frank Muscovitch, Mike Rosenblat, R. Steiman and others (13 Feb. 1914, 17, 7)

ROSENBLAT, Mrs. Nathan, is president of the Winnipeg Hebrew Ladies' Aid Society. The report of the annual Passover ball in Minuk's Hall, April 17, 1911, showed a net profit of $155.65 (16 June 1911, 14, 31)

ROSENBLAT, Mrs. Nathan, president of the Winnipeg Hebrew Ladies' Aid Society, sold $87 in tickets to the charity ball held Oct. 11, 1911. Other ticket sellers were:- Mesdames J. Blum, S. Bryier, M. Bronfman, J. Kluner, Abram Lechtzier, I. Portigal and Frank Rosenblat (12 Jan. 1912, 15, 9)

ROSENBLAT, Mrs. Nathan, was elected president of the Winnipeg Hebrew Ladies' Aid Society, which is located at the corner of Martha and Henry Sts. Other officers elected were:- Mrs. J. Blum, vice-pres.; Mrs. A. Lechtzier, treas.; Mrs. S. Bryier, sec.; Mesdames L. Markus, C. Bateman, I. Portigal, M. Huskolovitch and F. Rosenblat (27 Jan. 1911, 14, 11)

ROSENBLAT, Nathan, presided at a meeting in the Rosh Pina Synagogue held to discuss the Children of Israel Cemetery, situated in Elmwood, which was bought about twenty-eight years ago. "Since then committees have been appointed to look after it, which, however, proved unsatisfactory. It was, therefore, decided unanimously to appoint a committee of four, for the purpose of organizing a mass meeting to be held April 16, for discussion and adoption of plans, to improve the cemetery with grading, building, fence, trees, instal (sic.) a caretaker, etc. The committee appointed is Messrs. N. Rosenblat, J. Kluner, M. Raisky and J. Levine." (31 March 1911, 14, 20

ROSNER, Miss Sadie, is visiting her cousin, Miss Lillian (Lookye) Shragge (1 Oct. 1913, 16, 42-43)

SAMUEL, Rt. Hon. Herbert, the British Postmaster General, gave an address to the Canadian Club in Winnipeg on Mon. Sept. 8, 1913 (19 Sept. 1913, 16, 41)

SCHEINMAN, Mr., of Prince Rupert, passed through Winnipeg on his way home after a long trip out east (1 Oct. 1909, 12, 42)

SCHNEIDER, Miss Edith, of Milwaukee, is the guest of Mrs. A. Black (28 Jan. 1910, 13, 11)

SCHORR, Cantor Saul, conducted the children's Chanukah service held at Shaarey Shomayim Synagogue, on Sun. Dec. 12, 1909. Rev. J.K. Levin spoke to the children on the significance of the Chanukah Lights (17 Dec. 1909, 13, 5)

SCHRAGGE, Mesdames H., H. Steinkopf and Bercovitch and the Misses Hattie Robinson, Goldie and Claire Ripstein, Rae Coblentz, Annie Lyone and Ida Cohen, of Dauphin, Man. took part in the "Fete of all Nations" recently given in aid of the childrens hospital. (31 Dec. 1909, 13, 7)

SCHRAGGE, Mr. and Mrs. Alexander and family, of Kenora, Ont., spent the holidays in Winnipeg (1 Oct. 1909, 12, 42)

SEREBRIN, H., hon. secretary of the B'nai Zion Society of Winnipeg, wrote a letter to the Zionist Federation thanking A. Harris, National Fund chairman for addressing the society on Jan. 28, 1912 (9 Feb. 1912, 15, 13)

SEREBRIN, J., was elected president of the Hebrew Free Loan Association which held its first annual meeting last Sun. C. Frohman was elected secretary. The Association has 150 members (7 Feb. 1913, 16, 9)

SEREBRIN, R., is president of the B'nai Zion Society which held its annual Chanukah festival, Mon. evening, Dec. 26, 1910. D. Heitner was chairman of the evening (6 Jan. 1911, 14, 8)

SHAPIRO, Miss Mary, of Duluth, Minn., has arrived in Winnipeg to spend two months with her sister, Mrs. N. Ripstein (15 Sept. 1909, 12, 40)

SHRAGGE, Miss Irene, returned from an extended trip east (1 Oct. 1913, 16, 42-43)

SHRAGGE, Mr. and Mrs. B., are vacationing at Mt. Clemens, Mich. (28 Jan. 1910, 13, 11)

SHRAGGE Mrs. B., was elected president of the Esther Robinson Jewish Orphanage of Winnipeg Ladies' Aid Society on Mon. evening. Other officers elected were:- Mrs. H. Tessler, 1st vice-pres.; Mrs. B. Warhaft, 2nd vice-pres.; Mrs. Joel Pullan, sec.; Mrs. B.Z. Levinson, treas.; Mesdames B. Shragge and S.R. Levi, purchasing committee; Mesdames L. Booke, H. Tessler, B. Warhaft and E. Shechter, visiting committee. Meetings will be held at the Orphanage, 73 Robinson St., every Thurs. at 3 p.m. (31 Oct. 1913, 16, 47)

SILVERMAN, Mr. and Mrs. S.J. (née Constance S. Ripstein) have returned from their honeymoon (31 Dec. 1909, 13, 7)

SKALETER, Ald. A., is president of the Winnipeg Hebrew United Charities. Other officers are:- J. Schulman, sec. treas.; L. Berger, S. Bere, L. Seipp, B. Shragge and B. Whillins. The organization is affiliated with the Winnipeg City Associated Charities (24 Jan. 1913, 16, 7)

SKALETER, Alderman A., was responsible for the motion brought before city council protesting "...against the possible conviction of a Russian Jew now in prison at Kieff charged with ritual murder." After some hesitation the motion was passed and a copy forwarded to the Russian Consul in Montreal (10 Oct. 1913, 16, 44)

SOKOLOW, Nahum, arrived in Winnipeg on Wed. May 28, 1913 at 2.15 p.m. He was greeted by the president of the Zionist Council, S. Frankel, Alderman Skaleter, Rabbi Kahanovitch and other leaders including the Mayor of Winnipeg (6 June 1913, 16, 26)

SONNENSCHEIN, Edward, of Chicago, and Rabbi Dr. Deinard, of Minneapolis were in Winnipeg on Sun. June 27, 1909 to organize the B'nai B'rith Lodge. Forty charter members were installed. Local organizers are Max Steinkopf, a young barrister, and A.J. Bloomfield, formerly of Montreal. Officers elected were:- A.J. Bloomfield, pres.; S. Hart Green, vice-pres.; Max Steinkopf, monitor; I. Ripstein, treas.; J.K. Levin, sec.; R.S. Robinson, A.W. Myers and H. Weidman, trustees. On Mon. June 28, Rabbi Deinard was the guest at a banquet given by the Winnipeg Lodge. (16 July 1909, 12, 31)

SPITZER, Hugo, the Jewish evangelist, has not had much success. "The new anti-meshummed league of Winnipeg has been heckling Mr. Hugo Spitzer, who has charge of the mission to the Jews, to the verge of insanity. The indignation of the Jews of Winnipeg knows no bounds. The mission was originally intended for Jews. Spitzer was to get Jews in by any means and all means. It now takes ten policemen to keep Jews out. The young men find more amusement in the mission than in the theatre. A crowd of 400 gathered round the doors on Sunday last to express their indignation. The police were there to keep order and the meeting had to be called off...Poor fellow he has as much chance of converting a Winnipeg Jew to Christianity, as of converting an Eskimo into a roe's egg. He is therefore between the devil and the deep sea; for if he does not bring in the converts soon, his employers will dismiss him." (21 April 1911, 14, 23)

STEIN, L., is teacher of the Hebrew School, corner of Henry and Martha Sts. and Nathan Rosenblat is the principal. Student prize winners at the recent examinations were:- Abe Rosenblat, Aaron Genser, Alex. Gunn, Harry Colenski,

Louise, Dave and Willie Finkelstein, Morris Karduner, Mayer Fleishman, Julius Muscovitz, Alex. Colensko, Morris and Myer Bloom, Max Kimelman, Teddie Liss, Jake and Willie Jappenick, Harry and Frank Levi, Sam Wilder, Bennie Gherman and Sam Smilovitch (16 June 1911, 14, 31)

STEINKOPF, Max and A.J. Bloomfield have written to J. Seelenfreund, secretary of the Minneapolis District Grand Lodge about organizing a B'nai B'rith Lodge in Winnipeg. A meeting was held Thurs. June 10, 1909 to discuss the matter (18 June 1909, 12, 27)

STEINKOPF, Max and E.R. Levinson, who are both lawyers, are behind the move to form a club similar to the Montefiore Club in Montreal. A dinner meeting was held Thurs. Jan. 14, 1909 (15 Jan. 1909, 12, 5)

STERNBERG, S., contributed to the Zionist Land Fund (28 June 1912, 15, 29)

TAPPER, Mrs. J., has recovered from her recent illness and has left the General Hospital. "Mrs. Tapper is highly and universally esteemed for her kindness and philanthropy to the sick and poor and her numerous friends will be delighted to hear that she is once more able to get out." (17 Dec. 1909, 13, 5)

TOBIAS, Norman and Miss Ida Balcovsky appeared in a mock trial organized by the Young People's Hebrew Association last Sun. evening (2 May 1913, 16, 21)

VINEBERG, Mrs. M., was the first president of the Rosh Pinah Ladies' Society which was established in 1896, followed by Mesdames Isaac Rosen and Fannie Cohen. Out of this society grew the Winnipeg Hebrew Ladies' Aid Society which was formed seven years ago. Mrs. Nathan Rosenblat, was the first president. She was elected in 1907 and still holds that office. In 1908 the Rosh Pinah Society changed its name to its current title. In 1912, the WHLAS received its government charter and it has two hundred members. About $800. is distributed annually to the sick, old and needy. Current officers are:- Mrs. Nathan Rosenblat, pres.; Mrs. Etta Tapper, vice-pres. (who held office until her death in Nov. 1913); Mrs. R. Steiman, treas.; Mrs. Sarah Brier, sec.; Mrs. Clara Marcus, rec. sec.; Mesdames Atrubin, Annie Bateman, Clara Forgan, J. Kluner, A. Knelman, Frank Muscovitch, Papernick, Raisky and Solman (19 Dec. 1913, 17, 2)

WEIDMAN, H. and Rabbi J.K. Levin, B.A., convened a meeting Sun. Jan. 29, 1911, to discuss the formation of a Winnipeg United Jewish Charities. "The local B'nai B'rith Lodge is also taking a lively interest in the efforts towards federating the charities." (3 Feb. 1911, 14, 12)

WEINGARDEN, Mr. and Mrs. A.A., who were married Tues. June 22, 1909, are spending their honeymoon at Winnipeg Beach. They will reside in Dominion City, Man. (2 July 1909, 12, 29)

WILDER, H.E., president of the B'nai Zion Society and treasurer of the local B'nai Brith Lodge, gave a lecture on Zionism to the Montefiore Club (21 Feb. 1913, 16, 11)

WILDER, H.E., secretary of IOBB Winnipeg Lodge, will be at his office for the transaction of the Lodge's business. The permanent office of the Lodge is Room 6, Dominion Bank Bldg. 678 Main St. (22 Oct. 1913, 16, 46)

WODLINGER, Max, 66 Lily St., is in hospital with a compound fracture of the ankle sustained at his ranch which is a day's journey from Winnipeg (29 Oct. 1909, 12, 46)

YEWDALL, Mrs. H., of Prince Albert, Sask., is visiting her sister, Mrs. M. Finkelstein (1 Oct. 1913, 16, 42-43)

YOUNGHEART, Joseph, Louis Vineberg, William Hansher, Charles Cuppleman, Samuel Rosminsky, Jacob Marks, Samuel Shaffer, Samuel Valinsky, M. Salomon, Sidney Levine, M. Vineberg, B. Gardner and L. Zeigen were travellers from Montreal who spent the High Holy Days in Winnipeg (1 Oct. 1909, 12, 42)

ZIMMERMAN, Mrs. Sam, entertained in honor of Mrs. Meyers, of New York (1 Oct. 1913, 16, 42-43)

SASKATCHEWAN

ABRAMSON, J., formerly of Kingston, organized the Saskatoon Zion Herzl Society, assisted by B. Freedman. The society was formed on July 1, 1913 and has fifty members. Other officers elected were:- Joseph Abramson, hon. pres.; H. Lazuresco, pres.; Leon Goldman, vice-pres.; M. Volansky, treas.; S. Singer, Abraham Brunder and J. Volachaw, propaganda committee. The society applied for a charter to join the Zionist Federation (11 July 1913, 16, 31)

ACKERMAN, Mr. and Mrs., Mr. and Mrs. Gherman, and Mr. and Mrs. Mael are the three Jewish families living in the town of Melfort. During the High Holy Days, services were held at the home of Mr. and Mrs. Ackerman. Amongst those present were:- D. Book (Winnipeg), Mr. and Mrs. Book and family (Star City); Jack and Louis Carp (Manchester, Eng.), Mr. Cat (Edenbridge); Mr. and Mrs. Finkelman (Prince Albert); Mr. Friedman (Minneapolis); Prof. Herman (New York), Mrs. and Miss Isaacs (Winnipeg); Messrs. Kelly and Helfgot (Prince Albert), Mr. Shapiro (Boston); and I. Rapaport and J. Shriar (Quebec City) (15 Oct. 1913, 16, 45)

BARISH, I., of Weyburn, Sask., sent The Canadian Jewish Times a clipping from the Daily Province, which reads as follows:
"Estevan, Sask., June 24. - Committed for trial at the next sitting of the Supreme Court was the result of the preliminary hearing of the charge of attempted poisoning against Ivan Boszyn, hired man of a Jewish farmer, named Fishtrom, at Hirsch, who at a Shebuoth feast celebration on June 11th, is alleged to have placed strychnine in turkey soup with intent to kill the whole family. One of the girls on getting the meal ready noticed a peculiar smell, and remembered that Boszyn had been around the stove.
Five witnesses appeared to-day before Magistrate Hastings to prove that Boszyn would not touch food at Fishtrom's house for two days, he going to neighbours with the excuse that he had quarrelled with his employer. Dr. Charlton, provincial bacteriologist, sent down a sworn statement that there was sufficient strychnine in the soup to have killed every one who took a plateful.
Evidence was taken in Yiddish, and translated to the prisoner in Galician. He was not allowed to make a statement as he was not represented by counsel, the latter action being decided to prevent his incriminating himself. Sergeant-Major Lett, watched the case on behalf of the Crown. The prisoner will be taken by the Mounted Police tomorrow morning to Regina goal to await trial, which will probably take place in September." (4 July 1913, 16, 30)

FEINSTEIN, John, gave a report of the Jewish community in Saskatoon which organized a YMHA four months ago. The YMHA laid a charge of seditious libel against a Ruthenian school teacher who wrote an anti-Semitic article in Ruthinian in a Rosthern, Sask. newspaper. The author "...who probably thought that we are still living in Russia, has been committed to stand trial in May, before a jury, on the charge of seditious libel." (14 Feb. 1913, 16, 10)

FOGEL, Mrs. Sarah, presented a scarlet velvet mantle weaved with gold for the Sepher Torah, to the Agudath Yisroal Congregation of Saskatoon (27 June 1913, 16, 29)

LANDE, Israel, Sol. Lande and Moses Reubin had trees in the Herzl Wald purchased in their names at their Brith Milahs in Saskatoon

MORRIS, S., of Lipton, collected $1.65 for the National Fund at the wedding of P. Rachman (17 June 1910, 13, 31)

PERLMAN, S., is president of the recently formed congregation in Regina. Other officers are:- S. Prosterman, vice-pres.; B. Zarif, sec.; J. Kliman, treas.; J. Swarzfeld, head trustee; M. Hillman, Z. Nathanson and N. Shmirling, trustees. The congregation is building a synagogue this year. It will be thirty by sixty feet and when completed will be one of the most modern buildings in Regina. The building, which will have rest rooms and a swimming pool, will accomodate the Young Men's Society and other social organizations (1 Aug. 1913, 16, 34)

VICKAR, D., is the leader of a new Jewish farm colony at Edenbridge, established eighteen miles from Star City on the Canadian Northern Railway line. Mr. Vickar comes from Cape Colony, South Africa. "There are about sixty Jewish families here, and they are all fairly prosperous. The majority of them are from South Africa, and have emigrated here after the war. They have recently built a public hall, adjoining the synagogue, and have erected a cemetery. Mrs. Rutner was the first member of the colony who was buried there. Four marriages were recently solemnized. The crop has been fairly good, and Mr. Kauffman is advocating the formation among the colonists of a co-operative society to build granaries and flour and feed mills." (10 Jan. 1913, 16, 5)

ALBERTA

AARON, J., M. Durewsky, L. Goldberg, M. Gurewitch, Mr. Hazan and C. Malkin, all of Calgary, contributed funds to the Herzl Wald (28 June 1912, 15, 29)

ABRAMOVICH, H. J. Aron, Alex Bell, C. Benjamin, J. Berenson, I. Black, H.J. Cooper, F. Diamond, Jacob Diamond, M. Feinberg, H. Friedenthal, E. Geffen, B. Gurewich, J. Hart, M.B. Kranetz, Mr. Kuner, I. Kuisnick, H. Lipetz, H. Lozinsky, H. Margolis, Mrs. Murovich, J. Polsky, Joseph Rabin, N. Rabinowich, I. Rosenthal, H. Rudnick and M. Woolf, all of Calgary, donated funds to the Bezalel School in Palestine (26 Jan. 1912, 15, 11)

APPEL, J., of Spokane, who was in Edmonton for a few days on business, was responsible for the establishment of a new social organization known as the Young People's Hebrew Association. "Mr. Appel noted the absence of a club or social organization for the young Hebrews in the city, and immediately turned his attention to remedy this want." The club was formed at a meeting Sun. night held at the residence of Mr. Vourzell, 327 Seventeenth Ave. W. Officers elected were:- A.J. Allen, pres.; Sarah Greisman, vice-pres.; M. Kleiner, treas.; Cecilia Sereth, sec.; and F. Taube, sergeant-at-arms (18 Aug. 1911, 14, 40)

BALL, Nathan, J.S. Berkman, D. Boyaner, H. Brody, C. Claman, Sam Cohen, A. Cristall, J. Cristall, Rose and Bessie Cristall, Ruth Diamond, William Diamond, J. Epstein, Julius Erlinger, F. Fruchtman, J.S. Gariepy, A.H. Goldberg, J. Goldberg, A. Goldman, L. Goldsmith, D. Greenberg, H. Gurowitz, H.B. Kline, L. Kline, Max Lurie, Charles Lyons, H. Mayer, S.F. Mayer, M. Mickelson, I. Nelson, I. Nozick, I. Philipson, M. Philipson, P. Rabinowitz, Fred Romelson, R. Shaw, G. Silver, E. Stein, William Sugarman and L. Volansky, all of Edmonton, donated funds to the Bezalel School in Palestine (26 Jan. 1912, 15, 11)

BERCUSON, H., J. Bercuson, S. Bercuson, D. Cohen, M. Cohen, H.J. Cooper, H.L. Epstein, E. Geffen, S. Grinker, I. Kinsnick, K. Koren, C. Malkin, B.M. Margolis, M. Muscovitz, J. Polsky, J. Rabin, M. Rosen, H. Rudnick, M. Schachnowitz and I. Serot, of the Calgary Agudath Zion Society contributed a total of $60.70 to the Zionist National Fund (19 Dec. 1913, 17, 2)

BOYANER, Mrs. D. of Edmonton, chaired a meeting Tues. March 5, 1912, at the home of Mrs. M. Mickelson, 647 Clara St., to discuss the formation of the Edmonton Hebrew Ladies' Aid Society. Officers elected were:- Mrs. D. Boyaner, pres.; Mrs. M. Mickelson, vice-pres.; Miss Annie Kline, sec.; and Mrs. A. Greenberg, treas. (22 March 1912, 15, 19)

BOYANER, Mrs. D., president of the Edmonton Hebrew Ladies' Society, headed the charity ball committee which was held Jan. 6, 1914 in the Separate School Hall. Other committee members were:- Mesdames H. Brody, William Diamond, H. Goldberg, J. Goldberg, C. Lyons and I. Nelson. Two hundred people were present (13 Feb. 1914, 17, 7)

BOYANER, Mrs. D., was elected president (by acclamation) of the Edmonton Hebrew Ladies' Aid Society at the second annual meeting. Other officers elected were:- Mrs. W. Diamond, vice-pres.; Mrs. M. Michelson, sec.; Mrs. J. Goldberg, treas.; Mesdames Berg, H. Brody, Kasselman, I. Nelson, Ostry and Shragge (20 June 1913, 16, 28)

COOPER, H. and J.J. Goodman, of Calgary, collected $4.00 for the National Fund at the Brith Milah of the infant son of I. Krisnick (17 June 1910, 13, 31)

COOPER, H.J., of Calgary, is president of the Alberta Lodge, No. 201, Independent Order Western Star which had a social Sun. June 5, 1910. The Lodge, which has been in existence for almost a year, has 80 members (17 June 1910, 13, 31)

COOPER, H.J., of the Calgary Agudath Zion Society, remitted $13.00 in Federation fees from the society's twenty-five members to the Zionist Federation, Montreal (22 Oct. 1909, 12, 45)

COOPER, H.J., purchased ten Jewish Colonial Trust bearer shares and 215 National Fund stamps for the Calgary Agudath Zion Society (12 March 1909, 12, 13)

FEINSTEIN, D., of the Edmonton Zionist Society, visited the Zionist Federation office in Montreal this week (5 March 1909, 12, 12)

GEFFEN, E., of Calgary, collected $13.50 at the engagement of Hyman Rosenthal to Miss Kathie Rosenthal on July 7, 1912. Donors included Phillip Newman and Noah Rabinowitz (26 July 1912, 15, 33)

GEFFEN, E., of Calgary's the Palace Clothing House, has gone on a business trip out east (17 June 1910, 13, 31)

GEFFEN, E., president of the Agudath Zion Society of Calgary, is visiting Montreal. In an interview with The Canadian Jewish Times, he stated there are between 350 and 400 Jews in Calgary and that they have organized the Beth Jacob Congregation. Jacob Diamond is president of the congregation and Max Cohen is the treasurer. They plan to build a synagogue next summer. The community also has a Chevra Kadisha. The Zionist Society of Calgary was organized in Sept. 1907 with the help of M.B. Steine, of Montreal. H.J. Cooper is the society's secretary (15 Jan. 1909, 12, 5)

GEFFEN, E., was elected chairman of the Calgary Zionist Association at the annual meeting on Sun. Nov. 9, 1913. Other officers elected were:- M. Muscovitz, treas.; S. Grimker, sec.; M. Chaikin, propaganda commissioner; C. Malkin, National Fund commissioner; H. Rudnick, organization commissioner; and B.M. Margolis, collections supervisor. Dr. Lewin, field secretary of the Los Angeles Consumptive Relief Association, who was visiting Calgary for his organization, addressed the meeting (12 Dec. 1913, 17, 1)

GEFFEN, E., was re-elected president of the Calgary Agudath Zion Society. Other officers elected were:- H.J. Cooper, hon. sec.; and L. Goldberg, vice-pres. Others present at the meeting were:- C. Malkin, J. Serat, and J.J. Goodman, of Cochrane, Alta. (12 March 1909, 12, 13)

GOODMAN, J., of Edmonton, is president of the newly established Zionist society in Edmonton. Mr. Goodman "...is well-known as a very capable and indefatigable worker. He was at one time manager of the Maccabaean Publishing Co., of New York, the official organ of Zionism in the United States, and took a prominent part in the Movement in the latter country before coming to Canada." (30 June 1911, 14, 33)

GOODMAN, J., president of the Edmonton Hebrew Literary Institute, presented a silver mounted toilet service to Miss Bessie Cristal, the hon. sec. at a meeting Sun. Feb. 4, 1912. A.H. Goldberg, the executive chairman, read the annual report at the meeting (16 Feb. 1912, 15, 14)

GOODMAN, J., the first president of the Edmonton Hebrew Literary Institute, was honored at a banquet last night prior to his departure for England where he will attend his brother's wedding. Guests present included:- B. Abrams, W. Diamond, F. Fruchtman, A.H. Goldberg, J. Goldberg, Charles Horowitz, B. Kline, Max Lurie and M. Mohr. J.S. Berkman, J.P., chaired the banquet. Communicated by Miss Jennie Gurovitch (22 Nov. 1912, 15, 50)

GOODMAN, J., was re-elected president of the Edmonton Zionist Society at the semi-annual meeting. Other officers elected were:- F. Fruchtman, vice-pres.; W. Diamond, treas.; Miss Jennie Gurovitch, sec.; B. Abrams, J. Goldberg, D. Helman, C. Hurovitz, Max Lurie, M. Mohr, and Miss Lurie, committee members (11 Oct. 1912, 15, 44)

GREENBLAT, Monte and Leo A. Volansky were members of the floor committee at the first annual ball of the Edmonton B'nai Brith held in Empire Auditorium. Reception committee members included Mesdames Berkman, D. Boyaner and Greenblat (13 March 1914, 17, 11)

KEEL, A., on behalf of the Lethbridge Jewish community, sent $26.00 collected at the birthday party of Mr. and Mrs. H. Glassman's daughter on Dec. 8, 1912 to The Canadian Jewish Times, to be forwarded to the Chief Rabbi of Turkey, Pera, Constantinople for the material relief of Jews in the Balkan War. Donors were:- M. Bikman, B. Frishberg, H. Glassman, D. Goldstein, Rev. A. Goodman, M. Goodman, P. Heller, A. Israelovitch, L. Keel, L. Kling, S. Levine, I. Moscovitch, Max Moscovitch, I. Pinkas, B. Sadowski, W. Sadowski and Mr. and Mrs. Sam Fefferman (20 Dec. 1912, 16, 2)

KLINE, H.B., president of the Edmonton Zionist Society, chaired the general meeting held June 13, 1909. Miss A. Kline, the society's secretary, remitted $20.00 to the Zionist Federation in Montreal (9 July 1909, 12, 30)

KLINE, Mr. and Mrs. H.B., of Edmonton, celebrated their silver wedding anniversary on the last night of Chanukah with a banquet followed by a dance. Mr. Kline is vice-president of the Edmonton Hebrew Association. J.S. Berkman, treasurer of the Edmonton Hebrew Congregation was toastmaster. Madame Pevsner, of the Bezalel School of Arts in Jerusalem, addressed the gathering (5 Jan. 1912, 15, 8)

LEVINE, P., held a meeting at his home on Sun. Feb. 8, 1914 with the object of forming a Zionist society in Lethbridge. "After a few opening remarks by Mr. L. Keel, Mr. Levine delivered a very appropriate and stirring address, with the result that Zionism is, so far, richer by forty one new and ardent Zionists." (20 Feb. 1914, 17, 8)

MALKIN, C. and M. Muskovitz collected funds for the Zionist National Fund at the wedding of B. Gurewich, in Calgary. Guests also collected at the Pidyon Haben of the first born of Mr. and Mrs. Meyerowitz, at which Rabbi I. Kahanovitch, of Winnipeg, was present (26 July 1912, 15, 33)

MALKIN, C., was elected president of the Agudoth Zion Society of Calgary at a meeting held on Sun. May 29, 1910. Other officers elected were:- M. Cohen, treas.; J.J. Goodman, sec.; I. Serot, chairman of the National Fund; I. Rudnick, chairman, propaganda committee. "The newly-elected officers are all devoted Zionists of long standing, especially Mr. Goodman, who is an ex-vice-president of the Federation." (17 June 1910, 13, 31)

MIKELSON, Mr., of Winnipeg, is visiting H. Bercuson, of Calgary (17 June 1910, 13, 31)

PINSKY, Samuel, is president of the newly organized Young Judea club in Edmonton. Other officers are:- Bernard Cohen, 1st vice-pres.; Harry Gurvitch, 2nd vice-pres.; Daniel Boyaner, sec.; Jack Lyons, treas.; Martin Bloom, Louis Dun, Bennie Gumberg, Abraham Gurvitch, Morris Kline, Max Nickelson and Fred Shwartz, exec. committee. The young boy's club was organized by Dr. John Shayne when he was in Edmonton. Hon. presidents elected were:- Dr. Shayne, William Diamond, S. Freeman, H. Goldberg, N. Green, H.B. Kline and S. Malkin (27 March 1914, 17. 13)

RUBIN, Rev. S., was the principal speaker at the Herzl memorial meeting on July 7, 1912 which was organized by the Agudath Zion of Calgary. $1.50 was contributed for one tree in the name of Miss Fanny Malkin (26 July 1912, 15, 33)

SALZMAN, H., was elected chairman of the Agudath Zion Society of Calgary at the annual meeting held on May 28, 1911. Other officers elected were:- S. Grinker, vice-chairman; E. Geffen, treas.; D. Lazarus, sec.; H.J. Cooper, commissioner of the National Fund; H. Rudnick, commissioner of organization funds; and C. Malkin, advisory member (30 June 1911, 14, 33)

SHAW, J., was elected president of the newly formed B'nai Zion Club of Edmonton which has seventy-five members. Other officers elected were:- M. Lurie, vice-pres.; M. Mohr, treas.; S. Freeman, sec.; A. Aaron, William Diamond, H.A. Friedman, F. Fruchtman, H. Griesdorf and B. Shaw, committee

SILVERMAN, J.D., P. Bercusson, I. Falsin, A. Malkin, A. Ball, Mr. and Mrs. Gilfund and Mrs. Margolius purchased a total of fourteen trees for the Herzl Wald at a Herzl memorial meeting in Calgary held under the auspices of the Agudath Zion (4 Aug. 1911, 14, 38)

BRITISH COLUMBIA

ALEXANDER, Louis, Sol. Blackson, Harry Evans, Sam Gintzburger, H. Seigler, Paul Letvinoff and Miss Lena Letvinoff, all of Vancouver, contributed funds to the Bezalel School for Arts and Crafts in Jerusalem, Palestine (23 Feb. 1912, 15, 15)

BORONOW, Mrs. Robert (née Fleishman), of Vancouver, entertained for the first time since her marriage at her residence "Teader Cottage" on Oct. 8, 1910 (11 Oct. 1910, 13, 48)

DIRECTOR, I., of Prince Rupert, offered the use of his home for Rosh Hashanah services this year. The total Jewish population of about twenty people were present including women. H. Frome, of Winnipeg, assisted by M. Winestein and A. Simon, conducted the services. S. Hoffman sounded the shofar and delivered a short sermon (18 Oct. 1910, 13, 49)

DIRECTOR, Mr. and Mrs. I., of Prince Rupert, gave a progressive whist party on Jan. 2, 1910, on the occasion of the birthday of their little daughter, Rosalie. Among those present were:- Mr. and Mrs. Kauffman, Mr. and Mrs. Hoffman, Mr. and Mrs. D. Cohen, Messrs. Newman, Frome, Grossman, Zackon, Sheinman, Weinstein, Rosenberg and Guttstein. A toast was drunk to Mrs. Director's sister at the Soo, Miss R. Diamond and her groom who were married this day (21 Jan. 1910, 13, 10)

DIRECTOR, Mr. and Mrs. Isidore, Eleventh Ave., Prince Rupert, gave a dinner at their new home to celebrate their eighth wedding anniversary. Among those present were:- L. Lands, D. Scheinman, H. Rubinovitch, Mr. and Mrs. Gutstein, Mr. and Mrs. Herman, Mr. and Mrs. Scheinman, and Mr. and Mrs. Weinstein. During the dinner, Mr. and Mrs. Director's daughters, Rosalie, age five, and Zelna, age three, sang a few songs, accompanied by Master Stanley Director (7 March 1913, 16, 13)

FRIEDLANDER, Rabbi Elias, formerly of Shaar Hashomayim Synagogue in Montreal, and who subsequently occupied pulpits in Winnipeg and Vancouver, has received the call to Victoria. "Rabbi Friedlander who has been living in New York for several years past, leaves for the West this week to take up his new duties." (4 Nov. 1910, 13, 51)

GINTZBURGER, Mrs. Samuel, of Vancouver, called a meeting to organize a Whist Club. Members are:- Mesdames S.L. Robinson, H. Fruend, Wm. Goldbloom, M. Gintzburger, Louis Rostein, J. Rostein, S. Blackson, W.F. Gescheit, H. Lazarus, L. Ripstein, A.C. Fleishman, A. Goldberg, Merman, Melekov, S. Petersky and L. Frankenburg (29 Oct. 1909, 12, 46)

GINTZBURGER, S., was elected hon. president of the Young Men's Hebrew Association of Vancouver, at the semi-annual meeting, on Sun. evening, Jan. 30, 1910. Other officers elected were:- S. Petersky, M.D., C.M., pres.; R.L. Raphael, vice-pres.; William Petersky, sec.; H. Grossman, treas.; L. Hauseman, sergeant-at-arms; E. Morris, A. Petersky, W. Grossman and J. Morris, executive. S. Blackson, an hon. member of the Association, assisted by Mr. Brown, acted as returning officer (11 Feb. 1910, 13, 13)

GREINES, W., of Vancouver, contributed funds to the Bezalel Fund (28 June 1912, 15, 29)

GROSSMAN, A., E.A. Hillman, S.W. Rabinowitz, L. Silverman, Emma and Edward Gold, Horace and Rita Ripstein and L. Melekove, all of Vancouver, contributed funds to the Bezalel School for Arts and Crafts in Jerusalem, Palestine (22 March 1912, 15, 19)

GROSSMAN, Mrs. Harry, Harwood Ave., Vancouver, held her post nuptial reception Wed. aft. last week. Mrs. A. Grossman assisted in receiving. Other guests included:- Mesdames A.D. Goldstein, J. Lipstein, W. Gescheit, A. Freund, J. Meyer, M. Freed (Seattle), M. Mimoloch (Seattle), S. Gintzburger, A. Gintzburger, L. Frankenberg, S. Blackson, H. Alberta, C. Grossman, D. Grossman, M. Grossman, A.C. Fleishman, S. Petersky, D. Weinrobe, B. Simon, R. Farber, J. Harris and the Misses Clara Jonas and L. Weinrobe (30 Dec. 1910, 14, 7)

HOFFMAN, Mr. and Mrs. H., of Prince Rupert, had a son on Feb. 4, 1910. "Owing to the smallness of our numbers we are, unfortunately, not in a position to have a rabbi amongst us and the difficulty arose as to the Bris-Milah of Master Hoffman. After many tedious days, three months later, on the 29th May the Rev. Jacob Goldberg, of Vancouver, was persuaded to visit us and perform the ceremony. Every Jew within a possible radius was present and the Hoffman's residence was well filled and the host and hostess royally entertained their guests." Those present were:- Mr. and Mrs. M. Wainstein, of Victoria, B.C.; Mr. and Mrs. David Cohen; Mr. F. Frankenberg, of Vancouver; Mr. and Mrs. I. Director, Dr. Frieman, Dr. H.S. Ellison, J. Levy, H.L. Brin, C.J. Brin, D. Brin, A. Goldstein, Seattle; M. Sheinman, D. Rosenberg, H. Druck, J. Grossman, S. Soloman, A. Simon, A. Gurstein, J. Lozinsky, San Francisco; H. Hidzkin, Portland, Ore.; M.B. Jackson, Montreal; H. Goldberg, H. From, Winnipeg; I. Simon, Vancouver; Charles Cohen and J.C. Hoffman (17 June 1910, 13, 31)

LEVIN, Rabbi J.K., of Winnipeg, officiated at the dedication ceremony of the new synagogue of Congregation Sons of Israel of Vancouver, corner of Heatley Ave. and Pender St. E., on Nov. 19, 1911. Rabbi Levin thanked the congregation for giving him the honor of officiating at the dedication and complimented the Jewish community for establishing a synagogue. "The new synagogue, while small, was a beginning, he declared, and with the united efforts of the now large Jewish population should, in the near future, have a large and commodious edifice." Leon Melekov, the newly elected president thanked the congregation for electing him as its first president. He praised Mr. Seigler, the building committee chairman "...who, while not long a resident here, has devoted all his time and energies for the success of the undertaking." Mr. Melekov presented Mr. Seigler with an engraved gold key as a token of appreciation. A.J. Bloomfield thanked the speakers for their presence at the dedication (1 Dec. 1911, 15, 3)

LEVY, J., was elected president of the newly formed Young Men's Hebrew Association in Prince Rupert. Other officers elected were:- K. Brin, vice-pres.; M. Sosken, sec.; I. Director, N. Sheenman, M. Winestein, exec. council; M.B. Cohen, H. Hoffman and Mr. Rudnick, house committee. "There are at present nearly forty Jewish residents in the city, all of whom enrolled as members and are very enthusiastic. The object of the Ass'n is to cater to the physical, social, and intellectual welfare of the young men of Prince Rupert. The greater number of members are prominent merchants of the city." (25 Nov. 1910, 14, 2)

PETERSKY, Dr. Samuel, is president of the Young Men's Hebrew Association of Vancouver which was founded this month and has fifty-eight paid-up members. Other officers are:- L.A. Marshall, vice-pres.; Wm. Petersky, sec.; Harry Grossman, treas.; H. Lepsin, R.L. Raphael, H. Morris and M. Grossman, executive; M. Brown, sergeant-at-arms. " It seemed almost incredible to the young men themselves, that there are so many of them in Vancouver, and they regarded each other with astonishment, most of them having met for the first time, showing what a long felt want had been met. May this be a happy beginning of many Jewish organizations in the metropolis of the "Far West!"" (10 Sept. 1909, 12, 39)

PETERSKY, Dr. Samuel, president of the Young Men's Hebrew Association of Vancouver, and other members of the executive including William Petersky, Louis A. Marshall, Harry Grossman, M. Brown, H. Lipsin, H. Morris, R.L. Raphael and M. Grossman were responsible for organizing the successful Chanukah Ball on Tues. evening, Dec. 14, 1909. "The affair was largely attended; in fact, it is doubtful if the Jewish community have ever congregated in such large numbers on any previous occasion." (17 Dec. 1909, 13, 5)

SALMON, H.L., was elected president of the Hebrew congregation of Victoria at the annual meeting held in the pretty and spacious synagogue. "Dr. E. Friedlander, who was for many years the minister of the Montreal congregation, was re-elected for a further term of two years." Other officers elected were:- I.M. Nodek, vice-pres.; M.L. Platnauer, sec.; S. Lancaster, treas.; and M. Aaronson, H. Greensfelder and S. Glasau, trustees (13 Oct. 1911, 14, 48)

STEINE, M.B., of Montreal, vice-president of the Zionist Federation of Canada, lectured on Zionism to the Vancouver Junior Zionist Gate in the Sons of Israel Synagogue, corner Heatley and Pender Sts. B.W. Borovsky, president of the society, also spoke and gave an outline of the club's activities since its founding (25 April 1913, 16, 20)

WEINSTEIN, Mr., was elected president of Beth Israel Congregation, Prince Rupert. Other officers elected were:- H. Hoffman, vice-pres.; J. Levy, sec.; and I. Director, treas. Rosh Hashana and Yom Kippur services, with twenty-five people attending, were held at the home of I. Director (22 Oct. 1909, 12, 45)

INDEX

Aaron, A. 146, 184	Abrahams, Samuel (Mrs.) 60, 67, 78	Abremovich, L. (Mrs.) 120
Aaron, Adolph 60	Abrahams, Sarah (Miss) 30	Abremovich, Tess (Miss) 175
Aaron, J. 183	Abrahamson, Esther (Miss) 175	Acker, I. 22, 170
Aaron, Sadie (Miss) 164	Abrahamson, Mary (Miss) 175	Acker, Isidore 22
Aaron, Simon 60	Abrahamson, S. 175	Acker, S. 170
Aarons, A.S. 43	Abrahamson, Simon 175	Ackerman, Charles L. 13
Aarons, Mrs. 38, 154	Abramovich, A. 175	Ackerman, Hyman 61
Aaronson, Bennie 61	Abramovich, A.J. 175	Ackerman, L. 42, 81, 112
Aaronson, J. 60	Abramovich, H. 183	Ackerman, Milton 61
Aaronson, M. 185	Abramovitch, A.J. 179	Ackerman, Mr. and Mrs. 182
Aaronson, Rose (Miss) 60	Abramovitch, C. 175	Ackman, Anna (Mrs.) 27
Abecosis, Gabriel M. 60	Abramovitch, Ethel (Miss) 178, 179	Ackman, Ray (Miss) 27
Abelson, B. (Miss) 148, 150	Abramovitch, I. 175	Addelson, A. 61
Abelson, Birdie (Miss) 150	Abramovitch, J. (Rabbi) 57	Adelman, H. (Mrs.) 117
Abelson, H. (Miss) 150	Abramovitch, Leon (Mr. and Mrs.) 179	Adelman, Hiram 179
Abelson, Helen (Miss) 153	Abramovitch, M. (Mrs.) 179	Adelman, L. (Mrs.) 61
Abelson, Isidore (Master) 149	Abramovitch, Mr. and Mrs. 40	Adelman, Mr. and Mrs. 61
Abelson, J. 152	Abramovitch, Rabbi 57	Adelman, N. 170, 176, 178
Abelson, Jess 152	Abramovitch, S. 175	Adelman, S. 178
Abelson, Jesse H. 148	Abramovitch, Tessie (Miss) 179	Adelson, Anna (Miss) 27
Abelson, M. (Miss) 148	Abramovitz, D. (Mr. and Mrs.) 8	Adelson, Casper (Mrs.) 15
Abelson, Miss 149	Abramowich, A. (Mr. and Mrs.) 22	Adelson, Max 49
Abelson, W. 149, 150	Abramowich, Minnie (Miss) 22	Adelson, Mrs. 21, 61
Abelson, W. (Mrs.) 149	Abramowich, Morris 22	Adelson, R. 119
Abendorfer, Mrs. 166	Abramowich, Rachel (Miss) 22	Adelstein, H. 67, 127
Aberson, D. 42	Abramowitz, Herman (Dr.) 60	Adelstein, Harry 42
Abinovitch, Alice (Miss) 77	Abramowitz, Herman (Rabbi and	Adelstein, J.L. 106
Abinovitch, L. 49	Mrs.) 60, 100	Adelstein, J.L. (Mr. and Mrs.) 61
Abinovitch, L. (Mr. and Mrs.) 60	Abramowitz, Herman (Rabbi) 2, 3, 13-16,	Adelstein, J.L. (Mrs.) 77
Abinovitch, L. (Mrs.) . . . 60, 64, 98, 120, 146	19-26, 28, 29, 31-42,	Adelstein, Joseph (Mrs.) 152
Abinovitch, Libbie (Miss) 106	46, 48, 52, 59, 60, 61,	Adelstein, L. 106
Abinovitch, Mrs. 60	71, 72, 77, 78, 82, 89,	Adelstein, L. (Mr. and Mrs.) 8
Abinovitch, P. 60, 61, 115	102, 110, 115, 134, 149	Adelstein, Libbie (Miss) 42
Abinovitch, Phil 61	Abramowitz, J. (Rev.) 57	Adelstein, Louis (Mr. and Mrs.) 8
Abinovitch, Phil. 127	Abramowitz, Leon (Mr. and Mrs.) 8	Adelstein, M. 81, 115
Abinovitch, Philip 79, 88, 114	Abramowitz, Rabbi Herman 21	Adelstein, Max 42
Abinovitch, William 49	Abramowitz, Rev. 8, 10, 57	Adelstein, Michael (Mr. and Mrs.) 8
Abinovitz, Mrs. 20	Abrams, B. 183	Adelstein, P. 61, 106
Abinovitz, P. 60	Abrams, K. (Miss) 22	Adelstein, P. (Mr. and Mrs.) 42
Abinowitz, L. (Mr. and Mrs.) 2	Abrams, Lenard 49	Adelstein, Peter 61
Abinowitz, Philip 2	Abrams, Mrs. 17	Adelstein, Sara (Miss) 61, 77
Ableson, Miss 150	Abrams, Samuel 22	Adelstein, Sarah (Miss) 61
Abraham, R. (Bros.) 74	Abramsky. Joseph (Mr. and Mrs.) 169	Adelsteine, Joseph 34
Abrahams, A. 127	Abramsky, Alex. (Mr. and Mrs.) 8	Adilman, Anna (Miss) 27
Abrahams, A. (Mrs.) 60	Abramsky, Edith (Miss) 40, 41	Adilman, H. 178
Abrahams, A.A. 98	Abramsky, J. (Mr. and Mrs.) 41, 173	Adilman, H. (Mrs.) 61, 142, 143
Abrahams, Alfred A. 22	Abramsky, Joseph 155	Adilman, Mrs. 143
Abrahams, B. (Miss) 9	Abramsky, K. (Miss) 61	Adler, H. (Mr. and Mrs.) 41
Abrahams, Estella (Miss) 24	Abramsky, Katie (Miss) 154, 173	Adler, Herman (Rabbi) 7
Abrahams, Estelle (Miss) 13, 60, 77, 98	Abramsky, M.M. 22	Adler, Hetty (Miss) 41
Abrahams, G. 127	Abramsky, Miss 23	Adler, J. (Mrs.) 127
Abrahams, George 13, 60, 80	Abramsky, Mr. and Mrs. 156	Adler, Jacob P. 61
Abrahams, Grace (Miss) 13, 60, 67, 69, 70, 91	Abramson, A. (Mr. and Mrs.) 23	Adler, Julius 177
Abrahams, H.L. 60	Abramson, Anngene (Miss) 31	Adler, L. 61
Abrahams, I. 60	Abramson, Annie (Miss) 173	Adler, L. (Mr. and Mrs.) 109
Abrahams, I. (Mr. and Mrs.) 60, 107	Abramson, Anniie (Miss) 23	Adler, M.J. (Mrs.) 61, 125
Abrahams, I. (Mrs.) 67	Abramson, Aunyene (Miss) 39	Adler, Mr. 57
Abrahams, I.A. (Mrs.) 67	Abramson, Chaie (Miss) 41	Adler, Mrs. 146
Abrahams, L. 60, 155	Abramson, Chiae (Miss) 41	Adler, Samuel 22
Abrahams, Leonard 13, 24, 38, 60	Abramson, G. (Miss) 173	Aftel, Mrs. 61
Abrahams, M. 11	Abramson, Gussie (Miss) 31	Aftel, Stephanie (Miss) 61
Abrahams, Mack 13	Abramson, H. 173	Aftell, Miss 62
Abrahams, Miss 60	Abramson, J. 73, 173, 182	Agatson, Dr. 38
Abrahams, Misses 135	Abramson, J. (Mr. and Mrs.) 173	Agoos, S.L. 22
Abrahams, Mr. and Mrs. 60	Abramson, Joseph 61, 173	Agoos, S.L. (Mrs.) 22
Abrahams, Mrs. 91, 135	Abramson, Joseph (Mr. and Mrs.) . 31, 39, 41,	Ahrens, Mrs. 166
Abrahams, P. (Mrs.) 60	114, 173, 174	Aisenstein, Pauline (Miss) 22
Abrahams, Rosalind (Miss) 60	Abramson, L. 173	Alan, J.J. (Mrs.) 40
Abrahams, S. 60	Abramson, L. (Mr. and Mrs.) 173	Albert, A. 68, 136, 138
Abrahams, S. (Mr. and Mrs.) 60, 83	Abramson, Louis 173	Albert, Abraham 22
Abrahams, S. (Mrs.) 60, 108, 145	Abramson, M. 175	Albert, Beccie (Miss) 22
Abrahams, Sam 60	Abramson, Rae (Miss) 41	Albert, C. 47, 62
Abrahams, Samuel 13, 60	Abremovich, Ethel (Miss) 175, 180	Albert, Charles 22, 62

Albert, E.	Anthony, Louis	Ash, A.
.... 22	 13	.... 149, 150
Albert, F. 62	Anthony, M.O. 13	Ash, A. (Mrs.) 149
Albert, H. 13, 49, 57, 98	Antipetsky, H. 62	Asher, D. 156
Albert, H. (Mr. and Mrs.) 22, 92	Antipetsky, M. 162	Asher, H.S. 63
Albert, Harry 18	Antipetsky, Mr. 164	Asher, Isidore 63
Albert, J. 22, 62, 65, 68, 81, 138	Antipetsky, Mr. and Mrs. 33	Asher, J. 63
Albert, Jack 22	Antipitzky, Annie (Miss) 13	Asher, J. Mayer (Rabbi) 77
Albert, Joseph (Mrs.) 62	Antipitzky, Herman 13	Asher, Joseph M. 61
Albert, M. 19, 49, 62, 65, 68, 81, 96	Antipitzky, Lillie (Miss) 13	Asher, M. 106
Albert, M. (Mr. and Mrs.) 62	Antipitzky, Moses 13	Ashinsky, M.A. (Rev.) 175
Albert, M. (Mrs.) 78, 97	Antipitzky, Samuel 13	Ashkiloonay, N. 105
Albert, Moe 62	Apotheker, Ida F. (Miss) ... 46, 119, 138	Ashkins, Mrs. 56
Albert, Moe (Mrs.) 112	Apotheker, Ida Freda (Miss) 29	Ashofsky, H.A. 175
Albert, Morris 62	Appel, G. 162	Asner, B. (Miss) 94, 114
Albert, Moses 18, 22, 62, 87	Appel, J. 183	Asner, G. 61
Albert, Rebecca (Miss) 22	Appelbaum, E. 162	Asner, I. 107
Albert, S. (Mr. and Mrs.) 8	Apple, Molly (Miss) 23	Asner, J.D. 114, 130
Albert, Sam (Mr. and Mrs.) 8	Applebaum, Sidney 156	Asner, L. (Miss) 114
Albert, Samuel 22, 62, 68	Arakie Cohen, E. (Mr. and Mrs.) ... 8	Asner, Mrs. 139
Albert, Samuel (Mr. and Mrs.) 62	Arakie Cohen, Mrs. 101	Asner, S. 63
Albert, Simon 49	Arbess, H. 65	Asofsky, A. 180
Albert, W. 62	Arbess, Jacob 61	Asslie, C. 86
Albert, W. (Mr. and Mrs.) 22	Arent, Dorothy (Miss) 131	Assofsky, Chaene (Miss) 178
Albert, William 49	Arent, Mrs. 162	Ast, Anna (Miss) 22
Albert, William (Mrs.) 13, 77	Arent, Sactre (Miss) 164	Astor, Misses 154
Alberta, H. (Mrs.) 185	Arent, Sadie (Mrs.) 165	Astowski, Amelia (Miss) 154
Alder, L. 81	Arnovitz, J. 62	Astrof, H. (Mrs.) 121
Alexander, A.J. 106, 119	Arnovitz, S. 62	Astrof, Mrs. 78
Alexander, A.J. (Mrs.) 62, 109	Arnow, M. 22	Astrofsky, H. 63
Alexander, B. 154	Arnowitz, J. 62	Astrofsky, I. (Mrs.) 127
Alexander, George 119	Aron, A. 84	Astrofsky, J. 78
Alexander, George L. 5	Aron, A. (Mr. and Mrs.) 8	Astrofsky, S. 47, 63
Alexander, J. 62	Aron, Adolph ... 13, 62, 66, 84, 122, 144	Astrofsky, Samuel 63
Alexander, Joseph (Mr. and Mrs.) ... 8	Aron, Adolph (Mr. and Mrs.) 8, 62	Astrofsky, William 22
Alexander, Lewis 62	Aron, Emma (Miss) 13	Atkins, K. (Miss) 66
Alexander, Louis 185	Aron, H. 62	Atkins, Rhoda (Miss) 31
Alexander, M. 47, 62	Aron, J. 183	Atrubin, Abraham J. 179
Alexander, Maurice 5, 42, 62, 119, 125	Aron, L. (Mrs.) 65	Atrubin, David 175, 179
Alexander, Morris 62	Aron, Lewis 13	Atrubin, Messrs. 175
Alexander, Mr. and Mrs. 138	Aron, Louis 13	Atrubin, Mrs. 181
Alexander, Solomon 22	Aron, Milton 62	Atrubin, N. 175
Alexandor, A.J. 62, 119	Aron, Mr. 13	Atrubin, Nathan 175
Alexandor, Ada (Miss) 62	Aron, Simon 13	Audrus, C. 63
Alkovitzky, Liza (Miss) 154	Aron, Simon (Mr. and Mrs.) 125	Audrus, J. 63
Allan, Harry 22	Aronberg, Albert 62	Auerbach, Fischel 13, 63
Allan, J.J. (Mrs.) 173	Aronovich, A.H. 176	Auerbach, M. 63, 135
Allan, P. (Mr. and Mrs.) 22	Aronovich, A.H. (Mrs.) 175	Auerbach, Marcus 63
Allen, A.J. 183	Aronovich, Annie (Miss) 32	Auerbach, Marcus (Mr. and Mrs.) ... 63
Allen, Abel 11	Aronovitch, A.H. 175, 179	Auerbach, Mr. and Mrs. Z. 13
Allen, Rachel (Mrs.) 173	Aronovitch, D. 143	Auerbach, Mrs. 154
Allman, Joseph 22	Aronson, A. 62, 101	Auerbach, Z. 13, 109
Althaus, A. (Miss) 28	Aronson, A. (Miss) 139	August, Frances (Miss) 80
Althouse, S. 61, 81	Aronson, A. (Mrs.) 62	August, Jack 63
Altman, A. (Mr. and Mrs.) 178	Aronson, A.M. 47, 49, 50	August, Joseph (Mr. and Mrs.) ... 63
Altman, Hyman J. 43	Aronson, Aaron 137	Austin, B. (Mrs.) 154
Altman, Samuel 62	Aronson, Anna (Miss) 77	Averbuck, M. 151
Amder, R. (Mrs.) 10	Aronson, Annie (Miss) 109	Avner, L.W. (Mrs.) 19
Amdur (Rabbi) 16	Aronson, J. 145	Axbrod, I. 143
Amdur, B.L. (Mrs.) 56	Aronson, Jack 66	Axebrad, A. 107
Amdur, B.L. (Rabbi) 35	Aronson, Joseph 62	Axelrod, I. 74
Amdur, Belle (Miss) 56	Aronson, M. 65	Axelrod, L. 74
American, Sadie (Miss) 42	Aronson, Miss 121	Axfrad, Mrs. 115
Anchel, Mr. 57	Aronson, Mr. 47	Axlar, Annie (Miss) 39
Andrees, J. 62	Aronson, R. (Miss) 101	Azef, L. 81
Andrews, J. (Mrs.) 17	Asch, B. (Miss) 115	Azeff, L. 63
Anker, L.W. 22	Ascher, Albert G. 43	Baab, Isaac 56
Anker, Leonard 22	Ascher, D.D. 62	Bacal, A. 63
Anker, Mr. and Mrs. 22	Ascher, G.I. 43	Bacal, A. (Mr. and Mrs.) 8, 63, 119
Ansell, D.A. 62	Ascher, H.S.G. 37	Bacal, J. 63
Ansell, Daisy (Miss) 62	Ascher, J.G. 43	Bacharach, J. 63
Ansell, David A. 5, 20, 62	Ascher, Jacob G. 43	Bachrach, Michael (Master) 57
Anthony, Bertha Ollendorf (Mrs.) 13	Ascher, Miss 96	Bachrach, Rabbi 57
Anthony, J.R. 13	Ascher, Violet (Miss) 37	Bachrach, Rev. 57

189

Bachrack, B. 63
Bachrack, Jennie (Mrs.) 13
Bachrack, Maurice 13
Bachrak, M. 162
Backrack, Sadie (Miss) 154
Baer, Mrs. 92
Baere, Miss 63, 116
Bagan, Eli 74
Baile, M. 49
Baker, J. (Master) 137
Baker, Mr. and Mrs. 135
Baker, N. 162
Baker, Rev. 149
Balacan, Marguerite (Miss) 32, 35
Balacan, W. (Mr. and Mrs.) 35
Balcon, Anna (Mrs.) 132
Balcon, Joe (Mr. and Mrs.) 132
Balcon, W. 132
Balcover, Minnie (Miss) 29
Balcovske, D. (Dr.) 175
Balcovsky, Ida (Miss) 181
Bald, Anna (Miss) 41, 151, 152
Bald, Herman (Mr. and Mrs.) 41
Bald, I. 74, 114, 137, 138
Bald, Isadore 151
Bald, M. 91, 114
Bald, Mr. and Mrs. 173
Balinsky, Louis 22, 23
Balinsky, M. 23
Balinsky, Mr. and Mrs. 8
Balinsky, Rose (Miss) 22, 63
Balinsky, Toba (Miss) 22
Balkowsky, D. 175
Ball, A. 184
Ball, Nathan 183
Ballin, B. 63
Ballon, A. (Miss) 77
Ballon, Annie (Miss) 60, 63, 98
Ballon, D.H. (Dr.) 63
Ballon, David 5
Ballon, David (Dr.) 63
Ballon, David H. (Dr.) 63
Ballon, Dr. 63
Ballon, Ellen 42
Ballon, Ellen (Miss) 5, 42, 63, 103
Ballon, Florence 63
Ballon, Isidor 63
Ballon, Isidore 63
Ballon, Mamie (Miss) 63
Ballon, Mamie B. (Miss) 63
Ballon, Mamie Beatrice (Miss) 25
Ballon, Miss 63
Ballon, Misses 63
Ballon, Mr. and Mrs. 63
Ballon, S. 49, 59
Ballon, S. (Mr. and Mrs.) 63, 103
Ballon, Samuel (Mr. and Mrs.) 5, 25, 42
Balos, I. (Mr. and Mrs.) 33
Bamberg, Lillian 42
Banet, L. 158
Banks, Carrie (Miss) 63
Banks, N. 63
Banks, S. 64
Banon, Rabbi and Mrs. 65
Barash, Mr. 39
Baratz, Jack 22
Baratz, M. (Mrs.) 22
Barenblatt, Fanny (Miss) 37
Barenblatt, I. (Mr. and Mrs.) 37
Barish, A. 176
Barish, Alex. 177
Barish, I. 182
Barnett, E. 150
Barnett, J. 64
Barnett, J. (Mr. and Mrs.) 109
Barnett, Misses 64
Baron, G. 64
Baron, George 64
Baron, J. Ch. (Rabbi) 148
Barondess, Joseph 175
Barrett, A. (Mr. and Mrs.) 13
Barrett, Alexander 13
Barron, G. 64
Barsky, I.J. 40
Bartle, Miss 64
Bashein, Jacob 64
Bashien, J. (Mr. and Mrs.) 133
Baskewitz, Jacob 23
Baskin, L. 59
Baskin, Miss 166
Bateman, A. (Mrs.) 175
Bateman, Annie (Mrs.) 181
Bateman, C. (Mrs.) 180
Batson, J. (Mr. and Mrs.) 64
Bauer, S. 64
Bauet, S. (Miss) 27
Baulkind, Samuel 23
Baum, A.H. 86
Baum, Abe A. 64
Baum, B. 64
Baum, H. 64, 86, 99
Baum, H. (Lieut.) 64
Baum, H.A. 64
Baum, Harry 86
Baum, Harry A. 42, 48, 80
Baunbiger, Rebecca (Miss) 104
Bavitz, A. 28
Bavitz, M. 115
Baxt, Harry G. 23
Baxt, Mrs. 151
Bazar, Benjamin B. 8
Bazar, G. 66
Bazar, H. (Mr. and Mrs.) 63
Bazar, Mr. and Mrs. 12
Bazar, S. 64
Beamolt, Claire (Miss) 150
Beamolt, Miss 105, 150
Beamolt, P. (Miss) 105, 176
Beamolt, Pearl (Miss) 150
Bear, Mr. and Mrs. 8
Bear, Myer 8
Beber, Gertrude (Miss) 29
Beck, B.J. (Dr.) 22
Becker, H. 64
Becker, H.J. 64
Becker, H.L. 64
Becker, Harry I. 23
Becker, I. 2, 57, 58
Becker, I. (Mr. and Mrs.) 2
Becker, J. 64, 93
Becker, J. (Master) 88
Becker, L. 137
Becker, Master 2
Becker, Miss 64
Becker, S. (Miss) 88
Becker, T. 64
Beckerman, D. 175
Beckerman, Dave 175
Beckerman, H.M. 175
Beckerman, Mr. 177
Bedlier, Julia (Miss) 42
Beecher, B. (Miss) 114
Beecher, H. 64, 127
Beecher, N. 114, 137
Beecher, S. 120
Beer, Rose (Miss) 155
Beerman, M. 64
Beerman, Miss 124
Behr, A. 42
Behrends, A. 43
Behrer, Joseph 64
Beiber, E. (Mrs.) 149
Beiber, Kate (Miss) 154
Belanstein, S. 73
Belasco, Mr. 65
Belkin, G. 65
Bell, Alex 183
Bell, Angie (Miss) 40
Bell, B. (Miss) 34
Bell, I. 96
Bell, Miss 65
Bemak, Bella (Miss) 65
Bendarsky, Annie (Miss) 30
Bendarsky, I. 70
Bendarsky, Mr. and Mrs. 30
Bendarsky, R. (Miss) 70
Bender, Emanuel 65
Benihasker, Mr. 138
Benjamin, A. 65
Benjamin, Albert (Master) 149
Benjamin, Alfred D. 43
Benjamin, B. 114
Benjamin, C. 183
Benjamin, David 43
Benjamin, Dina (Miss) 65, 143
Benjamin, Dora (Miss) 65, 143
Benjamin, E. (Miss) 112
Benjamin, E.A. 42
Benjamin, Evelyn (Miss) 65
Benjamin, F.D. 166
Benjamin, Frank D. 43
Benjamin, Frank D. (Mrs.) 158
Benjamin, Goodman 42
Benjamin, H. 57
Benjamin, I. (Mrs.) 151
Benjamin, L. 65, 101
Benjamin, Miss 164
Benjamin, Moe 65
Benjamin, Morris 23
Benjamin, Mr. 65
Benjamin, Mrs. 66
Benjamin, S. 65
Benjamin, Samuel 42
Benjamin, T. (Mrs.) 65
Benjiman, Arthur 65
Benjiman, C.A. (Mrs.) 65
Benjiman, Miss 65
Benjiman, S.D. (Mr. and Mrs.) 65
Benmosche, H. (Rev.) 56
Bennett, A. 65
Bennett, A.B. 173
Bennett, Archie 173
Bennett, Archie B. 42
Bennett, Dave 173
Bennett, S. 173
Bennett, S. (Mr. and Mrs.) 174
Benowick, J. (Mrs.) 100
Benowick, Julius (Mrs.) 116
Benowick, Sylvia (Miss) 65
Benswanger, Mrs. 65
Berchansky, S. 175
Bercovich, A. 179
Bercovich, A. (Mrs.) 175
Bercovich, Dr. 175
Bercovich, H. 178
Bercovici, K. 134
Bercovici, Konrad 42
Bercovitch, A. (Dr.) 175
Bercovitch, B. 127

Bercovitch, Bernard 13
Bercovitch, H. 68
Bercovitch, H. (Mr. and Mrs.) 29
Bercovitch, Hyman (Mr. and Mrs.) 5
Bercovitch, Lyon 87, 141
Bercovitch, May (Miss) 29
Bercovitch, Mrs. 180
Bercovitch, Peter 5, 65, 93
Bercovitch, Peter (Mr. and Mrs.) 8, 65
Bercovitch, Peter (Mrs.) 65
Bercovitsky, Samuel 74
Bercowitz, Joseph (Mrs.) 65
Bercson, Annie (Miss) 39
Bercuson, H. 183, 184
Bercuson, J. 183
Bercuson, O. 112
Bercuson, S. 183
Bercuson, S. (Mr. and Mrs.) 33
Bercusson, Maxwell 61, 65, 141
Bercusson, O. 81
Bercusson, P. 184
Bere, Ethel (Miss) 175
Bere, May 175
Bere, May (Miss) 175, 179
Bere, S. 179, 180
Berenson, J. 183
Berg, A. 175
Berg, A. (Mrs.) 179
Berg, Benjamin 23
Berg, G. (Miss) 179
Berg, J.C. 175
Berg, Mrs. 183
Berg, S. 175
Berger, A. 23, 162, 175
Berger, Abel 154
Berger, E. 65
Berger, Eli (Master) 65
Berger, Emil 65
Berger, Emil (Mrs.) 65, 93
Berger, Hannah (Miss) 41
Berger, J. (Mr. and Mrs.) 23
Berger, J. (Rabbi) 24, 31, 38, 39, 148
Berger, J. (Rev.) 25
Berger, J.D. 148
Berger, J.D. (Mrs.) 65
Berger, Joseph (Rabbi) 31, 148
Berger, Joseph D. (Mr. and Mrs.) 65
Berger, Joseph D. (Rabbi) . . . 34, 65, 148, 149
Berger, Julius 23, 31, 65, 148-150, 154
Berger, L. 175, 176, 180
Berger, L. (Mrs.) 65
Berger, Miss 160
Berger, Mr. and Mrs. 154
Berger, Mrs. 154, 160
Berger, Rabbi 2, 34, 149
Berger, S. (Mrs.) 151
Berger, S. (Mr. and Mrs.) 41
Berger, Sarah (Miss) 65
Bergman, Barnet 65
Bergman, R. 178
Berk, Louis 23, 30
Berk, S. (Mrs.) 30
Berke, Louis 105
Berkman A. (Mrs.) 36
Berkman, A. 36
Berkman, J. 26
Berkman, J.S. 183
Berkman, Mrs. 183
Berkman, Sadie (Miss) 36
Berkovitz, Miss 169
Berkovitz, Rev. 8
Berkowitz, M. 81
Berlin, D. 78

Berlin, David 49
Berlin, F. 90, 108, 114, 115
Berlin, Felix 65
Berlin, H. 149
Berlin, Mr. 65
Berlin, Pauline (Miss) 65
Berlin, S. (Mrs.) 65
Berlind, H. (Mr. and Mrs.) 65
Berliner, E. 65
Berliner, E. (Mr. and Mrs.) 65
Berliner, E. (Mrs.) 77, 113, 144
Berliner, E.M. 65
Berliner, Edgar (Mr. and Mrs.) 65
Berliner, Mrs. 144
Berliner, Samuel 65
Bermak, Charles J. 175
Berman, A. 52, 65
Berman, A. (Miss) 65
Berman, Annie (Miss) 156
Berman, Archie 65
Berman, E. (Miss) 65, 77, 127, 170
Berman, Esther (Miss) 65, 66, 74
Berman, Gertrude (Miss) 40
Berman, Hannah (Miss) 42, 46
Berman, Harold 42
Berman, J. 48, 50
Berman, J. (Mr. and Mrs.) 66
Berman, J. (Mrs.) 96
Berman, L. (Mr. and Mrs.) 40
Berman, L. (Mrs.) 74
Berman, L.J. (Mrs.) 66
Berman, Martin 23, 97
Berman, Martin (Miss) 151
Berman, Miss 117
Berman, Mr. and Mrs. 128
Berman, Mrs. 144
Berman, R. (Miss) 65, 122, 127
Berman, Rose (Miss) 22, 65, 66, 74
Berman, S. (Mr. and Mrs.) 22
Berman, S. (Mrs.) 3
Bernbohm, Miss 164
Bernett, W. 148
Bernett, W. (Mrs.) 151
Bernfeld, M. 122
Bernfeld, Max 88, 98, 141
Bernfeld, S. (Dr.) 43
Bernfeld, W. 87, 122
Bernfeld, William 98, 141
Bernfield, Dora 61
Bernfield, M. 66
Bernstein, A. 88
Bernstein, A. (Mrs.) 66
Bernstein, Alexander 44
Bernstein, B. 66
Bernstein, B. (Miss) 88
Bernstein, B.H. (Mrs.) 66
Bernstein, Bertha (Miss) 162
Bernstein, Bessie 66
Bernstein, C. (Mr. and Mrs.) 36, 66
Bernstein, C. (Mrs.) 27
Bernstein, Clara V. (Miss) 66
Bernstein, D. 92
Bernstein, D.H. (Dr.) 66
Bernstein, D.H. (Mr. and Mrs.) 8
Bernstein, D.H. (Mrs.) 77
Bernstein, D.L. 66, 67
Bernstein, Daisy (Miss) 34
Bernstein, Dora (Miss) 32
Bernstein, Dr. and Mrs. 78
Bernstein, E. (Miss) 25, 66, 77, 109
Bernstein, E. (Mr. and Mrs.) 66
Bernstein, E.G. 66
Bernstein, E.G. (Mr. and Mrs.) 8, 66

Bernstein, E.G. (Mrs.) 66, 71, 89
Bernstein, Edna (Miss) 66
Bernstein, Elizabeth (Miss) . 3, 34, 36, 66, 67,
119, 147
Bernstein, Ettie (Mrs.) 44
Bernstein, Fanny (Miss) 141
Bernstein, Felix 132
Bernstein, H. 3, 43, 59, 66, 103
Bernstein, H. (Dr.) 71
Bernstein, H. (Mr. and Mrs.) . . 23, 27, 36, 66,
75, 125
Bernstein, H. (Mrs.) 77
Bernstein, Harry 23
Bernstein, Hattie (Miss) 27, 32
Bernstein, Hillel (Master) 8
Bernstein, Hyam 8
Bernstein, I. 67
Bernstein, Isidor 80
Bernstein, Isidore 23, 27, 103
Bernstein, J. (Mr. and Mrs.) 2, 23
Bernstein, Joe 139
Bernstein, Judah (Mrs.) 89
Bernstein, L. 57, 114, 115, 120
Bernstein, L. (Dr.) 66
Bernstein, L.H. 67
Bernstein, Leah (Miss) 35
Bernstein, Lew 66
Bernstein, Lily (Miss) 29
Bernstein, Lizzie (Miss) 66
Bernstein, Ludwig B. (Dr.) 66
Bernstein, M. 23, 32, 66, 67, 107
Bernstein, M. (Miss) 25, 47, 165
Bernstein, M. (Mr. and Mrs.) 35
Bernstein, M. (Mrs.) 60, 66, 67, 91, 109
Bernstein, M. Montefiore 66
Bernstein, Max 24, 27, 66
Bernstein, Minnie 43
Bernstein, Minnie (Miss) . . 34, 36, 43, 47, 66,
71, 77, 89, 102, 119, 168
Bernstein, Miriam (Miss) . 36, 45, 66, 119, 134
Bernstein, Misses 32, 66, 89
Bernstein, Misses 66
Bernstein, Mr. and Mrs. 8, 66
Bernstein, Mrs. 17, 66, 67
Bernstein, O. (Miss) 88
Bernstein, P. 67
Bernstein, Pauline (Miss) 66
Bernstein, Reba (Miss) 66
Bernstein, Rose (Miss) 139
Bernstein, Ruben 2
Bernstein, Ruth (Miss) 34
Bernstein, S. 23, 67, 101
Bernstein, Simon 119
Bernstein, T. 171
Bernstein, Tena (Miss) 18
Bernstein, V. (Miss) 67, 88
Bernstein, Violet (Miss) 27, 73
Bernstein, William 23
Bernzweig, Mr. and Mrs. 2
Bero, Stanley 43, 67
Berson, Bessie (Miss) 78
Berson, I. 49
Berson, I. (Mr. and Mrs.) 30
Berson, J. (Miss) 30, 67
Berson, M. 30, 91
Berson, M. (Miss) 88
Berson, Mabel (Miss) 30, 67
Berson, Mabyl (Miss) 30
Berson, Mary (Miss) 141
Berson, Mr. and Mrs. 30
Berson, Myer 67
Berson, R. (Mrs.) 30
Bertzovsky, Bernard 75

Besman, H. .61	Blackson, S. 185	Bloomfield, H. (Mr. and Mrs.) 61, 68
Besner, J.A. 131	Blackson, S. (Mrs.) 185	Bloomfield, Hannah Bessie (Miss) 8
Besner, Joseph A. 84	Blackson, Sol. 185	Bloomfield, Harry 62, 68, 138, 154
Besner, M. .67	Blankstein, Israel 148	Bloomfield, Harry (Mr. and Mrs.) . . 8, 68, 80
Bessler, S. .67	Blankstein, M. (Mr. and Mrs.) 8, 137	Bloomfield, M. (Rev. and Mrs.) 33, 40
Bessner, A. .68	Blankstein, M.I. 154	Bloomfield, M. (Rev.) 28
Bessner, H. 67, 94, 139	Blankstein, Max 23	Bloomfield, May (Miss) 33
Bessner, Harry 24, 46, 67	Blankstein, Mr. and Mrs. 80, 148	Bloomfield, Molly (Miss) 40
Bessner, Joseph 66	Blauss, R. (Miss) 22	Bloomfield, Ray (Miss) 40
Bessner, Joseph A. 81	Blaustein, Fannie (Mrs.) 13	Bloomfield, Rev. 15, 23, 117
Bessner, M. 61, 67	Blaustein, H. 68	Bloomfield, S. 23, 68
Bessner, Max 49	Blaustein, Mr. 154	Bloomfield, S. (Mrs.) 77
Bessner, Miriam (Miss) 40	Blaustein, S. 64, 68, 90, 134	Bloomfield, Sam 45, 81
Bessner, Miss 12	Bleekman, Miss 68	Bloomfield, Sam (Mr. and Mrs.) 68
Betcherman, M. 148	Bletcher, L. (Miss) 70	Bloomfield, Samuel . . 23, 68, 69, 73, 87, 122,
Betcherman, Mr. 149	Blitstein, P. 162	136, 138
Bezvinik, I. 162	Blitz, F. (Miss) 88	Bloomfield, Samuel (Mr. and Mrs.) 8
Bezwinik, Jacob 164	Blitz, Rabbi 141	Bloomfield, T. 72
Bieber, A. .81	Blitz, S. (Miss) 88	Bloomstein, Harry 112
Bieber, A. (Mr. and Mrs.) 67	Bloch, A.M. (Rabbi) 93	Bloomstone, H. 81, 89
Bierman, F. .67	Bloch, Edna (Miss) 68	Bloomstone, H. (Mr. and Mrs.) 69
Bikman, M. 183	Bloch, Jennie (Miss) 68	Bloomstone, Harold (Mrs.) 69
Bilsky, A. (Mrs.) 67	Bloch, Mabel (Miss) 68	Bloomstone, Harry (Mrs.) 69, 143
Bilsky, A.M. (Mr. and Mrs.) 8, 67, 85	Bloch, Mr. .68	Blout, E. 109
Bilsky, A.M. (Mrs.) 67, 85	Bloch, Mrs. .68	Blout, E. (Mr. and Mrs.) 69
Bilsky, Alec 67	Bloch, R. (Miss) 52	Blout, E. (Mrs.) 85
Bilsky, Alec (Mrs.) 67	Block, A. (Miss) 77	Blout, Emanuel (Mr. and Mrs.) 24, 69
Bilsky, Alec. (Mrs.) 67	Block, Anna 13	Blout, H.L. .66
Bilsky, Alexander (Mrs.) 67, 83, 84	Block, Aron 68	Blout, J. (Miss) 52
Bilsky, Annie (Miss) 67	Block, Caroline 171	Blout, J. (Mrs.) 90
Bilsky, David 149	Block, Edna (Miss) 168	Blout, Jeanette (Miss) 121, 128
Bilsky, E. (Miss) 67, 150	Block, Jennie (Miss) 68	Blout, Lena (Miss) 69
Bilsky, Etta (Miss) 67	Block, Joseph 13	Blout, Mildred 2, 50
Bilsky, Eva (Miss) 67, 149	Block, Julius 2, 61, 86	Blout, Miss .69
Bilsky, L. (Master) 122	Block, Katie (Miss) 68	Blout, Misses 135
Bilsky, Lucy (Miss) 84	Block, M. 68, 80, 93, 99, 106	Blout, Mr. and Mrs. 69
Bilsky, M. 149	Block, M. (Mr. and Mrs.) 2, 68	Blout, Mrs. 66, 69
Bilsky, M. (Mrs.) 149	Block, Mamie 49	Blout, Z. (Miss) 98
Bilsky, Miss 67, 84	Block, Mamie (Miss) 45	Blout, Zerlina M. 24
Bilsky, Mr. 149	Block, Mrs. 171	Blow, Mrs. 146
Bilsky, Mrs. 67, 85, 98	Block, Myer 86	Blucher, Marie (Miss) 69
Bilsky, R.M. (Mr. and Mrs.) 83	Block, Rhoda (Miss) 68, 147, 169	Blucher, Mary (Miss) 69, 124
Bilsky, Samuel 67, 148	Bloom, H. 172	Bluestone, Bella (Miss) 61
Binder, Joseph 61	Bloom, Harry 45, 171	Bluestone, J. (Dr.) 61
Bindman, C. 67, 68	Bloom, Ida (Dame) 45	Blum, J. (Mrs.) 69, 180
Bindman, E. 59	Bloom, Ida (Miss) 61, 86	Blum, Mrs. .69
Binswanger, H. (Mrs.) 68	Bloom, Jessie (Miss) 164	Blumberg, Becky (Miss) 24
Birch, S.H. (Mrs.) 179	Bloom, L. (Mrs.) 162	Blumberg, Frances (Miss) 86
Birk, L. 68	Bloom, Marguerite (Miss) 80	Blumberg, H. 69
Birke, H. (Miss) 96	Bloom, Martin 184	Blumberg, Hattie (Miss) 125
Birke, L. 68	Bloom, Morris 180	Blumberg, Isidore 24
Birkenthal, Camille (Miss) 68	Bloom, Mr. .66	Blumberg, Louis 87
Birkenthal, Helen (Miss) 154	Bloom, Mr. and Mrs. 33	Blumberg, Max 69
Birkenthal, Misses 109	Bloom, Myer 180	Blumberg, Max (Master) 76
Birmingham, A.H. 28	Bloom, R.A. 61	Blumberg, Miss 59
Birnbaum, H. 2	Bloom, S. (Mr. and Mrs.) 28	Blumberg, Mr. 69, 101, 114
Birnbaum, J. 61, 72, 137, 154, 156	Bloom, Sarah (Miss) 33	Blumberg, Mr. and Mrs. 69
Birnbaum, Rose (Miss) 154	Bloomberg, D. 70	Blumberg, S. (Miss) 85
Birnbaum, S.J. 42-45, 52, 154	Bloomberg, F. (Miss) 67	Blumberg, Sara (Miss) 69
Bishinsky, Benjamin 23	Bloomberg, Max 24	Blumenfeld, J. (Master) 137
Bishinsky, W. 68	Bloomberg, Max W. 42	Blumenfeld, Edward 107
Bismarck, Bernard 68	Bloomberg, Mrs. 104	Blumenstiel, C. (Mrs.) 171
Black, A. 173	Bloomer, David (Mrs.) 143	Blumenstiel, I. 171
Black, A. (Mrs.) 180	Bloomer, M. 68	Blumenthal, A. 45, 65, 69
Black, C. 158	Bloomfield, A.J. 175, 180, 181, 185	Blumenthal, A. (Ald. and Mrs.) 34
Black, Charles 154, 157, 168	Bloomfield, A.J. (Mr. and Mrs.) 175	Blumenthal, A. (Ald.) 111
Black, E. (Miss) 175	Bloomfield, A.J. (Mrs.) 175	Blumenthal, A. (Mr. and Mrs.) 23, 69
Black, Hugo (Mrs.) 154	Bloomfield, Celia (Miss) 37	Blumenthal, A. (Mrs.) 13
Black, I. 183	Bloomfield, D. 115	Blumenthal, Abraham 45
Black, Miss 166	Bloomfield, David 68	Blumenthal, Abraham (Ald. and
Black, Mrs. 25	Bloomfield, David (Mr. and Mrs.) 8	Mrs.) .69
Black, Rose (Miss) 154	Bloomfield, Dolly 175	Blumenthal, Abraham (Ald.) 69
Blackman, Max 123	Bloomfield, H. 65, 68, 138	Blumenthal, Alderman 131

Blumenthal, Alexander 60
Blumenthal, Annie (Miss) 35
Blumenthal, Dorothy (Miss) 60
Blumenthal, Esther (Mrs.) 13
Blumenthal, Florence (Miss) 34
Blumenthal, Florence Dinah (Miss) 35
Blumenthal, George 48, 51, 69, 81
Blumenthal, George (Mrs.) 70
Blumenthal, Gladys (Miss) . . . 24, 60, 69, 125
Blumenthal, H. 34
Blumenthal, I. (Mr. and Mrs.) . . 34, 69, 70, 125
Blumenthal, I. (Mrs.) . . 70, 108, 115, 135, 136
Blumenthal, Irene (Miss) . 60, 69, 70, 102, 121
Blumenthal, Irene (Mrs.) 69
Blumenthal, Isaac (Mr. and Mrs.) 35
Blumenthal, Isidore 107
Blumenthal, Israel 7, 69, 118, 144
Blumenthal, J. 172
Blumenthal, J. Leo 69
Blumenthal, J.H. 59
Blumenthal, Joe 35
Blumenthal, Joseph 2
Blumenthal, Jr., A. 69
Blumenthal, Lou 35
Blumenthal, M. 34, 138
Blumenthal, Mae (Miss) 115
Blumenthal, Maxwelll 35
Blumenthal, Miss 146
Blumenthal, Mr. 70
Blumenthal, Mr. and Mrs. T. 2
Blumenthal, Mrs. 67, 91, 136
Blumenthal, Muriel (Miss) 60, 125
Blumenthal, Myer 13
Blumenthal, Phil 84, 90
Blumenthal, Phillip 70
Blumenthal, R. 70
Blumenthal, R.H. 70, 84, 101, 109, 141
Blumenthal, R.H. (Miss) 69
Blumenthal, R.H. (Mr. and Mrs.) 69, 70
Blumenthal, R.H. (Mrs.) . . 17, 60, 66, 70, 135
Blumenthal, R.N. 70
Blumenthal, R.W. (Mrs.) 70
Blumenthal, Rev. 41
Blumenthal, Robert (Mrs.) 70
Blumenthal, S. 70
Blumenthal, S. (Mr. and Mrs.) 8, 70
Blumenthal, S. (Mrs.) 70
Blumenthal, Sam (Mr. and Mrs.) 70
Blumenthal, Samuel 23
Blumenthal, Samuel (Mr. and Mrs.) . . 70, 171
Blumenthal, T. (Mr. and Mrs.) 2
Blumer, A. (Mr. and Mrs.) 23
Blumer, D. 70, 81, 107, 122, 137
Blumer, D. (Mr. and Mrs.) . . . 8, 23, 70, 154
Blumer, David 112, 139
Blumer, L. 23
Blumer, L. (Mr. and Mrs.) 8
Blumer, L. (Mrs.) 143
Blumer, Lazar 23
Blumer, Lazare 70
Blumer, Moses 8
Blumer, Mr. and Mrs. 8
Blustien, S. (Mrs.) 172
Boas, A.B. 13, 70
Boas, B.A. 13, 90
Boas, B.A. (Mr. and Mrs.) . . 68, 70, 76, 121
Boas, B.A. (Mrs.) 70, 121
Boas, Bendix A. 70
Boas, Benjamin 70
Boas, Bernard 13, 70
Boas, Mr. and Mrs 65, 121
Bochenck, Joseph 154
Bochenek, J. 160
Bochenek, Joseph (Mr. and Mrs.) 154
Bochenek, Joseph (Mrs.) 154
Bochner, Rose (Miss) 156, 162
Bockar, I. (Mr. and Mrs.) 22
Bockar, Theresa (Miss) 22
Bockart, Theresa (Miss) 71
Bogatsky, Mrs. 154
Bogorad, S. 154
Bold, I. 23
Boltouch, I.W. 70
Boltuch, Isidore 42
Boltuck, Bessie (Miss) 70
Boltuck, Bessie D. (Miss) 70
Boltuck, D. 70
Boltuck, I.W. 70
Boltuck, J.W. (Master) 70
Bomberg, M. (Mrs.) 148
Bonavitskty, M. 2
Bonavitsky, M. 58
Bonder, A. 22
Book, D. 182
Book, Moses 70
Book, Mr. and Mrs. 182
Booke, L. (Mrs.) 180
Bookman, Eva (Miss) 38
Bookman, M. 70
Bookman, M. (Mr. and Mrs.) 38
Bookman, N. 70
Bookman, R. (Mrs.) 70
Booth, Eva (Miss) 33
Boronow, R. 71
Boronow, Richard (Mr. and Mrs.) 23
Boronow, Robert 23
Boronow, Robert (Mr. and Mrs.) 70
Boronow, Robert (Mrs.) 185
Borovsky, B.W. 185
Borshow, J. 65
Borts, A. 23
Borts, A. (Mrs.) 94, 115
Bottler, Myer 23
Boulkind, Mr. and Mrs. 71
Boulkind, S. 77
Boulkind, S. (Mr. and Mrs.) 8, 71
Boulkind, Samuel 23
Bouzensky, Irene (Miss) 34
Bowitch, I. 49
Boyaner, Bertha (Miss) 51
Boyaner, D. 183
Boyaner, D. (Mrs.) 71, 183
Boyaner, Daniel 184
Boyaner, I. 115
Boyaner, Jennie (Miss) 80
Boyaner, L. 56
Boyaner, Mrs. 165
Braderman, Fannie (Miss) 75
Brager, C. (Mr. and Mrs.) 23
Brager, J.L. 23
Brager, J.M. (Mrs.) 71
Brager, J.N. 23
Brager, Louis 56
Brager, Max 23
Braham, Alfred 45
Braham, Catharine (Miss) 45
Brahinski, Mr. 149
Brahinsky, Maurice 152
Braides, Mr. 66
Brainin, Bertha (Miss) 34, 71, 89
Brainin, Joseph 45
Brainin, Miriam (Miss) 34, 71, 89
Brainin, R. (Mrs.) 114
Brainin, Reuben . . . 4, 42, 45, 66, 71, 77, 78,
107, 111, 114, 148
Brainin, Reuben (Mr. and Mrs.) . . . 34, 71, 89
Brainin, Reuben (Mrs.) 71, 109
Brainin, Ruben 71
Brainin, Rubin 45, 71, 160
Brainin, Rubin (Mr. and Mrs.) 71
Brais, Philip 42
Brand, A. (Miss) 156
Brand, Millie (Miss) 154
Brand, P. 175
Brandes, Esther 132
Brandess, Esther 73
Brandt, Millie (Miss) 154
Brandwan, Fanny (Miss) 156
Brankstone, A. (Miss) 162
Braunstein, J. 175
Bravstein, H. 66
Brazer, B. (Miss) 65
Brazer, L. 65
Breebawm, Bessie (Miss) 165
Breeman, Racie (Miss) 165
Breitenbach, Mr. 30
Breitenbach, Richard Weimann 24
Breitman, Reuben (Master) 71
Breitshatz, J. 82
Brengelmann, Mr. and Mrs. 28
Brenner, N. 171
Brenner, Nathan (Mr. and Mrs.) 27
Breska, Esther 45
Breslau, Misses 160
Bresler, Mrs. 173
Breslin, Gertie (Miss) 34, 154, 155
Breslin, H. 154
Breslin, J. 154, 162
Breslin, Joseph 24
Breslin, L.J. (Dr.) 24, 154, 169
Breslin, Lena (Miss) 24
Breslin, Louis (Dr.) 154
Breslin, M. (Mr. and Mrs.) 155
Breslin, M. (Mrs.) 173
Breslin, Rose (Miss) 155
Breslin, S. (Mr. and Mrs.) 24, 165
Breslove, David 155, 157
Breslove, L. 155
Brier, Sarah (Mrs.) 181
Brill, A. 149
Brimm, Sheindel (Miss) 26
Brin, C.J. 185
Brin, D. 185
Brin, H.L. 185
Brin, K. 185
Broady, Pearl (Miss) 165
Brock, H.H. 71
Broder, Mr. 62
Broder, Nathan (Dr.) 93
Brodey, Abraham 157
Brodey, I. 155
Brodie, Annie (Miss) 77
Brodie, J. 24
Brodie, J. (Mr. and Mrs.) 86
Brodie, J.B. 155
Brodie, Jack (Mrs.) 103
Brodie, L. 61
Brodie, M. 114
Brodie, Miss 71
Brodie, Mrs. 71
Brodie, Rabbi 34
Brodski, Rae (Miss) 30
Brodsky, A. (Mrs.) 30
Brodsky, I. 49
Brodsky, Miss 160
Brodsky, R. (Miss) 155
Brodsky, Ray (Miss) 30
Brodsky, S. 122, 137
Brodsky, Samuel 24

Brody, D. 155	Bruker, Harry 118	Caplan, Lillie (Miss) 30
Brody, Esther (Miss) 57	Bruker, Maurice 118	Caplan, Lily (Miss) 30
Brody, F. 13	Brunder, Abraham 182	Caplan, M. (Rev.) 25
Brody, H. 57, 183	Bruser, H. (Mr. and Mrs.) 24	Caplan, Miss 72
Brody, H. (Mrs.) 183	Bruser, Michael 24	Caplan, R. 72, 82, 137
Brody, J.W. 163	Bryer, Mrs. 179	Caplan, Rev. 32, 38, 41, 156
Brody, Lilly (Miss) 57	Bryier, S. (Mrs.) 175, 180	Caplan, Roslyn (Miss) 103
Brody, Mr. 164	Buchan, Mrs. 72	Caplan, S. (Miss) 165
Brody, Mrs. 58	Buckey, D.L. 72	Caplan, Sam 152
Brody, S. 91	Buckey, Dan. L. 72	Caplan, Sarah (Miss) 30, 131
Broidy, A. 155	Budnitsky, Mr. 176	Caplan, Zusman 155
Broidy, J.I. 71	Budnitsky, S. 180	Caplin, A. (Mr. and Mrs.) 24
Broidy, S. (Mr. and Mrs.) 71	Budowitch, E. (Mrs.) 56	Caplin, Bessie (Miss) 148
Bronder, Miss 71	Budowitch, J. 56	Caplin, Emanuel (Master) 149
Bronfman, Allan 175	Budowitch, Myer 56	Caplin, Louis 152, 153
Bronfman, M. (Mrs.) 180	Budyk, D. (Miss) 72	Caplin, Miss Bessie 148
Bronfman, Mr. 176	Budyk, Dr. 62	Caplin, S. 151
Bronfman, Mr. and Mrs. 40	Budyk, H. 70, 72	Capolovitch, Israel 88
Bronstein, Mrs. 139	Budyk, Harry 50, 72	Capstein, Ed. 35
Broody, Z. 163	Budyk, J. 47, 77	Carousky, S.R. 72
Brooker, I. (Mrs.) 104	Budyk, J. (Dr.) 72	Carp, Jack 182
Brookstein, Hannah (Miss) 155	Budyk, J.A. 45	Carp, Louis 182
Brotman, C. 179	Budyk, J.C. (Dr.) 45	Carrell, M. 57
Brotman, E.A. 176	Budyk, J.F. (Dr.) 72	Carrick, J. 61
Brotman, M. 71, 176	Budyk, J.G. (Dr.) 146	Carsley, Charlotte (Miss) 72
Brotman, M.D. (Miss) 99	Budyk, J.H. 72	Carsley, Charlotte (Mrs.) 72
Brotman, M.H. 175, 176	Budyk, J.S. (Dr.) 137	Carsley, H.J. 115
Brotman, Mr. and Mrs. 137	Budyk, M. 47	Carsley, Israel 24
Brotman, R. (Miss) 67, 113, 122	Budyk, M. (Mrs.) 72	Carsley, M. 72
Brotman, R.C. (Miss) 99	Buegelersen, H.P. 72	Carsley, M. (Mrs.) 130, 144
Broudey, Miss 164	Bulfowitch, R. (Mrs.) 73	Cash, Alexander 45, 155, 162, 163, 165, 167-169
Broudie, Rev. 27	Bunnell, Master 165	Cashdan, E. (Mrs.) 40
Broudy, Helen (Miss) 155	Burman, A. (Miss) 88, 114	Cashdan, E. (Rabbi) 40
Broudy, Jack W. 71	Burman, G. (Mrs.) 79	Cashdan, E. (Rev. and Mrs.) 178
Broudy, Nellie (Miss) 154	Burman, R. (Miss) 67, 88, 114	Cashdan, E. (Rev.) 14
Broufman, A. 170	Burman, Rose (Miss) 72, 88	Cashdan, Elias (Rev.) 175
Browman, Saul 24	Burman, W. 137	Cashdan, Hyman 176
Brown, A. 24, 150, 154	Burman, William 72	Cashdan, Rev. 30, 176
Brown, A.J. (Mrs.) 23	Burnstein, Fanny (Miss) 72	Cashden, A. (Rev.) 39
Brown, Abraham 24	Burnstein, Harry 72	Cashden, Cantor 16
Brown, Albert 176	Burrows, Misses 72	Casner, Mildred (Miss) 40
Brown, B. 163	Burrows, S. 24	Casselman, Vaughan (Miss) 142
Brown, B. (Mr. and Mrs.) 35	Bye, Henry 52, 66, 72, 89, 115, 139	Cassil, Miss 124
Brown, Benjamin 154	Bye, Henry V. 2, 72	Cassils, Irene (Miss) 72
Brown, E. 49	Cadesky, D. 163	Cassils, Miss 72
Brown, E.A. 71	Cadesky, Miss 164	Cat, Mr. 182
Brown, H. (Miss) 57	Cadesky, Mr. 164	Caton, Mrs. 111
Brown, Hannah (Miss) 83	Cadisky, J. (Mr. and Mrs.) 23	Chachamowitz, Abraham 24
Brown, Hannah May (Miss) 23	Cadisky, Rose (Miss) 23	Chaikin, Avigdor (Rabbi) 7
Brown, Hilda (Miss) 57	Caffenberg, J. 72	Chaikin, M. 183
Brown, J. (Mrs.) 71	Caffenburg, A. 72	Champagnsy, Moses Clarence 8
Brown, Jenny (Miss) 35	Caffenbuy, R. 72	Champagnsy, Mr. and Mrs. 8
Brown, Jerome (Master) 71	Calashman, B. (Mrs.) 14	Chanaine, Ella (Miss) 173
Brown, Jessie (Miss) 164	Calof, Lena (Miss) 175	Chanaine, J. 173
Brown, L. 176	Camenetsky, Fanny (Miss) 176	Chanaine, Mr. 173
Brown, Leah (Miss) 77	Caminetski, F. (Miss) 176	Chanaine, Willie 173
Brown, M. 110, 157, 185	Caminetsky, Gertrude (Miss) 175	Charach, A. (Mrs.) 180
Brown, M.L. 92	Camintesky, Ira 176	Chariff, Moshe (Rabbi) 148
Brown, May (Miss) 39, 155	Camisher, B. (Miss) 87	Charles, Pauline (Miss) 24
Brown, Mr. 185	Canu, E. (Mrs.) 72	Charlton, Fannie (Miss) 98
Brown, Phillip 13, 176	Caplan, A. 149	Charminsky, A. 155
Brown, R. (Miss) 155	Caplan, A.H. (Mrs.) 149	Charwinsky, A. 156
Brown, T. 106	Caplan, B. (Miss) 148	Chasey, Lillian (Miss) 157
Browne, Miss 72	Caplan, Bessie (Miss) 153	Chaskelson, S. 66
Browne, Mrs. 72	Caplan, C. 149	Chaskelson, S. (Miss) 72
Brownstein, Clara (Miss) 38	Caplan, C. (Mrs.) 149	Chawkin, K. 24
Brownstein, Mr. and Mrs. 72	Caplan, Gordon (Master) 149	Chazanovitch, Mr. 72
Brownstein, N. (Mr. and Mrs.) 38	Caplan, H. 49, 59, 72, 81	Chechik, L. 177
Brownstein, Samuel 14	Caplan, I. 67, 68	Chelmnitsky, J. 178
Brownstone, S. 175	Caplan, I. (Mr. and Mrs.) 99	Cherniack, Joseph 175
Bruker, Charles 118	Caplan, L. (Mrs.) 76	Cherniak, A. 180
Bruker, D.S. (Mr. and Mrs.) 8	Caplan, Leslie (Miss) 153	Cherniak, F. 175
Bruker, Ernest 118	Caplan, Lessie (Miss) 29	Cherniak, L. 180

Cherniak, Mr. 175	Cohen, A. (Mr. and Mrs.) 8, 24	Cohen, H. 32, 60, 61, 73, 81, 87, 92, 136, 158
Chernoff, A. 81	Cohen, A. (Mrs.) 24, 74, 166	Cohen, H. (Mr. and Mrs.) 73, 74
Cherrin, William 57	Cohen, A.I. 45	Cohen, H. (Mrs.) 162, 165
Chertcoff, Y. 72	Cohen, A.J. 72	Cohen, H. (Rabbi) 112
Chessler, B. 24	Cohen, A.T. 87	Cohen, H.L. 73
Chessler, B. (Mrs.) 173	Cohen, A.Z. 62, 72, 146	Cohen, Harold 24, 40
Chiat, G. 158	Cohen, A.Z. (Mr. and Mrs.) 8, 24	Cohen, Harry 24, 67, 123
Chippen, A. 57	Cohen, A.Z. (Mrs.) 74, 98	Cohen, Harry B. 73
Chmelnitski, J.A. 175	Cohen, Aaron 167, 176	Cohen, Hattie (Miss) 73, 128
Chmelnitsky, Goldie (Miss) 176	Cohen, Abel 154	Cohen, Henry (Dr.) 155
Chmelnitsky, I. 180	Cohen, Abraham 24, 27	Cohen, Herman 49
Chmelnitsky, J. 176	Cohen, Abraham I. 57	Cohen, Hessie 49
Chmelnitsky, Mr. 175	Cohen, Adela (Miss) 134	Cohen, Hiam 14
Chodesh, Mr. 45	Cohen, Adelaide (Miss) 161, 168	Cohen, Hirsch (Rabbi) 3, 14, 15, 22-24,
Chopack, Hattie (Miss) 22	Cohen, Aida (Miss) 107	26-28, 31, 32, 34-37,
Chorlton, D. Marks (Mr. and Mrs.) 8	Cohen, Anna (Miss) 28, 35, 39, 73	39-41, 46, 49, 52, 59,
Chorlton, D.M. 72	Cohen, Annie (Miss) 36, 87	71, 74, 75, 77, 78, 80,
Chorlton, D.M. (Mrs.) 2	Cohen, Araki 177	87, 108, 110, 133, 141
Chorlton, David (Mrs.) 98	Cohen, Arakie (Mrs.) 101	Cohen, Horace 24, 61, 73, 74, 110
Chorlton, David M. (Mr. and Mrs.) . . 8, 72	Cohen, Arthur 5, 24, 157, 168	Cohen, Horace R. 42, 88, 114
Chorlton, David Marks (Mr. and Mrs.) 8	Cohen, Arthur (Mr. and Mrs.) 156	Cohen, I. . . 33, 73, 74, 78, 98, 107, 155, 173
	Cohen, Arthur E. (Master) 74	Cohen, I. (Cantor) 37
Churchill, Mrs. 175, 177	Cohen, B. 72	Cohen, I. (Mr. and Mrs.) 8, 86
Cipin, Joseph (Mr. and Mrs.) 8	Cohen, B. (Miss) 88, 112, 113, 134	Cohen, I. (Mrs.) 74, 96, 121
Circle, A. 173	Cohen, B.I. (Mr. and Mrs.) 135	Cohen, I. (Rabbi) 74
Circle, A. (Mr. and Mrs.) 174	Cohen, Barnet 156	Cohen, I. (Rev.) 26, 36
Citron, I. 57	Cohen, Barney 114	Cohen, Ida (Miss) 179
Citron, S.I. 57	Cohen, Beccie (Miss) 81	Cohen, Ida (Miss) 177, 180
Claman, C. 183	Cohen, Beckie (Miss) 73	Cohen, Isaac 27
Claman, Eva 2	Cohen, Beckie (Mrs.) 73	Cohen, Isaacson 14
Claman, Eva (Miss) 72	Cohen, Becky (Miss) 24	Cohen, Isidore 57
Claman, Florence (Miss) 28	Cohen, Ben 156	Cohen, J. . 49, 51, 72, 73, 114, 120, 131, 140,
Claman, Flossie 111	Cohen, Bernard 184	156, 165, 168
Claman, Flossie (Miss) 28, 72	Cohen, Bessie 61	Cohen, J. (Dr.) 74
Claman, H. 132	Cohen, Bessie (Miss) 24, 73	Cohen, J. (Miss) 163
Claman, Hilda Florence (Miss) 28	Cohen, C. 65	Cohen, J. (Mr. and Mrs.) 8, 73
Claman, Howard 2	Cohen, Cantor 38	Cohen, J. (Mrs.) 66, 74, 128
Claman, I. 24, 72	Cohen, Cecile (Miss) 156	Cohen, J.A. (Mrs.) 119
Claman, I. (Mr. and Mrs.) 72, 86	Cohen, Charles 175, 185	Cohen, J.S. (Mrs.) 156, 161
Claman, M. (Mr. and Mrs.) 28	Cohen, Charles (Mr. and Mrs.) 73	Cohen, J.W. 175
Claman, M. (Mr.and Mrs.) 28	Cohen, Charles (Mrs.) 61	Cohen, Jacob . 5, 14, 28, 32, 42, 61, 132, 155,
Claman, M. (Mrs.) 72, 90	Cohen, Charles H. 24	159, 163, 166
Claman, Morris 72, 94	Cohen, Clara (Miss) 170	Cohen, Jacob (Magistrate) 155
Claman, Mr. 72, 94	Cohen, Clarence J. 42	Cohen, Jacob (Mr. and Mrs.) 73
Clare, J. 65	Cohen, D. 163, 183	Cohen, Jacob S. 14
Clark, Mr. and Mrs. 72	Cohen, D. (Mr. and Mrs.) 185	Cohen, James 35
Clavir, Ben 167	Cohen, D. (Mrs.) 31	Cohen, Joseph 24, 49, 52, 73, 141
Clavir, Edith (Miss) 157	Cohen, David 24, 155	Cohen, Joseph (Mrs.) 156, 168
Clavir, Murry (Master) 157	Cohen, David (Mr. and Mrs.) 185	Cohen, Julian A. (Mr. and Mrs.) 73
Clayman, I. 176	Cohen, Dolly (Miss) 31	Cohen, Julius 61
Clayman, Isidore 176	Cohen, E. Arakie 176	Cohen, Julius A. 24
Clayman, Leah 27	Cohen, E.A. 16, 176	Cohen, K. 149, 152, 158
Clayman, Wolf (Mr. and Mrs.) 27	Cohen, E.A. (Mr. and Mrs.) 176	Cohen, K. (Mr. and Mrs.) 138
Cliff, Samuel 138	Cohen, E.A. (Mrs.) 177	Cohen, L. 56, 57, 73, 74, 103, 127
Close, L. (Miss) 154	Cohen, E.E. 49	Cohen, L. (Miss) 103
Coblentz, R. (Miss) 176	Cohen, Edith I. (Miss) 57	Cohen, L. (Mrs.) 57
Coblentz, Rachel (Miss) 177	Cohen, Elsie (Miss) 85	Cohen, L.H. 73, 90, 97, 98, 108
Coblentz, Rae (Miss) 180	Cohen, Ethel (Miss) 32, 38, 45, 46, 165	Cohen, L.H. (Mrs.) 74
Coblenz, Mr. and Mrs. 176	Cohen, Etta 35	Cohen, Laurie (Mrs.) 74
Cochenthaler, Carrie (Miss) 72	Cohen, Etta (Mrs.) 86	Cohen, Lawrence 14, 74
Cochenthaler, Joseph 70	Cohen, Ettie (Miss) 74	Cohen, Lawrence (Master) 83
Cochenthaler, M. 72	Cohen, F. 67	Cohen, Lawrence Z. 2
Cochenthaler, M. (Mrs.) 21, 72	Cohen, F. (Mrs.) 14	Cohen, Lazarus . 2, 3, 14, 25, 31, 32, 37, 42,
Cochenthaler, Miss 116, 123	Cohen, F. (Rev.) 25	59, 62, 73, 77, 78, 81,
Cochenthaler, Misses 116	Cohen, Fannie (Miss) 181	110, 115, 133
Cochenthaler, Mrs. 21, 116	Cohen, Fanny 66	Cohen, Lazarus (Mr. and Mrs.) . . . 31, 74, 75
Cochenthaler, Rebecca 72	Cohen, Fischel 14	Cohen, Lazarus (Mrs.) 31, 74, 140
Cochenthaler, S. (Mrs.) 14	Cohen, Fischel (Mr. and Mrs.) 75	Cohen, Levi 57
Codden, Etta (Miss) 178	Cohen, Frank 24	Cohen, Lewis 150
Coddon, Etta (Miss) 176, 179	Cohen, Frederick (Master) 155	Cohen, Lewis H. 98, 109
Cohan, Morris 155	Cohen, Fredie (Master) 71	Cohen, Libbie (Miss) 73, 128
Cohen, (Mrs.) 57, 162	Cohen, G. 72	Cohen, Louis 57, 114, 128, 152, 156
Cohen, A. . . . 14, 45, 61, 62, 72, 81, 151, 162	Cohen, G.M. 156	Cohen, Louis (Mrs.) 57

195

Cohen, Louis (Rev. and Mrs.) 8	Cohen, Sol 115	Corman, Miss 156
Cohen, Lyon . . . 3, 19, 25, 32, 42, 43, 45, 51, 61, 62, 67, 73, 81, 88, 90, 101, 107, 111, 114, 139	Cohen, Sol. 67, 73, 137	Corn, A. (Miss) 156
	Cohen, Sylvia (Miss) 139	Corn, Annie (Miss) 165
	Cohen, W. 148	Corn, Harry 156
	Cohen, W.M. (Mrs.) 73	Corn, S. 168
Cohen, Lyon (Mr. and Mrs.) . 2, 8, 40, 61, 74, 75, 89	Cohen, Walter 46	Cornfeld, Jack 25
	Cohen, William 24, 44, 74, 143, 148, 150, 151	Corper, Amelia (Miss) 34
Cohen, Lyon (Mrs.) 46, 74, 128	Cohen, William (Mrs.) 74	Corten, Philip (Mr. and Mrs.) 10
Cohen, M. 56, 68, 156, 169, 183, 184	Cohn, A. 157	Cossman, D. 58
Cohen, M. (Master) 88, 149	Cohn, Albert 166	Cossman, D. (Mr. and Mrs.) 2
Cohen, M. (Miss) 73, 86, 88, 114	Cohn, Arthur 157	Cossman, Dave (Mrs.) 75
Cohen, M. (Mr. and Mrs.) 74	Cohn, B. 165	Cossman, David (Mr. and Mrs.) 75
Cohen, M. (Mrs.) 100, 155	Cohn, B. (Miss) 156	Cossman, Eddie 2
Cohen, M.B. 185	Cohn, C. 155	Cossman, J. 75, 128
Cohen, Mabel (Miss) 45, 46	Cohn, David 156	Cossman, Jack 2, 25, 75
Cohen, Mamie (Miss) 156	Cohn, H. 156	Cossman, L. (Miss) 75
Cohen, Margaret (Miss) 80	Cohn, Harry 74, 156	Cossman, Lawrence 49
Cohen, Marguerite (Miss) 86	Cohn, Henry L. 74	Cossman, Leah (Miss) 75, 117
Cohen, Mark 14, 24, 43, 73, 166, 168	Cohn, I. 156	Cossman, Malca (Miss) 31, 75
Cohen, Mary (Miss) 26, 35	Cohn, J. 156, 175	Cossman, Malcah (Miss) 117
Cohen, Maurice 152, 162	Cohn, Joseph (Mr. and Mrs.) 27	Cossman, Master 58
Cohen, Max . . 49, 66, 73, 132, 134, 142, 183	Cohn, Louis 74	Costino, Annie (Miss) 75
Cohen, Maxwell 109	Cohn, M. 162	Costinsky, A. (Cantor) 156
Cohen, Meyer 30	Cohn, Mark G. 156	Cotersen, A.L. (Rabbi) 40
Cohen, Mildred (Miss) 73	Cohn, R. (Miss) 165	Cotzen, M.D. 25
Cohen, Minnie 45	Cohn, W. (Mr. and Mrs.) 156	Covecy, Jennie (Miss) 125
Cohen, Minnie (Miss) 46	Cohn, Willie 74	Covens, A. 176
Cohen, Miriam (Miss) 73, 81, 112	Cohon, P. 58	Coviensky, Anna (Miss) 32, 110
Cohen, Miss 32, 73, 169, 176	Cole, Mrs. 14	Coviensky, Annie (Miss) 75
Cohen, Mitchell 24	Colenski, Harry 180	Coviensky, L. 115
Cohen, Moe (Mr. and Mrs.) 24	Colensko, Alex. 180	Coviensky, Lionel 25, 75, 77, 78
Cohen, Montague N.A. (Rabbi) 46	Colle, C.M. 120	Coviensky, Lyon 32, 83
Cohen, Montague N.A. (Rev.) 74	Colle, Charles M. 70	Coviensky, M. (Mr. and Mrs.) . . . 32, 79, 110
Cohen, Moses M. 14	Colle, Chas. M. 122	Coviensky, M. (Mrs.) 14
Cohen, Mr. 40, 63, 74, 176	Colle, H.L. 73, 74, 101	Coviensky, Mr. and Mrs. 75
Cohen, Mr. and Mrs. 178	Colle, M. 66, 74, 137, 143	Coviensky, Ray (Miss) 32, 73, 81
Cohen, Mrs. 20, 74, 78, 98, 114, 127, 156, 167	Colle, M. (Mr. and Mrs.) 39	Covner, Dina (Miss) 75
Cohen, Mrs. Laurie 74	Colle, Sarah (Miss) 39	Cowan, Harry 75
Cohen, N. 47	Cooper, Abraham 2	Cowan, Leslie 75
Cohen, N.B. 47	Cooper, Amelia (Miss) 102	Cowan, Miriam (Miss) 75
Cohen, Naomi (Miss) 103	Cooper, B. 49	Cowan, Mrs. 75
Cohen, Nathan 57, 59, 73	Cooper, H. 183	Cowan, Willie 75
Cohen, Nellie 118	Cooper, H. (Mrs.) 74	Cowen, Jack 25
Cohen, P. 2, 166	Cooper, H.J. 183, 184	Cristall, Bessie (Miss) 183
Cohen, Percy (Mrs.) 141	Cooper, I. 162	Cristall, A. 183
Cohen, Perry (Mr. and Mrs.) 74	Cooper, I. (Mrs.) 156, 165	Cristall, Bessie 183
Cohen, Perry (Mrs.) 94	Cooper, J. 74	Cristall, J. 183
Cohen, Phil. 57	Cooper, Jacob (Master) 149	Cristall, Rose 183
Cohen, R. 66	Cooper, Jennie (Miss) 151	Cronstein, A. 78
Cohen, R. (Miss) 67, 73	Cooper, Julius 25, 28	Cross, J.B. (Mrs.) 44
Cohen, R. (Mr. and Mrs.) 26	Cooper, K. (Mr. and Mrs.) 37	Crossman, Hiram 75
Cohen, R. (Mrs.) 74, 84, 138	Cooper, M. 152	Crossman, Jack 75
Cohen, Rachel (Mrs.) 57	Cooper, Miss 81, 151	Crossman, Malca (Miss) 75
Cohen, Ray (Miss) 98	Cooper, Moses 2	Crowder, Mrs. 75
Cohen, Rebecca (Miss) 155	Cooper, Mr. 26	Crown, A. 162
Cohen, Rev. 24, 32, 34, 156	Cooper, Mrs. 49, 151	Crown, Abraham 118
Cohen, Richard 74	Cooper, Rebecca 154	Crown, G. (Miss) 64, 74
Cohen, Rose (Miss) 73, 135, 139	Cooper, Sara 149	Crown, Ida (Miss) 23
Cohen, Ruth (Miss) 106	Cooper, Sarah (Miss) 37	Crown, J. 11
Cohen, S. . . . 74, 90, 114, 143, 148, 149, 152	Cooperman, Dorothy (Miss) 32	Crown, Leah (Miss) 26
Cohen, S. (Miss) 176	Cooperman, J. (Miss) 81	Crown, M. 74, 81
Cohen, S. (Mr. and Mrs.) 8	Coopersmith, M. 74	Crown, M. (Miss) 64
Cohen, S. (Mrs.) 60, 64, 127	Copeman, Miss 34	Crown, M. (Mr. and Mrs.) 26, 80
Cohen, S.H. (Mrs.) 88	Coplan, A.H. (Mrs.) 151	Crown, Mary (Miss) 26, 69
Cohen, S.J. (Mrs.) 17	Coplan, Archie (Mrs.) 148	Crown, Meyer 26
Cohen, S.K. 56	Coplan, David (Master) 149	Crown, Moses (Mr. and Mrs.) 26, 80
Cohen, S.W. 74	Coplan, Mr. and Mrs. 35	Crown, Myer 65, 73
Cohen, Sadie (Miss) 56, 98	Copman, Mary (Miss) 156	Crown, Myer (Mr. and Mrs.) 80
Cohen, Sam 74, 138, 139, 171, 172, 183	Copper, R. (Mrs.) 74	Crystal, A. (Miss) 75, 114
Cohen, Samuel 24, 53, 74	Copper, S.M. 25	Crystal, Annie (Miss) 32, 75
Cohen, Samuel (Mr. and Mrs.) 8	Copper, Samuel F. 25	Crystal, B. 75
Cohen, Samuel W. 74	Corber, B. 74	Crystal, Bessie (Miss) 40
Cohen, Sarah (Mrs.) 35, 74	Corber, Bernard 67	Crystal, E. (Dr.) 75, 138

Crystal, E. (Mrs.) 75
Crystal, L. 75
Crystal, L. (Mr. and Mrs.) 32
Crystal, M. 75
Crystal, M.J. (Mrs.) 75
Crystal, Mr. 75
Crystal, Mrs. 27
Crystal, Rosaline (Miss) 27
Cumisher, B. (Miss) 88
Cuppleman, Charles 181
Curtis, J.B. (Mrs.) 75
Cutler, Tillie (Miss) 156
Czernak, Baruch 175
Czetzic, Meyer 175
Dachs, R. 114
Dainow, David 25, 46, 75, 82, 114, 141
Dalerofsky, P. 143
Dalgorf, Samuel 171
Dalton, Mr. 94
Dalzorf, Mr. 167
Daniel, L. (Mrs.) 75
Daniels, J. 115
Daniels, Miss 156
Daniels, Mr. 163
Daniels, Mrs. 154
Danielson, J. (Mrs.) 90
Danson, Flora (Miss) 165
Danson, Florence (Miss) . . 146, 152, 154, 156
Danson, Miss 164, 167
Danziger, Thina (Miss) 19
Darwin, J.A. 75
Darwin, M.P. 45
Darwin, M.P. (Mrs.) 45
Darwin, Maurice P. (Mr. and Mrs.) 75
Darwin, N.P. 75
Darwin, Paul 134
Darwin, R.A. . 3, 12, 63, 75, 77, 78, 115, 121
Darwin, R.A. (Mr. and Mrs.) 2
Darwin, R.A. (Mrs.) 46
Darwin, Robert A. 46, 75, 138
Darwin, S. (Master) 2
Dascal, D. 138
David, Goldie (Miss) 98
David, Jacob 25
David, Myer (Mrs.) 57
David, R.S. (Major) 75
David, Rosalie (Miss) 75
Davidovitch, H. 75, 168
Davidovitch, Harry 42, 51
Davidovitz, I. 172
Davidson, D.G. (Mr. and Mrs.) 157
Davidson, Elizabeth (Mrs.) 14
Davidson, H.M. (Mr. and Mrs.) 75
Davidson, L. (Miss) 149
Davidson, Leah (Miss) 36
Davidson, Lillian (Miss) 14, 148
Davidson, M. 14, 31
Davidson, Miss 150
Davidson, Misses 151
Davidson, Mr. and Mrs. 75
Davidson, Rose (Miss) 14, 31, 148, 150
Davidson, Sam 57
Davidson, W.M. (Mr. and Mrs.) 36
Davies, Rhoda (Miss) 156
Davis 76
Davis, A. 2, 14, 156
Davis, A. (Mrs.) 76, 143
Davis, Arthur 156
Davis, B. (Mrs.) 76
Davis, C.L. 75
Davis, C.W. 68
Davis, D. 14, 162
Davis, Dave 75
Davis, David 14, 45
Davis, E.R. 76
Davis, Eugene 76
Davis, Eugene H. 14
Davis, Gladys (Miss) 76
Davis, Gladys, (Miss) 76
Davis, H. 162
Davis, H. Lawrence (Mr. and Mrs.) 76
Davis, H.E. (Mr. and Mrs.) 76
Davis, Harry 76
Davis, Harry (Mr. and Mrs.) 76
Davis, Harry (Mrs.) 76
Davis, Harry E. 76
Davis, Harry E. (Mr. and Mrs.) 8
Davis, Hazel (Miss) 76
Davis, Henry 45, 166
Davis, Henry (Miss) 170
Davis, Henry (Mrs.) 156
Davis, Hilda (Miss) 175
Davis, Horace (Mrs.) 76
Davis, Isaac 44
Davis, J. (Miss) 33
Davis, J. (Mr. and Mrs.) 25, 127
Davis, J. (Mrs.) 128, 152
Davis, Jack 14
Davis, Jeanette (Miss) 8
Davis, Jennie (Miss) 148
Davis, L. (Miss) 173
Davis, L. (Mr. and Mrs.) 25, 150
Davis, L. (Mrs.) 150
Davis, Lawrence (Mr. and Mrs.) 76
Davis, Lily (Miss) 131
Davis, Lionel 45, 156
Davis, M. 59, 156
Davis, M. (Miss) 74
Davis, M. (Mr. and Mrs.) 76
Davis, M. (Mrs.) 76
Davis, M.B. 76, 90
Davis, M.B. (Mr. and Mrs.) 76
Davis, M.E. (Mr. and Mrs.) 76
Davis, M.H. (Mrs.) 13
Davis, Mabel (Miss) 76
Davis, Martha (Miss) 27
Davis, Maurice 76
Davis, Maurice (Mrs.) 76
Davis, Maurice B. 14
Davis, Maurice E. 76
Davis, Melvin (Mrs.) 76, 121
Davis, Miss 164, 167, 174
Davis, Morris (Mr. and Mrs.) 2
Davis, Mortimer (Mr. and Mrs.) 76
Davis, Mortimer (Mrs.) 76, 130
Davis, Mortimer B. . . . 14, 46, 59, 62, 76, 90, 100, 143, 146
Davis, Mortimer B. (Mr. and Mrs.) 76
Davis, Mortimer B. (Mrs.) . . 13, 18, 76, 115
Davis, Mr. 171
Davis, Mr. and Mrs. 28, 76, 127, 153
Davis, Mrs. 152
Davis, Nellie (Miss) 76
Davis, P. 174
Davis, R. 76, 136
Davis, R.G. 62
Davis, Rae (Miss) 76
Davis, S. 25, 90
Davis, S.W. 156
Davis, Samuel 14
Davis, Sol. 14
Davis, Violet (Miss) 155-157, 161, 162, 164, 165
Davis, Walter 25
Davis, William 27, 76
Davis, Z. (Mr. and Mrs.) 5
Davis, Z. (Mrs.) 100
Davis, Zelic 14
De Hart, J. 63
De Hirsch, Baron 5
De la Penha, I. (Rev. and Mrs.) . . . 14, 76, 77
De la Penha, I. (Rev.) 16, 18, 19, 39, 77, 118
De la Penha, Isaac (Mrs.) 76
de la Penha, Isaac (Rabbi) 33
De la Penha, Isaac (Rev.) 33, 38, 134
De la Penha, Mrs. Isaac 76
De la Penha, Philip 118
De la Penha, Philip (Master) 69, 76
De la Penha, S. (Miss) 76, 101
De la Penha, Sarah 14
De la Penha, Sarah (Miss) 14, 76, 140
De Levinne, Mrs. 17
De Pass, J. 77
De Silberg, H. 152
De Silberg, Mr. 149
De Sola Mendes, Rev. Dr. 38
De Sola Pool, Rev. 22
De Sola, Abraham (Rabbi) 77
De Sola, Belle Maud (Miss) 46
De Sola, Bram 77, 114
De Sola, Bram C. 77, 137
De Sola, Bram, C. 47
De Sola, Clarence 45
De Sola, Clarence (Mr. and Mrs.) . . 7, 77, 81
De Sola, Clarence (Mrs.) . . . 15, 77, 89, 130
De Sola, Clarence I. . 2, 3, 5, 32, 42, 46, 52, 62, 65, 68, 69, 73, 77, 81, 117, 118, 134, 139
De Sola, Clarence I. (Mr. and Mrs.) . . 8, 37, 77, 89
De Sola, Clarence I. (Mrs.) 77, 82, 109
De Sola, Jessica (Miss) 37
De Sola, Louise (Miss) 77
De Sola, M. (Mrs.) 77
De Sola, Meldola (Mrs.) . 6, 77, 129, 130, 147
De Sola, Meldola (Rabbi and Mrs.) 77
De Sola, Meldola (Rabbi) . . 3, 14, 15, 18, 19, 21, 26, 33, 38, 41, 42, 46, 59, 77, 125, 134
De Sola, Meldola (Rev.) 77
De Sola, Raphael 134
De Taub, Bella (Miss) 176
De Taube, Bella (Miss) 175
De Taube, Jean (Miss) 179
De Waltoff, Dr. 77
De Waltoff, F. (Miss) 77
De Young, Anna (Miss) 77
Deinard, Rabbi 32
Deinard, Rabbi Dr. 180
Dell, Edna (Miss) 41
Den Bow, N. 77
Denberg, N. 107
Denbow, N. 77
Denenberg, M. 11, 77, 115, 133
Denenberg, Moses 78
Denis, Lily (Miss) 26
Dennenberg, M. 78
Derosa, A. 78
Derosa, A. (Mr. and Mrs.) 24, 78
Derosa, A. (Mrs.) 18, 24, 78
Derose, A. (Mrs.) 121
Deskin, A. (Miss) 88
Deskin, K. (Miss) 88
Desroses, Alfred 46
Deutsch, S. 78, 80, 99, 116
Deutsch, Sender 86, 121
Deutsch, Solomon 25
Deutsch,S. 116
Diamond, B. (Mr. and Mrs.) 78
Diamond, B. (Mrs.) 78, 129

Diamond, Clara (Miss) 170	Docks, R. 82, 134	Dubrofsky, M. (Mr. and Mrs.) 3
Diamond, F. 183	Docter, F. (Mrs.) 36	Dubrofsky, M. (Mrs.) 65
Diamond, F. (Mr. and Mrs.) 9, 25	Docter, J. 36	Dubrofsky, P. 68
Diamond, Fanny (Miss) 78, 129	Doctor, L. (Rev.) 31, 34	Dubrofsky, P. (Mr. and Mrs.) 32
Diamond, G. 78	Doctor, Lyon (Rev.) 148	Dubrofsky, R. (Miss) 77
Diamond, Hilda (Miss) 78, 88, 129	Doctor, Rev. 38	Dubrofsky, Ray (Miss) 114
Diamond, I. (Miss) 78	Doctor, S. (Rev.) 34	Dubrofsky, Rose (Miss) 114
Diamond, Ida (Miss) 27	Dolgorf, Samuel 25	Duchan (Mrs.) 17
Diamond, J. 49, 64, 78, 139	Donnenfeld, J. 156	Ducoffe, M.A. 25
Diamond, J. (Mr. and Mrs.) . . 2, 78, 127, 174	Donnenfeld, J. (Mrs.) 156	Duefell, Miss 164
Diamond, J. (Mrs.) 128	Dorman, Mr. 171	Dukas, J. 78
Diamond, Jacob 2, 183	Dover, David 14	Dukas, Julius J. 78
Diamond, Joel 27	Dover, Esther (Miss) 30, 31, 78, 80	Dun, Louis 184
Diamond, Leah (Miss) 27	Dover, Fanny (Miss) 31	Dunkelman, Mr. 156
Diamond, Lena (Miss) 78	Dover, H. 148	Dunkleman, David 25
Diamond, M. 49, 157	Dover, Harry 14, 31, 78, 110, 111	Dunne, A. 170
Diamond, M. (Mr. and Mrs.) 27	Dover, Harry (Mr. and Mrs.) 30	Durewsky, M. 183
Diamond, Max 2	Dover, Hattie (Miss) 31, 78	Dushman, Prof. 155
Diamond, Miriam (Miss) 27	Dover, Hettie (Miss) 14	Dushman, S. (Dr.) 157, 162
Diamond, Mrs. 97	Dover, Jacob 14	Dushman, Saul 156
Diamond, P.R. 70	Dover, John 14, 31	Dushman, Saul (Dr.) 156
Diamond, R. (Miss) 78, 185	Dover, Joseph 14, 78, 148, 152	Dworkin, A.J. (Mr. and Mrs.) 9
Diamond, Ray (Miss) 78	Dover, Julius 14	Dworkin, E. (Mrs.) 157
Diamond, Rebecca (Miss) 27	Dover, Minnie (Mrs.) 14	Dworkin, Edward S. 25
Diamond, Rebecca Miriam (Miss) 170	Dover, Miss 152	Dworkin, H. (Mr. and Mrs.) 9
Diamond, Rhoda (Miss) 27, 170	Dover, Myer 14	Dworkin, Harry 157
Diamond, Ruth 183	Dover, Phillip 14	Dworkin, Henry S. 25
Diamond, S. 148	Dover, Sarah (Miss) 14	Dworkin, L. (Mr. and Mrs.) 9
Diamond, S. (Miss) 9	Dover, William 14	Dworkin, Messrs. 157
Diamond, S. (Mr. and Mrs.) 9, 27, 170	Dovia, I. 67	Dworkin, Mr. 148
Diamond, S. (Mrs.) 78, 79, 128, 152	Dovia, J. 139	Eason, S. 156
Diamond, Sam (Mrs.) 151	Dovia, S. (Miss) 112	Echenberg, A. 59
Diamond, Samuel 25	Dovia, Sarah (Miss) 106	Echenberg, Bertha (Miss) 78
Diamond, W. 183	Dovico, I. 67	Echenberg, Clara (Miss) 26
Diamond, W. (Mrs.) 183	Dovin, J. 94	Echenberg, M. 59
Diamond, William . . . 26, 39, 175, 183, 184	Draiman, A. 30	Echenberg, M. (Mrs.) 26
Diamond, William (Mrs.) 183	Draiman, Archie 78, 156	Echenberg, M.B. (Mr. and Mrs.) 26
Diamondstein, P.H. (Rev. and Mrs.) 25	Draiman, Charles (Mrs.) 158	Echenberg, R. (Miss) 67, 79, 92, 138
Diamondstein, William Benjamin 25	Draiman, Jennie (Miss) 165	Echenberg, Rebecca 52
Dickman, A. 157	Draiman, Miss 166	Echenberg, Rebecca (Miss) 79
Dickman, Adolf 156	Draiman, Mr. 166	Edelberg, V. 115
Dickman, Mr. 156	Draiman, W. 169	Edelman, Norman 176
Dickman, Simon 163	Draimin, A. 159, 169	Edelstein, A.M. (Mr. and Mrs.) 25, 27
Dickstein, M. 134	Draimin, Arch. 163	Edelstein, B. (Miss) 151
Dictar, Clara (Miss) 37	Draimin, Charles 25, 168	Edelstein, Becca (Miss) 27
Diner, H. 61	Draimin, Charles (Mrs.) 156	Edelstein, H. 46
Diner, I. 61	Draimin, Chas. (Mr. and Mrs.) 9	Edelstein, H. (Mr. and Mrs.) 148
Diner, Rachel (Mrs.) 177	Draimin, Jennie (Miss) 155, 157, 162	Edelstein, Harry 25
Diner, Simon 177	Draimin, M. 156	Edelstein, Harry (Mr. and Mrs.) 25
Dinnick, Misses 168	Draimin, Miss 164	Edelstein, Hyman 5, 46, 114, 148
Dinovitzer, J. (Mrs.) 64	Drainow, A. (Mrs.) 82	Edelstein, Joseph 148
Dinovitzer, Joseph (Mr. and Mrs.) 78	Draisin, Mr. 148	Edelstein, Mr. and Mrs. 79
Director, I. 185	Drapkin, A. 25, 149	Edelstein, R. 127, 151, 152
Director, I. (Mr. and Mrs.) 9, 185	Dreyfus, F. (Miss) 78	Edelstein, Ray (Miss) 25
Director, I. (Mrs.) 78, 176	Dreyfus, Isaac (Mr and Mrs.) 78	Edlestein, Hyman 46
Director, Isidore (Mr. and Mrs.) 185	Dreyfus, Theo. (Mr. and Mrs.) 78	Edlow, S. (Dr.) 79
Director, Rosalie 78	Dreyfus, Theresa (Miss) 78	Edlstein, Hyman 46
Director, Rosalie (Miss) 185	Drobkin, Mr. 46	Edlstein, Joseph 46
Director, Stanley (Master) 185	Druck, H. 185	Effinbine, Effie (Miss) 176
Director, Zelna (Miss) 185	Drucker, Fannie (Miss) 31	Egelnick, Charles 164
Disk, A. (Miss) 88	Drucker, P. (Mrs.) 78	Ehmann, Martha (Miss) 57
Dobrofsky, E. (Miss) 78	Druckman, S. 176, 177	Ehmann, S.L. (Mr. and Mrs.) 57
Dobrofsky, Edith (Miss) 78	Druckman, Sam 40	Ehmann, Sadie (Miss) 57
Dobrofsky, Joseph 78, 114	Druker, A. 56	Ehrenstein, H. (Mr. and Mrs.) 137
Dobrofsky, Joseph A. 78	Druker, Mrs. 58	Eidelberg, J. 65
Dobrofsky, M. 78, 81	Druxerman, B. 178	Eidelberg, Joseph 81
Dobrofsky, M. (Mrs.) 13, 66, 78, 100	Druxerman, Frank (Mr. and Mrs.) 178	Eidlow, Samuel 79
Dobrofsky, Mr. and Mrs. 78	Dubin, A. 162	Eighler, Rev. 27
Dobrofsky, Myer (Mrs.) 78	Dubin, Bertha (Miss) 139	Ein, G. 2, 58
Dobrofsky, P. 74	Dubinitsky, Joseph 132	Ein, J. 57
Dobrofsky, P. (Mr. and Mrs.) 37, 78	Dubinsky, Sarah (Miss) 25	Ein, P. (Mrs.) 57
Dobrofsky, R. (Miss) 73	Dubrofsky, D. 170	Ein, Sophie (Miss) 57
Dobrofsky, Rose (Miss) 37, 78	Dubrofsky, Jennie (Miss) 32	Eisen, Ike 25

Eisenberg, S. (Rabbi) 93
Eisenskin, J. (Mr. and Mrs.) 79
Eisenstadt, Ch. (Mr. and Mrs.) 25
Eisenstadt, Charles 64
Eisenstadt, Helena (Miss) 25, 128
Eisenstadt, Hillel 128
Eisenstadt, J.J. 25, 79
Eisenstadt, S.M. 25, 128
Eisenstadt, Solomon M. 25
Eisenstadt, Solonon M. 25
Eisenstat, C. .79
Eisenstat, Charles 79
Eisman, Julius 25
Eismer, R. (Miss) 156
Eissenberg, M. 157
Elbaum, Bella (Miss) 23, 79
Elias, L. 179
Elias, Leon .177
Eliasoph, Harry 14
Eliasoph, I. 79
Eliasoph, I. (Rev.) 37
Eliasoph, J.G. 49
Eliasoph, M.B. (Mrs.) 79
Eliasoph, M.I. (Rev. and Mrs.) . . . 14, 79
Eliasoph, M.I. (Rev.) 37
Eliasoph, R. (Mrs.) 133
Eliasoph, Rev. 27
Eliasoph, S. 77, 114, 129
Elisus, H. 158
Elkan, M. 79, 157
Elkhan, Mr. .79
Elkin, A. (Mr. and Mrs.) 26, 79
Elkin, A. (Mrs.) 79, 134
Elkin, Abraham A. 14
Elkin, Bessie (Miss) 26, 77, 79, 137
Elkin, Bessie (Mrs.) 46
Elkin, E.M. 79
Elkin, Isadore (Mrs.) 16
Elkin, Isidore 79
Elkin, J. 26, 49, 121
Elkin, J. (Mr. and Mrs.) 9, 79
Elkin, J. (Mrs.) 79, 98, 114, 121
Elkin, Jacob .26
Elkin, M. 88
Elkin, Max 26
Elkin, R. (Miss) 77
Elkin, Rose (Miss) 26, 79
Elkin, S. 75
Elkin, Samuel 26, 127, 144
Ellenberg, J. 106
Ellenson, Esther (Miss) 40
Ellenson, Ethel (Miss) 79
Ellenson, M. .40
Ellenson, Mordecai I. 174
Ellenson, Mordecai, I. 133
Ellenson, Moses (Mr. and Mrs.) 174
Ellinson, S. .158
Ellis, E. 70
Ellis, J.B. 68, 79
Ellison, A. 79, 112
Ellison, Annie (Miss) 36
Ellison, B. 34
Ellison, E. 79
Ellison, E. (Mr. and Mrs.) 9
Ellison, H. (Mr. and Mrs.) 36
Ellison, H.S. (Dr.) 185
Ellison, Hilda (Miss) 36
Ellison, J.B. (Mrs.) 62
Ellison, Joseph Bernard 91
Ellison, Kate (Miss) 79
Ellison, M. 79
Ellison, Miss .79
Ellison, Mr. 59

Ellison, Rebecca (Miss) 36, 126
Ellison, T. 79
Ellison, W. 79
Elman, E. 57
Elman, Mischa 79, 155, 176
Elman, Saul 176
Elstein, L. 51
Elzas, Barnett A. (Rev. Dr.) 5
Endelman, Ruth (Miss) 74, 79
Engel, A. 79
Engel, Adam .79
Engel, Beckie (Miss) 77
Engel, N.L. 26
Engel, Sarah (Miss) 77
Engelberg, A. 14
Engelberg, A.J. 14
Engelberg, Copel 70
Engelberg, Jennie (Miss) 32
Engelberg, Leah (Mrs.) 14
Engelberg, S. 14
Engle, E. (Miss) 40
Engle, J. (Miss) 173
Engle, R. (Miss) 40
Engleberg, Jennie (Miss) 32
Engleberg, S. (Mr. and Mrs.) 32
Engleman, H. 127
Engleman, Mrs. 85
Engleman, Pauline (Miss) 46, 79
Engleman, S. 79
Engleman, Solomon 46
Engler, Samuel 27
English, B. .117
Englsen, Miss 149
Enrich, S.M. .79
Enushevsky, I. 79
Enushevsky, Jennie (Miss) 157
Enushevsky, jr. I. 79
Enzer, I. 170
Enzer, J. 170
Enzer, Joseph 170
Enzer, M.S. (Mrs.) 64
Enzer, Mr. 79
Ephraim, Doris (Miss) 169
Eppenstein, Mr. and Mrs. 79
Epstein, D. (Rev.) 24
Epstein, D.H. (Mr. and Mrs.) 79
Epstein, D.H. (Mrs.) 72
Epstein, Dave 57
Epstein, David 2, 58
Epstein, Elizabeth (Miss) 161
Epstein, Gershon Abraham 9
Epstein, H. 79
Epstein, H.L. 183
Epstein, Harry 26
Epstein, Hilda (Miss) 131
Epstein, J. 183
Epstein, J. (Mr. and Mrs.) 9
Epstein, J. (Mrs.) 13
Epstein, Kate (Miss) 79
Epstein, L. 148, 150
Epstein, Libbie (Miss) 79, 148, 167
Epstein, Lillian (Miss) 161
Epstein, M. 171, 173
Epstein, M. (Mrs.) 79
Epstein, Max 79, 171
Epstein, Max (Mr. and Mrs.) 79
Epstein, Mrs. 79
Epstein, Misses 160
Epstein, Polly (Miss) 106
Epstein, R. (Miss) 173
Epstein, R. (Mrs.) 79
Epstein, S. (Mrs.) 151
Epstein, Sam 57

Epstein, Sarah (Miss) 106
Epstein, Sophie (Miss) 79, 156
Epstein, W. (Mrs.) 79
Erdilefsky, A. 26
Erdilefsky, Molly (Miss) 79
Erdrich, Jennie 118
Erdrich, Jennie (Miss) 134
Erdrich, Max (Master) 76
Erdrich, Mr. and Mrs. 79
Erdrich, S. .134
Erkheimer, A. 80
Erksheimer, A. 80
Erlinger, Julius 183
Ernstein, H. .68
Erron, Joseph 11
Ert, Michael (Mrs.) 39
Erxsheimer, A. 80
Eschenbaum, Mrs. 66
Eschner, Beatrice (Miss) 31
Espar, Edith (Miss) 165
Espar, Miss .23
Espar, Mr. and Mrs. 23
Esper, Esther 41
Etcovitch, William 65
Ettenberg, Bernard 46
Ettenberg, J. 49
Ettenberg, J. (Mr. and Mrs.) 71, 80, 120
Ettenberg, J. (Mrs.) 19, 103, 179
Ettenberg, Joseph 80
Ettenberg, Joseph (Mrs.) 147
Ettenberg, Mrs. 124
Ettson, Esther (Miss) 148
Evans, Harry 185
Evans, Harry (Mrs.) 86
Exler, J. 162
Ezekiel, Bert. (Mr. and Mrs.) 80
Factor, S. 158
Factor, Sam 157, 168
Factor, Samuel 154, 157, 167
Fainer, C.B. (Mrs.) 64, 78
Fainman, G. (Mr. and Mrs.) 160
Fairbank, Miss 80
Falick, A. 2
Falsin, I. 184
Farber, Max .59
Farber, R. 46
Farber, R. (Mrs.) 185
Farber, R. (Rabbi) 27
Farrar, W. 172
Faube, Mrs. 167
Fauman, Dave 172
Feather, J. .155
Fedderman, B. (Miss) 84
Fedderman, L. (Miss) 84
Feder, B. 57
Feen, Sarah (Miss) 80, 86, 139
Fefferman, Sam (Mr. and Mrs.) 183
Feiczewicz, D. (Mr. and Mrs.) 26
Feiczewicz, Rebekah (Miss) 26
Feiczweicz, L. 26
Feigelson, Annie (Miss) 35, 128
Feigelson, H. 74, 78, 143
Feigelson, H. (Mr. and Mrs.) 35
Feigleson, Annie (Miss) 35
Feigleson, David 35
Feigleson, H. (Mr. and Mrs.) 35
Feigleson, Hyman (Mr. and Mrs.) 35
Fein, M. 158
Fein, Samuel (Mr. and Mrs.) 97
Feinberg, B. (Mr. and Mrs.) 32
Feinberg, Bernard 80
Feinberg, H. (Mrs.) 80
Feinberg, Harry 26

Feinberg, Harry (Mrs.)	80	
Feinberg, L.	157	
Feinberg, Libbie (Miss)	32	
Feinberg, M.	183	
Feiner, P.	80	
Feingold, Louis	14, 42	
Feingold, N. (Mr. and Mrs.)	14	
Feinman, Annie (Miss)	28	
Feinstein, D.	183	
Feinstein, I.	57	
Feinstein, John	182	
Feinstein, Mrs.	158	
Feldheim, Martin	152	
Feldheim, Nellie (Miss)	20	
Feldman, A. (Mr. and Mrs.)	41	
Feldman, Ben	167	
Feldman, D.	63, 81, 114	
Feldman, I.J.	80	
Feldman, Ida (Miss)	80	
Feldman, J.	70	
Feldman, L. (Miss)	138	
Feldman, Libbie (Miss)	29	
Feldman, M.	80, 81	
Feldman, Minnie	42	
Feldman, Minnie (Miss)	128	
Feldman, Mr.	66	
Feldman, R. (Miss)	138	
Feldman, Rose (Miss)	29, 41, 74	
Feldman, S.	74	
Feldman, S. (Mrs.)	80	
Feldman, S.J.	80	
Feldman, Samuel H.	80	
Feldman, Sophie (Miss)	80, 128	
Feldstein, H.	81	
Feldstein, Harry	114	
Feldstein, I. (Mrs.)	114	
Feldstein, Ida (Miss)	22, 77	
Feldstein, M.	139	
Feldstein, M. (Mr. and Mrs.)	22, 23, 83, 116	
Feldstein, M. (Mrs.)	139	
Feldstein, Mr.	86	
Feldstein, Rose (Miss)	63, 77	
Feldstein, Rose Margaret (Miss)	22, 23	
Fels, A. (Mrs.)	80	
Fels, D.	59	
Fels, D. (Mrs.)	26, 99, 121	
Fels, Joseph	176	
Fels, Minnie (Miss)	80	
Fels, Mr. and Mrs.	80	
Fels, S.Z.	103	
Fels, Sarah (Mrs.)	14	
Felsen, M. (Mrs.)	13	
Felsen, O. (Mr. and Mrs.)	2	
Fencer, A.	37	
Fend, Sarah (Mrs.)	14	
Fenster, C. (Miss)	99	
Fenster, Carrie (Miss)	80	
Fenster, H.	81	
Fenster, H. (Mr. and Mrs.)	80	
Fenster, Issie	26	
Fenster, M.	81, 106	
Fenster, S.	63	
Ferber, Henry	167	
Ferguson, Ettie (Miss)	29	
Ferguson, Eva (Mrs.)	29	
Ferguson, Miriam (Miss)	148	
Ferierstock, Miss	157	
Ferstadt, Jennie (Miss)	167	
Fetzer, E.C.	156	
Fiderski, Ray (Miss)	80	
Fierst, Harry	80	
Figler, B. (Master)	137	
Filatreault, F.	130	
Fin, Miriam (Miss)	167	
Finberg, I.	168	
Finberg, Isidor	157	
Finberg, Isidore	157	
Finburgh, Alfred	80	
Finburgh, Alfred A.	80	
Finckle, Mr.	40	
Findlay, Miss	172	
Fine, B. (Miss)	149	
Fine, Becca (Miss)	153	
Fine, Beccie (Miss)	152, 153	
Fine, Beckie (Miss)	152	
Fine, Becky (Miss)	25, 149	
Fine, Elias	26	
Fine, J.	163	
Fine, Joseph	112	
Fine, M.	148, 149	
Fine, M. (Mr. and Mrs.)	25, 148, 149, 152	
Fine, M. (Mrs.)	149, 152	
Fine, Maurice	149	
Fine, Maurice (Mr. and Mrs.)	149, 160	
Fine, Maurice (Mrs.)	25, 157	
Fine, Morris	80	
Fine, Mr.	150	
Fine, Mrs.	152	
Fine, Ray (Miss)	40	
Fine, Rose (Miss)	25, 80, 148, 149, 151-153, 157	
Fineberg, A.	59, 78	
Fineberg, A. (Mr. and Mrs.)	26, 81	
Fineberg, A.H.	81	
Fineberg, A.J.	81	
Fineberg, Agnes (Miss)	3, 81	
Fineberg, Alfred	80	
Fineberg, Bess (Miss)	79	
Fineberg, F. (Miss)	81	
Fineberg, Fanny (Miss)	33	
Fineberg, H.	115	
Fineberg, H.A.	67	
Fineberg, H.S.	26, 66, 67, 81	
Fineberg, Harry	80, 145	
Fineberg, I.	169	
Fineberg, J.	80, 89, 139	
Fineberg, Joe	46	
Fineberg, Joseph	3, 65, 68, 81	
Fineberg, Lena (Miss)	46	
Fineberg, M.	46, 106	
Fineberg, M. (Mrs.)	79, 81, 128	
Fineberg, Max	122	
Fineberg, Max (Master)	81	
Fineberg, Max (Mr. and Mrs.)	75, 81, 110	
Fineberg, Maxie (Master)	81	
Fineberg, Moe	80	
Fineberg, Moses	42	
Fineberg, Mrs.	81, 139	
Fineberg, N.	60, 61, 111	
Fineberg, N.S.	34, 81, 88, 122	
Fineberg, Nathan	6, 122	
Fineberg, Nathan S.	81	
Fineberg, Nathaniel S.	6, 66	
Fineberg, Rose (Miss)	79, 81	
Fineberg, Rosie (Miss)	26	
Fineberg, S.	92	
Fineberg, Z.	6, 19, 45, 59, 81, 84, 115, 146	
Fineberg, Z. (Mr. and Mrs.)	80, 81	
Fineberg, Z. (Mrs.)	17, 45, 81	
Fineberg, Zigmond	81	
Fineman, N.	158	
Finemark, D. (Miss)	162	
Finemark, Dora (Miss)	167	
Finemark, Mr.	156	
Finesilver, G. (Miss)	179	
Finesilver, Goldie L.	177	
Finesilver, H. (Mrs.)	179	
Finestein, Harry	26	
Finestone, J.	49	
Finestone, M.	90	
Finestone, Mrs.	100	
Finestone, Ted	26	
Fingerhoot, Mr.	163	
Fink, Becky (Miss)	40	
Fink, Isidore	158	
Fink, L. (Mr. and Mrs.)	40	
Fink, Morris	26	
Finkelman, Charles	14	
Finkelman, H.	178	
Finkelman, Harry (Mr. and Mrs.)	9	
Finkelman, I.	14	
Finkelman, Mr. and Mrs.	182	
Finkelstein	180	
Finkelstein, A. (Miss)	68	
Finkelstein, B. (Mr. and Mrs.)	26	
Finkelstein, D.	157	
Finkelstein, D. (Master)	175	
Finkelstein, D.B.	171	
Finkelstein, Dave	176	
Finkelstein, H.	149, 152, 157, 158, 168	
Finkelstein, Harry	149, 157	
Finkelstein, Ida (Miss)	175	
Finkelstein, Joseph	177	
Finkelstein, K.	179	
Finkelstein, Louis	156	
Finkelstein, Louise	176, 180	
Finkelstein, M.	7, 152, 177, 179, 180	
Finkelstein, M. (Mrs.)	149, 176, 177, 181	
Finkelstein, M.J.	46, 176, 177	
Finkelstein, M.P.	87	
Finkelstein, Max	177	
Finkelstein, Max (Mr. and Mrs.)	81	
Finkelstein, Max J.	177	
Finkelstein, Moses	175	
Finkelstein, Moses Philip	42	
Finkelstein, Mr. and Mrs.	81, 82	
Finkelstein, Nathan	26	
Finkelstein, Rose (Miss)	26, 149	
Finkelstein, S.	149	
Finkelstein, T.	180	
Finkelstein, T. (Mr. and Mrs.)	177	
Finkelstein, T. (Mrs.)	177, 179	
Finkelstein, W.	63, 65	
Finkelstein, Willie	176, 180	
Finkleman, G. (Miss)	176	
Finkleman, Harry (Mr. and Mrs.)	9	
Finkleman, Isadore	14	
Finkleman, J. (Mrs.)	179	
Finkleman, Jacob	14	
Finkleman, Joseph	14	
Finkleman, S.	14	
Finklestein, H. (Mr. and Mrs.)	29	
Finklestein, Harry	157	
Finklestein, M.	177	
Finklestein, M. (Alderman)	177	
Finklestein, M. (Mrs.)	152	
Finklestein, Mr. and Mrs. M.	9	
Finmark, Doris (Miss)	38	
Finn, C.F.	149	
Finn, C.I. (Mrs.)	149	
Finn, L. (Miss)	148, 150	
Finn, Libbie (Miss)	81, 149, 150	
Finn, Miss	149, 150	
Finstein, J.	14	
Firerstock, Jennie (Miss)	164	
Firestein, Mrs.	146	
Firestone, H.	61, 136	
Firth, John S. (Mr. and Mrs.)	81	
Fischbein, Rose (Miss)	81	
Fischel, G.	81	

Fischel, G. (Mrs.) ... 64, 79, 81, 94, 115, 146
Fischel, Gus 14
Fischel, Gus (Mr. and Mrs.) 75
Fischel, Gus (Mrs.) 14, 65, 81, 115
Fischel, Gus. (Mr. and Mrs.) 65
Fischel, Gus. (Mrs.) 81
Fischel, Gustav (Mr. and Mrs.) 81
Fischel, Gustav (Mrs.) 93
Fischel, Gustave (Mr. and Mrs.) 2
Fischel, Gustave (Mrs.) 6, 93, 115, 128
Fischel, Leon 2
Fischel, Leon (Master) 81
Fischel, P. 98
Fischel, Rudolph 81
Fischel, S. 24
Fischel, S. (Mr. and Mrs.) 81
Fischel, S. (Mrs.) 15, 81, 146
Fischel, Sarah 81
Fischel, Sigmund 14, 90
Fischel, Victor 81
Fischman, Mr. and Mrs. 9
Fischman, Norman (Master) 81
Fischman, S. 81
Fischman, S. (Mr. and Mrs.) 149, 151
Fischman, S. (Mrs.) 81
Fish, A. (Mr. and Mrs.) 23
Fish, Abraham (Mr. and Mrs.) 23
Fish, Fannie (Miss) 23
Fish, J.B. (Dr.) 81, 111
Fish, Joseph (Dr.) 6, 89
Fishbein, Mr. and Mrs. 171, 172
Fisher, C. 81
Fisher, Charles 65, 68, 81, 112, 134, 139
Fisher, Chas. 45
Fisher, J. 81
Fisher, K. (Mrs.) 82
Fisher, Miss 82
Fisher, Misses 28
Fisher, Mr. and Mrs. 82
Fisher, R. (Miss) 169
Fisher, Rose (Miss) 161
Fisher, S. 26
Fisher, S. (Mrs.) 82
Fisherman, Mrs. 82
Fisherman, Norman (Master) 82
Fishkin, J. (Mr. and Mrs.) 39, 174
Fishkin, Minnie (Miss) 39, 174
Fishman, H. 86
Fishman, Harry 42
Fishman, M. 82
Fishman, P. 82
Fishman, P. (Mr. and Mrs.) 9, 82
Fishman, P. (Mrs.) 82
Fishman, Philip 26
Fishman, S. 149
Fishman, S. (Mr. and Mrs.) 40, 149
Fishtrom, Mr. 182
Fitch, Charles 26
Fitch, L. 47
Fitch, Louis ... 6, 25, 46, 47, 67, 81, 82, 111,
114, 157
Fitch, Louis (B.A.) 47
Fitch, O. (Mr. and Mrs.) 23
Fitch, Rebecca (Miss) 23
Fitzger, Miss 150
Flanders, A.H. 82
Flanders, F. (Miss) 64, 80, 99
Flanders, Fanny (Miss) 77, 80, 86
Flanders, Goldie (Miss) 79
Flanders, M. 64, 66, 72, 82, 131, 134
Flanders, M. (Mr. and Mrs.) 26
Flanders, Mary (Miss) 26, 80
Fleischman, William 82

Fleishman, A.C. 185
Fleishman, A.C. (Mrs.) 185
Fleishman, Arthur 155, 157
Fleishman, J. 23
Fleishman, Mayer 180
Fleishman, Pansy (Miss) 23
Fleisig, David 82
Fleisig, Rae (Miss) 82
Fleisig, Ray (Miss) 82
Fleisig, Samuel 82
Florence, A. 82
Florence, A. (Mr. and Mrs.) 26
Florence, A.E. (Mr. and Mrs.) 2
Florence, A.L. 34, 152
Florence, A.L. (Mr. and Mrs.) 24
Florence, A.L. (Mrs.) 149
Florence, D. 2
Florence, Jacob 2
Florence, Miss 82
Florence, P. 82
Florence, Philip M. 26
Florence, Sophie (Miss) 82, 106
Florin, B. (Mr. and Mrs.) 30
Florin, D. 109
Florin, J. (Mrs.) 30
Florin, Mrs. 101
Florin, Phil 101
Florin, Phillip 30
Florin, Sarah (Miss) 30
Fogel, Harry S. 177
Fogel, Sarah (Mrs.) 182
Fogle, J.R. (Mr. and Mrs.) 149
Fogle, Mrs. 150
Fogle, N. (Miss) 149
Fogler, Ben 157
Fogler, H.B. 168
Fogler, L. (Miss) 168
Forcimer, B. (Mr. and Mrs.) 30
Forcimer, Birdie (Miss) 30
Forcimer, E. (Mr. and Mrs.) 82
Forcimmer, B. (Mr. and Mrs.) 30
Forcimmer, Bertha (Miss) 30
Forcimmer, N. (Mrs.) 13
Forcimmer, Nathan 14
Forgan, Clara (Mrs.) 181
Forgan, Mrs. 180
Forman, E. (Miss) 149
Forman, Edith 42
Foss, A. 82
Foss, Alfred 113
Foss, J. (Mr. and Mrs.) 101
Foss, L. (Mr. and Mrs.) 82
Foss, Louis 14, 113
Fostovsky, B. (Master) 175
Fox, Bernard 81, 82
Fox, Brina (Miss) 26
Fox, J. (Mr. and Mrs.) 146
Fox, M. 101
Fox, Mr. and Mrs. 82
Fox, Mrs. 26
Fox, N. 170
Fox, S. 77, 78
Fox, S. (Mr. and Mrs.) 87
Fox, Samuel 171
Fox, T. (Mr. and Mrs.) 35
Fraenkel, H. (Mr. and Mrs.) 9
Fraenkel, Leo 157
Fraenkel, Leo (Mr. and Mrs.) 164
Fraenkel, Maurice (Mrs.) 157
Fraid, A. 40
Fraid, Beatrice (Miss) 29, 83
Fraid, Bertram (Master) 83
Fraid, Dave 49

Fraid, Dora (Miss) 40, 82
Fraid, Dora Z. (Miss) 40
Fraid, J.B. (Mrs.) 40
Fraid, Joseph 40, 82
Fraid, L. 40
Fraid, L. (Mr. and Mrs.) 82
Fraid, L. (Mrs.) 40, 105
Fraid, Lou (Mr. and Mrs.) 82
Fraid, Louis 2, 82
Fraid, Louis (Mr. and Mrs.) 83, 144
Fraid, Louis (Mrs.) 83
Fraid, Mollie (Miss) 40, 82
Fraid, Mr. 7
Fraid, Mr. and Mrs. 2
Fraid, Mrs. 83
Fraid, N. (Mr. and Mrs.) 74
Fraid, N. (Mrs.) 85
Fraid, N.J. 40
Fraid, N.J. (Mr. and Mrs.) 9
Fraid, N.J. (Mrs.) 83, 105
Fraid, Nathan 82, 83
Fraid, Nathan (Mr. and Mrs.) 82
Fraid, Nathan (Mrs.) 83
Fraid, Nathan J. 6
Frank, A. 149
Frank, Abraham (Mrs.) 171
Frank, Annie (Miss) 35, 134
Frank, David 118
Frank, David (Master) 76
Frank, Esther 118
Frank, F. (Miss) 67
Frank, Fannie (Miss) 33
Frank, Fanny (Miss) 118
Frank, Henry 157
Frank, Henry (Mrs.) 161
Frank, Khos. (Mr. and Mrs.) 33, 83
Frank, Khos. (Mrs.) 118
Frank, L. (Mrs.) 83, 151
Frank, Leah (Madame) 34
Frank, Louis 83
Frank, M. .. 67, 80, 91, 114, 115, 120, 130, 148
Frank, M. (Miss) 88, 112
Frank, Miss 38, 81, 83, 113
Frank, Mr. and Mrs. 83
Frank, Mrs. 136
Frank, Rose (Miss) 83, 86
Frank, S. 78
Frank, S. (Mrs.) 83
Frank, Thos. (Mr. and Mrs.) 79
Frankel, Carl 157
Frankel, Egmont 157
Frankel, Gottschall (Herr and Frau) ... 157
Frankel, H. 90, 162
Frankel, H.B. (Mrs.) 60, 83
Frankel, Herman (Mr. and Mrs.) 157
Frankel, Herman (Mrs.) 113
Frankel, Ike 157
Frankel, Ivan 157
Frankel, Joseph 157
Frankel, L. 68
Frankel, Leo 157, 158, 166, 168
Frankel, Leo (Mr. and Mrs.) 157
Frankel, Leo (Mrs.) 157, 161, 166
Frankel, Leo M. 157
Frankel, Louis 157
Frankel, Maurice (Mr. and Mrs.) ... 157, 166
Frankel, Maurice (Mrs.) 47, 157, 158
Frankel, Mrs. 157
Frankel, Roy 157
Frankel, S. 180
Frankel, S. (Mr. and Mrs.) 166
Frankenberg, F. 185
Frankenberg, L. (Mrs.) 185

Frankenburg, L. (Mrs.) 185
Frankenstein, F. 176
Frankenstein, M.L. 175, 177
Frankfurter, Ed. 179
Frankfurter, Edgar (Mrs.) 177
Frankfurter, G. 176, 179
Frankfurter, G. (Mrs.) 175, 177
Frankfurter, George (Mrs.) 179
Frankfurter, Roy (Mrs.) 176, 177, 179
Frankle, Minnie (Miss) 39
Frankle, Mr. and Mrs. 39
Franklin, Abraham 43
Franklin, Audrey Dorothy (Miss) 60
Franklin, Dora (Miss) 164
Franklin, Ellis 102
Franklin, F. (Mr. and Mrs.) 9
Franklin, H. 83
Franklin, H.B. (Mrs.) 13, 60
Franklin, H.M. (Mrs.) 60
Franklin, Harry B. (Mr. and Mrs.) 9
Franklin, Harry B. (Mrs.) 60
Franklin, J.A. 83
Franklin, J.L. 83
Franklin, M. 14
Franklin, Mr. 83
Franklin, Mrs. 60
Franklin, Simon 82
Franklin, W.A. (Mr. and Mrs.) 9
Franks, Cecile (Miss) 14
Franks, Mary (Miss) 35
Franks, Rose (Miss) 34
Franks, S.G. 139
Franks, Sadie (Miss) 30
Franks, Z. 34
Fred, Mr. and Mrs. 40
Fredin, Fanny (Dame) 83
Freed, Harry 26, 156
Freed, Harry (Mr. and Mrs.) 9
Freed, M. 58
Freed, M. (Mrs.) 185
Freedman, A. (Dr.) 83, 117
Freedman, A. (Mrs.) 22
Freedman, A.L. (Mrs.) 83
Freedman, A.O. (Dr.) 83
Freedman, Albert 26, 83, 134
Freedman, Albert (Mr. and Mrs.) 9
Freedman, B. 83, 182
Freedman, B. (Mr. and Mrs.) 2, 83
Freedman, B. (Mrs.) 83
Freedman, Barney (Mrs.) 128
Freedman, Celia (Miss) 103
Freedman, D. 83
Freedman, D.S. 83
Freedman, E. 88
Freedman, Eva (Miss) 83
Freedman, Fanny 42
Freedman, H. 59
Freedman, H. (Mrs.) 128
Freedman, H.M. (Mrs.) 95
Freedman, H.W. (Mr. and Mrs.) 9
Freedman, H.W. (Mrs.) 83
Freedman, Harry 49
Freedman, Harry (Mr. and Mrs.) . . 9, 83, 85
Freedman, Hiram 108
Freedman, Hiram (Mr. and Mrs.) 75
Freedman, I. 83
Freedman, I. (Mr. and Mrs.) 139
Freedman, I. (Mrs.) 67
Freedman, Isidore 83
Freedman, Isidore (Mr. and Mrs.) 83
Freedman, Isidore (Mr. and Mrs.) and daughter 118
Freedman, Isidore (Mrs.) 83
Freedman, J. 143, 149
Freedman, J. (Mrs.) 149-151
Freedman, Jennie (Miss) 150
Freedman, Leonore (Miss) 49, 103
Freedman, Levi 14
Freedman, Lewis (Master) 83
Freedman, Louis 2
Freedman, M. 83
Freedman, Margery Adele (Miss) 34
Freedman, Max 83
Freedman, May (Miss) 32
Freedman, Moe 83
Freedman, Mr. and Mrs. 9, 26
Freedman, Mrs. 166
Freedman, N.F. 157
Freedman, Nancy (Miss) 131
Freedman, Nathan 42
Freedman, Rachel 83
Freedman, Rebecca (Miss) 33
Freedman, S. 59
Freedman, S. (Mr. and Mrs.) 26
Freedman, Sadie (Miss) 103
Freedman, Sam 83
Freedman, Seymour (Dr.) 83
Freedman, Sid. 172
Freedman, T. (Mrs.) 83
Freeman, A. (Mrs.) 152
Freeman, Annie (Miss) 84
Freeman, H. 157
Freeman, H. (Miss) 98
Freeman, H. (Mrs.) 79, 115
Freeman, H.D. 84
Freeman, Hyalie (Miss) 67, 84
Freeman, Hyallie (Miss) 84, 128
Freeman, Hyman (Mr. and Mrs.) 9
Freeman, J. 179
Freeman, J. (Mrs.) 84
Freeman, K. 84
Freeman, K. (Mrs.) 84
Freeman, Kalman 15
Freeman, Kelman 15
Freeman, M. (Miss) 88
Freeman, Miss 32
Freeman, Mr. 169
Freeman, Mr. and Mrs. 25
Freeman, Myer (Mrs.) 84
Freeman, Nellie (Miss) 35, 165
Freeman, Pearl (Miss) 84, 150
Freeman, S. 84, 184
Freeman, Sadie (Miss) 84
Freeman, Sim. 84
Freemnan, Pearl (Miss) 84
Freidlander, Elias (Rev.) 84
Freidlich, A.M. 62
Freidman, Albert 122
Freidman, Eva (Miss) 84
Freidman, I. (Mr. and Mrs.) 84
Freidman, J. (Mr. and Mrs.) 160
Freidman, Louis 84
Freidman, Nolan 84
Freidman, Ralph 84
Freidman, Samuel 59
Freiman, A.J. 84, 149, 150
Freiman, A.J. (Mr. and Mrs.) . . . 10, 25, 149
Freiman, A.J. (Mrs.) . . . 31, 84, 149, 150, 152
Freiman, Archibald (Mrs.) 84
Freiman, Archie J. (Mrs.) 149
Freiman, H. 65
Freiman, H. (Mr. and Mrs.) 10, 84
Freiman, H. (Mrs.) 152
Freiman, H.J. 152
Freiman, Hyalie (Miss) 93
Freiman, Lawrence 149
Freiman, Mr. and Mrs. 79
Freiman, Pearl (Miss) 84
Fremers, I. 162
Fremes, A. (Mrs.) 165
Fremes, C. 167, 169
Fremes, Charlie 161
Fremes, Jennie (Miss) 161
Fremes, M. 169
Fremes, Max 161
Fremes, Miss 164
Fremes, Mrs. 156, 165, 167
Fremes, S. 161
Fremes, S. (Mr. and Mrs.) 157
Fremes, S. (Mrs.) 165
Fresco, James (Mrs.) 21
Fresco, Mrs. 21
Freund (Mr.) 15
Freund, A. (Mrs.) 185
Freund, Emil 84
Fridmann, S.M. 47
Fried, M. (Miss) 57
Fried, Max (Mrs.) 57
Fried, Miss 174
Friedberg, Mrs. 169
Friedenthal, H. 183
Friedland, Morris 15
Friedland, Mr. and Mrs. 15
Friedlander, E. (Rabbi) 93, 185
Friedlander, Elias (Rabbi) 185
Friedlander, Elias (Rev.) 47
Friedlander, Israel (Dr.) 84
Friedlander, J. (Rabbi) . . . 47, 168, 171, 172
Friedlander, J. (Rev.) 47, 171
Friedlander, J. Israel (Professor) 84
Friedlander, Joseph (Dr.) 171
Friedlieb, A.M. 122
Friedman, A. (Mr. and Mrs.) 22, 23
Friedman, A.L. (Mrs.) 128
Friedman, Abe (Mrs.) 129
Friedman, Adolph 15
Friedman, Albert 118
Friedman, Annie (Miss) 22, 23, 107
Friedman, Arthur 2
Friedman, B. (Mr. and Mrs.) 9
Friedman, B. (Mrs.) 85
Friedman, Bella (Miss) 155
Friedman, Benjamin 26
Friedman, Bertha (Miss) 107
Friedman, C. (Mr. and Mrs.) 84
Friedman, C.L. 98, 102
Friedman, C.L. (Mr. and Mrs.) 84, 85
Friedman, C.L. (Mrs.) 2, 85, 108
Friedman, Celia (Miss) 32
Friedman, Charles (Mrs.) 77
Friedman, Charles L. 109
Friedman, Charles L. (Mrs.) 144
Friedman, D. 107, 155
Friedman, D.F. 59
Friedman, D.S. 19, 20, 84, 113
Friedman, D.S. (Mr. and Mrs.) . . . 2, 77, 85
Friedman, D.S. (Mrs.) . . 40, 67, 85, 102, 146
Friedman, David 84
Friedman, Eli M. 88
Friedman, Eva (Miss) 60, 77, 84
Friedman, H. 84, 158
Friedman, H. (Mr. and Mrs.) 138
Friedman, H. (Mrs.) 85
Friedman, H.A. 184
Friedman, H.N. 60, 70
Friedman, Harry 157
Friedman, Hess. N. 84
Friedman, Hesse 84

Friedman, Hyman 15	Futrel, Annie (Miss) 149	Gelber, George (Mrs.) 86
Friedman, I. 78, 98	Futtrell, Annie (Miss) 152	Gelber, L. 154
Friedman, I. (Miss) 22	Fyne, S. (Mrs.) 151	Gelber, L. (Mr. and Mrs.) 23, 160
Friedman, I. (Mr. and Mrs.) 2, 85	Fyne, S. (Rabbi) . . . 9, 14, 25, 28, 31, 39, 42,	Gelber, L. (Mrs.) 119, 154
Friedman, Ida (Miss) 22	46, 47, 148-152	Gelber, Lipa 157
Friedman, Isaac 62, 98, 109	Gabriel, J.S. (Mr. and Mrs.) 9, 84, 112	Gelber, Lipa (Mr. and Mrs.) 157
Friedman, Isaac (Mr. and Mrs.) 85, 91	Gabriel, J.S. (Mrs.) . . . 85, 111, 112, 115, 149	Gelber, Louis 162
Friedman, Isidore 15, 25, 62, 84, 122	Gaetz, Rudolph 42	Gelber, Louis (Mr. and Mrs.) 9
Friedman, Isidore (Mrs.) 14, 85, 106	Gakky, Mr. 175	Gelber, M. 86, 154, 157, 162
Friedman, J. (Mrs.) 23	Galitzki, Mr. and Mrs. 85	Gelber, M. (Mr. and Mrs.) 23
Friedman, Jack 15, 26, 84	Gallay, R. (Miss) 80, 99	Gelber, Miss 37
Friedman, Jacob 26, 149	Gallay, Rose (Miss) 86	Gelber, Mr. 163, 169
Friedman, Joe 22	Gallen, Louis 57	Gelber, Mrs. 119
Friedman, L. 49	Gallen, Luis 57	Gelbman, M. 2, 45, 83, 86, 138
Friedman, L. (Mrs.) 84	Gallet, Joseph (Mrs.) 85	Gelbman, M. (Mr. and Mrs.) 86, 108
Friedman, Leah 66	Gallin, C. 152	Gelbman, M. (Mrs.) 45, 86
Friedman, Levy (Mrs.) 16	Gallop, Miss 85	Gelbman, Max 47, 61, 86, 112
Friedman, M. 171	Gally, Rose (Miss) 85	Gelbman, Reba (Miss) 107
Friedman, Malca (Miss) 106	Gameroff, B. 59	Geldsaler, B. 169
Friedman, Max 26, 84, 171	Gamsu, Lena (Miss) 85	Geldzaeler, Alfred B. (Master) 2
Friedman, Mr. 182	Garafe, Samuel 85	Geldzaeler, B. 156
Friedman, Mr. and Mrs. I. 2	Garbent, Mr. 169	Geldzaeler, B. (Miss) 168
Friedman, Mrs. 83, 91	Garber, E. (Mr. and Mrs.) 85	Geldzaeler, Ben 157
Friedman, N. 85	Garber, Ellie 26, 85	Geldzaeler, L. 157
Friedman, N. (Mrs.) 6, 83-85	Garber, Frank (Master) 157	Geldzaeler, M. (Mr. and Mrs.) 2
Friedman, Noel 48	Garber, I. 57	Geldzaeler, Miss 161
Friedman, Noel D. 84	Garber, L.E. 85	Geldzaeler, Mrs. 167
Friedman, Norman 2, 67	Garber, M. 47, 60, 61, 66, 88, 102	Geldzaeler, R. (Miss) 169
Friedman, Norman (Master) 77, 85	Garber, M. (Mr. and Mrs.) 157	Geldzaeler, Ray (Miss) 167
Friedman, Ralph 40, 85	Garber, Rabbi 85, 141	Geldzaeler, Rosa (Miss) 167
Friedman, Rebecca (Mrs.) 6	Garber, S. (Rabbi and Mrs.) 26, 133	Geldzaeler, Rose (Miss) 154, 161
Friedman, S.D. (Mr. and Mrs.) 85	Garber, S. (Rabbi) 85	Geldzaler, M. (Mrs.) 167
Friedman, S.D. (Mrs.) 37	Gardiner, B. 28	Geldzaler, Mr. and Mrs. 160
Friedman, Sara (Miss) 63	Gardiner, Jacob 157	Gelin, Annie (Mrs.) 15
Friedman, Sidney 171	Gardner, Adolph 86, 88	Gelin, M. 15
Friedman, W. 149	Gardner, B. 24, 49, 98, 181	Geller, G. (Mr. and Mrs.) 177
Friedman, Walter 85	Gardner, M. (Mr. and Mrs.) 177	Geller, G. (Mrs.) 65
Friefeld, G.H. 114, 134	Gardner, Mr. and Mrs. 39	Geller, George (Miss) 143
Friefeld, H.G. 72, 82	Gardner, N. 86	Geller, George (Mr. and Mrs.) 86
Friefeld, I. (Mr. and Mrs.) 30	Gardner, Yetta (Mrs.) 86	Geller, George (Mrs.) 86
Friefeld, Mildred (Miss) 30	Garfinkel, Mr. and Mrs. 23	Geller, George M. (Mrs.) 86
Frieman, Dr. 185	Garfinkel, S. 165	Geller, H. 108
Frieman, H. (Mr. and Mrs.) 107	Garfinkle, Annie M. (Miss) 47	Geller, Rhoda (Miss) 86
Friendly, Mr. 148	Garfinkle, E.T. 91	Geller, S. 66
Friendly, P. (Miss) 151	Garfinkle, J. 41	Geller, T. 131
Friendly, Pearl (Miss) 153	Garfinkle, J. (Miss) 84, 122	Geneson, M. 169
Frieze, Jack 26	Garfinkle, M. 80, 86, 91, 115	Geneson, Maurice 167
Frimes, Mr. 164	Garfinkle, Moe 67	Genesov, M. 157, 167
Frischling, Hattie (Miss) 85	Garfinkle, Mrs. 166	Genser, Aaron 176, 180
Frischling, L. 81	Garfinkle, P. 86, 91, 114, 122, 137	Genser, Claire (Miss) 37
Frischling, L. (Mr. and Mrs.) 85, 109	Garfinkle, T. 79, 80, 114, 115, 120, 130	Genser, E. (Mr. and Mrs.) 86
Frishberg, B. 183	Garfinkle, Ted 86	Genser, J. 40
Fritz, J. 85	Garfinkle, Teddy 67	Genser, Mae (Miss) 74
Frohman, C. 180	Garfunkel, Charles (Mr. and Mrs.) 157	Genser, Morris 164
Frohman, Jennie (Miss) 27	Garfunkel, J. 162	Gensor, Mary (Miss) 94
From, H. 185	Garfunkle, C. 161	Genzer, May (Miss) 94
Froman, D. 34	Gariepy, J.S. 183	Genzer, Mrs. 39
Frome, H. 185	Garmaise, A. 49	Gerlownin, Isaac Ben Naftali 177
Frome, Mr. 185	Garmaise, Anna (Miss) 140	Gerson, Mr. 172
Fromson, Abraham (Master) 2, 85	Garmaise, Hannah (Miss) 31	Gerson, Rachel (Miss) 80, 106
Fromson, M. 68, 79, 81, 85, 112, 114	Garmaise, Jacob 49	Gerstein, Anna (Miss) 31
Fromson, M. (Mr. and Mrs.) 2, 85	Garmaise, Miss 74	Gescheit, W. (Mrs.) 185
Fromson, S. 36	Garmaize, Hannah (Miss) 31	Gescheit, W.F. 185
Frooman, L.E. 47	Garrick, J. 91	Getz, L. (Mr. and Mrs.) 33
Fruchtman, F. 183, 184	Gart, Max 26	Getz, M. 86
Frueberg, Joe 66	Gart, Ralph 26	Getz, Max 119
Fruend, H. (Mrs.) 185	Gavrilowitz, Joseph Mendel (Mr. and	Getz, Misses 118, 119
Fuerst, Harry 35	Mrs.) 37	Getz, Rose (Miss) 33
Fuerst, Isidor 85	Gavrilowitz, Mary (Miss) 37	Getz, Tony (Miss) 33
Fuerst, Ph. 171	Geburtig, M. 157	Getzbun, Carl 26
Fundberg, Miss 163	Geffen, E. 86, 183, 184	Gevinsky, J. (Mrs.) 165
Furst, Ph. (Rabbi) 172	Geffen, M. 49	Gherman, Bennie 181
Futeral, A. (Mr. and Mrs.) 150	Gelber, G. 26, 162	Gherman, Mr. and Mrs. 182

Ghingold, Fannie (Miss) 22
Ghingold, S. 22
Ghitter, L. (Miss) 28
Ghitter, Leontina (Miss) 28
Ghitter, M. (Mr. and Mrs.) 28
Gilbert, A. 170
Gilbert, Bessie (Miss) 56
Gilbert, H. 56
Gilfund, Mr. and Mrs. 184
Gilled, M. (Mrs.) 134
Gillman, Harry 27
Ginns, N. 61
Ginsberg, A. (Miss) 99
Ginsberg, Anna (Miss) 80
Ginsberg, Annie (Miss) 86
Ginsberg, Arthur 66
Ginsberg, Belle (Miss) 86
Ginsberg, Helen (Miss) 86
Ginsberg, Hilda (Miss) 155
Ginsberg, I. (Miss) 157
Ginsberg, J. 86, 118
Ginsberg, J. (Mrs.) 86
Ginsberg, Jennie 42
Ginsberg, Jesse 69
Ginsberg, Jessie (Miss) 134
Ginsberg, Leba (Miss) 25, 37
Ginsberg, Leta (Miss) 86
Ginsberg, Libbie (Miss) 86
Ginsberg, Louis 86
Ginsberg, M. 17
Ginsberg, M. (Mr. and Mrs.) 25, 108
Ginsberg, M. (Mrs.) 62, 86
Ginsberg, Mendel 17
Ginsberg, Mrs. 99
Ginsberg, Rachel (Miss) 86
Ginsberg, Ray (Miss) 80
Ginsberg, Rose (Miss) 69
Ginsberg, Rosie (Miss) 134
Ginsberg, S. 61
Ginsberg, S. (Miss) 165, 169
Ginsberg, Selma A. (Miss) 86
Ginsburg, Annie (Miss) 158
Ginsburg, Belle (Miss) 100
Gintzburger, A. (Mrs.) 185
Gintzburger, M. 185
Gintzburger, S. 185
Gintzburger, S. (Mrs.) 185
Gintzburger, Sam 185
Gintzburger, Samuel (Mrs.) 185
Ginzberg, Jessie 118
Ginzberg, Rosie 118
Girdstone, Nathan 158
Gitson, A. 155
Gitson, Esther (Miss) 154
Gittelson, A.L. (Mr. and Mrs.) 86
Gittelson, E.G. 56
Gittelson, Eva (Miss) 67
Gittelson, J. (Mrs.) 57
Gittelson, J.L. (Mrs.) 121
Gittelson, Julius L. (Mr. and Mrs.) 86
Gittelson, Julius L. (Mrs.) 86
Gittelson, L. 86
Gittelson, Lawrence 86
Gittelson, Mr. 31, 148
Gittelson, Sarah 42
Gittelson, Sarah (Miss) 67
Gittleson, A. (Mrs.) 86
Gittleson, A.L. 49
Gittleson, A.L. (Mr. and Mrs.) 86
Gittleson, A.L. (Mrs.) 64, 141, 146
Gittleson, Abe L. (Mr. and Mrs.) 86
Gittleson, B. (Miss) 86
Gittleson, Eva (Miss) 77, 86, 98, 111

Gittleson, H. 130
Gittleson, H.L. 39, 149
Gittleson, J. (Mr. and Mrs.) 34
Gittleson, J.L. 49
Gittleson, J.L. (Mr. and Mrs.) . . . 120, 127
Gittleson, J.L. (Mrs.) 66, 86, 121
Gittleson, Julius (Mrs.) 86
Gittleson, L. 79
Gittleson, M. 148
Gittleson, Master 99
Gittleson, Mr. 34, 149
Gittleson, Sara (Miss) 77
Gittleson, Sophie 132
Glasau, S. 185
Glaser, Adolph 15
Glaser, Amy (Miss) 15
Glaser, Edwin V. 15
Glaser, Julius .15
Glaser, L. 123
Glaser, Lawrence 15
Glaser, Lewis .86
Glaser, Louis .15
Glaser, Morris 15
Glaser, Sigmund 15
Glaser, Simon (Rabbi) 86
Glaser, Walter 15
Glass, B. 137
Glass, Sidney H. 171
Glassberg, A. 157
Glassberg, Aaron 158, 163
Glassberg, Aaron (1st. Lieut.) 162
Glassbourg, E. (Mr. and Mrs.) 27
Glasser, Celia (Miss) 25
Glasser, David (Mr. and Mrs.) 25
Glassman, H. (Mr. and Mrs.) 183
Glassman, Joseph (Mrs.) 27
Glassman, Thomas 27
Glatt, Mr. 148
Glatt, Myer (Mr. and Mrs.) 149
Glazer, Louis .49
Glazer, Philip 34
Glazer, S. (Rabbi) 37, 86
Glazer, Simon (Rabbi) . 11, 13, 24, 27, 29, 30,
  34, 35, 39, 41, 46, 47,
  50, 86, 87, 141, 152
Glazer, Simon (Rev.) 39
Gleek, Samuel 158
Glenn, Samuel 27
Glesby, H. 180
Glickman, A. 47, 49, 50
Glickman, A. (Dr.) 34
Glickman, Alton 15
Glickman, B. 106
Glickman, B. (Mr. and Mrs.) 87, 89
Glickman, B. (Mrs.) 87
Glickman, D. .87
Glickman, D. (Miss) 87
Glickman, Ethel (Miss) 15
Glickman, I. 27
Glickman, I. (Mr. and Mrs.) 57
Glickman, J. 62
Glickman, L. 106
Glickman, Lawrence 2
Glickman, Lawrence (Master) 87
Glickman, Lillie (Miss) 87
Glickman, M. (Mr. and Mrs.) 141
Glickman, M. Oser 158, 168
Glickman, M.J. 77, 78, 87, 133
Glickman, M.J. (Mr. and Mrs.) 87
Glickman, M.J. (Mrs.) 20
Glickman, Mabel (Miss) 87, 150
Glickman, Marcus 47
Glickman, Miriam 72

Glickman, Moses J. 62
Glickman, Mr. 163
Glickman, Nathan 87
Glickman, Osher 15
Glickman, P. .87
Glickman, P. (Mr. and Mrs.) 87
Glickman, P. (Mrs.) 87
Glickman, P.B. (Mr. and Mrs.) . . . 9, 15, 87
Glickman, P.B. (Mrs.) 87
Glickman, Ph. 73
Glickman, Philip (Mr. and Mrs.) 9
Glickman, Phillip (Mr. and Mrs.) 87
Glickman, S. 163
Glickman, S. (Mr. and Mrs.) 87
Glickman, S.M. 87
Glickman, S.M. (Mr. and Mrs.) 9
Glickman, S.M. (Mrs.) 21
Glickman, T. 78, 81, 87
Glickman, T. (Mr. and Mrs.) 2, 87, 134
Glickman, T. (Mrs.) 87
Glickman, T.B. (Mr. and Mrs.) 87
Glickman, Tillie (Miss) 143
Glickman, Tobias 15, 62
Glicksman, Harry (Mr. and Mrs.) 36
Glicksman, Nathan (Mr. and Mrs.) . . .36
Glinzburg, B. (Miss) 109
Glosberg, Mr. 155
Glube, Phillip (Mr. and Mrs.) 178
Gluck, S. 150
Gluck, Samuel 27
Gluck, Samuel (Mr. and Mrs.) 9, 150
Gluck, Samuel (Mrs.) 151
Gluckman, David 27
Godel, Bessie (Miss) 27
Godel, M. (Mr. and Mrs.) 27
Godinsky, N.H. 45, 70, 81, 90
Godinsky, N.H. (Mr. and Mrs.) 9
Godinsky, N.H. (Mrs.) 74
Godinsky, N.U. 90
Godinsky, Nathan H. 87
Godner, A.J. (Mrs.) 64
Goglenug, Celia (Mrs.) 22
Gold, A. 87, 158
Gold, A. (Miss) 67, 92
Gold, Anna (Miss) 30, 87
Gold, Annie 86
Gold, B. 64
Gold, Dora (Miss) 87
Gold, Emma and Edward 185
Gold, Eva (Miss) 29
Gold, F. (Miss) 139
Gold, Fannie (Miss) 87
Gold, Fanny (Miss) 86
Gold, H. 87, 90, 114, 122, 127, 130
Gold, Hillie (Miss) 87
Gold, Hy. 86
Gold, I. 41, 158
Gold, I. (Mr. and Mrs.) 27, 29
Gold, Israel 167
Gold, J. (Mr. and Mrs.) 9, 87
Gold, Joseph .68
Gold, Katie (Miss) 87
Gold, Lillie (Miss) 86
Gold, Lina (Miss) 87
Gold, M. 47, 158
Gold, M. (Mrs.) 115
Gold, M.C. 155
Gold, Maurice 27
Gold, Maxwell 49, 87
Gold, Mr. 87
Gold, S. 87, 91, 158
Gold, S. (Mr. and Mrs.) 30
Gold, T. (Miss) 93

Name	Page
Gold, Tillie (Miss)	93
Goldbar, Fanny (Miss)	26
Goldbar, M. (Mr. and Mrs.)	26
Goldberg, , S.I.	87
Goldberg, A.	68, 158, 161, 185
Goldberg, A. (Miss)	114
Goldberg, A.H.	183
Goldberg, Abraham	27
Goldberg, Alex	80
Goldberg, Avigdor	27, 141
Goldberg, B.	47, 134
Goldberg, Ben (Master)	88
Goldberg, Bertha	39
Goldberg, Bertha (Miss)	88
Goldberg, David (Mrs.)	158
Goldberg, Dora (Miss)	88
Goldberg, Dora E. (Miss)	28
Goldberg, E. (Miss)	88
Goldberg, Edith (Miss)	38
Goldberg, Edythe (Miss)	38, 136
Goldberg, Fanny (Miss)	158
Goldberg, Gershon	15
Goldberg, Gittle (Mrs.)	15
Goldberg, Goldia (Miss)	29
Goldberg, Goldia Augusta (Miss)	29
Goldberg, Goldie	15
Goldberg, Goldie (Miss)	15
Goldberg, H.	70, 88, 121, 184, 185
Goldberg, H. (Mr. and Mrs.)	9
Goldberg, H. (Mrs.)	88, 165, 183
Goldberg, Harry	38, 41
Goldberg, Hyman (Mrs.)	158
Goldberg, Hyman (Rev.)	44
Goldberg, I.	61, 63, 122, 127, 139
Goldberg, I. (Mrs.)	139
Goldberg, I.L. (Mr. and Mrs.)	27
Goldberg, Isidore	15
Goldberg, Isidore (Mr. and Mrs.)	38
Goldberg, Israel	2, 15, 49
Goldberg, J.	183
Goldberg, J. (Miss)	67, 88
Goldberg, J. (Mrs.)	183
Goldberg, J.L. (Mr. and Mrs.)	88
Goldberg, Jacob (Rev.)	185
Goldberg, Jake	15
Goldberg, Julia (Miss)	15, 88
Goldberg, Julius	15, 29
Goldberg, K.	49
Goldberg, L.	28, 67, 68, 78, 183
Goldberg, L. (Mr. and Mrs.)	39, 106
Goldberg, L. (Mrs.)	88, 137
Goldberg, Larry	35
Goldberg, Leon (Master)	35
Goldberg, Lizzie (Miss)	88
Goldberg, M.	22, 32, 61, 73, 87, 90, 91, 114, 127, 136, 149, 171
Goldberg, M. (Miss)	87, 88
Goldberg, Max	15, 49, 88
Goldberg, Max (Mr. and Mrs.)	9
Goldberg, Moe	27
Goldberg, Morris	15, 67, 138
Goldberg, Mr.	66
Goldberg, N.	28
Goldberg, P. (Mrs.)	88
Goldberg, R. (Mr. and Mrs.)	88
Goldberg, Rabbi	30
Goldberg, Rose	88
Goldberg, Rose (Miss)	24, 38
Goldberg, S. (Mr. and Mrs.)	9
Goldberg, Sam (Mr. and Mrs.)	35
Goldberg, Samuel	22, 158
Goldberg, Sarah (Dame)	90
Goldberg, Saul	27
Goldberg, V.	66
Goldberg, W.	172
Goldberg, Z.	28, 88
Goldberg, Z. (Mr. and Mrs.)	2
Goldblatt, A.	47
Goldblatt, A. (Miss)	64, 88
Goldblatt, A.R. (Miss)	64
Goldblatt, Alta (Miss)	30
Goldblatt, Alta Rhoda (Miss)	30
Goldblatt, H.	61, 88, 111
Goldblatt, Harry	88
Goldblatt, M.	47
Goldblatt, P. (Mr. and Mrs.)	30
Goldblatt, Philip (Mr. and Mrs.)	30
Goldblatt, Rhoda (Miss)	86
Goldbloom, A.	97
Goldbloom, Alton	82, 88
Goldbloom, L.	176
Goldbloom, Mr. and Mrs.	30
Goldbloom, Wm. (Mrs.)	185
Golden, Abraham	27
Goldenberg, B.	47, 79, 88, 158, 161
Goldenberg, Benjamin	15
Goldenberg, Bernard	27
Goldenberg, Boyer	27
Goldenberg, D. (Miss)	77
Goldenberg, David	15
Goldenberg, Dorothy (Miss)	88
Goldenberg, I.	27
Goldenberg, J.	27, 41
Goldenberg, J.S. (Mr. and Mrs.)	9
Goldenberg, Jacob	15
Goldenberg, Joseph	15, 27
Goldenberg, Lottie (Miss)	15
Goldenberg, M. (Miss)	60
Goldenberg, M. (Mrs.)	83, 88
Goldenberg, Malca (Miss)	41
Goldenberg, Marion (Miss)	27
Goldenberg, Minnie (Miss)	27
Goldenberg, Miriam (Miss)	145
Goldenberg, Mirry (Miss)	77
Goldenberg, Moe (Mrs.)	88
Goldenberg, Molly (Miss)	15
Goldenberg, Mr.	92
Goldenberg, P.	49
Goldenberg, P. (Mr. and Mrs.)	27, 88
Goldenberg, P. (Mrs.)	15
Goldenberg, P.M.	15
Goldenberg, R. (Miss)	88
Goldenberg, Ruthie (Miss)	88
Goldenberg, S.	158, 163
Goldenblatt, Celia (Miss)	107
Goldenburg, Lillie (Miss)	34
Goldenburg, M. (Mr. and Mrs.)	9
Goldenburg, P. (Mr. and Mrs.)	34
Goldenstein, Dana	2
Goldenstein, I.G. (Mrs.)	109
Goldenstein, I.S.	15, 49, 88, 175, 177
Goldenstein, I.S. (Mr. and Mrs.)	2, 88
Goldenstein, I.S. (Mrs.)	77, 88
Goldenstein, Louis	27
Goldenstein, Louis (Mrs.)	137
Goldenstein, S. (Mrs.)	15
Goldfarb, L.	91
Goldfield, B.	148, 150
Goldfield, Ben	25
Goldfield, Benjamin	150, 151
Goldfield, M.	149
Goldfield, S.	87, 136
Goldfine, E. (Mr. and Mrs.)	27, 112
Goldfine, Elias	49
Goldfine, Gertrude (Miss)	32
Goldfine, L.	27
Goldfine, Mr.	66
Goldhamer, Charlie	47
Goldhamer, Sollie	47
Goldhar, Eva (Miss)	158
Goldie, James (Mrs.)	94
Goldie, Mrs.	39
Goldin, B.	134
Golding, Charles	178
Goldman, A.	106, 183
Goldman, Alex (Dr.)	89
Goldman, Arthur Zion	2
Goldman, H. (Mrs.)	89, 139
Goldman, Henry	47
Goldman, I. (Dr.)	88
Goldman, I. (Mr. and Mrs.)	89
Goldman, I. (Mrs.)	24
Goldman, J.	74, 88, 115, 117, 137, 139
Goldman, J. (Miss)	56
Goldman, Jack	27
Goldman, Jacob	27
Goldman, Joshua	15
Goldman, L.	81
Goldman, L. (Miss)	24
Goldman, L. (Mrs.)	71, 89, 114, 122
Goldman, Leon	15, 45, 47, 49, 51, 52, 66, 75, 80, 88, 89, 95, 112, 114, 182
Goldman, Leon (Mr. and Mrs.)	2, 22, 89, 98, 122
Goldman, Leon (Mrs.)	66, 77, 89, 109, 122, 124, 134
Goldman, M. (Master)	88
Goldman, M.H. (Mr. and Mrs.)	15
Goldman, Minnie	56
Goldman, Moe (Master)	89
Goldman, Philip	15
Goldman, Raya (Miss)	34, 48
Goldman, Raya E. (Miss)	52
Goldman, S. (Master)	88
Goldman, S.H.	27
Goldman, Samuel	47
Goldman, Tillie (Mrs.)	56
Goldman, W.	67, 88
Goldner, A.	68
Goldner, A. (Mr. and Mrs.)	9, 27
Goldner, A. (Mrs.)	98
Goldner, A.J. (Mr. and Mrs.)	9, 89
Goldner, L. (Mr. and Mrs.)	10
Goldner, L. (Mrs.)	92
Goldner, M.	39
Goldner, Mrs.	78
Goldner, R. (Miss)	132, 137
Goldner, Rose (Miss)	27, 77, 94
Goldner, Rosie (Miss)	35
Goldner, S.	62, 122
Goldner, S. (Mr. and Mrs.)	89
Goldreich, F.B. (Mrs.)	38
Goldreich, M.	168
Goldschlager, A. (Mrs.)	15
Goldsmidt, A.	131
Goldsmith, J. (Mr. and Mrs.)	113
Goldsmith, J. (Mrs.)	89
Goldsmith, Jack	153
Goldsmith, Jack (Mrs.)	90
Goldsmith, L.	183
Goldsmith, L. (Mrs.)	113
Goldsmith, Laura (Mrs.)	90
Goldsmith, Leo (Mrs.)	89
Goldsmith, Leon (Mrs.)	90
Goldsmith, Leopold	15
Goldsmith, Leopold (Mr. and Mrs.)	89
Goldsmith, M.	154
Goldsmith, Miss	164
Goldsmith, Perry (Mrs.)	158

Goldsmith, Samuel 27	Goldstein, Irene (Miss) . 36, 90, 147, 158, 168	Goldstein, William (Mrs.) . . 91, 100, 158, 170
Goldstein, A. 2, 90, 185	Goldstein, Isaac 15	Goldstick, Annie (Miss) 31
Goldstein, A. (Mr. and Mrs.) 91	Goldstein, J. 48, 61, 67, 73, 90, 102, 115, 146	Goldstick, Bettie (Miss) 167
Goldstein, A. (Mrs.) 82	Goldstein, J. (Miss) 67, 122	Goldstick, Betty (Miss) 158
Goldstein, A.D. 27, 28, 90	Goldstein, J. (Mr. and Mrs.) 3, 91	Goldstick, Dorothy (Miss) 25, 158
Goldstein, A.D. (Mr. and Mrs.) 27, 91	Goldstein, J. (Mrs.) 48, 77, 91, 108, 113	Goldstick, E. 157
Goldstein, A.D. (Mrs.) 185	Goldstein, Jake (Miss) 117	Goldstick, E. (Mrs.) 157
Goldstein, A.H. 87	Goldstein, Jessie (Miss) 60, 90, 91, 100	Goldstick, I. 48, 157
Goldstein, A.M. 74, 90, 122, 137	Goldstein, Joe 3, 171	Goldstick, Isidore 157
Goldstein, A.N. 136	Goldstein, L. 41, 90	Goldstick, Jennie (Miss) 158, 162
Goldstein, Abraham 72, 90	Goldstein, L. (Mr. and Mrs.) 178	Goldstick, L. (Miss) 154
Goldstein, Alice (Miss) 60	Goldstein, L. (Mrs.) 14	Goldstick, M. 158
Goldstein, Amy (Miss) 90, 91	Goldstein, Leo E. (Mrs.) 139	Goldstick, T. (Mr. and Mrs.) 158
Goldstein, B. 48, 81, 90, 151	Goldstein, M. 87, 90, 102, 177	Goldstick, William (Mr. and Mrs.) 31
Goldstein, B. (Miss) 139	Goldstein, M. (Mr. and Mrs.) . 3, 91, 139, 171	Goldstine, Ada Rose (Miss) 15
Goldstein, B. (Mr. and Mrs.) 26, 36, 90, 91, 145	Goldstein, M. (Mrs.) 68, 91, 139	Goldstine, Max (Mrs.) 176
Goldstein, B. (Mrs.) 17, 91, 125	Goldstein, M.L. 177	Goldstine, Mr. and Mrs. Max 15
Goldstein, B.J. (Mrs.) 90	Goldstein, Mabel (Miss) 36, 90	Goldstine, William 157
Goldstein, Baruch 176	Goldstein, Mabel Constance (Miss) 36	Goldstone, F. (Mrs.) 91
Goldstein, Bernard (Mr. and Mrs.) 91	Goldstein, Mabelle (Miss) 90	Goldstone, Mrs. 37
Goldstein, C.A. 90	Goldstein, Marjorie (Miss) 60, 90	Goldstuck, Betty (Miss) 158
Goldstein, Charles 91	Goldstein, Mary (Miss) 119	Goldvogel, Louis 91
Goldstein, Charles (Master) 91	Goldstein, Max 27, 90, 177	Goldwater, A. 59
Goldstein, Charles A. 88	Goldstein, Max (Mr. and Mrs.) 91	Goldwater, A. (Mr. and Mrs.) 3
Goldstein, Charlie 70	Goldstein, Max (Mrs.) 42, 91, 176-178	Goldwater, C. 66
Goldstein, Charlie (Master) 90	Goldstein, Maxwell . . . 5, 19, 48, 52, 90, 98,	Goldwater, Eliot 134
Goldstein, Clarence 119	102, 103, 111	Goldwater, Ephraim 3
Goldstein, Cyril (Master) 27	Goldstein, Maxwell (Mrs.) 91, 139	Goldwater, Ethel (Miss) 134
Goldstein, D. 27, 67, 183	Goldstein, Meyer 27	Goldwater, Gerald 134
Goldstein, D.A. (Mrs.) 27	Goldstein, Milton 158	Goldwater, I. (Mrs.) 24
Goldstein, Daniel 69	Goldstein, Miss 3, 66, 90, 125, 129, 160	Goldwater, Miss 66
Goldstein, David (Master) 153	Goldstein, Misses 90	Goldwater, Mr. 59
Goldstein, Dora (Miss) 34	Goldstein, Mr. 30, 52, 107	Goldwater, Ralph 27
Goldstein, Dorothy (Miss) 60	Goldstein, Mr. and Mrs. I. 15	Goldwater, S. 59
Goldstein, E. 27, 112	Goldstein, Mrs. 90, 91, 135, 160	Goles, L. 162
Goldstein, Ed 169	Goldstein, Muriel 2	Golland, L. 87, 136
Goldstein, Ed. 48, 51, 70	Goldstein, Muriel (Miss) 60, 90	Golowsky, Mr. 59
Goldstein, Edgar 3	Goldstein, N. 137	Golstein, E. 91
Goldstein, Edgar H. 127	Goldstein, N.W. 91, 114, 115	Golt, David L. 27
Goldstein, Edward 90	Goldstein, P. 49	Golt, F. (Miss) 67, 78
Goldstein, Edward (Mr. and Mrs.) 9	Goldstein, R. (Miss) 82, 177	Golt, Faiga (Miss) 92
Goldstein, Emanuel (Mr. and Mrs.) 178	Goldstein, R. (Mrs.) 175, 177	Golt, Fannie (Miss) 92
Goldstein, Emmanuel 27	Goldstein, Reuben 27	Golt, Fanny (Miss) 79
Goldstein, Estelle (Miss) 77	Goldstein, Rev. and Mrs. 90	Golt, Frances (Miss) 91
Goldstein, Esther (Mrs.) 15	Goldstein, Ruby (Miss) 177	Golt, I. (Miss) 79
Goldstein, Ethel (Miss) 164, 168	Goldstein, Rueben (Mr. and Mrs.) 11	Golt, J. 88
Goldstein, Ethel (Mrs.) 91	Goldstein, Ruth (Miss) 68, 90, 91	Golt, Joseph 91
Goldsmith, Eva (Miss) . 36, 69, 74, 90, 91, 124	Goldstein, S. 177	Golt, Moses 92
Goldstein, F. 27	Goldstein, S. (Mrs.) 91, 134, 142, 177	Golt, Rebecca (Miss) 92
Goldstein, Flossie (Miss) 26, 32	Goldstein, S. (Rev. and Mrs.) 34, 104	Golt, S. 92
Goldstein, G. (Mr. and Mrs.) 63	Goldstein, S. (Rev.) . . . 10, 12, 15, 19, 22-29,	Goltman (Mrs. (Dr.)) 17
Goldstein, G. (Mrs.) 139	31, 32, 34-37, 40, 46,	Goltman, A. (Mrs.) 92
Goldstein, G.A. 112	78, 91, 108, 110, 134	Goltman, A.M. (Mrs.) 92
Goldstein, G.E. 98	Goldstein, S.H. (Cantor) 177	Goltman, A.S. 92
Goldstein, G.E. (Mrs.) 66, 139	Goldstein, S.H. (Mrs.) 134	Goltman, C.E. (Mrs.) 92
Goldstein, George (Mr. and Mrs.) 91	Goldstein, S.J. (Mrs.) 90, 91	Goltman, Charles 16
Goldstein, George (Mrs.) . . . 68, 91, 138, 139	Goldstein, Salo H. (Rev.) 91	Goltman, Charles E. 16
Goldstein, George E. (Mr. and Mrs.) 91	Goldstein, Sam (Mrs.) 91	Goltman, Donald 134
Goldstein, George E. (Mrs.) 91, 139	Goldstein, Samuel 158	Goltman, Frances (Miss) 92
Goldstein, Gladys (Miss) 60, 90	Goldstein, Sarah (Miss) 27, 90	Goltman, M. (Dr.) 92
Goldstein, H. 90, 163, 171, 172	Goldstein, Siegfried 177	Goltman, Max (Dr.) 6, 16, 92
Goldstein, H. (Sergt.) 162	Goldstein, Sigmund 15	Goltman, Mrs. 72
Goldstein, Harold 15	Goldstein, Stella (Miss) 60, 91	Goltman, Reba (Miss) 107
Goldstein, Harry 139, 177	Goldstein, Sydney 38	Goltman, Robert 92
Goldstein, Harry (Master) 90	Goldstein, Sylvia (Miss) . . 27, 36, 60, 90, 98,	Goltman, Robert (Mr. and Mrs.) 9, 92
Goldstein, Herbert 90, 158	111, 135	Goltman, Robert (Mrs.) 77, 92, 134
Goldstein, I. 27, 32, 170	Goldstein, W. 166	Goltman, S. (Mr. and Mrs.) 92, 116
Goldstein, I. (Miss) 158	Goldstein, W. (Mrs.) 91, 97, 139	Goltman, S. (Mrs.) 16, 147
Goldstein, I. (Mrs.) 91, 128	Goldstein, Walter 91	Goltman, Samuel 19
Goldstein, I.J. (Mrs.) 91	Goldstein, William 91, 157	Goltman, Solomon 16, 92
Goldstein, I.S. 134	Goldstein, William (Miss) 90	Goltman, Stephanie (Miss) 92
Goldstein, I.S. (Mrs.) 42	Goldstein, William (Mr. and Mrs.) . 28, 36, 91,	Golub, Annie (Miss) 153
	139, 158	Golub, J. (Miss) . . . .

. . . .	151-152
Golub, J. (Mrs.)	150
Golub, Julia (Miss)	150
Golub, Miss	150
Golub, Mrs.	152
Golub, Nellie (Miss)	150
Golul, J. (Mr. and Mrs.)	33
Golul, Nellie (Miss)	33
Goniondzer, A.	48
Goodkowsky (Mrs.)	18
Goodkowsky, Mr. and Mrs.	92
Goodkowsky, N.	18
Goodkowsky, N. (Mr. and Mrs.)	92
Goodkowsky, N. (Mrs.)	22
Goodman, A. (Mrs.)	29, 129
Goodman, A. (Rev.)	183
Goodman, Aaron David	177
Goodman, Abraham (Mrs.)	43
Goodman, B.	48
Goodman, B.D.	167
Goodman, D.	168
Goodman, E. (Miss)	163
Goodman, Esther (Miss)	155
Goodman, Fannie (Miss)	154
Goodman, Fanny (Miss)	160, 161
Goodman, G.	162
Goodman, H.M.	158
Goodman, I.	78, 157
Goodman, J.	26, 28, 34, 39, 137, 163, 183
Goodman, J.A.	62
Goodman, J.J.	48, 92, 183, 184
Goodman, L. (Mr. and Mrs.)	158
Goodman, L. (Mrs.)	158
Goodman, M.	183
Goodman, Meyer H.	157
Goodman, Michael	28
Goodman, Miss	34
Goodman, Mr.	163
Goodman, Mrs.	92, 158
Goodman, R.	92
Goodman, R. (Miss)	82
Goodman, Ray (Miss)	36
Goodman, Samuel	28
Goodman, W.H.	155
Goodman, Will (Mrs.)	156
Goodson, A. (Mr. and Mrs.)	64
Goodson, Joe	92
Goodson, Joeseph	92
Goodstone, A.S	47, 92
Goodstone, Isidore	125
Goodstone, J.A.	47
Goodstone, Lucy	67, 132
Goodstone, S.	47
Goodwin, D.	30
Goodwin, Doris (Miss)	29
Goodwin, Michael	28
Goorovitz, N. (Mrs.)	57
Goorovitz, S.	57
Gordin, Jacob	51
Gordon, A.	158
Gordon, A.R.	155
Gordon, Alexander	158
Gordon, Annie (Miss)	23, 48, 92, 107
Gordon, Bessie (Miss)	37, 92
Gordon, D.	81
Gordon, D. (Mr. and Mrs.)	24
Gordon, D. (Mrs.)	92, 119
Gordon, David	92
Gordon, David (Mrs.)	92, 121
Gordon, E.	25
Gordon, E.C.	155
Gordon, E.M.	107
Gordon, E.M. (Mr. and Mrs.)	61, 92
Gordon, F. (Mr. and Mrs.)	28
Gordon, F. (Mrs.)	92
Gordon, Fanny (Miss)	57
Gordon, G. (Miss)	112
Gordon, H.	92, 93, 107
Gordon, H. (Miss)	61
Gordon, H. (Sergt.)	162
Gordon, Harry	23, 49, 73, 92, 125
Gordon, Hester (Miss)	23, 92, 158
Gordon, Hilda (Miss)	92
Gordon, J.	56, 92
Gordon, J. (Mrs.)	77
Gordon, J. (Rabbi)	155, 157, 158
Gordon, J. (Rev.)	24
Gordon, J.C.	24
Gordon, J.M.	158
Gordon, Lucky	134
Gordon, M.	155, 167
Gordon, M. (Mr. and Mrs.)	23, 107, 108
Gordon, M. (Mrs.)	158
Gordon, M. (Rev.)	30
Gordon, Malca (Miss)	92
Gordon, Max	22
Gordon, Miss	92
Gordon, Misses	160
Gordon, Moses	92, 107, 158
Gordon, Moses (Mr. and Mrs.)	23, 107
Gordon, Moses (Mrs.)	92
Gordon, Mr.	114
Gordon, Mrs.	92
Gordon, Nathan (Mrs.)	77, 92
Gordon, Nathan (Rabbi)	2, 6, 13-15, 17, 19, 23, 24, 26, 28-30, 32, 34, 36, 38, 42, 45, 48, 77, 92, 93, 111, 113, 159, 171
Gordon, Philip	28
Gordon, Rabbi	29, 33, 156, 159
Gordon, Rose (Miss)	23, 92, 93, 108
Gordon, Rose (Mrs.)	92
Gordon, S.	24, 93
Gordon, S.B.	61, 74, 115, 124, 137, 138
Gordon, S.E.	92
Gordon, S.E. (Mrs.)	93
Gordon, Sam	57
Gordon, Sara (Miss)	92
Gordon, W. (Rabbi)	25, 26, 28
Gordstein, M.	158
Goretzky, Rabbi	178
Gorfinkel, D.	151
Gorfinkel, David	151
Gorfinkel, Max (Mrs.)	93
Gorfinkel, Mr.	31, 148
Gorfinkle, M.	90
Gorfinkle, M. (Miss)	52, 93
Gorfinkle, Mildred (Miss)	3, 77
Gorfinkle, Mrs.	93
Gorn, A.	131
Gorofe, M.	138
Gorosh, S.	93, 108, 121, 138
Gostinsky, Mr.	156
Goteskind, Moses	159
Gother, A.	174
Gotkin, M.	158
Gotloeb, Yetta (Miss)	162
Gottlieb, Esther (Miss)	162, 165
Gottlieb, Henrietta (Miss)	154
Gottlieb, Julia (Miss)	154, 159
Gottlieb, Philip (Mr. and Mrs.)	165
Gottlieb, Saul	48
Gottlieb, Yetta (Miss)	162, 165
Gottloeb, Bessie (Miss)	165
Gould, A.	170
Gould, A. (Mrs.)	151
Gould, H.	30
Gould, M.	150
Gould, Miss	26
Gould, Mr. and Mrs.	26, 150
Gould, S. (Miss)	150
Gradenger, W.	23
Graefsky, A. (Miss)	88
Graff, J.B. (Mr. and Mrs.)	93
Gralik, M.	69
Granatstein S.	30
Granatstein, A.	159, 169
Granatstein, I.F.	162
Granatstein, I.M.	159
Granatstein, J.T. (Mr. and Mrs.)	159
Granatstein, Lillie (Miss)	159
Granatstein, Mrs.	35, 165
Granatstein, S.J. (Mr. and Mrs.)	159
Granklin, J.L.	93
Granovsky, Sophie (Miss)	175
Grassman, A. (Mrs.)	13
Gray, Miss	160
Gredinger, W.	81
Green, A.	57
Green, Adela (Miss)	93
Green, Arthur	57
Green, Clifford	93, 151
Green, H.	2, 57, 58
Green, H. (Mr. and Mrs.)	57
Green, Harry	93
Green, Helen (Miss)	93, 150, 152
Green, Isaac (Mr. and Mrs.)	57
Green, J.	93
Green, Jena (Master)	150
Green, Joseph	174
Green, L.	56, 148-152
Green, L. (Mr. and Mrs.)	87, 118, 150
Green, L. (Mrs.)	151
Green, Leon	81
Green, Lewis (Mrs.)	56
Green, Lily (Miss)	93
Green, Louis	6, 56
Green, Louis (Master)	9
Green, Louis (Mr. and Mrs.)	93
Green, Louis (Mrs.)	56
Green, M.	57
Green, Miss	56, 93
Green, Mr. and Mrs.	136
Green, Mrs.	93, 150
Green, N.	184
Green, N.L.	28
Green, Nathan (Mr. and Mrs.)	93
Green, S.	57
Green, S. Hart	6, 30, 93, 176, 177, 180
Green, S. Hart (Mr. and Mrs.)	9
Green, Sol.	57
Green, Solomon	57
Greenbaum, Ed.	28
Greenbaum, J.	59
Greenbaum, Mrs.	72
Greenberg, A. (Mr. and Mrs.)	23
Greenberg, A. (Mrs.)	94, 183
Greenberg, Abe	93
Greenberg, Abe (Mr. and Mrs.)	117
Greenberg, Albert	70
Greenberg, Albert (Mr. and Mrs.)	3
Greenberg, Annie (Miss)	26
Greenberg, B.	28
Greenberg, Benjamin	28
Greenberg, C.	28
Greenberg, Charles	28
Greenberg, D.	183
Greenberg, Dave	93

Greenberg, E. (Miss) 163	Greenspoon, Sarah (Miss) 41	Grossman, C. (Mrs.) 185
Greenberg, Essie H. (Miss) 93	Greenspoon, Solomon 49	Grossman, D. (Mrs.) 185
Greenberg, Esther (Miss) 28	Greenstein, C. (Master) 94	Grossman, Ethel (Miss) 33
Greenberg, F.F. De Young (Mr. and Mrs.) 9	Greenstein, H. (Miss) 94	Grossman, H. 94, 185
Greenberg, Gilbert (Master) 3	Greenstein, M. (Master) 94	Grossman, Harry 28, 185
Greenberg, H. 16, 57	Greenstein, M. (Mrs.) 94	Grossman, Harry (Mr. and Mrs.) 94
Greenberg, H. (Miss) 93	Greenston, Miss 94	Grossman, Harry (Mrs.) 94, 185
Greenberg, H. (Mr. and Mrs.) 28	Greenwood, Harry 28	Grossman, I. 49
Greenberg, H. (Mrs.) 57	Greines, W. 185	Grossman, Israel (Mr. and Mrs.) 33
Greenberg, Helen (Miss) 23, 93	Greisman, Francis H. (Miss) 94	Grossman, J. 185
Greenberg, I. 93	Greisman, H. 159, 162	Grossman, M. 28, 47, 119, 185
Greenberg, Isaac (Mr. and Mrs.) 177	Greisman, H. (Mrs.) 159	Grossman, M. (Mrs.) 185
Greenberg, J. (Mrs.) 162	Greisman, Mrs. 167	Grossman, Maxwell 94
Greenberg, Lionel 93	Greisman, Pearl (Miss) 34	Grossman, Mr. 159, 185
Greenberg, M. 61	Greisman, S. 162	Grossman, Mr. and Mrs. 28, 33
Greenberg, M. (Mr. and Mrs.) 9	Greisman, Sarah (Miss) 34, 183	Grossman, Mrs. 124
Greenberg, M. (Mrs.) 94, 141	Grew, Sophie (Miss) 33	Grossman, S.M. 162, 164
Greenberg, M.G. 155	Griesdorf, H. 184	Grossman, S.M. (Mrs.) 94, 159, 165
Greenberg, Miss 93	Griesman, Gertrude (Miss) 35	Grossman, W. 185
Greenberg, Misses 140	Griesman, Israel (Mr. and Mrs.) 35	Grossvogel, Mr. 159
Greenberg, Morris 28	Grimberg, Maurice (Mrs.) 148	Grover, Nachman 175
Greenberg, Moses 16	Grimker, S. 183	Grudginsky, Nathan (Mr. and Mrs.) 94
Greenberg, Mr. 66, 169	Grinker, S. 183, 184	Grumbacher, L. 94
Greenberg, Mr. and Mrs. 28, 93	Grinon, M.J. 94	Grundler, A. (Mrs.) 119
Greenberg, Mrs. 94, 129, 139	Groffer, Charles 28	Grupar, H. (Mrs.) 28
Greenberg, R. 155	Groner, B. (Mr. and Mrs.) 94	Grupar, Moses 28
Greenberg, Rosie (Miss) 36	Groner, B. (Mrs.) 77, 94	Gubbins, H. 114
Greenberg, S. (Mrs.) 36, 94	Groner, M. 64	Gubbins, W. 61, 91
Greenberg, Sophie (Miss) 16	Groner, Mr. 132	Guggenheim, Mr. 69
Greenberg, Soth (Miss) 94	Groner, R. (Miss) 60	Guilaroff, Dolly (Miss) 93
Greenberg, Tilley (Miss) 28	Groner, Ralph 145	Guilaroff, E. 3
Greenberg, Willie (Master) 149	Groner, Ruth (Miss) . . . 94, 102, 127, 135, 145	Guilaroff, Eugene (Mrs.) 95
Greenblat, H. 170	Gronin. J. 47	Guilaroff, Eugene and Annie 9
Greenblat, Monte 183	Gronin, J. 48, 73, 94	Guilaroff, O. (Miss) 94
Greenblatt, M. 94	Gronin, M. (Mr. and Mrs.) 94	Guilaroff, Olga (Miss) 73, 93
Greenblatt, Mr. 159	Gronin, Mr. 47	Guinsberg, Myer 142
Greenblatt, Mrs. 72	Grosman, S.M. 162	Guitess, B. (Miss) 148
Greenblot, M. 30	Grosman, S.M. (Mrs.) 154	Guitess, Bessie (Miss) 151
Greenbow, Bert 28	Gross, A. (Mr. and Mrs.) 28	Gulcau, M. 158
Greenfarb, Saul 94	Gross, Ada Bella (Miss) 24	Gumberg, Bennie 184
Greenfarb, Solomon 28	Gross, B. (Miss) 67, 70, 138	Gumbinsky, Mr. and Mrs. 173
Greenford, Isidore 3	Gross, B. (Mr. and Mrs.) 39	Gunn, Alex. 180
Greenford, S. 3	Gross, B. (Mrs.) 94	Gunn, W. 177, 178
Greenford, Sam 94	Gross, Bella (Miss) 46, 94, 137, 141	Gunn, William 177
Greenhood, J. 94	Gross, Bernard 94	Gunsberg, Rabbi 91
Greenhood, Joseph 94	Gross, C.J. 146	Gunther, Egmund 43
Greenhood, W. 94	Gross, C.J. (Dr.) 39, 71, 94, 101	Gupin, M. 74
Greenman, Charles (Mrs.) 74	Gross, Dr. 94	Gurewich, B. 183, 184
Greensfelder, H. 185	Gross, F. (Miss) 67	Gurewitch, M. 183
Greenshon, S. (Miss) 67	Gross, Fannie (Miss) 36, 39	Gurofsky, J.L. 163
Greenspan, B. (Miss) 88	Gross, Harry 87	Gurofsky, Joseph 159
Greenspan, Jennie (Miss) 94	Gross, Hyman 28	Gurofsky, L. 155, 163, 168
Greenspaun, A. 158	Gross, J. 121	Gurofsky, L.J. 155
Greenspon, Fannie (Miss) 94	Gross, J. (Miss) 94, 138	Gurofsky, L.S. 159
Greenspon, Ida (Miss) 23	Gross, Jennie (Miss) 39	Gurofsky, Louis 95, 159, 169
Greenspon, J. 69	Gross, L. 60	Gurovitch, Jennie (Miss) 183
Greenspon, Jennie (Miss) . . . 25, 82, 94, 135, 137, 141, 145, 149	Gross, L.M. 61	Gurowicz, Charles 170
	Gross, Louis 42, 85, 107	Gurowitz, H. 183
Greenspon, M. (Mr. and Mrs.) 23	Gross, M. 39, 120	Gurstein, A. 185
Greenspon, M. (Mrs.) 94	Gross, Martin B. (Mr. and Mrs.) 36	Gurvitch, Abraham 184
Greenspon, Rose (Miss) 94	Gross, Mary (Miss) 94	Gurvitch, Harry 184
Greenspon, Sadie (Miss) 157	Gross, Miss 94	Gutstein, Mr. and Mrs. 95, 185
Greenspon, Sarah (Miss) 94	Gross, Misses 145	Guttman, J.A. 28
Greenspoon, A. 28	Gross, Moses 42, 94	Guttman, Joseph A. 28
Greenspoon, Bella (Miss) 77	Gross, Mr. and Mrs. 3, 94	Guttman, Melanie (Miss) 153
Greenspoon, H. (Mr. and Mrs.) 41	Gross, Rose (Miss) 94	Guttman, R. (Miss) 129
Greenspoon, J. 94	Gross, Samuel 3	Guttman, Stephanie 153
Greenspoon, J. (Miss) 77	Gross, Sara (Miss) 94	Guttman, Stephanie (Miss) 146, 150, 153
Greenspoon, Jennie (Miss) 139	Gross, Sarah (Miss) 39	Guttman-Rice, Melanie (Mme.) 146
Greenspoon, M. 94	Grossman, A. 185	Guttstein, M. 185
Greenspoon, May (Miss) 77	Grossman, A. (Mr. and Mrs.) 94	Haas, Carolina (Miss) 16
Greenspoon, S.G. 94	Grossman, A. (Mrs.) 185	Haas, George 95
	Grossman, Benjamin 42	Haas, Henrietta 16

Haas, Max ... 95
Haas, Miss ... 95, 147
Haberman, H. (Mrs.) ... 37
Haberman, Ida (Miss) ... 37
Haft, Flossie (Miss) ... 74
Haid, Ada (Miss) ... 178
Haid, Clara (Miss) ... 16
Haid, M. ... 175-177, 179
Haid, M. (Mr. and Mrs.) ... 9, 16, 178
Haid, Mr. and Mrs. M. ... 9
Haid, Ray (Miss) ... 178
Haimowitz, D. ... 156
Haimowitz, Miss ... 156
Haines, A. ... 56
Halperin, Dorothy (Miss) ... 24, 73
Halperin, H. ... 70
Halperin, Hyman ... 42
Halperin, Jessie (Miss) ... 24, 73
Halperin, Jessie E. (Miss) ... 95
Halpern, A.E. ... 158
Halpern, Abraham ... 168
Halpern, B. (Mrs.) ... 95
Halpern, Bernard ... 28, 29
Halpern, Bernard (Mrs.) ... 95
Halpern, Ettie (Miss) ... 24, 167
Halpern, I. (Rev.) ... 24, 95
Halpern, Louis ... 28
Halpern, Mollie (Miss) ... 95
Halpern, Mrs. ... 156
Halpern, S. ... 29
Halpern, S. (Miss) ... 161, 165, 167, 169
Halpern, Susan (Miss) ... 154, 161
Halpern, Susie (Mrs.) ... 159
Halpert, H. ... 165
Halpert, Mrs. ... 165
Halpert, N. ... 162
Halpert, N. (Mrs.) ... 164
Halpin, J. ... 95
Halter, L. ... 179
Halter, Maurice (Mrs.) ... 178
Halter, Samuel ... 178
Halter, Samuel (Mr. and Mrs.) ... 9
Halter, Samuel (Mrs.) ... 178
Hamburg, B. ... 48, 57
Hamburg, Ben ... 57
Hamburg, H. ... 57
Hamburg, I. ... 57
Hamburg, Israel ... 57
Hamburg, M. ... 57
Hamburg, Ray (Miss) ... 57
Hamilton, John (Mr. and Mrs.) ... 95
Handleman, Minnie (Miss) ... 29
Handleman, Miss ... 95
Hanf, Miss ... 159
Hans, Maurice ... 158
Hansher, A. (Mrs.) ... 95, 118
Hansher, Charles ... 29
Hansher, Harry ... 29
Hansher, M. (Mrs.) ... 95
Hansher, Mr. and Mrs. ... 87
Hansher, Reuben (Master) ... 149
Hansher, S. (Mrs.) ... 118, 162
Hansher, S.M. ... 24
Hansher, S.M. (Mr. and Mrs.) ... 95
Hansher, William ... 181
Hansman, S. (Master) ... 174
Harbor, Sadie (Miss) ... 155
Harder, Miss ... 28
Harkness, Mrs. ... 95
Harle, R. (Miss) ... 67
Harris, A. ... 3, 23, 34, 41, 45, 81, 95, 110, 112, 145, 171, 180
Harris, A. (Miss) ... 64, 121

Harris, A. (Mr. and Mrs.) ... 3, 95, 119
Harris, A. (Mrs.) ... 96, 98, 160
Harris, Aaron ... 16, 95
Harris, Anna (Miss) ... 41
Harris, Bessie (Miss) ... 95
Harris, Bud ... 159
Harris, C. (Mr. and Mrs.) ... 39
Harris, C.A. ... 95
Harris, Charlotte (Miss) ... 41
Harris, David (Master) ... 95
Harris, Dora (Miss) ... 95
Harris, E. ... 11, 162
Harris, E. (Miss) ... 64, 98
Harris, Edith (Miss) ... 41, 102
Harris, Edythe (Miss) ... 136
Harris, Esther (Miss) ... 95
Harris, Eva (Miss) ... 39, 41, 102
Harris, Fannie (Miss) ... 16, 93
Harris, Felix (Mr. and Mrs.) ... 96
Harris, Felix (Mrs.) 45, 66, 88, 96, 105, 109, 142
Harris, G. ... 176
Harris, G. (Mr. and Mrs.) ... 9
Harris, G.B. ... 179
Harris, George (Mrs.) ... 179
Harris, H. (Mr. and Mrs.) ... 9
Harris, H. (Mrs.) ... 160
Harris, H.A. ... 155
Harris, Hannah (Miss) ... 116
Harris, Hesse (Master) ... 3
Harris, I. ... 171
Harris, I. (Mrs.) ... 114
Harris, J. ... 67, 106, 139, 162
Harris, J. (Mrs.) ... 185
Harris, Jack ... 66, 141
Harris, Jacob ... 3
Harris, Joe ... 66
Harris, Joseph ... 155, 168
Harris, Julius ... 95
Harris, L. ... 41, 171
Harris, L. (Miss) ... 121, 164
Harris, Lottie (Miss) ... 41, 95
Harris, M. ... 95
Harris, M. (Miss) ... 95, 104
Harris, M. (Mr. and Mrs.) ... 41, 121, 136
Harris, M. (Mrs.) ... 64, 76, 95, 96, 105
Harris, M.L. (Mr. and Mrs.) ... 121
Harris, M.L. (Mrs.) ... 96
Harris, Major Samuel ... 6
Harris, Max ... 61
Harris, Max (Miss) ... 95
Harris, Max (Mr. and Mrs.) ... 3, 71, 93, 95, 96, 140
Harris, Max (Mrs.) ... 95, 96
Harris, Maxwell ... 95
Harris, Maxwell (Mr. and Mrs.) 41, 96, 121, 136
Harris, Maxwell (Mrs.) ... 111
Harris, Misses ... 16, 95, 121, 135, 138
Harris, Mr. ... 74, 166
Harris, Mrs. ... 96
Harris, Nathan (Mr. and Mrs.) ... 6
Harris, R. (Miss) ... 95, 99
Harris, Rose (Miss) ... 41, 45, 66, 81, 95, 96, 99, 121, 142
Harris, Rosie (Miss) ... 95
Harris, Ruben ... 74
Harris, S. ... 96, 160, 171
Harris, S. (Major and Mrs.) ... 95
Harris, S. (Miss) ... 172
Harris, S. (Mrs.) ... 164
Harris, S.J. ... 96
Harris, Samuel ... 16, 96
Harris, Sarah (Miss) ... 95
Harris, Selina (Miss) ... 171, 172

Harris, Stella (Miss) ... 95
Harris, Theodor ... 96
Harris, Theodore (Master) ... 34
Harris, W. ... 73, 165
Hart, A.S. ... 56
Hart, Alan (Mr. and Mrs.) ... 96
Hart, Alan (Mrs.) ... 96
Hart, Alan J. (Mr. and Mrs.) ... 96
Hart, Allan (Mrs.) ... 96
Hart, Allen J. (Mr. and Mrs.) ... 9
Hart, Annette Lewis (Mrs.) ... 48
Hart, Arthur ... 33
Hart, Claude ... 96
Hart, Claude (Mr. and Mrs.) ... 96
Hart, Claude (Mrs.) ... 96
Hart, Claude B. (Mr. and Mrs.) ... 96
Hart, Cyril (Master) ... 96
Hart, D. ... 47
Hart, D. (Mrs.) ... 96, 144
Hart, D.A. (Dr. and Mrs.) ... 96, 127
Hart, D.A. (Mrs.) ... 96
Hart, David (Dr.) ... 130
Hart, David A. (Dr. and Mrs.) ... 96
Hart, David A. (Dr.) ... 96
Hart, David A. (Mr. and Mrs.) ... 29
Hart, David A. (Mrs.) ... 96
Hart, Dorothy (Miss) ... 69, 135
Hart, Dr. ... 96
Hart, Dr. and Mrs. ... 29, 75, 96
Hart, Evelyn K. (Miss) ... 33
Hart, F. (Miss) ... 82
Hart, Gertrude (Miss) ... 77
Hart, Gladys (Miss) ... 26
Hart, H. ... 68, 81, 96
Hart, H. (Mrs.) ... 73, 77, 96, 98
Hart, H.G. (Mr. and Mrs.) ... 9
Hart, Hellie (Mrs.) ... 91
Hart, Hillie (Mr. and Mrs.) ... 97
Hart, Hillie (Mrs.) ... 143
Hart, J. ... 183
Hart, John (Mr. and Mrs.) ... 33
Hart, L.M. ... 96
Hart, Lewis (Mr. and Mrs.) ... 33
Hart, Lewis A. ... 42
Hart, Lewis A. (Mr. and Mrs.) ... 26, 33
Hart, Louis A. (Mr. and Mrs.) ... 96
Hart, M. ... 67, 122
Hart, M. (Miss) ... 96
Hart, Mabel (Miss) ... 26, 33
Hart, Maurice ... 66
Hart, Mrs. ... 56, 96
Hart, Muriel (Miss) ... 33, 96
Hart, Philip ... 26
Hart, R. ... 96
Hart, R.E. ... 96
Hart, Reginald ... 96
Hart, Roslyn (Mr. and Mrs.) ... 160
Hart, Roslyn E. ... 29, 96
Hart, Roslyn E. (Mr. and Mrs.) ... 96
Hart, Rossyln ... 96
Hart, Rosyln ... 96
Hart, Rufus E. ... 29
Hart, Ruth (Miss) ... 96
Hart, S. ... 106
Hart, S. (Miss) ... 82
Hart, S. (Mrs.) ... 77
Hart, Sam (Mr. and Mrs.) ... 96
Hart, Samuel ... 143
Hart, Samuel (Mr. and Mrs.) ... 96
Hart, Samuel (Mrs.) ... 96, 145
Hart, Solomon ... 16
Hart, Stanley ... 134
Hart, Tillie (Miss) ... 96

Hart, Tilly (Miss) 77
Hart, V.S. (Mrs.) 96
Hart, William (Mr. and Mrs.) 96
Hartman, L. 155, 162
Hartman, Louis (Mr. and Mrs.) 160
Hartman, Louis (Mrs.) 160
Hartman, M. 160
Hartman, M. (Mrs.) 159, 160
Hartman, Mrs. 167
Hartman, Wiliam A. 29
Hartmann, William A. 48
Hashmal, A.B. 52
Haskell, Aaron H. (Mrs.) 17
Haskell, Fredelle Wilner (Mrs.) 48
Haskell, Miss 96, 166
Haskell, Mrs. 96
Haskell, Nellie (Miss) 167
Haskell, S. 81, 84, 96, 112, 134
Haskell, S. (Mrs.) 130
Hauman, Mrs. 171
Hauseman, L. 185
Havelock, Mr. 155
Hayes, B.J. 81, 96, 134
Hayes, B.J. (Mr. and Mrs.) 10, 96
Hayes, B.S. (Mrs.) 104
Hayes, E.J. (Mrs.) 141
Hayes, Eli 134
Hayes, Henrietta 16
Hayes, R.T. 56
Hayes, Solomon 134
Hazan, Mr. 183
Hazzan, Reuben 155
Hazzan, Rubin 156
Hecht, Amelia (Miss) 108
Hecht, Emily (Miss) 77
Hecht, Florence (Miss) 77, 94
Hecht, Harry 29
Hecht, M. (Miss) 132
Hecht, Milly (Miss) 94
Hecht, Nathan 29
Hecht, Nathan (Mr. and Mrs.) 96
Heft, Fanny (Miss) 96
Heft, H. 105
Heft, S. (Miss) 96
Heft, S. (Mr. and Mrs.) 96
Heilig, M. 178
Heilig, M.J. 105
Heilig, Ray (Miss) 105
Heillig, Fanny (Miss) 111
Heillig, I. 96
Heillig, J. (Miss) 61
Heillig, Jennie (Miss) 107, 128
Heillig, L. 29, 81
Heillig, Lyon 65, 96, 112
Heillig, M. 29
Heillig, M. (Mr. and Mrs.) 96
Heillig, M. (Mrs.) 91, 97
Heillig, M.J. (Mrs.) 98
Heillig, Mo. 122
Heillig, R. (Mrs.) 121, 141
Heillig, R.E. (Mr. and Mrs.) 97
Heillig, Rae (Miss) 29, 66, 142
Heillig, Ray (Miss) 66, 96, 128, 147
Heillig, Sadie 72
Heillig, Willie (Master) 128
Heim, J. 97
Heiman, J. (Miss) 178
Heimerdinger, Harry (Mr. and Mrs.) 97
Heimerdinger, Harry (Mrs.) 97
Heinsheimer, A. (Mrs.) 113
Heinsheimer, Art (Mr.and Mrs.) 97
Heinsheimer, Arthur (Mr. and Mrs.) . . 10, 97
Heinsheimer, E. 97
Heinsheimer, Elsie (Miss) 60
Heiser, Ida (Mrs.) 160
Heishorn, E. 119
Heisler, H. 97
Heitner, D. 180
Heitner, Jacob (Mr. and Mrs.) 175
Heitner, Mrs. 40
Held, A. 149
Held, E. 148
Held, Joe 150
Held, M. 63, 150
Held, Mr. 148
Helfand, L. 66
Helfgot, Mr. 182
Heller, A. 170
Heller, Beller (Miss) 36
Heller, David 29
Heller, Estelle (Miss) 100
Heller, G. 124
Heller, H.E. 162
Heller, I.E. 29
Heller, M.J. (Mr. and Mrs.) 97
Heller, M.J. (Mrs.) 46
Heller, Master 86
Heller, P. 183
Helman, Celia (Miss) 24
Helman, D. 183
Helman, Samuel 175
Helpern, Ettie (Miss) 160
Helpert, I. (Mrs.) 160
Helpert, Mrs. 165, 167
Helpert, N. (Mrs.) 160, 165
Hendler, Mr. and Mrs. 16
Henner, A. (Miss) 175
Hennessy, S. (Mrs.) 97
Henry, Harriet (Miss) 44
Hensher, S.M. (Mrs.) 160
Hensher, W. 160
Heper, A. 170
Heppner, Eva (Miss) 37
Heppner, Max 48, 67, 97, 115, 139
Heppner, Misses 178
Heppner, Mrs. 177
Herbert, I. (Mrs.) 164
Herbert, S. 38
Herbert, Sam (Mrs.) 164
Herbert, Samuel 29
Herbert, Samuel (Mr. and Mrs.) 160
Herbert, Sol. (Mrs.) 164
Herchorn, H.E. 114
Herdt, Joseph 97
Herkovitz, Ethel (Mrs.) 134
Herman, Annie (Miss) 175
Herman, B. 72
Herman, Bessie (Miss) 77
Herman, C. 114, 115
Herman, Charles 90, 91, 115
Herman, Gertrude (Miss) 24
Herman, H. 115
Herman, H.L. 97
Herman, L. (Mr. and Mrs.) 10
Herman, Lily (Miss) 158
Herman, M. 107
Herman, Mollie (Miss) 77
Herman, Mr. 114
Herman, Mr. and Mrs. 185
Herman, Mrs. 66
Herman, P. 154
Herman, Professor 182
Herman, R. (Miss) 160
Herman, R. (Mrs.) 97
Herman, Raby (Miss) 158
Herman, Ray (Miss) 97
Herman, S. (Rev.) 31
Herman, S.K. 97
Herman, S.L. 90, 97
Herman, W. 50
Hermann, L. (Miss) 177
Hermann, M. (Miss) 87
Hermant, Percy 29, 160
Hermant, Percy (Mr. and Mrs.) 10, 160
Hermant, Percy (Mrs.) 66
Herr, A. (Mr. and Mrs.) 117
Herr, B. 29
Herschel, J. 97
Herschkovitz, I. 134
Herschkowitz, H. 165
Herschman, Rev. and Mrs. 97
Herschorn, H. 47
Herschorn, H.E. 114, 140
Herscovitch, J. 29
Herscovitch, J. (Mrs.) 148
Herscovitch, L.E. 42
Hershberg, Bertram (Master) 97
Hershberg, Haskel I. 22
Hershberg, I. (Mr. and Mrs.) 22, 97
Hershberg, I. (Mrs.) 97
Hershberg, Isaac (Mr. and Mrs.) 22
Hershberg, Lottie (Miss) 22
Hershberg, Sam. (Mrs.) 97
Hershberg, Sol. M. 22
Hershfield, N. 42
Hershman, Mr. 160
Hershon, Ch. 60
Hershorn, Charles 61
Hershorn, H.E. 77
Hershorn, Mr. and Mrs. 97
Hershorn, S. (Miss) 131
Herskovitz, K. (Mrs.) 134
Hertz, Elizabeth (Miss) 97
Hertz, Emanuel (Mrs.) 160
Hertzberg, Mr. and Mrs. 97
Herzberg, M. 119
Herzberg, Mr. and Mrs. 39
Herzberg, Sara (Miss) 34
Herzberg, Sarah (Miss) 37, 39
Herzlich, M. 157
Herzlich, Mr. 169
Herzlich, S. 159
Herzog, Benjamin 29
Herzog, Bennie 29
Hess, Mrs. 177
Hess, S.E. 178
Hesser, S. 160
Heyman, Isaac (Mr. and Mrs.) 97
Heyman, Mrs. 91, 97, 143
Hide, Mr. and Mrs. 40
Hidzkin, H. 185
Higger, A. (Mrs.) 64, 98
Hilf, C. 34
Hilf, S. (Miss) 25
Hilf, Sadie (Miss) 34
Hilf, William (Mr. and Mrs.) 97
Hillels, Mrs. 167
Hillelson, J. 154, 157
Hillelson, J. (Mrs.) 164
Hillelson, Mrs. 167
Hillman, E.A. 185
Hillman, Gertrude (Miss) 97
Hillman, M. 182
Himmelrich, I. (Mr. and Mrs.) 97
Himmelrich, I. (Mrs.) 97
Himmelstein, Alfred Lewis (Mr. and Mrs.) 16
Himovitz, Mr. and Mrs. 28

Hindelman, T. 59
Hirsborn, H. 47
Hirsch, Arthur 97, 98
Hirsch, Elias 97
Hirsch, Essie 97, 98
Hirsch, Essie (Miss) 97, 98, 105, 108
Hirsch, H. (Miss) 67
Hirsch, I. (Mr. and Mrs.) 98
Hirsch, Isaac 61
Hirsch, J. (Mr. and Mrs.) 98
Hirsch, J. (Mrs.) 66, 98
Hirsch, J. Arthur 97
Hirsch, J.A. 97, 108
Hirsch, Jacob 97, 115
Hirsch, Jacob (Mr. and Mrs.) . . . 7, 20, 97, 98
Hirsch, Jacob (Mrs.) 13
Hirsch, Jacob L. 97
Hirsch, M. 84, 97
Hirsch, M. (Mr. and Mrs.) 98
Hirsch, M. (Mrs.) 98, 111
Hirsch, M.J. 98, 108, 109
Hirsch, M.J. (Mrs.) 98
Hirsch, Marcus 73, 97, 98
Hirsch, Marcus J. 97, 98
Hirsch, Michael 6, 61, 98, 102, 109, 111
Hirsch, Michael (Mr. and Mrs.) . . . 3, 97, 98
Hirsch, Michael (Mrs.) 98, 108
Hirsch, Miss 98
Hirsch, Misses 98
Hirsch, Percy (Master) 98
Hirsch, Percy T. 3
Hirsch, Robert 97, 98
Hirsch, S. (Miss) 146
Hirsch, S. (Mrs.) 64
Hirsch, Samson ben Raphael 5
Hirsch, Sophia (Miss) 97
Hirsch, Sophie (Miss) 97, 98, 101
Hirsch, T. Percy 97
Hirsch, W. (Mrs.) 98
Hirschberg, Abraham 160
Hirschberg, J. (Mr. and Mrs.) 157, 160
Hirschberg, J.B. 111
Hirschberg, Millie (Miss) 160
Hirschberg, Sam (Mr. and Mrs.) 160
Hirschberg, Samuel (Mrs.) 36
Hirschberg, Samuel (Rev.) 36
Hirschberg, Sol 29
Hirschberg, Sol (Mr. and Mrs.) 160
Hirschenbein, Moses 29
Hirschfelder, Maud (Miss) 160
Hirschfelder, Maude (Miss) 98
Hirschfield, F. (Miss) 112
Hirschfield, Miss 26
Hirschman, A.N. (Rev. and Mrs.) 98
Hirschorn, L. (Mrs.) 19
Hirschorn, M. 158
Hirscovitch, Fannie (Miss) 98
Hirscovitch, L. (Miss) 98
Hirscovitch, Mr. and Mrs. 98
Hirsenhorn, Benny 29
Hirshberg, H. (Mrs.) 98
Hirshberg, I. 129
Hirshberg, J.B. 98
Hirshberg, Lottie (Miss) 98
Hirshfelder, Maude (Miss) 160
Hirshfield, S.E. 98
Hirshman, A.C. 162
Hirshorn, H.E. 67
Hirshorn, M. 62
Hirskovitch, Hyman 29
Hirskovitch, Mrs. 29
Hofer, W. (Miss) 160
Hoffer, Benjamin 29

Hoffer, Charles 29, 152
Hoffer, I. 107
Hoffer, M. 170
Hoffer, Max 170
Hoffman, Bessie (Miss) 77, 99
Hoffman, C. 57
Hoffman, Charles (Mr. and Mrs.) 10, 25
Hoffman, H. 185
Hoffman, H. (Mr. and Mrs.) 185
Hoffman, Harry (Mr. and Mrs.) 10
Hoffman, Hazel (Miss) 98
Hoffman, I. 98
Hoffman, Ida (Miss) 99
Hoffman, Ida E. (Miss) 25
Hoffman, J.C. 185
Hoffman, Jack 29, 98
Hoffman, Lyon 8
Hoffman, Lyon (Mrs.) 77, 137
Hoffman, M. 99, 139
Hoffman, M. (Mr. and Mrs.) 98
Hoffman, M. (Mrs.) 99, 121
Hoffman, M.B. 98
Hoffman, Miss 99
Hoffman, Morrice 11
Hoffman, Morris (Mr. and Mrs.) 99
Hoffman, Mr. and Mrs. 99, 185
Hoffman, Mrs. 104
Hoffman, Nathan (Master) 98
Hoffman, Oscar 99
Hoffman, P. (Miss) 64, 94, 99
Hoffman, P.B. (Miss) 99
Hoffman, P.S. (Miss) 80
Hoffman, Pauline (Miss) 99, 106
Hoffman, Polly (Miss) 77, 86
Hoffman, R. (Miss) 64, 99
Hoffman, S. 185
Hoffman, S. (Miss) 178
Hoffman, S. (Mrs.) 99
Hoffman, S. Rachel 8
Hoffman, Sarah (Miss) 178
Hoffman, T. 99
Hoffman, T. (Mr. and Mrs.) 98, 99
Hoffman, T. (Mrs.) 74, 99, 104
Hoffman, T.H. (Mrs.) 139
Hohenstein, Rebecca 72
Hoichberg, Fanny (Miss) 138
Hoishberg, Mrs. 115
Holdengraber, A. (Mr. and Mrs.) 26
Holdengraber, Adolph (Mr. and
  Mrs.) 3, 99
Holdengraber, H. (Mrs.) 26
Holdengraber, Jacob 48
Holdengraber, Mr. 101
Holdengraber, S. 143
Holdengraber, S. (Master) 49
Holdengraber, S. (Mr. and Mrs.) 26
Holdengraber, S. (Mrs.) 99
Holdengraber, Simon 29
Holdengraber, Sol. 3
Holdengraber, Sol. (Master) 99
Holdengraber, Solomon 52
Hollander, Gertrude (Miss) 149
Hollander, Mildred (Miss) 25, 151
Hollander, Rachel (Miss) 149
Hollander, S. (Mr. and Mrs.) 25
Hollenburg, B. 170
Hollow, Edith (Miss) 153
Hollow, Regina (Miss) 153
Holofcener, I.D. 99, 148-150
Holofcener, I.D. (Mr. and Mrs.) 14
Holofcener, I.D. (Mrs.) 16, 150, 151
Holofcener, Mrs. 79, 99
Holofcener, S.M. (Mrs.) 77

Holstein, Beccie (Miss) 40
Holstein, Beckie (Miss) 40, 109
Holstein, E. (Mrs.) 60
Holstein, L. 49, 115, 139
Holstein, Louis 99
Holstein, Louis (Mr. and Mrs.) 40, 140
Holstein, Miss 12
Holstein, Nat. 51
Holstein, S.L. 40
Holtzman, Annie (Miss) 153
Holtzman, N. 56
Holtzman, Wm. 150
Holyman, A. (Miss) 152
Holyman, W. 152
Holzberg, F. 78
Holzberg, Rae (Miss) 26
Holzman, A. 149, 150
Holzman, A. (Miss) 150
Holzman, Annie (Miss) 148, 150
Holzman, F. 149, 150
Holzman, F. (Mrs.) 150
Holzman, H. (Miss) 152
Holzman, I.W. 150
Holzman, J. 25, 150, 152
Holzman, J. (Mr. and Mrs.) 150, 151
Holzman, J. (Mrs.) 149
Holzmann, Annie (Miss) 152
Honsberger, G. 99
Hoorvitch, L. 56
Horchover, Theo. 75
Horchover, Theodor 29
Horn, S. 148
Hornesteine, Mr. and Mrs. 133
Hornstein, J. 107
Hornstein, K.E. (Miss) 77, 99, 133
Hornstein, M. 61
Horowitz, Charles 183
Horowitz, Ethel (Miss) 23
Horowitz, Joe 73
Horsefall, H. 97
Horsfall, H. 67, 99
Horwitch, Sarah (Miss) 149
Horwith, Samuel 148, 149
Horwitz, A. (Mr. and Mrs.) 10
Horwitz, Albert 148
Horwitz, C. 25, 150
Horwitz, C. (Mr. and Mrs.) 177
Horwitz, Charles 24, 148, 150, 151, 153
Horwitz, Charles H. 150
Horwitz, Chas. 150
Horwitz, I. (Mrs.) 99, 164
Horwitz, Jessie (Miss) 177
Horwitz, Joseph 29
Horwitz, Josie 150, 152
Horwitz, Miss 178
Horwitz, Rachel (Mrs.) 21
Horwitz, S. 148
Horwitz, Sarah (Miss) 32
Howard, A. (Mrs.) 20
Hubert, Millie (Miss) 99
Huffman, Frank 175
Huffman, Frank (Mrs.) 179
Huffman, S. (Miss) 176
Huffman, S. (Mrs.) 180
Hugo, A. 22
Hurovitz, C. 183
Hurt, H. 67
Hurwitz, Charles 151
Hurwitz, H. 59
Hurwitz, Mr. and Mrs. 160
Husfeld, Hyman 176
Huskolovitch, H. (Mrs.) 180
Huskolovitch, M. (Mrs.) 180

Hyams, H. ... 99	Isaacs, Harry ... 176	Jackson, Harold (Master) ... 100
Hyams, Harry ... 29, 45	Isaacs, Henry ... 100	Jackson, M.B. ... 185
Hyams, Joseph ... 99	Isaacs, I. ... 56	Jackson, Minnie (Miss) ... 111
Hyams, S. ... 25, 122	Isaacs, Israel ... 16	Jackson, Miss ... 93, 135
Hyams, S. (Mr. and Mrs.) ... 99	Isaacs, J. ... 105	Jackson, Mr. and Mrs. ... 73
Hyams, Samuel ... 141	Isaacs, J. (Mrs.) ... 100	Jackson, Philip (Master) ... 100
Hyams, Samuel (Mr. and Mrs.) ... 99	Isaacs, Joel ... 160	Jackson, Sadie (Miss) ... 32
Hyman, Effie (Miss) ... 60, 99, 111	Isaacs, Joel D. (Mr. and Mrs.) ... 26	Jacob, Claude ... 178
Hyman, Ethel (Miss) ... 31	Isaacs, John ... 100	Jacob, Lottie (Miss) ... 30
Hyman, Florence (Miss) ... 99	Isaacs, Joseph ... 16	Jacob, Mrs. ... 166
Hyman, Flossie (Miss) ... 60, 84, 98	Isaacs, Jr., H. (Mrs.) ... 175	Jacob, S. (Rabbi) ... 160
Hyman, H. ... 99	Isaacs, Kathleen (Miss) ... 26	Jacobi, Mrs. ... 100
Hyman, H. (Mr. and Mrs.) ... 99	Isaacs, Kitty (Miss) ... 9	Jacobovitch, Etta ... 72
Hyman, H. (Mrs.) ... 100	Isaacs, L. (Mrs.) ... 100	Jacobs, "Doc" ... 51
Hyman, H.B. ... 99	Isaacs, L.J. (Mrs.) ... 14	Jacobs, A. ... 59
Hyman, H.J. (Mr. and Mrs.) ... 16	Isaacs, Lyle ... 100	Jacobs, A. (Mr. and Mrs.) ... 83, 101, 126
Hyman, H.J. (Mrs.) ... 100	Isaacs, Lysle ... 16	Jacobs, A. (Mrs.) ... 64, 65, 101, 125, 160, 165
Hyman, Harry B. ... 29	Isaacs, M. ... 52, 100	Jacobs, A.W. ... 100, 101
Hyman, Horatio ... 99	Isaacs, M.R. ... 100	Jacobs, Abraham ... 16
Hyman, Horatio (Mrs.) ... 100	Isaacs, M.R. (Mr. and Mrs.) ... 100	Jacobs, Abraham (Mr. and Mrs.) ... 126
Hyman, I. ... 25	Isaacs, Mildred (Miss) ... 16, 36, 128	Jacobs, Abraham (Mrs.) ... 101
Hyman, I.E. (Mr. and Mrs.) ... 3, 31	Isaacs, Miss ... 178	Jacobs, Al. (Mrs.) ... 102
Hyman, I.E. (Mrs.) ... 100	Isaacs, Mr. ... 56	Jacobs, Alex. Claude ... 48
Hyman, Isaac ... 99	Isaacs, Mr. and Mrs. ... 40	Jacobs, Annette (Miss) ... 38, 60, 67
Hyman, Isaac (Mr. and Mrs.) ... 100	Isaacs, Mrs. ... 65, 100, 161, 182	Jacobs, Annie ... 42
Hyman, Isaac (Mrs.) ... 100	Isaacs, Myer ... 15, 25, 29	Jacobs, Archie ... 61
Hyman, J. (Mrs.) ... 100	Isaacs, Prof. ... 171	Jacobs, Archie (Mr. and Mrs.) ... 97
Hyman, L. ... 150, 152	Isaacs, R. Irene (Miss) ... 100	Jacobs, Archie (Mrs.) ... 77, 98, 102
Hyman, Louis ... 99, 153	Isaacs, Ruby (Miss) ... 100	Jacobs, Arthur ... 31
Hyman, M. ... 47	Isaacs, Samuel ... 15	Jacobs, Arthur (Master) ... 101, 102
Hyman, Marcus ... 178	Isaacs, Sidney ... 25, 56	Jacobs, Arthur S. ... 102
Hyman, Margery (Miss) ... 100	Isaacs, Sydney ... 16	Jacobs, B. ... 73, 112
Hyman, Miss ... 3, 99, 100	Isaacs, W. ... 82	Jacobs, B.W. ... 100
Hyman, Misses ... 99	Isaacs, Walter B. ... 29	Jacobs, Ben W. ... 100
Hyman, Mr. ... 47	Isaacs, Zoe (Miss) ... 177	Jacobs, Benjamin ... 100
Hyman, Mr. and Mrs. ... 99	Isaacson, A. ... 156	Jacobs, Benjamin W. ... 98, 113, 142
Hyman, Mrs. ... 100	Isaacson, Rebecca (Miss) ... 41	Jacobs, Bernard (Master) ... 102
Hyman, Muriel (Miss) ... 99	Isaacson, S. (Mrs.) ... 155	Jacobs, Clara ... 72
Hyman, Nathan ... 100	Isaacson, W. (Mr. and Mrs.) ... 29	Jacobs, D. ... 100
Hyman, W. ... 63	Isaacson, William ... 29	Jacobs, Daniel ... 157
Hyman, William S. ... 16, 98	Isadore, J. ... 100	Jacobs, Dave (Mr. and Mrs.) ... 101
Hyman, Willie ... 100	Isbitz, Harry ... 29	Jacobs, Dorothea (Miss) ... 176
Hymans, S. (Mr. and Mrs.) ... 100	Iseman, Sarah (Miss) ... 23	Jacobs, E. ... 81
Hymowitz, B. ... 160	Iseman, W. (Mr. and Mrs.) ... 23	Jacobs, E. (Miss) ... 112, 127
Ibson, Miss ... 164	Isman, Charles ... 178	Jacobs, E.D. ... 73
Idder, Jacob ... 49	Israel, D. (Mrs.) ... 140	Jacobs, E.J. ... 100
Ilevitch, B. ... 63	Israel, Mrs. ... 100	Jacobs, E.W. ... 22, 59, 62, 90, 100, 101, 122
Illiewitz, A.B. ... 60	Israelovitch, A. ... 183	Jacobs, Eli ... 100, 122
Illivitch, J. ... 133	Israels, Clara (Miss) ... 158	Jacobs, Eli (Mr. and Mrs.) ... 101
Illwitz, B. ... 61	Issen, B. ... 30	Jacobs, Eli W. ... 113
Inclor, J.H. ... 115	Issen, B. (Miss) ... 30, 67, 138	Jacobs, Ernestina F. (Miss) ... 97
Ingentaft, Rose (Miss) ... 167	Issen, E. (Miss) ... 138	Jacobs, Ernestine (Miss) ... 98, 101
Ironstone, P. ... 114	Issen, E.L. (Miss) ... 30, 67, 112, 122	Jacobs, Estelle (Miss) ... 7
Isaacs (Mrs.) ... 16	Issen, Esther (Miss) ... 51	Jacobs, Fanny (Miss) ... 101
Isaacs, A. ... 82	Issen, J. ... 67	Jacobs, G.W. ... 98
Isaacs, A. (Mrs.) ... 36, 100, 128	Issen, Jack ... 29, 30	Jacobs, H. ... 60, 68
Isaacs, Abraham ... 20	Issen, Jack (Mrs.) ... 122	Jacobs, H. (Mrs.) ... 102
Isaacs, Alfred ... 16	Issen, Joseph (Master) ... 3	Jacobs, Hannah ... 16
Isaacs, Alfred (Mr. and Mrs.) ... 30	Issen, Mark (Mrs.) ... 3, 29	Jacobs, Hannah (Mrs.) ... 16
Isaacs, Alfred (Mrs.) ... 109	Issen, Max (Mrs.) ... 30	Jacobs, Harry ... 100, 107
Isaacs, B. ... 100, 122, 127	Issen, Sarah ... 61	Jacobs, Harry (Mr. and Mrs.) ... 101
Isaacs, Ben ... 29	Issenman, A. ... 67, 100	Jacobs, Henry ... 100
Isaacs, Benjamin ... 15, 100	Issenman, S. (Mr. and Mrs.) ... 10	Jacobs, I. ... 101
Isaacs, C. ... 86	Issenstadt, C. ... 100	Jacobs, I. (Miss) ... 101
Isaacs, Charles ... 29	Issenstein, Pauline (Miss) ... 100	Jacobs, I.W. ... 101
Isaacs, Charles Lopez ... 29	Isson, B. ... 74	Jacobs, I.W. (Mrs.) ... 176
Isaacs, Dolly (Miss) ... 9	Jackel, D. ... 89	Jacobs, J. ... 130
Isaacs, E. Miriam ... 42	Jackell, D. (Mr. and Mrs.) ... 75	Jacobs, J. (Mrs.) ... 98
Isaacs, Emmanuel ... 16	Jackell, Mr. ... 3	Jacobs, J.A. ... 59, 90, 101, 102, 111, 139, 143, 146
Isaacs, H. (Mrs.) ... 177	Jackson, A.E. (Mr. and Mrs.) ... 100	Jacobs, J.A. (Mr. and Mrs.) ... 10, 101, 147
Isaacs, H. Rufus ... 176	Jackson, A.H. ... 32, 49, 73, 81, 125	Jacobs, J.A. (Mrs.) ... 72, 77, 102, 113, 143
Isaacs, H.A. ... 176, 179	Jackson, A.H. (Mr. and Mrs.) 10, 32, 100, 138	Jacobs, J.H. ... 101
Isaacs, H.A. (Mrs.) ... 176	Jackson, A.H. (Mrs.) ... 100	Jacobs, J.L. ... 101

Jacobs, J.N. 98
Jacobs, J.W. 49, 101
Jacobs, Jack 100
Jacobs, Jacob A. 70, 101, 113
Jacobs, Jacob J. 62
Jacobs, Johnny 86
Jacobs, Jos. (Mrs.) 146
Jacobs, Joseph (Mrs.) 102, 108
Jacobs, Joseph H. 101
Jacobs, L. 47, 101
Jacobs, L.H. 98, 109
Jacobs, L.H. (Mr. and Mrs.) 88, 101
Jacobs, L.N. (Mrs.) 102
Jacobs, Lena (Miss) 98, 101
Jacobs, Libbie (Miss) 62, 100, 101
Jacobs, Lillian (Miss) 101
Jacobs, Lily (Miss) 142
Jacobs, Lionel 101
Jacobs, Louis 42, 171
Jacobs, Lyon 62, 101, 125
Jacobs, Lyon W. 30, 74, 101
Jacobs, Lyon W. (Mr. and Mrs.) . 10, 101, 109
Jacobs, Lysle 30
Jacobs, M. 60, 65
Jacobs, M. (Mrs.) 102
Jacobs, M. Nathan 132
Jacobs, Marvin 98
Jacobs, Mary (Miss) 101
Jacobs, Max (Mr. and Mrs.) 101
Jacobs, Max (Mrs.) 3, 97, 102, 126
Jacobs, Melvin (Master) 102
Jacobs, Melvyn G. 97
Jacobs, Mert 50
Jacobs, Miriam (Miss) 101
Jacobs, Miss 101
Jacobs, Miss Lena 101
Jacobs, Misses 100, 101
Jacobs, Morris 7
Jacobs, Morris (Mrs.) 102
Jacobs, Mr. 69, 101, 159
Jacobs, Mr. and Mrs. 97, 141
Jacobs, Mrs. 95, 102, 136
Jacobs, N. 120, 130, 171
Jacobs, P. (Miss) 101
Jacobs, R. 102
Jacobs, R.A. 102
Jacobs, R.F. 102
Jacobs, Rabbi 171
Jacobs, Ray (Miss) 164
Jacobs, Rea (Miss) 168
Jacobs, Robert 19, 102
Jacobs, Robert A. 102
Jacobs, Rose (Miss) 164
Jacobs, Rose (Mrs.) 34, 102, 126, 135
Jacobs, Ruth Hast (Miss) 8
Jacobs, S. 161
Jacobs, S. (Mrs.) 161
Jacobs, S. (Rabbi and Mrs.) . . . 101, 157, 166
Jacobs, S. (Rabbi) . . 13, 27, 29-31, 35, 36, 38,
44, 48, 102, 154, 156,
157, 158, 160, 161,
166, 168
Jacobs, S. (Rev.) 166
Jacobs, S.A (Mrs.) 102
Jacobs, S.A. 38, 59, 62
Jacobs, S.A. (Mrs.) 101, 102, 122, 135
Jacobs, S.W. . . . 5, 19, 42, 47-50, 52, 59, 62,
81, 88, 90, 101, 102,
106, 108, 139, 141
Jacobs, S.W. (Mrs.) 136
Jacobs, Sam 48
Jacobs, Samuel 51, 127
Jacobs, Sarah (Miss) 16, 100, 101

Jacobs, Simon 16
Jacobs, Sol (Master) 102
Jacobs, Sollie (Master) 102
Jacobs, Solly 67
Jacobs, Solly (Master) 102
Jacobs, Solomon (Mrs.) 102
Jacobs, Solomon (Rabbi) 42
Jacobs, Tena (Miss) 102
Jacobs, Theo. 122
Jacobs, Tina (Miss) 101
Jacobs, W. 85, 102
Jacobs, William 16
Jacobsohn, Landau (Mrs.) 103
Jacobsohn, Misses 103
Jacobson, A. 57
Jacobson, Alfred 103
Jacobson, Bertha 16
Jacobson, Bertha (Miss) 41
Jacobson, E. (Miss) 64, 80, 114
Jacobson, E.J. 103
Jacobson, Etta (Miss) 77
Jacobson, Fanny (Miss) 115
Jacobson, I. 155, 175, 180
Jacobson, J.J. (Mrs.) 103
Jacobson, Jennie (Miss) 22
Jacobson, Joseph, J. 103
Jacobson, L. (Miss) 138
Jacobson, Leah 42
Jacobson, M. 74, 149
Jacobson, Morisce 103
Jacobson, Mr. 49, 156
Jacobson, Nathan (Mrs.) 57
Jacobson, P. 114
Jacobson, Percy 118, 134
Jacobson, Peter 103
Jacobson, R. 20, 78, 81
Jacobson, R. (Miss) 114
Jacobson, Ruby (Miss) 28
Jacobson, S. (Mr. and Mrs.) . . . 23, 35, 103
Jacobson, Sophie (Miss) 23, 27, 35, 103
Jacobson, Violet (Miss) 41
Jaffe, K. 161
Jaffe, Mr. 132
Jampolsky, Arva (Miss) 22
Jampolsky, J. 71
Jampolsky, M. (Mrs.) 22
Jampolsky, Vera (Miss) 22
Jappenick, Jake 180
Jappenick, Willie 180
Jaslow, H. 103, 121
Jaslow, M. 34, 62
Jaslow, M. (Mr. and Mrs.) 34
Jaslow, Mollie (Miss) 34
Jasper, M. (Miss) 133
Jassby, A.H. 30
Jassby, Eva (Miss) 103
Jassby, N.A. 103
Jassky, A.H. 49
Jessel, M. .57
Jessell, M. .57
Jessell, M. (Mr. and Mrs.) 57
Jessell, Rebecca (Miss) 57
Joel, Minnie E. (Miss) 103
Joel, Rachel (Miss) 44
Johnson, Jenny (Miss) 35
Johnson, N. (Mrs.) 134
Jonas, Clara (Miss) 27, 185
Jonas, Freda (Miss) 103
Jonas, Meta (Miss) 103
Jones, E.W. (Mrs.) 135
Jones, Thomas 103
Jones, W.B. (Mrs.) 37
Joseffy, Miss 103

Joseffy, Raphael 42
Joseffy, Raphael (Mr. and Mrs.) 103
Josefo, Bertie (Miss) 31
Josefo, Ettie (Miss) 31
Josefo, Gertie (Miss) 31, 103
Josefo, John (Mrs.) 103
Josefo, Julius (Mr. and Mrs.) 10, 103
Josefo, Julius (mrs.) 103
Josefo, M. (Mr. and Mrs.) 144
Josefs, Julius 30
Josefs, Julius (Mr. and Mrs.) 103
Joseph, A. Pinto 30, 103
Joseph, Andrew C. (Mr. and Mrs.) . . . 3, 103
Joseph, B. 72, 127, 137
Joseph, Edward 30, 43
Joseph, Fanny (Miss) 103
Joseph, G.A. (Mr. and Mrs.) 103
Joseph, George 44
Joseph, George R. (Mrs.) 43
Joseph, Harry 49
Joseph, Henry 103
Joseph, Henry (Mr. and Mrs.) 103
Joseph, Henry (Mrs.) 103, 144
Joseph, Henry Abraham 43, 44
Joseph, Horace (Mr. and Mrs.) 3, 103
Joseph, Horace (Mrs.) 103
Joseph, Horace, Mr. and Mrs. 103
Joseph, Irene (Miss) 41
Joseph, J. 170
Joseph, J.N. 161
Joseph, Jack 103
Joseph, Jacob 3
Joseph, Judah George 42, 43, 45
Joseph, K. .47
Joseph, K. de S. 47
Joseph, L. (Miss) 103
Joseph, Louisa (Miss) 43
Joseph, M. 139
Joseph, M. (Miss) 30
Joseph, M. (Mr. and Mrs.) 3
Joseph, Marguerite (Miss) 130
Joseph, Michael Joseph 3
Joseph, Miss 123
Joseph, Misses 103, 138
Joseph, Montefiore 49
Joseph, Montefiore (Mr. and Mrs.) . . . 30, 41
Joseph, Montefiore (Mrs.) 103, 130
Joseph, Muriel (Miss) 103
Joseph, Muriel (Mrs.) 103
Joseph, Phyllis (Miss) 103, 130
Joseph, Rachel (Miss) 103
Joseph, Rosetta 42
Joseph, Rosetta (Miss) 41
Joseph, S. (Miss) 30
Joseph, S. (Mr. and Mrs.) 89
Joseph, Sybil (Miss) 130
Joseph, Theodore F. (Rabbi) 103
Josephi, K. (Miss) 161
Josephi, Kate (Miss) 161
Josephi, Miss 161
Josephson, F. (Mrs.) 13
Josephson, Frank (Mr. and Mrs.) 34
Josephson, I. (Mrs.) 138
Josephson, R. (Mrs.) 103
Josephson, Ray (Miss) 34
Jospe, J. 49, 81, 103, 178
Jospe, Mr. 103
Judah, H.H. (Mr. and Mrs.) 103
Judel, Sybil (Miss) 29, 103
Judelson, M.J. (Cantor) 137
Judelson, M.J. (Rev.) 29, 104
Judelson, Rev. 8, 23, 25, 26
Jurist, Carolyne (Miss) 104

Jurist, D. (Mrs.) 39	Kander, Myer 86	Kapstein, Edward M. 30
Jurist, David 104	Kandestin, Charles H. 30, 104	Kapstine, Edward (Mrs.) 178
Jurist, G. (Mrs.) 104	Kandestin, Ida (Miss) 38, 133	Karakofsky, Sam (Mr. and Mrs.) . . . 125
Jurist, Gustav (Master) 104	Kanovitz, Joseph (Rabbi) 49	Karduner, Morris 180
Jurist, M. (Miss) 99, 133	Kanter, M. (Miss) 176	Karn, Annie (Miss) 167
Jurist, M. (Mrs.) 104	Kaplan. M. (Rabbi) 31	Karn, B. (Miss) 167
Jurist, Maurice 104	Kaplan, A. (Mr. and Mrs.) 104	Karnow, Solomon 30
Jurist, Minnie (Miss) 39	Kaplan, Abraham 30	Karp, Mr. and Mrs. 10
Jurist, N. (Mrs.) 77, 104	Kaplan, Bernard M. (Rabbi and	Karp, W. 22
Kabalotsky, Samuel 49	Mrs.) 49, 104	Karrel, M. 57
Kadesky, Mr. 169	Kaplan, Blanche (Miss) 104	Kasel, Gabe 162
Kadishewitz, Dave 133	Kaplan, Blanche Lillian (Miss) 49	Kasky, Louis 104
Kaffenburg, Al 104	Kaplan, C. 149	Kasler, J.W. 170
Kahanovich, A. (Rabbi) 48	Kaplan, Edith (Miss) 149	Kassel, Deborah (Miss) 44
Kahanovich, Rabbi 179	Kaplan, Evelyn (Miss) 30, 167	Kassel, Harriet (Miss) 44
Kahanovitch, Fred 49, 52	Kaplan, F.R. 104	Kassel, Marx 43, 44
Kahanovitch, I. (Chief Rabbi) 178	Kaplan, Fannie (Miss) 99, 104	Kasselman, Mrs. 183
Kahanovitch, I. (Rabbi) 180, 184	Kaplan, H. 104, 154	Kassels, Irene (Miss) 104
Kahanovitch, Israel (Rabbi) 14	Kaplan, I. 115	Kassels, Miss 107
Kahanovitch, Israel J. (Rabbi) 175	Kaplan, I. (Miss) 172	Katz, H. (Dr.) 30
Kahanovitch, Rabbi 40, 175, 177, 180	Kaplan, I. (Mr. and Mrs.) 25, 30, 39	Katz, Hyman 158
Kahanovitch, Rabbi I. 27, 175	Kaplan, I. (Mrs.) 33	Katz, M. 169, 174
Kahanovitch, Sophie (Miss) 49	Kaplan, I.H. (Mr. and Mrs.) 104	Katz, M. (Dr.) 30
Kahn, Charles 30	Kaplan, Ida (Miss) . 30, 39, 104, 139, 161, 167	Katz, Maurice 118
Kahn, Chas. 30	Kaplan, Ida B. (Miss) 23, 161	Katz, Max 148, 151
Kahn, F. 161	Kaplan, Idel 175	Katz, Miriam (Mrs.) 27
Kahn, F. (Mrs.) 130, 161	Kaplan, J. 104	Katz, Mr. 135
Kahn, I.P. (Mr. and Mrs.) 36	Kaplan, J. (Mr. and Mrs.) 30, 99	Katz, Oskar 104
Kahn, J.J. 30	Kaplan, J. (Rev. and Mrs.) 23, 161	Katz, P. 72, 104
Kahn, Mr. and Mrs. 81	Kaplan, J.H. 104	Katz, P. (Mr. and Mrs.) 137
Kahn, P. 138	Kaplan, Jessie (Miss) 167	Katz, P. (Mrs.) 104
Kahn, Percy B. 176	Kaplan, L. (Miss) 161	Katz, Paul 141, 146
Kahn, S. 81	Kaplan, L.A. 56	Katz, Pearl (Miss) 27
Kahn, S. (Mr. and Mrs.) 30	Kaplan, Lillie (Miss) 167	Katz, S. 61, 149
Kahn, S. (Mrs.) 132	Kaplan, Lily (Miss) 154	Katz, Sarah (Miss) 26
Kahn, Samuel 30	Kaplan, M. (Rabbi) 30, 162	Katzman, Mr. 96
Kahn, Suzanne (Miss) 38, 104	Kaplan, M. (Rev.) . 11, 23, 28, 30, 32, 33, 35,	Katzva, A. 170
Kahne, Joseph 81	157, 164, 165, 167, 169	Kauffman (Mrs.) 16
Kaiser, Annie (Miss) 104	Kaplan, Miss 164	Kauffman, Anna (Miss) 25
Kaiserman, Sarah (Mrs.) 134	Kaplan, Misses 160	Kauffman, Bessie (Miss) 25, 105, 171
Kalin, Minnie (Miss) 74	Kaplan, Morris (Mr. and Mrs.) 177	Kauffman, Cora (Mrs.) 172
Kalish, Rose (Miss) 104	Kaplan, Mr. and Mrs. 25, 99, 104	Kauffman, Dora (Miss) 25, 171
Kallmeyer, Meyer (Miss) 161	Kaplan, Mrs. 167	Kauffman, Emma (Miss) 25, 171
Kallmeyer, Minnie (Miss) 161	Kaplan, Rev. 28, 156	Kauffman, H. (Mrs.) 30
Kallmeyer, Mrs. 161	Kaplan, Ruby (Miss) 25	Kauffman, Harry 30
Kalmanovitch, C. 74	Kaplan, S. 30, 169	Kauffman, J. (Mr. and Mrs.) 171
Kalmanovitch, Laura 132, 140	Kaplan, S. (Miss) 163	Kauffman, J. (Mrs.) 171
Kalmanovitch, S. 143	Kaplan, S.M. 30, 161	Kauffman, Jacob (Mr. and Mrs.) 25
Kalmanovitch, S. (Mr. and Mrs.) . . . 104	Kaplan, S.N. (Mr. and Mrs.) 161	Kauffman, Leo 35
Kalmanovitz, L.O. 64	Kaplan, Samuel 30	Kauffman, Leslie 171
Kalmanowitz, S. 122	Kaplan, Sol 30, 161	Kauffman, Maurice 35
Kalmon, P. 72	Kaplan, T. (Miss) 33	Kauffman, Max 16
Kalmonovitz, L. 137	Kaplan, Tessie (Miss) 30, 161, 169	Kauffman, Miss 105
Kamanoff, A. 123	Kaplan, Wolfe (Mr. and Mrs.) 104	Kauffman, Misses 171
Kaminsky, Abe 163	Kaplansky, A. (Mr. and Mrs.) 104	Kauffman, Moses 16
Kaminsky, B. (Sergt.) 162	Kaplansky, A. L. (Mr. and Mrs.) . . . 104	Kauffman, Mr. 182
Kaminsky, Clara (Miss) 149	Kaplansky, A.L. 104	Kauffman, Mr. and Mrs. 185
Kaminsky, E. (Miss) 151, 152	Kaplansky, A.L. (Mr. and Mrs.) . . . 3, 23, 30	Kauffman, Officer 49
Kaminsky, Ethel (Miss) 150	Kaplansky, David 134	Kauffman, P. (Mr. and Mrs.) 162
Kaminsky, Moses (Master) 149	Kaplansky, David (Master) 3	Kauffman, Saul 25
Kaminsky, R. (Miss) 151	Kaplansky, J. 104, 171	Kaufman, Ben 167
Kamisher, P. 122	Kaplansky, J.A. 104	Kaufman, Benny (Master) 167
Kamman, Clara (Miss) 30	Kaplansky, J.A. (Mr. and Mrs.) 104	Kaufman, D. 158
Kamman, Isidore 30	Kaplansky, Julius 104, 171	Kaufman, David 30
Kamman, J. 31, 167	Kaplansky, Julius A. 3, 104	Kaufman, Ethel (Miss) 25
Kamman, Julius 30, 161	Kaplansky, M. 30, 75	Kaufman, Harry 74
Kamman, L. 30	Kaplansky, Michael 104	Kaufman, I. (Mr. and Mrs.) 30
Kamman, Maurice 30	Kaplansky, R. 30	Kaufman, I.A. (Mr. and Mrs.) 131
Kamman, Maurice J. (Mr. and	Kaplansky, R.L. 30	Kaufman, L. 150
Mrs.) 10	Kaplansky, Rose (Miss) 23	Kaufman, Master 93
Kamman, Mr. and Mrs. 30	Kaplansky, Ruby 30	Kaufman, Max 16
Kander, Isaac (Mr. and Mrs.) 30	Kaplansky, William 3	Kaufman, Miss 66, 164
Kander, Meier 30	Kaplansky, Willie 69, 134	Kaufman, Philip 30, 162

Kaufman, R. 30	Kendenstein, Annie (Miss) 30	King, Herman Samuel 31
Kaufman, R. (Mr. and Mrs.) 10	Kenen, A.I. 156	King, J. 179
Kaufman, S. 114	Kenen, Augusta (Miss) 154, 158, 165	King, J.S. (Mr. and Mrs.) 162
Kaufman, Samuel 30	Kenen, Emanuel I. 155, 167	King, Joseph (Mr. and Mrs.) 106, 166
Kaufmann, Ethel (Miss) 23	Kenen, Emanuel I. (Mr. and Mrs.) . . . 157, 163	King, Joseph (Mrs.) 156, 169
Kauvar, H. (Rabbi) 61	Kenen, Emanuel J. 156	King, Leo 162
Kawin, M.R. (Mrs.) 161	Kenen, Esther (Miss) 158	King, M. (Miss) 161
Kay, Asna (Mrs.) 105	Kenen, Freda (Miss) 164	King, Mr. and Mrs. 158
Kay, Miss 105	Kenen, I.E. 162	King, Mrs. 167, 172
Kay, William (Mrs.) 105	Kenen, L.L. 156	King, Oscar 162
Kayton, Mrs. 19	Kenen, Miss 163	King, S. 106
Keces, S. 105	Ker, John (Mrs.) 105	King, Samuel 166
Keel, A. 183	Kerner, B. 105	King, Samuel (Mrs.) 162
Keel, L. 183	Kerner, H. 105	King, Theo 106
Keen, M. 105	Kerner, Mr. 105	King, Theo. 106
Keezel, Jacob 30	Kerner, O. (Mr. and Mrs.) 105	King, Theodore 106
Keir, J. (Mrs.) 127	Kerner, O.L. (Mr. and Mrs.) 26	Kinsky, I. 106
Keiser, Miss 105	Kerner, O.L. (Mrs.) 105	Kinsnick, I. 183
Kelf, Alexander 105	Kerner, S. 26, 99, 105	Kirsch, A. (Mrs.) 93, 106
Kellert, B. 105	Kerr, J. (Mr. and Mrs.) 105	Kirsch, Abraham (Mr. and Mrs.) 7, 31
Kellert, B. (Miss) 52, 98	Kerr, J. (Mrs.) 127	Kirsch, D. 98
Kellert, Beccie (Miss) 105, 128	Kert, A. 152	Kirsch, Dave 75
Kellert, Beck (Miss) 105	Kert, A. (Miss) 94	Kirsch, David 127
Kellert, Bessie (Miss) 29	Kert, A. (Mr. and Mrs.) 105	Kirsch, Edward (Master) 106
Kellert, Charles 49	Kert, A. (Mrs.) 105, 148, 149, 152	Kirsch, Malca 2
Kellert, Dorothy (Miss) 29, 77, 143	Kert, Charles 25, 105, 150	Kirsch, Rae (Miss) 117
Kellert, Ernest 105	Kert, Clara (Miss) 149, 150	Kirsch, S. (Dr. and Mrs.) 10, 75, 106
Kellert, Frances (Miss) 105	Kert, Clarabel (Miss) 150	Kirsch, S. 31
Kellert, H. 49, 106	Kert, E. 116, 127, 130	Kirsch, S. (Mrs.) 117
Kellert, H. (Mr. and Mrs.) 29, 83, 105	Kert, Ed. 98	Kirsch, Simon 6, 7, 31
Kellert, H. (Mrs.) 18, 83, 105	Kert, Eddie 73	Kirsch, Simon (Dr.) 31, 93, 106
Kellert, Harris 61, 118	Kert, Edward 105	Kirschberg, "Dollie" (Master) 76
Kellert, Hattie (Miss) 83, 105, 128	Kert, H.I. (Mrs.) 105, 142	Kirschberg, A. (Mrs.) 141
Kellert, I. (Mrs.) 105	Kert, H.M. 151	Kirschberg, Abraham 17
Kellert, J. 105	Kert, Hattie (Miss) 34	Kirschberg, Annie (Miss) 3, 17, 77
Kellert, J. (Mr. and Mrs.) 83	Kert, Hyman 150	Kirschberg, Bella 141
Kellert, J. (Mrs.) 105	Kert, I. 25, 61, 73, 77	Kirschberg, Bella (Miss) 17
Kellert, Jacob 61, 105	Kert, I. (Mr. and Mrs.) 16, 29, 34	Kirschberg, David 3, 68, 118, 134
Kellert, Jacob (Mr. and Mrs.) 105	Kert, Isaac 81	Kirschberg, Dollie 118
Kellert, Jacob (Mrs.) 77, 105, 143	Kert, J. 150, 152	Kirschberg, Dolly (Miss) 69
Kellert, Jake 105	Kert, Joe 148	Kirschberg, F. (Mrs.) 109
Kellert, Jake (Mr. and Mrs.) 105	Kert, Joseph 31	Kirschberg, I. 65, 81, 118
Kellert, Jake (Mrs.) 105	Kert, L. 51, 105, 114	Kirschberg, Isaac 17, 134
Kellert, Joseph (Mr. and Mrs.) 105	Kert, Levi 105	Kirschberg, J. (Mrs.) 109
Kellert, Joseph (Mrs.) 16, 40, 100, 107	Kert, M. 47	Kirschberg, Joseph 17
Kellert, Lillian (Miss) 29	Kert, Max 16, 31, 105	Kirschberg, Joseph (Mr. and Mrs.) 3
Kellert, Lillie (Miss) 105	Kert, Mr. 47, 148	Kirschberg, Joseph (Mrs.) 77
Kellert, Lily (Miss) 29, 98	Kert, R. (Miss) 105	Kirschberg, Miriam (Miss) 3, 17
Kellert, Michael 49	Kert, Rose (Miss) 25, 29, 36, 105	Kirshberg, Annie (Miss) 106
Kellert, Miss 105	Kessler, I. 107	Kirshberg, Miriam (Miss) 106
Kellert, Misses 40, 105	Keyfitz, Arthur 17, 31, 34, 105	Kishner, Ettie (Miss) 106
Kellert, Mr. and Mrs. 105	Keyfitz, Arthur (Mr. and Mrs.) 10	Kishner, Rachel (Miss) 51, 106
Kellert, Raphael 49	Keyfitz, E. 160	Kitz, Harry (Mr. and Mrs.) 10
Kellert, Rebecca (Miss) 83	Keyfitz, Esther (Miss) 17, 34, 167	Kizzel, Jacob 31
Kellert, Ruth (Miss) 119, 143	Keyfitz, Esther A. 34	Klein, A. 140
Kellert, S. 90	Keyfitz, Mark 17	Klein, A. (Mrs.) 106
Kellert, Sol 84, 105, 115	Keyfitz, Miss 105, 146, 161, 164	Klein, Abe M. 31
Kellert, Sol. 22, 73, 105	Keyfitz, Moses (Dr.) 17	Klein, Abraham 31
Kellert, Solomon 29, 67, 105, 143	Keyfitz, Mrs. 165, 167	Klein, Anna (Miss) 80
Kellman, E. 158	Keyfitz, Nathan 16, 34	Klein, Annie (Miss) 51
Kellnor, A. 105	Keyfitz, Rebecca (Mrs.) 34	Klein, I. 106
Kellnor, A. (Mr. and Mrs.) 22	Keyfitz, Samuel 17, 34	Klein, Israel 93
Kellnor, B. (Miss) 98	Kibrick, R. 66	Klein, Jacob 83
Kellnor, Esther 61	Kier, J. (Mrs.) 106	Klein, J. 80, 106
Kellnor, Etta (Miss) 105	Killer, Lipe 31	Klein, L. (Miss) 86, 99
Kellnor, Louis 3	Kimelman, Max 180	Klein, Lilian (Miss) 86
Kellnor, Mr. and Mrs. 3, 105	Kindestin, Annie (Miss) 31	Klein, Lillian (Miss) 80, 86, 106
Kelly, Mr. 182	Kindestin, Harry 31	Klein, Lily 42
Kelman, L. 158	Kindestin, Ida (Miss) 31	Klein, Moe 31
Kelsch, Helen 42	King, Arthur 124	Klein, Morris 31
Kelz, A. 155	King, Bertha (Miss) 25, 144, 168	Klein, Mrs. 24
Kempler, Sydney 64	King, Charles 162	Klein, R. (Miss) 64, 106
Kempner, J. (Mr. and Mrs.) 105	King, Harry (Mr. and Mrs.) 162	Klein, Rosa 49, 52

Klein, Rosa (Miss) 80, 86, 106	Kolber, S. 49, 81	Kronenberg, Henry 68, 105
Klein, Rose (Miss) 24, 77, 106	Koleski, Alex 176	Kronick, Gertrude (Miss) 41
Klein, Rosie (Miss) 80	Kollner, J. 106	Kronick, Joseph 31
Klein, S. 66	Komaroff, A. 134	Kronick, Mr. 149
Kleinberg, Annie (Miss) 84	Kominsky, Louis 56	Kronick, S. 30, 107
Kleinberg, L. (Mr. and Mrs.) 101	Konel, M. (Mr. and Mrs.) 10	Kronick, Sam 31
Kleinberg, N. 106	Konigsberg, T. 59	Kronick, Samuel . . 31, 155, 162, 164, 168, 169
Kleinberg, Otto 106	Konyer, Joseph (Mrs.) 130	Kronik, Mr. 166
Kleinberg, Sophie (Miss) 77	Kopel, Esther (Miss) 106	Kronik, S. 162
Kleiner, M. 183	Kopelowich, H. 175	Kronson, J. (Mrs.) 179
Kleiner, Morris 40	Koren, K. 183	Krugel, H. 156
Klezmer, R. 72	Korn, Anna (Miss) 22	Kruger, J. (Mr. and Mrs.) 107, 129
Kliman, J. 182	Korn, Annie (Miss) 162, 167	Kruger, Jean 107
Kline, A. (Miss) 183	Korn, F. (Miss) 165	Kruger, Jos. (Mr. and Mrs.) 107
Kline, Anna (Miss) 39	Korn, Fanny (Miss) 154	Kruger, Joseph 107
Kline, Annie (Miss) 183	Korn, I. (Mrs.) 179	Kruger, Joseph (Mrs.) . . . 90, 107, 123, 124,
Kline, B. 183	Korn, J. 152	129, 130
Kline, H.B. 183, 184	Korn, Louis (Mrs.) 13	Krukin, D. 115
Kline, H.B. (Mr. and Mrs.) 183	Korn, M. 149	Krulewitch, S. (Miss) 114
Kline, J.I. (Mr. and Mrs.) 178	Korn, Misses 160	Kruss, M. (Dr. and Mrs.) 107
Kline, L. 183	Korn, Rebecca (Miss) 22	Kubelick, M. 171
Kline, Lille (Miss) 106	Korn, S. 151	Kubelick, Mrs. 124
Kline, M. 106	Korn, S. (Mr. and Mrs.) 22	Kubelik, F. Max 31
Kline, Morris 184	Kornberg, Mr. 31	Kubelik, I. (Mrs.) 124
Klineberg, Adela (Miss) 107	Kornfeld, J. (Rabbi) 106	Kubelik, M. 107
Klineberg, L. (Mr. and Mrs.) 10	Kornfeld, Joseph (Rabbi and Mrs.) 10	Kubelik, Max 31, 107
Klineberg, O. 106	Kornfeld, Joseph (Rabbi) 93	Kubelik, Max (Mrs.) 100
Klineberg, S. (Miss) 60, 61	Kornfeld, Joseph S. (Rabbi) 93	Kuisnick, I. 183
Klineberg, Sophie 42	Kornreich, Abraham 31	Kuner, Mr. 183
Klineberg, Sophie (Miss) 37, 106	Korotkin, Mr. 155	Kuntz, Mr. and Mrs. 98
Kling, Gabriel 157	Korotkin, W. 17, 159	Kunz, Hugo (Dr.) 97
Kling, J. 64	Kortosk, B. 2, 90, 98, 101, 106	Kunz, Paul (Mrs.) 97
Kling, L. 183	Kortosk, E.H. 106	Kuppenheim, Helene (Mrs.) 17
Kling, Mr. and Mrs. 162	Kortosk, Mr. 43	Kuppenheim, J.D. 17
Kling, Mrs. 22	Kosawatski, Mrs. 66	Kuppenheim, Joseph 17
Kling, Oscar 31	Kotzon, Sara (Miss) 170	Kuppenheimer, J.D. 107
Klinsmith, S. (Mrs.) 14	Kotzon, W. (Mrs.) 170	Kuppenheimer, J.D. (Mr. and Mrs.) 107
Klopot, A. (Mrs.) 125	Kovansky, Mr. 175	Kuppenheimer, Joseph 107
Klopot, Adam (Mr. and Mrs.) 97, 124	Kowalson, Max (Mr. and Mrs.) 10	Kuppenheimer, Mrs. 107
Klopot, Adam (Mrs.) 19, 106, 117	Kowlson, Mr. 176	Kurtz, Sarah (Miss) 80
Kluner, J. 180	Kozinsky, J. 114	Kuschner, S. 59
Kluner, J. (Mrs.) 175, 180, 181	Kozlow, Sarah (Miss) 27	Kusner, H. 59
Knelman, A. (Mrs.) 175, 181	Kramer, E. (Miss) 24	Kussner, E. 115
Kobrinski, Solomon 175	Kramer, G. 24	Kussner, I. 17
Kochman, B. (Mrs.) 106	Kramer, Mrs. 107	Kussner, I. (Mrs.) 121
Koenigsberger, Stella (Mrs.) 97	Kranetz, M.B. 183	Kutner, Mr. and Mrs. 138
Koenigsberger, Sydney 97	Kraus, B. 31	Kutz, H. (Mrs.) 174
Koffman, I. 134	Kraus, Bernard 31	Kutz, Mrs. 174
Koffman, L. 108	Krauskopf, M. (Rabbi) 33	Labovitch, I. 178
Koffman, Rose (Miss) 69	Krawatz, Anna (Miss) 26	Lachman, Rose (Miss) 40
Kofman, L.J. 65	Krawatz, Jake 26	Lachman, S. (Mr. and Mrs.) 40
Kofman, Leon 98	Kredencer, S. 107	Lachovetiz, Jacob 47
Kofsky, Fannie (Miss) 28	Krehm, H. (Mr. and Mrs.) 10	Lachovitzky, B. 131
Kofsky, H. 158	Kreider, F. (Mr. and Mrs.) 36	Laff, William 174
Kofsky, Mr. 162	Kreiger, Joseph (Mrs.) 129	Lagowitz, S. (Mr.and Mrs.) 104
Kofsky, Sheshet 175	Kreinson, Jack 28	Laing, J. 82
Kohl, Alex. 161	Kreinson, L.M. 28, 107	Lalin, J. (Mrs.) 107
Kohl, D. 162	Kreinson, Louis 107	Lambert, C. 61, 90, 107
Kohl, H. 162	Kresner, Tessie (Miss) 93	Lambert, Charles 67
Kohl, Harry 162	Krevel, J.B. 17	Lambert, Mr. and Mrs. 107
Kohnstamm, Jacob 31	Kriger, F. (Miss) 27	Lancaster, S. 185
Kolber, Esther (Miss) 106	Kriger, Fanny (Miss) 38, 150	Landau, Charles 107
Kolber, Etta (Miss) 106	Kriger, L. (Miss) 151	Landau, J. 176
Kolber, F. (Mrs.) 91	Kriger, Leah (Miss) 38, 150, 151	Landau, L. 51, 107
Kolber, Fannie (Miss) 22	Kriger, Leah C. (Miss) 151	Landau, Michael 107
Kolber, Fanny (Miss) 106	Kriger, Miss 149	Lande, Francis (Miss) 107
Kolber, J. (Dr.) 106	Kriger, S. (Mr. and Mrs.) 27	Lande, G. 61
Kolber, Joseph 47	Kriger, Samuel (Mr. and Mrs.) 38	Lande, Gertrude (Miss) 84, 107
Kolber, Joseph (Dr.) 106	Krigle, Max 42	Lande, H. 37, 62, 78
Kolber, M. 67	Krischok, S. 129	Lande, H. (Mr. and Mrs.) 107
Kolber, M. (Miss) 124	Krisnick, I. 183	Lande, Harold (Master) 23
Kolber, M.M. 67	Krolick, Mrs. 14	Lande, I. 23, 81, 107
Kolber, Max 65, 88, 106	Krolik, M.Z. 47	Lande, I. (Mr. and Mrs.) 10, 107

Lande, I. (Mrs.)   23, 71, 92, 107, 108, 141, 158
Lande, Isaac 49, 112
Lande, Israel 182
Lande, J. (Mr. and Mrs.) 24
Lande, Mrs. 134
Lande, N. 89
Lande, N. (Mr. and Mrs.) 107
Lande, N. (Mr.and Mrs.) 75
Lande, N. (Mrs.) 84
Lande, Nathan 73, 122, 125
Lande, Nathan (Mr. and Mrs.) . . . 10, 74, 107
Lande, Nathan (Mrs.) 84
Lande, Rhoda (Miss) 23
Lande, Sol. 182
Landman, Isaac (Rabbi) . . 28, 31, 49, 93, 108
Landon, Miss .88
Lands, L. 185
Landsberg, A. (Mr. and Mrs.) 28
Landsberg, A. (Mrs.) 155, 165
Landsberg, E. (Miss) 162
Landsberg, J. 162, 163
Landsberg, Judith (Miss) 165
Landsberg, Mary (Miss) . . 28, 155, 157, 162,
                                   165, 168
Landsberg, Miss 27, 163
Landsberg, Mrs. 155, 156, 165
Landsberg, Ray (Miss) 154
Landskroner, S. 72
Landy, Mrs. 11
Lang, H. . . 3, 36, 45, 68, 71, 75, 78, 81, 83,
                              108, 112, 114, 115,
                              117, 121, 138
Lang, H. (Mr. and Mrs.) 3, 10, 65, 108
Lang, Harry (Mr. and Mrs.) 10
Lang, Jacob 65
Lang, Jacob David 3
Lang, Jesajahu Richard 3
Lang, Joshua Joseph . . . .·. .10
Lang, S. 68
Langeberg, H.F. 108
Lankofsky, Miriam (Miss) 107
Lapine, Mamie (Miss) 153
Lapine, Rose (Miss) 150
Lapkovitz, L. .59
Laredo, A. 108
Laredo, A.M. 108
Lasker, Lillian 72
Lasker, Lillian (Miss) 108
Lasker, Lily (Miss) 77
Lasker, M. (Mrs.) 19
Lasker, Mr. and Mrs. 108
Lasky, B. (Mr. and Mrs.) 10
Laster, B. 161, 162
Laterman, A. (Mr. and Mrs.) 22
Laterman, Rebecca (Miss) 22
Latsky, M. 86
Lauchman, J. (Mr. and Mrs.) 108
Lauchman, J. (Mrs.) 108
Lauchmann, Mr. and Mrs. 143
Lauderman, A.A. (Mr. and Mrs.) 108
Lauer, B. 108
Lauer, B. (Mr. and Mrs.) 108
Lauer, B. (Mrs.) 86
Lauer, Ben (Mr. and Mrs.) 10
Lauer, D. 60, 61
Lauer, David 106, 107
Lauer, Harold Isadore (Master) 10
Lauer, Louis (Master) 178
Lauer, M. (Mr. and Mrs.) 178
Lauer, M. (Mrs.) 35
Laurence, Barnett 43
Laurence, Rita (Miss) 168
Lauria, F.S. 126

Laurie, A.J. 108
Laurie, Dr. 108
Laurier, Wilfid (Sir) 42
Lauterman, Dinah (Miss) 108
Lauterman, Florence (Miss) 23
Lauterman, M. (Major) 7
Lauterman, M. (Mr. and Mrs.) 23
Lauterman, M.A. 114
Lauterman, M.A. (Rabbi) 25
Lauterman, Max (Dr.) 108
Lauterman, Maxwell (Dr.) 108
Lauterman, Misses 123
Lavat, L. 77
Lavine, Bessie (Miss) 39, 108
Lavine, D. 162
Lavine, D. (Mr. and Mrs.) 39
Lavine, D. (Mrs.) 155
Lavine, Harry 156
Lavine, J. 169
Lavine, Jack 167
Lavine, Jack (Capt.) 162
Lavine, Martha (Miss) 154, 156, 162
Lavine, Miss 126
Lavine, Morris 164
Lavine, Mrs. 162, 167
Lavine, Ray (Miss) 156, 162
Lavine, Sam 167
Lavoi, Mr. and Mrs. 28
Lavut, Bertha (Miss) 37
Lavut, I. (Mr. and Mrs.) 109
Lavut, Isaac 49
Lavut, M. 37, 78
Lavut, Menasseh 49
Lavut, Mr. 31
Lawe, N. (Mrs.) 79
Lawry, S. 157
Lax, Bertha (Miss) 87
Lax, H. (Mr. and Mrs.) 27
Lax, J. (Mr. and Mrs.) 27
Lax, M. 108
Lax, Rose (Miss) 27
Laxer, B. 137
Laxer, G. 26
Lazar, Mr. 70
Lazarovicz, L. (Mr. and Mrs.) 108
Lazarovitz, D. (Master) 108
Lazarovitz, L. 132
Lazarovitz, L. (Mrs.) 132
Lazarowitz, Louis 108
Lazarson, M. .42
Lazarus, B. 122
Lazarus, D. 184
Lazarus, D. (Mrs.) 108
Lazarus, Dora (Mrs.) 17
Lazarus, H. 108, 185
Lazarus, H. (Mr. and Mrs.) 72
Lazarus, H. (Mrs.) 91, 108
Lazarus, Hattie 49, 52
Lazarus, Hattie (Miss) 107
Lazarus, Hattie S. (Mrs.) 108
Lazarus, Henry 17
Lazarus, Henry (Mr. and Mrs.) 24, 108
Lazarus, Henry (Mrs.) 108
Lazarus, J. 171
Lazarus, J. (Mrs.) 171
Lazarus, J.L. (Mrs.) 171
Lazarus, Julius 171, 173
Lazarus, Julius (Mrs.) 144
Lazarus, M. 107
Lazarus, Maud (Miss) 24
Lazarus, Maude (Miss) 24, 66, 108
Lazarus, Maude (Mrs.) 108
Lazarus, Mr. and Mrs. 108

Lazarus, Mrs. 108
Lazarus, Rabbi 43
Lazuresco, H. 182
Leacock, Stephen (Professor) 123
Lean, Abraham W. 108
Lean, William 108
Leavitt, B. 108
Leavitt, E. 108
Leavitt, Emanuel 119
Leavitt, J. 73
Leavitt, Jacob 42
Leavitt, Joseph 49, 52, 108
Leavitt, O.L. (Miss) 69
Lebarsky, M. 179
Lebofsky, Annie (Miss) 162
Lechovitz, E. 148
Lechovitz, M. 148
Lechtzier, A. 178
Lechtzier, A. (Mr. and Mrs.) 178
Lechtzier, A. (Mrs.) 180
Lechtzier, Abram 180
Lechtzier, Barney 178
Lechtzier, Daisy (Miss) 178
Lechtzier, Elizabeth (Miss) 38, 178
Lechtzier, Hattie (Miss) 178
Lechtzier, Jack 178
Lechtzier, Jacob 178
Lechtzier, Lilly (Miss) 177, 178
Lechtzier, Moses (Mr. and Mrs.) . . . 38, 178
Lechtzier, P. 180
Lechtzier, Ph. (Mr. and Mrs.) 178
Lechtzier, Samuel 178
Lederer, Miss 102, 108, 142
Lederer, Theresa (Miss) 108
Lee, J. 108
Leeb, Irving 108
Leeser, Al. (Mrs.) 108
Leff, H. 170
Lefkovitch, S. (Miss) 88
Lefkovitz, H. (Mrs.) 80
Lefkovitz, L. .49
Lefkovitz, L. (Mrs.) 25
Lefkowitz, Dorothy (Miss) 109
Lefkowitz, Meyer 123
Lefkowitz, Meyer (Mr. and Mrs.) . . . 38, 109
Lefkowitz, Ruth (Miss) 109
Lefkowitz, Sarah (Miss) 38, 109
Lefson, Mr. 49
Lefson, Mr.) .51
Lehberg, Bernard 134
Lehberg, E. 178
Lehberg, Gladys (Miss) 134
Lehberg, J.L. 176
Lehberg, Mr. and Mrs. 10
Lehberg, Paula (Mrs.) 178
Lehberg, Ruth May (Miss) 10
Lehcovitz, M. 119
Lehman, Sol 152
Lehrer, Bernice Isabelle (Miss) 17
Lehrer, Gertrude (Miss) 24
Lehrer, H. 78, 81, 82
Lehrer, H. (Mr. and Mrs.) 24
Lehrer, H.M. 114, 134
Lehrer, L. 22
Lehrer, L. (Mr. and Mrs.) 10, 17
Lehrer, L. (Mrs.) 22
Lehrer, M. (Mrs.) 98
Leiboosky, L. 165
Leibovitch, Benny 70
Leibovitch, Bertha (Miss) 28
Leibovitch, P. (Mr. and Mrs.) 28
Leibovitz, R. (Miss) 88
Leikan, R. (Mrs.) 152

Leiken, Mrs. 151	Letomoff, Lena (Miss) 140	Levin, J. (Mrs.) 57
Leikin, Mrs. 149	Letvinoff, Lena (Miss) 185	Levin, J.K. 178, 180
Leishman, K. 112	Letvinoff, Paul 185	Levin, J.K. (Rabbi and Mrs.) 10, 178
Leiter, Jacob 81	Levay, Mrs. 140	Levin, J.K. (Rabbi) . 7, 14, 27, 29, 30, 33, 35,
Leiter, Mrs. 109	Levenhof, I.J. 49	39, 40, 46, 48, 49,
Lemlein, Bert 109	Levenson, A. (Dr.) 49	175, 176, 178, 180,
Lemlein, R. (Mrs.) 75, 101, 109	Levenstein, Ray (Miss) 109	181, 185
Lempert, Mr. 154	Leverenz, Otto 49	Levin, J.K. (Rev.) 179
Lennis, Mrs. 14	Leverson, H. 175	Levin, Jack 152
Leo, Dorothy (Miss) 3, 34, 66, 89	Levetus, H. (Mrs.) 109, 161	Levin, Jennie (Miss) 41, 149
Leo, J.S. 49, 109, 114, 134, 170	Levetus, H.G. (Mrs.) 157	Levin, L. 106
Leo, J.S. (Mrs.) 77, 109	Levetus, Lily B. (Miss) 163	Levin, Leon 106, 110
Leo, L.M. 103	Levetus, Mr. 168	Levin, Leon (Master) 110
Leo, Maitland 163	Levi, Anna (Miss) 179	Levin, M. 59
Leo, Maitland L. 42	Levi, Blanche (Miss) 38, 109	Levin, M. (Miss) 163
Leo, Mrs. 109, 134, 145	Levi, Bluma (Miss) 32, 109	Levin, M.A. (Rabbi) 110
Leon, Elias (Mr. and Mrs.) 178	Levi, Cassil 38	Levin, M.A. (Rev.) 3, 110, 163
Leon, Francis W. 61	Levi, D. (Mr. and Mrs.) 38, 109, 133	Levin, M.C. 178
Leonstroff, J. (Mrs.) 128	Levi, D. (Mrs.) 109, 131	Levin, M.L. 81, 106, 115, 122
Leopold, Felix 31	Levi, David 17, 62	Levin, M.L. (Mr. and Mrs.) 10
Leopold, Samuel 31	Levi, David (Mr. and Mrs.) . . . 7, 109, 131	Levin, Max 3, 122
Lepine, R. (Miss) 150, 152	Levi, David (Mrs.) 109	Levin, Max L. 32, 75, 110
Lepine, Rose (Miss) 77, 152	Levi, E. 163	Levin, Miss 150
Lepitzky, J. 109	Levi, Edward 22	Levin, Moses E. (Mr. and Mrs.) 150
Lepitzky, Mr. 28	Levi, Flora (Miss) 179	Levin, Mr. 24
Lepofsky, Fanny (Miss) 154	Levi, Frank 176, 181	Levin, N.C. 175
Lepsin, H. 185	Levi, Harry 176, 181	Levin, P. (Rev.) 57
Lerman, K. 59	Levi, Hilda (Miss) 38, 91, 109	Levin, Philip 32
Lerman, M. (Miss) 29	Levi, Irene (Miss) 38, 109, 133	Levin, Philip (Mr. and Mrs.) 10
Lerner, Annie (Miss) 37	Levi, J. 73, 90, 98	Levin, R. 61
Lerner, B. 139	Levi, Jack 34, 98, 102, 109, 126	Levin, Rev. 8, 10, 57
Lerner, E.M. (Mrs.) 151	Levi, L.H. (Mrs.) 178	Levin, S. (Dr. and Mrs.) 160
Lerner, J. (Mr. and Mrs.) 28	Levi, Leonard (Rabbi) 171	Levin, S. (Mr. and Mrs.) 40, 75, 110
Lerner, L. (Mrs.) 109	Levi, Lester 109	Levin, Sarah (Miss) 86
Lerner, M. 105, 152	Levi, Lyon 109	Levin, W. 112
Lerner, Ray (Miss) 28	Levi, Mattie (Miss) 109	Levin, Walter (Rabbi) 7
Lerner, Rhoda (Miss) 37	Levi, Maurice 109	Levin, William 178
Lerner, Sadie (Miss) 80, 86	Levi, Maurice (Mrs.) 109, 125	Levine, A. 62, 81, 90, 110, 135, 162
Lescnoff, S. 121	Levi, Michael 31	Levine, A. (Mr. and Mrs.) 32, 111
Lesner, L.M. (Mrs.) 150	Levi, Miss 109	Levine, A. (Mrs.) 74, 109, 111
Lesser, A. 109	Levi, Misses 178	Levine, A.A. 110
Lesser, A. (Mr. and Mrs.) 79, 109	Levi, Mrs. 180	Levine, A.S. 93
Lesser, A. (Mrs.) 77, 109, 145	Levi, P. 168	Levine, A.S. (Mr. and Mrs.) 111
Lesser, Al. (Mrs.) 119, 139, 144	Levi, Paul (Mrs.) 109	Levine, Annie (Miss) 150
Lesser, Ben (Mr. and Mrs.) 109	Levi, Percy 109	Levine, B. 110
Lesser, Benjamin (Mrs.) 60	Levi, Raphael (Mrs.) 109	Levine, Bella (Miss) 32
Lesser, Bennie 49	Levi, S.R. (Mrs.) 180	Levine, Bert (Mrs.) 81
Lesser, Bertha (Miss) 109	Levi, Sarah (Mrs.) 177	Levine, Bertha (Mrs.) 167
Lesser, C. (Mrs.) 146	Levi, W. 56	Levine, Cella 42
Lesser, H. (Mrs.) 109	Levi, W. (Mr. and Mrs.) 40	Levine, D. (Mrs.) 34, 165
Lesser, Julius 36	Levi, William 32	Levine, David 163
Lesser, L. (Miss) 139	Levi, William (Mr. and Mrs.) 10	Levine, Dr. 34
Lesser, Leah (Miss) 40, 77, 109	Levi, William (Mrs.) 109, 142	Levine, E. 110
Lesser, M. 49	Levi, William F. 61	Levine, E.C. 47, 111
Lesser, M. (Mr. and Mrs.) 26	Levin, A. . . 3, 32, 45, 49, 59, 65, 71, 78, 81,	Levine, E.C. (Dr.) 107, 114
Lesser, Moses (Mr. and Mrs.) 109	88, 106, 109, 110,	Levine, Emma (Miss) 100
Lesser, Mr. 163	112, 115, 146	Levine, Etta (Miss) 65, 77, 98, 111
Lesser, Mr. and Mrs. 109	Levin, A. (Miss) 152	Levine, Ettie (Miss) 111
Lesser, Mrs. 109	Levin, A. (Mr. and Mrs.) 3, 75, 110	LeVine, F. 40
Lesser, N. (Mrs.) 36	Levin, A. (Mrs.) 45, 110	Levine, Fanny (Miss) 19
Lesser, R. (Mrs.) 145	Levin, A. (Rev.) 112	Levine, Florence (Miss) 5
Lesser, R.E. (Mrs.) 64	Levin, A.A. (Mr. and Mrs.) 110	Levine, H.E.M. 111
Lesser, S. (Miss) 139	Levin, Abraham 110	Levine, H.M. 81, 111
Lesser, Sarah (Miss) 26, 40, 66, 77, 109	Levin, Anna (Miss) 150	Levine, H.M. (Mr. and Mrs.) 111
Lesser, Yetta (Miss) 135	Levin, Bertha (Miss) 40	Levine, H.M. (Mrs.) 19, 111
Lesses, I. 31	Levin, C. 59	Levine, Harry L. 32
Lesses, L. (Mr. and Mrs.) 174	Levin, D. (Mr. and Mrs.) 160	Levine, Herbert (Mr. and Mrs.) 111
Lesses, Max (Dr.) 174	Levin, D. (Mrs.) 154	Levine, Herbert (Mrs.) 111
Lessess, Dr. 174	Levin, E.C. 110	Levine, Irving 2
Lessess, L. (Mr. and Mrs.) 174	Levin, Emma (Miss) 57	Levine, J. 32, 67, 149, 180
Lessor, A. 62, 81	Levin, H. (Mrs.) 110	Levine, J. (Mrs.) 111
Lessor, M. 114	Levin, H.M. (Mrs.) 110	Levine, Jack 152, 153, 163
Lester, Sophie (Miss) 165	Levin, J. 98, 110	Levine, Lizzie (Miss) 97

Levine, Louis 22, 32	Levinson, Cecilia (Miss) 86, 112, 149	Levitt, Joseph (Mr. and Mrs.) 10
Levine, Louis D. 32	Levinson, Cecillia (Miss) 86	Levitt, M. . 7, 32, 66, 74, 81, 89, 92, 112, 143
Levine, Lyon 42, 88, 106	Levinson, D. (Miss) 177	Levitt, M. (Miss) 88
Levine, M. 162	Levinson, E.R. 32, 176, 178, 181	Levitt, M.B. (Mr. and Mrs.) 10
Levine, M. (Mr. and Mrs.) 36	Levinson, Ethel (Miss) 112	Levitt, M.B. (Mrs.) 27
Levine, M.A. 3, 25	Levinson, Etta (Miss) 176	Levitt, Manuel 112, 125
Levine, M.A. (Rev.) 111	Levinson, Eva (Miss) 77	Levitt, Moses 81
Levine, M.I. 111	Levinson, Goldie 17	Levitt, Mrs. 134
Levine, M.L. 73	Levinson, H. 107, 178	Levitt, R. (Miss) 88
Levine, Marcus 19, 97	Levinson, Harry 49, 51, 60, 73, 111, 112	Levitt, Ray (Miss) 32
Levine, Marcus A. 97	Levinson, Hattie (Miss) 112	Levitt, Rev. 49, 53
Levine, Mark 111	Levinson, I. (Mr. and Mrs.) 10	Levitt, Sam (Mr. and Mrs.) 112
Levine, Martha (Miss) 36, 111, 163	Levinson, I. (Mrs.) 98, 112	Levitz, S.L. (Mr. and Mrs.) 2
Levine, Max 112	Levinson, J. 47, 73, 93, 119	Levontin, D. 69
Levine, Mina (Miss) 111	Levinson, J. (Mr. and Mrs.) 61	Levy, A. 13, 112, 157, 158
Levine, Minnie (Miss) 111	Levinson, J. (Mrs.) 98	Levy, A. (Mr. and Mrs.) 166
Levine, Mr. and Mrs. 133, 163	Levinson, Joseph 61, 84, 111, 125	Levy, A. (Mrs.) 173
Levine, Mrs. 14, 30, 99, 111, 150, 163	Levinson, Joseph (Mrs.) 83, 112	Levy, A.M. 81
Levine, Myer D. 32	Levinson, Jr. Joseph 111	Levy, A.S. 163, 173
Levine, P. 156, 183	Levinson, Jr., J. 98, 111	Levy, Adolph 172
Levine, P. (Mrs.) 111	Levinson, Jr., Joseph 143	Levy, Adolph (Mr. and Mrs.) 171, 172
Levine, R. (Mrs.) 111	Levinson, L. 86	Levy, Adolph (Mrs.) 172
Levine, R.H. (Mrs.) 111	Levinson, Leah (Miss) 28, 29, 112	Levy, Anna (Miss) 33, 80
Levine, Rabbi 31, 172	Levinson, Lillian (Miss) 98, 128	Levy, Annie (Miss) 63
Levine, Rae (Miss) 36, 111	Levinson, Lily (Miss) 98, 112	Levy, Arthur 35
Levine, Ray (Miss) 111	Levinson, Lyon . . . 48, 51, 60, 73, 111, 112,	Levy, B. 112, 113, 136
Levine, Reba (Miss) 150	127, 144	Levy, Benjamin 171
Levine, Rhea (Miss) 97	Levinson, M. 86	Levy, Berthe (Miss) 112
Levine, Ruth (Miss) 111, 124	Levinson, M. (Miss) 112	Levy, Bessie (Miss) 37, 112
Levine, S. 32, 111, 183	Levinson, Mabel (Miss) 77	Levy, Blanche (Miss) 77, 163, 166
Levine, S. (Dr. and Mrs.) 10	Levinson, Mabyl (Miss) 112	Levy, C.J. 112
Levine, S. (Mr. and Mrs.) 36, 133	Levinson, Maxwell 32	Levy, Cecilia (Miss) 35
Levine, Samuel W. (Mr. and Mrs.) 97	Levinson, Miss 3, 112, 136	Levy, Celia (Miss) 34
Levine, Sidney 181	Levinson, Misses 111, 136	Levy, D. 81
Levine, Solomon (Mr. and Mrs.) 111	Levinson, Mr. and Mrs. 40	Levy, D. (Miss) 88
Levine, Walter (Rev.) 111	Levinson, Mrs. 112	Levy, D. (Mrs.) 74, 77, 112, 113
Levine, William 37, 111	Levinson, Myrtie (Miss) . . 98, 105, 111, 112	Levy, David 3, 22, 45, 78, 112
Levine, William M. 97	Levinson, Myrtle (Miss) 35, 60, 83	Levy, David (Mrs.) 77
Levine, Willie 111	Levinson, Mystie (Miss) 112	Levy, E. 158
Levinhoff, I. (Mrs.) 124	Levinson, N. 112, 163, 179	Levy, E.H. (Mrs.) 172
Levinne, D. (Mrs.) 163	Levinson, N. (Mr. and Mrs.) 28, 29, 76, 107, 112	Levy, Eva (Miss) 144
Levinne, Mr. 96	Levinson, N. (Mrs.) 107, 115	Levy, Evelyn (Miss) 24, 163
Levinne, William 111	Levinson, S. 32, 65, 81	Levy, Gabriel 17, 32, 172
Levinoff, H. (Mrs.) 115	Levinson, S. (Mr. and Mrs.) 37, 112	Levy, Gertrude (Miss) 26
Levinoff, H.M. 81, 111	Levinson, S. (Mrs.) 112	Levy, H. 65, 77, 78, 167
Levinoff, H.M. (Mr. and Mrs.) 111	Levinson, Samuel 166	Levy, H. (Mr. and Mrs.) 3
Levinoff, H.M. (Mrs.) 64, 80, 111, 123	Levinson, Sara (Miss) 60, 98, 112	Levy, H. (Mrs.) 98, 109, 122, 166
Levinoff, I. (Mrs.) 71, 111, 124, 159	Levinson, Sarah (Miss) 37, 112	Levy, H.L. (Mrs.) 36
Levinoff, Joseph 49	Levinson, Solomon 61	Levy, H.S. (Mr. and Mrs.) 34
Levinoff, R. (Mr. and Mrs.) 111	Levinson, Tillie (Miss) 60, 77	Levy, Herbert 112
Levinsky, D. (Mrs.) 117	Levinson, Tilly (Miss) 112	Levy, Herman (Mrs.) 172
Levinsky, E. (Miss) 163	Levinson, W. 112	Levy, Hiram 45, 49, 78, 81, 89, 112, 120, 133
Levinsky, H. 89	Levinson, Zave 49, 112	Levy, Hiram (Mrs.) 45
Levinsky, L. 160, 162, 165	Levinter, Etta (Miss) 161	Levy, I. (Mrs.) 173
Levinsky, L. (Miss) 163	Levinter, Etta Clara (Miss) 39	Levy, I. (Rev.) 169
Levinsky, Mrs. 165	Levinter, Mollie (Miss) 154	Levy, I.C. 157
Levinsky, S. 65	Levinter, S. 28, 162	Levy, Ida (Miss) 27, 112
Levinson. I. (Master) 112	Levinter, S. (Mr. and Mrs.) 39	Levy, Isaac (Mrs.) 20
Levinson, A. 118, 175, 179	Levinthal, J. 72, 137	Levy, J. 73, 112, 134, 157, 185
Levinson, A. (Miss) 98	Levinthal, J.M. 137	Levy, J. Leonard (Dr.) 171
Levinson, A. (Mrs.) 178	Levison, A. 152	Levy, J. Leonard (Rev. Dr.) 113
Levinson, A.H. 111	Levison, Dorothy (Miss) 178	Levy, Jack 81
Levinson, A.J. 46, 47, 111	Levison, J. 140, 171	Levy, Jacob 43, 157
Levinson, Annie (Miss) 28, 105, 111, 112	Levit, Mr. 169	Levy, Joe 173
Levinson, B. 176	Levitsky, L. 137	Levy, Jos. C.E. 112
Levinson, B. (Mr. and Mrs.) 10	Levitsky, M.L. 72, 137	Levy, Joseph (Mr. and Mrs.) 172
Levinson, B. (Mrs.) 112, 179	Levitt, Abraham (Rev.) 57, 58	Levy, Joseph (Mrs.) 163
Levinson, B.Z. 179	Levitt, B. (Miss) 88	Levy, L. 74, 108, 126, 173
Levinson, B.Z. (Mrs.) 123, 180	Levitt, B. (Mr. and Mrs.) 112	Levy, Lena (Miss) 172
Levinson, Ben 111	Levitt, Esther 61	Levy, Lewis (Mr. and Mrs.) 24
Levinson, Benjamin G. 32	Levitt, I.M. 134	Levy, Lillian (Miss) 73
Levinson, Bessie (Miss) 37, 111	Levitt, J. 66	Levy, Lily (Miss) 112
Levinson, Cecila (Miss) 112	Levitt, Joseph 112	Levy, Lily Lois (Miss) 112

Levy, Lou 161	Lewis, Mr. 28	Lightstone, Mr. 149
Levy, Louis 17, 32	Lewis, Mrs. 113, 167	Lightstone, Pauline (Miss) 127
Levy, Louis (Mr. and Mrs.) 37	Lewis, N. (Mrs.) 113	Lightstone, S. 32
Levy, Lulu (Miss) 168	Lewis, Nathan 70	Linder, Mr. 132
Levy, M. 32, 127, 163, 167, 171-173	Lewis, Nathan (Mrs.) 113, 147	Lipetz, H. 183
Levy, M. (Mr. and Mrs.) 172	Lewis, Netty (Miss) 31	Lipman, A. (Dr.) 174
Levy, M. (Rabbi) 158	Lewis, R. (Miss) 113, 152	Lipman, Arthur 114
Levy, M.A. (Rabbi and Mrs.) 27	Lewis, Rosalind (Miss) 98, 113, 128	Lipman, B. 114, 174
Levy, M.I. (Rabbi) 112	Lewis, Roslyn (Miss) 98, 113	Lipman, B. (Mr. and Mrs.) 114
Levy, M.M. (Mr. and Mrs.) 23	Lewis, S. (Mr. and Mrs.) 160, 163	Lipman, H. 87
Levy, Maurice 71, 112	Lewis, S. (Mrs.) 113, 154, 155	Lipman, Harris (Mr. and Mrs.) 114
Levy, Minnie (Miss) 171, 172	Lewis, S.B. (Mrs.) 107	Lipman, Max (Mrs.) 73
Levy, Miss 112, 120, 164	Lewis, S.D. (Mrs.) 56, 128	Lipschitz, H. 163
Levy, Misses 172	Lewis, Sam D. 56	Lipsey, Fannie (Miss) 114
Levy, Moe 35, 172	Lewis, Samuel (Mrs.) 16	Lipsey, Hyman 132
Levy, Mortimer 163	Lewis, Samuel D. 113	Lipsey, Joseph 50
Levy, Mr. 126	Lewiton, Louis 32	Lipsey, M. 47
Levy, Mr. and Mrs. 37, 71	Lexier, Elizabeth (Miss) 178	Lipshitz, Morris 138
Levy, Mrs. 29, 66	Lexier, Samuel 32	Lipsin, A. (Miss) 32
Levy, Pearl (Miss) 36, 160	Lhevinne, Mr. 109	Lipsin, H. 185
Levy, Pearl Evelyn (Miss) 36	Libovitz, Chazan 18	Lipsky, Louis 50
Levy, R. (Mrs.) 34	Lichtenhein, S.E. (Mrs.) 114	Lipstein, J. (Mrs.) 185
Levy, Rabbi 38	Lichtenhein, E. 90	Liss, Teddie 176, 180
Levy, Rene Ernest 17	Lichtenhein, E. (Mr. and Mrs.) 90, 113	List, H. 127
Levy, Rose (Miss) 171-173	Lichtenhein, E. (Mrs.) 82	Lithwick, Max (Mr. and Mrs.) 34
Levy, Rosette (Miss) 43	Lichtenhein, Ed. (Mr. and Mrs.) 89, 113	Lithwick, Max (Mrs.) 148, 150, 151
Levy, Ruth (Miss) 152	Lichtenhein, Edward (Mrs.) 113	Litner, G. (Miss) 65
Levy, S. 75	Lichtenhein, I.E. (Mrs.) 113	Litner, I. 139
Levy, S. (Mrs.) 13, 78	Lichtenhein, L. 113	Litner, Myer 50
Levy, S.L. (Mr. and Mrs.) 112	Lichtenhein, Louis 113	Litner, S. 65
Levy, Sol. L. 22	Lichtenhein, Philip (Master) 113	Litowitz, Israel 114
Levy, Theodore 156, 161	Lichtenhein, Phillip (Master) 113	Littner, G. 72
Levy, V. 160	Lichtenhein, S.E. 113, 114	Littner, Myer 50
Levy, V. (Mrs.) 113	Lichtenhein, S.E. (Mr. and Mrs.) 113	Litwick, Max (Mrs.) 11
Levy, Vera (Miss) 29	Lichtenhein, S.E. (Mrs.) 100, 113, 114	Litwick, Mrs. 150
Levy, W. (Mr. and Mrs.) 112	Lichtenhein, Sam. E. 70	Litwin, H. (Mr. and Mrs. H.) 10
Levy, William 32, 172	Lichtenhein, Samuel E. (Mrs.) 114	Litwin, Samuel 32
Levy, William (Mr. and Mrs.) 10	Lichtenstein, Clara (Miss) 42, 114	Litwin, Samuel (Mr. and Mrs.) 10
Lewin, A. (Mrs.) 163	Lieberman, B. (Miss) 150	Liveravet, Jacob 32
Lewin, Anna (Miss) 113	Lieberman, Harry (Mrs.) 104, 133	Liverman, Annie (Mrs.) 17
Lewin, Dr. 183	Lieberman, M. (Miss) 165, 169	Liverman, Louis 114
Lewin, Eina (Miss) 113	Lieberman, M. (Mrs.) 155	Liverman, M. 106, 114
Lewin, I.K. 154	Lieberman, Minnie (Miss) 161	Liverman, Max 32
Lewin, Mark 113	Lieberman, Miss 155	Liverman, May (Miss) 27, 75, 114
Lewin, Miss 113	Lieberman, Moe 161	Liverman, Mr. and Mrs. 27
Lewin, Mrs. 113	Lieberman, Mrs. 155, 167	Liverman, Thomas 17
Lewinsky, Mr. 166	Lieberman, Rebecca (Miss) 163	Livingston, H. (Mrs.) 114
Lewinson, A. (Mr. and Mrs.) 35	Liebling, D. (Mr. and Mrs.) 37	Livingston, H.H. (Mrs.) 114
Lewinson, Jerome (Mrs.) 113	Liebling, G. (Miss) 37	Livingstone, Gladys (Miss) 77
Lewinter, Mr. 164	Liekler, Nathan 81	Livingstone, H. (Mrs.) 77
Lewis, A. (Mrs.) 155	Lifchis, F. 162	Livingstone, H.H. (Mr. and Mrs.) 114
Lewis, A.P. 32, 160, 161, 163, 164, 168	Lifchis, M. (Miss) 165	Livingstone, H.H. (Mrs.) 79, 97, 98, 114, 128
Lewis, C. 162	Lifshitz, A. 149	Livingstone, Jennie F. 50
Lewis, F. 98, 114	Lighter, H. 57	Livingstone, L. 60
Lewis, F. (Mrs.) 136	Lighter, M. 57	Livingstone, L. (Miss) 60
Lewis, F.L. 32	Lightstone, B. 49	Livingstone, Leba (Miss) . 62, 77, 82, 111, 128
Lewis, Felix 30, 36, 62, 113	Lightstone, Bernard 7, 114	Livingstone, Leo 48, 51
Lewis, Felix (Mr. and Mrs.) 113	Lightstone, Dr. 114	Livingstone, M. (Miss) 165, 169
Lewis, Felix (Mrs.) 113, 139	Lightstone, Gordon 69, 118	Livingstone, Ruby (Miss) 77, 106
Lewis, G. (Mrs) 98, 103	Lightstone, H. (Dr.) 97, 114, 147	Livingstone, Ruth (Miss) 77
Lewis, George (Mrs.) 113	Lightstone, Harry 32	Livingstone, Sig. 179
Lewis, Grace (Miss) 60, 113	Lightstone, Hyman (Dr.) 114	Livingstone, T.H. 49
Lewis, H. 171	Lightstone, John Jacob 32	Livinson, A. Jacob 114
Lewis, H. (Mr. and Mrs.) 29	Lightstone, L. 29, 61	Livinson, A.H. 114, 115
Lewis, Helen (Miss) 113	Lightstone, M. . 60, 67, 93, 114, 118, 122, 134	Livinson, A.J. . . . 64, 71, 77, 80, 86, 88, 99,
Lewis, Jacob 172	Lightstone, Mamie (Miss) 111	114, 146
Lewis, Joseph 113	Lightstone, Max 32	Livinson, C. (Miss) 80
Lewis, L. 101	Lightstone, Maxwell . . 63, 83, 101, 106, 108,	Livinson, Cecilia (Miss) 115
Lewis, Louis 17, 90, 98, 113	114, 116, 146	Livinson, D. 67, 90, 114
Lewis, Louis (Mr. and Mrs.) 61, 113	Lightstone, Michael 7, 114	Livinson, Dave 73, 114, 127
Lewis, Louis (Mrs.) 61, 113	Lightstone, Michael (Mr. and Mrs.) 32	Livinson, David 91, 115
Lewis, Margaret (Miss) 113	Lightstone, Michael (Mrs.) 15	Livinson, Davis 90, 115
Lewis, Miss 113, 136	Lightstone, Minnie (Miss) 106, 114	Livinson, H.J. 98

Livinson, I. 115	Lubelsky, Sigmund 163	Malamuth, J. 134
Livinson, I. (Mr. and Mrs.) 85	Lubetsky, Habokuk 157	Malamuth, J.L. 115
Livinson, I. (Mrs.) 115	Lubetsky, L. 157	Maldaver, Oscar 33
Livinson, J. 73, 114	Lubetzky, H. 167	Malis, G. (Mrs.) 134
Livinson, Jack 67	Lubich, L. 32	Malis, S. 134
Livinson, Myrtie (Miss) 115	Lubich, Lawrence 33	Malkin, A. 184
Livinson, S.R. (Miss) 9	Lubin, Herbert 115	Malkin, C. 183, 184
Livinstein, J. 170	Lubin, Herbert (Mr. and Mrs.) 103	Malkin, Fanny (Miss) 184
Livshitz, J. (Mr. and Mrs.) 10	Lubinsky, J. 163	Malkin, S. 184
Lizenwitz, M. 156	Lubinsky, J. (Mr. and Mrs.) 24	Malkinson, J. 74, 115, 124
Lobitz, Miss 115	Lubinsky, Lena (Miss) 24	Malkinson, Jack 121
Lobitz, Mr. 115	Lubinsky, M. 162	Malkinson, Jean (Miss) 115
Lobschutz, Miss 115	Lublesky, Sigmund 163	Mallens, Max 33
Loeb, A. 115	Lumley, Isaac 45	Manaseveth, J.N. (Mrs.) 35
Loeb, Eda K. (Mrs.) 130	Lumley, Morris 45	Mandelstam, J. 59
Loeb, Morris (Dr.) 130	Lunenfeld, Mrs. 167	Manheim, Mrs. 159
Loebel, C. (Mrs.) 121	Lurie, C. 155, 163, 169	Manis, M. 115
Loebel, T. (Mrs.) 64	Lurie, Emma (Miss) 115	Manolson, J. 115, 137
Loeser, H.N. 157	Lurie, Fanny (Miss) 24, 115	Manolson, J. (Mrs.) 77, 98, 139
Loeser, H.S. (Mrs.) 166	Lurie, M. 184	Manolson, Jacob 49
Loeser, Herman (Mr. and Mrs.) 157	Lurie, Max 33, 155, 158, 164, 183	Manolson, Jacob (Mrs.) 18, 77
Loeser, Hilda (Miss) 168	Lurie, Miss 183	Manolson, S.E. 67, 115, 116
Loeser, Mr. 157	Lurie, Mr. 8, 57	Mansfield, A. 43
London, J. 176	Lusher, Harry 115	Manson, Mr. 169
London, Jack 175	Lustgarten, Eva (Miss) 77	Manuel, Louis (Mr. and Mrs.) 10
Lonn, David 32	Lustgarten, Mrs. 14	Manuel, Rosie (Miss) 27
Lonn, Dora (Mrs.) 115	Lustgarten, S. 14	Marcovitch, J. 136
Lonn, Frances (Miss) 32	Luxembourg, Freda (Miss) 60, 115	Marcus, A. 154
Lonn, H. (Mr. and Mrs.) 132	Luxenberg, Sam. 164	Marcus, Arthur 116
Lonn, H. (Mrs.) 77, 99, 115	Lyman, Sidney W. (Mr. and Mrs.) . . . 103	Marcus, B. 102
Lonn, Harris 32	Lyon, Alfred E. 115	Marcus, Bessie (Miss) 56
Lonn, Harris (Mr. and Mrs.) 17	Lyon, Jack 178	Marcus, Clara (Mrs.) 181
Lonn, J. (Mr. and Mrs.) 10	Lyon, Sara (Miss) 175	Marcus, E. (Miss) 24
Lonn, J.S. (Mr. and Mrs.) 10	Lyon, W.S. 115	Marcus, J. 56
Lonn, J.S. (Mrs.) 32	Lyone, Annie (Miss) 176, 179, 180	Marcus, Jennie (Miss) 57
Lonn, Martha (Miss) 17	Lyone, Sara (Miss) 179	Marcus, L. 163
Lonn, T.H. (Mrs.) 104	Lyons, Alfred 115	Marcus, L. (Mr. and Mrs.) 40
Lopsitz, Miss 115	Lyons, C. (Mrs.) 183	Marcus, L. (Mrs.) 175
Lorado, M.D. 115	Lyons, Charles 183	Marcus, M. 79, 116
Lorie, A. (Mr. and Mrs.) 163	Lyons, Esther (Miss) 175	Marcus, Marcel 73, 112
Lorie, Ella (Miss) 38, 165, 168	Lyons, Etta (Miss) 171, 172	Marcus, Mr. 132
Lorie, S. 157	Lyons, F.H. (Mr. and Mrs.) 3	Marcus, S. (Mrs.) 57
Lorie, S. (Mr. and Mrs.) 38, 163	Lyons, Harry 3	Marcuse, B. (Mr. and Mrs.) 37, 38, 116
Lorie, Zelina (Miss) 163	Lyons, J. 172	Marcuse, Berthold (Mr. and Mrs.) 33
Lorie, Zelna (Miss) 38	Lyons, Jack 184	Marcuse, Bertholde (Mr. and Mrs.) 33
Losinsky, E. .61	Lyons, Jake 164	Marcuse, Eliza (Miss) 37, 38, 116
Louis, Felix 115	Lyons, Jennie (Miss) 31, 171, 172	Marcuse, F. 172
Louis, Grace (Miss) 115	Lyons, Julius 172	Marcuse, F. (Mrs.) 82
Louis, J. 149	Lyons, Louis (Master) 172	Marcuse, Feodor 33
Louis, L. (Mr. and Mrs.) 115	Lyons, M. (Mr. and Mrs.) 115	Marcuse, L. 101
Louis, M. 162	Lyons, Pauline (Miss) 164, 168	Marcuse, M. (Miss) 67
Louis, Minnie D. (Miss) 115	Lyons, S. 171	Marcuse, Otto 116
Louis, Miss 115	Lyons, S. (Mr. and Mrs.) 115, 172	Margolese, Dr. 179
Louis, N. (Mrs.) 115	Lyons, S. (Mrs.) 172	Margolese, J. (Mr. and Mrs.) 116
Louis, Nathan (Mrs.) 115	Lyons, S.H. 172	Margolese, J. (Rev.) 36
Lowenthal, C. (Mrs.) 115	Lyons, Saul 35, 172	Margolese, L. 36
Lowenthal, F. (Miss) 115	Lyons, Saul (Mr. and Mrs.) 172	Margolese, L.S. 116
Lowrie, D. 170	Mack, Lou 172	Margolese, L.S. (B.C.L.) 116
Lozinski, H. 77, 115	Madorsky, Rebecca (Miss) 17	Margolese, L.S. (Mr. and Mrs.) 34
Lozinsky, A. 3, 45	Mael, Mr. and Mrs. 182	Margolese, L.S. (Mrs.) 102
Lozinsky, A. (Mrs.) 45	Maganett, M. 57	Margolese, Louis (Mr. and Mrs.) 126
Lozinsky, Adolph (Mr. and Mrs.) 3	Magder, J. (Mr. and Mrs.) 157	Margolese, Louis S. 50, 81
Lozinsky, E. .91	Maggid, Mr. and Mrs. 36	Margolese, Louis T. 59
Lozinsky, Ezra 3	Magid, J. 106	Margolese, Mr. 25
Lozinsky, H. 2, 81, 112, 115, 183	Magnes, J.L. 50	Margolese, O. (Dr.) 33, 36, 116
Lozinsky, H. (Mr. and Mrs.) 3, 115	Magonett, Sarah (Miss) 57	Margolese, O. (Mrs.) 116
Lozinsky, J. 185	Maher, S.M. 159	Margolese, Oscar (Dr. and Mrs.) 178
Lozof, J. 137	Mahimove, J. 43	Margolese, Oscar (Dr.) 33, 116
Lubchansky, Celia (Miss) 57	Maier, Max 115	Margolese, S. 68
Lubchansky, M. 2, 58	Maierbach, Mrs. 160	Margolese, S.L. 102
Lubelsky, Mr. 157	Maiser, M. 59	Margolese, S.L. (Mr. and Mrs.) 116
Lubelsky, Mr. and Mrs. 166	Makinoff, J. 65	Margolese, Sophie (Miss) 178
Lubelsky, S. 115, 155, 163	Malabar, T. (Miss) 177	Margolick, C. (Miss) 88

Margolick, G. (Mr. and Mrs.) 116	Markus, Ernest 3	Mehr, J. (Mrs.) 154
Margolick, M. 62, 78	Markus, H. 121	Mehr, Jacob 164
Margolick, M. (Miss) 88	Markus, Hortense (Miss) 102, 116	Mehr, M. (Mr. and Mrs.) 33
Margolies, G. (Mr. and Mrs.) 10	Markus, L. (Mrs.) 180	Mehr, M. (Mrs.) 155, 164
Margolies, Rosalind (Miss) 116	Markus, M. 52, 116	Mehr, Mr. and Mrs. 165
Margolies, S. 83	Markus, M. (Mr. and Mrs.) 3, 116, 145	Meinster, Elizabeth (Miss) 158
Margolis, B.M. 183	Markus, S. 57	Meinster, Lizzie (Miss) 157, 162
Margolis, G. (Mr. and Mrs.) 75	Maroff, D. 154	Meinster, Rose (Miss) 158
Margolis, H. 183	Marom, Morris (Mr. and Mrs.) 10	Meisels, S. (Rev.) 117
Margolis, J. 164	Marschoff, Rev. 149	Meld, M. 81
Margolis, Max 49	Marshall, L. 116	Melekov, Leon 185
Margolius, G. (Mr. and Mrs.) 179	Marshall, L.A. 185	Melekov, Mrs. 185
Margolius, George 179	Marshall, Louis A. 185	Melekove, L. 185
Margolius, George (Mrs.) 179	Marshall, M.A. 175	Melio, Mrs. 167
Margolius, J. 91, 114, 115	Marshall, R. (Miss) 176	Melkman, Solomon 117
Margolius, M. 91	Martin, A. (Mrs.) 18	Melon, Mr. 30
Margolius, Mrs. 110, 184	Martin, Abe 116	Meltzer, N. 56
Margolius, S. (Miss) 180	Martin, David (Mr. and Mrs.) 144	Melzer, L. 131
Margolius, Sophie (Miss) 179	Matloff, Issie 107	Mendel, B. 66
Margosches, Dorothee (Frau) 33	Matoff, Michael 50, 79	Mendel, C.M. 73
Margosches, Jacques (Dr.) 33	Matoff, Michael (Professor) 116	Mendel, David 110
Margosches, Max B. 33	Matts, B. 18, 116	Mendel, David Louis 49, 52
Margosches, Max B. (Mr. and Mrs.) ... 150	Matts, B.J. 116	Mendel, E. (Miss) 65, 73
Margosches, Max B. (Mrs.) 21, 150, 151	Matts, Benjamin 116	Mendel, G.F. 117
Margosches, Max. B. (Mr. and Mrs.) 10	Matts, Bessie (Miss) 77	Mendel, Joseph 117
Margosches, Salo 33	Matts, Edith (Miss) 106	Mendel, Miss 124
Markey, Fred (Mrs.) 93	Matts, Edythe (Miss) 116	Mendel, Sophie (Miss) 128
Markey, Mrs. 92	Matts, Emily (Miss) 116	Mendel, Wm. (Mrs.) 15
Markowitz, A. 163	Matts, Hattie (Miss) 65, 66, 105	Mendelowitz, Mrs. 117
Marks, A. 33, 73	Matts, L.J. 18	Mendels, Amy (Miss) 148
Marks, A. (Mrs.) 116	Matts, L.J. (Mr. and Mrs.) 116	Mendels, B. 151
Marks, Abraham 17	Matts, Miss 105, 116	Mendels, B. (Mrs.) 121
Marks, Alexander 17, 116	Matts, Misses 116	Mendels, Bernard 33
Marks, Annie (Miss) 80	Matts, Rose (Miss) 116	Mendels, Bernice (Miss) 148
Marks, B. 80, 86	Matz, Jacob (Rev.) 18	Mendels, Esther (Miss) 74
Marks, Bennie 106	Mauer. E. 52	Mendels, I. 117
Marks, David M. 116	Mauer, E. 47, 83, 92, 108, 114, 116, 138	Mendels, Isaac 18
Marks, Dorothy 106	Mauer, Elias 51, 103, 116, 121	Mendels, J. (Mrs.) 137
Marks, E. 168	Max, M. (Mrs.) 151	Mendels, J.H. 50
Marks, F. 116	May, Barney (Mr. and Mrs.) 116	Mendels, J.H. (Mrs.) 102
Marks, H. (Mrs.) 161	May, H. (Mrs.) 63	Mendels, Joseph (Mr. and Mrs.) 97, 117
Marks, I.H. (Mrs.) 116	May, Mrs. 116	Mendels, Joseph (Mrs.) .. 101, 102, 111, 117
Marks, J. 150	Mayback, Mr. and Mrs. 10	Mendels, M. 50
Marks, J.J. 33	Mayer, Emma (Miss) 164	Mendels, Misses 117, 124
Marks, J.J. (Mrs.) 151	Mayer, H. 183	Mendels, Mrs. 137
Marks, Jack 116	Mayer, Hedwig (Miss) 12, 39	Mendels, Sophie (Miss) 34, 74
Marks, Jacob 181	Mayer, J. 162	Mendelsohn, Annie (Miss) 117
Marks, L. (Mrs.) 16	Mayer, Julia (Miss) 157	Mendelsohn, Dolly (Miss) 117
Marks, Mary (Miss) 86	Mayer, Julius M. 116	Mendelsohn, E. (Mr. and Mrs.) 10
Marks, Mildred (Miss) 144, 168	Mayer, Max (Mr. and Mrs.) 116	Mendelsohn, Emile 129
Marks, Mira (Miss) 116	Mayer, Max (Mrs.) 116	Mendelsohn, H. 72
Marks, Miss 164	Mayer, S.F. 183	Mendelsohn, I. 65
Marks, Mr. 101, 166	Mayerbach, Mrs. 159	Mendelsohn, J. Felix 117
Marks, Mrs. 165	Mayers, Miss 116	Mendelsohn, M. 81, 117, 165
Marks, Myra (Miss) 2	Mayers, Mrs. 116	Mendelsohn, M. (Mr. and Mrs.) 10, 117
Marks, N. (Mrs.) 72, 116	Mazer, L. 49	Mendelsohn, M. (Mrs.) 31, 75, 117
Marks, Nathaniel 17	Mazur, William 50	Mendelsohn, Miss 164
Marks, P. (Miss) 80, 99	McClean, Alice (Miss) 33	Mendelsohn, Mr. 80
Marks, Pauline (Miss) 85, 86, 152	McFarlane, L.B. (Mr. and Mrs.) 117, 145	Mendelsohn, Mr. and Mrs. 2, 75
Marks, Philip 17	McFarlane, L.B. (Mrs.) 66	Mendelsohn, Mrs. 164
Marks, Phoebe (Miss) 116	McKinley, Adela (Miss) 138	Mendelsohn, N. 101
Marks, Polly (Miss) 86	McKinley, H. 138	Mendelsohn, R.M. (Mrs.) 50
Marks, R. (Mr. and Mrs.) 17, 109	McKinley, I. 68	Mendelsohn, Rae (Miss) 117
Marks, Rae (Miss) 2	McKinley, M. 83	Mendelsohn, Ray (Miss) 117
Marks, Samuel 93	McKinley, Mr. 63	Mendelsohn, Rebecca (Miss) 38
Marks, Samuel (Rabbi) 93	McKinley, Pauline (Miss) 138	Mendelson, E. 57
Markson, A. 152	McKinley, S. 75, 114, 117	Mendelson, M. 57
Markson, H. (Mrs.) 116	Mednedoff, M. (Rev.) 174	Mendelson, M. (Mr. and Mrs.) 106
Markson, Lena (Miss) 77	Mednick, J. (Mr. and Mrs.) 33	Mendelson, M. (Mrs.) 31
Markson, M. (Miss) 150	Mednick, Louis 33	Mendelson, Max 33
Markus, Arthur 59	Meeker, Miss 166	Mendelson, Mrs. 165
Markus, Arthur A. 116	Mehr, J. 159, 162	Mendelson, R. 61
	Mehr, J. (Mr. and Mrs.) 33	Mendelson, R. (Miss) 88

Mendelson, Ray (Miss) 117
Mendelson, S. (Mr. and Mrs.) 33
Mendelson, S.M. 33
Mendelson, W. 57
Mendelson, William 57
Mendelsshon, J. Felix 117
Mendelssohn, A. 117
Mendelssohn, C. 59
Mendelssohn, C. (Mrs.) 117
Mendelssohn, D. (Miss) 117
Mendelssohn, Dolly (Miss) 117
Mendelssohn, Felix 117
Mendelssohn, J. Felix 18, 98, 117
Mendelssohn, Joseph 33
Mendelssohn, Lillian (Miss) 169
Mendelssohn, Mr. 18
Mendelssohn, Mrs. 117
Mendes, Annie (Miss) 25
Mendes, Bram P. 117
Mendes, Florence (Miss) 37, 117
Mendes, L.P. (Mrs.) 77
Mendes, Leonard Pereira (Mr. and
  Mrs.) 117
Mendes, Marguerite (Miss) 75, 117
Mendes, Miss 118, 129
Mendes, P.L. (Mr. and Mrs.) 96
Mendles, J.H. (Mrs.) 19
Mercer, Rose (Miss) 157
Merin, S. (Miss) 164
Merker, Frances (Miss) 37
Merker, Francis (Miss) 165
Merker, Mr. 157
Merker, Mr. and Mrs. 37
Merker, S. 157
Merkin, Miss 166
Merkur, Mr. and Mrs. 166
Merman, Mrs. 185
Mernick, A. 158
Merson, F. 149
Merson, H. 148
Merson, H. (Mrs.) 127
Merson, H.S. 148
Merson, J. 114, 130, 146
Merson, J. (Mr. and Mrs.) 29, 93, 141
Merson, Joe (Mrs.) 115
Merson, Joseph (Mr. and Mrs.) 117
Merson, Joseph (Mrs.) 117, 141
Merson, Julius 117
Merson, M. 114
Merson, P. 67
Merson, Peter 117, 137
Merson, Peter H. 68, 105
Merson, S. 105, 117
Meshy, David 33
Metrick, N. 151
Metten, Jacob 101
Meyer, Abe 25
Meyer, Gertrude (Miss) 117
Meyer, Hans (Mrs.) 117
Meyer, J. 159
Meyer, J. (Mrs.) 185
Meyer, Leah (Mrs.) 18
Meyer, M. 117
Meyer, Max (Mr. and Mrs.) 117
Meyer, S. 162
Meyerowitz, Mr. and Mrs. 184
Meyers, Ben 164
Meyers, E.P. 117
Meyers, Ethel (Miss) 175
Meyers, H. 117
Meyers, H.E. (Mrs.) 72
Meyers, Minnie (Miss) 145
Meyers, Mr. and Mrs. 117

Meyers, Mrs. 117, 181
Meyers, Ray (Miss) 32
Meyers, S.F. 33
Miasnik, Annie (Miss) 175
Michael, Annie (Miss) 57
Michael, B. 2, 58
Michael, Mr. and Mrs. 164
Michael, N. 8, 57
Michaelis, V. 73
Michaels, A. (Mr. and Mrs.) 126
Michaels, Abe (Mr. and Mrs.) 118
Michaels, Abe. (Mrs.) 118
Michaels, Abraham 102, 117
Michaels, Abraham (Mr. and Mrs.) 118
Michaels, Abraham (Mrs.) 118
Michaels, Alfred 118
Michaels, Alfred (Mr. and Mrs.) 118
Michaels, Alfred (Mrs.) 77, 118
Michaels, Alfred Edward 33
Michaels, Beta S. (Miss) 115
Michaels, C. (Mr. and Mrs.) 10
Michaels, Ch. (Mrs.) 98
Michaels, Clarence 33, 118, 119
Michaels, Clarence (Mr. and Mrs.) 118
Michaels, Clarence (Mrs.) 118, 122
Michaels, Clarence I. 118
Michaels, John 33, 102
Michaels, John (Mr. and Mrs.) 118, 125
Michaels, John (Mrs.) 118
Michaels, M. 96
Michaels, M. (Mr. and Mrs.) 10, 118
Michaels, Michael 33, 134
Michaels, Michael (Mr. and Mrs.) 118
Michaels, Michael A. 33
Michaels, Michael A. (Mr. and
  Mrs.) 10
Michaels, Morris 70, 102, 118
Michaels, N. 118
Michaels, N. (Mrs.) 101, 102
Michaels, V. 118
Michaels, V. (Mrs.) 122
Michaels, Victor 102, 118
Michaels, Violet (Miss) 33, 118, 135
Michaelson, Harris 118
Michaelson, Isidore 147
Michaelson, J. 141
Michaelson, Jean (Miss) 60
Michaelson, Jennie (Miss) 118
Michaelson, M. 118
Michaelson, M. (Mr. and Mrs.) 118
Michaelson, M. (Mrs.) 98
Michaelson, Miss 118
Michaelson, Misses 92, 147
Michaelson, Mr. and Mrs. 118
Michaelson, Richard 51
Michaelson, Sara (Miss) 98
Michaelson, Sarah (Miss) 98, 118
Michalson, A. 56
Michalson, F. 56
Michalson, F. (Miss) 56
Michalson, Harris 118
Michalson, I. 118
Michalson, Israel 33, 118
Michalson, J. 118
Michalson, M. 49, 81
Michalson, M. (Mrs.) 118
Michalson, Minnie (Miss) 56
Michalson, Miss 92, 118
Michalson, Misses 88, 118
Michel, J.F. 118
Michelin, Mr. 45
Michelson, M. (Mrs.) 183
Michelson, Mr. 149

Michlin, Isidore 118
Michlin, Isidore (Mr. and Mrs.) 118
Michlin, S. (Dr. and Mrs.) 118
Mickal, B. 57
Mickelson, M. 183
Mickelson, M. (Mrs.) 183
Micklesburt, Elsie (Miss) 168
Midanik, A. 162
Midanik, Annette (Miss) 164
Middelstadt, Lionel 33
Midownik, S. (Mrs.) 87
Mikelson, Mr. 184
Millar, Beccie (Miss) 153
Millar, Bessie (Miss) 153
Millar, Blanche (Miss) 150-153
Millar, D.A. (Mrs.) 25
Millar, Dave 148
Millar, Dora (Miss) 153
Millar, H. 117, 152
Millar, L. 25, 105, 151
Millar, R.H. 151
Millar, Samuel 150
Millar, W. 152
Millar, Willie 150
Miller, A. 50
Miller, Adeline (Miss) 25
Miller, Alexander 44
Miller, Anna (Miss) 88
Miller, B. 115, 118
Miller, B. (Miss) 152
Miller, Beckie (Miss) 118
Miller, Bessie (Miss) 151
Miller, C. (Mr. and Mrs.) 119, 166
Miller, C.A. Morell 44
Miller, Coleman 44
Miller, Coleman (Mr. and Mrs.) 164
Miller, D. 59
Miller, D. (Miss) 152
Miller, D. (Mr. and Mrs.) 34
Miller, David (Mrs.) 11
Miller, Della (Miss) 168
Miller, Dora (Miss) 34
Miller, Dorothy (Miss) 34
Miller, Elsie (Miss) 29, 118
Miller, Etta (Miss) 34
Miller, F. 22
Miller, Fanny (Miss) 25, 118
Miller, G. 33
Miller, Gerson 34
Miller, H. 57, 152
Miller, H. (Mr. and Mrs.) 10
Miller, Harry 34
Miller, Harry (Mr. and Mrs.) 34
Miller, Herman 151
Miller, Hermann 151
Miller, Hyman 44, 164
Miller, I. 115, 118
Miller, Isadore (Mrs.) 164
Miller, Isidore 44, 118
Miller, Isidore (Mr. and Mrs.) 164
Miller, J. 118
Miller, J.B. 118
Miller, J.B. (Miss) 118
Miller, J.F. (Mr. and Mrs.) 29
Miller, Jacob (Alderman and Mrs.) 33
Miller, Jacob (Mrs.) 118
Miller, Jennie (Miss) 29
Miller, Joel 44
Miller, John (Mrs.) 118
Miller, Jos. 65
Miller, Joseph 65
Miller, Joseph (Mr. and Mrs.) 97
Miller, Julius 69

Miller, Julius B. 61	Mintz, Moses 50	Morris, Arthur C. (Mr. and Mrs.) 11
Miller, L. 73, 159	Mintz, Myer 18	Morris, Beatrice 106
Miller, L.E. (Mrs.) 164	Mintz, Nellie (Miss) 68	Morris, Beatrice (Miss) 50
Miller, L.J. (Mrs.) 179	Mintz, Sara (Miss) 172	Morris, Byrde (Miss) 173
Miller, Lawrence 44	Mintz, Sarah (Miss) 18, 171	Morris, C. (Mrs.) 136
Miller, Lazar 42	Mintz, Solomon 18	Morris, C.L. 68
Miller, Lewis 27	Mirewitz, Ida (Miss) 39	Morris, Cecil (Master) 172
Miller, Lillian (Miss) 159	Mirochnick, M. 167	Morris, D. (Miss) 169
Miller, Lucille (Mrs.) 164	Mirsky, B. 149	Morris, Dora (Miss) 119
Miller, M. 59	Mirsky, B. (Miss) 127	Morris, Dore (Miss) 119
Miller, Max .59	Mirsky, David 34, 151	Morris, Dorothy (Miss) 29, 119, 134
Miller, Max (Mr. and Mrs.) 118	Mirsky, H. 57, 58	Morris, E. 119, 185
Miller, Miss 118, 125	Mirsky, H. (Mr. and Mrs.) 27	Morris, E. (Miss) 77
Miller, Misses 151	Mirsky, J. (Rev.) 31, 34	Morris, Edward 37
Miller, Mr. and Mrs. 25, 109, 164	Mirsky, Lena (Miss) 27, 58	Morris, Eva (Miss) 35, 89, 154
Miller, Mrs. 45, 118	Mirsky, Libbie (Miss) 57	Morris, G. (Mrs.) 119, 130, 133, 136
Miller, Myron 179	Mirsky, M. (Rev.) 33	Morris, Gertrude (Mrs.) 37
Miller, N. 86	Mirsky, Myer 34	Morris, Gussie (Miss) 171-173
Miller, N. (Mr. and Mrs.) 22	Mirsky, R. (Miss) 152	Morris, H. 172, 173, 185
Miller, Naomi (Miss) 47	Mirsky, Rabbi 28, 31, 119	Morris, Harry 30, 171
Miller, Nathan 34, 118	Mirsky, Rev. 25, 38	Morris, Helen (Miss) 171, 172
Miller, R.C. .70	Mirsky, S. 57, 127	Morris, J. 172, 185
Miller, Rebecca (Miss) 27	Mirsky, S.D. (Mrs.) 151	Morris, J. (Mr. and Mrs.) 172
Miller, Rose (Miss) 25, 103	Mirsky, Sam 152	Morris, J. (Mrs.) 171, 172
Miller, Ruth (Miss) 69, 139	Mirsky, Sam (Master) 153	Morris, J.L. (Mr. and Mrs.) 157
Miller, S. 49	Mirsky, Sammie 153	Morris, Jake .3
Miller, S. (Miss) 114	Mirsky, Solomon 119	Morris, Joseph 61
Miller, S. (Mr. and Mrs.) 24, 31, 118	Mirsky, Tillie (Miss) 57	Morris, K. (Miss) 7, 77, 119, 125
Miller, S.D. (Mr. and Mrs.) 118	Mishkin, Adolphe 50	Morris, L. 119
Miller, Sadie (Miss) 25	Mishkin, Dora (Miss) 49	Morris, Leonard Henry 34
Miller, Samuel B. 118, 148, 151	Mishkin, Edward (Mrs.) 119	Morris, M.L. 49, 115, 119
Miller, Samuel David 33	Mishkin, I. .45	Morris, M.L. (Mr. and Mrs.) 29, 128
Miller, Sara (Miss) 118	Mishkin, I. (Mrs.) 45, 119	Morris, Margaret 18
Miller, Sarah (Miss) 31	Mishkin, J. 133	Morris, May (Miss) 37
Miller, Stella (Miss) 164	Mishkind, H. (Mrs.) 37	Morris, Miss 119
Miller, Tilly (Miss) 24	Mishkind, I. (Mrs.) 37	Morris, Misses 128, 172
Miller, W.C. (Corp.) 152	Mishkind, J. (Mrs.) 37	Morris, Moses 49
Miller, Winnie (Miss) 34	Mishkind, Leo (Master) 37	Morris, Mr. .28
Milliman, B. (Miss) 118	Misslow, Ruth (Miss) 160	Morris, Mr. and Mrs. 28
Millman, A. 18	Mitchell, M. (Mr. and Mrs.) 11	Morris, N.L. (Mr. and Mrs.) 29
Millman, Aaron 33	Mitnick, Fannie (Miss) 84, 119	Morris, Rae (Miss) 37
Millman, B. (Miss) 119	Mitnick, I. 74, 124, 137	Morris, Rosalie (Miss) 77
Millman, Bena (Miss) 18, 119	Mitnick, Isaac 34	Morris, S. 182
Millman, L. 18, 62	Mitnick, L. 105	Morris, T.L. 160
Millman, Miss 66	Mitnick, L. (Mr. and Mrs.) 34	Morris, Thomas 49
Millman, Rose (Miss) 18	Mitnik, L. 50	Morris, Y. (Mrs.) 131
Millman, S. (Mrs.) 18	Mittell, Harold (Master) 151	Moscovicz, Dora (Miss) 35
Millman, Saul 33, 119	Mittler, Elijah 179	Moscovicz, Sarah (Miss) 35
Millman, Solomon 18	Mizur, M. .59	Moscovitch, Ben 152
Millmutt, Abraham (Mr. and Mrs.) 175	Mochkowsky, Myer 86	Moscovitch, Bennie (Master) 153
Mills, H. 88, 146	Mohl, William 119	Moscovitch, Carolyn (Miss) 151, 152
Milmen, Mr. and Mrs. 40	Mohr, M. 183, 184	Moscovitch, Ephraim 179
Milmet, A. 180	Moldaver, Abraham 156	Moscovitch, Esther (Miss) 119
Milmet, A. (Mr. and Mrs.) 32	Moldaver, Mr. 169	Moscovitch, F. (Mr. and Mrs.) 119
Milmet, Abraham 179	Moldever, Mr. 155	Moscovitch, Harry 176
Milmet, Estelle (Miss) 32	Monason, Miss 119	Moscovitch, I. 183
Milmet, Esther (Miss) 40	Monasson, F. (Miss) 119	Moscovitch, Leon 176
Milstock, A. 61	Monblatt, Winnie (Miss) 73, 119	Moscovitch, M. 152
Mimoloch, M. (Mrs.) 185	Mond, Alfred (Sir) 119	Moscovitch, Maurice 152
Mimshewitz, Mr. and Mrs. 159	Moore, Kathleen (Miss) 119	Moscovitch, Maurice (Master) 153
Minkin, Fanny T. 50	Moore, W. (Mrs.) 119	Moscovitch, Max 183
Minkin, J.S. (Rabbi) 45, 164, 171	Morgan, Thomas M. 81	Moscovitch, S. 78, 138
Minkin, Jacob S. (Mrs.) 50	Morosnick, L. 71, 176	Moscovitz, Caroline (Miss) 149
Minkin, Jacob S. (Rabbi and Mrs.) 172	Morosnick, L.B. 179	Moscovitz, Dora (Miss) 119
Minkin, Jacob S. (Rabbi) . . 25, 35, 36, 46, 50,	Morosnick, Louis D. 179	Moscovitz, Dorothy (Miss) 35
51, 171, 172	Moroswich, L.D. 175	Moscovitz, I. 175
Minkin, Rabbi 164	Morris, A. .81	Moscovitz, J. (Mr. and Mrs.) 123
Mintz, Amelia (Mrs.) 18	Morris, A. (Mr. and Mrs.) 101	Moscovitz, J. (Mrs.) 119
Mintz, Clara (Miss) 26, 68, 83	Morris, A.E. (Mr. and Mrs.) 119, 125	Moscovitz, L. (Miss) 177
Mintz, H. 119	Morris, A.E. (Mrs.) 77, 102, 118, 119	Moscovitz, Mr. and Mrs. 40
Mintz, I. 172	Morris, A.I. (Mr. and Mrs.) 34	Moscovitz, Z. (Miss) 177
Mintz, Isaac 18	Morris, A.S. 68, 119	Moscowitz, Carolyn (Miss) 153
Mintz, Miss 164, 171, 172	Morris, Abe 35	Moses, Henry 61, 164

Moses, Henry (Mr. and Mrs.) 11, 28
Moses, Leanore (Miss) 29
Moses, Mr. and Mrs. 119
Mosher, A. 119
Mosher, Joseph 119
Moshovitch, M. 99
Moskovich, Joe 119
Moskovich, Tanna (Miss) 119
Moskovitch, Esther 18
Moskovitch, Esther (Miss) 119
Moskovitch, F. (Mrs.) 119
Moskovitch, Harry 3
Moskovitch, J. 67
Moskovitch, Joe 119
Moskovitch, Joseph 119
Moskovitch, Maude (Miss) 80
Moskovitch, Molly (Miss) 86
Moskovitch, S. 119
Moskovitch, S. (Mr. and Mrs.) 3, 119
Moskovitch, Sam 106
Moskovitch, Tanna (Miss) 119
Moskovitz, C. (Miss) 152
Moss, Charles 18
Moss, David 18
Moss, Hyam D. 18
Moss, I. (Mr. and Mrs.) 11
Moss, Sidney 118
Most, Florence (Miss) 158, 169
Most, Samuel 157
Mouer, E. 119
Mower, C. 68
Moyer, Carl 164
Mozore, J. (Mr. and Mrs.) 11
Muhlstock, A. 47, 67
Muhlstock, A.W. 77
Muhlstock, W. 88
Muller, Ray (Miss) 36
Mulstock, A.W. 119
Munn, A.H. 136
Munn, W.C. 74, 115, 138
Murick, Kate (Miss) 160
Murovich, Mrs. 183
Muscat, B. 119
Muscovitch, Frank (Mrs.) 180, 181
Muscovitz, B. 149
Muscovitz, B. (Master) 149
Muscovitz, Julius 180
Muscovitz, M. 183
Muscovitz, Mr. and Mrs. 28
Muscovitz, R. (Miss) 119
Muskovitch, S. (Mr. and Mrs.) 119
Muskovitch, Tanna (Miss) 119
Muskovitz, M. 184
Muskovitz, Maude (Miss) 119
Myer, Max 119
Myer, Max (Mr. and Mrs.) 119
Myer, S. (Miss) 119
Myers, A. 149
Myers, A.E. 102, 119
Myers, A.W. 35, 119, 180
Myers, A.W. (Mr. and Mrs.) . . . 80, 120, 179
Myers, A.W. (Mrs.) 120
Myers, Alfred 34, 102
Myers, B. 34, 57, 119, 149
Myers, Belle (Miss) 60
Myers, Ben 120
Myers, Ben (Mr. and Mrs.) 11, 120
Myers, Benjamin 34, 172
Myers, Benjamin (Mr. and Mrs.) 120
Myers, Benjamin (Mrs.) 144
Myers, Bernard 153
Myers, Eva (Miss) 119, 120
Myers, Fanny (Miss) 65

Myers, H. (Mrs.) 3
Myers, Henrietta (Miss) 153
Myers, I. 35
Myers, Isidore 119
Myers, J. (Mrs.) 120
Myers, J.F. 119
Myers, L.A. 119
Myers, M. 57
Myers, M. (Miss) 129
Myers, Marion (Miss) 120
Myers, Meyer 119
Myers, Miss 98, 120
Myers, Mr. and Mrs. 119, 120
Myers, Mrs. 20, 136
Myers, Myer 120
Myers, O.P. 120
Myers, P. (Mr. and Mrs.) 120
Myers, P. (Mrs.) 16, 94, 120
Myers, Philip 120
Myers, Philip (Master) 119
Myers, Philip (Mrs.) 96, 108, 120
Myers, Phillip 3, 120
Myers, Phillip (Mr. and Mrs.) 120
Myers, Phillip (Mrs.) 136
Myers, Ralph 34
Myers, Rosetta (Miss) . 35, 120, 165, 178, 179
Myers, S. 149
Myers, S.P. 35, 120
Myers, S.P. (Mr. and Mrs.) 3, 120, 124
Myers, S.P. (Mrs.) 120, 132
Myers, Sam 120
Myers, Samuel 119, 120
Myers, Samuel (Mr. and Mrs.) 120
Myers, Samuel (Mrs.) 100
Myers, Sophia (Miss) 120
Myers, Sophie (Miss) 65, 68, 120
Myers, Susie (Miss) 57
Myerson, J. 94
Myerson, J.I. 73
Myerson, J.J. 120
Myerson, J.W. 34
Myerson, M. 107
Myerson, M.H. 70, 120
Myerson, Moses 50
Myerson, W. 92
Myerson, William 34
Myerson, William (Mr. and Mrs.) 121
Myervitz, Philip 110
Myres, I. 30
Myres, Rosetta (Miss) 30
Myres, Sadie Sybil (Miss) 30
Myres, W. 30
Nachmanson, Benjamin (Mr. and
    Mrs.) 11
Nadler, H. 34
Nadler, Ida (Miss) 133
Nadler, Rebecca (Miss) 133
Naiman, I. (Mr. and Mrs.) 35
Naiman, Isabelle (Miss) 35
Nanniver, Gertrude (Miss) 162
Naphtalin, Ch. 170
Naravich, A. (Miss) 67
Narol, Miss 155
Narol, Mrs. 155
Naroll, Albert 163
Naroll, Master 164
Narovlansky, B. (Miss) 30, 120, 178
Narovlansky, Beck (Miss) 178
Narovlansky, Bee (Miss) 179
Narovlansky, Bella (Miss) 76, 179
Narovlansky, J. 120
Narovlansky, M. (Miss) 175
Narovlansky, Marguerita (Miss) 179

Narovlansky, Mr. and Mrs. 120
Narovlansky, P. 175
Narovlansky, R. (Miss) 179
Narovlansky, Rebecca (Miss) 120, 179
Narovlansky, Rose (Miss) 76
Narovlansky, S.H. 120, 179
Narovlansky, S.H. (Mr. and Mrs.) 179
Narovlansky, S.H. (Mrs.) 120
Narovlansky, Sarah (Miss) 76
Narovlansky, Sarah Leah (Miss) 179
Narrol, A.A. 164
Narrol, Ab. 167
Natenson, I. 57
Natenson, Joseph 57
Natenson, M. 57
Nathan, G. 85
Nathanson, Anna (Miss) 24, 158
Nathanson, B. . . 159, 160, 164, 165, 168, 169
Nathanson, B. (Mr. and Mrs.) . . . 24, 36, 164
Nathanson, Becky (Miss) 33
Nathanson, Emma (Miss) 36
Nathanson, Esther (Miss) 57
Nathanson, George M. 164
Nathanson, H. 66, 73
Nathanson, Henry 120, 141
Nathanson, I. (Mr. and Mrs.) 57
Nathanson, Israel 57
Nathanson, J. 58
Nathanson, Jacob 57
Nathanson, Joe 57
Nathanson, Joseph 50, 57, 58
Nathanson, L. 81
Nathanson, Mr. 168
Nathanson, Mr. and Miss 160
Nathanson, N. 57
Nathanson, Rebecca (Miss) 33
Nathanson, Reva (Miss) 24, 165
Nathanson, S.L. 33, 65, 120
Nathanson, S.L. (Mr. and Mrs.) 120
Nathanson, Yechiel (Master) 57
Nathanson, Z. 182
Naurm, Lillian (Miss) 29
Naurm, Samuel (Mr. and Mrs.) 29
Navarich, A. 66
Navarich, A. (Miss) 95
Nayov, Sonny (Miss) 23
Nayov, Z. (Miss) 23
Neamton, H. 137
Necktovitch, Lena (Miss) 30
Neidenberg, M. 154
Neiman, Sarah (Miss) 175
Neisser, Eugene Jacob (Dr.) 18
Nelson, I. 183
Nelson, I. (Mrs.) 183
Nepsky, Isaac 34
Nervich, H.P. 89
Nervich, Hyman P. 50
Nerwich, H.P. 81
Nerwich, Hyman P. 19, 120
Ness, A. (Mr. and Mrs.) 38
Ness, H. (Mrs.) 120
Ness, Harry 11
Ness, Jennie (Miss) 38
Ness, Mr. 25
Ness, Mr. and Mrs. 120
Ness, R. 120
Ness, R. (Mr. and Mrs.) 8
Ness, R. (Mrs.) 120
Ness, Robert 121
Neufeld, Elizabeth (Mrs.) 179
Neuhouse, H. 78
Neuman, Sydney 47
Neumann, A. (Mrs.) 64, 121

Name	Page
Neumann, Arthur	34
Neumann, J.	73
Neumann, J.N. (Mrs.)	66, 121
Neveren, L. (Mrs.)	35
Newark, Lillian (Miss)	170
Newman, D. (Mr. and Mrs.)	25
Newman, J.N. (Mrs.)	50, 121
Newman, Mr.	185
Newman, Mr. and Mrs.	80
Newman, Phillip	183
Newman, S.	156
Newman, Tillie (Miss)	25
Newmann, Harold	3
Newmann, J.N. (Mr. and Mrs.)	3
Nickelsburg, Elsa (Miss)	157
Nickelson, Max	184
Nieman, Mrs.	179
Nieman, S.	155
Nieto, Jacob (Dr.)	18
Nimerof, Annie (Miss)	121
Nissenholtz, S.	72, 137
Nissinholz, S.	72
Nitkin, Samuel	34
Nodek, I.M.	185
Nordheimer, Abraham	45
Nordheimer, Samuel	45
Norman, G. (Mrs.)	126
Norwitsky, D.	158
Novak, H.	131
Nozick, I.	183
Nurick, Kate (Miss)	157
Nurick, S. (Mrs.)	157, 160
Nurrick, L. (Mrs.)	24
Nurrick, Mollie (Miss)	24
O'Connor, Michael	179
Obendorffer, H.	121
Obendorffer, H. (Miss)	121
Obendorffer, Miss	121
Obendorffer, S.	173
Obendorffer, S. (Mrs.)	121
Ober, L.	74, 86, 122, 136
Ober, Louis	34, 50, 90, 121, 124, 137
Oberndorffer, Herman	121
Oberndorffer, Mr. and Mrs.	173
Oberndorffer, S. (Mrs.)	131
Oberndorffer, Simon	18
Oberneek, Frau	152
Oelbaum, Chas.	163
Ogulnick, L.M. (Mr. and Mrs.)	11
Ogulnick, P. (Mrs.)	78, 98
Ogulnick, Paul (Mrs.)	77, 146
Ogulnik (Miss)	19
Ogulnik, Blanche (Miss)	26
Ogulnik, E. (Miss)	121
Ogulnik, Edith (Miss)	37, 69, 76, 77, 111, 121
Ogulnik, Edythe (Miss)	26, 60
Ogulnik, Esther (Miss)	26, 162
Ogulnik, F.M. (Mrs.)	136
Ogulnik, Louis	26
Ogulnik, Mr.	121
Ogulnik, P. (Mrs.)	64, 79, 121
Ogulnik, Paul	26, 62
Ogulnik, Paul (Mr. and Mrs.)	26, 37, 80, 121
Ogulnik, Paul (Mrs.)	77, 107
Ogulnik, S.M.	121
Ogulnik, S.M. (Mr. and Mrs.)	11
Ogulnik, S.M. (Mrs.)	20, 109
Ogulnik, Sam (Mrs.)	77
Oielbaum, C. (Sergt.)	162
Oliver, May (Miss)	102
Ollendorf, Clarence	121
Oppenheimer, Alfred (Mrs.)	13
Oppenheimer, Mr. and Mrs.	121
Oppenheimer, Mrs.	70, 76, 121
Orenstein, H.	67
Orenstein, Harry	34
Orenstein, Joseph (Master)	82
Orenstein, O.	106
Orenstein, W.	79
Orken, H.B.	121
Orkin, Edward	42
Orkin, J.M.	90
Orkin, J.M. (Mr. and Mrs.)	125
Orkin, J.M. (Mrs.)	32
Orkin, M.J. (Mrs.)	113
Orkin, Nina (Miss)	32
Ornstein, Beckie (Miss)	151
Ornstein, David	121
Ornstein, I. (Mr. and Mrs.)	11
Ornstein, I. (Mrs.)	64
Ornstein, Isaac	18
Ornstein, J.	121, 143
Ornstein, J. (Mrs.)	152
Ornstein, Jacques	121
Ornstein, Jacques (Mr. and Mrs.)	121
Ornstein, Jacques (Mrs.)	121
Ornstein, M. (Mr. and Mrs.)	121
Ornstein, M. Jacques (Mrs.)	41, 121
Ornstein, Max (Mrs.)	121
Ornstein, Mrs.	119
Ornstein, O. (Mrs.)	119
Ornstein, Osias	18
Ornstein, Rebecca (Miss)	36
Ortenberg, Ben	37
Ortenberg, D. (Mr. and Mrs.)	34, 37, 132
Ortenberg, David	108
Ortenberg, Dr.	2, 3
Ortenberg, Rose (Miss)	37, 121
Ortenberg, S. (Dr.)	37, 66, 81, 121
Ortenberg, S. (Mrs.)	114
Ortenberg, Samuel (Dr. and Mrs.)	121
Ortenberg, Samuel (Dr.)	34, 71, 121
Osman, S. (Miss)	88
Osmiensky, Elsie	61
Osowsky, Judith (Miss)	51
Ostfield, M.L. (Mr. and Mrs.)	178
Ostro, J.	114
Ostrofsky, B.A.	139
Ostrofsky, Samuel	139
Ostrogursky, Joseph	3
Ostrogursky, Mr. and Mrs.	11
Ostry, Mrs.	183
Owens, C.	155
Palter, H. (Master)	167
Palter, H. (Mrs.)	28
Palter, Mrs.	164
Paltiel, A.D.	65, 81
Paltiel, B. (Miss)	64
Paltiel, Z. (Mr. and Mrs.)	65
Papernek, H.	162
Papernick, Elsie (Miss)	155, 164
Papernick, Harris	34
Papernick, Mrs.	181
Papernick, Sarah (Miss)	34
Pappenheim, Bertha (Miss)	121
Parent, Mrs.	121
Parnass (Mr.)	34
Parnass, B.	34
Parness, Mrs.	27
Pascal, Mrs.	61
Pashin, Bessie (Miss)	30
Pashin, J. (Mr. and Mrs.)	30
Pashovsky, Mrs.	121
Paskal, Clara	61
Pasternack, C.	155
Pasternack, Charles	162, 169
Pasternack, Gertie (Miss)	169
Pasternak, Charles (Mr. and Mrs.)	165
Pasternak, Chas.	163
Pasternak, Gertrude (Miss)	159
Pasternak, Mr.	158
Pasternak, Mrs.	167
Paube, Morris	165
Paul, L.	155
Pauline, Miss	156
Pauline, Mr.	156
Pawloswka, Madame	121
Payne, Bella (Miss)	106
Payne, Chester	121
Payne, S. (Mrs.)	121
Pchasias, N.	162
Pearl, B.	149
Pearl, B. (Mr. and Mrs.)	151
Pearl, Bella (Miss)	127
Pearl, Harold (Master)	149, 151
Pearl, Mr.	150
Pearl, Mr. and Mrs.	127
Pearl, Mrs.	150
Pearlman, D.	157
Pearlman, J.	165
Pearlman, M.	170
Pearlman, M. (Mrs.)	34
Pearlman, Mrs.	121
Pearlman, R. (Mrs.)	121
Pearlman, S.	156
Pearlstein, Miss	154
Pearson, L. (Miss)	88
Pearson, P. (Miss)	88
Pearson, Samuel (Mrs.)	121
Pearson, Simon (Mrs.)	121
Peavy, L.H. (Mrs.)	97
Pechet, L.	22
Pechet, S. (Mr. and Mrs.)	22
Pechet, S. (Rev.)	22
Pedlow, Isaac F.	121
Pedlow, Miss	121
Peerles, Jake	176
Pelof, B.	149
Penturn, Mrs.	160
Pepon, D.	49
Perchanok, J.	56
Perchanok, Jennie (Miss)	56
Pergament, J. (Mrs.)	121
Pergament, Miss	121
Perlman, D.	155
Perlman, S.	182
Perlson, J.G. (Mrs.)	62
Perlstein, Mr.	164
Perry, Hannah (Miss)	165
Persky, S.P.	78
Person, N.H.	49
Pesner, A.	61, 91
Pesner, Mr.	34
Pesner, Mr. and Mrs.	34
Petegorsky, L.	9, 150, 151
Petegorsky, L. (Mrs.)	151
Petegorsky, Leon	34, 148, 151
Petegorsky, O.	149
Petegorsky, Sam	151
Petegorsky, V.	151
Peterboro, Sam	162
Petergorsky, Leon	151
Petersky, A.	185
Petersky, D.	156
Petersky, S.	185
Petersky, S. (Dr.)	185
Petersky, S. (Mrs.)	185
Petersky, Samuel (Dr.)	185
Petersky, William	185

Petersky, Wm. 185
Peuesh, C. (Miss) 165
Pevner, I. 106
Pevsner, Bella (Madame) 172
Pevsner, I. 72
Pevsner, Madame 183
Philip, Mr. 87
Philips, Annette (Miss) 30
Philips, H. 137
Philips, J.F. (Mr. and Mrs.) 11
Philips, Mr. 175
Philipson, I. 183
Philipson, M. 183
Phillips, B. (Miss) 150
Phillips, Bertha (Miss) 60, 102, 122
Phillips, Dorothy (Miss) 36
Phillips, Emanuel (Mr. and Mrs.) 36
Phillips, F. (Mr. and Mrs.) 28, 91
Phillips, F. (Mrs.) 14
Phillips, Fannie (Miss) 28
Phillips, Fischel 40
Phillips, Fischel (Mr. and Mrs.) 40
Phillips, Frances (Miss) 33
Phillips, Frankie (Miss) 33, 119, 122
Phillips, Gordon 33
Phillips, Henry (Mr. and Mrs.) 122
Phillips, Horace 132
Phillips, J. (Miss) 73
Phillips, Jessie (Miss) 37, 40, 73, 81, 117
Phillips, L. 70, 165
Phillips, Lazarus 37, 51, 121
Phillips, Lazarus (Master) 122
Phillips, Miss 118
Phillips, Mr. 110
Phillips, Mr. and Mrs. 75
Phillips, N. 33
Phillips, N. (Mr. and Mrs.) 122
Phillips, N. (Mrs.) 122
Phillips, Nathan 157, 161
Phillips, Nathan (Mr. and Mrs.) 33
Phillips, Rebecca (Miss) 28, 40
Phillips, S. (Mr. and Mrs.) 118
Phillips, S. (Mrs.) 122
Phillips, W. 122
Pickleman, L. 122
Pierce, A. 82, 118, 122
Pierce, A. (Mrs.) 67, 142
Pierce, A.E. 106
Pierce, Ascher . . . 62, 111, 118, 122, 143, 146
Pierce, Ascher (Mr. and Mrs.) 122
Pierce, Ascher (Mrs.) 73, 98, 122, 123, 142, 146
Pierce, Asher (Mr. and Mrs.) 114
Pierce, Asher (Mrs.) 73, 123, 135
Pierce, B. (Miss) 122, 139
Pierce, Beccie (Miss) 66
Pierce, C. (Mrs.) 141
Pierce, Charles 51, 122
Pierce, Charles (Mr. and Mrs.) 39
Pierce, Isaac Kremeor 51
Pierce, J. (Mr. and Mrs.) 122
Pierce, Jacob (Mr. and Mrs.) 179
Pierce, M. 122
Pierce, M.A. 122
Pierce, Miss 98, 146
Pierce, Mr. 45
Pierce, Mrs. 118
Pierce, R. 122
Pierce, Rebecca (Miss) 39
Pierce, Richard 92, 122
Pierce, Sidney 118
Pierce, Sidney (Master) 114
Pierce, Sydney 67
Pierce, Sydney D. (Master) 122
Pikus, Mrs. 156
Pinchefsky, Harry 158
Pinchefsky, Lizzie (Mrs.) 158
Pinckes, Jack 122
Pinco, A. 151
Pine, Master 53
Pink, M.C. 157
Pinkas, I. 183
Pinkus, Joseph 28
Pinkus, Mr. and Mrs. 28
Pinkus, Pearl (Miss) 28
Pinsky, Samuel 184
Pinsler, A. (Miss) 67, 99, 122, 134
Pinsler, Alice (Miss) 25, 39, 122
Pinsler, H. 98
Pinsler, J. 67, 74, 124
Pinsler, Jack 39, 122
Pinsler, Miss 113
Pinsler, P. (Mr. and Mrs.) 39
Pinsler, Paul (Mr. and Mrs.) 25, 39
Pinsler, Regina (Miss) 39
Pionick, Maurice 157
Pionick, Maurice (Dr.) 34
Pius, D. (Mrs.) 179
Pivnik, Maurice 34
Platnauer, M.L. 185
Pliskow, Charles 35
Pliskow, Myer 34, 35
Plumm, William (Mrs.) 179
Polakewich, Dora 18
Polakewich, Emma 18
Polakewich, George 18
Polakewich, Isaac 18
Polakewich, Joseph 18
Polakewich, Joseph (Mrs.) 18
Polakewich, Louis 18
Polakewich, William 18
Polakewitch, L. 22
Polekswich, Dora (Miss) 122
Polin, N. (Mr. and Mrs.) 122
Polinsky, M. 175
Pollack, B.J. (Mr. and Mrs.) 122
Pollack, J. 122
Pollack, L. 157
Pollack, M. (Mrs.) 24
Pollak, Frank 35
Pollak, M. 164
Pollak, Tillie (Miss) 35
Pollin, Moe 122
Pollin, N. 122
Pollin, N. (Mr. and Mrs.) 89
Pollock, Frank 35
Pollock, G. 165
Pollock, K. 162
Pollock, M.A. 159, 169
Pollock, M.A. (Dr.) 165
Polloker, E. (Miss) 167
Polonsky, Billy (Mr. and Mrs.) 11
Polonsky, Fanny (Miss) 122
Polsky, J. 183
Pomerantz, Joseph 35
Pomerantz, M. 157, 167
Popkin, H. (Mr. and Mrs.) 11
Popliger, I. 66, 93, 122, 146
Popliger, Isidore 87, 122
Popliger, Mr. 46
Popliger, P. 59, 81, 107, 137, 139
Popliger, Philip 139
Popliger, S. 23, 62, 122, 137
Poplinger, Mrs. 122
Porteous, Dr. and Mrs. 123
Porteous, J. 123
Porteous, Miss 123
Portigal, H. 180
Portigal, I. (Mr. and Mrs.) 40
Portigal, I. (Mrs.) 179, 180
Portigal, S. 175
Portis, Carrie (Miss) 123
Portugal, Isaac (Mr. and Mrs.) 179
Poshertnick, J. 123
Posnanzki, Augusta (Miss) 36
Posnanzki, J. Edward (Mr. and Mrs.) 36
Posnanzki, Maurice 36
Posnanzki, Maurice A. 36
Posnanzki, Samuel 36
Potashner, Annie 42
Pottashner, Annie (Miss) 106
Poverin, M. 59
Povitch, Mary (Miss) 36
Powerin, M. 59
Poyaner, A. 49
Poyaner, A. (Mr. and Mrs.) 36
Poyaner, A. (Mrs.) 123
Poyaner, Esther (Miss) 35, 36, 41
Poyaner, Florence (Miss) 107, 123
Poyaner, Harry 35
Poyaner, M. (Mr. and Mrs.) 123
Poyaner, Meyer 35
Poyaner, Miss 123
Poyaner, Misses 123
Poyaner, Myer 35, 123
Poyaner, Myer (Mr. and Mrs.) 11
Poyaner, S. (Mr. and Mrs.) 119
Poyanor, A. 59
Poyas, A. 56
Poyes, L. 56
Pozner, A. (Mr. and Mrs.) 123
Pozner, L. (Mr. and Mrs.) 26, 123
Prager, E. (Miss) 165
Prager, Louis 156
Prager, Miss 164
Presner, A. 107
Presner, I. (Mrs.) 123
Presner, J. 35
Presner, J. (Mr. and Mrs.) 40
Presner, Louis 123
Presner, P. 69, 86, 176
Presner, P. (Mrs.) 179
Presner, Ph. (Mr. and Mrs.) 178
Presner, Philip 70
Press, A.S. (Mrs.) 37
Press, Gertie (Miss) 37
Press, Mrs. 146
Press, S. (Mrs.) 127
Presser, Phillip (Mr. and Mrs.) 11
Presser, W.F. (Miss) 113, 122, 123
Presser, Winnie F. (Miss) 123
Pressman, Mr. and Mrs. 123
Pressman, Tonnie 123
Pressner, Joseph (Mr. and Mrs.) 73
Pressner, M. 123
Pressner, P. (Master) 137
Pressner, Philip (Master) 46
Preston, J. (Mrs.) 123
Preston, L. (Mrs.) 116
Price, E.R. (Mrs.) 21
Prime, Mrs. 96
Pronoffsky, Fanny (Mrs.) 157
Prosky, Samuel 165
Prosterman, S. 182
Prusansky, J. 131
Pruzansky, Jacob 123
Pulaski, J. 123
Pullan, A. 2, 164, 165
Pullan, B. 24, 35

Pullan, Bessie (Dr.) 160, 164
Pullan, Bessie (Miss) 155, 162
Pullan, Bessie Thelma (Dr.) 38, 39
Pullan, D. 154
Pullan, D. (Miss) 165, 169
Pullan, D.E. 162
Pullan, Dora (Miss) 24, 154, 165
Pullan, E. 2, 154, 162, 169
Pullan, Elias 154, 155, 160, 169
Pullan, Elias (Mr. and Mrs.) 24, 165
Pullan, H. 169
Pullan, H. (Miss) 149
Pullan, H. (Mr. and Mrs.) 35
Pullan, H. (Mrs.) 151
Pullan, Harry 24, 35
Pullan, Henry (Mr. and Mrs.) 39
Pullan, Hilda (Miss) 39, 148, 151-153
Pullan, J. 179
Pullan, J.M. (Mrs.) 35
Pullan, Joel 33, 35, 61, 179
Pullan, Joel (Mrs.) 21, 33, 179, 180
Pullan, L.J. 123
Pullan, Louis I. 35
Pullan, Louis L. 35
Pullan, M. (Miss) 164
Pullan, M. (Mr. and Mrs.) 35, 38, 165
Pullan, M.D. (Mr. and Mrs.) 2
Pullan, Martha (Miss) 24, 150, 154, 165
Pullan, Miss 164
Pullan, Mr. and Mrs. 39
Pullan, Yetta (Miss) 156
Pullan-Singer, Bessie T. (Dr.) 165
Pullen, Dora (Miss) 167
Pulver, Adeline (Miss) 11
Puritzman, Bessie (Miss) 123
Puritzman, Sarah (Miss) 123
Puritzman, Sophie (Miss) 123
Pyes, Dave (Mrs.) 179
Pyes, David L. 35
Pyes, Mr. and Mrs. 179
Rabbinowich, George 66
Rabbinowich, S. 66
Rabin, A. 65, 81
Rabin, Harry 35
Rabin, J. 183
Rabin, Jennie (Miss) 35
Rabin, Joseph 183
Rabin, L. 62
Rabin, Louis 35
Rabinovich, Annie (Miss) 41
Rabinovich, R. (Mrs.) 85
Rabinovitch, A. 172
Rabinovitch, A. (Mrs.) 64
Rabinovitch, Aaron (Mrs.) 123
Rabinovitch, Annie (Miss) 123
Rabinovitch, Bessie (Miss) 35
Rabinovitch, Carl 132
Rabinovitch, Dr. 108
Rabinovitch, G. 64, 73
Rabinovitch, G. (Mrs.) 64
Rabinovitch, Gedaliah 92
Rabinovitch, George 81, 123
Rabinovitch, George (Mr. and Mrs.) 11
Rabinovitch, H. (Mrs.) 24
Rabinovitch, Harry 35
Rabinovitch, I. 11, 61, 161
Rabinovitch, Lazer 18
Rabinovitch, Lillie (Miss) 35
Rabinovitch, M. 64
Rabinovitch, M. (Dr. and Mrs.) 11
Rabinovitch, M. (Dr.) 74
Rabinovitch, M. (Mrs.) 77
Rabinovitch, Max 131
Rabinovitch, Max (Dr.) 35, 63, 123
Rabinovitch, Max (Mr. and Mrs.) 123
Rabinovitch, Olga (Miss) 24, 73, 78, 123
Rabinovitch, P. 18
Rabinovitch, Pauline (Miss) 77
Rabinovitch, S. 18, 64
Rabinovitch, S. (Mr. and Mrs.) 123
Rabinovitch, S. (Mrs.) 64, 77
Rabinovitch, Sam 131
Rabinovitch, Samuel 123
Rabinowich, N. 183
Rabinowitz, Aron 123
Rabinowitz, Max (Dr.) 123
Rabinowitz, Mr. 158
Rabinowitz, Noah 183
Rabinowitz, P. 183
Rabinowitz, Rabbi 74
Rabinowitz, S.W. 185
Raboo, I. (Mrs.) 134
Rachofsky, Minnie (Miss) 123
Rachofsky, Miss 123
Racko, M. 177
Racko, S. 177
Rackow, M. 177
Rackow, S. 177
Raefaelovitch, S. (Miss) 67
Rafel, A. 148
Rafelman, A. (Mr. and Mrs.) 165
Rafelman, A. (Mrs.) 165
Rafelman, Mrs. 165, 167
Rafelovitch, M. (Mrs.) 20
Rafelovitch, S. (Miss) 88
Raffalovitch, I. (Rev.) 151
Raffelman, A. (Mrs.) 165, 167
Rafolovitch, Lena (Miss) 123
Rafolovitch, M. (Mr. and Mrs.) 3, 123
Rafolovitch, Moses (Master) 3
Rafolovitch, Mr. and Mrs. 123
Rafolovitch, Sara (Miss) 123
Raginsky, A. 123
Raginsky, Pauline (Miss) 123
Raich, David 35
Rainblatt, Saul 81
Raiscubarg, I. 123
Raisky, M. 180
Raisky, Mr. 176
Raisky, Mrs. 181
Ram, A. 72
Ram, A. (Miss) 133
Ram, B. 37, 51, 81, 123
Ram, B. (Mr. and Mrs.) 18, 35, 79
Ram, Billy 51
Ram, J. 155, 162
Ram, Jacob 18
Ram, L. 61
Ram, Lawrence 87
Ram, Mr. 155
Ram, Sadie (Miss) 109
Ram, Samuel 35, 112, 123
Ramm, B. 120
Ramm, Harold 35
Ramm, Julius 155, 157, 162
Ramm, Norman 164
Ramsay, Miss 123
Rapaport, I. 182
Raphael, A. 18, 111
Raphael, Beatrice (Miss) 123
Raphael, Bertha (Miss) 19, 111, 123
Raphael, Claire (Miss) 123
Raphael, Clare (Miss) 124, 130
Raphael, Harry 19
Raphael, I. 172
Raphael, Julius 19
Raphael, Louis 171
Raphael, Louise (Miss) 124
Raphael, Mabel (Miss) 172
Raphael, Maurice 19
Raphael, Miss 124, 130, 156, 164
Raphael, Mr. and Mrs. 124
Raphael, Mrs. 124
Raphael, Nellie (Miss) 149
Raphael, Nettie (Miss) 151
Raphael, R. 118, 124
Raphael, R. (Mr. and Mrs.) 124
Raphael, R. (Mrs.) 107
Raphael, R.L. 185
Raphael, Ralph 124
Raphael, Ralph (Mr. and Mrs.) 124
Raphael, Ralph (Mrs.) 107, 131
Raphael, Randolph 19
Raphael, Rose (Miss) 171, 172
Raphael, Rudolph 124
Raphael, Samuel 19
Raphael, Walter 19
Raphael, William 18
Raphael, William (Mr. and Mrs.) . . . 123, 124
Raphalovitch, S. (Miss) 67, 146
Raphelowitz, Mrs. 49
Rapholovitch, R. (Mr. and Mrs.) 24
Rapholovitch, Sara (Miss) 24
Rapp, M. 49, 74, 124
Rappaport, A. 158
Rappaport, H. 115
Rappaport, Mr. 162
Rappaport, Mrs. 27
Rappelbaum, Leon 35
Rappoport, Mrs. 124
Rapport, Mr. 124
Rashofsky, J. 155
Rasin, Channah (Miss) 178
Raskin, P.M. 51
Rasminsky, D. (Mr. and Mrs.) 101
Rasminsky, D. (Mrs.) 64
Rasminsky, David (Mrs.) 99
Ratner, D. (Miss) 84, 112, 122
Ratner, Dora (Miss) 87
Ratner, Fanny (Miss) 65
Ratner, M. (Miss) 107
Ratner, Miss 71
Ratner, R. (Miss) 61
Ratner, Z. 81, 112, 124
Ratner, Z. (Mr. and Mrs.) 124
Rattner, Benjamin 178
Rattner, Chaiya (Miss) 178
Rattner, Deborah (Miss) 178
Rattner, Frida (Miss) 178
Rauner, A. (Mr. and Mrs.) 165
Rauner, W. (Mr. and Mrs.) 165
Ravitch, M. 46, 78
Rawson, H. 90, 91, 114, 115
Rawson, N. 115
Rawson, S. 87, 90, 91, 114, 115, 124, 137, 138
Rayhead, Nettie (Miss) 151
Redlich, C. (Mrs.) 106, 117, 124
Redlich, Charles 93, 124
Redlich, Charles (Mr. and Mrs.) 124
Redlich, Charles (Mrs.) 19, 97, 124
Redlich, Frank 124
Redlich, Frank (Master) 124
Redlich, J. (Mrs.) 124
Redlich, Joseph 124
Reim, Annie (Miss) 35
Reine, Annie (Miss) 35
Reinharz, David 124
Reisner, Mr. 114
Relkin, Edwin A. 165

Relkins, Edwin A. 158
Remach, G.K. 124
Rendon, S. 134
Resch, B. (Mr. and Mrs.) 40
Resch, E. (Miss) 40
Resch, M. 40
Resch, S. 122
Ressler, A. (Miss) 64
Ressler, H. 67
Ressler, Hyman 124
Ressler, I. (Mrs.) 19, 108, 130
Ressler, L. (Miss) 64, 99
Ressler, L. (Mr. and Mrs.) 81
Ressler, L. (Mrs.) 124
Ressler, Lillian 51
Ressler, Lillian (Miss) 80
Ressler, Lily (Miss) 87
Ressler, Louis 112
Ressler, S.A. (Miss) 99, 133
Ressler, Sadie (Miss) 122
Ressler, Sadie A. (Miss) 108
Ressler, Twinnie S. (Miss) 124
Ressman, Mr. and Mrs. 36
Reubin, Moses 182
Reudner, Abraham 53
Revoe, Miss 57
Rice, L. 175
Rice, Mr. 177
Richardson, R.L. 92
Richenburg, Annie (Miss) 124
Richman, Bessie 61
Richstone, A.S. 124
Richstone, Mr. 49
Richter, Frances E. (Miss) 124
Richter, Francis (Miss) 124
Richter, S. 149
Richter, S. (Dr. and Mrs.) 36, 124
Richter, S. (Mrs.) 124
Rider, Mr. 155
Riffenstein, Miss 124
Rigler, B. (Mr. and Mrs.) 141
Rigler, J. (Miss) 131
Rigler, Jennie (Miss) 124
Rigler, M. (Miss) 124
Rigler, R.E. (Miss) 124
Rill, A. (Mr. and Mrs.) 11
Rill, Abraham 19, 35
Rill, Abraham (Mr. and Mrs.) 11
Rill, Isidore 19
Rill, J.L. 124
Rill, J.L. (Mr. and Mrs.) 35, 179
Rill, J.L. (Mrs.) 30, 35, 178
Rill, Julius 19
Rill, Julius L. (Mrs.) 179
Rill, Louis (Mrs.) 19
Rincovar, Lewis 28
Rinder, Mr. 65
Ringel, G. 171
Rinkof, Solomon 51
Rinkoff, L. (Miss) 96
Ripstein, J. 179
Ripstein, Charles 176, 178
Ripstein, Charles K. 176
Ripstein, Claire (Miss) 179, 180
Ripstein, Constance S. (Miss) 180
Ripstein, Gertrude (Miss) 177
Ripstein, Goldie (Miss) 180
Ripstein, Goldye (Miss) 179
Ripstein, Horace and Rita 185
Ripstein, I. 175, 176, 180
Ripstein, I. (Mr. and Mrs.) 11
Ripstein, I. (Mrs.) 179
Ripstein, Isaac 179

Ripstein, Isadore 4
Ripstein, J. (Mr. and Mrs.) 38
Ripstein, Jerome (Master) 11
Ripstein, L. 185
Ripstein, Max (Mr. and Mrs.) 11
Ripstein, Misses 120, 178
Ripstein, N. (Mrs.) 180
Ripstein, Rose (Miss) 144, 175-177
Ripstein, Rose E. (Miss) 179
Ripstein, S.A. 175, 180
Ripstein, S.A. (Mr. and Mrs.) 4
Ripstein, S.A. (Mrs.) 177, 179
Ripstein, Sara Constance (Miss) 38
Ritberg, Rebecca (Miss) 178
Rittenberg, Alfred 4, 124
Rittenberg, Aubie (Master) 4
Rittenberg, B. (Miss) 167
Rittenberg, Belle (Miss) 124, 165
Rittenberg, E. (Miss) 167
Rittenberg, Eva (Miss) 164, 165
Rittenberg, I. (Mr. and Mrs.) 159, 165
Rittenberg, Isaac and Annie 19
Rittenberg, M. 46, 124, 130
Rittenberg, M. (Miss) 123
Rittenberg, M. (Mr. and Mrs.) 79, 124
Rittenberg, M. (Mrs.) 123-125
Rittenberg, Miss 107
Rittenberg, Misses 162
Rittenberg, Moe (Mr. and Mrs.) 4, 124
Rittenberg, Moe (Mrs.) 125
Rittenberg, Mr. and Mrs. . 4, 19, 94, 111, 124
Rittenberg, Mr. and Mrs. M. 124
Rittenberg, Phillip 19
Rittenberg, Riva (Miss) 26
Rittenberg, Sam 124, 125
Rittenberg, Samuel 19, 59, 125
Ritteneberg, Samuel 59
Rivenovitch, Annie 132
Rivenovitch, Annie (Miss) 125
Rivenovitch, Susie (Miss) 63
Roback, A. 47
Roback, A.A. 125
Roback, Abraham A. 51, 125
Roberts, B. (Mr. and Mrs.) 160
Robinson, B. (Miss) 36
Robinson, Dora (Miss) 179
Robinson, Dorothy (Miss) 179
Robinson, Esther 177, 180
Robinson, Esther (Miss) 22
Robinson, Fannie (Miss) 177
Robinson, Fanny (Miss) 176
Robinson, H. 56
Robinson, Hattie (Miss) 178-180
Robinson, J. 125
Robinson, Jennie (Miss) 80
Robinson, Louis 22
Robinson, Miriam (Miss) 60
Robinson, Misses 178
Robinson, Mr. and Mrs. R.S. 4
Robinson, Mrs. 125
Robinson, Nathan 180
Robinson, R.S. 40, 175, 176, 180
Robinson, R.S. (Mr. and Mrs.) 4
Robinson, R.S. (Mrs.) 177
Robinson, S.L. (Mrs.) 185
Robinson, S.R. 179
Robinson, Sydney 4, 180
Robitaille, K. (Miss) 22
Robitaille, M. 127
Robitaille, Mrs. 73
Robitaille, P. (Miss) 127
Robkin, Mrs. 158
Rock, Jack 165

Rockstein, Jacob 125
Roddin, Mr. and Mrs. 71
Rodin, Gertrude (Miss) 53
Roesner, Hilda (Miss) 125
Rogers, Mr. 19
Roggen, S. (Mrs.) 128
Roggen, Selig 35
Roggen, Selig (Mr. and Mrs.) 125
Roggen, Z. 36
Rogul, S. 154, 163, 167
Rogul, S. (Mr. and Mrs.) 11
Rohleder, W. 156
Rohr, Siegfried L. 42
Roman, Abraham 19
Roman, Marcus 19
Roman, Marcus (Mr. and Mrs.) 11, 125
Roman, Marcus (Mrs.) 131, 147
Roman, Mark (Mrs.) 116
Roman, Mrs. 20
Roman, Samuel 13, 19, 106, 117, 125
Roman, William 19
Romanovsky, Sara (Miss) 179
Rome, A.I. (Mr. and Mrs.) 36
Rome, Edythe (Miss) 36
Rome, H.J. 125
Rome, Hyman 36
Rome, I. (Mr. and Mrs.) 36, 125
Rome, J.L. 36
Rome, Jeannette (Miss) 36
Rome, Mrs. 66
Rome, Nathan 36, 66, 125
Rome, Nathan (Mr. and Mrs.) 125
Rome, Nathan (Mrs.) 66, 125
Rome, Philip 36
Rome, Sophie (Miss) 36
Romelson, Fred 183
Roodman, J. 149
Roodman, M. 152
Roodman, Mr. 148
Roodman, Z. 149
Roos, Miss 125, 136
Roscom, D. 125
Roscom, David 36
Roscom, Fannie (Miss) 125
Roscom, Misses 125
Roscon, L. 125
Roscow, J. 125
Rose, B. 65, 90, 124, 125
Rose, B.A. (Mrs.) 125
Rose, Ben 151
Rose, Bernard   36, 51, 62, 104, 107, 114, 115,
                                125, 136, 154
Rose, Della E. (Miss) 165
Rose, Henry H. 122
Rose, I. 7, 125
Rose, Isaac (Mrs.) 17, 77
Rose, J. (Mrs.) 109, 114
Rose, Joe (Master) 76
Rose, Lionel 134
Rose, M.I. (Mrs.) 62
Rose, M.L. 134
Rose, M.L. (Mr. and Mrs.) 125
Rose, M.L. (Mrs.) 13, 125
Rose, Miriam D. 51
Rose, Miss 125
Rose, Mr. 155
Rose, Mr. and Mrs. 129
Rose, Mrs. 30
Rose, R. 156
Rose, S. 125, 172
Rose, Samuel 125
Rose, Tylle (Miss) 172, 173
Rosen, B. 38, 61

Rosen, B. (Miss) 80
Rosen, Douglas 177
Rosen, E. (Mr. and Mrs.) 11
Rosen, H. 165
Rosen, H. (Miss) 177, 179
Rosen, H. (Mrs.) 125
Rosen, Harry 165
Rosen, Hattie (Miss) 177
Rosen, Hettie (Miss) 175
Rosen, Ida (Miss) 38, 110, 165
Rosen, Isaac (Mrs.) 181
Rosen, J. 125, 176
Rosen, J. (Mr. and Mrs.) 11
Rosen, J. (Mrs.) 139
Rosen, J.S. (Mr. and Mrs.) 11
Rosen, M. 165, 167, 183
Rosen, Miss 94
Rosen, Mr. 176
Rosen, Mr. and Mrs. 125
Rosen, Mrs. 139
Rosen, N. (Mr. and Mrs.) 129
Rosen, N. (Mrs.) 125
Rosen, R. 165
Rosen, R. (Mrs.) 38
Rosen, S. 162
Rosen, S. (Miss) 162, 176
Rosen, Sadie (Miss) 38, 165
Rosen, Sadye (Miss) 38
Rosen, Syd 175
Rosenas, F. (Miss) 36
Rosenas, Harry 36
Rosenback, S. (Mrs.) 15
Rosenbaum, B. 125
Rosenbaum, Beatrice (Mrs.) 19
Rosenbaum, C. (Miss) 82
Rosenbaum, Fanny (Miss) 165
Rosenbaum, Harry 19
Rosenbaum, J. 125
Rosenbaum, J. (Dr.) 125
Rosenbaum, J.H. (Mrs.) 43
Rosenbaum, J.J. 47, 51
Rosenbaum, Joseph 125
Rosenbaum, L. (Mrs.) 125
Rosenbaum, Mrs. 166
Rosenberg, A. 68, 125, 160
Rosenberg, A. (Mr. and Mrs.) 36
Rosenberg, A.G. 125
Rosenberg, Anna (Miss) 27
Rosenberg, Arthur H. 36
Rosenberg, B. 139
Rosenberg, C. (Mr. and Mrs.) 39, 126
Rosenberg, Carl 11, 81, 115, 131, 146
Rosenberg, D. 185
Rosenberg, E. (Mr. and Mrs.) 35
Rosenberg, Fred 164
Rosenberg, Gabriel 125
Rosenberg, H. (Miss) 47
Rosenberg, Hannah (Miss) . . 39, 59, 108, 125,
137, 139
Rosenberg, Helen (Miss) 36
Rosenberg, I. 36, 72
Rosenberg, Ida (Miss) 107, 125
Rosenberg, J. 36, 82
Rosenberg, J. (Mrs.) 126
Rosenberg, L. 86
Rosenberg, Lily (Miss) 35
Rosenberg, M. (Miss) 60, 61, 107, 111
Rosenberg, M. (Mrs.) 155
Rosenberg, M.J. 97
Rosenberg, M.J. (Mrs.) 28, 107
Rosenberg, Madge (Miss) 77, 106
Rosenberg, Merle (Miss) 165
Rosenberg, Mr. 185

Rosenberg, Mr. and Mrs. 102, 159
Rosenberg, Mrs. 102, 126
Rosenberg, N. (Mrs.) 164, 165
Rosenberg, Nathan (Master) 28, 107
Rosenberg, Norman (Mrs.) 165
Rosenberg, P. (Mr. and Mrs.) 160
Rosenberg, P. (Mrs.) 165
Rosenberg, R. (Miss) 126
Rosenberg, Rose (Miss) 36, 77, 79, 125
Rosenberg, S. 61, 137
Rosenberg, S. (Miss) 86
Rosenberg, Sadie (Miss) 106
Rosenberg, Sarah (Miss) 138
Rosenberg, W. (Mr. and Mrs.) 36
Rosenberger, M. 51, 126
Rosenberger, M. (Mr. and Mrs.) 11
Rosenberger, Mr. 51
Rosenberger, Rose (Miss) 98
Rosenblat, Abe 180
Rosenblat, Abie 176
Rosenblat, C.B. 175
Rosenblat, Charles B. 36, 126
Rosenblat, Chas. D. 126
Rosenblat, F. (Mrs.) 179, 180
Rosenblat, Frank (Mrs.) 180
Rosenblat, M. (Miss) 177
Rosenblat, M. (Mrs.) 175
Rosenblat, Mary (Miss) 116
Rosenblat, Mike (Mrs.) 180
Rosenblat, Miss 33
Rosenblat, Nathan 176, 180
Rosenblat, Nathan (Mrs.) 180, 181
Rosenblat, Pearl (Miss) 33
Rosenblatt, C.B. 126
Rosenblatt, E. (Miss) 33
Rosenblatt, Esther (Miss) 161
Rosenblatt, Gertrude (Miss) 177
Rosenblatt, H. 67, 126
Rosenblatt, H. (Mrs.) 126
Rosenblatt, Mr. 126
Rosenblatt, Pearl (Miss) 178
Rosenbloom, Dorothy (Miss) 126
Rosenbloom, E. (Miss) 114
Rosenbloom, Ethel (Miss) 32
Rosenbloom, I. 114
Rosenbloom, J. 59
Rosenbloom, J. (Mrs.) 142
Rosenbloom, Joseph 126
Rosenbloom, Joseph (Mr. and Mrs.) . . . 126
Rosenbloom, Joseph (Mrs.) 126, 143
Rosenbloom, L. 78
Rosenbloom, L. (Mr. and Mrs.) 126
Rosenbloom, Laz. 78
Rosenbloom, Louis 14, 114
Rosenbloom, Max 126
Rosenbloom, Mrs. 61
Rosenbloom, R. (Miss) 114
Rosenbloom, W. (Mrs.) 21, 87
Rosenbloom, William (Mrs.) 79, 143
Rosenbloome, J. 78
Rosenblum, Rose (Miss) 155
Rosenblum, Sam 156
Rosenburg, Bessie (Miss) 35
Rosenburg, L. 122
Rosenburg, N. (Mrs.) 35
Rosenburg, Philip (Mrs.) 35
Rosenes, H. (Mr. and Mrs.) 126
Rosenfeld, Annie (Miss) 29
Rosenfeld, B. (Mr. and Mrs.) 178
Rosenfeld, I. (Mr. and Mrs.) 29
Rosenfeld, Morris 51, 52, 165
Rosenfeldt, Mr. 66
Rosenfield, Charles 177

Rosenfield, Lillie (Miss) 158
Rosengarten, Sol. (Dr.) 100
Rosenseen, S. 119
Rosenshadt, Bertha (Miss) 172
Rosenshadt, J. 172
Rosenshadt, Jacob 172
Rosenshadt, Miss Bertha 172
Rosenshadt, Mrs. 172
Rosenshadt, T. (Mrs.) 172
Rosenstein, J. (Mrs.) 151
Rosenstein, Jacob 36
Rosensveig, Dora (Miss) 126
Rosensveig, L. 126
Rosensvieg, Dora (Miss) 126
Rosenthal, A. 7, 61, 126
Rosenthal, A. (Mr. and Mrs.) 36, 126
Rosenthal, A. (Mrs.) 33, 126, 151, 152
Rosenthal, A.S. (Mrs.) 36
Rosenthal, Aaron 18
Rosenthal, Adolph 126
Rosenthal, Arthur 19, 36
Rosenthal, Arthur (Mr. and Mrs.) 126
Rosenthal, B. 162
Rosenthal, B. (Miss) 99
Rosenthal, B. (Mrs.) 126
Rosenthal, Bella (Miss) 126
Rosenthal, Belle (Miss) 126
Rosenthal, Blanche (Miss) 160
Rosenthal, Dollie (Miss) 126
Rosenthal, Dora (Miss) 36, 38
Rosenthal, Edward Aaron 19
Rosenthal, Frieda 19
Rosenthal, H. (Mr. and Mrs.) 126, 146
Rosenthal, Harry 19, 38
Rosenthal, Harry (Mr. and Mrs.) . . . 126, 146
Rosenthal, Harry (Mrs.) 146, 147
Rosenthal, Hiram 19
Rosenthal, Hyman 183
Rosenthal, I. 183
Rosenthal, I. (Mrs.) 160
Rosenthal, J. 88, 126
Rosenthal, J. (Mr. and Mrs.) 36
Rosenthal, Jack 126
Rosenthal, Jake 126
Rosenthal, Joseph 126
Rosenthal, Joseph (Mrs.) . . 101, 160, 165, 169
Rosenthal, Kathie (Miss) 183
Rosenthal, M. (Mrs.) 92, 126, 146, 165
Rosenthal, Martin 19
Rosenthal, Master 60
Rosenthal, Maurice 19
Rosenthal, Miss 126
Rosenthal, Morton 36
Rosenthal, Mr. 126, 156, 160
Rosenthal, Mrs. 40, 66, 101, 166, 167
Rosenthal, Nellie (Miss) 22
Rosenthal, R. (Miss) 73
Rosenthal, Robert (Master) 126
Rosenthal, Rose (Miss) 165
Rosenthal, S. 152
Rosenthal, S. (Alderman) 126
Rosenthal, S. (Mrs.) 15
Rosenthal, Sam 163
Rosenthal, Sam (Mr. and Mrs.) 19
Rosenthal, Samuel 19
Rosenthal, Samuel (Alderman) 36
Rosenthal, Samuel (Mr. and Mrs.) 11, 126
Rosenthal, Sara 68
Rosenthal, Sarah (Miss) 83, 126
Rosenthal, Sr., A. (Mrs.) . . 20, 126, 149, 152
Rosenthal, Sr., Mrs. 126
Rosenthal, T. 59
Rosenthal, W. (Mr. and Mrs.) 165

Rosentsveig, F. (Miss) 131	Rothschild, Benjamin 127	Rubin, Jas. 36
Rosentzveig, I. (Mr. and Mrs.) 126	Rothschild, D. (Miss) 127, 138, 170	Rubin, Joseph D. 36
Rosenveesen, S. 131	Rothschild, David 42, 49, 51	Rubin, L.M. (Mr. and Mrs.) 127
Rosenveesen, S. (Mrs.) 121	Rothschild, Dora (Miss) 65, 71, 74	Rubin, M. 36, 51, 64, 96, 107, 111, 114,
Rosenweesen, Leo 134	Rothschild, E. 51	117, 127, 162
Rosenzveig, Jake 36	Rothschild, E. (Miss) 138	Rubin, Maurice 36
Rosenzwaig, P. (Miss) 121	Rothschild, Ethel (Miss) 32, 74	Rubin, Miss 174
Rosenzweig, Rebecca 66	Rothschild, Geraldine (Miss) 51	Rubin, Molly (Miss) 106
Roshkovsky, Benjamin 177	Rothschild, J. 127	Rubin, Mr. and Mrs. 78, 86
Rosin, Marcus 43	Rothschild, J. (Mr. and Mrs.) 127	Rubin, N. 25, 34
Rosin, R. (Mrs.) 40	Rothschild, J. (Mrs.) 19, 127	Rubin, S. 106, 128
Roskam, D. 98, 126	Rothschild, M. (Mr. and Mrs.) 127	Rubin, S. (Miss) 25, 152
Roskam, Dave (Mr. and Mrs.) 126	Rothschild, M. (Mrs.) 127	Rubin, S. (Rev.) 184
Roskam, David 36	Rothschild, Max 170	Rubin, Sadie (Miss) 34
Roskam, David (Mr. and Mrs.) 91, 126	Rothschild, Max (Mr. and Mrs.) 32, 127	Rubin, Sebina (Miss) 25
Roskam, Edward 126	Rothschild, Miss 127	Rubin, Sophie (Miss) 127, 152
Roskam, L. 126	Rothschild, Rose (Miss) 165	Rubinoff, Israel 36
Roskam, S. (Mrs.) 90	Rotkowitz, Harry 22	Rubinoff, Mr. and Mrs. 157
Roskom, Dave (Mr. and Mrs.) 126	Rotstein, A. 162	Rubinovich, A.I. 49, 128
Rosminsky, Samuel 181	Rotstein, A. (Mr. and Mrs.) 11	Rubinovich, A.I. (Mr. and Mrs.) 80, 128
Rosner, David 36	Rotstein, Mr. 164	Rubinovich, Erwin 128
Rosner, Sadie (Miss) 180	Rotstine Bros. 162	Rubinovich, Frieda (Miss) 128
Ross, H. (Mr. and Mrs.) 157, 160	Rottenberg, M. 167	Rubinovich, I.M. 36
Ross, Israel 167	Rouda, J. (Mrs.) 165	Rubinovich, I.M. (Mrs.) 100, 113, 128
Ross, J. 158, 168	Routten, S.L. 49	Rubinovich, Irwin 4
Ross, Joseph 162	Routtenberg, I. (Mr. and Mrs.) 11	Rubinovich, Irwin (Master) 119
Ross, M. 169	Routtenberg, Israel 36	Rubinovich, J.B. 128
Ross, Max 56	Rovin, Maurice L. 36	Rubinovich, J.B. (Mr. and Mrs.) 4, 128
Ross, Miriam (Miss) 35	Rowan, M. (Mrs.) 127	Rubinovich, J.B. (Mrs.) 128, 134
Ross, Miriam D. (Miss) 127	Rozine, Mr. 132	Rubinovich, Leona 178
Ross, Mrs. 150, 152	Ruben, J.H. 127	Rubinovich, Mr. 128
Ross, N. (Miss) 115	Ruben, L. (Mrs.) 96	Rubinovich, Sylvia (Miss) 128
Ross, S. 168	Ruben, L.M. 127	Rubinovitch, A. 68
Ross, S.W. 165	Ruben, L.M. (Mr. and Mrs.) 127	Rubinovitch, A.I. (Mrs.) 128
Rossin, Julius 45	Ruben, L.M. (Mrs.) 96, 127	Rubinovitch, F. (Mrs.) 128
Rossin, Marcus 45	Ruben, Ludovie (Mr. and Mrs.) 127	Rubinovitch, Frieda (Miss) 128
Rossin, Samuel 45	Ruben, Ludwig (Mr. and Mrs.) 127	Rubinovitch, H. 185
Rost (Mrs.) 14	Ruben, Mr. and Mrs. 96	Rubinovitch, I. (Mr. and Mrs.) 128
Rost, A. (Mrs.) 109, 127	Ruben, Mrs. 147	Rubinovitch, I. (Mrs.) 100, 113
Rost, Anna (Miss) 127	Rubenstein, B. 30	Rubinovitch, I.M. (Mr. and Mrs.) 11
Rost, Anna (Mrs.) 102, 115, 127	Rubenstein, E. 36, 134	Rubinovitch, Israel (Mrs.) 128
Rost, E. (Miss) 92	Rubenstein, Esther (Miss) 170	Rubinovitch, J. (Mr. and Mrs.) 128
Rost, Edith (Miss) 106, 127	Rubenstein, Hattie (Miss) 127, 170	Rubinovitch, J.B. 128
Rost, F. (Miss) 104	Rubenstein, Hettie (Miss) 30	Rubinovitch, J.B. (Mr. and Mrs.) 11
Rost, J. (Miss) 92	Rubenstein, I. 127	Rubinovitch, Leona (Miss) 128
Rost, Jane (Miss) 66, 100	Rubenstein, Israel 7	Rubinovitch, Mrs. 100
Rost, Jane B. (Miss) . . 36, 103, 127, 132, 145	Rubenstein, L. 68, 69, 114, 127	Rubinovitch, Sylvia (Miss) 128
Rost, Jean (Miss) 123, 127	Rubenstein, Lazarus 127	Rubinowitch, A.I. (Mr. and Mrs.) 25
Rost, Julius 36, 127	Rubenstein, Louis 67, 68, 98, 127, 137	Rubinowitch, J.B. (Mr. and Mrs.) 25
Rost, Julius (Mr. and Mrs.) 11	Rubenstein, M. 121, 138, 141	Rubinowitch, L. 25
Rost, Julius B. (Mrs.) 127	Rubenstein, Max 14	Rubinowitz, M. 100
Rost, Malca Esther (Miss) 11	Rubenstein, Messrs. 74	Rubinowitz, S. 100
Rostein, J. 185	Rubenstein, Miss 105, 106, 127, 146, 165	Rubinsky, Belle (Miss) 128
Rostein, Louis 185	Rubenstein, Moses 51	Rubinsky, Ethel (Miss) 128
Roston, J. 49, 81	Rubenstein, Rose (Mrs.) 134	Rubinsky, M. 103
Roston, J. (Mr. and Mrs.) 150	Rubenstein, S. (Miss) 77, 105	Rubinsky, M. (Miss) 128
Roston, J. (Mrs.) 128	Rubenstein, Samuel 36	Rubinstein, Mrs. 165
Roston, Mrs. 20, 120	Rubin, Abe 57	Rubish, Isaac Ben Mordecai 177
Rotblatt, Cantor 173	Rubin, Abraham 128	Rubner, J.A. 128
Rotblatt, H. (Rev.) 174	Rubin, B. 49, 118, 127	Rudnick, H. 183, 184
Rotenberg, L. 162	Rubin, Bertha (Miss) 36	Rudnick, I. 184
Roth, David Cecil 52	Rubin, C.S. (Mr. and Mrs.) 11	Rudnick, Mr. 185
Roth, I. 127	Rubin, C.S. (Mrs.) 127	Rudnikoff, John 83
Roth, Sarah (Miss) 155	Rubin, Dr. and Mrs. 79	Rudolfe, A. (Mr. and Mrs.) 32
Rothbart, I. 127, 138	Rubin, E. 152	Rudolfe, Bessie (Miss) 32
Rothblat, Cantor 173	Rubin, Gertie (Miss) 25, 36, 142	Rudolph, A. 23, 49, 128
Rothchild, M. 106	Rubin, Gertrude (Miss) 25	Rudolph, A. (Mr. and Mrs.) 19, 25, 128
Rother, Harry 36	Rubin, H. 127	Rudolph, A. (Mrs.) 128
Rothman, A. (Mr. and Mrs.) 11	Rubin, J. 36, 81	Rudolph, B. (Miss) 25
Rothman, Julia (Mrs.) 122	Rubin, J. (Dr. and Mrs.) 11, 34	Rudolph, Bessie (Miss) 128
Rothschild, Ben 127	Rubin, J. (Dr.) 90, 127	Rudolph, Jessie (Miss) 128
Rothschild, Ben (Mr. and Mrs.) 127	Rubin, J. (Mr. and Mrs.) 25, 33, 34, 36, 127, 152	Rudolph, M. 128
Rothschild, Ben (Mrs.) 127	Rubin, J. (Mrs.) 36, 65, 97, 128, 146	Rudolph, Misses 128

Schwab, W. 131	Segal, Moses 20	Serkan, Rebecca (Miss) 40
Schwartz, A. 37, 126, 131	Segal, Nathan 132	Serot, I. 183, 184
Schwartz, B.H. 68, 105	Segal, Nessie (Miss) 42, 72	Sessenwein, Belle (Miss) 132
Schwartz, Clara (Miss) 46, 68, 132	Segal, William 20	Sessenwein, Belle Leah (Miss) 3
Schwartz, D. 166	Segal, Z. 37	Sessenwein, C. (Mr. and Mrs.) 132
Schwartz, E. 61	Segall, B. 33	Sessenwein, C. (Mrs.) 3
Schwartz, Ettie (Miss) 132	Segall, Mr. and Mrs. 123	Sessenwein, Isaac 132
Schwartz, F. (Miss) 64	Segalowitz, H. 152	Sessenwein, L. 60, 132
Schwartz, F. (Mr. and Mrs.) 11	Segel, L. 178	Sessenwein, L. (Mrs.) 132
Schwartz, F.W. 131	Seibin, P.T. 156	Sessenwein, Leah (Miss) 38
Schwartz, Freda (Miss) 60, 77	Seiden, Antonio 118	Sessenwein, Louis 79
Schwartz, H. 67, 74, 116	Seiden, Henry 132	Sessenwein, M. 78, 106
Schwartz, Harriet E. (Mrs.) 24	Seiden, Regina 118	Sessenwein, M. (Mr. and Mrs.) 132
Schwartz, Ida (Miss) 60	Seidler, I.M. 37	Sevinoff, H.M. (Mrs.) 123
Schwartz, J. 131, 132	Seidman, M. 132	Shacher, N. (Dr.) 74
Schwartz, J. (Miss) 109	Seifert, C.E. (Mr. and Mrs.) 132	Shacofsky, M. (Mrs.) 171, 172
Schwartz, Joseph 37	Seifert, W. 132	Shaer, D. 132
Schwartz, L. 166	Seigal, B. (Mrs.) 57	Shafer, S. (Mrs.) 159
Schwartz, L.M. (Mrs.) 166	Seigal, I. (Mrs.) 159	Shaffer, B. 115
Schwartz, Leah (Miss) 33	Seigal, Mr. 169	Shaffer, Samuel 181
Schwartz, Louis 132	Seigel, B.R. 101	Shaffer, William 170
Schwartz, M. 132, 163	Seigel, D. 154	Shaffet, Conan 51
Schwartz, M. (Mr. and Mrs.) 33	Seigel, David 11	Shair, Adolf (Mrs.) 172
Schwartz, M.B. 132	Seigel, I. 80	Shakofsky, J. (Mr. and Mrs.) 32
Schwartz, Miss 164	Seigler, Bessie (Miss) 122, 132	Shakofsky, Mary (Mrs.) 32
Schwartz, Mr. and Mrs. 11	Seigler, H. 185	Shalasky, Samuel 73
Schwartz, Mrs. 19, 132	Seigler, Ida (Miss) 65, 132	Shaleck, Arthur 11
Schwartz, Pauline (Miss) 31	Seigler, M. (Mrs.) 132	Shalek, Mrs. 132
Schwartz, R. 61	Seigler, Mr. 185	Shalek, Ray (Miss) 132
Schwartz, Rachel (Miss) 41	Seilig, J. (Mrs.) 166	Shalett, S.J. 171, 172
Schwartz, Rose (Miss) 166	Seilig, Mr. and Mrs. 163	Shalinsky, A. 130
Schwartz, S. 159, 162	Seipp, L. 179, 180	Shalinsky, Abe 86
Schwartz, S. (Mrs.) 132	Seipp, Laurence 179	Shalinsky, David 4
Schwartz, Samuel 132, 166	Seleg, Misses 56	Shalinsky, J. 81, 133
Schwartz, Samuel (Mr. and Mrs.) 41	Selenger, Mr. and Mrs. 132	Shalinsky, S. 130
Schwartzman, Harry (Mr. and Mrs.) 11	Selichowsky, Pesach 178	Shalinsky, S.H. 120, 133
Schwarz, S. 150, 152	Selick, J. (Mrs.) 157, 167	Shalinsky, Sam 86
Schwarzbard, J. 37	Selick, Mrs. 155, 166	Shalinsky, Sam H. 67
Schwarzbard, J. (Mrs.) 132	Selicovitch, Meyer 139	Shalit, A.L. 133
Schwarzbard, Jacob 37	Selig, Rosie (Mrs.) 132	Shane, Mary 51
Schweisberg, M. (Master) 82	Seligman, M. 59	Shanfield, Beckie (Miss) 133
Schweizar, V. 175	Selinjee, H. 160	Shanfield, Joseph (Mrs.) 133, 142
Schweizberg, Samuel (Master) 132	Sellinger, I. (Mr. and Mrs.) 132	Shanfield, Mrs. 133, 143
Schwerin, Mrs. 109	Sempliner, J. (Mr. and Mrs.) 132	Shanikman, M. 37
Schwernki, A. 38	Serat, J. 183	Shanker, Bessie (Miss) 134
Schwernki, Monroe 38	Serbin, S. (Mrs.) 115	Shanker, Jennie (Miss) 134
Schwersenski, A.D. (Mrs.) 132	Serchuck, H. (Mr. and Mrs.) 26	Shanker, Louis 69
Schwersenski, Lizzie (Miss) 38, 132	Serchuck, Sadie (Miss) 26	Shankman, W. (Mr. and Mrs.) 11
Schwersenski, Mr. 132	Serchuk, Charles 132	Shankman, W. (Mrs.) 111, 133
Schwisberg, I. 72	Serchuk, Dorothea (Dolly) (Miss) . . . 37	Shankman, Wolf (Mrs.) 69, 133, 144
Schwisberg, Samuel 132	Serchuk, H. 132	Shapera, Charles (Mr. and Mrs.) 133
Sebag-Montefiore, Arthur (Mrs.) 132	Serchuk, Harry 37	Shapera, G. 175
Sechter, T. 59	Serchuk, M. (Mr. and Mrs.) 37	Shapera, Mrs. 37
Seelenfreund, A.B. 93	Serchuk, Miss 133	Shapira, G. 78
Seelenfreund, J. 181	Serchuk, W. 132	Shapira, K.L. 164
Segal, B.R. 73, 101	Serchuk, W. (Mr. and Mrs.) 131	Shapira, Rose (Miss) 114
Segal, Bella (Miss) 48	Serchuk, W. (Mrs.) 108	Shapiro, A. 68
Segal, Bernard R. 132	Serebrin, H. 180	Shapiro, A. (Mr. and Mrs.) 38, 133, 139
Segal, Bertha (Miss) 51	Serebrin, Isaac 178	Shapiro, A. (Mrs.) 119, 133
Segal, Billy Reuben 20	Serebrin, J. 180	Shapiro, A.H. (Miss) 166
Segal, Clara (Mrs.) 20	Serebrin, R. 180	Shapiro, Abe 37
Segal, D. 152	Serebrin, Reubrin 178	Shapiro, Annie (Miss) 31, 167
Segal, D.J. 114	Sereth, B.N. (Mr. and Mrs.) 40	Shapiro, Annie H. (Miss) 166
Segal, E. 26	Sereth, Cecilia (Miss) 22, 40, 132, 183	Shapiro, Aron 37
Segal, Ella (Miss) 39	Sereth, Clara (Miss) 40	Shapiro, B. 68
Segal, H. 34, 162	Sereth, Emily (Miss) 40	Shapiro, Charles 152
Segal, I. 74	Sereth, H.N. (Mr. and Mrs.) 22, 40	Shapiro, Charles (Mr. and Mrs.) 133
Segal, J. 37, 47, 51, 110, 111, 132	Sereth, H.N. (Mrs.) 132	Shapiro, D. 59, 138
Segal, J. (Master) 86	Sereth, N.H. (Mr. and Mrs.) 40	Shapiro, D. (Mr. and Mrs.) 64, 112, 133
Segal, Jean (Miss) 162	Sereth, Ruby (Miss) 40	Shapiro, D. (Mrs.) 20, 78, 98, 105
Segal, M. 162	Sereth, Sophia (Miss) 40	Shapiro, D.H. 20, 133, 135
Segal, M. (Mrs.) 72	Sereth, Sophie (Miss) 40, 132	Shapiro, D.H. (Mr. and Mrs.) 4, 28
Segal, Mendle 51	Serkan, A. (Mr. and Mrs.) 40	Shapiro, D.S. 49

Shapiro, Dave . . . 37
Shapiro, David . . . 20, 133, 178
Shapiro, David H. . . . 70
Shapiro, E. (Mrs.) . . . 4
Shapiro, Fanny (Miss) . . . 36
Shapiro, G. . . . 78
Shapiro, G. (Mr. and Mrs.) . . . 37
Shapiro, George J. . . . 37, 38
Shapiro, Gershon (Mr. and Mrs.) . . . 133
Shapiro, H. . . . 68
Shapiro, H. (Mr. and Mrs.) . . . 133
Shapiro, H.A. . . . 114
Shapiro, I. (Miss) . . . 73
Shapiro, I. (Mr. and Mrs.) . . . 79
Shapiro, I. (Mrs.) . . . 105
Shapiro, Ida (Miss) . . . 28
Shapiro, J. . . . 20, 136
Shapiro, Joseph . . . 20
Shapiro, Joshua . . . 17
Shapiro, Julius . . . 4
Shapiro, K.L. . . . 162, 166
Shapiro, L. . . . 64, 114
Shapiro, L. (Mr. and Mrs.) . . . 4
Shapiro, L. (Mrs.) . . . 133
Shapiro, Leah (Miss) . . . 86, 133
Shapiro, M. . . . 20, 37
Shapiro, M. (Mr. and Mrs.) . . . 4
Shapiro, Mary (Miss) . . . 178, 180
Shapiro, Minnie (Miss) . . . 141
Shapiro, Moses . . . 20
Shapiro, Mr. . . . 182
Shapiro, Mr. and Mrs. . . . 160
Shapiro, N. (Mr. and Mrs.) . . . 4
Shapiro, R.L. (Miss) . . . 114
Shapiro, S. . . . 172
Shapiro, S. (Mr. and Mrs.) . . . 4, 103, 133
Shapiro, Sam . . . 103, 133
Shapiro, Samuel . . . 4, 38
Shapiro, Sheppard . . . 52
Shapiro, Solomon M. . . . 61
Shapiro, Sophie (Miss) . . . 4
Shapiro, Theresa (Mrs.) . . . 166
Shapiro, Wilford . . . 38
Shapiro, Wilfred . . . 38
Shara, L. . . . 81
Shara, R. (Miss) . . . 60, 61
Sharkafski, Rose (Miss) . . . 133
Sharpe, Charles . . . 11
Sharpe, Myer . . . 11
Shatz, Alexander . . . 164
Shatz, D. . . . 164
Shatzky, Ella (Miss) . . . 167
Shaw, B. . . . 184
Shaw, J. . . . 184
Shaw, R. . . . 183
Shaw, S. (Miss) . . . 81, 82
Shaw, Sarah (Miss) . . . 133
Shayne, Alex. . . . 167
Shayne, Alexander . . . 167
Shayne, Alexander (Master) . . . 164
Shayne, Dr. (Mrs.) . . . 165
Shayne, John (Dr. and Mrs.) . . . 37, 133
Shayne, John (Dr.) . . 133, 155, 158, 162, 163, 167-169, 184
Shayne, Rose (Miss) . . . 131
Shayne, Roselyn (Miss) . . . 37
Shayne, Tilly (Miss) . . . 131
Shear, A. . . . 173
Shear, Kid . . . 127
Shear, Mrs. . . . 147
Shear, Philip . . . 163
Shearman, Eva (Miss) . . . 24
Shearman, H.P. . . . 109
Shearman, Lyon (Mr. and Mrs.) . . . 24
Shechter, E. (Mrs.) . . . 180
Shechter, M. . . . 56
Sheenman, N. . . . 185
Sheffer, M. . . . 165
Sheifer, J. (Miss) . . . 99
Sheifer, J.L. (Miss) . . . 133
Shein, Mrs. . . . 156
Sheinman, M. . . . 185
Sheinman, Mr. . . . 185
Shenker, Fannie (Miss) . . . 22
Shenker, Maurice . . . 22
Shenkman, W. . . . 151
Shenkman, W. (Mr. and Mrs.) . . . 150
Shenkman, W. (Mrs.) . . . 111, 133, 149, 151
Shenkman, Wolf . . . 133
Shenkman, Wolf (Mr. and Mrs.) . . . 133
Shenkman, Wolf (Mrs.) . . . 133, 151
Sher, A. . . . 163
Sher, Chas. . . . 163
Sher, P. (Mr. and Mrs.) . . . 164
Sherman, F. . . . 58
Sherman, Gertrude (Miss) . . . 108
Sherman, Mr. . . . 66
Sherman, Mr. and Mrs. . . . 97
Sherrin, H. . . . 171, 172
Shertzer, H. . . . 106
Sherwin, A. . . . 38, 109
Sherwin, A.H. . . . 38
Sherwin, Blanche (Miss) . . . 38
Sherwin, J. (Mr. and Mrs.) . . . 133
Sherwin, Miss, of New York . . . 38
Sherwin, Mr. . . . 109
Sherwin, Mrs. . . . 109
Sheuer, Edmund . . . 172
Sheurer, Blanche (Miss) . . . 32
Shevell, I. (Rev. and Mrs.) . . . 26
Shevell, Sarah (Miss) . . . 26, 133
Shieff, Edward I. . . . 38
Shildkraut, Rudolph . . . 133
Shiller, Carl (Mr. and Mrs.) . . . 32
Shiller, Eva (Miss) . . . 32, 133
Shiller, O. . . . 65
Shinbane, H. . . . 175
Shinbane, J. (Mr. and Mrs.) . . . 178
Shiner, M. . . . 49
Ship, A.P. (Dr. and Mrs.) . . . 133
Ship, A.P. (Dr.) . . . 133
Ship, Dr. A.P. . . . 38
Ship, F. . . . 49, 73
Ship, Fischel . . . 34
Ship, M.L. (Dr.) . . . 134
Ship, N. . . . 134
Shire, Blanche (Miss) . . . 172
Shirroff, Anna (Miss) . . . 175
Shleifer, F. (Miss) . . . 131
Shliefer, A. (Miss) . . . 134
Shliefer, F. . . . 134
Shliefer, F. (Mrs.) . . . 134
Shlossberg, L. . . . 2
Shlossberg, S. . . . 64
Shlossberg, W. . . . 58
Shmirling, N. . . . 182
Shneyer, K. . . . 134
Shomer, L. . . . 162
Shondling, Fannie (Miss) . . . 57
Shopira, Jacob . . . 123
Shor, Z. . . . 162
Shore, B. . . . 149
Shore, H. . . . 149
Shore, Harry . . . 38
Shore, Harry (Mrs.) . . . 149
Shore, P. . . . 162
Shore, S. . . . 180
Shore, Solomon . . . 179
Shore, Z. . . . 162
Shoster, A.L. . . . 67
Shoster, A.P. . . . 67
Shoster, Ethel . . . 61
Shragge B. (Mrs.) . . . 180
Shragge, A. . . . 180
Shragge, B. . . . 175, 179, 180
Shragge, B. (Mr. and Mrs.) . . . 40, 180
Shragge, Irene (Miss) . . . 179, 180
Shragge, Lillian (Miss) . . . 180
Shragge, M. (Mrs.) . . . 179
Shragge, Mrs. . . . 177, 183
Shragge, Muriel (Miss) . . . 40
Shragge, Muriel R. (Miss) . . . 40
Shriar, J. . . . 182
Shriberg, H. . . . 65
Shube, E. . . . 158
Shuker, Louis . . . 131
Shuleman, M. . . . 67
Shulemson, Abram . . . 132
Shulich, J. (Miss) . . . 134
Shulman, B. . . . 120
Shulman, Elsie (Miss) . . . 167
Shulman, Esther (Miss) . . . 158, 167
Shulman, Eva . . . 162
Shulman, H. . . . 154, 162
Shulman, J. . . . 51
Shulman, M. . . . 120
Shulman, P. . . . 157, 158, 162, 167, 168
Shulman, P. (Mr. and Mrs.) . . . 167
Shulman, Percy . . . 156, 157
Shulman, Sam . . . 132
Shumer, L. . . . 163
Shushelsky, Ida (Miss) . . . 134
Shuster, H. . . . 64
Shuster, Minnie (Miss) . . . 87
Shwartz, Fred . . . 184
Shweisberg, S. . . . 137
Sicher, Sophia (Mrs.) . . . 15
Sidel, Dorothy (Miss) . . . 31
Sidel, Dorothy M. (Miss) . . . 134
Sidenberg, Mr. . . . 149
Siderski, A. . . . 57, 58, 134
Siderski, Archie . . . 134
Siderski, H. . . . 171-173
Siderski, Miss . . . 134
Sidersky, A. . . . 57
Siegal, B. (Mrs.) . . . 57
Siegal, I.H. (Mrs.) . . . 167
Siegal, M. . . . 162
Siegel, Anna (Miss) . . . 134
Siegel, B. . . . 57
Siegel, D. . . . 167
Siegel, David . . . 164
Siegel, Dora (Mrs.) . . . 58
Siegel, I.H. (Mr. and Mrs.) . . . 11, 163
Siegel, I.H. (Mrs.) . . . 154, 160, 164, 167
Siegel, M. . . . 158
Siegel, Mrs. . . . 167
Siegler, B. (Miss) . . . 80
Siegler, Bessie (Miss) . . . 145
Siegler, F. (Mr. and Mrs.) . . . 4
Siegler, I. (Miss) . . . 60
Siegler, Ida (Miss) . . . 66, 100, 134
Siegler, Max . . . 4
Siegler, Mr. and Mrs. F. . . . 4
Siegler, Mrs. . . . 156
Siegler, S. . . . 68
Sieman, Frances (Miss) . . . 157
Sigal, Sam . . . 163
Sigler, Annie . . . 42

Sigler, G. . . . 66
Sigler, Ida (Miss) . . . 128, 134
Sigler, M. . . . 64
Sigler, Mrs. . . . 21
Sigler, S. . . . 59, 79, 81
Sigman, J. . . . 90, 91, 115
Sigman, Jack . . . 73
Sigmund, A. (Mr. and Mrs.) . . . 91
Sigmund, A. (Mrs.) . . . 134, 139
Sigmund, F. (Miss) . . . 134
Sigmund, Frances (Miss) . . . 46, 134
Sigmund, M. (Miss) . . . 134
Sigmund, Martha (Miss) . . . 134
Sigmund, Mr. and Mrs. . . . 91
Sigmund, Mrs. . . . 134
Signer, A. (Rev.) . . . 15
Signer, A.J. (Mr. and Mrs.) . . . 26
Signer, Gertie (Miss) . . . 26, 80
Signer, Gertrude . . . 88
Signer, Minnie (Miss) . . . 26
Signer, Moses . . . 51
Signer, R. (Mrs.) . . . 134
Signer, W. . . . 134
Silber, R. (Mrs.) . . . 36
Silberhertz, Moritz (Mr. and Mrs.) . . . 33
Silberman, B. . . . 160
Silberman, Harry (Mr. and Mrs.) . . . 11, 103
Silberman, Harry (Mrs.) . . . 103
Silberman, Susan (Miss) . . . 134
Silberstein, J. . . . 173
Silberstein, L. . . . 134
Silberstein, Oscar (Mrs.) . . . 16
Silva, J. . . . 134
Silver, A. . . . 156
Silver, Alexander . . . 4, 84
Silver, Alexander (Master) . . . 84, 135
Silver, B. . . . 63, 94, 119, 134
Silver, B. (Miss) . . . 67, 112, 122, 165
Silver, B. (Mr. and Mrs.) . . . 26, 38
Silver, B. (Mrs.) . . . 26
Silver, B.L. . . . 88
Silver, Benjamin . . . 49, 52, 108, 134
Silver, Benjamin (Master) . . . 134
Silver, Bessie (Miss) . . . 106, 155
Silver, E. (Miss) . . . 60
Silver, Edith (Miss) . . . 38, 102, 134, 135
Silver, Etta (Miss) . . . 77
Silver, G. . . . 183
Silver, H.J. . . . 134
Silver, J.H. . . . 134
Silver, Joseph . . . 134
Silver, Joseph (Mr. and Mrs.) . . . 135
Silver, L. . . . 134
Silver, L.P. (Mrs.) . . . 77
Silver, Lazarus . . . 38, 134
Silver, Lazarus (Mr. and Mrs.) . . . 11, 135
Silver, Lazarus P. . . . 38
Silver, Lazarus Pheneas . . . 52
Silver, M. . . . 60, 90, 134
Silver, M. (Mr. and Mrs.) . . . 94, 134, 135
Silver, M. (Mrs.) . . . 135
Silver, Mae (Miss) . . . 135
Silver, May (Miss) . . . 38, 135
Silver, Minnie (Miss) . . . 158
Silver, Moe . . . 38, 135
Silver, Moe (Mrs.) . . . 135
Silver, Mrs. . . . 135
Silver, N. . . . 49, 61, 72, 73, 122, 135
Silver, N. (Mr. and Mrs.) . . . 4, 74, 84, 135
Silver, N. (Mrs.) . . . 67, 74, 135
Silver, Nahum (Mr. and Mrs.) . . . 135
Silver, Nathan . . . 135
Silver, Nathan (Mrs.) . . . 109, 135
Silver, S. . . . 59
Silver, Sam . . . 38, 60
Silver, Y. (Miss) . . . 60
Silver, Yetta (Miss) . 77, 87, 98, 102, 122, 135
Silverberg, A. (Miss) . . . 131, 163
Silverberg, Ada (Miss) . . . 127, 135, 167
Silverberg, Eva (Miss) . . . 135
Silverberg, F. (Miss) . . . 122
Silverberg, Jacob . . . 145
Silverberg, Miss . . . 166
Silverberg, Rose (Miss) . . . 135
Silverman, A. (Miss) . . . 67
Silverman, A. (Mrs.) . . . 32, 133
Silverman, A.H. (Dr.) . . . 135
Silverman, Annie (Miss) . . . 135
Silverman, Arthur . . . 135
Silverman, B. . . . 79, 86, 115
Silverman, C. (Mrs.) . . . 140
Silverman, Charles . . . 4
Silverman, Dorothy (Miss) . . . 22
Silverman, E. . . . 38
Silverman, E.G. . . . 112
Silverman, Edwin L. . . . 135
Silverman, Elsie (Miss) . . . 60, 90, 135
Silverman, Elsie B. (Miss) . . . 38
Silverman, Elsie Rose (Miss) . . . 38
Silverman, F. . . . 167
Silverman, F. (Miss) . . . 113
Silverman, Frankie (Miss) . . . 135
Silverman, G. (Miss) . . . 98
Silverman, Gertie (Miss) . . . 98, 135
Silverman, Gertrude (Miss) . . . 38, 98
Silverman, H. (Mrs.) . . . 22, 133
Silverman, Harry . . . 22, 50
Silverman, Harry (Master) . . . 135
Silverman, Hattie (Miss) . . . 135
Silverman, I. . . . 170
Silverman, J. (Mrs.) . . . 135
Silverman, J.D. . . . 184
Silverman, J.S. (Miss) . . . 135
Silverman, L. . . . 2, 58, 155, 185
Silverman, L. (Mrs.) . . . 121, 135, 140
Silverman, Louis . . . 38, 178
Silverman, Louise (Miss) . . . 38, 102, 105
Silverman, Lyon (Mrs.) . . . 17, 38, 135
Silverman, M. . . . 3, 138, 172
Silverman, M. (Mrs.) . . . 172
Silverman, M.A. (Mr. and Mrs.) . . . 11, 101
Silverman, Mason . . . 132
Silverman, Miss . . . 135, 151
Silverman, Misses . . . 66, 103, 104, 135
Silverman, Moe . . . 173
Silverman, Moe (Mrs.) . . . 173
Silverman, Mr. and Mrs. . . . 135, 173
Silverman, Mr. and Mrs. J. . . . 4
Silverman, Mrs. . . . 67, 91, 135
Silverman, R. . . . 130
Silverman, S. . . . 61
Silverman, S. (Mr. and Mrs.) . . . 23, 135
Silverman, S. (Mrs.) . . . 135
Silverman, S.J. . . . 38
Silverman, S.J. (Mr. and Mrs.) . . . 4, 180
Silverman, Samuel . . . 4
Silverman, Solomon (Mrs.) . . . 3
Silverman, Susan (Miss) . . . 23, 135
Silverstein, Moses . . . 134
Silverstein, Mrs. . . . 101
Silverstein, Nell (Miss) . . . 178, 179
Silverstein, Shea . . . 134
Silverston, Ray (Miss) . . . 101
Silverstone, Alex. . . . 24
Silverstone, Alexander . . . 135
Silverstone, Annie (Miss) . . . 123
Silverstone, Charles . . . 27
Silverstone, Hiram . . . 21
Silverstone, J. (Mr. and Mrs.) . . . 27, 75
Silverstone, M. . . . 135
Silverstone, Mr. . . . 173
Silverstone, Mrs. . . . 120
Silverstone, P. (Mr. and Mrs.) . . . 127
Silverstone, R. (Miss) . . . 135
Silverstone, Rose (Miss) . . . 27
Silverstone, S. (Mr. and Mrs.) . . . 11, 22
Silverstone, S. (Mrs.) . . . 135
Silverstone, Samuel . . . 136
Silverstone, Sol. . . . 127, 136
Silverstone, Solomon . . . 38
Silverstone, W. (Mrs.) . . . 135
Silverstone, William (Mrs.) . . . 135, 136
Simand, R. (Mrs.) . . . 109
Simcoe, Mr. . . . 113
Simcover, Sam . . . 38
Simkevitz, Lily (Miss) . . . 36
Simkewitz, Miss . . . 31
Simon, A. . . . 119, 185
Simon, A. (Mr. and Mrs.) . . . 136
Simon, A. (Mrs.) . . . 136
Simon, Abraham . . . 38
Simon, Arthur . . . 38
Simon, Arthur (Miss) . . . 83
Simon, Arthur (Mr. and Mrs.) . . . 136
Simon, Arthur (Mrs.) . . . 93, 136
Simon, B. (Mr. and Mrs.) . . . 38, 136
Simon, B. (Mrs.) . . . 185
Simon, Bessie (Miss) . . . 73
Simon, D. (Miss) . . . 88
Simon, Doris (Miss) . . . 24, 167
Simon, Freda (Miss) . . . 136
Simon, George . . . 7, 136
Simon, George (Alderman) . . . 152
Simon, H. (Mr. and Mrs.) . . . 38, 136, 139
Simon, H. (Mrs.) . . . 116, 125, 136
Simon, Harry . . . 38, 109
Simon, Herman . . . 136
Simon, I. . . . 136, 185
Simon, I. (Mr. and Mrs.) . . . 139
Simon, I. (Mrs.) . . . 125
Simon, Isaac . . . 38, 132
Simon, Isaac (Mr. and Mrs.) . . . 7, 120
Simon, J. . . . 136
Simon, J. (Mr. and Mrs.) . . . 136
Simon, J. (Mrs.) . . . 95, 136
Simon, Jacob M. . . . 20
Simon, Jake (Master) . . . 4, 136
Simon, John . . . 136
Simon, John (Mr. and Mrs.) . . . 11, 41, 136
Simon, John (Mrs.) . . . 95, 96, 136
Simon, L. . . . 136
Simon, M. . . . 28, 136, 171
Simon, M. (Miss) . . . 30, 136
Simon, M. (Mr. and Mrs.) . . . 4, 136
Simon, Martin (Mrs.) . . . 77, 136
Simon, Miss . . . 112, 136
Simon, Mollie (Miss) . . . 136
Simon, Molly (Miss) . . . 136
Simon, Mr. . . . 136
Simon, Mr. and Mrs. . . . 95, 109
Simon, Mrs. . . . 121
Simon, Rosa (Miss) . . . 136
Simon, S. (Mrs.) . . . 88, 136
Simon, Sol . . . 136
Simon, Sol. (Mr. and Mrs.) . . . 136
Simon, Thelma (Miss) . . . 41
Simon, William . . . 38, 136
Simon, William (Mrs.) . . . 136
Simon-Burnschburg, R. . . . 136

Simons, Bessie (Miss) 29
Simons, I. (Mr. and Mrs.) 120
Simons, M. 173
Simons, M. (Mr. and Mrs.) 173
Simons, Moe (Mr. and Mrs.) 35
Simons, Mr. and Mrs. 29
Simons, Sylvia (Miss) 104
Simonski, A. (Mr. and Mrs.) 136
Simonski, A.A. (Mrs.) 159
Simonski, Albina (Miss) 154
Simonski, Arthur (Mrs.) 167
Simonski, I. 167
Simonski, Isidore 164
Simonski, L. 169
Simonski, M. 167
Simonsky, A.A. (Mrs.) 155
Simonsky, Arthur (Mrs.) 164
Simonsky, H. (Mrs.) 41
Simonsky, Harry 155, 156
Simonsky, I. 152
Simonsky, Isidore 167
Simonsky, L.I. 152
Simonsky, S. (Mrs.) 22, 167
Simonson, Mr. 37
Simonson, N. 68
Simonson, S. 136
Simowitz, M. 177
Simpson, Ernest A. 44
Simpson, Joseph 44
Simpson, Rupert M. 44
Simpson, Wilhelm 44
Simson, S. 136
Singer Israel (Mr. and Mrs.) 11
Singer, A. 28, 167, 169
Singer, A. (Mrs.) 168
Singer, Aaron (Mrs.) 137
Singer, Abe 161
Singer, Abraham 154, 167
Singer, B. (Miss) 67
Singer, Bessie 72
Singer, D.S. 38
Singer, D.Z. 164
Singer, Dr. 38, 166, 168
Singer, E. 136
Singer, E.F. 158, 167, 168
Singer, F. (Mr. and Mrs.) 136
Singer, F. (Mrs.) 137
Singer, Fannie (Miss) 38, 158
Singer, Fanny (Miss) 168
Singer, Frank (Mr. and Mrs.) 137
Singer, Fred 168
Singer, Fred (Mr. and Mrs.) 137
Singer, Fred. 136
Singer, Freda (Miss) 137
Singer, Frederick 136
Singer, Goldie (Miss) 28
Singer, H. 94, 106
Singer, H. (Mr. and Mrs.) 137
Singer, H. (Mrs.) 115, 137
Singer, Henry (Rev.) 168
Singer, Herman (Mr. and Mrs.) . . . 11, 137
Singer, I. 137, 139, 162
Singer, I. (Mrs.) 38
Singer, Israel (Mr. and Mrs.) 11
Singer, J. 159, 162, 163
Singer, J. (Mr. and Mrs.) 38
Singer, J. (Mrs.) 168
Singer, Joseph 154, 164
Singer, L. 168
Singer, L. (Mr. and Mrs.) 11
Singer, L.M. 154
Singer, L.M. (Mrs.) 35
Singer, Lily (Miss) 155, 162

Singer, Louis 38, 39, 160, 168
Singer, Louis M. 154, 158, 160, 163, 168, 169
Singer, Louis M. (Mrs.) 154, 168
Singer, M. 68, 90, 94
Singer, M. (Mr. and Mrs.) 11
Singer, M. (Mrs.) 137
Singer, M.J. 52
Singer, Mannie J. (Mrs.) 168
Singer, Max 38, 73, 87, 136, 168
Singer, Minnie (Miss) 28, 168
Singer, Miss 66
Singer, Mr. and Mrs. S. 166
Singer, P. (Mr. and Mrs.) 28, 168
Singer, Reba (Miss) 94, 136, 137
Singer, Riba (Miss) 137
Singer, S. 182
Singer, S. (Miss) 109
Singer, S. (Mr. and Mrs.) 73, 137
Singer, Sophie (Miss) 73, 77, 136, 137
Singer, Sylvia (Miss) 155
Singer, W. 74, 87, 138
Singer, William 39, 122, 137
Singer, William (Mr. and Mrs.) 137
Siskin, Julius 174
Siskind, E. (Miss) 173
Sissenwain, Louis 107
Sivitz, H.N. (Mr. and Mrs.) 11
Skafel, E.A. 175
Skaletar, A. 180
Skaletar, E.A. 175
Skaleter, A. (Ald.) 180
Skaleter, A. (Alderman) 179, 180
Skaleter, Alderman 180
Skaleter, E.A. 178
Skibelski, I. 112
Skibelsky, J. 71
Skibelsky, S. 66
Skiebelski, I.C. 81
Skiebelsky, M. (Master) 137
Sklover, P. 107
Sklower, J. 173
Skolnick, Abraham 39
Slabodsky, M. 164
Slabosky, M. (Mr. and Mrs.) 95, 128
Slabosky, M. (Mrs.) 95
Slabotsky, Esther (Miss) 137
Slabotsky, M. (Mr. and Mrs.) 137
Slabotsky, M. (Mrs.) 115
Slabotsky, Mr. and Mrs. M. 95
Slapcoff, Samuel 68
Slatken, S. 107
Slatkin, A. 101
Slatkof, S. 137
Slatkoff, S. 105
Slatkoff, S. (Mr. and Mrs.) 109
Slatkoff, Samuel 68
Slatkoff, Sophie (Miss) 85
Sloat, S. 170
Slobodsky, M. 68
Slobosky, M. (Mr. and Mrs.) 137
Slomensky, A. 137, 151
Slomensky, I. 137
Slomensky, Mr. 137
Slominsky, I. 137, 152
Slominsky, M. 149
Slomowitz, Joseph 39
Slonemsky, Alex. 150
Slonemsky, I. 25, 148, 149
Slonemsky, I. (Mr. and Mrs.) 152
Slonemsky, I. (Mrs.) 151
Slonemsky, J. 148, 152
Slonemsky, Jesse 150
Slonemsky, M. (Miss) 150

Slonemsky, May (Miss) 151, 152
Slonemsky, Mrs. 150
Slonemsky, Pearl (Miss) 149
Slonimsky, Cecil (Master) 149
Slonimsky, Mr. 148
Slotkin, B. 158
Slotkin, F. 158
Slotkin, H. 158
Slotkin, Sam 158
Slotkoff, S. (Mr. and Mrs.) 24
Slover, F. 29, 152
Slover, G. (Miss) 152
Slover, Gertrude (Miss) 29, 137
Sloves, A. 39, 108, 114, 137
Sloves, Abe 34
Sloves, B. (Miss) 82
Sloves, Bertha 20
Sloves, M. 114
Sloves, Max 34
Sloves, Moses 42
Sloves, N. 86
Sloves, N. (Mr. and Mrs.) 39, 108, 137
Sloves, N. (Mrs.) 20
Sloves, S. (Miss) 99, 114
Sloves, Sara (Miss) 137
Sloves, Sarah (Miss) 80, 86
Slovinsky, J. (Mr. and Mrs.) 28
Smalowitz, Lewis (Mrs.) 14
Smelinsky, Jacob 177
Smelzer, J.H. (Mrs.) 137
Smilovitch, Sam 176, 181
Smith, Annie (Miss) 168
Smith, B. (Miss) 152
Smith, B. (Mrs.) 151
Smith, E. (Miss) 137
Smith, Essie (Miss) 25
Smith, Fanny (Miss) 25
Smith, I.R. 159
Smith, Julius 153
Smith, Kalman 153
Smith, M. 164
Smith, M. (Mr. and Mrs.) 26
Smith, M. (Mrs.) 155
Smith, M.S. 175
Smith, Minnie (Miss) 161
Smith, Miss 140
Smith, Mr. and Mrs. 148
Smith, Mrs. 137, 152
Smith, N. (Mrs.) 155
Smith, Nathan (Mrs.) 168
Smith, R. 163
Smith, R. (Miss) 59
Smith, Rachel (Miss) 137
Smith, Rose (Miss) 161
Smith, S. (Miss) 92, 163
Smith, Wolf 39
Smithkin, Charles 177
Smofsky, Isaac 57
Smofsky, Lizzie (Mrs.) 57
Snare, I. 61
Sniderman, A. 57
Sniderman, I. 158
Snitsky, M. 158
Snow, Mr. 160
Sochter, J. 59
Society, Mr. and Mrs. 12
Sohmer, J. 72, 137
Sokolofsky, H. 175
Sokolow, Nahum 71, 168, 177, 180
Solberger, J. 137
Solin, J. 137
Solin, J. (Mr. and Mrs.) 88, 137
Solin, J. (Mrs.) 137

Name	Pages
Solin, M. (Mr. and Mrs.)	12, 137
Solin, M. (Mrs.)	88, 137
Solin, Maxwell	39
Solman, Mrs.	181
Solmon, E.	47
Soloman, E.	73
Soloman, J.	115
Soloman, S.	185
Solomon Engleman	46
Solomon, A.	61, 114
Solomon, A. (Miss)	92
Solomon, A. (Mr. and Mrs.)	12
Solomon, A. (Mrs.)	13, 138
Solomon, A.E. (Mr. and Mrs.)	12
Solomon, Annie (Miss)	27, 41, 76, 152
Solomon, Avner	39
Solomon, C. (Miss)	64
Solomon, Clara (Miss)	138
Solomon, D.	137
Solomon, D. (Mr. and Mrs.)	22
Solomon, Dayan	5
Solomon, E.	47, 90
Solomon, E. (Miss)	64
Solomon, E. (Mr. and Mrs.)	39
Solomon, E.S.	114
Solomon, Ed.	34, 137
Solomon, Edward	137
Solomon, Elias (Rev.)	22
Solomon, Esther (Miss)	22
Solomon, Eva (Miss)	138
Solomon, Evelyn (Miss)	138
Solomon, Freda (Miss)	22, 138
Solomon, Freida (Miss)	39
Solomon, G. (Mrs.)	27
Solomon, H.	39, 96, 137
Solomon, H. (Mr. and Mrs.)	138
Solomon, H. (Mrs.)	100
Solomon, Hyman	52
Solomon, J.	39
Solomon, J. (Master)	82
Solomon, Jennie (Miss)	39
Solomon, Julia (Miss)	138
Solomon, L.	137, 149
Solomon, Louis (Mr. and Mrs.)	138
Solomon, M.	68, 137, 138
Solomon, M. (Cantor)	43
Solomon, M. (Mr. and Mrs.)	22
Solomon, Mr.	138
Solomon, Mr. and Mrs.	28
Solomon, Nathan	122
Solomon, Ray (Miss)	138
Solomon, Rose (Miss)	107, 111
Solomon, S.	138
Solomon, S. (Miss)	60, 101
Solomon, S. (Mr. and Mrs.)	41
Solomon, S. (Mrs.)	145
Solomon, Sadie (Miss)	67, 111, 138
Solomon, Sam	87
Solomon, Samuel	26
Solomon, W.B.	138
Solomons, Louis	138
Solomons, Louis (Mr. and Mrs.)	12
Solomons, Louis (Mrs.)	138
Solomons, Reginald (Master)	12
Soloway, L.G. (Dr.)	168
Soloweizig, Myer	39
Solowsky, A.M.	178
Soltz, Rebecca (Miss)	160
Solvey, Dora (Miss)	138
Solway, L. (Miss)	165
Solway, Lena (Miss)	168
Solway, Leon J. (Dr.)	170
Solway, M. (Miss)	154
Solway, Misses	154
Somer, A. (Mrs.)	138
Somer, Sarah	67, 132
Sommer, A.	90, 138
Sommer, A. (Mrs.)	138
Sommer, Annie (Miss)	37
Sommer, B. (Mr. and Mrs.)	138
Sommer, D. (Mrs.)	37
Sommer, J.	120
Sommer, Kalman	20
Sommers, A. (Mrs.)	131
Sonnenschein, Edward	180
Soorovitz, S.	57
Sorkis, I.	26
Sorosky, Sals (Mrs.)	20
Sosken, M.	185
Soskin, A. (Mr. and Mrs.)	34
Soskin, Dr.	158
Soskin, I.	31, 39
Soskin, Leah (Miss)	34
Soskin, M.	87, 136, 138
Soskin, Milly (Miss)	66
Soskin, Mr.	168
Soskin, Tessie (Miss)	51, 52
Sourkes, A.	67, 94, 127
Sourkes, H.	52, 66, 67, 95, 139
Sourkes, H.L.	138
Sourkes, Harry	138
Sourkes, I.	67, 92, 94, 114, 139
Sourkes, I. (Mrs.)	98, 127
Sourkes, J. (Mrs.)	115
Spad, Louise (Miss)	168
Spain, Mrs.	167
Spaner, Jack	39
Spector, Abbie (Mrs.)	14
Spector, C.	81
Spector, D.	87, 138
Spector, N. (Mr. and Mrs.)	29
Spector, Sarah (Miss)	29
Sperber, D.	65, 137, 139, 141
Sperber, Dr.	62
Sperber, Leah	42
Sperber, M.N.	89
Sperber, Marcus	138
Sperber, Marcus M.	52, 138
Sperber, Maxwell	138
Sperber, Mr.	47
Sperber, N. (Mrs.)	25, 36
Sperber, S. (Miss)	66
Sperber, Sarah (Miss)	70, 74, 137, 138
Spergle, M.J.	169
Speyer, B.M.	63, 75, 114, 138, 152
Speyer, B.M. (Mrs.)	71
Speyer, Mr.	66
Spiegel, M. (Mrs.)	88
Spigler, Dorothy (Miss)	138
Spinner, M.	57, 58
Spira, Robert H.	127
Spittel, Mrs.	25
Spitzer, Hugo	180
Spitzer, V. (Dr.)	138
Spring, J.	168
Spring, Joe	168
Springer, J.	66
Springman, David	164
Springman, Millie (Miss)	177
Squire, Pearl	61
Squires, Abe	39
Squires, J. (Mr. and Mrs.)	39
Stahl, Montague	177
Stan, Nancy (Miss)	138
Stanley, H.	155, 156
Staples, Miss	138
Star, Mrs.	166
Starazumnik, H.	170
Stark, Adolphe	65
Stark, R.	47, 52, 121, 138
Stark, R.S.	92, 103, 138
Stark, Robert	39
Starke, A.	47
Starkoff, Mr.	175
Stei, E. (Miss)	61
Steiman, R. (Mrs.)	180, 181
Stein, Cyril (Miss)	60, 91
Stein, Cyrille (Miss)	138
Stein, D.	106
Stein, D. (Mr. and Mrs.)	138
Stein, E.	183
Stein, E. (Miss)	139
Stein, Elsie (Miss)	139
Stein, Esther (Miss)	79, 107
Stein, H. (Mr. and Mrs.)	139
Stein, Helen (Miss)	138, 139
Stein, Henrietta (Miss)	158
Stein, Herman	39
Stein, I. (Mrs.)	139
Stein, J. (Master)	138
Stein, J.I.	178
Stein, J.L.	177
Stein, John I.	177
Stein, Joseph (Mrs.)	68
Stein, L.	180
Stein, Lillian (Miss)	162
Stein, Lillie (Miss)	168
Stein, Luba (Miss)	37
Stein, M.	157
Stein, M. (Miss)	36
Stein, M. (Mrs.)	139
Stein, Max	141
Stein, Miss	91, 164
Stein, Morrie (Master)	138
Stein, Mr.	28
Stein, Mrs.	91, 139
Stein, Percy	155
Stein, Reginald (Master)	138
Stein, S. (Mrs.)	139
Stein, S.F. (Dr.)	68, 101, 138
Stein, S.L.	36
Stein, Sarah (Miss)	167
Stein, Seymour (Dr.)	138
Stein, Seymour F. (Dr.)	138
Stein, Seymour T. (Dr.)	138
Stein, Sydney (Mr. and Mrs.)	139
Stein, Sydney (Mrs.)	136, 139
Steinberg, A. (Miss)	28
Steinberg, Anna (Miss)	39
Steinberg, B. (Mr. and Mrs.)	168
Steinberg, D.	81
Steinberg, E. (Miss)	67
Steinberg, F. (Mrs.)	86
Steinberg, Frank (Mr. and Mrs.)	12
Steinberg, H.	34, 49
Steinberg, H.I. (Mr. and Mrs.)	39
Steinberg, Henry	20
Steinberg, Hyman	152
Steinberg, J.	59, 137, 139
Steinberg, J. (Mr. and Mrs.)	12, 139
Steinberg, Jacob	106
Steinberg, Joseph	20, 112, 139
Steinberg, Joseph (Mr. and Mrs.)	12
Steinberg, Julia Evelyn (Miss)	20
Steinberg, Kate (Miss)	131
Steinberg, L. (Miss)	28
Steinberg, Lillian (Miss)	131, 157, 160
Steinberg, Lily (Miss)	168
Steinberg, Lionel Montefiore	20

Steinberg, Max 39	Stern, N. 81	Strusser, J. 114
Steinberg, Miss 173	Stern, S. (Mr. and Mrs.) 113	Stuart, Joseph (Mrs.) 140
Steinberg, Moses 20	Stern, S. (Mrs.) 134	Stuart, Miss 140
Steinberg, Mr. 46, 162	Stern, Sam 168	Studner, M.A. (Mrs.) 179
Steinberg, Natalie C. 20	Stern, Samuel 44	Stutchinsky, Samuel 140
Steinberg, Peter 39	Stern, Seymour (Dr.) 139	Sugar, Sarah (Miss) 170
Steinberg, Peter (Mr. and Mrs.) 39	Stern, Sidney (Mrs.) 77	Sugarman, A. 152
Steinberg, Rose (Miss) 139	Stern, Sydney (Mr. and Mrs.) 136, 139	Sugarman, A. (Mr. and Mrs.) 23
Steinberg, S. 163	Stern, Sydney (Mrs.) 139	Sugarman, A.J. (Mr. and Mrs.) . 31, 140, 152
Steinberg, Sarah (Miss) 86, 139	Sternberg, John 40	Sugarman, Annie (Miss) 23
Steinberg, Victor (Mr. and Mrs.) 39	Sternberg, Mrs. 86, 145, 168	Sugarman, B. 157
Steinberg, Wolf Lion 20	Sternberg, S. 181	Sugarman, B. (Miss) 148, 150
Steinburg, Berde (Miss) 172	Sternberg, Wolff (Mr. and Mrs.) 139	Sugarman, Becca (Miss) 152
Steinburg, J. (Mrs.) 127	Sternberg, Woolf (Mr. and Mrs.) 139	Sugarman, Byrde (Miss) 144
Steinburg, Miss 166	Sternberger, Bertha (Miss) 43	Sugarman, E. (Miss) 151, 152
Steindler, J. 139	Sternberger, Leon (Rabbi) 43	Sugarman, E.H. (Miss) 150
Steine, Ben Zion 4, 139	Sterne, M.B. (Mr. and Mrs.) 140	Sugarman, E.R. 159
Steine, Ben Zion (Master) 4, 68	Sternklar, D. 81	Sugarman, Ephy 169
Steine, M.B. 52, 68, 94, 112, 137, 139, 183, 185	Sternklar, S. 68	Sugarman, Esther (Miss) . 30, 31, 140, 151-153
Steine, M.B. (Mr. and Mrs.) 3, 12, 139	Sternleib, J. (Mrs.) 132	Sugarman, Hattie (Miss) 151, 153
Steine, S. (Dr.) 59, 138	Stevenson, S. (Mrs.) 103	Sugarman, I. (Mr. and Mrs.) 122
Steine, Zusman Behr 12	Stockler, Max (Mrs.) 57	Sugarman, I. (Mrs.) 150, 151
Steiner, Bertha (Miss) 168	Stone (Miss) 31	Sugarman, Isidore 152
Steiner, Esther (Miss) 31	Stone, Annie (Miss) 140	Sugarman, Israel 152
Steiner, Herbert (Mrs.) 168	Stone, B. 162, 163	Sugarman, Rebecca (Miss) 150
Steiner, Herbert M. 39	Stone, Barnett . . 27, 140, 155, 159, 161, 163,	Sugarman, William 140, 183
Steiner, Newman Leopold 43	168, 169	Sugarman, William (Mr. and Mrs.) 169
Steiner, Wolfgang 43	Stone, D. 91, 107	Sugerman, Byrde (Miss) 179
Steinert, Minnie (Miss) 32	Stone, Kate (Miss) 140	Sugerman, Ephraim 157
Steinhouse, A. (Miss) 88	Stone, Katie (Miss) 16, 140	Sugsonitsky, I. 39
Steinhouse, Annie (Miss) 139	Stone, M. (Miss) 88	Sumeray, Minnie (Miss) 7
Steinhouse, B. 139	Stone, Mr. 166	Sundell, Gussie (Miss) 154
Steinhouse, Charles 139	Stone, Rebecca (Miss) 39	Superior, Celia 66
Steinhouse, J. 66	Stone, Samuel (Mr. and Mrs.) 140	Superior, J.H. 140
Steinhouse, Joe 139	Stone, Valentine 169	Superior, M.S. 81
Steinhouse, M. 139	Stone, W.R. 47	Superior, M.S. (Mr. and Mrs.) 140
Steinkopf, H. (Mrs.) 178, 180	Strachuran, A. 175	Superior, R.S. (Miss) 37
Steinkopf, Herman 180	Straither, David 39	Sushelsky, Ida B. (Miss) 87
Steinkopf, M. 176, 180	Strassburg, A. (Miss) 113	Susman, M. (Mr. and Mrs.) 174
Steinkopf, Max 39, 175, 180, 181	Straus, Adele (Miss) 169	Susman, Max (Mr. and Mrs.) 174
Steinkopf, Max (Mr. and Mrs.) 12	Straus, Bettie (Miss) 155	Susman, Mr. and Mrs. 173
Steinman, H. 65, 138, 139	Straus, E. 169	Susman, Mr. and Mrs.) 173
Steinman, I. 138	Straus, Julius 173	Susman, Mrs. 78
Steinman, M. 175	Straus, Leo 169	Susman, William 173
Steinman, R. (Mrs.) 175	Strausberg, Rose (Miss) 30, 161	Sussman, Beccie (Miss) 97
Steinsberg, E. (Miss) 67	Strausberg, S. (Mrs.) 30	Sussman, H. (Mrs.) 174
Steinsberg, J. (Mrs.) 115	Strauss, Adele (Miss) 21, 144	Sussman, M. 174
Steinsberg, R. (Miss) 115	Strauss, Alfred (Mr. and Mrs.) 169	Sussman, Rosalie (Miss) 97
Steinsburg, Bessie (Miss) 139	Strauss, Bettie (Miss) 144	Sutton, D. 171
Steinsburg, Eva (Miss) 139	Strauss, Betty (Miss) 169	Sutton, H. 171
Steinwortzel, William 167	Strauss, Daly (Miss) 173	Suzberg, Ralph 173
Steinworzel, Master 167	Strauss, Edna (Miss) 169, 170	Swartz, Cora (Mrs.) 15
Stekolsky, J. 56	Strauss, H. 140	Swartz, Eleanor (Mrs.) 15
Sterling, Sarah (Miss) 27	Strauss, J. 173	Swartz, H. 137
Stern, A. (Mrs.) 20	Strauss, J. (Mr. and Mrs.) 140	Swartz, Hattie (Miss) 119
Stern, Addie (Miss) 139	Strauss, Julius 173	Swartz, Jeanette (Miss) 119
Stern, C. (Mr. and Mrs.) 91	Strauss, L. (Mrs.) 171	Swartz, M. 159, 169
Stern, Charles 43	Strauss, Leo 39	Swartz, N. (Mr. and Mrs.) 35
Stern, Charles (Mr. and Mrs.) 139	Strauss, Leo. 173	Swartz, S. 162
Stern, Charles (Mrs.) 139	Strauss, Louis (Mr. and Mrs.) 173	Swartzman, H. 32
Stern, Dr. 52	Strauss, Miss 140, 147, 166, 169	Swarzfeld, J. 182
Stern, Edward (Sir and Lady) 139	Strauss, Misses 173	Sweedler, S. 114
Stern, Edward D. (Sir and Lady) 139	Strauss, Mr. and Mrs. 140	Sweedler, W. 87, 136, 138
Stern, Henry 20	Strauss, Mrs. 168	Sweedler, W.W. 138
Stern, Hirsch 49	Strauss, Oscar S. 39	Sweet, D. 171, 172
Stern, I. 139	Strauss, S. 108	Sweet, D. (Mr. and Mrs.) 171, 173
Stern, J.B. 139	Strauss, Therese (Miss) 144	Sweet, David 171-173
Stern, Joseph 52, 81	Streamer, Berthe (Miss) 144	Swisberg, S. 137
Stern, Joseph (Dr.) 42, 52, 139	Strean, S. 49	Swiss, S. (Miss) 158, 169
Stern, L. (Mr. and Mrs.) 139	Stremer, Mrs. 169	Swiss, Selina (Miss) 155
Stern, Miss 139	Stringer, Joseph (Mr. and Mrs.) 91	Switzman, F. (Mrs.) 145
Stern, Mr. 139	Strober, J. .39	Switzman, Morris 61
Stern, Mr. and Mrs. 91	Strober, Louis 39	Symonds, Daisy (Miss) 40

Symonds, R. (Mrs.) 40
Symonski, D. (Mrs.) 140
Taffert, Harold 39
Taillefer, Dora (Miss) 140
Takefman, H. (Mrs.) 39
Takefman, Louis (Mr. and Mrs.) 32
Takefman, N. 115
Takefman, Nathan 39, 86
Takefman, Rose (Miss) 32
Talpis, Hilda 132, 140
Talpis, I. (Mr. and Mrs.) 140
Talpis, J.H. 140
Talpis, J.H. (Mrs.) 140
Talpis, M. 3
Talpis, Mr. 45
Talpis, S. 17, 31, 52, 71, 87, 112, 140
Talpis, S. (Miss) 66
Talpis, S. (Mr. and Mrs.) 29, 140
Talpis, Sarah K. (Miss) 50
Tanenbaum, J. 115
Tannebaum, David (Dr.) 140
Tannebaum, Hannah (Mrs.) 98
Tannebaum, M. (Mr. and Mrs.) 140
Tannebaum, Miss 108
Tannebaum, Mrs. 127
Tannebaum, Rae (Miss) 98, 140
Tannenbaum , Rae (Miss) 66
Tannenbaum, Abraham 20
Tannenbaum, Benjamin 20
Tannenbaum, D. (Dr. and Mrs.) 140
Tannenbaum, D. (Dr.) 146
Tannenbaum, David 52, 140
Tannenbaum, David (Dr.) 39, 140
Tannenbaum, David (Mrs.) 77
Tannenbaum, Florence (Miss) 10
Tannenbaum, Harry 20
Tannenbaum, Hattie (Miss) 59, 69, 140
Tannenbaum, I. 127
Tannenbaum, Isidore 140
Tannenbaum, J. 78
Tannenbaum, L. 47, 77, 129, 132
Tannenbaum, L.M. 61
Tannenbaum, Lawrence 107, 110, 140
Tannenbaum, Lil (Mrs.) 72
Tannenbaum, Lillian (Miss) 98
Tannenbaum, Lillie (Miss) 98
Tannenbaum, Lily (Miss) 93, 121
Tannenbaum, M. 49, 59, 60, 140
Tannenbaum, M. (Miss) 60
Tannenbaum, M. (Mr. and Mrs.) 39
Tannenbaum, Michael 20
Tannenbaum, Miriam (Miss) . 77, 98, 107, 140
Tannenbaum, Miss 124, 140
Tannenbaum, Misses 72, 93
Tannenbaum, Morris 20
Tannenbaum, Mr. and Mrs. 59, 139, 140
Tannenbaum, Mrs. 72, 98, 104, 119
Tannenbaum, R. 61
Tannenbaum, Rae (Miss) 66, 140
Tannenbaum, Ray (Miss) 98, 140
Tanzman, Annie (Miss) 157
Tanzman, Yetta (Miss) 56
Taplitch, L. 49
Tapper, E. (Mr. and Mrs.) 178
Tapper, E. (Mrs.) 175
Tapper, Etta (Mrs.) 181
Tapper, J. (Mrs.) 181
Tapper, Jake (Mrs.) 178
Tapper, Mr. and Mrs. 40
Tapperberg, J. 67, 140
Tapperburg, J. 116
Tarantur, Mr. and Mrs. 35
Tarantur, P. 32
Tarantur, Rebecca (Miss) 35
Tartick, Florence (Miss) 36
Tashanskofsky, Mr. 140
Tastick, Florence 20
Taub, Annie (Miss) 40
Taub, Samuel (Mr. and Mrs.) 40
Taub, Sydney 140
Taube, F. 183
Taube, M. (Mrs.) 173
Taube, May (Miss) 167
Taube, Miss 164
Taube, Mrs. 165
Taube, S. 169, 171
Taylor, Fannie (Miss) 167
Taylor, Fanny (Miss) 158, 169
Taylor, I. 134
Taylor, Ida (Miss) 169
Taylor, Morris 52
Taylor, Morris (Master) 49, 52
Taylor, Mr. 169
Taylor, S. (Miss) 173
Tcherkow, H. 178
Tchwrenski, A. 69
Tebis, Norman 177
Tedman, Jacob Tuviah Ben Bazalel 177
Teich, Clara (Miss) 160
Teich, J. 155, 163
Teich, Joe 169
Teich, Miss 164
Teitelbaum, H. 140
Teitelbaum, Max 41, 140
Teitelbaum, Naphtali (Mr. and Mrs.) 175
Teitlebaum, Max 140
Temes, C. 158, 163
Temes, C.N. 167
Temes, Miss 155
Temmer, J. 74, 143
Teplitsky, L. (Mrs.) 20
Teplitzky, A. (Miss) 82
Teplitzky, Becky (Miss) 123
Teplitzky, Bernard Joseph (Master) 4
Teplitzky, L. 3, 49, 81
Teplitzky, L. (Mr. and Mrs.) 140
Teplitzky, L. (Mrs.) 4
Teplitzky, Lazarus 25
Teplitzky, Lazarus D. 20
Teplitzky, Lazarus David 20
Teplitzky, Rose (Miss) 123, 140
Teren, Joseph (Mr. and Mrs.) 39
Teren, Rosa (Miss) 39
Tessler, H. (Mrs.) 180
Tetchell, P. 61
Tewsley, Gertrude (Miss) 39
Thaler, A. 141
Thaler, Grace (Miss) 141
Thaler, Grace B. (Miss) 124
Thaw, Sonny (Master) 141
Thisber, Rachel (Miss) 41
Thisber, S. (Mr. and Mrs.) 41
Tichler, Becky (Miss) 77
Ticktin, Mrs. 165
Tieson, J. (Mrs.) 17
Tipograph, Carl M. (Mr. and Mrs.) 141
Tipograph, M. 52
Tipograph, Maurice 82, 141
Tipograph, Saul 82
Tobias, Ethel (Miss) 175
Tobias, Herbert 177
Tobias, L. (Mrs.) 27
Tobias, Minnie (Miss) 9, 27
Tobias, Mr. 87
Tobias, N.C. 176
Tobias, Nathan 39, 51
Tobias, Norman 181
Tobias, W. 175
Tobias, W.V. 175
Tobias, Will 179
Tobias, William 177
Tobin, Gertrude (Miss) 22
Todman, C. 175
Tolshinsky, H. 137
Tolzers, A.W. 52
Tolzes, A.W. 141, 150
Tolzes, I. 152
Tolzess, A.W. 141, 149
Tolzess, I.L. 149
Tolzess, Mr. and Mrs. 87
Tolzess, W.H. 141
Tomares, C. 173, 174
Tomares, Charles 173
Topless, A. (Mrs.) 151
Toplitski, Beccie (Miss) 106
Topp, I. 141
Toronto, H. (Master) 149
Toronto, Sarah 140
Torontow, Sarah 132
Tozman, R. 162
Trager, L. (Mr. and Mrs.) 37
Trager, Lizzie (Miss) 37
Trebeis, W. 178
Trefner, Joseph 39
Triller, M.W. 175
Tritt, G.S. 67
Tritt, J. (Mrs.) 141
Tritt, Jennie (Miss) 39, 80, 141
Tritt, jr., Saul 141
Tritt, M. (Miss) 138
Tritt, Mary (Miss) 46, 77, 83, 106
Tritt, S. 66, 77
Tritt, S.G. (Mr. and Mrs.) 71
Tritt, S.G. (Mrs.) 141
Tritt, Sam. 170
Tritt, Samuel Gerald 39
Tritt, Saul 114
Tshetchick, Mordecai Ben Myer 177
Tuck, J. 173
Tucker, Etta (Miss) 141
Tucker, M.H. 141
Tugendhaft, Rose (Miss) 155, 157
Tupper, Joe. 105
Turk, J. (Mr. and Mrs.) 173, 174
Turk, L. (Miss) 174
Turner, C. (Miss) 88
Turner, E. (Miss) 67
Turner, J.B. (Mr. and Mrs.) 27, 141
Turner, Mrs. 141
Turner, R. (Miss) 113
Turner, Ray (Miss) 27, 66, 141
Turofsky, H.A. 169
Turofsky, Harry Alfred (Dr.) 39
Turofsky, I. (Mr. and Mrs.) 39
Turofsky, L. 156
Turofsky, Mrs. 39
Uditsky, Max 141
Udow, David 141
Udow, Gertrude (Miss) 141
Udow, J. 141
Uhry, Paul 141
Undelman, A. (Mrs.) 134
Unger, Mrs. 25
Unterman, I. 167, 169
Ury, Hortense (Miss) 30
Ury, Irene (Miss) 30
Usher, Abe 80
Usher, Barney 132
Usher, Cecil 52

Usher, J. .49	Vineberg, Esther (Miss) 175	Vineberg, Mr. 66, 142
Usher, J. (Mrs.) 115	Vineberg, Eva (Miss) 142	Vineberg, Mrs. 143
Usher, M. 141	Vineberg, Frances (Miss) 142	Vineberg, N. 143
Usher, M. (Mrs.) 64, 115	Vineberg, Francis (Miss) 74, 86, 142	Vineberg, N. (Master) 88
Usher, Max 81	Vineberg, Gertie (Miss) 143	Vineberg, Nellie (Miss) . . . 4, 24, 31, 32, 40,
Usher, Peter 52, 86	Vineberg, Gertrude (Miss) 142	105, 117, 142
Usher, Peter (Master) 49	Vineberg, Goldie (Miss) 143	Vineberg, Norman (Master) 143
Valinsky, Mary (Miss) 51	Vineberg, H. 127, 139, 162, 177	Vineberg, Olive (Miss) 143
Valinsky, R. 66	Vineberg, H. (Dr. and Mrs.) 141	Vineberg, P. .67
Valinsky, Samuel 181	Vineberg, H. (Mr. and Mrs.) 12, 40	Vineberg, P. (Miss) 40, 176
Valinsky, Sarah (Miss) 50	Vineberg, H. (Mrs.) 21, 98	Vineberg, Pearl (Miss) 40, 175
Valoshin, Flo. (Miss) 178	Vineberg, H.L. 117	Vineberg, R. (Miss) 142
Valosky, A. 45	Vineberg, Harris . . 7, 20, 49, 52, 59, 81, 103,	Vineberg, Rae 77
Van Dusen, D.J. (Mrs.) 21	139, 141, 142	Vineberg, Ray (Miss) 135
Van Houton, Miss 166	Vineberg, Harris (Mr. and Mrs.) 33, 142	Vineberg, Rose (Miss) . 23, 30, 31, 33, 77, 98,
Van Raalte, Phineas 40	Vineberg, Harris (Mrs.) 33, 44, 77, 122	100, 142, 143
Van Raalte, S. (Rev. Mr. and Mrs.) 40	Vineberg, Harris E. 141	Vineberg, Rosie (Miss) 23, 32
Vechsler, Albert 92	Vineberg, Harry 40, 49	Vineberg, S. (Miss) 150
Vechsler, H. 173	Vineberg, Harry (Mr. and Mrs.) 128, 136	Vineberg, S. (Mr. and Mrs.) 40, 143
Veingust, Miss 133	Vineberg, Harry (Mrs.) 143	Vineberg, S. (Mrs.) 38, 143
Veld, Gertrude (Miss) 12	Vineberg, Henry (Mrs.) 143	Vineberg, S.L. (Mr. and Mrs.) 113, 143
Veld, H. (Rabbi) 93	Vineberg, Herbert 85	Vineberg, S.L. (Mrs.) 108, 143
Vender, Joseph 20	Vineberg, Hillel (Mrs.) 169	Vineberg, S.R. 114
Vender, Lazarus 20	Vineberg, Hiram (Mrs.) 112	Vineberg, Sadie (Miss) . . 4, 21, 24, 31-34, 61,
Vender, Rubin 20	Vineberg, Hyman (Mr. and Mrs.) 32, 142	105, 109, 134, 142, 178
Vender, S. 141	Vineberg, I. (Mr. and Mrs.) 32, 33	Vineberg, Sadie, (Miss) 73
Vender, Samuel 20, 141	Vineberg, I. (Mrs.) 36, 127, 133, 143	Vineberg, Sam 176
Vender, Sarah (Miss) 20	Vineberg, J. 130	Vineberg, Samuel 96
Vender, William 20	Vineberg, J. (Mrs.) 61, 143	Vineberg, Simon 20, 40, 90, 143
Venis, M. .40	Vineberg, J.H. 142	Vineberg, Simon (Mr. and Mrs.) 32
Venis, S. 40	Vineberg, J.H. (Mrs.) 78	Vineberg, Sol 21
Venis, S. (Mr. and Mrs.) 12	Vineberg, J.L. 7	Vineberg, Sol (Mrs.) 108, 143
Vexler, Fannie (Miss) 52	Vineberg, J.L. (Mr. and Mrs.) . . . 24, 41, 126	Vineberg, Sol S. 40
Vickar, D. 182	Vineberg, J.L. (Mrs.) 105, 143	Vineberg, Sol. 143
Victor, A. .81	Vineberg, Jack 142	Vineberg, Solomon 7, 20
Victor, J. 141	Vineberg, Jake 142	Vineberg, Solomon (Mrs.) 137
Victor, J.A. 40	Vineberg, Jennie (Miss) 117	Vineberg, Sydney 143
Victor, J.H. 81	Vineberg, Joseph 40, 142	Vineberg, T. 143
Victor, Jack 141	Vineberg, Joseph (Master) 143	Vineberg, T. (Miss) 88
Viener, A. 170	Vineberg, Joseph (Mrs.) 21, 61	Vineberg, T. (Mr. and Mrs.) 114
Viener, Freda (Miss) 169	Vineberg, Jr., Solomon S. 142	Vineberg, Thomas 143
Vigdur, Jeannette (Miss) 22	Vineberg, L. 142	Vineberg, W.L.A. (Mrs.) 75
Vilensky, Miss 67	Vineberg, L. (Miss) 142	Vinegarden, May (Miss) 169
Vineberg, A. 142	Vineberg, L. (Mr. and Mrs.) 86, 142	Vinegust, A. (Mr. and Mrs.) 39
Vineberg, A. (Miss) 61	Vineberg, L. (Mrs.) 101, 142	Vinegust, Leah (Miss) 39
Vineberg, A. (Mrs.) 143	Vineberg, Lawrence (Master) 40	Viner, A. 70, 107
Vineberg, A.B. (Mrs.) 143	Vineberg, Lilly (Miss) 77, 117, 142	Viner, A.K. 63, 127
Vineberg, A.H. 32, 141	Vineberg, Lily (Miss) 67, 84, 142	Viner, Annie (Miss) 29, 33, 143
Vineberg, A.J. 141	Vineberg, Louis20, 21, 40, 42, 67, 111, 142, 181	Viner, B. (Miss) 64
Vineberg, A.J. (Mrs.) 76, 143	Vineberg, Louis (Mr. and Mrs.) 40	Viner, Bessie (Miss) 126, 143
Vineberg, A.M. 62, 141, 146	Vineberg, Louis (Mrs.) 160	Viner, Dr. 143
Vineberg, A.M. (Mr. and Mrs.) . . 30, 91, 141	Vineberg, Louis I. (Mr. and Mrs.) 12	Viner, F. (Mrs.) 29
Vineberg, A.M. (Mrs.) 126, 143	Vineberg, M. 72, 106, 139, 162, 173, 181	Viner, H. (Dr.) 143
Vineberg, Abe 21, 141, 177	Vineberg, M. (Miss) 142	Viner, J. 52, 66, 73, 82, 143
Vineberg, Abe (Mrs.) 143	Vineberg, M. (Mr. and Mrs.) 86, 142	Viner, Jack 88
Vineberg, Abel 52, 141	Vineberg, M. (Mrs.) . . 33, 34, 40, 74, 86, 98,	Viner, Jacob 143
Vineberg, Abraham 20, 70, 141	131, 181	Viner, M.B. 143
Vineberg, Abraham (Mr. and Mrs.) 142	Vineberg, M.A. 142	Viner, Mrs. 143
Vineberg, Abraham M. 141	Vineberg, M.A. (Mr. and Mrs.) 143	Viner, Norman (Dr.) 62, 65, 125, 143
Vineberg, Albert 21, 70	Vineberg, M.A. (Mrs.) 74, 75, 99, 143	Vise, B. 167
Vineberg, Albert (Mr. and Mrs.) 142	Vineberg, M.J. (Mrs.) 139	Vise, Burney 164
Vineberg, Alf. (Mrs.) 143	Vineberg, Malca (Miss) . . 4, 31, 41, 117, 142	Vise, D. 161, 169
Vineberg, B. (Miss) 142, 149, 152	Vineberg, Malca (Mrs.) 142	Vise, Etta (Miss) 144
Vineberg, Beccie (Miss) 152	Vineberg, Malcolm 32, 40	Vise, I. 156, 169
Vineberg, Beck (Miss) 149, 152	Vineberg, Marcus 21, 70	Vise, J. (Mr. and Mrs.) 120
Vineberg, D. (Miss) 61	Vineberg, Mary (Miss) 142	Vise, Lillian 30
Vineberg, E. 23	Vineberg, Mary (Mrs.) 21	Vise, Matthew 30
Vineberg, E. (Mr. and Mrs.) 23	Vineberg, Max 49	Vise, Molly (Miss) 131
Vineberg, E. (Mrs.) 143	Vineberg, Max (Mr. and Mrs.) 143	Vise, Mrs. 166
Vineberg, Edward 67	Vineberg, Maxwell (Mr. and Mrs.) . . . 24, 86	Vise, Pearl (Miss) 169
Vineberg, Elias 20, 40	Vineberg, Moses 20, 143, 146	Voegler, Benjamin 143
Vineberg, Elias (Mr. and Mrs.) 23	Vineberg, Moses (Mr. and Mrs.) 143	Vogel, H. 143
Vineberg, Ellis (Mrs.) 143	Vineberg, Moses A. 62	Vogel, Isidore 40

Vogel, Marian (Miss) 22
Volachaw, J. 182
Volansky, L. 183
Volansky, Leo A. 183
Volansky, M. 52, 182
Volinsky, B. (Miss) 67
Volinsky, Rebecca (Miss) 34
Volk, A. (Mr. and Mrs.) 12
Volman, L. 143
Volushin, Flo (Miss) 179
Vosberg, E. (Mrs.) 64
Vosberg, H. 24, 81
Vosberg, H. (Mrs.) 138
Vosberg, Harry (Mr. and Mrs.) 143
Vosberg, Harry (Mrs.) 138
Vosberg, I. 137
Vosberg, S. (Mrs.) 64
Vourzell, Mr. 183
Vrenstein, P. 72
Vyse, Ena (Miss) 28
Wachman, Annie (Miss) 34
Wachman, Rosie (Miss) 39
Waghelstein, C. 74, 143
Waghelstein, Charles 138
Wagner, C. (Miss) 113, 122
Wagner, Hans 86
Wagner, Mrs. 146
Wagner, R. 61
Wainstein, M. (Mr. and Mrs.) 185
Waiser, D. 62
Waitelsky, Louis 174
Waitelsky, Mr. and Mrs. 174
Wald, P. 175
Waldman, J. (Rev.) 162, 163, 169
Waldman, J.H. 62, 143
Waldman, Joseph 70
Waldman, Joseph Hugo 52
Waldman, L. 162
Waldman, Louis 169
Waldman, Louis (Mrs.) 169
Waldman, Mrs. 144
Waldman, Rev. 175
Waldman, Sara (Miss) 77
Waldman, William 164
Walkem, R.T. (Mrs.) 144
Walker, Isaac 4
Wall, Thos. 108
Wallman, G. (Miss) 33
Walovich, V. (Mr. and Mrs.) 144
Walstein, Leonard 152, 153
Walters, M. 172
Walther, Mrs. 105
Warburg, Otto (Prof.) 110
Warhaft, B. (Mrs.) 180
Warnecke, J. 144
Warnick, Sam 176
Warrinsky, Ethel (Miss) 172, 173
Warshaft, Rev. 176
Warshawsky, H. 66
Wartell, H.B. 144
Wartell, H.B. (Mr. and Mrs.) 144
Wartell, Lewis 144
Wartelsky, Annie (Mrs.) 21
Wartelsky, L. (Mrs.) 21
Wartelsky, Mr. and Mrs. 174
Wartelsky, Sadie (Miss) 21
Wasserman, Miss 144
Wasserman, Mollie (Miss) 157
Wasserman, Mrs. 144
Waterman, H. 57
Watson, Josef K. 40
Waxler, Abraham 21
Waxler, Mr. 94
Waxman, S. (Mr. and Mrs.) 78
Webber, Annie (Miss) 156
Webber, Ben 167
Webber, Evelyn B. (Miss) 127
Webber, Ida (Miss) 154
Webber, Louis 52
Webber, Maurice 144
Webber, S. 169
Webber, W. 157, 167, 169
Webber, William 56
Weber, Bessie (Miss) 169
Weber, Gertrude (Miss) 169
Weber, Katherine (Miss) 169
Weber, Mrs. 169
Weber, S. 162
Weber, W. 169
Wechsler, Augusta (Miss) . . 30, 103, 104, 144
Wechsler, J. 82
Wechsler, M. 67
Wechsler, Maurice 66, 144
Wechsler, Paul (Mr. and Mrs.) 104
Wecksler, Fannie (Miss) 144, 165, 173
Wecksler, Fanny (Miss) 173
Wecksler, Misses 172, 173
Weeksler, Annie (Miss) 29
Weeksler, Augusta Rose (Miss) 29
Weeksler, Charles (Mr. and Mrs.) 29
Weeksler, Chas. (Mr. and Mrs.) 4
Weeksler, Fanny (Miss) 29
Weeksler, Gus (Miss) 29
Weeksler, Joseph 4
Weesberg, H. (Mrs.) 144
Weesberg, Joseph 144
Weichert, Clarice (Miss) 21
Weichert, Louis 21
Weichert, Sigmund 21
Weidman, A. (Miss) 176
Weidman, A.E. 175
Weidman, Annie (Miss) 175, 176
Weidman, B. (Miss) 176
Weidman, Buddy (Miss) 175
Weidman, Cynthia (Miss) 179
Weidman, Dorothy (Miss) 28
Weidman, H. 175, 179-181
Weidman, H.L. (Mr. and Mrs.) 28
Weidman, John 175
Weidman, M. 175
Weidman, N. 30, 179
Weidman, Neiman J. 40
Weil, Della A. (Miss) 144
Weil, Edgar 169
Weil, Edgar (Mrs.) 164
Weil, Henry 169
Weil, J. 144
Weil, Willie (Mr. and Mrs.) 169
Weinberg, A.M. (Mrs.) 66
Weinberg, Hillel 40
Weinberg, I. 62
Weinberg, I. (Mr. and Mrs.) 144
Weinberg, I. (Mrs.) . . . 66, 77, 109, 128, 144
Weinberg, Ike (Mrs.) 144
Weinberg, J. (Miss) 144
Weinberg, Jack 40
Weinberg, Marvin (Master) 144
Weinberg, Mrs. 30
Weinberg, P. (Mr. and Mrs.) 40
Weinberg, R. (Mrs.) 84
Weinburg, Isaac 144
Weiner, A. (Mrs.) 24, 144
Weiner, Annie (Miss) 29
Weiner, B. 71
Weiner, B.M. 81
Weiner, Benjamin 115
Weiner, Bernard M. 75
Weiner, H.L. (Mr. and Mrs.) 144
Weiner, Isidore (Mr. and Mrs.) 29
Weiner, L. (Miss) 88
Weiner, M.B. 114
Weiner, Mr. and Mrs. 94
Weiner, Sarah (Miss) 84
Weinfeld, H. (Mr. and Mrs.) 144
Weinfeld, Harry (Mrs.) 144, 147
Weinfeld, Henry (Mr. and Mrs.) 12
Weinfeld, Israel 21
Weinfeld, J.J. 62
Weinfeld, John J. 49, 119, 144
Weinfeld, Louis 40
Weinfeld, Otto 144
Weinfeld, Vera (Miss) 144
Weinfield, Abraham 52
Weinfield, Andrew 53
Weinfield, C. (Mrs.) 130
Weinfield, H. (Mr. and Mrs.) 144
Weinfield, H. (Mrs.) 130, 144, 147
Weinfield, Harry (Mr. and Mrs.) 144
Weinfield, Harry (Mrs.) 147
Weinfield, Henry 45, 59
Weinfield, Henry (Mrs.) 66
Weinfield, I. 131
Weinfield, I. (Mr. and Mrs.) 132
Weinfield, J.J. 65
Weinfield, John J. 40, 81, 112
Weinfield, John J. (Mr. and Mrs.) . . . 12, 144
Weinfield, John J. (Mrs.) 132
Weinfield, Mrs. 130
Weinfield, Otto 144
Weinfield, R. (Miss) 66
Weingarden, A.A. 40
Weingarden, A.A. (Mr. and Mrs.) 181
Weingarten, May (Miss) 165
Weingarten, Sadie (Miss) 155
Weinpohl, Mr. 144
Weinpohl, O. 144
Weinpohl, Otto 144
Weinreb, Rabbi 34
Weinrobe, D. (Mrs.) 185
Weinrobe, L. (Miss) 185
Weinroch, Joseph 4
Weinroch, L. (Mr. and Mrs.) 4
Weinstein, A. (Mr. and Mrs.) 26
Weinstein, Annie (Miss) 29
Weinstein, B. (Mr. and Mrs.) 21
Weinstein, Barnett 40
Weinstein, Celia (Miss) 29
Weinstein, E. (Miss) 74
Weinstein, Jennie (Miss) 50
Weinstein, L. 29
Weinstein, Maxwell 29
Weinstein, Mr. 177, 185
Weinstein, Mr. and Mrs. 185
Weinstein, N. 176
Weinstein, P. (Miss) 82
Weinstein, P. (Mr. and Mrs.) 12
Weinstein, Philip 40
Weinstein, S. (Miss) 82
Weinstein, Sarah (Miss) 26
Weinstein, Saul 21
Weinstock, J. (Mrs.) 152
Weinstock, Leah (Miss) 151
Weinstock, S. (Miss) 150
Weinstock, Sara (Miss) 151, 153
Weinstock, Sarah (Miss) 149, 152
Weintraub, Bella (Miss) 156
Weintraub, J. 144
Weintraub, J. (Mr. and Mrs.) 82
Weintraub, J. (Mrs.) 82

Weintraub, M. (Mr. and Mrs.) 12	Wener, Sam (Mrs.) 145	Willinsky, Ida 30
Weintraub, Milton 40	Wener, Samuel 49, 145	Willinsky, L. (Mr. and Mrs.) 31
Weintraub, Rabbi 156	Wener, Samuel (Mrs.) 145	Willinsky, M. (Miss) 161
Weisberg, Esther 66	Wener, Z. (Mrs.) 145	Willinsky, Minnie (Miss) 31, 164
Weisberg, Eva (Miss) 37	Weretnikow, Z. 170	Willinsky, Miss 166
Weisberg, Z. 66	Wershof, A. 170	Willinsky, S. 112
Weisburgh, Abraham 21	Wershof, Eli 150	Willinsky, S.R. (Mr. and Mrs.) 30, 31
Weisburgh, H. 21	Wershof, Mr. 150	Willinsky, Sadie (Miss) 169
Weisburgh, Nathan 21	Wershof, Rev. 34	Willoughby, MInnie (Miss) 165
Weisglass, S. 111	Wertheimer, J. (Miss) 109	Willus, Geo. E. (Mr. and Mrs.) 170
Weisman, J. 40	Wertheimer, Miss 89	Wilson, F. 81
Weisman, Mr. and Mrs. S. 12	Wetstein, B. (Mrs.) 103	Wilson, Frank 145, 162
Weisman, S. (Mr. and Mrs.) 12	Wetstein, L. (Miss) 132	Wilson, J. (Miss) 154
Weiss, A. (Mrs.) 144	Wetstein, Lillian (Miss) 66, 70, 125, 145	Wilson, M. (Miss) 92
Weiss, Adolph 144	Wetstein, Lily (Miss) 134	Wilson, Mr. 164
Weiss, Adolph (Mr. and Mrs.) 12	Wetstein, Louise 145	Wilson, T. 82
Weiss, Adolph (Mrs.) 144	Wetstein, Louise (Miss) 145	Wilson, Y. (Miss) 154
Weiss, Adolphe 144	Wetstein, Mrs. 121	Wineberg, Hal 41
Weiss, Adolphe (Mr. and Mrs.) 12	Wetstein, R. (Mrs.) 145	Wineman, L. 130
Weiss, Adolphe (Mrs.) 144	Wetstein, Ralph (Mrs.) 83, 140	Winer, A. 61
Weiss, Joseph 158	Wetstein, S. (Miss) 96	Winer, J. 61, 66
Weiss, L. (Miss) 82	Wexler, A. (Mr. and Mrs.) 24	Winestein, M. 185
Weiss, Louis (Rabbi) 21	Wexler, Fannie (Miss) 35	Winevoope, Maurice 115
Weiss, Paula (Miss) 166	Wexler, Lillian (Miss) 145	Wing, Ed. 67
Weissburgh (Mrs.) 4	Wexler, Louis 41	Wing, Tom 67
Weissburgh, E. 4	Wexler, Louis (Mr. and Mrs.) 12	Winkler, W.N. 158
Weissburgh, Isaac 4	Wexler, M. 2	Winsberg, Paul 41
Weissman, E. 41, 170	Wexler, Marcus (Mr. and Mrs.) 12	Winstock, J. 145
Weitzer, Hyman (Mr. and Mrs.) 28	Wexler, Mr. 138	Winstock, Miss 145
Weitzer, K. (Mr. and Mrs.) 28	Wexler, Mr. and Mrs. 145	Winstock, S. 145
Weitzer, Marie (Miss) 28	Wexler, O. 145	Winters, Mrs. 145, 168
Weitzer, Mary (Miss) 28	Wexler, Rebecca (Miss) 24	Wintraub, Miss 83
Weksler, Charles 169	Wexler, W. 67	Wirtz, George (Mr. and Mrs.) 12
Weksler, Charles (Mrs.) 169	Whillins, B. 180	Wise, Adolph (Mrs.) 145
Weksler, Mr. and Mrs. Charles 169	White, A. 167, 169	Wise, Bernard 167
Weldman, Dorothy (Miss) 28	White, Abraham 41	Wise, R. 162
Weldman, H. (Mr. and Mrs.) 28	White, B. 99	Wise, Stephen (Rabbi) 43, 170
Weler, Jacob 175	White, Bernard C. 41	Wiseman, A. 41
Welmertz, A. 144	White, Bernard L. 41	Wiseman, E. 170
Wendes, Misses 144	White, E. 41	Wiseman, Jacob 41
Wener, A. 106	White, E. (Miss) 163	Wiseman, M. (Dr.) 145
Wener, Albert 144	White, Esther 112	Wiseman, M. (Mrs.) 78
Wener, Albert (Mr. and Mrs.) 145	White, Louis 41	Wiseman, Master 53
Wener, Albert (Mrs.) 93	White, W. (Mrs.) 145	Wiseman, Max (Dr. and Mrs.) 12
Wener, Albert M. 144	Whitehouse, Joseph 58	Wiseman, Mrs. 71
Wener, B. (Mrs.) 71, 145	Whitehouse, Samuel 58	Wisenfield, Tillie (Miss) 24
Wener, D. 144	Wicks, Mollie (Miss) 108	Wisse, W. 115, 130
Wener, Edith 26	Wiener, B. 78	Wisse, W.H. 120
Wener, Edith (Miss) 71	Wigdor, Joseph S. 41	Wittal, Sarah (Miss) 75
Wener, Etta (Miss) 35, 36, 144, 145	Wilder, A.E. 177, 178	Wittenberg, N. 21
Wener, Fannie (Miss) 145	Wilder, Abraham E. 177	Wittes, S. 145
Wener, Florence 111	Wilder, C. 162	Witzling, Hannah (Miss) 36
Wener, Florence (Miss) 4, 35, 106, 111	Wilder, H.E. 175, 181	Witzling, P. 64
Wener, Gertie (Miss) 60	Wilder, Sam 181	Witzling, Phil 145
Wener, H. 35, 36, 49, 133	Wilence, B. 180	Wiznitzer, Anna (Miss) 145
Wener, H. (Mr. and Mrs.) 4	Wilensky, H. 94	Wladofsky, B. (Cantor) 169
Wener, H. (Mrs.) 77, 128, 145	Wilensky, Mr. 164	Wladofsky, Cantor 30, 34, 42, 159
Wener, Harry 96	Wilkinson, A. (Mrs.) 145	Wladofsky, Rev. 24
Wener, Harry (Mr. and Mrs.) 12, 128	Wilkinson, Amelia (Mrs.) 20	Wodlinger, A.D. (Miss) 176
Wener, Harry (Mrs.) 35, 128, 145	Wilkinson, H. (Mrs.) 139, 145	Wodlinger, Eva (Miss) 175
Wener, I. (Mr. and Mrs.) 145	Wilkinson, H.M. (Mrs.) 145	Wodlinger, H.A. 179
Wener, J. 106	Wilkinson, H.N. 145	Wodlinger, L. (Miss) 176
Wener, Jack 144	Wilkinson, H.N. (Mrs.) 145	Wodlinger, L.G. (Miss) 175, 176
Wener, Jack (Mrs.) 35	Willensky, Bertha (Miss) 75	Wodlinger, Lizzie (Miss) 179
Wener, Jacob (Mr. and Mrs.) 145	Willensky, S. 145	Wodlinger, Max 181
Wener, Julius 130	Williams, Golde (Miss) 56	Wohl, I.P. 145
Wener, L. 101, 133	Willinsky Lila (Miss) 30	Wohl, I.T. 145
Wener, Lawrence 4	Willinsky, A. 154	Wohl, Ida (Miss) 109, 145
Wener, Louis 144	Willinsky, A. (Mrs.) 154	Wohl, L. (Mrs.) 109
Wener, M. (Mr. and Mrs.) 145	Willinsky, A.I. (Dr.) 169	Wohl, Miss 146
Wener, Rose (Miss) 77	Willinsky, B. (Miss) 25	Wohl, Mrs. 146
Wener, S. 145	Willinsky, Gertrude (Miss) 31, 161	Wolf, Bernard 44
Wener, S. (Mrs.) 112, 128	Willinsky, I.A. (Dr.) 169	Wolf, David 146

Wolf, F.W. 146	Wolinsky, M. (Mr. and Mrs.) 34	126, 146
Wolf, Frank 146	Wolinsky, R. (Miss) 34	Workman, Mark (Mrs.) 144, 147
Wolf, Gertie (Miss) 43, 170	Wollenberg, A. 81	Workman, Marvie 48
Wolf, Minna (Miss) 44	Wollman, L. 74	Workman, Miss 136, 146
Wolf, N. (Mr. and Mrs.) 89	Wolman, W. 86	Workman, Misses 146
Wolfe, A. 146	Wolochow, A. (Mr. and Mrs.) 24	Workman, Nina (Miss) . 28, 60, 105, 117, 146
Wolfe, A. (Miss) 146, 149	Wolochow, Annie (Miss) 24	Workman, Ruth (Miss) 77, 102, 111, 146
Wolfe, A. Harry . . . 21, 33, 41, 90, 115, 146, 148, 152	Wolofsky, Aron (Mr. and Mrs.) 41	Workman, Winnifred (Miss) 146
Wolfe, A.H. 28, 41, 91	Wolofsky, Diana (Miss) 34	Wormser, Gertie (Miss) 155
Wolfe, A.H. (Corp.) 152	Wolofsky, Fanny (Miss) 41	Wormser, M. (Mrs.) 16, 147
Wolfe, Adele (Miss) 21, 146, 152, 153	Wolofsky, Felix 4	Wormser, Maurice (Mrs.) 16
Wolfe, Anna (Miss) 10, 33, 38, 146, 148, 152, 153, 170	Wolofsky, Felix (Mr. and Mrs.) 4	Wormser, Mrs. 147
	Wolofsky, H. 47, 50, 81, 84, 131	Wortsman, Dr. 2
Wolfe, Dorothy (Miss) . . . 21, 146, 148, 149, 152, 153	Wolofsky, L. 41	Woschsler, Miss 166
Wolfe, E. (Miss) 148, 150, 152	Wolofsky, M. 41	Wyman, C. 58
Wolfe, Essie (Miss) 24	Wolofsky, Mildred (Miss) 41	Wyman, Ch. 58
Wolfe, Esther (Miss) 21, 148-150, 152	Wolofsky, Philip 4, 41	Wyman, Charles 57
Wolfe, Florence (Miss) 35	Wolofsky, Philip (Master) 68	Wyman, Nathan 4
Wolfe, Gertie (Miss) 144	Wolofsky, Rosie (Miss) 41	Wynne, W.H. 114
Wolfe, Gladys (Miss) 21	Wolofsky, Sarah (Miss) 41	Wyse, Miss 147
Wolfe, H. 146, 151	Wolofsky, Sophie (Miss) 41	Yaffe, Mr. 168
Wolfe, H.A. (Mrs.) 150	Wolpaw, D. (Mr. and Mrs.) 174	Yampolsky, C. (Mr. and Mrs.) 25
Wolfe, Harry 150	Wolpaw, David 41	Yampolsky, Mr. 52, 137
Wolfe, J. 152, 153	Wolpaw, Mr. and Mrs. 173	Yampolsky, Rose (Miss) 25
Wolfe, Jay 21, 152, 153	Wolsey, H. (Mrs.) 141, 146	Yancovitch, Samuel Hirsch 147
Wolfe, Joseph R. 173	Wolsey, Hannah (Mrs.) 146	Yanover, J. 22, 162
Wolfe, L. (Mr. and Mrs.) 146	Wolsey, Mrs. 117	Yanower, Miss 29
Wolfe, L.H. (Mrs.) 165	Wolsey, S. (Mrs.) 146	Yaphe, F. (Miss) 99, 133
Wolfe, Louis (Mr. and Mrs.) 12	Wolsey, Samuel 21	Yaphe, Florence Ruth 21
Wolfe, M. 171	Wolsley, B. (Mrs.) 146	Yaphe, Jacob 50
Wolfe, M. (Mrs.) 151, 152	Wolstein, Leonard 153	Yaphe, N. (Mr. and Mrs.) 31
Wolfe, M.F. (Mrs.) 75	Woods, L. (Miss) 135	Yaphe, Rebecca (Miss) 31
Wolfe, Martin 41	Woolf, M. 183	Yaphe, S. 59
Wolfe, Max 21, 146	Woolf, Miss 88	Yaphe, Samuel 21
Wolfe, Max (Mr. and Mrs.) 33, 35, 41, 146, 151	Woolf, Mrs. 166	Yelkin, Isaac 41
Wolfe, Max (Mrs.) 76, 116, 146, 148, 151-153	Woolfson, I. 169	Yellin, L. 36, 78
Wolfe, Miss 146, 171	Woolfson, Mamie (Miss) 25	Yeruslawitz, M. 139
Wolfe, Misses 146, 150, 153	Woolfson, Rosa (Miss) 153	Yewdall, H. (Mrs.) 181
Wolfe, Mr. and Mrs. Max 146	Woolman, Irene (Miss) 146	Yolles, L. (Miss) 167
Wolfe, Mrs. 170	Woolman, L. (Mrs.) 146	Yoosprich, B. 170
Wolfe, Nadie E. (Miss) 21	Woolman, Mrs. 105	Yoshkovitz, Mr. 163
Wolfe, Phoebe (Miss) 33, 35, 61, 148	Workman Ed. 51	Youngheart, E. 47
Wolfe, Rachel 173	Workman, Abraham 21	Youngheart, E. (Mr. and Mrs.) 82
Wolfe, S. (Miss) 150	Workman, Abraham S. 70	Youngheart, E. (Mrs.) 147, 170
Wolfe, Sadie (Miss) 148, 151, 152, 165	Workman, C.A. 42, 146	Youngheart, Ed. (Mrs.) 131, 147, 166
Wolfe, Sadie E. (Miss) 146, 151-153	Workman, C.A. (Mr. and Mrs.) 146	Youngheart, Edward (Mr. and Mrs.) 147
Wolfe, Sadie Elenore (Miss) 33	Workman, C.A. (Mrs.) 16, 73, 95, 146	Youngheart, Edward (Mrs.) 43, 147
Wolfe, Sadie Elinore (Miss) 152	Workman, Charles 21	Youngheart, Edward Opoczynski 21
Wolfe, Teresa (Miss) 148	Workman, Charles (Mr. and Mrs.) 146	Youngheart, Felix 21
Wolfe, Teresa F. (Miss) 152	Workman, Charles A. 21	Youngheart, Joe 179
Wolfe, Teresa Frances (Miss) . . . 21, 33, 146, 153, 170	Workman, Charles A. (Mrs.) 95, 146, 147	Youngheart, Joseph 21, 147, 181
	Workman, Chas. (Mrs.) 147	Youngheart, Joseph (Mr. and Mrs.) 147
Wolfe, Tess (Miss) 179	Workman, Chas. A. 146	Youngheart, Joseph (Mrs.) 91, 147, 170
Wolfe, Theresa (Miss) 92, 146	Workman, Daisy (Miss) 60, 146	Youngheart, Mr. and Mrs. Edward 147
Wolfe, Theresa Frances (Miss) 53	Workman, E. (Master) 21	Youngheart, Mrs. 170, 172
Wolfe, Violet (Miss) 21, 153	Workman, Edward 42	Youngheart, Sybil 2
Wolff, Herbert 146	Workman, Elsa (Miss) 147	Youngheart, Sybil (Miss) 77, 147, 170
Wolff, M. (Miss) 164	Workman, Elsie 42	Yudell, Misses 147
Wolff, Martin 41	Workman, Elsie (Miss) 74, 147	Yudelmark, D. 65
Wolff, Martin (Mr. and Mrs.) 146	Workman, Flora (Mrs.) 147	Yuskewitz, Pincus (2nd. Lieut.) 162
Wolff, Maurice (Mr. and Mrs.) 146	Workman, Gertie (Miss) 146	Yuskovitz, Pincus 163
Wolff, Mrs. 39, 146	Workman, Gertrude (Miss) 28, 146	Zach, M.L. 123
Wolff, Rachel (Miss) 41	Workman, I. 21, 49	Zacharia, K. (Mrs.) 106
Wolff, S. (Rev.) 177	Workman, I. (Mrs.) 147	Zacharia, M. (Mrs.) 14
Wolffsohn, Herr 52	Workman, Isaac 21	Zack, J.C. 173
Wolfsohn, F. (Mrs.) 17	Workman, Jacob 70	Zackon, Mr. 185
Wolfson, E.I. 157	Workman, Lee 21	Zacks , Celia (Miss) 53
Wolfson, H. 57	Workman, Levi 21	Zacks, D. (Mr. and Mrs.) 174
Wolfson, M. 169	Workman, M. (Mr. and Mrs.) 146	Zacks, Harry 174
Wolfson, S. (Mrs.) 30	Workman, M. (Mrs.) 126, 147	Zacks, Hyman (Mr. and Mrs.) 173
Wolfson, Samuel 41, 178	Workman, Mark . . . 21, 59, 61, 90, 111, 112, 143, 146	Zacks, I. 147
		Zacks, J. 147
	Workman, Mark (Mr. and Mrs.) . . 28, 92, 93,	Zacks, J.C. 66, 73, 141, 147

Zacks, K. 173
Zacks, K. (Mr. and Mrs.) 174
Zacks, M. 174
Zacks, M. (Miss) 174
Zacks, Samuel 53
Zager, A. 162
Zaid, S. (Mr. and Mrs.) 12
Zakan, M. 49
Zakuto, Rev. 57
Zalzman, Israel 41
Zamenhoff, Ludwig (Dr.) 147
Zarakin, D. 81
Zarif, B. 182
Zavilansky, David 41
Zbar, B. 173
Zealin, L. 115
Zeaman, Mrs. 112
Zeamen, B. (Mrs.) 98
Zeamen, Bernhardt (Mrs.) 147
Zeeman, B. (Mrs.) 110, 147
Zeeman, Bernhardt (Mrs.) 147
Zeigen, L. 181
Zelchinhaw, M. (Rev.) 31
Zelecovitz, M. (Mrs.) 77
Zelicovetz, M. 137
Zelicovitch, Fanny (Miss) 77
Zelicovitch, Moses 131
Zelicovitch, Myer (Mr. and Mrs.) 147
Zelicovitz, M. 81
Zelicowitch, M. 66
Zeman, B. (Dr. and Mrs.) 12
Zeman, B. (Mrs.) 147
Zeman, Burnhardt 41
Zeman, Dr. and Mrs. 147
Zemmleman, David 110
Zernan, Dr. and Mrs. 96
Zhitlovsky, Ch. (Dr.) 128
Ziegler, Annie (Miss) 154
Ziff, Mrs. 156
Zigmond, A. (Mrs.) 98
Zimmerman, A. (Master) 175
Zimmerman, D. 178
Zimmerman, J. 175
Zimmerman, J. (Rev.) 27
Zimmerman, M. 66, 173
Zimmerman, Mr. 147
Zimmerman, Mrs. 173
Zimmerman, N. 175, 178
Zimmerman, Sam (Mrs.) 181
Zimmerman, W. 30
Zimmerman, W. Harry 177
Zimmerman, W.H. 178
Zivian, I. 174
Zivian, J. (Miss) 165, 169
Zivian, Jennie (Miss) 161
Ziwitz, A. 170
Ziwitz, Nachem (Mr. and Mrs.) 170
Ziwitz, Nachman 41
Ziwitz, Rabbi 170
Ziwitz, Rabbi and Mrs. 41, 170
Zolotkoff, Leon 145
Zoodick, A. 70
Zucker, M. (Mrs.) 147
Zucker, Max 41
Zuckerman, Mr. 147
Zuckes, A. 68
Zudick, G. 134
Zulauf, Bertha (Miss) 85
Zulauf, S. 106
Zusman, Abraham 41
Zweig, H. 158, 162
Zwibel, Louis (Master) 82
Zwieg, Harry 41